READER'S DIGEST
Illustrated Encyclopedia of
BRITAIN

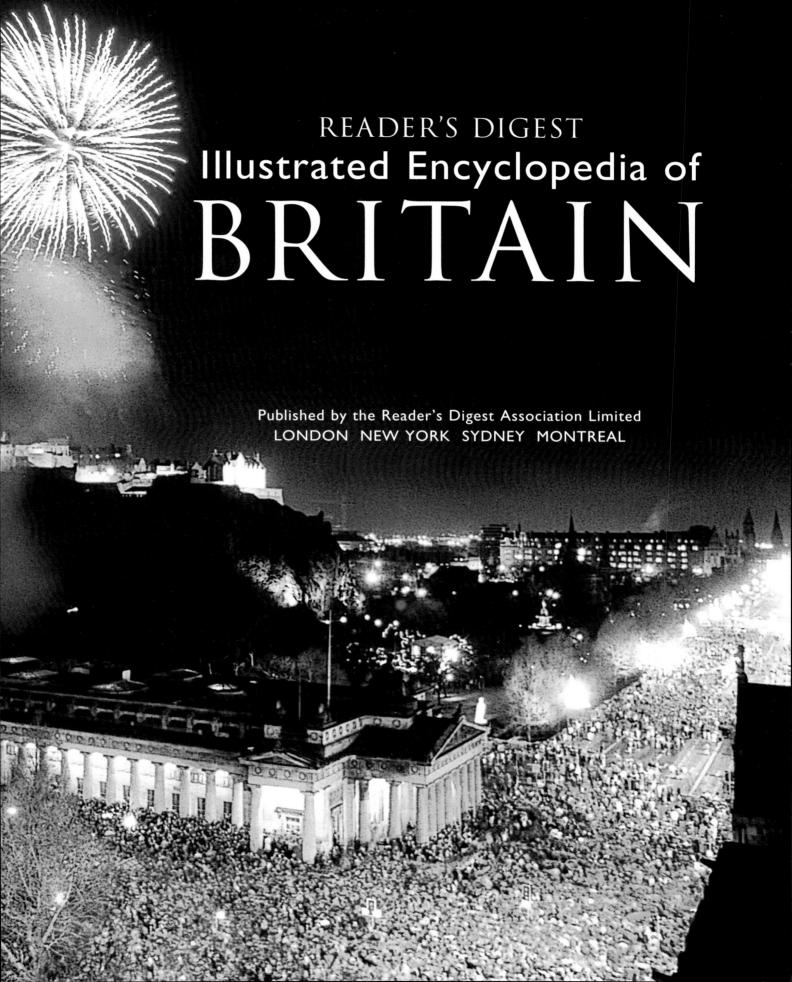

READER'S DIGEST
Illustrated Encyclopedia of
BRITAIN

Published by the Reader's Digest Association Limited
LONDON   NEW YORK   SYDNEY   MONTREAL

ILLUSTRATED ENCYCLOPEDIA OF BRITAIN
was edited and designed by
The Reader's Digest Association Ltd,
London

First edition copyright 1999
The Reader's Digest Association Ltd,
11 Westferry Circus, Canary Wharf,
London E14 4HE

www.readersdigest.co.uk

Copyright ©1999
Reader's Digest Association Far East Limited

Philippines copyright ©1999
Reader's Digest Association Far East Limited

Printed in Belgium

ISBN 0 276 42412 3

*Front cover: (top to bottom) London at night;
fox in winter; coronation procession of Charles II;
Eilean Donan Castle; Last Night of the Proms*
Spine: Geri Halliwell
*Back cover: (top to bottom) Liverpool;
path through bluebells, Wales; Angel of the
North, Gateshead; England football fans*
Half-title page: Spanish Armada
Title page: Hogmanay in Edinburgh
Pages 4-5: Poppy field

CONTRIBUTORS
Marcel Berlins
Joanna Bogle
Julia Bruce
William Burroughs
Anthony Burton
Michael Davison
Miranda Day
Ann Edwards
Michael Ellis
Jonathan Elphick
Fergus Fleming
Nigel Hawkes
Jonathon Grove
Simon Hemelryk
Godfrey Hodgson
Liz Hodgson
Charlie Hurt
Lawrence Joffe
Nicholas Jones
Rick Jones
Rhoda Koenig
Brendan Lehane
Tim Leigh
Anthony Livesey
Antony Mason
Roy Porter
Jonathan Rée
Richard Roberts
Nigel Rodgers
Stewart Ross
Hamish Scott
Rose Shepherd
Keith Spence
Rob Steen
Rachel Storm
Rosalyn Thiro
Katrina Tudor
Helen Varley
Stuart Walton
Andrew Williamson
Diana Winsor
Sue Wood
Michael Wright

EDITOR
Justine Scott-Macnab

ART EDITOR
Louise Bruce

DEPUTY EDITOR
John Andrews

ASSOCIATE EDITOR
Jonathan Bastable

ASSISTANT EDITORS
Alison Bravington
Alison Candlin
Celia Coyne
Malcolm Day
Chloë Garrow
Margaret Hotson
Marion Moisy
Rachel Warren Chadd

RESEARCHERS
Jane Egginton
Alastair McDermott
Michael Paterson
Rachel Weaver

EDITORIAL ASSISTANTS
Liz Jamieson
Rachel Robson

DESIGNERS
Kate Harris
Jane McKenna
Fay Singer
Rachael Stone
Austin Taylor

PROOFREADERS
Roy Butcher
Barry Gage

PICTURE RESEARCHERS
Carina Kelsey
Rosie Taylor

PICTURE MONTAGE
Ian Atkinson

INDEXER
Laura Hicks

EDITORIAL DIRECTOR
Cortina Butler

ART DIRECTOR
Nick Clark

EXECUTIVE EDITOR
Julian Browne

DEVELOPMENT EDITOR
Ruth Binney

PUBLISHING PROJECTS MANAGER
Alastair Holmes

PICTURE RESEARCH EDITOR
Martin Smith

STYLE EDITOR
Ron Pankhurst

Contents

Introduction

Where else can you find in one book a reconstructed Anglo-Saxon farmstead, a floorplan of the Houses of Parliament, a description of life on Hadrian's Wall, the history of tartans and the origin of place names – almost anything that makes these islands the rich and surprising place they are?

The *Illustrated Encyclopedia of Britain* is a unique and comprehensive guide to every aspect of our nation's life: wild Britain, with its hedgerows, fields and woods; urban Britain, with its Roman remains and its startling modern buildings by Richard Rogers; historical Britain, the land of Mary Queen of Scots, Churchill and Thatcher.

Here is Britain as our creative geniuses, such as Shakespeare and Turner, Elgar and Austen, have imagined it and mystical Britain – the land of Avalon, resting place of King Arthur, and the Avebury ring. Here is contemporary Britain, home of New Labour and the Millennium Dome. And here, not least, are the British themselves: the statesmen, the artists, the heroes, the villains, everyone who has helped to shape and define our nation.

ABOUT THIS BOOK

The great diversity of Britain's history, culture and natural environment made the choice of entries for this book an immense task. Many people – among them experts, editors and ordinary readers – were consulted. Every suggestion was carefully considered in the light of two fundamental criteria: importance and interest. We hope that the vast majority of entries in the book satisfy both, and that among them they cover all the information readers expect from a book of this kind.

A number of simple rules have been followed: for example, all major cities have their own entries, as do all the kings and queens of England since William the Conqueror. Most editorial decisions, however, were not so clearcut. Politicians and earlier monarchs were admitted only if particularly well known or of exceptional historical significance; artists, writers, musicians, books and television programmes only if they are either in the first rank of excellence or for some reason occupy a unique place in the national consciousness.

Features, charts and lists have been used throughout the book to complement individual entries and provide more comprehensive coverage of subjects. A complete list of prime ministers, their party allegiance and their terms of office, for example, can be found at the back of the book, and a list of all monarchs under Royal houses.

WHAT IS BRITAIN?

For the purposes of this book, 'Britain' has been taken to mean the United Kingdom of Great Britain and Northern Ireland. Events from Irish history that are also part of British history, such as the Battle of the Boyne and the Easter Rising, have been included. So, too, have Irish writers, thinkers and statesmen who made a contribution to mainstream British life in the days before political separation or who lived and worked primarily in Britain.

Similar criteria have been applied to people of other nationalities. Geniuses such as Handel, Marx, Popper and Wittgenstein are claimed for Britain on the grounds that they did significant work in this country or became leading figures in British intellectual or cultural life. Equally, many British-born people have made their mark abroad. Only those whose life's work also encompassed notable achievements in Britain have been given a place. So in the field of cinema, for instance, Alfred Hitchcock is included but Charlie Chaplin and Stan Laurel are not.

LOOKING UP SUBJECTS

The headwords reflect the most commonly used names of people, places and objects. Writers whose pseudonyms are better known than their real names (Lewis Carroll and George Orwell, for example) are listed under the former, and where titles are more familiar than forenames (Lord Byron and Mrs Beeton) these are used instead. Occasionally, where an author is best known for one particular work or character, this rather than the author's name is the headword – Biggles rather than W.E. Johns, for example. Acronyms are used sparingly and only where universally known, as in BBC and ICI.

ALPHABETICAL ORDER

Entries are ordered alphabetically, ignoring word breaks; therefore wool towns comes after Virginia Woolf. Fictional characters and nicknames (but not pseudonyms) are alphabetised on the first letter of the first name: James Bond appears under 'J', for instance.

HONOURS AND TITLES

Knighthoods and other honours and titles are mentioned at the start of entries. Thereafter the text generally omits titles, referring to 'Walter Raleigh' and not 'Sir Walter', 'Margaret Thatcher' and not 'Baroness Thatcher'.

POPULATION FIGURES

Figures are generally from the 1991 census, rounded up or down to the nearest 10.

MAP REFERENCES

All geographical entries appear on the maps at the back of the book. The page number of the map and a grid reference are supplied at the start of each entry.

CROSS-REFERENCING

References in small capitals appear within entries when other entries shed further light on a subject. Cross-references have also been inserted between entries in the alphabetical listing when the order of entries departs from strict alphabetical sequence.

ABBREVIATIONS

b. born
d. died
Pop. population
Est. established

kt knight
bn baron, baroness
visc. viscount, viscountess
bt baronet
CB Commander of the (Order of the) Bath
CBE Commander of the (Order of the) British Empire
CH Companion of Honour
DBE Dame Commander of the Order of the British Empire
MBE Member of the (Order of the) British Empire
OBE Officer of the (Order of the) British Empire
OM Order of Merit

EH English Heritage
NT National Trust
HS Historic Scotland
NTS National Trust for Scotland
Cadw Welsh Historic Monuments

ABERDEEN

• E Scotland (p.497 D3)   • Pop. 189 710

Scotland's third largest city has prospered in modern times from industry – mainly in the form of fishing and North Sea oil and gas – but its place as a centre of learning and Christianity goes back much further.

St Machar's Cathedral (14-15th century) in the old city commemorates a 6th-century Irish monk who converted the local Pictish population and is said to have built a chapel on the site. Although partly ruined, the cathedral is still in use.

Aberdeen's tradition of scholarship began in medieval times. King's College was founded in the 15th century to teach the 'rude and barbarous', and Marischal College in the 16th century. In 1860 they united as Aberdeen University.

Historic buildings include the 16th-century Provost Skene's House, where the duke of Cumberland stayed before the Battle of Culloden in 1746, and 18th-century houses of local pink granite that line the narrow 'wynds' (alleys). The art gallery holds works by Henry MOORE, Barbara HEPWORTH and Jacob EPSTEIN.

Robert ADAM: *see opposite page*

ADMIRAL'S CUP

• Biennial, August

Despite its maritime heritage, Britain has staged few international sailing events. But in 1957 the Royal Ocean Racing Club inaugurated the Admiral's Cup to attract foreign boats. Participating nations enter teams of up to three yachts in each of six races off the south coast of England. The competition coincides with the COWES WEEK yachting festival and culminates in the 609 mile Fastnet

CALM BEFORE THE STORM It is not all plain sailing for teams entering the Admiral's Cup. Conditions off the south coast can suddenly worsen. In 1979, storms cost 16 lives

ACTS OF PARLIAMENT

In Britain new legislation becomes law only after a proposal known as a 'bill' has been voted on and passed by both HOUSES OF PARLIAMENT, and received the monarch's assent. Until 1973, when Britain joined the Common Market (now European Union), an Act of Parliament was the highest law of the land. Since then, Acts have had to comply with European law, which takes precedence in cases of conflict.

The vast majority of bills are introduced by the government, which publishes a programme of proposed legislation at the beginning of every parliamentary session. Sometimes Green (discussion) or White (proposal) Papers are produced to aid debate. Individual MPs occasionally introduce bills called private members' bills, but these rarely succeed. Bills are usually read first in the House of Commons, though uncontroversial bills may go to the Lords first.

HOW A BILL BECOMES LAW

FIRST READING
Formal presentation to Commons; no debate

SECOND READING
Debate on bill's general principles

EXAMINATION BY STANDING COMMITTEE
Each word and clause is scrutinised and amendments made if necessary

REPORT STAGE
Further discussion and amendments. The government can use its majority to reverse amendments made in committee

THIRD READING
Final version is presented

HOUSE OF LORDS
Peers hold three readings. They can introduce amendments or reject the bill, in which case it is delayed and returns to the Commons, who may override the Lords

ROYAL ASSENT
Monarch approves the bill, which then becomes law

Race from Cowes on the Isle of Wight, around Fastnet Rock off the south-west coast of Ireland, and back to Plymouth.

A record 19 yachts took part in 1975, 1977 and 1979. Britain holds the overall record, having won the cup nine times up to 1997, once (1971) led by the prime minister Edward Heath in *Morning Cloud*.

ADMIRALTY

When the crimson flag of the Lord High Admiral, with its golden anchor emblem, was lowered over Admiralty House in Whitehall on March 31, 1964, it signalled the end of one of Britain's most ancient state departments. Britain has had some form of naval administration since medieval times. From the reign of

Charles II it was run by a civilian, political appointee (the First Lord of the Admiralty or Lord High Admiral) and a serving admiral (First Sea Lord), both consulting with the Board of Admiralty, consisting of more admirals.

A long list of Lords High Admiral includes Lord Howard of Effingham (1585), the earl of Sandwich (1763) and Winston Churchill (1911). George, earl Jellicoe, the last holder of the office, handed over to the Ministry of Defence, and Elizabeth II assumed the role of Lord High Admiral. Control now rests with the Navy Board, headed by the First Sea Lord who answers to the Minister of Defence.

AESTHETIC MOVEMENT

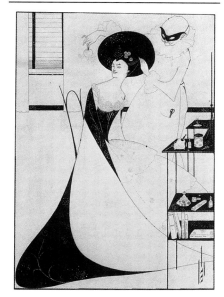

ELEGANT LINES Aubrey Beardsley's drawings captured the decadent spirit of Oscar Wilde's play *Salome*. Both artist and writer were influential in the Aesthetic Movement

In the late 19th century a group of artists and writers set out to shatter Victorian self-righteousness. Proclaiming 'art for art's sake', the Aesthetic Movement rejected the view that art should have a moral or social message, insisting instead on the pure value of beauty and form. Among the leaders were the artists Aubrey BEARDSLEY, Edward BURNE-JONES and James McNeill WHISTLER, and the writer Oscar WILDE.

INSTANT NOTORIETY
The Aesthetes first came to public attention in 1877 with the opening of the Grosvenor Gallery in London, where a painting by Whistler outraged the critic John RUSKIN. He accused the painter of 'flinging a pot of paint in the public's face'. Whistler sued for libel and won token damages of one farthing.

NEW SUBJECTS FOR ART
Aesthetic painters favoured exotic and decorative motifs remote from everyday life, such as peacock feathers and Japanese prints. Maintaining that life should imitate art, they carried the style over into dress and behaviour, becoming a popular target for parody. Despite excesses, the movement helped to change attitudes to art by rejecting the idea that pictures must tell a story and by simplifying aspects of design from interior decoration to women's dress.

Robert ADAM

• **Architect and interior designer** • **1728-92**

A three-year GRAND TOUR through France and Italy left the young Edinburgh architect Robert Adam buzzing with ideas. On his return he set up a London practice to put them into effect. His imaginative approach and the daring with which he mixed the Palladian style of the time with delicate decorative flourishes rapidly won him renown and popularity.

Of all the innovations that Adam brought to architecture, the way that he matched interior to exterior design is his most original contribution.

His vision was all-embracing, extending from the grand scheme of the whole building to the smallest detail. Some of his finest work on country houses can be seen at Kedleston Hall (1758-68), Syon House (1760-9), Harewood House (1761-71) and Kenwood House (1767-8).

During the 1770s Adam completed many town house terraces and adaptations to existing buildings. He also embarked upon the ambitious Adelphi project with his brothers, building houses, warehouses and wharves along the north bank of the Thames – but only narrowly escaped bankruptcy when this speculation failed.

It was destroyed in the 1930s but Adam's late style survives in Charlotte Square (1791) in Edinburgh and the clifftop mock-medieval Culzean Castle (1772-92), with its fine oval staircase and plaster ceilings now restored to their original colouring.

UNIFIED WHOLE From the plasterwork ceiling to the marble floor everything in Syon House reflects Robert Adam's vision and his meticulous attention to detail

Battle of AGINCOURT

• **Near Boulogne, France**   • **October 25, 1415**

The reputation of HENRY V as a fighting king was made with his dramatic victory at the Battle of Agincourt in northern France during the HUNDRED YEARS' WAR. Tired from a 40-day siege of Harfleur and a long march towards the Channel, Henry's men were forced into conflict again when the French army blocked the approach to Calais. Though heavily outnumbered, the English routed the French in a single day's fighting outside the village of Agincourt (now Azincourt). More than 5000 Frenchmen were killed; the English lost only a few hundred.

Heavy plate armour was the undoing of the French, who moved only slowly across the marshy ground. After an initial volley of arrows, Henry sent his archers into the fray with axes, mallets and swords to complete the slaughter.

AGRICULTURAL REVOLUTION

A rapid rise in argricultural productivity went hand in hand with the INDUSTRIAL REVOLUTION. For centuries there had been a slow drift to the towns, but as the city factories prospered they attracted ever greater numbers, creating a large urban workforce that needed to be fed.

Agriculture modernised rapidly to meet the demand and between 1700 and 1830 more capital went into farming than into industry and trade combined.

SCIENCE ON THE MARCH

The revolution occurred on many fronts. Crop rotation was introduced by Thomas COKE and Charles TOWNSHEND and scientific stock breeding was pioneered by Robert BAKEWELL. Mechanical devices such as Jethro TULL's seed drill further boosted output. The Enclosure Acts of the late 18th century reduced the amount of boundary waste, prevented soil erosion and above all gave greater scope for introducing new methods and machinery. Production swelled, and so did the population.

THE PLIGHT OF THE DISPOSSESSED

The changes fed the towns but brought misery to many country folk. Villagers lost their land to the enclosures and their jobs to machines. In areas such as the Scottish HIGHLANDS communities that had scraped a living on marginal land were displaced by more profitable inhabitants – sheep.

But a rapid population increase was also spurring change. By 1850, home production was feeding 6.5 million more people than a century earlier. To keep in step agriculture needed machines.

DASHING PRINCE When Victoria first met her cousin Albert at the age of 17 she thought him 'extremely handsome'. They were married in 1840 at St James's Palace

Prince ALBERT

• **Prince consort 1857**   • **1819-61**

The 19-year-old German Prince Albert Saxe-Coburg-Gotha had been in Britain only five days when his cousin Queen VICTORIA proposed marriage – her royal prerogative. It was the start of a devoted union of mutual benefit that lasted 21 years and produced nine children.

At first Albert was unpopular with the British public, and his interest in the arts, sciences, industry and social welfare set him apart from the Establishment. But his steady judgment soon began to show, as he steered Victoria towards a more constitutional role, leaving the business of government to politicians.

Albert helped to set the tone for his era: moral, dutiful, a doting if demanding father, committed to science and modernisation, he embodied the spirit of the VICTORIAN AGE. Among the projects he championed were the rebuilding of the House of Commons and the profitable GREAT EXHIBITION of 1851.

ALBERT MEMORIAL

• **Central London (p.499 A3)**   • **Built 1863-72**

After the early death of her beloved consort Prince ALBERT, Queen Victoria embarked upon a lengthy mourning. Of the many statues she erected in his memory, the 55 m (180 ft) high Albert Memorial in Kensington Gardens is the most elaborate. Designed by the architect George Gilbert SCOTT, it has a canopy encrusted with Venetian mosaic, glass 'jewels' and gilded statuary.

Around the base are 169 marble reliefs of artists, musicians, writers and allegorical figures representing Agriculture, Manufactures, Commerce and Engineering, and the continents of Europe, Africa, Asia and America.

ALBION

In a scene from *Henry V* William Shakespeare has the Duke of Britaine comment disparagingly on 'that nook-shotten isle of Albion'.

The ancient name for Britain most likely dates from Celtic times. In Gaelic Scotland is called *Alba*. Albion was mentioned in the 4th century BC by Pytheas of Massilia, a Greek navigator. The Romans assumed it came from *albus*, the Latin for white, and referred to the white cliffs of the south-east coast.

In his *Historia Regum Britanniae*, the 12th-century Welsh chronicler GEOFFREY OF MONMOUTH mentions Albion as an early name for Britain. Later writers have perpetuated its use in a poetic context. William BLAKE made Albion a giant personifying the national spirit of Britain. For him the stories of King ARTHUR were 'the acts of Albion, applied to a Prince of the 5th century', a time whose heroism he contrasted with the industrial age in which Britain's old free spirit lay buried in a wasteland of 'dark Satanic mills'.

ALCOCK AND BROWN

- **Aviators**
- **John Alcock; 1892-1919; kt 1919**
- **Arthur Brown; 1886-1948; kt 1919**

In 1919 two ex-war pilots made the first nonstop flight across the Atlantic. Flying a converted First World War bomber, John Alcock and Arthur Brown set off from Newfoundland at 1613 GMT, June 14. Alcock piloted the Vickers Vimy biplane while Brown navigated. After 1890 miles they landed near Clifden on the west coast of Ireland, having achieved an average speed of 115 mph. Extra fuel tanks enabled the plane to make the 16½ hour flight.

Alcock described the crossing as a 'terrible journey' and Brown had to climb out onto the wings to attend to the engines six times. But the achievement brought them instant fame, a £10 000 prize from the *Daily Mail* and a knighthood each.

ALDEBURGH FESTIVAL

- **Suffolk (p.495 K3)**   • **June**

The small resort town of Aldeburgh on the Suffolk coast was a cultural backwater until Benjamin BRITTEN took up residence after the Second World War and established an annual music festival. Most of his subsequent output of operas, cantatas and chamber music were written to be performed there.

The first Aldeburgh Festival was held in 1948 and for 20 years concerts took place in local village halls and churches. In 1967 Britten and his lifelong partner, the tenor Peter PEARS, bought the Maltings, a riverside barn in the nearby village of Snape, which they converted into a concert hall. It burned down on its opening night in 1969 but was rebuilt in time for the following year's festival. Aldeburgh is now an international event and place of pilgrimage for lovers of

HIGH IMPACT 'In sight of land' records Alcock and Brown's logbook (*right*). **A bumpy landing in an Irish bog 25 minutes later at 8.40 am concluded the first nonstop transatlantic flight**

Britten's music, which still predominates, although many other contemporary works have been premiered there. The Maltings also houses the Britten-Pears School of Advanced Musical Studies.

ALEXANDRA PALACE

- **N London (p.498 C2)**
- **Built 1873, rebuilt 1875**

Scarcely had the ornate glass and metal structure of the first Alexandra Palace been erected than it burned down. It was an inauspicious start but the exhibition centre – named after Alexandra, the Princess of Wales, wife of the future Edward VII – was rebuilt almost immediately. A new edifice, this time

in stone, opened in 1875. It contained a concert hall seating 14 000 and one of the world's largest organs. The grounds contained a racecourse and circus.

In 1936 BBC television studios opened at the palace and transmitted the world's first live scheduled broadcasts. The studios closed 20 years later, and in 1980 the building was once again gutted by fire. It was reopened in 1988 and has since been used as an exhibition hall and conference centre.

CAPTIVE AUDIENCE In 1914 the vast concert hall of Alexandra Palace provided shelter for tens of thousands of refugees from war-torn Europe. It later held German prisoners of war

ALFRED THE GREAT

• King of Wessex 871-99   • 849-99

When Alfred supposedly allowed the cakes to burn it was said to be because he was pondering the Danish invasions that were terrorising Wessex. In 878 his musing paid off and the Saxons vanquished the Danes at Edington. By the time he died the whole of southern England was under Alfred's control, and it was through him that the kings of Wessex eventually came to rule all of England, starting with Alfred's grandson, Athelstan, in 925.

KING ALFRED COIN (9TH CENTURY)

Alfred was an educated man and a thinker as well as a military commander. He issued a new code of laws, wrote and translated religious texts, and encouraged the creation of other books. He ordered the rebuilding of the Wessex capital Winchester as well as Oxford, Chichester and Wareham, with streets laid out in an orderly grid-pattern and massive walls to deter the Danes.

ALLOTMENTS

Today's Sunday gardener tending prize leeks on a council allotment may well be cultivating a plot that once kept a family from starving. The enclosure of more than 6 million acres of commonly farmed land during the AGRICULTURAL REVOLUTION of the 18th and 19th centuries created armies of landless poor unable to feed themselves. The Enclosure Act of 1845 sought to provide for them by 'allotting' land to grow food. In 1887 the Allotment Act required every local authority to provide 1000 m² (¼ acre) plots at low rentals.

MODERN TIMES

Mechanisation in the 19th and 20th centuries made food cheaper and self-sufficiency less important – until the Second World War when allotments once again helped to feed the nation. By 1943 1.5 million plots were being cultivated and city-dwellers became enthusiastic market gardeners, helped by advice from the BBC, which ran a 'radio allotment'. It was calculated that a dedicated allotment gardener could produce 66 kg (145 lb) of carrots, 94 kg (208 lb) of potatoes, 17 kg (37 lb) of peas and 270 lettuces a year.

There are now some 300 000 plots on more than 8000 sites throughout the country, most still conforming in size to the standard set out in 1887.

Lawrence ALMA-TADEMA

• Artist   • 1836-1912; kt 1899

Half-naked women, their bodies as smooth and white as the marble columns of the buildings around them, recline on gilded couches, or look down from flower-festooned balconies over the blue Mediterranean. With such opulent scenes Lawrence Alma-Tadema delighted

PRESERVED FOR THE PEOPLE Rich agricultural land around Winchcombe, Gloucestershire, produces bumper crops for allotment holders

his customers – typically hard-working Victorian industrialists. Later his paintings inspired Hollywood cinema epics such as *Ben Hur*.

Tadema was born in Holland and painted medieval scenes until a visit to Naples and Pompeii in 1863 inspired him with a passion for the ancient world. He developed a new style combining archaeological accuracy and a meticulous technique with two key Victorian principles: the pictures told a story and any eroticism was disguised – albeit thinly – in ancient Roman costume.

Alma-Tadema settled in London in 1870 and became both popular and wealthy, remodelling his luxurious house in St Johns Wood as a Roman villa.

After his death his work fell from fashion until a revival in the 1970s. Examples of his pictures can be viewed at Birmingham Museum and Art Gallery, and London's Tate Gallery.

ALMSHOUSES

In the Middle Ages the Church was the main provider for the needy, sheltering the poor in institutions such as the Hospital of St Cross (1136), which still stands in Winchester. But it was in the 17th century, as a new spirit of philanthropy emerged, that almshouses were first constructed in large numbers.

AN AGE OF PATERNALISM

Some were built by businesses for their aged workers; others were supported by private charities, or founded by people such as Henry Lucas, a 17th-century MP and mathematician, whose almshouses in Wokingham, Berkshire, still exist.

Among others still standing are the WREN-designed Trinity Almshouses (1695) in London's Mile End Road, for 'decayed masters and commanders of ships or the widows of such'.

Almshouses for ironmongers were paid for out of the will of Robert Geffrye, a former lord mayor of London – the 1715 building in Kingsland Road is now the Geffrye Museum of interior design.

THE TRADITION CONTINUES

Nearly 30 000 people live in almshouses today and new residences are still being built, financed privately or by charitable trusts. The Durham Mineworkers' Association, for example, has some 100 dwellings with plans for 500 more.

IN CLASSICAL MODE The combination of sensuality and archaeological accuracy in pictures such as *The Unconscious Rivals* (1893) made Alma-Tadema irresistible to Victorian art connoisseurs

ALNWICK CASTLE

• **Northumberland (p.496 B1)**
• **Built 11th-19th century**

A Norman castle built to command the Scottish border, Alnwick (pronounced 'Annick') was a vital stronghold against the Scots in the wars of the 14th century. Since 1309 it has been home to the Percy family, earls and later dukes of Northumberland, who ruled much of northern England. The family has made additions to the castle over the years, strengthening the walls, building a huge barbican to fortify the gatehouse and adding stone figures to the battlements.

Italian architects engaged by the 4th duke of Northumberland in 1854 took 11 years to transform the interior of the castle keep: some panels of the window shutters in the Red Drawing Room took a craftsman a year to carve. The gilded ceiling of the Music Room was inspired by St Peter's in Rome. Visitors to the castle can view Meissen and Sèvres china as well as paintings by Canaletto, Van Dyck and Turner.

ALTON TOWERS

• **Staffordshire (p.495 F2)** • **Built 19th century**

Today it is one of Britain's leading leisure parks, but Alton Towers has at its heart the ruins of a neo-Gothic mansion which, when completed in the mid 19th century, was claimed to be the largest private house in Europe. It was built for the 16th earl of Shrewsbury, and the ground floor covered an area of more than 2.4 ha (6 acres).

It was Charles Talbot, the 15th earl, who in 1814 began to landscape his estate with terraces, lakes, colonnades and gardens, and to embellish them with ornamental buildings, including a Chinese temple and a Swiss cottage. In 1980 a rollercoaster and other rides were built, including a 'Skyride' over the treetops to give visitors a bird's eye view of the park's attractions, old and new.

AMERICAN WAR OF INDEPENDENCE

• **1775-81**

Britain's American colonists would probably have remained peaceful subjects of the Crown had it not been for attempts to milk them for revenue after the financially disastrous Seven Years' War with France. The 1760s saw a battery of taxes imposed on the prosperous New World colonies, which curtailed their autonomy and aroused the indignant protest 'No taxation without representation'.

A tax on tea in 1773 led to the incident known as the Boston Tea Party, when colonists sneaked aboard three British ships, throwing their cargo of 342 chests of tea into Boston Harbour. In April 1775 armed conflict broke out and on July 4, 1776, the rebel provinces issued the Declaration of Independence. They enlisted French naval and military assistance and in 1781 forced a British surrender. Formal terms were agreed under the Treaty of Paris in 1783.

Though politically free, the American states were bankrupt and had to import many goods. Since Britain controlled the seas they had no choice but to resume trade links, replacing the bitterness of war with a pragmatic partnership.

Kingsley and Martin AMIS

• **Writers** • **Kingsley 1922-95; kt 1990**
• **Martin b.1949**

Although father and son, the two Amises could not be more different in their views of British life and manners, and in their novelistic style.

Kingsley cultivated a disenchanted and sometimes reactionary outlook. His satirical novel *Lucky Jim* (1954), about the university lecturer Jim Dixon's hopeless battle against pretension, earned Amis the journalistic badge of Angry Young Man. A stream of further novels combining caustic comedy with serious philosophical concerns confirmed his literary reputation. In 1986 *Old Devils* won him the coveted BOOKER PRIZE.

Satire of a darker and more violent sort characterises Martin Amis's novels of contemporary urban life, such as the bestsellers *Money* (1984) and *London Fields* (1990). He became notorious for the impressive £500 000 advance from Harper Collins for *The Information* (1995). He settled in New York in 1997.

Elizabeth Garrett ANDERSON

• **Doctor** • **1836-1917**

While her sister Millicent Fawcett was campaigning for women's rights through the SUFFRAGETTE movement, Elizabeth Garrett ('Anderson' after her marriage in 1871) was opening up another front. While she was a nursing student at the Middlesex Hospital she studied privately to be a doctor. Despite gaining the highest academic grades she was repeatedly refused permission to take the final qualifying examinations. Eventually her father threatened legal action and in 1865 she was licensed by the Society of Apothecaries, becoming the first woman to qualify as a doctor in Britain.

In 1866 she opened a dispensary for women and children at Marylebone, in London, which became a small hospital. It is now part of University College, still occupying the premises on Euston Road to which it was moved in 1888.

ANGLESEY

- **N Wales (p.494 C1)**   • **Area 276 sq miles**
- **Pop. 67 000**

The once-sacred Celtic stronghold of Anglesey (*Yns Môn* in Welsh, meaning 'end island') was the site of a fierce but doomed stand by the DRUIDS against the Romans in the 1st century AD.

The island is a focus for Celtic and Welsh cultural traditions and a popular venue for EISTEDDFODS. Over the years Anglesey's many prehistoric sites have generated countless myths and legends. One story says that Maen Pres (meaning 'brass stone'), in the north of the island, will reward anyone who can read its inscription (actually, natural crevices in the rock) by revealing a pot of gold.

> A tiny Anglesey village has one of the world's longest place names: *Llanfairpwllgwyngyllgogerych-wyrndrobwllllantysiliogogogoch*, which means 'St Mary's Church in the hollow of white hazel near a rapid whirlpool and the Church of St Tysilio near the red cave'

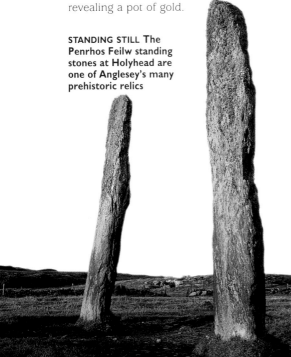

STANDING STILL The Penrhos Feilw standing stones at Holyhead are one of Anglesey's many prehistoric relics

A WOMAN'S PLACE Elizabeth Garrett Anderson faces the panel that finally qualified her as Britain's first woman doctor. She also became England's first woman mayor in 1908

ANGLICAN COMMUNION

One of the legacies of the British Empire is the presence today of 70 million Anglicans around the world. The 36 self-governing Churches of the Anglican Communion are spread across 500 dioceses in 164 countries.

Within broad adherence to the doctrines of the CHURCH OF ENGLAND, the Churches uphold the faith as set out in the Book of Common Prayer. Yet practices differ widely: by 1992, when the Church of England voted to permit the ordination of women, there were already at least 1400 women priests in other member Churches.

About 3000 people are added to the membership each day through baptism or conversion. The fastest growth is in the Southern Hemisphere.

ANGLING: *see opposite page*

ANGLO-CATHOLICISM

About a third of CHURCH OF ENGLAND members belong to Anglo-Catholic or 'High' Churches. Anglo-Catholics are Anglicans who either aspire to the reunification of the Church of England with the Roman Catholic Church, or who want to revitalise the Catholic aspects of its doctrine and practice. The form and ritual, such as the burning of incense, used in Anglo-Catholic services are essentially Catholic.

Anglo-Catholicism resulted from the OXFORD MOVEMENT, established in the 1830s by Oxford University theologians, including John Henry NEWMAN and John Keble. They viewed Protestantism as tainted with innovation and looked back to the period of Church history before the great splits of the Reformation.

ANGLO-SAXON CHRONICLE

- **c.890-1154**

Seven manuscripts compiled at different monasteries make up the *Anglo-Saxon Chronicle*, our main source of information on ALFRED THE GREAT and other ANGLO-SAXON kings. Unlike earlier ecclesiastical records, such as BEDE's 8th-century chronologies, the records are written not in Latin but Old English.

The *Chronicle* describes the Anglo-Saxon invasions, battles, Viking raids and the Norman Conquest, mingling events with verses and anecdotes on subjects ranging from Roman ruins to comets and miracles. Only one manuscript, the 'Worcester Chronicle', is on public display – at the British Library.

HOOK, LINE AND SINKER

**Though carbon-fibre rods and monofilament line have replaced
the hazel rods and white horse's tail of 200 years ago, the fundamentals
of fishing have changed little, and the sport's quiet pleasures
still reel in millions of enthusiasts every year**

WADDINGTON

BLUE CHARM

FURNACE DAPPING

PRAWN FLY

TUP'S INDISPENSABLE

GREEN HIGHLANDER

N *The Compleat Angler,* Izaac WALTON made an observation: 'Angling may be said to be so like the mathematics, that it can never be fully learnt.' His book, written in 1653, was the first fishing manual, and his comment remains as pertinent today as it ever was. It also perhaps explains the enduring popularity of a sport that attracts more than 3 million devotees in Britain and is one of the fastest-growing leisure pursuits.

Anglers fall into two schools: the canal-side enthusiast, or coarse fisherman, with his tub of maggots; and the fly-fisher, often spotted in the Highlands with a box of colourful, hand-tied lures. Both sports require a licence from the National Rivers Authority, which uses the money to maintain waterways. Open seasons for coarse or fly fishing depend on where you fish.

WITH BAITED HOOK

Practitioners of coarse fishing can be seen lining canals, lakes and ponds trying to capture still-water fish such as bream, roach, perch, carp, barbel and pike with baited hooks. Their devotion is obvious as they huddle under green umbrellas in the pouring rain, waiting for the tell-tale bobbing of a float or the tugging of the line through a ledger weight that indicates a bite. The fish is hauled in (sometimes after a considerable struggle), weighed, sometimes photographed (as irrefutable evidence) and then usually returned to the water.

Bait is big business, sold in packets and mixes and produced in seething tons in heat-controlled fly houses as the familiar maggot, or 'gentle'. Other snares include cheese, sweetcorn and luncheon meat.

TRICKING THE FISH WITH A FLICK OF THE WRIST

Fly-fishing is considered by many anglers to be the ultimate test of skill, requiring them to 'play' a fly across the surface of the water, or beneath the surface, to imitate an insect's movements. Their accomplices are Hairy Mary, Devon Dumpling, Chomper and a host of other bizarre and exotic lures designed to mimic the nymphs, mayflies and dragonflies of the fishes' natural diet. The aim of all the effort, practice and skill is to catch game fish (mainly salmon or trout), which, unlike most coarse fish, are delicacies for the table.

Salmon are migratory, spending most of their adult life at sea before returning to the river of their birth to breed. In their struggle to reach the spawning grounds they swim against rapids and waterfalls, leaping as high as 3 m (10 ft). It is during this time that they are at their best for sport, attracting thousands of anglers to rivers such as the Wye, Tweed, Tay, Spey and Dee.

Britain's native brown trout thrives in chalk streams such as the River Test and River Itchen in Hampshire – some of the finest, and most expensive, fishing in England. North American rainbow trout are stocked for sport in still-water reservoirs, but they are discouraged from entering streams and high lakes where they would create competition for the indigenous brown trout.

FLY TYING Nimble-fingered fly-fishers make lures out of tinsel, feathers, wool and hair. Their colourful creations are miniature works of art

WAITING GAME Whether casting a fly gently and accurately into water where fish are rising, or steadily bringing them to the landing net, angling requires both patience and skill

FOUNDERS OF ENGLAND

The Germanic tribes who colonised Britain from the 5th century were subsistence farmers, at home in wooden huts. Yet they bequeathed the nation its language, its first kings, some of its most exquisite jewellery and a new identity

WHEN THE last of the Roman legions left Britain's shores around AD 410, native rulers faced a new threat from Germanic tribes – Angles from southern Denmark, Saxons from the German coast and Jutes from Jutland, known collectively as Anglo-Saxons or sometimes just Saxons. Some came as raiders, others were invited as mercenaries by Roman-British warlords; all stayed on as settlers.

The dynamic pagan culture of the newcomers increasingly set them at odds with their Celtic and Christian hosts. Violence broke out in 456, when Saxon troops led by the semi-legendary brothers Hengist and Horsa seized control of Kent. Other battles followed and Anglo-Saxon influence expanded

steadily. By the 7th century seven kingdoms had emerged, controlling most of lowland Britain, and each in constant conflict with its neighbours. At times a king would claim sovereignty over all England, but it was not until the late 9th century that ALFRED, king of Wessex, eventually united the Saxon kingdoms.

HOW THE SAXONS LIVED

Saxon culture was very different from that of the Romans who preceded them. The Saxons were a rural people, who built in wood rather than stone – some thought the stone ruins the Romans left behind were the work of giants – and few Saxon buildings have been left standing. But in some ways they did more to

shape the face of the country, for it was the Saxon farmstead that laid the foundations of the English village.

BACK TO TOWN

Early Anglo-Saxon kings were warlords who typically had no single local power base but spent their time travelling with their courts between their many halls. But as the kingdoms became consolidated and established, old towns were revived. London, which had become a derelict community with the end of Roman rule, saw a busy

THE GREAT HALL Anglo-Saxon warlords, who ruled areas about the size of a modern-day county, held meetings and feasts with their warriors in aisled halls up to 25 m (80 ft) long, surrounded by trophies of their conquests – and perhaps toasted like the hero of the 8th-century epic poem *Beowulf*

PLOUGHING AND SOWING Pictures from an 11th-century Saxon calendar record the farming year. Narrow strips of land were allocated to individuals to cultivate barley, rye and wheat. In January, fields were ploughed with the help of oxen (*right*). The harvest at the end of summer was a communal activity

ESSENTIAL WOODLAND Most of Saxon England was wooded and managed as a valuable source of timber, fuel and fruit. The Saxon calendar shows men cutting wood in February (*left*)

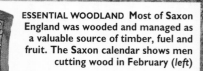

FAMILY HUT Buildings were generally made of timber, often with a planked floor over a storage pit or cellar. A central hearth, left to smoulder night and day, provided heat and light. In the absence of a chimney, the smoke seeped out slowly under the eaves or through the thatched roof

port develop around Covent Garden in the 7th century, and by Alfred's reign Winchester was effectively the capital of Wessex.

The need for protection from Viking raiders – a continual menace from the late 8th century – turned other places into towns. Exeter, Southampton and Warwick all started as walled townships, or 'burhs', built as much for refuge from the marauders as for administrative purposes.

THE INHERITANCE OF THE SAXONS

Saxon rule came to an end in 1066, but although the Norman invaders almost completely replaced the Saxon aristocracy many features of the old culture continued to shape life and attitudes in Britain. Shires and parishes, even parliament itself, all had Anglo-Saxon origins, while the expressive Germanic Anglo-Saxon tongue triumphed over Norman-French to become the dominant influence in the development of the ENGLISH LANGUAGE.

FIT FOR A KING

The prestige of a Saxon king rested on the splendour of his court as much as the heroism of his warriors. Lords wore fine mantles and robes; craftsmen came from far afield to fashion their prized jewellery.

HORN MOUNT *Kings drank from cattle horns decorated with silver mounts*

GILT SILVER *A bird adorns a finely cast cloak pin* (right)

SWORD POMMEL *Weapons often had exquisite ornamental fittings* (left) *wrought in silver and black inlay* (niello)

SILVER BUCKLE *Parade dress often displayed the art of cloisonné* (right), *in which coloured garnets are set in silver tracery*

ANGLO-SAXON HISTORY

c.450-c.600 First settlers arrive and begin to form small kingdoms

c.600 England is effectively divided into seven major kingdoms

c.630 The kingdom of East Anglia dominates Essex, including London

c.630-c.685 Northumbria extends its kingdom as far as the Firth of Forth

c.700-c.800 Rise of Mercia; King Offa rules over southern Britain (757-96)

800-99 Series of Danish invasions. Alfred the Great rules Wessex (871-99) and recovers Anglo-Saxon land

c.900-c.1000 Danes settle in north-east, Midlands and eastern England

c.1000-66 Anglo-Saxons and Danes vie for power until the Norman Conquest

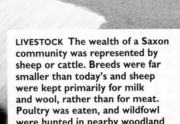

LIVESTOCK The wealth of a Saxon community was represented by sheep or cattle. Breeds were far smaller than today's and sheep were kept primarily for milk and wool, rather than for meat. Poultry was eaten, and wildfowl were hunted in nearby woodland

THE SAXON FARMSTEAD Rimmed by boundary ditches or fencing, early Saxon settlements were generally small, consisting of a few households and their slaves. Lords or thanes lived in large halls; churls, or free peasants, lived in smaller homes. The churls gave service to the thane by working in his fields and giving him a share of their crops. In return they were granted small plots of land.

Before the growth of trade and coinage, such communities were self-sufficient, producing their own food, weaving cloth, making pottery and fashioning tools and utensils in wood, iron or bone

LOCAL TRADE Roman roads, which linked long-deserted towns, were abandoned in favour of cross-country warpaths and unmade tracks. Traders and craftsmen, most of whom were itinerant, might be attracted to visit a settlement by the presence of a powerful magnate

BRITAIN IN THE MAKING (*map right*) In the two decades before Alfred the Great's reign from Wessex, the seven major Anglo-Saxon kingdoms still determined regional divisions in England, while Celts held fast in Cornwall, Wales and most of Scotland

ANGLO-SAXON KINGDOMS c.860

✝ Church
◆ Tower
◆ Archaeological find

CELTS

Monkwearmouth
Escomb
NORTHUMBRIA
Kirk Hammerton

Barton-upon-Humber
Stow
Barnack

Offa's Dyke
MERCIA
Brixworth
Earl's Barton
Great Paxton
EAST ANGLIA
Deerhurst
Wing
Sutton Hoo
ESSEX
Greensted
Bradwell
Bradford-upon-Avon
KENT
WESSEX
Breamore
Bosham
SUSSEX
Sompting

CELTS

ANNE

• Queen 1702-14 • 1665-1714

The Protestant daughter of Catholic JAMES II, who supported her brother-in-law WILLIAM III when he invaded England, Anne was the last Stuart sovereign. Her reign was marked by the Act of Union between England and Scotland in 1707 and military triumphs abroad under armies led by the 1st duke of MARLBOROUGH. Literature also flourished in the so-called AUGUSTAN AGE with writers such as Alexander Pope and Jonathan Swift.

Anne's private life was less fortunate. At 18 she married the young Prince George of Denmark. It was a happy match but the queen was dogged by poor health, contracting gout and becoming obese after 17 pregnancies. Her only child to survive infancy died aged 11 and at Anne's death, the throne passed to George I, elector, or ruler, of HANOVER and great-grandson of James I.

> Anne was the last British monarch to veto an Act of Parliament, the 1707 Militia Act, which would have given Scottish troops the same rights as English soldiers

ANTONINE WALL

• Central Scotland (p.497 C4)
• Built 2nd century AD

Just two decades after HADRIAN'S WALL was built to divide ROMAN BRITAIN from unconquered Scotland, emperor Hadrian's successor Antonius Pius attempted to push the boundary of the Roman Empire 70 miles northwards. He ordered the building of a new defensive barrier stretching from the Firth of Forth to the Clyde – the Antonine Wall.

Defending the 37 mile mound of turf were a deep ditch and a series of about 19 forts, but even so the wall proved impossible to secure. It is thought to have been abandoned around AD 190, when the legions retreated to Hadrian's Wall.

Most of the course of the ditch and parts of the wall itself can still be seen. **MAIN SITES • Fort and wall at Rough Castle • Bathhouse at Bearsden**

APPEASEMENT

In September 1938, Britain's prime minister Neville CHAMBERLAIN returned from meeting the German Chancellor Adolf Hitler in Munich to proclaim 'peace in our time...peace with honour'. He had just agreed to Hitler's annexation of the German-speaking Sudetenland – part of Czechoslovakia and the latest target of Nazi imperialism.

Appeasement originated as a way of compensating Germany economically for the vindictive terms of the Treaty of Versailles at the end of the First World War. Sceptics warned against the policy, arguing that it would only encourage Hitler's territorial demands in the Rhineland and later Austria, but most people – desperate to avoid another war – supported it. Appeasement ended in 1939 with the German seizure of the remainder of Czechoslovakia.

APPLEBY

• Cumbria (p.496 B3)

Every June hundreds of gypsies, farmers and tourists converge on Appleby-in-Westmorland for its horse fair – a highlight of the Romany gypsy calendar since the fair received its charter from James II in 1685. Deals are clinched between buyer and seller with a traditional slap of palms.

Other attractions include a Norman keep, the fine Moot Hall from 1596, the almshouses of St Anne's Hospital and the church of St Lawrence, which houses Britain's oldest organ, built in the 1500s.

Ron ARAD

• Furniture and interior designer • b.1951

Since he made his name in the early 1980s with raw concrete furniture and 'creative salvage' chairs and tables contrived from scaffolding poles and old car seats, Ron Arad has become one of Britain's best-known contemporary designers. Creations in stainless and raw steel have served as props in fashion shoots, pop videos and advertisements for Pernod. Limited edition pieces command five-figure bids from museums at auction; the Victoria and Albert Museum has several examples.

ARBOR LOW

• Prehistoric site
• Derbyshire (p.495 F1) • EH

The so-called 'Stonehenge of the North' stands on a windswept plateau with panoramic views over Middleton Moor. A prehistoric lead-mining community erected the stone circle in about 2000-1600 BC, and the site's importance is reflected in its vast size. The 60 huge slabs of local limestone lie prostrate on emerald grass surrounded by a ditched bank of earth 76 m (250 ft) in diameter and 4.5 m (15 ft) high in places.

Archaeologists believe that Arbor Low had a religious or ceremonial purpose, a theory supported by the presence of a burial mound built into the bank and by the existence of other barrows nearby.

HORSE-TRADING Dealers and gypsies in colourful caravans gather for a week of robust bargaining at Appleby-in-Westmorland's fair

Richard ARKWRIGHT

• Inventor and industrialist • 1732-92; kt 1786

Today Richard Arkwright is remembered as the inventor of the first successful cotton-spinning machine, which helped to establish the TEXTILE INDUSTRY of the early Industrial Revolution, but in his day he was esteemed particularly for his business achievements.

In 1769, while working as a barber and wigmaker, Arkwright patented a machine that could for the first time spin cotton thread strong and tenuous enough to be used as warp (the vertical threads in woven cloth). In 1771 he established a mill with water-powered spinning machines at Cromford, Derbyshire, where he produced the first cloth made entirely of cotton. But Arkwright's real talent lay in perfecting others' inventions and in manufacturing. He went on to set up cotton mills across Britain, pioneering large-scale production in factories whose conditions were exemplary for the times.

Machinery designed by Arkwright, including a water-powered spinning machine, can be seen at the Helmshore Textile Museum in Lancashire.

ARMISTICE DAY

The horror of the First World War finally ceased with an armistice that came into force on the 11th hour of the 11th day of the 11th month of 1918. November 11 subsequently became known as Armistice Day, marked with 2 minutes' silence at 11 a.m. to honour those who fell in Europe's bloodiest war.

After the Second World War commemorations for the dead of both wars were moved to Remembrance Sunday, the nearest Sunday to Armistice Day. A 2 minute silence is observed at the formal remembrance ceremony when veterans march past the Cenotaph in London, but the one on Armistice Day itself has generally fallen away despite an attempt to revive it in 1996. The poppies laid as wreaths and sold in aid of forces' charities are a reminder of the blood-red flowers that dotted the fields of Flanders, where so many soldiers met their deaths in the First World War.

The ARCHERS

In the 'austerity' years after the Second World War, when Britain was still living with rationing, the Labour government recruited the BBC to encourage farmers to grow more food. Godfrey Baseley, a Birmingham radio producer, had the idea of a drama series to deliver the propaganda message. Set in the Midlands 'Borsetshire' village of Ambridge, it told the story of a farming family, the Archers, and their neighbours.

The first episode was broadcast on January 1, 1951; more than 12 000 episodes later, *The Archers* is Britain's longest-running soap opera and the world's longest-running radio drama. The series lost its educational role in the 1970s but has continued to tackle topical issues such as organic farming and fox-hunting. Some 4 million people each week tune in to worry about the feckless Grundys, lap up the gossip at The Bull and despair over the doomed relationships of the younger Archers.

VOICE OF RURAL ENGLAND As Dan and Doris Archer, Harry Oakes and Gwen Berryman brought country concerns into homes across the nation

IN SELF-DEFENCE

**Arms and armour developed in tandem, each
vying for supremacy as better weapons necessitated better
body protection. Armour reached its heyday in the 1500s
but the use of guns prompted its decline**

PROTECTING THE HEAD

The helmet, developed in ancient Greece
and Rome, was the first full metal piece
of armour. Its form changed in response
to the weapons of each successive age;
when a knight faced arrows, lances and
swords, and armour was at its medieval
peak, a visor was attached to protect the
entire face. Armour declined but the
helmet lived on and survives to
the present day.

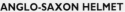

ANGLO-SAXON HELMET
*The iron helmet discovered
at Sutton Hoo resembles
those of the late Roman
period. For added
protection, it has a face
mask, neck guard and
cheek pieces*

THE GREAT HELM
*From the end of the
12th century, the
cylindrical great helm
protected the entire
head and was worn
in battle over a mail
hood and padded
arming cap. It was
still used for
jousting in the
15th century*

BASINET
*With its hinged visor
and round or pointed
apex to deflect
glancing blows, the
close-fitting basinet
was preferred in battle
from the late 13th century*

LOBSTER-TAIL HELMET
*When Cromwell formed his
New Model Army in 1645,
heavy armour had been
abandoned and a
more open style
of helmet was
adopted by
members of
the light
cavalry*

THE INVADING ROMANS and
after them the Normans
influenced British fighting
fashions. The Romans bequeathed
a style of helmet that protected
the face and neck, and also
invented the chain mail shirt
or 'hauberk' made of
interlocking iron rings.
Chain mail, developed by
the Normans, became the
most common medieval fighting
attire, worn with a padded tunic
or 'gambeson' underneath for
additional protection.

From the mid 1200s plates of metal
were added at vulnerable points such as
elbows and knees and extended until, by
the mid 15th century, the whole body
was encased. The metal plates defended
the wearer against arrows and lances
and were curved so that blows
glanced off them.

THE ART OF ARMOUR
Armouries developed throughout
medieval Europe and the
armourer's skill grew into a highly
developed art. Designs became
more elaborate as armour came to
be seen as a mark of social standing.
Rich English knights, influenced by their
European counterparts during the
Crusades, obtained custom-made suits
from the finest workshops of southern
Germany and northern Italy. Heraldic
devices were introduced in the 12th
century to distinguish one knight from
another, and displayed on shields,
helmets and 'ailettes' (shoulder pieces).

At around 20 kg (44 lb) in weight,
fighting armour was uncomfortable
and unwieldy. Even heavier suits
were developed for use in the jousts and
tournaments that became widely popular
in the 15th and 16th centuries.

The best English armour was made in
the reign of Henry VIII, who established
workshops at Greenwich; some of the
king's armour is on show in the TOWER
OF LONDON but the finest collection can
be seen at the Royal Armouries Museum
in Leeds. By the 1600s the use of armour

**GOLD PLATE This suit of late English armour,
gilt against a peacock-blue background, was
designed for show rather than battle. It was
made for the duke of Brunswick in about 1612
at the Royal Armoury at Greenwich**

was declining. Although fine armour
remained a symbol of prestige, it became
obsolete in battle as the use of cannon
and smaller firearms grew, and a new age
of war waged by trained armies dawned.

Thomas and Matthew ARNOLD

- **Thomas; educationalist; 1795-1842**
- **Matthew; poet and critic; 1822-88**

The culture of Britain's PUBLIC SCHOOLS was largely the creation of Dr Thomas Arnold. He became headmaster of Rugby in 1828 and immediately set about reforming the school. Steadfast ('muscular') Christianity and strength of character were his ambition for every boy. He rounded out the classical curriculum with modern languages, mathematics and science, and initiated the prefect system to give boys a say in running the school. Pupils revered him; one of them – Thomas Hughes – later portrayed him as the headmaster in his 1857 novel *Tom Brown's Schooldays*.

The poet Matthew Arnold was Thomas Arnold's eldest son and, like his father, a reformer and liberal. He was an inspector of schools by profession but made his name with poems such as 'The Scholar-Gipsy' (1853) and 'Dover Beach' (1867). In later years Arnold turned mainly to prose, taking English society to task for complacency and narrowness, and arguing in essays such as those of *Culture and Anarchy* (1869) for a broader outlook on the world.

ARRAN

- **North Ayrshire (p.497 B5)**
- **Area 200 sq miles • Pop. 4470**

The largest of the islands in the Firth of Clyde, south-west of Glasgow, Arran is often called 'Scotland in miniature' for its varied landscape of glens, rocks, mountains and lochs. Its rugged peaks rise to 873m (2866ft) at Goat Fell. The island's largest settlement is the port of Brodick, on the east coast.

ARSENAL

- **Founded 1886**

'The Gunners', as Arsenal fans call their football team, was founded by workers at the Royal Arsenal in Woolwich. It is the only team in England to have played in the First Division or Premier League continuously since the First World War.

The club moved to Highbury, north London, in 1913, since when it has won the League Championship ten times – a record exceeded only by LIVERPOOL FC. Five of those triumphs came in Arsenal's 1930s prime.

Until recently, Arsenal was frequently accused of being 'boring' and their victories dismissed as uninspired. But in 1997-8, under French manager Arsène Wenger, with new Continental players and English stalwarts such as Tony Adams and David Seaman, they became exciting again, repeating their League and FA Cup 'double' of 1970-1.

King ARTHUR

Experts agree that a historical Arthur almost certainly did exist – not a king but a warlord who led the Britons against Saxon invaders in about 490.

The first written reference to Arthur appears in 6th-century chronicles. The longer legends of adventure and romance do not appear until the 12th century *Historia Regum Britanniae* in Latin by GEOFFREY OF MONMOUTH – the basis for English and French versions by Layamon and Wace. Chrétien de Troyes then wrote five Arthurian romances (1170-90) that brought the tales huge popularity in France and introduced new Christian and chivalric elements. Chrétien's work also inspired the English poet Thomas MALORY, whose *Le Morte d'Arthur*, completed in 1470, has since been the basis of numerous retellings, from Alfred, Lord TENNYSON's series of poems *The Idylls of the King* (1859-85) to T.H. White's classic children's novel *The Sword in the Stone* (1937).

ON THE ARTHUR TRAIL

There are many sites associated with Arthurian legend. TINTAGEL in Cornwall is the king's traditional birthplace, and GLASTONBURY has been identified with AVALON, his final resting place, since the 12th century.

Caerleon, Winchester and Cadbury Castle have all laid claim to being the site of Camelot and local legend maintains that Arthur's father, Uther Pendragon, died at Pendragon Castle at Mallerstang in Cumbria.

HIGH ROMANCE By the time of the 15th-century *Roman de la Tristan* (below) Arthur and his knights had become models of chivalry and Christian virtue

KING ARTHUR A long way from his pagan warrior original, Arthur, the great and good king, dispenses wisdom at court. Around him are Guinevere and his knights

THE EPITOME OF CHIVALRY Galahad, the pure and perfect knight, who sought and found the Holy Grail, is armed with his sword

KNIGHT AND HIS LADY Lancelot's folly – falling in love with Guinevere – caused his downfall and destroyed the fellowship of the Round Table

THE HOLY GRAIL As Galahad takes his seat at the Round Table, the Holy Grail, the chalice used by Christ at the Last Supper, appears

ARTS AND CRAFTS

'Art made by the people, and for the people' was William MORRIS's ideal in establishing one of Britain's most influential aesthetic movements. Inspired by the teachings of the critic John RUSKIN and the architect Augustus Welby PUGIN, the Arts and Crafts Movement grew out of disillusionment with mechanisation, and the dehumanising effect of mass production and distaste for the lack of simplicity and honesty in 19th-century style. The aim was to re-establish the role and dignity of the artisan by emphasising the craftsmanship involved in art, design and architecture. For Morris, the key to good design was simplicity, exemplified by the Red House, built for him in Kent by architect Philip Webb, or later, by Charles Voysey's modest country houses.

The movement's impact spawned schools, guilds and societies across Europe, influenced the GARDEN CITY movement and paved the way for Art Nouveau. Even so, it failed to overcome the central contradiction that its objects were too expensive for the workers for whom they were intended.
MAIN COLLECTIONS • Victoria and Albert Museum, London • Kelmscott Manor, Oxfordshire • Ruskin Galleries, Sheffield

SHOWPIECE Charles Ashbee designed this inlaid writing cabinet in mahogany and holly for the 1899 Arts and Crafts Exhibition

ARTS COUNCILS

The 18th-century lexicographer, writer and critic Samuel Johnson derided the arts patron as 'a wretch who supports with insolence and is paid with flattery'. Modern-day patronage remains a sometimes thankless business.

Britain's first arts council was created by the economist John Maynard Keynes in 1945. The fine arts were the main recipients until the chairmanship of Lord Goodman (1965-72) when the focus shifted to more popular culture. In 1994

the national body became four regional councils for England, Scotland, Wales and Northern Ireland; they had the invidious task of awarding government grants of almost £240 million in 1998-9, and £200 million in NATIONAL LOTTERY funds to causes ranging from the Royal Opera to brass bands and village halls.

Awards for projects such as Anthony Gormley's 20 m (65 ft) statue *The Angel of the North*, or the record £2 million grant for a screen version of George Eliot's *Daniel Deronda* have aroused passionate public debate.

ARUNDEL CASTLE

• **West Sussex (p.495 G6)**
• **Norman foundations, rebuilt 19th century**

Romantics claim that Arundel's name comes from the French word *hirondelle*, (swallow), though it probably means 'the dell by the Arun'. Its castle, looming high above the town, has battlemented towers and gables giving it an air of medieval grandeur. But only the shell of the circular stone keep and a gateway survive from the stronghold built for Roger of Montgomery, William the Conqueror's powerful cousin.

In the mid 1500s Arundel passed into the hands of Thomas Howard, 4th duke of Norfolk; the Norfolks, England's leading Catholic family, have kept it ever since. Cromwell's forces destroyed it during the Civil War but it was rebuilt in the early 19th century. Its present look owes much to the 15th duke, who added baronial apartments in the 1880s.

Suits of armour, clocks, furniture and tapestries are displayed at the castle together with paintings by Canaletto, Gainsborough, Reynolds and Van Dyck.

ASCOT

• **Berkshire (p.495 G5)** • **Pop. 7540**
Nearly 300 years after Queen Anne founded a racecourse at this country town, the Royal Ascot HORSE RACING meeting, held over four days each June, is still one of the major occasions in the English sporting and social calendar. Its highlight is the 2½ mile Gold Cup, run annually since 1807. But the meeting,

traditionally attended by members of the royal family, is at least as well known for the extravagant fashions worn by spectators. Lavish headgear is a hallmark of Ladies' Day, the third day of the meet.

ASHES

• **Est. 1883**
The symbolic prize of TEST series between the CRICKET teams of England and Australia was set up after the visiting Australian team beat England for the first time in 1882. The *Sporting Times* posted a mock obituary notice for English cricket, announcing that, 'The body will be cremated and the ashes taken to Australia'. The following year, when the English team won a series in Australia, the captain was presented with an urn containing the ashes of burnt bails. Though Australia has won 'the Ashes' back many times, the trophy itself is kept at the MCC museum at LORD'S cricket ground in London.

Laura ASHLEY

• **Fashion and interior designer** • **1925-85**
The ruffled smocks and flower-sprigged prints that made Laura Ashley a high-street name had a beginning as homely as the dream they sold. In the early 1950s, Welsh-born Laura and her husband Bernard started making printed scarves and tea towels on their kitchen table in London.

They moved the business to rural Wales in 1961 and extended their range to flowing, floral garments in keeping with the 'flower power' mood of the time. The first shop opened in London in 1968, initiating a fashion empire which by Ashley's death extended to 220 stores in at least a dozen countries.

ASHMOLEAN MUSEUM

• **Oxford (p.495 F4)** • **Founded 1683**
Oxford University's art and archaeology museum began as a collection of 'curiosities' donated in 1677 by the antiquary Elias Ashmole, who had been left many of them by the TRADESCANT family. To house the pieces the university built Britain's first public museum, but with new acquisitions it became too small and the Old Ashmolean – now the

ETERNALLY ELEGANT
Refinement and lyricism defined the Ashton style – as the master at 65 could still demonstrate

Museum of the History of Science – was abandoned in 1845 for a new building designed by Charles Robert Cockerell. Exhibits include classical sculpture, drawings by Michelangelo and Raphael, Chinese porcelain, Egyptian artefacts, Saxon treasures, including the 'Alfred Jewel', and Pre-Raphaelite paintings.

Frederick ASHTON

• **Ballet dancer and choreographer**
• **1904-88; kt 1962**

British BALLET probably owes more to Frederick Ashton than to any other choreographer. *A Tragedy of Fashion* – created when he was just 21 – helped to found the Ballet Rambert. Five years later it was two Ashton ballets to music by British composers (*Façade* by William Walton and *Job* by Ralph Vaughan Williams) that established a distinct identity and lyrical style for the new Sadler's Wells Ballet (now the Royal Ballet). Ashton remained with the company for most of his long working life, first as resident choreographer and then as artistic director (1963-70).

Long after achieving world recognition as a choreographer he remained a working dancer, never losing touch with the physical craft. He disliked revivals but poured energy into new creations, saying 'Making a new ballet is like a love affair. Reviving one is too cold and calculated.'

Ashton choreographed more than 30 ballets, four operas and two films, which varied widely in style from the abstract plotlessness of *Symphonic Variations* (1946), developed for Margot FONTEYN, to the realism of *A Month in the Country* (1976), his last work. The choreography endures; his *Romeo and Juliet* (1955), *La fille mal gardée* (1960) and *The Tales of Beatrix Potter* (1971) are seldom out of the Royal Ballet's programme.

Herbert ASQUITH

• **Prime minister 1908-16**
• **1852-1928; earl 1925**

The last prime minister to preside over an exclusively Liberal government, Herbert Asquith led a radical reforming administration but lived to see his party replaced by Labour as the main alternative to the Conservatives. As chancellor in the government of Henry Campbell-Bannerman, Asquith pushed through a 'supertax' on incomes above £5000 and introduced noncontributory old age pensions. As prime minister he resisted votes for women, but introduced national insurance and curtailed the power of the House of Lords.

His most controversial policy, home rule for Ireland, was shelved with the outbreak of war in 1914. Faced with increasing Liberal discontent at his handling of the war, Asquith entered a coalition with the Conservatives and Labour in 1915, which further divided his own party. He resigned from office in December 1916 but remained leader of the dwindling Liberal party until 1926.

Nancy ASTOR

• **Politician 1919-45** • **1879-1964; visc. 1919**

The American-born wife of the newspaper proprietor and politician Waldorf Astor was the first woman to take her seat as an MP in the House of Commons. There her persistence contributed to the reform of the divorce law and the lowering of the voting age for women from 30 to 21.

But it was while entertaining at the Astor family home, CLIVEDEN, that she is said to have exercised most influence on government policy. Visitors included the prime minister, Neville Chamberlain, and other supporters of APPEASEMENT towards Nazi Germany. When war was declared in 1939, Lady Astor overcame her personal dislike of Winston Churchill to support his leadership.

FAMILY SEAT Vigorous campaigning won Plymouth for Nancy Astor after her husband resigned it to join the Lords

TALKING TACTICS Michael Atherton (*centre*), making his 1993 debut as England captain against Australia, briefs Graham Thorpe

ASTRONOMER ROYAL

When Charles II founded an observatory at Greenwich in 1676, he appointed John Flamsteed as the first ever Astronomer Royal and commissioned him to map the sky in unprecedented detail to help sailors to navigate at sea.

Flamsteed created the first great star map of the telescopic age, published in full six years after his death in 1725, by which time Edmund HALLEY had succeeded him in the post.

Astronomers royal were all directors of the Royal Greenwich Observatory until the 1940s, when the observatory moved away from Greenwich. The title is now honorary. A separate title, Astronomer Royal for Scotland, is held by the director of the Royal Observatory, Edinburgh.

ATHENAEUM

• Central London (p.499 C7) • Founded 1824

Established by John Crocker, a Secretary to the Admiralty, 'to unite persons of distinction in science, literature, the arts and the public services', the Athenaeum, situated on Waterloo Place, quickly became the most intellectually distinguished of all the gentlemen's clubs, and is still renowned for its outstanding library. Rudyard Kipling, an early member, described the studious atmosphere as like 'a cathedral between services'. Charles Darwin and Michael Faraday, the club's first secretary, were members.

Michael ATHERTON

• Cricketer   • b.1968; MBE 1997

In an era when leading the national cricket team became a dubious honour, Michael Atherton proved himself England's most resilient sportsman.

Although regarded as the most dependable of opening batsmen and a disciplined accumulator of runs, he was criticised, as England captain from 1993 to 1998, for the stubbornness that made him such an effective player. These qualities were demonstrated in a historic match against South Africa in 1996, when Atherton batted for two days, saving an apparently hopeless situation. The following year, with English cricket at one of its lowest ebbs, he led his country in a Test for a record 42nd time.

Richard and David ATTENBOROUGH

• Richard Attenborough; actor, producer and director; b.1923; CBE 1967; kt 1976; bn 1993
• David Attenborough; broadcaster and naturalist; b.1926; CBE 1974; kt 1985

Each half-century career would be remarkable on its own, but together the Attenborough brothers have clocked up an astonishing record in British film and television. Richard has worked on more than 50 films. His acting debut came in 1942 in *In Which We Serve*. From the 1960s he began to produce and direct as well, finding a vehicle for his personal idealism in films such as *Oh! What a Lovely War* (1969) and *Gandhi* (1982).

David joined the BBC in 1952, and made his first natural history filming expeditions for *Zoo Quest* (1954-64). His undiminished boyish enthusiasm continues to captivate – and educate – the public in series such as *Life on Earth* (1979), *The Trials of Life* (1990) and the perennial *Wildlife on One*.

Clement ATTLEE

• Prime minister 1945-51
• 1883-1967; 1st earl Attlee 1955

As Labour party leader and deputy prime minister in Winston Churchill's wartime coalition, Clement Attlee spent three years planning for a postwar society. A landslide Labour victory in 1945 allowed him to introduce profound economic and social changes. His government established the National Health Service and the welfare state, and nationalised the Bank of England and major industries such as coal, steel and the railways. India, Pakistan and Burma gained independence, marking the beginning of the end of Empire. By the time the Conservatives returned to power in 1951, Attlee had determined the shape of modern Britain. He led Labour in opposition until his retirement in 1955.

MAKING THE HEADLINES Clement Attlee led Labour to its first Commons majority in July 1945

W.H. AUDEN

• Poet • 1907-73

Lay your sleeping head, my love,
Human on my faithless arm...

LULLABY (1940)

It may not be shocking today that the lover in the poet's arms is a man or that the speaker seems to be admitting to less than wholehearted fidelity, but at the time Wystan Hugh Auden had set out to change attitudes and inject a dose of realism into English verse.

Throughout the 1930s he was a committed socialist and his early work is highly political, using anti-romantic industrial imagery to convey a sense of looming crisis in Europe. He wrote three political verse dramas with his fellow writer Christopher Isherwood.

In 1939 Auden changed direction. He converted to Anglicanism and moved to the USA. There he met Chester Kallman, who became his lifelong partner and collaborator. The poetry of this period became less political and more philosophical, concerned with ethical, artistic and religious questions.

AUDLEY END

• Essex (p.495 H4) • Built 17th century • EH

James I's Treasurer, Thomas Howard, dipped into the royal exchequer to build himself the grand home of Audley End, completed in 1614. Five years later he was dragged from its palatial comfort, convicted of embezzlement and sent to the Tower of London. After his release he returned, and died at Audley End in 1626. The Howard family found the enormous building so expensive to maintain that they eventually demolished half of it, but what remains is still one of the biggest houses in Britain.

Tall windows in the three-storey stone façade throw generous light into rooms whose styling reflects the changing tastes of 400 years: Jacobean wood panelling in the Great Hall, neo-classical rooms designed by Robert ADAM in the 1760s and a Georgian 'Gothick' chapel.

Outside are Victorian gardens and parkland landscaped by 'Capability' BROWN, with a Temple of Concord and other follies.

AUGUSTAN AGE

In the early 18th century the florid extravagance of Restoration literary style fell out of fashion. Writers turned instead to classical authors, taking Horace, Ovid and Virgil as their models. All three poets wrote during the reign of the Roman emperor Augustus (27 BC-AD 14), leading the writer Oliver GOLDSMITH to coin the term 'Augustan age' for the classical revival. The label became attached in particular to literary figures, including Alexander POPE and Jonathan SWIFT, although classical models were equally influential in other spheres of activity such as music and architecture.

AURORA BOREALIS

People in Britain, especially in the north, occasionally have the chance to see dramatic sheets and arcs of red, green and yellow light flashing across the night sky. The aurora borealis, or 'northern lights', is the result of electrically charged particles from the sun entering the Earth's atmosphere, where they are magnetically drawn to the poles.

The aurora borealis is much stronger in Scotland than in southern England. It is best seen a few days after the major solar storms that occur one or two years after the peak of the 11 year sunspot cycle. There was a sunspot peak between 1989 and 1991, so the next good displays are expected in 2001 and 2012.

LIGHTS FANTASTIC Electrical effects hundreds of miles above Earth cause the aurora borealis – here over central Scotland

Jane AUSTEN

• Novelist • 1775-1817

From the chit-chat of a drawing room in Regency Hampshire, where genteel ladies came to take tea, Jane Austen constructed six of the most perfectly crafted novels in the English language.

Confined within the narrow world of English provincial society, a typical Austen plot revolves around the minutiae of middle-class social intercourse. Growing up as the daughter of a rural clergyman in Steventon, her world was narrow; she appeared to care little for global events (the Napoleonic Wars receive no mention).

But her knowledge of people, their hopes, fears and subtle self-deceptions, was profound. Austen's books are masterpieces of observation and comic understatement, but it is for her characters that she is most revered, particularly her strong-minded, independent heroines Lizzy Bennet (*Pride and Prejudice*, 1813) and Emma Woodhouse (*Emma*, 1816).

In 1995, *Sense and Sensibility* (1811) was made into an Oscar-winning film; *Emma* followed in 1996, and *Pride and Prejudice* has been adapted for television.

The house at Chawton in Hampshire where Austen lived from 1809, and where she died, is now a museum.

FLYING MACHINES

The aeroplane has made travel more swift – and war more terrible.
Britain's contribution to the technology of flight has been crucial. Here
we compare the Sopwith Camel and the Hawker Harrier 'jump jet',
two aircraft in a fine flying tradition

THE BIRTHS of the Sopwith Camel and the Hawker Harrier (universally known as the 'jump jet') are separated by a mere 50 years, but in the short history of aviation that half-century represents aeons of technological evolution.

Both machines were built for aerial combat. The Camel was developed to counter the dominance of the Fokker fighters flown by German aces in the First World War. Introduced as the F/I, it was christened the 'Camel' when it arrived at the front in 1917. The name is probably a reference to the hump, housing two Vickers machine guns, which was situated in front of the pilot. The inelegant nickname was at first officially disapproved of, but it stuck. By the end of the war there were more than 2000 Camels in service.

A Camel pilot would be amazed by the performance of a Harrier, which has a maximum speed of over 700 mph, compared to just over 120 mph for the Camel. It can refuel in midair, giving it a range of around 3500 miles. Most of all, a Camel pilot would marvel at the Harrier's ability to ascend vertically from a standing position. The plane

GAS GUZZLER The thrust produced by a Harrier for vertical take-off consumes huge amounts of fuel, so for combat it generally uses a short take-off

THE WELL-DRESSED FLYER

The fighter pilot of the First World War had one overriding priority: to keep warm. Cockpits were open, the temperature at altitude is lower than at ground level and the air rushed past at more than 100 mph. In winter, the standard wear was a full-length leather coat, usually with fur collar, leather helmet and goggles to protect the eyes.

The Hawker Harrier pilot has the benefit of a controlled environment in a closed cockpit, but has to contend with G forces created by rapid acceleration and deceleration. He wears a pressurised G-suit to prevent his blood being dragged down by the forces, which would result in unconsciousness. The pilot's helmet carries headphones, a microphone, an oxygen mask to allow him to breathe if the cockpit is punctured, and usually two visors: one that is tinted for protection against glare, and a clear one which is kept down at all times to protect against injury if the cockpit were to shatter.

has rotating jet nozzles that are pointed down at the ground to provide the lift for take-off, and swivel back to the horizontal for normal flight. This ability is more than just a clever gimmick: VTOL (vertical take-off and landing) makes the Harrier ideal for use at sea, and means that it can operate from inaccessible places such as forest clearings.

The Camel, too, was known for its versatility in take-off. It sometimes went into battle from towed barges, and was even launched from airships. It was a difficult plane to handle but could make tight turns, an immense tactical advantage in the close combat of a dogfight. Its agility was partly due to its rotary engine, standard in the first models, which created a strong gyroscopic effect. The engine was also responsible for the Camel's handling problems. Pilots claimed that if they took their hands off the control column, the plane would start to loop the loop.

DOGFIGHTER The Camel accounted for 1300 enemy aircraft in the First World War, including the Fokker of Baron von Richthofen, the Red Baron, shot down by a Canadian pilot

OUTSTANDING BRITISH AIRCRAFT

EMPIRE FLYING BOAT *began duty for the Empire Air Mail Service in 1937. It had a cruising speed of 164 mph and carried up to 24 passengers. It could reach Australia in 9½ days, a journey that involved at least ten stops*

SUPERMARINE S6B *was designed for the specific purpose of winning the Schneider Trophy air race in 1931, which it did. It was powered by a Rolls-Royce engine, and could reach a top speed of 407.5 mph. The family resemblance to the Spitfire is already visible*

AVRO LANCASTER *was the most successful British heavy bomber of the Second World War. It took part in the Dambuster raids and in the sinking of the battleship Tirpitz. It was armed with up to ten machine guns as well as its bombs*

GLOSTER METEOR *was the only jet aircraft to see service with the Allies in the Second World War. Its great speed (550 mph was achieved by 1948) helped it to its major operational triumph, which was to shoot down V-1 flying bombs over England in 1944*

DE HAVILLAND COMET *made the world's first passenger jet flight in 1952. With its swept wings and graceful fuselage, it was a masterpiece of design. All Comets were grounded in 1954 when metal fatigue led to a series of crashes*

WESTLAND SEA KING *was developed for anti-submarine and search-and-rescue duties. Introduced in 1969, the helicopter has been a success for both the Navy and RAF. It can carry 22 people at speeds of up to 126 mph*

These control difficulties were compounded by the minimal training given to First World War pilots. It was not unknown for a flyer to go solo within half an hour of getting into a plane. W.E. Johns, whose fictional Biggles made his first appearance in *The Camels are Coming*, noted his own first effort: 'Time in air: five seconds. Height: 30 feet. Remarks: Crashed taking off.' Skill was all. The plane had little instrumentation, and guns were aimed by pointing the whole plane at the enemy.

The cockpit of a Harrier, by contrast, bristles with dials and displays, and even the most gifted flyer needs six months' training before taking to the skies. A Harrier pilot is the operator of a flying computer; he is not simply an airborne duellist like his distant predecessor in the Camel. The Harrier man needs to be able to cope with the latest in technology. A Doppler radar allows him to 'see' at night

and in bad weather. All the information he needs for flying is displayed on screens, including speed, altitude and wind direction.

The fire power that a Harrier pilot controls is immense. The weapons are themselves flying machines far more

sophisticated than the Camel or most of its descendants. A Harrier pilot has no need to point his plane at the enemy: Sidewinder air-to-air missiles, fitted to the Harrier as standard since the Falklands War in 1982, find their own way to the target.

BRITISH AVIATION LANDMARKS

1909 Charles Stewart Rolls is the first man to fly from England to France. Within a month he is the first Briton to be killed in an air crash

1919 John Alcock and Arthur Brown cross the Atlantic nonstop in a Vickers Vimy

1924 Imperial Airways, Britain's first national airline, is formed

1946 Heathrow airport opens

1952 A Canberra jet bomber makes the first there-and-back trip across the Atlantic in a single day

1999 Englishman Brian Jones and his Swiss flying partner, Bertrand Piccard, become the first men to circle the world in a hot-air balloon – made in Bristol

1900   **1910**   **1920**   **1930**   **1940**   **1950**   **1960**   **1970**   **1980**   **1990**   **2000**

1907 Horatio Phillips makes the first powered flight in Britain, covering a distance of about 150m (490ft)

1912 Royal Flying Corps is founded; in 1914 it adopts a roundel as its insignia

1920 Croydon is London's first air terminal

1936 A passenger is fined £10 in the first prosecution for smoking on an aircraft

1969 Britain's 002 Concorde prototype makes its first flight

1976 Two Concordes fly simultaneously from London and Paris – the first supersonic passenger services

SURROUNDED BY THE PAST The roads into Avebury follow four ancient causeways that cross a ditch, once up to 10 m (33 ft) deep, which was possibly a grandstand for prehistoric spectators

AVALON

In the mythology of the ancient Celts Avalon was an island where gods and heroes fed on the apples of immortality. In about 1136, the Welsh chronicler GEOFFREY OF MONMOUTH named Avalon as the resting place of King ARTHUR, and the idea caught on in medieval romance.

Arthur's last battle was supposed to have been in Somerset, and in 1191 monks at Glastonbury Abbey claimed to have discovered human remains and a cross conveniently inscribed 'Here lies buried the renowned King Arthur in the Isle of Avalon'. Despite this, and the fact that the area may once have been marshy, with islands, the monks' motives were probably not entirely unworldly. Pilgrims were the tourists of the medieval world and 'Arthur's tomb' would have been a popular and profitable attraction. Authentic or not, the site is still visible within the abbey ruins, and continues to attract visitors.

AVEBURY

• **Prehistoric site** • **Wiltshire (p.495 F5)** • **NT**
The 17th-century writer John Evelyn called the stone circle at Avebury a cathedral in comparison to the 'parish church' of STONEHENGE. When the circle was built in about 2500 BC, it consisted of some 154 upright boulders on a plateau of earth and chalk surrounded by a deep ditch forming a circle 348 m (1142 ft) across – the world's largest such site. Over the centuries, many stones have been taken for building materials and others may have become buried. Today only 27 are visible.

South of the circle, scattered stones mark the West Kennet Avenue, probably a processional route once lined by 100 pairs of standing stones. It stretches 1½ miles to marker stones indicating the Sanctuary, a circle near to the even earlier mound at SILBURY HILL. To the west are the Long Stones, two monoliths nicknamed Adam and Eve, which may have formed part of another avenue.

Who the builders of Avebury were remains a mystery. Its purpose – fertility rites or religious ceremonies, perhaps – can also only be guessed at.

AVIATION: see page 26

River AVON

Avon comes from the Celtic word for river, *afon*, and three important rivers of southern England are known by this name. The longest River Avon (96 miles) rises in Northamptonshire, flows through William Shakespeare's home town of Stratford-upon-Avon, waters the fertile Vale of Evesham and meets the River Severn in Gloucestershire. The second-longest Avon (75 miles) rises in Wiltshire and flows generally south and then west to join the Severn Estuary near Bristol. Ancient British peoples used it 4000 years ago to transport huge bluestones from Wales to STONEHENGE. The third Avon (60 miles) also rises in Wiltshire and flows south into Christchurch Harbour near Bournemouth.

Alan AYCKBOURN

• **Playwright and director** • **b.1939; kt 1997**
With more than 50 plays to his name, five once running simultaneously in the West End, Alan Ayckbourn is England's most prolific dramatist since Noël Coward. Tensions in middle-class life are typical Ayckbourn territory, particularly marital difficulties. 'My plays,' he says, 'are best appreciated if you've had at least one unhappy marriage'. Comedy is at the heart of his craft, touched by tinges of bitterness and regret.

Unusual sets are an Ayckbourn trademark. *How the Other Half Loves* (1969) put two households on the stage at the same time, and *Way Upstream* (1982) featured a full-size floating boat. *The Norman Conquests* (1974) constructs three plays out of the same events seen from the different viewpoints of garden, sitting room and dining room.

Since 1959 Ayckbourn has premiered his plays in the Stephen Joseph Theatre, Scarborough, where he is artistic director.

A.J. AYER

• **Philosopher and broadcaster**
• **1910-89; kt 1970**
At just 25 Alfred Jules 'Freddie' Ayer published one of the classics of 20th-century thought. *Language, Truth and Logic* (1936) was the first formulation in English of the Viennese science-based school of philosophy known as logical positivism. Ayer hoped to end the 'traditional disputes of philosophers' by imposing tough standards on which statements were to count as meaningful. He dismissed any that were impossible to disprove, which meant all of religion. But like all great philosophy his book provoked rather than quelled debate.

Ayer made many appearances on radio and television, where his lightning-quick responses and robust atheism turned him into a household name.

Charles BABBAGE

• Mathematician • 1791-1871

Charles Babbage designed and tried to build the world's first computer. His 1822 design for a 'difference engine', and the even more ambitious steam-powered 'analytical engine' a decade later, called for a mass of brass gear-wheels to carry out mathematical calculations. Punched cards, with holes representing data and instructions, were to be fed into the analytical engine, which would print out the results. The principle was sound, but making it work would prove too difficult for the next 100 years. The unfinished analytical engine and a working model of the difference engine are now on display at the Science Museum in London.

Impatient and tactless, Babbage was the typical frustrated inventor. When public money ran out for his machines, he worked on a system for betting on horses. He was helped by Ada Byron, Countess of Lovelace, daughter of Lord Byron and an amateur mathematician. In 1843 she published a defence of the analytical engine, which also predicted the development of an internal memory and a computer's future uses for composing music and producing graphic images. She is credited as being the first computer programmer, and in 1976 the US Department of Defense named a computer language, 'ADA', after her.

BACKBENCHER

Most Members of Parliament in the House of Commons are backbenchers, sitting behind the front-row benches of government ministers and opposition 'shadows'. Backbenchers rarely taste power, but wield great influence when a government majority is in doubt. Bills can be lost and governments fall by a single vote – the fate in 1979 of James Callaghan's minority Labour government, which lost a vote of confidence by one, ushering in 18 years of Conservative rule.

Despite their sometimes rowdy behaviour, backbenchers are expected to follow the party WHIPS, particularly if they want to rise to ministerial rank.

Conservative backbenchers have an influential forum of their own, the 1922 Committee, named for the year the party left Lloyd George's coalition government.

Francis BACON

• Philosopher and politician
• 1561-1626; kt 1603; bn 1621; visc. 1621

Lawyer, philosopher, parliamentarian and adviser to both Elizabeth I and James I, Francis Bacon's accomplishments were many. His political ambitions faded in 1621 when, as lord chancellor, he was convicted of corruption, stripped of his offices, fined and locked up in the Tower.

But public disgrace did nothing to dim Bacon's intellectual reputation. He aimed to overturn Aristotle's 2000 year grip on European philosophy and replace it with a 'new logic' of active experimentation that could support the fledgling sciences. Many of the principles he set out – such as the derivation of general laws from individual instances, and the need for reproducible experiments – still lie at the heart of modern scientific method.

Francis BACON

• Artist • 1909-92

Francis Bacon's pictures make uncomfortable viewing. Their typical subject is a lone, distorted figure. The emotion is anguish or despair, the only furnishing a rigid bed or chair, the background a box-like room. Yet many consider him the greatest British painter of his era, and Bacon's *Triptych 1975-77* broke all records in 1989 when it sold for $6.27 million – the highest price ever paid for a work by a living British artist.

Bacon was born in Dublin and taught himself to paint after working as an interior decorator. Edvard Munch and Vincent Van Gogh were influences, especially in their use of colour, broad brush strokes and thick pigment, as were the photographs of Eadweard Muybridge, whose 1880s studies of the body in motion were a constant source of inspiration for Bacon. Bacon's notorious *Screaming Popes* series of the 1940s and 50s were inspired by a Velázquez portrait of Innocent X.

Roger BACON

• Philosopher and scientist • c.1214-92

The 13th-century Franciscan friar Roger Bacon was one of the greatest medieval scholars in optics, medicine and mathematics. He studied in Paris and Oxford and was dubbed *doctor mirabilis* for the breadth of his learning. Three hundred years before it became generally accepted, Bacon argued that experiments were needed to prove a scientific argument. He believed the Earth was round – then a fantastic notion – suggested the use of magnifying lenses to help poor sight, and predicted powered flight and telescopes.

TRIPLE VISION *Study for Self-Portrait: Triptych (1985-6)* is just one of many three-part portraits by Francis Bacon. The contrast between the medieval form – traditionally used for religious subjects – and the artist's uncompromisingly modern style was intended to startle

Robert BADEN-POWELL

- **Founder of the Boy Scout movement**
- **1857-1941; bn 1929; OM 1937**

The Boer War turned Robert Baden-Powell into a national hero. For seven months he led the defence of Mafeking against the besieging Boers. He returned to huge acclaim, and to find a technical manual he had written on military scouting suddenly popular.

RALLYING CALL Baden-Powell summons Scouts with a blast from an antelope horn

Interest was so great that in 1907 Baden-Powell set up a scouting camp for boys and the following year founded the SCOUTS to promote active citizenship, outdoor skills and personal development. His book *Scouting for Boys* (1908) laid down the Scouts' principles of duty to God, country and others, and the well-known motto 'Be Prepared'.

BADGER

Brock, badget, bawson – badgers go by many names. They are social animals, living in complex groups in underground setts with chambers that are occupied for generations, sometimes for hundreds of years. The extinction of wolves in the 18th century left badgers as Britain's largest native land carnivore – up to about 1 m (3 ft) long – though their diet includes plant foods as well as beetles, earthworms, frogs and small mammals. There are at least a quarter of a million badgers in Britain, living in woodland and meadows and even in built-up areas, including parts of London. They are shy and, except in hot weather, nocturnal, so are not often seen.

Survival can be difficult for a badger. Some 50 000 die each year on roads and, despite legal protection, many thousands more are killed for sport. Since the 1970s around 1000 badgers a year have been culled by order of the government in the belief that they spread tuberculosis in cattle.

BADMINTON

- **First played c.1870**

A racquet game that mixes power with delicacy and disguise, badminton was once described as 'a poetic pastime for the Parish Hall' rather than a serious sport. Today tournaments are fiercely competitive, although the tradition of social play is still strong.

The sport is named after the home in Gloucestershire of the duke of Beaufort, where it supposedly developed from an ancient children's game. The small-headed, long-handled racquets strike a light, non-bouncing shuttlecock, made of plastic or cork with goose feathers, over a high net. The Badminton Association was formed in 1893 after army officers took the game to India and drafted formal rules. The first All-England Championships were held in 1899.

BADMINTON HORSE TRIALS

- **Three days in early May**

Horses performing delicate pirouettes, plunging down precipitous slopes carrying mud-spattered riders, and turning at speed to leap over a series of jumps – there is no greater equestrian test than the three days of dressage, cross-country and show-jumping of the Badminton Horse Trials, held each year in Gloucestershire.

Three-day eventing was largely a military sport until the duke of Beaufort, dismayed by the British performance at the 1948 London Olympics, launched an annual three-day event on his estate the following year. The challenge attracted increasing numbers of competitors and spectators, making stars of riders such as Lucinda Green (née Prior-Palmer), who won a record six times between 1973 and 1984, and Mark Phillips, who took four trophies between 1971 and 1981.

BAFTA

- **British Academy of Film and Television Arts**
- **Founded 1947**

The bronze Grecian-style masks handed out at the annual BAFTA awards are Britain's answer to the Oscars. More than 50 trophies – based on a design by the American sculptor Mitzi Cunliffe – are presented each April (for films) and May (for television), in categories that range from best film to best light entertainment performance.

BAFTA also screens new releases and holds master-classes and seminars at its headquarters in Piccadilly, London.

BAGPIPES

Though similar instruments are part of folk music tradition in many parts of Europe, Asia and Africa, the image of the bagpipes is inescapably associated with the Scottish Highlands. They became popular in Scotland in the 15th century, and by the next century they had displaced the harp in chieftains' households as the instrument of ceremony and entertainment, and were used for whipping up military fervour.

After the Scottish defeat at Culloden Moor in 1746, bagpipes were banned as part of a drive to stamp out the Scottish way of life. Their fortunes revived with the 19th-century 'rediscovery' of Scottish culture and customs.

The bag itself is leather or sheepskin, with one or two chanters – melody pipes – and up to three drones, or single-tone pipes. Fine piping today can be heard at HIGHLAND GATHERINGS.

NOT JUST FOR SCOTS The 14th-century Luttrell Psalter shows an Englishman with bagpipes

John Logie BAIRD

- **Electrical engineer • 1888-1946**

Television was born in 1924 when, using a tea-chest, hat box, bicycle lamp lenses, darning needles and old electric motors, John Logie Baird transmitted a flickering image of a Maltese cross on to a glass screen a few feet away. The Scottish engineer and inventor had already produced some failed innovations, including a glass razor and paper socks, before he began his experiments in 'pictures by wireless' in 1922. By 1927 he was sending pictures by wire from London to Glasgow, and by radio half-way across the Atlantic Ocean to the liner SS *Berengaria*. In 1928 he made the first transmission to North America.

Baird's system, based on mechanical image scanning, was used in experimental broadcasts by the BBC from 1929, but electronic scanning equipment developed by Marconi-EMI and tested by the BBC in 1936 gave a clearer image and his system was abandoned. Other inventions in Baird's creative career included infrared night-vision devices (1926), colour and stereoscopic (3-D) television (1928), and video recorders (1935).

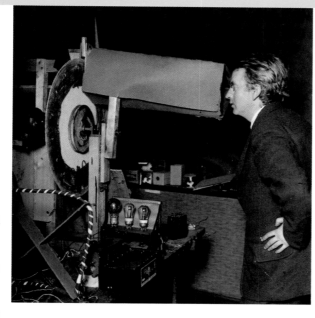

FAR-SIGHTED John Logie Baird in 1925 peers at a revolving cardboard disc punctuated with holes. This broke down an image into vertical lines that could be viewed on a screen

Janet BAKER

• **Opera singer** • **b.1933; DBE 1976; CH 1994**

When Dame Janet Baker announced her retirement from opera in 1982 she was only 49. But she quit at the top – the greatest postwar British mezzo-soprano, admired internationally for her natural acting, the dark intensity of her voice and the intelligence of her singing.

Baker made her debut in 1956 at Glyndebourne. She first sang at Covent Garden and in New York in 1966, and at the Salzburg Festival in 1973. From 1962 she regularly performed at the Aldeburgh Festival and became closely associated with Benjamin BRITTEN whose last work, the opera *Phaedra*, was written for her.

Robert BAKEWELL

• **Agriculturalist and livestock breeder**
• **1725-95**

Russian, French and British nobility were among those who flocked to Robert Bakewell's Leicestershire farm to learn from his revolutionary experiments in animal breeding. So impressive were Bakewell's results that today all British long-woolled sheep are descendants of his Leicesters – the first strain developed for meat as well as wool. In addition to

sheep, Bakewell specialised in longhorn cattle and strong, black draught horses. Unfortunately he was less astute financially than in animal husbandry and the generous hospitality extended to visitors eventually bankrupted him.

Stanley BALDWIN

• **Prime minister 1923-4, 1924-9, 1935-7**
• **1867-1947; earl 1937**

Behind the homely, pipe-smoking image he liked to cultivate, Stanley Baldwin hid sharply honed political instincts. After Cambridge, he joined the family iron and steel business, entering parliament as a Conservative MP only in 1908.

Power did not come until 1922, when Baldwin led a revolt that destroyed David LLOYD GEORGE's coalition government. A year later he succeeded Andrew Bonar Law as Conservative prime minister, but his term of office was brief. After the end of the short-lived 1924 Labour government, he returned to power, masterminding in 1926 the defeat of the GENERAL STRIKE. Baldwin's third term was marked by his skilful handling of EDWARD VIII's abdication.

On his retirement in 1937 Baldwin basked briefly in a glow of public admiration. Judgment was less kind after the Second World War broke out and he was blamed for appeasing Hitler and failing to rearm the nation in the face of mounting German aggression.

A.J. BALFOUR

• **Prime minister 1902-05, and philosopher**
• **1848-1930; earl 1922**

Although the epitome of the patrician Victorian public figure, Arthur James Balfour actually attained highest office in the more democratic Edwardian period. He was born into a Scottish landowning family, educated at Eton and Cambridge, and in 1874 became a Conservative MP. A sideline in philosophy bore fruit in 1879 with the publication of *A Defence of Philosophic Doubt*.

Balfour succeeded his uncle, Lord Salisbury, as prime minister in 1902. His Education Act of the same year set up the first coordinated national education system and in 1904 he settled long-held territorial disputes with France. Despite such successes Balfour lost the next election. Arguably his greatest impact was yet to come. In 1917, as foreign secretary in David LLOYD GEORGE's wartime Cabinet, he issued the Balfour Declaration, which promised British support for a Jewish state in Palestine.

BALLADS

Tales of highwaymen, adventure, love (often jilted) and dramatic events (usually tragic) are the stuff of ballads. With their simple tunes and memorable refrains they form an oral history going back as far as the 13th century.

The first ballad collections were published in the late 18th century. As industrialisation gathered pace so did interest in preserving the past; ballads were wildly popular in Victorian times. The form was even used for new songs, such as 'Home Sweet Home', idealising the simple life and selling song sheets by the million.

Lady Alice was sitting in her bower-window,
Mending her midnight quoif,
And there she saw as fine a corpse
As ever she saw in her life.

'What bear ye, what bear ye, ye six men tall?
What bear ye on your shoulders?'
'We bear the corpse of Giles Collins,
An old and true lover of yours.'

FROM THE BALLAD 'LADY ALICE'

MAGIC OF THE DANCE

Britain has brilliant ballet performers, choreographers and dance companies, both classical and experimental. And yet this most athletic and theatrical dance form was without British influence until the early 20th century

RUFFLED FEATHERS The modern British dance company Adventures in Motion Pictures shocked and thrilled audiences in 1995 by using male dancers to perform as the swans in the ballet *Swan Lake*

I N 1921 THE Russian impresario Sergei Diaghilev brought his Ballet Russe company to Britain. His visit sparked a passion for the precise style of dance that had originated in Renaissance French and Italian courts and reached an artistic peak in 19th-century Imperial Russia. Two Diaghilev-trained ballerinas, Marie RAMBERT and Ninette de Valois, established British ballet companies. In 1926 Rambert formed the Ballet Club, which became the Ballet Rambert, and in 1931 de Valois founded a company that became first the Sadler's Wells Ballet and then the Royal Ballet, based at the Covent Garden Opera House.

Another Diaghilev protégée, English ballerina Alicia Markova, formed the London Festival Ballet in 1935 to keep alive Diaghilev's ideas. In 1989 the London

DANCE CLASS Pupils join the Royal Ballet Upper School in West London at 16 for two years of hard training

Festival Ballet became English National Ballet, a touring company focusing on new productions of established works.

Ballet also thrives outside London. Manchester is home to the Northern Ballet Theatre, Glasgow has the Scottish Ballet, and the Sadler's Wells Touring Ballet left London for the Midlands to become the Birmingham Royal Ballet.

THE GOLDEN YEARS
The Royal Ballet was at its height in the 1960s. Choreography by Frederick ASHTON and the arrival of the sensational Russian dancer Rudolf Nureyev, who embarked on a dazzling partnership with Margo FONTEYN, brought a fresh popularity to ballet.

The Scottish choreographer Kenneth MACMILLAN then transformed classical ballet into 'dance drama' in works such as *Elite Syncopations* (1974), which is set to the ragtime piano music of American composer Scott Joplin.

MODERN BALLET

The impetus for a new free-flowing, less formal ballet came from the USA in the 1920s, led by the 'barefoot' ballet of the choreographer Martha Graham. But not until 1967, when Graham's pupil Robert Cohan formed the London Contemporary Dance Theatre, did Britain have an experimental dance company respected worldwide. Many independent, choreographer-led groups have followed, including the Cholmondeleys and Adventures in Motion Pictures, who alongside new dance works produce daring adaptations of classical ballets such as *Cinderella*.

NEW WAVE Ballet Rambert became the Rambert Dance Company in 1966 and dedicated itself to modern dance

BALLROOM DANCING

In the 18th and 19th centuries, the intricate dances of formal balls were central to the courtship ritual. With the 20th century came dance bands that played new rhythms and introduced dances from North and South America, including the foxtrot, tango, rumba and chachacha. In the 1940s, the jazz-inspired lindy-hop and jive began a move towards informal dancing, completed by rock'n'roll, which had no place for the rigidity of learned dance steps or appropriately dressed male 'leads' and female 'partners'.

Ballroom dancing declined as a social activity but grew as a competition event. Britain has thousands of ballroom clubs and classes, with the ultimate aim for many dancers of an appearance on the BBC television programme *Come Dancing*, first broadcast in 1950.

BALMORAL CASTLE

• **Aberdeenshire (p.497 D3)** • **Built 1852-5**
A profusion of pepper-pot turrets surrounds Balmoral's massive central tower, typical of the Scottish baronial style in which Prince Albert, husband of Queen Victoria, rebuilt the 15th-century castle that he had leased in 1848 and bought four years later. When Victoria first saw Balmoral (Gaelic *Bouchmorale*, 'majestic dwelling'), she fell in love with its setting on a curve of the River Dee. Subsequent monarchs have continued to cherish Balmoral as their Scottish holiday home.

The light grey granite of the walls sparkles in the least glimmer of sunlight and chases away any suggestion of Gothic gloom. The ballroom is open to the public and houses paintings and other exhibits from the Queen's collection. Albert himself laid out the gardens, overlooking wild moorland.

ARE WE NEARLY THERE? Traffic crawls to the Kent seaside resort of Margate on August Bank Holiday 1950

WHISKED OFF THEIR FEET Sequins sparkle and diaphanous fabric billows as a couple take part in an under-16s ballroom dancing championship

BAMBURGH CASTLE

• **Northumberland (p.496 B1)**
• **Built 12th century, restored 19th century**
The pink battlemented sandstone walls of Bamburgh Castle sprout upwards like a natural extension of the rocky outcrop on which it perches above Bamburgh Bay. By the 7th century the site was a stronghold of the Anglo-Saxon kings of Northumbria. Vikings sacked the fortress, which was later replaced by a Norman castle, of which only the keep remains. In the 14th century the castle fell into the hands of the Percy family of nearby ALNWICK, and in the Wars of the Roses 100 years later Bamburgh became the first English castle to fall to gunfire.

Victorian restoration gave Bamburgh a Great Hall with a hammerbeam roof of solid teak. The building contains displays of Dresden and Sèvres china, Fabergé animals, and arms and armour.

BANK HOLIDAYS

Before the Industrial Revolution, the Church encouraged people to rest on designated saints' days. But by the 1830s, with working hours on the increase, there were only two official public holidays: Christmas Day and Good Friday. In 1871, the banker and Liberal politician John Lubbock instigated the Bank Holidays Act to compel the Bank of England and clearing banks to close on Easter Monday, Whit Monday, the first Monday in August and Boxing Day. Other businesses followed suit and the days became recognised public holidays. New Year's Day and May Day, already holidays in Scotland (where January 2 is also a holiday), were added in 1975 and 1978. Northern Ireland also has St Patrick's Day (March 17) and July 12 to mark the Battle of the Boyne.

BANK OF ENGLAND

• **Central London (p.499 F2)** • **Founded 1694**
The United Kingdom's central bank was founded as a private company by merchants hoping to grow rich on loans to William III, who needed money to finance his war against France. This connection with the Crown soon brought semi-official status as the national bank, although it remained privately owned until nationalisation in 1946.

In 1734 the Bank moved from Poultry to Threadneedle Street in the CITY OF LONDON, where it now occupies a building designed by Herbert Baker and completed in 1939. A windowless wall, begun under the direction of John SOANE in 1788, encloses the site, which includes the Bank of England Museum. Until 1973 the premises had a military guard – a legacy of the 1780 GORDON RIOTS.

The 'old lady of Threadneedle Street' – Richard Brinsley Sheridan's phrase – sets interest rates and implements them through the Bank's financial market operations. It also prints the banknotes for England and Wales.

Joseph BANKS

• Botanist   • 1743-1820; kt 1781

Rich, handsome and talented, Joseph Banks could have chosen a life of ease and leisure. Instead he devoted himself – and his considerable fortune – to investigating the natural world. It was Banks who largely funded James COOK's 1768-71 voyage in *Endeavour*, which charted New Zealand and the east coast of Australia. Banks was a keen botanist and accompanied Cook, identifying and recording hundreds of new plants, and bringing specimens back to Britain.

NEW BLOOM The Australian *Banksia* genus is named after Joseph Banks

Banks befriended George III and became his scientific adviser. In 1773 he was made Honorary Director of the Royal Botanic Gardens at Kew, and for a record 42 years from 1778 he served as president of the Royal Society. Public honours never distracted him from practical experiments, particularly in transplanting flora and fauna from their native habitats. Banks took merino sheep from Spain to Britain and Australia, and tea plants from China to India. When sailors on the BOUNTY mutinied, it was Banks's scheme of taking breadfruit from Tahiti to the West Indies that miscarried.

Shortly before his death, Banks was in a coach accident that hastened the passage of a kidney stone. Scientist to the last, he offered it to a friend, noting its similarity to a piece of coral.

Roger BANNISTER

• Athlete and doctor   • b.1929; kt 1975

For the first half of the 20th century, running a mile in under 4 minutes was one of sport's great goals – though widely considered beyond human ability. On May 6, 1954, at the Iffley Road athletics track in Oxford, on a cool, overcast day with a gusting wind, the medical student Roger Bannister proved it was not. He made the distance in just 3 minutes 59.4 seconds.

Bannister was knighted for his work as a neurologist, and served as chairman of the Sports Council and Master of Pembroke College, Oxford.

Battle of BANNOCKBURN

• Stirling (p.497 C4)   • June 23-24, 1314   • NTS

The decisive victory of the Scottish king ROBERT BRUCE over EDWARD II at Bannockburn has resonated through the centuries as a symbol of Scotland's struggle against English domination.

The date and place were determined by a gentleman's agreement between Alexander Mowbray, governor of Stirling Castle and commander of the last major English garrison in Scotland, and Robert's brother Edward Bruce, who had laid siege to the castle. Unless Edward II brought an army north to relieve the garrison by Midsummer's Day (June 24), they agreed, the castle would be surrendered to the Scots.

On June 23 the English king arrived outside Stirling with an army of 20 000 men, to meet Robert and a force of fewer than half that number encamped in strategic positions above the road. After an initial skirmish, the Scots advanced, trapping the retreating English with a river and marshes to their rear. In battle the following day, 1000 English soldiers were killed and 500 knights seized for ransom, but Edward escaped. Despite his defeat, the English king, and then his son Edward III, refused to recognise Scotland's independence, and intermittent warfare continued for another 14 years.

The precise site of the battlefield is disputed, but is certainly very near the Bannockburn Heritage Centre memorial site south-east of the centre of Stirling.

BARBICAN CENTRE

• Central London (p.499 E2)   • Est. 1982

In the early 1960s an elaborate concrete structure began to take shape on a bombsite just north of St Paul's Cathedral. The Barbican Centre was commissioned by the Corporation of London to provide a combination of flats and arts venues. The complex is close to the old city walls and takes its name from a barbican, or watch tower, thought to have stood on the site.

The Barbican, designed by the Chamberlin, Powell and Bon company of architects, took 20 years to complete and is still the largest project of its kind in Europe. As well as 2000 apartments, the complex houses the Guildhall School of Music and Drama and the London Symphony Orchestra, and provides a metropolitan base for the Royal Shakespeare Company. Around 350 000 people a year visit the concert hall, two theatres – the main theatre, with the tallest fly tower in Europe, and the more intimate 200-seat Pit – three cinemas, two art galleries, a library and numerous conference suites, exhibition halls, bars and restaurants, all grouped around an ornamental lake.

ARTS CENTRE KEY

1 Foyers
2 Cinemas
3 Pit theatre
4 Roof-top conservatory
5 Fly tower
6 Barbican theatre

BARNARD CASTLE

- **Durham (p.496 B3)**
- **Built 12th-14th century** • **EH**

So dominant a feature was the castle begun around 1150 by the Norman baron Bernard de Bailleul that it gave its name to the market town that grew beside it. Even in ruin the 25 m (80 ft) hulk, built on a 30 m (100 ft) high rock above the River Tees, has a forbidding presence, which belies its affectionate nickname of 'Barney's Castle'.

The stronghold, built to defend a river crossing, gained a round keep in the 14th century and later passed to Richard III, whose emblem of a boar appears above an oriel window. After its capture by Oliver Cromwell during the Civil War the castle decayed.

The streets of the town still follow their medieval pattern and are linked by cobbled alleys. In contrast the Bowes Museum of European furniture, ceramics, tapestries, and paintings by Goya, El Greco and Canaletto, is housed in a chateau-like 19th-century building.

BARNARDO'S

- **Founded 1870**

Britain's biggest children's charity provides support for 30 000 young people and families, and finds homes for disadvantaged children with fostering and adoptive families. The organisation began in the 1860s when the Dublin-born evangelist Thomas Barnardo (1845-1905) arrived in London to train as a doctor. The plight of the thousands of street children he came across so moved him that he devoted himself to their care instead of practising medicine.

By 1870 Barnado had raised enough money to open – in Stepney – the first of many children's homes. They were strict institutions, where segregated, uniformed boys and girls were prepared for manual labour or domestic service. Under an emigration scheme, around 20 000 Barnado's children were sent to Canada between 1882 and 1914.

Residential care reached a peak in the mid 1930s when more than 8000 children were living in 188 homes. After the Second World War the charity concentrated on helping families to stay together. The last home closed in 1988.

GLORIOUS FOOD Boys clear their bowls in the refectory of an Essex Barnardo's home in 1926. On January 1, 1927 England and Wales legalised adoption, changing the fate of many orphans

BARONS' WARS

- **1215-17; 1263-6**

When King JOHN set his seal on the MAGNA CARTA in 1215, he had no intention of sticking to the limitations the barons had placed on his power. Many barons continued to oppose John, who in turn had the pope annul the treaty and excommunicate them. When John died in 1216 and the throne passed to the nine-year-old HENRY III, the barons offered the crown to Prince Louis of France. The French landed in May 1216 but were routed at Lincoln and Sandwich the following year – the first Barons' War.

In 1263 Henry himself caused the second Barons' War by disregarding agreed constitutional reforms. Rebel barons, led by Simon de Montfort, earl of Leicester, defeated the royalist forces at Lewes in May 1264. De Montfort took over the government of England, holding hostage the king's son, the future EDWARD I. Edward escaped and gathered an army that defeated the barons on August 4, 1265, at Evesham. De Montfort was killed and Henry III restored.

James BARRY

- **Surgeon** • **c.1795-1865**

A respected army surgeon, with dashing good looks and a fiery temper, James Barry maintained an astonishing lifelong secret – he was a woman. Already masquerading as 'James', Barry studied medicine at Edinburgh before entering the army as a hospital assistant in 1813. There she was promoted through the ranks to the position of Inspector-General in 1858. She served in the West Indies, South Africa and India and won a reputation as a skilled surgeon and formidable marksman.

Barry's double life remained a secret until a post-mortem examination finally revealed her sex. The War Department was acutely embarrassed, but with no clues as to her true identity she was buried as she lived – as James Barry.

William BATESON

- **Biologist and geneticist** • **1861-1926**

The self-proclaimed 'father of genetics' was a staunch early proponent of Charles DARWIN's theory of evolution. William Bateson was also a champion of the Austrian monk Gregor Mendel (1822-84), who in selective-breeding experiments with pea plants discovered the basic laws of heredity. In his lifetime, Mendel was largely ignored by other scientists but in 1900 Bateson published his work bringing it to a wider audience. His own work, based on that of Mendel, established links between the inheritance patterns of different characteristics, such as colour and pollen shape of flowers. In 1908 Bateson became Cambridge's and Britain's first professor of genetics.

BATH

- **SW England (p.494 E5)** • **Pop. 78 690**

The wealth of Bath rests upon the quarter of a million gallons of water that gush daily from its hot springs. According to legend, the city owes its origin to the ancient leprous King Bladud, who founded a settlement after being cured by bathing in mud pools at the site. What is more certain is that the springs were considered sacred by Iron Age Celts, who built a shrine to the water goddess Sulis at their source more than 2000 years ago.

In the 1st century AD the Romans constructed a massive temple complex at the site, which they called Aquae Sulis. It attracted pilgrims from across the empire. Visitors bathed, paid their respects in the adjoining temple and made offerings at the sacred spring. Their prayers were not always pleas for health – lead tablets imploring the goddess to strike an enemy with sickness have also been found at the site.

ONE CITY ON TOP OF ANOTHER

When the Romans withdrew, Bath fell into decay and it was probably the old reputation as a pagan shrine that inspired the abbey constructed among the ruins – possibly begun as early as the 7th century. By the 10th century, the building was a major Anglo-Saxon monastery.

The inhabitants were unaware of the Roman city buried beneath their feet, and during the Middle Ages Bath was known for its cloth weaving rather than as a watering place. But the springs still flowed, and began to attract visitors again after the visit of Elizabeth I in 1574.

FINE SWEEP Royal Crescent was built by John Wood the Younger in the early 1770s. No.1 is open to visitors

MIRROR IMAGE Shops flank Robert Adam's Pulteney Bridge (1774) over the Avon

'BEAU' NASH
After studying at Oxford, Swansea-born Richard 'Beau' Nash (1674-1762) tried careers in the army and the law. By 1705, when he arrived in Bath, he was making a living as a gambler.
He was appointed Bath's Master of Ceremonies and, with his combination of charm and biting wit, became the guiding spirit of the city. Despite his fame, he died a pauper but was buried in splendour in Bath Abbey.

A NEW GOLDEN AGE

The heyday of the city came in the 18th century. Wealthy invalids took the waters in summer and were joined by relations and friends, making it the most fashionable of all provincial centres.

John Wood the Elder (1705-54), a native of Bath, was the first of many architects to create new buildings. Palatial houses and public buildings such as the Assembly Rooms (1771) and Pump Room (1796) created a Georgian heritage that survived both wartime air raids and redevelopment in the 1960s.

Excavation of the Roman baths began in the 1880s – its remains are open to the public. A £6 million restoration scheme will bring the Georgian spa back into operation in the year 2001.

BATS: *see opposite page*

BATTERSEA DOGS' HOME

- **SW London (p.498 C4)** • **Founded 1860**

Mary Tealby, an elderly resident of Islington, began one of the noisiest, smelliest operations in London when she opened a Temporary Home for Lost and Starving Dogs in Holloway. Six years later, in 1866, the home was sheltering more than 35 000 dogs and by 1871 complaints about noise had prompted a move to Battersea.

The shelter, Britain's largest dogs' home, now takes in both dogs and cats. In 1996, a typical year, 8068 dogs and 1386 cats were received. Animals are never put down but are held for a week before rehoming, during which time 27 per cent are claimed by owners.

BATTERSEA POWER STATION

- **SW London (p.498 C4)** • **Built 1932-53**

This unique Art Deco industrial building, created by the architect Giles Gilbert Scott, attained grade II listed building status in 1980. Its four cream-coloured corner chimneys rise 102 m (337 ft) from a huge brickwork hulk, towering over its quays on the Thames. Londoners greeted the building grudgingly as a necessary evil to supply the growing need for electricity. As newer, more efficient stations took over, Battersea was phased out and ceased operation in 1983. It was saved from demolition the same year by plans to turn it into a leisure complex.

BAYEUX TAPESTRY

- **Completed c.1076**

The pictorial account of the Battle of HASTINGS of 1066, marking the beginning of Norman rule in Britain, was the documentary drama of its day. Bishop Odo of Bayeux, half-brother of the victorious William I and briefly earl of

BATS

The warmer southern coast of Britain is the most popular habitat for the country's 16 species of bat, which belong to two families: common (or vesper) bats and horseshoe bats.

Common bats have flattish bodies, fluttery flight and a fleshy lobe in each ear used for echo-location. They roost in crevices with their wings folded at their sides. Most common is the tiny pipistrelle, just 4 cm (1½ in) long, with a wingspan of up to 25 cm (9½ in). Other common bats can be much larger, such as Daubenton's bat, which hunts water flies and has a wingspan of up to 27 cm (11 in), or the brown long-eared bat, a woodland inhabitant with a wingspan of up to 28 cm (11½ in). One of the

ENDANGERED SPECIES Greater horseshoe bats can now be seen only in a few areas of south-west Britain

largest is the noctule, with a wingspan of 32-45 cm (12½-18 in).

Greater and lesser horseshoe bats have rounder bodies, horseshoe-shaped noses used for echo-location, broader wings and a slower flight. They roost in open spaces such as cellars, mines and caves, often wrapping their wings around their body.

Though common bats can be seen across most of the British Isles, bats of all species are declining, due to the use of insecticides that destroy the insects they rely on for food and the loss of

Many British bats live much longer than other small creatures. Tiny whiskered bats live for up to 23 years, while greater horseshoe and Daubenton's bats may survive for 30 years or more

habitats such as hollow trees. Since 1981, all British bats have been protected. It is illegal to disturb a colony, or to block up the bats' means of entrance and exit.

Kent, probably commissioned it from English nuns at Canterbury.

The 'tapestry' – actually an embroidery on a linen background – is 70.5 m (231 ft) long but just 51 cm (20 in) high. Odo hung it in Bayeux cathedral, in Normandy, for all to trace the battle through more than 70 illustrated scenes, assisted perhaps by a cleric reading the Latin captions. It is now displayed in its own museum near the cathedral.

Lilian BAYLIS

• Theatre manager • 1874-1937

As a girl, Lilian Baylis toured England and South Africa with her musical family as part of a performing troupe, eventually settling in Johannesberg. In 1897 she returned to London to help her aunt to manage the Royal Victoria Coffee and Music Hall, which she had bought to provide wholesome entertainment for working-class families.

In 1912, Baylis inherited the 'Old Vic' and turned it into a renowned Shakespeare venue. Though gauche and tactless (she long refused to give free tickets to reviewers), Baylis was revered for her devotion to the theatre that she ruled, it is said, as a benign autocrat. In 1925 she bought the derelict SADLER'S WELLS theatre for staging opera and dance, forming the origins of the English National Opera and the Royal Ballet.

Trevor BAYLIS

• Inventor • b.1939; OBE 1997

While watching a television documentary about AIDS in Africa in 1993, Trevor Baylis was struck by a comment that if Africans could afford to run battery-powered radios, advice on the disease could be more widely broadcast.

Baylis, whose career had included circus escapology and swimming pool design, conceived the idea of a clockwork radio that could run for an hour after 2 minutes' winding up. After a long struggle he found backing in South Africa, where in 1995 he helped to set up the BayGen factory staffed by handicapped workers. The company was soon selling 20 000 'Freeplay' clockwork radios a month, while Baylis set to work developing a clockwork computer.

BBC

• Est. 1922

Britain's public broadcasting service began life as a private company run by early radio manufacturers and broadcasters such as MARCONI. In 1927 the company became a public service corporation and its manager John REITH director-general.

Reith's belief in the duty of public broadcasting to 'educate, inform and entertain', free from commercial and

political pressure, set the idealistic agenda of the BBC – affectionately known for its improving tone as 'Auntie' – for the next 50 years.

Reith helped to draft the founding charter, under which the BBC may not advertise or broadcast sponsored programmes, and must be impartial in its treatment of current affairs and public policy. The licence fee, introduced by the private company, was retained, its level to be fixed each year by the government.

By the time of Reith's retirement in 1938 the framework for today's BBC had been laid. Live outside broadcasts were made from 1927, when an England v. Wales rugby match was broadcast from Twickenham. In 1932 the BBC acquired its own specialist news department to replace the often unreliable reports of

BUYING AIRTIME The 1922 BBC radio licence (below) cost 10 shillings

Hours of BBC television broadcast annually in Britain: **20 000**
•
Households with television licences: **21.5 million**
•
Income from licence fee: **£2000 million**
•
Income from programme sales: **£75 million**
•
Number of staff: **21 000 worldwide**
•
World audience for BBC World Service radio: **140 million**

outside news agencies. The BBC established the world's first TELEVISION service in 1936. Reith himself announced the death of George V in January; in December, Edward VIII's abdication was broadcast. A second channel, BBC2, started in 1964 and was the first to transmit in colour in 1967.

SHAKING UP AUNTIE

In the 1990s the director general, John Birt, pushed through a series of bold, often unpopular, reforms designed to increase commercial competitiveness, and the BBC has held on to 40 per cent of the television audience – a larger share than expected. The charter was renewed for another ten years in 1996, and the licence fee continues for now to finance the organisation, supplemented by sales abroad and spin-off products.

CUTTING EDGE In the 1990s the **BBC** introduced 'virtual reality' technology into programme-making, superimposing studio action on backgrounds generated by computer

BEACHY HEAD

• **East Sussex (p.495 H6)**
The Normans called Beachy Head *Beau Chef*, 'beautiful headland', but the sheer drop marking the end of the South Downs in East Sussex is also a notorious suicide spot, averaging one death a month.

The chalk cliffs suffer continuous erosion. The Belle Tout lighthouse, now a family home, was built 30m (100ft) from the edge in 1834; it was just 2.4m (8ft) from the brink when it was moved inland in 1999. Stunning views stretch to the Isle of Wight in the west and Dungeness in the east.

HEAD FOR HEIGHT Beachy Head rises 163m (535ft). Below it is the lighthouse that succeeded its cliff-top predecessor Belle Tout from 1902

BEAKER PEOPLE

Was ancient Britain once overwhelmed by Continental invaders? The theory arose in the early 20th century to explain the appearance of distinctive clay beakers in burial sites of about 2700 BC, quite unlike anything in earlier graves.

But although the earliest and finest beakers were Continental in origin, the theory of an invading race of 'beaker people' is now challenged by many archaeologists. Britain's insularity made early mass invasions highly unlikely, and the use of ceremonial sites such as Stonehenge is known to have continued uninterrupted.

A more likely explanation is that trade with groups on the Continent introduced a new cult and attractive foreign goods to prehistoric Britons who accepted the foreign influence willingly, prompting significant and peaceful social change.

Aubrey BEARDSLEY

• **Illustrator** • **1872-98**
With the sinuous lines of his black and white line drawings, stylised composition and preference for erotic or grotesque subjects, Aubrey Beardsley revolutionised late 19th-century book and poster design.

Illustrations for an 1893 edition of Thomas Malory's *Le Morte d'Arthur* were Beardsley's first major commission. They caught the eye of Oscar WILDE, who invited Beardsley to illustrate his play *Salome* (1894) and to design the literary *Yellow Book* magazine. Together with

Wilde, Beardsley was a prominent member of the AESTHETIC MOVEMENT. Although his life was short – he died of tuberculosis at 25 – he was prolific and his drawings are still widely reproduced.
MAJOR COLLECTION • National Art Library at the Victoria and Albert Museum

The BEATLES

• **Ringo Starr (Richard Starkey) b.1940; MBE 1965**
• **John Lennon 1940-80; MBE 1965**
• **Paul McCartney b.1942; MBE 1965; kt 1997**
• **George Harrison b.1943; MBE 1965**

Stepping on stage in 1962, four young men from Liverpool, all with pudding-basin haircuts and sharp suits, drove teenagers to hysterical excitement with their song 'Love Me Do', released earlier that year as their first single.

Beatlemania was a new phenomenon in the world of popular music. The Beatles' engaging personalities and the delicate harmonies of their MERSEYBEAT music appealed to all ages, and under the skilful guidance of their manager, Brian Epstein, a string of hits written by John Lennon and Paul McCartney led to 17 number one singles.

The group recorded 11 albums and acted and sang in five films, including *A Hard Day's Night* (1964) and *Help!* (1965). Increasingly influenced by the counter-culture of drugs and 'flower power', they took a new direction with the album *Sgt. Pepper's Lonely Hearts Club Band* (1967), an experimental adventure in music and technology capturing the psychedelic spirit of the time.

The beginning of the end came in 1968 after Lennon formed a relationship with the Japanese artist Yoko Ono. The group split up in 1970, though all four continued to compose songs. Hopes for a reunion were dashed in 1980 when Lennon was assassinated in New York.

NUMBER ONE HITS:

1963: 'From Me To You'; 'She Loves You'; 'I Want To Hold Your Hand'; 1964: 'Can't Buy Me Love'; 'A Hard Day's Night'; 'I Feel Fine'; 1965: 'Ticket To Ride'; 'Help!'; 'Day Tripper'/'We Can Work It Out'; 1966: 'Paperback Writer'; 'Yellow Submarine'/ 'Eleanor Rigby'; 1967: 'All You Need Is Love'; 'Hello Goodbye'; 1968: 'Lady Madonna'; 'Hey Jude'; 1969: 'Get Back'; 'Ballad Of John And Yoko'

JUMP FOR JOY
The Beatles rehearse for a performance in front of the Queen in 1963, the year of their first hits

Cecil BEATON

• **Photographer, designer** • **1904-80; kt 1972**
'Obviously amateur,' pronounced Edna Chase, editor of American *Vogue*, on first seeing Cecil Beaton's photographs. Although for years he used nothing but a basic Kodak camera, Beaton developed a unique style shooting family and friends. He became famous for society portraits in the 1920s while staff photographer for *Vanity Fair* and *Vogue*.

Beaton's pictures offered a glimpse of the high society in which he moved. He was a friend of the exiled duke and duchess of Windsor, and in 1939 Elizabeth, George VI's queen, asked him to photograph her at Buckingham Palace. The shoot was a success and he became an unofficial royal photographer.

Portraits of celebrities such as Marilyn Monroe and Winston Churchill were not Beaton's only skill. During the Second World War he took memorable photographs of burnt-out aircraft and exhausted soldiers. He also designed for stage and screen, winning Oscars for the sets and costumes of *Gigi* and *My Fair Lady*.

BEAULIEU

• **Hampshire (p.495 F6)**
• **Built 13th-19th century**
In 1204, King John founded a Cistercian abbey near his hunting lodge in the New Forest. This *Bellus Locus Regis*, 'beautiful place of the king', was later translated as 'Beaulieu' by French monks.

Only the lay brothers' living quarters survived the Dissolution of the Monasteries in the 16th century. The refectory became a parish church, and the gatehouse formed the core of Palace House, the home of the Montagu family since 1538. The present house dates mostly from the 1870s, when it was much expanded. Kim Philby, one of the CAMBRIDGE SPIES, worked as an instructor at the estate during the Second World War when its empty houses were used for training intelligence officers.

Lord Montagu opened Beaulieu to the public in 1952. A monorail gives a bird's eye view of the grounds, which contain the National Motor Museum. More than 250 vehicles are exhibited, including a Rolls-Royce *Silver Ghost* of 1909.

BEAUMARIS CASTLE

• **Anglesey (p.494 C1)** • **Begun 1295** • **Cadw**
The sophisticated defences of Beaumaris Castle on the *beau marais*, 'beautiful marsh', on the isle of Anglesey, mark it as the high point of military architecture in medieval Britain.

Beaumaris was to be Edward I's final link in a chain of castles defending English interests in Wales. Instead of the traditional Norman keep and bailey, two walls were built inside one another. A moat fed from the sea encircled the outer curtain wall; the inner wall, 13 m (43 ft) high, had six round towers and two gatehouses giving archers an open line of fire on every side. Yet the castle was left incomplete: during construction Wales was decisively conquered, and Edward's finances became stretched.

BEAUFORT SCALE

In 1805 Commander Francis Beaufort devised a way of measuring wind speed at sea based on the amount of sail a ship needed to carry. It lasted more than 100 years but as steam gradually replaced sail, the measurements were modified to register wind speed according to observable effects: at sea, scale 5 – a 'fresh breeze' – is described as 'moderate waves with white horses'. The scale became the international standard, but is now based on exact wind speeds.

FORCE	OBSERVABLE EFFECTS ON LAND
0	*Smoke rises straight up*
1	*Smoke drifts slightly*
2	*Leaves rustle*
3	*Flags extend*
4	*Paper blows about*
5	*Small trees sway*
6	*Umbrellas blow inside out*
7	*Difficult to stand up*
8	*Twigs break from trees*
9	*Roof tiles are dislodged*
10	*Trees are uprooted*
11	*Serious damage to buildings*
12	*Hurricane devastation*

CREATOR OF A CLASSIC The engineering draughtsman **Harry Beck** was paid just 10 guineas (£10.50) for his ground-breaking schematic map of the London **Underground**

BEAUMONT AND FLETCHER

- Playwrights
- Francis Beaumont c.1584-1616
- John Fletcher 1579-1625

Around 1609, sophisticated London theatregoers began to demand a greater refinement in their entertainment, including fewer lower-class characters, more regular verse and shorter, more compact plots. In response to this change in dramatic taste two up-and-coming playwrights, Francis Beaumont and John Fletcher, succeeded William Shakespeare as dramatists at the King's Men theatrical company.

The two worked together from about 1608, and are said to have shared everything – work, lodgings and even clothes. They produced a string of romantic comedies and tragicomedies, such as the sexually explicit and violent *Maid's Tragedy* (c.1611). Their plays depicted aristocratic manners and intrigues, with little of the clowning and politics of Shakespeare, and foreshadowed the comedy of manners of later RESTORATION drama.

Lord BEAVERBROOK

- Newspaper magnate and politician
- 1879-1964; kt 1911; bn 1916

The Canadian businessman Max Aitken came to London in 1910, and entered parliament later the same year as a Tory MP. When elevated to the peerage, he took the name of a Canadian stream, becoming Baron Beaverbrook.

His highest political office was in Winston Churchill's war cabinet in 1940, when he supervised aircraft production, but it was as an astute press baron that he was most prominent. In 1916 he bought control of the *Daily Express* and built it into the most influential popular newspaper of its day, with a circulation of more than 4 million. The *Sunday Express* was launched in 1918 and the London *Evening Standard* joined the stable in 1923.

Beaverbrook used his papers to campaign for conservative causes, such as free enterprise and British imperial interests, and seduced many left-wing journalists and politicians through well-paid jobs and lavish parties. The papers passed out of Aitken family control in 1979.

Harry BECK

- Graphic designer • 1901-74

The London Underground map that first appeared in 1933, a classic of graphic design, was the work of a young temporary engineering draughtsman. Harry Beck sketched a map of the network in 1931, in his own time. His brilliance lay in realising that it did not have to be to scale or follow the shape of the tracks, but only needed to show the order of the stations and where lines intersected. His schematic plan, still the basis of today's Underground map and a model for transport maps worldwide, shows junctions at 45 or 90 degree angles, with all stations evenly spaced.

Thomas BECKET

- Diplomat, cleric and politician
- 1118-70; archbishop of Canterbury 1162-70; canonised 1173

As chancellor to Henry II, Thomas Becket extracted heavy taxes from the Church. When the king added the position of archbishop to his trusted friend's duties, he envisaged that Becket would help him to curtail Church power, which provided a challenge to his authority.

Instead, Becket resigned as chancellor and vigorously defended Church rights. The two men became bitter enemies, and in 1164 Becket fled to France. Six years later, reconciled with Henry, he returned to England, but his first act was to excommunicate the bishops who had

A SAINT IN HEAVEN A 12th-century casket, made in France and now at the Victoria and Albert Museum, shows angels receiving **Thomas** Becket at the moment of death

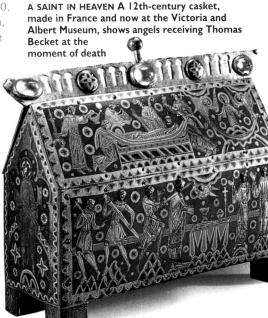

supported the king during his absence. Henry's outburst at the news – 'Who will rid me of this turbulent priest?' – led four knights to murder Becket in Canterbury Cathedral. Henry disclaimed responsibility, but Becket was instantly acclaimed a martyr. The road to his shrine became a busy PILGRIM ROUTE.

The Venerable BEDE

- **Monk and historian**
- **c.673-735; canonised 1899**

Although Bede probably never left the ANGLO-SAXON kingdom of Northumbria, his scholarship was recognised throughout 8th-century Europe and his *Ecclesiastical History of the English People*, one of the more reliable of the early HISTORIES OF BRITAIN, has been crucial to every later historian of England.

Bede grew up in monasteries at Wearmouth and Jarrow, where he wrote grammatical and scientific works and biographies of the saints. His *History* portrays Christianity as the force unifying the peoples of Britain and was the first instance of dating years from the birth of Christ. A synod posthumously awarded Bede the title 'Venerable' in 836.

BEDLAM

The first record of a lunatic asylum at the priory of St Mary Bethlehem, on the site of what is now London's Liverpool Street Station, appears in the early 15th century. By the following century, the renamed Royal Bethlehem (or Bethlem) Hospital had become one of the nation's most notorious institutions and 'Bedlam beggars', or destitute discharged patients, were a familiar sight. Visitors to the hospital would put a few pennies in the poor box for the privilege of gawping at the insane – a scene satirically depicted by the 18th-century painter William HOGARTH. Thus 'bedlam' passed into folklore as a byword for chaos.

A TERRIBLE PLACE?

An early inventory listed manacles, chains, locks and stocks, and there certainly were a few 'political prisoners'. The most colourful was the 17th-century Lady Eleanor Davies, who prophesied the death of Charles I some nine years before the event and was locked away to silence her. Revelations of neglect and

ABSOLUTE BEDLAM An inquiry into events at the Royal Bethlehem Hospital in 1815 revealed that one patient, James Norris, had been immobilised in irons for 12 years

other scandals were commonplace. But hospital archives mostly tell the story of an overworked institution attempting to cope with too many patients, decaying buildings, a shortage of trained staff, and above all, a profound ignorance about mental illness.

Gradually conditions improved. Bethlem moved to new premises in 1676, and, in 1815, to what is now the Imperial War Museum. By the mid 19th century, a new therapeutic regime brought in nourishing food, comfortable surroundings, games and work.

The hospital moved to its current site in Beckenham in 1930. With the creation of the National Heath Service in 1948, Bethlem was merged with the Maudsley, a pioneering psychiatric facility, and has so far survived the trend to close such institutions down.

Thomas BEECHAM

- **Conductor and impresario**
- **1879-1961; kt 1916; 2nd bt 1916**

The heir to the family chemical company, Thomas Beecham was largely self-taught as a conductor. The family fortune enabled him to fund whole seasons at the Royal Opera House, where he was principal conductor and artistic director in the 1930s, and to found the London Philharmonic Orchestra in 1932 and the Royal Philharmonic Orchestra in 1946. His biting wit and strong opinions frequently led to

accusations of arrogance – he dismissed J.S. Bach as 'too Protestant', and disliked the presence of women players in his orchestras – but his impassioned interpretations won him critical praise and popular devotion.

BEEF

The French consider us a nation of beef-eaters, *les Rosbifs*, but beef used to be a luxury – feeding cattle throughout the winter was expensive. In the 1700s, the AGRICULTURAL REVOLUTION provided cheaper fodder and improvements in breeding, and beef became more widely available. New London clubs such as the Beefsteak popularised a new cut, the steak, and beef established itself on British menus and farms. Today's breeds range from the ancient Hereford and Welsh Black to the French Charolais, first imported into Britain in 1961.

Crisis hit cattle farming in the late 1980s and 1990s as evidence emerged that beef from animals infected with bovine spongiform encephalopathy (BSE, or 'mad cow disease') was entering the food human chain, potentially causing fatal brain disease. Millions of cattle were destroyed and some farmers bankrupted.

BEEFEATER

Resplendent in their Tudor red and gold ceremonial uniform or red and dark blue everyday colours, the Yeoman Warders who guard the TOWER OF LONDON and assist tourists are as much an emblem of the capital as Buckingham Palace or double-decker buses. The nickname, 'Beefeaters', is thought to have arisen in the 17th century as an envious reference to their large rations; as late as 1813, the daily allowance for the 30 men on duty was a daunting 26 kg (58 lb) of meat.

The convoluted official title for the Beefeaters is 'The Yeoman Warders of Her Majesty's Royal Palaces and Fortress, the Tower of London, also members of the Queen's bodyguard of the Yeoman Guard Extraordinary'

The Warders were formed in 1485 as Henry VII's bodyguard in the Tower. Today's ceremonial force of between 35 and 40 Yeoman Warders is drawn from senior noncommissioned officers who have served 20 years in the army, air force or marines.

SWEET TASTE OF BITTER

Man has been fermenting wheat and barley to make alcoholic drinks for at least 4000 years. It was only towards the end of the Middle Ages – when herbs, berries and, most importantly, hops were added – that what we now know as beer evolved from basic ale

APART FROM a period in the early 18th century when gin was very cheap, and until tea became the staple drink of Victorian Britons, beer was the most popular British beverage. The ingredients – water and grain – were always plentiful and as early as the 12th century, towns on clean rivers, such as Burton upon Trent, were known for their beer. By the 16th century even the most modest peasant family was brewing its own supply.

THE BREWER'S ART

The basic technique of brewing is simple. Grains of barley or wheat are soaked in water until they begin to sprout, or 'malt', and are then roasted. The longer the roasting, the darker and richer the beer will be. The roasted malt is fermented in water with yeast, turning the sugar in the grain to alcohol. The longer the fermentation, the stronger the beer will be. Hops are added during fermenting as a preservative and to give the drink a distinctive, bitter flavour.

MILD OR BITTER?

Early ales were heavier than modern beers, as the brewer had little control over the malting process. Stout was the darkest and richest, but porter – a hoppy drink aged in the bottle – was traditionally considered the best, although it has now largely died out.

In hop-growing areas such as Kent, 'bitter' beer is the predominant brew. Northern bitters tend to be stronger than those from the south but are often lighter in colour and taste, as they use proportionally fewer hops.

'Mild' beers were developed in the industrial Midlands as a sweeter alternative to bitter. They are also less alcoholic, originally to make them a safe, thirst-quenching lunchtime drink for workers who had to operate machinery.

Pale ales became popular in the mid 1800s, brewed in Burton upon Trent for shipping to the outposts of the Empire and timed to be at their peak on arrival. India pale ale (IPA) found favour at home as well as abroad and was produced by many breweries.

Brown ales were launched in north-east England to rival Burton's pale ales. Probably the best-known is Newcastle Brown Ale, which is actually reddish in colour, with a flavour of nuts, fruit and malt.

OLD ALE RENAISSANCE

Since 1980 the pressure group CAMRA (the Campaign for Real Ale) has been lobbying for the return of the characterful 'old ales' of the past. Their efforts have successfully revived real ale breweries, including Bateman's, in Lincolnshire, and Ruddles, in Rutland.

HIGH-LEVEL HARVEST Hops are still grown supported by wires and poles, much as they were when introduced to England during the 15th century

A ROUND-UP OF ALES

The colour, density and character of an ale reflect the techniques and ingredients used to make it. When families brewed their own beer, probably no two barrels were ever the same. These five pints show the characteristics of the different styles of beer brewed in the British Isles.

GUINNESS STOUT

For almost 150 years, Guinness has been the dominant stout in Britain. The black beer with its roasted flavour and distinctive white head, was first brewed in Ireland in 1690

HIGHGATE OLD ALE

This Walsall brewery's 'winter warmer', available only in the winter months, is a rich, dark beer, in the style of early ales

ADNAMS

Local hops give this Suffolk bitter a dry, hoppy flavour. Bitters from the south tend to have very little head

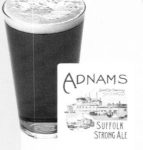

BODDINGTONS BITTER

Northern bitters, such as this one brewed in Strangeways Prison, Manchester, can be light and golden, with a creamy head that belies their alcoholic strength

INDIA EXPORT

Translucent amber pale ales were brewed with a high hop content to preserve them on the journey to India. The hops also gave the beer an antiseptic quality

Max BEERBOHM

• **Cartoonist and writer**
• **1872-1956; kt 1939**

'The incomparable Max', as the playwright George Bernard Shaw called him, specialised in satirising the writers and artists of his day such as Oscar Wilde and Aubrey Beardsley. He would sketch his subjects secretly, observing them in the reflection of his pocket watch as they drank at the fashionable Café Royal in London's Regent Street.

Beerbohm also wrote spoof essays and a comic novel, *Zuleika Dobson* (1911), in which the undergraduate population of Oxford University drown themselves for love of the unattainable Zuleika. Beerbohm's half-brother, the actor Herbert Beerbohm-Tree, gave Max the opportunity to move in theatrical circles, and in 1898 he succeeded Shaw as drama critic of the *Saturday Review*.

SELF-STYLED SWELL In a self caricature of the 1890s Beerbohm sent up his own dandyish dressing

BEES

In song, poetry and morality tales since Biblical times the hard-working bee has been held up as an example of industry and cooperation. Beekeeping has been going on almost as long. In Britain archaeological evidence exists of 1000-year-old Viking beehives, and the Romans almost certainly kept bees even earlier.

There are 35 000 beekeepers in Britain, tending around 12 million bees in 250 000 hives. In a typical hive as many as 500 000 honeybees live together

Long before sugar was known honey was loved as a sweetener and used as a preservative. Beekeeping and producing MEAD, an alcoholic drink made from fermented honey, were popular in the Middle Ages, especially in monasteries. Wax was also used in polish and candles.

There is only one species of honeybee in western Europe, *Apis melifera*, but almost 250 other types of bee are also found here, including 19 species of bumblebee. Bumblebees live in smaller groups than honeybees, in colonies of up to 150 insects. The other species lead solitary lives, nesting in soil, plant stems, loose mortar and other crevices, or are parasites.

Mrs BEETON

• **Cookery writer** • **1836-65**

The author of Europe's best-selling cookbook was not the mature housewife her name suggests but a fashionable young woman.

Isabella Beeton began writing at the suggestion of her husband, whose *Englishwoman's Domestic Magazine* featured fashion, fiction, food and gardening. By the age of 24 she had turned her monthly articles into *Beeton's Book of Household Management*, soon a bible in Victorian homes. For the first time food recipes listed quantities, cooking times, servings and cost. The book also included advice on managing houses, children, servants and husbands.

Mrs Beeton's book has sold more than 3 million copies and a revised edition is still published every 10 years.

BELFAST

• **Northern Ireland (p.497 B6)** • **Pop. 279 240**

Four hundred years ago Belfast was little more than a small fishing village. In the 17th century, Protestant settlers arrived from England and the Scottish Lowlands to secure the region's loyalty to the Crown. They were given land taken from native Irish Catholics – the origin of much hatred – but Belfast thrived.

The city's greatest expansion came with the Industrial Revolution, bringing first cotton spinning and linen weaving, and then shipbuilding to the area. The Harland and Wolff shipyard, which still dominates the city's docks, built the *TITANIC* in 1912.

When Ireland was divided in 1921, Belfast became the capital of NORTHERN IRELAND and has since been the focus of sectarian division, reflected in the graffiti-covered houses of the Falls and Shankhill Roads. Behind the war-torn façade is a different spirit, with live entertainment and music found from pubs and street corners to the Grand Opera House. To the south, the art gallery, botanic garden and Ulster museum offer a unique mix of Irish history, art and flora on one site.

Alexander Graham BELL

• **Scientist and inventor** • **1847-1922**

'Mr Watson, come here; I want you!' Alexander Graham Bell's curt summons to his assistant has gone down in history as the sentence that ushered in the era of the telephone.

Bell's interest in phonetics, acquired as a teacher of the deaf, led him to experiment with transmitting sound by electrical impulses. In 1876 he lodged a patent just hours before his rival Elisha Gray for 'transmitting vocal or other sounds telegraphically', which he refined into the instrument that brought Watson from an adjacent room.

The Edinburgh-born inventor was living in the United States when he made his breakthrough. He offered the rights to the Western Union Telegraph Company for $100 000 but in a historic miscalculation it turned him down, seeing no future in the 'phone. In 1877, Bell established the biggest private service organisation in the world: the Bell Telephone Company, now AT&T.

His later work in acoustics included a sound recording device. Bell also helped to develop a giant people-carrying kite, an iron lung and a hydrofoil that attained a record speed of 70.86 mph in 1919. He also developed a sheep strain disposed to multiple births.

MAKING THE CONNECTION Crowds turned out to hear Alexander Graham Bell open the New York to Chicago telephone line in 1892

Hilaire BELLOC

- **Writer and politician** • 1870-1953

For every time she shouted 'Fire!'
They only answered 'Little Liar!'
And therefore when her Aunt returned,
Matilda, and the House, were Burned.

('Matilda', *Cautionary Tales*, 1907)
Hilaire Belloc's comic admonishments to children with bad habits – like Matilda, who told lies – are still classics of the genre scores of years after their publication. But Belloc was also a serious author of biographies, histories, religious works and travel books – many coloured by his devout Roman Catholic faith.

Belloc was born in France but educated in England and in 1902 he became a British subject. From 1906 to 1910 he sat as a Liberal in the Commons, championing Roman Catholicism and attacking socialism for restricting personal freedom.

Alan BENNETT

- **Playwright** • b.1934

A bittersweet view of life, tinged by a sharp political edge, characterises the work of Alan Bennett for stage, radio and television. Bennett has always relished poking fun at the London literati who persist in viewing northerners as rough, tough and slightly uncouth. He both exploits the stereotype, proudly holding on to his Leeds accent, and turns it on its head, cultivating a witty, self-effacing, somewhat bookish image.

With Peter Cook, Jonathan Miller and Dudley Moore, Bennett developed the satirical revue *Beyond the Fringe*, which, at the 1960 Edinburgh Festival, launched all four careers and a new brand of COMEDY. He went on to work as an actor, dramatist and director in plays such as *Forty Years On* (1968) and *Habeas Corpus* (1973). For television he wrote the drama *An Englishman Abroad* (1983), about the spy Guy Burgess, and the *Talking Heads* monologues (1988 and 1998).

Arnold BENNETT

- **Writer** • 1867-1931

Although a novel about London high society, *Grand Babylon Hotel* (1902) first brought Arnold Bennett to public attention, his masterpieces are his tales of working life in the Midlands' Potteries region. Bennett moved to London at 22, but in novels such as *Anna of the Five Towns* (1902) and *Clayhanger* (1910) he wrote with affection about the area near Hanley, in Staffordshire, where he was born. Stylistically, he was an innovator, introducing techniques learned from French realist writers such as Guy de Maupassant and Emile Zola.

From 1912, Bennett turned mainly to plays, theatre criticism and newspaper journalism, including a column for the London *Evening Standard*. Regular post-theatre suppers at the Savoy Hotel conferred immortality in the form of omelette 'Arnold Bennett'.

Jeremy BENTHAM

- **Philosopher and reformer** • 1748-1832

The 'panopticon' – Jeremy Bentham's plan for a prison with inmates perpetually on view – embodied the ideal of complete clarity that also led him as a young man to give up studying law. The obscurity of legal language repelled Bentham, and he set out to simplify legal terms to ensure that every word referred directly to something plain.

In *Principles of Morals and Legislation* (1789) he proposed that the right action in all cases is the one that results in 'the greatest happiness of the greatest number'. This principle, which he called 'utilitarianism', was intended to make justice a matter of mathematical calculation rather than arbitrary human judgment, and provided the foundation for the philosophy of John Stuart MILL.

Bentham's body was preserved after death and his clothed skeleton remains on display at University College, London, which was founded on his principles in 1826. The body is regularly taken to Senate meetings, at which Bentham is recorded as being present but not voting.

BEOWULF

The oldest epic in the ENGLISH LANGUAGE is the tale of Beowulf, a story that probably originated in Denmark and came to Britain with the Angles, who invaded in the 5th century.

All that is known for certain is that the poem was recited at festivals from the 8th century. A written manuscript,

---

BEN NEVIS

- **Highland (p.497 C3)**
- **1343 m (4406 ft)**

The rounded granite mass of Britain's highest mountain rises south-east of Fort William, at the southern end of Scotland's Great Glen. Although it has no soaring peaks, rock buttresses and gullies make the north face a challenge even for experienced climbers. Up to 150000 visitors each year approach the top by the so-called 'tourist path', although even this has eroded into a fairly strenuous climb.

From the summit, views stretch 100 miles or more, on a clear day as far as the coast of Ireland. The uninterrupted vistas made Ben Nevis the site of a weather observatory in 1823. It closed in 1904 but ruins remain at the mountain top.

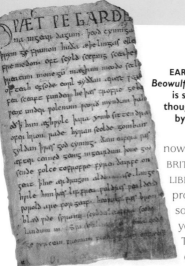

EARLY EPIC The Beowulf manuscript is still readable though damaged by fire in 1731

now in the BRITISH LIBRARY, was produced some 200 years later. The hero of the poem, the Swedish Beowulf, goes to the aid of a kingdom terrorised by the monster Grendel. Beowulf slays first Grendel and then his even more terrifying mother, before dying in a final conflict. In a blend of Christian and pagan influences, the poem upholds traditional warrior virtues but concludes by reflecting on the mortality of even the greatest heroes.

Bishop BERKELEY

• **Philosopher and cleric** • **1685-1753**

Early in life Irish-born George Berkeley's appetite for learning nearly killed him. He arranged to be hanged by the neck until he gave a signal to be cut down but, having waited until he was 'losing the use of his senses', had to be rescued as he was no longer able to ask for help.

In Berkeley, BRITISH EMPIRICISM took an unusual turn. As a cleric he hoped to reconcile science and religion. Like other empiricists, he believed that knowledge came from experience but, uniquely, he maintained that nothing existed but what was perceived – a theory expounded in his early works, such as *Essay Towards a New Theory of Vision* (1709). Far from being sceptical about external reality, this position was intended to give a central role to God – as the all-seeing eye that guaranteed the continued existence of the world.

BERKELEY CASTLE

• **Gloucestershire (p.494 E4)**
• **Built 1153-c.1350**

In 1327 the serene grey-pink walls of Berkeley Castle echoed with the screams of EDWARD II as he was tortured to death. Its largely untroubled past was only otherwise marred by an episode in the Civil War when Parliamentarian forces laid siege to the castle leaving a breach still visible in the massive wall.

As the residence of the FitzHardinge family since the 12th century, the castle became more a stately home than a stronghold: chimneys rose above the battlements and a terraced garden and Elizabethan bowling alley were created.

Annie BESANT

• **Feminist, socialist and theosophist**
• **1847-1933**

People who heard Annie Besant speak still recalled the brilliance of her oratory decades later. A passionate and fearless campaigner for many causes, she renounced religion after a brief, unhappy marriage to a clergyman, and became vice-president of the National Secular Society. With the founder Charles Bradlaugh she was prosecuted for a book on birth control – becoming at her trial in 1877 the first woman to defend contraception in public.

She became a socialist and a member of the FABIAN SOCIETY but in 1889 met Madame Blavatsky, head of the Theosophical Society, and abandoned socialism for mysticism. From 1895 she lived mainly at the society's Indian headquarters and by 1907 she was its international president. Still politically active, she joined the Indian National Congress and at 70 was interned for her passionate support of home rule.

Henry BESSEMER

• **Metallurgist and inventor** • **1813-98; kt 1879**

Steel built the bridges, rails and trains of the Industrial Revolution, but until Henry Bessemer developed a new process in the 1850s it was laborious to make. Cast iron had to be melted in furnaces to remove carbon, which was then reintroduced in precise amounts to make a strong, but not brittle metal.

As iron was needed in large quantities for guns in the Crimean War, Bessemer developed a much cheaper process of blowing air through molten iron – in the Bessemer converter – to burn off just enough carbon to leave behind steel.

But the process worked only with phosphorus-free ore. Manufacturers rapidly abandoned it but Bessemer persevered. He set up his own works in Sheffield, importing phosphorus-free iron from Sweden, and made a fortune supplying steel to railways worldwide.

George BEST

• **Footballer** • **b.1946**

Before tales of riotous living filled the gossip pages in the 1970s, George Best was lauded as Europe's most talented footballer for his mastery of the ball.

The Belfast-born winger made his debut at 17 with MANCHESTER UNITED and was soon one of their star players. He scored 137 goals in the 361 League games he played for the club, won two League championship medals (1965 and 1967), a European Cup medal (1968), and 37 caps for Northern Ireland.

Best was renowned for his partiality to alcohol and women, and entitled his autobiography *The Good, the Bad and the Bubbly*.

PLAYING THE FIELD Showmanship and skilful ball control, together with good looks and a roguish charm both on and off the pitch, made George Best a popular figure during the 1960s

John BETJEMAN

• Poet and essayist • 1906-84; kt 1969; poet laureate 1972

Phone for the fish-knives, Norman
As Cook is a little unnerved;
You kiddies have crumpled the serviettes
And I must have things daintily served.

HOW TO GET ON IN SOCIETY (1954)

The uniquely English voice of John Betjeman combines a deep love of the land and its traditions with gentle mockery of social affectations and manners.

By the time he died, Betjeman had been christened 'the people's poet', having seduced the nation with the charm and unpretentiousness of his verse. His first collection, *Mount Zion*, was published in 1932, and his softly ironic style reached a wider public during the 1950s, when he made television documentaries on British architecture, often with accompanying verse narrative.

With his portly figure and infectious laugh, Betjeman became immensely popular. His *Collected Poems* (1958, revised 1962) sold a million copies.

Aneurin BEVAN

• Politician • 1897-1960

'Nye', as the Labour politician Aneurin Bevan was known, started work at 13 in the south Wales coal mines and by 19 he was chairman of the local Miner's Lodge. He led the Welsh miners in the GENERAL STRIKE and went on to fight for jobs and better conditions for workers as MP for Ebbw Vale from 1929. Although Bevan was a brilliant and charismatic orator, his outspokenness often angered the Labour leadership. In 1939 he was briefly expelled from the party for proposing a 'Popular Front' against fascism.

The peak of Bevan's career came in 1948 when, as Clement ATTLEE's minister of health, he launched the NATIONAL HEALTH SERVICE. An uncompromising idealist, he resigned three years later when charges were proposed for false teeth and spectacles.

BEVERLEY

• East Riding of Yorkshire (p.496 D4)
• Pop. 23 630

A magnificent church stands at either end of Beverley's main street. The medieval Minster, with its graceful twin-towered west front, is renowned for intricate Gothic stone carvings and an unusual Saxon *fridstol*, a sanctuary chair, beside the altar, where criminals could claim protection from the law.

St Mary's Church, near North Bar, was built in the 14th century and is the sole survivor of the town's five medieval gates. The chancel ceiling was covered with cartoon-like paintings of English kings in 1445, and carvings in the church include a rabbit said to have inspired Tenniel's White Rabbit drawings for Lewis Carroll's *Alice in Wonderland*.

A market has been held on the cobbled main square, known as Saturday Market, for more than 700 years.

Ernest BEVIN

• Trade unionist and politician • 1881-1951

'A bit of a dreamer' whose best ideas came while cleaning his boots in the morning was how Ernest Bevin saw himself. To others he was a 'doer', who in 1920 won a guaranteed living wage for dockers by cooking for the board of inquiry a supposedly 'adequate' meal for a family of five on a docker's pay.

Orphaned at seven, Bevin started work at 11 as a manual labourer. Despite his lack of formal education he ended his career as foreign secretary, with a string of achievements behind him. In 1921 he amalgamated more than 30 TRADE UNIONS into the Transport and General Workers Union, the largest in the world; he helped to organise the GENERAL STRIKE in 1926; and in 1937 became chairman of the Trades Union Congress (TUC).

As foreign secretary, Bevin helped to organise the Berlin airlift of 1948-9 and took Britain into NATO.

BIBA

In the colour and excitement of 1960s London a new shop in Kensington had to be exceptional to make a splash. When it opened in 1964 Biba, with its palms, ostrich plumes and blood-red walls, became instantly famous.

The invention of the 28-year-old fashion designer Barbara Hulanicki and her husband Stephen Fitz-Simon, the shop sold an affordable 'total look' mimicking 1930s and 40s glamour. Biba dressed women in soft crepe and jersey in muted grey and lilac tones, accented by floppy hats, feather boas, black lipstick and brown eye-shadow. The clothes were modelled by Twiggy and worn by stars such as Julie Christie. In 1969 Hulanicki opened Big Biba, an opulent fantasy world selling everything from clothes to jewellery, satin sheets and wallpaper. Within two years the over-ambitious store had closed.

BIBA GIRL Art Deco glamour set the label's style – sold as a way of life, not just a look

English BIBLE

When John WYCLIFFE began translating the Bible into English in the late 14th century it was a revolutionary act. For the first time the text was accessible not just to scholars and clergymen but to those who knew no Latin. Books were still rare, though, and few could read, even in their native tongue.

THE WORD BECOMES PRINT

The invention of printing in the 15th century and growing anti-Catholic feeling after the REFORMATION led to a rash of new English Bibles, including William Tyndale's 1526 New Testament and Miles Coverdale's complete Bible of 1535. Henry VIII favoured Coverdale and soon every parish church had a copy.

AUTHORISED VERSION

In 1604 James I commissioned a new 'Authorised' version, based on Tyndale. The King James Bible, as it is also known, appeared in 1611 and for more than 300 years was the version most read in church and at home. The beauty of its prose enriched both literature and the ENGLISH LANGUAGE itself, giving us such expressions as 'gird one's loins' and 'salt of the earth'.

MODERN BIBLES

Numerous English Bibles have been produced in the 20th century. The Church of England uses mainly the 1952 Revised Standard Version and the New English Bible, published in two parts in 1961 and 1970.

BIG BEN

• Bell cast 1858

The clock tower at the northern end of the HOUSES OF PARLIAMENT is a symbol for London recognised the world over, rising to 98 m (320 ft) with four clock faces 7 m (23 ft) across.

Strictly, the name Big Ben applies to the biggest of the clock's bells, which sounds the hour. Weighing 13.5 tons, it was the largest bell in Britain when cast in 1858 and was probably named after the chief commissioner of works, Benjamin Hall.

The bell cracked soon after being installed, and had to be recast. Since 1923 its clear, deep boom, pitched to the note 'E', has resounded across the world as the time signal of the BBC.

FLYING ACE The invincible Biggles was always ready to battle his sworn enemy, Eric Von Stalhein. The books were written from first-hand experience, the author himself being shot down in 1918

BIGGLES

• Fictional pilot

James Bigglesworth ('Biggles'), air ace and hero of 96 novels, was the fictional creation of W.E. Johns (1893-1968), a First World War pilot.

Biggles's first appearance was in *Popular Flying* magazine in 1932. His daring exploits in 666 Squadron, and the fierce loyalty of Biggles and his fellow pilots Algie, Ginger and Bertie, made him a role model for generations of British boys. Although criticised for jingoism, Johns's tales brought the RAF many recruits in the Second World War.

BILLIARDS

While the shorter and faster and more recent game of SNOOKER has eclipsed billiards in popularity, aficionados maintain that the earlier game is more complex and therefore more interesting.

Billiards in France dates from at least the 15th century, and became popular in Britain during the 1800s. The game is played with three balls, one red and two white 'cue balls'. Points can run into thousands and are won by 'potting' or going 'in-off' another ball into a pocket, or making a 'cannon' – hitting both other balls with a cue ball.

BILL OF RIGHTS

When JAMES II was driven from England in 1688 he left behind a government weary from power struggles with the Stuarts. To avoid future wrangling a Bill of Rights was drawn up in 1689 by parliament for the new monarchs, WILLIAM AND MARY, asserting the rights and liberties of the people.

The bill restricted royal influence and introduced electoral reforms to ensure fuller public representation in parliament, laying the groundwork of the BRITISH CONSTITUTION. Prior to the 1997 election the Labour party pledged a new bill of rights to reform the country's democracy.

BINGO

'Two little ducks, 22', 'Legs 11' and the rest of the traditional Bingo chants regularly keep 3 million pairs of British eyes glued to their scorecards. Each card has 25 numbers between 1 and 90 or 99, printed in five rows. Players cover or score out numbers as the caller announces them, the aim being to fill a line, create a pattern or complete a card first, crying 'Bingo!' or 'Housey, housey!'.

Eighty per cent of the entry money is paid back in prizes and the chances of winning are significantly higher than in the National Lottery. Skilled players sometimes play several cards at once.

LUCKY NUMBERS Play halts as a steward checks out a winning Bingo card. Prizes can be as high as £2500 a game

LIFE ON THE WING

The British Isles, insulated by the warm waters of the North Atlantic Current, are a welcome landfall for millions of immigrant birds. These visitors from far-off lands join a wealth of indigenous species to provide a diversity of birdlife unmatched in continental Europe

ABOUT 270 SPECIES of bird are regularly seen in the British Isles, of which about 135 are regarded as year-round residents. Some are familiar inhabitants of gardens and parks, such as blackbirds singing from rooftop perches, blue tits busily examining garden nest boxes or searching for caterpillars on oak leaves, rooks nesting high in tall trees, and wood pigeons cooing 'take two teas taffy' throatily from afar. Others are less well known, including the common but unobtrusive dunnock (once misnamed the hedge sparrow), the rare Dartford warbler of southern heathlands, the ghostly barn owl in silent nocturnal flight, the red grouse of northern moorlands and the magnificent golden eagle presiding over the craggy peaks in the Highlands.

Most of these so-called residents are actually partial migrants: a proportion of their populations move around within the British Isles or even make the short sea crossing to and from the Continent. For instance, many British song thrushes that breed in the northern uplands choose to spend winter in southern parts of Britain and Ireland, with some, especially immature birds, even flying as far south as Spain. At the same time, some song thrushes that visit British gardens during winter will have travelled all the way from Scandinavia, central and eastern Europe and the Netherlands.

The real stay-at-home species that are generally reluctant to move more than a few miles from the place where they were hatched include the tree-dwelling tawny owl, nuthatch, treecreeper and coal tit, as well as the kingfisher and the magpie. Even residents such as these may travel farther afield, as young birds seek out new territories and adults disperse in winter to find food.

A number of exotic birds have also become residents. Pheasants were brought from southern Asia during the 11th century or earlier, the Canada goose was introduced from North America in the 17th century, little owls from the Continent in the 19th century and – perhaps the most exotic of all – ring-necked parakeets from India were first spotted in the wild in 1969. Thousands of these long-tailed green parrots now breed in Britain, mainly in south-east England, managing to survive the bleak British winters with the help of food provided at bird tables.

BRITISH RESIDENTS

RED KITE This supremely graceful and agile bird of prey has slowly built up its numbers in its mid-Wales stronghold. In recent years it has also been successfully reintroduced to parts of England and Scotland

ROBIN Associated with Christmas since the 1860s, the robin is the best loved of all garden birds. Fights between rival males are fierce and can end in death

BLUE TIT Up to 200 individual blue tits may visit a garden bird table in a single day, and up to 1000 over the winter

SCOTTISH CROSSBILL The only bird species unique to Britain, the Scottish crossbill is restricted to Highland pine forests. It tends to favour trees more than 70 years old

WREN The wren is the most widespread and abundant of all British birds. About 10 million breeding pairs live here

BARN OWL This bird has suffered a long-term decline in range and numbers due to modern farming methods, lack of nest sites, and road-kills

CHOUGH Our rarest member of the crow family, the chough is now found only on the wilder western fringes of the British Isles

GOLDEN EAGLE Over 400 pairs of golden eagle breed in Scotland each year, and there is one solitary pair in the Lake District. Eagles suffer from habitat destruction, deliberate poisoning, disturbance and egg-collecting, despite legal protection

AVOCET Symbol of the Royal Society for the Protection of Birds (RSPB), this elegant, boldly patterned wader is a rare breeder mainly in East Anglia

WHITE-FRONTED GEESE

FLYING VISITORS

Some 120 different migrant bird species regularly spend part of the year in Britain. Autumn brings geese, whooper and Bewick's swans, ducks, waders, redwings and fieldfares from Scandinavia, eastern Europe and Siberia. By this time summer visitors such as the osprey, Arctic and other terns, swifts, swallows, martins and warblers have left for the Mediterranean and Africa. Some birds, such as the curlew sandpiper and bluethroat, use the British Isles as staging posts on their journey between summer breeding sites in the Arctic and wintering areas in Africa.

SEASONAL MOVEMENTS

SPRING Winter visitors leave as summer migrants start to pour in. Passage migrants stop off on their way to breeding grounds as far north as the Arctic.

SUMMER Many birds have reared young, and some begin second or third broods.

AUTUMN Winter visitors start to arrive, including wildfowl, waders, thrushes, finches and starlings. Passage migrants pass through, heading south.

WINTER Winter visitors flock in, while local birds move around the country in search of food.

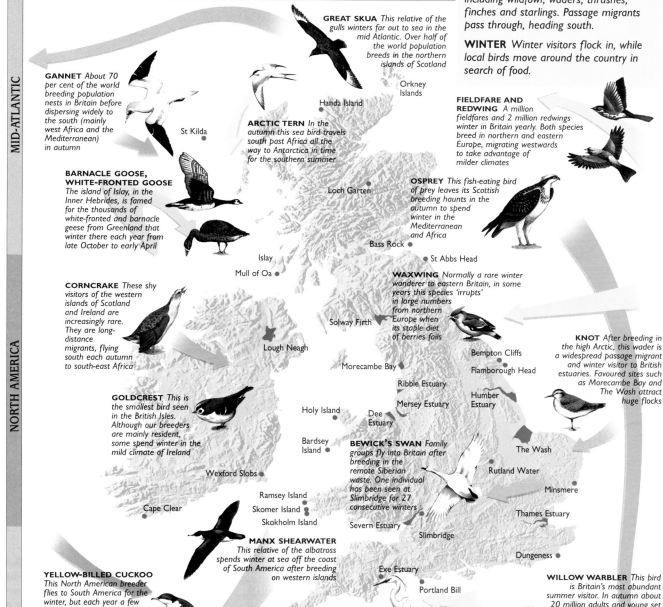

GREENLAND

GREAT SKUA This relative of the gulls winters far out to sea in the mid Atlantic. Over half of the world population breeds in the northern islands of Scotland

GANNET About 70 per cent of the world breeding population nests in Britain before dispersing widely to the south (mainly west Africa and the Mediterranean) in autumn

ARCTIC TERN In the autumn this sea bird travels south past Africa all the way to Antarctica in time for the southern summer

BARNACLE GOOSE, WHITE-FRONTED GOOSE The island of Islay, in the Inner Hebrides, is famed for the thousands of white-fronted and barnacle geese from Greenland that winter there each year from late October to early April

FIELDFARE AND REDWING A million fieldfares and 2 million redwings winter in Britain yearly. Both species breed in northern and eastern Europe, migrating westwards to take advantage of milder climates

OSPREY This fish-eating bird of prey leaves its Scottish breeding haunts in the autumn to spend winter in the Mediterranean and Africa

CORNCRAKE These shy visitors of the western islands of Scotland and Ireland are increasingly rare. They are long-distance migrants, flying south each autumn to south-east Africa

WAXWING Normally a rare winter wanderer to eastern Britain, in some years this species 'irrupts' in large numbers from northern Europe when its staple diet of berries fails

KNOT After breeding in the high Arctic, this wader is a widespread passage migrant and winter visitor to British estuaries. Favoured sites such as Morecambe Bay and The Wash attract huge flocks

GOLDCREST This is the smallest bird seen in the British Isles. Although our breeders are mainly resident, some spend winter in the mild climate of Ireland

BEWICK'S SWAN Family groups fly into Britain after breeding in the remote Siberian waste. One individual has been seen at Slimbridge for 27 consecutive winters

MANX SHEARWATER This relative of the albatross spends winter at sea off the coast of South America after breeding on western islands

YELLOW-BILLED CUCKOO This North American breeder flies to South America for the winter, but each year a few birds get blown off course and can end up in south-west England, where they are usually found suffering from exhaustion

LITTLE EGRET Until recently this member of the heron family was a rare wanderer to Britain in late summer. From the early 1990s onwards, increasing numbers from Europe have arrived on southern coasts and some have stayed to breed

WILLOW WARBLER This bird is Britain's most abundant summer visitor. In autumn about 20 million adults and young set off for Africa, stopping briefly in northern Spain and Portugal to refuel on a feast of berries and insects

SWALLOW After spending the summer in Britain swallows embark on a six to eight week journey to South Africa, where they stay for the winter

MID-ATLANTIC — NORTH AMERICA — SOUTH AMERICA — ARCTIC — EUROPE

Orkney Islands
Handa Island
St Kilda
Loch Garten
Islay
Mull of Oa
Bass Rock
St Abbs Head
Solway Firth
Lough Neagh
Bempton Cliffs
Flamborough Head
Morecambe Bay
Ribble Estuary
Humber Estuary
Mersey Estuary
Holy Island
Dee Estuary
Bardsey Island
The Wash
Wexford Slobs
Rutland Water
Minsmere
Ramsey Island
Skomer Island
Skokholm Island
Thames Estuary
Severn Estuary
Slimbridge
Cape Clear
Dungeness
Exe Estuary
Portland Bill
Isles of Scilly

As winter draws in there is a shuffling of Britain's bird population. Some species, such as fieldfares and redwings, are just arriving, while others, including swallows and Manx shearwaters, are departing for sunnier climes. This map shows where they are travelling to and from. A brown area or dot on the map indicates a good place to spot migrant birds.

AFRICA

BIRDWATCHING

Britain probably contains a greater number of birdwatchers for its size than any other country. More than a million people are members of The Royal Society for the Protection of Birds (RSPB).

The modern hobby and science of learning about birds through observation developed mainly in the 20th century. Before then, exceptional naturalists such as Gilbert WHITE (1720-93) and Charles Waterton (1782-1865) observed living birds, but most enthusiasts studied specimens only after shooting them.

The most fanatical birdwatchers are called 'twitchers', after their excited reaction to glimpsing a rare species. In 1989 a twitcher spotted a brightly coloured bird in a bush in Maidstone, Kent. On discovering that it was a scarce North American golden-winged warbler, he found it again in a car park, and set in train Britain's biggest ever twitch. Within days, 2500 twitchers were there, armed with binoculars and telephoto lenses.

BIRMINGHAM

• **W Midlands (p.495 F3)**   • **Pop. 965 930**
Modern development in the shape of a rebuilt Bull Ring shopping centre, the proposed Arena Central (at 245 m/805 ft, the tallest business tower in Britain) and a whirl of ring roads, have brought Birmingham's heritage of industry and grand exhibitions firmly up to date.

The restored water transport system recalls a busy past when canals more numerous than those of Venice linked nearby coalfields with factories and seaports. James WATT's rotary steam engine, made here in the 1780s, turned Birmingham from a market town into the hub of the INDUSTRIAL REVOLUTION and the heart of the manufacturing 'BLACK COUNTRY'. In 1838 one of the earliest railways in Britain, the London to Birmingham Railway, was built to link the two cities.

Wealth from industry enabled merchants in the late 19th century to finance grand building schemes, such as the Town Hall and the Museum and Art Gallery, which exhibits the city's prestigious jewellery collection. The City of Birmingham Symphony Orchestra, founded in 1920, won world status in the 1990s under the baton of Simon RATTLE.

Many of the old mills and factories have gone, but Birmingham remains at the forefront of commerce, with the motor industry playing a major part. It is home to the National Exhibition Centre, an international convention centre, and three universities. The city's Aston Villa Football Club won the European Cup in 1982 and the Edgbaston cricket ground hosts Test matches.

UP IN ARMS Harrison Birtwistle's *Punch and Judy (below)* **caused such outrage when the opera was premiered at the 1968 Aldeburgh Festival that Benjamin Britten walked out – and he had commissioned it**

Harrison BIRTWISTLE

• **Composer**   • **b.1934; kt 1988**
Once the enfant terrible of British music, Harrison Birtwistle is now part of the artistic establishment. He trained at the Royal Manchester School of Music in the 1950s and there met the composer Peter Maxwell Davies. Together they experimented with atonal music in the style pioneered in Vienna by Arnold Schoenberg and Alban Berg. In 1967 they formed the Pierrot Players, a group specialising in music drama.

Ritualistic and dramatic elements have always been a feature of Birtwistle's music and even in concert works he frequently dictates the positions and movements of the instrumentalists. In 1975 he became director of music for the National Theatre.

The composer's later works have become ever more innovative: the 1985 opera *The Mask of Orpheus* introduced computer sound technology for the stage. And Birtwistle can still shock audiences; his violent saxophone concerto *Panic* provoked widespread protest among the audience when it was premiered in the Albert Hall at the 1995 Last Night of the Proms.

James BLACK

• **Doctor and pharmacologist**   • **b.1924; kt 1981**
The high incidence of heart disease in his native Scotland led James Black to make one of modern medicine's most imaginative breakthroughs. Black deduced that if he could find a drug to block the action of hormones that stimulate the heart muscle, its rate could be better controlled. Success came in 1964 when he developed the now widely prescribed beta blockers. Black won the Nobel prize for physiology in 1988 for drug research founded on his analysis of the causes of disease.

BLACK AND TANS

In 1920, during the Anglo-Irish War, the British government drafted 12 000 ex-servicemen into southern Ireland to reinforce the Royal Irish Constabulary, who were under attack from the Irish Republican Army (IRA). Kitted out in a combination of khaki military and dark

police uniforms, the 'Black and Tans' as they were called – after a pack of Irish foxhounds – were an ill-disciplined force much hated by Republicans.

In 1920, the Black and Tans avenged the murder of 14 British agents in Dublin by firing on a crowd at a football match, wounding 60 and killing 12 – a day remembered as Bloody Sunday. Such atrocities shocked the British public and the force was withdrawn after the treaty creating the Irish Free State was signed in 1921.

HELL HOUND A weather vane at Bungay in Suffolk provides a daily reminder of a demon dog said to have appeared in the church in 1577 and wrung the necks of worshippers

BLACK COUNTRY

• **W Midlands (p.494 E2)**

The area north-west of Birmingham was christened the 'Black Country' in Victorian times, in reference to the grime produced by the metalwork factories and coal mines of the region. Charles Dickens's *The Old Curiosity Shop* records how local factory chimneys 'poured out their plague of smoke, obscured the light, and made foul the melancholy air', rapidly blackening rows of new houses.

Since the demise of coal-based industries and the introduction of clean air legislation in recent times, the Black Country has ceased to be black. A step back into the industrial past is still possible at the Black Country Museum in Dudley, where exhibits include glass-cutting and chain-making workshops in reconstructed buildings.

BLACK DOGS

In parts of southern England, medieval folklore warned that large dogs with pitch-black coats and eyes that glowed red or green prowled at night round graveyards and marshes. Anyone who saw one, it was said, was soon to die or to cause the death of a family member.

The howls of the dogs, often called Black Shuck from the Anglo-Saxon *scucca* (demon), were supposed to rise above the wildest storms. Travellers on lonely roads frequently reported icy breath on the back of the neck or the sensation of

a rough coat brushing past. During the Middle Ages, black dogs featured in witch lore even more than black cats. It was said that witches transformed themselves into black dogs in order to beset their victims, and also that the beasts were disguised demon lovers. Some women in the 16th century were hanged in Chelmsford in Essex for practising witchcraft, assisted by their familiars in the shape of dogs.

BLACKWELL'S

• **Est. 1879**

'The only bookshop to which I have become a life-long addict,' said the poet Stephen Spender of Blackwell's. Today an international bookselling and publishing business with a turnover of £350 million, it was begun by Benjamin Blackwell more than 100 years ago as a tiny secondhand shop in Broad Street in Oxford. The premises were so small that Blackwell's assistant had to go outside if there were more than two customers.

The business grew rapidly, supplying scholarly works to students and staff of Oxford University. Under Basil Blackwell, son of the founder, the business branched out into publishing in 1926, specialising in the humanities, social sciences and business and, from 1939, medicine and science.

As higher education expanded during the 1950s and 60s, Blackwell's started to supply university libraries worldwide, and became Britain's foremost academic bookseller. It remains an independent, privately owned family firm.

BLACKPOOL

• **Lancashire (p.496 A4)** • **Pop. 146 260**

Until the arrival of the railway in 1846, Blackpool was just a tiny fishing village with fewer than 500 inhabitants. But as holidaymakers started to pour in from the new industrial centres of Lancashire and Yorkshire the town grew and soon its 7 miles of sandy beaches were congested. In 1863 a pier was built to accommodate 3000 deck chairs but even this was crowded in high summer. Another two piers followed in quick succession.

In 1894 the town sprouted its Tower, imitative of the Eiffel Tower in Paris but about a third its height. Along the bustling Golden Mile is Blackpool's biggest attraction, the Pleasure Beach, with over 150 rides, including the world's fastest roller coaster and Europe's first 360° roller coaster, the Super Dooper Looper.

Electric trams carry weary revellers along the 7 mile promenade, festooned each autumn since 1912 with the celebrated 'Blackpool illuminations'.

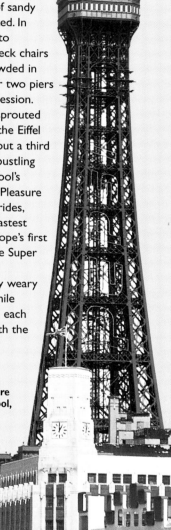

DEDICATED TO FUN Leisure is big business in Blackpool, which attracts nearly 17 million visitors every year

Tony BLAIR

- **Prime minister 1997-** • **b.1953**

In May 1997 Tony Blair at 44 became Britain's youngest prime minister since William Pitt, aged 24, in 1783. His youthful and direct style appealed to electors, who chose the 'new' LABOUR PARTY he represented as an alternative after 18 years of Conservative government.

As Labour leader from 1994, Blair, a barrister, set out to update its traditional socialism. A major step was the rewriting of Clause 4 of its constitution, which committed Labour to common ownership of the means of production. Blair stressed instead his party's support for private enterprise, a strategy that in the 1997 election won over even right-wing tabloid newspapers.

Blair continued to drive changes through after the landslide election victory, presenting parliament with a package of reforms, including Welsh and Scottish devolution.

The prime minister adopted a more informal personal style than his predecessors, inviting pop celebrities to parties and cultivating an image of Britain that is branded 'Cool Britannia'.

BLAIR CASTLE

- **Perthshire and Kinross (p.497 C3)**
- **Built 13th-19th century**

The whitewashed battlements and turrets of Blair Castle, set against the hills and forests of Strath of Garry, are all that a romantic could desire of a Scottish Highland fortress, but the imposing façade of the ancient home of the dukes of Atholl is a Victorian creation.

In 1746 Jacobite forces unsuccessfully besieged Blair Castle. It was the last siege of any castle in Britain

The original 13th-century tower remains, but Oliver Cromwell's army demolished most of its defences in the 1650s, and during Bonnie Prince Charlie's occupation in the 18th century it was little more than a country house. In the 1870s the 7th duke of Atholl remodelled the castle to restore its earlier splendour. The Atholl Highlanders, Britain's only private army, parade here each May before the Highland Gathering.

POET'S ART Blake engraved his own verses and printed them for private buyers. 'Infant Joy' (*left*) from *Songs of Innocence* is typical of his style

Peter BLAKE

- **Artist** • **b.1932**

The Beatles' *Sgt. Pepper* album cover of 1967 is perhaps Peter Blake's best-known work, but as early as the 1950s he was pioneering POP ART in Britain. His jagged realistic style, using scraps from comics, pin-ups and advertisements, creates colourful, jokey pictures.

Blake moved to the West Country in 1975 and with the artist Graham Ovenden formed the Brotherhood of Ruralists, producing dreamlike 'fairy paintings' of children, aimed at capturing the 'magical spirit of the countryside'.

William BLAKE

- **Artist and poet** • **1757-1827**

England's most eccentric poetic genius, William Blake used his art to cry out in passionate tones against the harsh materialism of the industrial age, with its brutalising effects on human feeling and relationships. He rejected conventional authority, religion and morality, holding instead to the teachings of nature and the spontaneous expression of human emotions. Much of his writing is obscure, mingling Christian imagery with personal mythology, but at its best – as

in *Songs of Innocence* (1789) and *Songs of Experience* (1794) – it has a startling emotional directness and moral insight.

Blake, who never went to school, earned his living as an engraver. He experimented with printmaking and painted watercolours on mystical and moral subjects, including scenes from the Bible and the works of BUNYAN, Dante and MILTON.

Although he lived and died in obscurity, Blake is now seen as a precursor of the ROMANTIC MOVEMENT, and has become one of the nation's best-loved poets. In his long poem *Milton*, Blake contrasts a vision of England as the promised land with the misery of the 'dark Satanic mills' of the Industrial Revolution. The words, set to music by Hubert Parry in 1916, have become the stirring hymn 'Jerusalem', a vital part of such patriotic occasions as the Last Night of the Proms.

BLENHEIM PALACE

- **Oxfordshire (p.495 F4)** • **Built 1705-22**

This vast and imposing country palace was built as a gift from Queen Anne to the 1st duke of MARLBOROUGH for his victory over the French at the Battle of Blenheim in 1704. Designed by the architect and dramatist John VANBRUGH, with the assistance of Nicholas HAWKSMOOR, Blenheim's magnificence, from the towering entrance hall to the 55 m (180 ft) long library with its Wedgwood blue ceiling, marks a high point of English baroque extravagance.

Construction was interrupted for several years when relations between the queen and the duke's wife became strained, and funds for the project dried up. The duke eventually completed the palace at his own expense, with his duchess acting as clerk of works.

The 890 ha (2200 acre) park was made over in 1764 by 'Capability' BROWN who created the lake and its island. Blenheim was the birthplace of Winston CHURCHILL, grandson of the 7th duke.

BLETCHLEY PARK

• Buckinghamshire (p.495 G3)

In August 1939, a month before war broke out, the codebreaking operations of British intelligence moved from the Foreign Office to the more discreet country estate of Bletchley Park. Here a team of military personnel, chess experts, linguists and mathematicians including Alan TURING worked at cracking German codes and radio communications between Adolf Hitler and his generals, probably shortening the Second World War by a year or more.

The work of the Government Code and Cypher School (GC&CS), as the group was known, developed from Polish prewar efforts to decode messages sent by the German Enigma cipher machine. In July 1939 the Poles passed details of their work to the British.

The GC&CS team built vast mechanical and electronic machines, including the world's first computers, to sift through the billions of ways the German cipher machines might operate, in order to decode their messages. Their work first became public in the 1970s. Bletchley Park is now a museum housing the machines used by the team.

William BLIGH

• Naval officer   • 1754-1817

Although unpopular with crews, William Bligh was probably not the tyrant of *Bounty*-film tradition. A pioneering navigator, he sailed on James COOK's

MUTINY AT DAWN William Bligh, set adrift in his nightclothes, swears revenge on *Bounty* mutineers. To his great satisfaction, three were later tracked down on Tahiti and arrested

second voyage around the world in 1772-4 before, in 1787, being given command of the *Bounty* on a journey to take breadfruit trees from Tahiti to Jamaica. After leaving Tahiti, the crew mutinied, reluctant to give up the idyllic island life and disaffected with Bligh's strict discipline. Their leader was the 23-year-old first mate Fletcher Christian, gallingly a personal friend of Bligh's.

Along with 18 loyal officers and crew, Bligh was bundled into an open longboat and set adrift. In a remarkable feat of navigation, all but one of the castaways survived a 3600 mile crossing to reach Timor in the East Indies. The mutineers returned to Tahiti and some sailed the *Bounty* to the Pitcairn Islands.

Bligh suffered another mutiny in 1797 during the French Revolutionary Wars, but he was never officially disciplined, ending his career a vice-admiral.

BLITZ

• September 7, 1940-May 10, 1941

'Don't tell me. I've got a bomb story too,' read a popular lapel badge during the Second World War bombing raids that battered the cities of Britain by night. Christened 'Blitz bombing' by the

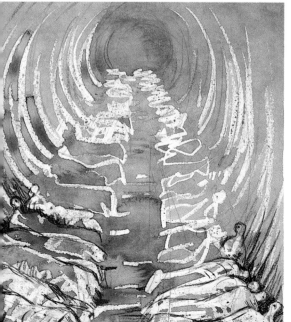

SAFE HAVEN The artist Henry Moore recorded the extraordinary sight of thousands of Londoners sleeping in Tube stations during the Blitz

Daily Express (from the German *blitzkrieg*, 'lightning war'), the Luftwaffe raids aimed to shatter civilian morale. London was bombed more intensively than most cities, with nearly 2000 people dying in the first night alone. In all some 3.5 million homes were hit, with the East End in particular suffering.

Despite the destruction, stoicism and grim humour prevailed. When Buckingham Palace was bombed the queen responded, 'I'm glad. It makes me feel I can look the East End in the face'. Gas masks, sirens and black-out curtains became part of everyday life as defiant Britons tried to carry on as normal. Even in Coventry, which lost its medieval cathedral in one raid, factories reopened after a couple of days.

BLOOMSBURY GROUP

Forty-six Gordon Square, in London's Bloomsbury district, was the meeting place for one of the country's most influential groups of 20th-century writers, artists and intellectuals. It was the home of the novelist Virginia WOOLF and her artist sister Vanessa Bell, whose regular visitors included the writers Lytton Strachey and E.M. FORSTER, the art critic Roger Fry, economist John Maynard KEYNES and like-minded aesthetes. The group began in 1905, united by their rejection of social and sexual convention and a passionate belief in the value of friendship and of beautiful objects.

BLUEBELL

Woodland carpets of intense blue nodding flowers, filling the late spring air with a sweet fragrance: this is the English bluebell. In the 16th century unsentimental Elizabethans used the starchy bulb to stiffen their elaborate ruffs, but in recent years bluebells have endured a different onslaught – large-scale and illegal uprooting for commercial gain. Even so, the plants remain widespread in Britain.

To a Scot, these flowers are wild hyacinths, since they are closely related to the cultivated hyacinth. The Scots' bluebell, known as a harebell in England, thrives not in woodland but in dry grassy places, its bell-shaped blooms dangling on a thin stem.

BLUE PLAQUES

Where can the American rock guitarist Jimi Hendrix be found next to George Frideric Handel? On adjacent houses in Brook Street, Mayfair, distinctive blue plaques commemorate the two musicians and show that, but for 240 years, they would have been neighbours. Since 1867, such signs have marked the London homes of a range of celebrities and are now set to spread elsewhere.

Responsibility for designating new blue-plaque sites rests with ENGLISH HERITAGE. A special panel considers nominations from the public and selects some 24 new buildings a year.

ENGLISH HERITAGE
JIMI
HENDRIX
1942~1970
Guitarist and
Songwriter
lived here
1968~1969

Enid BLYTON

• Writer • 1897-1968

Producing more than 30 books a year by the late 1940s, Enid Blyton became a household name for her creation of the 'Noddy', 'Famous Five' and 'Secret Seven' children's series. In the Noddy books, fantastical worlds with tiny houses and bluebells the size of trees are peopled by such characters as Big Ears and Mr Plod the Policeman. One of her

CRITICAL OPINION The rigorous standards of readers under 12 – including her own daughters – always came first for Enid Blyton

FIVE RUN AWAY TOGETHER
ENID BLYTON

most popular adventure stories, *Five on a Treasure Island*, involves children on holiday who witness the misdeeds of smugglers and thieves, triumphantly bringing them to justice.

In spite of huge success and more than 600 published titles, Blyton's books have been accused of reflecting too closely the racial and gender stereotypes of her time and class. With characteristic obstinacy, she claimed not to take any notice of critics over the age of 12, insisting that if libraries refused to stock her books children would go out and buy them with their pocket money.

BOAT RACE

• March/April

The first rowing race on the River Thames between Oxford and Cambridge universities took place at Henley in 1829 and was won by Oxford. The course ran from Westminster to Putney from 1836 until 1845, when steamboat congestion made it hazardous for the crews, and the race was moved to its present course of

MAKING A SPLASH Boat Race tradition rewards the winning cox with a dunking in the Thames

4 miles 374 yd from Putney to Mortlake. Cambridge holds the record for the fastest time – 16 minutes 19 seconds, set in 1998. Of the 145 races up to 1999, Cambridge has won 76 times and Oxford 68. In 1877 an Oxford rower broke his oar within sight of the finishing line, and the judge declared 'a dead-heat to Oxford by six feet'.

BODIAM CASTLE

• East Sussex (p.495 H5)
• Built 1385-9 • NT

In 1385 Edward Dalyngrigge, having distinguished himself fighting the French during the Hundred Years' War, built a defensive castle at Bodiam on the River Rother. The French never attacked it, and the battlemented walls, round towers and moat survive almost intact as one of Britain's finest examples of a late medieval fortress.

Unlike the earlier, more massive castles at BEAUMARIS and HARLECH, Bodiam was built when considerations of comfort were beginning to weigh equally with those of defence. The outlines of the great hall, chapel, kitchen and ladies' bower are still traceable inside the walls.

BODLEIAN LIBRARY

• Founded 1444

The scholarly calm at the 15th-century core of the Bodleian at Oxford University belies the technology used to run one of the largest libraries in the world. The Bodleian houses more than 6 million books on 100 miles of shelving, and as one of the nation's six copyright libraries is entitled to receive a copy of every book published in Britain.

A collection of 300 manuscripts given to the university in 1444 by the duke of Gloucester, younger brother of Henry V, formed the original nucleus of the library, but was dispersed. Thomas Bodley, an Elizabethan diplomat, devoted his retirement to restoring the collection, which reopened as the Bodleian in 1602.

Inside the building, the stone-vaulted Divinity School of 1426 is said to be Oxford's oldest lecture room. Later extensions include the 1749 Radcliffe Camera, designed by James GIBBS, and the 1940 New Bodleian, with its maze of underground passages. Among the Bodleian's treasures are a 7th-century manuscript of the Acts of the Apostles, later used by the Venerable Bede, and a copy of the *Anglo-Saxon Chronicle*.

BODMIN MOOR

• **Cornwall (p.494 B6)** • **Area 80 sq miles**

This high, treeless and rugged moor is rich in myth and legend. Huge stacks of weathered granite tors loom eerily like boulders heaped by ancient giants. The Hurlers – megalithic stone circles near Cheesewring – are said to be men turned to stone for not observing the Lord's Day. Jamaica Inn at Bolventor inspired Daphne du Maurier's tale of smuggling and murder. Nearby lies deep Dozmary Pool, which hid the water nymph who received King ARTHUR's sword Excalibur from his knight Sir Bedivere.

BOER WARS

• **1880-1 and 1899-1902**

In the brief South African war of 1880-1 the Boers asserted their independence from Britain in Transvaal and Orange Free State, but it was the discovery of gold and diamonds on Boer land that ignited the more serious conflict in 1899.

Britain assembled a force of some 500 000, including Australians, Canadians and 100 000 Africans. At the war's start, they outnumbered the Boers four to one but suffered a series of humiliating defeats – particularly shocking as this was the first conflict to be widely covered by the newspapers. Telegraph technology enabled reporters, including the young Winston CHURCHILL, to cable news home quickly, followed by photographs and film by sea. The public was horrified by

the suffering of soldiers and the poor health of working-class volunteers.

As the tide of the war changed in 1900, Boer commandos switched to a guerrilla campaign. The British response was to torch farmsteads and corral women and children into insanitary concentration camps where more lives were lost than in battle. The Boers eventually sued for peace under the Treaty of Vereeniging in 1902.

Anne BOLEYN

• **Second wife of Henry VIII and mother of Elizabeth I** • **1507-36**

Letters between Henry VIII and Anne Boleyn suggest that they were having a love affair for at least five years before they married, and certainly while Henry was negotiating his divorce from Catherine of Aragon, who had failed to provide a male heir.

In January 1533 the couple married secretly, and in May Archbishop Thomas Cranmer annulled Henry's marriage to Catherine, allowing Anne to be crowned queen in June – just three months before she gave birth to Elizabeth. Alas, when Anne, too, failed to bear a son she grew unpopular at court, and soon faced trumped-up charges of adultery and incest. She was convicted and beheaded.

BONFIRE NIGHT

• **November 5**

When James I's ministers uncovered the Roman Catholic GUNPOWDER PLOT to blow up parliament in 1605, they decreed that the failure of the conspiracy should be celebrated annually. All parish churches had to hold thanksgiving services on November 5, and townsfolk turned the event into a festive occasion burning effigies of Guy Fawkes.

In 17th-century London, the celebratory bonfires consumed cartloads of fuel and many guys, and the occasion came to include fireworks – popular in England since the reign of Elizabeth I.

The event remains traditional fun but in LEWES, Sussex, the guy has an added significance. Seventeen Protestants were martyred there during the reign of the Catholic Mary I, and every November 5 since 1679 the town has burnt an effigy of the pope to cries of 'No popery'.

Chris BONINGTON

• **Mountaineer** • **b.1934; kt 1996**

The peaks of Scotland were Chris Bonington's training ground in the 1950s before he turned his attention to the Alps. In 1962 he and his climbing partner Ian Clough became the first Britons to scale the north face of the 3970 m (13 025 ft) Eiger.

Bonington went on to lead the first ascent of the south face of Annapurna in the Himalayas in 1970, and of the south-west face of Everest in 1975. He was one of the first professional mountaineers and has also won success as a writer, photographer and television presenter.

BONNIE PRINCE CHARLIE

• **Charles Stuart, 'Young Pretender' to the British throne** • **1720-88**

The best chance the JACOBITES had of recovering the British throne since its loss in the 1688 GLORIOUS REVOLUTION fell to James II's grandson Charles – Bonnie Prince Charlie.

In 1715 his father, James Stuart (the 'Old Pretender'), fled to Rome where he sired two

FINAL FLING The romantic figure of Bonnie Prince Charlie rallied Scots to a last bid for the British crown

sons. The elder, Charles, aspiring to regain the crown, landed on the Scottish west coast in 1745 with just seven men.

His boldness won the hearts of soldiers and women alike. When Charles raised his standard in Glenfinnan, west of Fort William, an initial band of 1200 Highlanders swelled to 3000 to join him in the Jacobite FORTY-FIVE REBELLION. They quickly conquered Scotland and advanced as far as Derby, only to be routed at CULLODEN, near Inverness, on their retreat. The young prince, helped by Flora MACDONALD, escaped to France but was expelled as Louis XV sought peace with Britain. He died in Rome.

BOOKER PRIZE

• **Est. 1969**

Britain's oldest major literary award, the Booker McConnell prize for fiction, launched by the Booker food company, is given annually for a novel written in English and published that year by a British or Commonwealth author. Not until 1982, its 13th year, did a winner, Salman Rushdie's *Midnight's Children*, or even one of the six short-listed novels enter the best-seller lists. Today, with a prize of more than £20 000 and a televised award ceremony, the Booker prize is big business; the short list, issued six weeks before the final decision sparks activity in bookshops and bookmakers alike.

The selection is made by a panel of six literary figures. The final choice is often hotly debated by critics, readers and even the judges themselves – who have twice awarded the prize jointly.

> The first Booker prize was won by P.H. Newby in 1969 for his novel *Something to Answer For*. Newby beat Iris Murdoch and Muriel Spark to win the £5000 award

BORDERS

• **England-Scotland border (p.496 B1/B2)**
• **Area 1819 sq miles**

The rough heath between Hadrian's Wall and Scotland's southern uplands was a lawless frontier zone until James VI of Scotland inherited the English throne in 1603 (*see* JAMES I). Fitful 'Border Wars' between the Scots and English over 300 years had left Jedburgh, Kelso and MELROSE abbeys in ruins. Castles such as ALNWICK protected the so-called local 'robber barons' with their private armies; fortified farmhouses and towers, known as peel towers, guarded lesser magnates.

Forestry plantations cloak the Keilder and Redesdale moors but the landscape is little changed from the wilderness that inspired ballads such as 'Chevy Chase' and the tales of Walter SCOTT. In 1973 the counties of Berwick, Peebles, Roxburgh, Selkirk and part of Midlothian were merged to form the Borders administrative region.

RARE SIGHT In 1996 visitors to Kew botanic gardens were treated for the first time in 33 years to *Titan arum* in bloom

James BOSWELL

• **Writer** • **1740-95**

Writing the *Life of Samuel Johnson* (1791) was probably James Boswell's most ambitious task, but he was also a friend and travelling companion to the irascible lexicographer. Boswell was born in Edinburgh but left for London at the age of 20 in search of fame and pleasure. There, in a bookshop in 1763, he was introduced to JOHNSON, and set himself the task of recording the details of his life and table talk.

Boswell and Johnson made a tour of the Hebrides in 1773, about which both published accounts. Boswell fawned on the famous and conducted numerous affairs, but continued to write tirelessly. His journals, discovered in the 1920s, show him a sensitive man, winningly honest about his many weaknesses.

Battle of BOSWORTH

• **Leicestershire (p.495 F2)** • **August 22, 1485**

After more than 30 years of strife the WARS OF THE ROSES finally came to a bloody climax on a rough heath near the small town of Market Bosworth in Leicestershire. The Yorkist RICHARD III commanded 10 000 soldiers, twice as many as his challenger for the English throne, the Lancastrian Henry Tudor, newly returned from exile in France.

Already there had been defections to the Lancastrian side amid rumours that Richard had ascended the throne through murder and dishonour. On the march from Milford Haven, where he landed, to Bosworth, Henry added 3000 men to his original force of 2000.

As the battle began Lord Stanley, one of Richard's key supporters, defected to Henry's side and the earl of Northumberland's wing of the royal army stood back. Faced with betrayal and defeat, Richard threw himself into the battle to try to fell Henry with his own hand, only to be killed himself.

Richard's crown was plucked from a hawthorn bush where it had fallen and placed on his rival's head. The crown and the hawthorn became the emblem of the new king, HENRY VII, the first monarch of the TUDOR dynasty.

BOTANIC GARDENS

In 1732 a packet of seeds sent from CHELSEA PHYSIC GARDEN started North America's cotton industry. Numerous other plants – both commercial crops and decorative garden species – owe a similar debt to Britain's botanic gardens.

Gardens such as Chelsea, Kew and the Oxford Physic Garden – Britain's oldest, founded in 1621 – were offshoots of the age of exploration. As travellers and plant collectors started to send home specimens from increasingly exotic locations British botanists set up research gardens, often linked to universities. In the 18th century the gardens began to incorporate glasshouses for tropical species. Plants were investigated for their medicinal or commercial potential and new industries, such as pineapple-growing, opened up throughout the British Empire.

By Victorian times, botanic gardens had caught the public imagination; visitors flocked to see exhibits such as cactuses that flowered once in 100 years and waterlilies big enough to sit on.

Conservation is now a vital function of establishments such as KEW GARDENS in Surrey, the world's largest botanic garden, which grows ten per cent of all flora species and keeps around 6 million dried specimens.

Edinburgh's Royal Botanic Garden is also one of the world's largest, with some 35 000 plants. Others have specialist collections, such as the national collection of saxifrage at Cambridge, or the rhododendrons and azaleas of Liverpool Ness Gardens.

New gardens, such as the National Botanical Garden for Wales at Carmarthen and the EDEN PROJECT in Cornwall, aim not just to grow plants but to re-create as closely as possible their natural environment.

ALIEN ARTIST As the otherworldly Ziggy Stardust, David Bowie expressed the early 1970s fascination with outer space

Ian BOTHAM

• **Cricketer** • **b.1955; OBE 1992**

Flamboyant behaviour on and off the pitch kept Ian Botham in the news throughout his career. He made his debut with Somerset in 1974 but also played professional football with Scunthorpe United for four seasons from 1979.

'Beefy' Botham – nicknamed for his strapping physique – could single-handedly win a match either with his big hitting or his swing bowling. He was the first player to take more than ten wickets and score a century in one Test, hitting 114 and bowling 6-58 and 7-48 against India in Bombay in 1980. After the 1981 ASHES series, when his batting – coupled with Bob Willis' bowling – snatched victory from Australia at Headingley, Botham became a national hero.

In 102 Tests for England, before retiring in 1993, Botham scored 5200 runs, took 383 wickets and 120 catches.

BOUDICCA

• **Celtic warrior queen** • **Died c.AD 61**

'In appearance, terrifying, in the glance of her eye most fierce, and her voice was harsh; a great mass of the tawniest hair fell to her hips' – the Roman historian Dio Cassius paints a fearsome picture of Boudicca, the woman who led the largest British revolt against the Romans.

She was the wife of Prasutagus, the ruler of the Celtic Iceni tribe in what is now East Anglia. Roman law prohibited female inheritance, but Prasutagus left his lands equally to his two daughters and the emperor Nero. At his death in AD 60, the Romans sacked his palace, seizing Icenian land and his daughters' inheritance. Some reports say Boudicca was flogged and her daughters raped.

In fury, Boudicca swept south with a force of Celtic warriors, torching the Roman towns of Camulodunum (Colchester), Verulamium (St Albans) and Londinium (London). The Roman governor Suetonius Paullinus then rallied his troops and crushed the Iceni in battle. Boudicca reputedly poisoned herself.

Adrian BOULT

• **Conductor** • **1889-1983; kt 1937**

As founding conductor of the BBC Symphony Orchestra, established in 1930 as the world's first dedicated radio orchestra, Adrian Boult influenced the musical tastes of a generation.

Boult made a point of promoting British composers, especially Delius, Holst and Vaughan Williams, and was a noted interpreter of Elgar. Millions of people listened eagerly through the crackle to a regular programme of new works and classics for which he and the BBC earned worldwide acclaim.

Despite his fame and popularity, Boult shied away from public attention. He left the BBC in 1950 to become the conductor-in-chief of the London Philharmonic Orchestra, and continued to conduct regularly until the age of 92.

David BOWIE

• **David Jones** • **Pop musician** • **b.1947**

Reinventing himself with every changing trend has kept David Bowie's pop career alive for more than three decades.

His first hit, *Space Oddity,* coincided with the 1969 Moon landing. The 1972 album *The Rise and Fall of Ziggy Stardust and the Spiders from Mars* and the Ziggy persona inspired fellow 'glam rock' artists, such as Gary Glitter (see ROCK AND POP). Bowie discarded this image and eerie synthesised music for a more upbeat sound and attitude in the 1980s, when he also revived his earlier acting career with *The Elephant Man* on Broadway.

BOW STREET RUNNERS

A cry of 'Stop, thief!' and a chase by willing bystanders was the rough-and-ready way of catching criminals until 1748. Then the novelist and Bow Street magistrate Henry FIELDING established Britain's first organised POLICE force.

The name 'Bow Street Runner' was coined at the turn of the 19th century, by which time seven other groups based on the Bow Street model had started. The poorly paid volunteer 'Runners' grew increasingly corrupt and in 1829 Robert PEEL's Metropolitan force took over. The Runners were disbanded ten years later.

BOXGROVE

• **Prehistoric site** • **West Sussex (p.495 G6)**

The ancient cliffs and beaches unearthed at Boxgrove, now in inland Sussex, make up the largest preserved Stone Age site in Europe. Excavations began in a local gravel pit in 1985, and in 1993 a shinbone was found. 'Boxgrove Man', as the possessor was labelled, was dated to half a million years ago, making him one of the four oldest Europeans.

Shaped pieces of flint used for killing bison, deer and rhinoceros suggest that the rocks (which attracted gravel merchants to Boxgrove in the 1500s) had also drawn much earlier hunter settlers to the site.

BOXING

At amateur level boxers fight three 3 minute rounds in headguards, displaying their strength, stealth and skill. Professional titles are contested over 12 rounds, in more glamorous and unshielded bouts.

Boxing first featured in the ancient Greek games at Olympia in 686 BC, when competitors wore soft leather coverings on their hands to protect their fingers. It came to Britain 2000 years later as a bare-knuckle activity. The first recorded contest was held in 1681 between the duke of Albemarle's footman and a butcher. It was nearly 200 years before padded gloves, 3 minute rounds, the count to ten for a knockout, and a ban on wrestling were introduced with the Queensberry Rules, drafted in 1867 and still used.

Since 'Gentleman' James Corbett won the first world heavyweight title in 1892 Britain has raised many world champions, including the 'Mighty Atom', Welsh flyweight Jimmy Wilde (1916-21), and Scottish lightweight Ken Buchanan (1970-2), as well as popular heavyweights such as Henry COOPER and Lennox LEWIS.

GENTLEMEN'S CONTEST A well-attended fight between Messrs Broome and Hannan in 1841 carried a £1000 purse

Geoffrey BOYCOTT

• **Cricketer** • **b.1940**

A single-minded approach to run-making provoked criticism that Geoffrey Boycott sometimes put himself before the team. But his slow, determined style of play – at times he scored fewer than ten runs an hour – was a study in concentration and rock-steady technique. Over a 24 year first-class career with Yorkshire and England he scored a total of more than 48 000 runs, including 151 centuries.

Boycott is known for plain-speaking and as Yorkshire county captain in the 1970s caused friction in the club as a result of disagreements with fellow board members. This, and the team's lack of success, lost him the captaincy in 1978, though he was later reinstated when the board that had dropped him was voted out by his supporters.

Boycott retired from playing in 1986 to commentate for television and radio with characteristic bluntness.

Robert BOYLE

• **Physicist and chemist** • **1627-91**

'Nullius in verba' (nothing by mere authority) is the motto of the ROYAL SOCIETY, which Robert Boyle helped to found to promote experimental science; it was his own motto, too. A rigorous experimenter, he is best known for discovering in 1662 that the volume of a gas at constant temperature varies in inverse proportion to its pressure – now called Boyle's Law.

The many other investigations that Boyle made into the composition of matter and chemical compounds helped to establish chemistry as a pure science and to separate it from alchemy.

Boyle, the seventh son of the earl of Cork, was a devout Christian who had been terrified into belief as a young man by a tremendous thunderstorm. The Boyle Lectures, founded as his bequest to defend Christianity against sceptics, were given until 1941.

Battle of the BOYNE

• **Ireland, near Dublin** • **July 1, 1690**

The Battle of the Boyne was not especially bloody but it is unique – never before or since have two kings fought over the English throne on Irish soil.

In exile in France following the GLORIOUS REVOLUTION of 1688-9, the Catholic JAMES II sought to regain his crown from his Protestant successors WILLIAM AND MARY. In the summer of 1689 James and an army of French troops landed in Ireland, where they were welcomed by the numerous Catholic JACOBITE sympathisers.

William's troops rallied in the north and the king arrived to take personal command in June 1690. On July 1, James and 21 000 French and Irish troops faced William and his army of 35 000 in boggy ground on opposite banks of the River Boyne, 30 miles north of Dublin. Soon overcome by William's greater forces, James fled the battlefield for France, his hopes of reclaiming the British throne dashed.

Although the battle was fought on July 1, a new calendar adopted in 1752 added ten days to 17th-century dates and wrongly fixed the day as July 12. The ORANGE ORDER in Northern Ireland still celebrates the Protestant victory on July 12, the 'Glorious Twelfth'.

BP

• **Founded 1909**

Formerly British Petroleum, BP Amoco is now the third largest oil company in the world. BP was established in 1909 to exploit an oil discovery in Persia (now Iran), the first commercial oilfield in the Middle East. In 1914 the British government bought a 51 per cent share in BP, securing fuel for the Royal Navy at the start of the First World War. The government retained a substantial shareholding until 1987.

By 1930 the company had become a multinational with refining, shipping and marketing operations. It developed petrochemicals in the late 1940s, discovered gas in the North Sea in 1965 and established major oil finds in Alaska in 1969 and in the North Sea in 1970. BP merged with the American oil company Amoco in 1998.

Kenneth BRANAGH

• **Actor and director** • **b.1960**

At 23, Kenneth Branagh became the youngest actor to play Shakespeare's Henry V with the ROYAL SHAKESPEARE COMPANY. Three years later, in 1986, he founded his own Renaissance Theatre Company, but it was the television drama *Fortunes of War* (1987), in which he played opposite his future wife, Emma Thompson, that made him into a household name.

Together 'Ken and Em' were the nucleus of a glittering theatrical set in the 1980s. Branagh brought literary drama to popular attention, winning the approval of both audiences and critics and particular acclaim for his film versions of *Henry V* (1989), *Much Ado About Nothing* (1993) and *Hamlet* (1996).

Bill BRANDT

• **Photographer** • **1904-83**

With his photographs showing sleeping bodies stretching the length of a London underground tunnel, or the effects of bombs on the buildings of the capital, Bill Brandt helped to define our image of Britain at war.

SOCIAL SNAPSHOT **Bill Brandt was a master of intimacy, lovingly capturing details of everyday life, such as a teahouse scene in Bournemouth**

The German-born photographer settled in London in 1931 and established his reputation with richly printed, atmospheric black and white photo-documentaries of British life, published by magazines such as *Picture Post*, and in his book, *The English at Home* (1936).

After the war, Brandt turned from photo-journalism to portraiture, nudes and landscapes, using fish-eye lenses to create distorted, exaggerated effects.

Richard BRANSON

• **Businessman** • **b.1950**

Leaving Stowe public school at 16 to develop a magazine called *Student* was the first of many gambles for Richard Branson. He was still only 20 when he founded Virgin, a mail-order record business, in 1970. His style of management has always been 'hands-on' and personal. 'I chose [the name] because it reflected an inexperience in business,' he explained, 'and also a freshness and slight outrageousness.'

The Virgin group now has an annual sales turnover of around £3.1 billion from entertainment, publishing, retailing and travel. A natural showman, Branson is seldom out of sight for long and regularly courts publicity with world record bids. He achieved the fastest Atlantic crossing in his yacht *Virgin Atlantic Challenger II* in 1986, and was the first to cross the Atlantic (1987) and the Pacific (1991) by hot-air balloon.

BRAVE NEW WORLD

• **Published 1932**

Babies hatched in test-tubes, adults segregated by genetic structure, societies kept in a state of drowsy happiness by the drug 'soma', thought conditioning and mass production – such was the tainted utopia of Aldous HUXLEY's classic novel, *Brave New World*.

People born in the 'old-fashioned' way, such as the main characters,

AN INSTINCT FOR PUBLICITY **Richard Branson has injected humour into British business, launching Virgin's wedding service in person**

Linda and John, are seen by others as savages, reflecting a common fear during the 1930s that selective breeding could produce a 'master race'.

Brave New World parodied and grotesquely exaggerated English class divisions, contrasting a pampered elite with a brutal, ignorant sub-class. For neither was there any place for individual thought or feeling.

Black comedy or futuristic tragedy, *Brave New World* sold 23 000 copies in just two years and inspired many novels in similar vein, including George ORWELL's *Nineteen Eighty-Four*.

BRECON BEACONS

• **S Wales (p.494 D4)** • **Area 519 sq miles**

The million sheep that graze on the Brecon Beacons greatly outnumber the 2500 human inhabitants. The hilly moorland, including the Black Mountains to the east, was set aside in 1957 as one of Britain's NATIONAL PARKS. Caves and waterfalls dot the area, while Norman villages nestle in the valleys. Carreg Cennen Castle, reputedly a fortress since the time of King Arthur, was rebuilt in the 13th century but demolished in 1462. In Llanthony there are ruins of a 12th-century Augustinian priory.

At Dan-yr-Ogof a 10 mile cave complex with underground rivers and spectacular stalactites has been carved out of the limestone bedrock. The area also includes south Wales's tallest mountain, Pen y Fan, at 886 m (2907 ft).

BESIDE THE SEA Palace Pier still looks much as it did in 1896, when bathing machines would have crammed the beach

BRIGHTON

• **East Sussex (p.495 H6)** • **Pop. 124 850**

The transformation of Brighton from a fishing village into an elegant resort began when Richard Russell, a doctor, set up a surgery in 1754, proclaiming the healing powers of sea water. Visitors soon arrived to try the new craze for sea-bathing.

When the Prince of Wales, later GEORGE IV, became Regent he engaged the architect John NASH to turn his Brighton retreat into a palace to reflect his new status. Between 1815 and 1820 Nash created the Royal Pavilion, an exuberant Oriental fantasy of domes and spires. The kitchen ceiling is held up by palm-tree pillars and a Chinese influence pervades the building – dragons, lotus flowers and mandarin figures are much in evidence.

From 1841 the railway brought city dwellers in their masses to Brighton, earning it the nickname of 'London by the sea'. Its two piers – the West Pier (1863-6), saved from decay by a £14.2 million Lottery grant, and Palace Pier, renamed Brighton Pier in 1999 – were built with theatres and concert halls.

Beyond the grand, stucco-fronted Regency houses is the 'Lanes' area of Brighton – a vibrant mix of seaside amusements and narrow streets of antique dealers and junk shops.

ROYAL FOLLY Queen Victoria sold the Brighton Pavilion to the town, which opened it to visitors

BRIGHTON RUN

• **Veteran car rally** • **First Sunday in Nov**

Since 1927, entrants in the London to Brighton Veteran Car Run have coaxed their veteran (pre-1905) cars the 53 miles to the Sussex coast.

The 1927 event re-enacted the Emancipation Run of 1896, in which 33 drivers celebrated the repeal of the 'Red Flag' Act (*see* MOTOR CARS). On the 1996 centenary run, a record 660 cars took part, of which 540 finished. Speeds ranged from 7 mph by a 1896 Lutzman to 75 mph by a 1903 Mercedes.

BRISTOL

• **SW England (p.494 E5)** • **Pop. 407 990**

Even in medieval times Bristol was a busy port and by the 16th and 17th centuries its merchants were growing rich on trade. Until 1807, when it was outlawed, the slave trade contributed to their wealth. Ships went on a triangular run, taking slaves from West Africa to the West Indies and raw materials such as cotton, sugar and tobacco back to Britain, where new industries sprang up.

Bristol's shipyard produced the first propellor-driven ocean liner, Isambard Kingdom BRUNEL's SS *Great Britain* of 1843, now berthed and restored at the docks where it was built.

The city's cathedral dates back to the 12th century, and the Church of St Mary Redcliffe, admired by Elizabeth I as 'the fairest in England', has an 89 m (292 ft) spire and more than 1000 ornately carved roof bosses. The Theatre Royal of 1766 on cobbled King Street is Britain's oldest playhouse. To the west lies the Avon Gorge, spanned by Brunel's CLIFTON SUSPENSION BRIDGE, and the nearby Georgian suburb of Clifton.

Battle of BRITAIN

• **July-October, 1940**

'Never in the field of human conflict was so much owed by so many to so few,' said Winston Churchill to honour the Battle of Britain pilots who fought off German aerial attacks during 1940.

A string of early warning RADAR stations along the south coast alerted RAF squadrons to the approach of German bombing raids and allowed planes to be scrambled at short notice. People in south-east England grew used to seeing Spitfires and the more numerous Hurricanes battling overhead with the Focke Wulfs and Messerschmitts that flanked the German bombers.

The Germans had more than 1000 pilots to Britain's 600, but advance radar warnings gave Britain the advantage. Frustrated, Germany switched tactics in September and began the BLITZ on large cities, giving British aircraft factories a much-needed respite to re-equip the RAF. By October the battle had reached stalemate. The Luftwaffe had lost 2300 aircraft and Britain only 900; more importantly, Germany had to abandon any plans to invade England.

BRITANNIA

'Rule, Britannia, rule the waves;/Britons never will be slaves': set to music, the lines from James Thomson's masque *Alfred* (1740) have become a second national anthem and a feature of the Last Night of the PROMS.

The Romans bestowed the name 'Britannia', and the first female personification appeared on a

Falkland Islands. In June 1999 British troops were deployed as part of the NATO peacekeeping force in Kosovo. Front-line soldiers include the Royal Armoured Corps, Household Cavalry, Infantry and PARACHUTE REGIMENT, with combat support from groups such as the Royal Signals, Royal Logistics Corps and Intelligence Corps. Some regiments, including the Argyll and Sutherland Highlanders, are drawn from specific areas and have a strong local identity.

The British Army also plays a part in the delivery of humanitarian aid, and is deeply involved with state occasions such as TROOPING THE COLOUR.

BRITISH CONSTITUTION

Unusually for a democratic state, Britain has no single document prescribing the nature and functions of government. Instead, the British constitution is built on centuries of convention and Acts of Parliament. The requirement to hold a general election every five years, for example, is set out in the Parliament Act of 1911, while the monarch's speech at the state opening of parliament, outlining planned legislation, has been an established tradition since 1536.

The lack of a formal constitution can be a strength and a weakness, promoting flexibility but also, potentially, permitting governments to increase their powers without democratic consent. The 1997 referenda on DEVOLUTION in Scotland and Wales demonstrated the system's flexibility, making modifications without the lengthy amendment processes of countries with written constitutions.

BRITISH COUNCIL

• Est. 1934

Founded in a bid to promote a wider knowledge of Britain and the English language, the British Council, funded by the Foreign Office, works in more than 100 countries running language classes, arts sponsorship and libraries.

Since the 1960s, the council's role has expanded to support education, training and health programmes in developing countries. It promotes British educational materials and the work of British artists and performers overseas – sectors with an export value of £15 billion.

DANCE OF DEATH Life on the ground pauses for a while as vapour trails trace the balletic manoeuvres of two fighter planes, locked in a Battle of Britain dogfight over Kent

coin in AD 119. She was remodelled under Charles II, allegedly to a likeness of his mistress Frances Stuart, and coins were minted showing Britannia with an olive branch and spear – symbolic of peace and war. Under George III her spear was replaced with a trident to celebrate Britain's naval power, an image still found on the 50p piece.

BRITISH ARMY

Britain's first permanent army of paid soldiers – the New Model Army – was raised in 1645 by Oliver Cromwell. In 1689 the BILL OF RIGHTS brought the army under parliamentary control.

The army grew as Britain established standing forces overseas in the 17th and 18th centuries, and in the two world wars the ranks of professional soldiers were swelled by conscripts. Women were admitted in 1917, filling noncombat roles in the Women's Army Auxiliary Corps.

THE MODERN ARMY

Today's career soldiers are trained not only as fighters but also in one of more than 100 supporting professions and trades, including dentistry, electrical and mechanical skills, and veterinary science. Alongside the regular army of around 97 000 soldiers (7500 of them women) are the 65 000 part-time civilian volunteers of the Territorial Army.

In recent years, the army's largest operational commitment has been in Northern Ireland, but troops are also stationed in Brunei, Cyprus and the

BRITISH EMPIRICISM

Empiricism – the view that knowledge comes from experience rather than abstract reason – has influenced many British philosophers, notably John LOCKE, Bishop BERKELEY and David HUME. But just as many have taken the opposite standpoint and embraced rationalism.

Francis BACON, one of the first scientific thinkers, rejected both. 'The empiricists,' he said, 'are like ants, who simply heap things up and consume them. The rationalists, on the other hand, spin webs out of themselves like spiders. The best method, however, is that of the bee, who takes material from the flowers of the garden and the field, digesting it by his own powers.'

BRITISH GRAND PRIX

• **Silverstone (p.495 G3)**   • **July**

The British Grand Prix is one of the fastest of the races in the Formula One World Drivers' Championship. Drivers exceed 180 mph on the 741 m (810 yd) Hangar Straight and average 128 mph over the 192 mile race. Since the race was first held in 1948, venues have included Aintree, Brands Hatch and, since 1988, Silverstone. Brands Hatch has secured the race from 2002.

The most successful driver is the Scot Jim Clark, who won five times between 1962 and 1967 in a British-built Lotus.

BRITISH ISLES

- **Area** 120 478 sq miles
- **Population** 62 320 000
- **Northernmost point** Muckle Flugga lighthouse, Shetland Islands
- **Southernmost point** Les Minquiers islands, Channel Islands
- **Easternmost point** Lowestoft, Suffolk
- **Westernmost point** Rockall, 155 miles west of Dingle, Republic of Ireland
- **Highest point** Ben Nevis, Scotland (1343 m/4406 ft)
- **Lowest point** Holme Fen, Cambridgeshire (-2.22 m/-7.28 ft)

The geographical term 'British Isles' refers to the archipelago of islands separated from mainland Europe by the English Channel, the Straits of Dover and the North Sea. The 400-odd islands include the Channel Islands, the Isle of Man, the Isle of Wight, the Orkneys, Shetlands and Hebrides. It also includes the whole island of Ireland, although some citizens of the Irish Republic prefer the name North-west European Offshore Islands to avoid the ambiguous political connotations of the term 'British'.

CATHEDRAL OF LEARNING Three levels of desks make room for 500 people in the British Library's General Humanities reading room

BRITISH EMPIRE

Britain's overseas interests began when settlers landed in Virginia in 1607; in 1624, it was claimed as a royal province and other American colonies soon followed. They were lost during the AMERICAN WAR OF INDEPENDENCE but Britain expanded its territory in many other directions and, through a series of wars during the 18th and 19th centuries, took many Spanish and French colonies, too. By the 1930s, the British Empire was the largest the world had known. The costs were enormous but so were the benefits – both as a market for British goods and a supply of raw materials such as sugar, gold and diamonds.

In return Britain gave the colonies the ENGLISH LANGUAGE, schools, systems of government, Christianity, railways, modern water and power supplies – and millions of expatriates, who emigrated to man the huge colonial administration, farm or do business.

The empire began to be dismantled with the end of the RAJ and Indian independence in 1947. The 1950s and 60s saw most former colonies transformed into independent COMMONWEALTH states. Today, 13 overseas territories, ranging from Gibraltar to the Falkland Islands, remain under British control. Their inhabitants all have full citizenship and residence rights in Britain.

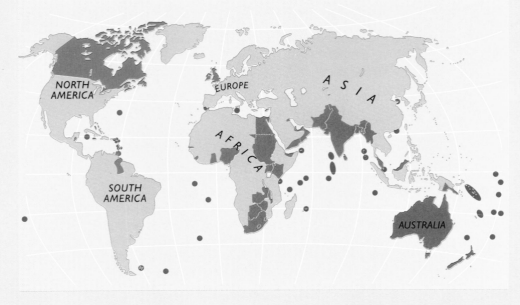

NORTH AMERICA
EUROPE
ASIA
AFRICA
SOUTH AMERICA
AUSTRALIA

THE SUN NEVER SETS In the 1930s about a quarter of the world was British, stretching in an almost unbroken band from east to west

BRITISH LIBRARY

• **Central London (p.499 D1)** • **Est. 1973**

In 1837 an Italian civil servant, Antonio Panizzi, became 'keeper of printed books' at the BRITISH MUSEUM. By 1857 he had ordered the museum's chaotic collection to found the library where writers and thinkers, including Rudyard Kipling, Karl Marx and George Bernard Shaw, studied and wrote in the domed Reading Room.

In 1973 the British Library became independent from the museum, although they continued to share premises in Bloomsbury. The library's long association with the museum finally ended in 1998 when the removal of its 12 million books to new, purpose-built premises in St Pancras was completed.

As one of six copyright libraries the British Library holds every book published in Britain. In addition to the reference division, it contains thousands of priceless first editions, documents and manuscripts, including the LINDISFARNE Gospels and ANGLO-SAXON CHRONICLE.

BRITISH MEDICAL ASSOCIATION

• **Founded 1832**

A burning desire to reform 19th-century medicine, and to free the profession from the grip of the Royal College of Physicians, drove the idealistic young doctor Charles Hastings to found the Provincial Medical and Surgical Association in 1832.

Renamed the British Medical Association (BMA) in 1856, the organisation campaigned through its mouthpiece the *British Medical Journal* against quackery and medical scandals, such as the high death rate of babies in public care.

Throughout the 20th century the BMA became less involved in issues of medical practice and more concerned with the status of the profession. It initially opposed the NATIONAL HEALTH SERVICE, which it feared would reduce doctors to the role of civil servants, but by the 1980s it was defending the NHS against government budget cuts and funding reforms. The BMA currently has 119 000 members, about 80 per cent of British doctors.

BRITISH MUSEUM

• **Central London (p.499 D2)** • **Opened 1759**

With around a million exhibits and a total collection of 6.5 million antiquities, from manuscripts and medals to marble statues and ceramics, the British Museum is Britain's largest. It is also the oldest public museum in the world and is funded entirely by government and private donation, never having charged an entrance fee.

An Act of parliament established the museum in 1753. Its nucleus was a collection of scientific books and manuscripts bequeathed to the nation by the physician and botanist Hans Sloane and originally exhibited in Montague House, in Bloomsbury.

The collection soon outgrew its home and today's premises with their imposing neoclassical entrance were built between 1823 and 1852 on the same site.

There are now 94 galleries, attracting more than 6 million visitors each year. Among notable exhibits are the ELGIN MARBLES, LINDOW MAN, the Rosetta Stone, the Portland Vase, Greek and Egyptian antiquities, and the SUTTON HOO treasure.

PRESERVED IN DEATH The British Museum houses dozens of human mummies, as well as dogs, cats, birds, snakes and crocodiles

BRITISH SUMMER TIME

• **Last Sunday in March to last Sunday in October**

The idea of advancing the clock by 1 hour during the summer was first suggested by the American statesman Benjamin Franklin in 1784 as a way to make best use of the long hours of daylight. But only in 1916 was the idea adopted by Britain, to save precious wartime fuel. The Second World War saw double summer time introduced, putting Britain 2 hours ahead of GREENWICH MEAN TIME during the summer and 1 hour in winter.

In 1968 and 1969 BST was continued through autumn and winter to bring British and European times into line, but the dark winter mornings proved unpopular, especially in Scotland, and so the scheme was dropped.

CLOSE HARMONY The partnership between the composer Benjamin Britten (*right*) and tenor Peter Pears lasted 39 years

Benjamin BRITTEN

• **Composer** • **1913-76; OM 1965; bn 1976**

The feast of St Cecilia, patron saint of music, proved an appropriate birth date for Benjamin Britten. He began writing music at the age of six but his fame rests particularly on the dozen operas he composed after the Second World War.

In 1937 Britten met the tenor Peter PEARS, beginning a musical and personal partnership that was to last to the end of his life. Many of Britten's leading male operatic parts, from Peter Grimes (1945) to Gustav von Aschenbach in *Death in Venice* (1973), were written for Pears's high, distinctive tenor.

From 1947 Britten and Pears lived in the Suffolk town of Aldeburgh where in 1948 they helped to found the ALDEBURGH FESTIVAL.

Britten's main inspiration came from poetry and drama but he also wrote purely instrumental works, such as the 1940 Violin Concerto, ballet scores and a War Requiem for the dedication of the new Coventry Cathedral in 1962.

BROADLANDS

- Hampshire (p.495 F5)
- Built 16th century, rebuilt 18th century

Lord MOUNTBATTEN, the last viceroy of India, owned this majestic house, and in 1981 his grand-nephew Prince Charles and Princess Diana spent their first three nights of marriage here. An exhibition covers Mountbatten's career as a statesman, sailor and sportsman, while a room is devoted to Lord PALMERSTON, the Victorian prime minister and a former owner of Broadlands.

The landscape gardener and architect 'Capability' Brown, aided by his designer son-in-law Henry Holland, transformed the 16th-century house. They created a square mansion in white brick with two fine porticoes and ornate plasterwork.

BROMPTON ORATORY

- Central London (p.499 B3) • Built 1884

Until the opening of Westminster Cathedral in 1903, Brompton Oratory was London's pre-eminent place of worship for Roman Catholics. The name derives from the 16th-century Oratory of St Philip Neri in Rome, whose priests are not committed for life to monastic vows such as celibacy. This system – the institute of the Oratory – was introduced to England by the theologian John Henry (later Cardinal) NEWMAN in 1846.

Unusually for its time, the Oratory was designed not in neo-Gothic style but in the florid Baroque of many Italian churches. The interior is dominated by huge 17th-century Carrara marble statues from Siena Cathedral, and a 60 m (200 ft) high dome, added in 1896.

BRONTË SISTERS

- Novelists • Charlotte 1816-55
- Emily 1818-48 • Anne 1820-49

Britain's great trio of literary sisters lived a mundane existence with their widower father and brother Branwell in a country vicarage in Haworth on the Yorkshire moors. Despite the social isolation they produced some of the most exciting and poetic fiction of the 19th century. Their first work was a joint collection of poems published in 1846 under the male pseudonyms Currer, Ellis and Acton Bell. The book sold just two copies but,

undeterred, each sister wrote a novel the following year and in total published seven novels between them.

The Brontës' books give little hint of the quiet life they led, expressing powerful passions and controversially challenging traditional feminine roles. Of Charlotte's four novels, *Jane Eyre* (1847) is one of the world's great literary love stories, suffused with mystery, terror and scarcely cloaked sexual passion. Emily's sole novel, the romantic masterpiece *Wuthering Heights* (1847), sets human passion against the dramatic landscape of the North York moors. The second of Anne's two novels, *The Tenant of Wildfell Hall* (1848), drew censure for portraying a married woman daring to leave her brutish and dissolute husband.

The sisters all worked as governesses. Charlotte was the only one to marry and then only in 1854, the year before she died, to her father's curate.

Rupert BROOKE

- Poet • 1887-1915

Although he never engaged in active combat, Rupert Brooke became one of the most popular of Britain's First World War poets, expressing an uncomplicated patriotism free of battle-weary cynicism.

By the time war broke out Brooke was already well known. After leaving Cambridge University, he settled down to writing poetry at the nearby village of Grantchester, publishing in 1911 a volume of verses romanticising rural

If I should die,
*   think only this of me:*
That there's some corner
*   of a foreign field*
That is for ever England.

RUPERT BROOKE 'The Soldier'

England. The popular subject and Brooke's celebrated good looks propelled him into London literary circles, where the novelist Henry James described him as 'A creature on whom the gods had smiled their brightest'.

Brooke joined up soon after war was declared in 1914, and wrote his war sonnets while in training. He sailed for the Dardanelles in February 1915 but just two months later died of blood poisoning on the Greek island of Skiros.

BROOKLANDS

- Surrey (p.495 G5)
- Motor racing and aviation centre, 1907-87

Britain's first purpose-built racetrack and testing ground grew out of frustration in the early years of the century with the national speed limit of 20 mph – a limit that remained in force until 1930.

In 1906-7 Hugh Locke-King, a Surrey landowner, paid £150 000 to build a concrete racetrack – the world's first – at Brooklands. It was 30 m (100 ft) wide, banked and oval in shape, and soon became a centre for innovation in motor racing. Racing reached a peak in the

BROOKLANDS FLIER In 1937 the Napier-Railton was regularly clocking more than 140 mph

1920s and 30s when drivers such as Malcolm CAMPBELL ruled the circuit, and the rich and famous frequented the plush clubhouse ('The right crowd, and no crowding').

From 1908 aircraft were tested on an aerodrome built within the circuit. Vickers opened a factory nearby in 1915 that produced fighter planes in the First World War, and Barnes WALLIS's Wellington bomber in the Second. Fear of detection by enemy aircraft in the 1940s signalled the end of Brooklands racetrack; some banking was demolished and trees were planted as camouflage. Despite this, aircraft production continued until 1987. Historic cars and planes are now displayed in the Brooklands museum.

> The world's first passenger flight ticket office opened at Brooklands aerodrome in 1911. For a few guineas people could take a 'joyride' above the grounds in a flimsy aircraft

'Capability' BROWN

• **Landscape gardener and architect** • **1716-83**
When Lancelot Brown was invited to view a grand estate, he would invariably comment, 'I see great capability of improvement here' – hence his nickname. He began as a gardener's boy in Northumberland, then moved to Buckinghamshire, becoming head gardener at STOWE under the direction of the architect and garden designer William Kent. Contact with visiting nobility at Stowe began to win Brown commissions, starting in 1751 with Croome Court in Worcestershire, where he designed both the house and gardens.

Kent had created a type of English garden more informal than the prevalent French style of orderly geometry, and Brown continued his work. He went to great lengths to create seemingly natural effects that blended in with the surrounding countryside, planting thousands of trees, creating serpentine lakes and gentle hills, and even removing entire villages to create an unplanned look.

Few 18th-century estates were untouched by Brown. Enthusiasm for his work was so great that George III made him 'Surveyor of his Majesty's Gardens', in charge of both Hampton Court and the botanic gardens at Kew.

Louise BROWN

• **'Test-tube' baby** • **b.1978**
On July 25, 1978, Louise Brown was born by Caesarean section at Oldham General Hospital, near Manchester – the world's first live delivery of a baby conceived outside the mother's womb. The technique used – called in-vitro (Latin for 'in glass') fertilisation (IVF) – was the work of the British doctors Patrick Steptoe (1913-88) and Robert Edwards (b.1925), and involved taking an egg from the mother, fertilising it and implanting the embryo into her womb.

IVF is now a standard infertility treatment. There are today at least 200 000 IVF babies worldwide.

Robert BROWN

• **Botanist** • **1773-1858**
Science owes two ground-breaking discoveries to the insight and sharp observation of Robert Brown. In 1828, while botanical keeper at the British Museum, he stumbled upon evidence for the existence of molecules, observing that pollen grains suspended in water moved in a rapid zigzag fashion. It took almost a century for science to reveal that what became known as 'Brownian motion' was caused by bombardment by liquid or gas molecules.

Brown also discovered the existence of a nucleus in plant cells, setting science on the track to uncovering the importance of the cell's control centre and its undreamed-of role as the storehouse of genetic information.

Elizabeth Barrett and Robert BROWNING

• **Poets** • **Elizabeth 1806-61** • **Robert 1812-89**
Love not only saved Elizabeth Barrett from a life of personal misery but rescued her poetic gift. She was just 14 when her first poems were published but illness, a domineering father and the accidental drowning of her brother stifled her talent. For years she lay confined to a sickroom, until in 1845 the poet Robert Browning visited her. They fell in love, secretly married and eloped to Italy, taking up residence in Florence.

Elizabeth's love poems, *Sonnets from the Portuguese* (1850), contain her best work, although wider issues also preoccupied her. *Aurora Leigh* (1856), a novel in verse, examines the place of artists and women in society, and 'The Cry of the Children' (in *Poems* 1844) denounces child labour.

Robert's finest works are dramatic monologues such as 'My Last Duchess' (1842) and fast-moving narrative poems such as 'How they brought the good news from Ghent to Aix' (1845) and 'Childe Roland to the Dark Tower Came' (1855).

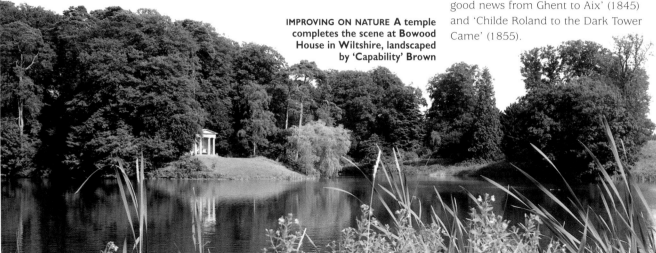

IMPROVING ON NATURE A temple completes the scene at Bowood House in Wiltshire, landscaped by 'Capability' Brown

ANXIOUS MOMENT Brunel, cigar in mouth, supervises one of many attempts in 1857 to launch the *Great Eastern* (*below*). It finally got afloat in January 1858

Isambard Kingdom BRUNEL

• Engineer • 1806-59

The little genius with the big cigar and the stovepipe hat was one of Britain's greatest engineers. Brunel's combination of singlemindedness and persuasive charm brought him early success. He had already assisted his French-born father Marc with the construction of the world's first underwater tunnel, running under the Thames from Wapping to Rotherhithe, when in 1831 his design for the CLIFTON SUSPENSION BRIDGE across the Avon at Bristol led to his appointment as chief engineer of the Great Western Railway (GWR).

It was an ambitious project: instead of the standard track gauge of 4 ft 8 ½ in, the line between London and Bristol was to have rails 7 ft apart. Natural obstacles were boldly overcome with

NATURE TAMED Nothing was permitted to stand in the way of Brunel's beloved GWR. He built the 1 ¼ mile Box Tunnel – in 1837 the world's longest – to drive the line through hilly Wiltshire countryside

tunnels, viaducts and bridges such as the massive Royal Albert Bridge carrying the Cornwall Railway 30.5 m (100 ft) above the River Tamar.

Not even the Atlantic Ocean could stop Brunel. In 1838 his first ship, the *Great Western*, steamed from Bristol to New York in 15 days. In 1845 the revolutionary *Great Britain* was the first big ship to have an iron hull and a propeller instead of paddle wheels.

Brunel's *Great Eastern* was the largest ship until the end of the 19th century but, underpowered, she almost sank after a boiler explosion. A week later the great engineer died of overwork and exhaustion.

BRUNEL SITES • GWR Museum, Swindon
• *Bertha* dredger, Exeter Maritime Museum
• Paddington Station, London • *Great Britain*, Bristol • Temple Meads Station, Bristol
See also RAILWAYS

Beau BRUMMELL

• George Bryan • Dandy and socialite
• 1778-1840

A visitor calling one morning on Beau Brummell, the setter of Regency fashion, inquired about a pile of crumpled but clean cravats. 'Oh, those are just today's mistakes,' replied the valet.

The high priest of dandyism was educated at Eton and Oxford, and after a spell in the army settled in London, where he set about spending his considerable fortune. Brummell was soon regarded as the most fashionable man in society, famed for a cutting wit and for exquisite dinner parties as well as sartorial perfectionism. He made the wearing of trousers acceptable in high society, preferring them to breeches.

Brummell became a favourite of the Prince of Wales, later prince regent and then GEORGE IV, but they quarrelled and Brummell fell from favour. In 1816, with his inheritance squandered, he fled into impoverished exile in France, never to return to Britain. He ended his days at Caen in an asylum for the insane.

John BUCHAN

• Writer and diplomat • 1875-1940; bn 1935

Throughout a distinguished diplomatic and political career John Buchan used every spare minute to pen some 50 books. He wrote histories, biographies and essays but it is as a storyteller that he is best remembered, particularly for adventure novels such as *Prester John* (1910) and *Greenmantle* (1916). *The Thirty-Nine Steps* (1915) introduced the reluctant hero, Richard Hannay, caught in a web of First World War espionage, involving frantic chases around the Highlands of Scotland.

Buchan's own life echoed the restless sense of adventure of his fictional characters. Passions for rock climbing and fishing in his native Scotland were fitted in around accomplishments that included winning the Newdigate poetry prize at Oxford and eight years as an MP.

A lover of wide, open spaces, Buchan spent two years helping to rebuild South Africa after the Boer War, and from 1935 to 1940 served as Governor-General of Canada – he signed the country's declaration of war on Nazi Germany.

BUCKINGHAM PALACE

- Central London (p.499 A8)
- Built 18th-19th century

Behind the austere façade of the British monarchy's headquarters is the mellow stone of an earlier Georgian building. This was the original Buckingham House, built in 1705 for the 1st duke of Buckingham and bought in 1762 by George III. It was remodelled for George IV by John NASH, who built a new west wing with opulent state apartments on its first floor. These rooms, open to visitors each August and September, include the 47m (154ft) Picture Gallery, which includes the work of artists such as Rembrandt and Rubens.

A year after George IV's death Nash was dismissed for exceeding his budget. The more practical but less talented Edward Blore took over and continued well into the reign of Queen Victoria, who made the palace her official London residence in 1837 in preference to ST JAMES'S PALACE. The existing buildings were inadequate for Victoria's family and her official duties, so Blore in the 1840s joined the two wings of the original house with a long east front facing The Mall. This left no room for Nash's MARBLE ARCH at the palace entrance, and in 1851 it was moved to the north-east corner of Hyde Park.

The Caen stone used for the east front deteriorated and in 1913 the architect Aston Webb added the present frontage. The palace is staffed by more than 300 people and has 600 rooms, including 52 royal and guest bedrooms, 188 staff bedrooms, 92 offices and 78 bathrooms and lavatories. The public can visit the Royal Mews, housing the State Coaches, and the Queen's Gallery, which displays art collected over 300 years.

ROOMS WITH A VIEW The ornate Centre Room (*above*) leads onto the balcony, where the royal family appear on public occasions. The west wing (*below*) overlooks the 16 ha (40 acre) gardens, scene of the annual summer parties attended by more than 20 000 people

BUCKFAST ABBEY

- Devon (p494 C6) • Rebuilt 20th century

For nearly 350 years after its dissolution in 1539, Buckfast Abbey, founded in 1018, remained a ruin set in the tranquil Dart valley. But in 1882 it attracted the interest of a French Benedictine order. In 1907 rebuilding was begun by a team of six monks – only one of whom had ever worked as a stonemason. Within 32 years they had erected a vast church of local limestone in 12th-century style, incorporating the original 48 m (158 ft) 14th-century tower. They added stained-glass windows and mosaic floors inlaid with semiprecious stones. The abbey is an active spiritual centre where monks farm, keep bees and make wine as well as performing religious duties.

BUDGET

The government's annual statement of plans for expenditure and income for the forthcoming year is presented to parliament in mid March by the CHANCELLOR OF THE EXCHEQUER in a tradition that goes back to the 17th century. The term 'budget' itself dates from the early 18th century when the chancellor kept his notes in a wallet called a 'bougette'.

In his budget speech the chancellor reviews the past year, makes forecasts for the coming year and announces taxation changes. Speeches are lengthy – William Gladstone's lasted 4½ hours in 1860 – but help is at hand in the form of alcohol. Gladstone took a cocktail of egg and wine, but whisky and soda is the more common tipple.

MONEY BAGS Gordon Brown shows off the red budget box in March 1998

BULLDOG DRUMMOND

- Fictional detective • Created 1920

'Sapper', otherwise known as H.C. McNeile (1888-1937), invented Bulldog Drummond as the dashing hero of a series of crime-detection novels. The first action-packed novel, *Bulldog Drummond* (1920), captured the imagination of postwar Britons, who warmed to its simple division of characters into heroic English and dastardly foreigners.

Hugh (Bulldog) Drummond was based on McNeile's friend Gerard Fairlie, an accomplished soldier, boxer and golfer, and on the author himself, who was awarded the Military Cross in the First World War. Relentlessly masculine, Drummond is an ex-army officer, with a liking for women, cigarettes, port and cars. A white gardenia buttonhole tops off his impeccable dress. Above all he is a natural leader whose prowess in the art of silent killing earns him undying loyalty from 'a number of civilians who acknowledge only two rulers – the King and Hugh Drummond'.

John BUNYAN

• **Writer and preacher** • **1628-88**

For 200 years from its publication (1678-84), John Bunyan's allegory *The Pilgrim's Progress* was, after the Bible, England's most owned and read book. Through the story of 'Christian' and his journey from the City of Destruction through testing territories such as Slough of Despond and Vanity Fair to the Celestial City, it presents human life as a search for God and truth in the face of enemies such as Giant Despair and Lord Hategood.

Bunyan was a tinker by trade. After a spiritual awakening in the early 1650s he began to preach around Bedford but in 1660 Charles II banned preaching without a licence and Bunyan was arrested. He spent some 12 years in Bedford prison where he wrote his autobiography *Grace Abounding to the Chief of Sinners* and the first part of *The Pilgrim's Progress*.

Anthony BURGESS

• **Novelist, critic and composer**
• **1917-93; born John Anthony Burgess Wilson**

The prodigious energy and erudition of Anthony Burgess produced a range of work unmatched by any other author, encompassing novels, literary criticism, biographies, screenplays, television scripts, opera libretti and even books for children. His novels range from thrillers and science fiction to the historical speculation of *Earthly Powers* (1980) and the comedy of the Enderby trilogy with its unlikely fat, flatulent poet of a hero.

MIXED MESSAGE Stanley Kubrick's 1971 film of *A Clockwork Orange* was accused by many critics of ignoring the moral complexity of Burgess's novel and of glamorising violence

Burgess was born into an Irish Catholic family in Manchester, a heritage that appears in his work as a preoccupation with themes of sin, damnation and free will. He came to

fiction relatively late when at 42 he was – wrongly – diagnosed with a fatal brain tumour. Wanting to provide an income for his first wife, he produced five books within a year, including *The Malayan Trilogy*, based on experience with the British Council in Malaya.

International fame came in 1962 with the dark comedy *A Clockwork Orange*, about the political manipulation of Alex, a violent young thug. Like much of Burgess's best work it combines extraordinary verbal inventiveness with philosophical and moral speculation.

BURGHLEY HOUSE

• **Lincolnshire (p.495 G2)** • **Built 1555-87**

As chief minister to Elizabeth I, William Cecil, Lord Burghley, wanted a house built on a scale to suit the most powerful of Tudor statesmen. The result is one of England's largest Elizabethan mansions. Constructed in an enormous 'E', in tribute to the queen, it has a 73 m (240 ft) frontage in local limestone topped by spires, domes, gilded weather vanes, tall chimneys and a balustrade.

The state rooms were refurbished in ornate Baroque style in the late 17th century for the 5th earl of Exeter who turned Burghley into a showcase for his treasures, including some 700 paintings.

Edmund BURKE

• **Politician and political theorist** • **1729-97**

At a time when the relative powers of monarch and parliament were still hotly debated, the forceful speeches and writings of Edmund Burke weighed in heavily on the side of elected politicians. His description of a political party as 'a body of men united, for promoting by their joint endeavours the national interest, upon some particular principle in which they are all agreed' is still accepted as definitive. His insistence, too, that MPs should be seen as representatives, not delegates, of their constituents has had enduring influence.

Burke was involved on the Whig, or liberal, side in many of the major issues of the late 18th century. Irish-born, he opposed discrimination against Roman Catholics. As an advocate of moderation he urged more liberal treatment of Britain's American colonies to prevent

rebellion. After the revolution in France, Burke favoured war against the new republican state, which alienated fellow Whig supporters. His *Reflections on the French Revolution* (1790) attacked the overthrowing of existing order and argued for preserving the monarchy, Church and private property – ideas that have remained as cornerstones of conservative thinking.

Lord BURLINGTON

• **Architect and arts patron**
• **1694-1753; 3rd earl 1703**

A tour of Italy fired young Richard Boyle, 3rd earl of Burlington, with enthusiasm for Roman buildings and the theories of the 16th-century architect Andrea Palladio, who revived the uncluttered, symmetrical style of ancient Rome.

On his return to London, Burlington sacked the Baroque-inspired James GIBBS as architect of his mansion, Burlington House, and replaced him with Colen Campbell, a Palladio disciple. For the next 30 years Burlington championed and popularised the PALLADIAN STYLE.

Burlington's own designs, carried out for friends or for himself, were few, although his architectural masterpiece, CHISWICK HOUSE (1725), survives. It was directly influenced by Palladio's Villa Rotonda near Vicenza, Italy.

Edward BURNE-JONES

• **Artist** • **1833-98; bt 1894**

Like his friend the artist William MORRIS, Edward Burne-Jones originally intended to become a priest, a spiritual orientation that led to the many Biblical references in his paintings. The mystical quality in his work also owes much to the PRE-RAPHAELITE painter Dante Gabriel Rossetti, with whom he and Morris worked on murals of Arthurian legends for the interior of the Oxford University Union building in 1856.

In 1861 Burne-Jones became a founder member of Morris's decorative arts firm, where he designed tapestries and stained glass for many churches, including the cathedrals of Birmingham and Christ Church, Oxford. A trip to Italy in 1862 brought exposure to Renaissance artists such as Alessandro Botticelli, and introduced a more ethereal style.

Burne-Jones became associated with the AESTHETIC MOVEMENT, with paintings such as *The Beguiling of Merlin* (1873-7), displaying a typical dreamlike eroticism. The best collection of his work is at Birmingham Museum and Art Gallery.

Robert BURNS

• Poet • 1759-96

On January 25, Scots the world over celebrate Robert Burns's birthday with songs, dancing, haggis and whisky. The poet was born into a poor tenant-farming family in Ayrshire, where he received little formal education but acquired an early love of reading.

Burns's first collection, *Poems, Chiefly in the Scottish Dialect* (1786), shows him as one of the few British poets to convey the true feeling of humble country life. A master of both lyric and comic verse in the Scots dialect of the time, Burns also collected and rewrote many hundreds of folk songs, including 'Auld Lang Syne' and 'Comin' through the Rye'.

Known as the 'ploughman poet', Burns became a celebrity in Edinburgh literary society, but, generous by nature and enthusiastic in his love life, he found it hard to live within his means. Having failed as a farmer he became an excise officer in 1791, but declining health in the final year of his life meant that he was often absent from work.

BURRELL COLLECTION

• Pollok Country Park, Glasgow (p.497 C4)

In one of the greatest bequests made to a city, the shipping magnate William Burrell in 1944 endowed Glasgow with 9000 artefacts and paintings. Alongside antiquities from Iraq, Egypt, Greece and Italy, such as the Roman Warwick Vase, were Oriental works of art, European medieval stained glass and tapestries, and paintings spanning 500 years. Highlights include a Rembrandt self-portrait (1632) and Degas' *Woman Looking Through Field Glasses* (c.1865).

The bequest stipulated that the works be displayed in a rural setting close to Glasgow. Since 1983, they have been housed in a museum, built from natural materials including ash wood and red sandstone, that lets in natural light and parkland views through high glass walls.

OTHERWORLDLY VISION The combination of a wistful Pre-Raphaelite scene and Botticelli-inspired figures caused a sensation when Burne-Jones exhibited his *Mirror of Venus* in 1877

Richard BURTON

• Explorer and Orientalist • 1821-90; kt 1886

Built like a prize fighter, a scholar and master of 25 languages, and with a fascination for Indian and Middle Eastern erotica, Richard Burton was far from a typical Victorian explorer. From 1842 to 1849 Burton served in army intelligence at the North-West Frontier of India. There he immersed himself in local customs and the Islamic religion, blending into bazaars in Indian dress, his face stained with walnut juice.

In 1856 he travelled to East Africa with John Hanning Speke to find the source of the River Nile. But at Lake Tanganyika Burton fell ill with malaria and it was Speke, continuing alone, who finally discovered the source at Lake Victoria.

Burton made a fortune from faithful, erudite translations of *The Perfumed Garden*, *Kama Sutra* and *Arabian Nights* even though the sexual material he included meant they had to be published privately. A new, even more explicit, edition of *The Perfumed Garden* and diaries and journals dating back 40 years were burnt after his death by his wife.

Richard BURTON

• Actor • 1925-84

Although critical acclaim came early in Richard Burton's acting career, it was his affair with Elizabeth Taylor during the filming of *Cleopatra* in 1962 and their two tempestuous marriages that brought him worldwide attention.

Burton was born Richard Jenkins into a south Wales mining family. He won a scholarship to Oxford and began acting in 1943. Christopher Fry's *The Lady's Not For Burning* (1949) established him as an actor and the 1954 radio narration of Dylan Thomas's *Under Milk Wood* as one of the greatest speakers of English.

Burton made many films, including *My Cousin Rachel* (1952), *Where Eagles Dare* (1969) and, with Elizabeth Taylor, *Who's Afraid of Virginia Woolf* (1966).

IN DISGUISE The explorer Richard Burton dressed as a Muslim holy man to infiltrate Mecca, a city forbidden to unbelievers

BURY ST EDMUNDS

• **Suffolk (p.495 J3)** • **Pop. 31 240**

'Shrine of a king, cradle of the law' proclaims the motto of this cathedral town which owes its origin to the Saxon king Edmund (d.870). Miracles were attributed to him and he was canonised, turning his abbey tomb into a major shrine in the Middle Ages.

It was here that King John's rebellious barons met in 1214, ostensibly to honour St Edmund's Day, but in fact to swear the oath that found expression in MAGNA CARTA, the charter of nobles' rights.

The abbey was dissolved by Henry VIII. All that remains are two massive gatehouses and some illuminated manuscripts, including the Bury Bible (*c*.1130), held at Cambridge University. In 1914 a 15th-century church in the abbey precinct was made a cathedral, the only one in Suffolk.

Darcey BUSSELL

• **Ballerina** • **b.1969**

More than any other modern dancer, Darcey Bussell has restored the reputation of Britain as a centre of classical BALLET. At a time during the late 1980s when the Royal Ballet's fortunes had slumped, its director, Kenneth Macmillan, spotted the 19-year-old Londoner. In 1989 he choreographed Benjamin Britten's *The Prince of the Pagodas* around her superb technique and elegance, establishing her international reputation overnight.

A classically lyrical English dancer, the tall Bussell is also one of the finest interpreters of the great American choreographer George Balanchine. Her humour and down-to-earth nature have made her a favourite with the public.

'Rab' BUTLER

• **Politician** • **1902-82**

No one ever failed so narrowly to become prime minister as 'Rab' (Richard Austen) Butler. He held the three top ministerial positions of chancellor, home secretary and foreign

LEAPING AHEAD Darcey Bussell – here dancing to Ravel's *Pavane pour une infante défunte* – injected new athleticism into British ballet

secretary, and three times deputised as prime minister. Although Butler never reached the top, his far-sightedness brought about Britain's postwar education system. His Education Act of 1944 provided free secondary schooling for children up to 15 years of age, and instituted the 'eleven plus' examination for grammar school entrance.

Butler encouraged the CONSERVATIVE PARTY to accept the principles of the welfare state introduced by Labour in 1945. His consensus approach to politics strove to find common ground between the Conservative left and the Labour right. It was so similar to that of the Labour leader, Hugh Gaitskell, that the term 'Butskellism' was coined jointly from their names.

BUTTERFLIES AND MOTHS: *see opposite page*

William BYRD

• **Composer** • **1543-1623**

The 'father of English music', as William Byrd is known, was both prolific and versatile, writing sacred and secular vocal and instrumental pieces.

Byrd's early life is obscure, but he became organist of Lincoln Cathedral in 1563 before joining his former teacher, Thomas TALLIS, at the Chapel Royal in London in 1572. Byrd was a founder of the English madrigal school that set English poetry to music in a style pioneered by Italian composers. His innovative music broke harmonic and rhythmic conventions, and influenced composers across Europe.

A staunch Roman Catholic, Byrd composed both for the newly formed

Anglican Church and for the Roman liturgy. He was a favourite of Elizabeth I, who granted him and Tallis exclusive rights to print and publish music.

Lord BYRON

• **Poet** • **1788-1824; 6th bn 1798**

In between writing some of the finest romantic and satirical poetry of his age, George Gordon Byron managed to fit in a good deal of worldly experience. His noble birth, good looks, literary success, lameness and romantic adventures turned him into a legend across Europe. At home, Regency drawing rooms were scandalised by his numerous love affairs – including one with his half-sister, Augusta, who bore a child that was almost certainly his.

Byron's literary accomplishments include the satires *Beppo*, *The Vision of Judgement* and *Don Juan* – a medley of wit, adventure, comedy, tragedy, philosophy, social comment and literary criticism, written in racy, intimate verse. He also wrote numerous letters and journals and some short lyrics.

From 1816 Byron lived on the Continent, befriending the SHELLEYs in Switzerland. In 1823 he joined the Greek struggle against Turkish rule but died the next year of marsh fever.

A FRAGILE BALANCE

Despite the creeping expansion of towns and cities and shrinking natural habitats, some 60 species of butterfly and 2400 species of moth occur in Britain, occupying environments ranging from the strand line of sandy beaches to city gardens and wardrobes

Cedar and lavender are kinder and sweeter-smelling moth deterrents than mothballs and proprietary insect killers, which even museums now refuse to use

THE BRIGHT yellow of the brimstone, then Britain's most numerous butterfly, is thought to have inspired the Anglo-Saxons to name the insects 'butterfloege'. From their time to our own, summer meadows with butterflies flitting from flower to flower have been one of the loveliest sights in Britain. But Britain's butterflies

PEACOCK *Wing markings like the eyes on a peacock's tail feathers warn off predator birds*

LARGE BLUE *After a morning spent patrolling its breeding ground at the bottom of south-facing hills, the male rests at midday, then reappears to drink nectar from wild thyme*

and moths are now under threat as human activities devour their habitats. Fens are being drained, heaths planted with trees, roads built on pastures, and ungrazed grassland is turning to scrub.

Gardens are an increasingly important refuge. Large gardens with a variety of flood plants such as buddleias and nettles will attract the widest variety of species. Even a small town garden may provide a valuable habitat for the more common butterflies and moths.

BRINGING BACK THE LARGE BLUE

The large blue butterfly became extinct in Britain in 1979 but has since been reintroduced into the West Country from Sweden – and with it one of the most remarkable life cycles in the animal world.

Young large blue caterpillars feed on wild thyme flowers, which causes them to exude a liquid that attracts a particular species of red ant (*Myrmica sabuleti*). The caterpillar inflates to resemble an ant grub and so deceives an ant into carrying it inside the nest.

There the caterpillar gorges on grubs until it has grown to a hundred times its original weight. After passing through the chrysalis stage the adult butterfly crawls out of the nest assisted by an excited group of ants.

HOW TO TELL A MOTH FROM A BUTTERFLY

There is no scientific basis for a division between butterfly and moth, though there are general distinguishing characteristics. Butterflies are day-flying, often brightly coloured, rest with their wings closed and held vertically over the body, and have antennae swollen at the ends like mini clubs. Moths are mostly nocturnal, drab in appearance, hold their wings either flat or closed like a roof over the body, and have hairlike or feathery antennae. Exceptions are the tigers and burnets that fly by day, are brightly coloured and, in the burnets' case, have clubbed antennae.

BUTTERFLY

MOTH

CONSERVATION

Vitally important for conservation is the network of sites of special scientific interest (SSSIs), national and local nature reserves, and RSPB reserves. Today 25 species of Britain's common butterflies and eight of its moths are protected. It is likely that before long over a fifth of all Britain's butterfly species will be found only in nature reserves.

BRIMSTONE *The year's first butterfly, the brimstone, appears in February*

LARGE WHITE *These butterflies frequent even Britain's most remote islands – provided they can find brassica plants to provide food for their caterpillars*

PAINTED LADY *Females lay their eggs on heathland thistles or nettles; when the caterpillars emerge they weave silk-fastened tents from folded leaves*

GARDEN TIGER MOTH *Dark brown-and-white fore-wings provide camouflage while red hindwings tell birds that the moth is poisonous*

PUSS MOTH *This common moth takes its name from the soft, cat-like hair that covers its body*

EMPEROR MOTH *This boldly patterned moth spins a silk cocoon – usually on heather or bramble*

CABINET

Each week the prime minister and senior ministers meet at No. 10 DOWNING STREET to decide government policy. The Cabinet, whose members are chosen by the prime minister, has its roots in the 17th century, when the monarch's most trusted 'privy' councillors, or ministers, were summoned for advice. By convention, Cabinet members make policy decisions collectively and must support them publicly.

In reality, many matters, particularly in key areas of economic and domestic affairs and defence, are agreed in smaller committees: in 1985 a committee decided to ban trade union membership at the GCHQ spy centre and the rest of the Cabinet was informed later in the House of Commons. Cabinet size since 1945 has varied between 18 and 23.

John CABOT

- **Mariner and navigator** • c.1450-98
While working for Venetian merchants trading in spices from the Orient, the Genoese-born John Cabot had the idea of trying to reach China by sailing west, across the Atlantic, rather than east. Finding no patron in Italy or Spain for such a venture, Cabot turned to England, settling there with his family in 1484.

Perhaps spurred by rumours of Columbus's discovery of the Indies, Henry VII offered patronage to Cabot, who set sail from Bristol in 1497. His English crew became the first Europeans since the Vikings to set foot on mainland North America, probably Newfoundland. His son, Sebastian (c.1475-1557), also a navigator, opened up British trade with Russia on expeditions in 1553 and 1556.

George and Richard CADBURY

- **Chocolate magnates and philanthropists**
- **George 1839-1922**
- **Richard 1835-99**
In 1861 George Cadbury and his brother Richard took over their father's modest cocoa and chocolate business, and set about turning Cadbury into a household name. But their ambitions were more than commercial: the Cadburys were also QUAKERS, and matched their business acumen with philanthropic zeal.

In 1879 the Cadburys decided to improve life for their workers by moving the factory from the heavy industrial environment of Birmingham to a rural site south-west of the city. Houses were added and by the 1890s 'Bournville' had become Britain's first planned town.

The Cadburys pioneered today's weekend by introducing the 5½-day

A BETTER LIFE Cadbury's Bournville factory initially employed only single women; wives and mothers were expected to stay at home

week, and closed the factory on bank holidays. Having no desire to be a landlord, George Cadbury set up common ownership of the village through a trust. Bournville's history and chocolate-making is explained in the village's Cadbury World museum.

Jack CADE

- **Rebel leader** • d.1450
Mystery surrounds the early life of the rebel Jack Cade, though some say he was an Irishman banished to France for murder. Whatever the truth, he crossed from France to England in 1450 and began to exploit the unpopularity of the Lancastrian Henry VI, whose reign had brought high taxes and defeat in the Hundred Years' War against France.

Cade let it be thought that he was related to the royal pretender, Richard, duke of York, and mustered a large army to march on London. After defeating a royalist force at Blackheath, Cade entered the capital and killed several ministers. His troops' unruly behaviour soon turned citizens against Cade and forced him to flee. He died soon afterwards in a skirmish in Rochester.

CAERNARFON CASTLE

- **Gwynedd (p.494 C1)**
- **Built 13th-14th century** • Cadw
The first breach in Caernarfon Castle's 700-year record of impregnability came in 1997 when burglars broke into a strongroom and stole a weekend's takings. Caernarfon was the mightiest of the CASTLES built by Edward I to guard his conquered territory in Wales. He modelled its soaring greystone walls, banded with red sandstone, on those of 5th-century Constantinople and gave it seven many-sided towers looking out to the island of Anglesey and inland to the peaks of Snowdonia.

The walls of Edward's castle join the gated town walls to enclose a gridiron pattern of narrow streets to protect its medieval inhabitants from the Welsh.

Taking nearly 50 years to build, the castle was a royal palace as well as a fortress and in 1301 Edward installed his son there as the first PRINCE OF WALES – a tradition maintained by the investiture of Prince Charles there in 1969.

CAERPHILLY CASTLE

- **Caerphilly (p.494 D4)**
- **Built 1268-c.1300** • **Cadw**

A crenellated tower that out-leans the famous Tower of Pisa interrupts the stern vertical lines of one of Europe's largest surviving Norman castles. The alarming 10 degree tilt dates from an attempt by Oliver Cromwell's forces to blow up the castle during the Civil War.

The first Caerphilly Castle was built by the Norman lord Gilbert de Clare as a defence against Llywelyn ap Gruffydd, the last Welsh prince of Wales, who threatened to reclaim south Wales from the Normans. Llywelyn destroyed the castle in 1270, but the following year Gilbert started work on a stronger fortress. Concentric battlements, artificial lakes and a moat combined to make it virtually impregnable. In the 19th century, the Bute family, owners of Cardiff's docks, restored the castle's formidable walls and towers.

James CALLAGHAN

- **Prime minister 1976-9** • **b.1912; bn 1987**

'Jim' Callaghan was successively chancellor of the exchequer, home secretary and foreign secretary before succeeding Harold Wilson as prime minister. It was on his advice that Wilson devalued the pound in 1967, but he is probably best remembered for his imperturbable calm as one crisis after another assailed his government, culminating in the industrial unrest of 1978-9 (the 'winter of discontent'). A vote of no confidence in 1979 led to election defeat by the Conservatives under Margaret Thatcher, and Callaghan's resignation as Labour party leader.

BRINK OF DISASTER Jim Callaghan returned from holiday in January 1979 to face industrial chaos and an increasingly hostile press

CALLANISH STONES

- **Prehistoric site**
- **Isle of Lewis, Western Isles (p.497 B2)** • **HS**

The tall, slender stones of this enigmatic prehistoric monument, set on moorland above a loch, form a cruciform pattern. At its centre, a 4.8 m (15 ft 7 in) monolith marks a small chambered tomb that is surrounded by a ring of 13 slabs from which rows of lesser stones radiate to north, south, east and west.

Built around 3000 BC, the monument is a little older than STONEHENGE and shows a similar preoccupation with celestial alignments, although attempts to reconcile such rough-hewn settings with modern astronomy have proved elusive.

CAMBRIAN MOUNTAINS

- **Central Wales (p.494 C3)**

What preserved Wales as a Celtic culture? More than anything else this formidable granite barrier enabled the local Ordovices and Silures tribes to halt the westward advance of the Roman army.

The distinctively round-topped range running 85 miles between Snowdonia and the Brecon Beacons is as remote as anywhere in Britain – the only likely sounds being the bleating of sheep and the mew of wheeling buzzards.

Except for conifer plantations, trees are few, owing to the attention of ubiquitous sheep, but deep lakes and hydroelectric plants lie concealed in the upland. Aran Fawddwy at 905 m (2970 ft) is the highest peak. The Wye and Severn rivers tumble from Plynlimon, which rises to 752 m (2468 ft).

BRIDGE OVER THE RIVER CAM Cambridge's tranquil waters invite relaxation in traditional flat-bottomed punts. Here, custom dictates that boats are steered from the flat end. At Oxford, punters stand on the sloping end

CAMBRIDGE

- **Cambridgeshire (p.495 H3)** • **Pop. 95 680**

Students fleeing from riots in Oxford in 1209 were the first scholars to come to Cambridge, a bustling medieval market town when in 1284 the bishop of Ely founded Britain's second university. It is now made up of 31 independently run colleges, 7200 members of staff and some 15 800 students, with the highest ratio of tutors to students in Britain.

The university has a worldwide reputation for pioneering scientific research in fields such as medicine, new materials and astronomy, conducted in laboratories such as the CAVENDISH LABORATORY. In the 1970s, Trinity College set up Britain's first science park to collaborate with industry on a number of research programmes.

ARCHITECTURAL GLORY

Of equal renown in Cambridgeshire's county town are its medieval and Tudor buildings, clustered in a sweep alongside the River Cam, fringed by lawns known as the Backs. The 1130 Round Church is one of only four medieval round churches in Britain, while the Gothic chapel of King's College, founded in 1441 by Henry VI, dominates the skyline with its vaulted 27 m (90 ft) high ceiling and turreted roof. Nearby is James Gibbs's neoclassical Senate House where degree ceremonies are held. The FITZWILLIAM MUSEUM contains one of Britain's major art collections.

OBSESSIVE PURSUIT Malcolm Campbell and his son Donald (pictured in 1933) named all their racing machines *Bluebird*. This car had recently allowed Malcolm to achieve a record 272 mph

CAMBRIDGE SPIES

- Anthony Blunt 1907-83
- Guy Burgess 1910-63
- Kim Philby 1911-88
- Donald Maclean 1913-83
- John Cairncross 1913-95

The members of a Soviet spy ring that penetrated to the heart of British intelligence met in the 1930s, as students at Cambridge, where the KGB recruited them. Like many at the time, they saw communism as a defence against rising fascism in Europe, and were sympathetic to the Soviet Union.

They worked in wartime British intelligence, passing on secrets and recruiting others. Kim Philby served as head of MI6 in Washington and chief liaison officer between the British and US intelligence services. In 1951 he tipped off Guy Burgess and Donald Maclean, who were working as diplomats, which allowed them to defect before they could be questioned.

Suspicion fell next on Philby, who was dismissed from MI6 in 1955 and fled to the USSR eight years later. Anthony Blunt and John Cairncross confessed secretly in the 1960s but were only later exposed – Blunt in 1979, by which time he had received a knighthood (later annulled) and had just retired as art adviser to the queen, and Cairncross in 1981.

TRAITORS (*clockwise from top left*) **Blunt** – at the heart of the Establishment when unmasked; **Burgess** and **Maclean**, who defected to the USSR in 1951; **Philby** in 1955 denying his role in the defections

CAMPAIGN FOR NUCLEAR DISARMAMENT (CND)

On Good Friday, 1958, 4000 marchers – from political activists to actors – set out from London to the Atomic Weapons Research Establishment at Aldermaston under the banner of the newly formed CND. The protest was the first of many against nuclear weapons by a movement whose founders included the philosopher Bertrand Russell and author J.B. Priestley.

In 1960 Russell led a breakaway group of more militant members to form the Committee of 100, dedicated to nonviolent civil disobedience. The announcement in 1980 that American Cruise nuclear missiles were to be sited at Greenham Common in Berkshire, inspired a march of 36 women from Cardiff to Greenham, ending with the setting up of a women's 'peace camp' outside the site. CND membership soon grew to around 100 000.

The Greenham women tried to block the first deployment of missiles in 1983 and many were still there to see the last of them removed in 1991.

Malcolm and Donald CAMPBELL

- Car and speedboat record breakers
- Malcolm 1885-1949; kt 1931
- Donald 1921-67; CBE 1967

A passion for speed on land and water united Malcolm Campbell and his son Donald. For 40 years they dominated world speed records, starting in 1924 with Malcolm's 146 mph run in the first *Bluebird* car. In the years that followed, it seemed that short courses and tyre trouble – one blow-out was almost fatal – would prevent him reaching his target of 300 mph, but in 1935 on the Bonneville salt flats of Utah he did it. Four years later he set a water-speed record of 141.75 mph that was to last his lifetime.

Like his father, Donald relished publicity. He broke the water-speed record seven times between 1955 and 1957, and the land-speed record in 1964 when he clocked more than 400 mph on the Lake Eyre salt flats in Australia. Competitive to the end, Donald reached an unofficial speed of 328 mph on Coniston Water, Cumbria, in 1967, before the turbo-jet boat overturned, costing him his life.

Edmund CAMPION

- Catholic martyr
- 1540-81; canonised 1970

In Elizabeth I's reign, when memories of the persecution of Protestants under Mary I kept alive a deep mistrust of Catholicism, it could prove fatal not to espouse the Church of England. For

Edmund Campion, a prominent deacon in the Church of England, to become a Catholic was courageous.

In the 1570s Campion travelled to Ireland and then to the Continent, where he joined the Jesuits, an order battling against the rise of Protestantism. Risking his life, Campion returned to England in 1580 with a Jesuit mission to restore Catholicism to his homeland. A year later he was seized, put in the Tower of London and charged with conspiracy. He was then tortured and hanged.

CANALS: *see page 76*

George CANNING

• Prime minister 1827   • 1770-1827

Enlightened reformer or scheming politician? George Canning used his skill as an orator to campaign against the slave trade, denounce Napoleon and support Catholic emancipation – yet he made enemies even within his own Tory party. His archrival, Viscount CASTLEREAGH, was so incensed when Canning blamed him for military blunders that he challenged Canning to a duel. Both survived, but were consigned to the back benches for ten years.

Castlereagh's later suicide left Canning the senior figure in government, and he served as prime minister for the last five months of his life.

CANTERBURY

• Kent (p.495 J5)   • Pop. 36 460

The seat of the Anglican faith has a tradition of Christian worship dating back more than 1400 years. In 597, when the Benedictine prior Augustine arrived in Kent on a papal mission to convert the English, Canterbury was already an important trading centre on the route to London. Augustine had intended to establish himself as archbishop of London but was so warmly received at Canterbury by Ethelbert, the Saxon ruler of Kent, and his Christian Frankish wife Bertha, that he made Canterbury his seat.

Augustine founded an abbey, now ruined, which became the greatest centre of learning in early medieval England. Another church became the cathedral, site in 1170 of the murder of Thomas BECKET, and twice destroyed by fire. The second rebuilding, begun in 1174, included a choir constructed in soaring Gothic style, and preserved the renowned 12th-century stained glass. Today it stands in a wide close, surrounded by medieval monastic buildings and the King's School, founded in 597. Its old boys include the playwright Christopher Marlowe, the physician William Harvey and the novelist Somerset Maugham.

ECCLESIASTICAL SUPREMACY

The martyrdom of Becket and his canonisation three years later made Canterbury a centre of pilgrimage – the inspiration behind Geoffrey CHAUCER's *Canterbury Tales*. Although there were claims for ecclesiastical primacy from Lichfield and York after the murder of Becket, Canterbury's authority was never again seriously challenged. After Henry VIII's break with Rome, the archbishop of Canterbury became the chief bishop of the Church of England and, later, of the worldwide Anglican Communion.

Archbishops of Canterbury are appointed on ecclesiastical advice by the

GLORY OF CANTERBURY The cathedral's great windows of early glass include a 13th-century panel of Thomas Becket's shrine

prime minister. Although they have use of a modest palace by Canterbury Cathedral, their official residence is at LAMBETH PALACE in London.

Modern Canterbury retains much medieval character. The Norman walls follow the lines of the Roman originals, and within them lies a grid pattern of narrow streets with medieval timber-framed houses. Kent county cricket is played at the St Lawrence Ground.

CANUTE

• King 1016-35   • c.997-1035

It took the Danish king Canute (or Knut) to bring stability to the emerging English nation. His defeat of Edmund II at Assandun, Essex, in 1016 ended five centuries of Anglo-Saxon dynastic rivalry and introduced a period of constancy. Canute was an astute ruler, keeping peace between his Danish and Saxon subjects by governing each according to their own laws and customs.

In 1019 Canute inherited the throne of Denmark, and in 1028 added Norway to his conquests, forging a Scandinavian empire. Though devoutly Christian, he maintained two wives, Aelfgifu, an English noblewoman, and Emma, widow of Edmund's father, Ethelred the Unready. Canute's sons were briefly kings of England but in 1042 the throne reverted to the Saxon house of Wessex.

RULING THE WAVES? Canute is misrepresented in the legend of the Danish king commanding the tide to stop it coming in. He was in fact demonstrating the limits of his power

ARTERIES OF INDUSTRY

The opening of the Bridgewater Canal in 1761 inaugurated a great new age of transport. Industrialists everywhere abandoned their horse-drawn wagons for narrowboats, and over the next 80 years, until the coming of the railways, constructed 2500 miles of canals across Britain

ARTIFICIAL WATERWAYS have existed in Britain since the Romans built dykes to drain parts of the Fens. In the Middle Ages, rivers were broadened and weirs bypassed to enable supply boats to reach inland ports. But when industrial towns emerged far from rivers in the 18th century, entrepreneurs had only the horse and cart for transport.

FIRST INDUSTRIAL CANAL

When the 3rd duke of Bridgewater realised that a horse hauling a barge could shift 30 tons of coal instead of a ton by cart along a rutted road, he commissioned the millwright and engineer James Brindley to build him a seven-mile canal from his coal mines in Worsley to his factories in Manchester. The canal opened triumphantly in 1761 and the aqueduct that carried boats 12 m (40 ft) above the River Irwell was the wonder of the age.

CANAL MANIA

Industrialists realised the potential of canals, and building activity peaked in the 1790s, known as the years of 'canal mania'. In just three years 39 new projects were approved for construction.

Canals formed the main system in Britain for bringing in raw materials and

CANALS OF BRITAIN 1790

- 1 Bridgewater
- 2 St Helens
- 3 Trent and Mersey
- 4 Stafford and Worcester
- 5 Birmingham
- 6 Coventry
- 7 Oxford

GRAND DESIGNS An ambitious scheme to link the four main estuaries of England – the Thames, Severn, Mersey and Humber – was realised in The Grand Cross, completed in 1790 by a series of seven canals

taking out finished products. No cargo was more important than coal, which fired the steam engines of factories and mills, and heated the houses of new towns, such as Stourport, that grew up around canal docks. Manufacturers lined the canal banks with massive warehouses to take advantage of the cheap transport. A city such as Birmingham depended on inland water transport – and ended up with 159 miles of canal.

MOVING WITH THE TIMES

The coming of the railways in the 1830s brought an end to canal building. The canal boatmen tried to compete by running boats day and night, but to no avail. Today, the working narrowboat has almost disappeared, and canals have a new use as routes for pleasure craft.

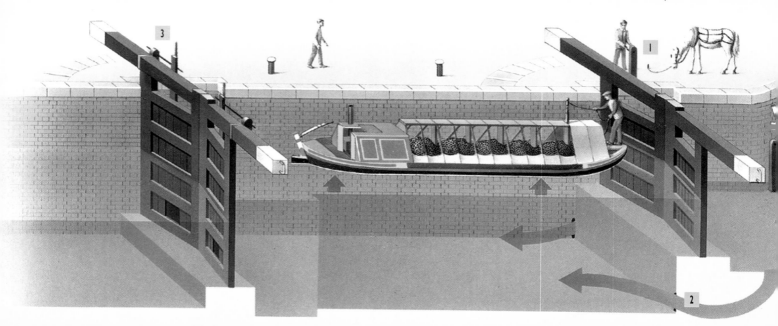

MARCH OF PROGRESS (*above*) As the Industrial Revolution gathered pace engineers devised ever bolder canal constructions. The Pontcysyllte Aqueduct took Thomas Telford ten years to build and carried the Shropshire Union Canal 37 m (121 ft) above the River Dee in Wales

COPING WITH CONTOURS (*left*) To transport Bath stone to London, the Kennet and Avon Canal, completed in 1810, had to scale Caen Hill at Devizes. The drop was so steep that even 21 locks could not prevent extreme rises and falls in water levels between the locks when their gates opened. To moderate the flow larger reservoirs were created by digging pounds to the side of the locks

WATERWAY DIGGERS

Once the engineers had finished surveying the line of a new canal the navigators, or 'navvies', were called in. At first they were recruited locally, but as the canal system developed a specialist work force emerged, mostly from the depressed areas of Ireland and Scotland. The work was done by hand, with heavy soil dug by pick axe and spade, and carried away in barrows. It was estimated that an experienced navvy could shift about 12 cubic metres, the equivalent of digging a trench 1 m (3 ft) by 1 m (3 ft) by 12 m (36 ft) every day.

They descended on an area in their hundreds, living rough with a reputation for working hard and drinking hard. Although steam power began to replace the burden of labour in the 19th century, some schemes such as the Manchester Ship Canal of 1894 (*below*) still relied on the muscle power of the navvy.

TAKING BOATS UPHILL By creating a 'staircase' of water, locks enable canals to ascend or descend a gradient. For a boat to travel uphill, the water level in the lock is raised to the level beyond the upper gate by means of a lockside paddle (1) that opens sluices (2) under the gate. To travel downhill, paddles in the lower gate (3) are opened to lower the water level in the lock to the level beyond the lower gate

CARATACUS

• **Celtic king**   • **c.AD 40**

The threat of a Roman invasion in AD 43 provoked Caratacus, king of the Catuvellauni tribe of south-east England, to muster British resistance. Although the Romans succeeded in conquering his kingdom, Caratacus emerged from hiding four years later to rally the Celtic tribes of mid Wales – the Ordovices and Silures. With their help he defied the Romans until AD 51, when he was betrayed by Queen Cartimandua of the Pennine Brigantes tribe, who had made an alliance with the Romans.

Legend has it that when Caratacus faced Claudius in Rome, he asked the emperor: 'Why do you wish to conquer my impoverished country when you already rule Rome?' Claudius was so impressed with his courage that he gave Caratacus the freedom of Rome, where he lived out the rest of his life.

CARD GAMES

It is thought that playing cards came to Europe from the East. The exact date of their arrival in Britain is unknown, but they were certainly here in the early 16th century, when they were called 'jack a naipes'. Such was their popularity that Henry VIII ordered all cards to be confiscated and burnt so that more time could be devoted to archery practice.

In 1628 Charles I granted the Worshipful Company of Makers of Playing Cards a monopoly on the manufacture of cards, and from then on the production and import of cards was always tightly taxed and controlled. In 1806 a certain Richard Harding was sentenced to death for the despicable crime of forging 2000 aces of spades.

John Suckling, a soldier, wit and poet of Charles I's court, is thought to have invented cribbage, but most card games evolved over the years. Whist (meaning silence) probably dates

COURT CARD Double-ended cards appeared in Britain soon after 1850. This one is from 1893

from around 1670 and formed the basis of bridge, a complex and highly sociable game with a large following. Brag, a simple three-card game, was the influence for poker. Loo was a favourite of late Georgian England, and patience a passion among Victorian solo players.

CARDIFF

• **S Wales (p.494 D4)**   • **Pop. 272 130**

Cardiff may appear to be a child of the Industrial Revolution, but its roots go back to Roman times. When the legions arrived in the first century AD, they built a fort beside the River Taff. This was strengthened in about 250 with 3 m (10 ft) thick stone walls. After the Norman Conquest, Lord Robert Fitzhamon used the walls as part of his castle. The Norman keep remains though much of the castle, with its lavish interior décor, is the result of a 19th-century restoration by William Burges.

Cardiff remained a modest town of no more than 1000 people until the 19th century, when it was catapulted to prominence by its excellent transport links with the coal-mining and iron-working industries of south Wales. The powerful Bute family saw the potential for trade and helped to finance the construction of a large dock complex in 1839.

In 1905 Edward VII turned the town into a city when he opened City Hall in Cathay Park, part of an impressive group of public buildings. Recent landmarks include an arts and leisure facility built in the old docks area and the International Arena, a venue for concerts and conferences. Cardiff, as capital of Wales, is home to the Welsh assembly.

For many Welshmen the true heart of Cardiff is the Arms Park rugby ground, rebuilt as the Millennium Stadium in 1999.

CARISBROOKE CASTLE

• **Isle of Wight (p.495 F6)**
• **Built 12th-16th century**   • **EH**

The hilltop site of Carisbrooke, situated at the centre of the Isle of Wight, was from Roman times the key to control of the island. The dominating feature is a Norman keep, about 18 m (59 ft) high on top of an artificial mound; under its protection are gathered the great hall and private apartments built by the Redvers family, rulers of Wight from 1100 to 1293. In the 16th century the castle, by then in royal hands, was refortified against the threat of Spanish invasion.

Charles I was imprisoned at the castle from 1647 to 1648, but enjoyed the privileges of his rank. Less fortunate prisoners turned the treadmill that draws water from the castle's 49 m (161 ft) well.

Will CARLING

• **Rugby union player**   • **b.1965; OBE 1992**

The leadership of Will Carling restored pride to English rugby in the late 1980s. His career took off early and fast. After resigning an army commission to devote himself to the game, Carling won his first England cap at 22, a powerful, clever centre with a crushing tackle. Within a year he was captain, a post he held for a world-record 59 times. Carling's behaviour off the field also made headlines. He was sacked in May 1995 after describing the Rugby Football Union

NICE TRY With Carling as captain the England rugby team was a powerful force, winning three grand slams in 1991, 1992 and 1996

committee as 'old farts', but two days later he was reinstated. He gained further press notoriety through his friendship with Princess Diana as well as his tangled love life.

CARLTON CLUB

- **Central London (p.499 B7)**
- **Founded 1832**

For more than 150 years the Carlton Club has been the London meeting place of right-wing politicians. It was founded by a group of Tories, including the Duke of Wellington, who had opposed the 1832 Reform Act and its extension of the right to vote. The original premises were in Carlton House Terrace, which gave the club its name. It is now in St James's Street.

Not all Conservative politicians like the Carlton, but few can do without it. In the early 1900s, Arthur BALFOUR complained, 'the Carlton is a beastly club ... but it must be suffered like long hours and constituents as a necessary though disagreeable accompaniment of a political career'. Women were not admitted as members until 1997, except for Margaret Thatcher, who joined when she became party leader in 1975.

Thomas CARLYLE

- **Historian and essayist • 1795-1881**

Thomas Carlyle offered moral certainties in an age of doubt and social upheaval, gaining influence and popularity that turned him into the leading intellectual pundit of his day. Although his emphasis on work, obedience and the individual's duty to society and its rulers ran counter to the growing liberal and democratic spirit of the time, it appealed strongly to a nation suffering the disruptive effects of the Industrial Revolution.

The son of a Calvanist Dumfriesshire stonemason, Carlyle achieved early success as a translator and interpreter of German Romantic literature. He turned to social commentary with the antimaterialistic *Sartor Resartus* (1833-4), a quirky, complex work.

In 1834 Carlyle settled in London, where his circle included the philosopher John Stuart MILL. In a notorious accident, Mill's maid burned the manuscript of the

IMAGES OF ALICE John Tenniel's Alice illustrations (*right*) were inspired by Lewis Carroll's own manuscript sketches (*below*)

first volume of Carlyle's *The French Revolution*. He rewrote it, and the three-volume work was published in 1837.

A series of lectures *On Heroes, Hero-Worship and the Heroic in History* was published in 1841, arguing for strong leadership, even benevolent dictatorship, as the best safeguard of personal freedom. Carlyle's house at 24 Cheyne Row, Chelsea, is now a museum owned by the National Trust.

CARNABY STREET

- **Central London (p.499 B5)**

Carnaby Street is associated with the swinging Sixties, when it was the trendiest shopping area in London. It had been lined with small traders since the 19th century, but its connection with youthful fashion began in the late 1950s, when John Stephens, John Vince and Andrea Spyropoulos opened 'Vince', a boutique selling flamboyant clothes to young people of both sexes. By the early Sixties, Stephens had opened half a dozen boutiques and the street became a mecca for teenagers anxious to embrace the latest fashion. Today, fashion has moved elsewhere, but tourists still flock in to buy the 'canned London fog' and Union Jack boxer shorts on offer there.

Lewis CARROLL

- **Pseudonym of Charles Lutwidge Dodgson**
- **Mathematician and children's writer**
- **1832-98**

The author of the classic children's book *Alice's Adventures in Wonderland* (1865), Charles Dodgson was also a brilliant mathematician. He adopted the pen name 'Lewis Carroll', constructed from Latinised versions of his Christian names, for his fictional writing to separate it from his academic publications.

Dodgson was a don at Christ Church, Oxford, and it was there in 1862 that he met Alice Liddell, the ten-year-old daughter of the college dean and the muse of the Alice stories. On a boating picnic with Alice and her two sisters, Dodgson invented a story about Alice falling down a rabbit hole in pursuit of a talking white rabbit – a tale he later developed into his best-loved book.

The Mad Hatter, the Cheshire Cat, the crotchety Queen of Hearts with her impatient, 'Off with his head!' – and the absence of moral instruction – delighted young readers. Dodgson wrote a sequel, *Through the Looking Glass* (1871), and several collections of nonsense verse, of which the best known is *The Hunting of the Snark* (1876).

CARRY ON FILMS

'Doctor, your mail.'
'Yes, and I can prove it too!'
Such double entendres pepper the script of *Carry On Doctor* and the 30 other films that became a byword for a uniquely British brand of bawdy humour.

The *Carry On* farces spanned 20 years from *Carry On Sergeant* in 1958 to *Carry on Emmannuelle* in 1978, ridiculing along the way the police, the National Health Service, the army, teachers, the British

WHAT A CARRY ON Shoestring budgets forced *Carry On* producers to be inventive. Snowdonia stood in for the Khyber Pass

Empire and historical figures from Cleopatra to Henry VIII.

All the films were created and produced by Peter Rogers, directed by Gerald Thomas and shot on small budgets (*Carry On Sergeant* cost just £72 000). One of the secrets of the series' success was its core of accomplished character actors, including Kenneth Williams, Sid James, Charles Hawtrey, Joan Sims, Barbara Windsor and Hattie Jacques. An attempt was made in 1992 to resurrect the genre with *Carry On Columbus,* but the new cast never quite recaptured the robust low humour of the original films.

Howard CARTER

• **Archaeologist** • **1874-1939**
'Marvels, marvels' was all Howard Carter could murmur when by the light of a candle he first set eyes on the antechamber of the tomb of the boy-pharaoh Tutankhamun. It was the find of a lifetime. For some 30 years Carter had been excavating the Valley of the Kings in Egypt but the tomb he opened at Thebes in November 1922 was unique. For once, he had arrived ahead of the looters, and the treasures were intact.

Before him stood shadowy figures of humans and animals carved in wood, chariots and chests, and the glint of gold. Twelve weeks later Carter entered the burial chamber itself, which yielded a sarcophagus containing three coffins, the innermost being of solid gold.

Although Carter's discoveries ignited a craze for Egypt in Britain, the artefacts themselves have remained in the Egyptian Museum in Cairo.

A legend arose that the tomb was cursed when Carter's sponsor the earl of Carnarvon died in 1923, but in fact the cause was a septic mosquito bite.

CARTOONISTS: *see opposite page*

STEPPING INTO THE PAST History yields its secrets as **Howard Carter** (*right*) and his **Egyptian assistant** prepare to enter the tomb of **Tutankhamun,** who died around **1325 BC**

CASTELL COCH

• **Cardiff (p.494 D4)** • **Built 1875-9** • **Cadw**
The 3rd marquess of Bute, who made his fortune from the docks of CARDIFF in South Wales, proved a generous benefactor to the town and surrounding area. He financed the restoration of Cardiff Castle, saved nearby Caerphilly Castle from ruin, and just outside the city built as his summer home Castell Coch – the name (literally 'red castle') referring to its rose-coloured stone walls.

The marquess fancied a design out of medieval romance and engaged the architect William Burges to build a fairy-tale castle. The site of a ruined medieval fortress was chosen, on a rocky ledge above a wooded gorge. Burges gave full rein to his eccentric imagination, creating a trio of towers topped with conical spires – a Victorian impression of King Arthur's legendary court at Camelot.

The buildings form a triangle around a cobbled courtyard approached by a working drawbridge and portcullis. Walls and ceilings are painted with birds, stars, monkeys, butterflies, and scenes from *Aesop's Fables* and classical mythology. The castle also has a mock dungeon.

Barbara CASTLE

• **Labour politician** • **b.1910; bn 1990**
One of the few women ever to become a cabinet minister, Barbara Castle has been a prominent figure in the Labour party since the 1940s. Educated at Oxford, she worked as a journalist before entering parliament in 1945 and was the youngest of 21 women MPs in Clement ATTLEE's new Labour government.

A supporter of Aneurin BEVAN in the 1950s, she went on to hold various posts in Harold WILSON's governments. Her significant achievements include introducing the breath test (1967); the publication of a controversial white paper, 'In Place of Strife', proposing new rights for trade unions (1969); the Equal Pay Act (1970); and launching the State Earnings-Related Pension Scheme (1978).

She opposed Britain's entry into the EUROPEAN UNION, but after retiring from government was a member of the European parliament (1979-89). She continues to argue for her version of socialism from the House of Lords.

QUICK ON THE DRAW

British cartoonists have been bringing pompous politicians and haughty monarchs down to earth for almost 300 years. Champions of the absurd and masters of allegory, they fight with the cruellest weapon of all: laughter

THE TERM 'cartoon', meaning a drawing, dates from the Renaissance, but modern cartoons satirising politicians or social behaviour developed in Britain only in the late 18th and early 19th centuries.

Inspired in part by the engravings of William Hogarth (1697-1764), the artists James Gillray (1757-1815) and Thomas Rowlandson (1756-1827) started a national tradition of often violent caricature, showing public figures such as George III and Napoleon Bonaparte in absurd situations.

Humour allowed the Regency artist George Cruikshank (1792-1878) to ridicule the fashions and vanities of the age in a way that would not otherwise have been tolerated. He portrayed a dissolute Prince Regent, the future George IV, as 'A Voluptuary in the Torments of

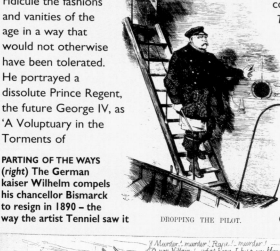

PARTING OF THE WAYS (*right*) The German kaiser Wilhelm compels his chancellor Bismarck to resign in 1890 – the way the artist Tenniel saw it

DROPPING THE PILOT.

Indigestion', with buttons bursting from his waistcoat, and double chins cascading down his neck.

A gentler tone, more in tune with Victorian decorum, was set by John Leech (1817-64) in political cartoons for *PUNCH* magazine. Leech was followed as chief cartoonist at *Punch* by John Tenniel (1820-1914), illustrator of Lewis CARROLL's children's books.

In the 20th century, the cartoon became an integral part of newspaper editorial comment, with *The Daily Telegraph*'s 'Garland', the *Evening Standard*'s 'Jak' and 'Giles' of the *Daily Express* serving up a daily diet of political and social satire.

The front-page 'pocket cartoon' first appeared in 1939 in the *Daily Express* where Osbert Lancaster (1908-86) developed a gallery of characters, including Lady Maudie Littlehampton, Father O'Bubblegum and Canon

NO SACRED COWS Crises over beef and the missing Downing Street cat in 1997 gave Steve Bell an excuse to ridicule the Blair style and smile (*above*). Matt (*right*) reflects on a regular occurrence at Wimbledon

Fontwater, with which to comically chart the ever-changing fads of the century.

Cartoons were used to great effect during wartime, as anti-German propaganda and to boost the country's morale. Symbolism, not always subtle, turned up everywhere – from the pugnacious Churchill bulldog to the ugly little Nazi 'Squander Bug', which tempted housewives to be spendthrifts.

The 1960s saw the revival of the Georgian tradition of grotesque character assassination – a speciality of Gerald Scarfe in the satirical magazine *PRIVATE EYE* – continued today by Martin Rowson in *The Independent* and *The Guardian* and, also in *The Guardian,* by Steve Bell's 'If...'.

Equally savage social satire plus lavatorial humour characterise the adult comic *Viz*, founded in 1979. Cartoon characters, drawn by Chris Donald and his team, include the feminist Millie Tant and Sid the Sexist and continue to attract a huge number of readers – mostly male.

SERIOUS COMMENT (*left*) To James Gillray in 1797 the introduction of paper money was nothing short of ravishing the Bank of England – the 'Old Lady of Threadneedle Street'

POLITICAL-RAVISHMENT, or The Old Lady of Threadneedle-Street in danger!

CASTLE HOWARD

- **North Yorkshire (p.496 C4)**
- **Built 1699-1726**

A palace in all but name, the huge Castle Howard is, with BLENHEIM, one of the two architectural masterpieces of John VANBRUGH. When his family home burned down in 1693, Charles Howard, the 3rd earl of Carlisle, commissioned Vanbrugh to rebuild it. Vanbrugh's assistant was Nicholas HAWKSMOOR, Christopher WREN's clerk of works during the building of St Paul's Cathedral. It is no coincidence that Castle Howard, like St Paul's, boasts a dome, the first to be built on a private house in England.

Everything about Castle Howard is grand. Beneath the dome a marble hall, restored after a fire in 1940, soars to 21 m (70 ft). The ceiling is painted with mythological scenes, ornately carved plasterwork covers the chimneypiece and on the walls are paintings by Rubens, Canaletto, Van Dyck and Holbein.

The Castle Howard estate is so vast that its entrance drive is 5 miles long. The stables house an exhibition of 3000 costumes dating back to the 17th century, and the grounds boast a 24 m (80 ft) obelisk, a domed Temple of the Four Winds and a circular mausoleum.

Viscount CASTLEREAGH

- **Statesman** • **1769-1822; visc. 1796; 2nd marquess of Londonderry 1821**

I met Murder on the way
He had a mask like Castlereagh

The poet Shelley was one of many who held Castlereagh, then leader of the House of Commons, responsible for the PETERLOO MASSACRE of 1819. But despite this charge, and unpopularity for his opposition to parliamentary reform, Castlereagh – born Robert Stewart – was an accomplished, even liberal politician who supported Catholic emancipation and opposed the slave trade.

Castlereagh served first in the Irish parliament and then in the government of William Pitt (1805-9). His major contribution was as foreign secretary (1812-22) under Lord Liverpool when he helped to reshape Europe after the Napoleonic Wars and at the Congress of Vienna argued against harsh treatment of France – a move that helped to secure several generations of peace in Europe. Castlereagh committed suicide, probably as a result of increasing depression and compulsive overwork.

CASTLERIGG

- **Prehistoric site** • **Cumbria (p.496 A3)** • **EH**

The ring of slate slabs known as Castlerigg or the Carles, is set on a low hill within a vast amphitheatre of Lakeland fells. But the prehistoric people who built the monument were possibly looking for more than a picturesque location; the panoramic views and clear horizon may have been chosen to aid astronomical observation.

The slightly flattened circle of 38 stones – all but five still standing – measures about 33 m (110 ft) across and has a curious rectangle of standing stones inside the eastern rim.

CASTLES: *see page 84*

CATHEDRAL CLOSE

While little more than a broad pavement separates most Continental cathedrals from the surrounding city streets, their English counterparts are usually snugly cocooned within a tranquil close or precinct. This is because England's medieval cathedrals – unlike most elsewhere – were often attached to monasteries and so were surrounded by cloisters, dormitories and other buildings. During the REFORMATION, monastic property was seized by the Crown and either sold to lay people or retained for cathedral staff, leading to the part-secular, part-religious composition of today's English cathedral close.

Notable examples include the close of Canterbury Cathedral, which displays a full sweep of English architecture, while Exeter Cathedral's yard is even graced by a hotel, the 18th-century Royal Clarence.

CATHEDRALS: *see page 86*

CATS

The first record of cats in Britain was a law of 936 protecting them. But by the Middle Ages they had become associated with the black arts and it was not unusual for a household pet to be burnt alive at the stake.

They regained their domestic niche in the 18th century but it was not until Victorian times that specialised cat-breeding began. The National Cat Club was formed in 1871 and held its first show at Crystal Palace for British Shorthair and Persian types.

There are now more than 40 distinct breeds and 8 million domestic cats in Britain, as well as many feral animals – domesticated cats gone wild – and in Scotland an indigenous wild cat (*see* WOODLAND). The most popular domestic breeds in 1998 were Persians (7815), Siamese (4596) and British Short Hair cats (4563).

CLASSIC CLOSE The Little Cloister of Westminster Abbey stands on the site of an 11th-century infirmary

CAVALIERS

By the beginning of the civil war in the 1640s the French word cavalier ('horseman') was being used to imply an arrogantly high-handed demeanour, and it took very little time for Parliamentarian Roundheads to begin using the epithet of their Royalist opponents.

The soberly dressed Puritans intended by the term to deride the Royalists for their long, curled wigs, foppish costumes, and air of disdain bred by belief in the divine right of kings. The strategy backfired, however, for with true cavalier insouciance the Royalists overlooked the intended insult and embraced the name.

Edith CAVELL

• **Nurse**   • **1865-1915**

NOBLE SPIRIT Edith Cavell faced death with the words '... patriotism is not enough. I must have no hatred or bitterness towards anyone'

When war broke out in 1914 a British nurse, Edith Cavell, was running the Berkendael Red Cross Hospital in Brussels. She kept the hospital open as German troops occupied the city, treating the wounded of both sides but secretly helping British and Allied soldiers to escape.

About 200 men found their way to Holland before Cavell was discovered and sentenced to death. After the war, her body was taken from Belgium and re-interred in Norwich Cathedral.

BIG SCIENCE A physicist in 1948 earths the proton source of a giant atom-smashing machine in the Cavendish Laboratory, site of much ground-breaking research into atomic structure

CAVENDISH LABORATORY

• **Founded 1871**

Cambridge University's world-famous physics laboratory is named after one of Britain's most eccentric scientists. Henry Cavendish was born in 1731, the son of aristocratic parents but unnaturally shy, especially of women. He lived in rigorous seclusion, working alone and communicating even with servants by means of notes. He was the first to demonstrate the existence of hydrogen (inflammable air) and carbon dioxide (fixed air) in 1766, and also published a theoretical study of electricity in 1771.

More than 60 years after the scientist's death in 1810, and using money donated by the Cavendish family, Cambridge University established a laboratory on a site at the centre of Cambridge. James Clerk MAXWELL was appointed to run it, and it was named after Cavendish. A succession of brilliant scientists worked there and the Cavendish soon became known as Britain's leading laboratory. It was there that J.J. THOMSON and his successor Lord RUTHERFORD made their great discoveries in subatomic physics, and there that in 1932 John COCKCROFT and Ernest WALTON succeeded for the first time in splitting the atomic nucleus.

Lawrence Bragg took over in 1938 and began to use X-ray crystallography to investigate molecular structure. It was as a direct result of his work that Francis CRICK and James Watson were able in 1953 to determine the helical structure of DNA (deoxyribonucleic acid) – carrier of the genetic code – marking the start of the new science of molecular genetics.

The working laboratory has now moved to the outskirts of Cambridge and is closed to the public, but the Whipple Museum, on the original site, houses a permanent exhibition of scientific instruments.

INVINCIBLE BASTIONS

The castles with which Edward I ringed Wales in the 13th century to subdue the turbulent principality are among the finest examples of military architecture in the world. They remained impregnable until well into the age of gunpowder

EDWARD I'S CHAIN of Welsh castles, built after his invasion of Wales in 1277, represent the peak of castle building in Britain, which had begun with the first fortified earth mounds dug by the Normans immediately after their conquest in 1066.

To put into action his master plan of building a series of stone fortifications around Wales, EDWARD I commissioned one of Europe's leading military architects, Master James of St George from Savoy. The fortresses, sited on clifftops or protected by moats, called for manpower, materials and money on an unprecedented scale.

Each castle required a workforce of hundreds of men — stonemasons, blacksmiths, carpenters and an army of labourers — for ten years or more. Workers faced gruelling conditions and seldom managed to raise the walls by more than 3 m (10 ft) a year.

STRATEGY FOR DEFENCE

James's designs were probably based on Byzantine and Saracen forts that Edward would have seen on crusade in the Holy Land. Their ingenuity lay in a double ring of defensive walls: if the enemy breached the outer curtain wall, they faced an even more formidable inner fortress.

Three-storey stone walls, up to 5 m (16 ft) thick, with towers at regular intervals gave archers on the battlements an all-round view. One or more massive gatehouses — superseding the square keep of a Norman castle — formed the ultimate bastion.

KEEP

BATTLEMENTS Archers shot arrows through the open sections, called embrasures, then sheltered behind the solid sections, or merlons

INNER CURTAIN WALL

GETTING INSIDE

Attackers adopted a battery of siege equipment to breach castle defences. Machines operated by rope mechanisms hurled rocks over the walls — or even putrefying animal carcasses to spread disease among the defenders.

Battering rams were used to try to break down the walls, and siege towers raised attackers to the level of the battlements for close, hand-to-hand combat. Mining below castle foundations could cause sections of the walls to collapse.

But Edward's forts were designed to withstand any siege and could be held by as few as 150 men. By the king's death in 1309, insurgents had only ever succeeded in

TOWERS Round towers superseded square Norman ones because they had no vulnerable corners to attack, and were more resistant to battering

taking CAERNARFON CASTLE — in 1295, when building works were incomplete.

Edward's castles were perhaps the greatest engineering achievement in Britain during the Middle Ages. As late as the Civil War, CONWY CASTLE was held by Royalists against Parliamentarian forces, and only voluntarily surrendered. Many of his castles are still largely intact.

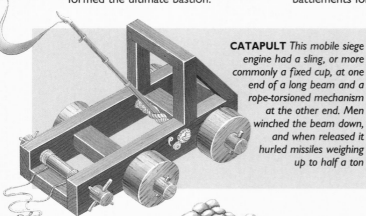

CATAPULT *This mobile siege engine had a sling, or more commonly a fixed cup, at one end of a long beam and a rope-torsioned mechanism at the other end. Men winched the beam down, and when released it hurled missiles weighing up to half a ton*

UNDERMINING THE CURTAIN WALL *In a long siege, castles built on earth mounds were most vulnerable. Attackers sometimes burrowed laboriously beneath their walls and then lit a fire there to burn down the beams supporting the roof of the mine. The ground collapsed and brought down part of the castle wall*

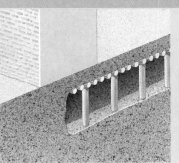

RAINING DEATH *Wooden 'hoardings' or stone platforms were sometimes built jutting out from the top of the walls, with apertures known as machicolations in the floor, through which defenders could drop stones onto attackers. Machicolations above a gateway would also enable defenders to pour water to douse fires set by attackers against the wooden door*

DRAWBRIDGE Beyond the outer wall was either a moat or a dry ditch cut from the rock, and crossed by a drawbridge. At the barbican, or castle gate, a section of this bridge could be raised by chains pulled up by men in the barbican towers, sealing off access to the castle

THE KING'S NEW CASTLES The earliest of Edward's castles were Aberystwyth, Builth, Flint and Rhuddlan – all started in 1277 during the first phase of the war between England and Wales. Edward's victory in 1282 precipitated building at Caernarfon, Conwy and Harlech. The construction of Beaumaris began in 1295

OUTER CURTAIN WALL

BARBICAN

GATEHOUSE At Harlech Castle and elsewhere, the gatehouse became the most important part of the castle; its elaborate B-shaped structure, favoured by Edward I, consisted of several towers and portcullises, and incorporated royal living quarters

HOW EDWARD'S CASTLES WORKED This reconstruction illustrates features typical of Edward's castles. Two concentric walls defended one or more gatehouse strongholds. If besiegers penetrated the barbican, they would be picked off by defenders stationed strategically along the battlements

BATTERING RAM *A tree trunk was slung from a cradle of ropes on a wooden framework, then swung back and forth to build up the momentum to batter holes in castle walls and gatehouses. Sometimes the beam was fitted with a sharp metal spike to ram into the mortar between stonework. A roof of hides protected the assault party from fire from the battlements above*

ARROW SLITS The openings for firing arrows from walls and towers were up to 2 m (6 ft) high but only inches wide. Behind them was a chamber designed so that up to three crossbowmen could shoot through a slit at the same time

SIEGE TOWER *A mobile siege tower was assembled out of range of the castle archers and then wheeled up against the walls. This brought the attackers onto a level with the defenders on the castle parapets, which they would try to storm from the bridge they lowered at the front of the tower*

THE MIGHTY CROSSBOW The defenders' most potent weapon was the crossbow, easier to use in a confined space than the longbow, and more accurate. The crossbow – mechanically cranked to a high tension – fired arrows or short bolts tipped with steel up to 325 m (350 yd) at a velocity much greater than bows tensioned by human strength alone

FAITH SET IN STONE

For the 500 years following the Norman Conquest, towns and monastic communities across Britain poured their wealth and skill into the creation of monuments to the glory of God. As each generation outdid the last, their cathedrals developed into extravagant displays of every style of medieval architecture

THE FOCAL POINT of a city is its cathedral, where the bishop has his *cathedra* (throne). Most of England's 43 Anglican cathedrals were built between the 11th and 16th centuries. Nearly all were the work of several centuries and display a blend of architectural styles. Despite the ravages of the Reformation, many retain some monastic buildings such as cloisters, and – a feature unique to Britain – each stands secluded in a green or precinct.

Arches, windows and vaults tell the story of their construction. Round Norman arches survive in cathedrals such as Winchester. By the late 12th century, arches had become pointed – cathedrals such as SALISBURY were influenced by the lighter structure of the new Cistercian monasteries in Yorkshire. This graceful style was named Early English.

An increasing technical mastery of stone by the mid 13th century led to more elaborate carving – a style that became known as Decorated, seen in the lavish ornamentation of Bristol and ELY.

A CHANGE OF DIRECTION

Many stonemasons were lost to the Black Death in 1348-9. As the labour force recovered, a uniquely English style of architecture emerged – Perpendicular. Large windows set in slender stonework,

such as the east window at Gloucester Cathedral, emphasised the spaciousness of the last flowering of medieval style.

Henry VIII's break with the Church of Rome in the 1530s brought building to an end. When it resumed in the 17th century, it celebrated the triumph of Protestantism. Its creators were no longer anonymous craftsmen, but architects such as Christopher WREN.

GRACEFUL ELEGANCE Delicate window traceries and intricate fan vaulting in the aisles behind the choir at Peterborough show the balanced proportions of Perpendicular design (*right*)

REALM OF ANGELS The Early English west front of Wells (*below*) displays nearly 400 statues of bishops and kings, the richest assembly of medieval sculpture in England

MAIN ENTRANCE

CLOISTERS

MAN AND BEAST Restored 12th-century carvings of humans, animals and distinctive Norman chevrons decorate the west doorway at Lincoln Cathedral (*right*)

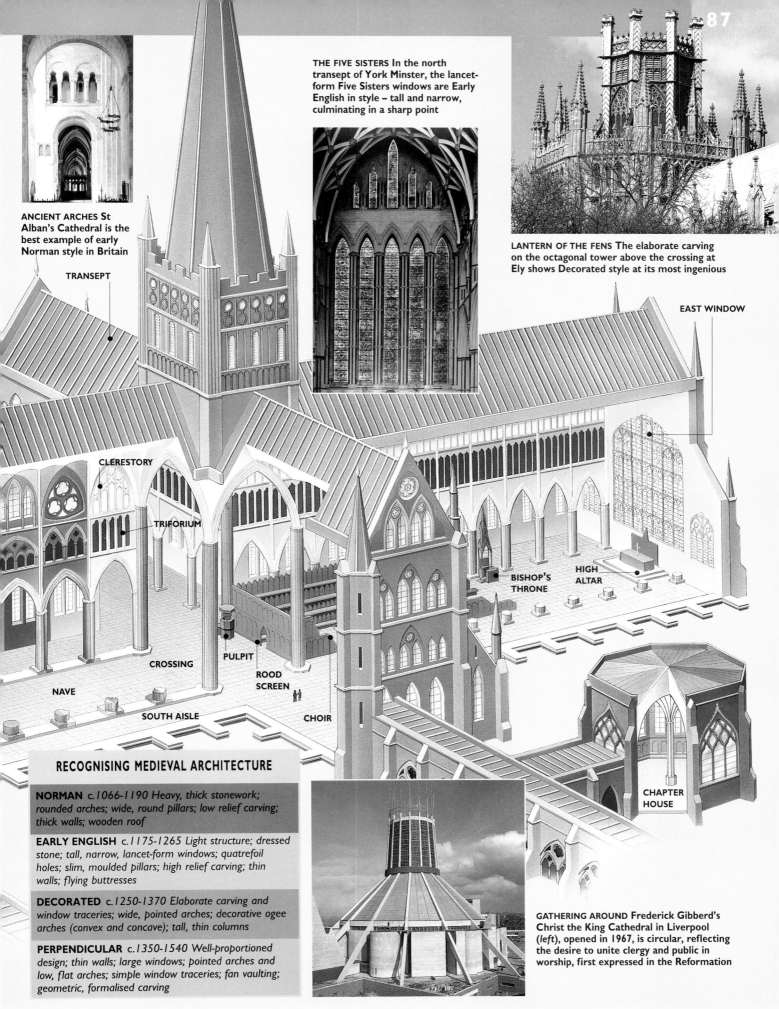

ANCIENT ARCHES St Alban's Cathedral is the best example of early Norman style in Britain

TRANSEPT

THE FIVE SISTERS In the north transept of York Minster, the lancet-form Five Sisters windows are Early English in style – tall and narrow, culminating in a sharp point

LANTERN OF THE FENS The elaborate carving on the octagonal tower above the crossing at Ely shows Decorated style at its most ingenious

EAST WINDOW

CLERESTORY

TRIFORIUM

BISHOP'S THRONE

HIGH ALTAR

PULPIT

ROOD SCREEN

CROSSING

NAVE

SOUTH AISLE

CHOIR

CHAPTER HOUSE

RECOGNISING MEDIEVAL ARCHITECTURE

NORMAN c.1066-1190 Heavy, thick stonework; rounded arches; wide, round pillars; low relief carving; thick walls; wooden roof

EARLY ENGLISH c.1175-1265 Light structure; dressed stone; tall, narrow, lancet-form windows; quatrefoil holes; slim, moulded pillars; high relief carving; thin walls; flying buttresses

DECORATED c.1250-1370 Elaborate carving and window traceries; wide, pointed arches; decorative ogee arches (convex and concave); tall, thin columns

PERPENDICULAR c.1350-1540 Well-proportioned design; thin walls; large windows; pointed arches and low, flat arches; simple window traceries; fan vaulting; geometric, formalised carving

GATHERING AROUND Frederick Gibberd's Christ the King Cathedral in Liverpool (left), opened in 1967, is circular, reflecting the desire to unite clergy and public in worship, first expressed in the Reformation

William CAXTON

• Printer • c.1422-91

As an English merchant operating on the Continent in the mid 15th century, William Caxton observed a booming trade in handwritten books. At the same time, Johannes Gutenberg was developing an early printing press in Germany, and Caxton quickly put the two ideas together.

Caxton acquired a press from Cologne and set up business in Bruges. In 1474 he produced the first book printed in English – his own translation of a French history of Troy. In 1476 he returned to Britain and established a press at Westminster. The first book ever printed in England was a translation of a French work, the *Dictes or Sayengis of the Philosophres* (1477).

By the time of his death, Caxton had published almost 100 books, entertaining and learned, religious and secular, including editions of early English works such as Geoffrey Chaucer's *Canterbury Tales* and Thomas Malory's *Le Morte d'Arthur*, which can be seen in the British Library. After Caxton's death, his assistant, Wynkyn de Worde, moved the printing business to FLEET STREET.

CEILIDH

Until recent times, social life in remote parts of rural Scotland centred on the ceilidh (a Gaelic word pronouced 'kayley' and meaning 'visit') – an informal gathering for conversation, music, dancing, singing and stories. Ceilidhs usually took place in crofters' homes as a way of keeping the community together and of passing on folklore from one generation to the next. Although the old traditions are now dying out, private ceilidhs still take place on the Scottish islands, mainly held in hotels and pubs.

CELTIC CHURCH

Dotted across Ireland, Scotland and Wales, ancient Celtic stone crosses provide a legacy of the earliest form of CHRISTIANITY in Britain. Roman missionaries probably brought the faith to the pagan Celts in the 2nd or 3rd century and Celtic Christianity built

on certain aspects of Celtic paganism. Colleges of druids were transformed into monasteries and pagan deities found new identities as Christian saints: Brigit, the Celtic goddess of fire, fertility and crafts turned into St Bride.

But the Celtic Church also strove for orthodoxy and developed a reputation for Christian piety. Missionary work, scholarship and asceticism – acts of self-mortification such as standing in icy streams – were all highly valued.

Christianity burned low during the Saxon invasions of the 5th century but survived through the efforts of St Patrick, who kept it aflame in Ireland. A century later, St Columba left Ireland to found a monastery on the Scottish island of IONA. From this centre missionaries such as St Aidan, founder of the LINDISFARNE monastery in 635, spread out, converting Scotland and re-establishing Celtic Christianity in England. But the decision to accept Rome as the central authority of the Church at the SYNOD OF WHITBY in 664 signalled the end of the Celtic tradition. By the 10th century the Celtic Church had been fully absorbed into Latin Christianity.

CELTIC CROSS, IONA

CELTIC LANGUAGES

The Celtic speech of the ancient Britons must have sounded strange to the Germanic ANGLO-SAXONS who invaded in the 5th and 6th centuries. They called the natives *wealas* (foreigners), the origin of the word 'Welsh'.

Celtic languages belong to two groups, the Brythonic languages of the main island and Goidelic, or Gaelic, spoken mainly in Ireland. Some Celtic tongues, such as Pictish, have died out; others have been artificially revived but have no real community of speakers – Cornish is one example – and a few are living languages in the full sense.

As Anglo-Saxon settlement spread westwards across Britain, Brythonic speakers were pushed into the farthest reaches of Wales and Cornwall. Some fled to Brittany in France, where their tongue evolved into the Breton language, which is still spoken in the region.

THE GAELIC TRADITION

Irish Gaelic, which has about 100 000 speakers, was taken to Scotland by 6th and 7th-century Irish invaders. By the 11th century, a separate Scots tongue had developed, but with the collapse of the clan system from the 18th century onwards English became the language of administration. Gaelic-speakers were marginalised but the language is still spoken by about 50 000-70 000 people.

The 20th century has witnessed a resurgence of interest in Celtic languages, inspired by poets such as Sorley Maclean in Scotland and T. Gwynn Jones in Wales.

LEGACY OF A LANGUAGE Relatively few Celtic words have passed into modern English. Those that have are mostly terms describing features of the landscape, now found in names of rivers and places

avon (river/water)	River Avon
bre (hill)	Brecon, Bredon
cumb (deep valley)	Wycombe, Cwmbran
pen (top/headland)	Penrith, Penarth
tor (peak/high rock)	Torcross, Torhill

CELTS: *see opposite page*

CENSORSHIP

The days are gone – though only since 1968 – when plays had to be submitted to the Lord Chamberlain, who would solemnly blue-pencil rude words. But even in liberal Britain there is no such thing as total freedom of expression. The laws of defamation, blasphemy, racial hatred, obscenity and many others all put limits on what may be said, shown or published. So do regulators such as the Press Complaints Commission.

On the whole, there is little pre-censorship in Britain and the authorities wait for publication before prosecuting. Films are an exception, being regulated before release. Occasionally the courts ban a book, article or television programme in advance on the grounds that it contains confidential material.

CELTS

When the Romans arrived in Britain they found an island populated by a tall race, with blue eyes and fair hair. These people, the Celts, are thought to have descended from migrants who travelled from Bavaria and Bohemia some time after 800 BC, and of other invaders who between the 5th and 1st centuries BC brought Iron Age culture to Britain.

Celtic communities were tribal, ruled by chieftains. The aristocracy devoted themselves to hunting, while people of lower rank tilled the fields and tended animals. Skilled craftsmen produced intricately patterned gold jewellery and weapons in bronze and iron. Celtic warriors were fierce and fearless – in battle, the front line often fought naked, and Celtic women were reputed to fight as hard as the men.

Before the arrival of Christianity the Celts practised pagan rites under the auspices of the DRUIDS. Until the 8th century they had no written language but passed on their history by word of mouth through the stories told by bards. Celtic myths typically involved the deeds of heroes, warriors and kings, and interwove natural and supernatural events. They survive today in the Irish tales of the Tuatha De Danaan and the Welsh stories of The MABINOGION.

HOME COMFORT Celtic dwellings were simple huts of wattle and thatch – crude constructions beside their fine gold jewellery. Historians have concluded that home was largely a place to sleep and shelter, while personal adornment had the status of art

CENSUS

A ten-yearly population survey has been part of British life since 1801 – except for 1941, when the country was at war. Early censuses were little more than a crude head-count, but over the years more and more information has been required of householders.

Questionnaires now probe everything from number of bathrooms to residents' incomes and, since 1991, ethnic origin. Census information is used by the government to forecast tax revenue, identify social trends and provide information for planners undertaking projects such as new roads, housing developments and schools.

James CHADWICK

• Physicist • 1891-1974; kt 1945

Until James Chadwick discovered the neutron in 1934, it had been thought that all atoms consisted of just two kinds of particle – negatively charged electrons and positively charged protons, discovered respectively by the scientists J.J. THOMSON and Ernest RUTHERFORD. In 1938, scientists used neutrons to penetrate the nucleus of an atom and trigger the first nuclear reaction, making Chadwick's discovery one of the most significant of the century. He won a Nobel prize in 1935, and led the British team on the Manhattan Project that created the atomic bomb.

CHALK FIGURES

For hundreds of years, the figures carved into the chalk downlands of southern England have baffled archaeologists – no one knows who created them, or why. The Uffington WHITE HORSE is one of many across Wiltshire, possibly carved by the Celts as a tribal emblem between 1400 and 600 BC. In Dorset, the Cerne Abbas Giant, a figure 55 m (180 ft) long, that is according to local legend, the outline of a wicked giant who once terrorised the area, may be 1500 years old or a 17th-century hoax. Some theories link the 70 m (230 ft) Long Man of Wilmington in Sussex with Norse mythology. The real origins of these figures are lost and their purpose remains a mystery.

SMASHING ATOMS James Chadwick discovered the neutron at the Cavendish Laboratory – a development that led to literally Earth-shattering consequences

Neville CHAMBERLAIN

• **Prime minister 1937-40** • **1869-1940**

In 1938 Neville Chamberlain was hailed as a hero whose diplomacy had prevented a war, only to be condemned the very next year as Adolf Hitler's dupe.

Chamberlain, a Conservative, succeeded Stanley BALDWIN as prime minister in 1937 and immediately encountered the German dictator's aggression. Like most people at the time, Chamberlain feared nothing more than a second European war. He pursued a policy of APPEASEMENT towards Germany, flying to Munich in 1938 to bargain with Hitler. The resulting Munich Pact allowed Germany to occupy part of Czechoslovakia, which Chamberlain thought would assure 'peace in our time'.

Winston CHURCHILL commented: 'England has been offered a choice between war and shame. She has chosen shame – and will get war'. It proved a prophetic utterance. On September 1, 1939, Hitler invaded Poland, and Chamberlain was forced to declare war. Support rapidly drained away from his uninspiring leadership and on May 10, 1940, he resigned in favour of Churchill.

CHANCELLOR OF THE EXCHEQUER

The minister in charge of the nation's finances, an office dating back to the reign of Edward the Confessor (1042-66), is today regarded as the most powerful person in government after the prime minister. As head of the Treasury, the chancellor approves government expenditure and arranges funding from TAXES, borrowing or the sale of assets. He announces his decisions each spring in a BUDGET statement to the Commons. Chancellors officially live at 11 Downing Street, and have the use of Dorneywood, a 45-room mansion in Buckinghamshire.

CHANNEL ISLANDS

• **English Channel (p.494 D7/E7)** • **Pop. 146 630**

Alderney, Guernsey, Jersey, Sark and the other islands off the coast of Normandy have been British since William the Conqueror united the dukedom of Normandy with the English throne in 1066. Islanders are of mixed French and British descent, and their loyal toast is made to 'The Queen, our Duke'.

The islands were occupied by Germany for five years during the Second World War, and coastal gun platforms and inland strongholds can still be seen.

Today the Islands are Crown dependencies of the United Kingdom, responsible for their own legislation and taxation. Alderney, Guernsey and Jersey have parliaments, but Sark is still run on feudal lines by a male 'Seigneur' or female 'Dame'. The mild climate makes tourism and agriculture profitable. Jersey potatoes, dairy products and flowers are exported internationally. Banking also brings in large amounts of revenue as a result of the islands' off-shore tax status.

CHANNEL SWIMMING

It is not the distance between England and France – 20½ miles at the narrowest point – that makes swimming the English Channel such a challenge, but the variable currents that can carry swimmers far off course.

Captain Matthew Webb was the first to swim to France in 1875 (in 21 hours 41 minutes), when the mayor of Dover declared: 'I do not believe that in the future history of the world any such feat

CHANNEL TUNNEL

Almost two centuries passed between the first proposal for an undersea route between England and France and the opening of the Channel Tunnel in 1994. Early plans included an 1802 design for a tunnel taking horse-drawn carriages, with ventilation shafts poking up above the waves. More feasible proposals for a railway link were made in the 1870s and a century later in the 1970s. In both cases construction work was started but soon abandoned for political reasons.

Work on today's three tunnels began in December 1987, with two teams burrowing towards each other from Folkestone and Sangatte. The service tunnel was completed three years later, and the two railway tunnels in 1991. Nearly 3 million passengers used the tunnel in its first year.

BREAKING THROUGH Three 31 mile tunnels were bored under the Channel: two for trains, 7.6 m (25 ft) wide, and a third, 4.8 m (15¾ ft) wide, as a service and escape route

will be performed by anybody else.' Of approximately 6000 attempts made since then, about 500 have succeeded. Record British swimmers include Thomas Gregory in 1988, the youngest to cross at 11 years old, and Alison Streeter, who has made the highest number of crossings – 37 by 1998.

CHARGE OF THE LIGHT BRIGADE

• **Balaklava, Crimea** • **October 25, 1854**
A simple mistake led to this legendary British disaster during the Crimean War, when Russian troops attempting to cut off British supplies met a British cavalry brigade at the Balaklava plain.

The British commander-in-chief, Lord Raglan, sent an instruction to Lord Cardigan, commander of the Light Brigade, to 'prevent the enemy taking away the guns' – ordering an assault on Russian artillery on the heights above the plain. Cardigan misunderstood, and ordered his cavalry, armed with only sabres and lances, to charge against further Russian artillery waiting in the narrow valley below. The British troops and their horses were exposed to gunfire on three sides – from the heights and from the valley ahead. Cardigan survived but 247 men perished.

CHARING CROSS

• **Central London (p.499 D6)**
The triangular area south of Trafalgar Square situated on a bend in the Thames was originally known as Cheringe, from an Old English word meaning 'big bend'. 'Cross' was added after Edward I erected an ELEANOR CROSS there in 1291, marking the penultimate resting place of

his wife's funeral procession. Distances from the capital are measured from the cross adjacent to the station, which is the estimated centre point of London. Charing Cross Road, which runs off to the north, is famous for its bookshops.

CHARITIES

Alms-giving goes back to medieval times when monasteries gave shelter and food to the poor – but it was the Victorians who institutionalised philanthropy on a national scale. Charity today is big business. In 1997-8 in England and Wales alone, 182 000 charities generated £18.3 billion and employed 400 000 people.

TOP TEN FUNDRAISING CHARITIES BY INCOME (1997/8)

	INCOME	PERMANENT EMPLOYEES
Oxfam	£96.5 m	1400
National Trust	£89.6 m	7250
Imperial Cancer Research Fund	£88 m	2150
Cancer Research Campaign	£74.4 m	820
Royal National Lifeboat Institution	£72.6 m	830
British Heart Foundation	£72.2 m	1200
Salvation Army	£66.7 m	5490
Help the Aged	£58.2 m	2160
Barnardo's	£58 m	5000
Royal Opera House Covent Garden	£56 m	560

Source: Charities Aid Foundation

INTO THE VALLEY OF DEATH The British Light Brigade rode straight into Russian guns at the Battle of Balaklava. Of 673 cavalry, 426 men and just 198 horses survived the slaughter

CHARLECOTE PARK

• **Warwickshire (p.495 F3)**
• **Built 1550s; restored 1830s** • **NT**
William Shakespeare is said to have been caught poaching in Charlecote Park. He would certainly have known the house, near to his home in Stratford-upon-Avon. The original gatehouse survives, and the house's bay windows, built by Thomas Lucy, are framed by towers and a gabled roof. A coat of arms above the door records a visit by Elizabeth I in 1572.

Much of the interior was renovated in 'Elizabethan Revival' style by George Lucy in the 19th century. The Lucys gave the house to the National Trust in 1946, though it continues to be their family home. Books, art and furniture collected by George Lucy are on view.

Prince CHARLES

• **Prince of Wales** • **b.1948**
What is the job of the heir to the throne? For Prince Charles, created PRINCE OF WALES in 1958, waiting to rule has not been sufficient. Instead he has assumed a role for himself, becoming known as a champion of causes ranging from the English language to spirituality and traditional architecture. His views have often found popular support. A proposed extension to the National Gallery was scrapped after the prince condemned it as 'a monstrous carbuncle on the face of a much-loved friend'.

The prince is also a dedicated environmentalist, and produces organic food on his estate at Highgrove. In 1976 he founded the Prince's Trust, which trains 100 000 young people a year and helps many into business. In addition, he is an accomplished watercolourist.

Charles was educated at Gordonstoun and Cambridge. He has said publicly that his childhood was unhappy and that his marriage in 1981 to Lady Diana Spencer (later DIANA, Princess of Wales) was made under pressure. The couple had two sons, William and Henry, but were divorced in 1996. Charles may remarry only with the permission of the sovereign and the archbishop of Canterbury.

CHARLES I

- **King 1625-49** • **1600-49**

The son of JAMES I grew from an artistic child into a high-minded king and a lover and patron of the arts. Politically, Charles's reign was less happy, marred by continual conflict with parliament, which finally flared into the CIVIL WAR that led to his execution.

An initial problem was the influence of the Duke of Buckingham, Charles's much-disliked chief minister. In 1628, Buckingham was assassinated, and parliament issued a Petition of Right to press for greater control over taxation and conscription.

In 1629 Charles dissolved parliament and for 11 years ruled alone, exercising his belief that kings had divine authority to rule. But in 1640 he was twice forced to recall parliament to raise funds. The second session – the LONG PARLIAMENT – responded by curbing his powers.

The king attempted to arrest five leading parliamentarians and in 1642 CIVIL WAR broke out. The Royalist forces were defeated and Charles was captured.

BROTHERS IN ARMS Jack Charlton (left) was known as 'the Giraffe' for his long neck. At 6ft 1½ in, he towers over his 5 ft 9 in brother, Bobby

In 1649 he was convicted of treason and, after a dignified final speech, beheaded in Whitehall.

CHARLES II

- **King 1660-85** • **1630-85**

As heir to the throne, Charles lived in exile in France during the CIVIL WAR. But in 1650, 18 months after the execution of his father, he returned to Scotland where he was crowned king and with COVENANTER support amassed an army. Charles marched south to take on Oliver Cromwell, but was defeated. He fled again into exile, until in 1660 disarray after Cromwell's death led parliament to seek his return. On his 30th birthday Charles was restored to the throne.

Charles supported the arts, revived cultural life and practised religious tolerance. His alliance with France led to war with the Dutch in 1672, and he rebuilt the Royal Navy for the task. He had many mistresses and fathered some 14 children – all illegitimate. Like his father, he dissolved a troublesome parliament, and ruled alone from 1681.

Bobby and Jack CHARLTON

- **Footballers**
- **Jack b.1935; OBE 1974**
- **Bobby b.1937; kt 1994**

If Bobby Charlton is British football's finest ambassador, his elder brother Jack (born John) is remembered as one of its most popular cult figures for his lanky physique and bluff personality.

At 19, Bobby played in the FA Cup final for MANCHESTER UNITED. He survived the 1958 Munich air crash that killed eight teammates, winning the first of 106 England caps two months later. His 49 goals for England are a record.

Jack played centre-half for Leeds United, helping them to win the League Cup in 1968, the League Championship in 1969 and the FA Cup in 1972. Both brothers played in England's WORLD CUP-winning team in 1966.

HANDSOME HORSEMAN Charles II enjoyed the public's support when he rode to Whitehall for his restoration to the throne

Jack went on to manage the Republic of Ireland side, earning a reputation for eccentric dictatorship. Bobby became a director of Manchester United in 1984.

CHARTISM

Britain's first genuinely national working-class political movement grew out of disappointment with the REFORM ACT of 1832, which left the vast majority of the population still disenfranchised. In 1838 a document called *The People's Charter*, drawn up by reformists such as Francis Place and William Lovett, demanded universal male suffrage – the vote – secret ballots and the removal of property qualifications for MPs.

Chartism drew support from groups ranging from hand-loom weavers to currency reformers. A petition in 1839 attracted 1.25 million signatures but was rejected by parliament, as were two further petitions. Chartism waned as economic conditions improved, though all its most important demands, such as the secret ballot, were subsequently met.

CHARTWELL

- **Kent (p.495 H5)**
- **Built 19th century, altered 1922** • **NT**

Winston CHURCHILL took a political back seat in the 1930s, disenchanted with Britain's policy of appeasement towards Germany, and spent more time enjoying his country home in Kent. During this political 'exile' he built a brick wall round the kitchen garden of Chartwell, the Victorian red-brick house he bought in 1922 and which remained his country home until his death.

The house, which has views over the Weald, still has a feeling of domesticity, with personal possessions on display. The desk at which Churchill wrote most of his *History of the English Speaking Peoples* is cluttered with family photographs. In the library is a model of Mulberry, the artificial harbour towed across the Channel after D-Day. Churchill's uniforms are kept upstairs, with gifts from foreign heads of state.

CHASTLETON HOUSE

• **Oxfordshire (p.495 F3)**
• **Built 1607-12 • NT**

Cotswold wool made a rich man of Walter Jones. The 17th-century merchant used his fortune to build a mansion fitted out with oak panelling, plasterwork ceilings, tapestries and fine furniture. Jones spent the last of his money supporting Charles I during the Civil War, leaving his heirs no means of altering the house.

Since 1991, the National Trust has preserved Chastleton's unique 'time-warp' quality. The garden is an additional attraction for croquet players; there in 1865 the official rules were formulated.

CHATSWORTH HOUSE

• **Derbyshire (p.495 F1) • Built 1687-1707**

Only landscaping on a grand scale could provide a fitting frame for the 1st duke of Devonshire's mansion. Columns along Chatsworth's classical frontage rise to a triangular pediment, like a windowed Parthenon set in a Derbyshire dale.

To achieve the best view across the 405 ha (1000 acre) park, 'Capability' BROWN diverted the River Derwent to flow past the house. The waters of the great Cascade, constructed in 1696, tumble down a hillside over a tall flight of steps, and the Emperor Fountain, added in the 1830s by Joseph Paxton, designer of Crystal Palace, shoots water nearly 90 m (300 ft) into the air. The

opulence of the gardens is reflected inside the house. Scenes from the life of Julius Caesar adorn the Painted Hall, decorated in 1694 by the French artist Louis Laguerre, and woodcarvings and wall hangings fill the State Rooms.

Geoffrey CHAUCER

• **Poet • c.1343-1400**

The poems of Geoffrey Chaucer sealed the victory of English over French as the language of literature in Britain and helped to establish southern English as the standard form of speech.

Chaucer became a royal page, probably through his father, a London wine merchant with connections at the court of Edward III. Later he undertook diplomatic missions to France and Italy, and moved in court circles – Edward's fourth son, John of Gaunt, was a relative by marriage – and the court was his main audience.

Chaucer's major work, *The Canterbury Tales* (c.1387-1400), presents a cross-section of 14th-century society, revealing the personalities of a group of pilgrims, including Chaucer himself, through the stories they tell along the way, from courtly romance, through parable and fable to downright bawdiness.

> The tradition of burying writers in Westminster Abbey began with Geoffrey Chaucer. More than 100 great names are now commemorated in Poets' Corner

CHEDDAR GORGE

• **Somerset (p.494 E5)**

The narrow canyon of sheer limestone cliffs known as Cheddar Gorge cuts 120 m (400 ft) deep into the MENDIP HILLS, which for 2 miles tower above the road to the village of Cheddar. The gorge was probably eroded by a river before the last Ice Age about 18 000 years ago, and later deepened by floodwaters from melting glaciers.

The cliffs conceal underground streams and some 400 caves, most accessible only to pot-holers. Gough's Cave, the largest, has been open to visitors since the 19th century. Its network of caverns, streams and pools and those of neighbouring Cox's Cave, are noted for stalactites and stalagmites. Stone Age tools and bones from the area are preserved in an adjoining museum.

CHEESE

Britain has produced cheese since before Roman times, and the varied nature of the farmland means there are now more than 1000 British cheeses. The flavour and texture of each depends on the animals that provide the milk, the quality of the grazing, the culture used and the ripening process.

REGIONAL FAVOURITES

CABOC
Scotland's oldest cheese dates from the early 1400s. Caboc is traditionally shaped into small logs and rolled in oatmeal. Its name derives from the Gaelic word for cheese

CAERPHILLY
Welsh manufacturers of Caerphilly were ruined by a cheese-making ban in the Second World War. Today it is made in England and Wales

CHEDDAR
This cheese, still made in the Cheddar area of Somerset, was first produced in the early 16th century

CHESHIRE
Cheshire is one of the oldest English cheeses. Its salty taste occurs naturally – the result of cattle grazing the grass of the Cheshire plain, which covers huge reserves of salt

DOUBLE GLOUCESTER
'Gloucester' is a breed of cattle: their evening milk is mixed with cream from the next morning's yield to make 'double' Gloucester, often flavoured with herbs

STILTON
Legend says the cheese was first sold in the early 18th century at the Bell Inn in Stilton, near Huntingdon. It is now made in Derbyshire, Leicestershire and Nottingham

WENSLEYDALE
Norman Cistercian monks held the freehold for grazing in the forest of Wensleydale. Their French recipe spread across the nearby dales

FLOWER POWER The central marquee at the Chelsea Flower Show is the largest in the world, enclosing an area of 1.5 ha (3½ acres) and the displays of 140 exhibitors

CHELSEA

• **W London (p.499 B4)**

Chelsea begins where the grandeur of Knightsbridge fades away, and ends at what was once working class Fulham. The borough has a long history.

Elizabeth I spent her childhood at Chelsea Manor, a house built on the River Thames by Henry VIII in 1536, and its main street, King's Road, once comprised part of Charles II's private route from Hampton Court to the city. In 1673, the CHELSEA PHYSIC GARDEN was founded on the banks of the Thames.

The success of the 18th-century Chelsea Pottery, one of Britain's first porcelain manufacturers, and the work of 19th-century residents such as Dante Gabriel Rossetti and Oscar Wilde, gave Chelsea an artistic, bohemian character that still survives. The clothes boutiques of King's Road have been a fashionable place to shop since they came to represent the epitome of style in the 1960s. In 1965 Chelsea merged with the adjoining borough of Kensington.

PENSIONERS ON PARADE The ceremonial dress and tricorn hats of the Chelsea Pensioners add colour to a Remembrance Sunday parade

CHELSEA FLOWER SHOW

• **Third week of May**

Each summer armies of builders and gardeners invade the grounds of Chelsea's Royal Hospital to prepare for the Chelsea Flower Show, organised by the ROYAL HORTICULTURAL SOCIETY since 1913. More than 700 exhibits, from prize vegetables to whole gardens, are housed on 4.5 ha (11 acres) of lawn.

Exhibitors range from nurseries and horticultural suppliers promoting plants and tools, or conservation societies reproducing mini-habitats, to charities and businesses with themed displays. Plants from around the world are brought in for national exhibits, and scientific stands cover subjects as diverse as water efficiency and genetic engineering. Coveted RHS medals are awarded for the best exhibits in five classes, judged on presentation, artistic effect and freshness.

Opening night is a huge event, often attended by members of the royal family and other celebrities. The show lasts four days and 170 000 tickets are issued. A bell is rung on the last day at 5pm, when remaining exhibits are sold to the public.

CHELSEA PENSIONERS

The military veterans who live in the Royal Hospital beside the Thames at Chelsea owe their home to Charles II, who commissioned the building to house retired soldiers in 1682.

Christopher Wren designed the hospital around three courtyards, with an arcade and central portico opening on to gardens leading to the banks of the Thames. The first Chelsea Pensioners

took up residence in 1690. Today the hospital houses more than 400 veterans, who are known for their distinctive 18th-century uniforms – red for summer, and blue for winter. The pensioners run a small museum which, with the hall and chapel, is open to the public.

CHELSEA PHYSIC GARDEN

• **W London (p.499 B4)** • **Est. 1673**

For more than 300 years staff at the Physic Garden in Chelsea have been studying and supplying medicinal plants. It was founded by the Society of Apothecaries at a time when most medicines were directly extracted from plants, and was Britain's third botanical garden.

The garden now grows some 6500 species from around the world on its 1.5 ha (3½ acre) site. It supplies plants for research to universities, museums and pharmaceutical companies, and has had some notable successes – some of Chelsea's digitalis and mandrake species were recently found to have cancer-fighting properties. Poisonous species are also grown – both for research and so that students learn to identify them.

CHELTENHAM

• **Gloucestershire (p.494 E4)** • **Pop. 91 300**

In 1718, a Gloucestershire landowner noticed birds pecking at salt crystals around the mouth of a spring in one of his fields. He fenced off the area, constructed a thatched building over the spring and invited people to sample – for a price – the health-giving waters. As other springs were found and more pump rooms constructed the town of Cheltenham came into existence.

A visit by George III in 1788 turned Cheltenham into a fashionable resort, and a rash of new building left the town with superb Regency terraces and an elegant promenade. The Pittville Pump Room, where the waters can still be taken, was added in 1825-30. Since 1853 Cheltenham Ladies' College has stood on the site of the original spring.

The Cheltenham Gold Cup steeplechase is run in March, with prize money of more than £1 million. The town also holds annual festivals of cricket, literature and music.

CHEQUERS

- **Buckinghamshire (p.495 G4)**
- **Built 16th century, restored c.1910**

The grand Elizabethan house and grounds of Chequers were bequeathed to the nation in 1917 by the heirless MP Arthur Lee, who wanted to see his restoration work appreciated. Lee set up a trust offering Chequers to the prime minister of the day as 'an inducement to spend two days a week in the high and pure air of the Chiltern Hills', in the hope that 'even the most hardened and least soulful politician would be humanised'.

Lloyd George in 1921 was the first to benefit from the bequest and since then 16 leaders have spent their weekends at Chequers. Once they depart from office, their coats of arms are placed in a window in the long gallery.

CHESIL BEACH

- **Dorset (p.494 E6)**

Ten miles of round pebbles make up the shingle bank known as Chesil Beach. It runs in a line parallel to the coast from Abbotsbury to Portland Island, enclosing on the landward side a long, thin lagoon called the Fleet, which is rich in animal and plant life.

As the shingle was washed up by the sea it created a pebble bank that is now a wildlife sanctuary supporting grasses, sea plants and nesting terns. The bank rises to nearly 15 m (50 ft) at the Portland end, and innumerable ships have been smashed against it by high winds. Shipwreck survivors have traditionally told their whereabouts by how large the stones were – from the size of chickpeas at West Bay near Bridport, a few miles north-east, to potatoes at Portland Island.

CHESTER

- **Cheshire (p.494 D1)** • **Pop. 80 110**

The heart of the ancient city of Chester has been enclosed by walls for nearly 2000 years, since the Roman town of Deva grew out of a marching camp beside the River Dee. Further medieval fortification incorporated the remains of the Roman walls and amphitheatre into the city walls visible today.

The streets in the city centre are lined with black and white timber-framed buildings. The Rows, first built in the 13th and 14th centuries, enclose galleried shops, and the 16th-century Bishop Lloyd's House is decorated with elaborate carvings. The grounds of the mainly 14th-century cathedral, which was restored in the 19th century, were once the site of a shrine containing relics of the Saxon abbess, St Werburga. Since the Middle Ages, they have been the setting for a five-yearly cycle of MYSTERY PLAYS.

G.K. CHESTERTON

- **Writer** • **1874-1936**

English detective fiction would not have been the same without Gilbert Keith Chesterton. His hero, the unassuming Roman Catholic priest Father Brown, who first appeared in 1911, established the tradition of the quirky, intuitive amateur investigator, and Chesterton's stylised settings and moral emphasis became hallmarks of the genre.

Chesterton was a huge, colourful man: absent-minded but quick-witted, with a delight in paradox and a hearty distaste for the modern world. His output was prodigious, from his early journalism to later novels and poems. Christian faith and love of religious ritual coloured every aspect of Chesterton's life and work, and led in 1922 to conversion to Catholicism.

CHESTNUT

The story of the chestnut is riddled with misconceptions. The charred floury morsels sold from street-corner braziers in winter are entirely unrelated to the conkers of schoolboy combat, though both come from trees known as chestnuts. Nor, despite the traditional associations of each, is either tree British.

Edible chestnuts come from the sweet or Spanish chestnut, probably introduced from the Mediterranean by the Romans. Its fruit seldom matures to full size in Britain, as the summers are too mild, but in south-east England, where the tree became naturalised, coppices produce wood for walking sticks and hurdles. Sweet chestnut trees can attain immense age and width: the trunk of the ancient Tortworth Chestnut in Gloucestershire is 11 m (36 ft) wide and bluebells grow inside the hollow core.

The conker-yielding horse chestnut was imported from central Asia in the mid 16th century. Its name may derive from the mistaken belief that horses liked the fruit, which is in fact inedible. The game of conkers developed in the 19th century. A world championship is held every October in the village of Ashton in Northamptonshire, which has a mile-long avenue of horse chestnuts.

CHEVIOT HILLS

- **English-Scottish border (p.496 B1)**

A long history of war and anarchy haunts the Cheviot Hills. The windswept granite peaks changed hands repeatedly as English and Scottish fortunes ebbed and flowed. Until about 300 years ago, raids, plundering and border strife gave the inhabitants of the Cheviots a reputation for lawlessness. Nowadays, the hills are mostly left to sheep, wild goats, blue hares, ravens, buzzards – and army training manoeuvres.

The fells and plateaux are cut by ravines with tumbling cascades of the North Tyne, Coquet and Rede rivers. The most rewarding views come not at the highest point, The Cheviot, soaring 816 m (2678 ft), but from its neighbour Hedgehope, 716 m (2349 ft) high, looking over east Northumberland, the Farne Islands and the North Sea.

OLD CHESTNUT The 18th-century tree specialist Peter Collinson dated the huge Tortworth Chestnut to the reign of the 9th-century King Edgar. His estimate remains unverified

CHICHESTER

• West Sussex (p.495 G6) • Pop. 26 570

Romans settled in Chichester in AD 43. They built a town called Noviomagus, enclosed by an 11-sided polygon of walls, with a symmetrical cross of four streets leading from the four gates. This pattern survives, with medieval walls standing exactly on the original lines, and the central meeting of the streets marked by an ornate market cross erected in 1501.

Dominating the city is the cathedral, consecrated in 1184. It has survived fires, Civil War damage, and the collapse of its spire in 1861. Nearby, four streets known as The Pallants are lined by Georgian buildings, including Pallant House, now an arts and decorative crafts gallery.

In July performers from all over the world take part in the Chichester Festivities, which include concerts and exhibitions, and from May to October the Festival Theatre, opened in 1962, stages productions with leading British actors.

Francis CHICHESTER

• Sailor and adventurer • 1901-72; kt 1967

Long before his seafaring achievements, Francis Chichester entered the record books as an aircraft pilot. In 1931 he was the first person to fly solo across the Tasman Sea east-west from New Zealand to Australia, a journey made in a Gypsy Moth biplane.

In middle age, this shy Englishman, with money from his map publishing firm, took up solo ocean sailing, winning the first single-handed transatlantic race in 1960 in the 12 m (40ft) ketch *Gypsy Moth III*. He then set out to emulate the 100-day trips made to Australia by 19th-century wool clippers such as *CUTTY SARK*, and aged 64

COPING SINGLE-HANDED In Sydney, Francis Chichester prepares for the second half of his round-the-world voyage in Gypsy Moth IV in 1967

set sail alone in *Gypsy Moth IV* on the first round-the-world single-stop voyage. He sailed from Plymouth to Sydney in 107 days and returned nonstop via Cape Horn in 119 days.

Elizabeth II knighted Chichester with the same sword that Elizabeth I used in 1581 to honour another great sailor, Francis Drake. *Gypsy Moth IV* can be seen in a dry dock near the *Cutty Sark* at Greenwich in south London.

Vere Gordon CHILDE

• Archaeologist • 1892-1957

Our view of PREHISTORIC BRITAIN owes much to Vere Gordon Childe, an Australian who spent most of his life teaching archaeology at the universities of Edinburgh and London. His reputation was made with the book *The Dawn of European Civilisation* (1925), which presented Bronze Age Britain as part of a distinctive and innovating European culture, based on individual artistic and technical skills, in contrast to the despotic Near East.

Childe led a number of digs at sites such as the 5000-year-old Orkney village of SKARA BRAE between 1927 and 1930. Eccentric and energetic, he liked to test his ideas in practice: in 1937 he organised the building and burning of a timber and stone wall to show how stone could be vitrified (turned to a glasslike material) by great heat. He retired to Australia.

CHILTERN VIEW Hawthorn trees stretch across windswept farmlands towards the distant 230 m (755 ft) high Ivinghoe Beacon, where the ancient Ridgeway and Icknield Way footpaths meet

CHILTERN HILLS

• Mainly Buckinghamshire (p.495 G4)

Over hundreds of millions of years a rain of tiny shells, falling through the ocean that once covered England, compacted into a carpet of chalk stretching from Dorset to Yorkshire. When the sea receded, erosion by wind and water left only a few uplands, including the Chiltern Hills. They run north-west from Goring-on-Thames in Oxfordshire to the turf-covered heights of Dunstable Downs in Bedfordshire, ending at Sharpenhoe Clappers, a wooded ridge north of Luton rising to 160 m (525 ft).

ANCIENT AND MODERN THOROUGHFARES

The hills are sliced through by railways and roads leading to London, running through gaps cut by long-dried-up rivers. Two of the roads – Akeman Street and Watling Street – were laid by the Romans. Much older is the Icknield Way, a path stretching the length of the Chilterns, which 4000 years ago was part of the route to the prehistoric religious sites at AVEBURY and STONEHENGE.

WORKING WITH WOOD

Many Chiltern hilltops and slopes are thick with beechwoods that in summer form a cool, shady canopy. In the 1700s beech wood became a valuable commodity for chair-makers, with wood-turners, known as 'bodgers', working throughout the Chilterns to make legs and spindles for the furniture manufacturers of High Wycombe.

CHILTERN HUNDREDS

It is one of the oddities of the British constitution that a member of parliament cannot resign from the House of Commons, but may quit by 'applying for the Chiltern Hundreds', a loophole found in 1751 by John Pitt, MP.

Pitt wanted to give up his Wareham seat in Dorset and stand in the election for nearby Dorchester. Resignations, however, had been banned since the early 17th century, when struggles between Charles I and parliament forced many MPs to resign rather than risk imprisonment, so compromising parliament's independence.

Another 17th-century rule barred employees of the Crown from standing as MPs as they might favour the monarch. Pitt realised that he would be disqualified from parliament if he could say he worked for the Crown, so he applied for the stewardship of the Chiltern Hundreds, three ancient Buckinghamshire districts that belonged to the Crown, ensuring his exclusion. After this he could resign the stewardship and stand again for parliament.

Pitt's precedent has proved ever since to be a convenient way for MPs to resign – often to avoid scandal or minimise embarrassment to their parties.

Thomas CHIPPENDALE

• **Furniture maker** • 1718-79

One of the few British furniture makers whose name is widely known, Thomas Chippendale was not as celebrated in his day as his reputation now might suggest.

A joiner's son from Otley in Yorkshire and a gifted carpenter, he set up a workshop in London in 1753 and developed a successful business. His clients included the architect and designer Robert ADAM, with whom he worked on the furniture for country mansions, including HAREWOOD HOUSE in Yorkshire. After his death, his son, also called Thomas, took over the firm.

Chippendale achieved lasting fame through his catalogue, *The Gentleman and Cabinet Maker's Director* (1754, 1755 and 1762), the first such collection of furniture designs.

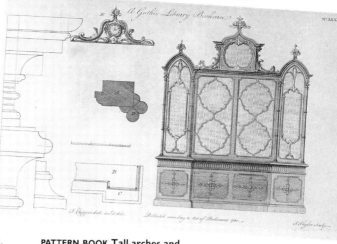

PATTERN BOOK Tall arches and carved pinnacles decorate a 'Gothic library bookcase' from Thomas Chippendale's *Director* catalogue, reflecting late 18th-century enthusiasm for medieval detail

Working mostly in red-brown mahogany, Chippendale mixed clean lines with Chinese, Gothic and rococo flourishes to produce strikingly elegant pieces. His furniture patterns set a standard of design and manufacture long after his death. Little so-called Chippendale furniture was actually made in his workshops, but was produced by others from the designs in the *Director*; copies of his chairs are still made.

CHIMNEYS

In medieval Britain most houses consisted of one room with an open fire and a hole in the roof through which the smoke could escape. Gradually, interior walls were erected to divide rooms, and fireplaces were created, with chimney flues to carry the smoke up to the roof.

ROOF-TOP SCULPTURE
The builders of grand houses in the early 16th century, influenced by Flemish and Dutch styles, began to use chimneys as a decorative feature. The shafts of chimney stacks were often put into clusters, as at HAMPTON COURT PALACE, and fancy brickwork became the favoured medium, shaped into cylindrical or octagonal columns. Patterning cut into the surface included scrolling, fluting, corkscrew and zigzag designs, often in combination.

Chimney shafts on Elizabethan and Jacobean houses, such as MONTACUTE HOUSE and LONGLEAT, continued to rise high above the roof, but eccentric brickwork went out of fashion, and chimney clusters became more unified.

The spread to 18th-century Britain of ancient Roman and Greek style imposed more refined and geometric designs, with flues gathered into one plinth-like stack.

A COMEBACK FOR CHIMNEYS
The architects Norman SHAW and Philip Webb, members of the ARTS AND CRAFTS movement,

FANCY WORK Tudor bricks (*below*) were shaped in moulds, usually on-site

led a late 19th-century revival of the tall chimney stack, and in the 1920s and 30s elaborate brickwork returned along the roofs of mock-Tudor suburban homes. Central heating made chimneys redundant, but in the late 20th century it became increasingly fashionable to unblock flues and reinstate fireplaces.

CLASSIC COLUMN A stone chimney (*left*) on a grand late-Tudor house shows the Renaissance influences that were beginning to enter Britain

CLEAN LINES A cream stuccoed plinth (*below*) meets the 18th-century aims of order and simplicity

HIGH AND MIGHTY In the early 1900s the architect Edwin Lutyens added towering geometric chimney stacks (*right*) to his country houses

SHORT AND SIMPLE By the Victorian age the urban chimney stack (*below*) had become a short, perfunctory projection topped by pots

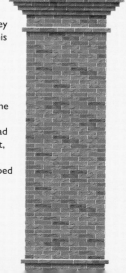

CHISWICK HOUSE

• W London (p.498 B4)   • Built c.1725-9   • EH

The 18th-century nobleman and architect Lord BURLINGTON saved his best work for himself when he designed his home Chiswick House. It is one of the finest examples of the PALLADIAN STYLE, inspired by the work of the 16th-century Italian architect Andrea Palladio and promoted in England by Burlington.

On either side of a low ground floor, external flights of stone steps lead to a colonnaded portico at the centre of a severely simple classical façade. Beyond rises the dome of the central octagonal hall around which all the main rooms are built. These include a gallery, designed by Burlington to show off his art collection, and the Blue Velvet Room and Red Velvet Room, sumptuously decorated by William Kent, with gilded ornamentation, lavish ceiling paintings and vibrant wall hangings. Kent was also involved in the design of the gardens.

CLASSICAL OUTLOOK The 18th-century Italianate orange tree garden at Chiswick House includes an obelisk and a miniature temple both modelled on examples from ancient Rome

CHRISTIANITY

The influence of Christianity pervades the landscape, language and culture of Britain, from architecture and literature to laws and morals. At the end of the 20th century more than 60 per cent of Britons claimed to be Christian, with about 10 per cent regularly attending a Christian church.

The teachings of Christ were brought to England by the Romans in the 3rd century but were usurped by the pagan Anglo-Saxon invaders in the 5th century. Celtic missionaries began the conversion of the British people in the next century, establishing monasteries in Scotland and northern England. In 597, on the bidding of Pope Gregory I, Augustine led a mission from Rome to England and established the English Church. Conflict between the CELTIC CHURCH and the English Church was resolved in favour of Rome at the SYNOD OF WHITBY in 664.

The English Church remained under papal authority until Henry VIII severed the ties in 1534, creating the CHURCH OF ENGLAND. The new Church splintered further in the 17th and 18th centuries into NONCONFORMIST groups such as Baptists, Independents, QUAKERS and Methodists, who still make up a small proportion of Christians, outnumbered by British Roman Catholics.

In the 19th century Charles DARWIN's theories on evolution rocked the Church, and subsequent scientific breakthroughs undermined much of the miraculous nature of Christian faith. Yet Britian is still officially a Christian country, with an established Church and a monarch who is the 'defender of the faith'.

Agatha CHRISTIE

• Writer of detective novels
• 1890-1976; DBE 1971

Millions of readers of Agatha Christie's murder-mystery novels have been challenged to compete with her characters, the plump Belgian detective Hercule Poirot or the inquisitive spinster from St Mary Mead, Miss Marple, to find out 'whodunnit?'

Christie is the biggest-selling fiction writer ever. She wrote 66 detective novels, many of which have been televised and filmed, including *Murder on the Orient Express* and *Death on the Nile*. She also wrote six novels under the pseudonym Mary Westmacott. Her play *The Mousetrap* has been performed continuously since 1952, making it London's longest running show.

In 1926 Christie created her own personal mystery, prompting nationwide concern, when she disappeared for ten days after learning of her husband's extramarital affair.

CHRISTMAS PAST Pagans put mistletoe and other evergreens on shrines to celebrate life surviving in winter

CHRISTIE'S

• Founded 1766

Christie's, founded in London by Scotsman James Christie, is the world's oldest fine art auction house. Among its most momentous auctions were the sale of Robert Walpole's collection to Catherine the Great of Russia in 1778 and that of the Russian crown jewels after the 1917 revolution.

By 1990, when Van Gogh's *Portrait of Dr Gachet* was bought for $82.5 million – then a world record sale – the auction house had become an international dealer, expanding into wines, cars and haute couture clothes. In 1998 this very British business was bought by a French entrepreneur for £721 million.

CHRISTMAS TRADITIONS

Christmas has developed out of two pagan traditions – the Norse festival of Yule and the Roman festivals of *Dies Natalis Solus Invicti* and Saturnalia. Yule was a 12-day festival when the yule log was burnt in fireplaces as a symbol of fire and light to mark the winter solstice on December 21 or 22. The Western Church replaced this with its own 12-day festival, and in the 5th century appropriated December 25, the culmination of the Roman festivities.

Christmas Day remained a day of feasting until it fell victim of the Puritan disapproval of merrymaking. In 1644 an ordinance was passed turning Christmas into a fast. The order lasted for 12 years but was often ignored. Puritans also denounced the eating of mince pies (originally made of chopped mutton) as idolatry and regarded plum porridge as popish. By the late 17th century the porridge had developed into the plum pudding, or Christmas pudding. At the same time turkey arrived from the New World, replacing pork or boar's head.

In the 19th century, new customs were added. The Victorians were the first to pull crackers, with sweets and a motto or poem, and from 1843 sent each other Christmas cards. The Christmas tree, long established in Germany, spread to Britain and was popularised by Prince Albert after his marriage to Victoria in 1840. Another import, this time from the USA, was Father Christmas, originally the Dutch *Sinterklaas* or St Nicholas.

Winston CHURCHILL

- **Prime minister 1940-5, 1951-5**
- **1874-1965; kt 1953; OM 1946**

With his bulldog jowls, fat Cuban cigar and two fingers lifted in a defiant 'V for Victory', Winston Churchill became the embodiment of Britain's indomitable wartime spirit. In addition to his 50 year, roller-coaster career in politics, he was also a fearless soldier, prolific historian and distinguished watercolourist.

Churchill was born at BLENHEIM PALACE, grandson of the duke of Marlborough and son of the Conservative MP Randolph Churchill and the American heiress Jennie Jerome. After army training at Sandhurst he fought in hand-to-hand combat with the Dervishes in the Sudan, and as a young reporter was captured by the Boers in South Africa, escaping with a £25 price on his head.

By nature a political maverick, Churchill became a Conservative MP in 1900, but four years later fell out with his party over free trade and joined the Liberals. Not yet 40, he helped to introduce labour exchanges, social insurance and other welfare reforms, and modernised Britain's navy in time for the First World War. Disgrace came in 1915 when his plans for an attack on Gallipoli, in western Turkey, ended in the futile loss of more than 300 000 lives.

CHURCH ARCHITECTURE

There are more than 19 000 churches in Britain, from huge CATHEDRALS to small parish churches and 'chapels of ease' — simple, spartan churches, built for remote communities. Despite the differences, they share many common structural elements, as well as religious and ornamental features.

The architecture of the Christian church developed in the 4th century, when Christianity became the official religion of the Roman Empire. The main body of most British churches is based on two styles: the Roman basilica — a colonnaded public hall — and the Celtic pattern of a cluster of cells.

In the Middle Ages, the basilica was often extended into a cross-shaped design, with transepts forming 'arms' at right-angles to the central body. Structurally, this divided the nave from the chancel and altar at the eastern end — a division usually reinforced by a carved rood screen. A bell tower was sometimes built above the crossing but in small churches the tower and spire above it were often at the western end.

In the 17th and 18th centuries, church design was influenced by the Italian Renaissance and Baroque architecture. Classical columns were introduced. Ornamentation increased with intricately carved capitals and pediments above grand entrance

porticos. The cruciform plan fell out of fashion and with it the central tower. Church architects of the late 18th and 19th centuries turned again to medieval models, reflecting the renewed interest in the Gothic design of the Middle Ages.

Church design in the 20th century tends to be divided between continued nostalgia for medieval styles and a modern ascetic simplicity.

THE MEDIEVAL PARISH CHURCH
The parish church began as a basilica-like assembly hall. Side chapels or a transept were later extensions

KEY
1 Tower and bells
2 Porch
3 Nave
4 Side chapels
5 Altars
6 Vestry
7 Pulpit
8 Rood screen
9 Chancel

THE CLASSICAL CHURCH
Eighteenth-century churches retain medieval elements, but elegant simplicity is the key

KEY
1 Portico
2 Entrance
3 Tower and bells
4 Nave
5 Pulpit
6 Altar rail
7 Vestries
8 Altar

Churchill rejoined the Conservatives in 1924 but his criticism of government indifference to the rise of communism and fascism in Europe, and to German rearmament, kept him out of office for most of the 1930s. The outbreak of the Second World War in 1939 vindicated his views, and in 1940 he succeeded Neville Chamberlain as prime minister. Through stirring radio broadcasts, his deep, plummy growl, superb command of English and unwavering confidence in victory inspired the nation.

In the postwar election of 1945 he was heavily defeated by the Labour party but returned to office in 1951. When, four years later, his powers began to decline he retired to CHARTWELL, his house in Kent, now a museum, where

he wrote his four-volume *History of the English-Speaking Peoples* (1956-8). There, he also painted landscapes and built brick walls, which had always helped him to escape from the cares of public life.

VICTORY SALUTE Churchill acknowledges the London crowds celebrating VE Day on May 8, 1945

CHURCH OF ENGLAND

England's state Church was created by legislation. The 1534 Act of Supremacy, passed after the pope refused to grant HENRY VIII a divorce from Catherine of Aragon, established the king as the leader of the Church, and the monarch still heads the Church of England today.

The new Church kept the Catholic structure of bishops, deans and parishes. Its faith, Anglicanism, was defined in the Thirty-nine Articles of 1563. In the 17th century the Church imposed a new translation of the BIBLE, the Authorised Version (1611), and a structure for services in the Book of Common Prayer (1662). The dignified, elegant prose of both has had an enormous influence on English literature and language.

A BROAD CHURCH

In the 18th century the Church of England priests John and Charles WESLEY founded the Methodist movement, preaching out of the pulpit directly to working people. The Church embraced this evangelical zeal in the 19th century and began to carry its mission into deprived areas, founding schools and sports clubs as well as places of worship, and abroad into the Empire.

An opposing tendency appeared in the 1830s. The OXFORD MOVEMENT campaigned for a return to the Church's Catholic roots and an end to political interference. In the 20th century this 'High Church' element vied for influence with the more liberal and modernising evangelical tendency.

In 1980 the Alternative Service Book was introduced to bring the language of the Church up to date, and in 1992 the GENERAL SYNOD, the Church's governing body, voted to ordain women priests, leading some traditionalists to defect back to Roman Catholicism.

About 1.5 million Britons are active members of the Church of England, and the Church remains wealthy, with assets of around £3.7 billion in 1998. It maintains a particularly strong influence in education, where it has a say in the running of more than 4800 schools.

CHURCH OF SCOTLAND

Unlike the Church of England, Scotland's official Church – known also as the Kirk – has no close links with the state or the British monarch.

The Protestant reformer John KNOX and others set up Scotland's Reformed Church in 1560. They rejected Catholic and Anglican hierarchy, where priests were chosen by bishops. Instead each congregation appointed its own minister, who was answerable only to a general assembly of elected ministers. Adherents became known as Presbyterians, after the presbyters, or elders, who governed churches at a local level.

After 17th-century struggles against Charles I, Oliver Cromwell and Charles II, who all wanted to impose the Church of England system on Scotland, the Presbyterian Church of Scotland was established in 1690. It has weathered various splits and reunions and now has some 850 000 members – around 17 per cent of the Scots population. Women were admitted as ministers in 1969.

CIDER

The Normans introduced fermented apple juice – cider – to Britain. Production rapidly took off in the Middle Ages in apple-growing areas such as Devon, Herefordshire and Somerset.

Soldiers traversing England during the Civil War helped to spread the reputation of cider until, according to the 17th-century agricultural writer John Worlidge, it was 'valued above the wines of France'.

PRESSING BUSINESS Cider makers build up a cheese – layers of pulped apples wrapped in hessian – which is pressed to extract the juice

Cider's standing was lowered in the 18th century by part-paying agricultural labourers with the drink, and in the 20th century by the mass-production of cheap cider for its intoxication value rather than taste.

And yet among Britain's 400 cider makers there are still farms and small breweries producing unfiltered 'real' ciders, including the potent and cloudy 'scrumpy', brewed in the West Country. Britain's apple orchards cover more than 4000 ha (10 000 acres) and produce 850 million pints of cider a year, 65 per cent of Europe's total output.

CINQUE PORTS

The Norman invasion of 1066 vindicated the Saxon fear of the vulnerability of England's south-east Channel coast to attack. Quick to learn the lesson they themselves had taught, the Norman kings appointed the five (*cinque*) ports of Dover, Hastings, Hythe, New Romney and Sandwich as providers of ships and sailors to form the basis of a royal fleet. Winchelsea and Rye were given the same status in the 12th century.

In return for their help the Crown allowed the towns to run their own affairs, exempted them from certain taxes and turned a blind eye to the wrecking and plundering of foreign ships.

The creation of an English navy in the 16th century, and the erosion or silting up of parts of the coastline, reduced the strategic role of the ports, although they retained their privileges until 1855. Only the honorary post of Lord Warden of the Cinque Ports, created in 1268, remains, with an official residence in the Tudor castle at Walmer, near Deal in Kent.

CIRENCESTER

• **Gloucestershire (p.495 F4)** • **Pop. 15 220**

Cirencester's magnificent largely 14th and 15th-century church of St John the Baptist, with its 40 m (132 ft) tower and unusual three-storey porch, proclaims the town's wealth and importance as a centre of the medieval wool trade. But Cirencester flourished long before that.

It began as the Roman settlement Corinium, and for a time in the 2nd century was the largest town in Britain outside London. Evidence of Roman

occupation survives in the form of the old wall near London Road, the grassy amphitheatre, the characteristic straight lines of Fosse Way, Ermine Way and Akeman Street, and the remains of Chedworth Villa 8 miles north of the town.

Cirencester continued to prosper in the Middle Ages – an Augustinian abbey, of which only a Norman arch remains, was founded in 1117 – and the town developed into one of the largest wool

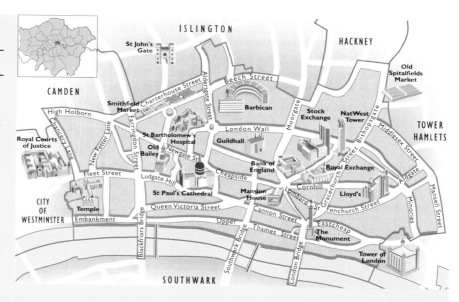

MELLOW FRUITFULNESS Vine leaves adorn Autumn on a 2nd-century Roman mosaic in Cirencester's Corinium Museum

markets in England, supplying around 150 local mills by the 12th century.

Cirencester's Royal Agricultural College, Britain's oldest, has produced new generations of farmers since 1845. Each May it holds a ball to rival the grandest of any Oxbridge college.

CIVIL LIST

Until 1697, when parliament voted a grant of £700 000 a year, royal household costs and civil state expenses – the 'civil list' – were borne by the Crown.

The current arrangement dates from a government agreement in 1760 to cover the whole civil list, including payment to the royal family of an annual sum to subsidise official duties. In return the government receives the profits of CROWN ESTATE property.

The grant pays for the work of the Queen, the Duke of Edinburgh and the Queen Mother. Since 1993 the Queen has paid for the official duties of other members of the royal family. Profits from the Crown Estate in 1997-8 came to a record £113.2 million, far outstripping the civil list payments of £7.9 million.

CIVIL SERVICE

A bowler-hatted man in a pinstripe suit striding into a Whitehall office is the popular image of the British civil servant. But in fact all government employees are civil servants – from a clerk at the local job centre to an MI5 agent.

The foundations of the civil service were laid in the mid 19th century by the statesman Stafford Northcote and the colonial administator Charles Trevelyan. In an age when patronage was the usual method of securing a government post, the Northcote-Trevelyan report of 1854 proposed recruitment by examination, promotion on merit, and pay according to salary grade. These principles still underpin the civil service, which employs about 500 000 people. Half of them are women and most work outside London.

About 4000 elite civil servants, expected to maintain political neutrality, are employed in and around Whitehall, preparing advice for government ministers. During the 1980s much of the business of Whitehall was transferred to 120 semi-independent agencies in an effort to improve efficiency.

CITY OF LONDON

• London financial district • Pop. 4140

Banks, insurance offices, stockbroking firms and commodity dealers now occupy the site of old Roman London – since the Middle Ages the financial and commercial heart of Britain. Known simply as 'the City', or the 'Square Mile' after the area it covers, it is London's smallest borough.

The City's proud tradition of independence, emphasised by the remains of high stone boundary walls, dates back at least to 1192, when King John granted the City of London the right to elect a LORD MAYOR. A mayor is still chosen every year and given an official residence at Mansion House, although the role is now a largely ceremonial one.

Within the City, with the BANK OF ENGLAND and the STOCK EXCHANGE at its heart, are the headquarters of Britain's major financial companies as

well as important branches of overseas banks and international firms. Despite its high-tech dealing rooms, the City still reeks of history. Money lenders from Lombardy, northern Italy, once did business in Lombard Street during the 12th century. Here too, in Great Tower Street, was LLOYD's coffee-

house, where the world's largest insurance underwriting business began in the 17th century. And the modern development of the BARBICAN (which includes a theatre, a concert hall and an art gallery) stands where once a lofty watchtower (barbican) is thought to have risen above the medieval walls.

WAR IN THE BACKYARD

The English Civil War began in 1642 and lasted almost ten years. It was the greatest domestic conflict in British history. Brother fought against brother, countryside and town were torn apart by divided loyalties, and the unthinkable happened – a king was executed by his people

THERE WAS nothing at all straightforward about the Civil War, fought between the Royalist forces of CHARLES I, known as CAVALIERS, and the Parliamentarians, or Roundheads, led by Oliver CROMWELL. It was a messy series of battles, sieges, negotiations and a good deal of changing sides. Allegiances were divided, inside families as well as within provincial areas such as Cornwall, where fierce local loyalties outweighed any feelings for king or parliament. Across all classes people had to decide whether to support Charles's belief in his divine right to rule, taxing, spending and punishing as he alone thought fit, or parliament, with its belief in individual freedom and no taxation without the consent of the people. Religion played its part: Charles I's Catholic sympathies provoked widespread hostility.

THE TENSION RISES

The trigger to conflict was Charles I's attempt to arrest five MPs for treason by leading 400 soldiers into the House of Commons on January 4, 1642. London was already inclined to the Parliamentary cause: aware of its outrage, Charles moved his royal standard to Nottingham.

Volunteer infantry units assembled across England, some rallying behind the king, some behind the Parliamentarians. The adversaries selected strong points, including houses and castles, around England as headquarters for their forces.

THE MARCH OF WAR

Local skirmishing culminated in the indecisive Battle of Edgehill on October 23, 1642, followed by clashes such as Newbury the following year. Charles I and his court moved to Oxford, attracting Royalist supporters from all around England. The Parliamentarians enlisted the paid help of the Scots, then occupying the north of England. Battle was joined at Marston Moor on July 2, 1644. It was a disaster for the king, but only a temporary one: less than two months later, on August 31, Cromwell's forces were defeated at Lostwithiel in Cornwall.

Cromwell made a decisive comeback at the Battle of Naseby on June 14, 1645. The king, stranded in Newcastle, was handed over by the Scots in January 1647 to the Parliamentarians, who guaranteed his safety. Negotiations followed: parliament wanted peace, but Cromwell's New Model Army had scented power and marched on London. In November Charles escaped to the Isle of Wight, where he signed an agreement with the Scots. He was then recaptured and imprisoned in Carisbrooke Castle.

A majority of MPs and much of the country were now behind the king, fearful of Cromwell's men and alarmed at Puritan destruction of property, including church furnishings such as 'Popish' altar rails and sacred paintings.

A TALE OF BATTLE AND SIEGE

KEY
1644 ✗	Parliamentarian victory
1642 ✗	Royalist victory
1642 ✗	Indecisive battle
✗	Parliamentarians under siege
✗	Royalists under siege
●	Parliamentarian stronghold
●	Royalist stronghold

UNLIKELY VICTORY At Dunbar, Cromwell, pinned against the sea and low on supplies, defeated Charles II's Scots army

CUTTING A DASH Charles I's nephew Prince Rupert led the Royalist cavalry at Powick Bridge. He was known as the 'Mad Cavalier' for his fearless charges

FIERCE BLOW Lord Fairfax led the New Model Army to a resounding victory in its first battle at Naseby

TO KILL A KING On January 30, 1649, Charles I was beheaded in front of the Banqueting House at Whitehall

LONG ODDS The Royalist Lady Bankes held Corfe Castle for six weeks in 1643 against 600 Parliamentarian troops

(Map labels: SCOTLAND, 1650 Dunbar, Newcastle, 1644 Marston Moor, York, 1648 Preston, Hull, ENGLAND, WALES, Severn, Trent, Nottingham, 1645 Naseby, 1651 Worcester, 1642 Powick Bridge, 1642 Edgehill, Gloucester, Colchester, Oxford, Thames, London, Bristol, Basing House, Taunton, Exeter, Lyme, Corfe Castle, 1644 Lostwithiel, Plymouth)

THE NEW MODEL ARMY

During the winter of 1644-5 Oliver Cromwell and his commander-in-chief Thomas Fairfax created their own army. They turned 22 000 men into a fighting force of 11 regiments of horse, each 600 strong, 12 regiments of foot, one regiment of dragoons and an artillery train. Officers were commissioned on merit, not social standing. Soldiers were supplied with red tunics, muskets, pikes and field guns, and were paid by parliament.

More than a third of the men were 'pressed' – forcibly made to enlist – but they were paid well: 8 pence a day for an infantryman, 2 shillings for a cavalry trooper and £1 for a colonel of foot. Cromwell insisted that the army must get rid of 'tapsets and decayed serving men' and recruit 'men of spirit'.

The New Model Army was a decisive factor in the winning of the Civil War, but its influence over parliament frightened the ruling class gentry. No army since has had a direct say in Britain's political system.

THE KILLER PUNCH

The Scots, now reluctantly on the Royalist side, were soundly beaten at Preston in August 1648 and Cromwell went on to Edinburgh to quash the terms they had made with the king. A 'purge' of moderate MPs left Cromwell a virtual dictator. He presided over only about 60 MPs, but enough to sign the king's death warrant.

Charles II was 19 and living in France when his father was executed in 1649. He planned to invade England with the help of the Irish, but Cromwell's ruthless suppression in Ireland forced him to turn to the Scots. He was defeated at Dunbar on September 3, 1650, but, undaunted, marched south, only to be routed at Worcester exactly one year later. It was the final engagement of a war that had claimed 120 000 lives, caused widespread destruction, and ousted the monarchy for the first and only time in English history.

CLANDON PARK

• Surrey (p.495 G5)   • Built c.1731-5   • NT

Lord Onslow chose the Venetian architect Giacomo Leoni to build his country house. Leoni gave him a unique blend of styles: onto the west front of a stark, red-brick block is grafted a classical centrepiece in white stone, while the windows facing the gardens are divided by tall columns that are more akin to an Italian palace than a Surrey mansion.

At the core of the house is a richly decorated, two-storey marble hall, with flamboyant chimneypieces and plaster figures of icing-sugar delicacy that hang precariously from an ornate ceiling. Other rooms contain fine 18th-century porcelain, furniture and textiles.

John CLARE

• Poet   • 1793-1864

The son of a farm labourer, able to turn his hand to hedging and ditching or minding the local ale house, John Clare delighted in common rural scenes, the changing seasons and country folk.

He wrote about what could be seen close to his beloved village of Helpston, near Peterborough. Places in his poems such as Sneap Green and Puddock's Wood are still there today. Birds, hares and foxes, observed with a countryman's sharp and unsentimental eye, and even the cruelty of badger baiting, are vividly brought to life. In 'Clock-a-Clay', Clare sees through the eyes of a ladybird:

> *In the cowslip pips I lye*
> *Hidden from the buzzing fly*
> *While green grass beneath me lies*
> *Pearled with dew like fishes eyes*
> *Here I lie, a clock-a-clay*
> *Waiting for the time of day*

SURREY SURPRISE A Maori meeting house in Clandon Park grounds is a reminder of the 4th earl Onslow, governor of New Zealand 1888-92

His life was shattered by depressive illness – called by Clare his 'blue devils'. He spent his last 23 years in an asylum, where he continued to write about lost love and past happiness.

CLAREMONT

• Surrey (p.495 G5)   • Created 18th century   • NT

A grassy amphitheatre overlooking a tranquil, tree-fringed lake is the central feature of Claremont, one of the earliest and most inspirational English landscape gardens. The amphitheatre is a folly, one of a number of whimsical eye-catchers, including a grotto and an island pavilion.

The garden was begun in 1715 by Charles Bridgeman and John VANBRUGH as the setting for the palatial home of the duke of Newcastle. Their naturalistic approach, which broke with the tradition of formal gardens, was continued by William Kent in the 1730s. When the estate passed to Robert CLIVE in 1768 'Capability' BROWN was brought in to embellish it and to build a new house.

CLARIDGE'S

• Central London (p.499 C2)   • Est. 1855

When William Claridge bought a hotel on Brook Street he followed a Georgian custom of naming it after himself. As a former butler to the aristocracy, he knew how to cater to the landed and titled classes. Offering a discreet and intimate home away from home for the blue-blooded soon became Claridge's stock in trade and earned the hotel the unofficial title of 'the Buckingham Palace annex'.

Claridge's was acquired by the Savoy Company in 1895 and rebuilt, but it kept its titled clientele and provided a home in exile for several European kings during the Second World War. Guests are now tended in Art Deco and Victorian splendour by more than 400 hotel staff.

CLARISSA

- **Published 1748-9**

At more than a million words, *Clarissa*, written by Samuel Richardson (1689-1761) entirely in the form of letters, is the longest novel in English. 'If you were to read Richardson for the story,' wrote the critic Samuel Johnson, 'your impatience would be so much fretted that you would hang yourself'.

Clarissa Harlowe is a well-bred young lady who falls for an unscrupulous rake, Robert Lovelace. Her parents object and confine her to her room (for 500 pages). Eventually she elopes with Lovelace. He rapes her and she dies of shame.

The high-life background of the novel was something that Richardson, a self-made printer and self-appointed guardian of morals, knew nothing of. But *Clarissa* was immensely successful reflecting the moral values of the emerging middle class at the time.

Arthur C. CLARKE

- **Writer** • **b.1917**

As a teenager, Arthur Charles Clarke mapped the surface of the Moon using a home-built telescope. His boyhood fascination with space was to inspire him to become one of the world's most prolific science fiction writers.

Clarke began writing stories while serving as a radar instructor in the RAF during the Second World War. His later space exploration novels, including *Earthlight* (1955) and *The Fountains of Paradise* (1979), brought him widespread success and acclaim. The director Stanley Kubrick turned Clarke's 1951 story *The Sentinel* into the Oscar-winning film *2001: A Space Odyssey* in 1968.

While still in the RAF, Clarke predicted that in the future rockets might launch satellites which could be placed in geostationary orbit, allowing

A MONUMENTAL EFFORT Cleopatra's Needle, a granite obelisk 18m (60 ft) high and weighing 186 tons, was towed by sea from Egypt on an iron pontoon

their position relative to the Earth's surface to remain constant. This idea is the basis for all of today's communications satellites.

CLEOPATRA'S NEEDLE

- **Central London (p.499 D6)** • **Erected 1878**

The accession of George IV in 1820 brought an unusual present to Britain – a huge obelisk inscribed with hieroglyphs, presented by Mohammed Ali, the Turkish ruler of Egypt. The obelisk, which stands on Victoria Embankment, was built around 1450 BC by Pharaoh Thutmose III for a temple at Heliopolis. It is one of a pair; the other, sent to the United States in 1880, is in New York's Central Park.

The monuments became known as Cleopatra's Needles in about 14 BC, when the Roman emperor Augustus removed them to grace the palace of Caesareum at Alexandria, the site of Cleopatra's supposed suicide in 30 BC.

Clarice CLIFF

- **Pottery designer** • **1899-1972**

At a time when ceramic designers were rarely credited for their work, Clarice Cliff had her signature on every piece and employed 150 pottery painters to copy her distinctive style. Born in Staffordshire, Cliff worked in local potteries before joining A.J. Wilkinson's pottery at Burslem. In 1927, asked to decorate old stock, she used Art Deco motifs to produce 'Bizarre', a series of bold, bright, geometric designs.

It was an instant success. Hundreds of other patterns followed, among them 'Crocus', which became her

CLASSIC CLARICE CLIFF Distinctive angles and bright geometric designs, such as this 'Melon' design, characterised Clarice Cliff's bold style

signature design. 'Bizarre' was manufactured until 1936, and her designs were produced by Wilkinson's Newport pottery until the 1960s.

CLIFTON SUSPENSION BRIDGE

- **Bristol (p.494 E4)** • **Built 1831-64**

The first major feat of engineering undertaken by Isambard Kingdom BRUNEL produced the longest, highest single-span bridge of its time – the 214 m (702 ft) long and 75 m (245 ft) high Clifton Suspension Bridge.

In 1829, a design competition for a crossing over the Avon gorge inspired Brunel to plan a bridge suspended between Egyptian-style towers. His scheme was chosen, but construction was held up due to fund shortages. After some modifications, work resumed, but Brunel died before its completion.

CLIMATE: *see opposite page*

CLIVE OF INDIA

- **Soldier, merchant and administrator**
- **1725-74; bn 1762**

The restless character of Robert Clive – energetic, but prone to depression – belied his military and administrative skill in laying the foundations of British rule in the Indian subcontinent.

While working in Madras as a clerk of the EAST INDIA COMPANY, Clive attempted to shoot himself, but the gun failed to fire. He felt destined to live. Desperate to thwart French expansion in India,

continued on page 106

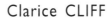

SUNSHINE AND SHOWERS

Britain is as close to the North Pole as chilly Newfoundland in Canada – its mild climate comes from the warm currents of the North Atlantic. The ocean also brings moist air, causing the rainy weather for which the island is known

BRITAIN'S CLIMATE is formed by water and air from thousands of miles away. The North Atlantic is warmed by the Gulf Stream, a current sweeping northwards from the Gulf of Mexico. Mild, moist air from above the ocean is carried across Britain by westerly winds, producing mild, wet winters and warm summers. The pattern is occasionally interrupted by static high-pressure systems – the meeting point of two opposing air currents – blocking westerly winds and causing freezing winters or hot summers.

Some scientists predict a move towards a new Ice Age in Britain as global warming melts polar ice caps. The water may dilute the North Atlantic Drift and move the Gulf Stream farther south, creating a chillier climate. But the effects could be less extreme, bringing more rain in the north and less in the south.

CHANGES AHEAD A depression – winds caused by low pressure – swirls around north-west Britain, bringing changeable weather as clouds are pushed eastwards across the country

REGIONAL DIFFERENCES

The western fringes of Britain experience the mildest winters because of the warming effect of the Gulf Stream, but the exposed north-west suffers more rain and stronger winds, and the sheltered south-east usually experiences the warmest summers. Four geographical areas (right) represent the basic differences in Britain's temperate climate.

KEY

- **North-west** *Cool, wet summers; mild, wet winters*
- **North-east** *Cool summers; cold, dry winters*
- **South-east** *Warm summers; cold, dry winters*
- **South-west** *Warm summers; mild, wet winters*

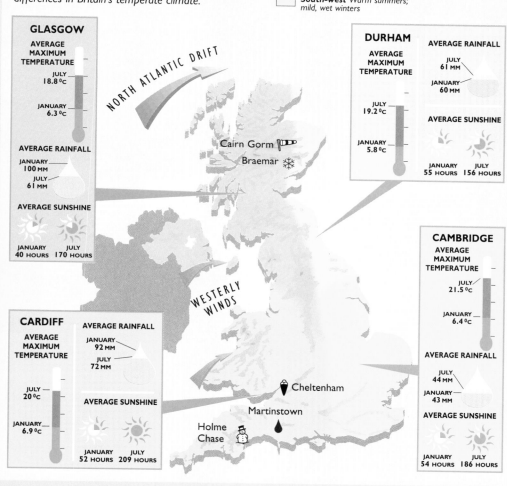

GLASGOW

AVERAGE MAXIMUM TEMPERATURE
JULY 18.8 °C
JANUARY 6.3 °C

AVERAGE RAINFALL
JANUARY 100 MM
JULY 61 MM

AVERAGE SUNSHINE
JANUARY 40 HOURS
JULY 170 HOURS

DURHAM

AVERAGE MAXIMUM TEMPERATURE
JULY 19.2 °C
JANUARY 5.8 °C

AVERAGE RAINFALL
JULY 61 MM
JANUARY 60 MM

AVERAGE SUNSHINE
JANUARY 55 HOURS
JULY 156 HOURS

CAMBRIDGE

AVERAGE MAXIMUM TEMPERATURE
JULY 21.5 °C
JANUARY 6.4 °C

AVERAGE RAINFALL
JULY 44 MM
JANUARY 43 MM

AVERAGE SUNSHINE
JANUARY 54 HOURS
JULY 186 HOURS

CARDIFF

AVERAGE MAXIMUM TEMPERATURE
JULY 20 °C
JANUARY 6.9 °C

AVERAGE RAINFALL
JANUARY 92 MM
JULY 72 MM

AVERAGE SUNSHINE
JANUARY 52 HOURS
JULY 209 HOURS

NORTH ATLANTIC DRIFT

WESTERLY WINDS

Cairn Gorm
Braemar
Cheltenham
Martinstown
Holme Chase

WEATHER RECORDS

HIGHEST TEMPERATURE
37.1 °C on August 3, 1990, at Cheltenham

LOWEST TEMPERATURE
-27.2 °C on January 10, 1982, at Braemar

HEAVIEST RAINFALL *(in 24 hours)*
279.4 mm on July 18, 1955, at Martinstown

HEAVIEST SNOWFALL *(in 24 hours)*
180 cm on February 16, 1929, at Holme Chase

HIGHEST WIND SPEED
150 knots on March 20, 1986, on the summit of Cairn Gorm

GREATEST HEATWAVE
1976 – Temperatures in excess of 32 °C were recorded in various parts of Britain for 15 consecutive days

HOTTEST SUMMER
1976 – Average central England temperature 17.8 °C

SNOWIEST WINTER
1947 – Snowfall was recorded in various parts of Britain for 55 consecutive days

COLDEST WINTER
1962-3 – Average central England temperature -0.3 °C

ICY SEA During the coldest winter in Britain's recorded history, in 1962-3, the sea froze over at Herne Bay in Kent – perhaps a portent of the colder weather some scientists predict for the country's future

GRANDFATHER TIME Longcase clocks such as this elaborate 17th-century James Clowes timepiece were designed to match contemporary furniture

he joined the military wing of the Company, where he excelled. He worked his way up to the governorship of Madras by securing south-east India for Britain.

In 1757 Clive's defeat of the nawab of Bengal at the Battle of Plassey – with 3000 troops against the nawab's 50 000 – earned him the governorship of the disordered state, which he then skilfully reorganised. He returned to England with a fortune and became Baron Clive of Plassey. Accusations of embezzlement, of which he was acquitted, finally led him to commit suicide, but he is remembered for his achievements as 'Clive of India'.

CLIVEDEN

• Buckinghamshire (p.495 G4)
• Built 1851   • NT

Its rakish associations with the 'Cliveden set' entertained by Nancy ASTOR in the 1930s and the PROFUMO AFFAIR of the 1960s now behind it, the former home of the millionaire Astors has become a hotel; three rooms are occasionally open to the public.

The architect Charles Barry designed the Italianate mansion for the 2nd duke of Sutherland in 1851. It took its name from an earlier house on the site called 'Cliefden', after an escarpment, or a 'clief', cut through by a valley, or 'dene'.

Visitors can still enjoy a brush with history in the 152 ha (376 acre) grounds. The gardens, embellished with fountains and sculptures in the Italianate style by William Waldorf Astor, take advantage of Cliveden's natural riverside setting with sweeping views towards the Thames and miles of woodland walks.

CLOCKS

England became the clockmaking centre of the world in the 17th century, led not by its native artisans but by skilled immigrants. Henry VIII employed craftsmen from the Continent to create his palaces, and his 16th-century clockmakers set high standards. A century later, the Clockmakers' Company gave its officers the power to destroy poor-quality work, and a drive for greater accuracy followed.

In 1658 a Dutch clockmaker living in England, Asahuerus Fromanteel, used the pendulum invented by the Dutch astronomer Christiaan Huygens to create the first longcase or grandfather clock. From 1650-1720, clockmakers and scientists such as William Clement, Joseph Knibb, Thomas Tompion and Robert Hooke pioneered new mechanisms. Tompion became England's supreme clockmaker, and in 1676 created an 'equation of time' clock, comparing mechanical with solar time. The clock is now in Bath's Pump Room.

Among later British innovators was the Scottish scientist Alexander Bain who, in 1843, was one of the first to use electricity in his clocks, and the inventor Louis Essen who built the first atomic clock, accurate to 1 second every 3 million years, installed at the National Physical Laboratory, Middlesex, in 1955.

CLOOTIE WELL

At St Mary's Well near Inverness the ancient tradition is maintained of tying 'clooties' or 'clouties' – small rags – to a nearby tree to make a wish. A further part of the ritual involved tossing a coin into the well and taking a sip of the water before making a wish.

The traditions are thought to have evolved from pagan offerings believed to invoke the assistance of gods and goddesses. The clooties were torn from the clothes of those suffering affliction and tied near wells to call upon the gods for a cure. At wells such as St Mary's and also St Boniface's Well near Munlochy, the tradition survived the disapproval of the early Christian Church, which throughout Britain rededicated many pagan wells to Christian saints.

CLOOTIE CRIMES Removing a rag from St Boniface's Well in Scotland is said to incur punishment – the affliction suffered by the rag's original owner transfers to the thief

River CLYDE

• S Scotland (p.497 C5)

From its source in the Lowther Hills, the River Clyde, a former centre of British shipbuilding, winds through Lanarkshire towards Glasgow. The Falls of Clyde near Lanark were admired by the poets Robert Burns and William Wordsworth; their flow has been reduced by a hydro-electric scheme, but impressive cascades remain at Cora Linn. GLASGOW was the site of the first fordable crossing above the Clyde estuary, and downstream, towards Clydebank, the largest shipyards in the world once produced great liners such as the QUEEN MARY. Beyond Erskine Bridge the estuary becomes the Firth of Clyde, a 60 mile waterway with a maze of sea-lochs reaching into the Highlands.

THE ESSENTIAL FUEL?

Just before the First World War, Britain was the world's biggest coal exporter. Of the 275 million tons mined in 1913, a quarter made its way abroad, and the coal industry accounted for 7 per cent of the country's economic output. Today, it accounts for less than 1 per cent

HE ROMANS were probably the first to mine for coal in Britain – the industry developed in Northumberland and the Forest of Dean. Production rose steadily between the 15th and the 17th centuries as the British population grew, but technical restrictions held back the potential of the fuel, and bad ventilation and flooding limited mining to shallow seams.

INNOVATION AND PROGRESS
Thomas NEWCOMEN devised a crude steam pump in 1712; by 1770 there were 100 such machines in Northumbrian mines alone, pumping water out of shafts. Dangers from explosive gases were reduced by John Buddle's exhaust fan and Humphry DAVY's safety lamp of 1815.

Aided by such inventions and by geological good luck, Britain's coal production soared from about 10 million tons in 1800 to 55 million tons in 1855. As steam technology swept through shipyards and railways, demand rose further. But the industry's rapid expansion produced social, environmental and political problems. The pollution from burning coal and the scarring of the landscape by mines changed the face of Britain. Mining

COAL IN DECLINE
Each helmet represents 10 000 miners employed by region in
- *1965*
- *1982*
- Former coalfields
- Coalfields in 1982

SCOTLAND
50 800
17 400

NORTH EAST AND CUMBERLAND
96 900
29 000

NORTH WEST AND STAFFORDSHIRE
64 000
20 800

SOUTH WALES
72 000
24 300

YORKSHIRE
108 400
60 700

NOTTINGHAMSHIRE AND DERBYSHIRE
43 700
33 000

SOUTH MIDLANDS AND KENT
25 800
15 700

HARD TIMES Between 1965 and 1982, 260 700 jobs were lost in the coal industry (*left*). Since 1982, more than 200 000 miners have faced redundancy

remained dangerous. Villages around the pits became toughened by hardship, and developed a politically militant, working class culture.

This militancy was tested after the First World War. Mine owners, who had invested little in new machinery, tried to reduce wages to keep British coal internationally competitive. Mine workers responded by spearheading the GENERAL STRIKE of 1926. As heavy industries declined between the wars, their position worsened.

The nationalisation of the coal industry in 1947 promised a better future, but cheap oil from the Middle East was already undermining sales. Between 1963 and 1973 coal production fell by 70 million tons to 130 million tons. An oil crisis, quadrupling prices that year, encouraged miners to strike and bring down the Conservative government, but a second strike in 1984 was defeated. As oil prices again declined, coal's economic importance has diminished still further.

A WAY OF LIFE Closeknit communities sprang up around working mines (*left*), facing hardship and danger together, including the risk of underground explosions or collapses

PIT PROTESTS Union banners demonstrated the traditional solidarity of mine workers in 1985 during a prolonged strike (*below*)

William COBBETT

• **Political reformer and writer** • **1763-1835**
Cobbett was a thorn in the flesh of
authority throughout his life. His journal
Weekly Political Register (1802-35)
campaigned for electoral reform and the
right of the poor to live off the land, and
railed against government corruption, the
patronage system and social injustice.
His mission to educate the literate poor
led him to write textbooks on subjects
from grammar to farming. In 1806,
he established a journal recording
parliamentary debates, later taken over
by Thomas HANSARD.

Cobbett, the son of an innkeeper, was
entirely self-educated. His travels around
southern England form the background
to his *Rural Rides* (1830), written in an
unaffected, pugnacious style, expressing
indignation at the conditions of country
life and the loss of COMMON LAND to the
rich during the enclosures.

John Douglas COCKCROFT

• **Nuclear physicist** • **1897-1967; kt 1948**
Working with fellow physicist Ernest
WALTON at Cambridge University in
1932, John Cockcroft designed the first
particle accelerator, or 'atom smasher',
and used it to turn one element into
another, creating the first artificial
nuclear transformation. He bombarded
the element lithium with subatomic
particles, breaking it down into helium.

Cockcroft never studied physics, but
his knowledge of electrical engineering
and mathematics made him a key
member of the CAVENDISH LABORATORY
team. He became the first director of the
Atomic Energy Research Establishment
at Harwell in 1946, where he designed
the earliest nuclear power stations, and
shared the 1951 Nobel prize for physics
with E.T.S. Walton.

COCKFIGHTING

The sport of fighting fierce gamecocks,
feathers ruffled and spurs strapped to
their ankles, was probably introduced
to Britain by the Romans.

In the 16th century, the popularity
of cockfighting soared when Henry VIII
had a cockpit built at Birdcage Walk in
Whitehall. As crowds gathered around

COFFEE AND CONTRACTS Merchants, ship owners and insurers frequented Lloyd's coffee house
in Tower Street, London, which eventually became the City's main market for marine insurance

the pit, a sunken arena, bird-owners,
bookmakers and successful gamblers
made their fortunes. The most vicious
variant became known as the 'battle
royal', in which many birds fought until
just one was left standing.

It wasn't until 1849 that a wave of
revulsion against animal cruelty led
parliament to ban the sport, which still
operates secretly in rural England.

COFFEE HOUSES

When the EAST INDIA COMPANY started
importing coffee, tea and chocolate into
Britain in the 17th century, enthusiasm
was so great that establishments
dedicated to serving the new beverages
quickly emerged. The first London coffee
house, the Sign of the Greek's Head,
opened in 1652 in St Michael's Alley in
the City. Within 50 years, 3000 coffee
houses had sprung up across the capital.

Charles II's government considered
them potential hotbeds of dissent, but
attempts to close them were abandoned
after a public outcry. Over time coffee
houses began to attract wealthy,
well-connected clienteles and acquired
the air of private clubs.

The oldest club in London, White's on
St James Street, began as a coffee house
while others became centres for business
transactions – the Stock Exchange, for
example, evolved from Jonathan's coffee
house on Change Alley.

Thomas COKE

• **Agricultural pioneer** • **1752-1842; earl 1837**
While serving as the Whig MP for
Norfolk in 1776, Thomas Coke inherited
the impoverished family estates at
HOLKHAM HALL near Wells-next-the-Sea.

Over the next 60 years Coke raised
the estates' annual income from £2000
to £20 000, tapping the brains of experts
at agricultural gatherings, or 'sheep
shearings', that became famous
throughout the country. He introduced
a system of crop rotation that raised
production, and he improved the size
and quality of his sheep and cattle by
selective breeding. Better crops and
richer harvests encouraged others to
follow his example.

COLCHESTER

• **Essex (p.495 J4)** • **Pop. 96 060**
The 1st-century capital of the Celtic king
Cunobelinus is reputedly England's oldest
town, situated on a ridgeway first settled
in the Bronze Age, around 1000 BC. The
town fell to the Romans in AD 44, who
rebuilt it with stronger defences after its
destruction by BOUDICCA in 60. Its name
means 'Fortress on the River Colne'.
Much of the old city wall remains,
including the largest surviving Roman
town gate in Britain.

Wool trade with the Continent
brought wealth to the town in the Middle

Ages, and Dutch refugees helped to establish a thriving textile industry from 1570. As a Royalist stronghold during the Civil War, the town was besieged for 11 weeks in 1648; the castle survived and is now a museum. Today, Colchester is renowned as a centre for rose growing, including the delicate Colchester Beauty.

Samuel Taylor COLERIDGE

• **Poet and critic** • **1772-1834**

Of the mysterious, dream-like poems written by Samuel Taylor Coleridge, the most vivid are 'Kubla Khan' (1816), a vision seen during opium-induced sleep, and 'The Rime of the Ancient Mariner', the first of a series of poems in the *Lyrical Ballads* (1798) produced with William WORDSWORTH. The mariner brings a curse upon his ship by shooting an albatross. Marginal notes describe parallel happenings in the spirit world, and how the curse is released by the mariner's response to the beauty of water snakes swimming nearby – 'A spring of love gushed from my heart, and I blessed them unaware'.

Coleridge's recorded table talk and notebooks show his wide-ranging and penetrating mind. His *Biographia Literaria* (1817) was the first English work of literary criticism. Ill health and depression led to his addiction to opium, which curtailed his poetic career.

Wilkie COLLINS

• **Writer** • **1824-89**

After his first job as a tea merchant, Wilkie Collins, the son of an artist, was called to the Bar in 1851. But he never practised law, as the experience of writing his first novel, *Antonina* (1850) – a historical tale – had already made him determined to live by his pen.

Collins' second novel, *Basil* (1852), demonstrated a flair for tightly plotted narrative in a story of mystery, crime and detection. *The Woman in White* (1860), *No Name* (1862), *Armadale* (1866) and *The Moonstone* (1868) followed. These novels of 'sensation', woven around dramatic events and guilty secrets, established detective stories as a new literary genre.

Aged 32 Collins set up house with Caroline Graves but had three children by another woman, Martha Rudd, an arrangement that shocked society. He wrote a further 15 novels, but his style deteriorated under the influence of opium, which he took for gout.

COMEDY AND COMEDIANS: *see page 110*

COMICS

On Britain's street corners in the 1840s, hawkers sold the earliest form of comics, called 'penny dreadfuls', the illustrated adventures of disreputable characters. The country's first regular comic, *Ally Sloper's Half-Holiday* (1884), continued the low tone with a lazy, gin-drinking hero. But one young publisher, Alfred Harmsworth, later the press baron Lord Northcliffe, decided to break the mould.

In 1892, Harmsworth created *Chips* and the halfpenny *Comic Cuts*, humorous broadsheets for children that set the style of future comics. By the 1930s the genre was well established. The rough-and-tumble antics of *The Beano* and *The Dandy* created lasting success for D.C. Thomson of Dundee – they are among the best-selling British comics of all time.

In the 1950s, the Hulton Press produced children's adventure comics with a more serious tone such as *Eagle*, introducing the futuristic pilot Dan Dare – read by a million children at its peak. Many outstanding children's comics died out in the 1960s, but today's best sellers still include *The Beano* and *The Dandy*, with a joint circulation of 300 000 copies a week, alongside *Thunderbirds*, *Rupert Bear and Friends* and adaptations from books and television programmes such as *Thomas the Tank Engine* and *Teletubbies*.

COMMON LAND

Many areas of uncultivated land, from the Southampton Marshes to Dartmoor, fall into the category of 'common land'. In medieval times peasants had the right to remove the 'products' of such ground, including wood, fish, peat and stones, and to graze stock and gather fallen fruit. But in the 12th century, lords of the manor began to claim direct ownership of common land, and from the 13th century areas were fenced off in a trend known as enclosure, which escalated in the 18th and 19th centuries.

Only 3 per cent of England and 9 per cent of Wales remains as common land (Scotland has none). A campaign to protect common land rights began in 1865. Since the Commons Registration Act a hundred years later, details of rights of way have been kept by county councils. A campaign to improve access is conducted by the Open Spaces Society.

COMIC CAPERS Dennis the Menace (right), launched in 1951 and still a star of *The Beano*, continues to delight youngsters in a tradition established by *Comic Cuts* and *Chips*, which sold their final copies in 1953

© D.C. THOMSON & CO. LTD. (The Beano)

FUNNY BUSINESS

The British have never taken themselves too seriously. For more than 100 years, a long line of music hall, radio and television comedians have been persuading the nation to have a good laugh at itself from biting satire to the pure silliness of a repeated catchphrase

TODAY'S COMEDIANS are born of a tradition which stretches back to the MUSIC HALL. The first comic routines were usually narratives, sung in character and costume. The mix of song and patter pioneered by the clog-dancing jester Dan Leno (1860-1904) has left its mark on comedy acts as diverse as Max Wall (1908-90), with his eccentric gait and lugubrious delivery, MONTY PYTHON and the 'Ministry of Silly Walks', all-round song-and-dance man Bruce Forsyth, and manic gag-teller Ken Dodd.

The music halls were mostly turned into cinemas, but their boisterous, boozy spirit haunts the stand-up pubs and comedy clubs of today. Another source of the modern alternative circuit is Max Miller, whose act was a lightning spiel of unrelated jokes. He was a master of innuendo, leading his audience on then scolding them for their dirty minds.

The comic sketch with its use of stock characters was created in the 1920s. Harry Tate, an early exponent, would play as many as 42 roles in his act. Radio lent itself to quickfire sketches (since costume changes were unnecessary), and in the 1940s, 50s and 60s shows such as *ITMA*, *The GOON SHOW* and *Round the Horne* drew millions of listeners.

Radio gave the nation the shared experience of the catchphrase: *ITMA* spawned at least a dozen, from 'Can I do yer now, sir?' to 'Don't mind if I do'. These were supplemented in the national consciousness by lines such as Kenneth Williams' 'Stop messin' about!'. In the 1990s, television made a cult of the catchphrase: Harry Enfield and Paul Whitehouse have built fine careers by repeating such harmless phrases as 'Loadsamoney', 'I'll get me coat' and 'Ooh! Suits you, sir'.

DON'T MENTION THE WAR!

British comedy is shot through with familiar themes, including embarrassment at sex and bodily functions, and a suspicion of 'funny' foreigners. Three of Britain's most popular sit-coms – *Fawlty Towers*, *Only Fools and Horses* and *Dad's Army* – focused on men (Basil Fawlty, Del Boy and Captain Mainwaring) whose unrealistic pretensions are exposed in situations of excruciating absurdity.

STAGE

MUSIC HALL

Dan Leno

1910

VARIETY SHOWS

1920

THE SKETCH

Harry Tate

STAND-UP COMICS

1930

Max Miller

'It's the way I tell 'em, lady'
Max Miller

1940

1950

'How tattifilarious!'
Ken Dodd

1960

Ken Dodd

1970

ALTERNATIVE COMEDY

1980

1990

Eddie Izzard

2000

RADIO

'After you, Claud[e]
No, after you, Ce[...]'
Tommy Ha[...]

RADIO VARIETY

'I thang-yew'
Arthur Askey

Bandwagon

'Jus' like that!'
Tommy Cooper

Tommy Cooper

It's That Man Again! (ITMA)

COMEDY SHOWS

'He's fallen in the water'
Bluebottle (Peter Sellers)

The Goon Show

Round the Horne

'Hallo, I'm Julian, and this is my friend, Sandy'
Kenneth Williams

'Manuel, this is a rat!'
'Is not rat, is filigree Siberian hamster'
Basil Fawlty (John Cleese) and Manuel (Andrew Sachs)

Fawlty Towers

'You plonker, Rodney!'
Del Boy (David Jason)

Only Fools and Horses

'Stupid boy!'
Captain Mainwaring (Arthur Lowe)

Dad's Army

MAD MANAGER *A stay at a chaotic Torquay hotel with the Monty Python team led John Cleese to create* Fawlty Towers *in 1975. Only 12 priceless episodes were made*

LUVVLY JUBBLY *The 'dodgy' Trotters of Peckham first appeared in 1981. More than 24 million saw the final show, in December 1996, the most watched TV sit-com ever*

ON PARADE *Dad's Army ran for nine series and 80 episodes from 1968 to 1977. Co-writer Jimmy Perry based Private Pike on his own experiences in the Home Guard*

TELEVISION

'Everybody out!'
Paddy (Miriam Karlin)

'A pint? That's nearly an armful!'
Tony Hancock

THE SIT-COM

The Rag Trade

SATIRE

SKETCH SHOWS

'You silly old moo!'
Alf Garnet (Warren Mitchell)

That Was The Week

WORKING-CLASS COMEDIES

Tony Hancock

Benny Hill

'All in the best possible taste!'
Kenny Everett

'Til Death Us Do Part

The Good Life

'Ooh! You are awful, but I like you!'
Dick Emery

SUBURBAN COMEDIES

'I do not believe it!'
Victor Meldrew (Richard Wilson)

Dick Emery

One Foot In The Grave

Spitting Image

Kenny Everett

Blackadder

ABSURD SIT-COM

'I have a cunning plan'
Baldrick (Tony Robinson)

'A mosquito's never bitten you, sweetie!'
Edina (Jennifer Saunders)

Absolutely Fabulous

'The last mosquito that bit me had to book into the Betty Ford clinic'
Patsy (Joanna Lumley)

Harry Enfield Paul Whitehouse

'Poptastic!'
Smashie and Nicey

COMMON LAW

Most English law is founded on ACTS OF PARLIAMENT, or 'statutes', but where there is no clear statute cases are decided on common law, rules based on custom and principles established by the precedent of previous cases as decided by judges.

Influenced by Norman practices, common law dates from the 12th century, when Henry II decided to replace local and ecclesiastical law with a 'common law for all'. Most COMMONWEALTH countries and the United States have legal systems based on English common law.

COMMONWEALTH OF NATIONS

A quarter of the world's population lives in one of the 54 member states of the Commonwealth of Nations. The name was coined by the politician Lord Rosebery in 1884, to reflect the BRITISH EMPIRE's changing nature as a group of equal sovereign states, rather than ruler and dependants. Only Mozambique, which joined in 1995, is not a former British colony, although many others, including Palestine, Yemen and even France in 1956, have tried and failed to join this exclusive worldwide club.

The Commonwealth promotes trade and alliance between its member states through political meetings and cultural events including the Commonwealth Games, held every four years. Until 1949 the British monarch was head of state in all Commonwealth countries. Today, she retains the position in just 16, and is symbolic head of the association.

Denis COMPTON

• Cricketer and footballer • 1918-97

A carefree nonchalance was Denis Compton's trademark. A cavalier and graceful batsman, he played for fun, took risks, and infuriated teammates and bowlers with his unorthodox shots – he once scored a 'four' one-handed after slipping in midstroke.

Compton represented England at both cricket and football but it was in cricket that he excelled. He played in 78 Test matches before retiring in 1957. In the 1947 season Compton scored 3816 runs and hit 18 centuries, records that still stand as highest annual scores. The following year he made the fastest ever triple century: in 3 hours 1 minute for MCC (Marylebone Cricket Club) against North Eastern Transvaal.

BRYLCREEM BOY Dashing, debonair and a first-class sportsman, Denis Compton found fame off the pitch as a 1950s advertising pin-up

CONCERT HALLS

As orchestral music developed in the 18th century, small chamber recitals began to give way to larger public concerts. Europe's first purpose-built concert hall, the Holywell Music Room, opened in Oxford in 1748, and still serves the city.

Britain now has a concert venue in most towns, from a converted malthouse at ALDEBURGH to Birmingham's 2260-seat Symphony Hall (opened in 1991).

London's concert halls include the ROYAL ALBERT HALL (1871), the gas-lit, 540-seat Wigmore Hall (1901), the Royal Festival Hall (1951) and the 1990-seat hall at the BARBICAN CENTRE (1982).

Among the major regional halls are St David's in Cardiff (1982) – acoustically one of the top five concert venues in the world – and Glasgow's Royal Concert Hall (1990), which rests on rubber pads to dampen noise and vibration from underground trains. Like many modern concert halls, Edinburgh's classical Usher Hall, built in 1914 by the brewer Andrew Usher, is also a conference venue.

CONCORDE

Almost 30 years after the first supersonic flight, by a US military aircraft in 1947, Concorde took to the skies as the first commercial airliner to break the sound barrier.

Concorde was an Anglo-French project begun in 1962. On January 21, 1976, simultaneous maiden commercial flights were made by British Airways from London to Bahrain and Air France from Paris to Rio de Janeiro.

Concorde's elongated profile, like a stork in flight, is now a familiar sight. British Airways' fleet of seven have made more than 37 500 flights at a cruising speed of 1350 mph – more than twice the speed of sound. American concerns about noise denied the plane landing rights in New York until 1978 but the transatlantic route is now its most popular. The flight from London to New York takes around 3 hours 40 minutes, about half the time taken by a conventional jet.

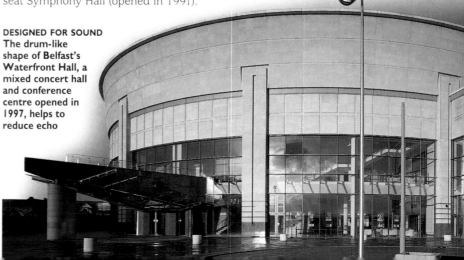

DESIGNED FOR SOUND The drum-like shape of Belfast's Waterfront Hall, a mixed concert hall and conference centre opened in 1997, helps to reduce echo

CONFEDERATION OF BRITISH INDUSTRY

• **Est. 1965**

A formal annual dinner addressed by the prime minister is the public face of the Confederation of British Industry (CBI). But the real work is behind the scenes, lobbying government ministers, civil servants and the media in Britain and Europe in the interests of British industry.

Members include more than 250 000 public and private companies, employing around 10 million people, as well as employer and trade associations.

Joseph CONRAD

• **Writer** • **1857-1924**

English was Joseph Conrad's third language but his highly atmospheric descriptions and sophisticated narrative techniques make his novels some of the most intense in the language.

Conrad was born Jozeph Teodor Konrad Korzeniowski in the Ukraine to Polish parents. At 17 he went to sea, and for 20 years served mostly on English merchant ships before settling in Kent in 1894 to write. His seafaring inspired stories such as *Lord Jim* (1900) and *Heart of Darkness* (1902).

Powerful themes attracted Conrad: fidelity, betrayal, isolation, idealism, corruption, courage, fear and the clash of primitive and modern cultures. His finest work, *Nostromo* (1904), a tale of greed and selfishness set during a revolution in South America, combines them all.

Terence CONRAN

• **Designer, retailer and restaurateur**
• **b.1931; kt 1983**

No one person has had more impact on British interiors since the 1960s than Terence Conran. His Habitat stores introduced such novelties as the duvet, and a modern style based on functional, well-designed – and affordable – goods.

Conran started a furniture-making company in 1952 and in 1956 set up a design group, as well as a fabric design company with his second wife, Shirley – who later wrote best-selling books such as *Superwoman* (1975). He opened his

HOME STYLE The 1980s boom of first-time buyers found everything they needed to set up home in Terence Conran's Habitat 'House Pack'

first Habitat on London's Fulham Road in 1964. By 1985, Habitat had 99 branches throughout Britain and abroad.

A love of French food inspired Conran to open the restaurant Bibendum in 1987. In 1990 he sold his retailing interests, which by then included BHS and Next, to focus on food. He opened six restaurants in the next seven years, including the Blueprint Café at the Design Museum, founded by Conran in 1989.

Conran's son Jasper (b.1959) has taken the family talent for design in other directions, primarily as a fashion designer but also, since the 1990s, as a creator of stage costumes.

CONSCIENTIOUS OBJECTORS

When conscription was introduced during the First World War, conscientious objection at once became a public issue. Religious and political pacifist groups had long existed, including the QUAKERS, but until 1916 bearing arms was voluntary. Once it was made compulsory, those who refused for reasons of conscience came to be resented, earning them the derogatory nickname 'conchies'.

Objectors who convinced a court of their sincerity were allowed to do non-combatant military or civilian service, but many refused any form of war work and were imprisoned. Anyone who joined up but refused to fight was likely to be seen as a deserter and risked execution.

The law was more liberal during the Second World War, and some 60 000 objectors were allowed some degree of exemption. Since 1968, recruits into the regular army have been allowed to resign freely on conscientious grounds within six months of joining.

CONSERVATION

A concern to preserve Britain's buildings as much from over-restoration as from destruction prompted William MORRIS to found the first formal conservation group, the Society for the Protection of Ancient Buildings, in 1877. Five years later, an Act of Parliament offered public protection to prehistoric monuments.

Efforts to protect Britain's wildlife and natural habitats soon followed. The Royal Society for the Protection of Birds was founded in 1889 to campaign against the slaughter of egrets and kingfishers to feather women's hats. The NATIONAL TRUST was founded in 1895, and in 1949 the first nature reserves and NATIONAL PARKS were created. In 1981 the Wildlife and Countryside Act was introduced to protect ENDANGERED SPECIES.

COMMUNITY EFFORT Conservation groups rely on local volunteers as much to help with practical projects, such as this bridge repair in Lancashire, as with fundraising support

CONSERVATIVE PARTY

A Tory defeat by the Whigs in the 1830 election led to the formation of the modern Conservative party, as Robert PEEL set about regrouping his members. The name reflected Peel's aims of conserving British traditions, although 'Tory' lived on as a nickname (*see* WHIGS AND TORIES).

From the 1860s Benjamin DISRAELI provided the party with a policy of imperialism and social reform, introducing the 1867 REFORM ACT which gave much of the urban working class the vote. Later leaders such as Winston CHURCHILL and Margaret THATCHER epitomised Tory belief in individual free enterprise, law and order, nation and monarchy. Divisions over the EUROPEAN UNION contributed to a heavy defeat in the 1997 general election; John MAJOR was succeeded by William Hague, at 36 the youngest-ever Conservative leader.

> Since its first victory in 1834, the Conservative party has had 78 years in government. The party has led Britain for two-thirds of the 20th century, including 18 consecutive years from 1979 to 1997

John CONSTABLE

• Artist • 1776-1837

'I should paint my own place best', declared John Constable, whose views of his native Suffolk are among the most archetypically English of all LANDSCAPE PAINTING, capturing timeless rustic scenes with honesty and naturalism.

Constable's great oil 'six-footers', such as *The Hay Wain* (1821) and *The Leaping Horse* (1825), inspired artists from Delacroix to the impressionists: never before had commonplace subjects been painted so majestically. In his later years, much saddened by his wife's death, he turned increasingly to painting stormy, gloomy scenes such as *Old Sarum* (1832). **MAJOR COLLECTIONS • Tate Gallery, London • Victoria and Albert Museum, London**

CONSTITUENCY

The size and shape of the area, or constituency, represented by a Member of Parliament – also known as a 'seat' – directly affects election results. In a town where a quarter of the population votes for the Labour party and lives in the town centre and the rest, Conservatives, live in the suburbs, four wedge-shaped constituencies would elect four Conservative MPs. One town centre and three suburban constituencies would give a more balanced result.

Constituency boundaries are set and regularly reviewed by the Boundary Commissions of England, Scotland, Wales and Northern Ireland. They take into account a range of non-political factors, such as local history and rivers that form natural boundaries, and aim to achieve an average number of electors in each constituency. After a review in 1995 Britain's 659 constituencies each had an average population of 88 000, but numbers vary greatly: 125 000 people live in the Isle of Wight, but only 29 600 in Scotland's Western Isles.

CONWY CASTLE

• N Wales (p.494 C1) • Built 1283-7 • Cadw

More than 15 000 men worked for four years building Conwy Castle, one of ten castles constructed by Edward I in his campaign to subdue Wales. When completed it was one of the most powerful castles in Western Europe.

The castle's might rests in eight towers, each 21 m (70 ft) high and with walls 4.5 m (15 ft) thick, but Edward's fortifications went further still. He also gave Conwy town a battlemented, 9 m (30 ft) high wall – some of which still stands – with 21 towers, three double-tiered gateways and 480 arrow slits.

HOSTILE RECEPTION At Botany Bay Captain Cook was met by spear-wielding natives but he respected the indigenous peoples he encountered and would win their trust and friendship

James COOK

• Naval explorer • 1728-79

In 1755, after an apprenticeship with a Whitby shipowner, James Cook joined the Navy, for whom he charted the eastern coast of Canada. In 1768 he was given command of the *Endeavour* and, with an astronomer and a party of naturalists led by Joseph BANKS, left on a three-year expedition to observe the transit of Venus over the south Pacific.

There, he mapped many of the Pacific islands and the coasts of New Zealand and eastern Australia. His party brought back some 1000 new plants and 1500 botanical drawings, and Cook's insistence on sailors eating as much fresh food as possible made this the first long voyage on which no one died from scurvy.

On his next voyage Cook became the first explorer to cross the Antarctic Circle, and on a third he sought a passage from the west around North America. He reached the Bering Strait before turning back to spend the winter of 1778-9 in Hawaii, where he was killed by natives in a dispute over a stolen boat.

Cook's birthplace at Marton, near Middlesbrough, is now a museum.

Peter COOK and Dudley MOORE

• **Actors and comedians**
• **Peter Cook 1937-95** • **Dudley Moore b.1935**

For six years between 1965 and 1971, the television partnership of Peter Cook and Dudley Moore in *Not Only... But Also* delighted comedy fans as their mournful 'Pete and Dud' dialogues scaled new heights of delusion and fantasy.

The pair first gained fame in 1960 when with Alan BENNETT and Jonathan MILLER they took a comedy revue, *Beyond the Fringe*, to the Edinburgh Festival. For each of them it launched a brilliant career but all agreed that it was Cook who revolutionised British comedy. 'His imitation of Harold Macmillan changed not only his life but the next 35 years of British humour,' said *The Guardian* – and Cook agreed. Cook's innovative brand of political satire provided the inspiration for *PRIVATE EYE* magazine, which he co-founded in 1961.

Moore is an acclaimed pianist and has composed film scores. He has also made a career in Hollywood, starring in *'10'* (1979), which turned him into a 'pint-sized' sex symbol, and *Arthur* (1981).

Thomas COOK

• **Travel agent** • **1808-92**

A pledge of temperance in 1833 turned out to be the defining moment of Thomas Cook's career. Eight years later he leased a train to take fellow temperance supporters on a day-trip from Leicester to Loughborough for a shilling each.

Soon Cook was organising regular temperance excursions, providing cheap – and teetotal – recreation for working people. In 1854 he devoted himself full-time to his new calling as a travel agent, catering for all classes of society. The following year he led his first trip abroad, to Paris via Cologne. His son, John Mason Cook, joined the business in 1864.

Cook's many innovations included an early form of traveller's cheque in 1874. When he died his agency was the world's largest. Cook's – German-owned since 1992 – now has 3000 branches.

Catherine COOKSON

• **Novelist** • **1906-98; DBE 1993**

'The best-paid bastard in the business' is how Catherine Cookson once described herself, referring to her illegitimacy and literary success. Born Kate McMullen, she was brought up in poverty by an alcoholic grandfather in the steel and docks town of Jarrow. When she died she was Britain's 17th richest woman, having sold some 100 million books in 17 languages. Her gritty, Tyneside novels consistently make up nine of the ten most borrowed books in British libraries.

Cobbled streets, violent men and hardened women, their roughness tempered by humour, provided Cookson's subject matter. She began writing at 44, as therapy against the illnesses that dogged much of her life. Her debut novel, *Kate Hannigan* (1950), was the first of 85 best sellers that she dictated at up to 15000 words a day.

Henry COOPER

• **Boxer** • **b.1934; OBE 1969**

At the height of his career, Henry Cooper was the acceptable face of a violent trade, as much a folk hero as a boxing champion. He held the British heavyweight title for a record ten years and five months, and took Commonwealth and European titles. But he won the nation's heart in a non-title

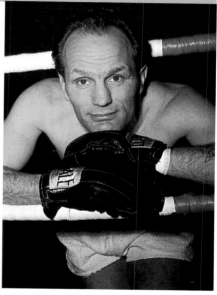

GENIAL GIANT Henry Cooper, pictured in the ring in 1961, was the British heavyweight champion from 1959 to 1970

fight at Wembley Stadium in 1963 when his fabled left hook, ''Enery's 'Ammer', flattened the cocky young American, Cassius Clay (later Muhammad Ali). Cooper was the first boxer to knock Clay down in the ring.

Though he never won the world title, Cooper earned respect and affection for his bravery, skill, humour and capacity to lose gracefully. He has remained in the public eye since his retirement in 1971, commentating for the BBC, working for charity and advertising 'Brut' aftershave. His choice of brand seemed ironic: 'Boxers', Cooper once asserted, 'are the most docile of men.'

CORFE CASTLE

• **Dorset (p.494 E6)**
• **Built 11th-13th century** • **NT**

The hilltop ruins of Corfe Castle's leaning towers dominate the village below. The original Saxon palace was replaced after William I bought it in 1080, making Corfe a secure fortress where King John imprisoned 24 French knights in 1203.

During the CIVIL WAR the Royalist Bankes family was twice besieged at Corfe by Parliamentary troops. Lady Bankes, with only five men and her maids, resisted the first attack in 1643. Three years later she was tricked into surrender by a treacherous attendant and the castle was ruined by a gunpowder

MANCHESTER. First Edition

HOLIDAY TOURS SEASON 1902

ORGANISED AND ARRANGED BY THOS COOK & SON LUDGATE CIRCUS, LONDON, E.C.

BROADENING HORIZONS Thomas Cook's early Continental tours cost about £10, and most working people could hope to save up for one

attack. Many of the cottages in the village are built of the local limestone, known as Purbeck marble. Quarrying for limestone reached its peak during the 19th century, after which it was replaced by the mining of china clay to be used in the making of local pottery.

CORN LAWS

No political issue of the 19th century so inflamed public opinion as the Corn Laws, a series of measures brought in between 1815 and 1842 to protect British farmers from competition by regulating grain prices and restricting imports. They soon came to symbolise aristocratic privilege, keeping bread prices high and profiting wealthy landowners at the expense of the poor.

Widespread hatred of the laws fuelled the call for parliamentary reform in 1819 in Manchester that ended in the bloody PETERLOO MASSACRE, when 11 protestors were killed and some 500 wounded. Twenty years later Lancashire cotton barons formed an Anti-Corn Law League, blaming 'agricultural protectionism' for industrial depression, as people could not afford manufactured goods.

In the end, the spur to the Corn Laws' repeal in 1846 was not public opposition but the Irish potato famine of 1845. Thousands starved and many of the young and able-bodied emigrated, forcing the prime minister, Robert PEEL, to remove import duties on grain.

ROYAL REGALIA **George IV designed elaborate costumes for himself and attendants at his coronation in 1821**

CORONATION

On a rainy June 2, 1953, Britain came to a halt. Anyone not lining the streets near Buckingham Palace and Westminster Abbey was in front of a television set – many bought for the day. The occasion was ELIZABETH II's coronation, the first to be televised.

The ceremony people saw had remained essentially unchanged for 1000 years, and it had been held at Westminster Abbey since William the Conqueror was crowned there in 1066.

WHAT HAPPENS AT A CORONATION

The ceremony begins with the new monarch swearing the coronation oath, promising to rule justly and to support the Church of England. He or she is annointed with oil. For 700 years the coronation chair held the STONE OF SCONE, on which ancient Scottish kings were crowned, but in 1996 the stone was returned to Scotland.

The regalia of office, the most significant CROWN JEWELS, are then presented: the coronation ring, a symbol of faith; the orb, representing worldwide Christianity; the sceptre, symbolising royal power; and the sword of state, for defending the Church and the people.

Next the archbishop of Canterbury crowns the monarch with St Edward's Crown, a 1661 replica of Edward the Confessor's 11th-century original, which was destroyed in 1649. Finally nobles and representatives of the clergy and commoners in turn swear loyalty.

> Each year, half a million *Coronation Street* fans tread the celebrated cobbles at the Granada Studios in Manchester, where the show's set is a major attraction

CORONATION STREET

As the camera pans over the terraced houses, a lone cornet plays the melancholy theme music announcing an episode of *Coronation Street*, the world's longest-running television soap opera.

In 1958 the writer Tony Warren presented an idea for a series about life in a working class street in the north of England. Granada Television placed the street in the fictional Manchester district of Weatherfield and broadcast the first episode on December 9, 1960. Although declared 'doomed' by the *Daily Mirror*, it quickly became a national institution, attracting 10 million viewers an episode by 1967.

Life in 'the street' centres on the Rover's Return pub, where matriarchs such as Annie Walker (Doris Speed) and Bet Lynch (Julie Goodyear) have presided over the pumps. Jean Alexander spent 23 years as the warrior-housewife Hilda Ogden but the longest-standing cast member is William Roache, who has played Ken Barlow since the show began.

John COTMAN

• **Artist** • **1782-1842**

His natural, unsentimental style, using flat planes of colour that prefigure the style of Cézanne, make John Cotman one of the most distinctive watercolourists of his era. Cotman probably had no formal artistic training but started drawing as a

ROUGH SEASCAPE John Cotman mixed rice paste with watercolour paint to add texture and movement to experimental paintings such as *Fishing Boats off Yarmouth* (1832)

child in Norwich. By 1803 he had toured Wales and was working in Yorkshire, whose scenery inspired paintings such as *Distant View of Greta Bridge* (1805). As well as watercolours he produced rich oil paintings, such as *The Drop Gate* (1826).

Cotman was a leading member of the Norwich school of early 19th-century artists, whose realistic landscapes were influenced by the Dutch school. He became president of the Norwich Society of Artists, the first provincial institution to hold regular exhibitions.

COTSWOLD HILLS

• SW Midlands (p.494 E4)

Clusters of honey-coloured limestone cottages and flocks of sheep dot the dells and dales of the Cotswold hills, which stretch in a 50 mile string between Bath and Chipping Campden.

At their highest point, Cleeve Cloud, near Cheltenham, the hills reach 329 m (1080 ft). A steep escarpment to the north-west cuts down into the vales of Gloucester and Evesham while, on the other side, the hills dip gently into the river valleys of the Thames and Avon.

The region's towns and villages, such as CIRENCESTER, Roman Britain's second-largest city, and Bourton-on-the-Water with its five stone bridges over the fast-flowing Windrush, prospered from the

wool trade between the 14th and 17th centuries. Many places have a Sheep Street, where flocks were once gathered for sale. Old-world charm and the 100 mile Cotswold Path, which weaves through the hills, have more recently brought prosperity from tourism.

Henry COTTON

• Golfer • 1907-87; MBE 1946; kt 1987

For most of his career Henry Cotton waged a lone battle against American domination of golf. In Britain it was largely an amateur game in 1934, when he won the first of his three Open titles. Disdain for those who played for a living even barred Cotton from club changing-rooms.

Fond of fast cars and five-star hotels, Cotton's health suffered from his extravagant lifestyle. Nevertheless, his successes earned the professional game respectability, and he was one of the first three professionals awarded honorary membership of the Royal and Ancient Golf Club at St Andrews, the game's traditional headquarters.

DRIVING AMBITION A high finish distinguished Henry Cotton's swing from others but he believed that strong hands were the secret

COUNTY

Traces of the Saxon system of dividing the country into local administrative districts remain in many of Britain's county names (*see map*, pages 492-3). The 'shire' of Gloucestershire, Yorkshire and others derives from the *scir*, a small region within ANGLO-SAXON kingdoms. The word 'county' itself is derived from a Norman term for the area administered by a lord.

Some ancient county posts still exist. The 'shire reeve', or sheriff, is pre-Norman; county-based justices of the peace date from the 14th century; and LORDS LIEUTENANT, created in the 16th century to administer regional law and order, still represent the monarch.

The Local Government Act of 1888 gave people the power to elect county councils to decide on local issues and administer services. When a 1972 Act disbanded many of the oldest shires there was fierce opposition from areas such as Rutland, whose historic boundaries meant more to local people than administrative borders. Further reorganisation of local government since 1996 has reinstated Rutland and created unitary authorities to serve large cities such as Bristol, Cardiff and Glasgow, while London remains divided into boroughs.

COUNTY HALL

• Central London (p.499 E8)
• Built 1909-33

The imposing colonnaded riverfront crescent of County Hall presents a stark contrast to the Gothic intricacy of the Houses of Parliament that face it across the Thames.

In 1908 the rapidly growing London County Council (LCC), which had wide-ranging responsibility for education, housing, planning control and the fire service in the capital, held a competition to design a new building, won by Ralph Knott. County Hall's 2390 rooms and 10 miles of corridor were opened by George V in July 1922.

Until 1986 the building was home to the LCC and its successor, the Greater London Council (GLC). Since the abolition of the GLC in 1986 County Hall has housed the London Aquarium, two hotels and other leisure facilities.

COUNTY SHOWS

The outsize village fêtes we know today as county shows grew out of a serious need in the 18th century to educate farmers in new techniques.

Until the time of the INDUSTRIAL REVOLUTION most British people were self-sufficient in food, but factories sucked the population into towns where growing food was no longer an option. The countryside was left depopulated but at the same time an equivalent AGRICULTURAL REVOLUTION was vital if the remaining farmers were to supply the urban demands.

To encourage farmers to adopt the new methods on display at shows, livestock and machinery competitions were held. A coveted gold medal would be awarded for the best – usually interpreted as the biggest – animal or vegetable in the class. In 1838, at the first Yorkshire Show, the prize for the best bull was £25.

Most counties still hold annual shows, where locally produced food and drink, and well-groomed pigs, sheep and cattle are exhibited. The Royal Welsh Show, held in Builth Wells each July, attracts up to 230 000 visitors, Edinburgh's Royal Highland Show (June) has more than 2000 exhibitors, and the Royal Show at Stoneleigh, near Coventry (July), displays some 7000 competing animals.

COURTAULD INSTITUTE

• **Central London (p.499 E6)** • **Founded 1931**
Textile manufacturing provided the wealth for Samuel Courtauld (1876-1947) to indulge his love of paintings. Courtauld started to buy Impressionist and post-Impressionist art in 1922 and amassed one of the world's most important collections. In 1931 he founded the Courtauld Institute of LONDON UNIVERSITY, Britain's first centre for studying the history of Western art.

Courtauld also donated his art collection to the university, providing the basis of the Courtauld Gallery, housed at the institute. Subsequent gifts and bequests from other sources have added paintings from the Renaissance to the 20th century to the collection.

Highlights include Manet's *Déjeuner sur l'Herbe* (1863), Renoir's *The Theatre Box* (1874), Gauguin's *Nevermore* (1897), Van Gogh's *Self-portrait with Bandaged*

Ear (1889), and Picasso's *Child with a Pigeon* (1901). The gallery also has works by Botticelli, GAINSBOROUGH and Modigliani, and rooms devoted to Rubens, Tiepolo and pre-16th century Flemish and Italian artists.

In 1990 the institute and gallery moved from Courtauld's original London home in Portman Square to the huge 18th-century neoclassical Somerset House, on the Strand.

COVENANTERS

In the 1630s Scottish Presbyterians came under threat from Charles I, who opposed their informal style of worship. Charles wanted the Scots to follow the English Church system, which included rule by bishops and use of the *Book of Common Prayer*. A group of Scottish Presbyterians drew up a National Covenant in 1638, pledging to uphold the doctrine of the CHURCH OF SCOTLAND. Some 300 000 Scots, almost a third of the population, signed.

These 'Covenanters' defied Charles I and in 1643 promised to support Oliver Cromwell in the CIVIL WAR, in return for the guarantee of an official Presbyterian Church in Scotland. Cromwell, and then Charles II following his restoration to the English throne in 1660, both failed to honour their pledges to the Covenanters, who finally took to arms to defend their beliefs. They were defeated by Charles's army at Bothwell Brig in 1679 and during the 1680s were rooted out as they worshipped secretly in the hills.

Covenanters remained suppressed until the Protestant monarchs WILLIAM AND MARY made Presbyterianism the established Church in Scotland in 1690.

COVENT GARDEN

• **Central London (p.499 D5)**
Each year, some 16 million people use Covent Garden Underground station. Most of them are visitors attracted by the street entertainers, shops, stalls and 350 restaurants on and around Covent Garden piazza.

The area takes its name from the quiet convent garden used by the monks of Westminster Abbey. After the Dissolution of the Monasteries the garden was bought by the 1st earl of

PRIZE BULL County show champions, such as this mighty Hereford at the 1988 Devon County Show, earn hefty stud fees for their breeders

Bedford. During the 17th century, the 4th earl engaged the architect Inigo JONES to design Britain's first piazza, surrounded by fashionable PALLADIAN STYLE town houses and the Church of St Paul's, now known as the actors' church.

A market, established in 1661, grew into London's main source of fruit, vegetables and flowers by the late 19th century. Shops and coffee houses drew a bohemian community of artists and actors after the Covent Garden Theatre was built in 1732, and from the ROYAL OPERA HOUSE when it opened in 1858.

When Covent Garden fruit and vegetable market moved to larger premises in Battersea in 1973, the old buildings found a new use selling crafts and antiques; the flower market became the London Transport Museum.

COVENTRY

• **W Midlands (p.499 F3)** • **Pop. 331 250**

The 11th-century legend of Lady GODIVA riding naked through the streets of Coventry secured the city's fame. Its other well-known association dates from the Civil War, when the city was a Parliamentary stronghold. Royalists captured in the Midlands were 'sent to Coventry', where they were imprisoned in the Church of St John.

Coventry established itself as a manufacturing town during the 19th century. Its links with the MOTOR CAR industry began in 1896 with the opening of factories to produce Daimlers and Humbers. The city is also the birthplace of the bicycle – the inventor James Starley's penny-farthing was made here from 1871.

The city's industrial importance turned it into a target during the Second World War, when it was a centre for armaments production. On the night of November 14, 1940, most of the city centre, including the

DRAMATIC DARLINGS Noël Coward's urbane comedy *Private Lives* (1930) was part of a long stage partnership with Gertrude Lawrence

14th-century cathedral, was reduced to rubble by German bombs.

A new cathedral, designed by the architect Basil Spence and joined to the ruins of the old, was consecrated in 1962. Inside are works by 20th-century artists. Graham SUTHERLAND's 23 m (75 ft) high 'Christ in Glory' tapestry hangs above the altar and a 26 m (85 ft) high stained-glass window by John PIPER forms the baptistry window.

Noël COWARD

• **Actor, dramatist and composer**
• **1899-1973; kt 1970**

'Specialise, dear, specialise' was Noël Coward's advice to aspiring actress Florence Desmond. He had no need to specialise, being not a jack-of-all-trades, but master of many. Coward wrote plays, poetry and short stories, acted, sang, produced films, performed cabaret, and composed music and lyrics such as 'Mad Dogs and Englishmen':

> *Mad dogs and Englishmen go*
> *out in the mid-day sun;*
> *The Japanese don't care to, the*
> *Chinese wouldn't dare to;*
> *Hindus and Argentines sleep*
> *firmly from twelve to one,*
> *But Englishmen detest a siesta.*

With his trademark smoking jacket and cravat, Coward set a refined, camp style. He became known when he was just 25, for his play *The Vortex* (1924), in which he appeared as a tormented drug addict. More typical are his comedies satirising polite English society at its most self-absorbed, such as *Hay Fever* (1925) and *Design for Living* (1933). His wartime and post-war screenplays, such as *In Which We Serve* (1942), *This Happy Breed* (1944) and *Brief Encounter* (1946), all directed by David LEAN, reveal a more sentimental side to his character.

GOOD OVER EVIL Jacob Epstein's *St Michael and the Devil* (1959) hangs outside Coventry Cathedral, facing the ruins of the city's medieval cathedral. Over both looms the steeple of 17th-century Holy Trinity church

COWES WEEK

• August

Nearly 1000 yachts in more than 30 classes enter the world's largest and oldest sailing regatta. Cowes, a modest Isle of Wight town on the estuary of the River Medina, where Queen Victoria and Prince Albert once whiled away their summers, has been a focus of attention since 1825, when a group of yachtsmen first staged a race there and founded the Royal Ocean Racing Club.

The centrepiece every second year is the Fastnet Race, begun in 1925 and since 1957 the final event of the ADMIRAL'S CUP. Competitors set off from Cowes on a course of 605 miles, round the Fastnet Rock on Ireland's south-west coast, and then head back to Plymouth.

Thomas CRANMER

• Archbishop of Canterbury • 1489-1556

Gentle and humane, Thomas Cranmer was a studious priest who became embroiled in political turmoil by the attempts of HENRY VIII to reconcile his personal desires with the responsibility of kingship. By supporting Henry in his bid to end his first marriage to Catherine of Aragon, Cranmer found himself swiftly appointed archbishop of Canterbury.

Although Cranmer believed in the Church of England and independence from Rome more profoundly than did Henry VIII, he surrendered almost entirely to the king's wayward will. Cranmer annulled Henry's first two marriages, divorced him from Anne of Cleves, and informed on Catherine Howard, who was then executed. Cranmer remained archbishop in the

SEA OF SAILS Although not part of the regatta, the Round-the-Island Race is the most popular event during Cowes Week, with a record 1813 yachts rounding The Needles in 1989

reign of EDWARD VI, and in 1549 completed the first *Book of Common Prayer,* which laid out the liturgy for public worship in English prose.

Cranmer's downfall came when the dying Edward persuaded him to assist in making Lady Jane GREY his successor. When the Catholic MARY I acceded to the throne less than two weeks later, Cranmer was arrested and under pressure signed seven recantations. He retracted them all as he was led to be burnt at the stake for heresy, and thrust the hand with which he had signed them into the fire, crying, 'This hath offended! Oh, this unworthy hand!'

Battle of CRÉCY

• N France • August 26, 1346

Soon after the outset of what turned into the HUNDRED YEARS' WAR with France, stunning news came from the village of Crécy: an army of English footsoldiers and archers had managed to destroy a French force at least three times its size, including many of Europe's finest mounted knights.

Pressing his claim to the French crown, EDWARD III of England had invaded Normandy in July 1346 with 17 000 men. As his army marched inland Edward's fleet, possibly mistaking orders, sailed for home, leaving the king at the mercy of Philip VI of France, who had assembled a 60 000-strong army.

At Crécy, 30 miles south of Boulogne, Edward was forced to prepare for battle. The English king drew up his men on a

ridge, placing archers on both sides of armoured footsoldiers.

Within a few hours some 21 500 French knights and soldiers lay dead, felled in a succession of disorganised French attacks by the relentless crossfire of English archers. The English suffered just 200 casualties. Edward, now secure, marched northwards and captured Calais, which remained in English hands until 1558. The tactic of combining footsoldiers with archers in defensive formation soon became standard practice, famously used at the Battle of AGINCOURT in 1415.

Francis CRICK

• Molecular biologist • b.1916

One evening in 1953 a jubilant Francis Crick burst into his local pub in Cambridge and announced that he had found the secret of life. People already knew that DNA (deoxyribonucleic acid) existed, but did not understand its structure or how it acted as a medium for transmitting genetic information from one generation to the next.

At Cambridge University, Crick and his American colleague James Watson were examining X-ray diffraction images of DNA crystals, produced by the London chemists Rosalind Franklin and Maurice Wilkins, when they discovered that DNA molecules were shaped like two entwined spiral staircases, or double helixes. With this information they were able to work out DNA's mechanism in replicating cells of the body. The Nobel prize was awarded to Crick, Watson and Wilkins in 1962 for their work, regarded as the most important 20th-century discovery in biology.

LEATHER ON WILLOW

'A chance to play the man and act the gentleman' was the traditional call to arms of the men in white flannels who still dot village greens in summer or tread the county cricket grounds of England

BATTLE OF WILLS To Archbishop William Temple, cricket was 'organised loafing', but taken seriously it is a tough duel between batsman and bowler, with balls reaching speeds of up to 90 mph

COUNTY CRICKET ROLL OF HONOUR
1890-1999

COUNTY	FOUNDED	CHAMPIONSHIP WINS
Derbs	1870	1
Durham	1882	-
Essex	1876	6
Glamorgan	1888	3
Glos	1871	1
Hampshire	1863	2
Kent	1859	7
Lancs	1864	8
Leics	1879	3
Middx	1864	12
Northants	1878	-
Notts	1841	4
Somerset	1875	-
Surrey	1845	17
Sussex	1839	-
Warks	1882	5
Worcs	1865	5
Yorks	1863	30

CRICKET AFICIONADOS still debate the origin of the game. Some claim that it was first played in 14th-century France, and that returning soldiers introduced it to Britain; others say the game started among shepherds in Kent and Sussex. The oldest surviving record of a cricket match describes schoolboys playing in Surrey around 1550, suggesting it began as a playground game.

THE MODERN GAME

Whatever its origin, a game called cricket, played with a bat and ball, had spread north by the 18th century to industrial areas. The game had also attracted wealthy patrons, and was championed by the public schools.

In 1760, the first major cricket club was formed at Hambledon, Hampshire,

where local innkeepers and farmers established the basic techniques for the eleven-a-side game. In 1835, the influential Marylebone Cricket Club drew up a formal set of laws, forming the basis of modern cricket. The first unofficial county championship matches took place in the 1860s, and the competition was

officially constituted in 1890. During the 19th century, as professional ranks grew, a class distinction developed between amateur 'gentlemen' and professional 'players'. Their meetings became the highlight of the county season, until the distinction was abolished in 1963.

YORKSHIRE PROWESS

During the 1930s, league cricket was highly competitive in the north of England and nowhere played with more passion than in Yorkshire. In cricketing terms, a successful Yorkshire has always meant a strong England, and the national side's decline over the past 25 years has been accompanied by an unprecedented fallow period for Yorkshire since the county claimed three consecutive championships from 1966 to 1968. In an attempt to raise the standard of English cricket, a more competitive two-division county championship is to start in 2000.

THE ONE-DAY THRILL

To make cricket faster and more exciting, and so attract more spectators, in 1963 county cricket clubs introduced the first major one-day tournament. Now called the NatWest Bank Trophy, its final in September is the climax of the cricket season, regularly drawing a packed house to the LORD'S ground.

See also ASHES, TEST MATCHES

UMPIRES: WARDENS OF FAIR PLAY

The expression 'that's not cricket' has long been common parlance for underhand behaviour, and still has its place in the sport that prides itself on fair play and good manners – standards that the umpire ensures players uphold. As well as supervising the game, the umpire watches players' conduct, and in Test cricket any dissent – in word or gesture – may result in disciplinary action.

All too often in England the umpire has to decide whether conditions are too wet or too dark for play. On one occasion the umpire Harold 'Dickie' Bird (left, looking after the bowler's hat and sweater) had to halt proceedings because a glass roof was reflecting sunlight into the batsman's eyes; a rare case of 'sun stops play'.

CRIMEAN WAR

• Black Sea peninsula • 1853-6

The first war to be covered by telegraph made grim news for readers of *The Times*. Atrocious conditions in Crimea on the Black Sea coast caused such fear for the state of the British army that Prime Minister Lord Aberdeen had to resign.

The Crimean War began amid rival claims to the Danubian provinces (modern Romania) in the Ottoman Empire. When Russia occupied the area in 1853, Turkey declared war. The following year Britain and France allied with Turkey, and sent forces to Crimea.

Action centred on the Russian naval base of Sebastopol, which the Allies besieged after their victory at the River Alma in September. After battles at Balaklava, which saw the disastrous CHARGE OF THE LIGHT BRIGADE, and Inkerman, Sebastopol fell in 1855 and the Russians negotiated peace at the Treaty of Paris the following year.

For the British forces, the war was a sobering experience: a number of military commanders were shown to be incompetent, soldiers poorly trained, the provision of supplies and medicine inadequate. Out of 22 200 British fatalities, the majority died of disease, which flourished in the insanitary conditions. One of the few beacons of light was the nurse Florence NIGHTINGALE, who by transforming the conditions on the hospital wards in Scutari saved the lives of many soldiers.

CROCKFORD'S CLERICAL DIRECTORY

• First published 1858

Until the 1980s each new edition of this biennial list of Anglican clergy was eagerly awaited for its provocative anonymous preface. In 1987 controversy over personal criticism of Archbishop Robert Runcie resulted in the suicide of the author, Canon Gareth Bennett. The anonymous preface was subsequently replaced by blander material such as a profile of the eponymous John Crockford (*c*.1823-65), about whom so little is known as to be safely uncontroversial.

John CROME

• Artist • 1768-1821

The rustic scenery of Norfolk was John Crome's inspiration. He seldom left his native county, becoming with John COTMAN one of the leading artists of the Norwich School of regional landscape painters. The son of a weaver and alehouse keeper, he worked for a time as a sign painter but became interested in Dutch landscapes and the early paintings of his fellow East Anglian Thomas GAINSBOROUGH.

Under their influence, Crome produced oil paintings such as *The Poringland Oak* and *St Martin's Gate*, *Norwich* that are both realistic and deeply romantic. He was an expert at catching the effects of moonlight on water and at lovingly depicting gnarled oak trees. Crome was also a highly accomplished painter of watercolours.

NORFOLK IDYLL *The Poringland Oak* **shows John Crome's mastery of depicting light in a landscape**

Oliver CROMWELL

• Soldier and statesman • 1599-1658

Contrasting reactions are still provoked by the name of Oliver Cromwell, whose passionate struggle to create a godly society was matched only by his ruthlessness as a military dictator. At the start of the CIVIL WAR, Cromwell, an East Anglian MP, joined the Parliamentarian side, and used his skills in leadership to help to form England's first trained, professional fighting force – the New Model Army – which crushed Charles I's forces at the Battle of Naseby in 1645.

After bringing the king to trial and execution in 1649, Cromwell suppressed political rivals by commanding absolute loyalty from the army. By 1653 he had routed the Scots' forces of Charles II and brutally suppressed Roman Catholic opposition in Ireland. His conquests established a single commonwealth of England, Ireland and Scotland.

When the government of the RUMP PARLIAMENT, the surviving MPs, fell short of his Puritan ideals, Cromwell dissolved it and appointed himself Lord Protector of the commonwealth, ruling as a military dictator until his death. Although initially popular, by 1658 political instability and high taxation to pay for the army had largely eroded his support. When Charles II was restored to the throne in 1660, Cromwell's body was dug up and his head displayed on a pole above Westminster Hall for 25 years.

Thomas CROMWELL

• Politician • c.1485-1540

Son of a clothworker, Cromwell first sought his fortune as a soldier in Europe, where he encountered Machiavelli's ruthless ideas on government. When he returned to England in 1514 he became the protégé of Cardinal WOLSEY, Henry VIII's powerful lord chancellor. By the time of Wolsey's arrest for treason in 1529, Cromwell had won the king's favour, and four years later became his chief adviser.

Cromwell's ambition was to break the power of the Roman Catholic Church. He supervised the Dissolution of the Monasteries, and by paving the way for Henry to make himself head of the Church in England delivered their wealth into Henry's hands. His Protestant beliefs led him to arrange the king's marriage in 1540 to the German princess, Anne of Cleves. Seeing her in the flesh, Henry furiously declared her a 'Flanders mare'. Cromwell's many enemies at court took the opportunity of this disaster to have him beheaded on London's Tower Hill.

CROQUET

Sunny afternoons on spreading lawns, punctuated by the clack of mallet on wooden ball – no sport shows the English upper classes at play better than the game of croquet.

The game is believed to be French, and the earliest record in this country is of it being played in the 17th century in London's Pall Mall – created originally as an alley for the purpose – where 'a round boxwood ball is struck through a high arch which he can that do at the fewest blows wins'.

The first national championships were held at Evesham in Worcestershire in 1867, and moved three years later to the All England Croquet Club in Wimbledon – although within ten years tennis had become the main spectator sport there. The centre of British croquet today is the Hurlingham Club in London.

CROWN ESTATE

Whether shopping in London's Regent Street or strolling along a beach, you may be treading on property owned by the Crown Estate. Land belonging to the monarch includes nearly 120 000 ha (300 000 acres) of forest and farmland, and about half the foreshore around Britain's coast; the monarch also has seabed extraction rights off much of the coastline. In 1997-8, the estate was estimated to be worth £3.02 billion.

The Crown Estate revenues were surrendered to the government in 1760 in exchange for annual payments known as the CIVIL LIST. The Crown Estate is now managed commercially by Commissioners and made a profit for the government of £113.2 million in

GENTEEL KNOCK Neither age nor dress is an obstacle to winning a game of croquet – skill and Machiavellian tactics are what count

1997-8, far outstripping the outlay required by the civil list – just £7.9 million – and the £55 million of additional state funding given to members of the royal family.

CROWN JEWELS

Britain's royal ceremonial jewellery has adorned monarchs ever since the coronation of Edward the Confessor in 1043. Among the most precious of the jewels are St Edward's Crown, used at most coronations since that of Charles II in 1661; the Star of Africa, the world's largest cut diamond; and the 109 carat Kohinoor diamond from Mughal India, made for the coronation of Elizabeth, the Queen Mother, in 1937.

Although now safely housed in the Tower of London, the jewels have had a precarious past. One of the oldest gems in Edward's crown, the Black Prince's

ruby, was nearly lost when Henry V wore it on his helmet during the Battle of Agincourt in 1415. In the turmoil of the Civil War, Oliver Cromwell ordered Edward's crown to be broken up. When the monarchy was restored in 1660, Charles II had it carefully reconstructed.

The only successful attempt to steal part of the crown jewels was made by Thomas Blood, an Irishman, in 1671. Disguised as a clergyman, Blood knocked out the warder and escaped with a crown, a sceptre and an orb before being confronted by a soldier coming down the road. His arrest was followed by a pardon from Charles II who also awarded him a pension for his audacity.

CRUFT'S DOG SHOW

When the champion dog at Cruft's goes on to a lucrative career in pet-food advertising, its owner is not bowing to modern commercialism but following the tradition of the event. Charles Cruft, who held his first show of 500 terriers in 1886, was a seller of 'dog cakes'. His annual show took his name in 1891, and ever since Cruft's has grown in size and complexity.

Cruft died in 1938, and the show was taken over by the Kennel Club, the body that classifies dog breeds, registers pedigrees and issues awards. From 1979 to 1990 the show was held at Earls Court Exhibition Centre in London, but it now takes place at the National Exhibition Centre in Birmingham, where more than 20 000 dogs representing up to 190 breeds compete each March on appearance, agility and obedience. The small cash prizes – £100 in 1999 for the best dog in the show – reflect the amateur sporting nature of the event, although individual dogs may later be sold for anything up to £40 000.

SLEEPING BEAUTY Every canine detail is crucial at Cruft's dog show. This patient Yorkshire terrier is having its hair curled in preparation for the beauty contest

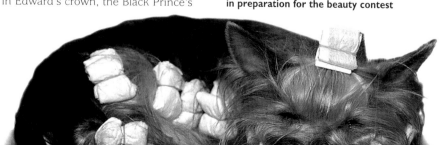

SPOILS OF WAR

For 200 years Britons fighting in the Holy Land encountered a civilisation more advanced than any they had experienced before. As well as earning privileges at home, returning Crusaders brought back new learning and exotic luxuries to a Britain emerging from provincial isolation

THE WORD 'CRUSADE' summons an image of Richard I, the Lionheart, sporting a red cross on white surcoat as he battles heroically with the Saracen Saladdin. But from the first Crusade in 1095 to 1291, when the West lost its last foothold in the Levant, tens of thousands of ordinary British folk, who had never before even held a weapon, 'took the cross' – a symbolic commitment to take part in the quest to recover the Holy Land from its Muslim conquerors.

Medieval Christians regarded the Saracens as infidels – unfaithful to the true religion – and encounters on

MODEL CONDUCT Psalters of the 12th century bore images of the Crusaders' chivalry and piety to inspire high ideals in the church flock

KNIGHTS HOSPITALLERS
Priests and knights under monastic vow formed the Order of the Hospital of St John of Jerusalem in the 11th century as a charity to care for sick pilgrims travelling to the Holy Land. When the Crusades started in the next century, the order developed a military role as well. Their head house in England was the Hospital or Priory of St John of Jerusalem in Clerkenwell, London, founded in 1144. The English branch closed in 1540 with the Dissolution of the Monasteries.

CARE FOR THE SICK The St John Ambulance Brigade, founded in 1887, was named after the Hospitallers

the battlefield were often hard-fought and bitter, but there were rich rewards to be won by survivors.

Pilgrims earned full remission of their sins – thought to be a passport to heaven – and enjoyed secular privileges too. Many Crusaders were tenants bound to a feudal lord who, obliged to support a Crusade, sent them as his proxies. On their return, he granted them freedom and land to farm.

THE WHITE KNIGHT'S BURDEN
Funding an expedition was expensive for a king or noble – Richard I once remarked that he would sell London if he could find a buyer. One source of finance was to offer the inhabitants of a town the chance to buy its charter, guaranteeing rights to graze livestock and hold market days.

A less welcome result of the Crusades was taxation, such as the 'Saladin tithe' of 1188, when Henry II levied a tax on every church parish in England, as well as on corporations and burghers. Its method of collection became the model for later taxation.

FRUITS OF CONQUEST
Arab civilisation was more advanced than that of western Europe, and returning Crusaders frequently brought back novelties from the East. Surgeons began to use anaesthetics in surgery, artisans learned how to make paper, and knowledge of dyeing came from Syria. People tasted exotic foods, including rice, almonds, dates and figs, sugar, and spices such as ginger and pepper.

PAYING THEIR DUES Pilgrims had to pay high taxes just to enter cities in the Holy Land that were held by the Saracens

Furnishings and clothes improved too. Luxurious tapestries were hung on castle walls, and carpets replaced rushes on floors. Those who could afford it took to wearing turbans, slippers, and flowing robes of silk and velvet brocade, while new perfumes brought an exotic whiff to dowdy baronial courts.

HERALDRY in warfare also developed during the Crusades. To distinguish one another in battle, knights wore surcoats embroidered with pictorial signs of family emblems over their armour.
See also CASTLES

SLEEP OF THE RIGHTEOUS Lying in Dorchester Abbey, in Oxfordshire, is the tomb effigy of a knight with crossed legs, indicating that he had 'taken the cross', meaning crusaded, to the Holy Land

CUCKOO

Probably no other bird delights and dismays the British public more than the cuckoo. For its mating call in April that heralds spring and draws excited letters to *The Times* is bad news for other birds, who will unwittingly foster the cuckoo's young.

The female's habit of laying an egg in the nest of a smaller bird of another species gave rise long ago to the notion of a cuckold, when neighbours would call 'cuckoo' to warn a husband that his wife was entertaining another man. As William Shakespeare writes in his play *Love's Labour's Lost*, come the spring,

The cuckoo then on every tree
Mocks married men; for thus sings he,
  Cuckoo;
Cuckoo, cuckoo; O Word of fear,
Unpleasing to the married ear.

Battle of CULLODEN MOOR

• **Highland (p.497 C3)** • **April 16, 1746**

On the night of April 15, 1746, Charles Edward Stuart (BONNIE PRINCE CHARLIE) trudged towards a bleak Scottish moor under cover of darkness in a last-ditch effort to defeat the British army and restore his family to the throne. The FORTY-FIVE REBELLION that he had led the previous year now found its final challenge as his 5500 JACOBITE followers faced 9000 troops led by George II's son, the duke of Cumberland.

Charles had hoped to surprise the enemy with an early morning attack but his troops were exhausted and in no condition to fight. When the end came the next day, it was quick and bloody. Cumberland had powerful artillery and fresh cavalry – in less than an hour the rebels were routed and a thousand Scots lay dead, though Bonnie Prince Charlie escaped to France with the help of the heroine Flora MACDONALD.

The duke of Cumberland earned the nickname 'butcher of Culloden' after

KING CHICK A young cuckoo soon outgrows its host, becoming as big as a pigeon when mature

he slaughtered battle prisoners and Jacobite sympathisers, set fire to their crops and began years of English repression in Scotland. The battle, the last to be fought on British soil, put an end to Jacobite aspirations to recover British sovereignty.

Nicholas CULPEPER

• **Herbalist and astrologer** • **1616-54**

When Nicholas Culpeper published *The English Physitian* (which was later reissued as *The Complete Herbal*) in 1653, he wanted to spread information about herbal remedies so that people who could not afford doctors could treat themselves 'with such things only as grow in England'.

Culpeper's mix of botanical, medical and astrological advice aroused strong opposition from the London College of Physicians, which controlled medical practice in England and preferred its knowledge to be kept secret. *The Complete Herbal*, though primitive by today's standards, was the first of its kind and is still in print.

CULZEAN CASTLE

• **South Ayrshire (p.497 C5)**
• **Built 1777-92** • **HS**

A huge mock-Gothic castle created for the 10th earl of Cassilis by the Scottish architect Robert ADAM dominates the clifftop skyline above the Firth of Clyde. Culzean (pronounced 'Cullane') contains some of Adam's best work, including an elegant oval staircase, created in what was once a central courtyard, and a circular drawing room within a tower on the seaward side.

The 200 ha (500 acre) estate that surrounds Culzean is now a country park with walled gardens, a fountain court and orangery, a swan pond, and 17 miles of woodland and field footpaths.

Samuel CUNARD

• **Ship owner** • **1787-1865; bt 1859**

When the Canadian ship owner and entrepreneur Samuel Cunard won the 1839 British tender to set up a trans-atlantic mail service, he created a shipping line that would set the style in gracious travel for the next 100 years.

After settling in Britain, Cunard launched his first ship, *Britannia*, from Liverpool in 1840. His mail ships, most built in Glasgow, plied the Atlantic route, running fortnightly services.

Not until after Cunard's death did the name become known for luxury ocean cruising. Tea dances, fancy-dress balls and cabarets entertained, while first class passengers could relax beside a marbled swimming pool sipping cocktails.

The *QUEEN MARY* and *QUEEN ELIZABETH*, both built in the 1930s, re-created a grand country house atmosphere on board, with baronial-sized drawing rooms and white-tie waiter service. The Cunard Line's swan song giant liner was the *Queen Elizabeth 2*, built in 1967.

DELIVERED IN STYLE Samuel Cunard's early ships were fast and modern for their day. The *Lusitania* met a tragic end when it was sunk by a German submarine in 1915

RARE TOURNAMENT Only when the ice has thickened to 20 cm (8 in) can a curling all-Scotland Grand Match take place, as happened in 1979 on Lake of Menteith, with 2400 competitors

CUTTY SARK

Of the clipper ships designed to race to Britain with fresh tea from China, the last to be built was the *Cutty Sark*, in 1869. Its sleek lines, steep bows and up to 3000 sq m (32 000 sq ft) of sail on three masts enabled the ship to race to market and, if the first clipper to arrive, charge premium tea prices.

Steamships travelling via the Suez Canal displaced the *Cutty Sark* from the tea trade in 1877 and it then began transporting wool from Australia in 1885. For ten years it was the fastest ship on the run, making a record 67-day passage (beating the next clipper by 12 days) from Sydney to London, with 5000 bales crammed into the hold.

After spending the rest of its working life in Portuguese ownership, the *Cutty Sark* was bought by Captain William Dowman. It was put into dry dock at Greenwich in 1954, since when the clipper has been open to the public.

CURLING

When the poet Robert Burns wrote 'Tam Samson's Elegy' in 1786, he referred to curling, a game of bowls on ice, as a winter tradition in Scotland:
> *When winter muffles up his cloak*
> *And binds the mire like a rock*
> *When to the loughs the curlers flock ...*

Curlers in Burns's day slid irregular-shaped stones across frozen lochs towards a target, or 'tee'. Today's curling stones are granite discs weighing on average 18 kg (40 lb). The sport is usually played between two teams of four players on a narrow ice rink, each sliding two stones to end up as close as possible to the tee. Players vigorously sweep the ice in front of the moving stones to control speed and direction.

The earliest evidence of curling is a challenge made at Paisley in 1541. In 1807 Scottish enthusiasts founded the Montreal Curling Club in Canada providing the impetus for international growth. The Scotch Whisky Cup in 1959 was the first international tournament. Scotland now has some 630 curling clubs with 19 000 members.

CURRY

A craze for eating 'curry' – as British colonials liked to call anything cooked in Indian style – swept through 18th-century Britain after it was introduced by employees of the East India Company.

Deriving from the Tamil *kari*, meaning sauce or stew, curry was misunderstood by Empire officers who brought home simplified versions of traditional Indian spice mixtures, and by the late 1700s a curry powder was marketed consisting of turmeric, cumin, coriander and red pepper.

In the late 1800s, an Englishman by the name of James Allen Sharwood imported a Bombay condiment, *catni*, anglicised to 'chutney', which so impressed Queen Victoria that she employed two Indian chefs to prepare a curry with chutney every day for lunch.

The curry trend did not extend to eating out until Bangladeshi immigrants opened restaurants in the 1960s, but with limited menus. Recent demand for real Indian food has brought regional variations among Britain's 8000 Indian restaurants, from the Mughal masala of north India to spicy vindaloos of south India.

CYCLE RACING

A ban on massed-start cycle races on public roads from 1888 to 1942 confined the sport to time trials on purpose-built tracks. The first major public road race was the 1951 amateur Tour of Britain, known from 1958 as the Milk Race. The race was relaunched in 1998 as a nine-day event running from Stirling in Scotland to London.

Thanks to the fitness boom, enthusiasts up and down the country have swelled cycling club memberships, bringing back mass cycle racing to British roads. The British Cycling Federation now has 1200 affiliated clubs, while the Cyclists' Touring Club, founded in 1898, boasts 47 000 members regularly taking part in race meetings.

RADICAL BIKE The light and strong Lotus bicycle frame, made from a single piece of carbon fibre, brought success for its rider Chris Boardman at the 1992 Olympics

DAFFODIL

The nodding yellow trumpet flowers of the wild daffodil – smaller than most garden varieties and sometimes called the Lent or Easter lily – have long been a symbol of spring in England.

Although the daffodil is the national flower of Wales (adopted, it is said, by those who found the leek too vulgar and smelly to wear), it is far rarer in the wild there than in England. Despite a decline caused by woodland clearance, the drainage of pasture and bulb theft (now illegal), wild daffodils can still be seen in large numbers in March and April in the damp woodland and meadows of southern England.

Roald DAHL

• **Writer** • **1916-90**

'The writer for children must be a jokey sort of fellow,' Roald Dahl once said, but it is a black humour, often with macabre overtones, that characterises his own writing. From his earliest short stories such as *Lamb to the Slaughter* (1953) – in which a guilty wife serves up the murder weapon (a leg of lamb) to the police – to his last book, *Matilda* (1988), his adults' and children's tales alike are fantasies with an unexpected twist.

Dahl wrote for adults for nearly 20 years before turning to children's books in 1961 with *James and the Giant Peach*, followed by *Charlie and the Chocolate Factory* (1964). Some of his books have been adapted for the screen, and in 1997 he was voted Britain's Favourite Children's Author.

MOCK-HORROR MASTERPIECE Illustrations by Quentin Blake brought Roald Dahl's *Dirty Beasts* rhymes luridly to life

John DALTON

• **Chemist** • **1766-1844**

The ancient Greek idea that all matter is composed of tiny particles (atoms) was given scientific expression for the first time by John Dalton in 1803. Although some of his proposals have since been disproved, his observations gave direction to modern atomic theory.

Dalton succeeded entirely by his own efforts, since as a Quaker he could not attend university, open only to members of the Church of England. He was the first person to describe colour blindness, from which he suffered. When presented to the monarch for his achievements, his Quaker faith forbade him to wear the scarlet ceremonial robes, but announcing that he could see no scarlet, he put on the robes and duly met William IV.

DANES

Despite the image of the Danes as ruthless pirates sacking monasteries and pillaging coastal towns, much of their occupation of England was peaceful, based on trade and agriculture. Gradually settling in the kingdoms of Northumbria and East Anglia from the late 8th century, the Danes were by 878 powerful enough to force a treaty with the Anglo-Saxon ruler ALFRED THE GREAT, granting them an area of self-rule, between the rivers Thames and Tees, that became known as the Danelaw.

A century later the Danes again raided English coasts. ETHELRED II tried to buy them off, raising a tax called Danegeld, first levied in 991, but in 1013 the Danish king Sweyn I conquered the entire country. From 1017 to 1042 England was ruled by Danish kings: Sweyn's son CANUTE and Canute's sons Harold and Harthacnut. Their dynasty ended with the succession to the throne of EDWARD THE CONFESSOR, son of Ethelred II.

DARTMOOR

• **Devon (p.494 C6)** • **Area 365 sq miles**

The characteristic mist, rain and bogs of Dartmoor can make it a forbidding place – as Arthur Conan Doyle realised when he chose it as the setting for his ghostly novel, *The Hound of the Baskervilles* (1902). Visitors might also see the softer nature of this National Park, with its sleepy villages and gurgling streams. Wild Dartmoor ponies graze heathered moors topped by tors, granite outcrops the highest of which is High Willhays at 621 m (2037 ft).

The ancient landscape still bears the mark of prehistoric inhabitants at sites such as Grimspound Bronze Age farm, an Iron Age hill fort at Hembury Castle, and Bronze Age stone rows on Harford Moor. Bowerman's Nose, 12 m (40 ft) high, is thought to be a druid shrine, and the legendary Hunter of the Moor is said to have been turned to stone here for hunting a witch disguised as a hare.

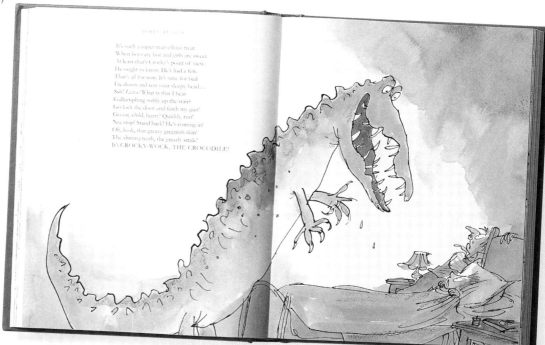

DARTMOUTH

• **Devon (p.494 D7)**   • **Pop. 5680**

Dartmouth has witnessed some historic naval expeditions from its estuarine vantage point. In 1190 Richard I's Crusaders set forth for the Holy Land from the Dart; 12 men-of-war weighed anchor in 1588 to harry the SPANISH ARMADA; the *Mayflower* sailed into harbour in 1620 before bearing the PILGRIM FATHERS away to the New World; and in 1944 nearly 500 ships massed in the estuary for the D-DAY landings.

The town's long history is reflected in some fine old buildings: the entrance to the harbour has been guarded since the 15th century by a castle, while 17th-century houses line The Butterwalk and the cobbled waterfront at Bayard's Cove. George V, George VI and Prince Charles trained at the Britannia Royal Naval College, which overlooks the harbour.

DARTS

The common name for darts, 'arrows', reflects the popular pub game's origins in the 12th-century 'butts' or 'flechettes' – an indoor form of archery. The modern game is credited to Brian Gamlin (1852-1903), a Lancashire carpenter who devised the circular segmented board and scoring system.

The inauguration of a world professional championship in 1978 owed much to the realisation by television executives that the sport provided relatively cheap, popular entertainment.

Charles DARWIN

• **Naturalist**   • **1809-82**

Fear of offending believers in the Biblical account of creation caused Charles Darwin to put off publishing his theory of evolution for more than 20 years. But in 1858 he was spurred into action by an essay sent to him by Alfred Russel WALLACE expounding similar views. The following year Darwin published *On The Origin of Species by Means of Natural Selection*, a book that would revolutionise the science of biology and become a subject of controversy for years to come.

EXOTIC EATING
Elizabeth David brought a Continental flavour to British cooking, introducing such obscurities as garlic and olive oil

Darwin started to form his ideas after visiting the Galápagos Islands during a voyage to South America as a naturalist aboard HMS *Beagle* from 1831 to 1836. But it was at Down House, his Kent home, from 1842 onwards, that Darwin fine-tuned his remarkable theory. The house is now a museum where visitors can view Darwin's private study and take part in an interactive science display.

Elizabeth DAVID

• **Cookery writer**   • **1913-92; CBE 1986**

Elizabeth David imported a sunny Mediterranean influence into Britain's bleak, postwar culinary climate. Her elegantly written books, focusing on simple, fresh ingredients, helped to transform the nation's attitude to food.

At 16 she went to study literature and history in France, and through the war travelled in Greece, Egypt (where she married) and India. Returning to a Britain of grey skies and even greyer, rationed food, she sought escape through writing. Books such as *Mediterranean Food* (1950) and *French Provincial Cooking* (1960) caught the imagination of her readers and were an instant success.

Humphry DAVY

• **Chemist**   • **1778-1829; kt 1812; bt 1818**

It is often said that Humphry Davy's finest discovery was the young Michael FARADAY, whom he took on as his assistant. But this is unfair to Davy, whose achievements include recognising the anaesthetic effects of nitrous oxide ('laughing gas') in 1799 and isolating several chemical elements, such as sodium and potassium. In 1815 he designed the safety lamp that bears his name for use in mines where explosive methane gas (firedamp) was present.

Charismatic but erratic, Davy was the first scientist to become a celebrity, attracting enthusiastic audiences to his lectures at the Royal Institution in London. He also wrote poetry, and corresponded with William Wordsworth and Samuel Taylor Coleridge.

Richard DAWKINS

• **Zoologist**   • **b.1941**

The first Professor of the Public Understanding of Science (1995) has for more than 25 years been one of Britain's most outspoken scientists. Apart from his firmly held atheist views, he is best known for his reinterpretation of Charles DARWIN's theory of evolution in terms of modern genetics. In *The Selfish Gene* (1976), Dawkins argued that it is genes – the units of heredity – that evolve, rather than individual organisms or species. Genes, he said, merely 'use' the bodies of the creatures they inhabit in order to propagate themselves.

He has also put forward the theory that cultural factors such as religious beliefs, ways of life and fashion similarly have an independent evolutionary existence, and are transmitted from generation to generation by 'memes' – the cultural equivalent of genes.

D-DAY

• June 6, 1944

The day that began the liberation of France and the opening of a second front in Europe was one of the most momentous of the Second World War. The timing was crucial, for Operation Overlord, as the Allied invasion of Normandy was code-named, required both a moonlit night and a low tide just after dawn. Possible dates were 5, 6 and 7 June, but bad weather put the mission in jeopardy until a break in the clouds allowed General Dwight Eisenhower, Supreme Commander of the Allied Forces, to authorise the assault on 6 June – ever after known as D-Day.

More than 6000 vessels crammed into south coast harbours, supported by 11 000 combat aircraft, 2300 transport aircraft and 2600 gliders. Military vehicles were concealed in woods, and 39 divisions – 20 US, 14 British, 3 Canadian, 1 Free French and 1 Polish – assembled in sealed camps as bogus tanks and landing craft acted as decoys.

Led by General MONTGOMERY, more than 150 000 men took part in the landing. Although over 10 000 were injured or killed, the mission achieved its aim and Paris was liberated by August.

DEAL CASTLE

• Kent (p.495 J5) • Built c.1540 • EH

When Henry VIII broke away from the Church of Rome he feared an invasion from France and Spain to re-assert the pope's authority. So in 1538 he began to

UNDER FIRE Deal Castle's two concentric rings of bastions, built around a central tower, allowed around 120 guns to be trained on an enemy

build a chain of more than 20 coastal forts. Deal was the most strongly fortified because of its strategic importance in defending the English Channel.

The low, squat castle, typical of Henry's forts, is shaped like a six-petalled rose – not to emulate the Tudor emblem but because rounded bastions gave the best defence against roundshot. It was besieged only once – in 1648, when held by Royalists. The basement today houses an exhibition on the history of England's coastal fortifications.

DEER

Once protected as the exclusive quarry of royal hunters, the wild deer of Britain are today the subject of great controversy. In 1997 the NATIONAL TRUST and the Forestry Commission banned stag-hunting with hounds on land they control, after evidence suggested that stags suffer extreme stress in the chase. The hunting fraternity saw it as another blow to their already beleaguered sport.

There are over a million deer in Britain. The red deer – Britain's largest wild mammal – roams the Scottish Highlands. The spotted fallow deer was the favourite of hunters in the Middle Ages, and those living in the ancient forests – including EPPING

D-DAY BRIEFING Pathfinder troops were the first Allied soldiers behind the lines

FOREST, the NEW FOREST, the FOREST OF DEAN, RICHMOND PARK and WINDSOR Great Park – are their descendants.

At just 60 cm (2 ft) tall, the roe deer is the smallest native species. It was almost hunted to extinction in the 18th century but was brought back in the 19th century. Another reintroduction is the reindeer, which died out thousands of years ago; a herd was brought from Scandinavia to Scotland in 1952. Our sika, muntjac and Chinese water deer are Asian, originally introduced into deer parks from which they escaped.

Daniel DEFOE

• Writer • 1660-1731

Widely regarded as the first true novelist in English, and noted for his mastery of sustained storytelling, Daniel Defoe came late to fiction writing, having led an eventful life as merchant, accountant, businessman, government spy and prolific pamphleteer and journalist. Defoe was nearly 60 when he wrote his best-known work, *Robinson Crusoe* (1719), a novel thought to be based on the true story of the sailor Alexander Selkirk, who had spent five years as a castaway on a Pacific island.

Defoe penned some 500 books, pamphlets and journals, many of which were published anonymously or under a pseudonym. His success lay in his use of realistic detail, as in *A Journal of the Plague Year* (1722), a fictional but truthful account the Great Plague of 1665.

Geoffrey DE HAVILLAND

• Aircraft designer • 1882-1965; kt 1944

Inspired by the Wright brothers' flight of 1903, de Havilland built his first aeroplane in 1908 and by 1910 had taught himself to fly. That year, the government employed him in aircraft development, and during the First World War he designed and produced five military aircraft, including a light bomber, the DH4.

In 1920 de Havilland formed his own AVIATION company, which produced a wide range of aeroplanes, from the Dragon Rapide airliner to the Tiger Moth. His lightweight Mosquito fighter-bomber was used in the Second World War. De Havilland revolutionised air travel with his Comet, the first jet-powered airliner, which entered service in 1952.

Frederick DELIUS

• Composer • 1862-1934

FINAL MOVEMENTS Though blind and paralysed for the last ten years of his life, Delius managed to work to the end by dictating his pieces

Although he was born and brought up in Yorkshire, Frederick Delius considered himself a cosmopolitan. His wealthy German wool merchant father tried to steer him towards a career in business, sending him at 22 to Florida to run an orange farm. But Delius succeeded only in playing the piano and learning Negro plantation songs that later found their way into his music.

In 1886 he went to Germany to study at the Leipzig Conservatory, where he was befriended and influenced by the Norwegian composer Edvard Grieg. From 1890 he lived in Paris where he fell in with playwright August Strindberg and the artist Paul Gauguin, and married the artist Jelka Rosen.

Nature was the inspiration behind many of Delius's scores – romantic, melancholy creations with lush harmonies. Although compositions such as *In a Summer Garden* (1908) and *On Hearing the First Cuckoo in Spring* (1912), are thought of as typically English, Delius composed firmly within the Germanic tradition and was for a long time little played in Britain. The conductor Thomas BEECHAM rescued him, premiering many of his works.

DEPRESSION

The crash of the US stock market in October 1929 triggered a worldwide economic crisis. In Britain, the effects of the Depression were felt for most of the 1930s, unemployment soaring to a record 3 million in 1932.

From 1931, the coalition government took draconian measures to stave off national bankruptcy. Income tax was raised, unemployment benefit cut and wages slashed. Soup kitchens and charitable handouts became a way of life, while people who fell through the welfare net, such as orphans, the mentally ill and single pregnant women, faced the harsh regime of the workhouse.

Amid this intolerable poverty, the government's policy of nosing out any scrap of undeclared earnings and trimming the dole accordingly was, for many, the final insult. Protests errupted, such as the JARROW MARCH, but little changed for the

FEELING DOWN One man tries some self promotion to boost his luck during the 1930s Depression

I KNOW 3 TRADES
I SPEAK 3 LANGUAGES
FOUGHT FOR 3 YEARS
HAVE 3 CHILDREN
AND NO WORK FOR
3 MONTHS
BUT I ONLY WANT
ONE JOB

unemployed. In 1936, having visited the stricken industrial areas of Wales, even the king, Edward VIII, was moved to remark: 'Something must be done to find them work.' Mass re-employment came only with heavy investment in rearmament and the outbreak of the Second World War.

DEVIL'S DYKE

The Devil provides many a colourful answer to bewildering features of the landscape. At Poynings in the Sussex Downs, it is said the Lord of Darkness planned to drown pious villagers in a dyke dug from the sea, but was interrupted when the light of an old woman's candle caused a cock to crow. The Devil fled in fear of the approaching dawn, leaving his half-completed work for all to see as a deep cleft through the chalk hill above the village.

There are many other Devil's Dykes, and local maps are rich in diabolical topography: the Devil's Punch Bowl sits in Haslemere in Surrey, his Beef Tub is outside Moffat in the Scottish Borders and he has a rocky Chair near Pennerley in Shropshire. Despite his supernatural advantages, he could seldom outwit local folk: one old woman even managed to trick him into building the Devil's Bridge over the Mynach Falls in north Wales.

DEVOLUTION

The transfer of some powers from central government to provincial assemblies in Scotland and Wales has become known as devolution. The Labour government proposed setting up a new Scottish parliament and a less powerful Welsh assembly in 1974. Referenda were held in 1979, with the Welsh voting against. The Scots narrowly voted in favour, but Westminster required the support of at least 40 per cent of the Scottish electorate, so nothing was done.

The intervening Conservative governments stood fast against devolution, but in 1997 the new Labour government moved swiftly to hold new devolution referenda. This time both countries voted in favour. The Scottish parliament and Welsh assembly, both elected in May 1999, received authority and legislative power over domestic issues, such as health, housing and social services, while central government at Westminster retained control over defence, economic policy, employment, taxation and foreign affairs.

Charles DICKENS

• Novelist • 1812-70

Along with his inventive humour and the flesh-and-blood vitality of his characters, Charles Dickens brought home to readers the injustices and harshness of life endured by many in Victorian England. His own childhood had been far from easy: at the age of 12 he was put to work in a blacking factory following his father's imprisonment for debt. In 1828 he started as a parliamentary reporter on the *Morning Chronicle*, and under the name of 'Boz' submitted short stories to the *Evening Chronicle*. These were collected and published in 1836.

NOVELS BY INSTALMENT

His reputation was established later the same year with the publication of the first chapters of the lighthearted *Pickwick Papers*, the first of 20 novels which were mostly published as serials in popular magazines. It was followed by the more sombre *Oliver Twist* (1837-8). Among the most popular of Dickens' novels are his own favourite, the semi-autobiographical *David Copperfield* (1849-50), and *Great Expectations* (1860-1).

PRIVATE LIFE

Dickens married Catherine Hogarth in 1836. They had ten children, but it was a troubled match and they divorced in 1858. Dickens longed to be an actor and his love of performance led him to undertake an exhausting series of dramatic readings between 1858 and 1870 in Britain and the USA. The strain is thought to have contributed to his early death, which left the novel *The Mystery of Edwin Drood* unfinished.

DIMBLEBY FAMILY

• Broadcasters • Richard; 1913-65
• David; b.1938 • Jonathan; b.1944

The Dimblebys have dominated the great occasions and big issues of British radio and television coverage for more than half a century. Richard Dimbleby was one of the BBC's star reporters in the

DIANA, Princess of Wales

• 1961-97

No one, the royal family least of all, imagined that Lady Diana Spencer would metamorphose into an international media star. The 1981 wedding of Prince CHARLES to Lady Diana Spencer, the 8th earl Spencer's bashful 20-year-old daughter, was hailed as a fairy tale come true, and Diana quickly produced 'an heir and a spare', Princes William (1982) and Henry, known as Harry (1984).

She soon became the world's most photographed woman and developed an ambivalent relationship with the press, using it to promote the many good causes and charities she espoused, while resenting any intrusion into her private life. Yet photographers continued to pursue her relentlessly.

Many people saw Diana as a victim of a remote, rather cold, royal family. The public pitied her lack of privacy, while devouring candid photographs and speculative stories about her private life once it became known that the marriage was unhappy.

Mismatched both emotionally and mentally, Diana and Charles separated in 1992, divorcing in 1996. In August 1997 Diana was killed in a car accident with her lover, Emad 'Dodi' Fayed.

Following a week of public emotional display, and a royal funeral service, Diana was buried at Althorp, Northampton, the seat of the Spencer family since 1508. The estate now includes a memorial exhibition on her life.

THE PEOPLE'S PRINCESS Diana's easy familiarity with children was in evidence at her visit to a Hindu temple in 1997

Second World War: it was his voice that listeners heard describing airborne forces taking off for Normandy, and the horror of the Belsen concentration camp.

His elder son, David, joined the BBC in 1960, working his way up as a reporter and documentary maker to present the current affairs programme, *Panorama* (1974-7 and 1980-2). He anchored the BBC's coverage of every

general election from 1979 to 1997, demonstrating a remarkable grasp of the minutiae of electoral politics.

His younger brother, Jonathan, has a more sensitive, even radical image. He has worked for ITV as well as for the BBC. Notable programmes include his report on the Ethiopian famine in 1973, and a 1994 documentary on Prince Charles, *Public Person, Private Man*.

LONDON DOCKS In 1910 the Upper Pool, upstream of Tower Bridge, was bustling with steamers, lighters, tugs and barges (*left*). The docks were still busy in 1947, receiving cargo from all over the world, including a shipment of baby elephants from Ceylon (*centre*). In 1950 the *Dominion Monarch* (*right*) became the largest ship to use King George V dry dock, and one of the last

Paul DIRAC

- **Mathematician and physicist** • **1902-84**

Born in Bristol of a Swiss father, Paul Dirac was a giant of quantum physics. He believed that an elegant equation was more likely to be right than one that had been adapted to fit imperfect data, and in 1930 deduced purely from mathematics that elementary particles ought to have antiparticle opposites, equal in mass but of opposite charge.

The idea of antimatter was derided at the time but in 1932 the positron, antiparticle twin of the electron, was discovered, and the following year Dirac received the Nobel prize for physics.

Benjamin DISRAELI

- **Prime minister 1868, 1874-80**
- **1804-81; earl 1876**

When Benjamin Disraeli entered parliament in 1837 he was seen as something of a dandy and his maiden speech was greeted by hoots of derision. 'The time will come when you will hear me!', he shouted. It seemed unlikely.

The Christianised son of a writer of Italian-Jewish origins, Disraeli was already known as a novelist when he turned to politics. He started out a radical, but when he entered parliament it was as Tory MP for Maidstone in Kent. Marriage to a wealthy widow brought further respectability, though his political novels, such as *Conningsby* (1844) and *Sybil* (1845), show his lasting desire to heal the divisions between rich and poor.

Disraeli first began to make his mark politically when in 1846 he led Tory opposition to the free trade policy of Robert PEEL over the CORN LAWS. He became prime minister briefly in 1868, then again in 1874-80. As leader of the party, Disraeli began laying the foundations of the modern Conservative party. His government pursued an aggressive foreign policy and introduced social, public health and trade union reforms at home.

'Dizzy' wooed Queen Victoria out of mourning and back into public life with his famous charm, and was instrumental in making her Empress of India in 1876. 'Everyone likes flattery,' he said, 'and when it comes to royalty you should lay it on with a trowel.'

DOCKLANDS

- **E London (p.498 D3)**

Dock-building started in earnest along the Thames in the EAST END of London in the early 19th century. Until then large ships simply anchored in the river, to avoid being grounded by low tides, and were loaded and unloaded by barges. West India Dock was the first to be built, cut by the canal engineer William Jessop through the Isle of Dogs peninsula in 1802. Many others followed, including Surrey Commercial (1807) and St Katharine (1828) sited just east of Tower Bridge and the nearest to the heart of London.

As ships got larger, the docks moved downstream, culminating in King George V Dock at Beckton in 1921. By the 1960s even these were proving unsuitable for the new container ships and supertankers, which required deeper and larger facilities, and one by one the docks closed. Today few ships venture farther up the Thames than the port of Tilbury in Essex.

In the 1980s the Dockland area was redeveloped for offices, housing and leisure, and acquired the tallest building in Britain, the 244m (800ft) Canada Tower at Canary Wharf (*see* MODERN BUILDINGS).

DOGGETT'S COAT AND BADGE

- **August**

The world's oldest sculling race was founded in London by an Irish actor and theatre manager, Thomas Doggett, in 1715, though the activity itself goes back to medieval times, when the wealthy first began to employ 'watermen' to man barges on the Thames. By the turn of the 18th century, with more than 40000 licensed watermen on the tidal reaches between Chelsea and Windsor, races were commonplace and betting heavy.

Doggett's Coat and Badge is contested each August by newly qualified bargees. Six men in separate sculls race from London Bridge to the site of the Swan Inn at Chelsea Pier to earn the right to wear the honoured coat and badge.

ALL DRESSED UP Past winners of Doggett's Coat and Badge turn out in their red livery and silver badge at the race every summer

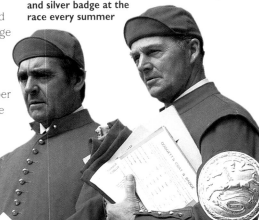

DOGS

Domestic dogs have been known in Britain for some 10 000 years. Early farmers exploited the herding instincts of the rough Scottish collie and the West Country Old English sheepdog. Sturdy, rough-coated terriers from Scotland and the north of England were prized for digging out burrowing rodents. They owe their name to the Romans, who called them *terrari* (from the Latin for 'earth'). Mastiffs, also here when the Romans came, hunted bears and wolves, and were used in battle.

NEW BREEDS FOR A NEW AGE

The real British love affair with dogs began in the 11th century, when Norman nobles brought in beagles and bloodhounds. The fleet-footed greyhound arrived at about the same time, and breeders produced deerhounds, foxhounds and wolfhounds for the chase. Bulldogs were developed for bull and bear-baiting from the 13th century, but when the practices were outlawed in 1835 their ferocity was bred out. Victorian miners produced the whippet – a scaled-down version of the greyhound.

WATERDOGS AND GUNDOGS

Spaniels, or 'Spanish dogs', arrived in the 16th century, and were used to flush out game for falcons; the small King Charles spaniel, named after Charles II, was also a favourite of ladies at court. Shooting succeeded falconry in the late 17th century, bringing gundogs such as pointers. Among the earliest of retrieving dogs were Labradors, which arrived from Newfoundland in the 1800s and are now Britain's most popular breed.

MODERN WORKING DOGS

Since the 1880s, dogs have helped police to track criminals. The first police-dog unit, made up of Airedales, was formed in 1908. Guide dogs for the blind have been trained in Britain since 1931 and dogs to assist the deaf since 1982. HM Customs and Excise employs gun dogs and border collies to detect illegal drugs and explosives.

DOMESDAY BOOK

In 1086 inspectors scoured England on the orders of WILLIAM I to assess the wealth of every landowner in the realm for tax purposes. Details of the size of every manor and the space devoted to arable crops, woodland or pasture were noted, alongside the number of priests, peasants and ploughs each estate contained. The result was a two-volume work, completed in 1087, which represents England's first land survey.

Recognising the financial implications of the survey, which were likened to the Day of Judgment, landowners called it Domesday, or Doomsday, Book. The original can be seen at the Public Record Office at Kew in Surrey.

John DONNE

• **Poet** • **1572-1631**

As the most complex and intellectual of the METAPHYSICAL POETS John Donne was out of favour throughout the Romantic period, which inclined towards emotion and simplicity. Not until the 20th century was his reputation restored by critics such as T.S. ELIOT and F.R. Leavis.

Donne's early works, such as *Elegies* (c.1590), deal with physical and spiritual experience through puns, paradoxes and images reflecting the academic disciplines and discoveries of the day. 'O my America! my new-found-land,' he exclaims as his mistress removes her clothes for bed.

Donne became an Anglican priest in 1615 and dean of St Paul's Cathedral in 1621. His later poetry and sermons have a profound and passionate intensity, and are preoccupied mainly with death and union of the soul with God.

IF OUR TWO LOVES BE ONE The Donne of the love poems – which he circulated privately – eschewed convention and revelled in sensuality, wit and philosophy

DORCHESTER

• **Dorset (p.494 E6)** • **Pop. 15 040**

Today, Dorchester, the county town of Dorset, is a place of pilgrimage for readers of the novels of Thomas HARDY, who come to see *The Mayor of Casterbridge* brought to life in buildings that appear in the book, such as the King's Arms.

During the Civil War the Roundheads turned Maumbury Rings, the site of Roman Dorchester's amphitheatre, into a gun emplacement. It was used as a place of public execution up to 1766

It is fitting that this was Hardy's home town, since the darker elements of his prose find an echo in the gloomier side of the town's long history. At the Old Crown Court in 1685 Judge Jeffreys held the Bloody Assizes following the failed Monmouth Rebellion, and it was there that in 1834 the TOLPUDDLE MARTYRS were sentenced to transportation.

Nearby are Stone Age burial mounds and remains of the Roman amphitheatre at Maumbury Rings; the massive Iron Age hillfort of MAIDEN CASTLE; and the mighty Cerne Abbas giant, a CHALK FIGURE carved into the downland.

DOVER

• **Kent (p.495 J5)** • **Pop. 34 180**

As the nearest port to France, just 21 miles away, Dover is the traditional gateway to England from the Continent. Its sheer white cliffs, rising like a giant shield, have been Britain's first line of defence ever since the Roman invasion.

A 24 m (80 ft) octagonal lighthouse survives as the tallest Roman building in Britain, although it is dwarfed by the Norman castle that looms from the clifftops. William the Conqueror's army sacked most of the Saxon town, although a 10th-century church still stands next to the Roman lighthouse.

Dover castle was begun in 1180 by Henry II. With its square-cut keep set within two concentric walls with towers, it is one of the earliest and most complete fortresses in Britain. In its day there were few more impregnable castles in Europe.

Several ferry companies operate out of Dover and in 1998 the port handled the passage of almost 23 million people on their way to and from the Continent.

John DOWLAND

• Composer • 1563-1626

The Elizabethan lutenist, John Dowland, built his career on melancholy, composing some 80 songs about death, sin, unrequited love and despair. Tunes such as 'Lachrimae' ('Flow My Tears') were hummed by courtiers and commoners alike, while his melody 'Walsingham' was used to accompany the play *Hamlet*. Today's lutenists consider his works high points of the instrument's repertoire.

Dowland spent his most prolific years in France, Germany, Italy and Denmark, where he served at the court of Christian IV. Dismissed for 'unsatisfactory conduct' in 1606, he returned to England in 1608. He wrote little after 1612.

DOWNING STREET

• Central London (p.499 C8)

The most famous front door in Britain is that of 10 Downing Street, the official residence of the prime minister. George Downing built numbers 10-12 in the late 17th century as private residences and George II took possession of them early in the 18th century.

The king gave number 10 to Robert Walpole in 1732, and prime ministers have lived there since 1735. The street is a cul-de-sac off WHITEHALL, about 360 m (400 yd) from the Houses of Parliament. Connecting doors link numbers 10, 11 (the chancellor of the exchequer's London base) and 12 (residence of the government chief whip), giving three of the most important people in government easy access to one another.

Traditionally crowds gathered in Downing Street on great occasions, but in 1979 iron gates were erected at the entrance to the street as a counter-terrorism measure and are now used to control access. People are still allowed in to welcome the prime minister on the morning after a general election.

DOWNS

• S England (p.495 H5/H6)

The Downs, named from the Celtic 'dun', meaning a hill, are rolling grasslands reaching a height of 300 m (1000 ft) and laced with dazzling white chalk paths. About 80 miles long, the North Downs form an arc from Guildford to Dover, while the South Downs stretch for about 70 miles from Winchester to end abruptly at the sheer cliffs of BEACHY HEAD on the Sussex coast.

Medieval pilgrims journeyed along the high dry ground from Winchester to Thomas BECKET's shrine in Canterbury, a route still known as the Pilgrims' Way.

ROLLING DOWNS The two popular walks of the North Downs Way and South Downs Way follow routes dating back to antiquity

D'OYLY CARTE COMPANY

• Founded 1879

The impresario Richard D'Oyly Carte (1844-1901) formed an opera company specifically to stage the light-hearted, satirical works of GILBERT AND SULLIVAN. The venture was so successful that by 1881 the D'Oyly Carte Opera Company was rich enough to build its own theatre, the Savoy, for a London home.

In 1982 government grants were cut and the company closed for six years until a legacy from D'Oyly Carte's granddaughter Bridget revived it. Since 1997 its headquarters have been the Grand Theatre in Wolverhampton.

Francis DRAKE

• Sailor and explorer
• c.1540-96; kt 1581

Britain's great seafaring adventurer Francis Drake set out on his first voyage in 1572, looting the Spanish territories of the Caribbean to bring home 30 tons of Spanish silver. The Spanish called him 'the master thief of the unknown world', but in the eyes of ELIZABETH I, who had long feuded with the Catholics in Spain and France, he could do no wrong.

In 1577, financed by Elizabeth, Drake set sail for the Spanish-occupied west coast of America. He claimed California for his queen and went on to circumnavigate the globe (the first Englishman to do so), returning in 1580 to a hero's welcome and a knighthood.

In 1587 Drake sailed into the port of Cádiz where he destroyed 33 Spanish ships to escape unscathed, having 'singed the King of Spain's beard'. A year later he played an important part in seeing off the SPANISH ARMADA.

what is now called product design. Dresser studied the manufacturing processes of objects including glassware, ceramics, metalware, linoleum, wallpaper and furniture, adapting his designs to mass production. The best collection of his work is at the Victoria and Albert Museum in London.

ANCIENT RITES Modern druids celebrate the solstices

DRAMBUIE

'Remember the gift of the Prince,' says the label on Scotland's pre-eminent liqueur. Legend has it that the recipe for Drambuie was given to one Captain John Mackinnon by BONNIE PRINCE CHARLIE in return for shelter on Skye after his defeat at Culloden in 1746.

The recipe for the whisky-based liqueur, flavoured with herbs and heather honey, has been in the hands of the Mackinnon family ever since. The name comes from the Gaelic *an dram buidheach*, 'the drink that satisfies'.

Christopher DRESSER

• **Designer** • **1834-1904**
The pioneer of industrial design, Christopher Dresser began his career lecturing in botany at the School of Design at Somerset House in London. In 1856 he produced a plate decorated with geometrical arrangements of flowers, which he contributed to *The Grammar Of Ornament*, an influential reference book compiled by the architect Owen Jones.

In 1860 Dresser received a doctorate from the University of Jena in Germany for his botanical research, but his interests turned rapidly to design. In 1862 he published *The Art of Decorative Design*, the first ever such manual, and quickly established himself as a specialist in

PRACTICAL DESIGN A spoon warmer designed by Dresser is both functional and pleasing to the eye

DRUIDS

The earliest druids were priests of a Celtic pagan religion that was suppressed by the Romans in the 1st century AD. Accounts by Caesar and Tacitus build a picture of them as judges and teachers of astronomy and oral poetry.

According to the Roman writer Pliny, the oak tree was sacred to the druids – 'druid' deriving from the Celtic words for 'oak' and 'knowledge' – and mistletoe found growing on oak trees was supposed to have magical powers. Druid ceremonies may have included human sacrifice – perhaps the fate of the LINDOW MAN – but their cruel reputation may owe much to Roman slander.

Antiquarians of later centuries revived interest in Britain's Celtic past and a new order, the Druid Circle of the Universal Bond, formed in 1717. Today there are many modern orders of druids, who practise a form of nature worship based on supposedly ancient druidic rituals.

DRURY LANE

• **Central London (p.499 D5)**
Named after the Drury family who had a large house there from Tudor times, Drury Lane became the heart of London's theatreland in the 18th century. Entertainment in the area dates from the time of James I when an old cockfighting venue was adapted for theatrical

purposes. When this burned down in 1619, a new theatre emerged from the ashes – the Phoenix, the first purpose-built theatre in the West End, which later succumbed to competition from the Theatre Royal in Drury Lane.

First built in 1662, the Theatre Royal was also destroyed by fire and rebuilt three times, most recently in 1812. Managed in the 18th century by the actor David GARRICK, it later became London's main pantomime venue. Since the Second World War it has staged mainly musicals.

John DRYDEN

• **Poet, dramatist and critic** • **1631-1700**
In all his writing John Dryden was a model of clarity and directness and master of the well-turned phrase. He had a powerful mind and a facility for many poetic forms, including couplets, songs, odes and blank verse. His formal, classical style had enormous influence on the literature of his age.

Most of Dryden's verse was in some sense public. His early *Astraea Redux* (1660) celebrated the Restoration of Charles II and *Annus Mirabilis* the war against the Dutch of 1666. He was appointed poet laureate in 1668 and historiographer royal in 1670. Perhaps his finest poem is *Absalom and Achitophel* (1681), a biting satire against Lord Shaftesbury and his support for the duke of Monmouth as Charles's heir.

Dryden also wrote verse dramas, including the comedy of manners *Marriage à la Mode* (1673) and the tragedy *All for Love* (1677). In later life he turned to verse translation, mainly from Latin authors such as Virgil and Ovid.

DRY-STONE WALLS

Much of Britain's agricultural landscape, including the Peak District, Yorkshire and much of Scotland, is criss-crossed with skilfully built walls held together not by cement but simply by the careful positioning of stones. Many are punctuated by 'throughs' – long stones extending right through the wall – and square 'creep' holes, big enough to allow sheep through while keeping cattle penned in.

Dry-stone walling is thought to be an ancient rural skill – some walls in Cornwall are at least 2000 years old. The AGRICULTURAL REVOLUTION of the 17th and 18th centuries created estates with miles of dry-stone walls built by professional squads. The craft is still practised, encouraged by the Countryside Commission and the National Trust.

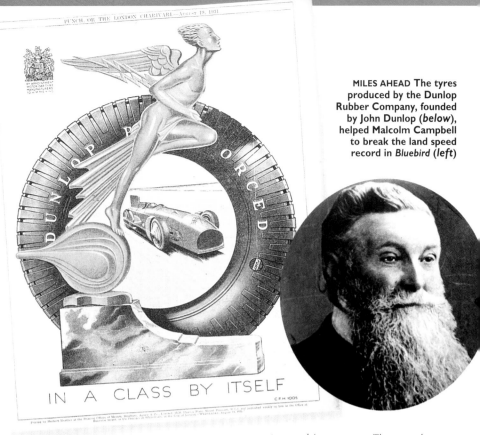

MILES AHEAD **The tyres produced by the Dunlop Rubber Company, founded by John Dunlop (***below***), helped Malcolm Campbell to break the land speed record in** *Bluebird* **(***left***)**

DUCKING STOOL

Women who were outspoken or scolded their husbands once received the same punishment as fraudulent tradespeople – a number of duckings underwater on a stool levered by a pivoted arm.

Ducking or cucking stools were a common sight in Britain in the 17th and 18th centuries. The last known woman to suffer the indignity was Jenny Pipes in 1809, ducked in the river near Kenwater Bridge in Leominster for being drunk and disorderly. The stool used can still be seen in the Leominster priory church.

DULWICH PICTURE GALLERY

• S London (p.498 D4) • Opened 1814

Britain's oldest public art gallery owes its existence to the partitioning of Poland. In 1790 the king of Poland commissioned Noel Desenfans, a French art dealer living in England, to collect paintings for his court. Desenfans duly acquired more than 300 works, but in 1795, before the collection was complete, the partition of Poland between Russia and Prussia forced the king to abdicate, leaving Desenfans without a buyer for his extensive collection.

Inspired by the idea of a national gallery for England, Desenfans set about rebuilding the collection to reflect his own taste. He sold many of the paintings and purchased others, with the help of his friend, the painter and Royal Academician Francis Bourgeois.

Bourgeois inherited the paintings when Desenfans died, and donated them to Dulwich College. John SOANE designed the gallery, which now displays works by Canaletto, Rembrandt and Rubens, and many fine 18th-century English portraits. A lantern top on the gallery roof inspired Giles Gilbert Scott's classic design for Britain's red telephone box.

DUNDEE

• E Scotland (p.497 D4) • Pop. 158 980

An Iron Age hill-fort overlooks the port of Dundee from a summit of volcanic rock. The site was once a Roman camp, and in 834 became the headquarters of Kenneth Macalpin, later king of the united Scottish people.

In the 19th century 'jute, jam and journalism' brought prosperity to the town. Jute arrived by ship from India and was made into cloth and sacking. Marmalade was first created in Dundee from an 18th-century shipment of Seville oranges too bitter to eat. The popular jam became a Scottish speciality. Journalism still survives in the form of D.C. Thomson, publishers of children's COMICS *The Beano* and *The Dandy*.

The Dundee shipyards of the 18th and 19th centuries built the exploration vessels of Robert SCOTT, *Terra Nova* and *Discovery*. The latter can still be seen at the port along with the oldest British ship still afloat, HMS *Unicorn* (1824). Since the 1970s, the port has played a major role in the North Sea oil industry.

John Boyd DUNLOP

• Inventor •1840-1921

When his young son complained about the bumpiness of riding a tricycle over cobbled streets, the Scottish vet John Dunlop set about finding an alternative to solid rubber wheels. His solution was an inflated rubber tube surrounded by a canvas jacket with rubber tread. In 1888 he patented his idea, and the following year he began ordering custom-made tyres from an Edinburgh factory and fitting them to tricycles made in Belfast.

But Dunlop's idea was not original as an earlier patent for the pneumatic tyre, registered in 1845 for horse-drawn carriages, caused legal difficulties. In 1896, the company was sold. Though it went on to manufacture car tyres as the Dunlop Rubber Company, Dunlop himself played no further part, and profited little from his enterprise.

John DUNS SCOTUS

• Theologian   • c.1265-c.1308

It is deeply unfair that the name of Scotland's greatest medieval scholar should have evolved into the word 'dunce'. His writings were mainly commentaries on Aristotle, the Bible and Thomism – the orthodox system of philosophy and theology developed by Thomas Aquinas, who stressed the role of reason in religious faith.

Duns Scotus, a Fransiscan friar, was known as Doctor Subtilis (the Subtle Doctor) because of his penetrating criticism of Thomism. He argued that an understanding of religious concepts such as the immortality of the soul is attained not by reasoning, but by acts of will and the gift of faith.

His views were attacked and since Scotism – as his doctrines were called – was opposed to the rational thrust of later Renaissance philosophy, by the 16th century his followers were being ridiculed and nicknamed 'dunces'.

Jacqueline DU PRÉ

• Cellist   • 1945-87

At the Wigmore Hall, London, in 1961, a 16-year-old cellist swayed energetically through her debut concert performance. Jacqueline du Pré, a pupil of Pablo Casals and Mstislav Rostropovich, became the leading cellist of her generation, while her passionate playing style was an instant trademark.

She married the pianist, and later conductor, Daniel Barenboim in 1967, but in 1972 her career was cut short by multiple sclerosis although she continued to teach. Her expressive renderings of Edward ELGAR's Cello Concerto are still among the most powerful on record.

DURHAM

• NE England (p.496 C3)   • Pop 36 940

When Danish invaders sailed across the North Sea to Britain in the 7th century, monks at the east-coast monastery of LINDISFARNE hurriedly made their escape

with the remains of their revered bishop, St Cuthbert. The saint's relics eventually came to rest at Durham, a town protected by a bend in the River Wear, and a shrine was created inside its Anglo-Saxon cathedral.

The Normans used Durham as their northern base, building the castle that is now part of the university. The shrine of St Cuthbert in the 11th-12th century cathedral still attracts pilgrims, as does the tomb of the Venerable BEDE.

As the county town of an agricultural, steel-manufacturing and coal-mining area, Durham flourished in the Industrial Revolution. Derwentcote Steel Furnace near Rowlands Gill is the most complete steel-making furnace to have survived.

DUTCH ELM DISEASE

Though seedling elms thrive in Britain's wooded countryside, hardly a single mature tree exists. Dutch elm disease – so-called because it first broke out in Holland – arrived in Britain in 1967, and over the next decade killed two-thirds of Britain's mature elms.

The culprit is a fungus, *Ceratocyctis ulmi*, carried by beetles. It attacks new ring-growth and blocks the flow of sap, causing leaves to wither and eventually the whole tree to die. The disease is still endemic, and the cure – spraying the beetles and injecting trees annually with fungicide – is too expensive to be practicable on a large scale.

Nature may provide a better solution. The roots of seedling trees infected by the fungus are remaining healthy, and every year new shoots grow a little taller – evidence of growing resistance.

James DYSON

• Inventor   • b.1947

Curiosity led the young designer and self-taught engineer James Dyson to investigate the poor performance of vacuum cleaners. He discovered that pores in the dust-collecting bag often became clogged long before the bag was full,

impeding suction. Dyson, who already had a portfolio of inventions under his belt, including the Ballbarrow, a wheelbarrow with a plastic ball instead of a wheel, set about designing a bagless vacuum cleaner. The result, his Dual Cyclone – invented in 1979 – uses centrifugal force to collect dirt.

Dyson set out on a sales trip around the world, but met with little success. By 1986 his revolutionary cleaner was being produced only in Japan. Production began in the USA but still Dyson could not find backing in Britain. In 1993, he set up his own company, Dyson Appliances, to produce his inventions. By the mid 1990s, it had become one of Britain's fastest-growing manufacturers, and by 1998, more than 4 million Dual Cyclones had been sold.

CLEANING UP The Dyson Clear uses two centrifuges or 'cyclones' to separate dirt from air and spin it into a plastic collection chamber. Its inner cyclone spins at up to 924 mph

PASSPORT TO PIMLICO Residents of Pimlico declare independence from Britain – and from post-war rationing – to the bemusement of civil servants in the Ealing Studios' 1949 classic comedy

EALING COMEDIES

To Britons tired of war and rationing, the comic films of the Ealing Studios offered a joyful, light-hearted view of themselves as a nation of formidable dowagers, bumbling eccentrics, affable bobbies and cheeky cockneys.

The great days of Ealing began when the film producer Michael Balcon took over in 1937 and set out to attract the finest comic actors and directors of the day. Alec GUINNESS, Stanley Holloway and Joan Greenwood were among those who trod the Ealing lots, making films such as *Kind Hearts and Coronets*, *The Lavender Hill Mob* and *Whisky Galore*, which captured the inimitable confidence and optimism of postwar Britain.

Ealing's golden age came to an end after *The Ladykillers* (1955), when the Rank Organisation, which owned the majority of the shares in the studios, sold them to the BBC. Film stages and offices were subsequently rented out for independent productions, and in 1995 the site was sold to the National Film and Television School.

EAST END

• E London

The tough reputation of the East End – from the grim fictional world of Charles Dickens's *Oliver Twist* to the real-life violence of Jack the Ripper and the Kray twins – has always been tempered by a strong sense of community and an acceptance of foreigners.

From the 17th century, London industries set up in the east to allow westerly winds to blow smells away from the city. Since ships could not pass above London Bridge, this was also London's docks and an initial landing place for immigrants.

Some of the first to come were HUGUENOT refugees in the 17th century who established a silk-weaving industry in Spitalfields. They were followed in the 19th and early 20th centuries by Jewish refugees from eastern Europe who settled in Whitechapel, and Chinese sailors who created an Asian community in Limehouse beside the Thames.

The Blitz of 1940-1 flattened much of the old East End and slum clearances from 1945-55 saw many families rehoused in Essex and Hertfordshire. The area is still ethnically mixed, but with the redevelopment of the DOCKLANDS a contrast is emerging between established East Enders and white-collar workers moving into exclusive new offices.

EASTER RISING

• April 24-29, 1916

On Easter Monday in 1916, 1600 Irish Volunteers and 200 members of the Irish Citizens' Army seized the General Post Office, courts, railway stations and other key sites in Dublin and proclaimed an Irish republic, independent from Britain.

The uprising, planned by the writer Patrick Pearse and other leaders of the Irish Republican Brotherhood, took the government by surprise, but was crushed in five days of heavy shelling and street fighting in which 450 people died. Two thousand rebels were imprisoned, and 15 of the leaders, including Pearse, were executed. The government's forceful response aroused deep resentment among Republicans that endured long after southern Ireland became the Irish Free State in 1921.

EASTER TRADITIONS: *see opposite*

EAST INDIA COMPANY

• 1600-1873

Britain's interests in India began as a purely commercial affair. Early in the 17th century a group of merchants formed the British East India Company and negotiated privileges with the Mughal emperors, fending off rival traders to reap rich profits from trading textiles in Bombay, Calcutta and Madras.

But politics and business soon mixed as company interests started to predominate in the region and influence local affairs. In the 18th century the BEIC, backed by British military might, was to become the most powerful force of government on the subcontinent.

In 1757, under Robert CLIVE, the British fought off French trading competition and seized Bengal. Officials began returning home with huge fortunes made from Bengal's trade revenue. The company became so powerful that in 1783 the British government took direct control. Civil rebellion in 1857 was quashed and the BEIC dissolved, but Britain declared India a Crown possession – the RAJ – in 1858, and retained power for nearly a century.

ECCENTRICS: *see page 140*

Arthur Stanley EDDINGTON

• Astronomer   • 1882-1944; kt 1930

As a young professor of astronomy at Cambridge University, Eddington boasted that only two people in the world really understood Einstein's theories of relativity – and the other was Einstein.

Eddington's own work was mainly concerned with investigating the structure of stars and the Universe. In 1919 an observation during an eclipse in West Africa brought him worldwide fame, for he noticed that the gravitational force of the Sun bent light rays passing close to it, confirming a prediction of Einstein's general theory of relativity.

Eddington was a skilful populariser, bringing his subject to life in early science best sellers such as *The Expanding Universe* (1933). He never married, declaring: 'falling in love is one of the activities forbidden that tiresome person, the consistently reasonable man'.

Anthony EDEN

• **Prime minister 1955-7**   • **1897-1977; kt 1954; earl 1961**

Despite three distinguished terms as foreign secretary and popularity as a moderate Conservative, it is for his one major failure – the SUEZ CRISIS – that Anthony Eden is primarily remembered.

Eden first served as foreign secretary under Neville CHAMBERLAIN but resigned in 1938 in protest over appeasement towards Italy. He returned to the post in 1940, working alongside Winston CHURCHILL throughout the Second World War, and again in 1951. In 1955 he succeeded Churchill as prime minister. The following year Eden faced an international crisis when President Nasser of Egypt nationalised the Suez Canal, threatening British interests. He intervened and seized the canal, but the economic and political consequences provoked condemnation at home and abroad. The crisis, and ill health, led him to resign in 1957.

EASTER TRADITIONS

When CHRISTIANITY arrived in pagan Britain, many local customs were incorporated into the new faith. The commemoration of Jesus's death and resurrection in the springtime coincided with pagan rituals celebrating fertility and new life, several of which were adopted by the Church.

According to the 8th-century historian BEDE, the name of the Christian festival, Easter, came from the pagan goddess, Eostre, whose feast day was celebrated in the spring.

THE EASTER BUNNY
The friendly rabbit who delivers Easter eggs derives from the hare, thought to be sacred to the pagan goddess Eostre.

DECORATED EGGS
The egg, an ancient symbol of new life, was adopted by Christianity as a symbol of the resurrection of Christ.

EGG ROLLING
Rolling Easter eggs down hills is said to have originated in pagan times as a symbol of the Sun's movement across the sky. Christian interpretation links the tradition with rolling the stone away from Christ's tomb at the Resurrection.

HOT CROSS BUNS
The Romans ate festive round buns marked with a cross to represent the four lunar quarters. Today's Easter buns represent the Cross on which Christ died.

LOST AT SEA At Easter in 1788, a landlady expecting her son home from the seas hung a hot cross bun, lucky for sailors, from the roof of her pub, since named The Widow's Son, in east London. He never returned, but her act became a local custom

EDEN PROJECT

• **Cornwall (p.494 B7)**

In 1998, in a disused china-clay pit at Bodelva near St Austell, construction work began on the world's biggest greenhouse. Nicholas GRIMSHAW's architectural firm designed a snaking structure of interconnecting domes up to 50 m (164 ft) high, to house ecosystems

continued on page 141

INSIDE EDEN The biomes of the Eden Project – galvanised steel frames covered with insulating air pillows of transparent foil – will use energy generated by the Sun and by wood-burning to supply two-thirds of their heating requirements

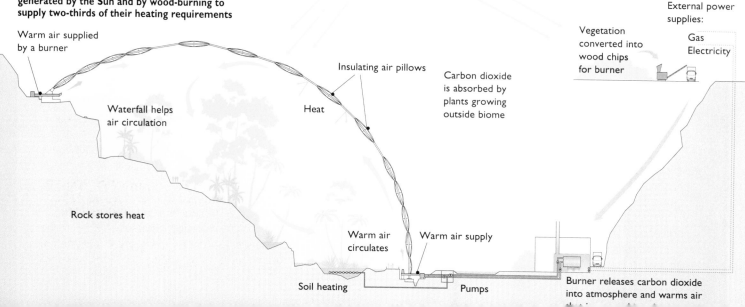

Warm air supplied by a burner

Waterfall helps air circulation

Insulating air pillows

Heat

Carbon dioxide is absorbed by plants growing outside biome

Vegetation converted into wood chips for burner

External power supplies:
Gas
Electricity

Rock stores heat

Warm air circulates

Warm air supply

Soil heating

Pumps

Burner releases carbon dioxide into atmosphere and warms air

NOWT SO QUEER AS FOLK

Even the most conventional Britons are a bit odd – discussing the weather, going potty about dogs and closing their pubs at 11pm. It is no wonder that the country has an abundance of eccentrics, from excruciating poets to spoof political candidates, food fanatics and reclusive scientists

BURIED DEEP in the British character is an admiration for people who cast off the shackles of convention. From the grotesque Miss Havisham in the Charles Dickens novel *Great Expectations* to the reclusive scientist Henry Cavendish, whose family founded the CAVENDISH LABORATORY, eccentrics in fiction and real life are something of a national obsession.

UPPER-CLASS TWITS

The aristocracy have the reputation of producing more than their share of oddballs, perhaps because they have the wealth and leisure to indulge their whims. The 5th duke of Portland built a palace beneath his ancestral home, which comprised more than 10 miles of passages and a railway to whisk meals from kitchen to dining room. On the rare occasions he emerged in public he wore a false beard and moustache, three frock coats and a 60 cm (2 ft) hat.

PLEASE YOURSELF

A key attribute of a true eccentric is a lack of concern for what other people think. At 26, 'Lady' Jane Lewson (c.1700-1816) lost her beloved husband. For the rest of her life she lived alone in Coldbath Square, London, never washing and refusing to part with any possessions. Her once-smart home fell into disrepair and

MAN WITH A MISSION Stanley Green, 'The Protein Man', conducted a single-handed dietary campaign in the West End of London for 25 years until his death in 1993

her clothes turned to rags. But far from succumbing to neglect, she lived on for 90 years.

A LIFE OUT OF THE ORDINARY

Britain's long history of tolerance has allowed alternative lifestyles to thrive. At his family seat of Longleat in Wiltshire the marquess of Bath (b.1932) has lived with more than 60 girlfriends, or 'wifelets', over the past 40 years in an arrangement more like that of a tribal chief than a member of the peerage. The marquess has otherwise led a normal life, conscientiously managing his estate and painting murals in his spare time.

BELIEVING IN YOURSELF

Many eccentrics are persuaded that they have a talent not evident to others. Margaret Cavendish, duchess of Newcastle (c.1624-74), posted servants on camp beds in an anteroom to take dictation during the night, should the poetic muse alight, undeterred by Samuel Pepys's verdict on her work: 'the most ridiculous thing that ever was wrote'.

No poet was more engagingly bad than The Great (William Topaz) McGonagall (c.1825-1902), whose doggerel earned him a cult following. He believed himself to be the greatest poet since Shakespeare, and a fine actor to boot. He made his stage debut as Macbeth, having paid to appear, but when attacked by Macduff, he refused to lie down and die. His work survives in libraries throughout Scotland.

PRICKING POMPOSITY

'Vote for insanity, you know it makes sense!' exhorted Screaming Lord Sutch (1940-99), founder of the Monster Raving Loony Party. At each election a handful

AFTER YOUR VOTE David Sutch (*centre front*) – a rock musician by trade – took political satire onto the streets in Monster Raving Loony Party election campaigns

of British voters do just that, allowing the party to sometimes hang onto its deposit. It now has imitators all over the world.

In 1997 it fielded a record 50 candidates and a manifesto that parodied the undeliverable pledges of serious parties by promising to tow Britain into the Mediterranean to improve the climate.

SERIOUS MONEY Audiences loved to bait The Great McGonagall at his readings, but the shrewd poet made money from his tormentors

From 'An Address to the New Tay Bridge'

*Beautiful new railway
  bridge of the silvery Tay,
With thy beautiful side-screens
  along your railway,
Which will be a great protection
  on a windy day,
So as the railway carriages won't
  be blown away,
And ought to cheer the hearts of
  the passengers night and day
As they are conveyed along thy
  beautiful railway . . .*

or 'biomes'. The structure will be supported by a light steel exoskeleton and covered with clear foil just 0.5 mm (0.02 in) thick, but strong enough to support the weight of a man.

Sent from botanical gardens across the world, many of the 10 000 species of plant that will populate the biomes are being grown and stored in nurseries and greenhouses nearby. The biomes will recreate two climates, humid tropics and warm temperate conditions, on 2.2 ha (5½ acres) of the 14 ha (34 acre) site.

Visitors to the project, when it opens in 2000, will find out about the world of plants through micro and time-lapse photography, and will be able to enter the biomes on walkways. The project also has a serious scientific purpose – to find new methods of conservation and sustainable farming that can be applied throughout the world.

EDINBURGH: *see p142*

EDWARD I

- **King 1272-1307**
- **1239-1307**

Civil war between HENRY III and his ambitious nobles led to the capture of his son, Edward, by Simon de Montfort, earl of Leicester, in the BARONS' WARS. Edward escaped in 1265, and set the stage for his own reign by defeating de Montfort in battle at Evesham.

Edward drew on his experience as a general soon after taking the throne with a campaign against the Welsh. After annexing Wales, he built a ring of massive CASTLES around the principality, including CAERNARFON and HARLECH.

The Scots also received some severe treatment. In 1296, after a victorious campaign, Edward removed the 'stone of destiny', on which Scottish kings were crowned. It was taken from SCONE near Perth and placed in Westminster Abbey. The ensuing wars dragged on for nearly 20 years, Edward eventually dying on his way to do battle with the newly crowned ROBERT BRUCE.

Edward's tomb in Westminster Abbey is inscribed 'Hammer of the Scots', but his more lasting achievements were his administrative and legal reforms. These included the introduction of compulsory trial by jury for criminal cases, which earned him the nickname 'English Justinian', after the 5th-century AD Byzantine emperor and lawgiver.

EDWARD II

- **King 1307-27** • **1284-1327**

The exclusive friendships of Edward II cost him the respect of both the court and his people. On his accession, he appointed his favourite – and probably homosexual lover – Piers Gaveston as earl of Cornwall, giving him considerable influence at court. Edward's furious nobles forced him to banish Gaveston but the king appointed his friend regent of Ireland and recalled him in 1312 – an event so unpopular that it provoked Gaveston's murder and a civil war. Edward's fortunes slumped further after his defeat by ROBERT BRUCE at BANNOCKBURN in 1314. In the disarray that followed, his cousin, Thomas of Lancaster, assumed government, campaigning against the king's new favourite, Hugh le Despenser. Lancaster was defeated in 1322 and Edward revenged Gaveston's murder with widespread executions.

> Edward II's favourite courtier, Piers Gaveston, created nicknames for the king's barons. The earl of Warwick became 'The Black Hound of Arden', the earl of Lincoln, 'Burstbelly', and the earl of Gloucester, 'Horeson'

Four years later his long-suffering queen, Isabella, returned from a visit to France, and with her lover, Roger Mortimer, deposed her husband. Edward was forced to abdicate in favour of his son. He died in captivity at BERKELEY CASTLE, reputedly murdered with a hot poker by order of his captors.

EDWARD III

- **King 1327-77** • **1312-77**

When Edward III inherited the throne of England, his mother Queen Isabella and her lover, Roger Mortimer, controlled the country. Three years later, the 18-year-old king imprisoned his mother and had Mortimer hanged to avenge the death of his father, EDWARD II.

Edward's claims on French territory led to the start of the HUNDRED YEARS' WAR in 1337. He extended the conflict in 1340 when he assumed the title 'King of France'. Victories at Sluys (1340), CRÉCY (1346) and Poitiers (1356) – where his son, EDWARD THE BLACK PRINCE, captured King John of France – led Edward to appear the epitome of European chivalry. Tournaments became popular and the Order of the Garter was introduced (c.1348).

The war with France dominated Edward's reign. Later, as the king aged and the Black Prince fell ill, power passed to Edward's younger son, JOHN OF GAUNT.

KING OF CHIVALRY
Edward III's tomb in Westminster Abbey is adorned with a striking bronze effigy of the ruler

EDWARD IV

- **King 1461-70 and 1471-83** • **1442-83**

Edward IV was born into a turbulent age. The HUNDRED YEARS' WAR continued to rage with France, while at home the WARS OF THE ROSES saw the rival houses of York and Lancaster bitterly contesting the English throne.

Edward revenged the death of his father, Richard of York, by defeating the Lancastrian HENRY VI at the Battle of Mortimer's Cross in 1461. With the backing of a powerful nobleman, the earl of Warwick, he was crowned king.

But Warwick's support did not last. Edward's marriage to a commoner, Elizabeth Woodville, enraged the earl, who with the aid of Henry VI's wife, Queen Margaret, deposed Edward in 1470 and restored Henry to the throne. Edward fought back and the following year Warwick died in battle. A month later, Edward defeated Margaret at Tewkesbury and killed her son, Prince Edward, delivering the final blow to the Lancastrian cause.

During his second reign Edward ended the other great conflict of the age and made peace with France. He died suddenly at the age of 40 but his widow lived to see their daughter marry the Lancastrian king HENRY VII.

SCOTLAND'S HUB

Edinburgh is one of Europe's most dramatic cities. The Georgian New Town is spread like a chequered tablecloth beneath the massif of the Castle Rock, and the medieval streets bear the marks of centuries of turbulent history

GILDED SIGN A 'gled' (kite) marks Gladstone's Land, a tall 17th-century merchant's house

ANCIENT TURRETS Now a museum, Canongate Tolbooth along the Royal Mile was built as a town hall in 1591

SCOTLAND'S CAPITAL is sited above the Firth of Forth, its buildings clinging to volcanic crags and straddling deep glacial canyons. Castle Rock has been occupied since the Bronze Age and was already called 'Dun Edin' in the 7th century when it was an Anglo-Saxon stronghold on the northern frontier of Northumbria.

The Scots took possession during the 10th century. By 1093 Edinburgh was a royal fortress, which was besieged, battered and rebuilt over successive centuries as Scotland fought to maintain its independence. Despite frequent English raids, the city expanded and by 1500 was the chief seat of the Scottish parliament. But in 1544 almost every building was burnt down by the

Earl of Hertford's army in the 'rough wooing' that followed Scotland's refusal to ratify the marriage between the infant Mary, Queen of Scots and Edward, only son of Henry VIII.

POWER RECEDES BUT THE CITY EXPANDS

The royal court left Edinburgh when Mary's son James VI became James I of England in 1603. Its parliament closed under the Act of Union a century later. But the city continued to flourish until its bustling High Street stretched down the ROYAL MILE from the castle to the palace of HOLYROODHOUSE, magnificently rebuilt in 1671-80.

With any further growth restricted by the old town's sheer topography and by a deep loch to the north, some tenements reached heights of 14 storeys and over-crowding was endemic. (The refurbished merchant's house Gladstone's Land, now a museum, dates from this time.) It was only when the loch was drained in the 1760s that the city could at last expand.

ELEGANCE AND STYLE

The New Town that developed over the next 60 years is a magnificent example of Georgian town planning, with a grid of beautifully proportioned terraces and squares. It is still the city's most exclusive residential area, while also housing offices and smart shops.

The north side of Princes Street, the main thoroughfare, is a hotchpotch of modern buildings but their plate-glass windows face one of the finest urban views in Europe – the clifftop castle and the jagged Gothic skyline of the Old Town. Bridges span the empty basin of the North Loch, now laid out as gardens to reach the Royal Mile and Edinburgh's historic heart, a labyrinth of

THE PREACHER'S HOME John Knox, leader of the Scottish Reformation, lived here on the High Street in the 1560s. His house is now a museum dedicated to his life and work

HEART OF MIDLOTHIAN
The heart marks the site of the Old Tolbooth jail

HOLYROODHOUSE The 17th-century royal palace is the British monarch's official residence in Scotland

cobbled lanes, steep twisting steps and secret, unexpected yards that, despite much 19th-century rebuilding, retain a dark medieval atmosphere.

FACING THE FUTURE

The city dubbed 'Auld Reekie' for the smoke that hung over it in the 19th century has had its sooty stonework cleaned. Today its prosperity is based on service industries. It is a banking and financial centre and houses Scotland's highest courts and government departments.

More than 30000 students attend the city's three universities and each summer visitors and performers from around the world make the Edinburgh Festival an international event and further boost the city's lucrative tourist trade. Its many galleries include the unique Museum of Scotland opened in 1998 – six galleries displaying 10000 artefacts that illustrate the story of the country and its people.

Most significant in Edinburgh's future is the Scotland Act 1998, which has paved the way for a devolved Scottish parliament in the year 2000 to be sited in a new government building beside the palace of Holyroodhouse.

ROYAL FORTRESS The walls enclose St Margaret's Chapel and the Renaissance palace where James I of England was born

THE EDINBURGH FESTIVALS

Every summer, the rhythm of the city undergoes a dramatic change. Visitors arrive in their thousands for a series of cultural events that pack the city's theatres, church halls, pubs and basements and spill exuberantly into squares and streets. These start with jazz and blues in July and continue with film, fringe theatre, books, art exhibitions and the world-renowned Edinburgh International Festival.

The events boost the city's cultural profile and bring in considerable revenue; in 1995-6 they generated £97.5 million.

FIRE MAN A juggler performs above the Royal Scottish Academy

PARTY ANIMAL The festival displays its light-hearted carnival atmosphere

MILITARY TATTOO Pipe bands from all over the world perform the tattoo on the Castle Esplanade every evening during the festival

EDWARD VI

• King 1547-53 • 1537-53

The delicate and studious Edward VI was the only son of HENRY VIII and just ten years old when he inherited the throne. For his short reign he was a pawn in a power game between his uncle, Edward Seymour, duke of Somerset, and John Dudley, duke of Northumberland.

Edward was too young to rule, so Somerset governed in his place, as Lord Protector. In 1549, after an uprising by 20 000 Norfolk peasants, Somerset was ousted by Northumberland and in 1552 he was executed. The king, manipulated even on his deathbed, altered the succession from his Catholic half-sister MARY to Lady Jane GREY, the Protestant daughter-in-law of Northumberland.

Despite religious turmoil, Edward's reign was a time of consolidation for the CHURCH OF ENGLAND. In particular, a creed and service structure were laid down in Thomas CRANMER's Book of Common Prayer (1549).

EDWARD VII

• King 1901-10 • 1841-1910

Queen Victoria's eldest son spent most of his adult life waiting to become king, and in disgrace with his mother for his frivolous behaviour. Victoria, believing that stress caused by Edward's scandalous love affair with an actress had contributed to Prince Albert's death in 1861, excluded her heir from state affairs. Instead he spent his time breeding racehorses, gambling in resorts around Europe, and pursuing numerous

affairs, even after his marriage to Princess Alexandra of Denmark in 1863. He was later cited in two divorce cases.

Edward was almost 60 when he took the throne, and his flamboyant style was a welcome contrast to his mother's severity. Abroad, his flair for languages and family ties with European royalty were a useful boost to British relations, particularly with France and Russia.

EDWARD VIII

• King 1936 • 1894-1972

The eldest son of George V gave up the throne after only 11 months to marry the woman he loved. Yet Edward had been groomed to rule. His public investiture as Prince of Wales at Caernarfon Castle in 1911 was the first since 1301.

After First World War service he toured the British Empire and joined Europe's high society. A trendsetting dresser, Edward popularised the trouser zip-fly and the 'Prince of Wales check'. Then, at a party in 1931, he met the divorced American socialite Wallis Simpson and they began an affair. When Edward became king he planned to marry her, but the prime minister,

OUT OF HARM'S WAY The former Edward VIII and his bride Wallis Simpson – Duke and Duchess of Windsor – spent the war years at Government House in the Bahamas, where he was appointed governor

Stanley BALDWIN, presented him with a stark choice: the Crown or Mrs Simpson.

Edward abdicated in December 1936 and the next year the couple married, living abroad for the rest of their lives, finally settling in Paris. A visit to Adolf Hitler in 1937 and suspicion of Edward's sympathies with aspects of Nazism have led some to believe that there may have been collusion with Germany in 1940-1.

EDWARDIAN STYLE

During Edward VII's reign and for a few years after – 'the long Edwardian summer' – Britain presided over a vast empire in a mood of self-confidence, ease and elegance, reflected in styles of dress, design and interior decoration.

It was the golden age of country house parties. At POLESDEN LACEY, the interiors were opulently reworked by the designers of London's RITZ HOTEL, with gilt-framed mirrors, crystal chandeliers and copious swags, pelmets and tassels. Further down the social scale the expanding middle classes moved into large semidetached suburban villas decorated with freizes, balustrades and columns. But the ultimate in Edwardian luxury was the ocean liner, a floating hotel for the wealthy. The sinking of the White Star company's palatial but ill-equipped TITANIC in 1912, and the horrors of the First World War, marked the end of a complacent era.

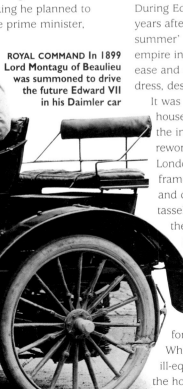

ROYAL COMMAND In 1899 Lord Montagu of Beaulieu was summoned to drive the future Edward VII in his Daimler car

Gareth EDWARDS

• Rugby player • b.1947; MBE 1975

Few rugby players have matched the speed, strength, vision, courage and all-round ability of Gareth Edwards, who could play at scrum-half, full-back or centre. Edwards was 19 when he made his debut for Wales in 1967, 20 when he became his country's youngest captain. He was a constant presence throughout Welsh rugby's golden age of the 1970s, playing in 53 consecutive internationals.

Edwards was a key figure in the British Lions victories in New Zealand (1971) and South Africa (1974). His try for the Barbarians against New Zealand in 1973 is often described as the finest ever seen in Britain, although others single out his solo effort against Scotland the previous year, when he dashed from his own 25 yard line to score.

EDWARD THE BLACK PRINCE

• Eldest son of Edward III • 1330-76

At the age of 16, Edward, Prince of Wales and heir to the throne, led one wing of the English army at the Battle of CRÉCY 'to win his spurs'. It may have been here that he first wore the black armour that gave him his sobriquet.

Edward became an outstanding military leader. At Poitiers in 1356 he defeated a much larger French army and took the French king prisoner. His chivalry became legendary when he then served the king supper on bended knee.

War with France flared again in 1369 and the next year Edward took the town of Limoges, whose violent sacking tarnished his noble image. Illness forced him back to England, where he took no further part in public life. He died shortly before his father; his young son became RICHARD II the following year, guided by Edward's younger brother, John of Gaunt.

EDWARD THE CONFESSOR

• King 1042-66 • c.1003-66; canonised 1161

Christian piety was responsible for Edward's nickname, his founding of Westminster Abbey and his eventual canonisation. It may also have helped to bring about the Norman Conquest, for

PRETTY AS A THOUSAND PICTURES The siting of Eilean Donan Castle on a tiny island where three lochs meet is probably the most romantic in Britain, but it was built by the Scottish king Alexander II in a strategic position and for a practical purpose: to keep out marauding Danes

an apparently celibate marriage left him without an heir at a time of confused and competing claims to the throne.

The son of Ethelred II and a Norman aristocratic mother, Edward represented both English and French interests and maintained a precarious hold on power despite numerous threats. Among the many thorns in his side was his father-in-law, Earl Godwin of Wessex, who staged a rebellion in 1051 and was briefly exiled before returning by force to become one of the most powerful men in the land.

On his deathbed Edward bequeathed the succession to Godwin's son, Harold, possibly going back on an earlier promise he had made to William, Duke of Normandy, soon to be WILLIAM I, the Conqueror, – a change of heart that led to the fateful events of 1066.

EILEAN DONAN CASTLE

• Highland (p.497 B3)
• Built 13th century, restored 1932

Familiar from countless calendars and shortbread tins, the crenellated tower house of Eilean Donan stands in lonely splendour on a rocky islet on Scotland's deeply indented west coast. A stone causeway and a three-arched bridge link the islet to the mainland.

In 1719 Eilean Donan, garrisoned by Spanish mercenaries fighting for the JACOBITE cause, was no match for the pounding guns of the English warship *Worcester*. The castle stood in ruins until it was restored between 1912 and 1932

by descendants of the Macrae family, who were once its hereditary constables.

Inside the 4.5 m (14 ft) thick walls are a banqueting hall with Jacobite relics, including drinking cups made from cannon balls, and soldiers' quarters with a spectacular curved stone ceiling and paintings of the feuding Highland clans.

EISTEDDFOD

The Welsh word *eisteddfod*, meaning 'a sitting', is used for the many competitive festivals of arts, crafts, music and poetry that celebrate the language and culture of Wales. They date back to 1176 when Lord Rhys is said to have held a gathering of poets and musicians at his castle in Cardigan. A chair from the lord's table was awarded to the best poet and musician, and winning artists today are still crowned in the 'bardic chair'.

The week-long National Eisteddfod, first held in 1880, takes place each August, alternating between venues in north and south Wales. Up to 170 000 visitors watch 6000 people take part in 200 events, from traditional choir and poetry recital competitions to more modern additions such as brass bands and disco dancing.

The International Musical Eisteddfod, held since 1947 each July at Llangollen in north Wales, attracts more than 6500 competitors from around the world. Events include both folk dancing and choral contests such as the Choir of the World Competition.

ELEANOR CROSSES

England's most notable act of devotion is marked by three tall, delicately carved medieval crosses at Geddington, Northampton and Waltham Cross. They alone remain from 12 crosses erected in 1290 by the grief-stricken Edward I to mark the final journey between Lincoln and London of his wife Eleanor of Castile, who had died of a fever. Edward and Eleanor were matched for political reasons, and yet they fell in love. Eleanor even joined her husband on Crusade in 1270 and is said to have sucked poison from a wound to save his life.

The final cross was raised in London at Charing Cross, where a replica now stands outside the railway station. Eleanor's tomb is in Westminster Abbey.

ELECTORAL REFORM

In the 1997 general election, the Liberal Democrats won 17 per cent of the vote but only 7 per cent of the seats in parliament. Labour took 63 per cent of the seats with just 44 per cent of the vote. This imbalance is part of the British 'first past the post' or 'simple majority' electoral system; no other Western European country uses it to elect a central government.

It has long been argued that a closer relationship is needed between share of vote and number of seats won, and that there should be electoral reform to bring about proportional representation, or PR.

The Electoral Reform Society was founded in 1884 to campaign for PR, and soon gained an additional role as independent scrutineer of elections.

PR was introduced for local elections in Northern Ireland in 1973, and the elections to the new Scottish parliament and Welsh assembly in 1999 used a system that included a form of PR. In 1997, the new Labour government announced it would hold a referendum on a new voting system for elections to the House of Commons.

Edward ELGAR

• Composer
• 1857-1934; kt 1904; OM 1911; bt 1931

Success eluded Edward Elgar as a young man. His father's music shop in Worcester gave him the means to teach himself to play various instruments, and in his 20s and 30s he gave violin lessons and played the organ as he struggled to achieve recognition for his compositions.

Elgar was 41 when the *Enigma Variations*, a set of musical portraits of his friends, made him the first British-born composer of international stature since Henry PURCELL 200 years earlier. The success was followed in 1900 with *The Dream of Gerontius*, an oratorio through which he expressed his deep religious convictions.

Elgar's music expressed the mood of turn-of-the-century Britain: outwardly confident yet inwardly perplexed by a growing sense of being out of step with the 20th century. Deeply depressed by the slaughter of the First World War, he wrote his most profoundly elegiac work, the Cello Concerto, in 1919.

A year later the composer's wife died and with her much of his inspiration. Of his unfinished third symphony Elgar said 'Don't let them tinker with it'. For more than 60 years he had his way but in 1998 the composer Anthony Payne completed it to great acclaim.

ELGIN MARBLES

The exquisitely carved Elgin Marbles – part of a frieze from the Parthenon in Athens – have been one of the prime attractions of the British Museum since 1816. Greece would like them returned.

The diplomat Lord Elgin removed the marbles in 1801, and later sold them to the British nation for £35000, much less than it cost him to transport them home. The frieze had been damaged when the Venetians bombarded the Parthenon in 1687, and Elgin, an art lover, was anxious to save the marbles from further damage.

The Greeks regard the marbles as plundered booty, which belongs to Athens. Successive British governments have steadfastly refused to return them, fearing that it would open the door to demands that would denude the nation's museums of their finest treasures.

CLASSICAL MODEL Marble panels from the 5th-century BC Greek Elgin Marbles, now held at the British Museum, display horsemen at a festival in honour of the goddess Athena

ENGLAND REBORN

Elizabeth I ruled for 45 years, from 1558 to 1603. In this time England evolved from a country on the periphery of Europe, still medieval in outlook and riven by religious and political struggles, into a confident nation that defeated mighty Spain and embarked on an age of exploration that would one day give birth to an empire

NEW HOPE DAWNS Elizabeth I was 25 years old when she was crowned Queen of England, succeeding her half-sister Mary I, who had once imprisoned her in the Tower of London. Elizabeth had less foreign blood than any previous monarch

WHEN ELIZABETH I came to the throne, she was versed in languages, history, mathematics, geography, science, music and religion. With a keen political instinct she chose wise advisers, including William Cecil, later Lord Burghley, who became her chief minister, followed by his son Robert, the first Lord Salisbury. Through them and her powerful personality Elizabeth unified and inspired the country, creating a strong sense of national identity.

SPIRITUAL AND TEMPORAL

Elizabeth established Anglicanism, with *The Thirty-nine Articles*, agreed in 1571, its statement of faith, as the national religion. She made churchgoing compulsory and ordered services to be conducted in English.

The economy grew, mixing state control with free enterprise, and even those at the bottom of the heap fared better, helped by the POOR LAW of 1601. A more flexible class structure gave wage-earners, businessmen and yeoman farmers a say in decision making.

ALL THE WORLD'S A STAGE

The theatre was the great cultural contribution of the Elizabethan Age, financed by enthusiastic noblemen. In 1576 the actor James Burbage built the first playhouse, followed 22 years later by the GLOBE, where William SHAKESPEARE acted and for which he wrote many plays.

RULING THE WAVES

Seafaring heroes such as Francis DRAKE, Martin Frobisher and Richard Grenville harried the Spanish, plundered treasure and, with the aid of the new mariner's compass, charted the oceans.

England itself was better mapped than ever before: between 1574 and 1579 Christopher Saxton produced 34 county maps and the first general map of Britain.

QUEEN OF THE WORLD In the Armada portrait of 1588 Elizabeth's hand rests on a globe, signifying England's new imperial ambitions, led by its seafaring might

A GREATER BRITAIN

Elizabeth secured Britain's position in Europe through treaties and alliances, and made capital out of defeating imperial Spain. Her speech before the approach of the SPANISH ARMADA inspired the nation. 'I have the body of a weak and feeble woman,' Elizabeth declared, 'but the heart and stomach of a king.'

WISE VIRGIN Two paintings of 1600 depict Elizabeth as a figure of worship. In the portrait (*above, left*), the serpent on her sleeve symbolises wisdom, the eyes and ears on her cloak her all-seeing and all-hearing political skill, and the loose hair and low-cut bodice her virgin status. A street scene (*below*) shows Elizabeth, in her favourite silver and white, carried in procession by her courtiers

ELSTREE STUDIOS

• Hertfordshire (p.495 G4)

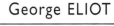

Films have been made at Elstree since cinema began. Neptune Studios opened there in 1914, choosing the rural location for its proximity to London. They closed in 1917 but were followed by a sprawling complex of studios that became known as the British Hollywood. In 1929 Alfred HITCHCOCK directed *Blackmail*, the first British 'talkie', there. At its peak in the 1930s, thrillers, comedies and musicals poured out of Elstree at the rate of about 15 a year.

ACTION! In 1927 the BIP studios at Elstree were as big as any in Hollywood

After the Second World War, Elstree continued to produce such British classics as the wartime adventure *The Dam Busters* (1954). It also drew American stars such as Gregory Peck (*Moby Dick*, 1954)

CULT TV
The 1960s *Avengers* series was produced at Elstree, where long-running TV programmes such as *Top of the Pops* and *EastEnders* are still made

and Cary Grant (*Indiscreet*, 1957). But when US investment dried up in the late 1960s Elstree struggled, although one American director, Stanley Kubrick, kept the studios busy with the epic *2001: A Space Odyssey* (1968).

In 1976 another American director, George Lucas, chose Elstree for *Star Wars*. With its sequels it became the world's most successful series, attracting American money to the three surviving studio lots for blockbusters such as *Who Framed Roger Rabbit?* (1987).

The runaway success of the British low-budget comedy *The Full Monty* (1997), shot at Elstree, signalled another revival in the studios' fortunes.

MAKING A BLOCKBUSTER
Steven Spielberg directs *Indiana Jones and the Temple of Doom* (1984), the second of the Indiana Jones trilogy, which all used the vast stages of Elstree

George ELIOT

• Pseudonym of Mary Ann Evans
• Novelist • 1819-80

George Eliot was the first English novelist to make a critical female consciousness the centre of her fiction. Her novel *Middlemarch* (1871-2), regarded by some as the finest English novel of the 19th century, is a complex story of provincial Victorian society, in which the heroine Dorothea learns the hard way the sacrifices that marriage can demand and the dangers of self-deception and over-idealism. *The Mill on the Floss* (1860) evokes the freshness of the novelist's own rural childhood.

A woman of formidable intellect, and already well known as a journalist and translator, George Eliot waited until the age of 38 before she turned to fiction, under the stimulus of the critic

TRUE TO HERSELF Ge[] Eliot's novels are vivi[] and realistic portraits provincial Victorian li[]

G.H. Lewes – her partner from 1853 until his death in 1878.

T.S. ELIOT

• Poet, critic and dramatist
• 1888-1965; OM 1948

In 1915 poetry woke up with a shock to find itself part of the modern world. The poet responsible was Thomas Stearns Eliot whose 'Lovesong of J. Alfred Prufrock' opened unromantically:

Let us go then, you and I,
When the evening is spread out against the sky
Like a patient etherised upon a table

Eliot, American-born but resident in Britain, created a second sensation with his 1922 masterpiece *The Waste Land* – a stark analysis of modern Europe, filled with unflattering comparisons to the great cultures of the past.

In 1927 Eliot took British citizenship and joined the Church of England. His faith heavily influenced the two major works of his later years, *Ash Wednesday* (1930) and *Four Quartets* (1935-42). As a critic, Eliot brought about a revaluation of the METAPHYSICAL POETS and the Jacobean dramatists, and he revived verse-drama with plays such as *Murder in the Cathedral* (1935). In 1948 he was awarded the Nobel prize for literature.

Queen ELIZABETH, the Queen Mother

- **Queen to George VI 1936-52** • **b.1900**

As a debutante in 1920 Lady Elizabeth Bowes-Lyon, daughter of the 14th earl of Strathmore and Kinghorne, met the younger son of George V. They were married three years later and had two daughters, Elizabeth and Margaret Rose.

After EDWARD VIII abdicated in 1936 Elizabeth's husband took the throne as GEORGE VI and she devoted herself to restoring the nation's confidence in the monarchy. Her Second World War visits to bomb sites won the enduring affection of the public. She took the title Queen Mother on the accession in 1952 of her daughter ELIZABETH II.

ELIZABETH I: *see page 147*

ELIZABETH II

- **Queen 1952-** • **b.1926**

When Edward VIII abdicated, his ten-year-old niece, Princess Elizabeth of York, became heiress presumptive. In 1947 she married Philip Mountbatten (*see* Prince PHILIP), and five years later became queen on the death of her father, GEORGE VI. She has four children: CHARLES, Anne, Andrew and Edward.

Elizabeth II has quietly updated the monarchy. Abroad, she has played an active role in transforming the Empire into a Commonwealth of equal states. At home, she has modernised the royal finances by agreeing to pay income tax, and has allowed the media unprecedented access to her family.

At a time of general decline in deference, criticism of the monarchy and of individuals within the royal family has seldom extended to the queen herself. She remains respected as a model constitutional monarch – hard-working, professional and dignified – who has been at the heart of British life through the governments of ten prime ministers.

ELSTREE STUDIOS:

see opposite page

ELY

- **Cambridgeshire (p.495 H3)**
- **Pop. 10 330**

Every approach to the market centre of Ely – over flat, waterlogged fenland – is dominated by its cathedral, built mostly in the 12th century. Around it are several well-preserved monastic buildings including the remains of the monks' guest hall and infirmary, and the 14th-century gatehouse.

Until the Fens were drained in the 1630s, Ely stood on an island – named after its plentiful eels – and could be reached only by boat or along narrow causeways. In 1070 the Anglo-Saxon rebel HEREWARD THE WAKE held off the Normans here, until betrayed by the monks.

EMANCIPATION ACT

Until the 1829 Act for the Relief of His Majesty's Roman Catholic Subjects, Catholics were barred from many aspects of British public life. Among other handicaps, they could not become an MP, a member of a lay corporation, or a Crown official.

Attempts at reform had been made since 1800 when, after the Act of Union between Britain and Ireland, William PITT tried to relax restrictions on Catholics, only to be thwarted by George III.

In 1828 the Irish politician Daniel O'Connell was elected as MP for County Clare. The law prevented him from taking his seat, but the Duke of WELLINGTON, then prime minister, saw that only the repeal of anti-Catholic laws would prevent civil war in Ireland, and the following year the Emancipation Act was passed. Some barriers remain. A Catholic cannot be lord chancellor, king or queen, or marry the monarch.

REACHING FOR HEAVEN The 14th-century octagonal tower of Ely cathedral soars 52 m (170 ft) above the nave and weighs 400 tons

ENCYCLOPAEDIA BRITANNICA

The world's largest English-language encyclopedia was conceived in 1768 by three Edinburgh printers – Andrew Bell, Colin Macfarquhar and William Smellie.

The first edition of the *Encyclopaedia Britannica* was published in 1771 and ran to three volumes and 2391 pages. It cost £12 to buy and attempted to replicate in English the achievement of the *Encyclopédie* compiled by the French philosopher Denis Diderot – himself inspired by the 1728 *Cyclopaedia* of the Englishman Ephraim Chambers.

The *Britannica* was bought by an American publisher in 1920 and has been published in the United States ever since. In 1994 it became the first encyclopedia available on the Internet.

THE LAST OF THEIR LINE?

Modern farming practices, industrial and urban development and the destruction of native woodland all threaten the survival of Britain's habitats and the plants and animals that live in them. Knowing which species are endangered is the first step to rescuing and protecting them

SOME SPECIES thrive in man-made habitats, such as herring gulls, which nest on the artificial 'cliffs' of city buildings. Others are increasingly threatened by humans.

Destroying habitats for building or industry is the main threat, but pollution by sewage, fertilisers and acid rain, and oil spills at sea are also damaging. Fishing, farming, illegal egg-collecting and hunting, and the introduction of new, non-native species can upset entire food chains.

Worldwide, there are around 5000 species listed as 'endangered' by the World Conservation Union. A species is included if there are fewer than 250 individuals in the wild (or 2500 in a single site), if it exists in only one place or if its population has halved in ten years or three generations. It is illegal to kill or harm an endangered species.

More than 100 British species became extinct during the 20th century. They include the greater mouse-eared bat, the short-haired bumble bee and plants such as hairy spurge and summer lady's tresses.

Conservation bodies such as English Nature work to prevent further species from disappearing. Creating nature reserves or SITES OF SPECIAL SCIENTIFIC INTEREST (SSSIs) helps to protect entire habitats. The species featured here highlight major threatened habitats, the reasons for declining numbers and some conservation success stories.

BITTERN *One of Britain's rarest birds, this secretive relative of the heron breeds in large reed beds. It has been threatened since the late 19th century by the destruction of its only habitat. The drainage of reed beds, use of pesticides and the effects of severe winters have reduced the bittern population to around 20 pairs*

RED SQUIRREL *The felling of mature native forests has led to a decline in red squirrels in the 20th century: only about 160 000 remain, mostly in Scotland and Northern Ireland. Their more adaptable, non-native grey cousins have helped to displace reds from their natural habitat*

DORMOUSE *The fragmentation of broad-leaved woodland has caused a drop in the numbers of this golden-brown rodent. It is small and shy, and lives in dense undergrowth, so its population is difficult to track, although a recovery programme was started by English Nature in 1992. This includes keeping a studbook to avoid inbreeding in captivity and is already showing success after release of dormice into the wild. They are now appearing in Cheshire woodlands, for instance, after an absence of nearly 100 years*

HIGH BROWN FRITILLARY *A 90 per cent decline in 50 years has made the high brown Britain's most threatened butterfly. It lives in open sunny areas with violets for caterpillars to eat and bracken for adults to cling to. Conservationists aim to re-establish the butterfly by 2005 at ten of the sites from which it has disappeared*

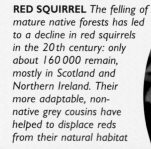

SKYLARK *The skylark's joyous song is increasingly a thing of the past in Britain. Numbers have more than halved in 25 years. A shift to autumn-sown crops has meant that stubble fields no longer supply winter food, and cutting spring grass for silage can destroy eggs and chicks, or expose them to predators*

LADY'S SLIPPER ORCHID *With the largest flowers of any orchid in northern Europe, the lady's slipper was a victim of its own beauty. It was once found scattered across northern England, but was devastated by intensive grazing of farm animals and theft. For 50 years just one lone plant survived in the wild, but the species is now becoming more widespread with the help of a reintroduction programme*

STAG BEETLE *The male stag beetle, Britain's second-biggest insect, is about the same size and weight as its smallest mammal, the pygmy shrew. Its huge jaws, shaped like a stag's antlers, give the insect its name. Larvae feed on dead wood for up to four years before reaching maturity. The species has become endangered by the clearance – in the name of tidiness – of rotting wood from forests*

SCOTTISH WILD CAT *Once found over much of Britain, the wild cat was extinct in England and Wales by the end of the 19th century, owing to persecution and habitat loss. By the early 1900s it had retreated north of Scotland's Great Glen. Since then it has begun to spread southwards in Scotland but is still threatened by shooting and trapping, as well as by crossbreeding with domestic cats*

GREAT CRESTED NEWT *The largest of the three British species of newts, the great crested is also the rarest, although Britain is one of its main strongholds in Europe. The newt population is threatened by the drainage and pollution of ponds. The increased use of pesticides has also destroyed many of the insects, worms and tadpoles that are the newt's main source of food*

ENGLAND

• **Area 50 871 sq miles**   • **Pop. 49.3 million**

Separated from the continent of Europe by the North Sea and English Channel, but sharing frontiers with Wales and Scotland, England has scarcely altered its boundaries in a thousand years.

The identity of southern England took shape in the centuries that followed the collapse of Roman rule. Germanic Anglo-Saxon tribes settled in England in the 5th and 6th centuries, gradually driving the native Celts into the west and north.

The Anglo-Saxon kingdoms had similar languages and culture but little sense of political unity. When Offa was recognised in 757 as overlord of England, other rival dynasties were merely paying lip service to the temporary supremacy of Mercia. Northumbria, north of the River Tees, was still independent, and Cornwall a free Celtic stronghold.

ONE ENGLISH NATION

It took raids by Norsemen and invasion by the Danes in the 9th and 10th centuries to create a sense of Anglo-Saxon solidarity, and the military and diplomatic skill of ALFRED THE GREAT to build a kingdom free of Danish control.

Nonetheless it was a Danish king, CANUTE, who in 1016 first united all of England, and a Norman, WILLIAM the Conqueror, who put an end to the dynastic squabbles of the Anglo-Danish royal house. After the Conquest England remained an independent state, but was governed by a Norman aristocracy that took generations to assimilate.

FORGING A UNITED KINGDOM

England was politically united with Wales in 1536 and with Scotland in 1707. Ireland was part of the Union from 1801 but in 1921 the south broke away, leaving today's political configuration.

ENGLISH CHANNEL

At its narrowest point, the Strait of Dover, the English Channel is 20½ miles wide. Now, it is the world's busiest sea passage, used by some 350 ships each day. The 350 mile stretch of the Atlantic Ocean sweeps around Britain's south coast, from Land's End towards Margate.

The Channel formed around 7500 years ago at the end of the last Ice Age, when melting ice cut Britain off from mainland Europe. Like a moat, it has defended Britain against many invasion attempts, including halting the Germans during the Second World War.

Crossing the Channel in new, unusual or faster ways is a popular challenge. The French aviator Louis Blériot was the first to fly across, in 1909, and swimmers have pitted themselves against the currents for more than a hundred years (*see* CHANNEL SWIMMING). When the CHANNEL TUNNEL opened in 1994 it became possible to go from Folkestone to France without leaving dry land.

ENGLISH HERITAGE

• **Founded 1983**

Protecting buildings and promoting the public's enjoyment and understanding of historic sites are key aspects of the work of English Heritage. Since its birth it has actively preserved hundreds of locations throughout Britain – from HADRIAN'S WALL to pub interiors and the wrought ironwork of Liverpool's Canning Street. It advises the government and manages

continued on page 153

WATER BEETLE In 1961 two Britons left Calais in a propeller-driven Volkswagen to cross the English Channel. After 10 miles, the crew were rescued as waves swamped the car

WORDS, WORDS, WORDS

English has the largest vocabulary of any language and is the international language of trade, science, technology, scholarship and communications. More than 300 million people worldwide speak it as their mother tongue and as many again as a second language

THE PRE-EMINENCE of English is not a matter of any natural superiority but of British power in the 19th century and American in the 20th. Even so, English does have certain natural advantages as an international language: it uses few inflected endings,

ANCIENT ALPHABET For many centuries English retained some letters from the runic Germanic alphabet, including the thorn, written 'þ' and sounded 'th'. It gradually came to look like 'y' though until the 19th century educated people knew that signs such as that below read 'the' not 'ye'. The 8th-century Ruthwell Cross in Scotland (*background, right*) bears a fragment of the poem, 'The Dream of the Rood', inscribed in the old runic alphabet

words such as 'egg', 'sky' and 'law', and even grammatical words such as 'they'.

FRENCH REFINEMENTS
That we refer to the Norman 'conquest' rather than a term derived from the Old English 'winwan' shows the influence of French on Middle English – the form of the language between 1100 and 1500.

Anglo-Norman, the French dialect of the new aristocracy, brought words to do with power and government, such as 'duke', 'judge' and 'prison'; and terms connected with refined life, such as 'curtain', 'plate' and 'poet' – as well as the more prosaic 'carry', 'face' and 'table'.

As the language of learning, Latin contributed formal and abstract words such as 'conspiracy' and 'transport'.

Ye Old Coffee Shoppe

making its grammar relatively easy to learn, and it has a wide and flexible vocabulary suitable for many uses – the result of a long mongrel inheritance.

FOREIGN ROOTS
At heart English is a Germanic language, related to German, Dutch and Scandinavian tongues. Its ancestor was the language of the Anglo-Saxon invaders of the 5th and 6th centuries. Core words such as 'he', 'is' and 'mother' go back to these beginnings.

English often has three near synonyms for one idea, a plain word from Old English or Old Norse, an elegant one from French and a more formal term from Latin roots: do – perform – perpetrate belly – stomach – abdomen take – seize – confiscate go – depart – vacate

But Old English, or Anglo-Saxon, the form used up to around 1100, now looks like a totally foreign language. Much of its vocabulary has been replaced by words borrowed from other languages, particularly French and Latin.

With the coming of Christianity in the 6th century the Anglo-Saxons adapted words from Latin such as 'candle' and 'tunic'. And from the Old Norse of the Vikings came everyday

NEW WORLDS, NEW WORDS
In the 15th and 16th centuries English experienced spectacular changes in pronunciation, in particular the so-called Great Vowel Shift. The result was Early Modern English – the language of Shakespeare and the King James Bible.

As the world opened up, words were borrowed from new sources: scientific and technical terms from Greek ('anonymous', 'caustic', 'system', 'crisis') and Latin ('genius', 'distil', 'lens') or both ('electricity', 'atmosphere'). From Italian came 'balcony' and 'opera'; from Spanish 'alligator' and 'bravado'; from the New World 'potato', 'tobacco' and 'chocolate'.

A LANGUAGE FOR OUR TIMES
Modern English started around 1700. It has two written standards, English and American, still vigorously importing and coining new words.

Slang is one source of innovation. 'Fun', 'cheat' and 'slang' itself were all thought vulgar at first. Cockney rhyming slang, a London variant dating from the 1840s, replaces words with rhyming phrases – 'trouble and strife' (wife) – or their contractions, 'titfer' (tit-for-tat, hat).

THE SENSE OF NONSENSE
New words also enter the language through literary invention and creative wordplay. 'Somehow,' says Alice of the nonsense poem 'Jabberwocky' in Lewis Carroll's *Through the Looking Glass*, 'it

MIND YOUR LANGUAGE

Accent (pronunciation) and dialect (grammar and vocabulary) vary greatly from region to region and between speakers of different social backgrounds. Bristolians sound the 'r' in words like 'heart',

a person from northern England might rhyme 'ample' and 'sample', and a Scot will disagree with an Englishman whether a vegetable is a swede or a turnip.

In her 1956 essay collection Noblesse Oblige, Nancy Mitford listed words as 'U' (upper class) and 'non-U', as a satirical guide to 'proper' speech. Using a word such as 'toilet' (non-U) instead of 'lavatory' (U) was an instant betrayal of one's background.

So-called 'BBC English', or 'received pronunciation' (RP), developed in 19th-century public schools, based on the upper-class speech of the capital. Now, many public figures – such as the Yorkshire politician John Prescott – proudly revel in their local accents.

LOST CONSONANT Dropping the 'h' at the beginning of words is common in every urban English accent except for the Tyneside Geordie

POOR LETTER H.
Tout Contractor (who has been paid a Shilling per Man, and sees his way to a little extra profit). "Now, look 'ere, you Two H's! The Public don't want yer—nor I don't, nor Nobody don't; so jist Drop them Boards, and then 'ook it!"

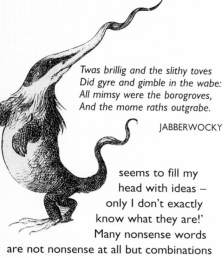

*Twas brillig and the slithy toves
Did gyre and gimble in the wabe:
All mimsy were the borogroves,
And the mome raths outgrabe.*

JABBERWOCKY

seems to fill my head with ideas – only I don't exactly know what they are!' Many nonsense words are not nonsense at all but combinations of 'sensible' words. As Humpty Dumpty explains, 'slithy means "lithe and slimy"… it's like a portmanteau – there are two meanings packed up into one word'. 'Brunch' (breakfast + lunch), 'electrocute' (electricity + execute) and 'smog' (smoke + fog) arose in a similar way.

Sets of words, such as computer 'bits', 'bytes' and 'bugs', enter the language with each invention. The *Oxford Dictionary of New Words* (1998) lists 2000 additions since the 1989 OXFORD ENGLISH DICTIONARY, including 'Blairism' and 'zero tolerance'.

ENGLISH THROUGH THE AGES
Four versions of Matthew 20.8 show how English has evolved. Flat accents mean a vowel is long, like the 'a' in 'car'; 'æ' sounds like the 'a' in 'bad' and 'þ' and 'ð' like the modern 'th'.

WEST SAXON BIBLE, OLD ENGLISH
Witodlīce on æfnunge cwæð se hlāford tō his wīcnere: 'Clypa ðās wyrhtan and āgyld him heora mēde. Fōh on ðām endenēxtan, oð þæt þū cume tō ðām fyrmestan.'

KENTISH BIBLE, MIDDLE ENGLISH
þo þet hiwel even, þo seide þe lord to his sergant: 'Clepe þo werkmen and yeld hem here travail. And agyn to hem þat comen last, and go al to þo ferste.'

KING JAMES VERSION, EARLY MODERN
So when even was come, the lord of the vineyard saith unto his steward: 'Call the labourers and give them their hire, beginning from the last unto the first.'

NEW ENGLISH BIBLE, MODERN ENGLISH
When evening fell, the owner of the vineyard said to his steward: 'Call the labourers and give them their pay, beginning with those who came last and ending with the first.'

---

more than 400 buildings, monuments and gardens under its direct care – from AVEBURY to AUDLEY END.

English Heritage also awards grants to help owners preserve buildings of note and recommends new additions to England's LISTED BUILDINGS. It provides an innovative range of services, including interactive discovery centres to explain the history of ancient sites. It also organises concerts and special events such as re-enactments of famous battles.

The Royal Commission for Historic Monuments of England was merged with English Heritage in April 1999.

EPPING FOREST

• **Essex (p.495 H4)** • **Area 2400 ha (6000 acres)**
Although enveloped by Greater London, Epping Forest remains a haven of green within the urban sprawl. It was a royal hunting ground until Tudor times, and Elizabeth I's lodge can still be seen at Chingford. The forest was opened to the public by Queen Victoria in 1873 and became a retreat for city-dwellers.

The largest of outer London's areas of parkland, Epping Forest has been protected from development since the Corporation of the City of London purchased it for £225 000 in 1882. It was already only a tenth its original size. The forest is one of Europe's oldest, with beeches and hornbeams that shelter a rare species of fallow deer, known for its dark, unspotted coat.

EPSOM DERBY

• **June**
'There is not a properer place in the world for this sport.' So an 18th-century enthusiast praised Epsom Downs, home of the Derby, the world's most celebrated horse race. The race, named after the

FIRST SIGHT Many who saw Jacob Epstein's alabaster *Adam* unveiled in Leicester in 1939 declared it both indecent and blasphemous

12th earl of Derby, has been run over the 1½ mile course in Surrey since 1780. The fashionable area around Epsom and its proximity to London gave the race prestige, and it became known as one of the five HORSE RACING 'classics'.

The greatest drama occurred in 1913, when a campaigner for votes for women, Emily Davison, ran onto the track to seize the reins of George V's horse. She was fatally injured when it trampled her.

Lester Piggott is the most successful Derby jockey: he won the race nine times between 1954 and 1983.

Jacob EPSTEIN

• **Sculptor** • **1880-1959; kt 1954**
After Jacob Epstein carved 18 nudes for the British Medical Association's London building in 1908, scandal greeted nearly all his work. He courted criticism in a Britain distrustful of radical influences. *Rock Drill* (1913), a robotic

A DAY AT THE RACES Each June around 100 000 horse racing enthusiasts don top hats and tails and fancy frocks to watch the Epsom Derby

torso mounted on a tripod drill, was dismissed by one contemporary as a 'kind of gigantic human locust'. Such distortions were a key element of VORTICISM, a movement with which he was briefly associated.

He carved Christian figures such as *Adam* (1939) in stone in the style of tribal models, and even his angels such as the monumental *Rima* (1925) in Hyde Park have a massive solidity. His prolific output of bronze sculpture includes *St Michael and the Devil*, which hangs as a parable of good triumphing over evil outside Coventry Cathedral.

ETHELRED I

• **King 866-71**   • **c.830-71**

The short rule of Ethelred I saw England under repeated and violent attack from Viking invaders. Ethelred's kingdom, Wessex, lay in the south and for a time

was relatively secure. But in 867 raiding forces swarmed through northern England and by 871 they were camped at Reading, part of Wessex.

Ethelred marched against the Vikings, taking care to have Mass said beforehand – 'God first, man later', he declared. Battle was joined at Ashdown, in Berkshire, and Ethelred's army drove the Vikings from the field. Ethelred died shortly afterwards from a wound received in a second battle with the Vikings and was given a martyr's burial at Wimborne in Dorset.

ETHELRED II (the Unready)

• **King 978-1016**   • **968-1016**

Ethelred was only ten when his retainers murdered his half-brother, Edward, so that he could become king. The appellation 'unready' does not refer to his premature accession to the throne but comes from the Saxon word *unraed*, meaning 'no counsel'. The name 'Ethelred' actually means 'good counsel'.

Ethelred ruled under the guidance of archbishop Wulfstan but grew into a weak monarch: uncertain of himself, ineffectual in war and mistrustful of his nobles. His subjects knew that he ruled as a result of a crime – the murdered Edward was widely regarded as a saint – and, when Danish raiding parties descended on England in 980, failed to unite behind him in resistance.

Ethelred tried to pay off the Danes with protection money – 'Danegeld' – but raids continued. In 1013 he fled to Normandy, but returned a few months later when the Danish king, Sweyn, died.

ETHNIC DIVERSITY: *see page 156*

ETON COLLEGE

• **Berkshire (p.495 G4)**   • **Founded 1440**

The King's College of our Lady beside Windsor – better known as Eton College – was founded by Henry VI to provide free education to 25 'poor and indigent'

SETTING A STYLE Tailcoats, initially red, have been worn at Eton since the late 1700s. The college has given its name to a ball game, a shirt collar, jacket and even a women's haircut

scholars. The school now caters for nearly 1300 paying pupils, known as 'oppidans', between the ages of 13 and 18, with an average 14 King's Scholarships awarded each year.

Eton's social standing as one of Britain's top PUBLIC SCHOOLS is secure, and with roughly one teacher for every nine pupils its academic standards are exacting. Places are still highly sought-after but the school's admission criteria are governed by merit rather than social connections. Boys can be registered as young as six months old but only one in four applicants gains a place.

The school has produced 18 prime ministers, and its pupils have included future monarchs, actors, writers such as George Orwell and Percy Bysshe Shelley, sportsmen and politicians, including the Duke of Wellington and Anthony Eden.

EUROPEAN UNION

When Britain joined the European Economic Community (EEC) in 1973, its members were a loose trade association – greatly strengthened by the free trade and free movement of labour achieved in the 1987 Single European Act. By 1993, when the Maastricht Treaty established the European Union (EU), 12 member states, led by France and Germany, wanted a closer political and economic union.

Margaret THATCHER, when prime minister, had negotiated an 'opt-out' clause in the 1993 treaty allowing Britain to agree in principle to the single European currency – the Euro, launched in 1999 – without actually joining the first wave.

> Some British measures such as pints of beer and milk have survived compulsory metrification, but selling a pound of sausages or sugar, or a gallon of petrol, is now illegal within the European Union

Although Britain is largely committed to a role 'at the heart of Europe', many in the country remain fiercely protective of its national sovereignty. As a result, Britain has used its right of veto to oppose changes on European issues such as border controls, taxation and defence.

A European parliament, with MPs from all member states, sets EU policy. Elections are held every five years and Britain has 87 of the 626 seats. Import taxes provide funds, and member states contribute according to their wealth: for 1999 Britain's share is about £2.5 billion.

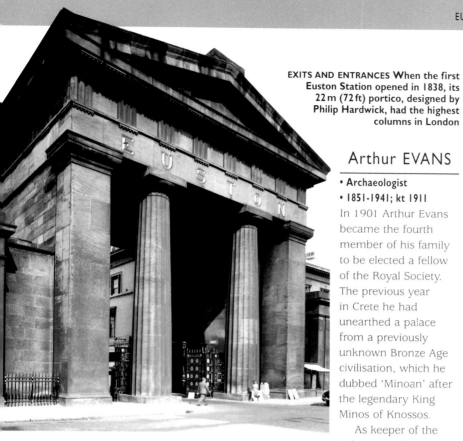

Arthur EVANS

- Archaeologist
- 1851-1941; kt 1911

In 1901 Arthur Evans became the fourth member of his family to be elected a fellow of the Royal Society. The previous year in Crete he had unearthed a palace from a previously unknown Bronze Age civilisation, which he dubbed 'Minoan' after the legendary King Minos of Knossos.

As keeper of the Ashmolean Museum in Oxford from 1884, Evans travelled widely. Two fortunes inherited in middle age helped to fund his many excavations, such as the Roman villa at Frilford, when public funding was scarce. He loved children and the outdoors and was an enthusiastic patron of the Boy Scouts, who trained in the grounds of his home in Youlbury, near Oxford.

EXETER

- Devon (p.494 D6) • Pop. 94 720

Exeter, the county town of Devon, rises above the left bank of the River Exe, the Norman twin towers of its cathedral jutting up from the horizon for miles around. Roads, including the Roman Fosse Way, radiate from the city, which was built at the lowest crossing point on the Exe, providing an entry to south-west England.

In Roman times Exeter prospered from local tin and later from sheep and cloth. The city survived attacks by Saxons, Danes, both sides in the Civil War, and German bombs, which in 1942 destroyed 16 ha (40 acres) of the city centre.

The Maritime Museum in the docks records the city's seafaring history: Francis Drake was said to drink at Mol's Coffee House in the Cathedral Close. Exeter's canal was one of the first in Britain, built in 1567 when large boats could no longer navigate the river.

EXMOOR

- Somerset and Devon borders (p.494 C5)
- Area 265 sq miles

Barrows and cairns commemorate the Bronze Age farmers who first settled on Exmoor. The moor is bleak and windswept, and only purple heather and bracken flourish in the poor sandstone soil. A plateau covers most of the moor, rising to 519 m (1705 ft) at Dunkery Hill, but oak trees line the richer valleys, or 'combes', around the edges.

The plateau, Exmoor Forest, has had no trees since prehistory. In medieval times 'forest' meant an area of open land and the place was a royal hunting ground. Red deer, Britain's largest native animal, are still plentiful here. The rugged Exmoor ponies that can also be seen roaming the moor belong to one of the oldest native British breeds.

In 1819 an industrialist, John Knight, bought 15 000 acres of the moor to farm, and though Exmoor has been a NATIONAL PARK since 1954, much of the land is still privately owned. Six hundred miles of footpath pass through unspoilt villages and 'Doone Country', the setting for R.D. Blackmore's novel, *Lorna Doone*.

EUSTON STATION

- Central London (p.499 C1)

The oldest mainline terminus in London, Euston opened in 1838. Its classical portico was a stately monument to the railway age and a fitting climax to Robert STEPHENSON's new London and Birmingham Railway.

For the first six years, departing trains had to be drawn up the hill to Camden Town on a winding cable powered by stationary steam engines; incoming trains coasted downhill. When the station opened, it had only two platforms: one for arrivals and one for departures. As goods and passenger traffic increased, Euston sprawled outwards, gaining more platforms and two hotels – the Victoria and the Euston.

In 1963, after the West Coast main line was electrified, British Railways defied a public outcry and demolished the Victorian station. The replacement, with dark glass walls and 6 ha (15 acres) of low, flat roof, opened in 1968 to widespread condemnation.

The discovery of the stones from the original portico in the River Lea, a Thames tributary, in 1993 sparked a campaign to rebuild the original arch, or a replica, to restore at least some of the station's former grandeur.

STONE AGE CROSSING Tarr Steps, a clapper bridge, crosses the River Barle near Winsford, on Exmoor. The structure is thought to date from prehistoric times

FACES OF A NATION

Britain is a culturally diverse society. Over the nation's long history invaders from the Continent, refugees from religious or political persecution and Commonwealth citizens seeking a new life in the 'mother country' have made their homes here, adding to and enriching the definition of Britishness

THE TERM 'ethnic minorities' is generally used to mean the groups who have come to Britain since the Second World War. But the history of these islands reveals that we have always been a mixed society, created since earliest times out of waves of migrants and invaders.

BIRTH OF A NATION

The Celtic tribes who resisted the Romans were the first people to call themselves Britons, yet they themselves were the descendants of central European migrants.

The Angles and Saxons, Germanic tribes who came after the Romans, gave their name to the south of the island (England is 'Angle-land'). Each warlike wave added to the ethnic mix. A sense of national identity, of Englishness, was forged in their struggles with the Danish Vikings who occupied the North, and was slowly transformed in the centuries following the victory of the French-speaking Norsemen (or Normans) who conquered England in 1066.

Britain remained an ethnically diverse nation throughout the next thousand years. The Jews, persecuted for their distinct culture and religion, were expelled from Britain in 1289, but returned under Oliver Cromwell.

French HUGUENOTS and other Protestant refugees fled to Britain from the Continent in the 16th and 17th centuries; African and Caribbean slaves worked in British cities by the 1560s, and at the height of Empire in the 19th century immigrants came from all over the British-ruled world.

THE TURBULENT 20TH CENTURY

At the beginning of the 20th century a new wave of Jews arrived, having been driven out of their homes in Russia and Poland. Many settled in the EAST END of London, an area with a long history of being the first staging-post for many settler communities.

As the century progressed, immigrant communities grew up in other British cities. Asian immigrants working in the clothing trade settled in sizable numbers in the Midlands and the north, and Chinese in Liverpool and Manchester.

After the Second World War, in which soldiers from all parts of the Commonwealth fought alongside British troops, the government sought workers from the West Indies to help to alleviate a labour shortage. The descendants of these pioneers are, even now, often called immigrants, though most of them were born in Britain to parents who arrived as British citizens assisted by the British government.

FOOD FOR THOUGHT

Diet is just one aspect of British culture to have benefited from the many peoples who have settled here. At the beginning of the 20th century immigrants from Hungary, Russia, Italy and Greece started to open restaurants in the Soho district of London. Later they were joined by Chinese and Indian businesses, which were often family-run, open late, reasonably priced and, as a result, highly successful. Today, our more than 7000 Indian and 8000 Chinese restaurants and takeaways generate more than £3 billion a year.

'Ethnic' foods are also big business for supermarkets. Sales of sauces, ready-made dishes and ingredients were valued at £451 million in 1998, with Indian, Chinese and Mexican varieties taking the major share. Booming sales of speciality fruit and vegetables show the increasingly cosmopolitan tastes of a population that in 1997 consumed more than 12 000 tons of avocados and 14 000 tons of mangoes.

FAMILY TIES Intermarriage is more common among some communities than others. One in five Afro-Caribbeans has a white partner

NEW COMMUNITIES Bradford (*right*) drew immigrants in the 1950s to its textile works. Now 16 per cent of the populace belongs to an ethnic minority

PART OF THE FAMILY Since Cromwell readmitted Jews to Britain in 1656 the community has grown to 300 000 – after France, the largest in Europe. The family unit is central to Jewish culture and tradition

MIXED FORTUNES

Many immigrants have thrived in Britain, but for some life here is still a struggle. Unemployment can be two to five times as high as among native Britons and some communities still have difficulty getting adequate housing, education or representation in public life. Since 1976 'incitement to racial hatred' has been a crime, and racially motivated crimes carry extra penalties, but discrimination is still a fact of life for many British citizens.

The Commission for Racial Equality, also appointed in 1976, has the power to investigate cases of discrimination and to issue codes of practice for employers, schools and medical professionals, significantly improving relations between peoples of different cultural backgrounds. By 1991 ethnic minorities constituted about 5.5 per cent of the British population, 3 million people in all. This includes about 825 000 people of Indian descent, 500 000 Pakistanis, 500 000 Afro-Caribbeans, 380 000 from African and other black backgrounds, 165 000 Bangladeshis, and 165 000 Chinese, mainly from the former British colony of Hong Kong.

Global upheavals have brought other, smaller groups to Britain: Vietnamese 'boat people', Kurds, Greek Cypriots, Bosnians, Somalis, Arabs, Ugandan Asians. As with every previous wave, from the woad-daubed Celts on, they have contributed something of themselves to the country: new foods, new fashions, new words and customs, a richer sense of what it means to be British.

FABIAN SOCIETY

• Founded 1884

By the end of the 19th century, many workers were enduring appalling, unsanitary conditions in factories and in overcrowded homes. In 1884, a group of left-wing intellectuals got together to call for improved working conditions and the creation of a democratic socialist state.

Among the Fabian Society's early members were the economists Sidney and Beatrice WEBB, and the writers H.G. WELLS and George Bernard SHAW. Believing that gradual reform was the key to lasting change, they named the society after a Roman general, Maximus Fabius, who used long-term harassment to wear down the forces of Hannibal, the

FIGHTING PRIVILEGE In words and images, the Fabians campaigned to topple the ladder of Victorian capitalism so that working people could reclaim the fruits of their labour

Carthaginian general. The Fabian Society gained recognition with its 1889 publication of the *Fabian Essays*, edited by Shaw.

In 1900 the society helped to create the Labour Representation Committee, the forerunner of the LABOUR PARTY. Today the society exists as an intellectual group within the Labour party, but its role in determining socialist policy has increasingly been taken over by specialist 'think-tanks'.

FACTORY ACTS

As the INDUSTRIAL REVOLUTION gathered pace in the early 19th century, the long hours imposed on factory workers spurred indignant reformers to introduce corrective legislation, known as the Factory Acts.

After the passing of two ineffectual Acts in 1802 and 1819, a movement of working-class groups and radical politicians brought about the first real change in 1833. Factory inspectors were appointed and a limit of 9 hours set on the working day for children in the textile industry, one of the largest employers, though 13 to 18-year-olds still worked an exhausting 68 hour week.

The working day for women and for children under 18 was finally limited to 10 hours in 1847, and legislation in the next decade restricted factories to operating 12 hours a day, confining working times for all employees. Reform has continued throughout the 20th century; the 1961 Factories Act laid down definitive regulations for health and safety throughout industry.

FA CUP FINAL

A jewel in England's sporting crown is the Football Association Cup Final. The world's first national FOOTBALL competition was devised in 1871 as a knock-out series for the 13 southern members and two guest sides of the fledgling English Football Association.

The inaugural winners in 1872 were Wanderers, who beat Royal Engineers at the Oval Cricket Ground, one of several venues used until a permanent home was opened in 1923 at WEMBLEY

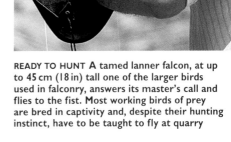

READY TO HUNT A tamed lanner falcon, at up to 45 cm (18 in) tall one of the larger birds used in falconry, answers its master's call and flies to the fist. Most working birds of prey are bred in captivity and, despite their hunting instinct, have to be taught to fly at quarry

stadium, north London. In the 1998-9 season 558 clubs entered the FA Cup competition. Manchester United hold the record of ten wins, but in an event devoted to romance and improbability, perhaps no achievement ranks higher than that by Tottenham Hotspur who became, in 1901, the only non-league side ever to win the Cup.

FAIRS AND FAIRGROUNDS:

see opposite page

FALCONRY

The practice of falconry, hardly changed since its introduction from Arabia and Asia in Saxon times, is enjoying a revival in Britain. Once the privilege of master falconers hunting on the king's land and other aristocratic estates, the sport is now taught in many parts of the Scottish moorlands, northern England and Wales.

Training of unpredictable falcons and other hawks is not for the faint-hearted. For several weeks, the falconer must spend hours each day carrying the bird on a gloved fist, talking to it gently and feeding it by hand to gain its confidence. It is then trained to feed from a lure, a padded weight to which meat is attached, and to fly towards the lure from increasing distances.

Eventually, the bird must kill for itself. When game, such as rabbit, grouse or pheasant, is flushed, the falconer casts the bird into the air and watches it swoop down for the kill at speeds of up to 120 mph. The bird should then return to the fist, and the falconer retrieves the prey from its talons.

This traditional method of hunting was frowned upon by Oliver Cromwell's Puritans, and after the advent of the more efficient shotgun birds of prey were nearly eradicated by gamekeepers and hunters. Many species are now protected, and working falcons have found a new role clearing airfields of birds. Falcons indigenous to Britain include the merlin and the peregrine.

Nick FALDO

• Golfer   • b.1957; MBE 1988

Watching the record-breaking American golfer Jack Nicklaus on television so inspired Nick Faldo that with single-minded determination he went on to become the most successful player ever to emerge from Britain.

He won Britain's Open in 1987 – the first of three Open titles – and the US Masters in 1989 and 1990, confirming him as the game's top player. Faldo's crowning glory came in 1996, when he overturned a six-shot deficit in the final round of the Masters to beat Australia's Greg Norman by five strokes. Although his coldly calculating style has won him more admiration than affection, no European has ever exceeded Faldo's record 23 Ryder Cup wins.

FAIRS AND FAIRGROUNDS

The Romans held trading fairs along Hadrian's Wall during their occupation of Britain, but most British fairs began with the new towns of the late Middle Ages. As shops were few and travelling difficult, yearly trading fairs became important as places where goods were exchanged with people from distant areas, and news and ideas swapped.

HOLIDAY TRADITIONS

Fairs usually began on the feast day of the local church, a holiday, and, like St Giles's at Oxford, were often dedicated to the church's patron saint. Others were named after the region's main product, such as the Cheese Fair held in Yarm, Yorkshire. Most lasted three days. Officially the right to hold a fair was established by a royal charter granted to a town, lord of the manor, monastery or bishop, who charged fees to traders; Elizabeth I granted a charter to Corby in Northamptonshire in 1585 after being rescued from a bog by men from the town.

Some fairs gained national and even international renown. Cattle and horses were brought to market from as far

FUN OF THE FAIR Climbing the greasy pole is one of the popular tasks at Egremont Crab Fair

CHANGING MARKET For more than 600 years geese were sold at Nottingham's annual October fair, but by the 1890s a huge funfair was the main attraction

MAJOR FAIRS THROUGH THE YEAR

• **King's Lynn Fair, Norfolk – February:** General trade, since 11th century; now also funfair. Lasts for 6 days

• **Appleby Horse Fair, Cumbria – June:** Horses, since 17th century; key event in Romany gypsy year (see page 18)

• **Honiton Fair, Devon – July:** Cattle and moorland ponies, since 13th century; now chiefly funfair

• **Egremont Crab Fair, Cumberland – September:** Crab apples and livestock, since 13th century; now chiefly funfair

• **Widecombe Fair, Devon – September:** Dartmoor ponies, since 19th century; now chiefly funfair

afield as Scotland and Ireland for the yearly fair at Barnet, Hertfordshire, established in the 13th century. At 'mop fairs', such as at Stratford-upon-Avon, people looking for jobs carried the symbols of their trade: shepherds with crooks, horsemen with whips, and maids with brooms or mops.

ROWDY ELEMENTS

Fairs brought crowds and wealth, but not everyone approved of them: along with traders, they attracted all manner of bawdy amusements and entertainers, gamblers, prostitutes and pickpockets. Fairs declined in the 18th and 19th centuries as roads, canals and railways brought goods to rural areas, and in 1871 a Fairs Act gave the government the right to abolish them as '... *the cause of grievous immorality ... and very injurious to the inhabitants of the towns where they are held'*. Transformed by the steam engine, many fairs turned into occasions for pure entertainment, with carousels and other fairground rides.

WORKING THE LAND

The prairie-like drained fens of East Anglia, the rolling downlands of the Midlands and South, and the rough hill pasture of the West and North have all been shaped by 6000 years of farming. Three-quarters of Britain's land area is still agricultural

BRITAIN'S AGRICULTURAL landscape is far older than most people realise. In areas such as Dartmoor and parts of the South Downs, traces of fields that were enclosed by ancient Britons as early as 4000 BC can still be picked out.

The combination of soil, temperature, rainfall, altitude and landform has always governed the best way to farm any particular piece of land. Arable (crop) farming on flat land using large machinery is most efficient with broad, open fields – hence the removal of old hedgerows in some areas. Dairy farms or mixed farms, where crops and grazing are rotated to prevent disease and obtain the best yields, can operate with traditional, smaller fields. Hill farming makes use of steep slopes that are inaccessible to machinery by grazing hardy breeds of sheep and cattle there.

Yet modern farming is more than simple husbandry. Today's farmer must have a good head for business, routinely balancing expenditure on feedstuffs, machinery, fertilisers and other chemicals against income from sales and subsidies. European Union quotas, setasides (subsidised noncultivation of fields) and government-backed conservation schemes all have an impact on the farming landscape. Intensive indoor methods of raising livestock – especially chickens, turkeys and pigs – mean that, in part, farming has become a semi-industrial process.

DIVISION OF THE LAND There are three main types of large-scale farming in Britain: arable and horticultural; lowland grazing (dairy farming and raising other livestock); and hill farming on rough, uncultivated pasture. Many farms practise a mixture, raising both livestock and crops

Hill farming | Mainly lowland grazing | Mixed arable and grazing | Mainly arable and horticulture | Forests | Urban areas

HILL FARMING

- **Rainfall:** heavy, 1500 mm (60 in) per year or more
- **Land:** hilly, up to 300 m (1000 ft) above sea level, with thin, infertile soil due to nutrients being washed by rain down into the valleys
- **Climate:** harsh, with cold, wet and snowy winters

The toughest farming country in Britain is in the uplands, where dry-stone walls divide fields of rough pasture. Lambs and beef cattle are the main produce, both usually sold to farmers in more lush lowlands to be fattened up for market. Wool is an important by-product, and older ewes are sold for a further few years' breeding in the lowlands.

On land in the valleys, hill farmers may grow crops to feed their stock in winter: grass for hay or silage, and swedes or turnips. A typical 90 ha (225 acre) hill farm might have 175-200 breeding ewes producing 250-300 lambs and 400 kg (8 cwt) of wool a year. It could also raise 20-30 steers and heifers for beef.

WELSH MOUNTAIN SHEEP Like other mountain breeds, this sheep is hardy and adapted to poor-quality grazing

BLACKFACE SHEEP This breed originated in Scotland but has become the most popular mountain breed in Britain

GALLOWAY STEER A popular choice with beef farmers, this is a fine example of British indigenous hardy hill breeds

LOWLAND GRAZING

- Rainfall: moderate, 750-1000 mm (30-40 in) per year
- Land: fairly flat or rolling, typically less than 100 m (300 ft) above sea level, with fertile, often rather heavy soil
- Climate: mild, often with wet winters

The rolling countryside of Devon and Dorset typifies agricultural Britain at its most lush. The relatively small, irregular fields are divided by hedges and fences, and the main crop is grass – some permanent, some 'ley' (temporary) – used for feeding dairy cattle.

Cows graze in the open during the summer, and in winter are kept under cover where they are fed a diet of silage (compressed, fermented grass) and perhaps some hay cut from fertilised fields.

On a typical 130 ha (320 acre) dairy farm, 150 cows may each produce almost 6000 litres (1320 gallons) of milk in a year.

HOLSTEIN-FRIESIAN COWS Making up 90 per cent of the British dairy herd, these yield more milk than other breeds

JERSEY COWS This breed yields rich, creamy milk. Like other cows, they each eat up to 70 kg (1 cwt) of grass a day

AYRSHIRE COWS This Scottish dairy breed is most often seen in Scotland and north-west England

ARABLE FARMLAND

- Rainfall: low, around 500-750 mm (20-30 in) per year
- Land: flat or gently rolling, less than 30 m (100 ft) above sea level, with large fields of fertile soil, often artificially drained
- Climate: sunny and mild, though often with cold winter winds

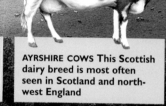

VEGETABLES 196 000 ha (484 000 acres) of farmland were used for growing sugar beet crops (15 per cent more than for potatoes) in 1997. Peas were grown on 98 000 ha (240 000 acres)

Carrot

Sugar beet

Cauliflower

Peas

Mechanised arable farming in giant fields reaches its peak in East Anglia, where drainage ditches rather than fences divide the fields. The major crops are wheat, barley, oilseed rape, sugar beet and potatoes. Where soil and climate are suitable high-value horticultural crops, such as fruits, vegetables, or even flowers for cutting, may be cultivated.

A typical 250 ha (600 acre) farm may yield 1000 tons of wheat, 225 tons of barley, 35 tons of oilseed rape and 1200 tons of sugar beet per year. Vegetables are harvested by machine and transported within hours to the supermarket or freezing plant.

Flax

ARABLE CROPS Wheat and barley are the most important British crops, covering two-thirds of all arable land. Oilseed rape, with its yellow flowers, produces seeds that are pressed for their oil. Flax is grown for the fibre in its stems, while its seeds yield linseed oil

Wheat

Barley

Oilseed rape

FALKLAND PALACE

- **Fife (p.497 D4)**
- **Built 15th-16th century** **NTS**

In the years following her return to Scotland in 1561 after a French upbringing and a brief marriage, the ill-fated Mary, Queen of Scots often visited Falkland Palace, riding, hunting and hawking among the Lomond Hills.

The palace was begun by James II of Scotland around 1440 and became a hunting lodge of the Stewart kings. A century later James V, Mary's father, embellished the nearby town of Falkland in Scottish Gothic style, with pepper-pot towers and twin-towered gatehouse. The palace's 16th-century real tennis court is one of Britain's oldest, and still in use.

FALKLANDS WAR

- **April 2-June 14, 1982**

One of the last remnants of the British Empire, the Falkland Islands of the South Atlantic have long been claimed by Argentina, though Britain has ruled there since 1833. On April 2, 1982, 5000 Argentinian troops seized the islands, and three days later Royal Navy vessels steamed south as Britain entered its first major conflict since Korea in the 1950s.

An early strike against the battleship *General Belgrano* claimed 350 Argentinian lives and caused controversy as the vessel was said to be heading away from the conflict. Argentina sank two British ships in retaliation, but by May 22 British troops had landed and on June 14, after a last-ditch defence at Tumbledown mountain, the Argentine forces surrendered.

In all, 255 Britons and 652 Argentines died, but the outcome could have been very different. The sinking of a vital supply ship meant that Britain might have had to withdraw if defeated at Tumbledown. Instead, victory marked a turning point in the fortunes of the prime minister, Margaret Thatcher, helping to secure her a second term of office.

Michael FARADAY

- **Physicist and chemist** **1791-1867**

From 1826, audiences packed into the Royal Institution in central London to hear Michael Faraday lecture on his discoveries in electricity. The son of a poor blacksmith, Faraday had little formal education, but as a bookbinder's apprentice he read avidly. He bound his own notes of the chemist Humphry Davy's lectures at the Royal Institution and sent them to Davy, who gave him a job as his assistant in 1813.

Faraday had no mathematical knowledge but an uncanny ability to construct physical images in his mind of the way things worked. As early as 1821 he had devised a simple electric motor. Ten years later he discovered electromagnetic induction – the principle behind the electric generator. By moving a magnet through a coil of wire, Faraday produced for the first time an electrical current, and so opened the way to unimaginable quantities of electricity.

A devout and principled man, Faraday refused to produce poison gas for use in the Crimean War, and modestly declined honours, requesting for his memorial 'a gravestone of the most ordinary kind'.

FARMING:
see page 160

FARNE ISLANDS

- **Northumberland (p.496 B1)** **NT**

Little of the wild archipelago of the Farne Islands, a few miles off the coast of Northumberland, has changed since the 7th-century hermit Cuthbert chose to live there in isolation. Now, as then, some 30 rocky islets are a sanctuary to thousands of wintering or summer-breeding birds.

'St Cuthbert's chickens', better known as eider ducks, are among the 17 or more species of sea bird which, with grey seals, regularly breed on the islands. The National Trust restricts visitors to Inner Island and Staple Island – and to spring and summer.

The dangerous waters of the islands were braved in 1838 by the consumptive Grace Darling, the lighthouse keeper's daughter, who rowed with her father to rescue storm-battered survivors of the wrecked *Forfarshire*.

FASHION: *see page 164*

BIRD TENEMENT
Sociable sea birds such as guillemot and gull use the stacks of the Farne Islands for nesting and roosting. More than 250 species of bird have been recorded in one of Britain's wildest nature reserves

FENS

• East Anglia (p.495 H2)
In the 17th century, the 4th duke of Bedford realised the agricultural potential of the huge expanse of waterlogged land, known as the Fens, stretching some 70 miles north to south from Lincoln to Cambridge and 35 miles west to east. The duke hired Dutch engineers experienced in reclaiming land from the sea to begin the first drainage scheme in the region since the Romans built dams and channels there. The peaty soil, kept drained by wind power, steam, and now electricity, has ever since provided Britain's best arable land for flowers, fruit and vegetables.

Wicken Fen, bought by the National Trust in 1899, was Britain's first nature reserve and is one of the few surviving fragments of original marshland. The fen preserves a wealth of the native plants and animals: 268 plant species; 212 different spiders, including Britain's biggest, the raft spider (up to 8 cm/3 in long); a third of Europe's winter population of Bewick's swans; and the reintroduced swallowtail butterfly.

Roger FENTON

• Photographer • 1819-69
Photographs taken of the CRIMEAN WAR by Roger Fenton in 1855 revealed how unglamorous war could be. As the first war photographer, Fenton travelled to the Crimea battle zone in a converted wine-merchant's cart, using it as both a caravan and a dark room. With camera technology still in its infancy, Fenton needed up to 20 seconds' exposure time, so could take only posed group shots.

As well as his war work, his pictures include still lifes, landscapes, architecture and portraits of the royal family, to whom he gave lessons in photography. In 1853 he founded what became the Royal Photographic Society.

Kathleen FERRIER

• Singer • 1912-53; CBE 1953
Most women who sing the lower parts in oratorio and opera are mezzo-sopranos, but Kathleen Ferrier was a true contralto, and one of the great British voices of the 20th century. She worked as a telephonist until 1937 when she won a singing competition, and went on to make her name during the war years, touring the country as a concert artist and performing with the Bach Choir.

After the war, Ferrier became one of the leading singers in Britain. She sang the title role in the world premiere of Benjamin BRITTEN's *The Rape of Lucretia* and was midway through a run of Gluck's *Orfeo* at the Royal Opera when illness cut short her career.

She died aged just 41, leaving behind recordings that are still considered classics, such as her 1949 interpretation of Mahler's *Das Lied von der Erde* and her renditions of English folk songs. Her instantly recognisable warm, deep voice was still being used in advertising in the 1990s. The annual Ferrier Award set up in her memory is Britain's most prestigious honour for young singers.

FESTIVAL OF BRITAIN

In 1951, a five-month celebration marked the end of postwar austerity and the centenary of the GREAT EXHIBITION. At the heart of the festival was an exhibition celebrating British achievements in science and the arts, using 11 ha (27 acres) of derelict ground on London's South Bank. Here were erected the Dome of Discovery, the world's largest dome at the time, the Skylon obelisk and Royal Festival Hall.

Two miles upriver at the Festival Pleasure Gardens in Battersea, visitors could enjoy a fanciful world of illuminated grottoes, Mississippi showboat rides, and a suspended tree-walk. Described as 'a gigantic toyshop for adults', the festival drew some 8 million visitors.

Regional and travelling spin-offs carried the celebrations to millions more around Britain. The only building designed to last was the Royal Festival Hall, nucleus of what became the SOUTH BANK CENTRE.

HIGH HOPES Postwar optimism took shape in London as a 90 m (295 ft) obelisk and a dome-covered exhibition of scientific discovery and global exploration

Henry FIELDING

• Writer and lawyer • 1707-54
Through the six rollicking volumes of *Tom Jones* (1749), Henry Fielding puts his hero through dozens of adventures, makes saucy and sarcastic asides to the reader, and energetically describes the fighting, hunting and amorous escapades of his robust characters.

Fielding's early career as a playwright ended abruptly in 1737, when his vigorous satire led to censorship that emasculated the theatre for more than two centuries. The novels he then wrote have the epic sweep, immediacy and developed characters of modern fiction.

A lawyer as well as a writer – and a great humanitarian – Fielding became a magistrate in 1748. While on the bench, he formed the BOW STREET RUNNERS, Britain's first police force.

CHIC OR FREAK?

When the British designers John Galliano and Alexander McQueen took over two Paris couture houses in the 1990s, fashion had not turned on its head but come full circle: the first couture house was founded by a Briton, Charles Frederick Worth, 140 years ago

DURING THE 19th and early 20th centuries, the clothes of wealthy British men, subtle tweeds and SAVILE ROW suits, were considered the height of elegance while British women, however well-off, were famous for being frumps.

In 1858 the British dressmaker Charles Frederick Worth opened a couture house in Paris, which produced the finest fashions. Worth began to revolutionise the industry, by introducing new techniques and designing spring and autumn collections of gowns, rich with beads, brocade, embroidery and feathers. The dresses, offered in a range of fabrics, were displayed on beautiful models, then made to order.

Before Worth, women bought lengths of fabric and paid a dressmaker to make a gown to their specification.

Worth's innovations went largely unnoticed in Britain where, for years, women regarded fashion as foolish and immoral – the main concern was that clothes be comfortable. When Christian Dior's 'New Look' was restyling postwar Parisians in the 1940s, its romantic, long skirts were frowned upon in rationed Britain as a waste of cloth.

The 1960s 'youthquake' finally shook off the image of

RICH SATIN Worth designed gowns to reflect the status, or aspirations, of his clients

English women as dowdy spinsters, with designers such as Mary Quant producing clothes that were youthful and sexy. The next two decades were quieter but by the mid 1990s British fashion was once again storming the catwalks of the world.

Graduates of such institutions as Central St Martin's College in London, including John Galliano, broke away from traditional English understatement, long the mark of such designers as the impeccably correct Hardy Amies. Instead they adopted styles that reflected the eccentricity, theatricality and wit of the British dandy.

SIXTIES STYLE REVOLUTION
• Mary Quant • b.1934

In 1955, when Mary Quant opened her first shop on the King's Road in Chelsea, young women dressed like their mothers, and no fashionable women anywhere dressed like the British. By 1966 London was the style capital of the world. Quant had chopped more than a foot off hemlines, raising them to fingertip length, and instead of cinching their waists and emphasising their bosoms, women donned short, tubular dresses, replaced stockings with tights, and pointy, 50s stilettoes with low-heeled ankle boots. Vidal Sassoon's layered, geometric bobs liberated women from curling and pinning, and intricate tailoring and expensive fabrics gave way to cheap and cheerful garments in stiff, simple paper-doll shapes. All of it meant freedom to move, to enjoy life and to be young.

SIMPLE ELEGANCE
• Hardy Amies • b.1909

When Hardy Amies opened his Savile Row couture house in 1946, he already had a royal client, the young Princess Elizabeth. Amies continued to dress the Queen throughout her reign in simple tweed suits and stately ballgowns. He opened a boutique in 1950 and in 1962 became the first couturier to design for men. Later, he became better known for his refined, understated gentlemen's tailoring than for the women's wear that made his name.

WOMAN OF HER TIME Mary Quant not only created the look of the 1960s, she was the look

HARDY AMIES (1961)

MARY QUANT (1967)

SOFT, STRUCTURED JERSEY
• Jean Muir • 1933-95

After working for Liberty and Jaeger, Jean Muir started her own company in 1966. Her classic style was instantly recognisable and changed little over the years she was designing. Muir worked with soft, draping fabrics such as jersey or sometimes crepe, tailoring them in gentle gathers at the shoulders or waist to create garments with a restrained but flowing line.

JEAN MUIR
(1990)

CLASSICS WITH A TWIST
• Paul Smith • b.1946

Paul Smith, Britain's most commercially successful designer, opened his first shop in Nottingham in 1974. His men's suits appear conservative, but show a flash of pink or violet in the tweed. Deep-coloured shirts, and socks and ties patterned with tiny, childlike drawings completed the quirky style. In 1994, seeing his men's shirts worn by women, he began to produce neatly tailored women's wear. Smith freed men from formality with an imaginative, smart but casual look, teaming chunky knits with an unusual take on traditional jackets and trousers.

PAUL SMITH
(1994)

DESIGNED TO SHOCK
• Vivienne Westwood • b.1941

Vivienne Westwood created the look of punk. During the 1970s, with Malcolm McLaren, manager of the punk band the Sex Pistols, she sold leather and rubber clothing with zips and chains suggestive of bondage and fetishism from a shop called 'Sex'. Eccentricity, humour and the boldness and wit of the cavalier now characterise her style. She makes unconventional use of traditional fabrics and styles, such as corsets, crinolines, tartans and Harris tweed – often all at once.

VIVIENNE WESTWOOD
(1993)

JOHN GALLIANO
(1993)

HIPPIE CHIC
• Zandra Rhodes • b.1942

Silks and chiffons patterned with lipsticks, cactuses or a distinctive squiggle were Zandra Rhodes's trademarks. She began as a fabric designer and established her own clothing firm in 1968. Rhodes's floaty, gossamer dresses with their zigzag hems, sometimes emphasised by wavy prints or stitched pearls along the edges, epitomised the romantic look of the early 1970s. She later coined a uniquely feminine version of Vivienne Westwood's punk style, with daintily slashed frocks held together by delicate safety pins.

ZANDRA RHODES
(1970)

CATWALK COSTUMES
• John Galliano • b.1961

John Galliano began his career designing slim, elegant bias-cut dresses with draped necklines. He then turned to whimsical, throwaway chic garments, such as transparent crinoline skirts made of telephone wire. After becoming director of Christian Dior in 1990, he settled into lavish theatricality, with heavy beading and striking contrasts of line, such as deep décolletages paired with chin-high chokers and barely-there hemlines.

FIELD OF THE CLOTH OF GOLD

• June 7-24, 1520

A meeting between HENRY VIII and Francis I of France, devised to cement peaceful relations between their two countries following the treaty of London (1518), gave rise to one of the last great displays of medieval chivalry.

The event was named after the splendour of the surroundings. Lavish temporary palaces of timber and canvas were created for the kings at Guînes, near Calais. The massed noblemen of England and France feasted at banquets and spent the days jousting and tilting.

Yet there was little diplomatic substance to the pageantry. Henry and Francis failed to achieve any rapport and in 1522 and 1523 English troops once more invaded France.

FINANCIAL TIMES INDEX

For businessmen and investors the indexes of shares traded that appear in the *Financial Times* are the traditional source of daily information on the state of the STOCK MARKET.

The oldest is the FT Ordinary Share Index, started in 1935 and compiled from the share prices of 30 companies broadly representative of British industry. However the FT-SE 100 Index (known as Footsie) is the index now normally quoted. Begun in 1984, it encompasses the 100 largest companies in Britain by market value, representing more than 70 per cent of total stock market value. Other indexes cover different sectors of the market – some are based on the size of companies, others on their sector of activity.

FILM INDUSTRY

From the era of silent films onwards, Britain's film industry has always been dwarfed by Hollywood's huge movie output and financial power.

In an early defensive move, the British government introduced in 1927 the Cinematograph Films Act to compel cinemas to show a quota of British films. At first this spawned more, but poor, silent films, but Britain's first sound production, Hitchcock's *Blackmail* (1929) – made at ELSTREE STUDIOS – was a huge success.

The Second World War saw the rise of classic films such as *Brief Encounter* and *In Which We Serve* (both directed by David LEAN and Noël COWARD). But in the 1950s, the industry declined as cinema attendance fell victim to television. The USA backed Hammer horror films but the CARRY ON FILMS and the gritty realism of *Room at the Top* (1959) and *A Kind of Loving* (1962) had little international appeal.

The industry suffered a further decline when quotas were abandoned in 1983. By 1992, only 4 per cent of films shown were purely British, and the USA had a 92.5 per cent market share. But in recent years British film talent has triumphed in movies such as *Notting Hill* and *Shakespeare In Love*.

MANPOWER Scottish actor Robert Carlyle struts his stuff in the box office hit *The Full Monty*

BIGGEST GROSSING BRITISH-PRODUCED FILMS (June 1999):	
The Full Monty	Over £50 million
Four Weddings and a Funeral	Around £28 million
Shakespeare In Love	Over £20 million
Bean	Over £17 million
Notting Hill	Over £15 million

FIRE OF LONDON

• September 2-5, 1666

The devastating inferno that became known as the 'Great Fire of London' began on a Sunday morning just before dawn in Thomas Farriner's baker's shop in Pudding Lane, just east of London Bridge. After the long, dry summer, the flames quickly engulfed the riverside, and then spread north and west.

They 'rushed like a torrent down Ludgate Hill' wrote one onlooker. People grabbed what belongings they could and fled by boat or on foot. Many camped at Moorfields; some sought refuge farther north on the hills of Hampstead and Highgate. The diarist Samuel Pepys wrote, 'It made me weep to see it. The churches, houses and all on fire and flaming at once; and a horrid noise the flames made and the cracking of houses at their ruin.' From Whitehall Charles II heard the cries of 'Fire, fire! God and the King save us!' and went to help the soldiers. The king had Scotland Yard unroofed to prevent the fire spreading, and ordered bread to be sent to the homeless.

When the flames subsided, 13 000 homes and 87 churches had been destroyed. Although it claimed only nine lives and largely rid London of the previous year's plague, the fire reduced

HEADING WEST A brisk east wind fanned the flames and kept them away from the eastern reaches of the city

PROGRESS OF FIRE

DAY 3
DAY 2
DAY 1

Cripplegate
Moorfields
Spitalfields
Smithfield
Moorgate
Bishopsgate
Aldersgate
London Wall
Newgate
Guildhall
Aldgate
River Fleet
CITY OF LONDON
Ludgate
St Paul's
Blackfriars
Pudding Lane (start of fire)
The Tower
River Thames
London Bridge

FIRST WORLD WAR *see page 168*

FISH AND CHIPS

London's East End boasts a shop with a plaque 'to mark 100 years of fish and chips', presented in 1968 by the National Federation of Fish Fryers. Mancunians, however, maintain that one John Lees may have been in business even earlier from his wooden hut opposite the Stamford Arms in Mossley.

Whatever its origins, fish and chip shops gave urban workers a cheap, nutritious meal and a place for gossip. Most shops also sold pickled eggs and onions and, in the North, mushy peas; many now offer pies, sausages, chicken, Chinese spring rolls, and in Scotland, deep-fried Mars Bars.

Despite the rising popularity of curries and pizzas as take-away meals, Britain's 8500 fish and chip outlets, ranging from corner shops to classy restaurants such as HARRY RAMSDEN'S in Yorkshire, still serve the nation's favourite dish.

FISHBOURNE ROMAN PALACE

• **West Sussex (p.495 G6)** • **Built c.AD 80**
In 1960, workmen laying water pipes found the largest, most luxurious domestic building of ROMAN BRITAIN yet discovered. Excavations revealed a huge complex of four wings covering a site of about 4 ha (10 acres) near Chichester, once the Roman town of Noviomagus. The building may have been the palace of Cogidubnus, a 1st-century British client king of the Romans. Although most of the villa was devastated by fire about 200 years after it was built, many of its elaborate floor mosaics and wall paintings survived.

Much of the palace now lies under roads and houses, but the remains of 15 rooms in the north wing and several of the 95 surviving mosaic floors can still be seen. Archaeologists have also been able to trace the layout of the palace gardens and partially reconstruct them.

Ronald Aylmer FISHER

• **Geneticist and statistician**
• **1890-1962; kt 1952**
As head of statistics at Rothampsted agricultural research centre, Harpenden, Fisher established important statistical methods for designing and analysing experiments. The work led him to study how genes vary in large groups of people and other organisms. As professor at London and Cambridge universities, he laid the foundations for the study of population genetics, combining heredity with DARWIN's theory of evolution.

FISHING INDUSTRY

With a coastline extending more than 3000 miles, Britain has always valued its fishing trade. In the 19th century the east coast herring fishery, fished from Lowestoft, Hull and Aberdeen, was Europe's largest, and deep-sea fishing was pioneered by whalers working out of British ports, such as Dundee and Hull.

But in the 20th century overfishing depleted fish stocks and led to international conflicts such as the 'cod wars' between Britain and Iceland in the 1960s. Recent European Union restrictions have led to cutbacks in fishing quotas and the size of fleets. Between 1995 and 1997 the number of British fishing vessels dropped from nearly 9200 to around 7800.

> In the 16th century Elizabeth I instituted 'fish days', when only fish could be eaten, providing an early form of government support for England's fishing industry

FITZWILLIAM MUSEUM

• **Cambridge (p.495 H3)** • **Opened 1848**
One of Britain's most important art treasure houses was founded in 1816 when Richard, 7th viscount Fitzwilliam of Merrion, bequeathed paintings, prints, books, medieval manuscripts and music autographs to Cambridge University, together with the sum of £100 000 for a building to house them.

The architect George Basevi won the competition to design it in 1834, and the Founder's Building opened in 1848.

The permanent collections include Egyptian, Greek and Roman antiquities; arms and armour; English furniture and clocks; ceramics; drawings by Picasso and Leonardo da Vinci; bronzes by Rodin and paintings by Titian, Rubens and Cézanne.

an area 1½ miles long by ½ mile wide to what a native of Westmorland described as 'just like our fells because there is nothing to be seen but heaps of stones'.

Within days Christopher WREN submitted plans for a monumental new London to be built in brick and stone on a grid plan, and parliament drew up tax legislation to pay for it.

But because many buildings survived at basement level, legal complications involving ownership of the land sabotaged the plan. The City was reconstructed within its existing layout but in brick and with improved access and sanitation. Wren also realised his finest edifice – St Paul's Cathedral. Eleven years later, in 1677, the 61.5 m (202 ft) Monument was erected to commemorate the fire on the spot where it started.

TINDERBOXES
Flames leapt across the narrow gaps between old wooden houses with their overhanging gables

BLAZING CITY It was a terrifying sight. The whole sky was 'like the top of a burning oven' wrote the contemporary diarist John Evelyn

THE GLORY AND THE PITY

**The Great War shattered bodies, minds and beliefs. At its end some 850 000
British servicemen lay dead; never again would boys go to war with the blithe optimism
of 1914's half-million volunteers. Historians are still struggling to gauge its legacy**

N O ONE COULD have imagined the horror and suffering to come. Britain had entered the war to curb the imperial ambitions of Germany, and had expected the Royal Navy to blockade the enemy into submission. But within a year, the realities of industrial warfare had emerged. Lines of heavily fortified trenches faced each other across the length of northern Europe.

Any movement above ground would be met by a hail of fire and impeded by barbed wire entanglements. Life in the trenches was miserably uncomfortable at best. It was plain that huge British reinforcements would be needed.

THE BATTALIONS OF LOCAL PALS

The 'New Army' raised by Lord KITCHENER, secretary of state for war, was largely made up of volunteers; often the younger men of entire towns would enlist. It was these 'pals' battalions who were thrown into action at the Battle of the Somme in July 1916, the biggest single action fought by the British army.

A bombardment was supposed to annihilate the enemy defences, allowing the heavily laden attackers to advance in parade ground formation. But as soon as the first wave of attackers went 'over the

THE ODDS Life was a lottery for servicemen's families – the terse War Office telegram (*above*) or the smile of those safely returned

top' they found that the barbed wire had not been cut, and the German machine-gunners emerged from their dugouts to inflict slaughter on a terrifying scale.

By the end of the first day, Kitchener's infantry had suffered almost 60 000 casualties, nearly half its force. One in three was dead. By the battle's end over four months later, in mid November, the British forces had sustained 400 000 casualties and advanced some six miles.

A BITTER VICTORY

The conflict dragged on for two more years. In 1918 an exhausted Germany was forced to ask for an armistice. Although political issues remained unresolved – Europe would go to war again little more than 20 years later – for Britain, four years of fighting had brought profound psychological and social change.

A generation had been stripped of husbands, fathers, sons. Millions of men who survived were scarred in body and mind. Women who had stepped into men's jobs would never again accept the

subservience of prewar years: in 1918, those over 30 were given the vote.

Nor would industrial workers, whose political power would rise as that of the old ruling classes diminished. And no one would ever again take orders out of unquestioning, dutiful patriotism.

CHANGING STATUS

Women's ability to turn their hands to traditional men's work paved the way to more social equality after the war. Close to the battlefront, they played a vital role as nurses but also proved capable of driving ambulances and supply trucks.

At home they did hard, physical work in agriculture and in the coalfields. By July 1916, some 766 000 women had directly replaced men at work – a figure which continued to rise until the end of the war. In the public services, women drove buses, operated railway signals, fought fires and joined the police.

BUILDING THE FLEET Women happily worked alongside men in the shipyards

HOME, SWEET HOME

An escape from the grinding misery of trench warfare was a basic need when serving men returned to Britain on home leave. Some sought it in the solace of their homes and families or in the tranquillity of the countryside. Others visited the music hall or went to watch the new 'movies'. Patriotic marching songs, such as the cheery 'Pack up your troubles in your old kit bag', were sung everywhere and the words were often printed on handkerchiefs and scarves for the civilian population.

Nº 1401 SIXEPENNY POPULAR EDITION (NO DISCOUNT ALLOWED)

*Prize Marching Song
in Francis & Day's 100 Guineas Competition*

PACK UP YOUR TROUBLES IN YOUR OLD KIT-BAG.

Written by
GEORGE ASAF.

Composed by
FELIX POWELL.

FLAGS

Flags first appeared in Europe during the CRUSADES, possibly copied from the armies of the Saracen enemy. The flag of St George with its red cross on a white background was adopted by England in the 13th century.

Since then Britain's four national flags have become potent symbols of history. Others, such as the Royal Standard used to denote the presence of the monarch, are used on special occasions.

The Union Jack combines the English, Scottish and Irish saints' crosses. The Welsh flag's fire-breathing dragon is absent – perhaps because it differs from the others' Christian imagery, speaking of an earlier, pagan tradition.

Equally distinctive is Northern Ireland's semi-official flag, adopted in 1953, depicting a red cross with, at

WELSH FLAG Its design dates from 1401 but the dragon emblem is ancient

its centre, a crowned, white, six-pointed star (for the six counties) and the Red Hand of the O'Neills, a symbol which is also included in the arms of the province of Ulster.

The ROYAL NAVY uses an entire lexicon of flag lore. A Royal Ensign flown upside down is a sign of distress. Dipped, it is a sign of honour and respect; lowered altogether it means surrender. The Royal Ensign also appears on the national flags of Australia and New Zealand.

FLEET STREET

- **Central London (p.499 F5)**

Named after the river that flows under it to the Thames, the street has centuries-old associations with the printed word.

It was already well endowed with taverns when, in about 1500, William CAXTON's assistant Wynkyn de Worde set up the first printing press 'at the sign of the Swan'. The street was also the site of London's first bank, established in 1671 at No. 1, one of the houses to survive the Great Fire of 1666.

By the early 1900s, Fleet Street and its surrounding alleys and courts had become the bustling heart of the national NEWSPAPER industry. The character of the

BUILDING THE FLAG OF UNITY
The crosses of St George and St Andrew joined forces for the first Union Jack in 1606 after James I had united England and Scotland under a single crown. The red cross of St Patrick was added when the second Act of Union drew Ireland into the United Kingdom in 1801

ST GEORGE, ENGLAND

ST ANDREW, SCOTLAND

FIRST UNION JACK, 1606

ST PATRICK, IRELAND

PRESENT UNION JACK, 1801

street changed significantly in the late 1980s as proprietors moved newspapers out of Fleet Street to break the stranglehold of print unions, who had resisted the introduction of new technology.

Alexander FLEMING

- **Bacteriologist**   • 1881-1955; kt 1944

In 1928, while working at London's St Mary's Hospital, the Scottish researcher Alexander Fleming made a chance discovery that has since saved hundreds of thousands of lives. He noticed that the mould *Penicillium notatum* had contaminated some of his bacterial cultures, stopped them from multiplying or even killed them – an effect known as 'antibiosis' (against life).

Realising the importance of his finding in an age when many minor infections were killers, Fleming managed to extract from the mould an effective antibiotic, which he called penicillin.

The drug became widely available in 1939, thanks to the work of the British biochemist Ernst Chain and Australian pathologist Howard Florey, who developed a method for its commercial production. They and Fleming were jointly awarded the Nobel prize for physiology or medicine in 1945.

Battle of FLODDEN

- **Northumberland (p.496 B1)**
- **September 9, 1513**

When the 21-year-old Henry VIII invaded France in 1512, Louis XII of France persuaded his ally James IV of Scotland to march south and attack England. By September 1513, James had gathered some 30 000 Scots, one of the largest Scottish armies ever seen. It included both Highlanders and Lowlanders, united in their desire to see the English vanquished. The English army marched north to meet them. It numbered some 10 000 fewer men, but the archers, pikemen and artillery were better armed.

The crafty English commander, the 70-year-old Earl of Surrey, tempted James down from a ridge into an ill-judged position on Flodden Field – sombre and desolate open land south of the Tweed in Northumberland. Then the arrows from English longbows rained down on the Scots. Ten thousand were

STEAM POWER London and North Eastern Railway's legendary express, the *Flying Scotsman*, leaves King's Cross Station in London on May 2, 1923, on its first trial run to the north

killed in 4 hours of hand-to-hand combat, including James and most of the leading Scottish nobles. An unparalleled tragedy, the battle was the heaviest defeat in Scottish history. The lament 'For the flowers of the forest are withered away' commemorates those who died.

FLYING SCOTSMAN

- **Steam locomotive** • **Built 1923**

Designed by Nigel Gresley, the *Flying Scotsman* was introduced by the London and North Eastern Railway to pull the new nonstop express service from King's Cross to Edinburgh in 1928. It was named after the service that first ran the London to Scotland route in 1862.

A powerful locomotive, it was capable of hauling up to 600 tons, and on a run from Grantham to Peterborough in 1934 it became one of the first steam locomotives in Britain to record a speed of 100 mph. The *Flying Scotsman* was retired from service in 1963, but after undergoing a £1 million restoration was restored to private service in 1999.

FOLK ART

From weathervanes to embroidered samplers, canal-boat painting and jewellery made by gypsies, Britain has a rich legacy of folk art. In some regions corn dollies are still made from the last sheaves to be harvested, and wells dressed with flowers (*see* WELL DRESSING) – both once part of pagan ritual.

From time to time there have been movements to popularise folk art. In the 18th century the 'primitive' was much admired, while the 19th century ARTS AND CRAFTS movement was a conscious revival of traditional techniques. Since the Second World War a wider concern with CONSERVATION has been linked with an interest in vernacular art.

There is no national museum of folk art in Britain, but it can be seen in many places. There are drawings and paintings by 'folk' artists in the British Museum, peasants' smocks in the

WELL DRESSED The ancient folk art of adorning wells with scenes made from flower petals is still practised in parts of rural England

Victoria and Albert Museum, toys in the Bethnal Green Museum of Childhood, and rural crafts in Reading University's Museum of English Rural Life.

Most local and rural museums keep some pieces. Coastal museums often exhibit sea art such as the carvings and figureheads sailors crafted to decorate their boats, and scrimshaw – engraved shells and ivory from sea mammals.

FOLK SONGS

'If a man were permitted to make all the ballads, he need not care who should make all the laws of a nation,' said a 17th-century Scottish politician who recognised that folk songs capture the people's mood and reflect universal themes of love, death, work and play.

Transmitted orally, and often evolved over the centuries, many British folk songs, which include 'The Lincolnshire Poacher' and 'Waters of the Tyne', were once in danger of being lost for ever.

Some survived through reworkings by medieval and Renaissance composers, but Thomas Percy made the first systematic attempt to set them down when he published his *Reliques of Ancient English Poetry* in the mid 18th century. The Percy Society, founded in 1840, continued his work.

More recently, Cecil Sharp (1859-1924) toured Britain collecting tunes, while Ralph VAUGHAN WILLIAMS (1872-1958) made numerous settings of folk melodies. The English Folk Dance and Song Society, based at Cecil Sharp House in London, teaches the old tunes at branches throughout the country.

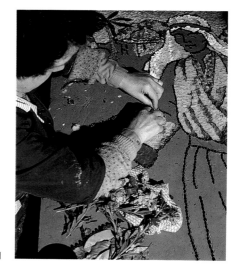

FLIGHTS OF FANCY

Two adjectives – useless and ornamental – could be used to describe more than a thousand architectural curiosities, in a wide variety of styles, that dot the landscape of Britain. In the 18th century a name was coined for them: 'follies'

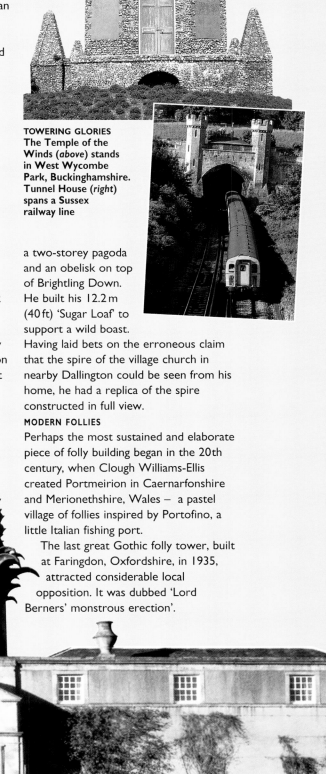

FOLLIES HAVE always served fantasy before function. In Britain, their origins may be traced back to the 16th century when Thomas Tresham built his Triangular Lodge (1597) at Rushton Hall, Northamptonshire, using a host of devices to symbolise the Holy Trinity – a defiant protest against years of detention for his Roman Catholic faith.

But the great age of folly building began in the 18th century, as part of the fashion for landscaping the grounds of country houses. Landowners believed that garden vistas would be enhanced by the addition of buildings in the classical style based on sights they had seen on their travels in Europe. Accordingly, Greek and Roman temples, arches, grottoes and sham ruins were strategically placed to crown a knoll, flank a lake, or draw the eye towards the end of a tree-lined avenue. More than 30 pseudo-classical and Gothic buildings are found at STOWE, where Richard Temple, 1st viscount Cobham, employed architects including William Kent, John Vanbrugh and James Gibbs.

ARCHITECTS OF CAPRICE

Some of the most individual and eye-catching follies, however, were built by landowners outside their own estates. These men set their whimsical obelisks, towers, cones and pyramids on any convenient hilltop or vantage point, simply to show off their ingenuity in the building's conspicuous placing and unconventional design.

The huge Gothic tower on Fish Hill, near Broadway in the Cotswold Hills, was built by the 6th earl of Coventry in 1797 just to give him something to look at from his family seat near Worcester, some 15 miles away.

Follies built in the early 19th century by the rich, eccentric 'Mad Jack' Fuller on wooded hills near Brightling Park in East Sussex include a circular temple,

TOWERING GLORIES The Temple of the Winds (*above*) stands in West Wycombe Park, Buckinghamshire. Tunnel House (*right*) spans a Sussex railway line

a two-storey pagoda and an obelisk on top of Brightling Down. He built his 12.2 m (40 ft) 'Sugar Loaf' to support a wild boast. Having laid bets on the erroneous claim that the spire of the village church in nearby Dallington could be seen from his home, he had a replica of the spire constructed in full view.

MODERN FOLLIES

Perhaps the most sustained and elaborate piece of folly building began in the 20th century, when Clough Williams-Ellis created Portmeirion in Caernarfonshire and Merionethshire, Wales – a pastel village of follies inspired by Portofino, a little Italian fishing port.

The last great Gothic folly tower, built at Faringdon, Oxfordshire, in 1935, attracted considerable local opposition. It was dubbed 'Lord Berners' monstrous erection'.

CAVE ART

The grotto, inspired by caves dedicated to the classical nymphs and muses, was a favourite feature of 18th-century gardening. The grotto at Painshill Park in Surrey, created for the painter and traveller Charles Hamilton and painstakingly restored in the 1990s, is a glittering example of this fanciful art. Artificial stalactites that reflect the water hang like great chandeliers, each crystal-like droplet formed from plaster over a wooden core.

RUGGED LINK A bridge of crystalline rock connects the two islets of Grotto Island at Painshill, Surrey

FRUIT SURPRISE The Pineapple folly was built in Dunmore Park, near Stirling, in 1761. It is said to have been a wedding present from the owner to his wife

THE BEAUTIFUL GAME

Football is our national game. It was invented in Britain as far back as the 12th century, became an organised spectator sport in the 19th century, and is now played in vast stadiums watched by tens of thousands of fervent supporters, or on Hackney Marshes by one man and his dog

FOOTBALL IS one of the few things that obsess the British. The tussle to direct a leather ball into an opponent's goal as frequently as possible within a 90 minute game is also our most significant contribution to world sport.

FROM STREET TO STADIUM

Richard II banned the fledgling game in the 14th century because it interfered with archery practice, but football thrived just the same, developing its modern form in 19th-century public schools.

The first club, Notts County, was formed in 1862, and the Football Association the next year, basing its rules on those devised by Edward Thring, headmaster of Oundle school, for what he called 'The Simplest Game'. The legitimate payment of players from 1885 prompted the formation of the

MATCH NOTES Some 99 000 fans saw Charlton Athletic beat Burnley 1-0 in the 1947 FA Cup Final. England played Scotland for the 100th time in 1982 – England won 1-0

Football League (1888), the Irish League (1890) and the Scottish League (1891). The Saturday 3 pm kick-off became a ritual, drawing huge crowds: nearly 119 000 went to a 'derby' between GLASGOW CELTIC AND RANGERS in 1939, and more than 41 million fans saw English league matches in the 1948-9 season. With floodlit pitches in the 1950s came the first midweek evening games.

The crowning glory for England fans was the 1966 WORLD CUP triumph at WEMBLEY, coinciding with the 'swinging 60s' that produced football's first sex symbol – George BEST.

THE FALL AND RISE OF FOOTBALL

League attendances went into sharp decline in the 1970s when England failed

FLYING CAPTAIN Between 1958 World Cup final games, England's Tom Finney, Maurice Setters and Bobby Charlton pick up Billy Wright, the first man to win 100 England caps

to qualify for two World Cup finals and violence between fans all too often marred matches.

In 1989, 96 fans, mostly from Liverpool, were crushed to death at an overcrowded FA Cup tie in Sheffield. The resulting Taylor Report forced clubs to end standing at matches and construct all-seater stadiums. Ticket prices went up, but more families joined the largely male crowds. In 1990 the England team reached the World Cup semifinal and rekindled a national passion.

Two events capitalised on the fervour. In 1991 Leeds United signed the French player Eric Cantona, who helped them to win the League then joined Manchester United the following season, heralding an influx of foreign stars into English and Scottish teams. In 1992 the English first division clubs broke away to form the Premier League and made lucrative deals with the satellite television service BSkyB. By the end of the century football was as popular as ever, but governed by business. Clubs were quoted on the stock exchange, and players paid more than £20 000 a week had pop star status.

FOOTBALLING GREATS

ACE STRIKER (*right*) Dixie Dean (1907-80) scored 349 goals in 399 games for Everton from 1925 to 1938. In 1927-8 he scored 60 league goals, the highest number in a single season

RECORD FEE (*left*) Trevor Francis was the first £1 million British player when he signed for Nottingham Forest in 1979. By 1999 the record stood at £15 million for Newcastle's Alan Shearer

SAFE HANDS (*right*) Pat Jennings played in goal 119 times for Northern Ireland from 1964 to 1986. His hands were said to be football's biggest

GOLDEN BOY (*left*) At 18 years, 59 days, Michael Owen in 1998 became the youngest England player of the 20th century. His goal against Argentina in the 1998 World Cup made him a national hero

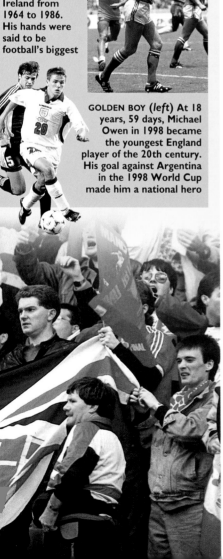

Margot FONTEYN

- Ballet dancer
- 1919-91; CBE 1951; DBE 1956

Margaret Peggy Hookham danced under her more sophisticated stage name for more than 30 years, and was probably the greatest ballerina of her time.

Her BALLET career began at the Sadler's Wells Ballet in 1934, later the Royal Ballet, where she became prima ballerina. Frederick ASHTON created some of his greatest choreography around her easy musicality and dramatic expressiveness. It was not until 1962, when her career seemed to be coming to an end, that she first performed with Rudolf Nureyev, 19 years her junior, in *Giselle*. The partnership rejuvenated Fonteyn's career and she continued dancing until the age of 60.

FOOTBALL: *see opposite page*

FOREIGN OFFICE

The Foreign Office implements the government's foreign policies and runs its diplomatic service. It is headed by the foreign secretary and housed in magnificent buildings designed in the 1860s by George Gilbert SCOTT. It backs conveniently onto DOWNING STREET.

The responsibilities of foreign and colonial (later Commonwealth) policy were first split between two secretaries of state in 1782; only in 1968 were the two offices merged into one, still officially named the Foreign and Commonwealth Office. Today, the department employs some 5800 staff, 2400 of them posted overseas, and 7600 local overseas staff.

FOREST OF DEAN

- Gloucestershire (p.494 E4)
- Area 35 sq miles

In a wedge formed by the Wye and Severn rivers, the remains of industrial and mining works dot the woodlands, commons and orchards of the Forest of Dean. Oak, beech, ash, birch and conifer

HIGH SOCIETY As well as having played all the ballerina roles of the classics, Margot Fonteyn also created many more, such as a society belle in Frederick Ashton's *Les Sirènes* (1946, *left*)

forests cluster in the centre, between Coleford, unofficial capital of the region, and Cinderford. Ancient Britons 2500 years ago used the wood to smelt iron, a practice that continued until Tudor times. Coal seams in the area were easily accessible and brought growing wealth, which peaked around 1900. Coal was deep mined in the forest until 1965.

In 1938 the Forest of Dean became England's first National Forest Park. Tourism now brings some 3 million people each year to the forest, many to walk or cycle on miles of nature trails where wildlife such as fallow deer, woodpeckers and 30 different species of butterfly may be seen.

FORESTS

When Neolithic farmers used timber to build the Sweet Track across a Somerset marsh 6000 years ago, they had plenty to choose from – Britain was largely covered by forest. For thousands of years, forests provided materials for fuel, carpentry and wickerwork. By the early 19th century, each man-of-war built at naval dockyards took 1000 mature oak trees, supplied by royal forests such as the NEW FOREST.

Such insatiable demand decimated the native woods, and as the vast forests of the Empire were exploited, there was no replanting of British WOODLAND. By the end of the First World War forests covered just 5 per cent of the country.

In 1919 the Forestry Commission was established to begin replanting, but its choice of fast-growing conifers instead of native broadleaved trees for new forests attracted criticism from conservationists. Today 65 per cent of Britain's forests are conifer, the rest are made up of old woods, mainly on private land, and broad-leaved planting by the Forestry Commission, whose policy is to develop woodlands as a sustainable economic resource, as a refuge for wildlife and to provide recreational opportunities such as forest trails. The Commission controls more than a million hectares of forest.

E.M. FORSTER

• **Writer** • **1879-1970; kt 1949; OM 1969**
Championing artistic freedom and opposing censorship were important themes in the life of Edward Morgan Forster, one of the liberal BLOOMSBURY GROUP of writers and artists, and the first president of the National Council for Civil Liberties in 1934.

Forster's early experiences left him with an abiding contempt for public school and upper middle-class snobbery.

REACHING FOR THE SKIES Fifty-seven workers lost their lives building the Forth railway bridge. The greatest fear was the momentum gained by objects falling from above – a spanner once fell 90 m (300 ft), punching a hole through a piece of timber 10 cm (4 in) thick

Travels in Italy and India between 1901 and 1922 led to lasting affection and respect for the culture of both countries. Contrasts between English and foreign society run through his novels, in which social issues are explored through personal relationships. Several of his books, including *Howard's End* (1910), *Maurice* (1912) and *A Passage to India* (1924), have been turned into films.

FORTH BRIDGE and RIVER

• **Central Scotland (p.497 C4/D4)**
• **Railway bridge built 1883-90**
The River Forth rises on the eastern side of Ben Lomond near Scotland's indented west coast and gathers tributaries from the Grampians, Ochill Hills and central Lowlands as it flows 120 miles towards the North Sea. Between Kincardine Bridge, below Stirling, and the Forth road and railway bridges, 14 miles to the east, it broadens to widths of up to 3 miles.

When it was built, the Forth railway bridge, designed by Benjamin Baker and John Fowler, was the world's longest bridge, with a steel superstructure and a cantilever system supporting most of its 1½ mile length. The bridge is legendary

for its continuous painting process – by the time work is finished at one end, it has to begin again at the other. This is likely to end in 2001 with the completion of a new coat intended to last for ten years. The road bridge to the west was opened in 1964.

Once past the railway bridge, the River Forth widens into the Firth of Forth at Edinburgh. The Isle of May and Bass Rock, with its tumult of gannets, mark its end as it meets the North Sea.

FORTNUM & MASON

• **Central London (p.499 B6)** • **Founded 1707**
William Fortnum and Hugh Mason made ideal business partners. Mason, a London shopkeeper, had retail experience, Fortnum had knowledge of courtiers' tastes, having worked in Queen Anne's household. The two men opened a grocery shop on Piccadilly, attracting the capital's well-to-do and importing exotic foods through the East India Company.

A special department serviced gentlemen's clubs, and soldiers on foreign postings came to rely on Fortnum & Mason to send provisions that could not be obtained abroad. The shop received royal approval when Queen Victoria sent a consignment of Fortnum & Mason concentrated beef tea to wounded soldiers during the Crimean War. By the time the present building was completed in 1925, the firm had expanded into furniture and clothes. The finishing touch came in 1964 with a new

THE FORTNUM & MASON CLOCK

clock above the entrance, adorned with figures of the store's founders, who turn to bow to each other on the hour. The shop's clientele includes the Queen, Queen Mother and Prince Charles.

FORTY-FIVE REBELLION

• 1745

More than 50 years after the deposition of his grandfather, JAMES II, in the GLORIOUS REVOLUTION, Charles Edward Stuart (BONNIE PRINCE CHARLIE) sailed from France to Scotland to make what became the final military attempt to restore a JACOBITE king to the throne.

Charles gathered an army of loyal Scottish clans, marched to Edinburgh, where his father was proclaimed James VIII of Scotland, and defeated the English at Prestonpans, east of the city. Charles then marched south and captured Carlisle, but as his men trudged farther south supplies dwindled and so did support; the troops reached Derby in December, cold and hungry, and now mocked by those they passed.

Charles began a bitter retreat, taking four months to reach Inverness. There, in April 1746, the 5000 exhausted and outnumbered Scots were routed by George II's army at the Battle of CULLODEN MOOR. Charles fled into the Highlands, his hopes of reinstating the STUART dynasty destroyed.

FOSSILS: *see page 176*

Norman FOSTER

• Architect
• b.1935; kt 1990; OM 1997; bn 1999

There is no better example of the ability of Norman Foster to design innovative structures than the Willis, Faber and Dumas headquarters in Ipswich. The building, completed in 1975, reflects the

sky and the tower of St Nicholas' Church in dark glass walls that follow the curve of the surrounding medieval streets.

With Richard ROGERS, his partner in the mid 1960s, Foster pioneered high-tech architecture. He builds lightweight steel structures covered with glass and metal cladding. Energy efficiency is a key objective – glass walls are often triple glazed for insulation. In the Hong Kong and Shanghai Bank (1986) – a skyscraper that brought Foster international recognition – reflecting screens filter natural light into the building. His latest work in Britain includes the 250 m (820 ft) long Canary Wharf Jubilee Line station (1999) and the Great Court of the British Museum (2000), both in London.

FOUNTAINS ABBEY

• North Yorkshire (p.496 C4)
• Built 12th-15th century • NT

The approach to Fountains Abbey through the gardens of the Studley Royal estate is a fitting introduction to what was once one of England's wealthiest monasteries. Its pointed Early English arches rise from the banks of the River Skell, and parts of the ruins span the water. The exceptionally long vaulted cloisters stretch 95 m (312 ft).

The abbey was founded in 1132 by monks from York whose income came

from the wool trade. But prosperity brought the abbey's downfall – it was one of the first to be sold by Henry VIII in the Dissolution of the Monasteries.

FOX

To farmers, Britain's most successful native carnivore is a pest capable of attacking lambs or killing every hen in a coop. But most foxes, hunting at night, live on rodents and insects, or scraps scavenged from dustbins. Foxes live anywhere, from salt marshes to urban areas, where they may even dig out their 'earth' beneath a garden shed. One family can occupy an area ranging from 20 ha (50 acres) in town to 15 sq miles in hill country. There are about 250 000 adult foxes in Britain.

The hunting of foxes has been a popular country pursuit since the 17th century. Although it attracts enthusiasts from a wide variety of rural occupations, it is often seen as the province of the rich and privileged, particularly on such illustrious hunts as the Belvoir and Quorn in Leicestershire.

Over the last century, concern that foxes suffer during a hunt has provoked clashes between animal welfare protestors and huntsmen. An attempt in 1998 to ban hunting with dogs failed through lack of government support.

TRADEMARK STYLE At night, the Willis, Faber and Dumas headquarters in Ipswich become transparent, revealing an open-plan interior characteristic of its designer, Norman Foster

FOSSILS

In 1811, 11-year-old Mary Anning was one of the first to discover, in a cliff near Lyme Regis, a dinosaur fossil. Scientists had just begun to realise that fossils were the petrified traces of creatures as old as the ROCK itself – knowledge that later led Charles Darwin to use fossils to support his theory of evolution.

Britain's diverse GEOLOGY has yielded many thousands of fossil species, from microscopic shellfish found extensively in chalk to an 18 m (60 ft) reptile unearthed near Peterborough. Dudley in the Midlands has revealed corals, sponges, starfish-like sea lilies and dragonflies from more than 300 million years ago, when the land lay in the tropics. Lulworth Cove in Dorset has fossilised stumps from prehistoric conifers.

GOOD SITES

Exposed faces of sedimentary rock such as limestone or shale are the best places to look. The age of the rock determines the fossil species found in it.

KEY

- Rock more than 570 million years old: fossils unlikely
- Rock 570-280 million years old: first plants and sea creatures
- Rock 280-65 million years old: first reptiles
- Rock 65-2 million years old: first mammals and birds

ACHANARRAS QUARRY, THURSO Numerous fish fossils (permits issued by Scottish Natural Heritage)

DUNBAR Corals and shells found in landslips at the cliff base

WHITBY Ammonites and plants at the cliff base

ISLE OF SHEPPEY Corals and molluscs washed up on beach

ISLE OF WIGH[T] Marine and mammal fossil[s] throughout th[e] north of the is[land]

PENARTH Marine fossils in fallen rocks at the cliff base

LYME REGIS AND CHARMOUTH Miles of cliffs containing a wide range of species; especially rich in ammonites

COMMON FINDS

The most plentiful British fossils are shelled sea creatures, such as sea urchins, early shrimp-like crustaceans called trilobites, and ammonites (distant relatives of today's squid). Also common are leaves and branches of trees, and teeth and bones of fish, mammals and birds.

| TRILOBITE | FERN | AMMONITE | SEA URCHIN | FISH |

George FOX

• Founder of the Quakers • 1624-91

In an age of religious turmoil during the Civil War, 19-year-old George Fox left his home and shoemaking apprenticeship to wander the country, preaching his belief that anyone could speak directly to God without the help of a priest.

His habit of interrupting church services, lambasting lawyers, priests and soldiers and denouncing trivial social convention and amusements frequently landed Fox in prison. Despite his unusual methods, his philanthropic and religious ideas attracted intelligent men and women. One of his earliest converts was Margaret Fell, whom he later married. It was at her Lancashire home in the 1650s that the Society of Friends, or QUAKERS, was formed.

The movement grew so fast that by 1656 nearly a thousand Friends were in prison for refusing to take the oath in court or for denouncing formal church services. Many more emigrated or became missionaries overseas to escape British restrictions. Fox continued to preach at home and abroad in Europe and North America for the rest of his life.

FOYLE'S

• Founded 1906

When William Foyle and his brother, Gilbert, both failed the civil service examination, they stumbled upon a career. The brothers advertised their unneeded textbooks and found demand so great that they went on to set up a bookshop in London's Charing Cross Road. By 1929, when Foyle's moved to its present premises across the road, it was London's leading bookshop. It now has 30 miles of shelves on four floors.

William's daughter Christina, who was managing director until she died in 1999, wrote to Hitler in the 1930s offering to buy the Jewish books he was burning. 'I would no sooner corrupt the morals of the British than those of the Germans', he replied. Christina ran the business traditionally, ignoring advances such as computerised billing even into the 1990s. Her passion was arranging Foyle's monthly literary lunches, held at the Grosvenor House Hotel, to celebrate a newly published book. Since 1930, the public and distinguished guests have been invited; past speakers include the philosopher Bertrand Russell and French statesman Charles de Gaulle.

John FRANKLIN

• Explorer • 1786-1847; kt 1829

No explorer came close to disaster more often than John Franklin. During his first expedition – a doomed attempt to sail to the North Pole in 1818 – his leaking ship nearly sank. The following year, he set out on a 5000 mile trek to find the Northwest Passage, the Arctic sea route connecting the Atlantic to the Pacific.

During the three-year odyssey his party ran out of food and one member resorted to cannibalism. Franklin chose to eat his boots. Of the 20 who set out, only nine returned. Seven years as Governor of Tasmania allowed Franklin time to plan a second attempt at the Northwest Passage. He set sail in 1845 with two of the Royal Navy's best-equipped ships, *Erebus* and *Terror*, carrying provisions to last the 138 men three years. He was never seen again, and none of the crew survived.

In dozens of unsuccessful rescue attempts, searchers mapped most of the unknown Canadian Arctic. But there was no trace of Franklin until 1859, when a sheet of paper found tucked into a cairn revealed that Franklin had discovered the Northwest Passage, but his ships had been trapped in ice, and he had perished without navigating it. Franklin, his ships and his diaries have never been found.

FREEMASONS

The largest secret society in the world originated among itinerant stonemasons of 14th-century Britain who developed secret signs and passwords to identify each other. As respected craftsmen, they were free to work anywhere in Britain, hence the term 'freemason'.

As cathedral building declined, stonemasons' guilds invited honorary members from outside the trade to join the all-male societies. By the 18th century, their local groups, or lodges, had become social clubs, retaining masonic tools for symbolic purposes. The Grand Lodge, founded in London in 1717, became the biggest in England.

Religious toleration and political compromise characterise the liberal thinking of the Freemasons, who also support charitable work. But their secrecy and commercial interests have invited criticism. Many freemasons hold influential positions. Members have included royalty (the Duke of Kent is the current Grand Master), judges and police officers. Some 700000 masons now belong to nearly 10000 lodges in the United Kingdom, and the society has more than 6 million members worldwide.

FAMILY HEIRLOOM The museum at Sigmund Freud's house contains his collection of books and antiquities, as well as his consulting couch

ENTERTAINMENT ON ICE In 1683-4, Charles II visited the colourful stalls of London's frost fair, set up on the thick ice of the Thames. For the event, hand presses published souvenir songs

Sigmund FREUD

- Psychoanalyst • 1856-1939

When he came to Britain late in 1938, a year before his death, Sigmund Freud had already pioneered the techniques and theory of psychoanalysis. A Jew, he sought refuge in London after Nazi Germany occupied Vienna, where he had established a private practice in 1886. Despite suffering from cancer, he continued to practise psychoanalysis at his Hampstead home, which opened as a museum in 1986.

Freud's children and grandchildren have also become public figures: his daughter Anna as a child psychoanalyst, his grandsons Lucian, as a painter of unsettling, candid nudes and portraits, and Clement, as a writer, broadcaster, Member of Parliament and chef.

FROST FAIRS

Before 19th-century engineering made them obsolete, narrow-arched bridges spanning the Thames slowed the flow of water to the extent that in cold winters the sluggish river sometimes froze from bank to bank. Townsfolk, tradespeople and travelling showmen were quick to take advantage, setting up fairs and festivities on the ice. Archery and dancing on the Thames were among the events recorded in the winter of 1564.

The last large frost fair took place in January 1814. Londoners gathered on 'City Road', a vast slippery walkway on ice stretching three-quarters of a mile from Blackfriars Bridge to London Bridge. It ended with a sudden thaw, and many stalls sank. Bank-to-bank ice became a thing of the past after 1831 when the old London Bridge was replaced.

Elizabeth FRY

- Prison reformer • 1780-1845

A visit to Newgate prison in 1813 horrified the QUAKER preacher Elizabeth Fry. She saw women detained with their children in cramped cells and filthy conditions and resolved to fight for reforms such as segregation of the sexes and female supervision for women.

Fry was deeply devout and had a captivating presence – an American minister at Newgate prison described how 'the wretched outcasts have been tamed and subdued by [her] Christian eloquence'.

Her philanthropy extended to arranging food and shelter for London's homeless, and self-help guidance for those willing to accept it. Her advice on prison reform was sought at home and abroad. She kept up her tireless work, in addition to bringing up several children, even after her merchant husband's bankruptcy wiped out the family fortune.

SITTING IN STYLE

Is there such a thing as a quintessentially British style of furniture? Surprisingly for a country that has long produced some of the world's finest pieces, almost every stylistic or technical development has foreign origins

THE STORY OF British furniture is a tale of 1000 years of foreign influences, from the Romanesque style that came with the Norman invaders in 1066 to the exotic materials and techniques from the great ages of exploration and Empire. But it was never a one-way process: British influence on furniture design has been felt worldwide, especially in Europe and the USA.

RARE TREASURES

Medieval homes – even the halls and manors of feudal lords – were sparsely furnished and little furniture from the period survives. Most pieces were of local woods, usually oak, and styles were plain and solid – functional stools and chests, armchairs and posted beds. Decoration took the form of simple carving, at first in Romanesque motifs.

From about the 12th century a more elegant variant – Gothic – started to emerge, with pointed arches, tracery and elaborate carved or painted decoration.

Medieval styles persisted for longer in Britain than in the rest of Europe but by the mid 16th century many Continental craftsmen were working in Britain, producing pieces with classically inspired motifs and ornamentation. Houses were larger and had rooms for specific purposes, requiring more furnishing.

Throughout Elizabethan and Jacobean times furniture was of four-square, solid construction, often panelled or carved, and accompanied by loose cushions.

BETWEEN TWO WORLDS Behind the elaborate carving and the revolutionary use of walnut and cane in this 1680s armchair, the basic square-set design of much earlier English styles is still evident. Just 20 years on all traces of this past were eclipsed

ELEGANCE AND REFINEMENT The 17th century brought a greater influx of skilled Continental craftsmen into Britain. French Protestant workers – HUGUENOTS – found refuge here in the Restoration period from 1660

MASTER OF MANY ARTS Thomas Chippendale (1718-79) showed matchless elegance in combining styles

THE CHANGING STYLES OF BRITISH FURNITURE

MEDIEVAL		ELIZABETHAN AND JACOBEAN			RESTORATION AND QUEEN ANNE		EARLY GEORGIAN
1500 1525 1550	1575 **1600** 1625 1650				1675 **1700**	1725	1750

Simple oak pieces with panelling and heavy carved decoration

Carved or panelled oak with architectural or naturalistic motifs; painted, gilded or ironwork decoration

PRESS CUPBOARD, 1610

Walnut veneers, marquetry, burr patterns and brass fittings; barley-twist or cabriole legs; some lavish carving; serpentine stretchers

CHIPPENDALE CHAIR, 1745   Rich styles often in mahogany; curved cabriole legs; ball and claw feet

OAK CHAIR, 1500

REFECTORY TABLE, 1600

SIDE TABLE, 1710

and others, both Dutch and French, under William and Mary in the last decade of the century. They brought a lighter foreign touch that finally ended the taste for massively solid styles.

MODERN MASTERPIECE Britain's reputation for individuality and craftsmanship has thrived in the industrial age. Contemporary design favours simplicity of line and form – made possible by modern materials and techniques. Ross Lovegrove's 1990s 'Magic Chair' is a moulded piece of polyurethane supported – as if by magic – on a single strip of steel tubing

Walnut began to rival oak in popularity, especially as a veneer, and delicate marquetry was used for ornamentation. The crowning achievement was the elegant simplicity of the QUEEN ANNE STYLE chair, with its restrained carving, curved back, slender cabriole legs and drop-seat.

British furniture-making of the 18th century ranked among the finest in the world, combining baroque and classical designs with unprecedented technical accomplishment. Pieces by William Kent, Thomas CHIPPENDALE, George HEPPLEWHITE and Thomas SHERATON are still endlessly copied.

MASS PRODUCTION AND MASTER CRAFTSMEN

In the 19th century taste started to favour heavier furniture again, first in the form of carved and gilded Regency pieces and later in yet more solid Victorian styles. The ARTS AND CRAFTS movement of 1870-90 reacted against the growing trend to mass production, calling for a return to traditional skills and simplicity.

British design in the 20th century was innovative and varied, ranging from the pragmatism of the 1940s Utility Furniture Scheme – set up by the Board of Trade to provide affordable furniture in wartime – to Pop Art pieces of the 1960s and flat-pack items from high street stores such as Habitat.

At the other end of the scale masters such as John MAKEPEACE and Ron ARAD have continued to produce pieces of such striking originality and quality that they amount virtually to works of art.

A TOUCH OF THE EXOTIC

Constant cultural and stylistic interchange between Britain and the rest of the world has left its mark on furniture materials, motifs and designs from all periods.

Romanesque arching arrived with the Normans in the 11th century but by the 12th was changing into more graceful Gothic.

In the reign of Elizabeth I Renaissance-style motifs such as columns and pilasters began to find expression in our formerly functional furniture and by the 1600s classical adornments such as acanthus leaves and winged cupids were commonplace. English explorers sailed to Russia, China, Japan and the Americas bringing back materials such as cane and tortoiseshell, ebony for inlays, and exotic techniques such as lacquering and japanning. London became a centre of world trade and a place where influences from many countries met.

Dutch and French craftsmen in the later 17th century brought a baroque style, making use of twists and scrolls, floral and seaweed-pattern marquetry, mirror panels and decorative veneers. Even the elegant furniture of the 18th century – a high point of British style – was an exotic mixture of Italianate baroque, French rococo, French Empire, Classical, Egyptian, Chinese and Indian styles.

Mahogany became increasingly popular in the 19th century and George IV introduced a vogue for mock-bamboo and Chinoiserie. The 20th century brought a return of European influence, particularly moderning movements such as Art Deco and Bauhaus.

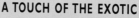

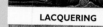
LACQUERING

MARQUETRY

VENEERING

ROCOCO

MOCK BAMBOO

ART DECO

BENT ON REFORM William Morris (1834-96) preached social change and a return to traditional craftsmanship

NEW STYLE Charles Rennie Mackintosh (1868-1928) developed a British version of Art Nouveau

BLURRING THE BOUNDARIES Works by Ron Arad (b.1951) are as much sculpture as furniture

0

LATE GEORGIAN	REGENCY	EARLY VICTORIAN	LATE VICTORIAN AND EDWARDIAN	BETWEEN THE WARS	POSTWAR	MODERN
1775	**1800** 1825	1850	1875 **1900**	1925	1950	1975 **2000**
Slender, restrained pieces with tapering legs and spade feet	Heavier forms with gilding, animal head and leg supports, and scrolled ends	Large ornate pieces, often in mahogany and imitating styles of other periods	Simple curvilinear shapes; stylised naturalistic designs of Art Nouveau	Geometric but asymmetrical forms; Art Deco	Contemporary styles; new, brighter colours	Space-saving, functional styles with minimal embellishment; new materials
SIDEBOARD, 1790	COUCH, 1805	CENTRE TABLE, 1850	SIDEBOARD, 1900	DRESSING TABLE, 1930	STACKING CHAIR, 1950	SOFABED, 1997

Thomas GAINSBOROUGH

• Artist • 1727-88

Society portraits made Thomas Gainsborough a living but LANDSCAPE PAINTING was his pleasure. He depicted his native Suffolk with a realism inspired by the Dutch school – the detail in every branch of *Cornard Wood* (1748) reflects his love of the area.

IDYLLIC STROLL Gainsborough painted an idealised view of nature and humanity in harmony in *The Morning Walk* in 1785

In 1759 Gainsborough moved to Bath to paint the aristocratic visitors to the spa. His rapid, light brush strokes created shimmering silks in works such as *The Blue Boy* (c.1770). He moved to London in 1774 where his exhibitions at the Royal Academy and portraits such as *Mrs Graham* (1777) attracted the attention of royalty. A commission to paint *George III* and *Queen Charlotte* (1781) ensured Gainsborough's reputation, and he displaced Joshua Reynolds as the court's most popular painter.

Francis GALTON

• Scientist • 1822-1911; kt 1909

Just as physical characteristics are hereditary, Francis Galton observed that mental attributes tended to run in families. He believed that encouraging people with desirable physical or mental attributes to breed and restraining those with serious defects would improve the human race. Galton considered his own heredity proof of the theory, which he called 'eugenics'. His cousin was Charles DARWIN, whose theory of evolution by natural selection had inspired him.

Galton's studies in heredity led him to develop the fingerprint identification system still in use, but his academic interests were wide. He identified the weather systems called anticyclones, designed the basis for weather maps, helped to set up the Meteorological Office, and invented an early telex machine and ultrasonic dog whistle.

GARDEN CITY

The unsanitary sprawl of growing cities after the Industrial Revolution prompted the town planner Ebenezer Howard to look for a better way of living.

Howard proposed building new towns from scratch in three concentric zones: public buildings in the centre; parks, schools and houses next; and factories and workshops in another ring outside. He coined a name for his vision in his 1902 book, *Garden Cities of Tomorrow*.

His aim was to combine the best aspects of town and country in an environment where all members of society had a place. He fixed populations at 32 000 and established green belts around the new cities to limit growth.

A VISION OF BRITAIN In Ebenezer Howard's plan, several garden cities with allotments, hospitals and leisure areas would cluster around a central metropolis

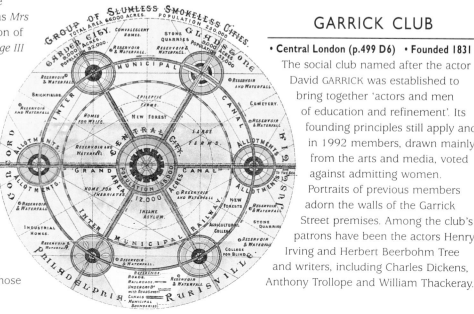

With the investment of George CADBURY and William Lever, who had built the 'factory towns' Bournville and PORT SUNLIGHT, Howard formed First Garden City Ltd. They bought a green-field site and began to build Letchworth, in Hertfordshire, in 1903. The new city prospered and others followed, including Hampstead Garden Suburb (1907) and Welwyn Garden City (1919).

Although Howard's ideas never won government backing, his principles of zoning were used in many of the NEW TOWNS built after the Second World War.

GARDENING: *see opposite page*

David GARRICK

• Actor, director and playwright • 1717-79

In 1741 the London debut in *Richard III* of David Garrick, one of the finest ever stage actors, was so sensational that crowds flocked from the West End to the East End playhouse to see it.

In 1747 he joined the management at the Drury Lane theatre in Covent Garden, where he set about modernising play-going. He introduced concealed lighting and banished the audience from the few privileged seats on stage.

Garrick was known not only for his productions of Shakespeare and his roles in contemporary tragedies, but also for his comedies, including his self-penned farce *A Peep Behind the Curtain* (1767). He retired in 1776 and is buried in Westminster Abbey. The GARRICK CLUB was named in his honour in 1831.

GARRICK CLUB

• Central London (p.499 D6) • Founded 1831

The social club named after the actor David GARRICK was established to bring together 'actors and men of education and refinement'. Its founding principles still apply and in 1992 members, drawn mainly from the arts and media, voted against admitting women.

Portraits of previous members adorn the walls of the Garrick Street premises. Among the club's patrons have been the actors Henry Irving and Herbert Beerbohm Tree and writers, including Charles Dickens, Anthony Trollope and William Thackeray.

TAMING THE WILD

Food for the table, herbs for health and flowers for simple delight filled the walled gardens of 11th-century monasteries. More than 800 years later, gardening – for pleasure and produce – is Britain's favourite hobby

TOPIARY BOX PEACOCK

WHEN BRITAIN was still largely forested, walls kept out the wilderness from medieval gardens. Inside, the emphasis was on order, with mazes of clipped evergreens, fruit trees trained on trellises and beds filled with medicinal plants, herbs and vegetables.

By the end of the 16th century more than 200 kinds of garden plant were being cultivated in Britain, including crocuses, hyacinths and tulips from the Middle East. The PLANT COLLECTORS of the 17th-century returned from voyages to the New World with North American species such as lupins, Michaelmas daisies and Virginia creeper. By the late 1830s more than 18 000 species were growing in British gardens and in the wild.

TRAINING NATURE

Hedges and arbours of roses and honeysuckles filled Elizabethan knot gardens – havens from the foul air and bustle of the growing cities. Herbs were trained into knot-like patterns inside low hedges of box, and topiaries added decoration, clipped into neatly shaped animals, particularly birds, and geometric motifs.

In the late 16th century, Renaissance ideals began to inspire garden design – tall trees and elaborate parterres gave large gardens an architectural look – and the Restoration of Charles II in 1660 ushered in a new era of formal style characterised by geometric forms defined with immaculately clipped hedges.

THE BIRTH OF THE ENGLISH GARDEN

The 18th century brought a wave of fresh opinion – a belief that the shaping of nature constrained its true beauty. A craze for LANDSCAPE GARDENING obliterated many structured, formal designs with more naturalistic vistas. The French named this 'natural' style the *jardin anglais* (English garden).

By the end of the 19th century, after the AGRICULTURAL REVOLUTION and the creation of ALLOTMENTS, food was no longer a priority in country gardens. Designers such as Gertrude JEKYLL encouraged informal, decorative layouts. The invention of the 20th-century GARDEN CITY gave urban dwellers the chance to indulge their green fingers, and gardening for pleasure – no longer the privilege of the wealthy – took root as a national obsession.

A CORNER OF PARADISE

There are 18.5 million private gardens in Britain and to most British people a home is not complete without one. Many are centred on a lawn – a concept introduced by the Tudor nobility to indulge their love of games such as bowls – but even where outside space is short, window boxes and flowering pots proliferate. Each year around £2.8 billion is spent in British garden centres.

The peculiarly British passion for gardening has led people to cultivate the most unlikely and unpromising places. On top of an office building in London, 30 m (100 ft) above Kensington High Street, is a 0.6 ha (1.5 acre) fantasy roof garden complete with ponds and pink flamingoes.

COUNTRY RETREAT High above the traffic, the city could be a million miles away from this tranquil London roof terrace

FLORAL FORMALITY Low box hedges separate herbs and bedding plants in the Knott Garden at New Place in Stratford-upon-Avon

MAKING A POINT Workers united in protest against pit owners during the General Strike while the middle classes turned to manual labour to keep the country running. At Paddington Station (right) women could be found driving goods lorries

Paul GASCOIGNE

• Footballer   • b.1967

The most captivating English footballer of his generation, Paul Gascoigne has made a career of polarising opinions. *The Observer* called him 'the most gifted git in football'. In 1991, radio listeners in Gascoigne's native Tyneside voted him 'Britain's biggest bore'.

An effervescent midfield player, 'Gazza' had great skill, speed and determination and could beat most defences at the height of his career. His talent was undeniable but he was characterised by the England manager, Bobby Robson, as 'daft as a brush' and became notorious for impulsive, ill-advised behaviour on and off the pitch. He injured himself making a wild challenge in the 1991 FA Cup final for Tottenham but it was his love of alcohol and parties that led to him being left out of the 1998 England World Cup squad for alleged lack of fitness.

EMOTIONAL DEFEAT Paul Gascoigne endeared himself to the nation by crying when England lost the 1990 World Cup semifinal

Mrs GASKELL

• Novelist and biographer   • 1810-65

'A woman of whose conversation I should never tire,' said Charlotte Brontë of her friend and later biographer Elizabeth Gaskell. Mrs Gaskell was a minister's wife in Cheshire. She lived near Manchester, with its mills and crowded, unsanitary slums, which became the focus of her fiction, beginning with *Mary Barton* in 1848.

Mrs Gaskell campaigned for better working conditions for factory girls, using books such as *Cranford* (1853) to expose the injustices of the mill owners. She wrote her long novels at the family dining table, interrupted by children, maids and gardeners; but despite these distractions her stories flow with natural ease and capture details of speech and behaviour with acute precision.

GENERAL STRIKE

• May 4-12, 1926

When Britain's miners were locked out of their pits by their employers on April 30, 1926, to try to force them to accept reduced wages, they turned to the TRADE UNION movement for solidarity. More than 2 million workers answered calls for a general strike in support of the miners. Stanley BALDWIN's Conservative government responded with a heavy hand. The military and some 200 000 special constables were mobilised to quell unrest and run essential services. Unexpected volunteers also came forward: peeresses drove newspaper lorries and tweed-clad undergraduates worked as railway signalmen.

The strike failed to cause the intended disruption, and after nine days union leaders acknowledged defeat and called off the protest. The miners fought on alone until November, when they went back to work, accepting the lower wages.

GENERAL SYNOD

Twice a year, more than 550 bishops and members of the clergy and laity comprising the General Synod meet to discuss doctrine and worship in the CHURCH OF ENGLAND. The synod was established in 1969 as the Church's governing body, and its clerical and lay representatives are elected every five years by Church members.

The General Synod is the only group outside Parliament with the power to initiate legislation, where it affects the Church. It also has a pastoral role and speaks for the Church on political, social and moral issues. In 1995 a synod committee urged the abandonment of the phrase 'living in sin'. Synod members voted to 'take note' of the request, but stressed the Christian ideal of marriage.

GEOFFREY OF MONMOUTH

• **Welsh cleric and writer** • c.1100-55

In his 12th-century *History of the Kings of Britain*, Geoffrey of Monmouth claimed to reveal the origins of Britain and chronicle the lives of the British kings over almost 2000 years.

His history included King LEAR and Cymbeline, and proved a rich source for legends of King ARTHUR. Captivated readers included the writers Milton, Shakespeare and Tennyson, who all used some of his stories.

Geoffrey cited his source as the 'most ancient book in the British tongue' – a book that only he had read. The only certainty is that he drew on a variety of historical texts, including the work of BEDE, and then gave free rein to his imagination. His account of British history was unchallenged for centuries, but although now accepted as fiction it is still admired as a literary work.

GEOLOGY: *see page 184*

GEORGE I

• **King 1714-27** • 1660-1727

A tough German soldier, George I spoke little English and showed no inclination to learn. When he became king he had already been Elector of HANOVER for 16 years. He felt no great fondness for his new realm, preferring to live in Hanover.

Despite George's lack of enthusiasm for Britain, he took seriously his duty to his adopted country. The writer Mary Wortley Montagu called him 'an honest blockhead' but others recognised George as a strong figurehead and the Hanoverian succession brought a period of stability to Britain.

With the support of the powerful WHIGS, the king shrugged off a JACOBITE uprising in 1715. George was a director of the slave-trading company at the centre of the SOUTH SEA BUBBLE financial fiasco of 1720, in which thousands of investors were ruined. Robert WALPOLE helped to limit the political scandal, and in 1721 George appointed him First Lord of the Treasury and put him in charge of Cabinet meetings – effectively making Walpole the first prime minister.

GEORGE II

• **King 1727-60** • 1683-1760

Like his father George I, George II much preferred Hanover to Britain. It was partly the threat to his homeland that drew Britain into the war of the Austrian Succession, in which George fought at the Battle of Dettingen – the last British sovereign to head an army in the field.

George II reigned over a stable and prosperous Britain and an expanding empire. At home, his troops suppressed a second JACOBITE uprising and defeated the Scots at the Battle of CULLODEN MOOR. Abroad he increased Britain's role in Europe during the Seven Years' War, and won control of most of Canada and parts of North America from France. In India, the British EAST INDIA COMPANY began to gain power.

George's son Frederick, whom he loathed, died in 1751 and he was succeeded by his grandson, George III.

GEORGE III

• **King 1760-1820** • 1738-1820

Raised in a secluded environment by his widowed mother and private tutors, George III grew up to be an awkward personality and an unworldly king. The diarist Fanny Burney, who spent time at court, found it a shockingly dull and decorous place.

George was the first Hanoverian king to be born in Britain and, unlike his predecessors, demanded personal involvement in the running of the country. He chose his own ministers to be responsible for policy and watched closely over military struggles such as the AMERICAN WAR OF INDEPENDENCE.

George III reigned through an energetic age of creativity and change, encompassing the Industrial Revolution, battles at Waterloo and Trafalgar, the Act of Union between Britain and Ireland, and the ROMANTIC MOVEMENT in the arts.

WORN BY AGE Joseph Lee depicted George III, near the end of his life, as Shakespeare's King Lear, who was also looked upon as mad

But while Britain flourished the king was struck by mental illness, now known to have been caused by the rare blood disorder porphyria. He suffered a last and permanent attack in 1810 and until his death in 1820 was considered mad, wandering the corridors of Windsor Castle in a purple dressing gown.

GEORGE IV

• **Prince Regent 1811-20; king 1820-30** • 1762-1830

The most dissolute of British monarchs, George IV rebelled against his disciplined father, George III, and led a scandalous life outside court. At 23 he secretly married a Roman Catholic widow, Mrs Fitzherbert. Still married, in 1795 he persuaded the king to settle his debts in return for marrying a German cousin, Princess Caroline of Brunswick.

In 1811 George was appointed regent, and in 1820 inherited the throne. He was self-indulgent and commanded little respect, but his rule was stable and he continued many of his father's policies.

George was the figurehead of REGENCY style and design. He brought fashion and prosperity to BRIGHTON, where he had the fanciful Royal Pavilion built, and left legacies of his taste in Regent's Park and Regent Street, in London, both designed by John NASH.

ROCK OF AGES

Nowhere in the world has such a wide diversity of landscape features and rock types in such a small area as Britain. The land we see now has evolved over millions of years and much of its history can be read in its geology

FOR MOST OF its 2800 million-year geological history, Britain was not a single entity. The regions above and below a line running roughly between Berwick-upon-Tweed and the Solway Firth were part of separate ancient continents until, some 350 million years ago, the two landmasses collided somewhere in the Southern Hemisphere. Under the force of the impact, the rocks crumpled and folded, pushing up high mountain ranges in Scotland and Wales.

TRIAL BY ICE AND FIRE

During Britain's 350 million-year journey north to its current position, parts of the country were flooded, turned to desert, and ravaged by ice, earthquakes and volcanoes. Evidence of these upheavals can be seen in the different ROCKS and scenery. The older, generally harder rocks of Wales, Scotland and the Lake District, which are not easily eroded, form rugged scenery such as the craggy GRAMPIAN MOUNTAINS. Farther south and east, the more rounded hills of lowland Britain such as the North and South DOWNS are composed of younger, softer rocks such as sandstones, clays and chalk: relics of past deserts and seabeds.

EVER-CHANGING LANDSCAPE

During the last ICE AGE, glaciers cut through the land, leaving wide valleys such as Glen Coe in Scotland. Rivers, weather and even people walking on the land continue to erode Britain's rocks. The east coast is changing most rapidly as waves undercut clay cliffs until they collapse. Wind and rain erode grains of rock from upland areas, which are carried by rivers towards their estuaries.

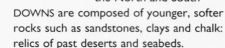

FOLDED ROCKS ON THE ISLE OF ARRAN

ICE SCULPTURE Glaciers gouged wide, U-shaped valleys in the rugged, ancient rocks of Britain. Scratches in the foreground show where the ice passed through on the Hebridean Isle of Skye

FAMILY RESEMBLANCE The rocks that compose the Shetland Islands are linked geologically with both Scottish rocks and formations of the same age and type in Greenland, Scandinavia and Spitsbergen

ROCKY ROAD Basalt forms the columns of the Giant's Causeway in Northern Ireland. Similar basalt columns of the same age can be seen around Fingal's Cave in the Inner Hebrides

HARD EDGE Sill, a ridge of dolerite, fo from volcanic juts up abov softer limest sandstones and s of the surrou count

ANCIENT REMAINS The hard, 230 million-year-old granite of south-west England weathers into distinctive formations called tors. Here, Haytor Rocks on Dartmoor dominate the landscape

Shetland Islands

Orkney Islands

Outer Hebrides

Loch Coruisk, Isle of Skye

Aberdeen

Fingal's Cave, Staffa

Glasgow   Edinburgh
Berwick-upon-Tweed

Giant's Causeway

Whin Sill

Newcastle upon Tyne

Belfast

Solway Firth

Liverpool   Manchester
                        She
Carlton-in

Birmingha

Cardiff

Haytor Rocks, Dartmoor

FOUNDATIONS OF THE LANDSCAPE

The oldest rocks in Britain form the mountains of Scotland; youngest are the soft clays in south-east England

SEDIMENTARY ROCKS

- Tertiary and marine Pleistocene. Clays and sandstones. Up to 65 million years old
- Cretaceous. Chalk, clays and sandstones. 65-140 million years old
- Jurassic. Limestones and clays. 140-195 million years old
- Triassic. Marls, sand and conglomerates. 195-230 million years old
- Permian. Magnesian limestones, marls and sandstones. 230-280 million years old
- Carboniferous. Limestones, sandstones, shales and coal. 280-345 million years old
- Devonian. Sandstones, shales, slates and limestone. 345-395 million years old
- Silurian. Shales, mudstones, greywacke. 395-445 million years old
- Ordovician. Shales and mudstone. Limestone in Scotland. 445-510 million years old
- Cambrian. Shales, slates and sandstones. 510-600 million years old
- Late Precambrian. Mainly sandstones and siltstones. 600-1000 million years old

METAMORPHIC ROCKS

- Proterozoic and lower Palaeozoic. Schists and gneisses. 500-1000 million years old
- Early Precambrian. Mainly gneisses. 1500-3000 million years old

IGNEOUS ROCKS

- Intrusive igneous. Mainly granite, gabbro and dolerite
- Extrusive igneous. Basalt, rhyolite, andesite and tuffs

PETRIFIED DUNES Red sandstones in the Midlands were part of a desert in the Triassic period, 200 million years ago. The area was then on the same latitude as the Sahara is today

Hemsby

London

SHAKY FOUNDATION The young clays on the coast of Norfolk are easily eroded. In places the coastline is receding by some 10 cm (4 in) a year

GEORGE V

- **King 1910-36** • **1856-1936**

Crisis and political turmoil dogged the reign of George V. His prime minister, Herbert ASQUITH, clashed with the House of Lords in 1910 over its right to veto financial legislation, and in 1914, amid threats of civil war, a bill was passed granting Home Rule to Ireland. The First World War was followed by the General Strike of 1926 and the Depression, and towards the end of his life George was troubled by his son Edward's relationship with the American divorcée, Wallis Simpson (*see* EDWARD VIII).

George was a quiet man with a love of the sea, who became heir to the throne after his brother Albert's death in 1892; a year later he married Albert's fiancée, Mary of Teck. He was reluctantly but inevitably drawn into politics, and proved a staunch and popular national figurehead. During the First World War George changed his family name from Saxe-Coburg to Windsor and in 1932 he began the tradition of the monarch's Christmas Day broadcast.

GEORGE VI

- **King 1936-52** • **1895-1952**

During the summer of 1936 Prince Albert, duke of York, was absorbed in the development of a network of boys' camps. By Christmas he was George VI, King of the United Kingdom and Emperor of India. Albert was the second son of GEORGE V, whose name he took as his regal title. He was a shy man with a stammer, which he learned to overcome, and a reluctant public figure.

He came to the throne amid scandal, on the abdication of his brother, EDWARD VIII, and devoted his reign to restoring the prestige of the monarchy. He married Elizabeth Bowes-Lyon, now known as Queen ELIZABETH, the Queen Mother, in 1923 and they had two daughters, ELIZABETH II and Princess Margaret. The king and queen earned the respect and affection of the public for staying in London during the BLITZ, and the king's steadfast leadership did much to preserve morale throughout the difficult war years.

Albert was an accomplished amateur sportsman, and played doubles in the 1926 Wimbledon tennis championships.

COMPARING NOTES Buckingham Palace was bombed nine times during the Blitz so George VI and Queen Elizabeth could empathise with other victims, which helped to boost morale

GEORGE CROSS

'For gallantry', reads the inscription on the George Cross. The civilian equivalent of the VICTORIA CROSS, the medal is the highest honour that can be bestowed. It can also be awarded to military personnel not on active service.

The silver cross depicting St George and the dragon hangs from a royal blue ribbon. George VI instituted the medal in 1940 to reward the heroism of those engaged in bomb disposal and mine clearance, and the people of Malta were collectively honoured in 1942 for gallantry under bombardment.

Only 45 George Crosses have been awarded, all of them to people who have knowingly placed their lives at risk for others. The lesser George Medal is awarded for risks taken on impulse, without such premeditation.

GEORGE CROSS MEDAL

IDEAL HOMES

During the 100 years following the accession of George I in 1714, British cities and country estates alike were transformed by a revival of the designs of ancient Rome and Greece. The most elegant solution to the restrictions of space imposed by urban living was the terraced town house

HIGH TIME Chinese-influenced designs embellish a longcase clock made in 1725

THE CONFIDENT new architecture commissioned from Georgian designers by their patrons was inspired by the European GRAND TOUR made by wealthy young men. The strict proportions of PALLADIAN houses championed by Lord BURLINGTON evolved into the more playful but no less classical interiors and exteriors of Robert ADAM and later the Regency crescents of John NASH.

The defining form of the period was the terraced town house. It epitomised Georgian style, from the measured elegance of its outward appearance to the lavish but strictly ordered interior.

The Georgian town house emerged because of foreign trade, which brought new wealth to the ports and major cities of Britain such as London, Edinburgh and Bristol. Aristocrats with estates on the fringes of these cities started leasing land to provide houses for the growing mercantile classes. Terraced housing was employed to maximise the use of space, and for a sense of grandeur buildings were developed around squares, and later circuses and crescents, most notably in BATH. The commercial impetus for the town house continued to sustain its development

throughout the reign of the four Georgian monarchs.

KEY SITES • London: Bedford Square; Berkeley Square; Fitzroy Square; Park Crescent • **Bath:** The Circus; Paragon; Royal Crescent • **Brighton:** Royal Crescent • **Edinburgh:** Charlotte Square

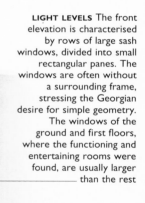

ANTIQUE PRINT Classical columns and urns decorate a printed wallpaper of the 1770s. Light and shade are used in a technique called 'chiaroscuro'

ORIENTAL TOUCH Hand-painted Chinese wallpapers (*see background*) were imported by the East India Company from the mid 18th century onwards for wealthy householders

TOWN LIVING

This house of about 1770 might accommodate a well-to-do family, including children and servants, with space for entertaining guests

INNER SANCTUM The private rooms of a Georgian house, including bedrooms, were simple in style, with plain doors and fireplaces

THE BEST ROOM The drawing room was the grandest room. It had an ornate fireplace, carved from wood or stone. Oak was used for the floorboards and oak or mahogany for the double doors. The cornice between the wall and ceiling is carved plasterwork, or stucco, introduced from Italy in the 1750s

EATING AREA The dining room was often on the ground floor to be close to the basement kitchen. By the mid 18th century floors were often covered by a rug or carpet. At the same time wood panelling above the dado became unfashionable. A candlestand (*inset*) or candelabra was the only source of night-time light in a Georgian home

LIGHT LEVELS The front elevation is characterised by rows of large sash windows, divided into small rectangular panes. The windows are often without a surrounding frame, stressing the Georgian desire for simple geometry. The windows of the ground and first floors, where the functioning and entertaining rooms were found, are usually larger than the rest

IMPOSING ENTRANCE Above the solid wooden panels of the front door is a fanlight, decorated with tracery. In some grander homes the entranceway might be developed into a portal, with two supporting columns and a triangular pediment

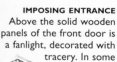

TIGHT FIT Space was at a premium in the building of town houses. Developers made the most of it with narrow 3 or 4-storey terraces, with additional basement and attic levels

Jean Paul GETTY I and II

• Oil tycoons and art collectors • Jean Paul I 1892-1976 • Jean Paul II b.1932; kt 1986

The American oil magnate Jean Paul Getty I was said to be the richest man in the world when he died at his mansion in Surrey, leaving a priceless collection of art. Although he lived in Europe from 1951 he bequeathed US$4 billion to the Los Angeles Getty Museum.

His third son, by the third of his five wives, worked for a time in his father's oil business and inherited one of the world's largest private fortunes. Jean Paul Getty II, who settled in Britain in 1972, is a shy and reclusive philanthropist whose gifts have included £50 million to the National Gallery in 1985, and who also supports charities for the homeless and young offenders. In 1997 his loyalty to his adoptive country was rewarded with British nationality.

GIANT'S CAUSEWAY

• Northern Ireland (p.497 B5) • NT

An extraordinary pavement of basalt columns along the north Antrim coast makes up the Irish end of the so-called Giant's Causeway. The giant in question was the mythical hero Finn MacCool, whose legendary home – Fingal's Cave on the Hebridean island of Staffa – displays a similar rock formation.

The causeway formed 50-60 million years ago as volcanic lava cooled and solidified into tightly packed bunches of polygonal columns. Most are hexagonal, although they can have between four and ten sides. Nearly 40 000 columns – the tallest of which, the Giant's Organ, is 12 m (39 ft) high – line the coast near Portrush and extend out into the Atlantic.

NATURE'S PRECISION The columns of the Giant's Causeway form such neat, geometric shapes they seem almost man-made

GHOSTS

Hysteria, hoax or hallucination – two in five British people claim to have seen a ghost. Britain has a strong tradition of folklore, and belief in ghosts, whether as divine messengers or unquiet spirits atoning for their sins or seeking vengeance, dates back to the Middle Ages. Thousands of spirits are said to inhabit pubs, churches, houses and dark lanes, and no other country has more reported hauntings than Britain.

One of the busiest British ghosts must be Anne BOLEYN, who was beheaded for adultery in 1536. She haunts seven sites, including her birthplace, Blickling Hall in Norfolk. On May 19, the anniversary of her death, Anne's headless wraith is said to ride up in a coach drawn by four headless horses driven by a headless coachman.

Reports of ghosts include sounds, smells and sightings but proof is elusive. If many of our old buildings have an eerie atmosphere, it may be that in Britain of all places the past is most real.

HAUNTED HOTSPOTS

• **Athelhampton Hall, Dorset**
Six resident ghosts

• **Fountains Abbey, Yorkshire**
A choir of chanting monks can be heard

• **Glamis Castle, Scotland**
Macbeth's castle, haunted by six ghosts

• **Longleat, Wiltshire**
Many ghosts, including a Green Lady

• **Morfa Colliery, Port Talbot, Wales**
The scent of roses can sometimes be detected at the coal face

At Borley Rectory in Essex, decades of unexplained incidents culminated in 1939 in a fire that destroyed the house. Strange lights were then reported in the ruins

Edward GIBBON

• Historian • 1737-94

A wealthy background allowed Edward Gibbon to devote himself to research, writing and travel. He spent most of his life on one great work, *The History of the Decline and Fall of the Roman Empire* (1776-88), inspired by his musings 'amidst the ruins of the Capitol' in Rome.

The first volume was an immediate success and the full six-volume work went on to cover 13 centuries. Through the example of ancient Rome, Gibbon explored many of the fears of the modern world, such as the fragility of civilisation. His chapters on Christianity provoked theological criticism but his scepticism and rational evaluations were typical of the critical approach of the Enlightenment, an 18th-century trend towards challenging accepted doctrines.

Gibbon once cynically dismissed history as merely 'a register of the crimes, follies and misfortunes of mankind'.

Grinling GIBBONS

• Woodcarver • 1648-1721

Intricate and brilliantly life-like wooden garlands of flowers and fruits, with small animals, birds and cherubs peering out from the foliage, were the hallmark of Grinling Gibbons's work. The delicate detail and realism of his work marked him out as the leading craftsman of his age and he became Master Carver in Wood to the Crown in 1693.

Gibbons worked for Christopher WREN on the decorations of St Paul's Cathedral and HAMPTON COURT Palace. His carvings also adorn BURGHLEY HOUSE in Lincolnshire and PETWORTH HOUSE in West Sussex.

Orlando GIBBONS

• Composer • 1583-1625

The most gifted keyboard player of the Jacobean period and a prolific composer, Orlando Gibbons excelled at both sacred and secular music, becoming organist of the Chapel Royal at the age of 21. He is remembered chiefly for his 40 church anthems – still sung today – and for numerous motets, and madrigals such as 'The Silver Swan'.

James GIBBS

• Architect • 1682-1754

For much of his professional life James Gibbs had to compromise his passion for the sensuous complexity of Italian baroque with shrewd pragmatism.

Disliking the plain style of PALLADIAN architecture that became popular in his day, Gibbs, a Scottish Roman Catholic, used ideas developed in Rome, where he studied architecture, for his 1714 design of the Church of St Mary-le-Strand in London. The Italian façade with ornate Corinthian and simpler Ionic orders stacked one above the other drew criticism, and Gibbs had to choose a plainer, though huge, form in his next commission from the Church of England, St Martin-in-the-Fields, London (1721-6).

Gibbs returned to his favoured Italian style in the most celebrated of his works,

Stick close to your desks and never go to sea
And you all may be rulers of the Queen's Navee

SIR JOSEPH PORTER, FIRST LORD OF THE ADMIRALTY,
IN GILBERT AND SULLIVAN'S *HMS PINAFORE* (1878)

the striking Radcliffe Camera library in Oxford (1737-48). Its dome tops a rotunda with carved stone garlands linking a series of Corinthian columns.

John GIELGUD

• Actor • b.1904; kt 1953; OM 1996

From his debut as a herald in Shakespeare's *Henry V* at the Old Vic in 1921, John Gielgud went on to become one of the outstanding classical actors of his generation, with a stage and film career lasting some 70 years.

Gielgud was as effective in comedy as in tragedy, and acted in plays by writers as diverse as Anton Chekhov, Somerset Maugham, Noël Coward, George Bernard Shaw and Harold Pinter. His versatile film performances include the spy in Hitchcock's thriller *The Secret Agent* (1936), Dudley Moore's valet in the romantic comedy *Arthur* (1981) – which earned him, in his 78th year, an Oscar for best supporting actor – and Prospero in *Prospero's Books* (1991), a fanciful version of Shakespeare's *The Tempest*.

GILBERT AND SULLIVAN

• William Schwenck Gilbert; librettist; 1836-1911; kt 1907
• Arthur Sullivan; composer; 1842-1900; kt 1883

When the impresario Richard D'OYLY CARTE brought together the composer Arthur Sullivan and librettist William Gilbert in 1875, he inspired a rousing 14-year run of comic operettas. The successful chemistry was a combination of Gilbert's comic wit and Sullivan's gift for melody and musical parody.

No aspect of society escaped their satire: the judiciary in *Trial by Jury* (their first operetta), women's emancipation in *Princess Ida*, the vogue for orientalism in *The Mikado*, Oscar Wilde in *Patience*, even Italian opera in *The Gondoliers*. Most of the pair's operettas were staged at London's Savoy Theatre, built specifically for them by the D'Oyly Carte Opera Company in 1881, and many ran for several hundred nights.

The Savoy Operas, as they came to be called, were particularly popular across the Atlantic. Gilbert and Sullivan fell out in 1889, reputedly over a choice of carpet at the Savoy. Attempts to reunite them resulted in only two further collaborations.

Eric GILL

• Sculptor, engraver, writer and typographer • 1882-1940

Unlike most sculptors of his day, Eric Gill carved the clean, simplified outlines of his monumental statues and relief sculpture direct – without preliminary clay models. In part, he was inspired by medieval religious attitudes to art, crediting divine inspiration for his work.

The eccentric artist, who lived a pseudomonastic rural life, began his career as a letter-cutter for tombstones before moving to sculpture. Among his finest works are the 14 relief carvings of the *Stations of the Cross* (1914-18) at Westminster Cathedral, commissioned after he had converted to Catholicism. Gill also created typeface designs for books, and hundreds of his wood engravings illustrate his many writings on the relationship between religion, art and the workman. Extracts from his diary, published in 1989, revealed a history of incest and paedophilia.

PRECISE CARVING Gill's huge stone sculptures, such as the figures of Prospero and Ariel at Broadcasting House (*background*), contrast with his fine engravings and typefaces. His Gill Sans Serif (*below*) is widely used today

AaBbCcDdEeFfGgHhIiJjKkLlMmNnOoPpQqRrSsTtUuVvWwXxYyZz

DEMON DRINK Gin-tippling reached epidemic levels in the 18th century, especially in London where some 6000 gin shops were open by 1736

GIN

Despite its image as the most English of spirits, gin originated in the Netherlands in the 16th century as a medicinal drink, good for relieving gout. British soldiers who served in the Thirty Years' War (1618-48) brought back a taste for it, and by the late 17th century gin was being made in London distilleries.

Low excise duty in the 18th century made gin cheaper than beer and turned it into the drink of the urban poor, and the widespread public drunkenness and crime that ensued led to the drink being made illegal briefly in the 1730s.

It took until the Victorian era for gin to recover its respectability. Mixed with quinine-rich tonic water, launched in the 1870s for its antimalarial properties, gin became the staple sun-downer for army officers in India.

The *GIN* Shop.

"— now Oh dear how shocking the thought is
They makes the gin from aquafortis

They do it on purpose folks lives to shorten
And tickets of un at two-pence a quartern."

William GLADSTONE

- **Prime minister 1868-74, 1880-5, 1886, 1892-4**
- **1809-98**

One of the great reformers of the 19th century, William Gladstone began his political life as a Tory MP in 1832 and ended it a radical Liberal. The son of a Scots merchant in Liverpool, Gladstone took a stand against aristocratic privilege in favour of free trade when he opposed the CORN LAWS in the 1840s.

In 1859 he joined the Liberals, and campaigned passionately against social injustice and in favour of home rule in Ireland and the British colonies.

As prime minister, Gladstone introduced wide-ranging reforms, including universal primary education, the disestablishment of

PEOPLE'S MAN William Gladstone's stance against privilege and protectionism won him the popular vote but also Victoria's enmity

the Irish Church, and the abolition of purchased commissions in the army that allowed wealthy but incompetent men to reach the highest ranks.

Gladstone's liberal policies alienated the aristocracy and drew him closer to the growing band of middle-class voters. But he never fulfilled his 'mission to pacify Ireland', and his attempts at pushing home rule through parliament split the Liberal party and twice caused his resignation from the premiership.

GLASGOW

- **W Scotland (p.497 C4)** • **Pop. 662 950**

Scotland's largest city – and Britain's third biggest – was founded around a church built by St Mungo in the 6th century, and by the 12th century the town was important enough to warrant a cathedral. The city's reputation for learning, gained from its 1451 university, began to change when mercantile activity expanded with the arrival of American tobacco in the 17th century.

It was the first import more convenient for a Scottish west coast than an east coast harbour, and Glasgow, with its location on the River CLYDE, dominated the trade. Sugar and cotton followed, and in the 19th century the area's vast coal and iron reserves turned Glasgow into a major shipbuilding and engineering centre. In the 100 years up

to the First World War its population grew tenfold and Glasgow became the British Empire's second city, but after the Second World War its major industries suffered a steep decline.

Glasgow's rich cultural inheritance includes a wealth of ornate Victorian architecture such as the opulent Renaissance-style City Chambers (1888), the art nouveau designs of Charles Rennie MACKINTOSH, and museums and galleries such as the BURRELL COLLECTION. The People's Palace, built in 1898 as a cultural centre, is now a museum of Glasgow's social history.

GLASGOW CELTIC and RANGERS

- **Rangers founded 1873** • **Celtic founded 1888**

Rivalry among Glasgow football fans between Protestant Rangers supporters and Roman Catholic Celtic fans has always been intense. Celtic claimed nine successive league titles from 1966 to 1974, and in 1967 became the first British team to win the European Cup. Rangers have held the whip hand since, winning ten championships from 1988 to 1999.

By the end of 1998 the two clubs had between them won 170 major domestic trophies – nearly twice as many as all the other clubs in Scotland put together.

GLASS

It was a Venetian glass-maker, Giacomo Verzelini, licensed by Elizabeth I in 1574, who introduced to England the method of manufacturing glass with water-like transparency. But the material was weak and broke easily until in 1674 the London glass-maker George Ravenscroft discovered that by adding lead oxide to the process the glass was strengthened and given extra brilliance.

GEORGIAN HEYDAY

By the early 18th century English lead 'crystal' was used to produce great quantities of graceful tableware, much of which was exported throughout Europe. New glassware was designed for every fashion in drink, from delicate glasses for tea-time cordials to the rummer, a peculiarly English vessel for beer, cider and punch. In the mid 1700s artists such as Michael Edkins in Bristol and the Beilby family in Newcastle upon Tyne emulated more established German artisans for their fine decorative enamelling, and English glass-cutters became so proficient that their chandeliers and other fittings were in demand all over the world.

The great age of British glass-making came to an end when the taste for the heavily ornate, colourful glassware of the Victorian period declined in favour of lighter, Continental styles.

CRYSTAL SPIRAL British glass-makers of the 1750s developed the art of narrow stems enclosing delicately twisted threads

GLASTONBURY

• **Somerset (p.494 E5)** • **Pop. 7750**
Associations with Christian and Arthurian legend make Glastonbury a magnet for visitors, especially New Age followers.

Legend says that St Joseph of Arimathea built a chapel there and housed in it the Holy Grail, the chalice containing drops of Christ's blood, in about AD 60. The Grail is said to rest beneath a spring on the Tor hill outside the town. Glastonbury Abbey was founded in the 7th or 8th century on the site of an earlier settlement of hermits, and bones discovered there in 1191 were said to be those of King ARTHUR.

The abbey was dissolved in 1539, and its ruins dominate the small market town, which is now also famous for its yearly three-day rock festival.

Massacre of GLEN COE

• **Highland (p.497 C4)** • **February 13, 1692**
A valley sheltering a peaceful community near Loch Leven was renamed Glen of Weeping after one of the most savage events in Scottish history.

William III, distrustful of Scots' loyalty after he had helped to overthrow his father-in-law, the Stuart James II, in the GLORIOUS REVOLUTION, required Scottish chieftains to swear allegiance to the Crown by the last day of 1691. Most obeyed, but the MacDonalds of Glen Coe delayed a few days into the next year.

William's government seized the opportunity to make an example of the recalcitrants, and dispatched a company of troops, mostly members of the Campbell clan – traditional enemies of the MacDonalds – with secret orders that 'they must all be slaughtered'. They took advantage of the MacDonalds' traditional Highland hospitality for two weeks, then one morning before dawn turned on their hosts, massacring the clan chief and 38 men, women and children.

GLEN MOR

• **Highland (p.497 C3)**
Also known as the Great Glen, the valley of Glen Mor cuts a deep gash through the Scottish Highlands, running in a diagonal line for 100 miles from the Firth of Lorn in the south-west to the Moray Firth in the north-east.

The glen, a geological fault line, was formed during massive upheavals of the Earth some 400 million years ago. The series of lochs along the fault line reach depths hundreds of feet below sea level.

In 1822 the Scottish civil engineer Thomas TELFORD built waterways to link the lochs and form the Caledonian Canal, allowing ships to pass between the east and west coasts of Scotland.

KING'S TOMB? High above a plain once flooded by the Bristol Channel rises Glastonbury Tor, the hill identified with the legendary Isle of Avalon, King Arthur's final resting place

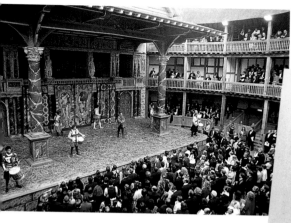

ALL THE WORLD'S A STAGE A packed house celebrates the opening of the rebuilt Globe Theatre in 1997. A rare sketch provided one of the few clues to its 17th-century appearance

The GLOBE on the Banke Side, where shakspere acted.
From the long Antwerp view of London in the Pepysian Library.

With the drawing from which this Cut was made I was favoured by the Reverend Mr. Henley STEEVENS.

GLOBE THEATRE

- **Central London (p.499 E3)**
- **Built 1598-9, rebuilt 1997**

Southwark, on the south bank of the Thames, was London's main theatre and entertainment district when the actor Richard Burbage and his brother opened the Globe there in 1599. One of the shareholders was William SHAKESPEARE, who acted at the theatre with Burbage and had 15 of his plays produced there.

The theatre, an octagonal building with an open centre, burned down in 1613 but was rebuilt the following year and flourished until 1642 when Puritans, disapproving of public entertainment, finally closed it down.

In 1970 the American film director Sam Wanamaker began fundraising to rebuild the Globe 180 m (200 yd) from the original site. A reconstruction of the second theatre, with seating for 1000 in the galleries and standing room for 600 around the stage, opened in 1997.

GLORIOUS REVOLUTION

- **1688-9**

In contrast to the bloody revolution that swept away the French aristocracy, the English people a century earlier simply swapped one king for another and introduced a constitution limiting the power of the monarchy.

After the death of CHARLES II in 1685, fears over the intentions and policies of the Catholic JAMES II encouraged opposition, especially when his Catholic second wife had a son in June 1688. This challenged the position of Mary, the Protestant elder daughter from his first marriage. Mary was married to William

of Orange, a leading Dutch political figure and a prominent Protestant.

Wishing to keep England from siding with France, William landed with troops in Devon on November 5, 1688. James did not fight and a power vacuum developed, but William initially claimed to have no designs on the crown.

Once James had been driven into exile, however, William actively sought kingship. Parliament therefore declared the throne vacant and invited WILLIAM AND MARY to occupy it as joint monarchs. Largely bloodless in England, the revolution led to civil war in Scotland and Ireland. The BILL OF RIGHTS passed by parliament in 1689 set out conditions under which monarchs could rule and declared that only a Protestant heir might succeed to the throne.

GLORIOUS TWELFTH

- **August 12**

The 'Glorious Twelfth' marks the opening of one of the great British countryside rituals. Every August 12, hundreds of guns take to the moors of Scotland and Yorkshire to seek the plump red grouse.

The date was set by the Game Act of 1831, brought in when overhunting threatened the survival of many species of game bird. The season ends on December 10. Most hunting is done in parties, with beaters to flush the birds from cover and into marksmen's view.

GLOUCESTER

- **Gloucestershire (p.494 E4)**   • **Pop. 114 000**

The city of Gloucester, the county town of Gloucestershire, has had a long, affluent past. Wealth was created in the 14th century from bell-founding, brewing and wool from Cotswold sheep, and in the 19th century through industry attracted to the city by newly built docks and a ship canal to the Severn.

The city's strategic location at the lowest bridging point on the Severn was recognised by the Romans, who laid out a grid pattern to which the streets of modern Gloucester still adhere. After the Romans left, the bustling river port became an important town of the Anglo-Saxon kingdom of Mercia.

Gloucester Cathedral is one of the finest in England. Edward II, murdered in 1327, was buried there, and Henry III was crowned there in 1216 – the only coronation of a monarch outside London. Choristers from the cathedral have sung in the THREE CHOIRS FESTIVAL, shared with Worcester and Hereford, since 1715.

GOTHIC WONDER Gloucester's cathedral cloisters, rebuilt in Perpendicular style in the 14th century, contain the earliest surviving example of fan tracery in Britain

PASTORAL THEME The rebuilt opera house preserves Glyndebourne's special atmosphere of space, air and intimacy

GLYNDEBOURNE

• **East Sussex (p.495 H6)** • **June-August**

In 1934 the wealthy eccentric John Christie (1882-1962) built an auditorium on his estate to stage an opera festival. Since then the annual Glyndebourne season has won international acclaim for its high standard of productions. Traditionally, patrons bring hampers for picnics in the gardens.

For their first season, Christie and his wife, the opera singer Audrey Mildmay, presented Mozart's *Don Giovanni*. Mozart remains the main focus for a now wider repertory, which has included premieres by Harrison BIRTWISTLE among its average of six productions each summer.

In 1994 the original 800-seat opera house was rebuilt as a horseshoe-shaped auditorium for up to 1150. After the festival, the productions go on tour.

Owain GLYNDWR

• **Welsh rebel leader** • **c.1359-c.1416**

Until the establishment of a Welsh assembly in 1999, Owain Glyndwr (or Owen Glendower) was the last leader of an at least partly independent Wales.

Glyndwr was a prince of Clwyd who studied law in London and was at first an ally of Henry Bolingbroke, later Henry IV. Appalled by the poverty he found on returning to Wales, in 1404 Glyndwr set up a Welsh parliament at Machynlleth and proclaimed himself prince of Wales.

His supporters won a series of skirmishes against the English until they were defeated at Harlech Castle in 1409, and the rebellion faded out. Glyndwr then lived in hiding until his death.

Lady GODIVA

• **English noblewoman** • **c.1040-80**

A 12th-century chronicle is the first to give an account of the virtuous Lady Godiva, said to have ridden naked through Coventry to help its townspeople.

Godiva had angered her husband, Earl Leofric of Mercia, complaining that the people were unable to bear his severe taxes. He promised her that, if she rode naked through Coventry on market day, he would change his tyrannical ways. To his surprise, she took up his offer, hiding her nakedness with her long hair.

Other accounts give differing reports of her modesty, one stating that the good

people of Coventry stayed indoors while Godiva rode through the town. A later addition to the story was 'Peeping Tom', who peered at her as she passed by and was struck blind. In 1949 a statue of Godiva was erected in Coventry.

GOG and MAGOG

The 12th-century historian Geoffrey of Monmouth told of Gog and Magog, the last survivors of a legendary race of giants who inhabited ALBION, the ancient name for Britain. The Trojan leader Brutus, great-grandson of the hero Aeneas, captured them and made them porters at his palace in Troynovant ('new Troy'), a site identified with London.

Gog and Magog appear in the Biblical book Revelation of St John, representing nations destined to fight one another at the Apocalypse. In the popular mythology of the 15th century the names Gog and Magog had come to refer generally to pairs of vast figures, especially pagan deities.

Statues of two giants have stood in London's Guildhall since the 16th century, and have been identified with Gog and Magog for at least 300 years. The first pair, made of wickerwork and pasteboard, were destroyed in the Great Fire of 1666 and replacements over 4m (12ft) high were made in 1708. These were then destroyed by bombing in the Second World War. The current figures, nearly 3m (10ft) high, were placed in the restored Guildhall in 1953.

LAST OF THE GIANTS A 19th-century representation depicts the second Guildhall statue of Gog, which was destroyed during the Blitz of 1940-1

GOLDEN HIND

The seafarer Francis DRAKE, the first Englishman to sail around the world, set off for his three-year journey in 1577 aboard the *Golden Hind*, one of his fleet of five ships. It was the only one to survive the voyage. Elizabeth I knighted Drake aboard the ship, and it remained in dock at Deptford, in south London, as a tourist attraction for a year after its return. Yet surprisingly little is known about the vessel itself. Neither the date nor place it was built are recorded.

The *Golden Hind* appears from contemporary illustrations to have been a modest vessel of about 21 m (70 ft) long with a 6 m (20 ft) beam, three masts, square-rigged on the fore and main masts, and a triangular sail on the mizzen. In spite of its small size, the ship accommodated Drake and some 80 men. It began life as the *Pelican*, and was renamed during the trip in honour of a shareholder in the venture whose emblem was a golden hind.

William GOLDING

• Novelist • 1911-93; kt 1988

With his first novel, *Lord of the Flies*, published in 1954, William Golding was marked out as one of the most distinctive and pessimistic voices in postwar British literature. For the middle-aged schoolteacher from Salisbury, the nature of evil and the inherent cruelty of man were dominant themes to which he returned obsessively in his later novels. *The Inheritors* (1955) tells of early man's extermination of his gentler Neanderthal cousins, and *Darkness Visible* (1979) looks inside the mind of a murderer.

A lighter, humorous side appeared in the three novellas of *The Scorpion God* (1971). Golding won the Booker prize for *Rites of Passage* (1980), the first of a trilogy set on a 19th-century convict ship sailing to Australia, and was awarded the Nobel prize for literature in 1983.

LAW OF THE JUNGLE William Golding's dark tale of a band of marooned schoolboys sees Piggy and Ralph failing to uphold reason and order against the savagery of their companions

Oliver GOLDSMITH

• Writer • c.1730-74

Let schoolmasters puzzle their brain,
With grammar, and nonsense, and
* learning,*
Good liquor, I stoutly maintain,
Gives genius a better discerning
(She Stoops to Conquer)

Blundering and vain on the one hand, kindly and generous, though simple, on the other – such is the description of Oliver Goldsmith in many anecdotes in James Boswell's *Life of Johnson*. Certainly Goldsmith's early years show an absence of common sense.

Goldsmith was the son of an Anglo-Irish clergyman and led a chequered career as a young man. After the Church rejected him, he studied medicine in Edinburgh, then wandered Europe before landing up destitute in London in 1756. While meagrely supporting himself as a poor physician he turned his hand to writing, and published a periodical, *The Bee*, in which he revealed his talent as a critic and essayist.

By 1761 he was writing the celebrated novel, *The Vicar of Wakefield*. The sale of the manuscript saved him from arrest for debt, although it was not published until 1766. He turned to the stage as a source of income, and in 1773 found success with his comic play, *She Stoops to Conquer*, in which a 'bashful and reserved' young suitor reveals his true character when he mistakes his potential father-in-law's house for an inn.

GOLF

Golf developed in Scotland, where it was a national game by the 15th century. So popular was it there that in the late 1400s it was frequently banned by authorities as interfering with the vital skill of archery. James VI of Scotland brought the game to England when he succeeded to the English throne in 1603.

The modern game and rules can be traced to the citizens of Edinburgh, who petitioned councillors in 1744 to supply a trophy for open competition. Soon afterwards the Royal and Ancient Club was founded in ST ANDREWS and became the sport's supreme authority. By 1779, the game had spread to America, where in New York the *Gazette* advertised golf clubs and 'veritable Caledonian balls'.

The Open, Britain's major golfing tournament, was first played in 1860 at Prestwick, in Scotland. Today some 3.5 million golfers play on nearly 2500 courses in Britain, but the game is still most popular in Scotland, where 1 in every 20 people plays.

PETER BROOK'S film of **LORD of the FLIES** from the novel by **WILLIAM GOLDING**

Produced by Lewis Allen   Directed by Peter Brook   An Allen-Hodgdon production   British Lion Presentation through BLC

Victor GOLLANCZ

- **Publisher and philanthropist**
- **1893-1967; kt 1965**

Concern for humanitarian issues drove Victor Gollancz to found a publishing company in 1928 to disseminate his views. Among the better-known authors published by his firm, Victor Gollancz Ltd, were George Orwell, Franz Kafka and H.G. Wells. In 1936 he founded the Left Book Club with the aim of alerting intellectuals to the growing threat of fascism. At the club's height in the early 1940s it distributed political books to some 50 000 members.

After the Second World War, although himself a Jew, Gollancz was opposed to the punishment of the German nation, and set up the Save Europe Now relief campaign to help starving populations in Europe. This campaign was extended worldwide when in 1951 he founded War on Want.

GOODRICH CASTLE

- **Herefordshire (p.494 E4)**
- **Built 12th-13th century   • EH**

The formidable red sandstone walls of Goodrich Castle, once an important border defence, soar upwards from a crag overlooking the Wye valley. The square Norman keep, built around 1170, commanded a strategic crossing of the Wye between England and Wales. A century later huge corner towers were added to protect the inner ward. Clearly identifiable remains of a suite of living rooms, including the great hall, chapel and kitchen, conjure up a vivid picture of conditions in a medieval castle.

During the Civil War, Goodrich was held by the Royalists, but its defences proved no match for the Parliamentarians with their 200 lb mortar, 'Roaring Meg'.

GOODWOOD

- **House, racecourse and motor-racing circuit**
- **West Sussex (p.495 G6)**

For nearly two centuries 'Glorious Goodwood' has been associated with horse racing – but it was for a different sport that the 1st duke of Richmond, son of Charles II, bought the original Jacobean manor and its estate in 1697. He enjoyed the new craze for hunting foxes, and used Goodwood as a base for riding with the local hunt.

In the 1790s the house was rebuilt in Sussex flint for the 3rd duke by the architect James Wyatt. The duke filled it with rich pickings from his travels, including a glittering collection of Sèvres porcelain. He designed the great ballroom as a gallery in which to display portraits of his ancestors by leading English painters such as Joshua Reynolds. Other treasures in the house were given as thank-you presents by kings, queens and tsars who stayed at Goodwood to watch the racing, which has been held annually on its breezy site 210 m (700 ft) up on the Sussex Downs since 1801.

The GOON SHOW

When Peter Sellers, Spike Milligan, Harry Secombe and Michael Bentine got together in a London pub run by scriptwriter Jimmy Grafton in 1949, they launched what became, as *The Goon Show*, the craziest of radio COMEDY programmes. 'I gave my sanity to that show', said Milligan, who wrote most of the Goons' scripts and songs.

With sketches like the 'Great Tuscan Salami Scandal', in which Milligan and Sellers, both playing deaf characters, argue about who should answer the door if the bell rings, the Goons were wildly and anarchically absurd. The show began in 1951 as *Crazy People*. It was renamed *The Goon Show* in 1952 – the year Bentine left – and lasted until 1960. An attempt to transfer the formula to television never quite succeeded.

BUNCH OF GOONS Weekly radio audiences of up to 7 million listened to the lunacy of (*left to right*) Peter Sellers, Harry Secombe, Spike Milligan and Michael Bentine

Charles GORDON

• Soldier   • 1833-85; CB 1864

A general, administrator and explorer, Charles Gordon served with distinction in the Crimean War of the 1850s and then spent four years in China leading a crack force that in 1864 crushed the formidable Taiping Rebellion, which had threatened European influence in the region. This achievement earned him the nickname 'Chinese Gordon'. He later served in Egypt, helping to suppress the slave trade, which used the River Nile.

Despite his success in public life, Gordon was a reclusive man who spent a year meditating in Palestine and another six caring for the poor of Gravesend, in Kent. In 1884 he departed on his final mission: to evacuate civilians and soldiers threatened by the Mahdi's Islamic revolutionaries in the Sudan, which was at the time a province of British-controlled Egypt.

Besieged in Sudan's capital, Khartoum, he survived for ten months with minimal resources. A relief column finally arrived, two days too late. Gordon had been one of the last to die, fighting off his attackers with swords and pistols before being hacked to pieces.

GORDON RIOTS

• June 2-8, 1780

Lord George Gordon, MP, probably did not foresee or intend the violence that ensued when he led an 'anti-Popery' rally in London on June 2, 1780. Gordon and an estimated 50 000 supporters marched on the House of Commons to protest against a bill of 1778 easing restrictions on Roman Catholic ownership of land.

The protesters first burned Catholic property, then went on to attack public buildings, including the Bank of England, and indiscriminately terrorised innocent citizens. They even forced their way into Newgate prison and released inmates.

After six days of mayhem, troops finally restored order, though at the cost of some 285 lives. The eccentric Gordon survived, was tried and aquitted of high treason, but was later convicted of

libelling Marie Antoinette, the wife of the French king, Louis XVI. He spent the last five years of his life imprisoned in Newgate, where he entertained his friends with lavish parties until he died of typhus in 1793.

GORDONSTOUN

• Moray (p.497 D2)   • Founded 1935

Set in a 60 ha (150 acre) estate in Elgin beside Scotland's Grampian Mountains, this independent boarding school has a reputation not so much for academic life as for a rigorous physical regime.

Its founder, the educationalist Kurt Hahn, fled from Nazi Germany in the 1930s and set up Gordonstoun with an emphasis on outdoor activities. One of its earliest pupils was Prince PHILIP, who later sent his son Prince CHARLES there. Inspired by Hahn's ideas, in 1956 Prince Philip launched the Duke of Edinburgh's Award scheme to give young people experience in sailing, mountaineering and orienteering.

Today, as well as schooling 465 pupils, Gordonstoun also runs summer courses for students of more than 30 nationalities with the aim of promoting international friendship.

HIGH GOTHIC Mary Shelley's *Frankenstein* elevated the gothic novel to the status of literature, using a macabre story to make a serious moral point

EMINENT VICTORIAN As governor of the Sudan in the 1870s, Charles Gordon once rode out on a camel to quell an uprising single-handed. He defused the revolt without violence

GOTHIC NOVEL

The writer Horace WALPOLE first coined the word 'gothic' to capture the medieval spirit of his novel *The Castle of Otranto* (1764), a dark and bloody tale in which the beautiful heroine, Isabella, desperately flees the tyrannical Prince Manfred, who is intent on marrying her. The book was so successful that it spawned a host of similar stories from other novelists, creating a new genre of literature closely associated with the ROMANTIC MOVEMENT.

Later writers in the genre emphasised the macabre over the historical. In Ann Radcliffe's *The Mysteries of Udolpho* (1794), a young woman is subjected to apparently supernatural episodes as well as attempted ravishment by an evil villain. In Mary SHELLEY's *Frankenstein* (1818), a scientist gives life to a monster assembled from parts of corpses, who then turns on his creator when his request for a mate is refused.

By the 1820s the appeal of these gruesome tales was beginning to wane. Jane Austen satirised the form in *Northanger Abbey* (1818), but it remained an influence on later writers, including the Brontë sisters, Charles Dickens and Bram Stoker, whose *Dracula* (1897) later inspired a succession of horror films.

FRANKENSTEIN.

MEDIEVAL INSPIRATION

In the late 18th century a new architectural style grew out of a romantic nostalgia for the art and literature of the Middle Ages. It took shape in the early 19th century and became an extravagant decorative expression of the prosperous Victorian age

EARLY ROMANCE Turrets, pinnacles and stained-glass windows adorn Strawberry Hill, Horace Walpole's elaborate neo-Gothic home

THE GOTHIC style of architecture with its elaborate grandeur – at its zenith in the Middle Ages – never died out entirely in Britain. Even through years of classical dominance in the 17th-18th centuries, its decorative form reappeared from time to time.

A full-scale revival began during the middle decades of the 18th century, influenced by a wider fashion for Romanticism and the medieval past, echoed in paintings of ruined medieval castles and abbeys, and in the novels of Walter SCOTT.

The writer Horace WALPOLE was an early enthusiast. From 1748, over a period of 20 years, he transformed his Twickenham home, Strawberry Hill, into a picturesque Gothic castle. Walpole also wrote one of the first Gothic novels – *The Castle of Otranto* (1764).

THE PROPHET OF GOTHIC
In the 19th century, Gothic forms were used increasingly in public buildings and became an alternative to the classicism then dominant. Architects began to design in both styles, according to the wishes of their client and the requirements of the site.

By 1840 the Gothic Revival was becoming more academic and ideological, studiously recreating the detail of original medieval buildings. The architect Augustus PUGIN was a key figure. For him Gothic was a form uniquely appropriate to the Victorian age. It was Christian and it was honest – no stucco

imitations here or plaster painted to look like marble. Above all it was English, said Pugin, as he urged architects to discard 300 years of 'foreign' influence and revive medieval style.

WESTMINSTER PALACE
Pugin was employed by the architect Charles Barry in the rebuilding of the HOUSES OF PARLIAMENT, which had been destroyed by fire in 1834. Barry preferred the neoclassical style, but Pugin's enthusiasm and persuasive zeal ensured that the internal detail, including wallpapers, carpets, furniture, glass and metalwork, was extravagantly Gothic. He even trained a team of craftsmen in the skills of their medieval counterparts.

The result is the most finely worked building of the Gothic Revival. Its influence was considerable, and the Revival moved on apace to its popular climax – High Victorian Gothic.

FLOURISHING FORM
George Gilbert SCOTT was among Pugin's most passionate disciples and became the foremost exponent of neo-Gothic style, designing government buildings and churches, restoring cathedrals and creating his most familiar structure, the ALBERT MEMORIAL. But the skills of Pugin and Barry's craftsmen were rarely matched. In other buidlings more ornament was piled on and the quality fell. In the 20th century, the style was used mainly for churches.

Good examples of Gothic Revival include: Strawberry Hill; the gateway of King's College, Cambridge (1824); Exeter College Chapel, Oxford (1859); and St Luke's Church in Chelsea (1824).

GOTHIC GLORY St Pancras Hotel in London, with ecclesiastical arches, decorative wrought ironwork and a magnificent sweeping staircase, was designed by George Gilbert Scott

GOWER PENINSULA

• S Wales (p.494 C4)

The dramatically lovely rolling plateau lies west of Swansea, stretching out some 15 miles into the Bristol Channel.

Popular with surfers for beaches such as Rhossili and with naturalists for its plant and bird life, the Gower Peninsula was designated Britain's first Area of Outstanding Natural Beauty in 1956.

Coves and limestone cliffs towering above crashing breakers line much of the south coast, extending as far as Mumbles, Swansea's seaside satellite at the eastern end of the peninsula. The resort is named after its two offshore islets, supposedly from the French *mamelles,* meaning 'breasts'.

Farther west, stretches of tall sand dunes have built up, notably at Oxwich Nature Reserve and also at Whiteford Burrows, in the north-west.

W.G. GRACE

• Cricketer • 1848-1915

The first cricketer to collect 2000 runs and 100 wickets in the same season, the first to amass 100 hundreds, and the first Englishman to score a Test century, Dr William Gilbert Grace single-handedly modernised and popularised CRICKET.

Ample of paunch, bushy of beard and effeminate of voice, 'W.G.' dominated the game for nearly half a century, elevating it from its rural origins and transforming

CONSUMMATE CRICKETER **W.G. Grace played with passion for England and Gloucestershire, the county side he captained for 28 years**

ENQUIRING MINDS Scientific specimens go under the microscope in 1950 at Manchester Grammar School, founded in 1515

GRAMMAR SCHOOLS

Britain's 163 grammar schools are in name descendants of the 300-400 schools created in the Middle Ages to educate clever boys of humble origins.

Like PUBLIC SCHOOLS they were privately endowed until the 20th century and, with public schools, the only source of secondary education. The 1902 Education Act established publicly funded grammar schools, which became part of a system of state secondary education that was later extended to all.

In the 1920s secondary school education was made compulsory and the 11-plus examination was established to determine which children went to grammar schools and which to new, less demanding 'secondary modern' schools.

In 1965 the Labour government, wishing to promote a more egalitarian system, called on local authorities to set up comprehensive schools to provide a broader education for children of all abilities. From 1974 public-sector grammar schools were increasingly aborbed into the comprehensive system.

However, because some believe that the system has lowered educational standards, places at the surviving grammar schools are still in great demand.

OLD SCHOOL CREST Uppingham School was founded in 1584 as a local grammar school

it into a national pastime. He played in 22 Tests, all against Australia, and led England in 13. He played his final Test at the age of 50 and still turned out for Gloucestershire at 60.

'He ought to be made to play with a littler bat,' urged one aggrieved rival. In an allusion to his notorious intimidation of umpires, Charles Kortright, the fearsome Essex fast bowler, once bowled him and cried: 'What, are you going, Doctor? There's still one stump standing.'

As a box-office attraction 'W.G.' had few peers in any sphere. Ground notices in the 1870s would announce 'Admission 3d...if Dr W.G. plays, 6d.' Thus was Britain's first sporting superstar born.

GRAMPIAN MOUNTAINS

• NE Scotland (p.497 C3/D3)

The mountain range runs from the Firth of Clyde to Aberdeenshire, forming a dramatic 'highland line' above Scotland's relatively lush and populated central belt. Once regarded as a terrifying wasteland, the area was popularised by Queen Victoria when she rebuilt the castle of BALMORAL near Braemar.

The many peaks rising above 900m (3000ft), called 'munros', include Cairn Gorm at 1245m (4084ft) and Ben Lawers at 1214m (3983ft). The Cairngorms national nature reserve, which lies between Braemar and

Aviemore is the largest in Britain, covering more than 27 000 ha (67 000 acres) of mountain, moor and woodland. Golden eagles breed on the high hills and capercaille live in the native pinewoods, while osprey have returned to nest on Spey-side, just outside the reserve.

The management of this wilderness can be controversial. Conservation has been managed so it does not conflict with the demands of landowners, hill-walkers and the thriving skiing industry around the resort of Aviemore.

GRAND NATIONAL

• April • Est. 1839

Some think it the most thrilling of all horse races; others say it should be banned on grounds of animal cruelty. The Grand National's allure is, however, undeniable. In 1998, a typical year, 15 million people – most of whom otherwise never gamble – bet around £70 million on the outcome of the race.

The 4½ mile steeplechase – since 1839 held annually at Aintree, near Liverpool – is the most severe test of jumping and stamina in British horse racing, encompassing two circuits and 30 fences, including The Chair, the highest at 1.57 m (5 ft 2 in). Red Rum was the only horse to gain three wins (1973, 1974 and 1977) in an event that habitually makes a mockery of the odds. One exception was Rough Quest, who in 1996 became the first favourite to triumph for 14 years. 'After that sex is a bit of an anticlimax', said his jockey, Mick Fitzgerald.

Apart from interruptions during the First and Second World Wars, the Grand National was a fixture largely untroubled by outside incident until in 1997 an IRA bomb warning halted the race before it could start, forcing a postponement until the following Monday. In 1993, when mass confusion set in after a false start, there was no second attempt.

Past owners of Aintree had periodically threatened to sell the racecourse, jeopardising the Grand National's future, but in 1983 donations from the public helped the Jockey Club to buy Aintree and save the event.

GRAND TOUR

First introduced in Elizabethan times, the Grand Tour reached its height of popularity during the 18th century. By then it had become accepted as the ideal finishing school for young aristocrats. Despatched to the Continent in the charge of a tutor, they would complete their education and acquire a knowledge of art, history, foreign languages and classical civilisation.

A Grand Tour could last up to two years. There was no set route, although Paris and Rome were usually included, and the journey would be punctuated by stays in cities along the way.

The Tourists returned with art to hang in their stately homes, and their trips also inspired the adoption of the neoclassical style of architecture. The Grand Tour was halted by the Revolutionary Wars in Europe in 1792, and ended by the arrival of the steam train and the modern hotel.

GRAVES: *see opposite page*

POETIC VOICE OF ANCIENT ROME Robert Graves' *I, Claudius* is an imaginative eye-witness account of historical events, narrated by the emperor

Robert GRAVES

• Poet and novelist • 1895-1985

Although Graves is perhaps best known for his historical novels *I, Claudius* and *Claudius the God*, both published in 1934, he always regarded himself as a poet who wrote prose only to make money. In fact, he was remarkably prolific, producing novels, biographies, essays, works for children and critical pieces.

He wrote his first poems, *Over the Brazier* (1916) and *Fairies and Fusiliers* (1917), mainly in reaction to the horrors of the First World War, during which he was once left for dead in a heap of corpses. His autobiography, *Goodbye to All That* (1929) perfectly voiced postwar disillusion and became an instant classic.

Graves, who settled in Majorca in 1946, had a series of 'muses' who inspired him, including the American poet Laura Riding. He was never part of any literary movement and is held to be one of the century's most classical poets.

FATAL FALL In the 1989 Grand National, Brown Trix, ridden by David Pitcher, falls at the formidable Becher's Brook

IN MEMORIAM

Britain's graveyards, cemeteries, mausoleums and the tombs and memorials within churches, chapels and cathedrals offer a unique insight into country and urban life stretching back over centuries and embracing people of every class

WEATHERED GRAVESTONES, wild flowers, yew trees and a lich gate in a quiet country churchyard make up the idealised image of our final place of rest. The reality is rather different.

Most people are not now buried in churchyards; cemeteries have taken their place. And some of Britain's oldest tombs are not outside but within a church or family chapel. In the Middle Ages the most favoured places, high up by the altar, went to aristocratic families; carved tombs, brass plates and effigies announced their wealth and rank. The poorer folk were laid in the ground with only wooden markers on their graves.

SAINTLY SHRINES

From early medieval times, the tombs of saints and martyrs became places of PILGRIMAGE. Among the most popular were the shrines of Thomas Becket at Canterbury; St Cuthbert at Durham; and St Edward the Confessor at Westminster Abbey.

By the 17th century, headstones came into general use, giving ordinary people lasting memorials. Some might show the tools of trade of the deceased – the barber's scissors or the gamekeeper's rifles and rods. Others were embellished with decorative symbols – the globe for Mortality or the hourglass for Time.

THREAT TO HEALTH

With his 'Elegy Written in a Country Churchyard' of 1751, Thomas GRAY reinforced the pastoral image – and was himself buried in St Giles' churchyard in Stoke Poges, Buckinghamshire.

But as the population grew, churchyards could no longer cope with the burden of dead. They became overcrowded, with graves jammed close together, posing health risks. In the early 19th century Charlotte Brontë noted that there was barely a wisp of grass between the slabs in the graveyard at her father's church.

The government realised that bigger burial grounds were essential as industrial cities expanded. Large tracts of land were bought on the edges of towns and public cemeteries were opened. These were not connected with any church, although there was always a chapel at the centre.

YOUNG DEATH A child's memorial from the early 20th century rises from the undergrowth of a graveyard in Wales

LANDMARK GRAVES

Among the best-known burial grounds is west London's Kensal Green Cemetery, where the novelist Anthony Trollope, the engineer Isambard Kingdom Brunel and the trapeze artist Blondin are buried. In north London Karl Marx's grave is an attraction at HIGHGATE Cemetery.

Although a host of illustrious figures lie in Westminster Abbey or St Paul's Cathedral, some of the greatest are found elsewhere. Florence Nightingale is buried in the churchyard at St Margaret's, East Mellow, Hampshire; the poet Robert Burns lies in St Michael's churchyard, Dumfries; Lord Mountbatten of Burma is buried at Romsey Abbey, Hampshire; and Winston Churchill's grave is at Bladon in Oxfordshire.

THE STONEMASON'S ART

As stone was used increasingly from the 17th century to mark graves, the mason's art flourished. Gravestones told stories, proclaimed occupations and were arrayed with decorative symbolic imagery.

WARRIOR'S TOMB An effigy and a tombstone beside it inscribed with Celtic symbols (left) marks the burial place of an 18th-century Scottish soldier in Old Luce, Galloway

IMAGES OF DEATH A slab from a medieval tomb chest (above) now stands outside Keills Chapel in Argyll

A MASTER'S TRIBUTE An unusually fine tombstone (left) was erected by the earl of Suffolk and Bradon in 1720 to commemorate Scipio Africanus, his young black servant

LIONISED The king of the beasts slumbers atop a tomb (right) in Highgate Cemetery, erected in memory of George Wombwell, described as a 'menagerist', who died in 1860, aged 83 years

LIFE IN DEATH The Tree of Life (below) adorns a 19th-century gravestone to a young man buried in St Ethelbert's churchyard, Littledean, Gloucestershire

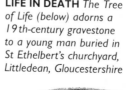

HERE Lieth the Body of SCIPIO AFRICANUS Negro Servant to y Right Honourable Charles William Earl of Suffolk and Bradon who died y 21 December 1720 Aged 18 Years

Thomas GRAY

- **Poet** • **1716-71**

The curfew tolls the knell of
parting day,
The lowing herd wind slowly
o'er the lea,
The ploughman homeward plods
his weary way,
And leaves the world to darkness
and to me.

Elegy Written in a Country Churchyard
(1751)

With its evocative detail, nostalgic tone, ballad rhythms and dignified description of common life, Gray's *Elegy* has a universal appeal. For the writer and critic Samuel Johnson it 'abounds with images which find a mirror in every mind, and with sentiments to which every bosom returns an echo'.

Despite the *Elegy*'s enduring success, Gray wrote few poems, and taught history at Cambridge University for most of his life. His writing is dominated by themes of nostalgia, regret and the inexorable passage of time. From solitary country ramblings, he derived images of nature's simultaneous beauty and cruelty.

A true son of the Enlightenment, Gray cleverly combined the Roman meters of Horace and the Greek Pindaric ode with Norse mythology and Britain's own Celtic traditions.

Later Romantic poets such as Wordsworth and Coleridge found Gray sentimental and stylised. Yet without the example of his richly imaginative use of language, the ROMANTIC MOVEMENT might never have blossomed as it did.

GREAT BRITAIN

- **Area 88 685 sq miles** • **Pop. 55.9 million**

The term Great Britain was introduced after the 1707 Act of Union formalised the unification of Scotland with England and Wales under the rule of Queen Anne.

It is still the correct name for the landmass encompassing the three countries that, together with the six counties of the province of Northern Ireland, form the UNITED KINGDOM – often known simply as 'Britain'.

However, the term 'Great Britain' is frequently used to describe the nation including Northern Ireland in contexts such as international sports events.

GREAT EXHIBITION

- **May 1-October 15, 1851**

Originally billed as a display of 'the Works of Industry of all Nations', the Great Exhibition, held in Hyde Park, was in fact a showcase for Britain's supreme industrial skills.

Prince ALBERT was its patron and Queen Victoria opened it – and went back to visit 34 times. In the 9.5 ha (23 acres) encased by the glass of Joseph Paxton's huge structure – dubbed the Crystal Palace by *Punch* magazine – more than 100 000 exhibits were displayed, including the Koh-i-Noor diamond, now part of the CROWN JEWELS. Many of the works of art found new homes, including a statue of Richard I (the Lionheart), which was re-erected outside the Houses of Parliament.

When the Great Exhibition closed, the Crystal Palace was reassembled in Sydenham. It became the central feature of an amusement park until destroyed by fire in 1936.

CRYSTAL SPLENDOUR Confounding its early sceptics, the Great Exhibition was a huge success, attracting more than 6 million visitors

GREAT ORMOND STREET HOSPITAL

- **Central London (p.499 D1)** • **Founded 1852**

Paediatrics was in its infancy and children were officially excluded from general hospitals when Charles West and Henry Bence Jones founded the Hospital for Sick Children in 1852. It was housed at 49 Great Ormond Street in

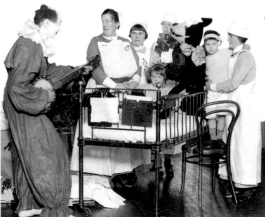

London's Bloomsbury district, once the residence of Richard Mead, physician to Queen Anne. But it soon expanded next door as its work increased, thanks to early support from patrons such as Queen Victoria, Charles Dickens and the earl of Shaftesbury.

In 1929 James Barrie gave the lucrative copyright of *Peter Pan* to the hospital; in 1987, special parliamentary authority was granted to extend the copyright in perpetuity.

The 300 bed hospital currently treats some 22 000 inpatients a year and around 78 400 outpatients, offering the widest range of paediatric specialities in the world. From 1946 it has also been the headquarters of the Institute of Child Health of the University of London, devoted to research and teaching.

PAIN RELIEF A Christmas clown performs at Great Ormond Street Hospital in 1925. Keeping children happy is an integral part of its care

GREAT STORM

• Night of October 15-16, 1987

On a late autumn night, the normally sheltered south-east of England was battered by ferocious winds reaching speeds of up to 115 mph.

The 'great storm' uprooted some 15 million mature trees from rain-saturated ground. Its severity astonished the Meteorological Office. The wind speeds exceeded anything recorded since 1703 – touching 95 mph even in central London.

The death toll of 18 was mercifully low but insurance losses to property amounted to some £800 million. The ecological damage, however, seemed even more costly. At the Royal Botanic Gardens at Kew, the storm destroyed 500 trees and damaged 1000 others. Losses included rare specimens, mature trees over 30 m (100 ft) high and two that were more than 200 years old.

THE MORNING AFTER Wind-torn buildings on a landscape strewn with uprooted trees left parts of England looking like a battlefield

GREAT TRAIN ROBBERY

At the time it was the biggest and most successful heist in British history. In the early morning of August 8, 1963, a band of armed men held up a Royal Mail train in Buckinghamshire and got away with mailbags containing £2.6 million in old, untraceable banknotes. The 58-year-old train driver was clubbed over the head during the raid and never fully recovered

SMASH AND GRAB The audacity of the 'Great Train Robbery' – a name borrowed from a 1930s silent film – appealed to the public, though its violence shocked them

from his injuries. Within a couple of years the culprits were caught and sentenced but not before they had hidden the money, little of which was ever recovered.

Two years later one of the gang, Ronnie Biggs, escaped from Wandsworth prison and picked up his share of the haul. He then made his way to Brazil, which did not have an extradition treaty with Britain, and remains there to this day.

One of his collaborators, 'Buster' Edwards, served his time and on his release became the subject of a film. However, in 1994 he was found hanged and an open verdict was recorded.

GREAT YARMOUTH

• Norfolk (p.495 K2) • Pop. 56 190

A port for more than 1000 years, the town has also flourished as a seaside resort since Victorian times. Its herring fishing industry brought prosperity in the early 20th century; later, North Sea oil and gas exploration generated new trade.

Yarmouth's medieval past survives in the narrow alleys of The Rows, the Tolhouse and the restored 12th-century church of St Nicholas. The Anna Sewell House marks the birthplace of *Black Beauty*'s author and, south of the town, a 44 m (144 ft) pillar honours Lord Nelson.

GREEN BELT

The 1930s idea of a 'green belt' – a strip of countryside round cities on which building would be restricted – was adopted as a reaction to postwar pressure to enlarge towns considered by many to be big enough already.

The object was to limit urban sprawl, preserve the character of the countryside and of historic towns, and to keep neighbouring towns distinct.

Green belts have no statutory authority and their demarcation is under constant challenge from the conflicting interests of developers, agriculture, nature conservation and existing

residents. In spite of this, the amount of green belt land doubled during the 1980s and in 1998 accounted for 1.5 million ha (3.7 million acres) of England and 145 700 ha (360 000 acres) of Scotland.

However, increasing calls for more housing in Britain threaten future reductions in the green belt area.

Graham GREENE

• Novelist • 1904-91

Despair and failure fill Graham Greene's novels. Moral dilemmas and the betrayal of trust are constant ingredients. Greene, for 50 years among Britain's most popular authors, introduced his dominant theme, which he called 'the appalling strangeness of the mercy of God', in *Brighton Rock* (1938), with its seedy gangsters and destruction of innocence.

Having converted to Roman Catholicism in 1926, Greene spent the rest of his life struggling with his faith. His fiction addresses the agonies and doubts of religion, questioning the meaning of good and evil.

Though Greene spent much of his life in the south of France, it is his extensive travel to countries riddled with political corruption that is reflected in his novels. Their exotic locations and the despair of the characters who inhabit them were dubbed 'Greeneland' by his critics.

His major works include *The Power and the Glory* (1940), *The Heart of the Matter* (1948), *The Third Man* (1950) and *The Honorary Consul* (1973).

LEAFY LORD The fronded face of the Green Man lives on in pub signs and has become a new symbol for the environmental movement

GREEN MAN

This mysterious figure is usually regarded as a folk character or as a pagan fertility deity of the woodlands. He appears in Middle Eastern myths and in European legends as a wild, gypsy-like figure representing the birth of new life in spring.

The medieval motif of a disembodied head, half human, half tree, may represent this spirit of unruly nature. Entwined with greenery, leaves sprouting from his mouth and nostrils, he is carved on rood screens, pillars or misericords in many British churches and cathedrals – including Canterbury, Exeter, Norwich and Sheffield.

Some say that the craftsmen who executed the images were incorporating their traditional pagan beliefs into their handiwork. The Green Man may be the same figure as the Green George or Jack in the Green who traditionally leads MAY DAY processions. He has also been associated with ROBIN HOOD, and the strange figure in the 14th-century epic poem *Sir Gawain and the Green Knight*.

GREENWICH

• **S London (p.498 D4)**

The borough of Greenwich, which lies just south of the Thames, included a royal palace between the 15th and 17th centuries where HENRY VIII, MARY I and ELIZABETH I were born. Greenwich played a prominent role in Britain's maritime history and has some fine architecture as a result of its past prestige.

Richard Chancellor and Hugh Willoughby set off from Greenwich to seek a north-east passage to China in 1553. Francis Drake was knighted there and it was there that the order to attack the Armada was signed.

Among its finest buildings is the Queen's House designed by Inigo JONES in the early 1600s and now part of the National Maritime Museum, whose collection includes the coat worn by Lord NELSON at TRAFALGAR. Until 1998 the old Greenwich Hospital, designed by Nicholas HAWKSMOOR and Christopher WREN, housed the Royal Naval College.

In dry dock, two vessels recall past voyages – the elegant tea clipper *CUTTY SARK* and *Gipsy Moth IV*, in which Francis CHICHESTER completed in 1967 the first solo circumnavigation of the world.

A huge dome of steelwork and fabric, designed by Richard ROGERS, has been erected on a derelict riverside site as part of the millennium celebrations.

GREENWICH MEAN TIME

The time at the ROYAL GREENWICH OBSERVATORY – Greenwich Mean Time (GMT) – sets the time for the world. GMT came into wide use in the 18th century as an accurate time-keeping system to help astronomers to plot the position of the stars.

REAL TIME The clock outside the observatory gates has displayed Greenwich Mean Time to the public since 1852

In 1759 John Harrison, an English clockmaker, fixed Greenwich at the centre of the world when he built a timepiece that could keep time at sea. Sailors could now calculate their longitude, the distance east or west from a line through Greenwich, by comparing the 'Greenwich time' on the clock with local time, set by the position of the sun.

From 1833, a large red 'time-ball' on the roof of the observatory dropped each

GRETNA GREEN

• **Dumfries and Galloway (p.497 D5)**

A little village on the Scottish border has been the goal of eloping couples since an Act of parliament in 1754 banned 'irregular' marriages in England, in which couples made vows before witnesses with no legal preliminaries.

Runaways could be married in the village inns, the tollhouse or private houses, although the most popular venue became the forge. A change in the law in 1857 required one of the partners to be resident in Scotland for 21 days before a licence was granted, and from 1940 a minister or registrar was necessary. Even now Scottish law allows people as young as 16 years to marry without parental assent, while elsewhere in Britain the minimum age is 18 years.

Several thousand couples each year still choose to marry with complete legitimacy in one of the chapels or registry offices at Gretna Green.

FORGING A UNION More than 500 couples each year still make their marriage vows – before a minister or registrar – over the anvil (*left*) at the old blacksmith's (*above*) in Gretna Green

day at 1300 hours to provide navigators on the Thames with a time signal. Until then, 'local time' took noon as the moment when the sun was directly overhead and varied from place to place. Standard time became essential when places were first linked by rail from the 1830s, so that timetables could be drawn up.

GMT was officially adopted by parliament in 1880. Global recognition followed in 1884 at the International Meridian Conference in Washington DC, establishing the line through Greenwich as the prime meridian for a system of 24 time zones around the world.

HIGH-TECH TERMINAL Nicholas Grimshaw's best-known work, the futuristic yet functional Waterloo International terminal, opened in 1994 for the start of the Channel Tunnel rail link

Lady Jane GREY

• Queen July 10-19 1553 • 1537-54

The bookish 15-year-old who became queen for nine days was a brilliant linguist and student of classics. Her claim to the throne was remote – through her grandmother, a daughter of HENRY VII – and she became a tragic victim of political manipulation.

First she was unwillingly married to the duke of Northumberland's son, then she was named heir to the throne when Northumberland persuaded the dying EDWARD VI to set aside the claim of his elder sister MARY in favour of the strongly Protestant Lady Jane.

Crowned on July 10, 1553, her reign was brief. Mary was furious and, by popular acclaim, became queen nine days later. Northumberland was executed. Lady Jane spent six months in the Tower of London before she was beheaded for treason in February 1554.

GREYHOUND RACING

Greyhound racing was devised in the 19th century as a humane alternative to dogfighting. The sport is derived from coursing, in which dogs pursue hares by sight instead of scent, but takes place on a track where spectators can watch.

A mechanical hare was used for the first-ever

'Ravage Again', the fastest British greyhound on record, ran at 39.38 mph over 250 m (273 yd) in May 1990 at Belle Vue racetrack in Manchester

'simulated coursing' on a straight track in Hendon, north London, in 1876. The oval track was pioneered by Owen Patrick Smith, an American, in California in 1919; betting on the dogs was started by his compatriot, Charles A. Munn.

Munn then sold the idea back to England, where the first purpose-built oval track – at Manchester's Belle Vue – opened in 1926. The appeal was self-evident – cheap gambling and a night out for working-class townsfolk.

From a peak of some 34 million in 1946, the audience has waned. The 1960 Betting and Gaming Act opened up other forms of gambling. Today, 4 million people each year bet a total of approximately £2000 million on the 35 000 dogs which race at Britain's 32 greyhound tracks.

GRIME'S GRAVES

• Prehistoric site • Norfolk (p.495 J2) • EH

In 1868 excavations uncovered what may well be Europe's first large-scale mines. They were first dug more than 4500 years ago by Neolithic flint miners who began chipping at the earth near Thetford Forest, using deer antlers as picks.

Cutting slowly through chalk and seams of flint, their work lit by lamps fuelled with animal fat, they sank more than 360 pits and shafts – the deepest dropping nearly 14 m (46 ft). It is estimated that 25-30 million flint axes were produced during the life of these mines.

Much later, the barren stretch of land with its strange, shallow hollows became known as Grime's Graves – the digging place of 'Grim', the Devil. One of the ancient shafts is now open to the public.

Nicholas GRIMSHAW

• Architect • b.1939

The Waterloo International rail terminal in London with its vast, sinuously curving glass roof is one of a number of eye-catching structures from the influential architectural practice of Nicholas Grimshaw and Partners. Others include the restoration of the 18th-century spa in Bath, an innovative Sainsbury's supermarket in London and the British Pavilion for Expo 92 in Seville, Spain.

After studying in Edinburgh and at the Architectural Association in London, Grimshaw went into partnership with the architect Terry Farrell from 1965 until 1980, when he set up his present practice.

His guiding principle is that structures should serve their users – with a built-in flexibility to accommodate changing requirements. Some of his buildings have interior walls that are movable like screens, and structural elements that are replaceable when they wear out.

GROG

In 1740 sailors in the Royal Navy learned that their daily ration of half a pint of full-strength rum, to which they had been entitled since the 17th century, would henceforth be diluted with water by four parts to one. The order came from Admiral Edward Vernon, who was concerned at the lack of discipline and the health problems associated with the consumption of such large quantities of strong drink.

The admiral's nickname, Old Grog – derived from his shipboard cloak of grogram, a coarse waterproofed fabric – was duly shortened into contemptuous naval slang to christen the new mixture. Sailors continued to enjoy a ration of rum until August 1970.

GUILDS

In the centre of many large towns and cities is a guildhall, once the meeting place of guilds: organisations of self-employed artisans or merchants formed in the Middle Ages to regulate the price and quality of products such as ironwork and cloth. The name 'guild' comes from the old Germanic word *gelth*, meaning pay – in this instance, the subscriptions paid by the guild members.

HIGH CHAIR This master's throne was used in the 17th century by the Framework Knitters guild

BOGEY MAN Before the Gulf War began, Iraqi leader Saddam Hussein vainly tried to win world approval by posing with the British boy Stuart Lockwood

Iraqi TV Taped Broadcast

By the end of the 12th century, guilds governed not only standards and pricing but also wages and apprenticeships – the seven-year training essential to learn the 'mystery' of a craft such as barrel-making. Then at the age of 23 a man could become a paid journeyman or master craftsman.

Guilds wielded great power to protect their members and the standards of their trade or craft, in much the same way as 20th-century TRADE UNIONS. Some became so influential and inflexible that laws were passed in 1437 and 1504 forcing guilds to submit to local judicial and civic authorities. By the end of the 16th century guilds had lost most of their commercial influence in the face of the growth of entrepreneurial capitalism.

Alec GUINNESS

• **Actor** • **b.1914; kt 1959**

At school London-born Alec Guinness was told by his headmaster that he would 'never make an actor'. His first job was writing advertising copy for products such as radio valves and lime cordial, but he did not give up his dreams of the stage. With the advice of John Gielgud he took voice and drama lessons, and by 1938 he was playing Hamlet at the Old Vic, the colleague of Gielgud and Lawrence Olivier.

A chameleon-like ability to play a vast range of characters – the actor Peter Ustinov called him 'the outstanding poet of anonymity' – gained Guinness many film roles. He was a memorable Fagin in *Oliver Twist* (1948), the first of four films he made with director David LEAN. In the second, *Bridge on the River Kwai* (1957), his portrayal of a British prisoner-of-war officer won him an Oscar.

Guinness was a stalwart of the 1940s and 50s EALING COMEDIES, including *Kind Hearts and Coronets* (1949), in which he played eight members of the d'Ascoyne

family, and *The Lavender Hill Mob* (1951). He received an Oscar nomination for his role as the wise old warrior Obi-wan Kenobi in *Star Wars* (1977), and in 1979 was awarded an honorary Oscar 'for advancing the art of screen acting'.

GULF WAR

• **January 17-February 28, 1991**

The war against Iraq and its dictator Saddam Hussein was one of the shortest conflicts involving British troops. It achieved the aim of liberating Kuwait from Iraqi troops, but Hussein and much of his arsenal, including chemical weapons, have continued to be a threat.

BRITAIN JOINS THE FRAY

The war began when Iraq, which had invaded neighbouring Kuwait in August 1990, refused a United Nations demand to withdraw by January 15, 1991. Two days later, forces from a coalition of 28 countries, including Britain, bombarded Iraqi industrial and military targets with 'smart' bombs – computer-directed missiles that could, even when launched from hundreds of miles away, target a specific doorway or window.

On February 24, coalition forces launched an all-out ground offensive against Iraqi troops. It lasted four days, with a death toll of 234 allied soldiers, of which 42 were British, and at least 50 000 Iraqis.

The war was over but its indirect effects persisted. Symptoms that ranged from fatigue to respiratory problems – the so-called 'Gulf War syndrome' – were said to have affected thousands of veterans, possibly causing some 150 deaths. Pesticides used by the forces, vaccines against germ warfare agents and Iraqi nerve gas were blamed, but the causes have remained unclear.

The force Britain mobilised for the Gulf War was one of its largest since the Second World War. More than 45 000 troops, 160 aircraft, 26 ships and 15 000 support vehicles were sent

---

GUNPOWDER PLOT

It was the most audacious of British conspiracies: Catholic zealots plotting by candlelight to blow up the Houses of Parliament as JAMES I, the Lords and Commons gathered for the opening of a new session. The conspirators, including the aristocratic ringleader Robert Catesby and the soldier Guy Fawkes, were disillusioned by James's failure to provide equal rights for Catholics. The explosion was intended to spark a rebellion after which James's nine-year-old daughter Elizabeth was to be installed as head of a Catholic state.

THE PLOT THICKENS

A year before the target date of November 5, 1605, the plotters rented a tiny house in the parliament precincts. It had a storehouse at ground level under the House of Lords, where they deposited barrels of gunpowder that were camouflaged with firewood and coal. But the plot was undermined. An anonymous note sent to Lord Monteagle, possibly by his brother-in-law Francis Tresham, one of the conspirators, warned Monteagle not to attend the state opening. The note was passed to Robert Cecil, James I's chief minister, and the Houses of Parliament were searched. Guy Fawkes was found alone in the cellar on the night of November 4, 1605.

Fawkes and those of his colleagues not killed resisting arrest were hanged for treason. English Catholics were discredited and any hope of their playing an active part in public life was dashed for the next 200 years. The discovery of the plot is still celebrated each year on November 5, BONFIRE NIGHT.

Nell GWYN

• Mistress of Charles II • c.1650-87

Nell Gwyn was a favourite of the people as well as of the king. One day in London a crowd jeered at her coach, thinking an unpopular Catholic royal mistress was inside. Nell turned the insults to laughter as she waved and

THE KING'S PLEASURE Nell Gwyn was 19 when she became the mistress of Charles II, who rewarded her with a house in Pall Mall. She bore him two children

shouted, 'Pray, good people, be civil, I am the Protestant whore!'.

Born in Covent Garden, Nell Gwyn sold oranges at the theatre in Drury Lane and was an actress by the age of 14. She was said to have kept faithful to Charles, replying when propositioned, 'Shall the dog lie where the deer once couched?'. Charles's dying wish, 'Let not poor Nellie starve', was honoured by his brother, James II, who gave Nell a pension for life.

GYMKHANA

Every summer in villages across the land young riders and their ponies, most of them members of one of Britain's 300 pony clubs, compete in the egg and spoon, balloon sticking and apple ducking races of the annual gymkhana. Originating around 1860 in the India of the RAJ, 'gymkhana' is a composite Latin and Hindi word coined by the British for a meeting of sports such as badminton and tennis. Horse and pony races were added and the idea was imported into English villages.

The gymkhana season climaxes with the Prince Philip Cup held in Wembley at The Horse of the Year Show every September.

GYPSIES

There are more than 50 000 gypsies in Britain. Their forebears arrived in about 1500, originally coming from India where they began their nomadic life 500 years before. In 1530 gypsies performed for James V of Scotland and gained a reputation as fine dancers and musicians. They were also rumoured to be cannibals and kidnappers and many gypsies were hanged – some accused merely of 'being Egyptian', the origin of the name 'gypsy'.

The persecution of gypsies declined in the late 18th century, and their open-air life and lack of convention became romanticised by writers such as John Keats in his poem 'Old Meg'.

Old Meg she was a Gipsy,
And liv'd upon the Moors:
Her bed it was the brown heath turf
And her home was out of doors

Some gypsies still use the traditional Romany language and continue customs such as telling fortunes and burning the possessions of the dead.

HORSE PLAY Thelwell's gymkhana cartoons epitomise the love affair between young girl and frisky pony

HABEAS CORPUS

Applying for a writ of habeas corpus – Latin for 'you must have the body' – is a way of demanding under English common law the release of someone held against his or her will. For centuries the principle has been a symbol of the freedom of the citizen not to be unlawfully imprisoned. It dates back to before the Magna Carta, sealed by King John in 1215, when it was a petition made to the sovereign. Today application is made to a High Court judge.

Habeas corpus is today used mainly in cases of immigrants and asylum-seekers kept in detention for long periods while their claim is considered.

J.B.S. HALDANE

• Biologist and geneticist • 1892-1964

As a pioneer in the field of genetics in the 1920s, John Burdon Sanderson Haldane put forward the then radical, but now widely accepted, theory that primitive life arose spontaneously from a chemical 'soup' billions of years ago.

He also investigated the genetic control of enzyme actions and tackled ventilation problems in submarines and mines. During the Second World War he used himself as a guinea pig to investigate the effect of extremes of temperature and high concentrations of carbon dioxide on the body in studies for the Royal Navy.

Haldane came from a family of scientists and was an outspoken Marxist and atheist. From 1940 to 1949 he chaired the editorial board of the Communist party newspaper *Daily Worker*. He left the party over Stalin's interference in scientific research and in 1957 emigrated to India as a protest against British action in the Suez Crisis. He became an Indian citizen in 1961.

GIVING A LEAD Peter Hall directs Peggy Ashcroft, buried up to her neck in sand, in the 1975 National Theatre production of Samuel Beckett's absurdist play *Happy Days*

HADRIAN'S WALL

• N England (p.496 B2) • Built 2nd century AD

'I have sent you... socks, and from Sattia two pairs of sandals; and two pairs of underpants.' To Romans unused to either socks or underwear, winters at Hadrian's Wall were a chilly experience, and gifts from home – such as these to a soldier at Vindolanda fort – much appreciated.

Stretching for 73 miles across northern England from the Solway Firth in the west to the mouth of the River Tyne in the east, Hadrian's Wall is one of Britain's greatest building projects. Nearly 2000 years on, wall sections, defensive ditches and fortifications can still be seen.

LIMIT OF EMPIRE

The emperor Hadrian visited 'Britannia' around AD 122 and ordered the building of a wall to defend the northernmost outpost of his empire against the 'barbarian' tribes of what is now Scotland. It was finished by 136 and occupied until the early 400s, when the Roman withdrawal began.

The wall that the troops left behind was about 4.5-6 m (15-20 ft) high, and up to 3 m (10 ft) thick. Sixteen major forts defended it, as well as 'milecastles' at

IMPOSING ENTRANCE The east gate at Birdoswald fort, one of the 16 front-line forts, includes a double entrance with gate jambs, pivot holes and part of an arch

COLD COMFORT A carving at Housesteads – one of the best preserved sites – shows three gods wrapped against the harsh climate

Birdoswald Poltross Burn Cawfields Housestea

HALTWHISTLE Vindoland

A6071 Irthing A69

BRAMPTON

A74 A689 A689

Solway Firth

BOWNESS-ON-SOLWAY Eden

CARLISLE

M6

MAIN SITES

- Milecastle
- Fort
- Settlement
- Line of wall (no longer visible)
- Remains of wall

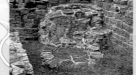

MASS CATERING The oven in the north-west corner of Poltross Burn milecastle would have been used to feed a garrison of up to 30 men

FOOD STORE Stone piers at Housesteads fort provided ventilation for the granary and protection against rats

Peter HALL

• **Theatre director** • b.1930; kt 1977

As a stage-struck Suffolk schoolboy, Peter Hall, the son of a railway worker, travelled to London to queue for cheap seats in the 'pit', to see actors such as John Gielgud, Laurence Olivier and Peggy Ashcroft. By his early 20s he was running London's Arts Theatre, staging challenging new plays, including Samuel Beckett's *Waiting for Godot*. At the age of 29 he became director of the Royal Shakespeare Company, working with his idols Olivier and Ashcroft.

NEW LIFE FOR THE NATIONAL

In 1973 Hall succeeded Olivier as director of the NATIONAL THEATRE, steering it through its move from the Old Vic to the South Bank and producing new plays such as Harold Pinter's *No Man's Land* and Peter Shaffer's *Amadeus*. Since 1988 he has run his own company.

Hall has worked extensively in opera. He has been artistic director of the Royal Opera (1969-71), and has staged many works for Glyndebourne. He has also made films and television dramas.

WANDERER OF THE SKY The most recent appearance of Halley's comet (*right*, viewed from Joshua Tree, California) was in 1986; it will not be seen again from Earth until 2061

Edmond HALLEY

• **Astronomer and mathematician** • 1656-1742

In 1682 Edmond Halley, who had written extensively on planetary orbits and catalogued the stars of the Southern Hemisphere from the island of St Helena, observed the comet that would bear his name. When he studied the movements of past comets, he noticed similarities between that of 1682 and those of 1456, 1531 and 1607. They were the same comet, returning every 75 to 76 years.

Halley published the claim in 1705, and 15 years later he was made ASTRONOMER ROYAL. Before he died, he wrote that if the comet 'should return again in about the year 1758, candid posterity will not refuse to acknowledge that this was first discovered by an Englishman'. The comet was duly sighted on Christmas Day 1758.

Halley's comet has punctuated history. In 240 BC it was noted in Chinese and Mesopotamian records, and in AD 451 it appeared before the first defeat of Attila the Hun. The comet coincided with the Norman Conquest in 1066 and is recorded in the Bayeux tapestry, where Saxons gaze skywards to see the heavenly portent of their imminent defeat.

---

every Roman mile (1686 yards) and turrets at every one-third of a Roman mile between them. To the north of the wall was a ditch 8 m (27 ft) wide and 3 m (10 ft) deep; to its south lay the Stanegate road and the *vallum*, another ditch, about 6 m (20 ft) wide at the top and 3 m (10 ft) deep, between turf banks.

LIFE ON THE WALL

Each fort was assigned to one of the three legions based in Britain, although the wall was normally garrisoned by up to 12 000 lower-paid and less well-equipped auxiliary soldiers, recruited from all over the empire and from the local Celtic tribes. They spent most of their 25 years' service not fighting but training, making repairs and carrying out other mundane duties.

The soldiers were relatively well fed. At Vindolanda fort provisions included barley, garlic, wine, beer and fish sauce, and the shops of the nearby Celtic village probably supplied pork and venison. Many soldiers married local women. One, Barates, a Syrian standard-bearer, married Regina, a freedwoman from north of London. Her tomb was found at South Shields while Barates, who outlived her, was buried 25 miles away at Corbridge.

BUSY THOROUGHFARE The main street of Corbridge was lined with columns. The lion, a monument from a grave, was found being used as a fountain in 1907

NEWCASTLE UPON TYNE

North Sea

North Tyne

rrawburgh   Chesters   A68

South Tyne   Corbridge

A69   HEXHAM   CORBRIDGE   A69   Tyne   A695   PRUDHOE   B6318   WALLSEND   SOUTH SHIELDS   GATESHEAD   A184

A1   A194   A19

CONTOUR LINE A section of the wall snakes over the top of an escarpment near Housesteads fort

ROMAN PLUMBING In the bath house at Chesters fort, two drains carried away waste water from the cold plunge room. The changing room, with alcoves for soldiers' uniforms and equipment, can still be seen

HALLOWEEN

• October 31

The autumn celebration of witches, ghosts and demons originated in the Celtic festival of Samhain, when fires were lit to mark the end of the year and ensure the renewal of life after the sleep, or death, of winter that began on the first day of November. This was the Celtic month of the dead, and mischief-making evil spirits were thought to appear after dark. Dressing in disguise was seen as a way of avoiding the spirits' attention.

As Christianity spread in Britain from the 4th century AD, the church absorbed many pagan elements, including the month of the dead. November 1 was dedicated to the saints in heaven as All Saint's Day, or All Hallows Day, and October 31 became All Hallows Eve – the origin of 'Halloween'.

Customs such as lighting bonfires and telling fortunes recall the festival's pagan roots. 'Trick or treat', where children wear ghoulish dress and knock on doors hoping to be given sweets, originates in a Celtic form of 'guizing', where children and adults would dress up and call on houses to collect money, food and drink, perhaps singing or dancing in return.

HALLMARKS

Any item made in Britain of gold, silver or platinum should have hallmarks – punch marks giving information on its age, standard and provenance. Hallmarks were introduced as an official guarantee of metal quality around 1300, when any silver item of the standard of the coinage or higher – 92.5 per cent silver or more – and gold items of 19.2-carat gold or more, were struck by an assayer from Goldsmiths' Hall, thus the term 'hallmark'. The uniform standard for silver allowed for silver objects to be made into coins, and coins into silver objects, as the economy demanded.

MARKS OF RESPONSIBILITY

From 1363 gold and silversmiths had to add an identifying mark to make them accountable for poor quality. Symbols were used at first, but initials appeared from the late 15th century.

The system was open to abuse: an assayer might be bribed to mark a substandard piece, which if melted down for coins would undermine the currency. So in 1478 a 'date letter' was added to identify the year and assay master.

The London assay office at Goldsmiths' Hall briefly came under royal control in 1544 and a fourth mark, the 'sterling lion', was added. In 1697 the silver standard was raised to 95.84 per cent – above the silver standard for coins – and makers were identified by the first two letters of their surname. On silver the Britannia figure replaced the sterling lion, although from 1720 the sterling mark and 92.5 per cent standard were used once again.

GOLD AND PLATINUM

In 1798 18-carat gold was introduced, followed over the next 100 years by further measures of purity to satisfy the demand for gold products.

The Hallmarking Act of 1973 added platinum to the system; its mark is an orb and cross inside a pentagon. The Act was amended in 1999, adding more gold, silver and platinum standards, and making it voluntary to mark the date letter and traditional standard symbols.

SOLID SILVER This 18th-century ornate table centrepiece has four hallmarks stamped by the London assay office

MASTER'S MARK The inverted initials 'NS' denote silversmith Nicholas Sprimost

DATE LETTER The 'm' shows that the piece was made between 1747 and 1748

STERLING LION A mark of authenticity guaranteeing at least 92.5 per cent silver

ASSAY STAMP The leopard's head is the official stamp of the London assay office

HAM HOUSE

• Surrey (p.498 B4)   • Built 1610   • NT

As the home of one of Charles II's most powerful ministers, John Maitland, duke of Lauderdale, Ham House had its heyday in the 1670s, when courtiers gossiped and intrigued in its drawing rooms. The red-brick Thames-side villa belonged to the duke's wife, Elizabeth, who as Countess of Dysart had used her influence with Oliver Cromwell to save Maitland's life during the Civil War.

Elizabeth, described in her day as 'profuse in her expense', lavished money on refurbishments to make Ham House a fit centre of court life. The entrance hall is surrounded by a picture gallery; beside it the Great Staircase, adorned with bronze-painted panels, links two floors of rooms that retain much of the original extravagant furniture and vibrant red and yellow textiles. A spiral staircase from the duchess's bedchamber leads to a Bathing Roome – the latest thing in the 1670s.

The gardens, restored in the 1990s to their original layout, have grassy squares, gravel paths and summer houses framed by clipped hornbeam hedges.

MAKE YOURSELF AT HOME The Queen's Bedchamber at Ham House was decorated for the visit of the queen of Braganza in 1680. It was used as a drawing room from the 1790s

PROLIFIC POSER When Emma Hamilton met the artist George Romney he became obsessed with her beauty and used her as a model for some 50 paintings

Emma HAMILTON

- **Mistress of Lord Nelson**
- **c.1765-1815**

From humble beginnings as the daughter of a Cheshire blacksmith, Emma, born Emily, or Amy, Lyon, became a high-society courtesan, the wife of a diplomat and lover of the naval hero Lord NELSON.

She moved to London as a girl and worked in service until her beauty was noticed by the quack-doctor James Graham, whose clients included the Prince of Wales. She posed as a Greek goddess in his 'Temple of Health' and was spotted by the 20-year-old Harry Fetherstonhaugh, owner of Uppark House in Sussex. Still only 15, she became his mistress, gaining a reputation for posing in diaphanous costumes and dancing on the dining-room table at Uppark House.

Emma was dismissed, six months pregnant, in 1781, only to be rescued by a young aristocrat, Charles Greville, who

had met her at Uppark. He in turn disposed of Emma to pay off his debts, trading her to his uncle William Hamilton, British envoy in Naples. In 1791 they married, settling in Naples, where Emma first met Horatio Nelson.

It was love at first sight. Hamilton appears to have tolerated the affair, and for a year all three lived together in England, where in 1801 Emma gave birth to Nelson's daughter, Horatia. Their ménage à trois was short-lived. Hamilton died in 1803, and Nelson at the Battle of Trafalgar two years later. Both men left Emma large sums of money, but she spent it all by 1814. To escape debtors' prison she fled to Calais, where she died.

HAMPSTEAD

- **N London (p.498 C3)**

Renowned and parodied as the epitome of literary London – and 'champagne Socialism' – the hill-top 'village' of Hampstead lies only about 4 miles north of the capital's heart and yet has the air of a country town. Its grand Georgian and Victorian houses and small workers' cottages were separated from the city by farmland until the late 19th century.

That rural link remains in the 320 ha (791 acre) Hampstead Heath, one of London's largest open spaces, where sheep grazed until 1952. On the Heath's edge is KENWOOD HOUSE, remodelled by Robert Adam in the 1760s and 70s.

Rural Hampstead first began to change in the early 18th century when visitors came to take its supposedly beneficial well waters. Long after the well became disused, Londoners continued to make day trips to Hampstead Heath for its fairgrounds and its pubs. They include the Spaniards Inn, a watering-hole of the highwayman Dick TURPIN, and Jack Straw's Castle, named after a leader of the Peasants' Revolt of 1381.

From the early 1800s writers and artists have been drawn to Hampstead. John Keats, whose house is now a museum, fell in love with his neighbour Fanny Brawne and wrote his ode 'To a Nightingale' there. The artist John Constable, buried at St John's Church, painted local views. The psychiatrist Sigmund Freud died at 20 Maresfield Gardens, now a Freud museum.

HAMPTON COURT PALACE

- **SW London (p.498 B5)**
- **Built 16th-18th century**

Cardinal Wolsey built Hampton Court to impress. The result was so glorious that he prudently handed it to Henry VIII rather than appear to outshine his monarch. Since then a succession of royal owners have made the palace a showcase of architecture and decoration.

Beyond Tudor red-brick courtyards topped by corkscrew chimneys are Henry VIII's Great Hall and Chapel Royal, beneath which the immense 16th-century royal kitchens are laid out as if a saint's day feast were being prepared. The King's Staircase, its walls and ceilings covered with allegorical paintings by Antonio Verrio, leads to state apartments designed for William and Mary by Christopher WREN and further embellished for Queen Anne.

Windows look out upon the radiating avenues of the Fountain Garden, and beyond it the Long Water created by Charles II. The ornamental Privy Garden was restored in the 1990s to the elegant symmetry of its 1702 design, and the maze, planted around 1690 and celebrated in Jerome K. Jerome's *Three Men in a Boat*, continues to baffle.

Hampton Court's real tennis court, built c.1530 by Henry VIII, a keen tennis player, is the oldest in the world still in use. The court has altered little since Charles II rebuilt it in the 17th century

PROLIFIC OUTPUT Handel wrote 32 oratorios. A page from his last, *Jephtha* (1752), includes a frustrated footnote about his failing eyesight

George Frideric HANDEL

• **Composer**   • **1685-1759**

When the Elector of Hanover became George I of England in 1714, his fellow-German and former employee George Frideric Handel had already settled in London, staging Italian-style operas. He composed 46, with huge success.

But audiences tired of opera in the 1730s and Handel turned to oratorios – choral works on Biblical subjects, including *Saul* (1739), *Solomon* (1749) and *Messiah*, composed in six weeks and first performed in Dublin in 1742.

Handel gave an admiring foreigner's perspective to an invigorated Britain and its new empire, which he expressed in the triumphal grandeur of pieces such as his Royal Fireworks music and *Zadok the Priest*, a coronation anthem for George II.

A fierce temper and huge appetite bestowed on Handel the nickname 'Great Bear'. His generosity was on an equal scale. He gave the *Messiah* manuscript to London's Foundling Hospital for children, a popular charity of the day, and performed many charity concerts.

House of HANOVER

• **British royal house**   • **1714-1901**

Queen Anne, the last STUART monarch, died childless in 1714, but a Protestant succession was assured when her distant cousin George, ruler of the German

FIERY SCOT Keir Hardie, a keen pacifist, speaks at a peace rally in Trafalgar Square in 1914, when he was MP for Merthyr Tydfil

kingdom of Hanover, came to the throne. The Hanoverians – George I to IV, William IV and Victoria – ruled Britain for the next 200 years.

The male Hanoverians were kings of both Hanover and Britain, but Victoria had to forfeit the crown of Hanover because under the Salic law that applied in Germany women could not inherit land. Nor could she pass the family name of Hanover to her son, Edward VII. On Victoria's death in 1901, he took his father Prince Albert's family name of Saxe-Coburg-Gotha.

HANSARD

• **Est. 1811**

Each member of parliament receives a free daily copy of Hansard, which details the debates from the previous day's business in the House of Commons and House of Lords.

The publication, described by the 20th-century statesman Lord Samuel as 'history's ear, already listening', is named after the official printers to the House of Commons, Luke Hansard (1752-1828) and his son Thomas Hansard (1776-1833). Thomas produced the first reliable reports of Westminster debates in 1806 for publication by William COBBETT in his journal *Parliamentary Debates*. Thomas bought out Cobbett in 1811 and he and his successors reported and published the debates throughout the 19th century.

Hansard reporters record debates verbatim, audiotyping at a minimum of 180 words a minute when an MP or peer speaks. They have licence only to tidy up ungrammatical expressions.

The Stationery Office has distributed Hansard since 1855.

Keir HARDIE

• **Politician**   • **1856-1915**

There was no middle ground with James Keir Hardie. His fierce, often unpopular convictions meant contemporaries either loved him or hated him. He was raised in poverty, started work aged seven and spent 12 years in the Lanarkshire coal mines. Scandalised by the miners' poor pay and conditions, he agitated on their behalf and was sacked.

Hardie became a journalist in 1878 and began to champion the socialist cause. He founded and edited the hard-hitting *Labour Leader*, which boosted his influence, and in 1892 was elected as an independent MP for West Ham South. A year later he helped to found the Independent Labour Party, which merged with other socialist groups in 1900 to form a new party, named the LABOUR PARTY in 1906.

The tweed-suited, cloth-capped and outspoken MP, whose socialist brief also embraced women's suffrage and temperance, shocked the gentlemanly sensibilities of parliament. But no one questioned his sincerity. He paved the way for the first Labour government, formed nine years after his death.

TOWERS OF POWER For seven years in the 1460s, a Lancastrian garrison held Harlech Castle against besieging Yorkists in the Wars of the Roses. The struggle is said to have inspired the stirring song 'Men of Harlech'

HARDWICK HALL

• Derbyshire (p.495 F1) • Built 1591-7 • NT

Hardwick Hall stands as a memorial to a remarkable woman, Elizabeth, countess of Shrewsbury, or 'Bess of Hardwick'. She outlived four rich husbands and at 70 poured her wealth into a hilltop mansion. Her estates yielded most of the raw materials – sandstone, timber, lead, iron. Bess even had her own glassworks: the huge windows of Hardwick earned it the contemporary epithet, 'Hardwick Hall, more glass than wall'.

Three floors of splendour reflect Bess's personal tastes and the skill of her architect, Robert Smythson. A staircase, with low risers for easy ascent by a septuagenarian, sweeps through the house. On the top floor is the High Great Chamber, with a plasterwork frieze illustrating the story of Diana, goddess of hunting. From the parapets of the house the initials 'ES', 'Elizabeth Shrewsbury', shout proudly in letters 2 m (6 ft) tall.

Thomas HARDY

• Writer • 1840-1928; OM 1910

Mighty but usually vain struggles against poverty, the restrictions of society and the cruelty of chance characterise Thomas Hardy's novels. Their country setting – called Wessex – was based on Dorset. Hardy spent most of his life there, and though his ashes were interred in Westminster Abbey his heart was buried in a Dorset churchyard.

Hardy's popularity was established by his novels, including *Far from the Madding Crowd* (1874), *The Return of the Native* (1878) and *The Mayor of Casterbridge* (1886). Though his language was always discreet, Hardy angered many people by his rejection of Victorian prudishness and sentimentality, dealing with subjects such as rape in *Tess of the D'Urbervilles* (1891) and infanticide in *Jude the Obscure* (1895).

Discouraged by criticism, Hardy gave up fiction and devoted himself to poetry, of which he published eight volumes, including the deeply moving love poems of *Satires of Circumstance* (1914), written after the death of his first wife, Emma. Hardy's simple poetic style reflects his distate for 'the jewelled line'.

HAREFIELD HOSPITAL

• NW London (p.498 A2)

Public attention focused on Harefield Hospital in 1980 when the first heart transplants in Britain were performed there by the surgeon Magdi Yacoub.

Harefield was established during the First World War on the site of the home of Thomas Wakley, founder of the medical journal, *The Lancet*. Initially it cared for wounded soldiers and then became a centre for the treatment of tuberculosis. A new hospital was built in 1937 featuring curved blocks and ample window space to allow maximum light, believed to be beneficial in TB cases.

Averaging around 100 heart and lung transplants a year, Harefield has the largest transplant programme in Britain. Patients of all ages – the youngest ten days old, the oldest 71 years – have received new hearts there.

HAREWOOD HOUSE

• W Yorkshire (p.496 C4) • Built 1759-71

A fortune made in the West Indies from sugar by Edwin Lascelles, 1st lord Harewood, was lavished on the building and decoration of Harewood House by some of the greatest talents of the day. John Carr of York designed the building in Palladian style. Robert ADAM created the interiors, including the 23m (76ft) long moulded gallery ceiling, with its paintings of gods and goddesses, a library covered with 17th-century Spanish leather, and a drawing room hung entirely with paintings by Venetian masters such as Titian and Tintoretto.

Thomas CHIPPENDALE made the furniture: among his triumphs are carved pelmets that imitate the cloth of the curtains. To the north of the house is the park, landscaped by 'Capability' BROWN.

HARLECH CASTLE

• Gwynedd (p.494 C2) • Built 1283-90 • Cadw

No castle could have seemed more impregnable than Edward I's stronghold at Harlech, on a promontory once lapped by the sea. Protected on the seaward side by a sheer cliff, it was defended on the landward side by a twin-towered gatehouse, a ditch and a strong wall.

In 1294 a garrison of only 37 men held off a Welsh rebellion, but the stronghold was destined to change hands several times, earning it the title 'castle of lost causes'. Owain GLYNDWR seized Harlech in 1404, turning it into the headquarters of his campaign against the English; it was retaken five years later.

During the Civil War the castle was the last Royalist stronghold in Wales until it fell in 1647. The building subsequently deteriorated, though its gatehouse and four enormous corner towers remain largely intact after 700 years.

HARLEY STREET

• **Central London (p.499 C2)**
A reputation for elite medical practice makes Harley Street – named after the ground landlord Edward Harley, 2nd earl of Oxford – a sought-after address by doctors. The street became a fashionable residential area in the 18th century. For no clear reason, by the late 19th century 36 physicians had chosen Harley Street premises, including Dr Alfred Garrod, the world expert on gout. By 1900, 157 brass plates adorned the street's medical premises – one belonging to Dr Elizabeth Blackwell, the first woman doctor to practise openly. Fifty years later, 1000 doctors worked there, and since then applications for premises from medical practitioners have been encouraged.

HAROLD II

• **King 1066   • c.1022-66**
The adroit opportunism of Harold Godwineson, earl of Wessex, led him to the heights of power, but ultimately caused the downfall of the Anglo-Saxon monarchy. Harold ingratiated himself with EDWARD THE CONFESSOR, and on the king's death in January, 1066, announced himself as the chosen successor, staging his own coronation the next day.

Within months, the rival claimants, Harald Hardrada of Norway and Duke William of Normandy – to whom, according to Norman sources, Harold had pledged allegiance – invaded England. Harold defeated Hardrada at Stamford Bridge in September, then dashed 250 miles to meet William near HASTINGS in October, where he died in battle. One scene from the BAYEUX TAPESTRY may show him being struck in the eye by an arrow.

Bomber HARRIS

• **Head of RAF Bomber Command 1942-6**
• **1892-1984; bt 1953**
Arthur Harris has been described as both a hero and a demon of the Second World War. He rejected precision attacks in favour of wide-ranging 'area bombing' against German cities. In 1943, 40 000 people in Hamburg were killed by bombs dropped from British planes. The same tactics killed hundreds of thousands in other German cities, at a cost of the lives of thousands of British aircrew.

Harris's defenders claim that he helped to undermine the German war effort. Critics maintain that his attacks on civilians went beyond moral bounds, and that the bombing affected German industrial production and morale no more than the Blitz affected the British.

HARRODS

• **Central London (p.499 B3)   • Founded c.1849**
Britain's most prestigious department store began life as a grocery shop. When the tea merchant Charles Henry Harrod took over the business in the mid 19th century, the weekly turnover was just £20. His energetic son, Charles Digby Harrod, expanded its floor space and range of goods in the 1860s, increasing the turnover to £1000 a week. He sold the shop as a successful business in 1889.

London's first escalator was installed at Harrods in 1898 – staff waited at the top with smelling salts to revive the nervous. Construction of the present store began on the same site in 1901. Pampered customers were offered a banking hall, nursery and lending library. The store still contains a bank – now

SIGN OF DISTINCTION
Today's Harrods logo was designed in 1988

joined by an estate agent, a personal tailoring service, the largest hair and beauty salon in Europe, a vast food hall and 19 bars and restaurants. At night its façade is adorned by 11 500 light bulbs. The store – regarded as a British institution – was sold to the Egyptian Al-Fayed brothers in 1985 for £615 million.

HARRY RAMSDEN'S

At one of the largest, most luxurious fish and chip restaurants in the world, a million customers each year enjoy supper in opulent surroundings. But the monogrammed carpets, stained-glass windows and chandeliers of Harry Ramsden's at White Cross in Guiseley, Yorkshire, are a surprising contrast to Harry's original premises.

Ramsden started his enterprise in White Cross in 1928 with a loan of £150, serving FISH AND CHIPS from a wooden hut. Business boomed, and in 1931 he opened the swankiest 'chippie' that Britain had ever seen.

In 1989 Ramsden's became the first fish and chip restaurant to be floated on the stock market. There are now 27 branches in Britain and five overseas, all in the style of the White Cross premises.

HARVEST FESTIVAL: *see opposite page*

William HARVEY

• **Physician   • 1578-1657**
The courage to question orthodoxy was the key to William Harvey's discovery of the circulation of the blood. Since the 2nd century, scientists had accepted the authority of the Greek physician Galen, who believed that blood ebbed and flowed in arteries and veins.

Harvey's open mind set him apart. Unlike Galen, Harvey dissected many bodies, and saw that the valves in the

HARVEST FESTIVAL

The British custom of leaving bread and vegetables around church altars at Harvest Festival – usually held between August and October – has its origin in earlier, less sedate celebrations. Before machines took over harvesting in the 19th century, the gathering of the corn was a labour-intensive job. Passers-by were expected to make a donation to the labourers. If sufficient, the gift would be met with the 'hollering of largesse' – a raucous shouting of thanks and blowing of horns. When the last load had been gathered, the farmer rewarded the harvesters with a feast – the Harvest Home – and the harvest lord, or chief labourer, was crowned with a wreath.

The drunkenness encouraged by the Harvest Home celebration made it a clear target for the Victorian temperance movement, and in the 1840s two clergymen from the West Country introduced a quieter alternative – a Harvest Festival church service, followed by a tea.

As farming methods changed, the old customs died out. Today the festival is largely centred on the church in services of thanksgiving for the fruits of the earth, later distributed to the needy. One of Britain's most spectacular harvest festivals is led by PEARLY KINGS AND QUEENS at St Martin-in-the-Fields in Trafalgar Square, London, on the first Sunday in October.

The last sheaf of the harvest held great significance. Often it was made into a corn dolly, dressed up and led in the harvest procession. It might also be ploughed back into the land in January to ensure good crops

A JOB WELL DONE The last load of the harvest was dressed with flowers and ribbons and accompanied by dancing and singing in readiness for the Harvest Home feast

heart and veins allowed blood flow in one direction only. His treatise explaining this, *De Motu Cordis et Sanguinis in Animalibus (On the Motion of the Heart and Blood in Animals)* (1628), is a masterpiece of clear reasoning.

Despite his position as royal physician to Charles I, Harvey found his work was dismissed. But his methods – using observation rather than assumption – created a new way forward for medicine, and he lived to see his theories accepted.

Battle of HASTINGS

• **East Sussex (p.495 H6)** • **October 14, 1066**
In September 1066 WILLIAM, duke of Normandy, made landfall in Sussex with an invasion force of 8000 men. His aim was to seize the English throne from HAROLD II, whom he regarded as a usurper. Within three weeks Harold, fresh from a hard-fought victory over Norwegian invaders, had raced south from Yorkshire. The English king drew up his army on a ridge near Hastings, barring William's route to London.

The armies were of similar size, but the English were footsore and without cavalry or sufficient archers. Despite this advantage, and reckless pursuits down the hill by ill-disciplined English militia, the Normans could not take the narrow ridge throughout a day's savage fighting. The light was failing when Harold was wounded, possibly by an arrow in the eye, and at last the Normans poured through the English defences. William was crowned in Westminster Abbey on Christmas Day.

HATFIELD HOUSE

• **Hertfordshire (p.495 H4)** • **Built 1607-11**
Robert Cecil, 1st earl of Salisbury and chief minister to James I, created Hatfield House – a masterpiece of red-brick walls and mullioned windows – to reflect his high status. Behind its façade, elaborate interiors reflect the continuing eminence in public life of the Cecil family, who have lived there ever since.

The oak ceiling and minstrels' gallery above the chequerboard floor of the Marble Hall are, like the Grand Staircase, fine examples of Jacobean wood carving. The stairs lead to a succession of state rooms containing paintings, furniture,

INSTRUMENTS OF DEATH English housecarls, armed with lethal two-handed axes, clash with Norman cavalry at the height of the Battle of Hastings, as shown in the Bayeux tapestry

tapestries and armour. In the garden, furnished with European plants by the botanist John TRADESCANT, the young Elizabeth heard of her accession to the throne on the death of Mary Tudor.

Lord HAW-HAW

• **William Joyce** • **Traitor** • **1906-46**

The tagline 'Germany calling...' crackled over Britain's airwaves throughout the Second World War, in an upper-class accent that earned the broadcaster the nickname Lord Haw-Haw. The words introduced a German propaganda slot, broadcasting rumours and lies about Britain, beamed from Radio Hamburg by an ardent Nazi, William Joyce.

Joyce was born in the USA but came to Britain as a child, and later obtained a British passport by falsifying his application. In 1933 he joined Oswald Mosley's British Union of Fascists, only to be expelled four years later for his extremism. He fled to Germany in 1939.

Joyce was captured by the British in 1945 and tried as a traitor. His defence, that he was an American citizen, was rendered invalid by his British passport, which expired nine months into the war. He was condemned and hanged.

Stephen HAWKING

• **Theoretical physicist** • **b.1942**

In 1988 a book called *A Brief History of Time* entered the best-seller lists and remained there for three years. Its popularity was remarkable because of its difficult subject matter – the physical laws which govern the Universe – explained in layman's terms by its author, Stephen Hawking.

After reading physics at Oxford, Hawking studied cosmology at Cambridge, where he suffered the first symptoms of the crippling motor neurone disease. Despite this, he secured a fellowship at Cambridge and began studying phenomena such as black holes – caused when stars collapse under their own gravitational force. He also investigated the origins of the Universe – his calculations support the Big Bang theory that the Universe began as a dense mass that

GEOMETRIC EXACTITUDE Nicholas Hawksmoor was appointed surveyor for 50 new London churches, commissioned by the Tory administration of 1711. He designed six of them himself, including the elegant Christ Church in Spitalfields

exploded, forming stars and galaxies. Hawking became Lucasian Professor of Mathematics at Cambridge in 1980. His disease has robbed him of speech and mobility, but he continues his work using a voice synthesiser and wheelchair.

Nicholas HAWKSMOOR

• **Architect** • **1661-1736**

Christopher WREN's young draughtsman Nicholas Hawksmoor was indispensable to the architect on projects such as Hampton Court and St Paul's Cathedral. Few major English Baroque buildings are without his influence.

Hawksmoor's skill also guided the untrained playwright-turned-architect John VANBRUGH through two highly ambitious projects – CASTLE HOWARD and BLENHEIM PALACE. His own work includes Castle Howard's Renaissance-inspired rotunda mausoleum, the twin west towers of Westminster Abbey, and the Northamptonshire mansion Easton Neston, but he is best known for four of his six London churches, commissioned in 1711 by the Fifty New Churches Act: Christ Church, Spitalfields; St Anne's, Limehouse; St George's, Bloomsbury; and St Mary Woolnoth, in the City.

The Tuscan columns and arches of Christ Church and the Egyptian interior of St Mary Woolnoth are examples of Hawksmoor's ability to draw on a wide range of architectural styles to create his unique version of ornamental Baroque.

HAY-ON-WYE

• **Powys (p.494 D3)** • **Pop. 1410**

Britain's town of books owes its fame to Richard Booth, who opened his first second-hand bookshop in the town's old fire station in 1961. His talent for publicity turned it into the biggest second-hand bookshop in the world, and revitalised the area's flagging economy.

Booth bought the town's ruined Norman castle and converted it into a home. A loathing of bureaucracy and central power led him to declare Hay's independence from

BROWSER'S PARADISE The 'honesty' bookshop in the grounds of the castle at Hay-on-Wye holds just part of the town's combined stock of more than a million books

Britain and to crown himself king of Hay in 1977. In this role, he champions rural self-sufficiency. The town has benefited from his enterprise and notoriety, and holds a festival of literature every May.

Hay now contains more than 30 bookshops, and has begun a trend – 20 'Book Towns' across the world copied its success, and more are joining Booth's International Book Town movement.

William HAZLITT

• Essayist • 1778-1830
Few authors as prolific as Kent-born William Hazlitt have left behind so much material of such a high standard. He made a large part of his living from critical essays – a feat that no other English writer had achieved.

Hazlitt's father, a Unitarian minister, intended his son for the ministry, but William's visits to his artist brother encouraged him to paint and read. He made some money as a portraitist, but it was his meeting with the poet Samuel Taylor Coleridge in 1796 – recorded in *My First Acquaintance with Poets* – that inspired him to pursue a literary career.

He wrote on miscellaneous subjects, from *Political Essays* on Britain's social ills – expounding strong liberal views – to literature. His *Characters of Shakespeare's Plays* (1817-18) is still widely read. His best-known essays include his profiles of well-known men such as William Wordsworth and Charles Lamb in *The Spirit of the Age* (1825).

Seamus HEANEY

• Poet • b.1939
Seamus Heaney was born in rural County Derry, the son of a Catholic farmer. Increasingly disturbed by the troubles in Northern Ireland, he moved to the south in 1972.

Heaney's poems are deeply rooted in his background and his times, and above all in the verdant, peaty landscape

The lough waters
Can petrify wood:
Old oars and posts
Over the years
Harden their grain,
Incarcerate ghosts...

'RELIC OF MEMORY' (1969)
SEAMUS HEANEY

of his native land, reflected in *Death of a Naturalist* (1966) and *Door into the Dark* (1969). Later works such as *Wintering Out* (1972) and *North* (1975) explore the tensions in Northern Ireland, with particular concern for the problems of maintaining artistic detachment from the situation. His work is also intensely personal – *Stations* (1975) looks back to his childhood and relationships with his parents and friends.

Heaney became Professor of Poetry at Oxford in 1989. He won the Nobel prize for literature in 1995. Later poetry collections include *Seeing Things* (1991) and *Spirit Level* (1996).

Edward HEATH

• Prime minister 1970-4 • b.1916; kt 1992
The negotiation of Britain's entry into the European Economic Community (now the European Union) in 1973 was the lasting achievement of Conservative prime minister Edward Heath. His other promises – to boost Britain's flagging economy and legislate to curb the power of the unions – proved unattainable in the face of growing economic crisis.

In an attempt to remedy increasing unemployment and inflation caused by a quadrupling of oil prices, Heath froze workers' wages in 1973 – a technique used by the previous Labour government. The unions responded with two miners' strikes, and

energy shortages forced Britain into a three-day working week to conserve coal supplies. The Conservatives failed in two general elections in 1974, and Heath lost the party leadership to Margaret Thatcher the following year.

HEATHROW

• W London (p.498 A4) • Opened 1946
More than 60 million passengers a year use Heathrow, the world's busiest airport, a far cry from its beginnings as a strip of grass on Hounslow Heath used for test flights and as a transport base in the Second World War.

In the postwar years, civil aviation took over, and Heathrow displaced Croydon as London's major airport in the late 1940s. Its check-in tent was replaced in the 1950s by the first of four terminals, the fourth opened in 1986. A planned fifth terminal would enable Heathrow to cope with another 30 million passengers a year. More than 90 airlines use Heathrow's two runways.

HEATHS AND MOORS: *see page 216*

HEBRIDES

• Western Isles (p.497 A/B1-4)
• Area 1119 sq miles • Pop. 28 880
Despite their windswept isolation and rocky landscape, evidence scattered across the Hebrides tells of a long history of human settlement. Monuments span vast tracts of time, from prehistoric standing stones at CALLANISH on Lewis to a medieval cathedral on IONA.

From the 8th century, Norse Vikings colonised and maintained the Hebrides as an independent kingdom until a 12th-century Islay chief, Somerled, and his descendants began to regain control. The Norsemen ceded sovereignty in 1266, and the Somerled clan ruled as Lords of the Isles until suppressed by the Scottish throne in 1493.

There are more than 250 Hebridean Islands – only 32 are inhabited today, and about half the total population live in Stornoway on Lewis. Islands near the mainland such as SKYE and MULL depend on tourism, but on the Outer Hebrides Gaelic culture is preserved – crofting, fishing and tweed weaving still form the basis of a self-sufficient way of life.

RICH WASTELANDS

Forest clearance has left Britain a legacy of open grassland. Purple heather spreads across the heaths of southern England and the moors of the northern uplands. The two habitats are very similar, but contrasting climates create distinctive differences in their wildlife

EXPANSES OF WILD grassland cover nearly 5000 ha (12 350 acres) of Britain, from the Scottish Highlands to the Hampshire Basin. The damp upland moors of the north and west British Isles support dwarf shrubs, grasses, sedge and heathers. Each area has its own character – the CHEVIOT HILLS and the North York Moors belong to the red grouse and the mountain sheep; on EXMOOR, red deer roam between bleak plateaus and valleys dense with oak woods.

The sandy, gravelly soils of southern England's lowland heaths are less remote, often lying close to major towns. Bracken, gorse and heather form rich habitats for insects, birds and reptiles. Heathland has been drastically depleted in the 20th century – most of Norfolk's Breckland has been lost to commercial forestry plantations, and housing development in Surrey has overtaken the 'sandy desert' once described by Daniel Defoe.

MERLIN FALCON
In search of prey on the moors

WET AND WINDSWEPT MOORS

Moors such as Rannoch Moor in Scotland (*above*) are characterised by peaty, boggy soil. They are exposed, and wildlife must endure harsh winters.

RED GROUSE This species of game bird is found only in the British Isles. It nests in moorland grass and feeds on heather and bilberry shoots

MOUNTAIN HARE The blue-grey summer coat of the mountain hare turns white in cold winters to provide camouflage in snowy settings

RED DEER Britain's largest native animals stand up to 1.2 m (4 ft) at the shoulder, weigh up to 127 kg (20 stone) and live wild in Scotland, Devon, Hampshire and Cumbria

DRY AND DUSTY HEATHS

Southern lowland heaths such as Winfrith Heath in Dorset (*left*) were created by prehistoric forest clearance. Heather and bracken have colonised what was once woodland floor – an ideal habitat for birds and reptiles.

MONTAGU'S HARRIER Only about ten pairs are known to nest each year, although migrant visitors are often seen in Norfolk during spring and summer

SAND LIZARD This lizard lays its eggs in the summer in the sand on the dry heaths of Dorset, Surrey and Norfolk

SMOOTH SNAKE The rarest of Britain's snakes is a timid creature. It emerges from underneath stones to prey on lizards and small rodents

DARTFORD WARBLER (*right*) Despite its name, this small bird is most common in eastern Dorset. It nests in dense gorse bushes for protection against predators

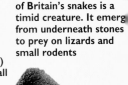

HEDGEROWS: *see page 218*

Lost Gardens of HELIGAN

• Cornwall (p.494 B7)

In February 1990, entrepreneurs looking for land to start a rare breeds farm stumbled across the remains of 63 ha (157 acres) of gardens and woodland, neglected for half a century. Soon, one of Britain's most ambitious restoration projects was under way.

The Tremayne family, who still own the Heligan Estate, created the gardens between 1780 and 1914. But the First World War brought ruin – 16 of the 22 estate workers were killed, and new tenants after the war could not afford to maintain the grounds. The restoration has re-created gardens that include the world's largest rhododendron, 25 m (82 ft) across, exotic fruit trees, tree ferns and palms. In 1998, Heligan welcomed more than 290 000 visitors, making it the most visited private garden in Britain.

HENLEY ROYAL REGATTA

• First week in July

The oldest rowing regatta in Europe, founded in 1839, Henley takes place on an idyllic, straight stretch of the Thames and attracts the finest international crews. As many as 550 entrants compete in several hundred races over five days.

To some, the occasion is less about sport than fashion and high society. The crowds of spectators watching events such as the Grand Challenge Cup (a race for crews of eight first held in 1839) or the equally coveted Diamond Sculls, dating from 1884, were once summed up by Frank Keating in *The Guardian*: 'Henley is full of haughty happiness, hats, haves and very few have-nots.'

HENRY I

• King 1100-35 • 1068-1135

The youngest son of William the Conqueror inherited his father's fiery ambition. Henry succeeded his brother, WILLIAM II, who died in a hunting accident – possibly arranged by Henry. Three days later, with his other brother Richard away on Crusade, Henry had himself crowned. He created Richard Duke of Normandy in compensation,

but in 1106 Henry took Normandy back and imprisoned Richard for life. Henry made tax collection more efficient to fund his subsequent defence of Normandy, and reformed the law courts. He also defended his right to appoint bishops against the archbishop of Canterbury, St Anselm.

After the death of his son, Henry made his barons swear allegiance to his daughter, Matilda. But he quarrelled with Matilda before he died, allowing STEPHEN, his nephew, to seize the throne.

HENRY II

• King 1154-89 • 1133-89

The first king of the PLANTAGENET royal house, son of the Empress Matilda and grandson of HENRY I, ended the chaos of the reign of STEPHEN through his administrative genius. He won the support of the powerful nobility and created a system of common law, uniformly applied throughout England, which survived for centuries.

His attempt to control the Church was less successful. When he appointed Thomas BECKET, previously his trusted chancellor, as archbishop of Canterbury, Becket surprised the king by passionately defending the rights of the Church. Henry's anger led his supporters to murder Becket, and the reprisals damaged the king's reputation.

Henry ruled much of France through his wife, Eleanor of Aquitaine, and his inheritance from his father, Geoffrey of Anjou. He expanded his influence in Britain and invaded Ireland in 1171. Two years later, he crushed power struggles within his own family over the division of his estates, but the respite was temporary. Throughout Henry's final years, he was vigorously opposed by his youngest son, the future RICHARD I.

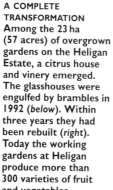

A COMPLETE TRANSFORMATION Among the 23 ha (57 acres) of overgrown gardens on the Heligan Estate, a citrus house and vinery emerged. The glasshouses were engulfed by brambles in 1992 (*below*). Within three years they had been rebuilt (*right*). Today the working gardens at Heligan produce more than 300 varieties of fruit and vegetables

NATURE ON THE EDGE

Forming natural corridors through the rural landscape, hedges protect and nurture a rich variety of flora and fauna. Modern farming methods and encroaching development have caused the loss of many centuries-old hedgerows, a trend that is at last being slowed down

CRISSCROSSING FARMLAND and snaking along country lanes, hedgerows have for centuries played a vital role in the British landscape. They divide fields, mark boundaries and shelter livestock, wildlife, flowers and saplings.

Some hedges are older than the most ancient cathedrals, dating back to Anglo-Saxon days, or even the Bronze Age, and some are like ghosts of the ancient wildwood, rich in wildlife. Others are self-seeded, springing up on the edges of fields or untended areas where saplings have established themselves.

In the last 600 years there have been several waves of deliberate hedge-planting. In the 14th and 16th centuries they were cultivated to enclose sheep for the flourishing wool trade, and during the Agricultural Revolution of 1750-1850, the greatest period of land enclosure of fields, 200 000 miles of hedges were planted.

Although predominantly hawthorn and blackthorn, but also beech, holly, field maple, dogwood and elm, hedges also attract other species. Seeds, blown by the wind or carried by birds, lodge and root in them. This leafy network of interconnecting corridors helps wildlife to move from woodland, marsh or meadow, safe from predators and farm machinery. In effect, they are linear nature reserves, home to many birds, including warblers and redwings, fieldfares, finches and song thrushes. Mammals such as hedgehogs, field mice, voles and shrews, as well as their hunter, the fox, find shelter under the protective branches, and the ditches below harbour frogs, toads and newts. The hedgerow is also a larder for wildlife, providing fruits such as blackberries, elderberries, hazelnuts and crab apples.

And yet, this natural habitat is now under threat: since the Second World War up to 40 per cent of Britain's hedgerows have been ripped out to make bigger fields, or clear ground for development. In an attempt to stop the destruction, parliament introduced the Hedgerow Regulations 1997, and today more hedges are being planted than destroyed. However, the use of mechanical trimmers to prune hedges down to a stubble does little for their conservation. Coppicing and laying them by hand every 20 to 30 years is the favoured form of maintenance.

BLUEBELLS Bursting into bloom in late spring, bluebells make the most of the sunlight before it is obscured by leaf cover

PRIMROSE Low-growing *Primula vulgaris* brings a splash of spring yellow to the hedgerows

RED CAMPION An estimated 600 species of flowering plants colonise the hedgerows

WILD AT HEART

Hedgerows, such as that pictured here near Chew Valley Lake in Somerset, form a remarkable, self-contained wildlife sanctuary harbouring as many as 20 species of mammals, 65 species of birds and 1500 species of insects.

COMMON FROG (below) *Ditches often run along the base of the hedgeline and provide a sheltered habitat for water-loving creatures, including the common frog, toads and newts*

BANK VOLE (above) *Small mammals such as voles and hedgehogs find refuge from predators in the tangled undergrowth of hedges*

GARDEN SPIDER (above) *Birds and mammals find hedgerows a rich hunting ground for numerous varieties of insects*

WARBLER (WHITETHROAT) *With berries, insects and nesting materials in ample supply, Britain's hedgerows support a large bird population. The whitethroat (left) is a summer visitor*

...YING A HEDGE

...e best way to maintain hedges is to lay ...em by hand every 20 to 30 years. Using ...billhook, the hedgelayer cuts part way ...rough the main stems (pleachers), bending ...em at an angle of 30-45 degrees and ...lding them in position with stakes and ...ngths of pliable wood (binders), along the ...o and sides. The stakes and binders give ...e hedge rigidity while it grows back thicker ...an before. Bodies such as the British Trust ...r Conservation Volunteers are helping to ...vive hedgelaying skills.

HENRY III

• King 1216-72 • 1207-72

Eldest son of King JOHN, Henry succeeded to the throne aged nine. The government fell to a succession of noble courtiers until Henry took control in 1236. One of his aims was to recover the territories on the Continent lost by his father. He failed, but the cost of the expeditions, together with his promotion of foreign favourites and his attempts to ignore constraints that MAGNA CARTA put on his power, caused a series of crises.

The most serious started in 1258, when a strong baronial movement tried to impose a governing council to limit royal authority. Henry was forced to agree to the Provisions of Oxford, but went back on his oath, provoking the civil war between the king's faction and nobles led by Simon de Montfort known as the second BARONS' WAR.

In 1264 de Montfort defeated and captured the king at the Battle of Lewes. A year later, Henry's son Edward, later EDWARD I, defeated and killed de Montfort at the Battle of Evesham.

Henry's last years were spent as titular ruler. Pious, well-meaning but ineffectual, he was content to involve himself in the rebuilding of Westminster Abbey, which was completed in 1269.

HENRY IV

• King 1399-1413 • 1366-1413

Henry IV took the surname Bolingbroke from the Lincolnshire castle where he was born. He was the eldest son of JOHN OF GAUNT, duke of Lancaster, who ruled England as lord protector while his nephew, RICHARD II, was a child.

In 1398 Richard exiled Henry, and when John of Gaunt died in 1399 he seized the Lancastrian possessions. Richard's autocratic rule angered the nobles, and when Henry invaded in 1399 he had sufficient support to force the king to retract. Parliament declared Henry king, having deposed Richard, who died four months later.

Henry's 14 year reign was plagued with threats of invasion by the French and rebellions in Scotland and Wales.

Parliament exacted a heavy price for its financial support, and the Prince of Wales, later HENRY V, fostered discontent against his father. By 1409 there was relative peace, but Henry had suffered a series of strokes. He died in 1413.

HENRY V

• King 1413-22 • 1387-1422

Shakespeare shows Henry V inspiring his troops through appeals to their patriotism. He was perhaps the first king to promote a sense of English nationhood, and certainly the first to use the English language in his letters. His war with France was highly successful.

BITTER BATTLE Arrows from the feared English longbows 'fell so heavily that no one durst uncover or look up', wrote a French knight about the Battle of Agincourt in 1415

Henry's campaign in 1415 culminated in the stunning victory at AGINCOURT, where his 6000 foot soldiers destroyed a 20 000-strong army including the flower of the French cavalry. By 1420 the French king Charles VI was forced to recognise Henry as his heir and allow him to marry his daughter Catherine. But in 1422, only weeks before the French king died, Henry himself lay dead at Vincennes, a victim of dysentery.

His body was brought back to Westminster Abbey with great ceremony. Despite complaints about the taxation needed to pay for his wars and unrest caused by the early Puritan sect called the Lollards, Henry's dynamic reign was long recalled as a golden age – especially during the disastrous rule of HENRY VI, the one-year-old son he left behind.

HENRY VI

- King 1422-61, 1470-71 • 1421-71

Henry was only eight months old when he inherited the crown on the death of his father, HENRY V. He was raised by the Lancastrian Beaufort family, to the fury of the rival house of York, and his uncles governed as regents until 1437.

Timid, highly strung and pious, Henry hated war, thought hunting cruel and had little interest in politics. To evade the responsibility of national debt, corruption and the HUNDRED YEARS' WAR, Henry busied himself founding religious and educational establishments, including Eton and King's College, Cambridge.

In 1444 he married Margaret of Anjou, a formidable queen who stepped up the feud that became the WARS OF THE ROSES. Henry was defeated in 1461 and the Yorkist EDWARD IV proclaimed king. Margaret continued to fight and in 1470 Henry was briefly reinstated, but the Yorkists successfully fought back and Henry was murdered the following year.

HENRY VII

- King 1485-1509 • 1457-1509

Integrity and business sense made Henry VII one of England's strongest kings. He traced his claim to the throne through his mother Margaret Beaufort, a descendant of John of Gaunt, the fourth son of Edward III, and became the first TUDOR monarch after defeating RICHARD III at BOSWORTH in 1485. He soon set to work healing a country scarred by the WARS OF THE ROSES, marrying Elizabeth, daughter of the Yorkist Edward IV, to unite the warring dynasties.

Henry secured internal order and external peace, built up trade and regulated the judicial system. From such stability, England looked to new horizons, embarking on an age of exploration with voyages such as John CABOT's expedition to north America in 1497.

HENRY VIII

- King 1509-47 • 1491-1547

In his youth, Henry VIII was tall and handsome, an accomplished musician, sportsman and scholar: a true Renaissance prince. He married his brother's widow, Catherine of Aragon, to protect an important alliance, but it was an inauspicious start to married life for an idealistic youth. Only one of their six children, the future MARY I, survived, which Henry saw as divine displeasure at an unnatural union.

DEFENDER OF A NEW FAITH

Henry had been a pious man, writing a treatise in 1521 against the Protestant reformer Martin Luther, which so impressed the pope that he conferred upon him the title 'Defender of the Faith'. But in 1533 he defied Rome by divorcing Catherine without papal approval and marrying Anne BOLEYN, thus precipitating permanent political and religious change in Britain. In 1534, with the Act of Supremacy, Henry proclaimed himself head of a new CHURCH OF ENGLAND and two years later began to close the monasteries and sieze their wealth.

FLATTERING FACE The king probably looked much older than his image when Henry VIII was painted by Hans Holbein around 1537

REFINED STYLE Simple elegance marks George Hepplewhite's designs. His use of the Prince of Wales's feathers as a decorative feature was copied by Regency chair makers

A MAJESTIC MONARCH

Henry was an ostentatious king who revelled in expensive pageantry, and was the first British monarch to be addressed as 'majesty'. He reformed state powers to create a more centralised national government and built a powerful navy, including the great warship the MARY ROSE, whose sinking he witnessed. But he was unsuccessful in war and left a weakened economy and many debts when he died.

George HEPPLEWHITE

- Furniture maker • d.1786

Little is known of the man himself, but the delicate chairs George Hepplewhite designed characterise his work today.

Hepplewhite was influenced by the architect Robert ADAM in his use of light-coloured woods, neoclassical motifs and painted decoration or inlays. In turn, he inspired many later craftsmen with his book of designs, the Cabinet Maker and Upholsterer's Guide, published by his widow in 1788. The Guide later became the standard Regency style manual for a wide range of simple domestic furniture.

A Hepplewhite chair is distinguished by the shape of its back: usually an oval, hoop, heart or shield. Within the back he carved designs such as leaves, lyres, swags, urns and wheatsheafs.

HENRY VIII'S WIVES, DATES AND FATES		
Catherine of Aragon	m.1502	divorced May 1533
Anne Boleyn	m. Jan 1533	beheaded May 1536
Jane Seymour	m. May 1536	d.1537 (in childbirth)
Anne of Cleves	m. Jan 1540	divorced July 1540
Catherine Howard	m. July 1540	beheaded 1542
Catherine Parr	m.1543	d.1548 (natural causes)

PICTURES OF RANK

The art of heraldry began during the medieval Crusades, when knights – anonymous behind their helmets – adopted pictorial emblems to distinguish them in battle. The system became known as heraldry after the heralds, or messengers, whose duty it was to identify the knights

I N AN AGE when not everyone could write, a seal bearing a noble's crest carried all the authority of his signature. Having a coat of arms became so fashionable in 13th-century England that lions, eagles and roses were no longer sufficient to meet the demand for unique arms. A bizarre menagerie of mythical creatures came into use and by the 14th century a complex system of rules had evolved, governing the colours, divisions and patterns on each shield.

BADGE OF ARISTOCRACY

Coats of arms were originally assumed by rulers and then by nobles and knights, who wore them in battle and at tournaments, and became regarded as symbols of gentility. Colleges of heralds, or arms, adjudicated between rivals for the same emblem, drew up coats of arms and dispensed mottoes.

When in 1417 Henry V decreed that coats of arms could be used by those entitled to them by legitimate ancestry through a male line, or by a royal grant, arms began to be issued to eminent people who were not from the old nobility – lawyers, clerics, even merchants – and corporate bodies such as guilds and towns. In 1484 England's heralds were incorporated by Richard III

as the College of Arms, and authority to grant arms passed to the senior heralds, or kings of arms.

NATIONAL PRIDE

The college still does brisk business from its London premises in Queen Victoria Street – a site it has occupied since 1555; on average, it grants some 200 coats of arms every year. Requests are examined by officers with such curious titles as Rouge Dragon (a reference to the royal Tudor badge of a red dragon) and Portcullis (family symbol of Margaret Beaufort, mother of Henry VII).

Modern-day applicants, particularly life peers honoured for their work in a specialist field, continue to introduce new heraldic symbols in their coats of arms. 'Supporters' (see illustration of Bristol's city arms below) are now almost as likely to be scientists as they were once lions and dragons.

BASE ELEMENTS OF THE SHIELD

Strictly speaking, a coat of arms is contained within a shield, but through common usage the term has come to include the full armorial bearings, including elements outside the shield – known as an 'achievement of arms'.

A few simple patterns and symbols, such as those below, still form the basis of most coats of arms. Colours are limited and have special heraldic names. Dexter (the right) and sinister (the left) refer to the view of the person carrying the shield.

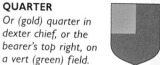

CHIEF
Gules (red) bar across the top of the shield. Anything 'in chief' is in the shield's top portion

QUARTER
Or (gold) quarter in dexter chief, or the bearer's top right, on a vert (green) field.

CHEVRON
Purpure (purple) chevron on argent (silver) field. Silver is represented as white

BEND
Or diagonal band on azure (blue) field runs from dexter chief to sinister base

FESS
Broad horizontal band across the centre of the shield. The fess point is at the centre

DANCE
Sable (black) zigzag across the centre of the shield. Also known as a fess dancetty

LION RAMPANT
The lion was at first the main heraldic animal. This one is 'rampant', rearing up

STAG'S HEAD
This stag's head is 'cabossed', or shown from the front without the rest of the body

A PROUD CITY

Bristol's coat of arms dates from the 13th century, when the shield was first used as a seal. Its other pictorial elements were added in 1569, its motto in the 18th century.

HELMET Supports a crest. Designs vary: this is a tournament helmet, granted to corporations

SUPPORTERS Accorded to peers, knights and those with a royal grant. Any living beings can be used; unicorns pay homage to the virtuous

MOTTO Although often seen on coats of arms, mottoes are seldom officially granted, and several coats of arms might share the same one

CREST A wreath on the helmet supports the crest. Here, the arms rising out of the clouds signify that all good things come from above; the scales represent good judgment and the serpent, wisdom

MANTLING A helmet is always adorned by mantling

SHIELD A merchant ship and castle reflect Bristol's history as a fortified port. The figures used on a shield are called 'charges'; the background (Bristol's is gules, or red) is the 'field'

COMPARTMENT The base beneath the supporters

VIRTUTE · ET · INDUSTRIA

Barbara HEPWORTH

• Sculptor • 1903-75; CBE 1958; DBE 1965

In 1939 Barbara Hepworth and her husband, the painter Ben NICHOLSON, joined the colony of artists living in ST IVES, in Cornwall. Hepworth's distinctive sculptural style was to make her one of the key figures in the development of abstract art in Britain.

Her early works were naturalistic, but in 1931 she began – like Henry MOORE, who was her contemporary – to lend an extra dimension to her sculptures by piercing holes in them. Working mainly in wood, Hepworth progressed to purely abstract, hollowed-out forms, often strung with wires and resembling musical instruments. Every shape, she believed, had an inside and an outside; her sculptures aimed to explore both.

During the 1950s and 60s Hepworth began to work with metal in projects such as the steel structure *Apollo*, made for a 1951 stage production of Sophocles' *Electra*, and *Single Form*, a memorial, cast in bronze, to Dag Hammarskjöld, secretary general of the United Nations from 1953 to 1961. She died in a fire at her St Ives studio, which is now a museum dedicated to her work and includes some unfinished pieces in stone.

MAKING WAVES
The wood carving *Pelagos* ('the sea', 1946) was inspired by sculptor Barbara Hepworth's view of St Ives Bay, in Cornwall, from her home

HERALDRY: *see page 221*

HEREFORD

• Herefordshire (p.494 E3) • Pop. 54 330

Cider and cattle are the two things most associated with the county town of Herefordshire, but Hereford also has two rare medieval relics, both held in the Norman cathedral. One, the *Mappa Mundi*, is a map of the world painted on vellum in about 1275, with Jerusalem at its centre and its margins filled with fantastic creatures imagined by the artist. The other relic, the Chained Library, contains some 1500 early books and manuscripts – some dating from the 9th century – which were chained to the shelves to deter thieves.

Hereford was founded by Saxons in the 7th century to defend England against the Welsh and stands on the River Wye, in the WELSH MARCHES. High Town, the city's main street, retains a half-timbered building, the Old House, dated 1621. There is a museum of cider on Grimmer Road, near the cathedral.

HEREWARD THE WAKE

• 11th-century rebel

According to legend, the Lincolnshire landowner Hereward the Wake ('the watchful') travelled around the country performing unspecified noble deeds. He entered history when he helped to stir up an anti-Norman uprising in 1070.

Around The Wash, Danes were rousing an insurrection against England's new rulers. The locals, already angered by the appointment of a Norman abbot in Peterborough, needed little urging to revolt. Under Hereward's command, a Danish and Anglo-Saxon force sacked Peterborough monastery.

When Norman soldiers retaliated, Hereward retreated to the Isle of ELY. A year later, he disappeared across the marshes. Subsequent legend cast him as an early Robin Hood and a symbol of English resistance to the Norman Conquest. He might equally have been no more than a troublemaker with a fondness for church silver.

STAR MAN By the age of 75, the astronomer John Herschel had discovered double stars, star clusters and nebulae in their thousands

HERSCHEL FAMILY

• Astronomers
• William 1738-1822; kt 1816
• Caroline 1750-1848
• John 1792-1871

In 1781 the amateur stargazer William Herschel discovered Uranus, the first planet not known to the ancients, from his garden in Bath. He wanted to name it Georgium Sidus ('George's star') after George III, but the tradition of naming planets after Greek gods prevailed, and it was named for the father of Saturn. Nevertheless, the king was flattered by Herschel's wish and made him court astronomer in 1782.

Herschel, a musician by trade, moved to Britain from Germany in 1757 and in 1772 was joined by his sister, Caroline, who shared his passion for astronomy. Unable to obtain a good telescope, they

made their own, grinding the lenses themselves to make the best instruments of the day. With Caroline as his assistant, Herschel made an extensive catalogue of the stars, in the course of which he discovered more than 5000 new nebulae.

His son John was also a distinguished astronomer. He devised a system for measuring the brightness of stars and was the first astronomer to map the stars of the Southern Hemisphere as his father had in the north.

HEVER CASTLE

• **Kent (p.495 H5)**   • **Built 1270, restored 1903**
This story-book castle is surrounded by a wide moat, reached by a drawbridge and sealed with a portcullis. It was here that Henry VIII courted his second wife, Anne Boleyn. Her father, Thomas Boleyn, had enlarged the original 13th-century castle and built a Tudor house within the protective medieval walls.

Henry seized Hever after Thomas died and later gave it to his fourth wife, Anne of Cleves, on their divorce. From the late 16th century the castle fell into decay but was restored in 1903 by the American millionaire William Waldorf Astor. He built a village of Tudor-style cottages, joined to the castle by a covered bridge across the moat.

Astor landscaped the grounds, and diverted the River Eden through a 14 ha (35 acre) lake dug from the surrounding marshland and meadows. The castle and grounds opened to visitors in 1963.

HIDCOTE MANOR GARDEN

• **Gloucestershire (p.495 F3)**
• **Created 1907-47**   • **NT**
Packed borders and rambling hedgerows flourish alongside precise topiary and still ponds at Hidcote Manor Garden. The garden was the creation of Lawrence Johnston, an American who in 1907 bought a 4 ha (10 acre) site high on the Cotswold escarpment. He spent the next 40 years turning the wilderness into one of the most influential gardens of the 20th century, inspiring gardeners such as Vita SACKVILLE-WEST.

Clipped hedges of beech, box and yew screen delicate plants and divide the garden into themed plots, like open-air rooms, such as a circle of lilacs and hellebores, and thick drifts of lilies and azaleas.

HIGHGATE

• **N London (p.498 C2)**
Although long absorbed by the capital's urban spread, until the late 1700s Highgate was a hilltop village surrounded by farm land. It used to lie on the main road out of London, and a tollgate at the road's highest point gave the village its

SHRINES OF THE TIMES
The monolithic tomb of Karl Marx in Highgate cemetery draws visitors from around the world. Victoriana marks the older section of the cemetery (*left*)

name. A roadside stone on Highgate Hill marks the spot where, according to folklore, Dick Whittington was stopped by the sound of the Bow bells and returned to become London's lord mayor. Highgate was by-passed in the 19th century, and the sloping High Street with its elegant Georgian buildings retains a village atmosphere.

Highgate has attracted many artistic inhabitants, from the Romantic poet Samuel Taylor Coleridge to the pop singer George Michael. Among the many famous people buried in Highgate cemetery are the scientist Michael Faraday and the writer George Eliot.

HIGHLAND CLEARANCES

In the 19th century, large-scale eviction of Scottish crofters and their families, known as the Highland Clearances, left much of the HIGHLANDS depopulated.

The crofters, tenant smallholders who raised cattle, oats and root crops, had almost no rights over their land. When it became apparent that sheep farming or commercial deer hunting could yield

CIRCLE OF CALM The still waters of the ornamental pool at Hidcote Manor Garden mirror the hedges and trees that shelter it. Topiary birds flank the path to the fuchsia garden beyond

HIGHLAND GATHERINGS

Bagpipes, Highland dancing, trials of strength and hill races, combined with tartan and a dash of Gaelic, are the essential ingredients of the gatherings or 'games' that take place wherever Scots are found, from Caithness to Tasmania.

The origins of the games are believed to lie in a contest held at Braemar by the 11th-century king of Scotland, Malcolm III. He called clansmen to a series of trials to choose warriors and postal runners for the royal service. But it was only in the 19th century that the tradition took firm root and spread, popularised by Queen Victoria.

Gatherings are now held throughout Scotland every summer and attract contestants from around the world. Many villages hold less formal games where locals compete in a spirit of amateur enthusiasm. The main features of gatherings include dancing, tossing the caber, throwing the hammer, and wrestling and piping events.

HIGHLAND DANCING
The precise formality of many dances stems from rough origins. The Sword Dance (*Gille Callum*) was invented by Malcolm III when he pranced in triumph over his weapon crossed with that of a vanquished foe. The Highland Fling is based on the antics of a rutting stag, and the Reel of Tulloch is said to have been first danced by a group of men trying to keep warm outside the kirk while waiting for their minister.

No champion has ever rivalled Donald Dinnie. He could toss a caber, throw the hammer, wrestle, jump, dance and run the hill race, and come first in each. When he retired, aged 73, in 1910, he had won 11 000 contests

TOSSING THE CABER Said to have derived from foresters launching logs from riverbanks, this demanding trial of strength and skill is the most spectacular of the heavy events. The caber (*cabar* in Gaelic), is usually 5.8 m (19 ft) long and weighs 68 kg (150 lb). It must be lifted and thrown to turn a perfect arc, landing in the straightest possible line

MAJOR GATHERINGS
• **Inveraray** – held at the castle of Clan Campbell chieftains; mid July
• **Fort William** – includes an arduous hill race up Ben Nevis; late July
• **Lonach, Aberdeenshire** – features a 'March of the Clansmen' in warrior regalia; August
• **Cowal, Dunoon** – noted for piping and dancing; late August
• **Braemar, near Balmoral** – last games of the season; early September

much greater returns than their rents, they were at the mercy of greedy landlords, who included both Englishmen and their own clan chieftains.

Thousands of crofters were evicted, leaving their homes to crumble, and the land was turned over to sheep and deer that destroyed most of the ancient Caledonian pine forest. In the 1880s many of the remaining crofters turned to violence in the so-called Crofters' War, until they achieved security of tenure by an Act of parliament in 1886.

HIGHLANDS

• N Scotland (p.497 C3)
• Area approx. 60 000 sq miles

The Scottish Highlands embrace snow-topped peaks and subtropical gardens; mighty castles and modest crofts. Making up the northern half of Scotland, above a line drawn from the Firth of Clyde to the town of Stonehaven, the region is thinly populated but inhabited by a wide variety of wildlife, including golden eagles, red deer, wildcats and salmon. Its granite mountains rise to Britain's highest peak, BEN NEVIS, at 1343 m (4406 ft).

The inhospitable landscape made the Highlands difficult to penetrate by Roman and Norman invaders. Highland tradition survives in gatherings (*see left*) and the annual Mod festival of Gaelic music, dance and storytelling. The area around Aviemore, in the Cairngorms range, has been developed for winter sports.

SNOWY SUMMITS On some Highland peaks, such as the 1010 m (3314 ft) Saddle above Glen Shiel (*centre*), there is snow all year round

STAND AND DELIVER

During the 17th and 18th centuries, theft of anything worth more than a shilling was a capital offence. Nevertheless, masked highwaymen on horseback stalked the roadside shadows, robbing travellers and disappearing into the night, beyond the reach of the law

The wind was a torrent of
darkness among the gusty trees,
The moon was a ghostly galleon
tossed upon cloudy seas,
The road was a ribbon of
moonlight over the purple moor,
And the highwayman came riding -
riding - riding -
The highwayman came riding, up
to the old inn door.

THE HIGHWAYMAN (1913), *Alfred Noyes*

ALFRED NOYES had a romantic, modern view of highwaymen, but even in their own time outlaws were a popular subject of literature, such as Jonathan Swift's 18th-century poem 'Tom Clinch', based on the real-life robber Thomas Cox.

Highwaymen concentrated on the wealthy, who were increasingly travelling on the regular stagecoaches that began to link Britain's major towns in the 17th century. Gallows strung with highwaymen lined the waysides, but still there were thieves everywhere. One of the most notorious was Dick TURPIN, from Essex, a cattle rustler turned highwayman.

ARMED ROBBERY

The first of the legendary highwaymen were Royalist officers, who 'took to the road' when they were outlawed during the Commonwealth in the 1650s and were familiar with the relatively lightweight pistols that had recently been introduced. Knives and swords offered little protection against their guns and soon every stagecoach had a guard, armed with a blunderbuss, designed for use at close range.

'One is forced to travel,' wrote Horace Walpole in 1751, 'even at noon, as if one were going into battle.' By 1780 he could barely persuade friends to dine with him at home in Twickenham, so dangerous was the journey from London.

NOWHERE TO HIDE

Roads often crossed large, deserted areas of open heath or common land where travellers were hopelessly vulnerable to attack. The diarist John Evelyn tells how

TOOLS OF THE TRADE
Most highwaymen carried small pistols; coach drivers defended themselves with the powerful blunderbuss (*top*)

HOLD UP A carved tree stump off north London's Finchley High Road marks the spot where, in the early 18th century, Dick Turpin accosted travellers on Finchley Common

he was robbed by highwaymen near Bromley one hot day in June, 1652. 'Two cut-throats started out, and striking with long staves at the horse, and taking hold of the reins, threw me down, took my sword, and hauled me into a deep thicket, some quarter of a mile from the highway, where they might securely rob me, as they soon did.'

Highwaymen gangs were as organised as any gangs today. Jonathan Wild, a London magistrate, secretly ran a whole network of highwaymen, thieves and harlots. His exposure, trial and execution in 1725 inspired John Gay to write *The Beggar's Opera* three years later.

The Enclosure Acts of the late 18th and early 19th centuries, when more than 6 million acres of common land and heath were hedged into enclosed fields, did much to impede the activities of highwaymen. By the 1850s, helped by the establishment of an effective police force, highway robbery was a thing of the past.

WICKED LADY
A woodcut and pub sign show Kathleen Ferrers, a 17th-century aristocrat who robbed travellers in Nomansland, Hertfordshire, just for the thrill of it

SHOCK OF THE NEW
Damien Hirst's 1991 exhibition of his first preserved animal, a tiger shark, caused a sensation with its frighteningly lifelike form, apparently suspended in death

Graham and Damon HILL

- Motor racing drivers
- Graham 1929-75 • Damon b.1960

Before dawn on October 13, 1996, 7 million Britons switched on their television sets to watch Damon Hill win the Japanese Grand Prix, a victory that made the Hills the first family to celebrate two generations of world motor racing champions.

Graham Hill became Grand Prix champion in 1962 and 1968. Slow to emulate his father's success, Damon did not win his first grand prix until nearly 33 years of age, and then won the next two races in the 1993 calendar. The next season at Silverstone he achieved what had always eluded his father – victory in the BRITISH GRAND PRIX.

Nicholas HILLIARD

- Painter • 1547-1619

The most decorative of all miniature portraitists trained as a jeweller before he found his true vocation. In 1570 he was appointed by the court, and painted portraits of Elizabeth I and many of her

LITTLE GEM Nicholas Hilliard's miniature *Youth Leaning against a Tree among Roses* (1588) is seen here at half its real size

courtiers, including Walter Raleigh, Francis Drake and Philip Sidney. Hilliard conveyed the individuality of his sitters with remarkable vividness, never painting shadows, which he believed detracted from the purity of line and colour. The intense but romantic air of his portraits resembled the character of Elizabethan madrigals and poems, and the wide appeal of his subjects earned Hilliard commissions beyond the court circle.

In his later years Hilliard's fame was eclipsed by that of his former pupil Isaac Oliver, and he died in debt. More than 200 of his exquisite miniatures have survived, and an extensive collection is exhibited in the Victoria and Albert Museum in London.

Damien HIRST

- Artist • b.1965

Winning the 1995 Turner prize confirmed Damien Hirst as the most successful and controversial young artist in Britain. At the associated exhibition he displayed *Mother and Child Divided* – a cow and a calf bisected and preserved in formaldehyde inside a glass tank – which enraged animal lovers and traditional art lovers alike. Hirst intends his 'conceptual'

art to convey ideas about life and death using unconventional media. Other works include cabinet installations, with ordered displays on shelves, and 'spin-painting', where centrifugal force spatters paint across canvas on a spinning table.

HISTORIES OF BRITAIN

For more than 1200 years histories such as these have shaped the British nation's sense of identity.

731 BEDE: *History of the English Church and People* – reliable account of Anglo-Saxon settlement and early Christianity

9TH-12TH CENTURIES *Anglo-Saxon Chronicle* – main source on events up to the Norman Conquest

12TH CENTURY Geoffrey of Monmouth: *History of the Kings of Britain* – legends rather than facts about national origins

1577 Ralph Holinshed: *Chronicles* – source for Shakespeare's history plays

1849-55 Thomas Macaulay: *History of England* – best-selling defence of constitutional monarchy of 1688-1700

1944 G.M. Trevelyan: *English Social History* – popular work, written in a readable, nostalgic style

1954 G.R. Elton: *England Under the Tudors* – authoritative on the Tudors

1956-8 Winston Churchill: *A History of English-speaking Peoples* – four-volume history of the British Empire

1965 A.J.P. Taylor: *English History 1914-45* – definitive world wars account

Alfred HITCHCOCK

- **Film director and producer**
- **1899-1980; kt 1980**

'The Master of Suspense', known for his portly profile and his cameo screen appearances, kept audiences on the edge of their seats in 53 feature-length films in as many years. He was an outstanding exponent of the director's craft, yet never won an Oscar for Best Director.

Hitchcock made his first British talkie, *Blackmail*, in 1929, and commercial success followed with *The Thirty-Nine Steps* (1935) and *The Lady Vanishes* (1938). He developed a distinctive thriller style that worked well in Hollywood, where between 1954 and 1964 he made his memorable spine-chillers such as *Dial M for Murder*, *Psycho* and *The Birds*.

When Hitchcock returned to Britain to make *Frenzy* in 1972, he was greeted with acclaim as a London boy made good. He made his final film, *Family Plot*, in 1976 – the only director from the silent era still working.

Thomas HOBBES

- **Philosopher • 1588-1679**

Controversy and hostility dogged Thomas Hobbes for most of his life, but hindsight shows him to be the first moral and political philosopher in England. His view that only an absolute ruler could ensure the security of the state made him an enemy of anti-Royalists during the Civil War, while his denial of the divine right of kings alienated Royalists – though not Charles II, whom he tutored in exile. Hobbes' stay in Europe enabled him to dispute with great minds of the day, such as Descartes and Galileo.

Hobbes returned in 1652, the year after the publication of his greatest work, *Leviathan*, to find he was under attack from the Church for asserting that morality had no religious basis. Despite official disfavour, Hobbes had his works published abroad, where he was lionised as the greatest living philosopher.

HOCKEY

Besides being the first team sport for women, hockey was the forerunner of all stick-and-ball games. Drawings on Nile Valley tombs suggest a 4000-year history, though the modern game was not played in Britain until Victorian times.

Organised hockey was first played by men at Blackheath, London, in the mid 19th century and by women when the Hockey Association was formed in 1886. Enthusiastic army officers made the game popular in India in the 1880s. Meanwhile, London clubs formed the rules of the modern game.

Unlike most major team games, hockey has remained an amateur sport. Great Britain's gold medal for hockey at the 1988 Olympics in Seoul, South Korea, is a reminder of the country's past dominance of the game.

David HOCKNEY

- **Painter, etcher and set designer • b.1937**

The bold simplicity of David Hockney's bright acrylic paintings so caught the spirit of London in the 1960s that he became the fashionable young painter of his generation. Despite living in California since the 1960s, this affable Yorkshireman remains in touch with his home town of Bradford, putting on exhibitions and painting local scenes.

As a student of the Royal College of Art in London, Hockney won prizes for POP ART, though he never accepted that label. In the late 1960s he adopted a representational style, which included the snapshot-like swimming-pool paintings. Much of his Californian work is a frank celebration of homoeroticism.

Hockney has also created photograph montages and designed dazzling operatic sets and costumes, including productions at Glyndebourne of *The Rake's Progress* (1975) and *The Magic Flute* (1978).

Dorothy HODGKIN

- **Chemist • 1910-94; OM 1965**

In 1928, when few women went to university and even fewer studied science, Dorothy Hodgkin read archaeology and chemistry at Oxford University's Somerville College.

She went on to pioneer methods of beaming X-rays through crystals to reveal their structure, and in 1956 discovered the composition of penicillin. In the 1950s, Hodgkin used computers to determine the structure of vitamin B_{12} (to prevent anaemia) and insulin. In 1964 she won the Nobel prize for chemistry.

> In 1965, Dorothy Hodgkin became the first woman since the nursing and hospital reformer Florence Nightingale to receive the Order of Merit

Howard HODGKIN

- **Artist • b.1932; kt 1992**

Most of Howard Hodgkin's paintings, from *Dinner at Westhill* (1964-6) to *Rain* (1984-9), appear to be abstract, yet in fact they depict specific events and encounters with real people.

Hodgkin's art, generally small in scale and brilliant in colour, shows the influence of his travels in Asia, and the decorative border arabesques and flat colouring of his works resemble the style of Persian and Indian miniatures of the Mughal age (*c*.1500-1750). Hodgkin won the Turner prize in 1985.

URBAN DREAMSCAPE In *Salt's Mill* (1997) David Hockney celebrates a Victorian endeavour to create an ideal community in a Bradford suburb. The mill now houses work by Hockney

William HOGARTH

• Painter and engraver • 1697-1764

In his satirical engravings William Hogarth provided the definitive image of the underside of 18th-century England – the poverty, vice and hypocrisy just beneath the gilded elegance. The moral tales of vice receiving its due punishment in his series of engravings, *A Harlot's Progress* (1732), *The Rake's Progress* (c.1735) and *Marriage à la Mode* (c.1753), made Hogarth's fortune, selling in tens of thousands of copies. His *Gin Lane* series of engravings, showing the ill effects of cheap gin, led to new legislation.

If engravings made Hogarth rich, his less known portrait paintings, such as *Captain Coram* (1740) and *The Shrimp Girl* (c.1759), revealed him as the first great British-born artist. Hogarth had no immediate followers, his true heirs being the CARTOONISTS Cruikshank and Gillray.

HOGMANAY

The Scottish New Year has been celebrated for centuries with bonfires, bagpipes and haggis (offal cooked inside a sheep's stomach). But it is to the 18th-century Scottish poet Robert Burns that Britain is indebted for the climax of festivities, the singing in of the New Year with 'Auld Lang Syne', the song recalling the good old days of long ago.

A popular superstition of Hogmanay (the origins of the name are obscure), and of northern England, is 'first footing', in which the first visitor to enter a house after the New Year is supposed to bring a gift, traditionally a piece of coal, to symbolise the promise of warmth for the coming year. In Scotland, a dark-haired, male first-footer, bringing food and fuel, or a sprig of mistletoe, was believed to bring good luck to the household.

Hans HOLBEIN

• Artist • 1497-1543

No other painter captured the spirit of Tudor England better than Hans Holbein. German by birth, Holbein left the austere environment of Reformation Switzerland and came to England in search of patronage. Henry VIII was so impressed with the accuracy of his work that he appointed him court painter in 1536, and sent him back to Europe to produce likenesses of prospective wives.

His *Study of Christina of Denmark* (1538) shows a mature artist. Instead of the lavish details that adorned his earlier paintings, such as *The Ambassadors* (1533), he uses simple light and shade to reveal the princess's personality. His 1540 rendering of Henry is one of the best-loved portraits of the monarch, and his paintings still inspire artists of our own time such as Peter BLAKE.

HOLIDAY CAMPS

'Is everybody happy?', 'You bet your life we are!': the good-natured, organised, collective fun of the holiday camp has been part of British life since the 1930s.

Above all, holiday camps were affordable, even in the Depression. Billy Butlin opened his first site in 1936 at Skegness in Lincolnshire, where a week's stay for a family in a chalet with full board cost £3. Butlin's formula of non-stop games, food, cabaret and child care – coordinated by uniformed attendants called 'Redcoats' – was so successful that it was soon being copied on a large scale. British camps reached a peak of popularity in the 1950s, and in the 1960s Fred Pontin took the concept abroad to Spain with his 'Pontinental' holidays.

By this time holiday camps were starting to seem old-fashioned and were facing competition from package tours. However, Rank plc bought Butlins in 1972 and the company has successfully modernised the camps while retaining the exuberant communal atmosphere, with some 9000 campers staying each week at Skegness in the summer – the same total as in 1939.

HOLKHAM HALL

• Norfolk (p.495 J2) • Built 1734-62

'An Englishman's house is his castle' was one of the legal pronouncements of Edward Coke, James I's Lord Chief Justice and founder of the Coke family fortune. Edward's 18th-century descendant Thomas Coke created for the Cokes their own family 'castle' of Holkham.

The architect William Kent designed a Palladian mansion with a symmetrical stone frontage 104 m (340 ft) long and a

STATELY BUT SUBVERSIVE Diplomats appear confident amid fine trappings in Holbein's *The Ambassadors*. But closer scrutiny of the foreground reveals a distorted skull and the painter's view that all our pomp ends in death

BUTLINS SKEGNESS HOLIDAY CAMP

WINDSOR HOUSE

BUTLINS HOLIDAY CAMP

CHEAP FUN
Butlins holiday camps in coastal towns began to thrive in the late 1930s, when holidaymakers could splash in the pool at Skegness (*above*) and pedal around the camp at Clacton-on-sea (*right*)

central columned portico. The austere façade belies Kent's sumptuous interior. In the marble entrance hall, modelled on a Roman temple, fluted alabaster columns rise towards a coffered ceiling. The principal state room is a 10 m (32 ft) high saloon of dark red velvet and gold, and all the rooms have magnificent 18th-century ceilings and works of art.

Thomas Coke built Holkham Hall on reclaimed dune and marsh. No doubt an inherited talent inspired his great nephew, also Thomas COKE, to pioneer advances in agriculture, including crop rotation, which earned him the title of 'Coke of Norfolk'.

HOLLY AND IVY

These two evergreen emblems of continuing life in winter have an ancient history as magical plants. Long before Christianity made the association between blood-red berries and spiky leaves and Christ's crown of thorns, Britons were bringing holly into their homes to ward off evil. Ivy, worn by Bacchus, the Roman god of wine, was seen as an antidote to drunkenness.

To pagan people the prickly holly signified man, the clinging, easily bending ivy, woman. Two traditional

The holly and the ivy
When they are both full grown,
Of all the trees in the wood
The holly bears the crown.

15TH-CENTURY CAROL

characters in English Shrovetide dances were the 'holly boy' and 'ivy girl'. Songs linking the two may have started out as fertility dances.

Holly and ivy are believed also to have medicinal uses. Chilblains may be relieved with holly sprigs, while ivy is said to be a cure for warts, corns and verrucas, and worn as a wreath on the head it may prevent hair loss.

Gustav HOLST

• Composer • 1874-1934

To Gustav Holst's dismay, his orchestral suite *The Planets* (1914-16) turned him into a celebrity, the Mars and Jupiter movements becoming among the most frequently performed British classical music. The composer was gratified when later works such as the opera *Savitri*, inspired by Hindu mysticism, puzzled his more superficial admirers.

Holst, of Swedish descent, dropped 'von' from his name during the First World War. His enthusiasm for folk and choral music – a passion shared by his lifelong friend Vaughan Williams – inspired his teaching methods at St Paul's Girls' School and Morley College, and influenced music education across England.

HOLYROODHOUSE

• Edinburgh (p.497 D4) • Built 1501-1679

Mary, Queen of Scots spent most of the six troubled years of her reign as Scottish sovereign at the palace of Holyroodhouse. Here in 1566 her jealous husband, Lord Darnley, and a group of conspirators stabbed to death her Italian secretary David Rizzio.

The Renaissance palace known to Mary was built by James IV of Scotland when he made EDINBURGH his capital. He chose the site for the volcanic cliffs of Salisbury Crags that form the palace's magnificent background. The building was largely reconstructed by Charles II to the designs of William Bruce, and it was in this new palace that Bonnie Prince Charlie held his brief but dazzling court in 1745. When George IV visited Holyroodhouse in 1822 he dazzled in his own way by appearing in pink silk tights and an extremely short kilt.

HORSE RACING

Mounted races go back to at least the 14th century, when Richard II rode a winner at Smithfield. The sport of kings is now mass entertainment. With an annual turnover in the billions, horse racing is Britain's sixth largest industry

WHEN A former managing director of Epsom racecourse spoke of the Derby as 'a national day out for the aristocrats and artisans, gypsies and generals, viscounts and villains', he might have been talking about horse racing in general. For the sport made for medieval kings, and still a bastion of wealth, privilege and power, appeals to people from all walks of life – some 5 million people now attend races each year.

Horse racing in Britain developed in the Middle Ages as private 'match' races in which prosperous owners pitted mounts against one another and made side bets. By 1660, Charles II was encouraging competition by holding races open to the public, with substantial prizes. The first was the NEWMARKET Town Plate, which the king himself won twice.

The nature of racing changed dramatically in the 18th century when three Arab stallions were brought to Britain and crossbred with local horses, giving rise to the first thoroughbred racehorses. The first of the one-off 'dash' races, replacing those run in heats, was held in 1776 at Doncaster over a distance of 2 miles.

When off-course betting shops were legalised in 1961, the tote business ballooned. In 1997-8, turnover for the industry reached a record £4.6 billion

RAISING THE STAKES At race meetings, signalling by hand is the quickest way for bookmakers' agents, or 'ticktack men', to show changes in the odds on horses before the start of the race

RACING ON THE FLAT
The Doncaster race became known as the St Leger, and was the first of England's five principal flat races (those with no jumps), known collectively as the Classics. The Oaks at Epsom followed in 1779, the EPSOM DERBY in 1780, and in 1809 and 1814 the Newmarket 2000 Guineas and 1000 Guineas. The races were supervised by the Jockey Club, founded in 1750 by noblemen with a common interest in the turf, which made the sport professional.

HONOURS LIST

Every year, some 3000 Britons receive official honours for outstanding civilian or military service to the country. Recipients come from all backgrounds and include civil servants, industrialists, scientists and entertainers. The prime minister and the Cabinet review suggestions from the public before proposing candidates to the sovereign, who has the final say.

Awards are announced twice a year – at New Year and on the sovereign's official birthday in June. Additional honours may be awarded at the end of each parliament and for special events, such as a monarch's jubilee year.

Honours in the personal gift of the sovereign are, in ascending order of precedence, the Royal Victorian Order, Order of Merit, Order of the

RECOMMENDED BY THE PRIME MINISTER

ORDER OF ST MICHAEL AND ST GEORGE
Established in 1818 mainly for diplomats; maximum 2252 members

ORDER OF THE BATH
Established in 1128 for military or civil distinction; maximum 2500 members

ORDER OF THE BRITISH EMPIRE
Established in 1917; three ranks in ascending order of importance: OBE (Officer); MBE (Member); CBE (Commander); 120 000 living recipients

Thistle (exclusive to Scotland) and Order of the Garter. Knighthoods are awarded within different Orders and holders may use the title Sir or Dame before their name.
See also GEORGE CROSS, VICTORIA CROSS

Frederick HOPKINS

• Biochemist • 1861-1947; kt 1925

It is largely thanks to Frederick Gowland Hopkins that vitamins are now known to be essential for health – a discovery for which he shared a Nobel prize for physiology or medicine in 1929.

As early as 1906 Hopkins realised that even a balanced diet of protein, carbohydrate and fat, if artificially produced, could not keep animals alive. Artificial milk fed to rats did not help them to grow unless small amounts of cow's milk were added. Hopkins deduced that unidentified 'accessory food factors' – the substances now called vitamins – must be present in natural foods.

Hopkins's other discoveries spanned a wide field within biochemistry, including the chemical composition of butterflies' wings and the role played in muscle metabolism by lactic acid – the

No horse has ever won all the Classics in a single season, but in 1902 a horse called Sceptre took four of the five. The jockey's record is held by Lester PIGGOTT, who achieved 30 Classic wins.

STEEPLECHASING

At about the same time as flat racing developed, a cross-country variation was being run with a distant church steeple as the winning post. Riders chose their own course, jumping whatever obstacles lay in their path. The first such 'steeplechase' was run in 1752 in County Cork, Ireland, over a distance of 4 miles. Soon racecourses were being designed to imitate the terrain with fences, ditches and water jumps.

The National Hunt Committee, founded in 1866 to regulate steeplechasing, was amalgamated with the Jockey Club in 1968. Local hunts run an amateur version of steeplechasing called point-to-point.

STARTER'S ORDERS Jockeys line up their horses at Epsom's starting gates (*top*), ready for the off. Race meetings test a horse's fitness to the limit. Strenuous exercise routines include wading through equine pools (*above*)

cause of athletes' aching muscles. The laboratories he set up at Cambridge University are now pre-eminent in the world for biochemical research.

Gerard Manley HOPKINS

• Poet   • 1844-89

An intensely private man, Gerard Manley Hopkins published little during his lifetime and it was not until 1918 that his work was seen into print by his friend and confidant, the poet Robert Bridges. His influence on 20th-century poetry since then has been profound.

Born into a wealthy middle-class Anglican family, Hopkins converted to Roman Catholicism in 1866. He burnt all his early poems when he became a Jesuit priest in 1877. His earliest surviving piece, and also his longest, is 'The Wreck of the *Deutschland*', which commemorates the death of five nuns in a shipwreck in 1875. All Hopkins's work

is deeply personal, tracing his inner conflicts and doubts about his spiritual relationship with God. Some poems are dark and intense, but many are full of a sense of wonder, celebrating nature and God's infinite beauty and variety:

> *Glory be to God for dappled things –*
> *For skies couple-coloured as a brinded*
> *cow . . .*
>
> 'Pied Beauty'

Hopkins was deliberately experimental, making use of archaic and dialect words and the rhetorical power of speech – what he called 'sprung rhythm'. He produced startling effects with diction, as where he expresses the idea that for all humans, whatever their faults, there is the promise of eternal life:

> *This Jack, joke, poor potsherd, patch,*
> *matchwood, immortal diamond,*
> *Is immortal diamond.*
>
> 'That Nature is a Heraclitean Fire'

HORSES: *see page 232*

HOUSEHOLD CAVALRY

Resplendent in gleaming breastplates and helmets, plumes bobbing on parade, the Household Cavalry is a classic part of British pageantry.

It dates back to 1661, when troops who had followed Charles II into exile (the Life Guards) joined the Royal Horse Guards, or 'Blues', as the sovereign's mounted guard. These two regiments – the senior units of the BRITISH ARMY – merged with the Royal Dragoons in 1969 to form the Blues and Royals.

The Household Cavalry is the mounted arm of the Blues and Royals, most of which forms mechanised armoured units.

QUEEN'S ESCORT The guardsmen of the **Household Cavalry** fulfil more than a ceremonial role; at any time, half of them are involved in armoured exercises

IN YOKE AND HARNESS

**Whether pulling a hackney carriage or ploughing a field, leading a
cavalry charge or giving chase, horses have partnered mankind ever since
the Iron Age. Britain is second only to Russia in the number of native
breeds developed for their different purposes**

**UFFINGTON WHITE
HORSE**

BRITAIN'S MOST ANCIENT wild
horses include Exmoor and
Shetland ponies, which roamed
wild at least 10 000 years ago during
the last Ice Age when a land bridge
connected Britain with the Continent.
Stone Age people hunted horses for their
meat, and perhaps even milked them, but
horses were probably not domesticated
until the Iron Age, the period preceding
the Roman era. They may have been
revered as religious cult symbols in some
areas, as suggested by the WHITE HORSE
figures carved into the Oxfordshire and
Wiltshire countryside.

THE WARHORSE

The Romans brought cavalry horses to
Britain, and crossed them with small,
nimble native breeds much like today's
Welsh mountain ponies to produce fine
warhorses praised by Julius Caesar. But
the heyday of military horses began in the
Middle Ages, when
much heavier animals

than those used by the Romans were
bred from horses imported by the
Normans in the 11th century. The
development of the longbow meant that
ever stronger horses were needed to
carry a knight and his (also his mount's)
armour, typically weighing more than
200 kg (31 stone).

The 16th-century 'Great Horse of
England' was renowned as the sturdiest
of warhorses, but it was still a good deal
smaller than later heavy horses such as
the Shire. With the development of
firearms, speed became paramount, and
cavalrymen rode into battle on horses
much like today's heavy hunters.

THE WORKHORSE

Until the 18th century, most ploughs
were pulled by oxen, while donkeys and
mules carried out the more mundane
farm jobs. Where
speed was vital,
such as for hauling
carriages and
stagecoaches, horses
were preferred, and
by the 19th century
they had become the
main source of
motive power in

both countryside and town, with most
farming machinery powered by horse.
The best-known British heavy breeds,
such as the Shire, Suffolk Punch and
Clydesdale, date from this period. At
the same time, Shetland ponies hauled
waggons in coal mines and millions of
cross-bred animals pulled hackney
carriages, delivery vans, buses and trams
in every town and city until motor
vehicles took over.

Today, apart from police and
ceremonial military horses, some hauling
brewer's drays, and a few others in
forestry and farming, most horses are
bred and kept for sport and recreation.
Of the 570 000 horses
in Britain, about 88
per cent are
privately owned.

At just 1 m (39 in)
high, Shetland ponies
– also called 'shelties' –
are among the smallest
horses in the world, and
the strongest for their
size. They can easily
carry an adult

BRED FOR TOIL (*above*) Shetland ponies were
crossed with other breeds to produce larger
ponies such as the Eriskay, ideal for carrying
heavy loads of peat across Scottish moors

HORSEPOWER (*main picture*)
Some farmers still prefer
plough horses, such as
this Clydesdale in
Northumberland, to
the modern tractor

HOUSES OF PARLIAMENT: *see p.234*

A.E. HOUSMAN

• Poet   • 1859-1936

The publication of *A Shropshire Lad* in 1896, at Alfred Edward Housman's own expense, turned the impecunious classics scholar into one of the most successful poets in Britain. The nostalgic collection is filled with longing for an imaginary, idealised Shropshire of the mind – the 'blue remembered hills of . . . the land of lost content'. Old country ballads form the basis of the poem's 63 verses, many of which are addressed to or spoken by a farm boy or soldier – a factor that made the book especially popular during the First World War.

Unaccountably, Housman failed his final exams at Oxford University, despite his brilliance as a scholar. An unrequited homosexual love affair at Oxford turned into an anguished longing that may have inspired the impassioned lament for lost youth expressed in his poems. He continued translating Latin authors in his spare time while working as a clerk, and by 1911 held professorships at London and Cambridge universities.

HOVERCRAFT

In 1950 the electrical engineer and boatbuilder Christopher Cockerell began investigating the 'ground effect' reported by aircraft pilots, who found that less lift was needed to raise an aeroplane near the ground than at greater heights.

Five years later, Cockerell patented an idea for a craft using downwards-directed fans to raise it off the ground while the propellers of a single engine drove the vessel forwards with a minimum of friction over ground or water.

The first hovercraft, SR-N1, was a modest 9 m (30 ft) vessel that crossed the English Channel in 1959. A ferry service began in 1968, capable of carrying 250 passengers and 30 cars at speeds of up to 70 knots (80 mph). Since then, capacity has nearly doubled.

With their ability to glide smoothly over water and rough terrain, hovercrafts also have military applications as landing craft and in anti-mine operations.

HOXNE TREASURE

The village of Hoxne in Suffolk is known for two unrelated archaeological finds. The discovery by landowner John Frere in 1797 of Stone Age flint tools among bones of lions and rhinoceros revolutionised opinions about early humans. He was one of the first people to suggest that such tools must have been made long before the civilisations described in the Bible, regarded in his day as an accurate record of the past. It is now known from the SWANSCOMBE SKULL discovery that the Hoxne artefacts were made up to 500 000 years ago.

The second find came in 1992 when a local labourer was searching for lost tools with a metal-detector. He came across one of the most important hoards of Roman treasure ever found in Britain – sets of silver tableware, gold jewellery and some 15 000 coins dating from AD 393 to 411, their wooden chest long since decayed. The hoard, declared as treasure trove, was acquired by the British Museum for £1.75 million.

TEST FLIGHT Cockerell's prototype hovercraft could take just three passengers at low speed when it crossed the English Channel in 1959

Fred HOYLE

• Cosmologist   • b.1915; kt 1972

For half a century Fred Hoyle has illuminated cosmology with provocative theories, some brilliant, others far-fetched. In 1948, he was part of a small team who proposed the steady-state theory of the creation of the Universe, suggesting that as it expanded new material was constantly created so that the overall density remained unchanged. Despite vigorous defence, the theory eventually lost out to the rival 'Big Bang' theory – a term Hoyle had coined derisively – put forward by Martin RYLE.

A more successful theory has been Hoyle's explanation of the origin of chemical elements, according to which light elements could in stages create heavier ones through thermonuclear reactions. Perhaps Hoyle's most controversial notion is that life began not on Earth but in space in gas clouds, that comets brought it to Earth, and were also the source of viruses such as flu.

BURIED TREASURE The late-Roman hoard found at Hoxne included 19 gold bracelets, among them three pierced with intricate lace-like patterns

SEAT OF GOVERNMENT

Britain is ruled from the Palace of Westminster, whose vast site includes more than 1000 rooms and over 2 miles of corridors. It is the hub of power, a bustling community and also a very fine club

THE THAMES-SIDE SITE at Westminster has been closely linked with government since EDWARD THE CONFESSOR built a royal palace there and made it his main home in 1050. The last king to live there was HENRY VIII and parliament moved into the palace in the mid 1500s.

By then parliament had established its 'bicameral' structure with two debating chambers – the House of Commons and the House of Lords – designed to ensure that each checked the other to deter the abuse of power or poor lawmaking.

In the late 1600s, as the power of the king and the aristocracy waned, the Commons became the more powerful of the two chambers. Today it is made up of 659 members (MPs) directly elected by the British people. Whichever political party leader can command a majority of MPs in the House is appointed prime minister by the monarch.

PEERS OF THE REALM

Members of the House of Lords are not elected. Most are hereditary peers, who have taken up the seat with their title – a privilege inherited by their heirs. The others, apart from a handful of senior churchmen and law lords, are life peers

and peeresses, created by the monarch on the recommendation of the prime minister. The fact that most of the hereditary peers are Conservative has consistently denied the Labour party a majority in the Lords – one factor in its determination to reform the so-called Upper House.

The Lords debate bills passed to them for scrutiny by the Commons (*see* ACT OF PARLIAMENT) and occasionally a bill is initiated in the Lords. The peers lost the power to veto financial legislation in the Parliament Act of 1911, but can

SOVEREIGN ROLE For the opening of Parliament the monarch enters through the arch of Victoria Tower

THE ARCHITECT
The neo-Gothic palace of Westminster was the work of the Victorian architect Charles Barry and Augustus Pugin, who assisted him. Fire devastated the original ancient buildings in 1834, and rebuilding was largely completed by 1860. A statue of Barry stands near the central lobby.

Serjeant at Arms Offices
St Stephen's Entrance
Peers' Corridor
St Stephen's Hall
Opposition
Black Rod
Peers' Entrance
State Off Cour
Prince's Chamber
Chancellor's Court
Royal Gallery
Royal Cour
Victoria Tower
Sovereign's Entrance
Queen's Robing Room
Victoria Tower Garden
Lord Chancellor's Department

still delay non-financial bills for a year under the Parliament Act of 1949.

A GRAND PLACE TO WORK

Pomp and ceremony survive, particularly in autumn when the monarch arrives in full regalia to open parliament after the long summer recess.

When parliament is in session, MPs sometimes work almost round the clock and Westminster becomes their club and home-from-home. Its numerous facilities include bars and restaurants, a hairdressing salon, a chess room, a gymnasium and even – in the House of Lords – a shooting range.

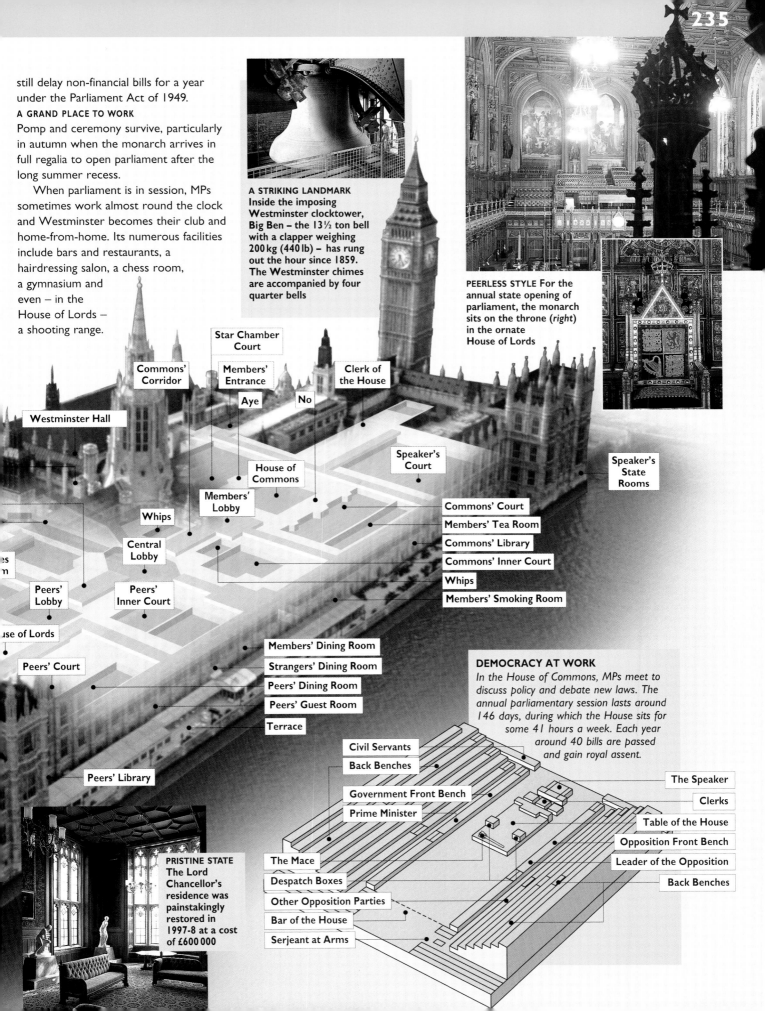

A STRIKING LANDMARK
Inside the imposing Westminster clocktower, **Big Ben** – the 13½ ton bell with a clapper weighing 200 kg (440 lb) – has rung out the hour since 1859. The Westminster chimes are accompanied by four quarter bells

PEERLESS STYLE For the annual state opening of parliament, the monarch sits on the throne (right) in the ornate House of Lords

Star Chamber Court

Members' Entrance

Aye

No

Clerk of the House

Commons' Corridor

Westminster Hall

Speaker's Court

Speaker's State Rooms

House of Commons

Members' Lobby

Whips

Commons' Court

Members' Tea Room

Commons' Library

Commons' Inner Court

Whips

Members' Smoking Room

Central Lobby

Peers' Lobby

Peers' Inner Court

use of Lords

Peers' Court

Members' Dining Room

Strangers' Dining Room

Peers' Dining Room

Peers' Guest Room

Terrace

Peers' Library

DEMOCRACY AT WORK
In the House of Commons, MPs meet to discuss policy and debate new laws. The annual parliamentary session lasts around 146 days, during which the House sits for some 41 hours a week. Each year around 40 bills are passed and gain royal assent.

Civil Servants

Back Benches

Government Front Bench

Prime Minister

The Speaker

Clerks

Table of the House

Opposition Front Bench

Leader of the Opposition

Back Benches

The Mace

Despatch Boxes

Other Opposition Parties

Bar of the House

Serjeant at Arms

PRISTINE STATE The Lord Chancellor's residence was painstakingly restored in 1997-8 at a cost of £600 000

Henry HUDSON

• **Explorer**   • **c.1565-1611**

In 1607 Henry Hudson set off from England with a crew of just 11 men. His destination was the Arctic Ocean; this was the first of four attempts to find a north-west passage to the 'islands of spicery' and the golden lands of China and Japan believed to lie beyond the North Pole. Hudson never found a way to the East, but on his third voyage in 1609 sailed 150 miles up the river to which he gave his name.

In April 1610 he headed north once again as far as Hudson Bay, which was also named after him. He intended to move on in the spring after the ice had broken. But his crew mutinied, claiming that he had withheld food rations, and Hudson, his son John and seven of the crew were cast adrift in a small boat, never to be seen again. A passage to the East was finally found in the 1850s, more than 200 years after Hudson's last fateful voyage.

Ted HUGHES

• **Poet**   • **1930-98; poet laureate 1984-98**

A pretty, golden-green pike with deadly jaws; the hawk whose 'manners are tearing off heads'; and a greedy crow 'screaming for blood' – the savage beauty of nature and mysterious lives of animals are recurrent themes in the poetry of Ted Hughes.

Hughes was born in Yorkshire and became fascinated with wildlife on childhood hunting trips. Literary recognition came early with his first volume, *The Hawk in the Rain* (1957). *Crow* (1970) was acclaimed his best work, until the publication of *Birthday Letters* in 1998, just before he died. These intimate poems, written over many years, meditate on Hughes' relationship with Sylvia Plath, his first wife, who committed suicide in 1963. More copies were sold than any other volume of verse in Britain in the 20th century.

SILKEN THREADS The highly skilled Huguenots produced many fine fabrics in the patterns and colours of the age

HUGUENOTS

The largest influx of French settlers into Britain was not at the time of the Norman Conquest, but during the 16th and 17th centuries. The first wave of 'Huguenots', as they were known (the word's origins are obscure), arrived in the middle of the 16th century, fleeing persecution by the Catholic authorities. Many thousands more followed in 1685, when Louis XIV revoked an edict of 1598 that guaranteed religious freedom for Protestants.

Most Huguenots settled in the south and east where they set up thriving businesses that benefited the British economy. The renowned Spitalfields silk was the work of Huguenot weavers and they were also expert silversmiths. Huguenot churches survive in London and Norwich, while Canterbury Cathedral has a Huguenot chapel.

HULL

• **NE England (p.496 D5)**   • **Pop. 266 800**

Once a byword for stagnation and urban decay, the port of Hull on the River Humber estuary is being transformed. In 1991 a shopping centre opened on stilts above the water of the landlocked Prince's Dock, and the adjoining dock is now a marina. The city's lottery-funded project, 'The

Deep', is set to open in 2001. It features a marine research station and, through a series of exhibits, explains the origins of life in the oceans.

Much of old Hull was destroyed by bombing in the Second World War, but there are still some houses dating from the 18th century and earlier. William WILBERFORCE was born in one of them in 1759. Now called Wilberforce House, it has been turned into a museum. Another famous inhabitant was the poet Philip LARKIN, who from 1955 to 1985 was librarian at Hull University.

HUMBER BRIDGE

• **NE England (p.496 D5)**   • **Built 1972-80**

At the time of its official opening in 1981, the Humber Bridge was the longest single-span bridge in the world, stretching 1410 m (4626 ft) between the 155.5 m (510 ft) towers, to an overall length of nearly 2220 m – about a mile and a

A BROAD SPAN The Humber Bridge cost some £96 million to construct

half. Because of the bridge's vast length, the two supporting towers had to be set out of alignment by 36 mm (1½ in) to allow for the curvature of the Earth. Its record length was beaten in 1998 by the Akashi-Kaikyo bridge in Japan, which has a 1911 m (6268 ft) suspended main span.

Cardinal HUME

- **Archbishop of Westminster**
- **1923-99; OM 1999**

As head of the Roman Catholic Church in England and Wales from 1976 until his death, Basil Hume consistently fostered closer ties with the Church of England. In 1981 he became the first Roman Catholic priest for 400 years to take part in a British royal wedding. While regarded as a liberal by Rome, he was uncompromising on moral and doctrinal issues, speaking out against the loss of Christian values in modern society.

Much of Hume's life was spent at Ampleforth – both the public school (as pupil and teacher) and the abbey. Born George Hume, he was brought up in the Roman Catholic faith of his French mother and entered the Benedictine Order in 1945, taking the name Basil. After being ordained in 1950, he returned to Ampleforth to teach and was elected abbot in 1963. In 1976 he became archbishop of Westminster and was made cardinal a few months later.

David HUME

- **Philosopher** • **1711-76**

As a student at Edinburgh University aged about 12, David Hume discovered his natural bent for scepticism and by implication atheism. He decided to explain his

dangerous views in a bold work of philosophy, eventually completed many years later. *The Treatise of Human Nature* (1739) set out to establish empirically a science of human faculties and also suggested that moral judgments are expressions of approval or disapproval.

Hume applied this principle to science, arguing that all thought was based in habits of feeling rather than logic. Concerning philosophy, he noted, 'Errors in religion are dangerous, those in philosophy only ridiculous'.

Hume enjoyed a comfortable income as a writer, and his six-volume *History of Great Britain* (1754-62) was well received. He detested England and spent his last years growing ever fatter among Edinburgh's dining circles. He died as he lived, a cheerful atheist, on his deathbed upsetting James Boswell by proclaiming immortality 'a most unreasonable fancy'.

HUNDRED YEARS' WAR

- **1337-1453**

This long, intermittent war between England and France dragged on as generations of English kings laid claim to the French throne. The original dispute, over the status of Aquitaine, was exacerbated in 1340 when EDWARD III of England claimed the throne through his mother, Queen Isabella, daughter of King Philip IV of France. Edward was thus a grandson of Philip IV, while the reigning French king, Philip VI, was a nephew.

English victories at CRÉCY (1346) and Poitiers (1356) forced France to accept an unfavourable peace in 1360. But by 1375 England had lost most of its gains.

HENRY V renewed the war in 1415, defeating the French at AGINCOURT, but by 1453, following French victory at the Battle of Castillon, the English were expelled from all France save for the port of Calais. The war did not finally end until 1558, when Calais was stormed and taken. In spite of this, English monarchs continued to call themselves kings of France until 1802.

John HUNT

- **Mountaineer** • **1910-98; kt 1953; bn 1966**

Experiences as an army officer in the mountains of Europe and India gave John Hunt the training that equipped him to

MACABRE COLLECTION When he died John Hunter had amassed more than 13 000 human and animal anatomical specimens

be leader of the first expedition to conquer Mount Everest, the world's highest mountain. The gruelling trip was made in 1953 with Edmund Hillary and Tenzing Norgay. 'We climb mountains,' Hunt reasoned later, 'because we like it.'

John HUNTER

- **Surgeon, anatomist and pathologist**
- **1728-93**

The so-called 'founder of scientific surgery' gained most of his training by helping his brother William (1718-83), a lecturer and obstetrician, and by attending classes at Chelsea and St Bartholomew's hospitals, where he developed a fascination with anatomy.

Bodies for medical research were in short supply, and Hunter resorted to conducting research on himself and, notoriously, on bodies 'resurrected' from fresh graves by robbers. His thirst for interesting examples was so well known that one unusually tall man arranged to be buried at sea in an (unsuccessful) attempt to avoid becoming a specimen.

More than 3000 of John Hunter's specimens can be seen at the Hunterian Museum of London's Royal College of Surgeons. Another Hunterian Museum in Glasgow holds the anatomical collection of his brother William.

HURST CASTLE

- Hampshire (p.495 F6)
- Built 16th century   • EH

A mile of water separates the pebble spit on which Hurst Castle stands from the shore of the Isle of Wight. Henry VIII chose this spot as the site of an elaborate fort, one of many built to protect his realm against the threat of French invasion after his breach with Rome.

The invasion never came, but during the Civil War the castle was occupied by Parliamentarians who kept Charles I prisoner there on his way to trial and execution in London. The 12-sided central tower is surrounded by a curtain wall with three semicircular bastions, all overlaid with Victorian brickwork.

Len HUTTON

- Cricketer   • 1916-90; kt 1956

Undeterred by an accident in an army gym that left one arm shorter than the other, Len Hutton became the bedrock of the England batting order. Shy, wry and sparely built, the Yorkshire opener came to the forefront in 1938 when he made 364 runs in a match against Australia. It stood as a Test record for two decades and remains the highest score by an Englishman. In 1952 he again broke fresh ground as the century's first professional England captain.

His finest hour came in 1954-5 when he became the first of only three England captains in the 20th century to regain, then successfully defend, the ASHES.

RECORD RUNS Len Hutton is cheered off the field at The Oval in August 1938 after scoring 364 in the 5th Test against Australia

TAKING THE PLUNGE Hardy bathers in 1932 prepare for a dip in the Serpentine at Hyde Park, a favourite haunt of winter swimmers. A race for the Peter Pan Cup is held on Christmas Day

HUXLEY FAMILY

- Thomas Henry; biologist; 1825-95
- Julian Sorrel; biologist; 1887-1975; kt 1958
- Aldous Leonard; writer; 1894-1963

The Huxley family is one of those extraordinary British dynasties, like the Rothschild family, whose members became eminent in several fields.

T.H. Huxley, who had only two years' formal schooling, taught himself five languages. He made discoveries in zoology, palaeontology, geology and anthropology, and championed Charles DARWIN's ideas on evolution. He was a prolific writer and lecturer, and coined the term 'agnostic'. His grandson, Julian Huxley, also a biologist, made important contributions to ornithology and the study of embryonic development.

Huxley's second grandson was the novelist Aldous, whose *BRAVE NEW WORLD* (1932) described a gloomy vision of the future. He also wrote a series of novels satirising English society, including *Point Counter Point* (1928) and *The Doors of Perception* (1954), an account of his experiences under the influence of the hallucinogenic drug mescalin.

HYDE PARK

- Central London (p.499 B3)
- Created 16th-19th century

When Henry VIII seized the manor of Hyde from Westminster Abbey during the Dissolution of the Monasteries, he turned it into a private park where he hunted hares, partridges and pheasants. James I opened it to a privileged few, and in 1637 Charles I allowed the public in. It became the scene of aristocratic recreations such as horse racing and duels: the mile-long track of Rotten Row, 'Route du Roi', was a favourite parade of the fashionable in their carriages. The Serpentine lake was formed from the River Westbourne, a Thames tributary, for Queen Caroline, the wife of George II.

In the Victorian age Hyde Park became a centre for popular orators, and in 1872 the north-east corner of the park became the officially recognised soapbox site of SPEAKER'S CORNER. Hyde Park and KENSINGTON GARDENS together form the largest of central London's royal parks, covering 257 ha (634 acres).

HYMNS

The first important collection of hymns in the Anglican Church was published in 1861 as *Hymns Ancient and Modern*. It was enduringly popular, selling some 100 million copies in 90 years. The oldest hymn in the collection is 'Veni Creator Spiritus', which dates from the early Latin Church.

Half a century later came the equally successful *English Hymnal*, compiled and edited by Ralph VAUGHAN WILLIAMS. Most significantly, it recorded folk melodies such as the Welsh 'Ay hyd y nos' ('All Through the Night') and 'Monks Gate' ('He Who Would Valiant Be').

The first collection of recent times was *100 Hymns for Today* (1969), which has been followed by ecumenical collections such as *Mission Praise* (1987), which embraces an informal style of worship with handclapping songs such as 'Our God Reigns' and 'Servant King'.

ICI

- **Founded 1926**

Twentieth-century life is unimaginable without polythene, Perspex and polyester. They were all introduced by Imperial Chemical Industries (ICI), one of the world's largest chemical companies with a worldwide staff of 60 000 and a turnover of around £11 billion.

ICI began in 1926, with the merger of four giants of the British chemical industry, in order to compete better internationally, especially with dynamic German industries.

In 1993 a demerger led to a new company, Zeneca, handling drugs, agricultural chemicals and seeds, while ICI itself continued to produce acrylics, adhesives, lubricants, explosives and the world's widest range of decorative paints.

ICKWORTH

- **Suffolk (p.495 J3)**
- **Built 1795-1830** • **NT**

The huge oval rotunda, modelled on the Pantheon in Rome, is the most arresting feature of Ickworth. Round the building, below its 30 m (100 ft) high dome, runs a finely carved frieze of scenes from Homer. Curving corridors link the rotunda to two flanking pavilions.

Frederick Augustus Hervey, the 4th earl of Bristol and bishop of Bristol, designed the rotunda in the late 18th century as his living quarters and the pavilions as galleries for his art treasures. His plan misfired: while he was in Rome, Napoleon's forces occupied the city and seized most of his art collection, and in 1803 the earl died, long before the house was finished.

The earl's heirs adapted the pavilions as living quarters and made the rotunda the setting for family portraits, fine furniture, porcelain and a collection of Georgian silver.

TRANQUIL SETTING The rotunda at Ickworth is surrounded by a park landscaped by 'Capability' Brown. The grounds also contain a formal Italianate garden

IDEAL HOME EXHIBITION

- **March-April**

Upwards of half a million people flock to the Ideal Home Exhibition held at Earl's Court in London each year, in search of the latest home comforts on sale there from the 650 stands. The exhibition has become famous for its spectacular displays, such as a full-size house of the future and the world's biggest bathtub. The exhibition was launched by the *Daily Mail* as an advertising ploy in 1908 and has reflected changing tastes ever since.

ICE AGE

The most recent ice age began less than 2 million years ago and exposed Britain to intermittent periods of glaciation separated by long intervals of warmth, known as interglacials. Even though the last ice advance ended some 12 500 years ago, it is possible that the ice age proper is not yet over and that there are further glaciations to come.

The ice sheet that covered Britain in glacial periods was as thick as 1½ miles in places, and had a huge impact on the landscape. U-shaped valleys, such as Glen Coe in Scotland, are typical, formed by the movement of enormous glaciers. Scratches in the rock face such as at the Pass of Llanberis, north Wales, show the direction of the flow of ice. The weight of the ice pressed the Earth's crust down, and even now the Highlands and Ulster are minutely, year by year, rising back to their preglacial levels.

ANIMALS FROM ABROAD

During glacial periods, large amounts of water were locked up in ice sheets, with a consequent lowering of sea levels all over the world. While the ice remained, Britain was joined by land to the Continent, allowing animals to cross to and fro. Among them were those adapted to life in icy conditions, such as woolly rhinoceroses, mammoths, giant Irish elks and arctic hares and foxes.

When the ice eventually melted, the sea level rose and Britain was again cut off, ending the migration of animals.

GLEN COE, FORMED BY ICE AGE GLACIERS (*below*)

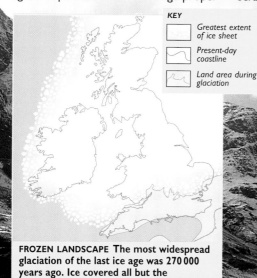

KEY

- Greatest extent of ice sheet
- Present-day coastline
- Land area during glaciation

FROZEN LANDSCAPE The most widespread glaciation of the last ice age was 270 000 years ago. Ice covered all but the southernmost parts of Britain, which was joined by land to the Continent

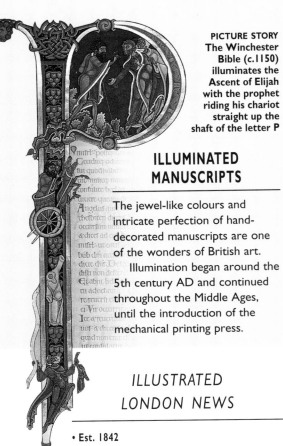

PICTURE STORY
The Winchester Bible (c.1150) illuminates the Ascent of Elijah with the prophet riding his chariot straight up the shaft of the letter P

ILLUMINATED MANUSCRIPTS

The jewel-like colours and intricate perfection of hand-decorated manuscripts are one of the wonders of British art. Illumination began around the 5th century AD and continued throughout the Middle Ages, until the introduction of the mechanical printing press.

Illustrations took the form of initial letters, which could contain a complete scene; small pictures, or miniatures, embodied in text; and borders that held decorative motifs. The purpose was educational as well as artistic, serving to convey information to a society that was predominantly illiterate.

SACRED AND SECULAR
Most early manuscripts were religious works written in Latin, such as the LINDISFARNE Gospels (698), now in the British Library. Monks painstakingly copied out the text onto parchment or vellum and for illuminations applied gold leaf and paints from natural sources such as iris sap (green) and madder root (red).

As the Middle Ages progressed, styles became more elaborate. Scribes working outside religious orders could charge a fortune for their work. In the 13th century, a book by Nicholas Parchmenter, a secular illuminator from London, cost £40 – the price of a house. Some of the finest secular work were the scenes of country life in the 15th-century *Bedford Hours*.

FADING LIGHT
Simpler, less luxurious books, often made from paper instead of vellum, appeared from the 14th century on.

Increasingly, books were in English rather than Latin and some early works of English literature, such as Chaucer's *Canterbury Tales,* were illuminated (a 15th-century 'The Miller's Tale' is in the John Rylands Library, Manchester). But the high point was already past and the art largely died out after William CAXTON introduced the printing press in 1476.

ILLUSTRATED LONDON NEWS

• Est. 1842

The first journal to use pictures to illustrate news stories was the idea of the printer Herbert Ingram. He began his ground-breaking *Illustrated London News* in 1842, sending artists around the world to capture important events, rather as photographers did later. Their drawings were rushed home and turned into engravings for reproduction in the *News*.

The tradition continued into the 20th century, with artists such as Brian de Grineau covering the two world wars. Another speciality was cutaway drawings of aircraft carriers, tanks, bombers and other military hardware.

The *Illustrated London News* now appears every second month and has a reputation for outstanding photography.

INDUSTRIAL REVOLUTION

The transformation of Britain's traditional agrarian economy into one based on manufacturing and machines was one of the most profound upheavals the nation has experienced.

Change began in the 18th century with technological innovations such as the flying shuttle and spinning jenny that revolutionised the TEXTILE INDUSTRY. The pace was soon accelerated by the factory system, which required labourers to work under one roof using machinery powered from a single source.

That source was initially water. Early factories were all built next to rivers but with the advent of the steam engine, perfected by James WATT in the 1760s, they could be sited anywhere. Better transport links via canals and then railways brought further industrialisation.

WORKSHOP OF THE WORLD
Between 1800 and 1850 Britain's coal output rose fourfold, cotton eightfold and pig iron 2000 per cent. Industrial centres grew up around the coalfields close to Manchester, Birmingham and Newcastle, which sprawled into huge conurbations.

DARK SATANIC MILLS
For those with money or ideas opportunities were unlimited. But for the new 'working class' who manned the factories life was far from rosy. Hours were long, wages low and conditions dangerous. 'Hell is a city much like London – A populous and a smoky city', wrote Percy Bysshe Shelley in 1819, referring to the darker side of the revolution: overcrowded tenements, pollution spewing from the factory chimneys, and 12 hour shifts.

Manufacturing dominated British trade until the mid 20th century when the traditional industries such as mining, shipbuilding and textiles became less profitable. Most of the vast Victorian mills of the north of England are now derelict. But a slice of old industrial life can be seen in the museums and historical sites at IRONBRIDGE GORGE in Shropshire, the first place where iron was successfully smelted using coke.

INFLATION

When prices go up and money buys less economists speak of inflation – the declining value of a currency and a sign of general economic weakness, sometimes described as 'too much money chasing too few goods'.

Inflation has been a major fear of British chancellors since the 1970s, when the quadrupling of oil prices in 1973-4 led to massive price hikes. By 1977 some staple foods were costing three times as much as they had ten years before.

AVERAGE FOOD PRICES (pence)		
	1967	1977
Potatoes (1 lb)	1.6	4.2
Milk (1 pint)	4.2	8.5
Pork sausages (1 lb)	16.3	46.1
Eggs (dozen)	19.8	38.6
Tea (¼ lb)	7.8	10.5
Sugar (2 lb)	7.0	22.8

Inflation is now curbed by the BANK OF ENGLAND's control of interest rates and the government's fiscal policy. As prices and incomes do not rise equally, some benefit from the system and some lose.

GLOWING EMBERS When Frederick Daniel Hardy painted *The Clergyman's Visit* in 1887, inglenooks were back in fashion as part of the late 19th-century vogue for cottage style

INGLENOOK

Before the mid 16th century, few dwellings in Britain had CHIMNEYS. Instead, a central room called a hall or firehouse was built with an open hearth and a roof opening for smoke to escape. Smoke was directed upwards through a fireproofed timber hood resting on a beam crossing the firehouse at ceiling height. The space beneath the beam was called the ingle (from a Gaelic word meaning 'house fire').

The Elizabethans enclosed the open hearth in a chimney stack built of brick or stone, with a fireplace that was tall and deep enough to allow a wooden seat to be built in the chimney corner or 'inglenook'. By the 18th century, inglenooks were replaced by more efficient flues serving several small fireplaces. They reappeared in the late 19th century, more as a fashion than for practical purposes.

INLAND REVENUE

• Founded 1849

'Inquisitorial' was parliament's verdict on the proposal of the prime minister William PITT to levy income tax in 1797. But the French Revolutionary Wars had to be financed, and to raise the millions needed by other means would have meant taxing almost everything. There were already taxes on salt, sugar, glass, soap, paper and tea.

So, pledging to repeal the measure when the war was over, Pitt imposed an income tax in 1799. It raised £15 million and was still resented in 1811 when a cartoon depicted the tax as a fiery comet being snuffed out by John Bull. Income tax was abolished in 1816, but no government has been able to do without it since its reintroduction in 1842.

A LICENCE TO EXTRACT MONEY

The Board of Inland Revenue was formed in 1849 to administer and collect all taxes. In 1908 the Board of Customs and Excise took over the collection of indirect levies, such as that on alcoholic drinks, and, from 1973, value added tax (VAT). The Inland Revenue collects direct TAXES, which include stamp duty, income tax, inheritance and corporation tax. Though exempt, the Queen has paid income tax voluntarily since 1992. In 1998-9 the Inland Revenue collected around £126.1 billion.

INNS OF COURT

• Central London (p.499 D2 & F5)
• Est. c.14th century

In the Middle Ages, the Inns of Court were places where law students lived, ate and studied. The four Inns (Middle Temple, Inner Temple, Lincoln's Inn and Gray's Inn), in Holborn and off Fleet Street, are today a combination of workplace and dining club for barristers.

The Inns are remarkable for their resplendent dining halls, elegant lawns and atmosphere of quiet, secluded old-worldliness within yards of traffic-ridden streets. Visitors are normally admitted to the grounds but not to the gardens.

PROPPING UP THE BAR

All barristers must be admitted to one of the Inns before thay can practise, and many have offices there (known as 'chambers'). Traditionally, they must eat a number of dinners at the Inns before they qualify, or are 'called to the Bar'. The Inns also have reponsibilities for training would-be barristers and the administration of the Bar, but their influence over the profession is waning.

The Scottish equivalent of the Inns of Court is the Faculty of Advocates in Edinburgh, founded in the 16th century.

ROOM AT THE INNS The tranquil gardens of Gray's Inn are a stone's throw from the bustling City of London. 'The Walks' are said to have been laid out by Francis Bacon, a member of the Inn

BRIGHT AND BEAUTIFUL

There are more species of insects in Britain than all our other plants and animals put together. Life would be unsustainable without these tiny creatures. They pollinate flowers, clean up debris, provide food for birds and small mammals – and some of them even prey on other pest species

ON A CALM SUMMER evening it is impossible to miss the presence of insects: clouds of midges dancing in the last few rays of the setting sun, the buzzing of bees as they make their final collections of nectar, butterflies floating from flower to flower, a chorus of chirping crickets. But insects are always there – 22 500 different species in Britain – making a living in almost every imaginable habitat.

No British insect is deadly poisonous but some can give a nasty sting or bite. Most are more sinned against than sinning, though, under threat from farming practices that are rapidly destroying their habitats. Since the 1950s, three kinds of dragonfly have disappeared from Britain, and the number of common bumblebees has halved to just six.

HARNESSING INSECT POWER
Some insects are natural enemies of others, a fact gardeners have learned to use to their benefit. Unlike chemicals, biological control affects only the target pest. It is now common for British gardeners to protect greenhouse crops from whitefly with the help of *Encarsia formosa*, a small parasitic wasp that attacks young whitefly. Other allies include ladybirds, which feed on aphids, and ground beetles, which prey on slugs, root aphids and vine weevils.

BUTTERFLIES AND MOTHS *Drab or vividly coloured, most* BUTTERFLIES AND MOTHS *are harmless, though some (such as clothes moths) are pests. They are some of nature's most effective pollinators*

DRAGONFLIES AND DAMSELFLIES
These slender, often brilliantly hued insects are seen over British streams and ponds, though their winged life may be brief. Dragonflies, for example, spend three years under water as immature nymphs and just eight weeks as airborne adults

Death's-head hawk moth (caterpillar and adult)

Common darter dragonfly

Common field grasshopper

Rose aphids

Black ants herding aphids

Greenbottle

BUGS *Notorious garden enemies such as aphids and capsid bugs belong to a group known as 'bugs'. They do damage with sharp rostrums, or beaks, that pierce plants and suck up the juices*

ANTS *Though they are tiny, ants live in large, complex communities. The wingless workers tend to the queen, forage for food and protect the nest. Winged (fertile) females and males leave the nest to mate*

FLIES *Britain has more than 5000 species of fly, many of which spread disease. Greenbottles lay their eggs in dead animals and the eggs hatch into maggots. A rat carcass can feed 4000 maggots*

GRASSHOPPERS AND CRICKETS *Enlarged hind legs enable these insects to jump great distances. Unlike their relative, the African locust, British species rarely do serious damage to crops*

Common wasp

Silverfish

Woodlouse

BEES AND WASPS *Britain has both solitary and social bee and wasp species. Some are scavengers, others are pollinators and some are parasites, laying their eggs inside other insects. See also* BEES

OTHER SPECIES *Creepy crawlies with more than six legs are not strictly insects though they look similar. They include spiders, mites, woodlice and centipedes. Britain has 640 species of spider. Some, like the garden spider, spin 'orb' webs; others make funnel webs and some, like the zebra spider, do not spin webs at all*

BEETLES *About 4000 beetle species live in Britain, the great diving beetle being one of the largest at 3 cm (1¼ in). Its larval form has huge jaws with which it kills tadpoles and even small fish. The adult carries a supply of air under its wing case*

WINGLESS INSECTS *Some primitive species, such as silverfish, never have wings at any stage in their life cycle. Also, unlike most insects, they do not undergo metamorphosis as they mature into adults*

Great diving beetle

Common centipede

Garden spider

INSTITUTE OF CONTEMPORARY ARTS

• **Central London (p.499 C7)** • **Founded 1947**
In the words of one of its founders, the art critic Herbert Read, the ICA was intended to be '. . .an adult play centre, a workshop where work is a joy, a source of vitality and daring experiment.' Its first exhibition, 'Forty Years of Modern Art', which opened on February 9, 1948, included works by Braque, Dali, Matisse, Magritte, Kandinsky, Klee, Picasso, and Britons BACON and MOORE, setting the tone of its work for the next half century.

The institute holds about six exhibitions a year. It also provides a forum for contemporary music and literature, independent films and videos as well as hosting conferences. In 1991 Damien HIRST's *Cow in Formaldehyde* was put on display, creating shock waves throughout the art world. Other recent exhibitors include the equally provocative Chapman brothers.

INVERARAY CASTLE

• **Argyll and Bute (p.497 C4)** • **Built 1746-80**
The 3rd duke of Argyll, chief of the powerful Clan Campbell, built Inveraray Castle after the 1745 Jacobite rebellion. The blue-grey castle was built by Roger Morris in Gothic Revival style, with corner towers and pepper-pot turrets.

The magnificent interior by Robert Mylne includes a state dining room and drawing room with decorated ceilings, panelled walls, fine tapestries, a wealth of furniture, and paintings by Thomas Gainsborough, Henry Raeburn and Edwin Landseer.

INVEREWE

• **Highland (p.497 B2)**
• **Created 1862-1952** • **NTS**
On a latitude more northerly than Moscow, exotic trees and plants from warmer climes flourish in a garden formed by the vision and toil of a single dedicated man, Osgood Mackenzie. In acquiring in 1862 a barren sandstone headland on the shore of Loch Ewe, Mackenzie put his faith in the warming effect of the North Atlantic Drift, which washes the coast of north-west Scotland. He started by planting windbreaks of Corsican and Scots pines, and replacing the acid black peat soil with blue clay brought up from the shores of the nearby sea-loch.

Rhododendrons from the Himalayas, pines from California, eucalyptuses from Tasmania, pink orchids from Madeira, an umbrella tree from Japan and rare plants from Italy and China now provide varied foliage and colourful blooms for most of the year in this 20 ha (50 acre) oasis.

INVERPOLLY NATURE RESERVE

• **Highland (p.497 B2)**
Covering 10 800 ha (27 000 acres) of heather moor and mountain wilderness, Inverpolly is Britain's second-largest nature reserve. The bare rock slopes and peaty bogs scattered with small lakes are inhospitable to man, but home to countless forms of wildlife, including red deer, otters, pine martens and wild cats.

Birds such as red-throated divers breed on the lakes and barnacle geese graze on the offshore islands in the winter. A nature trail leads past lichens, mosses and rare plants, and the red sandstone of Knockan Cliff.

HIGH POINT The 849 m (2786 ft) Cul Mor overlooks Inverpolly Nature Reserve

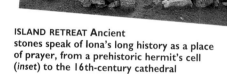

ISLAND RETREAT Ancient stones speak of Iona's long history as a place of prayer, from a prehistoric hermit's cell (*inset*) to the 16th-century cathedral

IONA

• **Argyll and Bute (p.497 B4)** • **Area 3 sq miles**
• **Pop. 98**
The Scottish novelist Walter Scott found the island of Iona, off the south-west coast of Mull, 'desolate and miserable', but for many it has been a place of pilgrimage and a source of religious inspiration. In AD 563, the Irish evangelist Columba (*see* SAINTS) chose Iona as the site for a monastery, and from its shores Christian missionaries travelled throughout pagan Scotland.

The end of the 8th century brought disaster. Norse invaders murdered 68 monks, and in 807 they returned and burnt the monastery. But because of its connection with St Columba, the island remained a sacred place, and became a burial ground for Scottish, Norse and Irish kings until the 11th century.

In 1203 a new monastery was founded, and in the 16th century its church served as the cathedral of Argyll. The cathedral has been restored by the Iona Community, a religious brotherhood founded in 1938, who live on the island.

It is reached by car ferry from Oban to Mull, then across Mull by bus or car to Fionnphort, from where a boat trip to Iona takes 5 minutes. The remoteness may be part of the attraction, for today Iona receives 200 000 visitors a year.

IRISH QUESTION

Who rules Ireland? – the Irish Question – has long poisoned Anglo-Irish relations. Henry II landed in Dublin in 1171 and established control over land in south-east Ireland that formed a 'pale', a fenced-off area, of English settlers. In the next century ULSTER was seized by the English to be ruled by vassal Irish earls.

Tudor monarchs extended English influence by 'planting' Protestant colonists on land confiscated from Irish chieftains. The Reformation did not penetrate Roman Catholic Ireland, which created a religious divide between the native Irish and the English settlers.

BRITAIN TAKES CONTROL

The character of the north of Ireland was changed in 1607 when more than 100 Ulster lords, tired of the restrictions imposed on them, fled to Europe. This allowed the mass settlement of the province by Protestant Scots and English.

Irish revolt during the Civil War was put down by Parliamentarian forces, led at the bloody sackings of Drogheda and Wexford in 1649 by Oliver Cromwell. In 1689 Catholics rose again, supporting James II's attempt to regain the English throne. They besieged Londonderry, confirming the Ulster Protestants' fear of Catholics, but were beaten at the Battle of the BOYNE. For the next century Anglo-Irish Protestants ruled Ireland, until a nationalist revolt in 1798 led to the abolition of the Irish parliament and unification in 1801 with Britain. Resentment of British rule intensified in 1845 when the potato harvest failed and a million Irish died.

ROAD TO INDEPENDENCE

The Emancipation Act of 1829 allowed Catholics to sit in parliament and agitate for Irish autonomy. Violence was added to this peaceful protest from the 1850s by the Irish Republican Brotherhood, a forerunner of the IRA.

The Liberal prime minister William GLADSTONE made repeated attempts to pass Irish home rule bills in the late 19th century, but failed each time. This handed the initiative to the Irish nationalists, who led the EASTER RISING of 1916 and fought the British army after the First World War.

In 1921 the Irish Free State was formed, with six Ulster counties becoming Northern Ireland. Links between Britain and Ireland were weakened further by a tariff war in 1936 and by Irish neutrality in the Second World War. In 1949 Britain recognised the new Republic of Ireland but the position of Northern Ireland remained a vexed issue (*see* NORTHERN IRELAND).

IRISH REPUBLICAN ARMY

• Created 1919

The Good Friday Agreement of 1998 promised to end almost 80 years of violent protest in NORTHERN IRELAND by the paramilitary Irish Republican Army (IRA), formed during the Anglo-Irish conflict after the First World War.

The IRA has always consisted of warring factions. In 1921 IRA members opposed to the creation of the Irish Free State fought the Irish government. With the formation of the Republic of Ireland in 1949 the IRA targeted Northern Ireland and split again in 1969 into an 'official', more moderate wing, and a 'provisional' militant wing – the 'Provos'.

In 1994 the Provisional IRA agreed to a temporary ceasefire that allowed SINN FÉIN, its political wing, to join peace talks.

IRONBRIDGE GORGE

• Shropshire (p.494 E2)

The story of Ironbridge Gorge, birthplace of the Industrial Revolution, begins with the humble cooking pot. The ironmaster Abraham Darby I took over an ironworks in Coalbrookdale, near the River Severn in Shropshire, and in 1709 implemented a new method for casting iron pots using coke, a coal by-product, rather than charcoal to smelt the iron ore, thus reducing the dependency on limited timber supplies.

The process proved a great success and Darby's son and grandson carried on the business: Darby iron was used in James WATT's new steam engines, Richard TREVITHICK's steam locomotive, and the world's first iron bridge, which gave the place its name.

The coal mines thrived and Ironbridge soon had other industries, including brick and tile works, and the Coalport Pottery. The historical remains of these industries make up the Ironbridge Gorge Museums, and include Darby's first furnace.

Next to the Coalport China Works Museum is the Hay Inclined Plane, on which boats were hauled 63 m (207 ft) along a sloping railed track to connect the Severn with the Shropshire Canal.

OLD CHINA In 1828 even Coalport milk jugs reflected the romance of industry

BUILT TO LAST Abraham Darby III's iron bridge of 1779 has a span of 30 m (100 ft) and rises 14 m (45 ft) above the River Severn

Henry IRVING

• **Actor and impresario** • 1838-1905; kt 1895

John Henry Brodribb, who took the stage name of Henry Irving, was the first actor to be knighted. From 1878 to 1902, in association with the actress Ellen Terry, he managed London's Lyceum Theatre, where he rekindled popular enthusiasm for Shakespeare with performances as King Lear and an over-age Romeo.

Irving introduced portable scenery and, preferring a dark stage, pioneered the use of subtle stage lighting. The critic Max Beerbohm noted his 'incomparable power for eeriness, for stirring a dim sense of mystery'. George Bernard Shaw disapproved of his cavalier attitude to the text, commenting, 'He does not merely cut plays, he disembowels them.'

ISLE OF MAN

• **Irish Sea (p.497 C6)** • **Area 226 sq miles**
• **Pop. 74 790**

The Isle of Man's 13th-century three-legged coat of arms represents its motto: 'Whichever way you throw me I will stand'. A crown dependency but not part of the United Kingdom, the island is governed by the Court of Tynwald, founded in AD 979 and one of the world's oldest parliaments.

The island's motorcycle race, the TT (Tourist Trophy), is also one of the oldest, held each summer since 1907 on a 37¾ mile circuit. At the harbour town of Laxey is the world's largest waterwheel – 22 m (73 ft) wide – built in 1854.

Early inhabitants of the island built the Meayll stone circle around 2000 BC. Few people today speak Manx, Man's Celtic tongue, but many are drawn to the island by the low taxes that make it an offshore banking haven.

ISLE OF WIGHT

• **English Channel (p.495 F6)**
• **Area 147 sq miles** • **Pop. 125 100**

The Romans, Jutes, Saxons and Danes all crossed the Solent to occupy the Isle of Wight. The capital, Newport, was sacked by the French in the Hundred Years' War and saw Charles I imprisoned at CARISBROOKE CASTLE. The island came to prominence again in the Victorian era when the queen and Prince Albert built

NATURAL BOUNTY Wild daffodils carpet the Scilly Isles, which export more than 1000 tons of commercially grown flowers each spring

OSBORNE HOUSE there in the 1840s. Tourists are the main source of income for the island, filling resorts such as Ryde, Shanklin and Ventnor, while in August the week-long regatta at COWES, home of the Royal Yacht Squadron, attracts sailors from around the world.

Along the coast, deep wooded ravines called chines, once cover for smugglers, cut through the cliffs. At the west tip of the island, the chalk stacks of The Needles thrust like teeth out of the sea near the multicoloured Alum Bay cliffs.

ISLES OF SCILLY

• **SW Cornish coast (p.494 A6)** • **Pop. 2000**

No fools, the islanders introduced a silent 'c' into the name of their home four centuries ago. Aided by a temperate climate, they also replaced traditional vocations such as fishing, smuggling and piracy with tourism and flower growing.

According to legend, the islands, 28 miles from Land's End, are King Arthur's

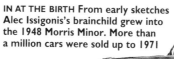

IN AT THE BIRTH From early sketches Alec Issigonis's brainchild grew into the 1948 Morris Minor. More than a million cars were sold up to 1971

lost kingdom of Lyonesse. Only five out of more than 150 – some no bigger than rocks – are inhabited, with most people living on the largest, St Mary's.

The island of TRESCO, ringed by sandy beaches, has a Victorian Gothic castle and the subtropical Abbey Gardens.

Alec ISSIGONIS

• **Car designer** • 1906-88; kt 1969

Two masterpieces of car design owe their existence to Alec Issigonis. Both the Morris Minor and the Mini came from his drawingboard, and both caused a sensation. Not only did they look unlike any other car but they provided much more space within a small frame.

Issigonis was Turkish-born but came to Britain in the 1920s, and studied engineering. In 1936 he joined Morris and 12 years later launched the Minor, with advances such as independent front suspension and rack and pinion steering that improved roadholding.

The Mini first appeared in 1959 and is still in production. It set new standards of comfort in a small car, yet handled better than most sports models, with its front-wheel drive, transverse engine and independent rubber suspension.

Although shy and reserved, Issigonis was fiercely independent, earning the nickname 'Arrogonis'.

Tony JACKLIN

• Golfer • b.1944; CBE 1990

'Maybe I am tougher mentally than most,' Tony Jacklin once said, displaying the un-English lack of humility that helped to restore prestige in British golf and revive the game in Europe.

SWEET VICTORY Tony Jacklin clutches the 1987 Ryder Cup. The USA had never before lost at home

Jacklin honed his golfing skills in the USA, where in 1970 he became the first British player for 50 years to win the US Open. A year earlier he had won the British Open, the first home victor since 1948. By the 1980s his star was waning, but he was made the nonplaying captain of the European Ryder Cup team against the USA. An astute tactician, Jacklin led his team in 1985 to its first cup win in 28 years and retained it two years later.

JACK THE RIPPER

'The Whitechapel murderer', as Jack the Ripper was also called, is Britain's most notorious killer. In the autumn of 1888 he terrorised London's East End, cutting the throats of six women and mutilating their bodies. All but one were prostitutes.

Despite an extensive investigation, the police never found the killer, although many suspects have since been suggested, including the artist Walter Sickert, Queen Victoria's son the duke of Clarence and her physician, William Gull. The attention that the case focused on the poverty and filth of the Whitechapel area led the writer George Bernard Shaw to wryly nominate his own candidate for the Ripper: a social reformer.

JACOBEAN STYLE

At the start of James I's reign in 1603 the profession of architect was not yet established in Britain, and houses were built by surveyors and craftsmen still using medieval techniques.

Jacobean style differed from that of the Elizabethan age only in subtle detail. Classical architectural motifs had infiltrated Britain from Italy, but more as decoration than integral components, adapted as they moved with craftsmen through France, Germany and Flanders.

And yet, classical forms did begin to appear. The red-brick façades of new houses displayed an elegant symmetry, often with corner turrets topped by pointed 's'-shaped domes, as at HATFIELD HOUSE. Hatfield also had the curved 'Dutch' gables that most distinguish Jacobean buildings.

Interiors were exuberant. Flemish craftsmen gave vent to their enthusiasm for intricate and elaborate detail. Every surface was carved and patterned, as in the gallery at Blickling Hall in Norfolk, where the heavily carved oak panelling contrasts in tone only with the ceiling of extravagant plaster-like cake icing.

JACOBITES

When the Roman Catholic JAMES II was declared to have abdicated in 1688 and the crown given to William of Orange, many supporters of the old Stuart regime vowed to restore James or a descendant. Although largely Catholic, the Jacobites, as they called themselves – from Jacobus, Latin for James – also drew support from Protestants who could not accept the new king.

In 1689 James made an attempt to recover the throne, landing in Ireland where he was joined by Jacobite sympathisers. After his forces were defeated at the Battle of the BOYNE, Scotland became the centre for Jacobite resistance, boosted later by opposition to the union with England and to the succession of the Hanoverian George I.

In 1715 the earl of Mar led a doomed rising, joined belatedly by James's son 'the Old Pretender'. The cause was then left to James's grandson, BONNIE PRINCE CHARLIE – 'the Young Pretender' and architect of the FORTY-FIVE REBELLION. He got as far as Derby, but without English support was defeated in 1746 at CULLODEN MOOR, leaving Jacobitism little more than a romantic ideal.

JAMES I

• James VI of Scotland 1567-1625; king of England 1603-25 • 1566-1625

The only son of MARY, Queen of Scots, James became king of Scotland at the age of one after his mother's abdication. He was 37 and the ruler of a settled nation when he inherited the English crown from his cousin, Elizabeth I.

His English subjects at first welcomed the novelty of a royal family with three children and a handsome queen, Anne of Denmark. They were less happy with James's fondness for attractive young men such as the duke of Buckingham, with whom he shared his power as king.

James upheld Protestantism and commissioned the 'Authorised' BIBLE. He tolerated Catholics but angered them by his failure to champion their cause and was the intended target of the 1605 GUNPOWDER PLOT.

The English parliament proved far less obedient to James than had the Scottish, and an increasingly intense debate on the roles of the king, parliament and the judges in deciding taxation and the law

KEEP IT UNDER YOUR HAT Portraits of James I did not reveal his physical handicaps, which included fragile legs racked by arthritis, and a tongue that was too big for his mouth

foreshadowed the conflicts of the CIVIL WAR. James believed in the 'divine right' to rule and imbued his son, the future CHARLES I, with the same conviction.

JAMES II

• King 1685-8   • 1633-1701

The last of the Stuart kings, James II (James VII of Scotland) lacked the charm and judgment of his brother Charles II. Conversion to Roman Catholicism in 1671 cost him his position in the navy, and marriage to Mary of Modena, a formidable and bigoted Catholic, almost lost him the succession.

When James did take the throne he faced a revolt by the duke of Monmouth, the illegitimate son of Charles II. The duke was defeated and executed, and hundreds of his followers were hanged or transported. James then moved to revoke anti-Catholic laws, and prosecuted seven bishops who opposed him. The bishops were acquitted to public acclaim, which further weakened James's position.

When in June 1688 a son was born to James, a number of politicians invited William of Orange, James's Protestant son-in-law, to invade. In the GLORIOUS REVOLUTION that followed, James fled to France and William took the throne. James's one attempt to retrieve the crown ended in defeat at the Battle of the BOYNE in 1690.

JARLSHOF

• Shetland (p.497 D2)   • HS

In the 1890s, a violent storm reshaped the sand dunes of Sumburgh Head, the southernmost tip of Shetland, partially uncovering the remains of settlements dating from Bronze Age houses of the 8th century BC to a 16th-century hall.

Excavations revealed Iron Age remains from about 500 BC and a broch, or stone watchtower, built some 500 years later. From the 3rd to 8th century AD, builders used stones from the broch to construct wheelhouses – circular, turf-roofed dwellings divided by stone piers projecting like wheel spokes around a central hearth. A Viking settlement established in the 9th century was later replaced by a medieval farmstead and in the 16th century a hall was built, which was abandoned by the 17th century.

JAMES BOND

For 50 years the unflappable fictional secret agent Commander James Bond – the '00' of his code name 007 giving him licence to kill – has been an emblem of Britishness the world over. The resourceful, daring and witty superspy who conquers both beautiful women and villains bent on world domination first appeared in the 1953 novel *Casino Royale*, by Ian Fleming (1908-64).

Fleming wrote 12 Bond novels, the locations and espionage plots given authenticity by his experience as a naval intelligence officer and time as a Reuters correspondent in central Europe. Tens of millions of Bond books have been sold, some written by authors other than Fleming, including Kingsley Amis.

LICENSED TO THRILL

The Bond films began in 1962 with *Dr No*. This introduced Sean Connery, a relatively unknown 32-year-old Scottish actor, as a suave but rugged and ruthless Bond, enjoying acerbic encounters with his boss, M, unconsummated flirtations with M's secretary, Miss Moneypenny, and the deployment of fantastic and lethal gadgets invented by the boffin, Q.

Connery was replaced by George Lazenby for *On Her Majesty's Secret Service* (1969), the only film in which Bond marries. Roger Moore played a laconic Bond in seven films, and two more actors, Timothy Dalton and Pierce Brosnan, have followed in the role.

WORDS AND PICTURES The cover for the first Bond novel (*right*) hints at his amorous nature. Less subtle is the fleshy poster for the film *You Only Live Twice* (1967)

The film formula includes explosions, chases involving cars, boats or stranger vehicles, and 'Bond girls' such as Pussy Galore (Honor Blackman) in *Goldfinger* (1964) and Solitaire (Jane Seymour) in *Live and Let Die* (1973). The films are still popular but the Britishness has been diluted: Bond is as likely to drive a BMW as a home-made Aston Martin.

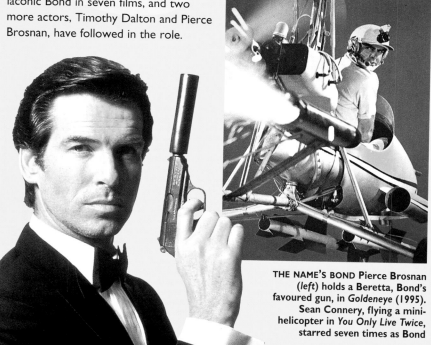

THE NAME'S BOND Pierce Brosnan (*left*) holds a Beretta, Bond's favoured gun, in *Goldeneye* (1995). Sean Connery, flying a mini-helicopter in *You Only Live Twice*, starred seven times as Bond

JARROW MARCH

Only 200 men marched from Jarrow, near Newcastle, to London in October 1936, but they made more impact than other, larger hunger marches during the DEPRESSION. The public imagination was caught by the plight of a once-thriving community of steel and ship workers enduring an unemployment rate of more than 80 per cent. Jarrow became known as 'the town that was murdered'.

The 300 mile march, taken in stages of 15-20 miles each day, was well planned. The marchers and the public knew the route in advance, food and shelter were provided at the end of each day, and stewards prevented begging, drunkenness or other bad behaviour.

The arrival of the march in London was an anticlimax. A petition of 12 000 signatures was presented to parliament, then the men returned to Jarrow by train. The march did little to relieve unemployment but became a symbol of the suffering that the Depression caused.

JAZZ

Jazz began in the USA but it became Britain's most popular music for much of the 20th century, its infectious rhythms making dancing a popular pastime and a liberating way of courtship.

American soldiers brought jazz to Britain during the First World War. After the visit of the Original Dixieland Jazz Band to London in 1919, home-grown bands such as the Savoy Orpheans swung to dances like the Charleston and Black Bottom through the 1920s.

In the 1930s British bandleaders such as Ted Heath and Ray Noble emulated the big brass sound of American 'swing', and in the Second World War GIs introduced the athletic jive and jitterbug dances. At the same time American musicians had developed bebop – improvised jazz with complex rhythms. In Britain this was embraced only in the bars of London's Soho, where the two fathers of modern British jazz, saxophonists Ronnie Scott and John Dankworth, played in the decade after the war. In 1959 Scott opened his jazz club, RONNIE SCOTT'S.

Jazz, ousted by ROCK AND POP as Britain's dance music, became the preserve of enthusiasts. Some kept faith with the New Orleans style of 'trad jazz', or took to the 'mainstream' jazz of bandleaders such as Humphrey Lyttelton and Chris Barber. In the 1990s, a new genre – 'crossover' – combined jazz with classical music and pop.

JEDBURGH ABBEY

- Borders (p.497 D5) • Built c.1120-1220

The magnificence of the red sandstone ruins of Jedburgh Abbey attest both to its medieval spiritual importance and to its vulnerable position close to the border with England.

David I founded the abbey in 1118, and the nave was completed in 1200. The abbey was burnt by the English in 1523, sacked 20 years later and finally ruined during the reformation of the Scottish Church in 1559. Jedburgh's 12th-century castle endured so many attacks that it was pulled down in 1409.

Gertrude JEKYLL

- **Garden designer and writer**
- **1843-1932**

Failing eyesight in middle age diverted Gertrude Jekyll from a career as a painter to designing and writing about gardens. She produced 13 books on horticulture and helped to plan some 350 gardens, applying her painter's eye for composition and colour to the seemingly informal grouping of flowers that emulated the charm of cottage gardens. 'I try to paint living pictures with living flowers,' she said.

GREEN FINGERS Gertrude Jekyll tends her garden in a cartoon drawn by Edwin Lutyens around 1896

A HAPPY PARTNERSHIP

Jekyll's most celebrated work was carried out in a long collaboration with the architect Edwin LUTYENS, including the walled garden of the remodelled LINDISFARNE Castle in Northumberland. The two planned houses and gardens as a single entity, red-brick walls and grey roofs being softened and complemented by close-set splashes of colour in courtyards, beside steps and along hedged pathways.

The architecture and crafts of Jekyll's native Surrey were reflected in her designs of features such as pergolas, summerhouses and wells. Hatchlands (NT), East Clandon, and Goddards, near Dorking, all have Jekyll gardens, and the garden at her Lutyens-built Surrey home of Munstead Wood has been restored.

War of JENKINS' EAR

- **1739-40**

This was a small, contrived war. Spain, which had colonised much of the Caribbean, suspected British ships of

CAPED CRUSADER Ellen Wilkinson was the Labour MP for Jarrow and the voice of its marchers. As education minister, she introduced free school milk in 1945

illegally trading in its waters, and Spanish coastguards regularly searched them. In 1738 Captain Robert Jenkins protested to parliament, displaying what he said was his severed ear, cut off by a Spanish cutlass.

George II's chief minister, Robert WALPOLE, was opposed to action against Spain, but, with public feeling running high, war was declared. The capture of Portobello, Panama, in 1739 was a rare British success. The war merged into the War of the Austrian Succession, with Spain, Britain and France sucked into a conflict between Prussia and Austria that lasted until 1748.

OUT OF THIS WORLD The 76 m (250 ft) wide Jodrell Bank telescope, now named the Lovell Telescope, still maps radio sources in the sky

Even the USSR, realising the importance of independent corroboration, arranged in 1959 for confirmation of the arrival of *Luna 2* at the Moon to come from Jodrell Bank, not Moscow.

Edward JENNER

• **Doctor and immunologist** • **1749-1823**
A smallpox epidemic in the 1780s in his Gloucestershire practice started Edward Jenner on the path to developing the process of immunisation. The highly infectious disease was often fatal, and at best left patients permanently scarred; but country lore held that milkmaids who had caught the less virulent cowpox from their cows were immune.

In 1796 Jenner tested the theory by scratching some cowpox fluid into the arm of an eight-year-old boy, and later inoculating him with smallpox. The child developed cowpox but resisted smallpox. Jenner named his process 'vaccination', after the Latin *vaccinus*, meaning 'from cows'. His discovery was accepted only after a year of fierce opposition.

Jerome K. JEROME

• **Writer** • **1859-1927**
'I have a kink in my brain, I suppose. I can't help it.' That kink won Jerome Klapka Jerome fame as a humorist, especially for the whimsically hilarious *Three Men In A Boat* (1889), an account of three men and a dog called Montmorency on a boat trip up the Thames from Kingston to Oxford.

Jerome was born in Walsall but brought up in east London. He worked as an actor, teacher and journalist, and although hailed as one of the most amusing novelists of the time, he

considered himself foremost a playwright, an area in which he proved unmemorable. His humour hid a serious, compassionate nature. Jerome served as a volunteer ambulanceman with the French army in the First World War and, during the 1920s, took an early and unfashionable stance against racism.

JODRELL BANK

• **Cheshire (p.494 EI)**
The determination of one man – Bernard LOVELL – led to the building of the world's first giant radio telescope at Jodrell Bank, south of Manchester, now the site of the Nuffield Radio Astronomy Laboratories. Lovell lectured on physics at Manchester University in the 1930s, then spent the Second World War working on airborne radar for blind-bombing and anti-submarine warfare. After the war, he agitated for the building of a huge telescope to start research into radio sources in the sky.

He finally got the go-ahead in 1951, but the project ran well over budget. Lovell was saved by the launch of the Soviet satellite *Sputnik 1* in 1957, which the new telescope tracked as it orbited Earth. Suddenly Lovell was a visionary, not a spendthrift.

INWARD GAZE Gwen John painted this haunting self-portrait two years before she moved to Paris in 1904 to be close to Auguste Rodin

Gwen and Augustus JOHN

• **Artists** • **Gwen 1876-1939**
• **Augustus 1878-1961**
Britain's greatest sibling artists could not have been more different in either their personalities or work. Gwen spent most of her life in France, becoming the mistress of the sculptor Auguste Rodin, a relationship that led to her near-breakdown. In 1913 she converted to Catholicism. Her delicate portraits and quiet interior scenes reveal the influence of her teacher, James McNeil WHISTLER, and reflect the reclusiveness of her life.

Augustus, flamboyant, bohemian and handsome, painted exuberant pictures of gypsies or landscapes of his native Wales that displayed superb draughtsmanship and French post-impressionist influences. Some of his boldest and most colourful works were portraits of renowned figures, such as the poet Dylan Thomas and the soldier T.E. Lawrence.

MAIN COLLECTIONS • **National Gallery of Wales, Cardiff** • **Tate Gallery, London**

Barry JOHN

• Rugby player • b.1945

During the victorious 1971 British Lions rugby tour of New Zealand, a player expressed surprise when Barry John used the door to leave a room rather than vanishing through the wall, so often did the Welshman ghost through tackles from men twice his size.

'The King' to his teammates, John was the most dazzling talent to emerge from the Welsh fly-half 'factory' of the 1960s and 70s. He was a deceptive, gliding runner whose kicking – whether for position or goal – made him the master of his position. With scrum half Gareth EDWARDS, his partner in all but two of his 25 games for Wales, John formed the most respected of all British half-back pairings. John scored a huge 180 points on the 1971 Lions tour but, uneasy with adulation, he retired at 27.

Elton JOHN

• Pop singer and songwriter • b.1947; kt 1997

Of all pop stars, Elton John was expected to have the least staying power. Born Reg Dwight, he was overweight, wore glasses and went prematurely bald. Yet by the early 1970s he was the world's most successful solo pop artist, at one point having four albums in the US top ten, the first artist since the Beatles to do so.

On stage he played to audiences in excess of 100 000, wearing outrageous clothes and bizarre spectacles. After drug and alcohol problems in the 1980s, John bounced back in 1995 to win an Oscar for his songwriting on the Disney film *The Lion King*. Two years later he adapted his 1974 release 'Candle in the Wind' – a tribute to the actress Marilyn Monroe – for the funeral of Princess Diana. The record quickly sold more than 33 million copies and became the world's biggest-selling single, adding to his British tally of 24 top ten singles.

King JOHN

• King 1199-1216 • 1167-1216

Few kings have a worse reputation than John, although this is not entirely justified. Cruel and disloyal, he was also hard-working, judicious and a crafty diplomat. The youngest and favourite son of HENRY II, John was sent to oversee Ireland in 1185 but his autocratic behaviour alienated natives and settlers alike. Later he joined his brother, the future RICHARD I, in a rebellion that hastened the king's death.

A compulsive plotter, John intrigued with Philip II of France against Richard, and in 1203 had Arthur of Brittany, his nephew and pretender to the crown, killed. The French, supporters of Arthur, seized most of John's empire in France.

His obsession with French territory meant resources were squeezed from the English nobility, whom John regarded with suspicion. The pope also joined the list of John's enemies, excommunicating him in 1209 for blocking the papal choice of archbishop of Canterbury. Philip of France was ordered by the pope

GLAM ROCKER The flamboyant pop star Elton John turned up to his 50th birthday party in a dazzling 18th-century fop's ensemble, topped by a silver galleon, reputedly costing £50 000

to depose John, who hung onto the throne by bowing to papal authority. Another failed war in France pushed many English nobles into rebellion, and in 1215 they forced John to seal the MAGNA CARTA. With papal backing, John ignored the nobles, who in 1216 invited the French dauphin to invade. John died soon after, possibly poisoned.

JOHN OF GAUNT

• Son of Edward III • 1340-99

*This royal throne of kings, this sceptred isl
This earth of majesty, this seat of Mars,
This other Eden, demi-paradise,
This fortress built by Nature for herself
Against infection and the hand of war,
This happy breed of men, this little world,
This precious stone set in the silver sea...*

The resounding words of John of Gaunt from William Shakespeare's *Richard II* have sealed his place as an English hero. The power-broking prince, younger brother of EDWARD THE BLACK PRINCE and the begetter of two royal dynasties, rarely used the name Gaunt, taken from his birthplace, Ghent, in Holland. He was known instead as Duke of Lancaster, a title inherited from the father of his first wife, Blanche of Lancaster.

When his father, EDWARD III, died, John became virtual ruler of England, acting as protector for his ten-year-old nephew, RICHARD II. After John's death, and the deposing of Richard II by parliament, his son became HENRY IV, the first king of the House of LANCASTER. Another dynasty, the TUDORS, descended through John's eldest son by his marriage to his mistress, Katharine Swynford.

JOHN O' GROATS

• Highland (p.497 D1)

The windswept village of John o' Groats is not, as is often thought, the most northerly point of the British mainland. Nearby Dunnet Head reaches more than 2 miles farther north into the Pentland Firth. This has never bothered long-distance walkers arriving from Land's End in Cornwall, 876 road-miles away.

The village is named after Jan de Groot, a Dutchman who lived here as a farmer and a ferryman 500 years ago.

HIGH FLYER Amy Johnson prepares to board her plane in 1932 before making a record solo flight to Cape Town and back in 4 days, 6 hours and 56 minutes

Amy JOHNSON

• Aviator • 1903-41

When Amy Johnson flew single-handed to Australia in 1930, the first woman to do so, she had never before left England. She was born in Hull, where her father was a fish merchant. After university she worked as a secretary in London and joined the London Aeroplane Club, receiving her pilot's licence in 1929 and becoming the first woman to be granted a ground engineer's licence.

On May 5, 1930, Johnson set off from England in her tiny Gipsy Moth aircraft, *Jason*, and six days later arrived in Karachi. She reached Port Darwin on May 24 and flew on to Brisbane, where a poor landing wrecked the plane. Johnson returned home a national heroine, and £10 000 the richer, thanks to a prize from the *Daily Mail* newspaper.

At the outbreak of the Second World War, Johnson joined the Air Transport Auxiliary, but lost her life when she bailed out over the Thames estuary during a delivery flight.

Samuel JOHNSON

• Writer, lexicographer and critic • 1709-84

'A woman's preaching is like a dog's walking on his hinder legs. It is not done well; but you are surprised to find it done at all.' Samuel Johnson, known mostly as Dr Johnson, is remembered best for the

scornful wit and worldly wisdom recorded by his biographer and friend James BOSWELL.

Johnson was born in Lichfield, the son of a bookseller, and moved to London in 1737 with his wife – 20 years his senior – and a former pupil, the actor David GARRICK. He scraped a living writing parliamentary reports, poems and reviews and in 1747 began his English dictionary, published nine years later and the forerunner of all English dictionaries. He continued to struggle financially, writing his moral tale *Rasselas* in one week in 1759 to pay for his mother's funeral.

A pension of £300 a year granted in 1762 ended Johnson's financial worries. He became the centre of a social circle of which the artist Joshua Reynolds and playwright Oliver Goldsmith were members, and turned to literary criticism, including *The Lives of the Poets* (1779-81) and an edition of Shakespeare.

Inigo JONES

• Architect and designer • 1573-1652

Only a handful of Inigo Jones's buildings survive, but he ranks alongside Christopher Wren and Robert Adam as one of the greatest British architects. He embraced and imported the neoclassical Roman style, which later dominated British architecture for two centuries.

HUMBLE BEGINNINGS

Little is known of Jones's early life beyond his birth in London, the son of a Smithfield clothworker, and his two journeys to Italy. After the first, he was employed by James I as a costume and stage designer for the masques of playwright Ben JONSON. On the second trip he was inspired by the 16th-century architect Andrea Palladio's revival of the styles of ancient Rome. Back in Britain, Jones became surveyor of the king's works and a disciple of PALLADIAN STYLE.

ROYAL PATRONAGE

The series of buildings that Jones designed for Charles I from 1616 broke with the prevailing JACOBEAN STYLE. The Queen's House at Greenwich was the first British classical building, with a geometric symmetry, colonnaded loggia (open gallery) and roofline balustrade.

This was followed in 1619-22 by the Banqueting House at Whitehall, Jones's finest surviving work. With the onset of the Civil War in 1642, Jones's career suffered a decline but he later worked for the Parliamentarian Lord Pembroke.

WORK OF TWO GENIUSES The ceiling of Inigo Jones's Banqueting House was painted for Charles I by Rubens. It was a magnificent addition to the medieval Whitehall Palace

Ben JONSON

• Dramatist and poet • 1572-1637

At the Mermaid Tavern near Blackfriars in London Ben Jonson held court, a huge man with a fearless wit. Among his literary disciples, the 'Sons of Ben', was William Shakespeare, who acted in Jonson's first great success, *Every Man in his Humour* (1598), a satire on the various forms of human folly represented by different 'humours'.

In 1605 Jonson started writing for the court of James I, producing MASQUES with elaborate scenery and costumes designed by the architect Inigo JONES. His lyric poetry includes 'Drink to me only with thine eyes'.

Jonson's masterpieces are his mature comedies *Volpone* (1606), *The Alchemist* (1610) and *Bartholomew Fair* (1614), bitingly satirical plays in which vices such as greed and lust are held up to merciless scrutiny, and human nature is found wanting. The plots – tightly woven webs of intrigue and deceit – lead to the downfall of the villains with a compelling relentlessness.

James Prescott JOULE

• Physicist • 1818-89

What sort of man would take a thermometer on honeymoon to measure the temperature of the water at the top and bottom of a waterfall? James Prescott Joule – a man obsessed with precise measurement – did just this, hoping to show exactly how the energy of falling water was converted into heat.

The wealth of Joule's brewing family financed his scientific experiments. His discovery of the mechanical equivalent of heat proved fundamental to the science of thermodynamics, which relates heat to other forms of energy, and to the design of engines.

Joule never held an academic post, and at first found himself ignored and denied publication. But in 1847 William Thomson, later Lord KELVIN, recognised his exceptional skill as an experimental scientist and enlisted him as an assistant. They jointly discovered the cooling effect of the expansion of a gas, a principle now applied in refrigerator design. In honour of his work, Joule's name was given to the international unit of energy.

JUDGES

> The customs governing legal dress were set down in the Judges' Rules of 1635. Wigs were assumed in the 1680s. Judges are addressed according to their position in the judicial hierarchy:
>
> • **Appeal Court and High Court judge:**
> My Lord/Lady or Your Lordship/Ladyship
>
> • **Circuit and district judge:**
> Your Honour
>
> • **Magistrate:** Your Worship

In England, judges were first appointed by William the Conqueror in the late 11th century. Magistrates, usually unpaid lay people also known as justices of the peace or JPs, were created by 1388 to replace judges in trying less serious offences.

The head of the judiciary, the LORD CHANCELLOR, recommends judges for appointment, choosing them from the ranks of practising lawyers. The hierarchy of judges follows the same pattern as that of the LAW COURTS. At the most senior level they are mainly former barristers; the junior end of the judiciary has more solicitors.

COLOUR-CODED Black robes with lilac facings are the ceremonial dress of circuit judges. In court, they wear blue bands for criminal cases

The profession has been a traditional bastion of the Establishment – 88 per cent of judges studied at Cambridge or Oxford universities. The first female judge was appointed in 1962, and women remain a minority. In 1999, there were seven women High Court judges, compared with 92 men, and of 561 circuit judges only 36 were women.

JULIAN OF NORWICH

• Mystic author • c.1342-c.1413

On May 8, 1373, a young woman of 30 lay perilously ill receiving the last rites. As the priest left, he set a crucifix before her and told her to draw comfort from Jesus. She did not die, but the next day had mystical visions, and when she recovered took up residence as a hermit in the church of St Julian in Norwich.

Many years later Dame or Mother Julian, as she became known, described her visions in the book *The Revelations of Divine Love*. It offered assurances of divine love, and that 'all shall be well and all manner of things shall be well' – unusual at a time when plague and Church rifts led clergy to stress God's more wrathful and awesome qualities.

Julian's outlook and her references to God's 'motherhood' have made the *Revelations* – the first book written in English by a woman – popular with many modern spiritual thinkers.

JURY SYSTEM

Is it a bulwark against oppression, or an outdated and expensive method of trial, overdue for reform? Either way, trial by one's peers for serious offences has been a part of the criminal justice system since Norman times.

Today, a jury consists of men and women between 18 and 70, chosen at random from the electoral roll. In England, 12 jury members decide upon a verdict of 'guilty' or 'not guilty'. Ideally, the decision should be unanimous, but a majority verdict of 10 to 2 may be acceptable. In Scotland, 15 jurors decide the verdict by simple majority, and have a third option, 'not proven', which has the same practical effect as an acquittal – the accused is free and cannot be tried again for the same crime – but leaves a lingering doubt about innocence.

John KEATS

• Poet • 1795-1821

In the few productive years before tuberculosis claimed his life at the age of 26, John Keats wrote some of the finest poems of the ROMANTIC era. His genius lay in a sensuous style and a purity of language worthy of comparison with William Shakespeare.

Keats's creative powers peaked in 1819 – a year marked also by a series of sad events in his life, including the death of his brother and an unhappy love affair with Fanny Brawne, his neighbour. When health permitted, Keats worked incessantly, producing in the space of two months his third and final volume of verse, containing the odes 'To Autumn', 'To a Nightingale', 'On a Grecian Urn' and 'On Melancholy'.

In 1820 Keats moved to Rome, where he died and is buried. His house and that of Fanny Brawne in Well Walk, north London, are now joined as a museum.

KEDLESTON HALL

• Derbyshire (p.495 F2) • Built 1759-65 • NT

As a showcase of the work of the Scottish architect and designer Robert ADAM, Kedleston Hall has few equals. Fresh from his Grand Tour of Europe, Adam was called in by Nathaniel Curzon, 1st baron Scarsdale, in 1760, to continue the work begun by the architect James Paine on remodelling his family home.

Adam designed a south front based on the triumphal Arch of Constantine in Rome; inside the house, he poured his creativity into a series of state rooms, including a Great Hall with Corinthian columns supporting a coved ceiling.

Objects collected by the 1st marquis Curzon while viceroy of India from 1899 to 1905 are housed in Kedleston's Eastern Museum, and an exhibition displays architectural drawings by Adam.

Walter KEELER

• Potter • b.1942

The inventive work of Walter Keeler has been at the forefront of a resurgence of interest in domestic tableware. He trained at the Harrow School of Art to which he returned to teach a studio pottery course, experimenting with kilns and firing techniques.

Keeler's salt-glaze stoneware is inspired by the work of 17th-century English potters. He is also fascinated by the clean lines of traditional tin vessels such as oil and watering cans, the forms of which he has translated into practical clay pots of sophisticated modernity. He still teaches and is now professor of ceramics at the University of the West of England in Bristol.

KELMSCOTT MANOR

• Oxfordshire (p.495 F4) • Built 16th century

It was the garden at Kelmscott that first won the heart of the Victorian designer and craftsman, William MORRIS. He rented the Cotswold Tudor house as a country retreat from 1871 until his death

NOT WHAT MEETS THE EYE The potter Walter Keeler translates the simple lines, gleaming surfaces and pronounced joins of a watering can into an unusual teapot

GARDENS AND GABLES William Morris used his woodcut of Kelmscott Manor as an illustration in his utopian fantasy, *News from Nowhere*

in 1896, and it has altered little since his time. The house is decorated in the ARTS AND CRAFTS style. Its grandest piece of furniture is Morris's four-poster bed, with hangings designed and stitched at the family embroidery workshop run by his daughter, May.

Morris and his wife, Jane, shared Kelmscott with the painter and poet Dante Gabriel Rossetti for a time. Jane bought the house after Morris's death, and built a group of cottages nearby in 1902 as a memorial to him. Morris is buried in the village churchyard.

The house and its contents are now owned by the Society of Antiquaries, which has re-created the garden as Morris first saw it.

KELSO ABBEY

• Borders (p.497 D5) • Founded 1128 • HS

An imposing west porch and a few fragmentary ruins are all that remain of what was once the greatest abbey in the Scottish Borders.

The Scottish king David I founded the Benedictine abbey, when the area was known as 'Calkou' (chalk hill). It enjoyed four centuries of wealth and influence, but eventually paid a heavy price for its proximity to England. After the Scottish defeat at the Battle of FLODDEN in 1513, the monastery was raided three times by the English. In the last attack, led by the earl of Hertford in 1545, 100 monks and lay brothers were mercilessly butchered and the buildings razed.

Lord KELVIN

- Mathematician and physicist
- 1824-1907; kt 1866; bn 1892

Though no single discovery can be solely attributed to William Thomson – later Lord Kelvin – he was the outstanding physicist of his day.

Kelvin entered Glasgow University at the age of ten and Cambridge at 16 where, to his dismay, he came only second in his finals, despite one examiner remarking to another, 'you and I are just about fit to mend his pens'. By the age of 22 he was professor of natural philosophy at Glasgow.

Kelvin went on to research a huge range of topics, from thermodynamics to electricity and magnetism. He also constructed the absolute scale of temperature now used by scientists and calibrated, in his honour, in degrees Kelvin. His work on the first transatlantic cable in 1857-8, in which he went against conventional thinking by predicting that a fast rate of signalling could only be achieved by using very small currents, earned him a knighthood.

John KENDREW

- Molecular biologist   • b.1917; kt 1974

The science of molecular biology developed largely in Britain after the Second World War. One of its chief pioneers was John Kendrew, who with the Austrian-born biochemist Max Perutz founded the Unit for Molecular Biology at Cambridge University in 1946.

Kendrew had returned to science after a wartime job at the Ministry of Aircraft Production. With Perutz, he studied the structure of proteins in the body using X-ray diffraction, and discovered the structure of myoglobin, responsible for transporting oxygen in the muscles. Kendrew and Perutz shared the Nobel prize for chemistry in 1962.

KENILWORTH CASTLE

- Warwickshire (p.495 F3)
- Built 12th-16th century   • EH

In 1575, Elizabeth I visited Kenilworth, the home of her favourite, Robert Dudley, earl of Leicester. The 19 days of pageantry that welcomed her included plays, fireworks and acrobatics. The

PLAIN SAILING Londoners in 1959 gather at the Round Pond of Kensington Gardens, created in 1728 when the gardens were the private grounds of Kensington Palace, still a royal residence

castle was enjoying its heyday as one of the grandest fortified palaces in Britain.

Geoffrey de Clinton, treasurer to Henry I, founded Kenilworth in about 1120, making it strong enough to withstand a six-month siege during the BARONS' WAR of 1263-6. In the 1390s the duke of Lancaster, JOHN OF GAUNT, converted it, adding a banqueting hall and living quarters. The keep was badly damaged in the Civil War, and the castle has been unoccupied for 350 years. The extensive red sandstone ruins include remains of the 14th-century Great Hall. The castle was the setting for Walter Scott's novel *Kenilworth*.

KENSINGTON PALACE AND GARDENS

- Central London (p.499 A3)
- Palace built c.1605, remodelled 1689-96

William III found that the traditional Whitehall residence of the Tudor and Stuart monarchs made his asthma worse. In 1689, he and Queen Mary sought alternative accommodation – the earl of Nottingham's Kensington house, which they bought for £14 000.

Christopher WREN made alterations, and successive monarchs updated the decoration. Queen Caroline, wife of

George II, extended the grounds of the palace and the adjoining HYDE PARK. Her Serpentine lake (1727), called the Long Water, inside Kensington Gardens, unites the two. The public was admitted from 1841, and within its 110 ha (274 acres) lie some of London's most familiar sights, such as the ALBERT MEMORIAL and George Frampton's statue of Peter Pan.

When George III moved to the newly acquired Buckingham House in 1762, royal relatives took rooms at the Kensington property. Queen VICTORIA was born at the palace. It is still a secondary royal residence, and was the home of DIANA, Princess of Wales.

KENWOOD

- Hampstead Heath, N London (p.498 C2)
- Remodelled 1764-99   • EH

The brewing magnate Edward Guinness saved Kenwood from demolition in 1920. On his death in 1927, he left the house to the nation with his collection of paintings by artists such as Rembrandt, Vermeer and J.M.W. Turner.

The original late 17th-century brick house which stood on the site was remodelled by Robert ADAM into a majestic villa with a neoclassical façade for the Lord Chief Justice, Lord Mansfield. Inside, a succession of light-filled rooms include Adam's magnificent library in pink, blue and gold. Gilt mirrors reflect the surrounding parkland, sloping down to a lake and a shell-shaped concert bowl used for waterside concerts in summer.

John Maynard KEYNES

• **Economist** • 1883-1946; bn 1942

In 1936, in the depths of the DEPRESSION that affected Britain for most of the 1930s, John Maynard Keynes suggested that employment and growth could be created by the government offsetting the depths of the economic cycle through investment in public works. His ideas, which he presented in his book *The General Theory of Employment, Interest and Money*, established Keynes as the most influential economist of the 20th century.

Until then, governments had seen the economy as a self-regulating mechanism, which they could do little to manipulate.

But the Second World War compelled them to invest in the armed forces – and the Depression seemed to end.

During the war, Keynes served as economic adviser to the chancellor, helping to plan the postwar international financial system. In 1944 he played a leading part in the establishment of the International Monetary Fund.

Postwar Western governments applied Keynesian policies, with apparent success. But by the 1970s they seemed powerless against inflation caused by simultaneous wage and price rises, and experiments began with monetary policies designed to control inflation.

Captain KIDD

• **Pirate** • c.1655-1701

Terror of the seas or political scapegoat? The story of Captain Kidd is a mysterious one. Born in Scotland, he emigrated to America where he was a merchant

skipper in New York. In 1695 he was given a royal commission to operate as a privateer against pirates in the Red Sea.

Among the vessels captured and looted by Kidd were two merchant ships, and on his return to America in 1699 he was charged with piracy and murder. At his trial in England, Kidd claimed in his defence that his orders had specifically permitted attacks on French shipping, and that his victims had both been carrying French papers. But the papers were not produced at the trial, and Kidd was convicted and hanged.

Around 1910 a historian found two documents in the Admiralty records: the French papers that could have saved Kidd's life. Kidd may well have enriched himself through piracy, but he had been financed by a consortium – including Cabinet ministers – which shared in his profits. The discovery of the papers suggested that he was sacrificed to avoid a scandal.

KEW GARDENS

• **SW London (p.498 B4)** • **Est. 1759**

In 1759 the Prince and Princess of Wales began planting a 3.6 ha (9 acre) BOTANIC GARDEN at their estate beside the Thames at Kew. After George III inherited the gardens in 1772 and added them to his neighbouring estate at Richmond, the botanist Joseph BANKS, an early director, sent collectors all over the world in search of plants of economic, scientific and horticultural interest.

The gardens were handed to the nation in 1840, and opened to the public the following year as the Royal Botanic Gardens. By 1904, further royal gifts of

land increased Kew to its present size of 120 ha (300 acres). The gardens now contain the largest, most eclectic collection of plants in the world, with some 40 000 species descended from seeds culled from as far afield as the Congo, Antarctica and Himalayas.

Botanists from all over the world come to Kew to examine rare specimens and consult its collections, which include 6 million dried plants and fungi and a library of more than 120 000 books. Research in Kew's laboratory and herbarium investigates the potential of plants as medicine, food and fuel. But to the public Kew is also, more simply, a beautiful place, with a springtime carpet

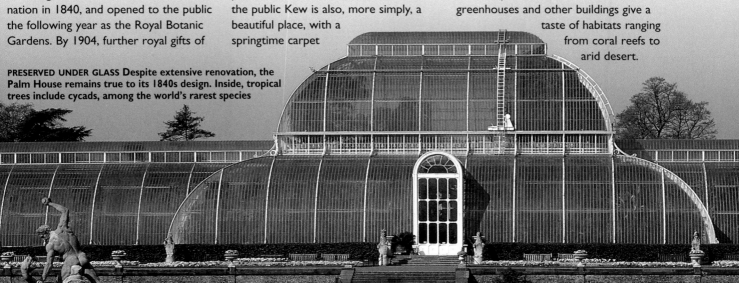

HOME FROM HOME A 2 m (6 ft) elephant's ear thrives in the 'wet tropics' section of the **Princess of Wales Conservatory**

of more than a million crocuses, bluebell glades, a rhododendron dell designed by 'Capability' BROWN and specialist areas for plants such as bamboos and heaths. Artificially maintained climates in greenhouses and other buildings give a taste of habitats ranging from coral reefs to arid desert.

PRESERVED UNDER GLASS Despite extensive renovation, the Palm House remains true to its 1840s design. Inside, tropical trees include cycads, among the world's rarest species

KING'S CROSS STATION

• **Central London (p.499 D1)** • **Built 1851-2**
Britain's largest railway station and London's main point of departure to the north was built to designs by the architect Lewis Cubitt that were both grand and functional. Two enormous arched train sheds – one for arrivals, one for departures – were fused along their 240 m (800 ft) length. At the southern end, the sheds were fronted by a brick façade with a central Italianate clock tower; at the northern end, tracks led the way to Newcastle, Edinburgh and Aberdeen.

POSTER OF THE 1930s FOR KING'S CROSS STATION

An average of 189 000 people now use the station each day, and there are plans for an extensive redevelopment of the whole King's Cross area, including the neighbouring ST PANCRAS station.

KING'S LYNN

• **Norfolk (p.495 H2)** • **Pop. 41 280**
The poet John Betjeman described the walk along the streets of King's Lynn, with their mixture of medieval, Elizabethan and Georgian buildings, as one of Europe's finest architectural experiences. The town, tucked away beside the Great Ouse river, can look back on centuries of maritime prosperity, though silting long ago took away its easy access to the sea. A stone compass set into the quay is inscribed with the names of famous locally born sailors – among them Lord Nelson.

The town (known to the locals simply as 'Lynn') was called Bishop's Lynn until Henry VIII renamed it when he began the Dissolution of the Monasteries in 1536.

Lynn's medieval wealth is reflected in its two 15th-century guildhalls, Holy Trinity, built in a chequerboard of dark and pale stone, and the huge St George,

the most complete merchants' guildhall in England. Its upper floor was once a theatre – a tradition carried on each July, when King's Lynn holds a week-long festival of music and drama.

KINGSTON LACY

• **Dorset (p.494 E6)**
• **Built 17th century, remodelled 1835-41** • **NT**
William John Bankes, who inherited Kingston Lacy in 1834, gave the building much of its character. Bankes spent his youth travelling and collecting treasures. While abroad, he met the architect Charles Barry, who transformed the 17th-century Dorset home into an Italianate palace clad in grey-green Chilmark stone. It was a fitting home for Bankes's Egyptian relics and paintings, including works by Titian and Rubens.

Bankes fled to Italy in 1841 to escape prosecution for homosexuality, but he continued to commission carvings and to send treasures home. Visible from the balustraded terrace is a granite obelisk from Philae on the Nile, which took Bankes 24 years to transport to Britain.

Rudyard KIPLING

• **Writer** • **1865-1936**
In short stories, novels and poems Rudyard Kipling more than any other author captured the spirit of British India. Every level of RAJ society finds a place in his work, from English soldiers and civil servants to Indian royalty, tradesmen, mystics and beggars. Native animals inspired the two *Jungle Books* (1894 and 1895) and the *Just So Stories* (1902).

Kipling hated high-flown literary pretension and chose instead to write in the language of ordinary people. In his *Barrack-Room Ballads* of 1892 he combined a strong sense of rhythm with a sharp ear for dialect:

> *Elephants a-pilin' teak*
> *In the sludgy, squdgy creek,*
> *Where the silence 'ung so 'eavy you*
> *   was 'arf afraid to speak!*
> *On the road to Mandalay...*
>
> ('Mandalay')

Kipling was hugely popular in his day and in 1907 he became the first English-language poet to win the Nobel prize for literature. When the Empire faded he fell out of favour but his reputation has been rising since the 1980s. His poem 'If' was voted the nation's favourite in 1997.

Lord KITCHENER

• **Soldier and statesman** • **1850-1916; kt 1894; bn 1898; visc. 1902; earl 1914**
The First World War army recruiting poster, 'Your Country Needs YOU', made Horatio Herbert Kitchener the best-known face in British military history. Kitchener joined the

MERCHANT MARINE King's Lynn's splendid Custom House and Exchange of 1683 reflects the town's days of mercantile eminence

army in 1870 and served in the Middle East, Africa and India, earning admiration for his victory at Omdurman – which secured the Sudan for the British Empire – and for rebuffing French ambitions on the Upper Nile in 1898.

As commander-in-chief in the second BOER WAR, his strategy of destroying farms and interning women and children in concentration camps brought the Boers to their knees, but lost him popular support at home.

He redeemed himself as secretary of state for war in 1914. Almost alone in predicting that the war would last for years, he recruited some 3 million men. He died before the war ended, on board a ship that struck a mine off the Orkney Islands.

KITEMARK

The kite-shaped emblem (*right*) of the British Standards Institution (BSI) is an official mark of approval for manufactured goods. The BSI was founded in 1901, the world's first national standards body. Tram rails were the first to carry the Kitemark the following year. The mark is now given to some 500 categories of products, from toasters, kettles and children's car seats to radiator valves, bricks and manhole covers.

KNEBWORTH HOUSE

- **Hertfordshire (p.495 G4)**
- **Built 15th-19th century**

In 1843 the Victorian novelist Edward Bulwer-Lytton gave a romantic face-lift to the exterior of his family's Tudor house. New turrets, domes and battlements encrusted with gargoyles turned Knebworth into a Gothic palace.

Robert Lytton founded the family's fortune fighting for Henry VII during the Wars of the Roses in 1485. Inside the house are 17th and 18th-century paintings and furniture, and relics and manuscripts of Bulwer-Lytton. A British Raj exhibition celebrates the service of a previous owner, Robert Bulwer-Lytton, as viceroy of India from 1876 to 1880.

The vast grounds include a deer park, a formal garden laid out by Edwin LUTYENS, and a herb garden designed by Gertrude JEKYLL.

KNOLE

- **Kent (p.495 H5)** • **Built 1456-1608** • **NT**

Seen from outside, Knole's long walls and jumble of roofs and chimneys are more reminiscent of a village than of a single country house. A fabled total of 52 staircases and seven courtyards connect its 365 rooms, including three long galleries, a ballroom and a great hall.

Thomas Bourchier, a 15th-century archbishop of Canterbury, built Knole, and successive archbishops used the palace until it was handed to Henry VIII in 1538. Elizabeth I 28 years later gave it to Thomas Sackville, 1st earl of Dorset, her cousin and the Lord High Treasurer.

Sackville renewed the interior of the house in 1605-8, using craftsmen who worked for James I. Inside, visitors can see carpets, tapestries, portraits and 17th-century furniture from the royal palaces.

John KNOX

- **Protestant reformer** • **c.1514-72**

John Knox seemed destined for a quiet life as a Scottish Catholic priest until he was converted to Protestantism by the religious reformer George Wishart in 1545. When Wishart was burned at the stake for heresy in St Andrews the following year, his scholarly follower emerged as a passionate preacher for the Scottish Protestant cause.

In 1547 Scottish Catholics and their French allies beseiged St Andrews and Knox was captured, spending 19 months as a galley slave on French ships. The Protestant government of Edward VI secured his release and Knox settled in England, where he helped to revise the Book of Common Prayer.

When Mary I began to burn English Protestants in 1553, Knox went to live in Geneva, where he ministered to Protestant refugees and wrote a bitter pamphlet against female rule, *The First Blast of the Trumpet Against the Monstrous Regiment of*

Women (1558). He returned to Scotland in 1559, determined to see the Church reformed on strict Protestant lines. In 1560, with aid from England, Scottish Protestants prevailed and, largely determined by Knox, the foundations of the CHURCH OF SCOTLAND were laid. The Edinburgh house Knox is believed to have lived in is now a museum.

Alexander KORDA

- **Film producer** • **1893-1956; kt 1942**

The audacity and imagination of the Hungarian-born Alexander Korda gained international recognition for British film making in the 1930s.

Korda left Hungary during the political turmoil that followed the First World War, eventually directing films in Hollywood. Disillusioned with the studio system there, he came to Britain in 1932 and set up his own production company and studio at Denham, Buckinghamshire.

He was immediately successful, receiving huge acclaim for *The Private Life of Henry VIII* (1933), starring Charles Laughton. But he spent so lavishly on historical epics such as *Catherine the Great* (1934) and *Rembrandt* (1936) that his backers took over the studio in 1938.

In 40 years Korda made almost 150 films and established the film careers of actors such as Laurence OLIVIER and Vivien Leigh. He was the first film producer to be knighted.

STAND BY! Assistants record script changes as Alexander Korda directs the filming of Oscar Wilde's *An Ideal Husband* in 1946

LANDSLIDE FOR LABOUR Tony Blair joins the crowds cheering the Labour election victory in 1997, which brought the party back into power for the first time in 18 years

LABOUR PARTY

• **Founded 1900**

On February 27, 1900, trade unionists and socialist groups, including the FABIAN SOCIETY and Keir HARDIE's Independent party, met in London as the Labour Representation Committee. Their goal was to raise the living standards of the poor and to obtain better representation in parliament for working people.

The committee renamed itself the Labour party after gaining 29 seats in parliament in 1906, and in 1918 the party's constitution committed it to socialist policies. Ramsay MACDONALD became the first Labour prime minister in 1924, but it was the party's first majority government under Clement ATTLEE in 1945 that initiated social change, with nationalisation of industries, free education for children up to 15 and the creation of the WELFARE STATE.

Later Labour governments under Harold WILSON and James CALLAGHAN were dogged by inflation and struggles with the powerful trade unions. By 1979 Labour had lost the support of the electorate, and under Neil Kinnock set about eliminating many of the party's more radical policies. A 'New Labour' emerged in 1994 under Tony BLAIR, who distanced the party from rigidly socialist policies and the trade unions – a strategy that won Labour the 1997 general election with a majority of 179.

LADYBIRD

The familiar red and black beetle has a variety of names – ladybird, ladybeetle, ladybug, ladycow and ladyfly – reflecting an association with the Virgin Mary. The seven spots of the most common type of ladybird were said to symbolise the Virgin's seven joys and seven sorrows, and the red wings her cloak. There are more than 40 species of ladybird in the British Isles, welcomed by farmers and gardeners alike for feeding on insect pests such as aphids.

The children's chant 'Ladybird, ladybird, Fly away home, Your house is on fire And your children all gone' probably refers to their flight when fields were fired after the harvest.

LAKE DISTRICT

• **Cumbria (p.496 A3)** • **Area 880 sq miles**

North-west England's rugged wilderness of mountain ridges and deep valleys, established as the Lake District National Park in 1951, provides some of the most dramatic scenery in Britain. Its 16 major lakes, formed in the ICE AGE when glaciers gouged valleys through volcanic rock, include Coniston Water, Derwent Water and Ullswater. The largest is Windermere (10½ miles long), the deepest Wast Water (79 m/259 ft). The park also includes England's highest mountain, Scafell Pike (977 m/3205 ft).

The area was once a Roman frontier, defended by forts such as Hardknott,

west of the small resort town of Ambleside. Subsequent Viking and Saxon invasions have left a legacy of Norse and Saxon place names.

LAMBETH PALACE

• **Central London (p.499 D3)**
• **Built 12th-19th century**

Proximity to the king was all-important to the power brokers of medieval England. It was no accident that Lambeth Palace, the main residence of the archbishop of Canterbury, was built a short ferry ride from the monarch's London residence. Even when control of the Church passed from pope to Crown, the archbishop, a member of the House of Lords, spent long periods in the capital.

The palace was built on land bought by Archbishop Baldwin in about 1185. It was damaged during the Peasants' Revolt, and was used as a prison during the Civil War. The mix of architectural styles dates back to the 13th century. Only the palace's 14th-century Church of St Mary, the parish church of Lambeth borough, is open to the public.

House of LANCASTER

• **English royal house** • **1399-1461**

The House of Lancaster came to power when Henry Bolingbroke, son of JOHN OF GAUNT, duke of Lancaster, returned from exile enraged by the seizure of his late father's lands by RICHARD II. Taking

TROUBLED CROWN On his deathbed, Henry IV, the first king of the House of Lancaster, begged forgiveness for usurping the throne

temporary advantage of Richard's absence in Ireland, Bolingbroke rallied support, deposed his cousin and took the throne as HENRY IV.

The House of Lancaster – Henry IV, his son HENRY V and grandson HENRY VI – ruled for 62 years. The throne was seized by the House of YORK in the WARS OF THE ROSES, but when Henry Tudor – of Lancastrian blood – defeated RICHARD III, he married Elizabeth of York thus uniting the two warring houses.

The LANCET

• **Founded 1823**
The practices of the early 19th-century medical establishment so enraged one surgeon, Thomas Wakley (1795-1862), that he began a journal with the aim of 'incising the abscess on the medical body politic'. In *The Lancet*, Wakley savaged the medical world for its exclusiveness and nepotism, exposing misdiagnoses and botched operations.

The journal's abusive tone – the Society of Apothecaries appeared as the 'Old Hags of Rhubarb Hall' – made its editor unpopular with the professional elite, as did his unauthorised transcripts of their lectures. But it gave voice to the reform-minded within the medical profession, and by 1825 circulation had climbed to 4000. Later editors lacked Wakley's bite, but by then the journal

NATURAL CREATION In 1814 the landscape gardener Humphry Repton retained the dramatic backdrop of hills behind Endsleigh House in Devon, but framed the original garden (*inset*) with elegant terraces

was well established. With a weekly circulation of more than 30 000, *The Lancet* is the world's leading independent journal of medical science and practice.

LANDMARK TRUST

• **Founded 1965**
Cottages and castles, old mills and elaborate follies across Britain have all been transformed by the Landmark Trust from neglected ruins into unusual holiday homes.

Rental income from holidaymakers pays for the ongoing maintenance of the restored historic buildings, of which there are some 160 throughout Britain, four in Italy and one in the USA. They include the lighthouse on LUNDY ISLAND and the Gothic temple, one of Britain's most distinctive FOLLIES, at STOWE.

LANDSCAPE GARDENING

In the 18th century, British enthusiasm for the sweeping vistas encountered on the GRAND TOUR and the idealised landscapes of painters such as the Frenchman Claude Lorrain led to a new kind of gardening. The formality that had dominated garden design since Tudor times was replaced by a fervour for turning landscapes into living works of art. Projects were ambitious.

LIVING IN THE PAST Holidaymakers with a yen for the Elizabethan can rent 16th-century Beamsley Hospital, near Skipton in Yorkshire, refurbished by the Landmark Trust

The architect and designer William Kent (1685-1748) took three years to transform the terraces around Rousham House, Oxfordshire, into a romantic landscape of winding paths and glades, with added lakes, hills and follies.

Kent's work was developed by 'Capability' BROWN, who created wilder landscapes in a style known as 'picturesque', and Humphry REPTON, who planned carefully informal classical gardens. The late 19th century saw a greater emphasis on the flower garden, culminating in Gertrude JEKYLL's deceptively free-form groupings.

A VISION OF BRITAIN

Landscape painting has shaped our view of the British countryside,
captured in the works of artists such as John Constable and J.M.W. Turner.
But pictures of the natural world have not always enjoyed such
prestige, and do not always serve such idyllic ends

WHEN THE fashionable portrait artist Thomas GAINSBOROUGH died in 1788, his house was filled with unsold landscapes. In the 18th century, landscape painting was perceived to be an inferior art, suitable for amateurs. But a distinct British landscape school was already emerging, and within a generation attitudes were transformed, partly under the impact of the ROMANTIC MOVEMENT.

At first, British painters such as the Welsh artist Richard Wilson (1714-82) were influenced by 17th-century Italian landscapes – idealised views of the Italian *campagna*, dotted with imaginary sunlit classical buildings, snapped up by aristocratic British visitors to Rome as souvenirs of the Grand Tour. The popularity of Claude Lorraine (1600-82), a French painter working in Rome, inspired the LANDSCAPE GARDENING revolution of the 18th century.

The Dutch tradition of topographically faithful 'real' scenes influenced the early works of Gainsborough, such as *Cornard Wood* (c.1748). Gainsborough moved to Bath in 1760, where he adopted a more elegant, artificial treatment of nature, but his love of the countryside of his native East Anglia was shared by the founders of the Norwich school of landscape painting, John COTMAN (1782-1842) and John CROME (1768-1821). Their direct approach attracted many followers – in 1823 the Norwich Arts Society exhibited paintings by 323 artists, marking an original group outside the influence of the Royal Academy.

Independent of Norwich and the London art world, John CONSTABLE (1776-1837) drew on the Dutch

LAND AND SEA Constable's *Kitchen Garden* (*main picture*) shows man at harmony with a landscape that is under his control. In constrast, Turner's *Keswick Lake, Cumberland* (*left*) shows the immense Lake District scenery towering over its human inhabitants. Colours melt into one another, the darkness over the lake suggesting the approach of bad weather

approach, but wanted to raise the genre to new heights. In his paintings of southern England, he tried to capture the 'light-dews-breezes' bloom-and-freshness, not one of which has yet been perfected on the canvas of any painter'. This freshness is most visible in his sketches, executed in the open air, some of which anticipate the colours and unrestrained brushwork of the French Impressionists.

Constable's domestic landscapes contrasted with the more epic works of his contemporary, J.M.W. TURNER (1775-1851). Turner roamed Europe in the wake of the Napoleonic Wars, a restless visionary searching for inspiration in dramatic Alpine vistas. But he could detect the same stirring qualities in an English landscape: his melodramatic views of the Lake District show huge, craggy mountains looming over valleys and lakes.

Turner endowed landscape with the heroic qualities reserved by earlier artists for historical or religious subjects. His human figures are often dwarfed by the terrible majesty of nature. In *Rain, Steam, Speed* (1844) the forms dissolve into pure colour and light – a technique that baffled contemporaries, but appeals to a modern eye used to abstract composition.

THE DEATH OF THE HEROIC VISION

By the time Turner died, landscape painting was again going out of fashion. The Victorian taste was for narrative painting, often with a moral message. One exception was James McNeill WHISTLER (1834-1903) whose *Nocturne* (1870), a melting, blue-green view of the Thames, is a dream-like abstraction reminiscent of Turner. Whistler's urban landscapes comment on the alienating

effect of the modern city. By now the Industrial Revolution was destroying the bucolic way of life recorded by Constable in works such as *The Haywain* (1821).

The 20th century saw a revival of landscape painting. In the First World War, artists such as Paul NASH (1889-1946) found themselves in places where the human presence was not just insignificant, but had been annihilated. His bomb-shattered moonscapes are a bitter testimony made more striking by the pastoral associations of the genre.

The gentle attraction of the British landscape reasserted itself in later decades. Ben NICHOLSON (1894-1982) used bare, clean lines to depict the play of light on the Yorkshire moors; Graham SUTHERLAND (1903-80) made landscape romantic and intimate in works such as *Entrance to a Lane*; and Victor Pasmore (1908-98), influenced by Whistler, painted naturalistic views of the Thames.

At the turn of the century, enthusiasm for landscapes declined, though painters such as Dennis Creffield (b.1931) and Peter Prendergast (b.1946) still take inspiration from Britain's countryside.

WHERE TO SEE THE LANDSCAPE ARTISTS:
- **British Museum** **National Gallery**
- **Tate, London** **Victoria and Albert Museum**

FIELD OF THE DEAD Nash's *We Are Making a New World* (1918) turns landscape into a political statement. Tree stumps stand in the blasted terrain like tombstones, and the bright sunrise over the hills is as ironic as the title

Edwin LANDSEER

• Artist • 1803-73; kt 1850

Queen Victoria admired Edwin Landseer; she bought his pictures and thought him 'very good-looking but rather short'. Typical of the artist's romantic view of nature is *Monarch of the Glen* (1851), portraying a noble stag in the Highlands.

Landseer painted portraits, groups of animals and landscapes in oils. Adapting to popular taste, he began to give his animals more human expressions, notably the dog in *Dignity and Impudence* (1839), which is held at the Tate Gallery, London. His work was greatly valued, but to modern eyes seems uncomfortably sentimental. Landseer also sculpted animals, including the bronze lions in TRAFALGAR SQUARE.

LAND'S END

• Cornwall (p.494 A7)

Land's End is England's most westerly point – a turf-topped granite mass where heathery moorland slopes down to craggy cliffs and a spectacular coastline with rocky islets, weathered by wind, spray and Atlantic waves.

Coastal paths to the north and the south-east, round Gwennap Head, offer walkers views as far as the Isles of Scilly on a clear day. More strenuous hikers often set off from here to JOHN O'GROATS, 876 road-miles away in northern

LITERARY CONTRADICTION Although he was a pessimist who loathed many aspects of modern Britain, Philip Larkin wrote some of the finest British poetry of the 20th century

Scotland. Remote Land's End, known to the ancient world as *Bolerium* and in Cornish as *Penwith*, has its own theme park, relating local history and legend.

Philip LARKIN

• Poet • 1922-85

Sexual intercourse began
In nineteen sixty-three
(Which was rather too late for me) –
Between the end of the Chatterley ban
And the Beatles' first LP
       'Annus Mirabilis' (1967)

The sadness of lives out of joint with their times is a recurring theme in Philip Larkin's poetry, often infused with a cynical and melancholy wit. He delighted in breaking taboos, contrasting slang and profanity with formal rhythms and consciously poetic themes such as eternal longing and, in *High Windows* (1974), death and transience.

LAW COURTS

The House of Lords is the highest court in Britain, but it hears fewer than 100 cases a year. Beneath it, in England and Wales, is a dual system of civil and criminal courts with a strict hierarchy.

PAYMENT TO FIT THE CRIME

In Anglo-Saxon times justice was mainly decided in county, or shire, courts with no distinction between civil and criminal cases – even for murder the penalty was often a fine – while crown courts dealt with crimes against the king's interests. Over time moral wrongs were separated from infringements of personal rights leading to a distinction between criminal and civil offences, and two types of court.

THE SCOTTISH SYSTEM

Scotland has its own court structure. Its lowest criminal court is the district court, dealing with minor crimes, punishable by up to 60 days in prison. Most criminal cases are heard in Sheriff courts, but serious offences such as murder and rape go to the High Court of Justiciary. Sheriff courts hear most civil claims, but appeals and serious or complex cases go to the Court of Session and then to the Lords.

HIERARCHY OF LAW COURTS IN ENGLAND AND WALES

CIVIL   CRIMINAL

HOUSE OF LORDS
Lords of Appeal in Ordinary, or 'Law Lords'
Highest of the British law courts. Hears appeals concerning points of law of public importance

COURT OF APPEAL
Lords Justices of Appeal
Hears appeals from High Court cases

COURT OF APPEAL
Lords Justices of Appeal
Hears appeals from Crown Court cases

HIGH COURT
High Court Judges
Split into three divisions:

Family division takes on divorce disputes and the legal protection of children

Chancery division deals with company law, tax, probate and other financial or property issues

Queen's Bench division hears serious civil cases and challenges to government decisions

CROWN COURT
Circuit Judges
Hears serious criminal cases, with trial by jury if the accused pleads not guilty. Appeals from Magistrates' Court

MAGISTRATES' COURT
Magistrates
The lowest criminal court hears 95 per cent of criminal cases

COUNTY COURT
Circuit and District Judges
Hears most civil actions and holds 'small claims' arbitrations for amounts of up to £5000

SCALES OF JUSTICE The figure of Justice tops the Central Criminal Court at the Old Bailey, in London, a crown court where 1800 cases are heard each year

Larkin lamented the narrowness of ordinary lives in *The Whitsun Weddings* (1964), gently mocking the working-class tastes of the wedding guests in the title poem. He lived a quiet life as university librarian at Hull and also published novels, and criticism of his two favourite subjects: literature and jazz.

LAVENHAM

- **Suffolk (p.495 J3)** • **Pop. 1230**

The passage of time seems suspended in Lavenham. The town did not recover from the decline in its wool and clothmaking trades in the 16th century until, during the Second World War, the traditional pubs attracted American bomber crews from nearby bases. Since then its charm has ensured new, continuing prosperity from tourism.

The riches that wool brought to the town have left their mark in the guildhall of 1529, the huge parish church dating from 1480, and the ornate plasterwork, or pargeting, of the half-timbered houses.

LAW COURTS: *see opposite page*

D.H. LAWRENCE

- **Writer** • **1885-1930**

The uninhibited language and explicit sex scenes of David Herbert Lawrence's last novel, *Lady Chatterley's Lover* (1928), challenged the British sense of propriety. Human passions, the natural world and the stultifying effects of social convention were major themes for Lawrence, whose daring prose brought new vigour to the English novel.

His first commercial success was the semi-autobiographical novel *Sons and Lovers* (1913), set in a Nottinghamshire mining community. His next novel, *The Rainbow* (1915), introduced the sisters Ursula and Gudrun, who reappeared in *Women in Love* (1916), which was declared obscene and suppressed. With his German-born wife, Frieda, Lawrence travelled widely, collecting material for his writing and searching for a climate to cure his tuberculosis.

When PENGUIN BOOKS published an un-cut edition of *Lady Chatterley's Lover* in 1960, they were prosecuted under the obscenity laws. The case was a landmark in establishing freedom of the press.

ARABIAN KNIGHT T.E. Lawrence adopted the dress and habits of the Bedouin, making use of his knowledge of the Middle East as an Allied agent during the First World War

T.E. LAWRENCE

- **Archaeologist and soldier** • **1888-1935**

'Lawrence of Arabia', as Thomas Edward Lawrence became known, left his career as an archaeologist in the Middle East to become a guerrilla figher during the First World War.

DESERT WARRIOR

The dashing soldier-scholar, often seen in Arab dress crossing the desert on a motorcycle, was an avid lover of Arabia and led the Arab revolt against the Turkish Ottoman empire in 1918. He was thrilled by the adventures of war, which he recorded in *Seven Pillars of Wisdom* (1926).

RELUCTANT HERO

In 1921 Lawrence took a post as Arab adviser to Winston Churchill, in the Colonial Office. He enlisted in the RAF in 1922 under the name of Ross, and later changed his name to Shaw in attempts to shed his fame as a war hero. But he had become a popular legend, later to inspire plays, novels and, in 1962, the film *Lawrence of Arabia*.

He died in a motorcycle accident near his home, Cloud's Hill, in Dorset, now owned by the National Trust.

LAWYERS

Barristers and solicitors, collectively known as lawyers, were once quite distinct as the senior and junior branches of the legal system. Solicitors, who out-number barristers by about nine to one, were general practitioners of law while barristers specialised in court advocacy.

In 1993 the first solicitor joined the ranks of High Court JUDGES. Since 1994 others have become qualified to argue cases in the higher LAW COURTS. But most solicitors are still the first port of call for clients seeking advice on matters such as wills, divorces, house buying and civil and criminal disputes. A minority in City practices advise large companies on legal aspects of finance and commerce.

Barristers – known as 'advocates' in Scotland and distinctive in their wigs and gowns – work for themselves from premises called chambers. They conduct cases in the higher courts representing clients referred by solicitors and are also called upon to give specialist legal advice.

Around 10 per cent of barristers are designated 'QC' or 'Queen's Counsel' – 'KC' when the monarch is a king – by the Lord Chancellor for their expertise.

Bernard LEACH

• Potter   • 1887-1979

The Japanese concept of pottery as art, rather than a craft, as disseminated by Bernard Leach in *A Potter's Book* (1940), was a major influence on modern ceramics, and the inspiration for the 'studio pottery' movement in Britain.

Leach studied pottery in Japan and in 1920 he founded a pottery in St Ives, in Cornwall, with the Japanese potter Shoji Hamanda. There he produced tableware and vases of stoneware or earthenware, relying on simple forms and decoration with subtle glazes and often an isolated, bold motif. This style, influenced largely by Japanese tea ceremony ware, was a departure from the European tradition of translucent, patterned porcelain.

Many later artists, including Lucy RIE, cite Leach as their major inspiration. The Leach Pottery and Tate Gallery in St Ives display collections of his work.

EASTERN INFLUENCE Many vases made by Bernard Leach show the inspiration of the ceramic styles of the Chinese Sung dynasty

LEAKEY FAMILY

• Anthropologists   • Louis 1903-72
• Mary 1913-96   • Richard b.1944

Investigations made by the husband-and-wife anthropologists Louis and Mary Leakey from the 1930s onwards, and later by their son Richard, established East Africa as the probable 'cradle' of the human race. It had been thought that humans evolved in Asia, where some of the oldest fossils were unearthed, but finds by the Leakeys, notably in Olduvai Gorge in Tanzania, showed that early humans had inhabited Africa long before Asia. In 1976 Mary Leakey discovered footprints at Laetoli, in Tanzania, proving that human-like creatures were already walking 3.7 million years ago.

DAVID LEAN

• Film director   • 1908-91; kt 1984

David Lean grew up in the era of silent films, and began his career at the Gaumont Studios as a runner and tea boy. From there he went on to command higher pay than any director of his generation. Lean's secret was his meticulous attention to detail and the use of lavish sets and locations in such Oscar-winners as *The Bridge on the River Kwai* (1957) and *Lawrence of Arabia* (1962). Although his films were not always well received by critics – *Doctor Zhivago* (1965) was described as 'tortuous' by the critic Leslie Halliwell – the public flocked to see them.

Lean was a mass of contradictions: ruthless, demanding, self-deprecating and generous. He helped to set up a home for leprosy sufferers in India and was utterly dedicated to his craft, once remarking, 'I hope the money men don't find out that I'd pay them to let me do this.'

SEIZING THE DAY David Lean (*centre*) and his crew waited almost a year on Ireland's west coast for storms big enough to shoot the climactic scene of *Ryan's Daughter* in 1970

Edward LEAR

• Writer and painter   • 1812-88

'How pleasant to know Mr Lear!'
Who has written such volumes of stuff!
Some think him ill-tempered and queer,
But a few think him pleasant enough.

So Edward Lear introduced his *Nonsense Songs* of 1871, the volume that included 'The Dong with the Luminous Nose', 'The Owl and the Pussy-Cat' and other nursery favourites. Much earlier, in *A Book of Nonsense* (1845), written for the grandchildren of his patron the earl of Derby, Lear had popularised the limerick.

Lear is also known for the charming watercolours that illustrate many of his rhymes and record his visits to Egypt and India. He travelled widely and after 1871 settled in San Remo, in Italy.

King LEAR

The King Lear myth, although based on ancient folklore, was largely created by the 12th-century writer GEOFFREY OF MONMOUTH. He took the name 'Lear' from 'Llyr', a Celtic deity that featured in the Welsh tales of *The MABINOGION*.

Geoffrey's story of Lear, driven mad by disputes with his daughters over the division of his kingdom, was related in chronicles, turned into a play around 1590 and again dramatised by William SHAKESPEARE about 1605. Shakespeare drew on several different sources for his version of the tale, which includes graphic scenes of the king's madness and subplots of treachery, illegitimacy and war with France.

John LE CARRÉ

• Pseudonym of David John Cornwell
• Writer   • b.1931

As a member of the British Foreign Service, David Cornwell had to write under a pen name. As John Le Carré his first success was *The Spy Who Came in from the Cold* (1963), a radical departure from the traditional spy story and the first of a stream of best sellers.

Unlike the James Bond-style figures of other espionage fiction, Le Carré heroes, who specialise in the shabbier side of spying, have little glamour. Typically, a mild-mannered agent, such as George Smiley, the best known, becomes enmeshed in a convoluted plot played out in a bleak, Cold War setting.

LEEDS CASTLE

• **Kent (p.495 J5)** • **Built 12th-19th century**

A 9th-century Saxon lord called Leed built a wooden fortress here, and traces remain of a stone castle, that replaced the Saxon fort in 1119. But most of the mellow stone buildings that now rise dramatically from two islands in a lake fed by the River Len are the result of extensive renovation in 1822.

The castle was bought by Edward I in 1278 and remained in royal hands for nearly 300 years. Henry VIII turned the fortress into a palace, rebuilding the Gloriette – a separate keep connected to the main island by a covered stone bridge – and adding the Maiden's Tower to house the royal maids of honour.

Leeds is often called the Ladies' Castle because it was the home of six medieval queens. Two rooms in the Gloriette have been restored as they might have looked in the time of Catherine de Valois, the queen of Henry V.

LEICESTER

• **E Midlands (p.495 F2)** • **Pop. 318 520**

Leicester has royal connections both legendary and historical. The mythical King LEAR is said to have lived in the city, possibly called 'Llyrcester'. More reliably, in 1485 the new king Henry VII rode triumphant into Leicester after his victory over Richard III at nearby BOSWORTH.

Many relics of the town's rich past lie hidden by modern developments. The city grew up as a Roman settlement

LEEDS

• **N England (p.496 C4)** • **Pop. 424 190**

In spite of modern redevelopment, the centre of Leeds remains a monument to 19th-century industrial and civic pride. The Town Hall of 1858, crowned by a lofty central tower and elegant dome, is just one of the stately buildings that dominate the city. Its Victorian glory was captured on film in 1888 by a local photographer, Louis le Prince, who filmed Leeds traffic in what is thought to be the world's first motion picture.

Leeds' prosperity, won from clothing manufacture and the wool trade, is reflected in its sumptuous Victorian shopping arcades, flooded with light streaming through glass domes. They have recently been restored to their original brilliance after years of decay and are alive with restaurants and shops.

The city is also a thriving centre for the arts. Opera North is based at The Grand Theatre, and the works of the Leeds-born sculptor Henry MOORE are exhibited at the City Art Gallery and Henry Moore Institute. Vaudeville lives on at the Leeds City Varieties, Britain's oldest music hall.

SERENE BUT SECURE Leeds Castle occupies one of the most romantic settings of any fortress in Britain. The natural lake and island near Maidstone provided an ideal defensive site

called Ratae, where the Fosse Way crossed the River Soar. The 9 m (30 ft) remains of the Jewry Wall near the Guildhall, built of narrow bricks and flint around AD 150, is thought to have been part of either the forum or Roman baths.

The tall spire of St Mary de Castro, the chapel of the now ruined medieval castle, dominates the south-west side of the city. It was in the castle in 1264 that Simon de Montfort, the earl of Leicester, forced his brother-in-law, Henry III, to hold the nation's first parliament.

The hosiery industry, Leicester's traditional source of wealth, is explained at the Newarke Houses Museum. Coal later brought increased prosperity, and Leicester is still a thriving city producing footwear, hosiery and knitwear.

Lord LEIGHTON

• Artist   • 1830-96; kt 1878; bn 1896

Step inside the house created by Frederick, Lord Leighton, near Holland Park in London, and you enter a world of fountains, Moorish arches, statues and lavish decoration on almost every surface. Leighton House, now a museum, is a work of art comparable with anything the artist created on canvas.

Leighton's paintings, many of which can be seen in the house, interpreted neoclassicism with a sensuality influenced by the AESTHETIC MOVEMENT. In pictures such as *Elijah in the Wilderness* (1874) or *Captive Andromache* (1888) youths and maidens pose nobly against antique backdrops, their nudity made acceptable by the fabulous contexts. Later works such as *The Garden of the Hesperides* (1892) display a more explicit erotic languor.

Leighton was dedicated to raising the social status of the artist. Fittingly, he received a peerage, barely a month before his death. He remains the only British artist honoured in this way.

Peter LELY

• Artist   • 1618-80; kt 1680

The sleepily voluptuous, bejewelled court ladies and heavy-jowled, cynical-looking courtiers of Lely's portraits provide the definitive images of Restoration England.

Lely was born of Dutch parents in Germany, and moved to England around 1641 where he became principal painter to Charles II in 1660. Much of his work is still in the royal collection at Hampton Court. He soon had a studio turning out

glossy portraits of aristocratic beauties clad in exquisite silks, and noblemen so heavily bewigged that it can be hard to tell them apart. In truth, Lely's assistants would often paint all but the heads of the sitters, who could select poses and settings from already-sketched canvases.

LEVELLERS

For many ordinary men recruitment into Oliver Cromwell's New Model Army during the CIVIL WAR meant not just a job but a heady taste of power. A number of pressure groups emerged from the ranks of the worker-soldiers, of whom the Levellers were the most powerful.

Their aim was to 'level' inequality through reforms, including an elected parliament, free trade and the end of the monarchy. The men defended honest hard work but, as one of the leaders, Gerrard Winstanley, said, being told 'the poor shall inherit the earth' did not compensate for inadequate pay.

The Levellers incited mutiny in the lower ranks of Cromwell's army and in 1649 the movement was suppressed before achieving any of its aims.

LEWES

• East Sussex (p.495 H6)   • Pop. 15 380

Lewes, the county town of East Sussex, has largely escaped the ravages of modern development. Its main streets and the steep, narrow lanes or 'twittens' leading off them are lined with houses in a jumble of styles, from Tudor half-timbering to the traditional Sussex combination of brick and flint.

Ruins of a Norman castle stand at the high point of the town; below it, at Southover, are the remains of a medieval priory. The sprawling Tudor house given to Anne of Cleves by Henry VIII after their divorce in 1540 is now a local history museum with a fine collection of old Sussex ironwork.

Lewes is also the scene of spectacular November 5 festivities, when bonfires blaze and an effigy of the pope is burned to commemorate 17 local Protestants burnt as heretics by Mary I.

MOORISH MOSAICS Tiles designed by **William de Morgan** decorate the Arab Hall in Leighton House. From 1864-89 Leighton spent £4000 – a small fortune – to build and furnish his home

C.S. LEWIS

• Scholar and writer • 1898-1963

To those who shared his academic world, Clive Staples Lewis was a bluff, no-nonsense Oxford don. A fellow of Magdalen College for nearly 30 years, he had a distinguished career as a scholar, critic and teacher. He wrote influential academic texts, including *The Allegory of Love* (1936), about medieval courtly love and literary form, and *English Literature in the Sixteenth Century* (1954).

But Lewis found international fame explaining his Christian faith in books such as *The Screwtape Letters* (1942), a witty dialogue between a senior devil and his more junior colleague putting a persuasive case for belief in God. The seven *Narnia* novels, beginning with *The Lion, the Witch and the Wardrobe* (1950), present the tenets of Christianity in allegorical form for children.

TRIUMPH OF LOVE C.S. Lewis married at 58 and was devastated when his wife, Joy, died after four years. His Christian faith sustained him and resulted in a profound book on grief

Lennox LEWIS

• Boxer • b.1965

The first British-born world heavyweight boxing champion of the 20th century, Lennox Lewis won his title in unorthodox circumstances. In 1992, the American holder, Riddick Bowe, gave up his World Boxing Council championship belt rather than face losing to Lewis. Just the presence of the 6 ft 5 in heavyweight seems to strike fear into his opponents; during a 1997 fight he reduced the American Oliver McCall to tears. But in March 1999, Lewis lost a bid to become the undisputed world champion when, controversially, his 12 round bout against Evander Holyfield was ruled a draw.

LIBERAL DEMOCRAT PARTY

The 'third force' in British politics, the Liberal Democrats support better public services, strong links with Europe, a tax to pay for education and DEVOLUTION. Proportional representation is another key policy – with 17 per cent of the vote in 1997 but only 46 seats in parliament (less than 7 per cent) the 'Lib Dems' clearly lose out under the current 'first past the post' system.

The party is the result of a merger in 1988 between the Liberal Party and the Social Democratic Party. Its first leader was Paddy Ashdown, a former soldier and diplomat, who held the position until he stood down in summer 1999.

THE LIBERAL INHERITANCE

Liberal thinking took shape under GLADSTONE in the second half of the 19th century as part of a Europe-wide political phenomenon. Broadly speaking, liberalism stood for individual freedom, peace and political reform – ideals promoted in the 20th century by leaders such as David LLOYD GEORGE, David Steel and, since 1988, the Liberal Democrats.

LEY LINES

In 1921 a Herefordshire businessman, Alfred Watkins, had a mystical vision in which he saw glowing lines stretching across the landscape of his home county. When he consulted maps of the area he noticed that many religious sites – from ancient, Neolithic barrows and standing stones to churches and chapels built on pre-Christian sacred sites – were aligned with one another and with natural features such as hilltops.

In his book *The Old Straight Track* (1925) he called the lines linking these sites 'leys', the Saxon word for open ground or woodland clearings. He believed they coincided with prehistoric trading routes, which used the sites and hilltops as navigational landmarks.

During the 1930s water diviners began to claim that leys represented currents of 'earth energy' and ley hunters today often use dowsing to trace their path.

The alignment of sites on the St Michael ley line, which crosses southern Britain, can be seen by the diagram below (not to scale). The line passes exactly through many of the sites and only narrowly misses several others. The disproportionate number of churches dedicated to St Michael gave the route its name.

ST MICHAEL'S CHURCH, HOPTON

BURY ST EDMUNDS

ST MICHAEL'S CHURCH, CLIFTON HAMPDEN

STOKE ST MICHAEL'S CHURCH

AVEBURY RING

The rings and avenues of standing stones at Avebury once constituted a pre-Christian temple larger and more complex than Stonehenge

The abbey shrine of the martyred 9th-century king Edmund made Bury an important pilgrim centre. The current cathedral is adjacent to the ruins of its medieval predecessor

From St Michael's Tower at the top of Glastonbury Tor, the ruined church of St Michael on Burrowbridge Mump can be seen. Glastonbury has been regarded as a sacred site since ancient times

GLASTONBURY TOR

BURROWBRIDGE MUMP

ST MICHAEL'S CHURCH, OTHERY

St Michael was revered during the Middle Ages. Pilgrims travelled from all over Europe to shrines such as St Michael's Mount

CHEESEWRING

ST MICHAEL'S CHURCH, TRULL

ST MICHAEL'S CHURCH, BRENTOR

ST MICHAEL'S MOUNT

CARN LÉS BOEL

The pile of weathered rocks known as the Cheesewring, on the edge of Bodmin Moor, is thought by some to have been an ancient druid shrine

CONNECTING FORCE The St Michael Line is the longest ley line in Britain, stretching from the Cornish coast to East Anglia, past many churches and ancient sites. At dawn on May Day, an observer looking east along the line will see the sun rise above it

LIBERTY'S

• Central London (p.499 A5) • Est. 1875

From a small shop in Regent's Street in 1875, Arthur Lasenby Liberty started selling ornaments and shawls from China, India and Japan. The decorative objects, particularly those from Japan, appealed to artists of the AESTHETIC MOVEMENT, who bought fabrics and props from Liberty's shop. As business grew he added Oriental carpets, china and printed silks in fluid patterns that influenced the ARTS AND CRAFTS movement led by William MORRIS.

Liberty's began selling ladies clothes in 1884, and soon became the most fashionable shop in London. To meet the demand, Liberty began dying imported Indian silks at the turn of the century.

The company now has outlets in France, the USA, Japan and Kuwait. It supports contemporary design while still stocking its characteristic floral patterns.

LIFEBOATS

After a ship foundered off South Shields, on Tyneside, in 1789 a group of local businessmen offered 2 guineas for the best design for a rescue boat. The winner, named the *Original,* was stationed on the Tyne and although not self-righting, as modern lifeboats are, it nevertheless proved unsinkable.

The service offered by the *Original* was so successful that lifeboat stations staffed by volunteers sprang up all around Britain's coast.

In 1824 the National Institution for the Preservation of Life from Shipwreck was founded, later to become the Royal National Lifeboat Institution (RNLI). Its 304 boats at 222 stations now cover all British waters, funded entirely by donation. In 1999 this reached a figure of around £80 million.

Thomas LINACRE

• Physician • 1460-1524

Before Thomas Linacre proposed the idea of licensing physicians there was no way of telling whether a doctor had any training. The result was a haphazard system of medical care that Linacre aimed to reform.

In 1518, under a charter from Henry VIII, Linacre established the Royal College of Physicians. Operating initially from his London home, he assessed and licensed physicians, remaining president until his death. Linacre himself studied at Oxford, where a graduate college was founded in his name in 1962.

LINCOLN

• Lincolnshire (p.495 G1) • Pop. 80 280

Earthquake, storm and fire have all struck Lincoln's cathedral. The current, pale gold structure was started in 1185 after an earthquake destroyed its 11th-century predecessor.

Lincoln stands on a limestone ridge above the River Witham overlooking the Fens. Cloth, including the so-called 'Lincoln green' worn by Robin Hood, was, from the 14th century, the city's main product. By the time of the Norman invasion, wool trade with Europe had made Lincoln the fourth most important city in England. Among many surviving medieval buildings is the 12th-century Jew's House on Steep Hill.

Since the Industrial Revolution Lincoln has manufactured agricultural machinery, and during the First World War military TANKS were developed and built there.

LINDISFARNE

• Northumberland (p.496 B1) • Pop. 180

In AD 793 the peace of Lindisfarne, or Holy Island, was shattered by a band of raiding Vikings. They murdered monks, slaughtered cattle and stole treasures from the monastery, which had stood on the remote island since 635.

The monastery, missionary centre of the CELTIC CHURCH, reached its greatest glory under St Cuthbert from 664 to 676. In honour of his canonisation in 698 the monks produced the Lindisfarne Gospels (*see* ILLUMINATED MANUSCRIPTS), now kept in the British Museum.

The Viking attack left a lasting terror, and the prospect of Danish invasion drove the monks away in 875; the monastery is now in ruins. The castle (NT), which dominates the island's skyline, was built during the 16th century to defend against the Scots and was converted into a private house in 1903 by the architect Edwin LUTYENS.

The island is linked to the mainland by a 3 mile causeway, built in 1954, which is exposed at low tide.

BYGONE STYLE The Liberty's building looks old but was built in 1924 using Elizabethan timber. The small, floral 'Sungleam' 1930s design is typical of the company's fabric patterns

LINDOW MAN

In 1984, the 2000-year-old remains of a man were discovered in a peat bog in Lindow Moss, Cheshire. The airless, waterlogged conditions of the bog had preserved the body and kept the skin intact, although dark and leathery. Naked except for a fox-fur armlet, the man, who was in his early 20s, had manicured nails and a trimmed beard. With his skull fractured and throat cut, he had been garrotted and laid face-down in water.

The form his death took and the presence of MISTLETOE pollen in his stomach suggest that Lindow Man was a victim of ritual sacrifice, perhaps by DRUIDS. He is the best-preserved British example of such 'bog people' and his remains are kept in the British Museum.

LINNEAN SOCIETY

• **Founded 1788**

In 1858 Charles DARWIN and Alfred Russel WALLACE chose a meeting of the distinguished society in Piccadilly to announce the theory of evolution.

The Linnean Society – the world's oldest devoted to biological science – is named after the Swedish botanist, Carl Linnaeus, who founded the modern system of classification. Its archive was formed from his papers and specimens, which were bought after his death by the English naturalist James Smith. Today the society, with over 2000 members, still documents the world's flora and fauna.

Joseph LISTER

• **Surgeon**   • **1827-1912; bt 1883; bn 1897; OM 1902**

Before Joseph Lister, postoperative infections such as gangrene were claiming the lives of nearly half of all surgical patients. As head of the surgical wards at Glasgow Royal Infirmary and a staunch advocate of prevention rather than cure, Lister set out to find a way to destroy the germs identified by Louis Pasteur as the cause of infection.

Carbolic acid was the breakthrough. Lister used it to clean wounds, dressings and instruments, and introduced his antiseptic techniques to surgery. His wards were soon free of infection and his methods were universally adopted.

LISTED BUILDINGS

What do Battersea Power Station, a Birmingham prefab, Blair Castle and the Royal Greenwich Observatory have in common? They are all buildings listed as being of architectural or historical interest. The system began in 1945 to preserve Britain's architectural heritage amid postwar rebuilding.

Most buildings from before 1840 and all those before 1700 were automatically listed, encompassing architectural styles up to the Regency period. Post-1840 buildings were chosen on the basis of design, craftsmanship and technical innovation, or for association with a person or event of national importance.

MAKING THE GRADE

Three grades of listing were set: grade I being most important, followed by II* and II. Around 95 per cent of listed buildings are grade II, 4 per cent grade II* and only 1 per cent grade I. Planning consent must be granted before a listed building is altered in any way that would affect its character, even painting.

Around 450000 buildings have been listed in Britain and ENGLISH HERITAGE, Scottish Heritage and Cadw in Wales advise the government on new

TEMPORARY ACCOMMODATION Prefabs were put up as emergency postwar housing but in 1998, 16 Birmingham homes were grade II listed for their historical importance

additions, particularly if they are under threat. Works by prominent modern architects are often listed, such as Frederick Gibberd's Metropolitan Cathedral in Liverpool (grade II*) and Richard Seifert's Centrepoint (grade II), both built in the 1960s.

WHAT IS A BUILDING?

The range of structures has diversified since the 1970s to include airfields, dockyards, factories, public houses, restaurants and cinemas, even village pumps, milestones and bus shelters.

The system now acknowledges the social history of buildings as well as their architectural importance. The entire village of Saltaire in Yorkshire, built by the wool magnate Titus Salt to house his factory hands in the 19th century, is listed – as much for the insight it gives into the lives of the workers as for the buildings.

Pottery kilns in Derbyshire, the Penguin Pool at London Zoo, the 1960s' swimming baths at Coventry and the signal box at Birmingham New Street station all preserve details of life and leisure in a public, living museum.

FORM AND FUNCTION The Palladian-style bridge at Prior Park, near Bath (1755), is an ostentatious river crossing, while the windmill at Sibsey (1877) is starkly functional. Both are grade I listed, the bridge for its design, the windmill for its social and industrial significance

A LITERARY PILGRIMAGE

Travel through Britain and at every turn you will find places whose names evoke writers or works of literature that made them famous – Thomas Hardy's Dorset or the Lake District celebrated in the poems of William Wordsworth – and landscapes that bring their words to life

SCOTLAND

1 ERISKAY In Compton Mackenzie's 1947 novel *Whisky Galore!*, the inhabitants of the small Hebridean island of Eriskay find themselves happily awash with whisky after a merchant ship founders offshore

2 WESTERN ISLES James BOSWELL, friend and biographer of Samuel JOHNSON, was born in Ayrshire. In 1773 the pair toured Scotland and the Western Isles, writing two very different accounts of the journey

3 MULL The shores of Mull offered safety to David Balfour in Robert Louis STEVENSON's novel *Kidnapped* (1886). He is washed up there after a shipwreck

4 ALLOWAY The original 'Brig o' Doon' across which Tam o' Shanter leapt in Robert BURNS' swashbuckling poem, spans the Doon river in Alloway, near Ayr

5 TANTALLON CASTLE The cliff-top castle Tantallon featured in Walter SCOTT's 1808 poem 'Marmion', which culminates with the battle of FLODDEN. Scott lived in Abbotsford, in a fanciful, castellated house where he wrote romantic, historical novels

6 BORDERS The anonymous 15th-century border ballad 'Chevy Chase' is an epic account of a bloody battle between two landowners over hunting rights

NORTHERN IRELAND

36 LONDONDERRY Seamus HEANEY draws on the landscape, language and life of his native Londonderry particularly in his early poetry, such as 'Digging' (1965), in which he recalls his father cutting peat

37 BELFAST In his poem, 'Valediction' (1934) Louis MacNeice celebrates the hard-edged industry of his home town:
See Belfast, devout and profane and hard,
Built on reclaimed mud, hammers playing in the shipyard,
Time punched with holes like a steel sheet, time
Hardening the faces, veneering with a grey and
speckled rime

38 MARKETHILL Jonathan SWIFT was a clergyman in Dublin but visited Markethill after the death of Stella, his intimate friend and subject of his *Journal to Stella* (1710-13). Natural features in the area include Swift's walk, chair and well, where he wrote during his stay

NORTH

7 GRASMERE William WORDSWORTH and Samuel Taylor COLERIDGE idealised the Lake District landscape in their verse. Wordsworth and his sister Dorothy retired to Dove Cottage, near Grasmere, in 1799

8 WINDERMERE Arthur RANSOME set *Swallows and Amazons* (1930) on Lake Windermere, which the children in his novel imagined as a wide sea, stretching from the unexplored Arctic to the Antarctic and inhabited by sea monsters and pirates

9 WHITBY A cross near the abbey *(see map)* commemorates the 7th-century shepherd Caedmon, who is said to have received the gift of song in a vision. Bram Stoker knew Whitby well and had Count Dracula visit the fishing port in his 1897 vampire classic

10 KNUTSFORD Tatton Park *(right)* was the home of Mrs GASKELL, and featured as 'Cunnor Towers' in her novel *Wives and Daughters* (1864-6), Knutsford appearing as 'Cranford'

CENTRAL

11 STOKE-ON-TRENT Tunstall, Burslem, Hanley, Stoke-upon-Trent and Longton were the Turnhill, Bursley, Hanbridge, Knype and Longshaw of Arnold BENNETT's 'five towns', now grouped together as Stoke-on-Trent

12 EASTWOOD D.H. LAWRENCE's novels were often part autobiography, set in Nottinghamshire. Eastwood is the 'Bestwood' of *Sons and Lovers* (1913) and 'Beldover' of *Women in Love* (1920)

13 NEWSTEAD ABBEY Once an Augustinian priory, Newstead Abbey was the BYRON family seat and the poet's childhood home. He inherited the house in 1798 and wrote his elegy on the deserted and ruined priory *(right)* in 1807

14 HALL GREEN The Valley of Cole, near Birmingham, where J.R.R. TOLKIEN lived, was the inspiration for Hobbiton, the enchanted land of *The Hobbit* (1937)

15 MALVERN HILLS William Langland was born in around 1330 near Malvern. His poem, *PIERS PLOWMAN* (c.1362) begins with the narrator falling into a reverie on the hills

16 WENLOCK EDGE A.E. HOUSMAN wrote a collection of poetry called *A Shropshire Lad* (1896) but his background was in Worcestershire. The Midlands landscape, such as Wenlock Edge, features in much of his work

WILD FRONTIER The battles over the bleak land between England and Scotland from the 13th to 16th centuries are recounted in the narrative poems known as **Border Ballads**

THE SCOTTISH PLAY Fairy-tale turrets at Glamis Castle belie the scenes of murder related in the story of *MACBETH*. The castle was the setting for William Shakespeare's play but was built 300 years after the death of Malcolm

EARLY BARD A cross in Whitby honours Caedmon, the bottom of the four figures, as 'the father of English sacred song'

SOUTH-EAST

20 ADLESTROP
Yes, I remember Adlestrop –
The name, because one afternoon
Of heat the express-train drew up there
Unwontedly. It was late June.
Edward Thomas, 'Adlestrop' (c.1917)

21 BEDFORD John BUNYAN wrote his spiritual allegory *The Pilgrim's Progress* (1678-84) while in prison at Bedford

22 GRANTCHESTER The poet Rupert BROOKE lodged at Orchard House in Grantchester while studying at Cambridge. He was one of many writers, including E.M. FORSTER, A.A. Milne, J.B. PRIESTLEY and Virginia WOOLF, to take tea in the gardens

23 CANTERBURY The shrine of Thomas Becket in Canterbury Cathedral was the destination of the pilgrims, including the monk (*right*), in Geoffrey CHAUCER's 14th-century masterpiece *The Canterbury Tales*

24 ROCHESTER When Mr Pickwick and Snodgrass catch sight of Rochester Castle in Charles DICKENS's *Pickwick Papers* (1837), their companion, Jingle, contradicts their wonder by revealing the decay within

25 PENSHURST Ben JONSON idealised the grand home of the 16th-century poet Philip SIDNEY in his 1616 ode 'To Penshurst' as the model of gracious country living, imagining fish leaping into nets to be caught and trees weighed down with fruit

26 READING Oscar WILDE was imprisoned in Reading prison for homosexual practices and wrote of the misery of incarceration in 'The Ballad of Reading Gaol' (1898)

Ah, fine place! …
glorious pile –
frowning walls –
tottering arches –
dark nooks –
crumbling
staircases –
Charles Dickens, *Pickwick Papers* (1837)

ADLESTROP

Ah God! to see the branches stir
Across the moon at Grantchester!
To smell the thrilling-sweet and rotten
Unforgettable, unforgotten
River-smell, and hear the breeze
Sobbing in the little trees.
Rupert Brooke, 'The Old Vicarage, Grantchester', 1912

Bronte Parsonage Museum, Haworth

Shakespeare's birthplace, Stratford-upon-Avon

Bunyan Meeting House and Museum

LONDON

Jane Austen's House, Chawton

COTTAGE INDUSTRY Jane Austen wrote her six novels at the family home in Chawton

LONDON

P 17 GOUGH SQUARE Samuel JOHNSON's house is just off Fleet Street, near his local inn, Ye Olde Cheshire Cheese

Q RUSSELL SQUARE The Osborne and Sedley families, in THACKERAY's 1847 novel, *Vanity Fair*, lived in this square

R 12 BUCKINGHAM STREET Samuel PEPYS lived in this house between 1679 and 1688

S 221b BAKER STREET The fictional detective SHERLOCK HOLMES lived here; a few doors away is a museum to the sleuth

K KEATS HOUSE, HAMPSTEAD John KEATS wrote many of his poems, including 'Ode to a Nightingale' (1819), at his north London home

L 23 FITZROY ROAD, PRIMROSE HILL The Irish poet W.B. Yeats and Ted HUGHES' wife, Sylvia Plath, both lived here

M 46 GORDON SQUARE The BLOOMSBURY GROUP regularly met here during the 1920s

N 48 DOUGHTY STREET Charles DICKENS' house in Holborn is now a museum

O MERMAID TAVERN, BREAD STREET John Keats wrote 'Lines on the Mermaid Tavern' (1818) about the hostelry popular with writers from Shakespeare, Jonson and Donne to Beaumont and Fletcher

Hampstead Heath

Regent's Park

Hyde Park

Thames

Museum

On Wenlock Edge the wood s in trouble;
His forest fleece the Wrekin heaves;
The gale, it plies the saplings double,
And thick on Severn snow the leaves.
A.E. Housman, *A Shropshire Lad*, 1896

WALES

17 ABERYSTWYTH Two 14th-century manuscripts, 'The White Book of Rhydderch' and 'The Red Book of Hergest', kept in Aberystwyth, contain the medieval Welsh legends of *The MABINOGION*

18 STRATA FLORIDA ABBEY Burial place of Dafydd ap Gwilym, the 'Welsh bard' who introduced European themes and techniques to 14th-century Welsh poetry

19 LAUGHARNE The Llareggub of Captain Cat, Organ Morgan and Nogood Boyo in Dylan THOMAS's radio play *Under Milk Wood* (1954) is based on Laugharne, where Thomas lived and is buried

THOMAS HARDY SITES

A 'Tor-upon-Seas' (Torquay)
B 'Exonbury' (Exeter)
C 'Tivworthy' (Tiverton)
D 'Emminster' (Beaminster)
E 'Ivell' (Yeovil)
F 'Abbots Cernel' (Cerne Abbas)
G 'Casterbridge' (Dorchester)
H 'Budmouth' (Weymouth)
I 'Sandbourne' (Bournemouth)
J 'Melchester' (Salisbury)

SOUTH-WEST

27 BATH The refined society of 19th-century Bath was the setting for many of Jane AUSTEN's novels. The city has attracted many other writers, including Johnson, Sheridan and Thackeray

28 WINCHESTER Although the first of Antony TROLLOPE's Barchester Chronicles, *The Warden* (1855), was inspired by Salisbury Cathedral close, he based 'Barchester' on another cathedral city, Winchester

29 BOURNEMOUTH The poet Percy Bysshe SHELLEY's heart is buried in Bournemouth with his wife Mary Shelley, who wrote the GOTHIC NOVEL, *Frankenstein* (1818)

30 DORSET Thomas HARDY used Dorset as the model for his fictional county of Wessex. Hardy was born near Dorchester and lived there for much of his life

31 LYME REGIS Jane Austen's Louisa Musgrove slipped and fell on the Cobb (*left*) at Lyme Regis in *Persuasion* (1818) but the wild danger of the curved harbour wall was most vividly captured by John Fowles in *The French Lieutenant's Woman* (1969)

32 OTTERY ST MARY The poet Samuel Taylor COLERIDGE recalled the church bells of his birthplace in 'Frost at Midnight' (1798). A memorial plaque in the local churchyard features the albatross from 'The Rime of the Ancient Mariner' (1798)

33 OARE A plaque in Oare church honours R.D. Blackmore, who set the wedding of Lorna Doone there in his 1869 novel. Locals know the surrounding area as Doone Valley

34 JAMAICA INN The old coaching inn on bleak Bodmin Moor made an isolated retreat for smugglers in Daphne du Maurier's 1936 novel

35 ST IVES Virginia WOOLF spent her childhood summers in St Ives, at a house overlooking the bay. Godrevy lighthouse (*below*) inspired her novel *To the Lighthouse* (1927)

SPIRIT HOUSE Jamaica Inn is said to be haunted by the ghost of a sailor who was murdered there

LIVERPOOL

• **NW England (p.496 A5)** • **Pop. 481 790**

Although Liverpool's history as a port goes back to King John's charter of 1207, the modern city's growth began in the late 17th century when a west coast location favoured the flourishing new trade with the New World and Africa.

BOOM AND BUST

Commerce, first in slaves and sugar, then serving Lancashire's cotton industry, made Liverpool one of the world's most thriving ports in the 18th century. Shops and businesses prospered as emigrants to North America and Australia came from all over northern Europe to board steamships built at docks which, by the late 19th century, stretched 7 miles along the banks of the River Mersey.

But as Britain's manufacturing industries declined after the Second World War, and transatlantic passengers increasingly used much cheaper air travel, Liverpool's port and shipyards suffered a steep downturn.

MODERN TIMES

In the 1960s, a growing Irish-Catholic population – many of them descendants of Irish refugees from the potato famines of the 1840s – led to the building of a Roman Catholic cathedral, a modernist concrete and aluminium funnel illuminated by a stained-glass lantern tower designed by John PIPER. The Anglican counterpart is a red-brick, neo-Gothic design by Giles Gilbert Scott, begun in 1904 but, owing to two world wars, not completed until 1978.

The warehouses around 19th-century Albert Dock now house museums and galleries, including the TATE GALLERY Liverpool, and a BEATLES exhibition.

LIVERPOOL FC

• **Founded 1892**

After its manager Bill Shankly took Liverpool into the first division in 1962, the 'Reds' became the toast of English FOOTBALL. By far England's most successful football club, Liverpool has won the league championship a record 18 times since 1901.

If Shankly turned Liverpool FC into a national institution, proclaiming – tongue only partly in cheek – that football was more important than life and death, his successor Bob Paisley (1974-83) made it the most feared side in Europe, guiding it to European Cup triumph three times in five years.

The club's home ground, Anfield, carries on its gates the motto 'You'll never walk alone' – the title of a song in the musical *Carousel*, which club fans turned into a popular football anthem.

LIVERY COMPANIES

Since the 14th century, the government of the CITY OF LONDON has been largely run by members of the livery companies, which originate from the powerful craft GUILDS of the early Middle Ages, and of which there are more than 80 today. Workers of a common trade banded together in guilds, based in often grandiose guildhalls and financed by subscriptions, to train apprentices, set wages, resolve disputes and ensure high standards of workmanship.

Street names such as Ironmonger Lane recall the areas where guild members were once focused, wearing their distinctive gowns or 'livery', similar to monks' habits. To such early livery companies as the Goldsmiths, Merchant

FOR EVER RED Liverpool FC's most passionate fan, and manager from 1959 to 1974, Bill Shankly was the cornerstone of its success

Taylors, Vintners and Grocers have been added in modern times Engineers, Air Pilots and Chartered Accountants. The companies still have an influence on trading standards, but their work today is more concerned with charity and City government – their members elect the LORD MAYOR and sheriffs.

David LIVINGSTONE

• **Missionary and explorer** • **1813-73**

From 1840 until his death, David Livingstone made the exploration and conversion of Africa his life's task. A Scottish doctor turned missionary, he travelled and evangelised in southern and central Africa, discovering both the Victoria Falls and Lake Nyasa.

Livingstone's disappearance in 1866 caused widespread concern, but in 1871 he was tracked down near Lake Tanganyika by the journalist Henry Morton Stanley. The meeting gave rise to Stanley's greeting, 'Doctor Livingstone,

EDWARDIAN PIER HEAD Liverpool's waterfront is dominated by the 1910 Royal Liver Building (*left*). Its twin towers are topped by statues of the mythical Liver Birds (pronounced lie-ver) after which the city is said to be named

I presume?'. Livingstone was dedicated to the abolition of slavery, and thought that the only way to counter it and stop the tribal wars it caused was to introduce commerce and European settlement. In opening up the African interior to Europeans, he helped to make possible the continent's colonisation.

David LLOYD GEORGE

- **Prime minister 1916-22**
- **1863-1945; earl 1945**

Known as the Welsh Wizard for his fiery oratory and introduction of welfare support to the sick, old and unemployed, David Lloyd George was, at the height of his career, one of the most popular politicians Britain had ever had.

He courted controversy from the first, when, as Liberal chancellor of the exchequer, he introduced the Pensions Act of 1908. A year later his 'People's Budget' proposed taxing the rich to fund new welfare schemes, including health and employment insurance.

THE WIDER STAGE

As the FIRST WORLD WAR sapped British strength, Lloyd George offered solid leadership and in 1916 replaced Herbert ASQUITH as prime minister. His declared aim of making Britain 'a land fit for heroes' won him a landslide election victory at the war's end in 1918.

Lloyd George helped to negotiate the peace settlement the following year, and established the Irish Free State in 1921. But he could not maintain full support from his coalition government, and after allegations of 'selling' titles to boost Liberal funds, he resigned in 1922, never to hold office again.

LLOYD'S

- **Central London (p.499 F2)** • **Est. c.1688**

'If Lloyd's won't insure you, no one will' ran the motto of the world's largest insurance market. Its prestige grew over the 300 years since shipowners began organising insurance for their vessels and cargo at Edward Lloyd's coffee shop in London in the late 1680s.

From these meetings, syndicates of underwriters (known as 'names') formed the modern Lloyd's, backing ventures, in theory, with their entire personal wealth. The system nearly collapsed in the

RICH MAN'S TOLL The Lutine Bell at Lloyd's was rung once for good news, twice for bad, and an unprecedented three times in 1996 to herald its restructuring after its financial crisis

early 1990s when an exceptional combination of man-made and natural catastrophes led to heavy losses, bankrupting many members. Lloyd's was then restructured to allow underwriting on a limited liability basis.

Andrew LLOYD WEBBER

- **Composer** • **b.1948; kt 1992**

The curtain never falls on an Andrew Lloyd Webber show before it has risen on another somewhere else in the world. He is Britain's most successful composer of musicals of all time.

In collaboration with the lyricist Tim Rice he co-wrote his first three hit shows: *Joseph and The Amazing Technicolor Dreamcoat* (1968, originally a cantata for a London boys' school), *Jesus Christ Superstar* (1970) and *Evita* (1978). Then followed *Cats* (1981), based on T.S. Eliot's children's verses *Old Possum's Book of*

NESSIE: FACT OR MYTH? A model of the prehistoric plesiosaurus epitomises the popular perception of the Loch Ness Monster

Practical Cats, the roller-skating musical *Starlight Express* (1984) and *The Phantom of the Opera* (1986). None of these has run for less than a decade and all are still selling out in London.

LOCH NESS MONSTER

The 6th-century monk St Columba was the first reported witness of a monster in the loch that lies in Glen Mor, in the Scottish Highlands. Since then legends of a 'water kelpie' have persisted, with thousands of sightings reported.

No more than a mile wide but 22 miles long and in places more than 230 m (750 ft) deep, Loch Ness has inspired explanations of the mystery ranging from the survival of a colony of aquatic dinosaurs to rotting logs and seismic waves. Tourist attractions inspired by the monster include the Monster Exhibition at Drumnadrochit, and there are good views over Loch Ness from the ruined Urquhart Castle.

John LOCKE

- **Philosopher** • **1632-1704**

Two years after William of Orange acceded to the British throne in 1688, John Locke returned from political exile in Holland to publish two epoch-making books. His *Two Treatises of Government* endorsed the ousting of James II in 1688 by asserting that citizens have a right to refuse to be governed when basic rights, such as life and liberty, are violated.

In *An Essay concerning Human Understanding*, Locke set out the principles of BRITISH EMPIRICISM – the philosophy that experience rather than intellectual reasoning is the root of human knowledge.

CAPITAL GROWTH

London was born as a Roman garrison on the strategic north bank of the Thames. The city has been inhabited almost uninterruptedly for two millennia, and in that time it has grown to cover 610 square miles. Britain's capital is now among the world's largest cities – and its historically and culturally richest

THE GHOST of Roman Londinium can be seen on any map of London. The limits of the modern CITY OF LONDON correspond almost exactly to the Roman wall. A vibrant trade centre under the Romans, London fell into disrepair after their departure and was razed more than once by Viking marauders. But its strategic position as a crossing point on the Thames ensured its recovery and by 1066 when the Normans invaded it the city was effectively England's capital.

SEEDS OF MODERN LONDON

The Normans enhanced the prestige of the 1000-year-old city with stone-built churches and monasteries. They also erected a fortified palace – the TOWER OF LONDON – hard against the eastern wall of the city.

Although the medieval city was not much bigger than that of the 1st century, the power centre of today's London was already taking shape. To the west, on marshy land that was once known as Thorney Island, the seat of government grew up around the court of Edward the Confessor (c.1003-66). His palace, called WESTMINSTER, became the meeting place of parliament under

Edward I, establishing the nation's political heart a little more than a mile away from the commercial centre in the old Roman City district.

FLOURISHING WEST END

During the 17th and 18th centuries foreign trade brought vast wealth to London. Entrepreneurs leased plots to build grand residences in areas north of Westminster and west of the City. Developments included the regular

REGENT'S STREET John Nash designed London's most elegant street for the Prince Regent. It remains intact except for the colonnades, dismantled in the 1920s

1830

CRYSTAL PALACE Joseph Paxton's 488 m (1600 ft) iron and glass conservatory was erected in Hyde Park to house the Great Exhibition

1851

ST PANCRAS STATION 1872 The neo-Gothic faciade enclosing the station was erected in 1872 as part of George Gilbert Scott's Midland Grand Hotel

BRITISH MUSEUM Robert Smirke's classically inspired edifáce replaced the museum's first home, Montagu House

1852

TRAFALGAR SQUARE Charles Barry laid out the square south of the National Gallery in 1838. Nelson's Column was added in 1843

1838

WESTMINSTER ABBEY Edward the Confessor's 11th-century Romanesque abbey was rebuilt in English Gothic by Henry III in 1245. Hawksmoor completed the west towers in 1745

1066

ROYAL ALBERT HALL Public subscription financed the huge domed tribute to Prince Albert

1870

BUCKINGHAM PALACE In 1825 John Nash made a three-sided court out of Buckingham House for George IV. An east front was added in 1847

1829

HOUSES OF PARLIAMENT The medieval House of Lords (A), Commons (B) and Westminster Hall (C) were destroyed by fire in 1834, and rebuilt in neo-Gothic style

1647

NATURAL HISTORY MUSEUM The vast Romanesque-style temple to science was built at the height of Victorian confidence

1881

CHELSEA ROYAL HOSPITAL The magnificent riverside home for veteran soldiers was designed by Christopher Wren

1692

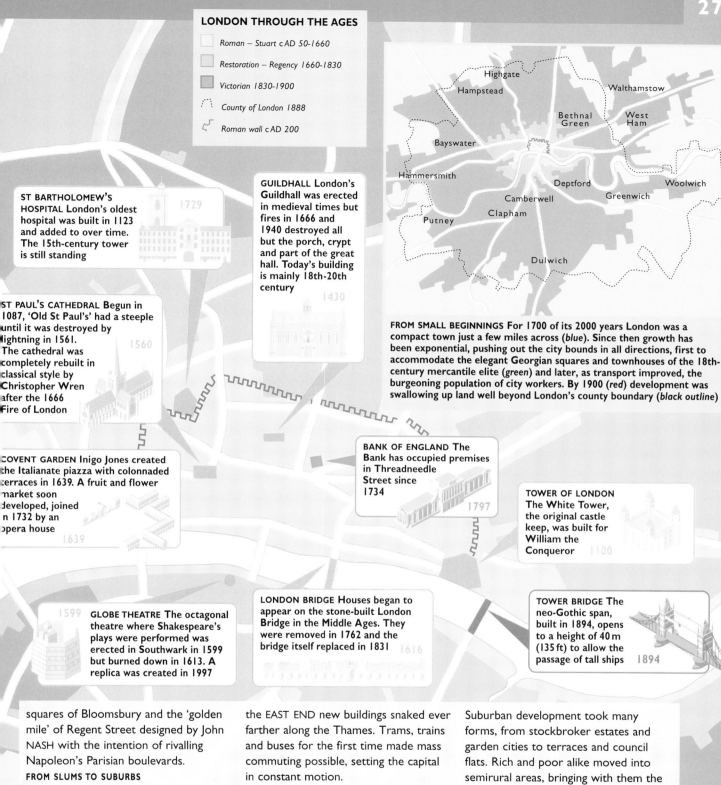

LONDON THROUGH THE AGES

Roman – Stuart c AD 50-1660

Restoration – Regency 1660-1830

Victorian 1830-1900

County of London 1888

Roman wall c AD 200

ST BARTHOLOMEW'S HOSPITAL London's oldest hospital was built in 1123 and added to over time. The 15th-century tower is still standing
1729

GUILDHALL London's Guildhall was erected in medieval times but fires in 1666 and 1940 destroyed all but the porch, crypt and part of the great hall. Today's building is mainly 18th-20th century
1430

ST PAUL'S CATHEDRAL Begun in 1087, 'Old St Paul's' had a steeple until it was destroyed by lightning in 1561. The cathedral was completely rebuilt in classical style by Christopher Wren after the 1666 Fire of London
1560

FROM SMALL BEGINNINGS For 1700 of its 2000 years London was a compact town just a few miles across (*blue*). Since then growth has been exponential, pushing out the city bounds in all directions, first to accommodate the elegant Georgian squares and townhouses of the 18th-century mercantile elite (*green*) and later, as transport improved, the burgeoning population of city workers. By 1900 (*red*) development was swallowing up land well beyond London's county boundary (*black outline*)

COVENT GARDEN Inigo Jones created the Italianate piazza with colonnaded terraces in 1639. A fruit and flower market soon developed, joined in 1732 by an opera house
1639

BANK OF ENGLAND The Bank has occupied premises in Threadneedle Street since 1734
1797

TOWER OF LONDON The White Tower, the original castle keep, was built for William the Conqueror
1100

GLOBE THEATRE The octagonal theatre where Shakespeare's plays were performed was erected in Southwark in 1599 but burned down in 1613. A replica was created in 1997
1599

LONDON BRIDGE Houses began to appear on the stone-built London Bridge in the Middle Ages. They were removed in 1762 and the bridge itself replaced in 1831
1616

TOWER BRIDGE The neo-Gothic span, built in 1894, opens to a height of 40 m (135 ft) to allow the passage of tall ships
1894

squares of Bloomsbury and the 'golden mile' of Regent Street designed by John NASH with the intention of rivalling Napoleon's Parisian boulevards.

FROM SLUMS TO SUBURBS

The size and shape of London evolved further as growing industrialisation through the 19th century, with its slums and polluted air, turned the middle classes away from the inner city.

Quiet villages such as Clapham, Chiswick and Hampstead were rapidly absorbed into the red-brick landscape. Development engulfed the relatively unbuilt areas south of the river and in

the EAST END new buildings snaked ever farther along the Thames. Trams, trains and buses for the first time made mass commuting possible, setting the capital in constant motion.

London's population, which has fluctuated with pestilence and prosperity since its foundation – it was just 14 000-18 000 in 1066 – reached a peak of more than 8.6 million in 1939. After the war, development increasingly spread outwards into suburban areas and density decreased slightly. The 1991 census put the population of greater London at 7.6 million.

Suburban development took many forms, from stockbroker estates and garden cities to terraces and council flats. Rich and poor alike moved into semirural areas, bringing with them the trappings of urban life such as roads, shopping centres and cinemas.

Within the city itself, housing became an urgent priority and the postwar years brought waves of new development. The process of reshaping London still goes on, primarily in the east of the city, where the disused wharves and warehouses of the old docks are rapidly being reclaimed for offices and homes.

LONDON BRIDGE

• Central London (p.499 F3)

London Bridge made headlines in 1968 when it was sold for more than £1 million to an American who thought he was buying Tower Bridge.

Now a tourist attraction in Arizona, the 19th-century structure was one of many bridges that have spanned the River THAMES at this point since Roman times. The first were of timber but around 1200 a stone bridge was built supported by 19 arches. It soon became lined with houses but these were pulled down for a widening scheme in the 18th century.

The present bridge, which opened in 1973, is a cantilever design with three prestressed concrete spans.

LONDONDERRY

• Northern Ireland (p.497 A5)   • Pop. 95 370

Christened Derry from the Irish *doire*, meaning 'a place of oaks' (and still called Derry by Nationalists), Northern Ireland's second largest city grew up around a monastery founded by St Columba in 546 and now a ruin.

In 1604 the town was granted its first charter and in 1613 it was given to the City of London as a 'plantation' to be colonised, funds for which were raised by the London livery companies – hence the new name Londonderry.

It was besieged in 1641 and 1649 by Royalist forces during the Civil War. In 1688-9, it held out for 105 days against JAMES II; a feat recalled annually by Unionists in the Apprentice Boys' March.

Londonderry has huge 17th-century city walls, a Church of Ireland cathedral dating from 1633, and a Roman Catholic cathedral on a hilly site opposite it.

LONDON LIBRARY

• Central London (p.499 B7)   • Founded 1841

Silence reigns in St James's Square in the world's largest private library, which has more than a million books on all subjects, particularly the humanities. The London Library was conceived by the historian Thomas CARLYLE who, weary of noise and long waits in the British

SPEED AND SKILL Longbowmen help John Chandos to secure an English victory at the Battle of Auray in Brittany in 1346

LONGBOW

Of Welsh origin and probably used for hunting in the 12th century, the longbow was incorporated into the English armoury by EDWARD I. For the next two centuries it was to prove a potent weapon, enabling England to triumph at battles such as Poitiers, CRÉCY and AGINCOURT.

Longbows comprised 1.8 m (6 ft) staves of YEW or elm, tensioned by a bowstring. They could propel a 92 cm (36 in) steel-tipped arrow with great accuracy up to 256 m (280 yd), decimating enemy ranks from afar.

The weapon's great advantage was the speed with which highly trained archers could fire it – up to ten arrows a minute. Also, because they fired facing sideways, the ranks of longbowmen took up relatively little space.

By contrast, the crossbow, a Continental weapon, was fired facing ahead. Although it was accurate, high-powered and had a similar range, it was more unwieldy because it had to be wound up before firing, allowing one shot a minute at most.

Museum Reading Room, interested a group of intellectuals, including the historian Henry Hallam and philosopher John Stuart Mill, in founding an alternative funded by public subscription.

The institution, which has some 8000 subscribers, moved to its present site in an 18th-century house in 1845.

LONDON MARATHON

• April

He paced Roger Bannister to the first 4 minute mile, and won an Olympic 3000 metres steeplechase gold in 1956, but Chris Brasher's most lasting mark was in establishing the London Marathon as the world's largest city marathon.

Inspired by competing in the New York marathon, the fiercely idealistic Brasher challenged London, in the columns of *The Observer*, to have 'the heart and hospitality' to stage a similarly ambitious festival.

Brasher's enthusiasm rubbed off on city authorities, police and public alike; some 20 000 runners applied to enter the first race, on March 29, 1981, of whom 7747 were accepted.

By the late 1990s, the annual field had swelled to over 30 000, divided between the elite men's and women's fields, club runners, competitors in wheelchairs and hordes of 'fun runners'. By 1999 the event, which covers 26 miles 385 yd from Blackheath to the finish on The Mall, had raised some £100 million for charity.

LONDON UNIVERSITY

London University is Britain's largest, with more than 96 000 internal and nearly 22 000 external students. It is a federation of colleges and institutes, with outposts such as the British Institute in Paris and a marine research department on the Clyde estuary. As a result of its external programme, London University degrees are accessible to students throughout the world.

Administration and funding are controlled from the Senate House in the university's heartland close to the British Museum in Bloomsbury. Academically, the colleges, including the 'big five' – University College, King's, Imperial, Queen Mary and Westfield, and Royal Holloway – are largely self-governing.

Senate House is also home to the School of Slavonic and Eastern European Studies, and the university library, which holds more than 1 250 000 books.

LONG-DISTANCE ROUTES

Britain's public rights of way, which anyone has the right to walk, extend for more than 140 000 miles. Among these are now hundreds of long-distance routes from 30 miles to 600 miles in length, on which walkers have freedom to roam without diverting onto roads.

Most are regional routes maintained by the local authorities whose boundaries they cross. The government looks after the 15 national routes, the oldest of which is the 256 mile Pennine Way, established in 1965 by the Countryside Commission, the body in charge of access and landscape conservation. England and Wales have a total of 11 national trails, the longest of which is the 600 mile South West Coast Path.

In Scotland, where a much greater freedom of access reduces the need for formal paths, Scottish Natural Heritage has established three long-distance paths. In Northern Ireland the Ulster Way does a round tour of the entire province.

LONGLEAT

- **Wiltshire (p.494 E5)** • **Built 16th century**

In 1949 the Elizabethan manor of Longleat became the first of Britain's stately homes to be opened to the public on a commercial basis. Its tourist appeal was enhanced in 1966 by converting part of the parkland landscaped by 'Capability' Brown into a drive-through safari park. Here the 'Lions of Longleat' and other exotic animals bring the sights and sounds of Africa to 240 ha (600 acres) of Wiltshire countryside.

The great house, partly the work of Robert Smythson – architect of HARDWICK HALL and WOLLATON HALL – was begun in 1568 by John Thynne. Its colourful present owner, Alexander Thynne, the 7th marquess of Bath, has added his own touches, including the Kama Sutra Room mural, to the opulent Renaissance décor of the interior.

LONG PARLIAMENT

- **1640-60**

Britain's longest parliament lasted 20 years, although there was a break from 1653 to 1659 when Oliver CROMWELL instituted his military regime. The

THE NATIONAL ROUTES
The 11 national trails in England and Wales, and the Ulster Way in Northern Ireland, are indicated by an acorn symbol. The three official long-distance routes in Scotland are waymarked with a thistle. Regional routes also have their own distinctive signs.

KEY
1 **Speyside Way** *45 miles*
2 **West Highland Way** *95 miles*
3 **Southern Upland Way** *212 miles*
4 **Pennine Way** *256 miles*
5 **Cleveland Way** *110 miles*
6 **Wolds Way** *79 miles*
7 **Peddars Way and Norfolk Coast Path** *94 miles*
8 **Thames Path** *180 miles*
9 **Ridgeway** *85 miles*
10 **North Downs Way** *141 miles*
11 **South Downs Way** *106 miles*
12 **South West Coast Path** *600 miles*
13 **Pembrokeshire Coast Path** *186 miles*
14 **Offa's Dyke Path** *182 miles*
15 **Ulster Way** *570 miles*

parliament was summoned by CHARLES I in 1640 to raise cash through taxation after 11 turbulent years during which he had tried to rule alone.

Immediately, its members moved to strip Charles, and all future monarchs, of many of the sovereign's powers. They abolished the ancient Star Chamber, which had allowed the king arbitrary freedom to punish opponents. They then took command of the king's finances and the army and navy, winning popular support but alienating conservatives.

Charles tried but failed to resist, and in 1642 was forced to leave London; the CIVIL WAR had begun. By the end of the war, all moderate members of the parliament had been purged by Cromwell; the king's death warrant was signed by a mere 59 MPs – members of the RUMP PARLIAMENT.

LOOK BACK IN ANGER

- **Play by John Osborne** • **1956**

When *Look Back In Anger* was first staged, at the Royal Court Theatre, London, John Osborne was – to his annoyance – labelled an 'angry young man'. But its rage at English hypocrisy and philistinism was not the only emotion depicted in the play. Centring on the marital conflicts of the well-educated, working-class Jimmy Porter and his wife, Alison, a colonel's daughter, the play also expressed, with melancholy and lacerating wit, the disappointment of postwar youth. *Look Back in Anger* marked a turning point in British theatre, ushering in a sequence of works by writers such as Osborne and Arnold Wesker that dealt realistically with the problems of working-class people.

LORD CHANCELLOR

The Lord Chancellor – whose high office of state dates from the 12th century – combines executive, legislative and judicial functions. He is a senior member of the CABINET, responsible for the administration of justice and the courts. He is also head of the judiciary and Speaker of the House of Lords where, by centuries-old tradition, he sits on the 'woolsack', a red bag stuffed with wool symbolising Britain's prosperity.

Lords Chancellor have included figures such as Thomas BECKET, Cardinal WOLSEY and Thomas MORE. Since 1997 the post has been occupied by Lord Irvine of Lairg, who has been pivotal in the Labour government's constitutional reform programme, including Scottish and Welsh devolution and new human rights legislation.

LORD MAYOR

In England and Wales, if a large town is designated a city by royal charter, it has a lord mayor rather than a mayor as its civic leader. Like mayors, they are usually councillors who have given long service to the local authority and are voted into the office by fellow council members for a year, during which they wear the town's chains of office to local events and civic ceremonies.

The post is largely ceremonial. The lord mayor may have the casting vote when debates result in deadlock, but true power rests with the leader of the largest political party on the city council.

This may change. In some countries mayors are directly elected by voters as a chief executive of the local council. Following a referendum in 1998, London voters are due to elect a mayor in 2000; in the future, other cities may follow suit.

LORD'S

• N London (p.499 B1)   • Founded 1787

Like Ascot and Wimbledon, Lord's – the home of CRICKET – is part of the fabric of an English summer. Although the Test match in late June is the centrepiece, the London ground also stages various cup finals and a multitude of other fixtures, including Eton v. Harrow – first held at Lord's in 1805, when Lord Byron played in the losing Harrow side.

Lord's was named after Thomas Lord, a Yorkshire entrepreneur, who opened a private cricket ground in Dorset Square in 1787 and founded the Marylebone Cricket Club (MCC). Lord's moved once in 1811 and to its present site in 1814. One match in every English Test series has been played there since 1884.

The ground's entrance gates, a memorial to W.G. GRACE, were designed in 1923 by Herbert Baker, who also rebuilt the grandstand and added the cast-iron weathervane depicting Father Time. Lord's now holds 30 000 spectators following the opening of a new grandstand in 1998 – the year the MCC voted to permit women members.

LORDS LIEUTENANT

Lords lieutenant are appointed by the Queen as her permanent representatives in the 97 counties and metropolitan districts of the United Kingdom. The office was created in 1557 when MARY I needed trusted aids to keep peace in the provinces.

Their role is now largely ceremonial. Traditionally peers, baronets or military officers, lords lieutenant are selected on the recommendation of the prime minister and attend royalty during official visits to their district or act on the Queen's behalf. In England, Wales and Northern Ireland, they also make recommendations to the LORD CHANCELLOR for the appointment of magistrates.

LORD MAYOR'S SHOW Each November, the new Lord Mayor of London rides to the Law Courts in his 18th-century coach to swear an oath of allegiance

LOUGH NEAGH

• Northern Ireland (p.497 B6)

Five of Northern Ireland's six counties share the shoreline of Lough Neagh – the largest lake in both Ireland and Britain, spanning 170 sq miles.

According to legend the lake was the water-filled cavity left when the mythical figure Finn MacCool (the giant of the GIANT'S CAUSEWAY) hurled a lump of mud out to sea, which became the Isle of Man. More probably it is a hollow left when molten basalt welled up 50 million years ago to cover much of Antrim.

Ten rivers converge to form the lough, which supplies water to a third of Northern Ireland's homes. Its thriving eel industry yields 700 tons a year. It also attracts many waterbirds, best observed from Shane's Castle and the national nature reserve on Oxford Island.

Bernard LOVELL

• Astrophysicist and writer   • b.1913; kt 1961

Enthralled by radio technology as a child, Lovell went on to explore the Universe by means of RADAR – a method of detection using high-frequency radio waves.

He had developed airborne radar systems in the Second World War and, after 1945, took war-surplus radar equipment to JODRELL BANK, open land owned by the University of Manchester, to investigate radio signals from space.

Lovell's discovery of meteor showers secured him funding to build the world's largest radio telescope at Jodrell Bank – a 76 m (250 ft) diameter parabolic dish that could track across the sky. It was used to detect many new quasars, pulsars and red dwarfs deep in space.

L.S. LOWRY

• Artist   • 1887-1976

Lawrence Stephen Lowry painted the northern industrial cities of Britain, especially his native Lancashire. In his pictures small stick-like figures scurry to work at factories or mills beneath grey, overcast skies, suggesting the alienation of human beings powerless before the juggernaut of industrialism.

This loneliness is the hallmark of Lowry's art, depicted in his distinctive naive, flat style, which was not self-taught as – contrary to popular belief – he had studied at several art schools.

Lowry was a part-time artist until retiring from clerical work in 1952, and his pictures – many of them painted in Salford, which now holds the main collection of his work – only gradually became widely known. His first major retrospective exhibition was not until 1976.

Nowadays Lowry's works command high prices. In 1998 *Piccadilly Gardens* was sold for £563 000.

CITY SCENE Even water becomes part of the industrial landscape in L.S. Lowry's *The Pond*, denuded of colour and neatly ringed off

LOYALISTS

In 1886 the prime minister, William GLADSTONE, introduced the first Home Rule bill, aiming to repeal the 1800 Act of Union between Britain and Ireland, and allow a parliament in Dublin.

The bill was fiercely resisted by many Protestants in the nine counties of ULSTER in the north of Ireland. They became known as Unionists, or Loyalists, maintaining absolute loyalty to Britain and forming an alliance with the Conservative party, still formally known as the Conservative and Unionist Party.

The term was also used to refer to Americans who stayed loyal to Britain in the AMERICAN WAR OF INDEPENDENCE. After the war, some 100 000 Loyalists fled, many of them settling in Canada.

LUDDITES

Faced with unemployment and starvation, so-called Luddites broke into Nottinghamshire textile factories in 1811 and smashed the new industrial machines that they perceived were putting them out of work. The violence quickly spread to neighbouring counties.

It was not clear if the General Lud from whom they took their name, was a real figure or a cover for the activists, many of whom were hanged or transported overseas in 1813.

A further outbreak was suppressed in 1816 and the term has lived on to mean all those who oppose technical progress.

LUDLOW

• Shropshire (p.494 E3)   • Pop. 9040

Once a thriving wool centre, the hillside town of Ludlow is remarkable for its well-preserved old buildings, such as the large 15th-century parish church, the ornate half-timbered Feathers Hotel and the Georgian houses lining Broad Street.

Ludlow's streets were laid out in the Middle Ages, outside the rose-pink stone walls of its Norman castle – a ruin since the 18th century and now the main venue of the annual Ludlow festival.

Built high above the River Teme, the castle was part of a chain of strongholds that guarded the English borders against marauding Welsh tribesmen and later belonged to the powerful Mortimer family, who feature prominently in Shakespeare's historical plays.

LULLINGSTONE

• Kent (p.495 H5)   • Built c.AD 80   • EH

Excavations in 1949 revealed the remains of an opulent Roman house, destroyed by fire in the 5th century AD.

Built in the 1st century AD above the River Darent, Lullingstone became increasingly luxurious. From the 3rd century, rooms with underfloor heating were added and later a reception room was decorated with classical mosaics – parts of which survive. Fragments of frescoes from its chapel – now in the British Museum – provide some early evidence of Christianity in Britain.

LUNDY ISLAND

• **Bristol Channel (p.494 B5)** • **Pop. 20** • **NT**

The dramatically wild Lundy Island – some 11 miles off Devon's Hartland Point and just three miles long and half a mile wide – is largely uncultivated plain, hills, bays and massed anarchic jumbles of granite. Its cliffs plunge 122 m (400 ft) into the sea in places.

The piratical clan De Marisco held Lundy in Norman times, and built a castle near the island's only landing spot. The Turks, French and Spanish later took turns controlling Lundy – all briefly; it was also an occasional government garrison. The scattering of buildings, most of which date from the 19th century, includes a church, an inn and three lighthouses.

Now managed by the LANDMARK TRUST on behalf of the National Trust, Lundy supports sika deer, soay sheep, wild ponies and wild goats. There are seals and a rich tally of fish and aquatic plants in surrounding waters. More than 400 bird species have been recorded, but the

SACRED STONES Early Christian memorial stones stand in the cemetery below a lighthouse on Lundy Island

puffin, which gave Lundy its Norse name *lund* – meaning 'puffin island' – is in sharp decline. Access to Lundy is by boat from Bideford or Ilfracombe in Devon.

Edwin LUTYENS

• **Architect** • **1869-1944; kt 1918**

His expressive, grandiose approach made Edwin Lutyens the Edwardian establishment's favourite builder. Early in his career Lutyens was influenced by the ARTS AND CRAFTS movement and specialised in country houses, such as Munstead Wood in Surrey, commissioned in 1896 by the garden designer Gertrude JEKYLL.

Later he designed a number of public buildings and the Cenotaph in Whitehall, London (1919-20). Lutyens' masterpiece was the planning of the British imperial capital of New Delhi, India. This included the magnificent Viceroy's House (now the presidential palace; 1913-30), which he personally designed.

LYME REGIS

• **Dorset (p.494 D6)** • **Pop. 3850**

In Saxon times, Lyme belonged to the monks of Sherborne Abbey, who came to its shores to distil salt from sea water. Lyme gained the title 'Regis' in 1284, when the little harbour town was granted a royal charter by Edward I, who used the port as a base for wars against the

French. In 1588 five ships sailed to fight the Spanish Armada from the Cobb, the town's massive sickle-shaped stone breakwater, made famous in the novels *Persuasion* by Jane Austen and John Fowles' *The French Lieutenant's Woman* (1969), made into a film in 1981.

The town became a fashionable seaside retreat in the late 18th and early 19th centuries. The area around Lyme Regis is also known for its fossils; the skeleton of a prehistoric marine reptile known as an ichthyosaurus, discovered in nearby cliffs in 1811, is displayed in the Dinosaurland museum. To the east is Golden Cap, at 191 m (626 ft) the highest cliff on Britain's south coast.

Vera LYNN

• **Singer and Second World War forces' sweetheart** • **b.1917; DBE 1975**

Vera Lynn made a name for herself in the 1930s with the dance bands of Joe Loss and Bert Ambrose. But she is chiefly remembered for the concerts and broadcasts during the Second World War that raised the morale of British troops and helped spur the Allies to victory.

The London-born entertainer's best-known hits were 'We'll meet again' and 'There'll be blue birds over the white cliffs of Dover', songs of hope that promised warm hearths and faithful sweethearts to those in the front line.

LYONS' CORNER HOUSES

In 1908 the catering entrepreneur Joe Lyons opened his first Corner House in Coventry Street, near London's Piccadilly Circus, with 4500 seats. It filled a gap in the market between tea shop and high-class restaurant, offering quality food at low prices in bright surroundings with snowy white cloths and fresh flowers on every table. Others quickly followed in London and the provinces.

The pretty, smartly dressed waitresses (the first to be employed on such a large scale) earned the name 'Nippies' in the 1930s when a guest at a banquet for 7500 at Olympia remarked, 'They're not waitresses – they're too nippy.'

The Lyons' chain survived decades of change until fast food restaurants started to boom in the 1970s.

The MABINOGION

Compiled in the 14th century, the Welsh collection of tales known as *The Mabinogion* (a title thought to derive from *mabinogi*, Welsh for 'youth') is widely believed to have been written down by monks. They replaced the ancient deities with knights, and even clerics, although the tales themselves clearly predate CHRISTIANITY.

Reading between the lines unravels a rich Celtic mythology, the central theme of which is the conflict between the Children of Llyr and the Children of Don – perhaps relating to the underworld and sky deities.

The Mabinogion is divided into four main sections. In the second the gigantic Bran – so vast that when he lies across a river an army can march over his back – wades across the Irish Sea leading the Britons to war against the Irish.

Mortally wounded in the final battle, Bran commands his head to be cut off and taken to the White Hill in London – to remain there for decades undecayed, staring out to the Continent in order to protect the kingdom from invaders.

John McADAM

• Road builder • 1756-1836
John McAdam did not set out to be a road builder. Born in Ayr, he went to New York aged 14 and became a wealthy businessman.

On his return to Scotland in 1783, McAdam was appointed deputy lieutenant of Ayrshire and introduced local road improvement schemes. He went to Bristol as an adviser in 1789 and experimented in different road building techniques. From 1815, as surveyor-general of the Bristol Roads Trust, he put his new methods to work.

McAdam built roads with a slight camber, using layers of small, carefully graded stones, which became compacted with use – a technique that was widely adopted from 1827 when he became surveyor-general of roads in Britain. Later, the stones were bound with tar to create 'tarmacadam' or 'tarmac'.

Thomas MACAULAY

• Historian   • 1800-59; bn 1857
With his *History of England* (1848-61) Thomas Macaulay was the first English historian to reach a mass market. For 20 years he wrote brilliantly for the *Edinburgh Review* and was also a lawyer and reformer whose work had a lasting

MOCK-ADAM-IZING – the Colossus of Roads.

KING OF THE ROAD When John McAdam was appointed surveyor-general of British roads in 1827, his achievements and wealth were gently mocked by the caricaturist Henry Heath

impact on British and Indian law. An ardent Whig, he was elected MP for Calne, Wiltshire, in 1830 and then for Leeds. From 1834 he worked for four years in India, where he helped to structure Indian criminal law and reformed the education system.

Back in London he wrote the popular *Lays of Ancient Rome* (1842). He was elected MP for Edinburgh and began the *History of England*. Well researched and eminently readable, it brought Macaulay great wealth and, in due course, a seat in the House of Lords.

MACBETH

• King of Scotland 1040-57 • 1005-57
To many, Macbeth is no more than the doomed murderer of Shakespeare's tragedy – a play better known than the man himself. In reality, he was a wise and successful monarch whose name translates from the Gaelic as 'son of life'.

Having seized the Scottish throne from Duncan I, Macbeth ruled for the next 17 years, bringing such prosperity that, during a pilgrimage to Rome in 1050, he was said to have scattered money 'like seed corn'.

Both Macbeth and his queen, Greoch (Shakespeare's Lady Macbeth), had legitimate claims to the throne, being descended from earlier monarchs. But they were ousted by Malcolm, the son of Duncan, who won victories at Dunsinane in 1054 and at Lumphanan in 1057, where Macbeth was killed. Macbeth was briefly succeeded by his stepson Lulach 'The Simpleton' and Malcolm became king of Scotland in 1058, as Malcolm III.

HARBINGERS OF DOOM The three witches of Shakespeare's *Macbeth* – forever overshadowing historical reality – are vividly evoked in an oil painting by the 18th-century artist Henry Fuseli

Flora MACDONALD

• **Scottish heroine** • **1722-90**

At the age of 22 Flora Macdonald won fame for saving the life of BONNIE PRINCE CHARLIE after the Scottish Jacobite army's defeat by English forces at the Battle of CULLODEN MOOR in 1746.

A respectable young woman brought up by Lady Clanranald, wife of the chief of the Macdonald clan, she met the dashing young Charles – on the run from the English army – as she was travelling from Benbecula in the Outer Hebrides. Flora arranged for him to be disguised as her Irish maid, 'Betty Burke', and to travel with her to her home on SKYE.

After the prince's escape, she was imprisoned for a year in the Tower of London. She married in 1750 and emigrated with her husband to North Carolina in 1774, later returning to Skye.

Ramsay MACDONALD

• **Prime minister 1924, 1929-35** • **1866-1937**

James Ramsay MacDonald was Labour's first prime minister. Although his initial period of office in 1924 lasted a mere nine months, he established Labour as a competent governing party.

Born in Lossiemouth, Scotland, he joined the Independent Labour Party in 1894, and was elected MP for Leicester in 1906. In Parliament, his oratorical powers proved outstanding; he became leader of the LABOUR PARTY in 1911.

However, his ardent opposition to the First World War, for which he was vilified in the press, lost him his parliamentary seat. Later his stand won respect and in 1922 he returned to parliament and resumed leadership of the party.

MacDonald won the 1929 election but the Depression frustrated plans for social reform. In 1931 impending national bankruptcy compelled him to form the National Government, a coalition with the Liberals and Conservatives. He remained in power until 1935.

WATERPROOFS Charles Macintosh and his partner Thomas Hancock manufactured an extensive range of novel rubber products

FRESH NEW LOOK Style defies age in the drawing room of the Hill House near Glasgow, which Charles Rennie Mackintosh created for the publisher Walter Blackie in 1904

Charles MACINTOSH

• **Industrial chemist** • **1766-1843**

It was a passion for science that led Macintosh to discover a process of waterproofing fabric and to develop the garment that bore his (misspelt) name.

Born in Glasgow, he abandoned an early clerical job to experiment with dyestuffs, alum, steel and bleaching powder. His 'mackintosh' material was a chance discovery while he was trying to find a use for the solvent coal naphtha, a by-product of the gas industry.

Macintosh hit on the idea of dissolving India rubber in naphtha and using the solution between two layers of cloth to create a water-repellent material. He patented the idea in 1823 and the first material came into use in 1824.

Though remembered chiefly for this achievement, it was for other pioneering work in chemistry that he was made a fellow of the Royal Society in 1823.

Charles Rennie MACKINTOSH

• **Architect and designer** • **1868-1928**

Charles Rennie Mackintosh was one of the most notable exponents of Art Nouveau. In 1896 he won the contest to design the new Glasgow School of Art and created a building of square-cut stone, iron and plate glass with a sparkling but stark interior that won him international acclaim.

His interior work with rectilinear, often inlaid furniture – especially his high-backed chairs – also gained him a considerable following on the Continent, although he was less influential in Britain. He created elaborate tearooms on a variety of sites around Glasgow – most now destroyed or disused – and some remarkable house interiors. In 1913 he broke with his architect colleagues and moved to London in 1923. There his practice failed and he retired to the south of France.

Kenneth MACMILLAN

• **Choreographer** • **1929-92; kt 1983**

When stage fright ended his BALLET dancing career in the 1950s, Kenneth MacMillan turned to choreography. Born in Scotland, he joined Sadler's Wells Ballet as a teenager, remaining with the company, which became the Royal Ballet in 1956, until the end of his career.

He succeeded Ninette de Valois and Frederick ASHTON as the company's principal choreographer in 1953 and modified its classical style to incorporate modern dance techniques. He set his first three ballets to music by Stravinsky.

For Rudolph Nureyev and Margot FONTEYN, he choreographed a notable *Romeo and Juliet* in 1965. In 1970, he succeeded Ashton as director of the Royal Ballet

MUD-
RESISTANT
BOOT

SEA HOOD

LIFE BUOY

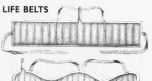

LIFE BELTS

BUCKET

WATERPROOF
TENT

and forged strong links with American companies. In 1977, he resigned to concentrate on choreography. His major works include *Rite of Spring* (1962), *Manon* (1974) and *Requiem* (1977).

MACMILLAN FAMILY

The great-grandfather of Britain's 44th prime minister, the Conservative Harold Macmillan (1894-1986), was a poor Scottish crofter. However, he made sure that his son Daniel was educated and apprenticed him to a bookseller.

Daniel later set up a bookshop in Cambridge with his brother Alexander and in 1843 founded Macmillan and Co., publishers, in London – a company which was solidly successful. When they died, the House of Macmillan was run by three of their sons and expanded rapidly, signing writers of the calibre of Thomas Hardy and W.B. Yeats.

In 1920 Harold Macmillan joined the firm, eventually becoming senior partner with his brother Daniel. In 1924 he was elected to parliament. As minister of housing in the 1951-4 Conservative government, he oversaw the building of

300000 houses a year. In 1957 he succeeded Anthony Eden as prime minister and led the party to a third successive victory with the slogan 'You've never had it so good'.

As prime minister he supported independence for British colonies in Africa and introduced Polaris missiles. His bid to take Britain into the European Community was blocked in 1963, when ill health forced him to resign.

MADAME TUSSAUD'S

• **Central London (p.499 B2)**
• **Founded 1835**

Beside the busy Marylebone Road, Oscar Wilde keeps company with boxer Frank Bruno, model Naomi Campbell and former prime minister Margaret Thatcher.

The history of the gallery that displays famous and infamous wax figures is gruesome. It stretches back to 1770 in Paris, where Madame Tussaud learnt to model with wax, tutored by her uncle, Dr Philippe Curtius. During the French Revolution, she was forced to turn her hand to making the death masks of aristocrats sent to the guillotine.

In 1802 Madame Tussaud came to Britain with a travelling exhibition of effigies and artefacts from the revolution and the Napoleonic Wars, which seized the public imagination. In 1835 the exhibition found a permanent home in London's Baker Street, moving a short distance to its present site in 1884. Some of Tussaud's original work and earlier relics, including death masks and a guillotine blade, are on display in the 'Chamber of Horrors', a ghoulish display that includes the likenesses of the murderers Dr Crippen and John Christie.

Around 365 characters inhabit Madame Tussaud's. Every year 15 new famous figures replace fading stars – each costing around £30 000 to produce

MAES HOWE

• **Prehistoric site** • **Orkney (p.497 D1)** • **HS**

At 35 m (115 ft) wide and 7 m (23 ft) high, Maes Howe, built around 3000 BC, is the largest chambered tomb in north-west Europe. Housed in a cone-shaped mound, from which it takes its old Norse name, it is also one of the best surviving constructions of PREHISTORIC BRITAIN.

Outside, the mound is surrounded by a bank and a ditch; inside, there is a central chamber, side chambers and an upward-sloping passage leading to the entrance. At the winter solstice in late December, the setting sun streams down the passageway to illuminate the back wall of the main chamber, marking the turning point of the year – perhaps a time of religious significance for the Neolithic people who built the tomb.

The tomb was later raided by Vikings, who left runic inscriptions mentioning treasure. If gold and silver were ever present in the tomb, none now remains.

MAGNA CARTA

In June 1215, when King JOHN sealed the 63-clause charter presented by rebellious barons at Runnymede, he did so to buy time. Neither he nor his opponents, angry at his high-handed government and lack of leadership, realised how influential the charter would be.

The charter contained something for everyone – narrow clauses protecting baronial property, and sweeping provisions guaranteeing the rights of all freemen. Clause 39 asserted the right of a freeman to be tried 'by the lawful judgment of his peers or by the law of the land' before any punishment could be imposed, which formed the basis of the HABEAS CORPUS principle still in force today.

There are four surviving copies of the original 1215 charter, one in Salisbury Cathedral, one in Lincoln Cathedral and two in the British Library.

DRIVING GLOVES

RAILWAY CUSHION

INFLATED GLOBE FOR SENDING LETTERS BY SEA

BOAT CLOAK

BOAT CLOAK INFLATED

DIVING SUIT

MAIDEN CASTLE

- **Dorset (p.494 E6)** • **EH**

Overlapping earthworks 2.7 m (9 ft) high conceal the entrances to Maiden Castle, making it one of the largest hill-forts in western Europe. The ramparts were built in about 300 BC on a site first settled in 4000 BC. The fort was occupied for 40 years after the Roman invasion, perhaps by the invaders, and also contains the remains of a 4th century Romano-Celtic temple. When the archaeologist Mortimer WHEELER began excavating the 19 ha (47 acre) site in 1934, he uncovered an ammunition dump of 22 000 sling stones and a cemetery, where the remains of 52 people – one with a Roman spearhead in its spine – have so far been found.
See also PREHISTORIC BRITAIN

John MAJOR

- **Prime minister 1990-7** • **b.1943**

John Major was not obvious prime minister material. He was born in Merton, south-west London, the son of a former trapeze artist, and left school at 16 with few qualifications. He worked in banking and as a Conservative councillor in Lambeth, and in 1979 he became MP for Huntingdon. In a giddy rise to high office, he was appointed in 1989 as, first, foreign secretary and then chancellor of the exchequer, enforcing the monetarist policies of the prime minister, Margaret THATCHER. When she resigned in 1990, he won the party leadership.

As prime minister, Major pledged to create a classless society. He launched the Citizen's Charter to raise the standard of public services, took Britain into the 1991 GULF WAR, and against the odds won the 1992 election, his unassuming manner appealing to voters.

Deep divisions in the Tory party over the EUROPEAN UNION, particularly

ART AND CRAFT John Makepeace used more than 800 pieces of ebony to create the Mitre chair in 1978

its goal of a single currency, blighted Major's government, and it was rocked on September 16, 1992, by the Black Wednesday financial collapse.

Major brought peace in Northern Ireland closer in 1993 with the Anglo-Irish Downing Street Declaration, but the splits over Europe and scandals involving Conservative MPs seriously weakened his government. His election defeat in 1997 was the heaviest of the 20th century.

John MAKEPEACE

- **Furniture designer** • **b.1939; OBE 1988**

A towering figure in British design, John Makepeace has led a late 20th-century revival in furniture-making. He combines native hardwoods such as mulberry, sycamore, oak and holly with leather, metals and stone in functional yet painstakingly constructed tables, chairs and cabinets.

Makepeace made his first furniture in 1957, inspired by the work of William MORRIS. He bought Parnham House in Dorset in 1976, where he established a school for craftsmen. His forest-based Hooke Park campus aims to educate furniture makers in converting native timbers into mass-market products.

MALLARD

- **Steam locomotive** • **Built 1938**

On July 3, 1938, an elegant, streamlined steam engine, with the incongruous name of *Mallard*, hauled a train of seven coaches at 126 mph, establishing a world speed record for steam locomotives. It has never been broken.

Mallard was designed for the London and North Eastern Railway (LNER) by its chief mechanical engineer, Nigel Gresley. It was one of a class of powerful engines called 'A4 Pacifics' – following on from the 'Atlantics' – the first of which, *Great Northern*, appeared in 1922. *Mallard* is now displayed at the National Railway Museum in York.

Thomas MALORY

- **Writer** • **d.1471**

Romance and derring-do envelops the figure of Thomas Malory, just as they do the characters in *Le Morte D'Arthur*, his collection of Arthurian legends and the finest English prose narrative of the late Middle Ages. Speculation surrounds his identity, but he was probably Sir Thomas Malory of Newbold Revel, Warwickshire. The writer was repeatedly put in prison, where he wrote most, if not all, of his great work, and repeatedly escaped.

In 1485 William CAXTON printed *Le Morte D'Arthur*. His version remained the standard edition until 1934, when a superior 15th-century manuscript was found in Winchester College library.

NO UGLY DUCKLING The 1938 *Mallard* engine, with its sweeping Art Deco curves, is still capable of working up a head of steam. It was retired from service in 1963, after covering almost 1.5 million miles in 25 years

Thomas MALTHUS

• **Economist and demographer** • **1766-1834**

The pamphlet 'Essay on the Principle of Population' shocked Britain's intellectual elite in 1798. It was published anonymously by Thomas Malthus, a curate, and his message was simple: given that populations increase as food supplies increase, and that there is a limit to how much food can be produced, the rise in population must soon outstrip the food available. Only infanticide, disease, famine and war could keep numbers down. His pessimistic ideas clashed with philosophers of the day who believed that reason could solve human problems.

In 1805 Malthus was made professor of political economy at the East India Company's college, where he made his reputation as an economist. An advocate of late marriage and birth control to slow population increase, he married at 38 and limited himself to three children.

MALVERN HILLS

• **W England (p.494 E3)**

The 9 mile Malverns range, formed by volcanic action 300 million years ago, rises unexpectedly from the Midland Plain to divide Herefordshire and Worcestershire. Its highest point is the 425 m (1395 ft) Worcestershire Beacon.

The many springs dotted about the hills made Malvern Wells a fashionable spa town in the 19th century. Queen Victoria visited the baths and pump room, and Elizabeth II always travels with a supply of Malvern water.

MANCHESTER

• **NW England (p.496 B5)** • **Pop. 402 890**

Natives of England's third-largest city are called Mancunians – a distant link with the Romans who built a fort there in AD 79 called Mamucium. Manchester's prosperity started in the 1300s when Flemish weavers settled there to work in wool and linen, but the city's 18th-century growth coincided with the mechanisation of the cotton industry, which transformed a rural area into one dotted with mill towns, such as Bolton

and Blackburn. Manchester dominated them all, overrunning Salford, across the River Irwell, merging with Stockport, and in 1894 linking with the sea 35 miles away along the Manchester Ship Canal.

Victorian wealth is reflected in the city's public buildings, such as the Gothic town hall. Another 19th-century legacy is the *Manchester Guardian* newspaper, now *The Guardian*, founded in 1821 by city liberals.

Manchester is, after London, England's greatest centre of education, with four universities and some 50 000 students.

Manchester's glass-and-steel-fronted Bridgewater Hall – the base for the Hallé Orchestra, founded in 1857 – was built in 1996 on giant springs to muffle noise and vibrations from nearby railway stations

IT'S ALL IN THE GAME Bobby Charlton scores against Benfica in Manchester United's 4-1 European Cup Final victory – the first by an English team – in 1968. Thirty years on, sales of United strips help to boost the profits of the world's richest football club

MANCHESTER UNITED

• **Founded 1878**

Adored by millions who have never seen a match at its Old Trafford ground, Manchester United is the world's best-known and richest football team. The club became a consistent football force in the 1950s, thanks to the perceptive Scottish manager Matt Busby, whose 'Busby Babes' were England's first European Cup representatives in 1956.

In 1958 eight of the players died in an aircrash at Munich while returning from a European Cup tie in Belgrade. Busby survived to build an even better team containing football icons such as Denis Law and George BEST. United again dominated English football in the 1990s,

managed by Alex Ferguson. Between 1993 and 1998 the team won four league championships, including two 'doubles' – league and FA Cup victories. In 1999 United again won the league and FA Cup, then added the European Cup to become the first British team to win the 'treble'.

MANOR

England's villages, parishes, country houses and rural social structures owe much to the medieval landholding system of the manor. This was a district owned and administered by a lord, who held regular courts in the great hall of his manor house to deal with minor local offences. His farmland was worked by serfs – unpaid peasant farmers who were virtually the lord's slaves.

From the time of the PEASANT'S REVOLT in 1381, the manorial system came under increasing pressure, and by the 17th century it had given way to a pattern of landholders and tenant farmers that is little changed today.

Lordships of the manor are still eagerly sought after whenever they are sold at auction. Although stripped of any purpose, they often include ancient perks such as local fishing or mineral rights.

MARKETS

Most British communities larger than a village began as market towns. The Romans had markets at Lindum (Lincoln) and Glevum (Gloucester), and the Cotswold 'Chippings' such as Chipping Campden and Chipping Norton were the Saxon 'cepings' or 'cheapings', where goods were bought and sold. In Norwich the wide street of Tombland gets its name from the Saxon 'toom', meaning an open marketplace.

UNDYING TRADITION

Medieval kings raised much revenue from selling royal charters for markets to local lords or bishops. From 1200 to 1400 more than 5000 charters were issued to towns such as Market Harborough, which has had both a general and a cattle market since 1203, and King's Lynn, whose two main squares are still known as Tuesday Market and Saturday Market.

LONDON MARKETS

The capital's giant wholesale food markets include Smithfield meat market, still on its original site – once a 'smooth field' – and Billingsgate, which traded in fish for 400 years near London Bridge before moving to the Isle of Dogs in 1982. Open-air markets enliven more

ANTIQUE ROAD SHOW Every Saturday a mile of stalls stretches along London's Portobello Road, selling everything from junk to genuine antiques. The market began in the 1870s

than 100 streets. Petticoat Lane, near Liverpool Street Station, was originally a place where the poor could buy the cast-off clothes of the wealthy. Camden Lock, the trendiest of London's markets since the 1970s, is a complex of restored warehouses crammed with ethnic clothes and arts and crafts, books and records. Brick Lane, off Bethnal Green Road, offers everything from frozen meat to old DIY tools in a bedlam of bustle and noise.

COME AND BUY The market held every Wednesday and Saturday in St Albans, Hertfordshire, was founded around the late 10th century to supply the abbey

MARBLE ARCH

• Central London (p.499 B2) • Built 1827

At the junction of Oxford Street, Park Lane, Edgware Road and Bayswater Road traffic teems around the incongruous Marble Arch monument. It was designed as an equal to the Arch of Constantine in Rome by John NASH in 1827 to stand in front of BUCKINGHAM PALACE. But royal carriages were too wide to pass through the arch, so it was moved to its present site as an entrance to Hyde Park. In 1908 road expansion left it marooned in the middle of an island.

The ground the arch stands on is the site of Tyburn, which from 1196 to 1783 served as the place of public execution for condemned prisoners at Newgate prison. On the adjacent traffic island a concrete circle inlaid with brass lettering identifies the spot where the gallows stood. Only senior members of the royal family and the King's Troop Royal Horse Artillery may pass through the finely wrought gates of Marble Arch.

MARBLE HILL HOUSE

• SW London (p.498 B4) • Built 1724-9 • EH

The grand rooms of Marble Hill House presented a glittering social scene in the 18th century when Henrietta Howard, countess of Suffolk, the well-rewarded mistress of George II, played hostess in her Thames-side villa to a salon of artists and statesmen. Writer and wit Horace Walpole dropped in from his nearby home in Twickenham; the poet Alexander Pope helped to design the parkland; and aristocrats arrived by river with the latest gossip from court.

The elegant, cube-shaped house was designed in the PALLADIAN STYLE by Roger Morris and Henry Herbert, 9th earl of Pembroke. The columned entrance hall is based on the central court of a Roman house, and rising through the upper two floors is the Great Room, with sumptuous gilded carving.

Twenty years of detective work and craftsmanship restored the house in 1986 to the splendour of the 1740s and 1750s. Wallpapers were recreated from faded fragments; tables lost for 150 years were found in Australia; and Roman scenes painted for Lady Suffolk were recovered from New York and France.

FIELD OF BATTLE A daring cavalry charge into the heart of the French army won Blenheim for the Duke of Marlborough. Four out of five French troops were killed or taken prisoner

Guglielmo MARCONI

• Physicist and inventor • 1874-1937

The wife poisoner Dr Crippen had Guglielmo Marconi to blame for his arrest in 1910 on the SS *Montrose*. The Italian-born Marconi had developed in Britain the first practical system of sending messages through the air by electromagnetic wave, enabling the captain of the ship to contact Scotland Yard – the first use of wireless telegraphy in a murder hunt.

Marconi made his first experiments in Italy in 1895, but when he failed to win support there he came to Britain and in 1897 established his Wireless Telegraph Company. In 1898 he sent a radio signal across the Channel and three years later in Newfoundland, Canada, he received a Morse code message sent from Cornwall. Within 20 years his invention had made it possible to broadcast speech and music on radio waves.

Marconi received the Nobel prize for physics in 1909. When he died the BBC maintained a 2 minute radio silence.

MARKET GARDENING

A 1086 Domesday Book listing of eight cottars – peasants with a small piece of land – in the manor of Fulham growing vegetables, and no doubt supplying London, is the first mention in Britain of market gardening: the cultivation of fruit and vegetables for sale.

Market towns provided the outlet for gardeners' produce, and the demands of urban dwellers, particularly from the Industrial Revolution onwards,

RADIO HAM Guglielmo Marconi (*far right*) stands in 1901 beside the first road vehicle to be fitted with radio. The tall tube on the roof is the aerial

brought gardeners to bustling city markets such as Covent Garden in London. Today, flowers and fresh fruit and vegetables, such as Norfolk parsnips, Devon broad beans, Kent apples, pears and cherries, and Scottish raspberries, are cultivated by market gardeners for stalls, shops and supermarkets in a business worth more than £3 billion.

MARKETS: *see opposite page*

MARKS & SPENCER

• Founded 1894

'Don't ask the price, it's a penny' was the slogan when Michael Marks, a Jewish Russian-Polish refugee and Leeds market stallholder, joined Tom Spencer, a cashier from Skipton, in a business that became 'M&S', Britain's biggest clothing retailer.

Marks passed on his 60 'penny bazaars' in 1907 to his son, Simon, who recruited his friend, Israel Sieff. Each married the other's sister. In the 1920s they took the radical step of buying goods direct from manufacturers, allowing them the control over quality and price that defined the M&S appeal. This was not lost on the government in the Second World War when it relied on M&S to produce high-quality, low-cost utility clothing.

The famous St Michael trademark first appeared in 1928, and in 1930 the flagship store on London's Oxford Street opened. A year later food departments appeared in some large branches.

In 1975 the first stores outside Britain were opened in Paris and Brussels, part of a chain that now includes more than 400 outlets in 30 countries. But in 1999 M&S showed that it was fallible by announcing a surprise net loss, despite having a turnover of £8.2 billion.

Duke of MARLBOROUGH

• Soldier • 1650-1722; bn 1682; duke 1702

John Churchill was 51 when Queen Anne made him commander-in-chief of her army during the War of the Spanish Succession (1701-14). He won every battle he fought, including Blenheim (1704), demonstrating his gifts as a great British general and daring military strategist. In thanks, Anne named him 1st duke of Marlborough.

Churchill was born into a Devon Royalist family bankrupted by the Civil War, but bought his way into the Guards with £5000 charmed out of the duchess of Cleveland, a mistress of Charles II. He was soon a colonel and in 1677 married Sarah Jennings, an attendant of the young Princess Anne, later queen.

After William III's succession, rumours of Jacobite sympathies halted Churchill's career until Anne came to the throne in 1702. After the victory at Blenheim she granted him an estate at Woodstock, near Oxford, and £100 000 of public money to build BLENHEIM PALACE.

Churchill was accused of embezzling public funds in 1711 and dismissed. He returned to favour under George I but never saw Blenheim completed.

SEASIDE REDOUBT The Martello tower at Aldeburgh in Suffolk was the only one to be built in a quatrefoil, or four-lobed, pattern. It has been restored by the Landmark Trust

Karl MARX

• Political philosopher • 1818-83

An attendant at the British Museum was once asked to recall Karl Marx, who had studied in the reading room. 'Well,' he said, 'he worked away, year in year out, until one day he never came back, and nothing was heard of him since.'

The German-born Marx, whose philosophy helped to shape 20th-century communism and socialism, had urged the overthrow of the bourgeoisie with his *Communist Manifesto* (1848). After the republican uprisings of that year failed across the Continent he was banned from most European countries and settled in London. He eked out a living as a journalist while working on the first volume of *Das Kapital,* completed in 1867, which savages capitalism and advocates an ideal form of communism.

When Marx died, his collaborator, Friedrich Engels, completed and published the second and third volumes. Marx was buried in Highgate Cemetery.

Christopher MARLOWE

• Playwright • 1564-93

'A kind of cross between Oscar Wilde and Jack the Ripper' is how the poet Seamus Heaney described Christopher Marlowe, the most important English playwright before William Shakespeare.

In plays such as *Tamburlaine the Great* (1587-9) and *Dr Faustus,* first staged in 1592, Marlowe took the dramatic form of tragedy and infused it with blood and vengeance, and central characters whose towering passions dictate the action of the play and their own destruction.

Marlowe's life was melodramatic, full of rumours of political, religious and sexual irregularity. He was killed at a Deptford pub in an argument over a bill.

MARTELLO TOWERS

In 1794 the British army captured a small, squat tower on Corsica's Cape Mortella. Its defensive capabilities were so impressive that the design was copied in Britain and some 100 'Martello' towers were erected between 1805 and 1812 along the English coast from Seaford in Sussex to Aldeburgh in Suffolk.

The low, thick-walled towers, each with a 24-pounder cannon and a garrison of 25, were cheap to build and reassured the public that steps were being taken against an anticipated French invasion.

The invasion never happened and many of the towers became redundant, but some Martellos were used as coastguard stations up to the 1980s.

MARTYRS

The religious and political turmoil of British history is marked by the names of those who were martyred for their beliefs. The first English martyr was St Alban, a Roman soldier put to death around AD 200 for sheltering a fugitive Christian at Verulamium, which was renamed ST ALBANS in his honour.

KING AND MARTYR

In 978 the 15-year-old Saxon king Edward was killed at Corfe Castle by order of his stepmother. From 1001 he was known as Edward the Martyr and his remains were said to have miraculous powers.

KNIGHTLY REBEL

Critics of the papacy and the English Church of the 14th and 15th centuries, known mockingly as Lollards, from a Flemish word for 'mumbler', were led for a time by John Oldcastle. He transcribed the works of the religious reformer John WYCLIFFE and fought in France for Henry IV. After the accession of Henry V he was 'hanged burning' in 1417. He may have been the model for the Shakespearean character Falstaff.

TUDOR TYRANNY

Henry VIII and his daughter MARY I martyred many an Englishman. In 1536 Robert Aske, a Yorkshire lawyer and leader of the Pilgrimage of Grace, a Catholic protest at the Dissolution of the Monasteries, was hanged by Henry along with many of his followers. Henry also executed the statesman Thomas MORE and Bishop John Fisher for their refusal to acknowledge him as supreme head of the English Church.

Mary I had more than 300 people burned at the stake for the heresy of being Protestant.

In the 1550s John Foxe, a Protestant scholar, compiled his history of Protestant martyrs, known as *Foxe's Book of Martyrs,* which stirred up religious bigotry for years to come.
See also Thomas BECKET

ULTIMATE SACRIFICE A window in the Saxon church at Greensted in Essex shows the martyrdom of St Edmund, the last king of East Anglia, killed by Danes in 869

MARY,
Queen of Scots

- Queen of Scotland 1542-67
- 1542-87

Mary Stuart was six days old when she became queen of Scotland on the death of her father, James V. Her mother, Mary of Guise, became regent and the princess, a great beauty, was educated at the French court. At 16 she married the French king's eldest son, later Francis II of France.

In 1561 Mary returned to Scotland as a widow and stated her ambition to take the English throne, repeating the Catholic view that ELIZABETH I was illegitimate.

UNSUITABLE ALLIANCES

In 1566 Mary married her cousin, Lord Darnley, who demanded a share in the Scottish throne, was refused and killed her chief adviser David Rizzio. Mary was implicated in Darnley's murder the following year, along with the earl of Bothwell, who then married her. The outraged lords of Scotland rose against Mary and she and Bothwell were parted.

Forced to abdicate in favour of her son, who became James VI, Mary raised an army but was defeated near Glasgow. She fled to England, where Elizabeth I held her prisoner for 19 years, although she kept her own household as she moved from castle to castle.

Mary never ceased to conspire against Elizabeth, who eventually ordered her death. On the scaffold at Fotheringhay Castle, Mary behaved with regal charm. The executioners asked her to forgive them, and she replied, 'I forgive you with all my heart, for now, I hope, you shall make an end of all my troubles'.

MARY I

- Queen 1553-8 • 1516-58

The only child of Henry VIII and Catherine of Aragon to survive infancy, Mary was one of England's most unhappy sovereigns. She was ten when Henry first sought to annul his marriage to Catherine, and in 1534 he declared her illegitimate.

After Henry's death, Mary's half-brother took the throne as EDWARD VI, and on his death in 1553 the throne was

QUEEN'S HOBBY While held in custody on the Derbyshire estates of the earl of Shrewsbury, Mary, Queen of Scots filled her time with works of embroidery. The cat and mouse motif reflected her vulnerable situation

offered to the Protestant Lady Jane GREY. With wide support in the country, the devoutly Catholic Mary swiftly removed Grey to the Tower of London and was proclaimed queen.

At first she was welcomed, but her resolve to return England to Roman Catholicism was unpopular with many people. She further tilted feeling against her by marrying Philip II of Spain, who dragged England into a war against France in which Calais, a possession for 200 years, was lost.

Mary appointed Catholic bishops and let the pope interfere in English affairs, leading to the persecution of Protestant 'heretics'. Some 300 people were burned at the stake, including Thomas CRANMER, archbishop of Canterbury, in 1556, earning Mary the nickname 'Bloody Mary'. She died childless, broken-hearted and hated by her people.

MARY ROSE

- Henry VIII's flagship • Built 1509-10

In July, 1545, the Mary Rose, the pride of Henry VIII's navy, set sail to engage a French fleet. About a mile off Portsmouth harbour the wind and tide combined to swamp and sink her.

The ship was discovered by divers in 1836, but it was not until 1982 that a major project was undertaken to lift the remains. It was a delicate operation, as the oak timbers had suffered 400 years of erosion, but salvagers were able to raise one entire side of the ship and parts of the deck. The open hull of the

Mary Rose is now exhibited in Portsmouth dockyard, together with artefacts, from thimbles and musical instruments to longbows and cannon.

MASQUE

In the early 17th century, the royal court staged spectacular masques – aristocratic entertainments combining music, poetry, dance, pageantry and elaborate scenery. Some were written by Ben JONSON and designed by the architect Inigo JONES. All the performers wore masks, with a noble participant unmasked in the final act.

Masques first appeared in England in the 14th century and reached the height of fashion in the reigns of James I and Charles I, for whom John MILTON wrote the masque Comus, first performed at Ludlow Castle in 1634.

The outbreak of civil war in 1642 put an end to the masque, although its opulent sets influenced opera and ballet.

SHIP AHOY! The Mary Rose remains are lifted from the sea 437 years after she sank. The timbers were kept wet for two years to stop them disintegrating when exposed to air, then treated with preservative chemicals

MASTER OF THE ROLLS

The second most senior judge in Britain, below only the Lord Chief Justice, takes his title from duties dating back to the 13th century as the custodian of court records, and of the list, or roll, of solicitors in England and Wales. Only vestiges of these functions remain, and the Master of the Rolls now heads the civil division of the Court of Appeal (the Lord Chief Justice deals with the criminal division). Until 1958 he also presided over the Public Records Office, which is now the responsibility of the LORD CHANCELLOR.

The best-known holder of the office in modern times was Lord Denning (1899-1999). He became a national figure in the 1960s and 70s for his keen sense of justice. Denning had the last word on the PROFUMO AFFAIR, concluding in his 1963 report that the relationship between John Profumo, the Secretary of State for War, and the call girl Christine Keeler had not compromised government security.

Stanley MATTHEWS

• **Footballer**   • **b.1915; kt 1965**

For more than half a century, Stanley Matthews, 'The Wizard of Dribble', inspired boyhood dreams of footballing prowess. He tormented fullbacks with his skill as a mesmeric right-winger, winning more than 80 caps for England – the first at the age of 19 and the last at 41.

Matthews spent his career at two unfashionable clubs, Blackpool and Stoke City, and domestic honours proved elusive until the 1953 FA Cup final when one of his crosses set up the winning goal for Blackpool against Bolton Wanderers. The game became known as 'The Matthews Final'. Returning to Stoke in 1961, he underlined his durability by becoming, at 50, the oldest player to appear in an English League match.

The inscription on the statue of Matthews in his home town of Hanley, Stoke-on-Trent, encapsulates

CULTURE CLASH Far Eastern travels inspired Somerset Maugham to write about the differences between quintessential Englishness and the colourful exuberance of the tropics

his enduring appeal: 'His name is symbolic of the beauty of the game, his fame timeless. A magical player, of the people, for the people.'

Somerset MAUGHAM

• **Writer**   • **1874-1965**

The compelling narratives of Somerset Maugham explore themes from his own life as a doctor, author and wartime secret agent. He was orphaned at the age of ten, and his autobiographical novel *Of Human Bondage* (1915) portrays an unhappy childhood – the hero's clubfoot represents Maugham's severe stammer.

Most of his short stories and the novel *The Moon and Sixpence* (1919) are set in the South Seas and South-east Asia, following the fortunes of European people experiencing exotic cultures. His other works deal with the clash between conventionality and independent-mindedness in upper and middle-class England, and his plays depict social climbing and adultery in high society.

Maugham narrates in a smooth, urbane style. Criticised for cynicism, he claimed that 'cynic' is another name for 'realist'. His best novel, *Cakes and Ale* (1930), is his least characteristic: an affectionate portrait of a country girl who marries a writer but continues to love where she pleases.

MAUNDY MONEY

On Maunday Thursday, the day before Good Friday, pensioners selected for service to their church and community attend an alms-giving ceremony, held at Westminster Abbey. They receive three small, symbolic gifts of coins from the Queen. The first two are for clothing and food, and the third is specially minted Maundy coinage: fourpenny, threepenny, twopenny and penny pieces.

The tradition derives from a 13th to 17th-century ceremony, when the sovereign washed the feet of the poor in remembrance of Christ washing the disciples' feet at the Last Supper.

James Clerk MAXWELL

• **Mathematician and physicist**   • **1831-79**

Not much 19th-century physics remains unmodifed, but the equations of the Edinburgh-born James Clerk Maxwell explaining the behaviour of electricity and magnetism still hold true.

In 1873 he proved that light is a form of electromagnetic radiation, showing that there must be other undetected forms of radiation with different wavelengths. The discovery of radio waves and X-rays later in the century proved that he was right. At Cambridge University in 1871 Maxwell became the first director of the CAVENDISH LABORATORY. He died young of cancer, but his advances in the areas of electromagnetism and thermodynamics ensured his reputation as the most important theoretical physicist of his day.

Robert MAXWELL

• **Publisher**   • **1923-91**

The irrepressible Robert Maxwell – a charmer to some, a bully to others – was by turns a refugee, war hero, publisher, Labour MP, newspaper magnate and embezzler.

Maxwell was born Jan Hoch in Czechoslovakia. He joined the British army in 1940 and won a battlefield commission for gallantry. In 1951 he founded Pergamon Press, which published scientific journals, in Oxford. Twenty years later, the

continued on page 293

LIGHT THE GOODLY FIRES

May Day festivals mark the arrival of the British summer with processions and dancing. In the 17th century, disapproval of such pagan behaviour by a Puritan government brought a temporary end to the celebrations, but local customs – never forgotten – have since been revived

O N MAY EVE between the 5th and the 1st century BC, the hilltops of Britain burned brightly with pagan bonfires welcoming the return of the sun.

The Celtic festival of Beltane – often interpreted as meaning 'bright fire' or 'goodly fire' – marked the beginning of open pasturing: flocks were turned out to graze and bonfires lit to ward off evil and make the coming year fruitful. Fertility rituals involved dancing around the flames and driving cattle through or between two fires. These and other ceremonies such as burning the 'Beltane hag' – a cake – may have survived from earlier animal, or human, sacrifice, and continued to inspire May Day festivities for centuries; Beltane fires were lit in the Highlands up to the 1830s.

GATHERING AROUND THE MAYPOLE
In the more lighthearted medieval May Day festivities, branches were gathered from the woods and brought home at sunrise to welcome the summer. From this practice derived the maypole, originally a flowering tree set up in each village around which the May Queen, sometimes with her male counterpart, the May King, would dance with her followers. Later celebrations became more elaborate, with the MORRIS DANCE (first recorded in Britain in the 15th century) and formal ribbon dancing around the maypole.

ALL DRESSED UP Jack-in-the-Green, a tree-like figure often taken to represent rebirth and the coming of spring, leads the May Day morris dance in Oxford

COURTING DISAPPROVAL
May Day celebrations were frowned upon by the Puritans – at the height of their influence in 1644, parliament banned maypoles as a 'heathenish vanity'. But when Charles II was restored to the throne in 1660 maypoles were erected as a mark of loyalty to the crown – a 41 m (134ft) high pole graced the Strand in London for the next 50 years.

By the 19th century one of the most notable May Day rituals was the annual procession of chimney sweeps, led by the Jack-in-the-Green, although this was seen by some as an urban debasement of an old rural festival. A wave of Victorian nostalgia for traditional customs led to a revival of May games. Today the ancient sports, plays and dancing take place in many towns and villages.

MILKMEN, MAIDENS AND MAYPOLES On the May bank holiday, the 'Old Scholars' of Ickwell Green in Bedfordshire – villagers who have taken part in the May Day festival since they were children – dance around the village maypole. Their milkmen and milkmaid outfits represent English traditional dress

CURIOUS LOCAL CUSTOMS

HOBBY HORSE
Animal guisering – dressing up in an animal disguise – may derive from Maytime animal sacrifices. The tradition continues at Padstow in Cornwall and Minehead in Somerset, where men in boat-like horse costumes dance through the streets.

JACK-IN-THE-GREEN
After taking part in morris dancing, a man dressed as a tree with a flowered crown is ceremonially 'beheaded' at Hastings Castle on May bank holiday. The falling foliage is gathered for luck.

OXFORD MAY MORNING
At 6am on May Day morning, the tower of Magdalen College in Oxford echoes to the sound of 'Te Deum Patrem Colimus' ('God and Father, we worship thee'). The more reckless revellers have been known to jump off Magdalen Bridge into the icy water of the River Thames.

SAND TIPPING
At the May Day festival at Knutsford in Cheshire, sand is funnelled into patterns in the street. King Canute is said to have forded the nearby river, then tipped sand from his shoes in the path of a wedding party, wishing them joy and as many children as grains of sand.

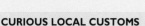

HOBBY HORSE
The Red Ribbon 'Oss is led through Minehead by a 'Teaser' with a stick

MAKING HAY

In early summer, Britain's meadows are a riot of colour, their mixture of grass and wild flowers providing a home for birds, insects and small mammals. But intensive agriculture threatens this unique habitat, and its preservation has become a key concern of Britain's conservation groups

SINCE THE Anglo-Saxons settled in some of England's river valleys in the 5th century, meadows – wild, unploughed fields of grass – have provided pasture and hay harvests for livestock.

Wild meadows produce nutritious hay because of their mixture of grass and other wild plants such as clover – bacteria on its roots process nitrogen that enriches grass.

CLOUDED YELLOW BUTTERFLY

The grasses False brome and quaking grass suit the dry, chalky soils of the Downs, the Cotswolds and other uplands, and timothy grass and meadow fescue thrive on the damp, clayey soils of East Anglia and other lowlands.

TECHNICAL PROGRESS

In the 16th century the first flood meadows were created near rivers, using labour-intensive irrigation methods to preserve pasture over the winter period. Sluicegates were opened in December to flood the meadow, covering the vegetation with water to protect it from frost and keep it nourished. When the floods were drained in February, the grass fed the first spring lambs.

In the 20th century, the area of ancient meadowland in England reduced by 97 per cent. Many meadows have been turned into arable land, intensively farmed to produce larger yields of hay or silage. In many areas, cultivated rye-grass, which grows vigorously, has suffocated other species of grass. The use of chemical fertilisers and herbicides threatens wildlife with extinction, and plants such as the pepper-saxifrage and the corky-fruited water dropwort have become rarities.

PRESERVING THE PAST

The conservation body English Nature preserves natural meadowland habitats at National Nature Reserves such as Upwood Meadows in Cambridgeshire, Mottey Meadows in Staffordshire and North Meadow in Wiltshire – a water meadow that turns purple in the spring with blooms of snakeshead fritillaries.

BENEATH THE GRASS

Meadows support rich insect life and a wealth of tiny mammals such as shrews, voles and mice. The unploughed land is perfect for mole burrows and ant-hills. Birds such as corncrakes and partridges nest on the ground or in surrounding hedges.

MEADOW PIPIT *The shrill 'pheet, pheet, pheet' call of the meadow pipit is often heard in moorland meadows*

HARVEST MOUSE *One of Britain's smallest mammals, the 6.5 cm (2½ in) long harvest mouse, weaves together living leaf blades in rushes and reed beds to make a suspended, ball-shaped nest*

TIGER BEETLE *Burrows tunnelled 30 cm (1 ft) deep into sandy meadowland soils by tiger beetle larvae store their captured prey*

A COLOURFUL CARPET

Wild meadowland contains a huge variety of plant life in a single habitat. Untouched pasture can be identified by flowers such as cowslips, yellow rattle and meadowsweet.

TIMOTHY GRASS

Timothy grows up to 1 m (3 ft) high on damp, clayish soils. It is named after the American agriculturist, Timothy Hanson, who promoted its use as cattle fodder

SNAKESHEAD FRITILLARIES

This chequered flower could be seen in the wild in 27 counties before 1930. Within 40 years intensive farming had halved that number

PYRAMIDAL ORCHID

Conical pink flowers blossom in chalky meadows in July. The flowers have a foxy odour and their nectar attracts moths

QUAKING GRASS

Chalk and limestone meadows are the ideal habitat for shimmering purple-green quaking grass

YELLOW RATTLE

The semiparasitic yellow rattle has roots that wind around those of other plants to draw nutrients. Dry seeds inside the flowers rattle when shaken

Department of Trade and industry investigated the company's finances and found Maxwell unfit to be a director of a public company. He fought back and built a business empire, acquiring the British Printing Corporation and the *Daily Mirror* in the 1980s.

Maxwell drowned off his yacht near the Canary Islands. The subsequent discovery that he had embezzled hundreds of millions of pounds from his companies and their pension funds led to suspicions of suicide or murder – but probably he simply fell overboard.

Peter MAXWELL DAVIES

• **Composer** • **b.1934; kt 1987**

The aggressive and confrontational style of much of the work of Peter Maxwell Davies demonstrates his belief in the relationship between music and theatre. One of his works, *Vesalii Icones* (1970), requires a pianist to perform naked.

In 1967 Maxwell Davies formed 'The Pierrot Players', an avant-garde music group, with Harrison BIRTWISTLE. When Birtwistle left in 1971, they reformed as 'The Fires of London', directed by 'Max' from his new home on the island of Hoy in the Orkneys until they disbanded in 1987. On Hoy, he found the solitude he needed to compose. A search for inspiration for an Antarctic symphony led him to visit the South Pole in 1997. His works include the theatrical *Eight Songs for a Mad King* (1969) about George III, the operas *Taverner* (1972) and *The Lighthouse* (1979) and the ballet score *Caroline Mathilde* (1991).

MAY DAY: *see page 291*

MAYFAIR

• **Central London (p.499 A6/A7)**

Mayfair stands as the capital's bastion of wealth and grandeur, confined by the major thoroughfares of Oxford Street, Regent's Street, Piccadilly and Park Lane. Bond Street is the principal commercial centre, its shops offering fine clothes, jewellery, antique rugs and rare books, with a concentration of commercial art galleries clustered around Cork Street.

Mayfair's beginnings were less auspicious. The area grew up around the site of a popular May Fair in the late 17th century – 15 days of bawdy, drunken revelry, brought to a close in 1764 when the sensibilities of the local gentry reached breaking point.

Names such as Albemarle Street, Curzon Street and Berkeley Square recall the six huge estates that covered 18th-century Mayfair. As estate land was leased to developers, fashionable London society moved to the district, close to the royal parks. Lawrence Sterne, author of *Tristram Shandy*, breathed his last on Bond Street, and in the adjacent Brook Street George Frideric Handel and Jimi Hendrix were neighbours, though separated by more than 200 years.

MAZES

Mazes cut from turf – mizmazes – have survived since medieval times at Breamore in Hampshire and Wing in Leicestershire, but they were at their most fashionable during the Renaissance. The geometric layout and ambitious topiary of Renaissance gardens led to more complex designs. The finest maze of the period, planted at Hampton Court in the reign of William III, still intrigues hundreds of thousands of visitors a year. For those who find it baffling, there is a simple key: go left on entering, then right and right again, then always turn left.

Fine mazes were constructed at Somerleyton Hall in Suffolk and Hever Castle in Kent in Victorian times, but the longest and most complex in the world, built in 1975, is at LONGLEAT in Wiltshire.

PERPLEXING PATTERNS The centre of the mizmaze at **Breamore** is said to symbolise Paradise. Its origins are a mystery

MEAD

When the Romans arrived in Britain they brought mead, an alcoholic drink made from fermented honey and water. Bowls of mead later became a centrepiece of Anglo-Saxon feasts, and the drink continued to be made throughout the Middle Ages. A spiced Welsh version, metheglin, also became popular.

The late 17th-century cookery book of Kenelm Digby includes 100 recipes for honey-based drinks. But the recent arrival of cane sugar from the West Indies had already led to a decline in honey production, and ale and sweet wine became more popular. Mead is now made only by small producers such as St Aidan's at Lindisfarne in Northumberland.

MEADOWLAND: *see page 292*

MELROSE ABBEY

• Borders (p.497 D5)
• Built 12th-14th century • HS

Cistercian monks from RIEVAULX ABBEY in North Yorkshire founded Melrose in 1136. Its wealth attracted the attention of marauding English armies in the 14th century, leading to its destruction. The Scottish king ROBERT BRUCE restored the building in 1326 and bequeathed his heart to the abbey. Rebuilding after further attacks in 1385 introduced

PRACTICE MAKES PERFECT At the centenary concert of the Berlin Philharmonic, yoga enthusiast Yehudi Menuhin conducted part of Beethoven's Fifth Symphony with his feet while performing a headstand

elaborate Renaissance stonework. A gargoyle of a pig playing the bagpipes is one of several unusual pieces of carving, preserved largely through the efforts of the writer Walter Scott, who campaigned for the building's repair when living nearby at Abbotsford.

Excavations in the chapterhouse in 1921 revealed a casket believed to contain the Bruce's heart. The casket was reburied in the abbey grounds in 1998.

MENDIP HILLS

• Somerset (p.494 E5)

A gigantic, flat-topped chunk of carboniferous limestone stretches 24 miles from Frome towards the mouth of the Severn. The Mendips are 6 miles across at their widest, and rise to 325 m (1067 ft) at Blackdown, the highest point. Drystone walls outline sheep-grazed fields, heathland covers outcrops of sandstone, and broad-leaved woods hang on the steep slopes, edged by cliffs and ravines such as CHEDDAR GORGE.

Thousands of tons of Mendip rock are quarried annually for road building. The range is riddled with hollows where rain has dissolved the stone leaving holes, tunnels and underground caves hung with stalactites that once sheltered Stone Age communities. Now they attract cavers and potholers and – at WOOKEY HOLE, Cox's Cavern and Gough's Cave – hordes of tourists.

Yehudi MENUHIN

• Violinist and conductor
• 1916-99; kt 1965; OM 1987; bn 1993

At the age of ten, Yehudi Menuhin could hold his own as a solo violinist against any symphony orchestra in the world. At 16, he recorded Edward Elgar's Violin Concerto under the baton of the composer himself. Menuhin grew up in San Francisco, taking up the violin at four years old. In his teenage years, he performed on tours across the world. After the Second World War, he was the first Jewish performer to play in Berlin. He sympathised with Palestinian rights and spoke up for Wilhelm Furtwängler, who conducted the Berlin Philharmonic throughout the Nazi regime.

As Menuhin grew older, his musical tastes diversified, and he became known

for performing contemporary classical music. He worked with the French jazz violinist Stephane Grappelli and the Indian sitarist Ravi Shankar.

In 1959 Menuhin moved to London. Four years later he established a boarding school for musically gifted children in Surrey, where today around 50 boys and girls are educated. The violinist Nigel Kennedy is a former pupil.

MERCHANT IVORY

In the 1980s the independent film company formed by Californian-born James Ivory (b.1930) and Indian-born Ismail Merchant (b.1936) became associated with adaptations of classic English novels. Their films exploit the visual delights of period costume and settings, and the nuances of English middle-class behaviour.

The company was formed in the 1960s, but the golden age of Merchant Ivory began in 1985 with a film version of E.M. FORSTER's *A Room With a View*. *Howard's End* (1992), another Forster adaptation, and *The Remains of the Day* (1993), from a novel by Kazuo Ishiguro, were among their box-office hits, which have earned them nine Oscar wins out of 33 nominations.

The refined period style of Merchant Ivory films has been criticised for its repetitiveness, but attempts to move away from the formula with films such as *Jefferson in Paris* (1994) and *Surviving Picasso* (1997) led to mixed reviews.

MERCHANT NAVY

Trade ships and their sailors gained the title Merchant Navy in 1922, an honour conferred by George V in recognition of the sacrifices of the First World War, in which 9 million tons of British shipping were sunk; by then, Britain was the leading mercantile power. Although its shipping was in decline, in late Victorian times it had owned half the world's tonnage. Steamships built in British shipyards circled the globe and brought prosperity to ports such as London, Bristol, Liverpool and Glasgow.

Until the 16th century, ships were small and vulnerable, and generally kept close to land. But the development of ocean-going vessels made possible

AS OTHERS SEE US Helena Bonham-Carter plays Helen Schlegel in *Howard's End*, one of the Indian-American partnership Merchant Ivory's successful film adaptations of literary classics

voyages of discovery to the Far East and the New World. By the 17th century EAST INDIA COMPANY ships were as big as 1000 tons, and trade in commodities such as cotton, sugar and tobacco (and until 1833 slaves) added to the British Empire's wealth.

The 19th-century dominance of the British merchant navy proved brief. Even before the two world wars, competitors from Germany, USA and Japan were catching up. The war losses were never replaced, SHIPBUILDING moved overseas and by 1986 Britain's share of world tonnage was just 3 per cent.

MERLIN

Who was Merlin – a magician, a mystic or simply a wise old man? According to the 12th century writer GEOFFREY OF MONMOUTH, King ARTHUR's magician transported vast stones from Ireland to Salisbury Plain to create Stonehenge in just one night so great were his powers.

The character of Merlin in Geoffrey's legends of King Arthur may have been inspired by Myrddin, a legendary 6th-century Welsh bard said to have the gift

MAGICAL PRISON In one legend, Merlin is trapped in thorny branches by a sorceress

of prophecy. In Geoffrey's account Merlin's intervention brings about Arthur's birth; later sources credit the magician with creating the Round Table and the palace at Camelot. In *Le Morte D'Arthur* the medieval writer Thomas MALORY developed Merlin, associating him with the miracle of the sword Excalibur and the quest for the Holy Grail.

Merlin has become an enduring figure of English folklore, appearing as a bard, druid or wise prophet in later literature such as Lord TENNYSON's *Idylls of the King*.

River MERSEY

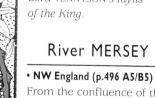

• **NW England (p.496 A5/B5)**
From the confluence of the Tame and Goyt rivers at Stockport near Manchester, the River Mersey flows 70 miles westwards, reaching the Irish Sea downstream of LIVERPOOL.

In the 18th century, ocean-going ships used the Mersey to reach Liverpool and, on the opposite bank, Birkenhead. In 1894 a canal was built giving access all the way to Manchester. The Laird shipyards in Birkenhead produced battleships and passenger

liners until a decline in SHIPBUILDING after the two world wars. Today the port, while still important to the area's economy, has declined and the shipyards undertake mainly repairs.

In 1934 a 2½ mile underwater tunnel, at the time the longest in the world, opened beneath the Mersey, joining Liverpool to Birkenhead by road.

MERSEYBEAT

Pop groups playing in and around Liverpool on the River Mersey during the 1960s developed their own distinctive, upbeat musical style influenced by American music – particularly rhythm and blues. One group, the Merseybeats, gave its name to the new sound, which by 1963 was shared by 300 bands.

Liverpool's Cavern Club played host to many of the bands, including The BEATLES, The Searchers, and Gerry and the Pacemakers – whose 1963 hit 'You'll Never Walk Alone', taken from the musical *Carousel*, became the anthem of Liverpool Football Club.

METAPHYSICAL POETS

The 18th-century writer and critic Samuel JOHNSON coined the term 'metaphysical' to disparage a generation of 17th-century poets, including John DONNE, who sought new methods to make their verse arresting. The poets drew on images from alchemy, law, mathematics, science and philosophy, as in *Definition of Love*, by Andrew Marvell (1621-78):

> As lines, so loves oblique may well
> Themselves in every angle greet:
> But ours so truly parallel,
> Though infinite, can never meet.

To this was linked 'wit': acuteness of mind, and the power to conceive unforeseen connections. Johnson deplored their 'metaphysical conceits', which he described as 'heterogeneous ideas yoked by violence together'.

The metaphysical poets did not form a single movement, and ranged from secular poets such as Donne and Marvell to religious writers such as George Herbert, Richard Crashaw and Henry Vaughan. Their work has had a profound influence on many 20th-century poets, including T.S. ELIOT and W.B. YEATS.

SPACE-AGE STRUCTURES

Modern architecture, once synonymous with the concrete eyesore, is now one of Britain's boom industries. Revolutionary change in the last 20 years has transformed urban landscapes all round the nation, particularly in London

EMIGRÉS FROM across Europe first brought the Continental influence of architectural modernism to Britain in the 1930s. It was promoted by groups such as MARS (Modern Architectural Research Group) and Tecton, founded by the Russian-born architect Berthold Lubetkin and creators in 1933 of London Zoo's Penguin Pool.

Traces of these pioneers are still clear in the work of Britain's two most successful architects of the present day, Richard ROGERS and Norman FOSTER. So is the avant-garde spirit of postwar 'New Brutalist' architects such as Peter and Alison Smithson, who exposed the raw materials of their buildings.

A STYLE BATTLING TO BE BORN

Making modernism acceptable in a country where tradition counts for so much has not been easy. Innovators have often been treated with suspicion – a legacy from the 1950s and 60s when British cities suffered a rash of soulless offices and tower blocks.

Many designers have had to prove themselves abroad before winning major contracts at home. Land, especially in the south-east, is in short supply, and new constructions must fit in with their surroundings, which may include buildings from many different periods.

But since the late 1970s a new spirit of creativity and confidence has emerged and buildings are now being constructed with unprecedented boldness and to unsurpassed technical standards.

Three areas have led the way: museums and exhibition spaces, housing – perhaps the most controversial since it involves social experimentation – and office development.

ON SHOW: MUSEUMS AND EXHIBITION SPACES

SAINSBURY CENTRE FOR VISUAL ARTS, NORWICH (1977-91)
NORMAN FOSTER

Foster's rectangular glass-ended structure is a flexible building designed to meet many different needs. As well as space for temporary exhibitions it houses a permanent collection of art and sculpture and a school of fine arts. It was built in two stages, the first creating one clear span, steel structure and the second an underground extension – the Crescent Wing – whose only visible feature on the surface is a sloping glass roof drawing light into a gently curving basement corridor (right).

THE ARK, EARTH CENTRE, DONCASTER (2002)
ARCHITECTS AT FUTURE SYSTEMS

A unique combination of high techology and environmentally sensitive design is the hallmark of the prizewinning firm Future Systems. Their biggest project to date is The Ark exhibition arena at the Earth Centre in Doncaster, a millennium project based on the theme of sustainability and built on the site of a disused coal pit. The building, due for completion in 2002, consists of a low-lying, 3-tiered structure resembling from above the compound eyes of an insect. The hardworking 'eyes', made of superplastic aluminium scoops, allow natural light to enter the building and support photovoltaic cells that generate more than half the power needed for its 9000 m² (97 000 sq ft) area.

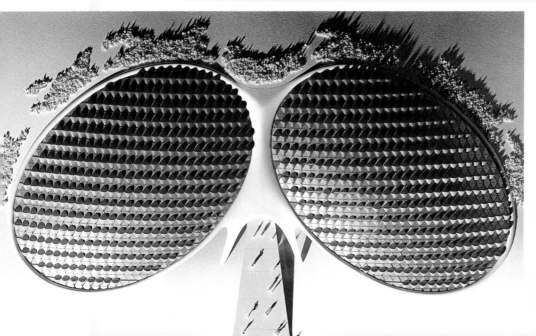

NO PLACE LIKE HOME

HAUER-KING HOUSE, LONDON (1994)
JAN KAPLICKY AND AMANDA LEVETE (FUTURE SYSTEMS)

Ever since Le Corbusier described a home as a 'machine for living in' houses have been a hot-bed of architectural innovation, inspiring many modernist experiments. A structure made almost entirely of glass was not the most obvious solution for a narrow site between the end of a listed Georgian terrace and a listed 19th-century pub, but the Hauer-King house in north London was an overnight success. It makes use of surrounding trees to preserve privacy – essential, since clear glazing sweeps to floor level at the back of the house.

ARCHITECT'S RESIDENCE, LONDON (1997)
SETH STEIN

Stein converted stables and a builder's yard to create his home in Kensington. Adding an extension of his own design formed a central Japanese-style courtyard, paved in green Spanish limestone. Its glass walls allow natural light to penetrate the interior while maintaining privacy.

BUILDINGS THAT WORK

LLOYD'S BUILDING, LONDON (1978-86)
RICHARD ROGERS

Britain was largely responsible for developing the 'High Tech' school of architecture, in which the appearance of a building is determined by its structure. Lloyd's Building in the City of London has spawned imitations all over the world. Metal struts and pipes, corrugated container boxes, service cranes and the building's industrial framework are all clearly visible. Ducts and ventilation shafts remain exposed and glass lifts travel up and down the exterior.

ONE CANADA SQUARE, LONDON (1991)
CESAR PELLI

The DOCKLANDS development at Canary Wharf is the largest of its kind in Britain, with more office space than the whole business district of Edinburgh. Its defining symbol – the 244 m (820 ft) pyramid-topped, steel Canada Tower – is the tallest building in Britain, and was designed by an Argentinian-born American architect.

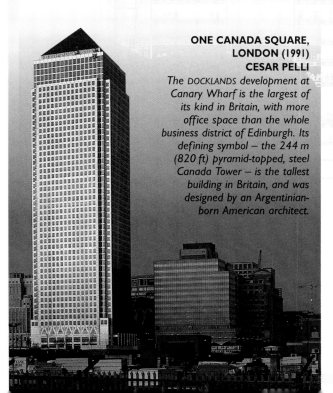

John Stuart MILL

• **Philosopher** • 1806-73

Brought up by his philosopher father to be a reformer and rational thinker, John Stuart Mill was arrested at the age of 17 for distributing pamphlets on birth control. In the same year he started preparing the philosopher Jeremy BENTHAM's chaotic notes for publication.

At the age of 21, Mill revolted against this life as a 'dry, hard, logical machine', and fell under the spell of German Romantic philosophy. For the rest of his life he strove to unite the demands of reason with freedom of imagination.

Mill worked at the East India Company in London from 1823 to 1858, writing articles and books in his spare time, including the *System of Logic* (1843) and *Principles of Political Economy* (1848). But his most original works were conceived in partnership with Harriet Taylor, whom he loved for 20 years before they married in 1851 – Mill insisting that she retain 'the same absolute freedom of action as if no such marriage had taken place'.

After Harriet's death in 1858 Mill decided he must accomplish 'some things which she wished done'. The result was the final flowering of *On Liberty* (1859) – the classic defence of individual freedom. An MP briefly in the 1860s, he published *The Subjection of Women* in 1869, which demanded equal rights for women, and completed his painfully revealing *Autobiography* in 1873.

Jonathan MILLER

• **Theatre director** • b.1934; CBE 1983

Cambridge University endowed Jonathan Miller with two careers, qualifying him as a medical doctor and – through the Footlights revue – giving him his first taste of the stage. Miller came to public attention as a political satirist as part of the 1960 *Beyond the Fringe* team, but it is for his work as a director of theatre and

CIVIC ART Wendy Taylor's *Octo* sculpture is dedicated to Llewelyn Davies, co-designer of Milton Keynes, and is one of 200 public works of art in the city

opera that he is best known. Outstanding productions have included *The Merchant of Venice* (1970), with Laurence Olivier as Shylock, and the innovative *Rigoletto* for English National Opera (1982) – displaced from its time, like other Miller productions, and set among the mafiosi of 1950s New York.

He has also written and presented programmes for the BBC, including the medical series *The Body in Question* (1977), which also became a bestselling book, *States of Mind* (1982) and *Opera Works* (1997) – masterclasses in opera direction. He is noted for his eclecticism, imagination and the intellectual rigour of his approach and in *Subsequent Performances* (1986) outlined his original views on directing opera and the theatre.

John MILTON

• **Poet** • 1608-74

'...of the Devil's party without knowing it,' said William Blake of his fellow poet John Milton – and many readers of *Paradise Lost* agree. For despite taking 10 565 lines to 'justify the ways of God to Men' Milton's poem about the Fall ends up with Satan as its most interesting and beguiling character.

Milton began writing early, experimenting with different styles. *L'Allegro* (1631) reflects on poetic inspiration, *Comus* (1634) is a MASQUE and *Lycidas* (1637) an elegy on the death of a young man.

Between 1639 and 1660 Milton largely gave up poetry for political and religious pamphleteering. He supported Cromwell in the Civil War and campaigned on issues ranging from divorce and freedom of expression to republicanism and the right of people to remove tyrannical rulers. But overwork damaged his sight, and by 1651 he was blind.

Deeply disillusioned after the Restoration of 1660, Milton returned to poetry, this time tragic in tone and monumental in scale. Alongside *Paradise Lost* stand the two other late masterpieces, published in 1671, *Paradise Regained* and *Samson Agonistes*.

MILTON KEYNES

• **Buckinghamshire (p.495 G3)** • Pop. 156 150

Britain's largest NEW TOWN – 33 sq miles, in area – Milton Keynes was designed to encompass countryside and existing villages, and provide a huge shopping complex, factories, offices and homes. The result – tree-lined roads, footpaths and cyclepaths laid out to a neat plan of grid squares – allows motorists to travel anywhere in the grid in 15 minutes. The initial plan, completed in 1967, allowed for expansion. By its 25th birthday in 1992, more than 45 000 homes had been built and 66 000 new jobs created, and it is still growing.

A programme of public works of art gave the town many sculptures, including six concrete cows standing in an open field. The town is also home to the OPEN UNIVERSITY – established there in 1971.

MISTLETOE

A parasitic evergreen, mistletoe may have gained its ancient magical reputation from its ability to flourish in winter on a bare tree. Druids revered mistletoe growing on the sacred oak, harvesting it with golden sickles for religious rites. In medieval times the plant was used to cure epilepsy, safeguard crops and bring prosperity.

The CHRISTMAS TRADITION of kissing under mistletoe may stem from Norse legend. In one account Balder the Good was killed by a mistletoe-tipped arrow but his mother, the goddess Frigga, restored him. In her joy she kissed all who passed beneath the mistletoe and the kiss became a token of good luck.

MITFORD SISTERS

- **Nancy 1904-73** • **Pamela 1907-94**
- **Diana b.1910** • **Unity 1914-48**
- **Jessica 1917-96** • **Deborah b.1920**

Few sisters can have had more colourful lives than the six daughters of the 2nd baron Redesdale.

Nancy, a novelist, provoked debate with her guide to polite usage *Noblesse Oblige* (1956), with its 'U' (upper class) and 'non-U' distinctions – 'dinner' (non-U) and 'luncheon' (U) for the midday meal, or 'toilet' (very non-U) and 'lavatory'. Deborah married the future duke of Devonshire and made Chatsworth a huge commercial success.

Jessica, a communist, went to the USA in 1939 and became a writer and journalist. Her autobiography, *Hons and Rebels* (1960), recollects their unconventional upbringing. Diana, a great beauty, left her first husband for the politician and fascist leader Oswald MOSLEY; Adolf Hitler was a guest at their wedding. Divided by their politics, Diana and Jessica never met again after the start of the Second World War.

Unity shared Diana's politics and was infatuated with the Führer, attempting to commit suicide when war was declared.

Only Pamela – described by the poet John Betjeman as 'gentle Pamela, most rural of them all' – was content to stay out of the limelight.

MODERN BUILDINGS: *see page 296*

MODS AND ROCKERS

The two rival youth gangs of the 1960s were instantly recognisable by their appearance. Mod (short for modernist) style had its roots in the art and fashion schools of the late 1950s. Youths wore narrow shoes and thin ties, girls short skirts and pale lips. both reflecting Italian trends and riding Lambretta and Vespa motor scooters. Some male mods even wore make-up. In 1964, The Who were launched as the first 'mod' pop group.

Rocker style was the antithesis to mod. Rockers took as their model the aggressive American cult of the Hell's Angels, riding heavy motorbikes. They kitted themselves out in studded leather jackets and grease-stained jeans, and slicked back their hair. They aimed not to flatter but to alienate. The groups are remembered for their violent seaside confrontations, particularly in south-coast resort towns on Bank Holidays.

MOLE

Soil thrown up by the constant burrowing of moles is the bane of the gardener's life. Methods of deterrence range from buried garlic bulbs to half-buried bottles that create an eerie hooting in the wind.

Mouldiwarps, as they are known in northern England, are certainly prodigious diggers. An adult animal just 15 cm (6 in) long and weighing less than 115 g (4 oz) can shift ten times its weight of soil in less than 5 minutes. The result of this labour is an extensive network of tunnels and chambers for living. breeding and foraging.

With poorly developed senses of smell and sight, moles find their food – mostly earthworms, insect larvae and slugs – by touch and hearing, which has helped to create their secretive and bumbling reputation.

DRESSED FOR THE BEACH A group of mods, part of a late-1970s revival of the clothes-conscious tribe, stride out on Brighton beach, the scene of violent clashes in the early 1960s with rockers (*right*), here preparing their bikes outside the Ace café in London

IN THE CLOISTERS

Modern monks and nuns are as likely to be found at a computer terminal or doing social work in the inner cities as tending the fields or praying, yet in the essentials a life dedicated to God has changed little in 1500 years

LEARNED MONK Monastic seclusion produced pioneering scholars such as the Venerable Bede at Jarrow

BRITAIN'S FIRST monasteries were established by the CELTIC CHURCH in Scotland, Wales and the far west of England. They were usually no more than a church and a cluster of monks' cells within a defensive wall, though IONA, founded by St Columba off the west coast of Scotland in 563, was internationally renowned.

The monasteries of the Middle Ages were conceived on a far grander scale. Guidelines for a life of prayer within an enclosed community had been drawn up by St Benedict of Nursia in his *Rule*, written in about 540 at Monte Cassino in Italy. In 598 St Augustine, who had been sent by Pope Gregory the Great to bring Roman Christianity to Britain, founded a monastery in CANTERBURY. It marked the beginning of a flowering of art and scholarship that lasted until raids by Vikings in the 8th and 9th centuries brought widespread destruction.

Monasticism revived under the protection of the Saxon Wessex kings, such as ALFRED THE GREAT, who founded two new communities, one for men and one for women. Under the influence of St Dunstan, who became abbot of GLASTONBURY in about 943, Benedictine monasteries spread throughout southern Britain.

FAITH AND WEALTH

In the 12th and 13th centuries the wealth of the monasteries rivalled that of the Crown. They had been granted huge estates, on some of which they pioneered new agricultural techniques. In an era before the foundation of universities, they had a near monopoly on learning, their scribes writing and illuminating the only available books. Their abbots frequently became close royal advisers. By the beginning of the 15th century there were nearly 850 religious houses in Britain, but decline had already set in. Using the religious reforms of the REFORMATION as a pretext, Henry VIII was able to represent them as corrupt and worldly.

PILLAGE AND MURDER

In 1534 Henry declared himself head of the Church in England. The following year he ordered a valuation – the Valor Ecclesiasticus – on all Church property, and in 1536 dissolved all religious houses with an income of less than £200 a year,

FORTIFYING THE SPIRIT The monks of Buckfast Abbey have been making tonic wine infused with maté, coca leaves and vanilla to the same basic recipe since 1897

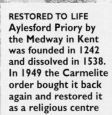

RESTORED TO LIFE Aylesford Priory by the Medway in Kent was founded in 1242 and dissolved in 1538. In 1949 the Carmelite order bought it back again and restored it as a religious centre

1	Gatehouse
2-5	Shrines and chapels
6	Library
7	Kitchens
8	Guest house
9	Great courtyard
10	Administrative office
11	Friars' quarters

RELIGIOUS ORDERS

About 1200 British monks and nuns are Benedictines – the largest order – and thousands more belong to other orders. Each has its own dress and character, and emphasises particular aspects of religious life such as teaching, healing or meditation.

CISTERCIAN 'White' monks favour simplicity and manual labour

CARTHUSIAN Monks live in cells in a charterhouse, and emphasise prayer

DOMINICAN The 'black' friars study and teach, mostly in towns

POOR CLARE These Franciscan nuns are still an enclosed order

BENEDICTINE The original order imposes austerity and strict discipline

THE DAILY ROUND OF DEVOTION

The everyday life of a nun or monk revolves around 6½ hours of religious observance. This starts with Prime, a service at 6 am, continuing with Morning Mass, High Mass, Nones, Vespers, Compline, Night Office and Lauds.

Eight hours are allocated to sleep, but the time is broken into three periods, including an hour at midday.

The rest of the day is taken up with personal study, reading, meals and work – which can range from cooking, cleaning and agricultural labour to teaching, social work or other service to the wider community.

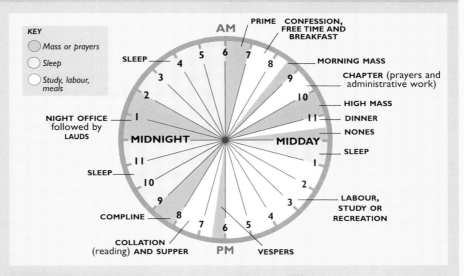

KEY
- Mass or prayers
- Sleep
- Study, labour, meals

AM
PRIME CONFESSION, FREE TIME AND BREAKFAST
SLEEP
MORNING MASS
CHAPTER (prayers and administrative work)
HIGH MASS
DINNER
NONES
SLEEP
MIDDAY
LABOUR, STUDY OR RECREATION
VESPERS
PM
COLLATION (reading) AND SUPPER
COMPLINE
SLEEP
NIGHT OFFICE followed by LAUDS
MIDNIGHT

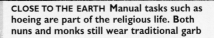

CLOSE TO THE EARTH Manual tasks such as hoeing are part of the religious life. Both nuns and monks still wear traditional garb

THE MONKS RETURN

Today there are more than 40 communities of monks and nuns in the British Isles, most founded in the 19th century when the rights of Roman Catholics were restored. Some, like Downside in Somerset, date back to the 18th century, when refugees fled to Britain to escape the French Revolution. A few are Anglican but the majority are Catholic and mainly Benedictine.

There are still some enclosed orders of contemplative monks and nuns, but most are active in the world outside, running schools, teaching, nursing or doing social work. Friars retain their essentially unenclosed character, taking Christianity to the secular world.

Some monasteries, such as Downside, run independent schools while the monks of Caldey Island, Cardiff, make perfume and world-famous pottery comes from Prinknash, Gloucestershire. At BUCKFAST ABBEY, built by French monks on the site of a medieval monastery, honey and wine are best-selling products. Other monasteries have produced chart-topping recordings of plainsong, the traditional melody of the Western Christian Church.

REACHING OUT Monasteries are increasingly turning to the Internet to spread their Christian message. Many now operate their own Web sites

transferring their assets to the Crown. A serious rebellion in the north of England, the Pilgrimage of Grace, was bloodily suppressed, and Henry's propaganda campaign began to attack the larger and wealthier monasteries. Soon their treasures were also seized and their communities dispersed.

Many abbey churches were demolished and their stone used for other buildings. Some were incorporated into private houses. The riches and lands of the monasteries passed to the Crown or to favoured courtiers. In 1540 the last monastery, Waltham Abbey in Essex, surrendered. In less than half a decade a thousand years of monastic tradition had been destroyed.

MONEY

After Roman money stopped circulating in Britain in the 5th century, simple bartering took over until Anglo-Saxon settlers in the next century struck the first English coins for official payments.

The silver penny – abbreviated to 'd', after the Roman *denarius* – became currency in the Anglo-Saxon kingdom of Mercia in the 8th century when King Offa achieved political unity. About the same time, a pound in weight of silver was first melted down to mint 240 Saxon coins – later called sterlings – hence the term pound STERLING.

The Normans introduced a new penny after their Conquest of 1066. As the market economy grew, demand for smaller denominations brought the silver halfpenny and

farthing (fourth of a penny) into circulation in 1279. As Latin remained the language of government, the English pound, shilling and penny were denoted as *libra*, *solidus* and *denarius*, after Roman coinage, and led to the use of the symbols £, s, d until decimalisation in 1971 rationalised the currency to pounds and pence.

Treasure from the Americas increased the supply of bullion in the 16th century, and Britain suffered high inflation as Tudor kings struck new coins, introducing gold sovereigns and crowns, silver shillings and sixpences.

High-value coins were replaced by more practical banknotes, certifying the bearer's promise to pay, in the 17th century. Notes issued by the BANK OF ENGLAND gradually supplanted others, though in Scotland four private banks still issue notes. *See also ROYAL MINT*

SILVER PENNY
Tenth-century Viking lords had coins bearing the pagan symbol of a raven struck at York, which the Vikings intermittently controlled as a centre of trade. Their coins were often made by minters who had worked for the defeated Anglo-Saxon kings

SILVER SHILLING
Artistic developments during the 15th-century Renaissance led to coin designs for the first time bearing realistic portraits of kings. England's first silver shilling, known as a testoon (from the Latin testa, 'head') was struck in c.1504 bearing a likeness of Henry VII

COPPER FARTHING
England and Scotland were making coins out of copper by the 17th century. Widespread counterfeiting caused the English government to abandon royal farthings during the Civil War of the 1640s, and thousands of private local issues replaced them

GOLD SOVEREIGN
A general reform of British currency in 1816 set the pattern for the next century with new silver coinage, and gold as the currency standard. Gold sovereigns valued at £1 sterling were introduced the following year, typically depicting St George slaying a dragon

MONTACUTE HOUSE

• **Somerset (p.494 E6)** • **Built 1588-1601** • **NT**
Golden-hued blocks cut from the local limestone of Ham Hill have mellowed in time to make Montacute House one of the most beautiful of Elizabethan country mansions. The house is H-shaped with projecting gabled wings, mullioned windows and balustraded parapets.

The builder of the 1590s, intent on thus parading his wealth, was Edward Phelips, who later became Speaker of the House of Commons, and the house

remained in his family's ownership until 1931. On the second floor a 52 m (172 ft) gallery, built for indoor exercise on wet days, runs the entire length of the building and is hung with Tudor portraits.

Many rooms have original panelling, chimneypieces and heraldic stained glass, and contain furniture and Gothic tapestries dating from the 15th century. An unusual feature of the Great Hall is a plaster frieze depicting the punishment of a local man who was carried round the parish tied to a pole – for drinking while on baby-sitting duty.

Field Marshal MONTGOMERY

• **Soldier** • **1887-1976; kt 1942; visc. 1946**
Few British commanders have aroused such conflicting opinions as Bernard Montgomery. Known as 'Monty' by his troops, he raised the morale of all who served under him, but his intolerance of the opinions of others made enemies among his fellow officers.

In 1939 he led the 3rd Division of the British Expeditionary Force to France, culminating in the evacuation from Dunkirk. His meticulous planning as commander of the Eighth Army in North Africa, and insistence on superiority in armour before fighting, led to Britain's first major victory, the defeat of the German general Rommel at El Alamein in 1942, followed by the expulsion of all Axis troops from North Africa.

The following year Montgomery commanded the Allied land forces for the D-DAY invasion of Normandy, but did not see eye to eye with the supreme commander General Eisenhower and was less successful in the later campaign. Montgomery's trademark beret bore two cap badges: one denoting his rank of general, the other the corps he esteemed above all – the Royal Tank Regiment.

MONTY PYTHON

• **Comedy team**
''E's not pinin'!', Cleese retorted to the pet-shop owner, ''E's passed on! This parrot is no more! 'Is metabolic processes are 'istory!'. The dead parrot sketch in *Monty Python's Flying Circus* is a classic of British COMEDY. With such surreal scripts John Cleese – one of the Monty Python author-performers – staked his claim to be the funniest man of his generation in Britain.

The Monty Python humour stems from the performance by John Cleese and Terry Chapman at the Cambridge University Footlights Revue in 1963. After a successful debut with the BBC in the late 1960s, Chapman and Cleese teamed up with Eric Idle (also at Cambridge), Terry Gilliam, Terry Jones and Michael Palin to form Monty Python in 1969. The show used visual gags, improbable scenarios, silly songs, silly

COMPLETELY DIFFERENT **Performers in the Monty Python team included** *(from left)* **Palin, Chapman, Cleese** *(in announcer's suit),* **Idle and Jones in their second television series in 1970**

walks and animation in intentionally unrelated sketches, introduced by the catchphrase, 'and now for something completely different'. Although nearer to an undergraduate review than mass entertainment, it kept millions of viewers entertained for 48 episodes.

The first film, *Monty Python and the Holy Grail*, appeared in 1975, followed four years later by *The Life of Brian*, a parody of the life of Christ. *The Meaning of Life* was screened in 1983.

Bobby MOORE

• Footballer   • 1941-93; OBE 1967

In the age of the 'professional foul' during the 1960s and 70s, when defenders became increasingly less scrupulous about playing by the rules, Bobby Moore was the last vestige of a sporting ideal. This blond, handsome and self-assured East Ender enjoyed the highest profile of any British sportsman in the 1960s, captaining West Ham United to the FA Cup and the European Cup-Winners' Cup, and then England to its 1966 WORLD CUP triumph.

Goalkeepers aside, no player has won more England caps (108), or more universal respect. Though lacking in pace, Moore compensated with timing, alertness and coolness. An uncanny ability to 'read' the game usually kept him one move ahead of the opposition.

CASTS OF THOUSANDS **Henry Moore's sculpture was once described as 'the most pervasive artistic status symbol in the developed world'. In 1983, while working on a model for** *Large Reclining Figure* **(right), Moore had exhibitions at 77 venues worldwide**

Henry MOORE

• Sculptor   • 1898-1986

Gaping voids in huge humanoid shapes positioned dramatically in bleak landscapes are typical of Henry Moore's sculpture. The awesome primitiveness and monumental scale of such works as the stone *Recumbent Figure* (1938) and bronze *Family Group* (1948-9) have made Moore one of the most admired sculptors of the 20th century.

Moore's sculptures were usually based on natural forms, such as reclining human figures, mother-and-child combinations, or bones and shells, but he experimented in the 1930s with abstract ideas, rejecting traditional concepts of beauty. During the Second World War he drew Londoners sleeping in air-raid shelters (*see* BLITZ), and in 1948 won the International Sculpture prize at the Venice Biennale.

There are about 75 Moore sculptures standing in open-air sites in Britain, and more than 30 next to his studio in Much Hadham in Hertfordshire, where the Henry Moore Foundation has converted a barn to exhibit them.

Patrick MOORE

• Astronomer   • b.1923

The presenter of the BBC's second longest-running television series, *The Sky at Night*, launched in April 1957, is a man who has no degree in astronomy and, except for a brief directorship at the Armagh Planetarium in Northern Ireland, has no professional experience. But Moore's infectious enthusiasm and erudition have made him a national celebrity. Educated privately because of poor health, he trained aircraft pilots until 1952 when he decided to turn his hobby into a career and become a full-time writer on astronomy.

Moore is the author of dozens of books, all written on a 1908 typewriter, and has presented more than 500 television programmes.

Thomas MORE

• **Statesman and writer**
• **1478-1535; kt 1521; canonised 1935**
In an age beset with political corruption Thomas More became a beacon of moral courage, a virtue he paid for with his life. More made known his views on the need for a just and rationally governed society in 1516 when he published his great work *Utopia* – a word he coined from the Greek for 'no place' and 'good place'. In it, he describes a perfectly run, imaginary island where there is religious toleration and equal education for boys and girls, contrasting with the England of his day.

As lord chancellor from 1529, More could not reconcile his Catholic faith with a duty to support Henry VIII, who was taking his first steps in establishing a Church independent of papal authority, and he resigned after three years. Although a close friend of the king, More refused to accept Henry's 1534 Act of Supremacy. Imprisonment followed by a show trial led to More's conviction for high treason and he was beheaded.

AESTHETIC PATTERNING William Morris scribbled instructions to the printers on his pencil and watercolour vine pattern for wallpaper, designed in 1873

MORECAMBE AND WISE

• **Television comedians**
• **Eric Bartholomew (alias Eric Morecambe); 1926-84; OBE 1976**
• **Ernest Wiseman (alias Ernie Wise); 1925-99; OBE 1976**
A wartime youth talent show brought together the duo that kept television audiences laughing for nearly 20 years. Their first series, in 1954, was panned by the critics, but they persevered with their trademark act, developed from music hall COMEDY tradition: Ernie as stuffed-shirt, older-brotherish and embarrassed; Eric chirpy, puckish and embarrassing.

In 1961, after the pair gave the second of their four Royal Variety Performances, the *Morecambe and Wise Show* began its 17 year television run. They poked fun at show guests and each other, and developed routines and catchphrases: 'There's no answer to that', and 'What do you think of it so far? Rubbish!'

Desmond MORRIS

• **Zoologist and anthropologist**   • **b.1928**
The genial zoo keeper and presenter of Granada's *Zoo Time* wildlife series in the 1950s gained new prominence a decade later when he published his controversial books *The Naked Ape* (1967) and *The Human Zoo* (1968). Desmond Morris applied techniques of animal observation to people, interpreting human behaviour in terms of hunting and territorial instincts and stress reactions caused by overcrowding.

Many academics criticised Morris's views as simplistic, but his books, including studies of cats and dogs, sold in millions and later works, such as *The Human Animal* (1994), have been made into popular television series.

DOUBLE ACT Cheery buffoonery won the nation's heart for Eric Morecambe (*far left*) and his 'buddy Ern' – 28 million people watched their 1977 Christmas show

William MORRIS

• **Craftsman, designer and writer**   • **1834-96**
'Man's expression of his joy in labour' was how William Morris defined art. A utopian socialist, Morris dedicated his working life to reviving traditional craftsmanship threatened by mass production. In 1861 he founded the firm Morris & Co to produce handmade fabrics, furniture, tiles and wallpapers. The objects he designed with the PRE-RAPHAELITE painter Edward BURNE-JONES are some of the finest examples of 19th-century decorative arts. Many are still reproduced.

Morris extended his design principles to books and printing in 1890 when he founded the Kelmscott Press, named after KELMSCOTT MANOR, his country home in Oxfordshire. His romantic fantasy *News from Nowhere*, depicting an idyllic nonindustrial society, reflected his socialist ideology, but his politics were less influential than his aesthetics, which inspired the ARTS AND CRAFTS movement in the 1890s. His childhood home in Walthamstow, north-east London, is now a museum dedicated to his work.

MORRIS DANCING

The folk dance known as the morris dance has been performed in England since at least the 15th century, traditionally as part of the celebrations on MAY DAY, at Whitsun and Christmas.

Its obscure origins have been linked to sword dances, but its name is associated with the Spanish Moors, perhaps because performers had their faces blackened.

Morris dancing had become nearly extinct by the late 19th century, until Cecil Sharp (1859-1924) travelled England recording FOLK SONGS and dances. Morris dancing varies between towns, especially in the Midlands, where it is most common, but usually involves male dancers, dressed in white and wearing bells around their shins, who wave handkerchiefs and strike sticks.

Oswald MOSLEY

• **Politician and fascist** • 1896-1980; bt 1928

During the Depression years of the 1930s, Oswald Mosley, a member of a wealthy and titled family and a magnetic, skilful orator, urged people to join his British Union of Fascists (BUF). Many supported his calls for state intervention in the economy and a strong system of government, but in the end his party failed to gain a single seat in parliament.

Mosley had become a Conservative MP in 1918, then moved to Labour, before founding the BUF in 1932. His admiration of Hitler, his antisemitism and parades of uniformed followers in Nazi-style black shirts won derision more than support, particularly after a rally in London in 1934 when fascist stewards brutally suppressed hecklers. When, two years later, Mosley marched 1900 thugs down Cable Street, a Jewish area of the East End, public sympathy was with the Jews, who repelled them by throwing cobbles dug up from the road.

The government interned Mosley and his second wife, Diana MITFORD, during the Second World War as a threat to national security, and dissolved his party.

Stirling MOSS

• **Motor racing driver** • b.1929; OBE 1957

He never won the World Drivers' Championship, yet Stirling Moss was runner-up four times between 1955 and

BRITISH FASCISM Oswald Mosley organised Nazi-style parades of his followers, hoping to inspire a national movement, but from 1934 increasing violence and antisemitism alienated the public

1958, and was one of the most admired and charismatic figures to grace Formula One. The first Englishman to win the BRITISH GRAND PRIX (1955), he insisted patriotically on driving uncompetitive British cars for much of his career. A crash at the Goodwood circuit put an end to his racing career in 1962, after which he became a journalist and broadcaster.

MOTOR CARS: *see page 306*

MOTORCYCLES

From the 1920s to the 1960s British motorcycle manufacturers led the field with makes such as BSA (Birmingham Small Arms), Norton and Triumph. After Colonel Henry Holden had successfully powered a bicycle with a petrol engine to produce the world's first 4-cylinder motorbike in 1889 – capable of a

dizzying 20 mph – he was joined by others eager to develop this invention.

Among the first were the Collier brothers, who began making their Matchless motorcycles in London in 1899. One of the firm's machines won the single-cylinder event at the inaugural Isle of Man TT RACE eight years later, while the twin-cylinder event went to Norton, founded in 1902. BSA, originally a gun manufacturer, graduated from building bicycles to motorcycles in 1905, and by the 1950s was the world's leader, turning out more than 75 000 reliable machines a year.

The Brough Superior, advertised as the Rolls-Royce of motorbikes, broke speed records in the 1920s and 1930s, and each new Brough came with a guarantee that it had been tested at 100 mph. Among many famous owners was T.E. Lawrence, who owned several and was killed riding one.

Increased competition after the Second World War from Italian scooters and Japanese motorbikes sent the British industry into decline, and by the 1970s all the major names had gone bankrupt or been merged into conglomerates. In the 1990s new models from Triumph signified new shoots of recovery.

BORN FOR SPEED Stirling Moss, who won 222 of his 506 races before retiring, returned to the track for a 1977 historic car race at Brands Hatch

A DRIVING PASSION

Motoring changed the face of Britain: throughout the 20th century a network of metalled roads spread across the landscape, bringing traffic jams and speed cameras in its wake. Cars became symbols of success and prized possessions, and by the 1930s building them was Britain's biggest industry

A CAR FOR THE PEOPLE *In 1921 Herbert Austin designed the first car intended to bring motoring to the masses. The cheapest and most popular version of his Austin 7, the 'Baby' (left), sold for £118 and was followed by the Singer Junior for £150 and the first £100 car, the Morris Cowley, in 1931. But all were still out of the reach of the majority of people; in 1936, the year of the Jarrow March, 60 per cent of Britons took home less than £130 a year*

THE CAR was born in Germany but from the earliest days Britain was its adopted home. Motor Mills in Coventry, one of the first British car factories, was the world's largest when it began production in 1897 for the German company Daimler.

The British industry was held back by the 1865 'Red Flag' Act, which required a pedestrian to carry a warning flag, or a lantern at night, ahead of each vehicle to warn other road users. Speed was limited to a walking pace of 4mph on the open road and 2mph in towns.

After the Act was repealed in 1896 the British industry began to expand, with scores of tiny firms emerging, run by enterprising engineers such as Frederick Lanchester. Within 20 years most of the famous British marques were well established in production: Bristol, Humber, Morris, Riley, Rover, Singer, Standard, Sunbeam and Wolseley, using designs by Herbert Austin. By 1930 car ownership in Britain exceeded a million.

After the Second World War overseas trade became vital for rebuilding the economy and cars were Britain's biggest export. In 1950 Britain was exporting three-quarters of its cars – more than any other country in the world. The

After the 1896 repeal of the 'Red Flag' Act's speed restrictions the engineer F.W. Lanchester produced a motorised vehicle in 1898 capable of a hair-raising 28mph

same entrepreneurial spirit that inspired so many small brands was to prove the industry's downfall. In other countries fewer but larger companies had been developing. By the 1950s foreign firms such as Fiat, Renault, General Motors, Ford and later Nissan, Honda and Toyota from the Far East were producing cars cheaper and faster than their smaller British competitors.

COMBINED FORCES

In 1952 Austin and Morris merged as the British Motor Corporation (BMC). Morris brought with it the designer of the hugely successful Minor, Alec ISSIGONIS, and with BMC he produced his most revolutionary car, the Mini. By placing the engine sideways with the gearbox underneath it Issigonis built a tiny car that could hold four adults.

The Mini hit the streets in 1959 and had instant, cheeky appeal. Forty years on, it is the most successful British car ever, with more than 5.25 million sold.

Major mergers in the 1960s brought together BMC, the Jaguar Group and Standard-Triumph to become British Leyland (BL). Leyland had 30 factories and 200000 employees, and supplied

POLE POSITION Superb roadholding made Minis as popular on the racetrack as in town. They won the Monte Carlo Rally three times in the 1960s, and races such as this one at Crystal Palace in 1966 made exciting sport. When three 'starred' in the film *The Italian Job* in 1969 the Mini's cult status was secured

SPIRIT OF INDULGENCE
The 1907 Rolls-Royce Silver Ghost is a symbol of faultless quality and sumptuous luxury – attributes that the company still proudly upholds

BONE SHAKER Early cars such as the Lanchester offered bare comfort

MOTORING MILESTONES

1894 The first British car is built by Frederick Bremer

1902 A garage in Newcastle upon Tyne offers a breakdown-truck rescue service

1905 The Automobile Association (AA) is founded. Patrolmen salute to warn members of speed traps ahead

1914 A roadside petrol pump is installed in Shrewsbury

1914 A 'motorway' from London to Liverpool is proposed in parliament

1926 Electric traffic lights (*right*) are installed in Piccadilly, London

1934 Percy Shaw invents 'cat's eyes'

1935 Driving tests become compulsory

1948 The Land-Rover four-wheel-drive (*right*) combines utility with roadworthiness

1958 The Preston bypass opens, Britain's first motorway, followed by the M1 (*below*) in 1959

MADE IN BRITAIN, BUILT TO LAST

From the industry's infancy, skilled craftsmanship attracted firms such as Daimler to build their vehicles in Britain and earned British-made cars a reputation for quality. The world's wealthy travelled in style in British vehicles such as the Rolls-Royce Silver Ghost, first produced in 1907.

The glamour of MOTOR RACING, both at home circuits such as BROOKLANDS and abroad with the Le Mans endurance race, sparked a desire for cars that would offer speed and excitement on the road. British engineers responded with style. At one end of the range was the MG, the two-seater sports car produced by Morris Garages in 1928. At the other were the 1927 4½ litre Bentley with a top speed of 90 mph, which won at Le Mans in 1928, and the majestic, 1931 8 litre Bentley tourer.

Britain still produces a wider range of luxury and high-performance cars than any other nation, including long-established marques such as AC, Aston Martin, Jaguar, Lotus, Morgan and TVR. Despite the foreign ownership of several of these companies, much of the engineering is distinctively British. Often hand-built, such cars retain a flavour of the industry's original spirit, offering not just a mode of travel but a driving experience.

GLAMOUR PUSS Sleek good looks and a top speed of 150 mph combined to make the British 1961 Jaguar E-type one of the most desirable cars ever built

DESIGNER MOTORING British engineers continue to produce individualistic cars such as the 1997 Lotus Elise. A small team of skilled designers and craftsmen build 3000 vehicles each year at the company's Norfolk works

40 per cent of the British market. Car ownership doubled in a decade to nearly 12 million but Britain's most popular car was the Escort, from US-owned Ford.

By 1972 BL dominated the British-owned car industry. Within the conglomerate, marques lost their individuality, and worker morale and build quality began to suffer. Two years later, hit by the 1973 oil crisis, strikes and high import taxes, BL was bankrupt.

AN INDUSTRY IN DECLINE

With the aid of public finance BL continued production into the 1980s when it was broken up and sold to British and foreign companies. Despite the loss of British-owned firms, cars remain the country's biggest industry: 1.7 million are produced annually, more than half of them for export. In 1998-9 Rover Group, Britain's largest manufacturer, made £3200 million in overseas sales.

Even the quintessentially British brand Rolls-Royce was sold in 1997 to the German firm Volkswagen, but the national obsession with the car remains. Throughout the 1990s car ownership in Britain grew faster than the population to more than 25.5 million vehicles.

1960 MOT tests and traffic wardens (*left*) are introduced

1964 The Forth Road Bridge opens, at 1 mile the longest road bridge in Europe

1967 The breathalyser is introduced

1973 The Middle East oil crisis causes fuel prices to quadruple

1983 Wearing seat belts in the front seats of cars is made compulsory; deaths and serious injuries from road accidents drop by 20 per cent as a result

1986 The M25, a 121½ mile motorway around London, is completed

1992 Speed cameras (*right*) are introduced

MOTOR RACING

Cars have been raced almost from the moment they were invented, and Britain has produced some of the towering heroes of this dangerous sport. The open road was the first venue for racing, and this form of competition survives in fossilised form in the BRIGHTON RUN. But the sport soon moved to the specially built circuits with which it is now associated. The first of these was BROOKLANDS, which opened in 1907. Brands Hatch and Silverstone, BRITISH GRAND PRIX courses, opened after the Second World War.

In 1958 Mike Hawthorn became the first British world champion, beating Stirling MOSS by one point. This heralded a brilliant decade; Formula One saw four British world champions in the 1960s: Jim Clark (1963, 1965), Graham HILL (1962, 1968), John Surtees (1964) and Jackie STEWART (1969). James Hunt, Nigel Mansell and Damon HILL carried forward a noble motor-racing tradition.

Lord MOUNTBATTEN

• Statesman and naval officer
• 1900-79; 1st earl Burma 1947

As a great-grandson of Queen Victoria Louis Mountbatten was born with the title Prince Louis of Battenberg, but assumed the more English-sounding Mountbatten in the First World War.

In the Second World War he was supreme Allied commander of South-east Asia. He led the defence of India and the campaign to expel the Japanese from Burma. In 1947 he became the last viceroy of India, overseeing the end of the RAJ. In later years he commanded the Mediterranean fleet, was First Sea Lord, and chief of defence staff.

Mountbatten was an influential and well-loved elder member of the royal family, especially close to Prince Charles. His death was violent: in 1979 he was killed on his boat by an IRA bomb.

MULL

• Argyll and Bute (p.497 B4)
• Area 340 sq miles • Pop. 2700

With mountains, moors and 300 miles of wild, ragged shoreline, Mull is a microcosm of the western Highlands. Less than two miles separate it from the mainland, yet the island has its own long history and distinctive character.

In the 4th century AD Mull was one of the first areas settled by Irish invaders who called themselves Scots, and was

EYE-CATCHING The 200-year-old cottages lining Tobermory's harbour were built when the capital of Mull was a busy fishing station

the scene of many battles with the native PICTS. It was later ravaged by the VIKINGS, but following their defeat formed part of the Lordship of the Isles (a confederation of the Hebridean chieftains). In the 15th and 16th centuries the Macdonalds and the Campbells fought bitterly for possession, culminating in an invasion by the Campbells, led by the earl of Argyll, in 1674.

The capital, Tobermory, was first established as a fishing station in the 1780s, though today its main industry is tourism; it hosts the Highland Games in July. Regular boat trips go to Fingal's Cave and IONA from Fionnphort.

MUMMERS

Mummers are the actors in folk dramas known as 'mumming plays'. Wearing masks and disguised with strips of cloth or paper sewn over their clothes, mummers stand silent (mum) in a semicircle before delivering set speeches and returning to their places. A fight follows, usually between St George (perhaps originally the GREEN MAN) and an infidel knight. One of the combatants is slain but is miraculously revived by a doctor.

Mumming has its roots in pagan ritual, although the earliest references to the dramas date from the 18th century. There are nearly a thousand versions of the British mumming play, but all of them deal with the symbolism of death and new life, and the renewal of the natural world. In Christian times, the plays were adapted to encompass the doctrine of Christ's Resurrection.

Mummers often perform outdoors, usually at Christmas time, Easter or Halloween. Marshfield in Gloucestershire and Church Crookham in Hampshire are regular venues for the performance of this ancient rite.

GOODBYE GOVERNOR Crowds bid farewell to Lord Mountbatten on his retirement in 1948. As viceroy and governor general, he oversaw India's transition from colony to independent state

Iris MURDOCH

• **Writer and philosopher** • 1919-99; DBE 1987

'Writing is like getting married. One should never commit oneself until one is amazed at one's luck.' So wrote Iris Murdoch, who began her career as a philosopher, lecturing at Oxford (1948-63). Her first published work was *Sartre, Romantic Rationalist* (1953). She started writing fiction as a hobby, penning *Under the Net* in 1954.

Murdoch concerned herself with the inner lives of her characters, dealing with complex moral and psychological issues. Common themes are sexuality and good versus evil. Her best-known works include *The Bell* (1958), *The Black Prince* (1973) and *The Sea, The Sea*, which won the 1978 Booker prize.

MUSIC HALL

In Victorian and Edwardian Britain music halls served audiences with drink and entertainment in equal measure. Soon music hall came to refer simply to the entertainment itself, which consisted of ballad, communal and patter songs, selections from operetta, female impersonators, comedians and variety acts such as jugglers and conjurors.

MY LORDS, LADIES AND GENTLEMEN

A master of ceremonies ushered the artists on and off from a desk at the side of the stage and a pianist accompanied the singers. The audience, sitting at tables, behaved informally, often exchanging banter with the artists. At the turn of the century there were 50 music halls in London; at the top of the bill would be stars such as Vesta Tilley (1864-1952), a male impersonator, the comedian George Robey (1869-1954), dubbed the 'prime minister of mirth', and the singer Marie Lloyd (1870-1922) with witty songs such as 'A little bit of what you fancy does you good'.

END OF AN ERA

Music hall fell into decline after the First World War, faced with competition from the cinema and record industries. A few venues still provide music hall acts, most notably the Players Theatre in London where, as tradition demands, 'Down at the Old Bull and Bush' has been sung at the end of the show since 1937.

See also COMEDY AND COMEDIANS

MYSTERY PLAYS

• **14th-16th century religious dramas**

One Thursday every June the towns of medieval England came alive with noise and pageant. For this was Corpus Christi, a religious festival, and traditionally the day of the annual mystery plays.

The mystery plays, or miracle plays, are composed of 'cycles' of dramatised Biblical stories. These short plays in rhymed verse have been performed since around 1350, and possibly earlier.

The name comes from the 'mysteries' or craft guilds, which sponsored and acted in the plays (drapers doing Adam and Eve, for example). Four complete cycles survive: from York, Chester, Wakefield and 'N-Town', possibly in East Anglia. The plays are rarely performed today, although York has included its cycle in its millennium celebrations.

MUSHROOMS AND TOADSTOOLS

The familiar field mushroom that heralds the approach of autumn in the countryside is only one of more than 3000 larger types of fungi found in Britain. Unlike plants, fungi have no need of sunlight, drawing their nutrition from decaying matter. In speeding up the process of decay they play a vital role in nature's cycle of regeneration. Some types of fungi, however, are not so beneficial: honey fungus (also known as bootlace fungus) destroys living trees, while dry rot attacks houses.

Rich in folklore, wild mushrooms are traditionally distrusted in Britain. The disparaging term 'toadstool' is commonly employed, even for species considered to be delicacies in most European countries. But this attitude is changing, with around 25 British species regularly collected for consumption. Favourites include the blewit, parasol, chanterelle and horn of plenty. In spring gourmets seek out the rare morel that grows in scrub and open woodland. It has a convoluted, honeycombed cap, resembling a brain, yet it is a delicious addition to meat dishes.

As well as edible species, many British mushrooms are poisonous, even deadly. Before eating always check their identity carefully in a reliable field guide.

FLY AGARIC The blood-red cap and white spots of this toadstool spell danger. Its traditional association with fairies could be connected to hallucinogens present in its highly toxic flesh

FIELD MUSHROOM
A circle or dense clusters of field mushrooms is a common sight on British grassland. Purple-brown gills and a pleasant mealy smell identify this edible species, but it can be confused with the deadly death cap (*see below*)

GIANT PUFFBALL
This edible fungus can grow to 30 cm (1 ft) across. It is found in open fields, gardens and woodland and is best eaten while it still has firm, white flesh. Older, yellow-fleshed fungi can cause indigestion

CEP
Known as 'penny bun' because of its brown cap, this mushroom is highly prized for its nutty flavour. It grows in all types of woodland, often in dense grass. It has a thick stem and spongy pores instead of gills

DEATH CAP
This is the world's most deadly fungus. Even though its gills are pale and it has a nasty taste, it is sometimes mistaken for a field mushroom. Other identifying features include a grey-green cap and a sheath at its base

NANNIES

The first nannies were mere servants in well-off households who dressed the children, corrected their speech and taught them prayers and simple lessons. But by the 19th century the nursemaid employed to look after the children had evolved into Nanny, an authoritative head of the nursery (usually a suite of rooms at the top of the house).

Nannies had special responsibility for the youngest child and, in upper class families, nursery maids to assist them. Parents would see their children only at set times of the day, so Nanny was the centre of many young people's lives – surrogate mother, teacher and nurse.

Most Victorian nannies were unmarried women from poorer backgrounds, who had begun as nursery maids and were experienced but untrained. The fictional nanny, Mary Poppins, may have been a different breed, however. She was perhaps a Norland Nurse, trained at the first nannies' college, the Norland Institute, which opened in London in 1892.

Today Norland takes up to 40 girls a year on its two-year residential course, leading to a Diploma in Nursery Nursing (from the Nursery Nursing Examinations Board). Trainees can still be seen wheeling their old-fashioned prams in Denford Park, Berkshire.

NORLAND KNOW-HOW Budding nannies learn the ropes in 1956 at the most respected of British nanny schools. Today, a Norland diploma virtually guarantees a job

COUNTING BONES Napier mechanised his logarithmic tables into a simple form of slide-rule. Made out of bone or ivory, the device became known as Napier's bones

John NAPIER

• Mathematician • 1550-1617
Nothing was drearier, wrote the Scottish aristocrat John Napier, 'than the multiplications, divisions, square and cubical expansions of great numbers, which, beside the tedious expense of time, are subject to many slippery errors'.

After 20 years of experiment he came up with a solution – logarithms – that was to last 350 years until the arrival of calculators. Logarithms reduced complex operations to addition and subtraction by expressing numbers as exponents to a base with the aid of special tables. Napier was also the first to use and popularise the decimal point.

John NASH: *see opposite page*

Paul NASH

• Artist • 1889-1946
Paul Nash was an individualistic English artist in the tradition of Blake and Turner, whom he admired. While keenly aware of the latest developments on the Continent, he always retained an English feeling for landscape and form.

Nash studied at the Slade School of Fine Art before fighting in the First World War and, in 1917, becoming an official war artist. Tortured landscapes of the Western Front were his first distinctive pieces. In the 1920s he came under the influence of Surrealism and in 1936 he helped to organise the First Surrealist Exhibition in London, at which Salvador Dali appeared in a diving suit.

Nash's later works were mostly pastoral landscapes until, in 1939, he was again appointed a war artist. *Totes Meer* (Dead Sea) and his other war pictures specialised in aircraft wrecks in a style that uniquely united Surrealism, landscape and the horror of war.

NATIONAL ANTHEMS

Thomas Arne wrote the music for the first official rendition of *God Save the King* (or Queen) in 1745, although both words and music were more a matter of evolution than the inspiration of any one man. The *English Hymnal* labels it 'origin obscure'.

The tune was at one time used by at least 20 different countries including Denmark, Russia and the USA (where it is known as *America* and sung to the words 'My Country 'tis of Thee'). It is still the national hymn of Liechtenstein.

Constituent nations of the British Isles have their own anthems: Wales has *Land of My Fathers* (1856) and Ireland sings *Sinne Fianna Fáil* (1926). Scotland remained aloof to the idea until unofficially adopting the celtic-flavoured *Flower of Scotland* (1971), composed by a popular folk duo called The Corries.

NATIONAL DEBT

The national debt is the total outstanding borrowings of a government. British governments that cannot raise sufficient revenue from taxation to meet their commitments borrow the difference, from both home and overseas in return for gilt-edged securities, index-linked gilts, Treasury bills and National Savings products. This is administered by the Debt Management Office – an executive agency of the Treasury.

The British national debt really started to grow at the end of the 17th century, when the government borrowed from the newly formed BANK OF ENGLAND, and governments ever since have lived beyond their means. By 1999 the debt

THE ONLY WAY IS UP Britain's National Debt has never been paid off. It dropped briefly during the latter half of the 19th century when British industry dominated the markets of the world

YEAR	DEBT (£ million)
1691	3
1741	49
1791	243
1841	790
1891	616
1941	10 366
1991	225 120

John NASH

• Architect • 1752-1835

By the end of the 18th century, John Nash had already achieved some success with stucco-fronted houses in London and a collection of country abodes, where he worked in partnership with the landscape gardener Humphry REPTON. The picturesque evocation of a medieval castle at Luscombe in Devon (1800) and the Italian-influenced villa at Cronkhill, Shropshire (1802), are an indication of his range and diversity.

Flamboyant and worldly in his personal style, Nash was a natural choice for the patronage of the Prince Regent (later GEORGE IV). Together they produced an intriguing array of work in which Nash used a miscellany of styles from Gothic to neoclassical, via Italian Renaissance and English Palladianism. His best-known work for the Prince is the exotic BRIGHTON Pavilion (1815-21). Its roof-line of domes playfully recalls the Taj Mahal while its lusciously ornate interior is in oriental style bedecked with golden Chinese dragons and sumptuous silks.

Away from the heady seaside air, Nash's attention turned in London to the redevelopment of a large tract of the West End. His design encompassed REGENT'S PARK, which he linked with St James's Park by a great, curving line of terraces, streets and circuses, known as the Nash Sweep. The area included the Quadrant, Regent Street (rebuilt in 1923) and Piccadilly Circus. Carlton

CLASSICAL STYLE Cumberland Terrace (1827) was built as part of Nash's redesign of the West End. Its skyline statuary and giant columns are best viewed from Regent's Park

House Terrace (1827-32) at the southern end of the scheme stretches along the Mall, and now houses the Institute of Contemporary Arts, the Royal Society and the Mall Galleries.

The majestic route passes one of Nash's most charming works, All Souls Church at Langham Place (1822-4), a small counterpoint to his master plan. Within his enormous scheme, the ageing but vigorous Nash had plans for a new square to be laid out to the north-east of Carlton House Terrace, but he died before this got fully underway. Charles Barry took up the mantle, developing Nash's plans into Trafalgar Square.

stood at £300 billion. About 10 per cent of the British national debt is owed to overseas creditors. Like domestic holders, they receive interest that is either at a fixed rate or linked to the rate of inflation, depending on the type of debt they have bought.

NATIONAL EXHIBITION CENTRE

• Birmingham (p.495 F3) • Opened 1976

More than 4 million visitors pass through the NEC's 20 halls each year, making it Europe's busiest exhibition centre. They

come to attend a wide variety of events, from trade fairs and shows to major sporting occasions like the World Figure Skating Championships, and concerts by famous orchestras and bands.

The centre is situated on the outskirts of Birmingham, England's 'second city', and the site comprises a massive 314 ha (775 acres), hosting up to 160 exhibitions a year. In total there are around 158 000 m² (1.7 million sq ft) of exhibition space, but there are plans to open four new halls, taking the capacity up to 190 000 m² (2 million sq ft). The largest venue is the Arena, with a seating capacity of 12 600.

NATIONAL GALLERIES OF SCOTLAND

• Edinburgh (p.497 D4)

The National Gallery of Scotland, Scottish National Portrait Gallery and Scottish National Gallery of Modern Art are housed in three distinctive buildings.

The first and oldest stands on the Mound between EDINBURGH's medieval old town and Georgian new town. The building, designed by William Henry Playfair, opened to the public in 1850.

The gallery houses a large collection of European paintings and sculpture spanning the Renaissance to post-Impressionism. As well as old masters such as Rembrandt's *Woman in Bed* and Titian's *Three Ages of Man*, it holds some outstanding Scottish paintings, including Henry RAEBURN's *Reverend Robert Walker Skating on Duddingston Loch* (1784).

The Portrait Gallery opened in 1889. It tells the history of Scotland through portraits of famous patriots, from Mary, Queen of Scots to Sean Connery.

The Gallery of Modern Art, in the west of the city, opened in 1984 with a collection strong on surrealism, German Expressionism and French art. Its grounds provide a setting for work by Henry MOORE and Barbara HEPWORTH.

NATIONAL GALLERY

• Central London (p.499 C6)   • Founded 1824

The gallery's handsome neoclassical building, designed by William Wilkins, houses more than 2300 west European paintings dating from 1260 to 1900, including John CONSTABLE's *The Hay Wain* (1821), Van Gogh's *Sunflowers* (1888) and the *Arnolfini Portrait* (1434) by Jan Van Eyck. In the main vestibule a series of mosaics by Russian-born Boris Anrep, completed in 1952, uses famous people as embodiments of such qualities as Defiance (Winston Churchill) and Delectation (Margot Fonteyn).

The gallery was founded in 1824 when parliament set aside £57 000 for the purchase of 38 pictures from the Russian emigré financier John Julius Angerstein. This job lot included *The Raising of Lazarus* by Sebastiano del Piombo and Rembrandt's *Adoration of the Shepherds*. The gallery's collection has been increased over the years by government grants, bequests and gifts, including a donation of £50 million by Jean Paul GETTY in 1985.

A northern extension opened in 1975, and the Sainsbury Wing, funded by the SAINSBURY family and designed by Venturi, Rauch and Scott Brown of Philadelphia, opened in 1991 to house the early Renaissance collection.

NATIONAL FILM THEATRE

• Central London (p.499 E7)   • Est. 1952

The National Film Theatre (NFT) screens some 2000 film, television and video productions a year, ranging from the early silents to contemporary avant-garde productions and Hollywood blockbusters. The theatre developed from the Telekinema designed for the 1951 FESTIVAL OF BRITAIN as a model for the cinema of the future. After the festival, the British Film Institute took over the Telekinema, renaming it the National Film Theatre in 1952. It moved to its current premises at the SOUTH BANK CENTRE in October 1957, with the launch of the first London Film Festival. In 1970 a second theatre, NFT2, was built, devoted to arthouse

AT THE FLICKS
The NFT stages an annual film festival that attracts serious film buffs, as well as more light-hearted events such as 3-D shows requiring special glasses (*below*)

films, and in 1988 the Museum of the Moving Image (MOMI) was added. State-of-the-art technology is presented next to cinematic antiques, but the main attraction of this modern museum is its interactive displays. Visitors are encouraged to participate and can even see themselves 'on camera' reading the news.

NATIONAL HEALTH SERVICE

• Est. 1948

After the hardship of war and with the memory of the 1930s recession still fresh, the British public in 1948 greeted the arrival of the National Health Service (NHS) enthusiastically.

Free medical care was first proposed by the economist William Beveridge in his visionary 'Beveridge report' of 1942. Doctors initially opposed the idea, fearing loss of professional autonomy, but they were eventually won over and the scheme was successfully introduced by Aneurin BEVAN, health secretary in the postwar Labour government.

The founders of the NHS expected it to reduce demand for healthcare by ensuring that illness was treated early. In fact, demand has grown relentlessly from the day the NHS began and the trend is set to continue as life expectancy increases and medical advances make new – and often very expensive – treatments available.

The NHS is potentially a financial black hole: with a staff of 1 million (Europe's largest employer), it faces growing expectations and rising demand. The budget for 1998-9 was £37 billion.

Governments struggling to fund the service have steadily increased charges: a prescription cost 20p in 1971, by 1998 the price had risen to £5.80. The Conservative administration of the 1980s tried to create an 'internal market', giving hospitals and GPs the option of running their own budgets, but the results were at best patchy and led to accusations of a 'two-tier' service and of covert privatisation. The 1997 Labour government has announced plans to modernise the NHS.

NATIONAL INSURANCE

Ensuring a decent standard of living for all is a relatively new government function. The first scheme, covering unemployment in a few selected industries only, was introduced by David LLOYD GEORGE in 1911. Employees paid 4d, employers 3d and the state 2d per person per week – 'Ninepence for fourpence' as it was advertised.

In 1999/2000 only people earning more than £64 per week were liable to pay National Insurance. The National Insurance fund was split between the NHS (10 per cent) and benefit allocation (90 per cent). Retirement pensions took up 75 per cent of the benefit allocation and 25 per cent went into state benefits.

NATIONALISATION AND PRIVATISATION

A swathe of British industry passed into public ownership (nationalisation) under the Labour government of 1945-51, including the gas, water, electricity, coal, iron and steel industries, as well as railways and road haulage. The government was motivated partly by an ideological commitment to public ownership, but also by the fact that the industries were run down after the war.

The process was reversed under Margaret THATCHER's radical Conservative administration of the 1980s. A steady programme of privatisation sold off such companies as British Aerospace, Britoil,

FREE FOR ALL Aneurin Bevan prepares for the launch of the National Health Service in July 1948. He resigned three years later when charges were brought in for dentures and spectacles

Sealink, British Gas, the electricity boards, the water authorities, the coal industry and the railways.

Privatisation reduced government subsidies and raised revenues, while sales of shares to the public created a new class of small shareholders. Labour opposed the policy but since coming to power in 1997 has not reversed it.

NATIONAL LOTTERY

Since the opening draw on November 19, 1994, the first national lottery for more than 200 years has proved controversial. It has been called disguised taxation, little better than legalised fraud.

The 14 000 000-to-1 odds of winning the jackpot have not stopped 90 per cent of the population entering at least once, and heavy demand led to a Wednesday draw starting on February 7, 1997.

From every £1 ticket sold, 50p goes towards prizes. The New Opportunities Commission receives almost 6p, the arts, sport, charities and heritage fund each get just under 4p and the Millennium Commission gets slightly less. The organisers and retailers each get 5p and the taxman takes the remaining 12p.

NATIONAL MUSEUM OF PHOTOGRAPHY, FILM AND TELEVISION

• **Bradford (p.496 B4)** • **Founded 1983**
This museum houses the world's first photographic image; 6000 pictures by the English pioneer of photography, William Henry Fox TALBOT; Louis le Prince's 1896 film of Leeds Bridge, one of the earliest surviving moving pictures; and the first television footage.

A permanent exhibition displays 150 years of photography of everyday life, and a new wing is dedicated to electronic imaging, virtual reality and interactive special effects. Visitors can operate a television camera, see themselves read the news and view films on a 16 m × 20 m (52 ft × 64 ft) screen.

BLUE PRINT Early images at Bradford's Museum of Photography include an 1840s 'cyanotype' of a fern, created by using salts that turn blue on exposure

NATIONAL PARKS

Ten areas of England and Wales are designated as national parks: the BRECON BEACONS, DARTMOOR, EXMOOR, the LAKE DISTRICT, Northumberland, the North York Moors, the PEAK DISTRICT, the Pembrokeshire coast, SNOWDONIA and the Yorkshire Dales. The Norfolk Broads have a similar status and there are plans to add the NEW FOREST and, in Scotland, LOCH LOMOND and the TROSSACHS.

The parks were set up to preserve the scenic beauty and wildlife of large areas (10 per cent of England and Wales) and to protect the livelihoods of those who farm on hills, mountains and wetlands.

Some £40 million a year of public money supports the national parks. Most of the land is in private hands and includes farms, villages and small towns, although the total population of all national park land is just 250 000.

NATIONAL PORTRAIT GALLERY

• Central London (p.499 C6) • Founded 1856

Around 10 000 oil paintings, miniatures, sculptures, caricatures, silhouettes, photographs and videos of the people who have shaped the history and culture of Britain fill the National Portrait Gallery (NPG). Early treasures include Hans Holbein's *Cartoon of Henry VIII*, and the 'Ditchley' portrait of Elizabeth I. Since 1996, 19th and 20th-century portraits such as that of the Brontë sisters by their brother Branwell, and Vanessa Bell's of Virginia Woolf have hung in new galleries designed by the architect Piers Gough.

'A gallery of portraits of the most eminent persons in British history' was proposed by the 5th earl Stanhope. It opened in Westminster in 1856 and 40 years later moved into the present Italian Renaissance-style building. The NPG has been the scene of many controversies, such as the 1998 commissioning of a group portrait marking the peace process in Northern Ireland, which included the Sinn Féin leader Gerry Adams.

NATIONAL SERVICE

Until the First World War, Britain relied on volunteer forces to fight its wars. But the slaughter on the Western Front caused a shortage of fighting men and in February 1916 the government brought in conscription for men between 18 and 40 – later raised to 50.

Compulsory military service ended in 1918, but as war loomed in 1939 it was reintroduced under the National Service Act for men between 18 and 41 – later 51. From 1942 unmarried women joined those available for service. The 'call-up' continued after the Second World War until 1960 for men of 18, who had to do 18 to 24 months' service.

More than 5 million conscripts served from 1939 to 1963. Some 2500 died after 1949, fighting in places such as Korea and Malaya.

NATIONAL THEATRE

• Central London (p.499 E7) • Est. 1963

Britain's national theatre had a long gestation. It was first mooted in the 18th century by the actor David GARRICK, backed by parliament in 1949 and the foundation stone of the present building laid in 1951. It was another decade before the National Theatre company was formed, under the directorship of Laurence OLIVIER.

The opening production in 1963 was *Hamlet*, with Peter O'Toole, and the same play, with Albert Finney as the Prince, was the last before the company moved in 1976 from the Old Vic to its present home in the SOUTH BANK CENTRE.

NEW DIRECTIONS

From 1973 to 1988 Peter HALL directed the theatre, encouraging the production of new plays and successfully defending a charge of indecency brought by Mary Whitehouse over the portrayal of homosexual rape in *Romans in Britain*.

Hall was replaced by Richard Eyre in 1988 and the company was given the title 'Royal' to mark its 25th anniversary. In the same year Alan Bennett's double bill *Single Spies* contained the first British stage portrayal of a living monarch.

Trevor Nunn was appointed director in 1997. The productions he oversees are watched by some 690 000 people a year.

NATIONAL TRUST

• Founded 1895

A 1.8 ha (4.5 acre) clifftop site above Barmouth in Gwynedd was the first purchase of the National Trust, a charity founded to conserve Britain's landscape and historic buildings. The Clergy House in Alfriston was bought the next year for £10 and in 1907 Barrington Court in Somerset became the trust's first stately home.

Today, the trust is Britain's largest private landowner, with 244 000 ha (603 000 acres) and more than 300 houses and gardens open to the public. The trust also owns 575 miles of coastline, as well as prehistoric sites,

SONG AND DANCE In 1982 *Guys and Dolls* was the first large-scale musical staged at the new National Theatre. It ran for 370 performances and was watched by more than 390 000 people

woodland, farms, villages and such oddities as a former council house in Liverpool where Paul McCartney of The Beatles grew up.

Founded when conservation drew little interest, the trust now has more than 2.5 million members and had an income in 1997-8 of over £210 million.

NATURAL HISTORY MUSEUM

• W London (p.499 A4) • Opened 1881

In January 1860 the trustees of the BRITISH MUSEUM resolved to move their natural history collection. Land was bought in South Kensington and 21 years later a buff and blue terracotta-faced building designed by the architect Alfred Waterhouse in German romanesque style opened on west London's Cromwell Road. The interior, roofed in glass and steel, is as spectacular as the exterior, full of delicate carvings of animals and plants.

The Natural History Museum's 5.7 ha (14 acre) site has more than 68 million specimens, including some 28 million insects, 27 million animals, 9 million fossils and 3200 meteorites

OUT OF THIS WORLD The central hall of the Natural History Museum is dominated by the 26 m (85 ft) long skeleton of a diplodocus

The 'Life' and 'Earth' galleries house displays on dinosaurs, mammals – including a 27.5 m (90 ft) long blue whale – insects, rocks and fossils, and an earthquake simulation. Almost 2 million people visit the museum each year.

Lord NELSON

• Naval commander • 1758-1805; visc. 1801

Despite having a weak constitution, Horatio Nelson, Britain's most enduring maritime hero and the son of a Norfolk clergyman, joined the navy aged 12 and served in North America and the West and East Indies. As a commander in the wars against revolutionary France, Nelson survived the loss of his right eye in an attack on Corsica in 1794 and his right arm in an assault on Tenerife in 1797, by which time he was already a rear admiral.

In 1798, Nelson destroyed most of the French fleet at the Battle of the Nile, leaving Napoleon and his army stranded in Egypt. Returning in triumph to Naples, he began a love affair with Lady Emma HAMILTON, the wife of the British envoy, which was to continue until his death.

I SEE NO SHIPS

When Denmark joined battle against Britain in 1801, Nelson defeated its fleet at Copenhagen. It was there that he disobeyed an order to retreat by putting a telescope to his blind eye and claiming he could not read the signal flags.

After a year in London with Lady Hamilton, during which his daughter Horatia was born, Nelson was made commander of the Mediterranean fleet. In October 1805 he confronted the French and Spanish fleets off Cape Trafalgar. Nelson flew a signal from the masthead of his flagship, HMS VICTORY, that read: 'England expects that every man this day will do his duty'. This they did, and the victory might have been complete had not a French sniper put a bullet through Nelson's spine. His last words were not 'Kiss me, Hardy', but 'Thank God, I have done my duty'.

NEWCASTLE UPON TYNE

• NE England (p.496 C2)   • Pop. 189 150

Newcastle has a longer history than most British industrial cities. It stands where the Romans built a bridge and fort – Pons Aelius – near the end of Hadrian's Wall, and where the Normans erected a 'new castle' in 1080. From the 16th century, the city's coal exporting led to the saying 'carrying coals to Newcastle', meaning an unnecessary activity.

A 15th-century crown-shaped spire tops Newcastle's cathedral and overlooks the classical façades of Grey Street. This, and civic buildings such as the Central Station and Theatre Royal, were the fruits of the city's 19th-century shipbuilding and engineering boom. It was here that George STEPHENSON built his steam locomotive, *Rocket*, in 1829.

Six river bridges, including Robert Stephenson's High Level Bridge (1849) and the huge single arch of the Tyne Bridge (1928), are Newcastle transport

FULL HEAD OF STEAM The Black Country Museum at Dudley has a working replica of Thomas Newcomen's pumping engine of 1712. An original Newcomen engine is preserved at Dartmouth in Devon

arteries, as is the A1(M) motorway, overlooked at Gateshead by the *Angel of the North* – a gigantic 20 m (65 ft) high and 54 m (177 ft) wide sculpture.

Thomas NEWCOMEN

• Engineer   • 1663-1729

The steam engine built in 1712 by the blacksmith-turned-engineer Thomas Newcomen to pump water from the deep shafts of a West Midlands coal mine made possible the INDUSTRIAL REVOLUTION, for 50 years later James WATT used it as the basis for his new engines to power factories.

In 1698 the inventor Thomas SAVERY patented the first steam pump. Newcomen developed it into a more efficient machine. It was known as an atmospheric steam engine because it used air pressure at the top of the cylinder in which steam was condensed to create a vacuum and force a piston down to activate a pump.

Newcomen was born and worked in Dartmouth in Devon, where he made tools for local miners.

Harry 'Brusher' Mills, a New Forest snake catcher, is said to have caught and sold 30 000 snakes before he died in 1905. He seized them with a long pair of tongs

NEW FOREST

• Hampshire (p.495 F6)   • Area 150 sq miles

The New Forest is less wooded than it was when roamed by Saxon hunters 1000 years ago, but no less remote in places. William the Conqueror declared the forest a royal hunting ground in 1079, and made poaching a capital offence and the disturbance of deer punishable by blinding.

The Normans gave grazing rights and other privileges to the local people. These are still guarded by forest officials, called 'verderers', who have held a court in Lyndhurst since the 12th century.

When other royal forests were sold in the 16th century, the New Forest remained Crown land and became an important source of timber for the navy. Lord Nelson's first command, the *Agamemnon*, was one of many warships built from New Forest oak trees at Bucklers Hard on the Beaulieu river. Aside from woodland, the forest includes large areas of heath and grassland now grazed by some 1500 fallow deer and 3000 ponies.

Cardinal NEWMAN

• Theologian and poet   • 1801-90

'Lead, kindly light', one of the 19th century's best-loved hymns and read to Queen Victoria on her deathbed, was composed by a fever-struck John Henry Newman on an orange boat sailing from the Mediterranean in 1833. In the same year he helped to found the OXFORD MOVEMENT, dedicated to returning the CHURCH OF ENGLAND to its Catholic roots.

The movement's beliefs were defined in the *Tracts of the Times*, 90 pamphlets written between 1833 and 1841, many by Newman. In the final tract, Newman argued that the 'Thirty-nine Articles' – the Anglican standard of faith – could be read so as not to contradict Catholic doctrine. The ensuing controversy brought the tracts to an end. In 1845 Newman converted to Catholicism, and in 1879 was made a cardinal.

Newman also wrote poetry, which included 'The Dream of Gerontius', set to music by Edward Elgar in 1900.

HOLD THE FRONT PAGE

Newspapers evolved in the 18th century to satisfy the need for business, political and legal information. Two hundred years on, the British thirst for news, including sports and celebrity gossip, is slaked by 'quality' and 'tabloid' titles battling it out for a slice of the 26 million readership

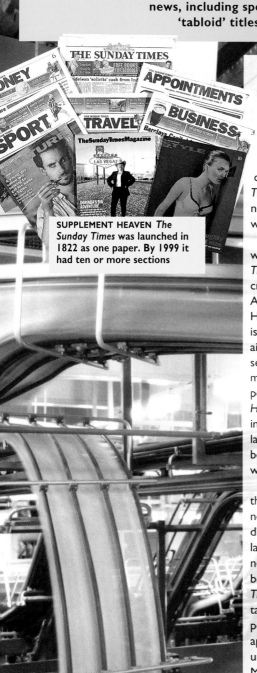

SUPPLEMENT HEAVEN *The Sunday Times* was launched in 1822 as one paper. By 1999 it had ten or more sections

I N THE 18th century, London's merchant community wanted up-to-date information on its markets, and the governing class required the latest political and legal news. *The Daily Universal Register*, first published by John Walter, a bankrupt coal merchant, in 1785 and renamed *The Times* in 1788, satisfied these needs, combining impartial information with editorial opinion.

By the mid 19th century the paper was outsold by cheaper rivals such as *The Daily Telegraph* in a single market created by quick rail delivery. On April 4, 1896, the editor Alfred Harmsworth, later Lord Northcliffe, issued the first edition of the *Daily Mail*, aimed at the office worker. It led to a series of lively, fiercely competitive mass market papers with differing political allegiances, notably the *Daily Herald*, pro-Labour, the *Daily Express*, imperialist, and the *Daily Mirror*, first launched as a women's paper before becoming the first to speak for the working masses.

After the Second World War these titles all struggled with newsprint shortages, anticompetitive distribution agreements and high labour costs. In 1969 an Australian newspaper publisher, Rupert Murdoch, bought the *News of the World* and then *The Sun*, which he relaunched as a tabloid, turning it into Britain's most popular title. With his ruthless approach to the printing unions and unashamedly commercial approach, Murdoch began to modernise the British newspaper industry, moving his titles, including *The Times* and *The Sunday Times*, acquired in 1981, from FLEET STREET to a non-unionised plant at Wapping, in London's East End.

In 1993 Murdoch cut the price of *The Times* from 45p to 30p, starting a price war that increased broadsheet readership, while tabloid sales remained steady. At the end of the 20th century the British still loved their newspapers.

NEWSPAPER TIMELINE

1791 First issue of *The Observer*, Britain's oldest Sunday paper

1800

1785 First issue of *The Daily Universal Register*

1821 First issue of *The Manchester Guardian*

1825

1855 *The Daily Telegraph* first published

1850

1888 *The Financial Times* printed on pink paper

1875

1890 The first tabloid paper – the *Daily Graphic*

1900

1903 Britain's first paper for women, the *Daily Mirror*, published

1925

1962 *The Sunday Times* publishes the first Sunday colour supplement

1950

1975

1986 *Today* is the first paper to use colour photography. *The Sunday Sport* and *Independent* are published

SECOND SPY INSIDE GCHQ

1995 A 10p edition of *The Sun* sells 4 898 118 copies – the most ever

2000

HOT OFF THE PRESS
A printing press at full speed runs off copies of *The Financial Times* in 1990. Modern computer technology replaced labour-intensive printing techniques in the 1980s

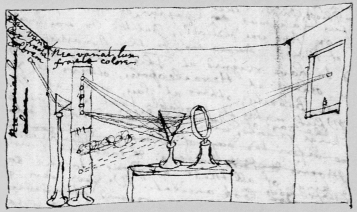

SECRETS OF LIGHT Sunlight is refracted through a prism in a diagram sketched in one of Isaac Newton's notebooks

Isaac NEWTON

- Scientist and mathematician
- 1642-1727; kt 1705

For a scientific colossus, Isaac Newton had an unpromising start. His father died three months before he was born – a baby so small 'they could put him in a quart pot' – and his mother left him to be raised by his grandmother.

At King's School in Grantham, Lincolnshire, Newton did not at first excel. But after a physical triumph over a school bully he turned into an intellectual whirlwind, drawing in his notebook Copernicus' Solar System, and diagrams of how to make a sundial and a model of a windmill.

PRECOCIOUS TALENT
After Newton gained a Cambridge degree in 1665, he retired to his mother's home of Woolsthorpe Manor, near Grantham, to escape the Plague. Here, in what he called his 'wondrous year', he developed the basis for differential calculus – used by physicists and mathematicians ever since – and his

theories on the properties of light and gravitation. Legend has it that the theory of gravity was inspired by the fall of an apple in his mother's orchard, although Newton never pretended that it hit him on the head.

GREAT ACCLAIM
At 27 Newton was elected to a professorship at Cambridge, and three years later to the Royal Society. His secretive and pugnacious nature led to disputes with other scientists, including Robert Hooke, who accused him of plagiarising his own gravitation theories.

Newton's greatest work was *The Mathematical Principles of Natural Philosophy*, better known as *Principia*, since it was written in Latin. It was published in 1687 and won him world fame. Newton had ushered in an age in which it seemed possible that every problem could be solved by intellectual endeavour.

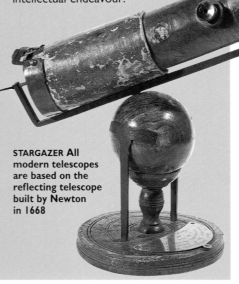

STARGAZER All modern telescopes are based on the reflecting telescope built by Newton in 1668

NEW TOWNS

Britain's 28 new towns, which have a population today of more than 2 million, were the world's most ambitious urban planning experiment. Born partly of idealism and partly of practicality, the new town concept was developed after the Second World War, when the need to rehouse many of Britain's city dwellers was seen as a chance to create better living and working conditions.

The idea, inspired by Ebenezer Howard (1850-1928), a visionary of town planning, whose first GARDEN CITY, Letchworth in Hertfordshire, was founded in 1903, was to build satellite towns around London and other cities. Each would be self-sufficient, divided into housing neighbourhoods with their own shops, schools, factories, services and open spaces for recreation.

The New Towns Acts of 1946, 1947 and 1950 established 15 towns, including Basildon, Stevenage, Hemel Hempstead and Harlow close to London, Cumbernauld near Glasgow and Cwmbran in Wales. A second wave of new towns in the 1960s included Washington, Runcorn, Telford and the largest, MILTON KEYNES.

Ben NICHOLSON

- Artist • 1894-1982

A pioneer of abstract art in Britain, Ben Nicholson was not converted to the new form until he spent 1933 in Paris, studying Cubists such as Georges Braque. Two years later he painted *White Relief*, the first of a series of geometric works using layered reliefs of right angles and circles. It was influenced by the Dutch abstract painter Piet Mondrian, whom Nicholson had met in Paris.

In 1939 Nicholson moved with his second wife, the sculptor Barbara HEPWORTH, to the Cornish fishing town of ST IVES, where they founded an artists' colony. Although some of his later work is more figurative, he declared 'the kind of painting I find exciting is not necessarily representational but both architectural and musical'.

The best collections of Nicholson's work can be seen in the TATE galleries in London and St Ives.

NEWMARKET

- Suffolk (p.495 H3) • Pop. 16 500

Newmarket has been dominated by HORSE RACING since James I helped to instigate the first meetings there in 1605. He also began at Newmarket the practice of breeding thoroughbred horses using imported Arab stallions and English mares.

Charles II introduced spring and autumn meetings at the Rowley Mile course, so called after his nickname,

'Old Rowley', itself derived from the name of his favourite horse. These are still staged and include the first two classics of the flat racing season – the 1000 and 2000 Guineas – and the Cambridgeshire and the Cesarewitch that launch the season. Races in July and August are held on the July Course. The Jockey Club, founded in 1750, is still based in Newmarket, which is home also to the National Horse-racing Museum.

NEWSPAPERS: *see page 317*

BRAVE NEW WORLD A family inspects the first batch of houses built at Crawley new town in Sussex. Work began at Crawley, the only new town south of London, in 1947

NIGHTINGALE

That certain night, the night we met,
There was magic abroad in the air.
There were angels dining at the Ritz
And a nightingale sang in Berkeley
Square.

Even if a nightingale were to sing in a London square on a warm May evening, the lovers of the 1940 song would find it hard to spot. It is an inconspicuous, shy brown bird, with a long tail and white breast, about the size of a blackbird.

The nightingale is a summer visitor from north Africa to south-east Britain. Its unforgettable song – a mixture of liquid and harsh notes in a wonderful variety of phrases, and remarkably loud for such a small bird – is the male territorial and mating call, and is best heard in the stillness of night. Few bird songs have inspired so many poets, including Andrew Marvell, John Keats and William Wordsworth.

Florence NIGHTINGALE

• Hospital reformer • 1820-1910; OM 1907

Florence Nightingale made her name as a hospital reformer in the CRIMEAN WAR. When she arrived with 38 nurses in Scutari, the British army's base in Turkey, in 1854 the main hospital lacked beds, blankets and medical supplies, and men lay naked on floors that were filthy with excrement. Almost half of them died.

MATRONLY FIGURE The elderly Florence Nightingale sits at the centre of a group of London nurses in 1886. Her handbook, *Notes on Nursing*, was published in 1860

Initially dismissed as a meddler, Nightingale single-handedly organised beds and clothing for the sick, arranged proper laundry facilities, and improved army food, helped by two French chefs. Within six months of her arrival the death rate had fallen to little more than 2 per cent. Her noctural ministrations to the wounded earned her the name of 'The Lady with the Lamp'.

Despite war fatigue and a near-fatal illness in 1857, Nightingale raised £50 000 by public subscription to open training colleges for nurses at St Thomas' and King's College hospitals in London. Her efforts transformed British hospitals and in 1908 she became only the second woman to be given the Freedom of the City of London.

NONCONFORMISTS

After the RESTORATION of the monarchy in 1660, Charles II and the re-established CHURCH OF ENGLAND attempted to suppress the more radical Protestant groups that had flourished under Oliver Cromwell's Commonwealth, such as the Baptists, Congregationalists, QUAKERS and Presbyterians. Threats of fines or imprisonment led many to emigrate to North America in search of religious freedom; those who stayed and who refused to conform to the prescribed form of Anglican worship came to be known as 'Nonconformists'.

The 1689 Toleration Act lifted some restrictions but Nonconformists were barred from university and civil, political or military office until the Emancipation Act of 1828. By 1851 a religious census showed that Nonconformist church attendance nearly equalled that of Anglican services.

THE FINAL CONQUEST

WILLIAM THE CONQUEROR SILVER PENNY

The most famous date in our history marks the last successful invasion of Britain. After 1066, the Normans displaced the aristocracy, reordered society from top to bottom, and built castles and cathedrals on a scale never seen before

THERE WAS no clear law of succession in 11th-century England and when EDWARD THE CONFESSOR died childless on January 5, 1066, he left behind him at least five competing claimants to the throne. The English nobility overwhelmingly supported HAROLD, the brother of Edward's queen, and he was quickly crowned on January 6.

But Duke William of Normandy (see WILLIAM I)

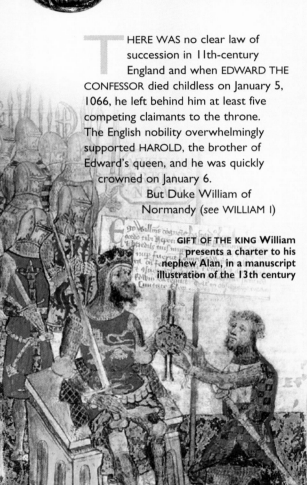

GIFT OF THE KING William presents a charter to his nephew Alan, in a manuscript illustration of the 13th century

claimed, with some justification, that both Edward and Harold had promised him the succession. With Church backing he assembled an army of around 7000 men.

BRITAIN'S LAST INVASION
Fate played into William's hands. As Harold prepared for the Normans, news came that his half-brother Tostig and the Norwegian Harald Hadrada had invaded northern England. Harold sped to Yorkshire, and on September 25 defeated them at Stamford Bridge.

Three days later William landed at Pevensey, Sussex. Harold came swiftly south and on October 14 confronted the invaders at Senlac Hill, near HASTINGS. The fight lasted all day, Anglo-Saxon footsoldiers defending the hill against repeated assaults from the mounted Normans. The issue was decided in the late afternoon, when Harold was killed and the bulk of his dispirited army lost the will to fight on.

CONSOLIDATING POWER
The battle marked only the beginning of the Norman Conquest. William circled London, via Dover, Canterbury and Winchester, before receiving the capital's

submission at Berkhamsted. After his coronation he set about removing Harold's supporters and building a network of royal castles to secure his power. But William's overlordship was not readily accepted. Following revolts in Kent and the south-west, a huge swathe from Dorset to the Tees rebelled.

William's reaction was swift, decisive and brutal. He systematically ravaged northern counties, leaving the region almost

MONKS AT WORK The Cistercians had 40 monasteries by 1154

CHURCH REORGANISATION
The Normans brought the English Church into line with Continental practice. They established a hierarchy of officials, built imposing new Romanesque cathedrals and encouraged monasticism.

ARISTOCRACY
William redistributed land to his followers and by 1086 only two Englishmen were left in the first rank of nobility. In 20 years Norman England had become a two-tier society.

THE CHANGED FACE OF ENGLAND
As well as reintroducing rabbits – and later ferrets to catch them – the Normans affected just about every aspect of life.

LANGUAGE
In 1066 most people in England spoke Old English, or Anglo-Saxon, but the Norman ruling class brought a new tongue, Anglo-Norman. It was never learned by ordinary folk, but survived as the language of the upper classes until the later Middle Ages and continued to be used for law reports until the 17th century. Its impact on modern English is largely seen in legal and administrative terms – and in quirks such as 'beef' (boeuf) from animals the common people called 'cows'.

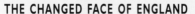

DOMESDAY BOOK *The great catalogue was commissioned by William in 1085 as a monumental survey of who owned what, in what capacity, and how much it was worth. It was considered as comprehensive as the Last Judgement, or Doomsday.*

DEATH OF A KING
The Bayeux tapestry records Harold's death ambiguously. Was it caused by an arrow in the eye (*left*) or a sword blow (*right*)?

SLEEPING GUARDS The rare bronze piece (*left*), was probably part of a 12th-century Holy Sepulchre scene

entirely depopulated, and throughout the land replaced English nobles with Norman.

THE DUAL INHERITANCE
William died in 1087, leaving Normandy to his oldest son, Robert, and England to his second son, William – known as Rufus for his red hair. Robert and his supporters coveted the English throne and WILLIAM II was frequently at war until in 1096 Robert mortgaged Normandy to him to finance a Crusade.

Robert was still abroad when William died under suspicious circumstances in 1100, which allowed the Conqueror's third son, the ruthless HENRY I, to take the crown. Henry defeated Robert in 1106, reuniting his patrimony. But Henry died in

WILLIAM RUFUS His 13-year reign was marked by broken promises and corruption

1135 and civil war broke out yet again, this time between his daughter, Matilda, and nephew, STEPHEN. Matilda abandoned England for Normandy in 1148, and on Stephen's death the entire Anglo-Norman inheritance passed to her son, HENRY II, the first Plantagenet king.

ON THE CELTIC FRINGE
By 1067 Norman barons were carving out private lordships in Wales, then a region of small independent kingdoms. A castle was built at Cardiff in the early 12th century but not until the late 13th century did Anglo-Norman influence make much impact outside the south and the borderland Marches.

Scotland was different, for in 1072 William I forced Malcolm III of Scotland to accept Norman overlordship. Thereafter, although the Normans did not occupy Scotland, their influence was far-reaching. Its most notable effect came during the reign of the Norman-educated David I (1124-53), who invited Anglo-Norman barons such as Bruce, Stewart and Balliol to modernise his realm.

BRITAIN'S NORMAN LEGACY

The Normans built to last, and hundreds of their constructions lie scattered across the length and breadth of Britain. This map shows a selection of some of the finest of each type.

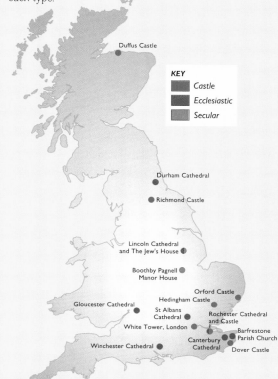

KEY
- Castle
- Ecclesiastic
- Secular

Duffus Castle
Durham Cathedral
Richmond Castle
Lincoln Cathedral and The Jew's House
Boothby Pagnell Manor House
Orford Castle
Hedingham Castle
Gloucester Cathedral
St Albans Cathedral
Rochester Cathedral and Castle
White Tower, London
Barfrestone Parish Church
Canterbury Cathedral
Winchester Cathedral
Dover Castle

ST MARY'S, IFFLEY

FEUDAL SYSTEM

The Conqueror's new ruling house and aristocracy were bound together by ties of mutual responsibility. The monarch granted land to tenants who swore to serve him and were granted protection in return. This pattern was repeated throughout society, the tenants granting land to their followers and so on down to humble serfs working for the lord of the local manor. Although such lord-master relationships existed before 1066, afterwards they were almost universal.

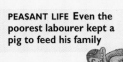

PEASANT LIFE Even the poorest labourer kept a pig to feed his family

ARCHITECTURE

Although there was 'Romanesque' architecture (harking back to ancient Rome) in pre-Conquest England, the Normans used it so prolifically that it is often known as 'Norman'. Its chief features are huge rubble-filled pillars, rounded arches and carved decoration, often using the chevron motif. Dozens of CASTLES were built, with massive square keeps, and vast, imposing CATHEDRALS such as Ely, Durham, St Albans and the rebuilt Canterbury.

CASTLE RISING, NORFOLK

DURHAM CATHEDRAL

NORMAN TRADEMARKS Rounded arches, carved chevron patterns and square towers are all characteristic features of Norman style

NORTHERN IRELAND

• **Area 5206 sq miles** • **Pop. 1.6 million**

Twenty-six counties of Ireland, now the Republic of Ireland, achieved independence from Britain in 1921. The remaining six counties in the north-east – Antrim, Armagh, Down, Fermanagh, Londonderry and Tyrone – stayed within the United Kingdom. Now subdivided into smaller administrative units, these six counties constitute the province of Northern Ireland. Together with three in the Republic, they make up the ancient province of ULSTER.

BEYOND THE TROUBLES

Long associated with sectarian violence (Protestants make up 51 per cent of the population and Catholics 38 per cent), Northern Ireland nevertheless attracts large numbers of tourists to sights such as the extraordinary hexagonal basalt columns of the GIANT'S CAUSEWAY and the volcanic cliffs of the north-east coast.

BELFAST is the capital and industrial centre of the province. In the 1600s it was settled by Protestants from England and Scotland. Fortunes were made in cloth and shipbuilding, the latter still an important activity. Derry, the second largest city, dates from 546 when St Columba founded a monastery there.

Politically, the IRISH QUESTION has dominated the late 20th century. The province's assembly at STORMONT was suspended in 1972 as violence escalated between unionists and nationalist groups calling for the reunification of Ireland. The 1990s saw a popular will for reconciliation, making possible the Good Friday peace agreement in 1998.

RUGGED OUTLOOK Northern Ireland's Mourne Mountains rise up from the coast in the south-east county of Down. The granite slopes are popular with walkers and climbers

NORTH SEA

Once called the 'German Ocean', the North Sea lies between Britain's eastern coast and mainland Europe. It covers 222 000 sq miles and reaches depths of 661 m (2170 ft).

The North Sea is a busy shipping lane, a rich fishing ground and a major source of fossil fuels. Gas was discovered under the sea in 1965 and oil in 1969. There are now more than 170 North Sea gas and oil fields pumping out at least 350 000 tons of fuel a day, making Britain the world's ninth largest producer. More than 30 000 people work in these offshore industries.

The sea's highest tidal range is 4-6 m (13-20 ft) near The WASH between Norfolk and Lincolnshire. High tides and storm force winds occasionally raise water levels to dangerous heights, causing flooding of British and Dutch coastal areas.

NORWICH

• **Norfolk (p.495 J2)**
• **Pop. 171 300**

During the medieval heyday of the East Anglian wool trade, Norwich was England's second city after London. Its riches and reputation attracted skilled immigrants from Europe between the 14th and 16th centuries. It is now the county town of Norfolk, situated on the Wensum River, 20 miles from the North Sea.

A large 12th-century castle – now a museum and art gallery – overlooks the city, including sections of the 14th-century city wall, the medieval cobbles of Elm Hill and more than 30 medieval churches. The art gallery is noted for works by the 19th-century Norwich

School of landscape artists, including John CROME (1768-1821).

Norwich Cathedral, which has a spectacular fan-vaulted roof, dates mainly from the 15th century. It was founded in 1096 and built of white stone imported from Normandy. Its spire, rising to 96 m (315 ft), is England's second tallest after Salisbury.

The University of East Anglia, founded in 1963, lies north-west of the city. Norwich City football club is known as the Canaries after the Norwich canary, a breed reared in the city.

NOTTINGHAM

• **E Midlands (p.495 F2)** • **Pop. 270 220**

An 11th-century castle overlooking the River Trent provided the nucleus around which the county town of Nottingham developed. Charles I raised his standard on the castle in 1642, marking the start of the English Civil War. The castle was demolished in 1651. Its replacement, a stately home known as 'The Castle', is home to the city's museum.

Nottingham's industrial growth in the 18th and 19th centuries was based on lace, hosiery, bicycles and tobacco. One of Nottingham's major employers today is the Boots Company, built up in the mid 19th century by Jesse Boot. He created a successful business by buying toiletries and herbal remedies in bulk and selling them at low prices. He began to manufacture pharmaceuticals in 1888 and by 1933, two years after his death, the 1000th 'Cash Chemist' was opened. As Lord Trent, Jesse Boot helped to establish University College, now the University of Nottingham.

Jesse Boot took over a small herbalist shop in Nottingham in 1877, which he developed into 'Boots Cash Chemists'. In 1999 Boots' profits were almost £561 million

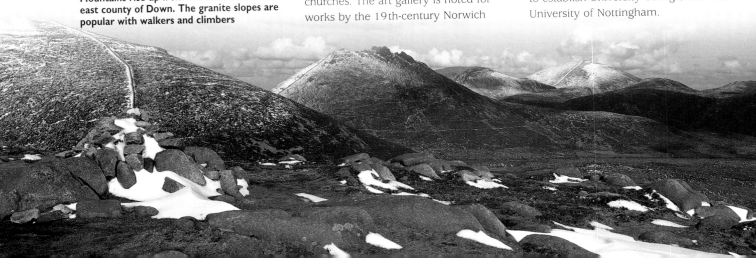

CARNIVAL TIME Every summer London throbs to the sound of steel bands as the **Notting Hill Carnival** winds through the capital's streets. The magnificent costumes and floats are based on the traditional Trinidadian carnival

The city's churches include the 15th-century church of St Mary's in the Lace Market, and the Gothic Revival Roman Catholic cathedral designed by A.W. Pugin (1840-2). On the banks of the Trent are the Trent Bridge cricket ground, and the football grounds of Nottingham Forest and Notts County, England's oldest club, founded in 1862. Nottingham's annual Goose Fair, which dates from the Middle Ages, is held in October.

NOTTING HILL CARNIVAL

• **W London (p.498 C3)**   • **August Bank Holiday**
The largest street festival in Europe has its origins in a street party held in 1964 for the children of Trinidadian immigrants who had settled in the area during the 1950s. Two years later, the party developed into a regular local event. Steel bands provided the music, and food and drink were donated by local traders. During the 1970s the carnival grew into a spectacular event.

Steel bands, costume parades, floats, processions, dancers, food stalls and sound systems transform Notting Hill into a dazzling spectacle attended by more than a million people over the two-day festival. A parade of children's floats still takes place on Sunday.

The carnival's popularity was originally boosted by many of London's indigenous street festivals having been closed down in the 18th and 19th centuries to prevent crime and disorder. Violence broke out at the Notting Hill Carnival in 1976 after tension escalated between black youths and police. Some 250 people were injured but, despite attempts to take the carnival off the streets, it has since flourished peacefully in its original form.

Ivor NOVELLO

• **Actor, composer and dramatist**   • **1893-1951**
Versatility must have been Ivor Novello Davies' motto. He began publishing songs in his teens, and 'Keep the Home Fires Burning', written when he was only 21, became the hit song of the First World War.

From his infancy in Wales, Novello lived and breathed music and the stage. His mother, a respected singer, sent him to Magdalen College School in Oxford as a chorister. In the 1920s, the handsome Novello became a matinée idol, starring in silent films produced by Michael Balcon and D.W. Griffith. In 1926 he appeared in Alfred Hitchcock's thriller *The Lodger*.

Using the stage name Ivor Novello, at 29 he set about making a mark as a stage actor. He part wrote, managed and acted in *The Rat* (1924), the first of several successful plays. Songs, films and plays were followed by musicals, and in 1935 Novello wrote the script and score and played the lead in *Glamorous Nights*, a glittering romantic operetta. He

followed it with *The Dancing Years* (1939), *Perchance to Dream* (1945) and *King's Rhapsody*, which ran on stage for almost a decade from 1949.

Lord NUFFIELD

• **Businessman and philanthropist**
• **1877-1963; bt 1929; bn 1934; visc. 1938**
William Richard Morris, 1st viscount Nuffield, was a pioneer of the British motor industry. He started his career as a bicycle mechanic in Oxford, and in 1912 began to build Morris Oxford cars in a shed at Cowley, just outside the city. The first car, launched in 1913, cost £175.

The Morris Oxford and the Morris Cowley (1915) were the foundation of the British mass-production car industry, and made motoring an everyday activity for millions. Morris Motors, formed in 1919, soon became Europe's largest car manufacturer. An amalgamation with the Austin Motor Company in 1952 produced the British Motor Corporation, of which Morris became chairman.

Morris was a leading philanthropist: he established Nuffield College at Oxford University in 1937, and the Nuffield Foundation, a charitable trust, in 1943, which he endowed with £10 million of shares in his company.

JUST MOTORING Lord Nuffield sits at the wheel of an early Morris Oxford, nicknamed 'Bullnose' for the shape of its front end

OAK

No tree is more closely associated with Britain than the majestic, long-lived English oak (*Quercus robur*) and its cousin, the sessile oak (*Quercus petraea*), more common in Scotland and Wales. Spreading craggy branches over the fields, surviving lightning strikes and dying off into distinctive 'stag head' branches at the top, oaks symbolise British doggedness and power. 'Heart of oak are our ships/Heart of oaks are our men,' wrote the Georgian actor David Garrick, and for centuries the British navy depended on oaks for the building of its ships, from Henry VIII's *Mary Rose* to Lord Nelson's *Victory*.

Most English villages have an oak at least 250 years old and many trees live more than 500 years. The Robin Hood

Oak in the heart of Sherwood Forest, Nottinghamshire, beneath which the gallant outlaw reputedly gathered his merry men 800 years ago, still stands. An oak at Eardisley, near Hereford, with a girth of 10 m (34 ft) is said to be more than 1000 years old. The oak is more likely than any other tree to survive future climate changes, thanks to its drought-defying deep roots.

OAST-HOUSE

Oast-houses – strictly known as 'oasts' – are among the most distinctive industrial buildings of rural Britain, especially in Kent and Sussex. They were built of brick to dry hops for making beer, and usually had a circular section with a conical roof where the hops were dried by hot air from a furnace. A wooden cowl on top turned with the wind to draw out the hot air. In a rectangular extension to one side, the dried hops cooled on a wooden floor and were then bagged for transport to the brewery.

Many such oast-houses were built in the mid 19th century. Some earlier buildings were square in section. Today, most hops are dried using oil burners, and some oast-houses have been converted into homes.

The Hop Farm Country Park in Beltring, Kent, has a large group of oast-houses, which forms a museum.

OFFA'S DYKE

• Welsh-English border (p.494 D3)

In the course of a long reign (757-96) King Offa of Mercia extended his rule from what is now Yorkshire in the north to the coast of East Anglia, and to Hampshire in the south. Recalcitrant Wales he decided not to conquer but to hold at bay by building an earthwork – Offa's Dyke – extending along most of its boundary from north to south.

The earthen barrier is the largest archaeological monument in Britain, reaching a height of 6 m (20 ft) and a width of 18 m (60 ft). There are gaps where the dyke had to cross a river and today only about 80 miles of the earthwork remain. After 1200 years the barrier diverges surprisingly little from the present Welsh-English border.

A waymarked LONG-DISTANCE ROUTE – the 182 mile long Offa's Dyke Path – follows the earthwork across wild and spectacular countryside. It also passes through the town of Knighton in Powys, where an interpretative centre gives information on the dyke.

OFFICIAL SECRETS ACT

The law intended to protect the nation by forbidding government employees from passing sensitive information to others is known as the Official Secrets Act. Passed by parliament in 1911 during an anti-German spy scare, its catchall section two made it an imprisonable offence to give or receive information relating to the function of government. In theory, that meant a civil servant could be jailed for describing the colour of his or her office carpet – as could the person to whom they spoke.

Controversy over the powers within the Act raged in the 1980s, when two civil servants – Sarah Tisdall and Clive Ponting – were prosecuted for leaks to the media. The Act became discredited in 1987, when the government used it to seek a ban on the publication of *Spycatcher*, the memoirs of Peter Wright, a former spy, even though the book was on sale outside Britain. As a result, it was replaced with the Official Secrets Act of 1989, which more closely defined the types of information that could be treated as official secrets.

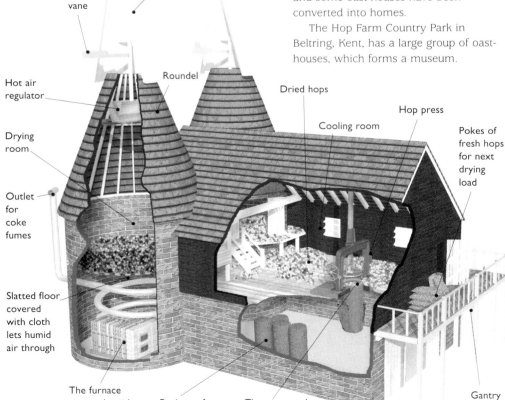

Wind vane

Cowl

Hot air regulator

Roundel

Drying room

Outlet for coke fumes

Slatted floor covered with cloth lets humid air through

The furnace creates humid air to dry hops

Pockets of pressed hops

The press packs hops into pocket

Dried hops

Cooling room

Hop press

Pokes of fresh hops for next drying load

Gantry

OLD BAILEY

- **Central London (p.499 E2)** • **Opened 1907**

Britain's Central Criminal Court, the Old Bailey, is built on the site of Newgate prison, whose medieval inmates were rounded up and brought before a temporary court held in hired premises. In 1539 the first Sessions House was built next to the prison. It stood beside London's medieval bailey (defensive wall), after which it is named.

There was a serious risk of catching typhus from infected prisoners and so, when the courthouse was rebuilt after the Great Fire, it was left open at one end. This was later boarded up, but with fatal consequences. More than 60 people were killed by typhus during the 'Black Assize' of 1750, including the lord mayor. After that, prisoners were washed down with vinegar before being brought to trial and judges armed themselves with posies of sweet-smelling flowers.

Newgate was demolished in 1902, and from the land rose an imposing new courthouse surmounted by a 6 m (20 ft) high bronze figure of Justice. The Old Bailey has seen many high-profile trials, including Dr Crippen (1910), J.R. Christie (1953) and Peter Sutcliffe (1981).

OLD KING COLE

The identity of Old King Cole, the 'merry old soul' of one of Britain's most popular nursery rhymes, has long been the subject of speculation. Originally he may have been the ancient British ruler Cunobelinus or Cymbeline, the founder of Colchester, who in medieval tradition became 'Coel'.

Later legend identified the jolly king with Thomas Cole, a wealthy Reading clothier murdered in Buckinghamshire and thrown into a stream; both the river Colne and the town of Colnbrook were said to be named after him.

Another hypothesis makes him 'Old Cole the Splendid', a warlike leader of southern Scotland in the 5th century AD. According to the novelist Walter Scott, 'Auld King Coul' was the father of the legendary giant Finn MacCool. Both theories might account for the song's popularity in Scotland; the poet Robert Burns made a transcript of one version, and said he had heard many more.

STAGE COUPLE Laurence Olivier cast himself as Antony and his wife Vivien Leigh as Cleopatra for the staging of Shakespeare's *Antony and Cleopatra* in 1951

Laurence OLIVIER

- **Actor and director**
- **1907-89; kt 1947; bn 1970; OM 1981**

Laurence, the son of a clergyman, won his first critical notice at the age of ten when the actress Ellen Terry praised his performance in a school play. He went on to become one of the finest classical actors of his generation – 'The greatest of them all,' according to the film star Spencer Tracy. A dominating presence and commanding diction marked his stage performances, especially in the great Shakespearean roles.

MATINEE IDOL

Olivier also made the transition from stage to screen, playing a smouldering Heathcliff to Merle Oberon's Cathy in the 1939 Hollywood version of *Wuthering Heights*, followed the next year by Alfred Hitchcock's *Rebecca*, before cutting a dash as Mr Darcy in *Pride and Prejudice* in 1940. He costarred as Lord Nelson with his new bride, Vivien Leigh, in *Lady Hamilton* in 1941. His screen versions of *Henry V* and *Hamlet*, in which he starred and directed, revolutionised the filming of Shakespeare. He returned to the stage to acclaim in John Osborne's *The Entertainer* in 1957.

Olivier was the first director of the NATIONAL THEATRE, and he was the first actor to be made a life peer. His last roles were mainly on television and in films.

OLYMPIC GOLD MEDALLISTS

Britain won 56 gold medals at the 1908 Olympic Games in London, but the phenomenal international growth of sport that followed stiffened the competition dramatically. Since 1980, British competitors have won gold medals for the following events:

1980

MOSCOW *(summer)*
Allan Wells *100 m*
Steve Ovett *800 m*
Sebastian Coe *1500 m*
Daley Thompson *Decathlon*
Duncan Goodhew *100 m breast stroke*
LAKE PLACID *(winter)*
Robin Cousins *Figure skating*

1984

LOS ANGELES *(summer)*
Sebastian Coe *1500 m*
Tessa Sanderson *Javelin*
Daley Thompson *Decathlon*
Richard Budgett, Martin Cross, Adrian Ellison, Andrew Holmes, Steve Redgrave *Rowing: coxed fours*
Malcolm Cooper *Shooting*
SARAJEVO *(winter)*
Jane Torvill, Christopher Dean *Ice dance*

1988

SEOUL *(summer)*
Adrian Moorhouse *100 m breast stroke*
Andrew Holmes, Steve Redgrave *Rowing: coxless pairs*
National team *Men's hockey*
Malcolm Cooper *Shooting*
Mike McIntyre, Bryn Vaile *Yachting*

1992

BARCELONA *(summer)*
Matthew Pinsent, Steve Redgrave *Rowing: coxless pairs*
Jonny Searle, Greg Searle, Garry Herbert *Rowing: coxed pairs*
Chris Boardman *Cycling*
Linford Christie *100 m*
Sally Gunnell *400 m hurdles*

1996

ATLANTA *(summer)*
Matthew Pinsent, Steve Redgrave *Rowing: coxless pairs*

SEBASTIAN COE

STEVE REDGRAVE AND MATTHEW PINSENT

OPEN UNIVERSITY

• Founded 1969
Britain's largest teaching institution enrolled more than 150 000 students in 1997 alone and awarded some 10 000 degrees. The idea of an open university that would enable mature students without formal academic qualifications to study to degree level was launched by Harold Wilson on becoming leader of the Labour party in 1963. The Open University (OU), based in Milton Keynes in Buckinghamshire, began its courses in 1971, since when it has awarded more than 200 000 first degrees.

The advantage of the Open University for mature students is that they can study in their spare time using distance-learning methods, without having to attend classes daily. Students use interactive course books, tapes, videos, radio and television programmes, computer software, the Internet, and home experiment kits in their studies. They discuss course work with locally based academic tutors and attend seminars and tutorial sessions.

The OU offers vocational courses leading to certificates, diplomas, BA and BSc degrees in humanities, science and social science subjects, higher degree courses, and research degrees.

> The Open University Business School (OUBS), founded in 1983, is Europe's largest. It has more than 25 000 students in the UK and 19 other countries

House of ORANGE

In the Middle Ages, Orange was a small, independent principality to the north of Avignon in southern France. The title Prince of Orange was inherited in the 16th century by William the Silent, leader of the Dutch in their fight for independence from Spain. William, Prince of Orange and stadholder, or chief magistrate, of the Netherlands, whose landing in England in 1688 led to the GLORIOUS REVOLUTION to depose JAMES II, was his great-grandson. With his wife, Mary, he became joint monarch of England (see WILLIAM AND MARY).

When William defeated James in his attempt to regain the English crown at the Battle of the BOYNE in 1690, the name Orange became synonymous with Protestant supremacy, and 'King Billy' a hero to the Protestant settlers of the northern counties of Ireland. The ORANGEMEN, their 'lodges' and marches are still part of life in NORTHERN IRELAND.

ORANGEMEN and the ORANGE ORDER

At the end of the 18th century the prime minister William Pitt's plans for Catholic emancipation following a union of Britain and Ireland alarmed ULSTER Protestants. Having benefited from a code of laws biased against Catholics, they saw a threat to their privileges and jobs. Sectarian fights broke out.

In 1795 a battle in Armagh was won by Protestants, who marked the event by forming an 'Orange Society' (later the Orange Order), named after Prince William of ORANGE, who became William III in 1689 after the Catholic JAMES II was ousted. The new

organisation infiltrated the British army, helped to suppress the 1798 nationalist rising, and following the union of Ireland with Britain in 1801 set itself up to maintain Protestant supremacy.

In the 20th century the Orange Order retained a firm grip on the defiantly Protestant government of the new United Kingdom province of NORTHERN IRELAND, and organised the paramilitary Ulster Volunteer Force. It exerts a strong influence within the Ulster Unionist Party, at the heart of unionism.

ORDNANCE SURVEY: *see opposite page*

ORKNEY ISLANDS

• N Scotland (p.497 D1)   • Pop. 15 130
Lying 6 miles north of mainland Scotland, the Orkneys comprise about 90 islands and islets, totalling 377 sq miles. They have been occupied for 6000 years and 18 of them are still inhabited. Remains of a Stone Age settlement have been found at SKARA BRAE on Mainland island, and standing stones can be seen at Stenness and Brogar.

The islands were settled by Vikings in the 9th century, and they belonged to Norway for 300 years before they were acquired by Scotland in 1472. Today, much of the population is still of Scandinavian descent.

During the two world wars the islands were used as a base by the Royal Navy. At the end of the First World War the trapped German fleet scuttled itself in SCAPA FLOW, between the islands of Mainland, Hoy and South Ronaldsay, rather than fall into British hands.

Kirkwall, capital of the Orkneys, on Mainland, has a 12th-century cathedral, St Magnus. Cattle farming, fishing and the North Sea oil industry are the main sources of the islands' revenue.

Joe ORTON

• Playwright   • 1933-67
Censors became apoplectic when they read Joe Orton's scripts, but his audiences collapsed in fits of laughter. Moral corruption, sexual repression and domestic violence are his themes, presented in a blackly comic style.

His subversiveness still has the power to shock: he sees selfishness and

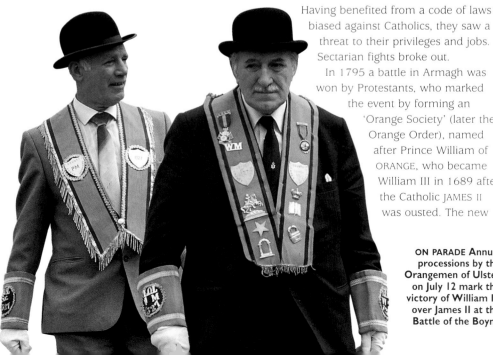

ON PARADE Annual processions by the Orangemen of Ulster on July 12 mark the victory of William III over James II at the Battle of the Boyne

SHOOTING STAR In 1964, when this picture of Joe Orton was taken, he lived on £3 10s a week National Assistance. Three years later, when he died, his plays were the toast of the town

stupidity as the predominant human characteristics, and explores them in vividly surrealistic language.

Orton's plays include *Entertaining Mr Sloane* (1964), *Loot* (1966) and *What The Butler Saw* (performed posthumously in 1969). A homosexual who courted danger, Orton was beaten to death at the height of his fame by his lover Kenneth Halliwell, who then killed himself.

George ORWELL

• Pseudonym of Eric Blair • Writer • 1903-50

Probably one of the most widely read English authors of the 20th century, George Orwell wrote in a style plainer than that of most newspapers. Despite his Eton education and service in the

Indian Imperial Police in Burma in the 1920s, he was a staunch socialist: when his early writing, mainly fiction, was poorly received, he took to living as a

tramp, chronicling this period in *Down and Out in Paris and London* (1933). In 1936 he was commissioned to report the effects of the Depression on the poor; the result, *The Road to Wigan Pier* (1937), depicted the wretchedness of the coal-mining towns.

Acting on his principles, Orwell fought for the Republicans in the Spanish Civil War. He was shot, and later risked arrest by trying to free a political prisoner. His experiences appear in *Homage to Catalonia* (1938).

Orwell's novels include the literary and financial struggles of Gordon Comstock in *Keep the Aspidistra Flying* (1936) and his two warnings against totalitarianism, *Animal Farm* (1945) and *Nineteen Eighty-four* (1949). He was also a prolific reporter and critic; he wrote penetrating essays on Charles Dickens and P.G. Wodehouse, as well as on crime stories and cartoons.

ORDNANCE SURVEY

Today we think of Ordnance Survey (OS) as a supplier of leisure maps, with their familiar symbols indicating features such as windmills, bridges, railway cuttings and embankments. But the word 'ordnance' means military supply and equipment, and gives a clue to the origins of the name.

Britain's national mapping agency was established in 1791, when, following the French Revolution, and fearing an invasion from Europe, the government ordered its Board of Ordnance to map the south coast of England so that defences could be planned.

For its first 50 years Ordnance Survey worked from the Tower of London. Following a fire in 1841 it moved to Southampton, where it is still based. The OS retains its military title, but has been a civilian government department since 1983, employing around 1850 people.

RELIABLE PATHFINDER

Ordnance Survey produces the most detailed maps of Britain. Its National Topographic Database (NTD) is now the definitive map of Britain, recording on computer more than 200 million features of the British landscape – everything from

a telephone kiosk or private garage to the outline of forests, copses, lakes and stately homes. Updated daily using the latest technology, NTD is the prime source for the creation of a range of products at different scales, including traditional paper maps and atlases for ramblers and motorists.

Alongside the latest updated information, Ordnance Survey also maintains an extensive archive of almost 1 million maps dating from its creation two centuries ago, including its first map (of Kent), published in 1801 and dedicated to the soldier Lord Cornwallis.

ORDNANCE SURVEY "ONE-INCH" MAP

Hertford & St. Albans
Mounted on Linen

FIELDWORK Surveying has changed markedly since the 1930s. Using Global Positioning Satellite systems, Ordnance Survey staff rarely get their feet wet today

ROYAL RETREAT Osborne House was Queen Victoria's favourite home, where she enjoyed family picnics (*left*). She made the house her main base in the 40 years following Albert's death

OSBORNE HOUSE

- **East Cowes, Isle of Wight (p.495 F6)**
- **Built 1845-51** • **EH**

Prince ALBERT, consort of Queen Victoria, designed Osborne House as a seaside retreat where the royal family could enjoy a private life. The style of the house was influenced by villas Albert had seen on the Bay of Naples, which reminded him of the Solent.

Osborne was built by Thomas Cubitt, with two tall towers resembling Italian bell towers flanking the long three-storey façade, one bearing a flag and the other a clock. Inside, a Grand Corridor lined with sculptures links the two main wings, and more grandeur abounds in the state rooms and banqueting hall. The family character of the house is evident in the queen's sitting room, with its brass-edged writing tables where Victoria worked at state papers, and the bedroom in which she died in 1901.

The grounds contain terraced gardens, a miniature Swiss chalet built in the 1850s for the royal couple's nine children, and the elaborate bathing machine from which the queen had her first experience of sea bathing.

River OUSE

- **E Midlands and East Anglia (p.495 H2)**

Of the several English rivers named 'Ouse', from the Sanskrit word for 'water', the 160 mile Great Ouse is the longest. From its source in Northamptonshire, it flows east through Bedford, passes Godmanchester and enters Fenland. Two parallel channels, 20 miles long, were cut by order of the earl of Bedford in the 17th century between Earith and Downham Market to improve drainage and contain winter floods, releasing land for corn-growing. The river passes Ely and at Brandon Creek fuses with the Little Ouse, entering The Wash below King's Lynn.

Wilfred OWEN

- **Poet** • **1893-1918**

What passing-bells for those who die as cattle?
Only the monstrous anger of the guns.
Only the stuttering rifles' rapid rattle
Can patter out their hasty orisons.

With its startling combination of almost sensual language and grimly realistic subject matter, Wilfred Owen's 'Anthem for Doomed Youth' brought home to a wide reading public the horror and pitilessness of modern warfare.

Owen's early work was dreamily romantic, recalling the poetry of John KEATS, but the experience of the First World War transformed his style. The poems that followed his return to the Western Front just before his death have shaped our view of the war: some were chosen by Benjamin BRITTEN for the text of his choral work *War Requiem* in 1962.

OWL

The quizzical, open-faced gaze; the silent, wraith-like dusk flight; the nocturnal hooting or shrieking; all add to the mystique of the 'wise old owl'. In fact, owls are no more intelligent than other birds of prey. They are efficient nocturnal hunters, thanks to their large eyes and binocular vision (enabling them to see in dim light and to judge distances accurately), their soft wing feathers (which allow silent flight), their powerful talons and sharp, hooked bill.

Owls kill large numbers of mice, rats and other vermin, and are protected. The barn and tawny owls are the best-known species; both are widespread but tawnies are more common in southern and eastern counties of England. There are four other British owls: the day-hunting little owl; the long-eared and short-eared owls, with tufts of feathers that look like ears, both of which are more common in the north of Britain; and the larger, rare white snowy owl, up to 60 cm (2 ft) tall, a winter visitor to north Scotland.

OXFORD: *see opposite page*

OXFORD ENGLISH DICTIONARY

The *Oxford English Dictionary* is a monument to the creativity of English speakers over 800 years and the energy of a self-educated tailor's son from Scotland, James Murray (1839-1915).

The first edition, completed in 1928 after his death, runs to some 16 000 pages and contains 240 165 main words, around 400 000 entries, and 1.5 million quotations. It covers English vocabulary since 1150, including variant spellings, dialect usage and details of each word's origins. The second edition in 1988 has more than 500 000 entries.

Murray, the driving force behind this enterprise, worked as a teacher and bank clerk. His spare time was devoted to study and to the Philological Society in

STREET THEATRE The 'Queen of Time' is returned to the façade of the Selfridges store on Oxford Street in 1954. It had been removed in 1953 to make way for decorations to mark the coronation of Elizabeth II

London. Preparatory work on a dictionary on historical principles was started in 1858. In 1879 the project was taken over by the Clarendon Press in Oxford and Murray was appointed editor. He organised thousands of amateur helpers, laid down the principles and methods, and edited more than half the final work. He was knighted in 1908.

OXFORD MOVEMENT

The Oxford Movement was initiated in 1833 by a group of Fellows of Oriel College, Oxford – John Keble, Edward Pusey, John Henry NEWMAN and Richard Hurrell Froude. Its aim was to reanimate the CHURCH OF ENGLAND with the faith and fervour of the Church fathers who had dominated early Christianity. In effect they created a powerful Anglo-Catholic party within the Church.

Newman brought the movement's views to the public's attention with a series of 'Tracts' about the historic basis of Church doctrine. In 1841 his argument in 'Tract 90' that the Thirty Nine Articles expressing Anglican doctrine were Catholic in spirit caused such an outcry that many members (Tractarians), including Newman, converted to Rome.

OXFORD STREET

• Central London (p.499 A5/B5)

When the 18th-century traveller Thomas Pennant described Oxford Street as 'the lurking place of cutthroats,' it was two centuries too early to be referring to the successful haggling tactics of the illegal perfume and souvenir street traders that are now features of Europe's busiest shopping street.

Following a Roman road west, the old road to Oxford got its name more by coincidence than logic when Edward Harley, 2nd earl of Oxford, bought the neighbouring land in 1731. Today,

Oxford Street attracts 200 million bargain hunters a year from all over the world to more than 300 shops between Marble Arch and Tottenham Court Road.

Development to alter what was once a residential area began in 1739 with the building of theatres and entertainment halls. The 20th century marked the arrival of the department stores. Gordon Selfridge, a Wisconsin retail merchant, bought a site and built Selfridges, which opened in 1909. This palatial store, the largest in London after Harrods, leads the Oxford Street shops in the crowd-drawing tradition of dressing up their windows for Christmas.

OXFORD

• Oxfordshire (p.495 F4) • Pop. 118 800

Cloistered colleges, magnificent honey-coloured stone buildings, and punts drifting lazily on the River Cherwell are all part of the character of this university town. Oxford was first settled by Saxons at a ford in the River Thames, 50 miles north-west of London. Its university is the oldest in England, dating back to at

least the 12th century, and has one of the world's finest libraries, the Bodleian. The university's chief area of learning has long been the humanities, although it also excels in the sciences. There are 36 colleges in and around the town.

Every narrow street reveals some new architectural treasure, including Christ Church, founded in 1546, the chapel of which serves as the city's cathedral, and Christopher Wren's Sheldonian Theatre. The ASHMOLEAN

MUSEUM, founded in 1683, is noted for its collection of antiquities. Oxford also has one of the earliest botanic gardens, laid out by the earl of Danby in 1621.

Car manufacturing, printing and publishing are among the city's largest employers. The county of Oxfordshire is mainly agricultural with industries concentrated around Oxford itself, Banbury and Didcot.

ROOFTOP VIEW The Oxford skyline inspired Matthew Arnold's lines: 'That sweet city with her dreaming spires'

PADDINGTON STATION

• **Central London (p.499 A2)** • **Built 1854**
'An enormous conservatory in a railway cutting' was Isambard Kingdom BRUNEL's vision for the London terminus of his Great Western Railway. What he designed was far grander: a cathedral to steam, enclosed by a glazed, triple-arched roof, decorated by the architect Digby Wyatt. Paddington was also the starting point in 1863 for the world's first underground railway, the Metropolitan, which ran to Farringdon Street.

The station is known worldwide for a fictional piece of left luggage. *A Bear Called Paddington* (1958) was the first of almost 40 children's stories written by Michael Bond about the hapless Peruvian bear in sou'wester and duffle coat.

Thomas PAINE

• **Political theorist and writer** • **1737-1809**
Dangerous eccentric or reformer ahead of his time? Thomas Paine polarised opinion with his radical ideas. He left for America in 1774, a year before the American War of Independence, and published *Common Sense*, a pamphlet advocating autonomy from Britain.

Paine returned to England in 1787 and wrote his best-known work, *The Rights of Man* (1791-2), a defence of the French Revolution, democracy and republicanism in which he supported graded income tax and free education. Its ideas horrified Georgian England, and Paine was charged with treason. He fled to France, where he composed much of *The Age of Reason* (1795), a bitter attack on conventional Christianity that finally lost him any friends he had left.

PAISLEY

• **Renfrewshire (p.497 C4)** • **Pop. 75 530**
Silk and cotton manufacture brought prosperity to Paisley during the late 18th century. In 1805, mills began weaving copies of shawls brought back from India by soldiers, with a pattern mimicking the shape of Kashmiri almonds. Thriving on this trade, Paisley was in the mid 1800s Scotland's third largest town, and the local museum and art gallery has many examples of the fabrics produced.

Paisley has now been largely engulfed by the sprawl of Glasgow. During the 20th century its textile industry declined, although it is still one of the world's main producers of cotton thread.

Ian PAISLEY

• **Protestant minister and politician** • **b.1926**
The strident oratory of this towering clergyman, delivered in his rasping Armagh accent, has resounded through Northern Irish politics since the 1950s.

Ian Paisley is revered by his supporters as the hardline leader of the Democratic Unionist Party and loathed by opponents for his intransigence. His political rival John Hume once told him: 'If the word "no" were taken out of the English language, you'd be speechless.'

When not on the political podium, Paisley, ordained in 1946 into the Free Presbyterian Church of Ulster, which he founded, delivers fire-breathing sermons in the south Belfast Martyrs' Memorial church. His militant campaigning has twice landed him in prison but as MP for North Antrim he is known for serving his constituents well, whatever their religion.

ITALIAN SPIRIT The Diocletian window (*top*), Venetian window (*middle*) and triangular pediment over the door of Peckover House in Cambridgeshire are features of Palladian style

PALLADIAN STYLE

The Palladian architectural style was inspired by the 16th-century Italian architect Andrea Palladio. He drew on the formal principles of classical building, imitating the style of ancient Rome.

Inigo JONES brought Palladio's ideas to Britain after a trip to Italy in 1614, with designs such as the Banqueting Hall on London's Whitehall marking a dramatic break with the JACOBEAN STYLE of the time. The crisp simplicity of Ionic and Corinthian columns made his the first truly classical buildings in Britain.

PAISLEY PATTERN Although weaving is no longer an important local industry, the Scottish town of Paisley still gives its name to the distinctive fabric pattern that was mass-produced there

However, Palladianism took hold widely only during the 1720s, under architects such as Colen Campbell and Lord BURLINGTON. Theirs was a pared-down version of Palladio's vision. Both Campbell's and Burlington's imitations of Palladio's Villa Rotonda, at Mereworth and CHISWICK HOUSE respectively, have a restrained elegance. In Burlington's building, lines are chiselled in stone as clearly as ink on paper, showing a puritanical element in the English style.

Samuel PALMER

• Painter • 1805-81

A meeting with William BLAKE in 1824 filled Samuel Palmer with visionary zeal and he settled in the Kentish village of Shoreham to paint views of an England transported to heaven. He described Blake's engravings as 'visions of little dells and nooks, corners of Paradise', but his own watercolours of Shoreham and the Darenth valley were equally sublime.

In works such as *The Harvest Moon* (1830-1) trees explode into blossom, sheep wander like clouds on impossibly steep hills and a huge moon gleams. It was a vision too brilliant to last and by 1833 Palmer's work was becoming repetitively sentimental. Since a revival of interest during the 1920s he has come to be regarded as one of the truest ROMANTICS. Many of his early pieces are in the Ashmolean Museum in Oxford.

Lord PALMERSTON

• Prime minister 1855-8, 1859-65
• 1784-1865; 3rd visc. 1802

'Firebrand Palmerston', born Henry John Temple, dominated mid 19th-century politics. As a Tory MP he served as junior Lord of the Admiralty and secretary of war before defecting to the Whigs in 1828. As foreign secretary, he astounded Britons and foreigners alike with his assertiveness and readiness to interfere in other nations' affairs.

As prime minister he steered Britain through many diplomatic crises. What Palmerston wanted above all was to promote the interests of Britain, not any particular set of political ideals.

Palmerston's love of parties and a succession of romantic entanglements earned him the nickname 'Cupid'.

PANTOMIME

The popular Yuletide entertainment of pantomime has its roots in the chaotic Roman feast of Saturnalia, when men and women exchanged clothes, and slaves and masters swapped roles. Until the 1880s, pantomime was elaborate mime, with harlequins and fools borrowed from the Italian commedia dell'arte theatre.

The Victorians then made pantomime their own, developing it into a uniquely British entertainment. For a few weeks around Christmas, pantos turned the song, dance, topical gags and acrobatics of music halls into a fairytale enchantment for the family.

The formula is predictable. The hero, or principal boy, is played by a woman; a dame, grotesque in wig and bloomers or the height of camp glamour, is played by a man; and two hapless fools struggle

HANKY PANKY Some pantomimes, such as this one from 1901, are no longer known. Others have lasted a century or more

for coordination in the costume of a horse or cow. In strict Victorian England when women's legs were never seen, the dress of the principal boy was considered quite titillating.

Characters such as the slapstick Widow Twankey in *Aladdin* and Buttons in *Cinderella* have now become perennial favourites. Other popular pantomimes include *Dick Whittington*, *Babes in the Wood* and *Puss in Boots*.

SONG AND DANCE The pantomime of *Jack and the Beanstalk* is based on the folk tale about a plucky boy who outwits a fearsome giant, but there is still a part for a comic stage cow

PANKHURST FAMILY

• Suffragettes • Emmeline 1858-1928
• Christabel 1880-1958 • Sylvia 1882-1960
• Adela 1885-1961

'Deeds, not words' was Emmeline Pankhurst's motto for the Women's Social and Political Union, which she and her daughter Christabel founded in 1903, to fight for electoral votes – or suffrage – for women.

Newspapers tried to belittle them by calling them SUFFRAGETTES, but Emmeline had a flair for creating 'news'. She and her followers set out on a campaign of law-breaking. Dramatic acts, such as invading the House of Commons and chaining themselves to the railings in Downing Street, usually led to violent clashes with the police followed by arrest and publicity. Emmeline and Christabel both served time in prison, gaining further attention by going on hunger strike.

Campaigning stopped with the First World War, Emmeline and Christabel supporting the conflict, Sylvia and Adela opposing it. Women over 30 were given the right to vote in 1918 in recognition of the part they played in the war. Only in 1928 was the franchise extended to give women the same rights as men.

PARACHUTE REGIMENT

**'UTRINQUE PARATUS'
READY FOR ANYTHING**

The infantrymen of the 1st British Airborne Division, Britain's premier airborne formation, had their finest hour in a losing cause during the Second World War. Some 10 000 soldiers were dropped behind enemy lines at Arnhem, in the Netherlands, in September 1944, and although they were cut off they managed valiantly to hold their positions, unaided, for nine days instead of the two that had been planned.

The division was established by the prime minister, Winston Churchill, in 1940. The regiment now has 4000 infantrymen who still wear the red berets that led their German foes to nickname them the 'Red Devils'.

PARISH

England's parishes, the areas served by local churches, have been central to the organisation of local communities for more than a thousand years. Medieval parishioners paid tithes to the church to maintain the buildings and support the running of the parish. Before the advent of social security the parish, through its vicar and church wardens, was a source of relief to the poor. Since 1538 details of all baptisms, weddings and burials in the parish church have been kept in parish records.

The practice of beating the bounds, in which children were once led around the parish limits and beaten at landmarks to encourage them to remember the boundaries, survives as a ceremony in some areas (without actual beatings).

Parishes gained an administrative role distinct from the church with elected councils set up in 1894 to govern local or 'parochial' issues such as lighting and parking. Some 10 000 parishes now cover all of England and Wales.

Nick PARK

• Animator   • b.1959; CBE 1996

Two endearing Plasticine characters, Wallace and Gromit – one man and his dog inhabiting a timeless England – have won the animator Nick Park wide acclaim. Wallace, in his jumper and slippers, is an unlikely hero. In the films *A Grand Day Out* (1989), *The Wrong Trousers* (1993) and *A Close Shave* (1995) he and Gromit fly to the Moon in search of cheese and outwit villains, but are always home in time for a cup of tea.

Park graduated from the National Film and Television School in 1983 and won an Oscar in 1991 with a 5 minute film, *Creature Comforts*, about zoo animals, using the synchronised voices of real people. Park shoots just 3 or 4 seconds of film a day but his efforts have been rewarded with many accolades, including two further Oscars.

Charles PARNELL

• Politician   • 1846-91

If Charles Parnell had lived a longer life and a chaste one, the history of modern Ireland might not have been written in so much blood. The Irish nationalist

PRECISION IN PLASTICINE The minute attention to detail Nick Park pays to his miniature sets and models, even down to newspaper headlines, makes his films painstaking to produce but a delight to watch

leader was elected to parliament in 1875, and in a career spanning only 15 years brought the issue of Irish self-government through home rule to the forefront of British politics.

Parnell was president of the Land League, whose methods of resisting eviction of tenant farmers included ostracising landlords until they relented – a practice that came to be named after one such landlord, Captain Boycott.

Parnell's support helped William GLADSTONE, who supported Irish home rule, to become prime minister, but in 1890 a colleague sued his wife, Kitty O'Shea, for divorce, on the grounds that she was Parnell's mistress. The scandal caused Parnell to be thrown out of office.

PASSPORT

Originally passports were little more than letters bearing the sovereign's signature to ensure safe conduct for subjects travelling abroad on royal business, and for foreigners entering the

British Isles. One of the earliest to survive was issued on June 18, 1641, and signed by Charles I. Records exist of each British passport issued from 1794, but not until 1858 did states agree to issue passports only to their own nationals.

Passports became compulsory for international travel when the First World War broke out, the passport photograph was introduced in 1915, and in 1920 a League of Nations conference established the booklet format. Despite national pride in the old blue United Kingdom passports, since 1988 they have been smaller and burgundy in colour, in line with the rest of the European Union. In Britain, passports are issued by the United Kingdom Passport Agency, part of the Home Office.

LOCAL ROYALTY Pearly kings and queens, resplendent in their buttoned finery, are found only in London. Their sons and daughters – pearly princes and princesses – inherit their titles

Joseph PAXTON

• Gardener and architect • 1801-65; kt 1851

Few have benefited more from a lucky break than Joseph Paxton. He was on the point of emigrating to America in 1826 when the duke of Devonshire asked him to manage his gardens at CHATSWORTH HOUSE in Derbyshire. Paxton leapt at the opportunity, for the duke was a keen and wealthy horticulturist.

The work at Chatsworth culminated in the construction of a huge glasshouse between 1836 and 1840, on which Paxton modelled his proposal for the 1851 GREAT EXHIBITION. His iron and glass conservatory, 563 m (1850 ft) long, 140 m (460 ft) wide and 33 m (108 ft) high, was chosen above 232 other designs and the 'Crystal Palace' was so successful that Paxton was knighted.

PEAK DISTRICT

• Derbyshire (p.496 B5) • Area 555 sq miles

There are no peaks in the Peak District. The upland region of limestone dales and peat moors at the southern end of the PENNINES takes its name from the Pecsaete tribe who lived there in prehistoric times, and from the Old English 'peac', a knoll or hill. The highest point is Kinder Scout plateau, at 636 m (2088 ft), dotted with gritstone tors.

The area was designated as the first NATIONAL PARK in 1951. The Peaks are popular with hikers, potholers who explore the underground caves in the

limestone hills, and climbers. Half of England's population lives within easy reach of the Peaks and 22 million people visit each year. The local tradition of WELL DRESSING is still a popular annual event, with the most spectacular displays in the towns of Buxton and Tissington.

PEARLY KINGS AND QUEENS

According to folklore, in around 1880 a boat spilled its cargo of Japanese pearl buttons when it foundered in the Thames. Henry Croft, a north London roadsweeper decorated his suit, hat and stick with his share of the salvage, making himself the first of the so-called 'Pearly Kings'.

Soon, every London district had its own pearly royalty – usually leading costermongers (fruit and vegetable street traders) who protected the interests of others and helped to raise money for the needy. When Croft died in 1930, some 400 'pearlies' followed his coffin to St Pancras Cemetery.

There are now about 100 pearly kings and queens – they have become a glittering symbol of London. Pearlies decorate their own suits using thousands of buttons to create elaborate flower motifs, horseshoes or other symbols of good luck, and a borough crest or

landmark. The costermongers' HARVEST FESTIVAL at St Martin-in-the-Fields church, off Trafalgar Square, attracts dozens of pearlies in their full regalia.

Peter PEARS

• Operatic tenor • 1910-86; CBE 1957; kt 1978

From their first meeting in 1936, Peter Pears became the constant companion of the composer Benjamin BRITTEN, who went on to compose many of his greatest works for Pears's distinctive, high, vibrant tenor voice. Pears took the leading role in operas by Britten, including Peter Grimes (1945) and Death in Venice (1973).

Joint recitals by Britten and Pears were a feature of the international concert circuit. Pears also collaborated with Britten in establishing, in 1948, the international music festival at ALDEBURGH, where they are buried, side by side, in the parish churchyard.

PEASANTS' REVOLT

• June 1381

The rising of the English peasantry in 1381 followed the imposition of a POLL TAX of 1 shilling per adult, the third time in four years that a tax was levied to fund the Hundred Years' War. This was the final straw for people already penalised by wages fixed for many years and the ancient manorial law of serfdom, which prevented peasants from seeking work elsewhere.

Peasants from Essex and Kent, led by Wat TYLER and John Ball, marched on London. Most dispersed after the 14-year-old RICHARD II agreed to reforms such as fair rents and the abolition of serfdom. Some rebels reached the Tower of London, where they attacked and killed the archbishop of Canterbury, the treasurer and other officials; Wat Tyler was beheaded following a fight with the mayor of London. Richard's concessions were swiftly revoked and the tax was levied.

Robert PEEL

- **Prime minister 1834-5, 1841-6**
- **1788-1850; 2nd bt 1830**

Every 19th-century criminal knew who Robert Peel was. As Tory home secretary, he had created London's Metropolitan POLICE force in 1829, who became popularly known as 'Peelers'.

Peel was a political pragmatist, first resigning in protest against Catholic Emancipation then returning to office to implement it. After the Tories failed to block the Reform Act of 1832 extending the right to vote, Peel reformed the party into a new CONSERVATIVE PARTY that accepted necessary reforms.

During his first term as prime minister, Peel presided over a minority government. He was soon forced out, but when he returned in 1841 it was with a decisive victory. He reduced import duties in his drive for free trade, but his repeal of the CORN LAWS in 1846 was opposed by the majority of his party and he was removed. His defence of the interests of ordinary people against an aristocratic minority earned him lasting respect.

PEERAGE

The ranks of the British aristocracy are collectively known as the peerage. The highest rank is duke, followed by marquis, earl, viscount and baron. Peers are not allowed to vote in general elections, but gain the right to speak and vote in debates in the House of Lords, which helps to shape legislation.

Until the introduction of life peerages in 1958, titles were hereditary and few could be inherited by women. Hereditary honours are now seldom granted – the last was in 1984, when the former Conservative prime minister Harold Macmillan received an earldom.

In the 1650s there were some 130 peers, but their ranks swelled during the 18th and 19th centuries as businessmen and industrialists were honoured for their work. By May 1998 there were 1272 peers, 479 of them life peers.

The undemocratic and Tory-leaning composition of the House of Lords drove the Labour party to call for reform. In 1997 the new Labour government pledged to remove the voting rights of hereditary peers and redress the balance of party support.
See also HOUSES OF PARLIAMENT

PELAGIUS

- **Heretical theologian**   • **c.360-c.420**

Pelagius' belief in free will brought him excommunication by two popes in 417 and 418. Little is known of his life (his name is probably a Greek translation of the Celtic Morgan), but he was an educated man who left Britain for Rome in

around 400. His doctrines were strongly opposed by the Church because they affirmed the individual's capacity to achieve redemption by leading a virtuous life. This ran counter to the orthodox belief that everyone is tainted by Adam's 'original sin' and must therefore achieve redemption through God's Divine Grace.

Pelagianism had a powerful influence on early Christian thinking, especially in Britain. Twice in the early 5th century St Germanus, the forceful bishop of Auxerre in France, was sent to Britain to counter the heresy. Even so, echoes remained strong in Celtic and early English Christianity for several centuries.

PEMBROKE CASTLE

- **Pembrokeshire (p.494 B4)**
- **Built 13th century**

A round keep almost 25 m (80 ft) high with walls 5 m (16 ft) thick dominates and protects Pembroke Castle. It was built around 1200, when Pembroke was a key fortress in the English settlement of Wales. The tower adjoining the gatehouse was, in 1457, the birthplace of Henry Tudor, later Henry VII.

During the 13th century the castle walls were extended to enclose the town, and some stretches of these walls survive. Pembroke was a Parliamentary stronghold during the Civil War, but in 1648 the governor changed sides, invoking the fury of Cromwell, who besieged the castle in person. Cannonfire destroyed much of the outer enclosure before the garrison surrendered – the first time that the castle had fallen.

NATURAL DEFENCES The steep river banks on three sides of Pembroke Castle combine with its curtain wall and stout towers to make the fortress a formidable challenge to attackers

PENDENNIS CASTLE

- Cornwall (p.494 B7)
- Built 16th-17th century   • EH

The compact size of Pendennis Castle belies its role as a bastion of England's defence for four centuries. Strategically sited on a headland at the mouth of a natural harbour, Pendennis commands wide views across the harbour and seaward to Falmouth Bay.

Henry VIII built the squat, cylindrical keep, together with its neighbour at St Mawes across the River Fal, as part of a chain of coastal fortresses. After his break with the Roman Catholic Church he feared invasion from France, in support for the Church of Rome.

In Elizabeth I's time the castle was enclosed within a star-shaped fortress in case of invasion by Spain. Pendennis was strengthened again by Royalists in the Civil War, and withstood a five-month siege before yielding.

LOCAL STONE The limestone used to build houses and walls in the Pennines is only thinly cloaked by grass and heather. Rocky scars, such as this near Malham, dot the landscape

PENGUIN BOOKS

FIRST EDITION Ariel was the first Penguin paperback, and helped to bring literature to a much wider readership

In 19th-century France paperbacked books were sold for readers to have bound for themselves; in Britain, however, they were often associated with dubious subject matter. But in July 1935 Allen Lane, managing director of the publisher Bodley Head, issued ten paperback books at sixpence each under his new Penguin imprint. The books, which were all reprints of existing works, included titles by Agatha Christie, Ernest Hemingway and Compton Mackenzie.

Lane had forecast that, in the depths of an economic slump, readers would appreciate cheap, quality fiction in a bright, convenient format. A year later, Penguin sales had exceeded 3 million and a nonfiction list, Pelican, was launched with H.G. Wells's Short History of the World. In 1941 Worzel Gummidge, by Barbara Euphan Todd, became the first of the Puffin children's list.

In 1960 Penguin was prosecuted for publishing an uncut version of D.H. LAWRENCE's sexually explicit novel Lady Chatterley's Lover. After intense publicity Penguin won a historic victory against censorship. The book sold 2 million copies in six weeks, overtaking E.V. Rieu's 1946 translation of Homer's Odyssey as the best-selling Penguin.

In the early 1970s Penguin was bought by the Pearson information and entertainment group. Today, the company sells books in more countries than any other publisher and has one of the most diverse lists, including a huge back catalogue of literary classics and also controversial works such as Peter Wright's Spycatcher (1987) and Salman Rushdie's The Satanic Verses (1988).

William PENN

- Quaker colonialist   • 1644-1718

The Society of Friends, or QUAKERS, was regarded as a noisy and troublesome movement when William Penn, the son of a wealthy admiral, joined in 1666. Refusing to exploit his father's influence, Penn was imprisoned four times for his beliefs and for writings such as The Sandy Foundation Shaken (c.1667), which attacked orthodox Christian doctrines.

After the admiral's death, Charles II awarded Penn a grant of land in North America, in settlement of debts owed to his father. In 1682 Penn founded Pennsylvania (Penn's Woodland) and began planning Philadelphia as the capital of a colony with religious tolerance as its first law. Card playing and play-going, however, were prohibited as 'evil sports and games'.

Penn returned to England in 1684, where he worked towards freeing some 1200 imprisoned Quakers. He made only one more visit to Pennsylvania, between 1699 and 1701, but financial mismanagement forced him to remortgage the colony and he spent his last years in England, harassed by debt.

PENNINES

- N England (p.496 B3/B4)

The so-called backbone of England, the Pennine Chain stretches 150 miles down the centre of Britain from the CHEVIOT HILLS in the Scottish Borders to the Vale of Trent and the PEAK DISTRICT. The limestone bedrock of the mountains is riddled with networks of underground caves and tunnels carved out by streams and rainwater – all the major rivers of northern England rise in the Pennines as rapid streams, or 'becks'.

The hills themselves are not dramatic: the highest is Cross Fell at 893 m (2930 ft). Together they form a long, flat-topped ridge, highlighted by spectacles such as the 73 m (240 ft) cliffs and slabs of limestone pavement at Malham Cove, in North Yorkshire.

The challenging 250 mile Pennine Way long-distance walk links Edale in Derbyshire to Kirk Yetholm over the Scottish border.

PENRHYN CASTLE

• **Gwynedd (p.494 C1)** • **Built 1820-45** • **NT**

On a coastline studded with castles dating from the time of Edward I, Penrhyn looks as medieval as any – but in fact was built only in the early 19th century. It was designed by the architect Thomas Hopper for the Pennant family, using slate quarried from local mines in which the Pennants had invested their fortune. The battlements, including a square keep 35 m (115 ft) high and 18 m (60 ft) wide, rival or even surpass those of many a real fortress.

The neo-Norman style continues inside. The Great Hall is three storeys high, arched and vaulted, with a polished sandstone floor modelled on Durham Cathedral. Lavish decoration throughout includes wall panelling and plasterwork by Hopper and paintings by old masters including Rembrandt and Canaletto.

The stables contain a museum of industrial locomotives, and the grounds enclose a Victorian walled garden.

Samuel PEPYS

• **Diarist** • **1633-1703**

The diaries of Samuel Pepys (pronounced 'peeps') painstakingly record the events of almost a decade. Pepys wrote the diaries from January 1, 1660 to May 31, 1669, when he abandoned it for fear of failing eyesight, although he continued his naval career and rose to Secretary to the Admiralty in 1672.

Pepys wrote in a mix of shorthand, French and Spanish, which was only deciphered in 1825. The personal details he records, in particular his extramarital affairs, have led scholars to speculate that he was afraid of his wife discovering the notebooks.

His accounts of the Great Plague of 1665-6 and the 1666 Fire of London reveal important historical details, but the more mundane aspects of 17th-century life are just as fascinating. Pepys waged a lifelong battle against poverty and wrote in 1666, 'I do find that I am worth more than I ever yet was, which is £6200, for which the Holy Name of God be praised'.

Fred PERRY

• **Tennis player** • **1909-95**

In 1936, when he won the men's singles title at the Wimbledon championships for the third time in succession, Fred Perry could not have foreseen that he would be the last Briton to do so for the rest of the century. He was the first player to win all four major tennis singles titles, and at the height of his fame 'Fred' was all the introduction he needed.

Perry fell abruptly out of favour when he joined the first professional circuit in California after the 1936 season. Earning a living from the sport remained forbidden by the game's ruling bodies for a further three decades. He was one of the first sportsmen to brand himself when he designed a line of sportswear, which is still popular, under his own name.

PLAYING TO WIN Fred Perry cut a willowy figure on the tennis court but he played with a singular confidence and aggression, and hit a notoriously powerful running forehand drive

STATE CONTROL The campaigners for civil liberties on the platform cannot protect the crowd from the cavalry's brutal attack in George Cruikshank's 1819 cartoon of the Peterloo Massacre

PERTH

• **Perth and Kinross (p.497 D4)** • **Pop. 41 450**

During the Middle Ages, when English kings fought to conquer Scotland, Perth was an important strategic stronghold on the west bank of the River Tay. The city was seized by the Scottish leader Robert Bruce in 1311 and was the Scottish capital until the murder of James I of Scotland in 1437, after which James II took his court to Edinburgh.

The Scottish Reformation, which led to the dissolution and destruction of the city's monasteries, began in Perth in 1559. The Calvinist John KNOX preached his influential sermon against Catholic idolatry in the Kirk of St John, which still stands in the city centre.

Glass, whisky and the manufacture of dyes are Perth's main industries but a 14th-century house in the city became a tourist attraction when Walter Scott made it the setting of his novel *The Fair Maid of Perth* in 1828.

PETERLOO MASSACRE

• **August 16, 1819** • **Manchester**

Times were bleak for many ordinary people in England in 1819. The Industrial Revolution was under way and new machines were making many manual jobs redundant. In the countryside bad harvests and the CORN LAWS, introduced to prevent the import of cheap grain, had caused the price of bread to soar.

Unrest was growing and the government of Lord Liverpool was unnerved.

On August 16, 1819, a crowd of more than 80 000 gathered at St Peter's Fields in Manchester to hear a speech by the politician Henry 'Orator' Hunt, a fiery advocate of parliamentary reform. Local magistrates, alarmed at the size of the crowd, ordered Hunt's arrest and sent in the yeomanry to quell the angry – although unarmed – protesters.

In the confusion the regular cavalry charged the crowd with sabres. Eleven people were killed and some 500 injured. With the Battle of Waterloo still recent, the *Manchester Observer* called the conflict the 'Peterloo Massacre'. But the government praised the magistrates and brought in further restrictions (the Six Acts) on public protests, which only gave weight to the reform movement.

PETER PAN

• **Published 1904**

The story of Peter Pan, the boy who would not grow up, was one of the first plays written for children and quickly attained the status of classic fairy tale. The name coined by the Scottish playwright J.M. Barrie (1860-1937) for the character Wendy was soon a popular first name for girls.

In the play, Peter Pan shows the children of the Darling family how to fly, and takes them on night-time adventures from their Bloomsbury home to Never Never Land, populated by fanciful characters such as the fairy Tinker Bell and the flamboyant pirate Captain Hook.

In 1929 Barrie donated the royalty rights to the play to the GREAT ORMOND STREET HOSPITAL for children.

PETITION OF RIGHT

The document known as the Petition of Right, presented by parliament to CHARLES I in 1628, has been called the most significant advance in the BRITISH CONSTITUTION since the MAGNA CARTA. Charles had been king for only three years but had already clashed with

parliament over his marriage to a French Roman Catholic princess, the influence of the powerful 1st duke of Buckingham and his extravagance on everything from war to wine.

When parliament curtailed Charles's spending he retaliated by imposing his own taxation and imprisoning those who refused to pay. In reply, the Petition of Right was drawn up, stating that any tax unauthorised by parliament was illegal, that there should be no imprisonment without trial, no enforced billeting of troops and no martial law.

The reluctant king accepted and his financial grant from parliament was restored, but he later reneged on the agreement and his powers were cut once more. The BILL OF RIGHTS of 1689 further increased restrictions on the monarchy.

Flinders PETRIE

• **Archaeologist** • **1853-1942; kt 1923**

Before Flinders Petrie, Egyptian archaeology was driven more by the market for artefacts than by scholarship. From childhood visits to the British Museum Petrie developed an interest in Egyptology. He spent most of 1880 to 1926 digging in Egypt, returning to England each year to write up his work and from 1892 to teach as Professor of Egyptology at London University.

From 1880 until 1882 Petre carried out a detailed survey of the pyramids in Giza, but his main contribution was to impose order in a field where anarchy reigned. He showed that archaeology was more the collation of tiny fragments of evidence than the unveiling of marvels, and recorded every minute stage of research. He devised a dating system, based on associations between sites, the sequence of layers of debris, and changes in the designs of artefacts, and established scientific field work methods that form the basis of those used by archaeologists today.

SCIENCE OF HISTORY Flinders Petrie pioneered archaeological classification. He systematically catalogued the pottery he unearthed in Egypt into types such as Class D – decorated (*below*)

PETWORTH HOUSE

• **West Sussex (p.495 G5)**
• **Built 17th century** • **NT**

For a man such as the 6th duke of Somerset, nicknamed the 'Proud Duke', only a house as stately as Petworth would do. He expected to be served on bended knee, and his children had to stand when addressing him. The house, most of which was completed in 1696, announces its grandeur with a 100 m (300 ft) long west front of classical simplicity facing lawns and a broad lake.

Among the treasures added by the duke's successors is the superb Carved Room, decorated by the woodcarver Grinling GIBBONS. His delicate flowers and fruit stand out from the walls in intricate detail.

The house is rich in sculpture, fine furniture and paintings, and has one room entirely devoted to works by the artist J.M.W. Turner, who was a frequent visitor. In the 1830s Turner painted a series of landscapes of the 280 ha (700 acre) deer park, which was laid out by 'Capability' BROWN during the 1750s.

Nikolaus PEVSNER

• **Art historian** • **1902-83; kt 1969**

A two-decade study, the *Buildings of England* (1952-74), recorded with scholarly precision in 50 volumes, is German-born Nikolaus Pevsner's most enduring legacy. He came to Britain in 1933 as a refugee from Nazism and began lecturing and writing on art history, holding professorships at Cambridge University and Birkbeck College, London.

The success of his 1942 book, *An Outline of European Architecture*, allowed Pevsner to undertake his county-by-county architectural tour of England. His publisher, Penguin Books, lent him a 1933 Wolsley Hornet car and gave him a permit for 30 gallons of petrol. With his wife at the wheel, the professor spent his university holidays researching the most comprehensive catalogue of England's buildings ever made.

FLY AWAY HOME A rush of pigeons released from crates marks the start of a race. Breeding and training have produced racing birds that fly at speeds up to 100 mph – twice that of a wild pigeon – over distances of up to 600 miles

Prince PHILIP

• Duke of Edinburgh   • b.1921

Friends of Prince Philip, husband of ELIZABETH II, describe him as forthright, others as tactless. He has referred to himself as a man without a job, but has made it his task to give the Queen his loyal support throughout her reign.

The son of Prince Andrew of Greece and Princess Alice of Battenburg, Philip was educated at GORDONSTOUN in Scotland, then enlisted with the Royal Navy on the advice of his uncle, earl MOUNTBATTEN. During the Second World War, Philip courted Princess Elizabeth, and they married in 1947.

As royal consort, he founded the Duke of Edinburgh Award Scheme in 1956, running outward-bound courses for youngsters, and is president emeritus of the wildlife charity WWF International.

PICCADILLY

• Central London (p.499 B6)

Beneath the tarmac of Piccadilly lies an ancient highway that leads due west from the city of LONDON. When a tailor who excelled in making fanciful ruffs known as piccadills built a country home along this route in the 17th century, the house, and the roadway by association,

became known as Piccadilly. By 1820 John NASH had laid out the imposing Piccadilly Circus as a road junction with Regent Street. Piccadilly, sandwiched between Mayfair and St James's Palace, turned into a smart area of London. Mansions such as Burlington House, now housing the ROYAL ACADEMY, still grace the road, as do the luxurious 1906 RITZ Hotel and 1925 FORTNUM & MASON.

A rash of neon signs at Piccadilly Circus illuminate Alfred Gilbert's 1892 statue of the Angel of Charity, which quickly became better known as Eros, the winged messenger of love.

PICTS AND SCOTS

Third-century Romans in Britain referred to the indigenous tribes living north of the ANTONINE WALL, the frontier of their empire, as 'picti', perhaps meaning 'painted people'. The evidence of place names suggests that their language was of Celtic origin; little remains of Pictish culture except some intricately carved stones and early Christian crosses, metalwork and jewellery.

During the 4th century, Gaelic-speaking Irish tribes – Scots – settled in Argyle, and over the next three centuries expanded across Pictish lands by war, treaties and dynastic intermarriage.

In 843, partly in order to repel Viking raids, the Picts united with the Scots under the Scottish king Kenneth Macalpin. The new kingdom, north of a line from Strathclyde to Northumbria, was at first known by its Gaelic name, Alba, and soon became entirely Scottish as the Picts were assimilated.

PIERS PLOWMAN

With enthusiasm and vigour, William Langland (born c.1330, probably in Herefordshire) inveighed against the corruption of materialism – especially within the Church – in one of the great allegorical poems of the Middle Ages.

In *Piers Plowman* Langland presents a series of 'dream visions', beginning as a social satire and developing into a quest for Truth as a guide to virtue and the heavenly realm. Written in alliterative verse, the poem mingles the symbolic with vivid glimpses of ordinary lives, as in the image of Envy:

...beetle-browed and babber-lipped,
with two bleared eyes,
And as a leatheren purse
lolled his cheeks.

Binding the whole is the figure of Piers the Plowman – at first a humble servant of God, then a leader in the search for Truth, and finally as Christ incarnate.

PIGEON RACING

Once described as the 'poor man's racehorse', the homing pigeon has provided sport for the working men of the North since the 19th century. In Britain today, there are around 8 million racing pigeons and 100 000 loft owners – including Elizabeth II.

Races take place in summer, when lorries bearing crates of pigeons from all parts of Britain gather at a 'liberation' point. As the flaps go up, the birds make for home. As each bird arrives its coded ring is put into a sealed clocking device, which is later opened at a pigeon-racing club and the bird's speed calculated. Prize winners, sold for their breeding potential, can fetch thousands of pounds.

Lester PIGGOTT

• Jockey • b.1935

The doyen of British jockeys rode his first winner at the age of 12 and was still galloping home ahead of the field 47 years later. A master tactician and shrewd judge of horses, Piggott was champion jockey 11 times, and for eight consecutive seasons from 1964.

After winning a record 29 classics, including nine Derbys, he retired from HORSE RACING in 1985 to train horses. A conviction for tax evasion two years later jailed him for a year, but Piggott returned to the saddle and in 1992 won his 30th classic, the 2000 Guineas.

PILGRIM FATHERS

It was in the 19th century that the first English settlers of Massachusetts, in the north-eastern area of America that became known as New England, were given the name Pilgrim Fathers.

In 1607, fleeing religious persecution, a group of 35 Puritans from Scrooby in Nottinghamshire left England to settle in Leiden, in the more tolerant Netherlands.

In September 1620, realising their Englishness would be better preserved in the New World, the separatists joined a group of London merchant adventurers heading for America, and set sail from Plymouth in the *Mayflower*. Two months later, the group of 102 men, women and children made landfall in Cape Cod Bay, naming their new settlement Plymouth.

PILGRIMAGE

In the 6th century, Pope Gregory I, the Great, sent to England 'all things necessary for the worship of the Church', including relics of the Apostles and martyrs. Relics and sites associated with saints developed a reputation for curing illness and performing miracles, and soon pilgrims were visiting shrines the length and breadth of the country.

Pilgrims travelled in groups for safety, and before returning home bought the badge of the shrine they had visited as proof of their journey. From the 8th century, the practice of imposing pilgrimage in place of public penance for sin fuelled its later popularity.

By the 15th century, according to the standards of those who wanted to reform the Church, the religious value of pilgrimages seemed to be diminishing. The conviviality of the poet Geoffrey Chaucer's pilgrims in the *Canterbury Tales* would not appear to be very religious by the standards of some.

Pilgrimages were greatly reduced after Henry VIII broke with the Catholic Church and established the Church of England, sanctioning the Dissolution of the Monasteries by 1540. All the shrines were destroyed except that of Edward the Confessor. Anglo-Catholicism in the 19th century prompted a revival within the Church of England, and today Walsingham, LINDISFARNE and IONA attract large numbers of pilgrims.

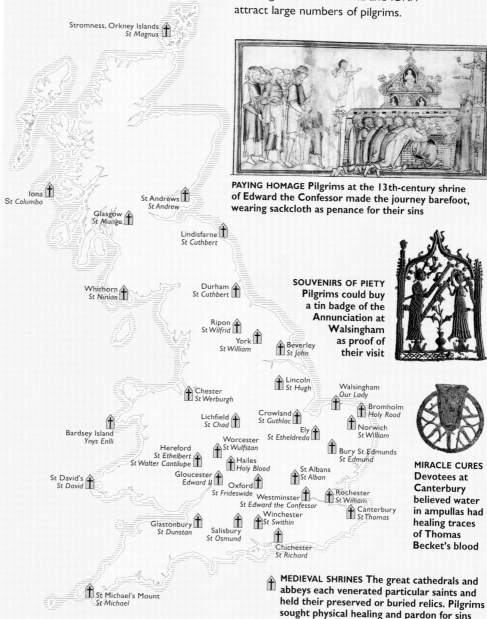

PAYING HOMAGE Pilgrims at the 13th-century shrine of Edward the Confessor made the journey barefoot, wearing sackcloth as penance for their sins

SOUVENIRS OF PIETY Pilgrims could buy a tin badge of the Annunciation at Walsingham as proof of their visit

MIRACLE CURES Devotees at Canterbury believed water in ampullas had healing traces of Thomas Becket's blood

Stromness, Orkney Islands
St Magnus

Iona
St Columba

St Andrews
St Andrew

Glasgow
St Mungo

Lindisfarne
St Cuthbert

Whithorn
St Ninian

Durham
St Cuthbert

Ripon
St Wilfrid

York
St William

Beverley
St John

Lincoln
St Hugh

Chester
St Werburgh

Walsingham
Our Lady

Crowland
St Guthlac

Bromholm
Holy Rood

Lichfield
St Chad

Ely
St Etheldreda

Norwich
St William

Bardsey Island
Ynys Enlli

Worcester
St Wulfstan

Bury St Edmunds
St Edmund

Hereford
St Ethelbert
St Walter Cantilupe

Hailes
Holy Blood

St Albans
St Alban

St David's
St David

Gloucester
Edward II

Oxford
St Frideswide

Westminster
St Edward the Confessor

Rochester
St William

Winchester
St Swithin

Canterbury
St Thomas

Glastonbury
St Dunstan

Salisbury
St Osmund

Chichester
St Richard

St Michael's Mount
St Michael

MEDIEVAL SHRINES The great cathedrals and abbeys each venerated particular saints and held their preserved or buried relics. Pilgrims sought physical healing and pardon for sins

PILLORY AND STOCKS

Every market town and most villages in medieval England had a pillory or stocks where offenders could be punished. The pillory was a vertical pole with a crossbar that contained holes to fasten head and hands. Stocks lay on the ground allowing legs, and sometimes hands, to be secured through holes. As well as enduring discomfort, usually for an hour on market day, culprits had to suffer abuse and a pelting from passersby.

Stocks were used by the Romans in Britain, and an order of 1350 prescribed the punishment for unruly artisans. The pillory, introduced in Anglo-Saxon times, was used for more serious crimes, such as forgery and perjury, as defined in a statute of 1256.

The writer Daniel Defoe was pilloried in 1703 for his satirical pamphlet *The Shortest Way with Dissenters*. He was well treated by onlookers, however, who threw flowers at him. Pillorying was abolished in 1837, but stocks were used as late as 1865 in Rugby.

PILTDOWN MAN

In 1912 Charles Dawson, a lawyer, sent to the British Museum the remains of a skull of modern type complete with an ape-like jaw, which he claimed he had found in a gravel pit at Piltdown, near Lewes in East Sussex. His find was hailed by experts as the 'missing link' between man and his ape ancestors, and the skull named after him – Dawson's dawn-man.

In 1953 British Museum experts proved the 'find' to be a hoax. The skull was human but only about 600 years old, and the jaw belonged to a modern orang-utan. Both had been modified and stained to make them look ancient.

PIMM'S

Summer garden parties and occasions such as Royal Ascot or Henley Regatta would not be the same without the ritual drinking of Pimm's No.1 Cup. The gin-based fruit drink was devised in the 1820s by James Pimm, owner of an oyster bar in the City of London, who sold it by the pint over the bar. By 1859 it had become so popular that it was being mass-produced and sold in bottles for 3 shillings. Six years later Pimm sold the business but his name was retained.

The reputation of Pimm's as a refreshing drink in hot weather assured its success wherever the British were serving abroad. Today, overseas orders account for half of sales.

The recipe, blending gin, liqueurs, fruit extracts and spices, is a tightly guarded commercial secret. Pimm's is traditionally served on ice, topped up with lemonade and garnished with mint, borage leaves and sliced apple and citrus fruits. There is also a Pimm's Vodka Cup.

PINEWOOD STUDIOS

• **Buckinghamshire (p.495 G4)**   • **Est. 1936**
With the aim of establishing the most advanced film studio in the world, the wealthy builder Charles Boot bought Heatherden Hall, at Iver near London, in 1934, and named his enterprise after the tall pines in the grounds. He went into partnership with the entrepreneur

DOUBLE TAKE The technique of filming actors against a prerecorded background, which avoided expensive location shoots, was skilfully applied at Pinewood in the mid 1970s

J. Arthur RANK and within two years they had constructed the studio. Using an innovative 'unit system' by which several films could be made simultaneously, Pinewood made more films in its first year than any other studio in the world, and achieved blockbuster successes after the Second World War with *Oliver Twist* and *The Red Shoes*, both made in 1948.

Attracted by lower production costs and facilities often superior to those in Hollywood, in the 1960s American production companies began making films at Pinewood. To keep pace with the fast-moving film, televison and commercial industry, more studios were built, and there are now 18 stages on the 40.5 ha (100 acre) site. On a typical day some 2500 people work at Pinewood.

Pinewood's productions include the *CARRY ON* and JAMES BOND film series, *The Day of the Jackal*, *Batman* and *Mission Impossible*, and television productions such as *Minder* and *Poirot*.

Harold PINTER

• **Playwright**   • **b.1930**
Audiences at Harold Pinter's early plays in the late 1950s and early 60s were shocked, worried and confused, which was his intention. Most of his best work, including *The Birthday Party* (1958) and *The Caretaker* (1960), is set in the claustrophobic atmosphere of a single room, where unspoken tensions build up among emotionally isolated individuals. In *The Dumb Waiter* (1958) two inarticulate hitmen wait nervously for their instructions in a seedy boarding house. With great skill, Pinter manipulates the lines of pointless everyday talk to create an intense, grim 'comedy of menace'.

Pinter has also written works for television, radio and cinema, including the screenplays of *The Servant* (1963) and *The French Lieutenant's Woman* (1981). Other than short pieces, Pinter wrote no stage dramas from the late 1970s to the early 90s, and has recently concentrated on directing and acting.

MAN FOR ALL SEASONS In four stained-glass windows designed for the Ipswich School Library, John Piper symbolises man's oneness with nature: (*from left*) spring and youth, summer and adulthood, autumn and middle age, winter and old age

John PIPER

• Painter and designer   • 1903-92

Although he had been one of Britain's foremost abstract artists in the 1930s, John Piper had turned to figurative art by the outbreak of the Second World War. A series of darkly evocative paintings of bombed buildings, such as *Somerset Place, Bath,* firmly established him in a tradition of landscape painting which he analysed in his 1942 book, *British Romantic Artists.*

After the war Piper concentrated increasingly on designing stained glass, such as the large windows for Liverpool Metropolitan Cathedral and Coventry Cathedral. He also collaborated with the composer Benjamin BRITTEN, creating stage sets for seven of his operas.

Augustus PITT-RIVERS

• Ethnographer   • 1827-1900

While serving with the Grenadier Guards, Augustus Pitt-Rivers grew fascinated with the types of weaponry used in different places and times. After building up a huge collection, he focused on costume, toys, jewellery, musical instruments, religious artefacts and household objects from far-flung civilisations.

On retiring from the army in 1882 Pitt-Rivers donated his collection – some 15 000 objects – to Oxford University to form the core of an ethnographic museum, established in 1885. The Pitt-Rivers Museum displays Zulu baskets, Native American baby carriers and Peruvian feather headdresses, shrunken heads and one of the world's largest collections of musical instruments.

PITT THE ELDER and PITT THE YOUNGER

• William Pitt   • Prime minister 1766
• 1708-78; earl 1766
• William Pitt   • Prime minister 1783-1801, 1804-6   • 1759-1806

The two Pitts could hardly have been more different: the father, a socialite, a formidable orator and firm war leader; the son, a private, backroom 'fixer' who preferred peace. Yet both in different ways became champions of the people.

As secretary of state, Pitt the Elder led the country in the Seven Years' War (1756-63) against France. His strategy to win Canada and India for Britain confirmed him as a great war leader. He was appointed prime minister in 1766, but illness soon lost him the office.

Unlike his father, the younger Pitt cared more for modernising government than directing war. At 24, he became the youngest prime minister Britain has ever had, and held the office continuously for 17 years. Pitt's mastery of public finance and support for free trade brought prosperity, and lowering customs duty made smuggling largely unprofitable.

Avoiding hostilities with France until it declared war in 1793, Pitt was hailed as saviour of Europe after Lord Nelson's victory at Trafalgar in 1805. To pay for the war, Pitt introduced income tax.

PLACE NAMES

TOWN NAMES AND THEIR MEANINGS

-beck (*OS*) eg Troutbeck	stream trout stream
-by (*OS*) eg Whitby	village or settlement white village
-combe (*OE*) eg Ilfracombe	narrow valley valley of Alfred's people
-ham (*OE*) eg Feltham	village, manor village in a field
-ing (*OE*) eg Reading	people of people of Reada (a local chieftain)
-ley (*OE*) eg Horsley	glade, wood horse's glade
-minster (*OE*) eg Axminster	monastery, church church by River Axe
strat- (*OE*) eg Stratford	Roman road, street street by river ford
-ton (*OE*) eg Wilton	village or settlement village among willows

OE: Old English
OS: Old Scandinavian

British place names can be a source of wonder and delight – Maggots End, Matching Tye, Nether Wallop, Steeple Bumpstead, Ugley – and most have a traceable history. The cluster of towns, for example, ending with '-by' north of Great Yarmouth in Norfolk (Hemsby, Ormesby, Scratby) point to a Norse-speaking Viking settlement.

Names may reflect local agriculture, as in Flax Bourton and Toller Porcorum (pigs), or past industries, such as Glass Houghton and Iron Acton. Most place

PLAGUE

In July 1348, a ship arrived from France at the Dorset port of Weymouth. It delivered not only trading goods but also rats bearing fleas infected with the bacterium *Pasteurella pestis* – the terrible plague known as the Black Death. No one knew the disease was transmitted to humans by flea bite, and over the next two years the plague swept through Britain, killing almost a quarter of the country's 4 million population.

WIDESPREAD EPIDEMIC

The fleas lived on rats but could infest bundles of cloth and wool, England's staple products. Wherever merchants from Weymouth made a sale they unleashed the disease and the plague spread relentlessly along trade routes

ALL FALL DOWN The game Ring-a-ring o' roses is thought to refer to the plague – the first symptom being a ring of rosy spots. People believed that pomanders of herbs (*right*) kept the disease at bay

until 1350, when severe winter cold began to kill the fleas. It reappeared sporadically for another 300 years, taking its final toll in the 1665 Great Plague of London, at the height of which up to 6000 people a week were dying.

THE DREADED SYMPTOMS

The most common form of the illness was bubonic plague, starting with the irritation of a flea bite. Within days, egg-sized swellings, or 'buboes', appeared, followed by fever and delirium. Death came to 70 per cent of those infected. The rarer pneumonic plague, in which the disease attacks the lungs, could also be spread simply by coughing, and was always fatal.

STRANGE REMEDIES

Many ways to treat the plague were tried. Ten-year-old treacle mixed with diced snake was one bizarre prescription. Homes were fumigated with burned herbs, and doctors wore beak-like masks filled with fragrant flowers.

After the 1665 Great Plague, effective quarantine measures and rodent control rid Britain of the disease, which is now treatable with antibiotics.

DEADLY MENACE Woodcuts made during the 1665 Great Plague of London show people fleeing the city (*top* and *bottom*); the dead were tipped into mass graves (*centre*)

names indicate either their landscape or a settlement, and are a mix of Celtic, Anglo-Saxon and Norse, with a few from Norman French and Latin. Cricket, in Somerset, is named from the Celtic *cruc* (hill) and the Norman suffix *et* (little).

Most names have altered since they were first comprehensively recorded in the DOMESDAY BOOK, and their true meaning can be masked. The 'hamp' in Northampton means 'home', while in Southampton it means 'water meadow'; the forms were different in Anglo-Saxon.

PLAID CYMRU

• Founded 1925

The 1997 DEVOLUTION referendum, which promised Wales its first measure of political autonomy since Owain GLYNDWR's 1404 parliament, only partly fulfilled the goal of the Welsh nationalist party, Plaid Cymru (the Party of Wales).

Plaid Cymru's original aim was to preserve Welsh culture by ensuring that the language was taught in schools, but by the 1930s it was seeking to secure full self-government for Wales and a democratic Welsh state, based on socialist principles. The party won its first parliamentary seat in 1966, but has never had more than four MPs.

In the May 1999 Welsh assembly election, Plaid Cymru won 17 seats, second only to the Labour party's 28.

PLANTAGENETS

• English royal house • 1154-1399

When HENRY II succeeded King STEPHEN in 1154, he became the first of the Plantagenet dynasty that ruled England for 245 years (*see* ROYAL HOUSES). The name derives from the sprig of broom plant (in French, *plante genet*) that Henry's father, Geoffrey of Anjou, habitually wore in his cap.

Henry's widespread inheritance formed an empire stretching from the Pyrenees to Scotland, but the empire proved too large for the Plantagenets to manage. In 1259 HENRY III renounced all claims to French land, except Gascony.

The Plantagenets provided eight kings, but the dynasty crumbled in 1399 with the deposition of Richard II by Henry Bolinbroke (HENRY IV), and it split into the Houses of LANCASTER and YORK.

CRAZE FOR THE EXOTIC

Today's gardens would look very different were it not for five centuries of botanical exploration. No azaleas, rhododendrons or red roses; no geraniums, gladioli, tulips or in fact the vast majority of our garden plants – all 'exotics' we owe to a special breed of explorer

NORTH AMERICA
LUPINS
MAIDENHAIR FERN
MICHAELMAS DAISIES
VIRGINIA CREEPER

EUROPE
GLADIOLI
LILACS
MADONNA LILY
MARIGOLDS

HIMALAYAS
AZALEAS
BLUE POPPY
RHODODENDRONS

MIDDLE EAST
ANEMONES
CROCUSES
HYACINTHS
RED ROSE
TULIPS

SOUTH AMERICA
MONKEY PUZZLE TREE
ORCHIDS
RUBBER PLANT

SOUTHERN AFRICA
PELARGONIUMS

GREEN FINGERS Plant hunters, such as Ernest Wilson (1876-1930, *right*), spent years penetrating uncharted territory in their search for new species. Through expeditions to China, Japan, Australia, India and Africa, Wilson introduced 1000 species to cultivation

TWO THOUSAND years ago the Romans brought marigolds, Madonna lilies and other Mediterranean plants to Britain, but imports on a much grander scale began in the 16th century as trade and exploration opened up the world.

WEALTH FROM THE NEW WORLD
The 17th-century royal gardener John TRADESCANT the Younger introduced from the North American colonies such now-familiar plants as lupins, Michaelmas daisies and Virginia creeper. At about the same time, tulips first reached Britain from the Middle East via the Netherlands, where fortunes were made and lost gambling on 'tulipomania' – the craze for growing these novelties.

But the biggest influx came in the 19th and early 20th centuries, when the Empire was at its height and gardening was becoming popular with the middle classes. Two types of collector were at

work: those sent by public bodies such as the ROYAL HORTICULTURAL SOCIETY and KEW GARDENS, and those working for commercial nurserymen.

DEDICATED GARDENERS
Most collectors were gardeners, although some were qualified botanists. All had a sense of adventure – essential when travel was slow and often dangerous.

Robert Fortune, one of the founders of the Indian tea industry, fought off pirates to smuggle tea seeds from China to Calcutta in 1848-51. In 1876 Henry Wickham smuggled 70 000 rubber-tree seeds from Brazil – with the connivance of the British consul – to Kew; fewer than one-twentieth germinated but it was enough to establish a Malayan industry.

ON THE ORCHID TRAIL
No plants were more valuable than orchids from the jungles of South America and South-east Asia, and in some cases collecting amounted to

plunder as thousands of specimens were uprooted and shipped home. Plant collecting on such a scale largely stopped with the outbreak of the First World War but horticultural explorers still search the world for new garden plants and, increasingly, for medicinal species.

COLLECTOR'S ITEM The Wardian case – a kind of miniature greenhouse – was invented by Dr Nathaniel Ward in the 1830s for transporting tender plants on long sea voyages

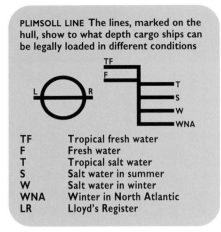

PLIMSOLL LINE The lines, marked on the hull, show to what depth cargo ships can be legally loaded in different conditions

TF	Tropical fresh water
F	Fresh water
T	Tropical salt water
S	Salt water in summer
W	Salt water in winter
WNA	Winter in North Atlantic
LR	Lloyd's Register

Samuel PLIMSOLL

• **Social reformer** • **1824-98**

The line that bears Samuel Plimsoll's name is not one but a series of marks on the hull of cargo ships showing the safe levels to which they can be loaded in different conditions.

For Plimsoll, a coal trader who had seen four ships wrecked during a voyage in 1864, shipping safety was a crusade – vigorously pursued when he became MP for Derby in 1868. In 1869, the National Life Boat Institution (NLBI) reported 177 ships wrecked in calm or near-calm conditions. Every day seamen and even paying passengers died in overloaded, unseaworthy ships.

But vested interests opposed reform and it took Plimsoll six years to get his safety measure, contained in the Merchant Shipping Bill, made law. Backed by seamen and the NLBI, it was finally passed in 1875.

PLYMOUTH

• **Devon (p.494 C7)** • **Pop. 245 300**

Plymouth's seaport, known as Sutton in Domesday, embodies centuries of maritime history. A statue of Francis DRAKE, who sailed from its harbour in 1588 to defeat the SPANISH ARMADA, stands prominent on the grassy expanse of Plymouth Hoe.

Other great navigators who sailed from the port on voyages of discovery include Walter RALEIGH and Captain COOK. In

the harbour, the Mayflower Memorial commemorates the PILGRIM FATHERS, who set sail for America in 1620.

At the western end of the Hoe is the Citadel, built by Charles II to deter the French and to intimidate the people of Plymouth who had supported Oliver Cromwell in the CIVIL WAR. Nearby is John Smeaton's lighthouse of 1759, which originally stood on the treacherous Eddystone Rocks 14 miles offshore.

Plymouth, which has the naval base of Devonport to its west, was savagely bombed in the Second World War – only the cobbled Barbican above the port and nearby streets survive from the old town. The new city, laid out on a grand scale, centres on Armada Way – a thoroughfare that leads inland from the Hoe.

PLYMOUTH BRETHREN

The Brethren are adherents of an early 19th-century evangelical Christian sect originating in Ireland who took their name from the branch founded by John Nelson Darby (1800-82) in Plymouth, Devon, in 1830. Rigorous Puritans, they believe implicitly in the Scriptures

and, based on a literal interpretation of a passage from Revelations, await the return of Christ and his saints to reign on Earth for a thousand years.

In 1848 when Darby and an associate split over a doctrinal difference, the group divided into Exclusive Brethren (or Darbyites), under a central authority, and Open Brethren, whose congregations are independent units. The Brethren, mainly found in English-speaking countries, now number about 100 000, of whom two-thirds are Open Brethren.

POET LAUREATE

The official title of Poet Laureate, conferred for life, was established in 1688. It had inauspicious beginnings, having been bestowed by James II on John DRYDEN only months before James was toppled in the Glorious Revolution. Dryden was also replaced.

Since then the list of Poets Laureate has been remarkable for its mediocrity. Who now remembers Laurence Eusden (1688-1730), William Whitehead (1715-85) or Alfred Austin (1835-1913)? The few major poets to hold the post include William WORDSWORTH, Lord TENNYSON and Ted HUGHES, but only Tennyson, Queen Victoria's favourite, could be seen as a 'national poet'.

Hughes' death in 1998 led to a heated debate on who should succeed him as laureate. Andrew Motion (b.1952) was eventually appointed in May 1999 for a ten-year term on an annual salary of £5000 – a considerable increase on the previous £70 and case of wine.

POETS' CORNER

In the south transept of Westminster Abbey is one of the most prestigious burial spots in the world – Poets' Corner. Burials date back six centuries to 1400, when Geoffrey CHAUCER was interred

FINAL TRIBUTE A section of Poets' Corner in Westminster Abbey commemorates some of the greatest British poets, including Milton, Tennyson and Wordsworth

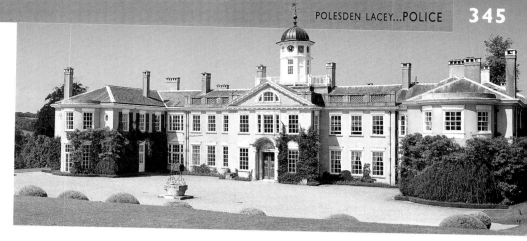

A STYLISH HOME For nearly 40 years Mrs Greville entertained the rich and famous at Polesden Lacey. At her death in 1942, she left the house and its estate to the National Trust

there as a special honour. In 1599 Edmund SPENSER was buried near Chaucer, whom he much admired, as other poets threw poems into his grave.

By the time Ben JONSON was near death in 1637, space was already a problem. Jonson said he needed only two feet square so he was buried upright, with the epitaph 'Oh rare Ben Johnson'.

John DRYDEN and Samuel JOHNSON were also buried in the abbey but 19th-century poets such as Lord BYRON, Percy Bysshe SHELLEY and John KEATS were rejected for many years because they were judged to have led immoral lives.

When they were finally accepted, there was only room for commemorative plaques, which were also accorded to Jane AUSTEN, Charlotte BRONTË, Thomas HARDY, T.S. ELIOT and the actor Laurence OLIVIER. Nowadays in the abbey, space even for plaques is severely limited. The most recent memorial – to John BETJEMAN, a former poet laureate – was unveiled in November 1996.

POLESDEN LACEY

• Surrey (p.495 G5) • Built 1823 • NT

Set high on the North Downs with views of valley and woodland, Polesden Lacey was built on the site of the playwright Richard Brinsley SHERIDAN's country home. It is a two-storey building set round a courtyard, with an exterior that still resembles the original Regency villa designed by Thomas Cubitt.

From 1906, however, the house was extended and the interior reconstructed by Ambrose Poynter to turn it into the comfortable Edwardian country home of a celebrated society hostess – the Hon Mrs Ronald Greville. Edward VII

was a guest at Polesden Lacey, and the Duke and Duchess of York – later George VI and Queen Elizabeth – spent part of their honeymoon there.

Mrs Greville's tastes are reflected in the crimson silk brocades that decorate the dining room, the English, French and Chinese furniture, Georgian silver, porcelain and English portrait paintings. Even more personal are the snapshots of Mrs Greville's favourite dogs and signed photographs of her guests.

The grounds include a tranquil walled rose garden, and statues set to catch the eye among clipped hedges and bushes of box and yew. An open-air theatre at the house opens for a summer season.

POLICE

The British police force has its roots in the BOW STREET RUNNERS, a volunteer group set up in London in the 1750s to catch thieves. The first organised force – a forerunner of the Royal Irish Constabulary – was created in Ireland in 1814 by Robert PEEL, after whom its members were dubbed 'peelers'.

When Peel as home secretary went on to found London's Metropolitan Police in 1829, they were called 'bobbies' – a nickname later extended to all other British policemen. The London force, now known as 'The Met', is headed by a commissioner still under the control of the home secretary, with headquarters at New SCOTLAND YARD. There are 27 000 Met officers, with 14 000 civil staff, to police about 800 sq miles of London.

The Met's detective department – founded with eight officers in 1842 after two attempts on Queen Victoria's life – was reorganised as the CID (Criminal Investigation Department) in 1878. The Special Branch was established in 1883 to

combat terrorism in Ireland, and the Central Robbery Squad, formerly the Flying Squad, set up in 1920 to control crime in the more dangerous parts of London.

From the mid 19th century each county in Britain formed its own police force, although some neighbouring forces have now merged. There are 43 forces in England and Wales, eight in Scotland and one in Northern Ireland.

Regional forces are each accountable to a police authority, which consists of local councillors and magistrates who appoint a chief constable, responsible for operational control of the force. There are around 150 000 police officers in the UK.

FROM BOBBY TO MARKSMAN The traditional image of the police (above) was cosily reassuring. But by 1999 armed officers in England and Wales were being called out to almost 12 000 incidents a year

PUBLIC REVOLT Under the 'poll tax' a duke paid the same as a dustman for council services. Violent protests broke out in 1990, including this one in Trafalgar Square

POLL TAX

The unpopular flat-rate 'community charge' for local government services brought in by Margaret THATCHER's Conservative government in 1989-90 soon became known as the 'poll tax'. Levied by 'poll', or head of population, the intention was that every adult in an area should pay the same. Under the old rates system, which it replaced, people paid a fee related to the value of their property and one in four was exempt.

Ministers hoped that the community charge would discourage councils from overspending, but critics warned that the tax was hard to administer and that people would drop off the council-held voting register to evade payment.

Public opposition and unease over the policy among Conservative MPs contributed to the removal of Thatcher as party leader and prime minister in 1990. Her successor, John Major, moved swiftly to abolish the system, replacing it in 1993 with a 'council tax'.

POLO

Polo, the oldest equestrian sport, is a pastime associated with nobility and the rich, just as it was when the Persian poet Firdausi described the game around

600 BC. Prince Charles and Prince Philip are both notable devotees.

The British discovered polo in the 1850s in Assam, India. The game, played by two teams on horseback wielding long mallets to drive a small ball through a goal, became a favourite with army officers, who established clubs and fostered interest among Indian princes.

The exclusive Hurlingham Club in west London, founded soon after the first polo match was staged in England – in 1871 between the army regiments of the 9th Lancers and the 10th Hussars – instigated the modern rules and became the focal point of the European game. In recent years, however, its English Champions Cup has been largely dominated by foreign teams.

POOLE HARBOUR

• **Dorset (p.494 E6)**

With 60 miles of shoreline, the natural harbour of Poole is one of the largest in the world. It was formed after the last ice age by a river that flowed into The Solent from melting glaciers in the west.

During the Iron Age and Roman period the area was noted for its potteries, an industry that still continues in the town of Poole. With a maze of hidden creeks backed by wild heathland, the harbour was notorious for its smugglers in the 18th century.

The old quayside is well preserved and the harbour is now popular for water sports. The southern shores remain lonely mud flats, with nature reserves at Arne and Studland. Brownsea Island, the site of Robert Baden-Powell's first scout camp in 1907, contains the last colony of red squirrels in southern England.

POOR LAWS

A surge in unemployment in Tudor times brought about Britain's first legal measures to help the poor. The problem was partly caused by a sharp rise in the population – from 2.26 million in 1525 to 4.1 million in 1601 – but the enclosure of COMMON LAND in the 16th century had also begun to deny the poor the means to graze animals, catch fish and collect firewood.

As bands of penniless beggars began to threaten law and order, local communities gradually

JET-SET SPORT Polo matches at Windsor Great Park attract an international elite; many of today's top players are from Argentina

evolved a system of relief for the poor, based on the PARISH network and enforced by local justices under the supervision of the PRIVY COUNCIL.

The Poor Law Act of 1601, which codified all the earlier local laws, remained the basis of relief for the next 200 years. Hardship in the early 19th century prompted a new Poor Law Act in 1834, setting up WORKHOUSES in which able-bodied paupers laboured in return for food and housing.

A Royal Commission investigated the system in 1909, and the last Poor Law in 1930 marked a radical shift from local to national provision for the poor.

In 1948 the Labour government introduced comprehensive social security benefits that were paid out by a National Assistance Board and funded by taxation rather than rates.

Alexander POPE

- **Poet and essayist** • 1688-1744

An invalid from the age of 12, and deprived of public positions because of his Roman Catholic faith, Alexander Pope devoted his working life to writing.

He published his first verses when a youth and at 21 produced the didactic *Essay on Criticism*, a poetic discussion of the laws by which a critic should be guided. It coined such phrases as 'Fools rush in where angels fear to tread' and 'A little learning is a dangerous thing', and provided Pope with an introduction to London literary society.

Pope was a master both of classical form and of satire. His 1712 *The Rape of the Lock* combined the two to lampoon fashionable pretensions in high-flown style. He translated Homer's epic *Iliad* (1715-20) and *Odyssey* (1725-6) to great acclaim and between 1728 and 1743 published *The Dunciad*, ridiculing dull writers. That, and the philosophical poem *An Essay on Man*, secured him an international reputation.

Karl POPPER

- **Philosopher** • 1902-94; kt 1965

When Karl Popper came to England in 1946, he was already a well-known iconoclast who had attacked first Marxism and psychoanalysis in his native Vienna, and then the simple faith in scientific certainty of the positivists. Scientific theories, Popper argued, could be disproved but never proved.

Popper left Austria for New Zealand in 1936, and spent the war years writing philosophical attacks on both fascism and communism. The remainder of his life was spent in Britain, where from 1949 to 1969 he held court at the London School of Economics, offering an exotic alternative to mainstream philosophy with his emphasis on the creative side of scientific discovery.

PORT

The British might never have developed a taste for port – a wine fortified with brandy during fermentation – but for a tariff war with France that began in the mid 17th century. Seeking wines to replace French claret and burgundy, which were banned and then punitively taxed, British merchants turned instead to the robust red wines of the Portuguese Douro valley.

Two merchants are said to have been the first Englishmen to taste port, at a monastery in 1678. The wine was named after the town of Oporto, where British vintners were established by 1703, when Britain and Portugal signed a tariff treaty that lasted for 150 years.

After early overproduction, the industry was regulated and fortification techniques were refined. In the Victorian era, a range of styles were developed, such as tawny, which is aged in cask for longer than classic, vintage-dated port.

PORTCHESTER CASTLE

- **Hampshire (p.495 F6)**
- **Completed c.1120** • EH

The castle stands high above Portsmouth Harbour, enclosed by the longest and best-preserved Roman wall in northern Europe. On this site in the 3rd century AD the Romans built a fort to defend the shore against Saxon pirates.

The flint walls of the fort form a great quadrangle, and in the early 12th century Henry I built a castle inside; its tall square keep survives. At the end of

NAKED CHARM 'Just what is it that makes today's homes so different, so appealing?' asked the pop artist Richard Hamilton in the title of his satirical 1959 collage

POP ART

Pop art was fun art – with a touch of satire. Rejecting any distinction between good taste and bad, it cheerfully embraced emblems of the modern world – comic books, advertisements, chairs and kitchen sinks, television and cinema images.

The origins of pop art have been traced to Dadaism and surrealism. The movement emerged in Britain in the late 1950s, representing the art of the present, unconcerned with precursors. Pop artist Richard Hamilton defined it as 'popular, transient, low-cost, mass-produced, young... sexy, gimmicky'.

Peter BLAKE's collages, including his album cover for The BEATLES' *Sgt. Pepper's Lonely Hearts Club Band*, epitomised the spirit of the Sixties. When the era ended, so did pop art.

the 14th century Richard II turned the castle into a small palace, whose hall, kitchen and great chamber remain.

Edward III set forth from Porchester to fight at Crécy and Henry V rallied troops there before victory at Agincourt. In Napoleonic times, 4000 French prisoners were held in the keep.

A MODEL OF SOCIAL PLANNING Replacing rundown housing (*above*), factory owner William Hesketh Lever built Port Sunlight (*right*) for his workers – a village of attractive houses fronted by unfenced garden plots

PORT OF LONDON AUTHORITY

• Founded 1908

After a critical Royal Commission report in 1902, parliament created the Port of London Authority (PLA) to control the proliferating dock companies competing for trade along the tidal reaches of the Thames, and also to promote the authority as a commercial concern.

The modern PLA is a self-financing public trust, responsible for the 95 miles from Teddington to the outer estuary, including the riverbed and foreshore. It is responsible for dredging the river to keep it navigable and oxygenating the water to encourage river life, and has steadily reduced pollution levels.

It supplies pilots, navigation and harbour services for visiting ships, sets buoys and licenses everything from moorings to 'mudlarks' – people who search the shores with metal detectors.

PORTSMOUTH

• Hampshire (p.495 G6)   • Pop. 174 690

Its strategic position on the narrow peninsular of Portsea Island, with major harbours to the east and west, has made Portsmouth the most important English naval port since Tudor times.

The city was granted a charter in 1194 by Richard I, and established as a naval dockyard in 1540 by Henry VIII – a role it has retained ever since.

The city, whose famous natives include Charles Dickens and the engineer Isambard Kingdom Brunel, has an old town of narrow streets and also includes the resort and beaches of Southsea.

Its vast naval base has Portsmouth's principal tourist attractions – HMS *VICTORY*, the ship on which Lord NELSON died in 1805 at the Battle of Trafalgar, and Henry VIII's warship the *MARY ROSE*, which sank off Portsmouth in 1545. Its wreck was raised in 1982, restored and put on display.

POSTAL SYSTEM

More than 6 billion first-class, and 10 billion second-class letters are posted in Britain every year. The now vast and complex operation began with a public service established by Charles I in 1635.

For the first 150 years, letters were delivered between 'posts' by boys on horseback. Then, from 1784, the first mail coach service plied up and down between Bristol and London via Bath.

Uniformed letter-carriers, dubbed 'postmen', first appeared on London streets in 1793; in 1830 the new Manchester-Liverpool rail service began to carry mail. Postage was paid

PILLAR BOX RED Pillar boxes were painted green until 1874 when they were standardised as red

by the recipient of mail until 1840, when the world's first postage stamps – the Penny Black and the Twopenny Blue – were introduced.

Senders took their letters to receiving houses until the early 1850s. In 1852, at the suggestion of the novelist Anthony Trollope who worked for the Post Office, four roadside pillar boxes were set up in St Helier, Jersey, and were introduced throughout Britain from 1853.

Since 1927, mail has been shuttled across London on underground rail tracks. The Post Office Underground Railway, rechristened Mail Rail in 1987, has 50 computerised trains on 23 miles of track, carrying more than 6 million bags of mail each year.

Airmail got off to a flying start on June 14, 1919, when ALCOCK AND BROWN carried 96 letters with them on the first non-stop flight across the Atlantic Ocean.

More than 790 million international letters a year are now posted from Britain. The Post Office, a government department until nationalisation in 1969, now includes Royal Mail Letters, Post Office Counters and Parcelforce.

SORTED In 1998, Royal Mail invested £200 million in high-tech machinery to enable more than 4 million letters to be sorted per hour across the nation

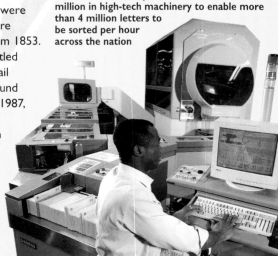

PORT SUNLIGHT...POSTAL SYSTEM...POSTCODES...POTTER...POTTERY AND PORCELAIN...POWELL AND PRESSBURGER...POWER...POWIS CASTLE

349

PORT SUNLIGHT

• Wirral (p.496 A5)   • Pop. 3020

When the Victorian soap-maker
William Hesketh Lever founded his
factory at Port Sunlight in 1888, he
was enlightened enough to build a
garden village to house workers.

It still survives, its layout and
character little changed since it
was completed in 1914, though
residency is no longer restricted to
company workers or pensioners.

The landscaping of the village
includes a curved valley called the
Dell, dotted with trees and flower-
beds and spanned by a saddle-backed
stone bridge. For 18 months, Lever –
later 1st viscount Leverhulme – lived in
Bridge Cottage, one of the larger homes.

He created the Lady Lever Art Gallery
in memory of his wife, who died in
1913. It is noted for its 18th-century and
Pre-Raphaelite paintings. A heritage
centre tells the story of the village.

POSTAL SYSTEM: *see opposite page*

POSTCODES

In the 19th century London grew so
large that the Post Office could no longer
treat it as one area. In 1857 Rowland
Hill, who designed the first stamp,
divided the capital into ten postal
districts, coded by location – W = West;
SE = South-east, for example – and gave
each its own sorting office.

By 1912 the cities of Liverpool,
Manchester, Sheffield and Dublin had
followed suit. But London continued to
grow, and during the First World War
the Post Office had to subdivide the
original postal areas into 77 numbered
districts such as W1, E3 or N6.

In the 1950s, mechanised mail-sorting
demanded more sophisticated coding,
and in 1959 Norwich was chosen for
coding experiments. Its system proved
successful, and by 1974 the whole of
Britain had been allocated postcodes;
there are now around 1.8 million codes.
Foreign consultants declared it the
world's best postcode system but the
public had to be persuaded to use it.
Luckily, by the 1990s more than 70 per
cent of all mail posted had the correct
postcode address.

Beatrix POTTER

• Author and illustrator   • 1866-1943

Beatrix Potter attributed her originality to
never having gone to school. Educated
by governesses, she taught herself
drawing and painting – skills that she
later used to embellish her whimsical
books about the highly anthropomorphic
lives of little animals.

The Tale of Peter Rabbit, recounting
the mishaps of naughty Peter and his
well-behaved sisters, Flopsy, Mopsy and
Cottontail, was published with Potter's
illustrations in 1901, at her own expense.
Her other books include *The Tailor of
Gloucester* (1902), *The Tale of Squirrel
Nutkin* (1903), *The Tale of Tom Kitten*
(1907) and *The Tale of Jemima Puddle-
Duck* (1908).

Potter devoted her last 30 years to
countryside conservation and left
1620ha (4000 acres) in the Lake
District to the National Trust.

POTTERY AND PORCELAIN:
see page 350

POWELL AND PRESSBURGER

• Film-makers
• Emeric Pressburger 1902-88
• Michael Powell 1905-90

The 19 films Powell and
Pressburger made from
1939 to 1957 were
among the most
influential and
daring in British
cinema history.

UP TO HIS EARS Mischievous Peter
Rabbit – in trouble again – was one of
Beatrix Potter's earliest creations. The
character first appeared in 1893 in an
illustrated letter to a governess's son

Rejecting realism, they explored
the realms of fantasy, dreams,
emotions and the inner life. *A
Matter of Life and Death* (1946) was
set inside the mind of the central
character, played by David Niven.

Their other films include *The
Life and Death of Colonel Blimp*
(1943), starring Roger Livesey;
Black Narcissus (1947), a daring
treatment of a nun's passion;
and *The Red Shoes* (1948).

After the partnership broke up, Powell
struck out alone with *Peeping Tom* (1960)
– condemned for bad taste at the time
but later applauded for its realistic
commentary on the voyeurism of film.

POWER: *see page 352*

POWIS CASTLE

• Powys (p.494 D2)
• Built 16th-17th century   • NT

A Welsh prince built the earliest fortress
high on a crag above the Severn valley
around 1200. The present dramatic
castle in rose-pink limestone was built
later, and in 1587 became the home of
the Herbert family.

They embellished the
exterior with mock-military
towers and battlements, and
built the Long Gallery with its
fine plaster ceiling. In 1784
Lord Clive – the son of Clive
of India – married into the
family, and the Clives
enriched the castle with
paintings, furniture and
treasures from India.

The castle's four Italianate
terraces are part of one of
Britain's finest 17th-century
formal gardens. They drop
in steep steps adorned with
shrubs and classical statuary,
then descend a grassy bank
to a broad lawn.

**DANCE CLASSIC Moira Shearer
starred as a love-torn ballerina
in *The Red Shoes*, filmed by
Powell and Pressburger**

THE POTTER'S ART

Inspired by pieces imported from China, the potters of 17th-century Europe were busily experimenting in a bid to discover the secret of porcelain. Caught up in this creative wave, Britain's craftsmen were soon employing the unique variety of native clays to produce innovative pottery and, later, china

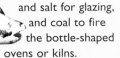

THE FIRST British attempts to produce quality ceramics began in the 1600s as potters in London began to make 'delft' – tin-glazed earthenware – imitating a technique used in the Netherlands.

Their market was the middle classes who wanted something resembling the exquisite but costly porcelain from China, which Europeans were as yet unable to replicate. Though relatively thick and opaque, the blue-and-white delftware became popular and potteries were opened in Bristol, Dublin, Glasgow, Liverpool and Wincanton.

Stoneware, originally imported from Germany, was made in England by the late 1600s in Staffordshire and London. The pottery was fired at a high temperature and the wares were then glazed by means of salt thrown into the kiln at its hottest, resulting in an 'orange peel' texture to the surface.

From the 1640s lead-glazed earthenware, decorated with liquid clay or 'slip', was made at many centres including Bristol, Devon and Staffordshire, which by the first half of the 18th century had established itself as the centre of the British ceramics industry. This was due to the fortuitous combination of local clay deposits suitable for pottery making, lead

PÂTE-SUR-PÂTE VASE
The decorative piece (c.1893) was designed at Minton by French artist Louis Solon

COW CREAMER
Lowestoft (1757-1802) specialised in simple soft-paste china tableware

and salt for glazing, and coal to fire the bottle-shaped ovens or kilns.

From the 1720s flint was introduced into the clay body to produce stronger ware. This was combined with white clay, transported to Staffordshire from Devon by sea, river and packhorse, to form both the white salt-glazed stoneware and the lead-glazed creamwares and pearlwares.

GREAT STAFFORDSHIRE NAMES

Thomas Whieldon, one of the most respected of the mid-18th century potters, made both ornamental and useful wares, including figures, toys, snuff boxes and tea services. Josiah SPODE was apprenticed to Whieldon and Josiah WEDGWOOD was his partner for five years. In the 1760s and 1770s Wedgwood introduced new stonewares – the unglazed black basaltes and jasper ware.

By the late 18th century large numbers of figures were being made. Several members of the Wood family, including Ralph, Enoch and John, made fine models in pearlware from the 1770s including superb examples of that peculiarly British vessel, the Toby jug.

From the 1750s, both pottery and porcelain could be decorated with

DRINKING MAN The Staffordshire Toby jug was named either after Shakespeare's character Sir Toby Belch or after a famed Yorkshire toper, featured as Toby Fillpot in the song 'The Brown Jug'

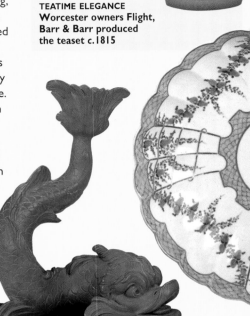

TEATIME ELEGANCE
Worcester owners Flight, Barr & Barr produced the teaset c.1815

ORNAMENTAL CANDLESTICK
The basalt and rosso antico candlestick was made around 1820 by Josiah Wedgwood II

printed designs by taking a paper print from inked and engraved copper plates, then pressing it onto the surface of the pottery – a method still used at Spode.

ENGLISH POTTERS INVENT BONE CHINA

It was also in the mid 18th century that factories across the country began to produce the first English porcelain, made from a soft translucent paste. The Bow factory in London was the first to introduce large quantities of bone to soft paste porcelain but it was not until the late 1790s, at the Spode factory in Staffordshire, that bone ash was used to produce the first commercially successful British porcelain, bone china.

Authentic hard paste porcelain, first produced in Europe in 1710 at Meissen in Germany, required the use of china clay and china stone – also called kaolin – found in abundance in Cornwall, and first used in Plymouth around 1768.

GOLD-GROUND SAUCER
Robert Chamberlain's
Worcester, c.1800, was
outstanding for its beauty

COFFEE POT The
piece was made
by Whieldon or
Wedgwood c.1760

STAFFORDSHIRE TEAPOT
The salt glaze used on
the teapot,
c.1755, has
created its
typically pitted
appearance

BRILLIANT BIRDS
Staffordshire potter
George Jones
produced the finely
painted bone china
dessert plate, part
of a set, c.1887

FUDDLING CUP
Made in Bristol
or London c.1740,
such a piece was
used to challenge
drinkers not to spill
the contents of its cups

EARLY WORCESTER
The fluted saucer-dish,
c.1770 is transfer printed
with a hop trellis design

TRAGIC LOVE DEPICTED ON A PLATE

The Chinese imagery of the blue-and-white willow pattern is possibly the best known of all ceramic decorations. Imitative of the oriental designs that were hugely popular in the 18th century, it is thought to have been first produced by Thomas Minton in about 1780 for Caughley in Shropshire.

The essential components are a stylised willow tree, a Chinese temple, a bridge with figures on it, a boat and a distant island. The pattern was often fancifully interpreted as a tragic tale of doomed young love and grew ever more elaborate as it was taken up by other factories including Davenport, Wedgwood and Spode in Staffordshire. At the height of its popularity, the pattern was even copied in China and exported back to Europe.

Other porcelain factories of the 18th century included Bristol; the Salopian Porcelain Manufactory at Caughley Shropshire; Chelsea, London; Derby; Longton Hall, Staffordshire; Liverpool; Lowestoft and Worcester. Most factories favoured the oriental blue-and-white style of decoration, and each had its own secret recipe for its porcelain.

By 1775 the London factories of Chelsea and Bow had been acquired by William Duesbury, who took the moulds and tools to his Derby factory, which continues today as the Royal Crown Derby Porcelain Company. Other 18th-century names that continue to flourish include Worcester, Minton and Spode.

ORNAMENTATION GOES WILD

Stone china – a hard white earthenware – caught the public imagination in the early 1800s. The best known was Mason's Patent Ironstone China with strong bright colours in oriental designs, which was made into durable tableware, vases, fire surrounds and even bed posts. Styles changed in the early Victorian period prompting new, often overly ornate patterns.

Multicolour transfer printing was developed in the 1840s, while companies such as Minton made Italian-style Majolica wares, tiles, marble-like Parian ware and ceramic monstrosities, including fountains and a complete staircase.

MODERNIST STYLES TO REFLECT A NEW ERA

The 20th century brought a revolution in production methods and increased productivity but the industry is still largely dependent on individual craft skills. Traditional styles remain popular but a succession of new designers have made their mark. Clarice CLIFF expressed the exuberance of the 1920s Jazz Age. Susie Cooper dominated the 1930s with her clean-cut modernism, joining forces with Wedgwood in 1966. Her pieces and those of postwar designers such as Janice Tchalenko and Terence CONRAN are already eminently collectable.

20TH-CENTURY STYLE
Produced for the Designers'
Guild in 1986, the Dartington
vase (left) was made to a
design by Janice Tchalenko. The
modern Wedgwood teapot is
a reproduction of a 1930s Susie
Cooper style

PLUGGED IN

At the flick of a switch energy pours into our homes, factories and offices, generated by huge power stations and distributed through a complex supply grid. British ingenuity over 150 years has made this possible, from the discovery of electricity to the harnessing of the wind and sun for power

WE TAKE IT for granted that electrical power is always available, and that a device that works in one house will work just as well in another. Yet for a century after Michael FARADAY first demonstrated in 1831 how magnetic forces could be converted into electric current this was not the case.

INITIAL SPARK
The first practical application of the new power came in 1858 when a small steam-powered generator provided electricity for an arc lamp at South Foreland lighthouse in Kent.

The next step forward came in the 1870s with the invention by Joseph SWAN in Britain and Thomas Edison in America of the light bulb. Its use in street lighting demanded something far bigger than a lighthouse generator: it called for a power station. The first in the world was built in 1882 at Holborn Viaduct in London.

Two engineers – Sebastian Ferranti and Charles Parsons – brought together the elements for the mass-generation of power. Ferranti argued the case for big power stations serving wide areas. He designed such a plant at Deptford for the London Electric Supply Corporation, founded in 1887 with what was then the huge capital of £1 million. The plant was powered by the steam turbine, perfected by Parsons in 1884 at his Newcastle works. The turbine still dominates the generating industry today.

CURRENT DEBATE
By the beginning of the 20th century, everyone could see the importance of electricity for lighting, heating and powering machinery, but no one could agree on how it was to be supplied and who would supply it. Some favoured

alternating current (AC) supply – the type we have in our homes today – others direct current (DC), the electricity we usually get from batteries. And suppliers produced different voltages. In London alone in 1917 there

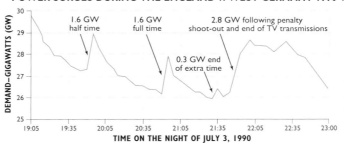

POWER SURGES DURING THE ENGLAND v. WEST GERMANY 1990 WORLD CUP SEMI-FINAL

1.6 GW half time

1.6 GW full time

2.8 GW following penalty shoot-out and end of TV transmissions

0.3 GW end of extra time

DEMAND–GIGAWATTS (GW)

TIME ON THE NIGHT OF JULY 3, 1990

When the English football team was knocked out of the 1990 World Cup just after 9.30 pm on July 3, 1990, millions of people turned from television to kettle and light switch, causing a massive power surge of 2.8 gigawatts

were 70 generating stations, using 50 different systems. Some rich people even had personal power plants, a few of which have survived. Charles Parsons had one at Cragside, his country house in Northumberland, and the writer Rudyard Kipling had a hydroelectric plant at Bateman's, his home in East Sussex.

Into this confusion stepped the Central Electricity Board, established by the government in 1926, with the duty of setting up a 'national grid' of electricity supply. The system brought high-voltage electricity from the power station, stepped down through secondary transmitters and sub-stations until it reached the customer at a comparatively low voltage. This final supply was not standardised at 240 volts AC until 1946.

NEW FUELS
At this time, nearly all power stations were using coal to raise steam to drive turbines, apart from a few hydroelectric schemes in Scotland and Wales, where water was abundant. Then, in 1956, the first nuclear power station, Calder Hall

in Cumbria, began to feed power into the grid. Today, coal-fired stations and gas-fired stations each provide just over a third of Britain's power, and nuclear energy, making a contribution of more than a quarter, supplies the rest.

ALTERNATIVE SOURCES
Fossil fuel power stations are a major source of greenhouse gases, and nuclear power creates radioactive waste. But there are alternatives: more than 40 British wind farms produce enough electricity for 200 000 homes, and wave power and solar energy have been harnessed. In 1998 the government pledged to provide 10 per cent of Britain's power from renewable sources.

WIND AND FIRE The 103 turbines of the Llandinam wind farm in Powys (*above*) produce up to 31 megawatts. The coal and gas-fired Didcot A power station (*left*), with six 99 m (325 ft) high cooling towers, has a capacity of 2000 megawatts

PREHISTORIC BRITAIN: *see page 354*

PREMIUM BONDS

In 1956 premium bonds were introduced by Harold Macmillan, the chancellor of the exchequer, to raise government capital. The bonds accrued no interest but were entered into a weekly draw, with prizes of up to £1000.

Now investors can hold a maximum of 20 000 bonds in £1 units, with tax-free prizes ranging from £50 to £1 million. One bond in every 24 000 wins a prize each month, when there are more than 500 000 prizes, which add up to a total in excess of £30 million.

The winning numbers are selected by ERNIE – Electronic Random Number Indicator Equipment – a device that cannot hold information on numbers or bond holders. Some £4 billion has been distributed since the scheme began.

PRE-RAPHAELITE BROTHERHOOD

The mysterious initials 'PRB' appeared on three canvases at the Royal Academy summer exhibition in 1849. The letters stood for 'Pre-Raphaelite Brotherhood' and portended an artistic revolution that looked back to the Middle Ages but also portrayed social issues such as emigration and industrial life.

Formed in September 1848, the Brotherhood had three leading members: William Holman Hunt, John Everett Millais and Dante Gabriel Rossetti, son of an Italian revolutionary. Fired by the critic John RUSKIN's book *Modern Painters* (1843) they rejected art as taught by the Royal Academy as repetitive, vulgar and frivolous, and looked instead to Italian art before Raphael (1483-1520), then considered the most perfect artist but whose work they considered insincere.

In 1850 the Brotherhood published *The Germ*, a literary and artistic magazine. Its failure, and the secretiveness of the PRB, invited

criticism. The novelist Charles Dickens described the young Christ in Millais' *Christ in the House of His Parents* (1850) as 'a hideous, wry-necked, blubbering, red-headed boy, in a bed gown'.

BROTHERS NO MORE

The movement soon disintegrated. Millais broke the circle by becoming an associate member of the Royal Academy in 1853. Hunt left for Palestine in search of backgrounds for his biblical paintings.

Rossetti continued to use the Pre-Raphaelite name, painting dreamy medieval scenes such as *The Tune of the Seven Towers* (1857). Among his disciples were the young artists William MORRIS and Edward BURNE-JONES, whose designs and paintings perpetuated the neomedievalism of the Pre-Raphaelites almost into the 20th century.

MAIN COLLECTIONS • Ashmolean Museum, Oxford • Birmingham City Art Gallery • Manchester City Art Gallery • Tate Gallery, London • Walker Art Gallery, Liverpool

WATERY GRAVE Elizabeth Siddal, Dante Rossetti's lover, posed fully clothed in a bath for *Ophelia* (1852), painted by the Pre-Raphaelite John Everett Millais

PRESS GANGS

As the ROYAL NAVY expanded from the mid 17th century to support Britain's trading and territorial ambitions abroad, the shortfall of recruits was made up through increasingly desperate methods. These included bribery, conscription of prisoners and, most notorious of all, the press gang – a band of armed sailors that went ashore to 'impress', or force, unsuspecting young men into service. Their methods ranged from painting unrealistic pictures of navy life to violent kidnapping. Although use of the press

gang declined after the Napoleonic Wars of the early 1800s, only when seamen were given proper contracts of service in 1853 did it finally become redundant.

PRESTON NORTH END FC

• **Founded 1881**

Preston North End football club was a founding member of the Football League in 1888 and within two years had won the first two league championships and an FA Cup. It is the only founder to play at its original ground, Deepdale, now the site of a new national football museum.

Tom Finney, one of football's most versatile forwards, spent his entire career from 1946 to 1960 at North End, scoring 187 goals in 433 games, and 30 goals in 76 games for England.

J.B. PRIESTLEY

• **Writer** • **1894-1984; OM 1977**

'I may not be a genius, but I've got a hell of a lot of talent,' John Boynton Priestley once asserted. He wrote more than 100 novels, plays and essays, and gave hundreds of radio talks attracting up to 20 million listeners.

Priestley was born in Bradford, served in the First World War and studied at Cambridge University. His journalism and criticism after 1922 reflected his interest in the idea of 'Englishness', and included studies of English humour and fiction.

Rollicking novels, such as *The Good Companions* (1929) about an acting troupe's cross-country journey, brought Priestley popularity but were tempered with studies of a nation in the grip of the Depression, as in the city-by-city account *English Journey* (1934).

In plays, such as the psychological dramas *Dangerous Corner* (1932) and *An Inspector Calls* (1947), Priestley was concerned with the enigma of time and the strange workings of the mind. He also wrote more light-hearted domestic comedies, including *Laburnum Grove* (1933) and *When We Are Married* (1938), and several volumes of autobiography.

ANCESTRAL LANDS

We know the earliest Britons not through written records but through their archaeological remains. Standing stones and ceremonial sites provide enigmatic clues to their ancient way of life

I N PALAEOLITHIC TIMES Britain's earliest human visitors were migratory hunters whose remains have been discovered at sites such as BOXGROVE and SWANSCOMBE. But a series of ICE AGES rendered most of the country uninhabitable until about 8000 BC when temperatures began to improve. Trees recolonised the tundra and life returned, and by about 6000 BC Mesolithic hunter-gatherers inhabited the wooded island of Britain, leaving scattered traces of their nomadic lifestyle at Star Carr in Yorkshire and Gough's Cave in CHEDDAR GORGE in Somerset.

THE FIRST FARMERS

One of the earliest known farming settlements appeared in Britain around 3500 BC at Windmill Hill. Over the next 2000 years, the hunters turned to large-scale agriculture, clearing forests, cultivating cereals and herding cattle, sheep and pigs. Settlements were still largely impermanent – the remains of permanent houses at SKARA BRAE on Orkney are unusual for this period.

Collective burials – chambered tombs such as MAES HOWE and WEST KENNET LONG BARROW – suggest the strong ties that existed between the living and their ancestors.

CALLANISH Four standing stone avenues lead to this stone circle, which contains the remains of a chambered tomb

SKARA BRAE A distinctive feature of the prehistoric houses at Skara Brae on Orkney is a stone 'dresser' – possibly used for storage – situated behind a central hearth (above). The ten houses are linked by stone passageways

MAES HOWE A 9 m (30 ft) passageway (above) leads into a tomb with three side chambers and a vaulted roof. At the winter solstice, the setting sun shines down the passageway into the main chamber. Outside, the tomb is covered with turf (below, right)

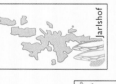

JARLSHOF Inside the wheelhouses (below), late Bronze Age stone implements for grinding grain were discovered, their ends worn away through use (left)

Callanish

Jarlshof

Skara Brae

Maes Howe

THROUGH THE AGES

PALAEOLITHIC *(Old Stone Age) Before 8000 BC Climate fluctuating between temperate and polar. Britain joined to the European mainland, but only visited by hunter-gatherer bands in warmer periods. Glaciers intermittently cover all but the far south*

MESOLITHIC *(Middle Stone Age) 8000–4000 BC English Channel forms as ice cap melts back into the oceans. Trees recolonise the tundra and hunter-gatherer bands return*

NEOLITHIC *(New Stone Age) 4000–2000 BC Forest clearances and the beginnings of farming appear. Life is still mainly nomadic. Communal burial mounds and stone circles are erected*

BRONZE AGE 2000–700 BC *Metalwork is introduced, forest clearance continues and permanent settlements appear. The population rises and society becomes more complex. Individual burials are more prevalent*

IRON AGE 700 BC–AD 43 *Introduction of iron improves weaponry and tools. Hillforts of increasing size are built. The Romans invade Britain in AD 43*

——— *Prehistoric trackway*

——— *Modern long-distance route*

NOTE: The dates of prehistoric ages and monuments are approximate. The map shows the date of the main activity at a site

SIGNS OF THE TIMES

Permanent settlements slowly began to appear, and a more complex Neolithic society left its mark on the landscape. The purpose of monuments such as STONEHENGE, CASTLERIGG stone circle and SILBURY HILL – one of the many prehistoric monuments near AVEBURY in Wiltshire – cannot be known for sure, but they may have been used for meetings or ceremonies, or to celebrate the changing of the seasons.

A GRADUAL TRANSFORMATION

The introduction of metalwork to Britain around 2000 BC boosted craftsmanship and trade – the exchange of fine bronzework may have been an expression of political power. The culture we refer to as the Bronze Age constructed community settlements such as Grimspound in Devon, but individual burials suggest an increasingly hierarchical society, which may have encouraged rivalries. By 1000 BC, boundaries of earth and timber fences straddled the countryside.

The process of land division continued, and well-defended roundtower farmsteads, or brochs, were constructed in some areas. Monumental hill-forts such as MAIDEN CASTLE mark the final stage of prehistory. In AD 43 the Romans invaded Britain, establishing roads, towns and their own gods and cultural life, which transformed the country.

STAR CARR A sickle or hide-scraper (far left) and barbed bone spear tips (left) were found in a temporary Mesolithic hunter-gatherer settlement in the Vale of Pickering

WEST KENNET LONG BARROW At least 46 people were buried in the barrow at West Kennet. Inside, a passageway with side chambers leads to a larger, central chamber

CASTLERIGG STONE CIRCLE The small rectangle of stones in the centre of this Cumbrian monument – a feature unique to this circle – has never been explained

GRIME'S GRAVES Prehistoric mines (right) in use during the late Neolithic and early Bronze Age provided tons of flint for knapping. A goddess figure (far right) was discovered in a shaft where the flint had run out

LINDOW MAN Scientists dated the body of a man preserved in a peat bog at Lindow Moss in Cheshire to the late Iron Age or soon after the Roman occupation. He had been garrotted and drowned, indicating that he may have been a victim of ritual sacrifice

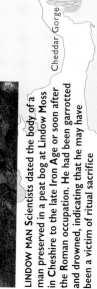

MAIDEN CASTLE This well-defended Iron Age fort in Dorset (below) is built on the site of an earlier Neolithic camp

Castlerigg
Lindow Moss
Star Carr
Grime's Graves
Swanscombe
North Downs Way
Boxgrove
Ridgeway
Windmill Hill
Avebury
Stonehenge
Silbury Hill
West Kennet
Cheddar Gorge
Maiden Castle
Grimspound

Joseph PRIESTLEY

• Scientist • 1733-1804

When the Yorkshire-born Presbyterian minister-turned-scientist Joseph Priestley heated mercuric oxide he found a gas was liberated that made a candle burn more brightly. This gas was oxygen, a discovery that Priestley shared with other scientists.

A meeting with the American physicist Benjamin Franklin in the 1760s led Priestley into science. In 1794 he left London to settle in America, having been driven out of his house in Birmingham by a mob three years earlier for his support of the French Revolution.

Priestley also coined the name 'rubber' for the elastic material found in a tropical tree. He did so only for the banal reason that it could erase pencil marks by rubbing.

PRINCES IN THE TOWER

• Edward V; 1470-83
• Richard, duke of York; 1473-83

The fate of Edward V and his brother Richard is a mystery. Edward, son of EDWARD IV and Elizabeth Woodville, succeeded to the throne in April 1483, aged 12. His uncle, Richard, duke of Gloucester, seized first Edward and then Richard, confining them to the Tower of London. Gloucester made himself Lord Protector and postponed the coronation.

In June, Gloucester intimated that the princes were illegitimate. Parliament urged him to take the throne and he was crowned RICHARD III in July. The princes were never seen again.

When Henry Tudor (Henry VII) took the throne in 1485, he encouraged the story that Richard had had the princes killed. In 1674 the bones of two young boys were found in the Tower and buried as those of Edward V and Richard of York in Westminster Abbey .

PRINCESS ROYAL

The title Princess Royal, the highest honour that can be bestowed on a female member of the royal family, is a non-hereditary gift of the monarch to his

PRINCE OF WALES

'I shall give you a prince who speaks no English', declared Edward I to the conquered Welsh, and made his baby son, later Edward II, Prince of Wales. Or so the story goes. In fact, Prince Edward was 17 when invested with the title in 1301. The previous Prince of Wales, the last Welsh ruler to use the title, had been Llywelyn ap Gruffydd, killed in battle in 1282. Ever since, the title has been conferred on the English monarch's eldest son. Only Owain GLYNDWR reclaimed the title for Wales when rising against the English in 1404.

The prince has at times focused opposition to a monarch, notably when George, later Prince Regent, quarrelled with his father, George III, and set up a rival court at Brighton and Carlton House, London.

FEATHERS IN THE CAP
The motto 'Ich dien' on the Prince of Wales' emblem means 'I serve'

CROWNING MOMENT Prince Charles was invested as Prince of Wales by his mother Elizabeth II at Caernarfon Castle in 1969

or her eldest daughter. It was first conferred by Charles I on his daughter Mary and was revived by George II for his daughter Anne, and then by Queen Victoria, Edward VII and George V.

In 1987 ELIZABETH II conferred the title on her only daughter, Anne, the present Princess Royal and eighth in line to the throne of Britain. Anne had excelled as a sportswoman, competing in the Montreal Olympics in 1976 as a member of the British three-day event team, and as an active patron of a number of charities, including the presidency of the Save the Children

Fund. Princess Anne's marriage to Mark Phillips, an army captain, ended in 1992, and shortly after she married Tim Laurence, a naval commander.

PRISONS

Britain has more than 140 prisons and just over 20 establishments for young offenders. And yet, until 19th-century reforms established a national penal system, offenders were more likely to be fined, executed, put on a prison hulk or transported than be sent to prison.

In 1166 HENRY II introduced a circuit of county courts, which required jails, often in the local castle, to hold suspects until trial by a royal justice. In London, prisons such as Fleet, Marshalsea and Newgate were built from the 12th to 14th centuries to hold state prisoners and debtors. By the 17th century petty offenders were being locked up in houses of correction, with a fierce regime of hard labour.

Two prison reformers, John Howard and the Quaker Elizabeth FRY, fought to change the chaotic system. In 1777 Howard reported on the appalling sanitation and rampant disease in prisons, and on the practice of jailers charging prisoners for bedding, food and water. As a result wages for jailers and better conditions were introduced. Fry agitated for single-sex prisons and shortly after her death in 1845 a prison for women was built in London at Holloway, one of the many Victorian jails, such as Pentonville and Strangeways, still in use.

PRIVATE EYE

• Founded 1961

Started as a scruffy, impertinent rag by half a dozen Oxford and Cambridge university graduates, including Paul Foot, Christopher Booker, Richard Ingrams and Willie Rushton, the satirical magazine *Private Eye* has lampooned British politics and society for four decades and remains a popular publication. National newspapers have habitually aped its nicknames and slang, such as 'hacks' for journalists, 'Lord Gnome' for newspaper owners, or 'my learned friends' for lawyers.

The *Eye* thrived in the satire boom of the early 1960s, and survived many near-ruinous libel actions. Contributors have included writers Christopher Logue, Barry Humphries and Auberon Waugh, and cartoonists Nicholas Garland, Gerald Scarfe and Ralph Steadman.

Ian Hislop, who took over from Richard Ingrams as editor in 1986, has maintained the *Eye*'s irreverent tone, portraying Tony Blair as the oily vicar of St Albion, and achieved a fortnightly circulation of up to 180 000.

PRIVY COUNCIL

There are more than 400 Privy Council members, including archbishops, judges and ambassadors. Once the monarch's closest advisers, they now have a largely symbolic role, assembling in full council only for the proclamation of a monarch's death or marriage.

Medieval monarchs ruled with the help of a 'great council' of England's most powerful subjects. It grew too large and in the 1530s was replaced by a Privy Council of around 20, which for nearly a hundred years administered the State. When the Privy Council itself became too big, Charles II resorted to a 'cabal' of close advisers. Under Anne this cabal became known as the CABINET.

The lord president of the council is still a Cabinet member, and the council's judicial committee acts as a court of appeal for dependent British territories, the Isle of Man and the Channel Islands.

PROFUMO AFFAIR

In the early 1960s the secret service hit on a plan to compromise Yevgeny Ivanov, the Soviet assistant naval attaché to Britain, who was involved with a call-girl, Christine Keeler. The plan ran into trouble when it was discovered that she was also the mistress of John Profumo,

LAST NIGHT FEVER At Proms concerts a section of the audience is allowed to stand. Some promenaders queue all night for the privilege of getting a spot in front of the stage

secretary of state for war. Profumo denied the liaison in the House of Commons but resigned in 1963 when the truth emerged, contributing to the downfall of the Conservative government of Harold MACMILLAN.

Profumo quit politics to devote himself to charitable works, for which he was awarded the CBE in 1975. The greater victim of the case was Dr Stephen Ward, in whose flat Keeler lived with another call-girl, Mandy Rice-Davies. Ward was arrested and tried on trumped-up charges of living from immoral earnings. Faced with ruin, he committed suicide.

PROFUMO FALL-OUT The 18-year-old Mandy Rice-Davies (*above*) leaves the Old Bailey in July 1963 after giving evidence in the trial of Stephen Ward. Five months later Christine Keeler (*left*) was jailed for perjury

The PROMS

• **Royal Albert Hall, Central London (p.499 A3)**
• **July-September**

The BBC Henry Wood Promenade Concerts – the Proms for short – are one of the world's most popular music festivals, running nightly for two months. Most concerts are performed by BBC orchestras, though soloists and groups from around the world also appear every year. In the 100th season in 1994, 240 000 people attended 72 concerts at the rate of nearly 3500 a night.

The Proms were founded in 1895 by the conductor Henry WOOD and the impresario Robert Newman. Then, as now, both classics and new works were performed.

The BBC became sponsors in 1927, and the Albert Hall was adopted after the Queen's Hall was bombed in 1941. Malcolm SARGENT became principal conductor in 1950 and introduced the patriotic tone of the Last Night.

PUBLIC RECORD OFFICE

• **Kew, SW London (p.498 B4)** • **Est. 1838**

The Domesday Book, Guy Fawkes's confession and Napoleon's post-mortem results can all be consulted in the Public Record Office (PRO), the official archive for the United Kingdom.

Until the 19th century more than 200 sites, including the Tower of London and Westminster Abbey, were used to store records. Parliament acted to centralise the storage of documents in 1838, and the Rolls Chapel in Chancery Lane, where the Rolls, or records, of the central courts of law were kept, became the first collective repository for public records.

In 1977 they were moved to Kew. The PRO has 90 miles of shelving and 89 000 visitors a year, who can examine records dating from the 11th century. After a 30 year embargo, most government files can be read.

FOR RICHER OR POORER Most pupils at Christ's Hospital in Sussex, founded in 1552 by Edward VI as a school for the London poor, do not come from privileged backgrounds. Parents pay only what they can afford or no fees at all

PUBLIC SCHOOLS

Britain's first public school, Winchester College, was founded in 1382 to feed students into New College, Oxford. Unlike schools attached to churches, monasteries or hospitals, Winchester was self-governing. It employed a warden, ten fellows, two schoolmasters and three chaplains. Out of some 100 pupils, almost three-quarters received free tuition.

Other schools followed, ETON in 1440 offering free instruction in 'the rudiments of grammar' to anyone except 'bastards' and the 'unfree'. Standards –

always variable – reached a low point in the early 19th century when the schools were doing little more than teaching Latin and Greek to the sons of the rich.

In 1828 Thomas ARNOLD, headmaster of Rugby, imposed religious observance, a modern curriculum, and a prefect system to maintain discipline. Arnold's regime was copied by both established public schools and new ones set up to educate the children of the growing business and professional classes.

There are now some 2500 public schools in Britain – about 10 per cent of the total – charging up to £5000 a term.

THE OLD SCHOOL TIE

Traditionally an education at an elite public school such as Eton or Harrow has eased the passage to a position of power and influence in government, judiciary, church or armed forces. Of Britain's 51 prime ministers, 38 went to public school – 18 to Eton, 7 to Harrow. In the Labour-filled parliament of 1997, 30 per cent of MPs were public school old boys, three times the 10 per cent national average.

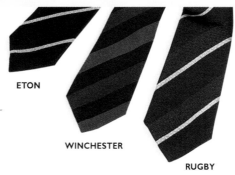

ETON / WINCHESTER / RUGBY / HARROW / FETTES / CHARTERHOUSE

PUBS: *see opposite page*

A.W.N. PUGIN

• Architect and designer • 1812-52

A fanatical Roman Catholic convert, Augustus Welby Northmore Pugin had a vision of English life very different from the factories and slums of the industrial age into which he was born. His passion was for an idyllic medieval past, which he revealed in his book *Contrasts* published in 1836.

Working in his father's drawing office instilled in Pugin a reverence for the Gothic style, particularly the high Gothic of late 13th-century churches. He was the first GOTHIC REVIVAL architect to realise the level of craftsmanship in carving, glass and metalwork needed to achieve its intricate detail. Few big

BACK TO GOTHIC Pugin took six years to create the lavish interior of St Giles's Church in Cheadle

commissions came his way, but his visionary imagination ran riot in a series of Gothic churches, including Nottingham Cathedral (1841) and St Augustine's, Ramsgate (1846), with their vividly decorated interiors. His patron for a great deal of this work was the 16th earl of Shrewsbury, who employed Pugin on the chapel and great hall of ALTON TOWERS.

Charles Barry's plans for the HOUSES OF PARLIAMENT gave Pugin his greatest challenge. He designed the whole interior, from stained glass, furniture and wallpapers, to hatstands and inkwells.

Pugin's stormy personal life included being shipwrecked and losing two of his three wives within 12 years. In 1852, his health failing, he spent some time in an asylum: he died shortly afterwards of a stroke at his house in Ramsgate.

PUNCH

Jokes from the pages of *Punch*, such as the obsequious curate pronouncing his egg 'good in parts', or Mr Punch's advice on marriage ('Don't'), have become part of British culture. But *Punch*, founded in 1841, was a radical as well as a satirical journal under its first editor, Mark Lemon. A co-founder was Henry Mayhew, author of *London Labour and the London Poor*, a survey of deprivation in the capital. Early contributors included the novelist William THACKERAY, who mocked English snobbery in 'The Snobs of England'.

Punch was a showcase for British CARTOONISTS such as John Tenniel, illustrator of *Alice in Wonderland*, George du Maurier, E.H. Shepherd – illustrator of *Winnie the Pooh* – and H.M. Bateman, whose 'The Man Who' series turned gaffes into an art form.

The eccentric Christian moralist Malcolm Muggeridge edited *Punch* in the 1950s, but its popularity declined in the 1960s, hit by the rise of its rival, *PRIVATE EYE*. *Punch* closed in 1992, but was revived – in name at least – in 1996.

PUNCH AND JUDY

Punch is the English name for Pulcinella, a mischievous peasant character of 16th-century Italian commedia dell'arte. He arrived in England as a marionette in the next century, when puppet shows became popular after the Restoration.

The 18th century saw puppet theatres thriving in London and Bath, and puppeteers travelling the country giving shows from collapsible booths. Punch evolved into a glove puppet with a hunchback, a hooked nose and a wife called first Joan, then Judy.

But the heyday of the puppet show was in Victorian times, when Punch and Judy – by now the familiar bullying braggart and nagging, battered wife – became regulars of every seaside resort.

PUNK ROCK

'God save the Queen, and her fascist regime,' snarled the *Sex Pistols* in 1977 as an antidote to the Royal Jubilee. A year before their single, 'Anarchy in the UK', had confirmed the arrival of punk – Britain's most subversive contribution to popular music.

Aggressive, anti-establishment lyrics, and stunts such as 'pogoing' – a frenzied solo dance mimicking a pogo stick – and 'gobbing', or spitting, at audiences shook new life into the rock industry.

The music was matched by a nihilistic lifestyle and the punk look of spiked hair, ghoulish make-up and ripped clothes held together with safety pins.

PUNK PIN-UP Lead singer of *The Sex Pistols* John Lydon acquired the name Johnny Rotten because of his bad teeth. He led the band onstage for the first time in November 1975

PUBS

For travellers far from home the medieval inn, or public house, provided refuge from the dangers and discomfort of the road, even if the quality of home-brewed ale could leave much to be desired.

Domesday Book of 1086 recorded more than 40 commercial ale brewers, who could be fined or ducked in a pond for selling substandard ale. In 1267 Henry III issued a decree controlling the price and quality of ale – at this time brewed mostly by women, known as 'ale-wives' or 'brewsters'. Enforcement began in earnest a century later with the appointment of official ale tasters but it was not until 1552 that 'tippling houses' had to be licensed.

ONE FOR THE ROAD

Publicans were quick to spot a new source of income as STAGECOACH traffic increased in the 1600s and with it passing trade. They created a network of highly efficient and competitive coaching inns, but the stagecoach was killed off in the 19th century by the arrival of the railways. The growth of cities created a need for town-centre pubs, met by the Victorian and Edwardian 'gin palaces', where workers could drink in often elaborately decorated surroundings.

Pubs throughout Britain were given a new lease of life when people took to the road again in cars. The changing times are reflected in the story of the Haycock at Wansford, near Peterborough. Built around 1630 as a coaching inn with stabling for 150 horses, it was later starved of custom and became a farm in 1887. It reopened as a pub in 1928 and is now a hotel.

A NATIONAL TREASURE

There are more than 60 000 pubs in Britain, a significant decline from the peak of 75 000 in 1985. But many remain the centre of village life, and the hub of city socialising. In the 1990s new pubs were still opening, some, such as the Counting House in Glasgow, in converted banks or other business premises.

CITY PRIDE The ornate glass, tiles and woodwork of Belfast's Crown Liquor Saloon date from 1849

SIGNS OF THE TIMES

Medieval pubs had to identify themselves by simple pictorial signs as most people could not read. Written names were added from the 19th century onwards.

SWAN A sign that could be understood by anyone, the swan has hung outside pubs since the 14th century. Both Edward III and Henry VIII used a swan in their royal coat of arms

ROYAL OAK More than 500 Royal Oaks celebrate the escape of Charles II after his defeat in 1651 at the battle of Worcester, when he hid in an oak tree at Boscobel House in Shropshire

RED LION Britain's most popular pub name refers to the emblem of John of Gaunt, son of Edward III; it is also a heraldic reference to Scotland

OLD BULL The name was originally given to pubs next to abbeys; the Latin word 'bulla' meant a monastery seal

Henry PURCELL

• Composer • 1659-95

Despite his death at only 36, Henry Purcell was the greatest 17th-century British composer, marrying new Italian styles such as opera to traditional English music. He was a chorister of the Chapel Royal and by 1677 had a place at the court of Charles II. Within five years he was organist at Westminster Abbey and then at the Chapel Royal.

Purcell's prolific output included music for plays and masques such as *King Arthur* (1691) and *The Fairy Queen* (1692), and the opera *Dido and Aeneas* (1689). He composed music for the coronations, birthdays and funerals of five monarchs and died on the eve of St Cecilia, the patron saint of music and the subject of one of his finest odes.

David PUTTNAM

• Film producer • b.1941; CBE 1983; kt 1995

After successful careers in advertising and photo-journalism, London-born David Puttnam made his first film, *S.W.A.L.K.* in 1971. Within 15 years he was Britain's most successful producer.

From 1978 to 1986 Puttnam had a string of cinema hits, including *Midnight Express* (1978) – two Oscars – *Chariots of Fire* (1981) – four Oscars – and *The Killing Fields* (1984) – three Oscars.

In 1986 he was the first Briton to take control of a major US studio – Columbia Pictures. He returned to independent cinema in 1990.

QUAKERS

The Society of Friends – popularly known as Quakers – has more than 19 000 members in Britain and Ireland. It was founded in the 1650s by George FOX, who preached that God communicates by means of an 'inward light', which does not require ministers or sacraments. His stern bidding to 'tremble at the word of the Lord' may have led to the Quaker name.

Many sect members emigrated to north America, including William PENN, who in 1682 founded Pennsylvania. In the 18th and 19th centuries Quaker industrialists such as the chocolate magnates Joseph Fry and George CADBURY pioneered better working conditions for factory employees.

QUEEN ANNE STYLE

In the reign of Anne (1702-14) French and Dutch HUGUENOT craftsmen brought a new furniture style to Britain. Their elegant chairs had wide seats for the full skirts of the time, and backs shaped to fit the body, often with a carved cockleshell motif. Surfaces were plain and smooth,

ELEGANCE IN WOOD Cabriole legs (curved with an ornamental foot) and walnut veneer were typical of **Queen Anne** furniture

using veneers and lacquers – a style later adapted by Thomas CHIPPENDALE.

'Queen Anne' is applied also to a style of architecture, popular in the 1870s and 80s. It drew on English and Flemish buildings of the 17th and 18th centuries, characterised by Dutch gables, grouped chimneys, steep-tiled roofs, terracotta ornament, and pedimented doors and windows. The leading exponents were Norman SHAW and W.E. Nesfield, whose Dutch lodge in Kew Gardens is an early example of the style.

QUEEN MARY and QUEEN ELIZABETH

• Passenger liners

The *Queen Mary* and *Queen Elizabeth*, the transatlantic flagships of the CUNARD Line, were launched on Clydeside in 1934 and 1938 by their namesakes, Mary, wife of George V, and Elizabeth, wife of George VI. *Queen Elizabeth* was the longer, at 314 m (1031 ft), although *Queen Mary* was the quicker, managing 30 knots even in high seas. Both served as Second World War troopships, the *Queen Elizabeth* transporting a total of 750 000 troops 500 000 nautical miles.

By 1947 both ships were again plying the Atlantic, but cheaper air travel took passengers away from them; in 1967 the *Queen Mary* became a floating hotel. In 1972 an arson attack gutted the *Queen Elizabeth*. The last Cunard liner, the *Queen Elizabeth 2*, was launched in 1967.

The LENGTH of the "QUEEN MARY" COMPARED WITH THE HEIGHT OF FAMOUS TALL STRUCTURES THROUGHOUT THE WORLD

CHICAGO, ILL BOARD OF TRADE 609 FEET

DETROIT, MICH. PENOBSCOT BLDG. 557 FEET

PHILADELPHIA, PA CITY HALL 548 FEET

BOSTON, MASS. CUSTOM HOUSE 496 FEET

SEATTLE, WASH. SMITH TOWER 462 FEET

LOS ANGELES, CAL. CITY HALL 438 FEET

SAN FRANCISCO, CAL RUSS BUILDING 435 FEET

HIBERNIA BANK BUILDING NEW ORLEANS, LA. 355 FEET

RHODES-HAVERTY BUILDING ATLANTA, GA 250 FEET

EMPIRE STATE BUILDING (THE WORLD'S TALLEST BUILDING) NEW YORK CITY 1248 FEET

"QUEEN MARY" 1018 FEET

EIFFEL TOWER PARIS 984 FEET

WASHINGTON (U.S.) MONUMENT 555 FEET

PYRAMID of CHEOPS, EGYPT 461 FEET

ST. PATRICK'S CATHEDRAL NEW YORK 328 FEET

WESTMINSTER TOWER LONDON 310 FEET

COLOGNE CATHEDRAL (GERMANY) 524 FEET

· The "QUEEN MARY," MEASURED ALONG THE WATERLINE IS THE WORLD'S LONGEST SHIP ·

QUEEN OF SHIPS The vast *Queen Mary*, later surpassed in size by her sister ship, carried more than 2000 passengers on ten decks, with shops, a ballroom and two swimming pools

RABBIT

The Romans first brought rabbits to Britain for food and fur. They died out and were reintroduced by the Normans but became a pest, consuming crops and damaging young trees. The viral disease myxomatosis was introduced in the 1950s and wiped out 99 per cent of rabbits. Most of the remainder developed a resistance and, thanks to breeding habits that mean a female is fertile from four months and bears 20 young a year, by the 1990s rabbit damage was costing farmers around £100 million a year.

Rabbits, whose grazing also helps to maintain habitats such as heath and chalk grassland, burrow in hedgerows, embankments, fields, heaths and sand dunes. They have no legal protection and can be shot or trapped without a licence.

RADAR

In 1934, while working on the use of radio anti-aircraft 'death rays', Robert Watson-Watt of the National Physical Laboratory realised that waves reflected from an aircraft should be detectable.

On February 26, 1935, pulses from a transmitter at Daventry detected a bomber eight miles away. The new technique was called Radio Direction Finding (RDF). The term radar, standing for radio direction and ranging, was coined later by American scientists.

When war broke out in 1939, radar stations were built around Britain's coast to give early warning of German air attacks. In February 1940 the physicists John Randall and Henry Boot invented the cavity magnetron, a device little bigger than a fist that sent a beam of microwaves, more powerful than radio waves. Aircraft were fitted with versions that were able to detect German submarines and produce images of the ground for navigation and bombing. The cavity magnetron was later adapted to power microwave ovens.

RADIO BROADCASTING

The voice of the singer Nellie Melba launched radio as an entertainment medium in 1920. A year before, the MARCONI company had made the first broadcasts, and in November 1922 the BBC went on air from Savoy Hill to begin its 50 year domination of British radio.

In the Second World War, broadcasts of news, comedy and the speeches of Winston CHURCHILL bound the national audience together. After the war, radio entered a golden age of entertainment with comedy such as *The GOON SHOW*, the thriller *Dick Barton, Special Agent* and soap operas like *Mrs Dale's Diary*.

In 1964 the BBC's monopoly was threatened by the 'pirate' stations such as Radio Caroline, which broadcast pop music from the North Sea. The BBC countered with Radio 1, its own pop station, and in the late 1960s introduced a network of local stations.

OPTICAL ILLUSION The trompe l'oeil mural that covers 465 m² (5000 sq ft) of wall and ceiling at Ragley Hall was begun by Graham Rust in 1969 and took 14 years to complete

In 1971 the BBC lost its monopoly when 60 commercial radio stations were set up. In the 1980s a new wave of commercial FM stations was created, including Classic FM, which competed with the BBC's Radio 3 (launched as the Third Programme in 1946), although Radio 4, the former Home Service, has few rivals in its current affairs coverage. *See also* THE ARCHERS, COMEDY AND COMEDIANS, TODAY

Henry RAEBURN

- **Artist • 1756-1823; kt 1822**

Until he married a rich widow in 1780, Henry Raeburn, the leading Scottish portraitist of the late 18th and early 19th century, earned a living as a jeweller. His early painting, epitomised by the informal and light-hearted 1784 portrait of *The Reverend Robert Walker Skating on Duddingston Loch*, was influenced by the work of Joshua REYNOLDS.

After two years of study in Italy, Raeburn settled in Edinburgh in 1787 and captured the leading figures of the 'Athens of the north' at its zenith. His technique of painting directly onto canvas without preliminary drawings led him to develop a vigorous broad-brushed style suited to depicting rugged Scots lairds like *The Macnab* (1813).

MAIN COLLECTION • National Gallery of Scotland, Edinburgh

RAGLEY HALL

- **Warwickshire (p.495 F3)**
- **Built 17th-18th century**

The visitor who ascends the south staircase at Ragley Hall is met by the unusual spectacle of recent members of the Conway-Seymour family, owners of the house since it was built in 1680, looking down from the first-floor balcony. The group is part of *The Temptation*, a huge mural that follows the staircase up to a dome painted on the flat ceiling.

Ragley Hall was designed by Robert Hooke in Palladian style. It was embellished in the 18th century by the plasterwork of James Gibbs, a classical portico by James Wyatt and parkland laid out by 'Capability' Brown.

RAJ

The largest, most elaborate colonial administration the world has ever seen was the British raj – from the Hindi word *rajati*, 'he rules' – set up in 1858 when India was declared a Crown possession. The raj held sway over more than 350 million people and was ruled by a viceroy, the monarch's representative. He was supported by a bureaucracy of some 1000 senior civil servants and an army of around a million men, mostly Indian, protecting a captive market and source of raw materials that was vital to Britain.

THE FACE OF EMPIRE

Outwardly, the raj manifested itself in glittering panoply. Huge parades, such as the Delhi Durbar of 1911, including turbanned warriors and jewel-studded elephants presided over by George V and Queen Mary, convinced Britons and Indians alike of the raj's permanence. A well-organised social life involved colonial military officers, civil servants and their families in amusements of Indian origin such as BADMINTON, POLO and the GYMKHANA, or perhaps gathering for a tea party or tiffin – a snack that might include CURRY.

THE ONLY WAY TO TRAVEL Elephants carry European dignitaries on a tiger hunt during George V's tour of India in 1911

INDIAN INFLUENCE Along with lime juice cordial, many drinks and foods familiar in Britain began with the raj, including tonic water, mulligatawny soup and kedgeree

THE VENEER OF STABILITY

The mainstay of the raj was the Indian Civil Service, a British-dominated body that astutely appointed Indians to administer India on behalf of the colonial power. Beyond this elite, many Indians disliked the raj, and after the First World War an independence movement gained widespread support. From the 1920s the English-educated lawyer Mahatma Ghandi provided a focus for nationalist sentiment. In 1947 Britain gave India its independence, overseen by Earl MOUNTBATTEN, the last viceroy.

The raj's legacy included the English language, newspapers, a government and legal system, railways and palaces in New Delhi designed by Edwin LUTYENS.

RAILWAYS: *see page 364*

Walter RALEIGH

• **Explorer and writer**   • 1552-1618; kt 1584

The adventurer Walter Raleigh had shown skill as a sailor and soldier, including the quashing of an Irish revolt, when he became a favoured companion of Elizabeth I in 1582. He remained a favourite, naming the American colony of Virginia after the 'virgin' queen.

Raleigh was rewarded with Sherborne Castle in Dorset and estates in Ireland, where he planted both tobacco and the potato, which he had brought back from his explorations of the New World.

When Elizabeth I died, Raleigh was rumoured to be plotting against James I and spent 13 years in the Tower of London, making chemical experiments and writing his uncompleted *History of the World*. He was released in 1616 to look for gold in South America, but the expedition ended in disaster, including the loss of his son. On his return, Raleigh was beheaded for treason.

Marie RAMBERT

• **Dancer and choreographer**
• 1888-1982; DBE 1962

Marie Rambert was a driving force behind the establishment of BALLET in Britain. She was born Cyvia Myriam Ramberg in Warsaw and in 1912 joined Sergei Diaghilev's Ballet Russe company, dancing with Vaslav Nijinsky in Igor Stravinsky's *Rite of Spring*.

In 1914, she settled in London and married the playwright Ashley Dukes. In the late 1920s she started her own dance school, which in 1931 became the Ballet Rambert company. Her productions were stylish, witty and poetic, and she encouraged talented dancers, designers and choreographers, including Frederick ASHTON. In 1966 the Ballet Rambert changed its name to the Rambert Dance Company and dedicated itself to new ballet and experimental techniques.

J. Arthur RANK

• **Film producer**   • 1888-1972; bn 1957

Britain's most successful movie magnate began his career in his father's flour milling business. As a Methodist Sunday school teacher, Joseph Arthur Rank first became interested in film as a new way of preaching the Gospel. By the 1930s he had built up the Rank Organisation into a company that controlled film production and distribution, and ran cinemas. It dominated the British industry for 40 years with films such as *Henry V* and *Great Expectations*, its trademark a bare-chested man beating a giant gong.

When filmgoing declined in the 1950s Rank diversified into hotels, bowling alleys and bingo. It still owns Odeon cinemas and PINEWOOD STUDIOS.

Arthur RANSOME

• **Writer and journalist** • **1884-1967**

'If not duffers, won't drown' – with this gruff endorsement from their father the children of Arthur Ransome's book *Swallows and Amazons* (1930) set off on their first sailing and camping adventure in the Lake District. They appeared in a further 11 novels, blending believable adventure with an imaginary world of exploration: the mountain the children climb is the Old Man of Coniston, but they call it Kanchenjunga.

Ransome turned to children's stories in his 40s while recovering from stomach ulcers. His own adventurous life included reporting on the 1917 Russian revolution; he married Evgenia, Trotsky's secretary. He later reported from China and the Middle East for the *Manchester Guardian*.

Terence RATTIGAN

• **Playwright** • **1911-77; CBE 1958; kt 1971**

Terence Rattigan's first successes, in the late 1930s, were light comedies, but it was the more sombre works of the next decade that made his name. *The Winslow Boy* (1946) and *The Browning Version* (1948) both deal with boys' public schools in ways not entirely complimentary to the institutions: the first is concerned with injustice, the second with loneliness and treachery. Both plays, and the later *Separate Tables* (1954), were made into successful films.

In the late 1950s, when younger and more outspoken playwrights such as John Osborne were in the ascendancy, many critics dismissed Rattigan's work and its sensitive emotions as feeble and phony. But in the 1990s he began to be

RATIONING

'There's a war on, you know' was the automatic response to any complaint about shortages during the SECOND WORLD WAR. The rationing of food, clothes, petrol and furniture was seen as the fairest way to share Britain's resources.

Slogans encouraged national self-sufficiency. 'Dig for Victory' encouraged every spare acre of land to be given over to vegetable growing. 'Is your journey really necessary?' made people think twice before using fuel. Utility clothing, commissioned from designers such as Norman Hartnell, won approval from women, and 'no frills' design was extended to household goods and even jewellery. Rationing outlived the war and did not end until June 1954.

MAKING DO The weekly food ration for an adult might include three pints of milk and two lamb chops. To save clothes coupons, women had stockings painted onto their legs (*below*)

WARTIME WARDROBE
On June 1, 1941, each British person was given 66 clothes coupons to last a year. Later the number varied. Husbands and wives could give coupons to each other or to their children. Secondhand clothes were not rationed and utility clothes required no coupons

Two handkerchiefs	1 coupon
Stockings	2 coupons
Pair of socks	3 coupons
Blouse	5 coupons
Women's shoes	5 coupons
Men's shoes	7 coupons
Skirt	7 coupons
Woollen dress	11 coupons
Man's overcoat	16 coupons
Three-piece suit	26 coupons

taken more seriously than ever, his plays seen as powerful commentaries on the isolation and suffering implicit in human existence.

Simon RATTLE

• **Conductor** • **b.1955; kt 1994**

Son of a music shop proprietress and a jazz musician, the conductor Simon Rattle was reading orchestral scores at the age of eight. As a schoolboy he took percussion and piano lessons and played in the Royal Liverpool Philharmonic Orchestra. In 1970, at the age of 15, he founded the Liverpool Sinfonia, which was committed to playing new music. A year later he went to the Royal Academy of Music to study conducting.

Aged 21 Rattle was the youngest conductor to appear at the Proms and four years later was appointed principal conductor of the City of Birmingham Symphony Orchestra. He turned it into one of the world's leading orchestras, with a choice of music that was always adventurous and never predictable.

Rattle resigned in 1998 so that he could conduct with other of the world's top orchestras. In 1999 the players of the Berlin Philharmonic, the most prestigious orchestra of all, elected him as their senior conductor.

John RAY

• **Naturalist** • **1627-1705**

Together with Gilbert WHITE, John Ray was the father of British natural history. He was a keen observer of nature in action and a meticulous recorder of the physical structure and appearance of plants and animals. The son of an Essex blacksmith, Ray studied at Cambridge and in 1660 published a flora – a catalogue of plants – of the Cambridge area with precise descriptions of habitats, many of which are still recognisable.

Ray also classified plants and animals systematically and was the first to define a species, laying the groundwork for taxonomists such as the Swede Carl Linnaeus (1707-78) who developed the first scientific classification system.

THE GREAT WAY ROUND

**Railways were born in Britain. Trains made travelling easy and swift
as lines spread like a net across the landscape. From its beginning in 1841, the Great
Western was one of the most glamorous and popular lines, stretching into the west
of England and Wales from London. Its story is the story of the railways**

GWR WAS God's wonderful railway to devotees, the great way round to those who despaired at the less-than-direct route the line took between London and Bristol. The Great Western Railway inspired enthusiasm and affection in its passengers more than any other line. The company played on this by producing promotional travel guides and even jigsaw puzzles and added glamour to its trains by giving them exotic names such as the *Cheltenham Flyer* and the *Cornish Riviera Express*. To travel by GWR meant adventure, romance and speed.

BRAVE NEW WORLD
The story of GWR began in 1832, when four Bristol merchants appointed a young engineer, Isambard Kingdom BRUNEL, to build them a railway to transport their goods to London.

Railway construction was already steaming ahead in the north of England, led by George and Robert STEPHENSON, using the old colliery track measure of 4 ft 8½ in. But for the fast, smooth trains Brunel envisaged, a wider gauge was required. His 7 ft wide, 'GWR broad gauge' was the standard until 1892.

AT THE END OF THE LINE Railway posters of the 1930s and 1940s, by some of the finest poster artists, tempted travellers to take the train

A 1¾ mile tunnel under Box Hill, near Bath, alarmed critics, who declared passengers would never survive the journey. For the first years of operation travellers could go over the top by coach rather than risk suffocation. The brick viaduct over the Thames at Maidenhead was also declared 'unsafe', but after minor adjustments still carries trains over the widest brick arches ever constructed.

By the time the Bristol to London line opened in 1841, the GWR empire was already spreading. By the 1850s, trains from the London terminus, Paddington Station, could travel to Penzance in Cornwall.

In time, GWR lines stretched throughout south-west England, as far north as Liverpool and through most of Wales. It was Britain's largest railway company, with 900 more miles of track than its nearest rival, the Midland.

SPEED AND GLAMOUR
It was typical of the youthful zeal of GWR that the company employed a 21-year-old, Daniel Gooch, to design its locomotives. His job was to provide the fast trains for Brunel's smooth track. In 1840 his engine *Firefly* took a directors' special train from Reading to London at an average speed of 50 mph, an astonishing four times faster than the previous average of 12 mph. A succession of great GWR engines followed, including *City of Truro*, the first locomotive to record a speed of over 100 mph, and the 'Castles' and 'Kings'

WESTON SUPER-MARE in Smiling Somerset

WALES

SPEED TO THE
CORNWALL DEVON SOM

of the 1920s with their dashing green livery and sparkling brass chimneys.

THE MODERN AGE

Railways brought a new pace to life; they even affected the time of day. Local time was still determined by sundial in the 1840s, and Cornwall time differed from London time by about 20 minutes. Starting in 1852, a daily signal was sent out from Paddington at 10am down newly erected telegraph lines to every station to synchronise the network.

In 1923 four regional companies were formed to rationalise a network that had sprawled across Britain, with some companies running the same routes. The new giants were GWR; London and North Eastern Railway; London, Midland and Scottish; and Southern Railways.

SLEEK AND SWIFT Streamlined locomotives such as this one belonging to London, Midland and Scottish hauled express trains in the 1930s

The GWR came to an end, in name at least, in 1948 when the railways were nationalised. Now the network has been privatised and fragmented again, but the grandeur of the GWR in its heyday lives on. Lines such as the Severn Valley Railway and the Paignton and Dartmouth Steam Railway, and the Didcot Railway Centre keep the old trains running.

IS THAT SINGLE OR RETURN?

Buying a ticket was once a complicated business. The clerk had a book – hence the term 'booking office' – where he logged in triplicate the passenger's name and details of the journey. One copy was given to the traveller, one was kept in the office and the third went to the guard.

In 1832 the Leicester and Swannington Railway experimented with brass tokens, which passengers returned to the guard at the end of their journey. In 1838 Thomas Edmonson, the stationmaster at Brampton Junction in Norfolk, began stamping the names of the most popular destinations on numbered slips of cardboard. The process was later mechanised, including the addition of a device to print the date, and the modern ticket was born.

Season tickets for frequent travellers date back to the 1830s. The earliest were partly handwritten, handsomely engraved documents, sometimes backed with leather.

1837 A first-class ticket, handwritten and personalised with the name of the traveller

EARLY 1900s Machine-printed tickets for third-class travel

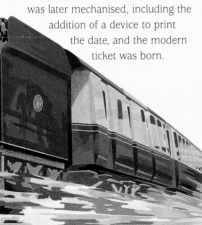

1923 First-class season ticket enclosed in an enamel fob

1997 Computer-printed ticket with information stored on a magnetic strip on the back

TRAIN TIMETABLE

1804 Richard Trevithick designs a steam locomotive that runs on rails

1825 The Stockton and Darlington becomes the first public railway to use steam locomotives

1829 Robert Stephenson's *Rocket* wins the Rainhill Trials to become the locomotive used by the Liverpool and Manchester Railway

1839 The first railway timetable is published by George Bradshaw

1846 In a year of 'railway mania', parliament approves the construction of 273 new lines

1863 The Metropolitan Railway, the world's first underground line, opens in London from Paddington to Farringdon

1883 An electric railway opens in Brighton

1886 The Severn tunnel opens. Britain's longest railway tunnel, at 4 miles 628yd, it cost £5 million

1890 The first electric Tube train runs in London from Monument to Stockwell

1904 *City of Truro* hauling the 'Ocean Mail' is said to have exceeded 100 mph

1913 The first London-Paris trains run

1923 Britain's 123 railway companies are amalgamated into four regions

1931 The first diesel locomotives enter service in Britain

1933 The first main line is electrified from London to Brighton

1938 *Mallard* sets a world record speed for steam locomotives at 126 mph

1948 The railways are nationalised

1952 Britain's worst passenger train accident at Harrow kills 112

1960 The last steam locomotive, *Evening Star*, goes into service

1963 Dr Beeching's plan recommending the closure of many lines is accepted

1973 A prototype high-speed train (HST) reaches 143 mph. It becomes widely used as the 'Intercity 125'

1987 The Docklands Light Railway (DLR) opens in London with computer-controlled, driverless trains

1994 The Channel Tunnel opens

1997 The privatisation of the rail network is completed

INTERNATIONAL EXPRESS Eurostar trains streak from London Waterloo to Paris Gare du Nord in 3 hours, reaching a top speed of 186 mph

EST GWR WALES

REDGRAVE FAMILY

- **Actors**   • Michael 1908-85; kt 1959
- **Vanessa b.1937**   • **Corin b.1939**
- **Lynn b.1943**

Theatre must be in the Redgrave genes. Michael was born into a family of stage and circus performers. After working as a teacher he joined Liverpool Rep and showed a flair for sensitive, cerebral characters. He became celebrated for roles in Chekhov and Shakespeare, and for his intense performances in the films *Dead of Night* (1945) and *Mourning Becomes Electra* (1947).

The Redgrave children also took to the theatre. Vanessa, a committed socialist like her father, made her stage debut in 1958 in *A Touch of the Sun* and continues to 'tread the boards', although she is best known for her film work. She was nominated for an Oscar for *Morgan, a Suitable Case for Treatment* (1966), and received an Oscar for *Julia* (1977). Lynn won an Oscar nomination for her role as the title character in *Georgy Girl* (1966), and Corin's film credits include *Four Weddings and a Funeral* (1994). Corin's daughter Jemma, and Vanessa's daughters Natasha and Joely, also act.

Carol REED

- **Film director**   • 1906-76; kt 1952

Childhood in a theatrical environment – he was the son of the actor-manager Herbert Beerbohm Tree – and an early career as an actor gave Carol Reed two essential qualities for an accomplished director: tact and sensitivity.

Reed learned to direct at Ealing studios, where two of his films – *The Stars Look Down* (1939) and *Night Train to Munich* (1940) – attracted rave reviews and an offer of work from the film magnate J. Arthur RANK. He soon left Rank's employ to begin a long association with the Hungarian director Alexander KORDA. Their most popular films – *The Fallen Idol* (1948), a detective story, and the thriller *The Third Man* (1949) – showed Reed's mastery of storytelling, but it was his talent for handling child actors that won him an Academy Award as Best Director in 1968 for the musical *Oliver!*

REFORM ACTS

- **1832; 1867; 1884; 1918; 1928; 1969**

Within the space of just over 50 years, three Acts of parliament changed the electoral map of Britain. The first Reform Act, passed in 1832 by Earl Grey's Whig administration, emerged from widespread unrest over the corrupt parliamentary system. 'Rotten Boroughs' – constituencies with few electors and with MPs elected by undisguised bribery of the voters – were rife.

The Act abolished these boroughs and redistributed their parliamentary seats to new industrial towns. It also extended the vote to the prosperous middle classes by giving it to householders who owned or rented premises at an annual cost of £10 or more. The Reform Acts of 1867 and 1884 further extended the franchise to include about 63 per cent of the adult male population.

Though these Acts transformed the electoral scene, giving 6 million people the vote, they still left 30 million unrepresented. The 1918 Act ended the property qualification and enfranchised women aged 30 or over. More than 21 million people could now vote. In 1928 both sexes could vote at 21 and in 1969 the minimum voting age for men and women was lowered to 18.

REFORMATION

In the 16th century many Christians across Europe wanted to see the Church purged of corruption. The more radical followed Martin Luther in Germany and John Calvin in Switzerland. Like the 14th-century English theologian John WYCLIFFE they challenged the Catholic Church's use of tradition. Their insistence on the Bible's authority over that of the Church sparked a split across Europe.

In England 'reformation' did not begin for theological reasons. HENRY VIII, to secure his dynasty, wished to divorce, but could not get the Pope's approval, so he appointed himself head of the CHURCH OF ENGLAND in the 1534 Act of Supremacy. Church lands were seized with the Dissolution of the Monasteries, and under EDWARD VI and ELIZABETH I much church art was destroyed.

Scottish reformation began in 1560 when the priest John KNOX founded presbyterianism, forming the basis of a new CHURCH OF SCOTLAND.

REFORM CLUB

- **Central London (p.499 C7)**   • **Founded 1836**

In the years after the 1832 Reform Act extended the right to vote, Whig supporters of the bill established the Reform Club to rival the Tory CARLTON CLUB. The club became a meeting place for politicians who later established the Liberal party.

Thanks to the expertise of the French chef Alexis Soyer the club became a popular venue for lavish banquets, such as the ceremonial breakfast held in April 1864 for Guiseppe Garibaldi, the hero of Italian nationalism. Though its political

TENDER SOUL Michael Redgrave (*left*) stars as a working-class hero made good in **Carol Reed's** first major film, *The Stars Look Down* (1939), a story about life in a troubled mining community

RELIGIOUS FAITHS

Britain is the most religiously diverse country within the European Union. The dominant religion is Christianity (including Catholicism, the Orthodox Church and Protestantism), but many others are represented, from Buddhism to Zoroastrianism.

Membership of Christian churches has been in decline since the 1970s and continues to fall. The Islamic religion, second only to Christianity in the size

MEMBERSHIP OF RELIGIONS IN BRITAIN 1995 (millions)	
Anglican	26.1
Roman Catholic	5.7
Presbyterian	2.6
Methodist	1.3
Muslim	1.2
Baptist	0.6
Sikh	0.6
Church of Scientology	0.5
Orthodox	0.5
Hindu	0.4
Jewish	0.3

EASTERN ELEGANCE
The diversity of religions practised in Britain is reflected in its places of worship. In London, Muslims can attend the Central Mosque in Regent's Park (right). North of the city in Neasden, the largest Hindu temple outside India opened in 1997

of its membership, is growing fast. Between 1980 and 1995 the number of Muslims in Britain doubled, and there are now more than 600 mosques. Britain's Jewish community, dating from 1656, is the largest in western Europe outside of France.

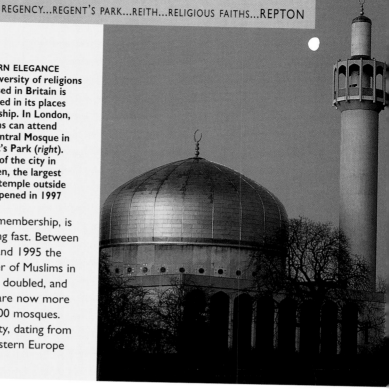

activity has declined, the club maintains its gastronomic traditions. In 1981 it became the first traditional gentlemen's club to admit women as members.

REGENCY

• 1811-20

In 1811, GEORGE III was regarded as deranged and incapable of transacting business. His son George, Prince of Wales, was appointed regent. Despite his extravagant lifestyle, he made no great change to his father's policies. His influence was chiefly felt in the elegance and exuberance of early 19th-century English art and architecture, which became known as 'Regency' style.

One of the Prince Regent's most frivolous legacies is the onion-domed BRIGHTON Pavilion. Its flamboyant interiors combine neoclassical and oriental designs. His patronage of the architect John NASH resulted in London's Regent Street and REGENT'S PARK, with its 'wedding-cake' terraces.

REGENT'S PARK

• Central London (p.499 B1)   • Opened 1835

During the REGENCY of Prince George the architect John NASH won a competition for the remodelling of Marylebone Park, a 16th-century royal hunting preserve. By the time it was opened to the public, the prince was George IV.

Nash planned the layout of the 166 ha (410 acre) park and designed the elegant stuccoed terraces that still flank it. The sinuous curves of his artificial lake give an impression of a greater body of water.

One of Britain's finest collections of roses can be seen in Queen Mary's Garden, and there is a tree-fringed open-air theatre. Zoological gardens laid out by Decimus Burton in 1828 took in animals from royal menageries at Windsor and the Tower of London, and opened to the public in 1847. As London Zoo, it now accommodates thousands of animals from more than 650 different species.

Lord REITH

• Director-general of the BBC 1927-38
• 1889-1971; kt 1927; bn 1940

At 6 ft 8 in, the craggy-jawed presbyterian John Charles Walsham Reith cut an imposing figure in the offices of the private British Broadcasting Company when he became general manager in 1922. Over the next 16 years Reith was to dominate public service broadcasting.

Reith, who began his career as an engineer, seized the challenge of steering the BBC with a mixture of enthusiastic energy and fierce idealism, fuelled by a commitment to high standards. His announcers were required to appear in full evening dress, and he fired anyone whose integrity was in doubt – this included those who divorced.

Reith fought to retain the BBC's freedom from political and commercial pressure, and stood by these principles when the company became publicly owned in 1927. He left the BBC in 1938.

In 1948 the corporation established the Reith Lectures in his honour with a series of radio broadcasts by Bertrand Russell on 'Authority and the Individual'. The lectures, given by a different figure each year, are transmitted on Radio 4.

Humphry REPTON

• Landscape gardener   • 1752-1818

After the death of the garden designer and architect 'Capability' BROWN, Humphry Repton inherited the mantle of Britain's finest 'landscape gardener' – a term coined by Repton himself.

Repton was an amateur painter with a passion for watercolour landscapes – a skill he put to good use when setting up his garden design business in 1788. Though influenced by Brown's love of the picturesque, Repton would blend buildings into his gardens, linking them with terraces and steps.

For each client Repton painted before-and-after pictures. The paintings for gardens at Antony House in Cornwall, Sheringham in Norfolk and Attingham in Shropshire survive in about 70 of his *Red Books*. These were bound in red morocco leather and presented to each client.
See also LANDSCAPE GARDENING

VALLEY OF POWER Many of Snowdonia's rivers were dammed in the 1960s. The four 90 megawatt pump turbines at Llyn Stwlan Reservoir, beneath the peaks of Moelwyn Bach, provide electricity for the national grid

RESERVOIRS

Britain's natural reservoirs – its rivers and lakes – could not cater for the huge rise in demand for water in the Victorian era. As the population expanded and the first lavatories and baths were installed in private houses, man-made reservoirs became essential – seven were built to supply Edinburgh alone in 1847-57.

Today more than 30 per cent of our water comes from man-made reservoirs, but many provide more than just storage. The four reservoirs in the Elan Valley in Wales, dammed between 1892 and 1952, draw visitors for their views. Rutland Water, built in the 1970s and with the largest area of any British man-made reservoir, caters for water sports and birdwatching. The Queen Mary Reservoir in Staines, opened in 1947, is on a bird migration route, and became a Site of Special Scientific Interest in 1955.

RESTORATION

• 1660-8

General public enthusiasm greeted the restoration of CHARLES II to the throne in 1660. Church traditions and simple pleasures suppressed during Oliver CROMWELL's puritanical Commonwealth returned with the monarchy. Bishops and prayer books reappeared in churches. MAY DAY and CHRISTMAS celebrations were no longer frowned upon. The Restoration came to represent a new era in cultural and social life.

The opening of VAUXHALL GARDENS in London in 1660, with tree-lined walks and supper rooms, symbolised the new mood. Restoration comedy – cynical, witty plays such as *The Country Wife* (1675), by William Wycherley, and *The Way of the World* (1700), by William Congreve – caught the optimistic atmosphere, which lasted until JAMES II was overthrown in 1688.

REUTERS

• Est. 1851

Founded by the German-born Paul Julius Reuter, the world's biggest supplier of news and market information originated as a telegraph agency near London's Stock Exchange, sending prices to Paris. Soon Reuters began to sell general information, breaking the news to Europe of Lincoln's assassination. Business expanded rapidly as telegraph cables were installed worldwide.

Its investment in modern computer technology to monitor international finance dramatically increased Reuters' profitability; it became a public company valued at £700 million in 1984 and now employs some 3500 staff in 74 countries.

SQUEEZED FOR SPACE Subeditors on a Reuters newsdesk in the 1930s tilt their typewriters to gain more room for writing

Joshua REYNOLDS

• Artist • 1723-92; kt 1769

When Joshua Reynolds received his knighthood, he fitted his visit to St James's Palace between portrait sittings. Such organisation was typical of the supreme classicist of British art.

Reynolds, the son of a Devon clergyman, travelled in Italy from 1749 to 1752. The work of Michelangelo and Raphael overwhelmed him, and on his return to England he tried to raise the humble status of 'face painting' (portraiture) by adopting the 'Grand Manner' of the Italian artists' lavish historical scenes.

Reynolds established himself in London and by 1760 he was earning £6000 a year for painting 150 portraits. He is said to have painted some 2000 portraits in all. In 1768 he was appointed the first president of the ROYAL ACADEMY, where he gave influential 'discourses', or lectures, on classical art.

Cecil RHODES

• Politician and entrepreneur • 1853-1902

At the age of 17, Cecil Rhodes was sent to South Africa for the sake of his health. Despite persistent heart and lung problems his energy for business was unbounded. In 1888 he founded the De Beers mining company to exploit newly discovered diamond mines in Kimberley. By 1891 the company controlled most of the world's diamond output; it remains the largest diamond company.

Rhodes was driven by a passion to expand the Empire. 'If there be a God,' he said, 'I think what he would like me to do is paint as much of Africa

THE GRAND MANNER Joshua Reynolds adapts classical themes in his portrait of three society ladies, the Montgomery sisters, as Greek maidens in *Three Ladies Adorning a Term of Hymen*

British-red as possible.' He championed imperial interests in Africa, settling a new colony, which he called Rhodesia, now the independent state of Zimbabwe.

By 1895, Rhodes was prime minister of Cape Colony, but resigned after his raid into the Boer state of Transvaal indirectly started the BOER WAR of 1899-1902. He did not live to see the end of the war, in which Britain won control over southern Africa.

Cliff RICHARD

• Pop singer   • b.1940; kt 1996

When skiffle band singer Harry Webb decided to sing rock'n'roll with The Drifters, he began a career in pop music that has so far spanned four decades.

A change of name to Cliff Richard and some lip-snarling, hip-thrusting Elvis Presley imitations helped 23 successive singles reach the top ten between 1960 and 1965, including six number ones. His 1963 B-side hit 'Bachelor Boy' turned out to be prophetic of his lifelong bachelorhood, which he ascribes to his Christian faith.

Though he acted in teenage musical movies such as *Summer Holiday* (1963), it was not until the age of 57 that Richard fulfilled his lifetime ambition

of playing the hero of Emily Brontë's novel *Wuthering Heights*, in the stage musical *Heathcliff*.

CHART TOPPERS 1959: 'Living Doll'; 'Travelling Light'; 1960: 'Please Don't Tease'; 'I Love You'; 1962: 'The Young Ones'; 'The Next Time'; 1963: 'Summer Holiday'; 1965: 'The Minute You're Gone'; 1968: 'Congratulations'; 1979: 'We Don't Talk Anymore'; 1986: 'Living Doll'; 1988: 'Mistletoe and Wine'; 1990: 'Saviour's Day'

RICHARD I

• King 1189-99   • 1157-99

During his ten-year reign, Richard I – known as 'the Lionheart' for his courage – spent a total of six months in Britain. He grew up in France with his mother, Eleanor of Aquitaine, and developed a violent temper and a strong will, rebelling against his father, HENRY II.

England was well administered when Richard succeeded to the throne. Within a year, he left on the Third Crusade to recapture Jerusalem from the Muslims. Richard defeated Saladin, the sultan of Egypt, but failed to take the Holy City. On his way back to England, a quarrel led to his seizure by Leopold V of Austria.

The huge ransom demanded for Richard's return – 150 000 marks – was raised by his English subjects. He

returned in 1194, but soon set out to defend his lands in France and was killed while attacking a castle at Chaluz.

RICHARD II

• King 1377-99   • 1367-1400

EDWARD III's eldest son, the Black Prince, died before his father, leaving the succession to his son, Richard. As a young king, Richard displayed courage during the PEASANTS' REVOLT of 1381, confronting the rebels in person. But he was still a minor, and power belonged to his uncle, JOHN OF GAUNT.

When Richard turned 18, his attempts to exert authority were frustrated by ambitious barons, who in the power struggle that followed executed or exiled his supporters. A compromise was then reached, and the king stifled his desire for revenge for eight years.

In 1397, hostility to his foreign policies finally provoked Richard to engineer the death or exile of his rivals. He forced subjects into giving loans and terrorised opponents with his army of Cheshire guards. He unwisely left England for Ireland in 1399, giving Gaunt's son, Henry Bolingbroke, a chance to claim the throne as HENRY IV. Richard rushed back, but found little support. He was forced to abdicate and died in prison at Pontefract Castle.

RICHARD III

• King 1483-5   • 1452-85

The reign of Richard III was one of the shortest in English history, but the jailing of his royal nephews – the PRINCES IN THE TOWER – and their disappearance provoked William Shakespeare's characterisation of Richard as a hunchbacked murderer.

Richard's physical deformity is a myth. He was a courageous soldier, an able administrator and totally loyal to his brother, EDWARD IV. After Edward's death, Richard became lord protector to the 12-year-old Edward V. But within three months, Richard had the young king and his brother imprisoned in the Tower of London, arguing that they were illegitimate.

Parliament offered Richard the crown. His acceptance, combined with rumours of the deaths of his nephews, alienated many of his supporters. The duke of Buckingham transferred his support to Henry Tudor, a descendant of Edward III. Buckingham was crushed, but Henry returned from exile, killed Richard at the Battle of BOSWORTH, and took the throne as HENRY VII.

Ralph RICHARDSON

• Actor • 1902-83; kt 1947

'Never tell them how it's done, cocky,' Ralph Richardson advised his younger, greener colleagues – despite his success as a classical actor, he was the least self-important of men.

Richardson began his career at the Birmingham Repertory Company in 1926, but first came to wide public notice in the 1930s while working at the Old Vic alongside Laurence Olivier. He excelled at playing ordinary men and turning them into characters of intriguing

TRAVELLING IN STYLE Ralph Richardson could often be seen in London making his way to rehearsals on his BMW motorbike

depth. In his later years, he brought the same complexity to parts in modern plays such as Hirst in Harold Pinter's *No Man's Land* (1975) – often acting opposite John Gielgud.

Although seldom taking the lead role in films he often outshone the stars. He received two Oscar nominations, one for *The Heiress* in 1949, the second for his role as Tarzan's grandfather in *Greystoke: The Legend of Tarzan*, released a year after his death.

RICHMOND PARK

• Surrey (p.498 B4) • Created 1637

In 1637 Charles I built a wall to enclose his hunting ground near the palaces of Richmond and Hampton Court. But in the 1750s a local brewer organised a mass trespass and won the right of free access to Richmond Park. Walls still surround this royal piece of countryside – Britain's largest urban park.

The park's 1000 ha (2500 acres), a varied landscape of hills, woodland gardens and grassland dotted by ancient oak trees, are home to 700 red and fallow deer – descendants of those hunted by Charles – and 100 species of birds. Its 18th-century White Lodge was the birthplace of Edward VIII, and Pembroke Lodge, now a restaurant, was the childhood home of the philosopher and mathematician Bertrand Russell.

The RIDGEWAY

• S England (p.495 F4)

An ancient trackway, in use for at least 6000 years, runs 85 miles from near Avebury in Wiltshire to Ivinghoe Beacon in Buckinghamshire. It follows chalk downland along what was once the Great Ridgeway, a network of routes linking the Norfolk coast to the English Channel and the West Country.

The track was one of the main routes of PREHISTORIC BRITAIN and is punctuated by monuments such as the 40 m (130 ft) mound at SILBURY HILL and the WEST KENNET LONG BARROW nearby. Iron Age tribesmen carved a WHITE HORSE near Uffington, and added several hill-forts.

As traders, drovers and armies trod its course over the centuries, the Ridgeway spread into a maze of paths across the hills until the 18th-century

Enclosure Acts defined a right of way. It remains one of Britain's oldest and greenest LONG-DISTANCE ROUTES.

Lucie RIE

• Potter • 1902-95

British postwar cultural life was enriched by many artists who took refuge in Britain from Nazi persecution, among them Lucie Rie, who was born in Vienna into a wealthy Jewish family. She studied ceramics under Michael Powolny, the leading ceramic artist of the Viennese Secession decorative arts movement, and soon developed her trademark – a pitted 'volcanic' glaze.

BOTTLE VASE WITH FLARED LIP BY LUCIE RIE (1982)

Nazi attacks on her family led Rie to emigrate to Britain in 1938. She met the potter Bernard LEACH in 1939 and was influenced by the Japanese style of his work, but developed a sophisticated style in contrast to Leach's rustic designs. The work she produced in the 1970s – modern, simple and elegant vases and bowls – is considered her best. Her work can be seen at the Victoria and Albert Museum in London.

RIEVAULX ABBEY

• North Yorkshire (p.496 C4)
• Built 12th-13th century • EH

The grassy strip of Rievaulx Terrace, laid out in the 1750s, provides a vantage point over the remaining three-tiered arches of Rievaulx Abbey. The secluded abbey, hidden in the wooded foothills of the North Yorkshire moors, was founded around 1131 – the first in Yorkshire to be built by Cistercian monks.

By 1225-30, when the choir was added, Rievaulx had become a flourishing community of 140 monks and more than 500 lay brothers who worked in the wool trade. But by the early 14th century the monastery was heavily in debt, and when Henry VIII dissolved the abbey in 1539 it had declined to a mere 22 monks.

RIGHTS OF WAY

Members of the public are entitled to travel unhindered along any route where there is right of way – bridleways, footpaths, byways and public roads. The right is enshrined in the Highways Act of 1980, but existed in other statutes and in common law for centuries before that.

A total of 130 000 miles of rights of way were mapped in the 1950s, shown on today's ORDNANCE SURVEY maps as red or green dotted lines. Most roads are clearly marked and identifiable on the ground, but this is not always the case with paths and bridleways that cross fields or private land. Where no path has been mapped but members of the public wish to assert their right of way, they must prove that the route in question has been used unfettered by the public for the previous 20 years – a test laid down in the Rights of Way Act 1932.

RIOT ACT

The expression 'to read the riot act' is a reminder of a time when magistrates did just that. The Riot Act was passed in 1715 as part of the government's harsh response to the threatened JACOBITE rebellion in support of James Stuart's claim to the throne.

Unruly public gatherings were common in the 18th century, for they were the only way people of low social status could express discontent. The Riot Act could be invoked when 12 or more people disturbed the public peace; they were required to disperse upon a magistrate's proclamation, and refusal could result in life imprisonment.

In practice the Act was infrequently used. Of 41 riots recorded in Devon in the 1790s, only one resulted in the proclamation being read. The Act was repealed in 1967.

RITZ HOTEL

• **Central London (p.499 A7)**   • **Opened 1906**
César Ritz (1850-1918), the greatest hotelier of the Victorian and Edwardian eras, worked his way around the fashionable cities and resorts of Europe, earning a reputation for excellence and a loyal clientele. In 1898 he received financial backing for a hotel in his own name: the Ritz in Paris.

The project was a success, and his backers began searching for similar hotel sites in other major cities. In London they acquired a prime location on Piccadilly and hired Ritz's favourite architectural team, Charles Mewès and Arthur Davis. The result was a Parisian-style building with luxurious Louis XVI interiors and an arcade along Piccadilly reminiscent of the Rue de Rivoli.

Guests at the London Ritz have included royalty and the literati. Unlike the SAVOY HOTEL, it did not encourage the custom of stage and screen stars. The hotel was mobbed by crowds during Charlie Chaplin's 1921 visit, and the manager vowed 'never again'.

RIVERS: *see page 372*

ROADS

Britain's first road network was built by the Romans. Their straight, well-drained stone thoroughfares, covering thousands of miles, were still in use in medieval times, and some stretches can still be walked along today (*see* ROMAN BRITAIN).

Packhorse and wagon traffic increased over the 16th and 17th centuries, and by 1663 tolls were introduced to pay for road maintenance and building. By the 1840s, Britain's road network extended over 126 000 miles.

Toll roads were phased out as local government took over road management at the end of the 19th century. By the late 1930s, 3 million MOTOR CARS filled British roads and in 1958 a new era of motorways began with the opening of the Preston bypass, now part of the M6. By the end of 1997, of the 229 800 miles of roads in Britain, more than 2000 miles were motorway.

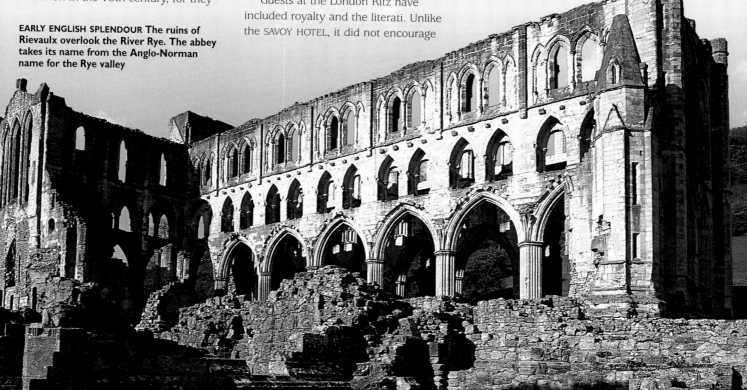

EARLY ENGLISH SPLENDOUR The ruins of Rievaulx overlook the River Rye. The abbey takes its name from the Anglo-Norman name for the Rye valley

WATER OF LIFE

Britain's rivers provide three distinct habitats on their journey to the sea. Torrents rush down mountains and hillsides through the steeper valleys, and finally slow to a gentle ooze through fertile lowland plains. Wildlife has ingeniously adapted to each condition

RIVERSIDE HABITAT depends in part upon the pace of the water's flow. Most rivers begin at a spring or meltwater, usually on a hill or mountainside – though some in southern and eastern England, such as the Thames, have little or no upland habitats. The upper reaches of a river broaden as tributaries join the stream, carving out valleys in the foothills where rapids alternate with quiet pools.

The middle reaches meander across lowlands, and good examples of this can be found in the winding channels of the Tamar and the Forth. In the waterlogged Lincolnshire Fens, Norfolk Broads and Somerset Levels, sections of many rivers have been straightened by man to drain surrounding farmland.

In the lower reaches at the river's estuary, SHORE LIFE habitats emerge.

THE TORRENTS

Mountain torrents are plentiful in northern Britain at the source of rivers such as the Dee in Scotland, and the Eamont and Kent in the Lake District. They are populated by small creatures that can grip the riverbed. The current is too fast for flowering plants to settle, but green carpets of moss cover the damp waterside.

FOUNTAIN BLADDER SNAIL *The finger-like projections of the bladder snail's mantle grip the sides of its shell. The snail survives underwater on air taken in at the surface and stored in a single lung for hours*

CADDIS FLY LARVAE *These soft larvae construct a case of sand and sticks 3-4 cm long (1 ¼-1 ½ in) for protection in fast-flowing streams*

THE TORRENTS

VALLEY STREAMS

LOWLAND CHANNEL

VALLEY STREAMS

Well-oxygenated, fast streams sustain brown trout in rivers such as the Wye, the Severn and the Spey – the valley stretch is sometimes called a troutbeck. The habitat encourages hardy plants such as lichens and liverworts.

LIVERWORT *Branches of this lettuce-like plant grow up to 20 cm (8 in) long. Carpets of liverwort provide food for aquatic animals and shelter for their eggs*

SALMON *Mature fish can jump 3 m (10 ft) out of the water over fast-flowing rapids, making their way upstream to spawn in unpolluted rivers such as the Tay and the Dee*

DIPPER *This small bird walks upstream on the riverbed, using the force of the current to stay underwater, searching for larvae and crustaceans*

LOWLAND CHANNEL

Silt from upstream is deposited on the riverbed and banks by slower currents in the lowlands. Vegetation settles in the fertile soil, alders and willows overhang the water, their roots strengthening the banks, and animals may find good nesting sites and food supplies.

EEL *Adult eels spawn at sea, but the elvers swim upstream from the estuary to mature*

WHIRLIGIG BEETLE *The legs of the whirligig work like oars, turning the beetle in circles as it swims. Its eyes are divided in two, enabling it to see above and below the surface at the same time*

BULRUSHES *The brown seed heads of bulrushes are a common sight from July until February, when they burst and spread their seeds across the water*

HERON *After waiting patiently in the shallows of the river, the heron uses its dagger-sharp beak to skewer fish*

OTTER *Hunting and pollution depleted the otter population during the 20th century. They became a protected species in 1978, and are now successfully breeding again in the wild*

ROBERT BRUCE

• **Robert I of Scotland 1306-29** • **1274-1329**

The Bruces were a Norman family with vast estates on both sides of the Scottish border, and Robert spent part of his youth at the court of EDWARD I. Though he swore fealty to the English king in 1295, his loyalties were changeable: he is thought to have supported the Scottish independence fighter William WALLACE in a rebellion against the English in 1297.

Robert's true intentions became clear in 1306 when his ambition to take the Scottish throne led him to murder a rival claimant, John Comyn. His supporters crowned him at Scone in March in defiance of Edward, but within three months English reprisals drove him into refuge on Rathlin, an island off the coast of Ireland. It is here that he is said to have taken inspiration from a spider persistently building a web, and vowed to continue the fight for independence.

After the death of the English king in 1307, Robert regrouped his forces to win a series of victories culminating in the defeat of Edward II at BANNOCKBURN in 1314. But it was not until the Treaty of Northampton in 1328 that Scotland's independence and Robert's claim to the throne were recognised.

ROBIN

The British robin, happy searching for worms in the company of a gardener, is much less timid than those on the Continent. Robins are year-round residents, but traditionally associated with winter, when males perform their mating display and fight over territory.

The robin's distinctive red breast has earned it a place in British folklore. In Welsh legend, the bird burnt its feathers when it tried to pour water on a fire. According to Breton tradition, the robin stained its chest with blood when it plucked a thorn from the brow of the dying crucified Christ. Killing such a kind and compassionate bird is said to bring bad luck.

TREASURED RELICS Even centuries after death, Robert Bruce continued to inspire his Scots countrymen. A bronze cast of his skull (*above*) is kept at the Scottish National Portrait Gallery. His heart is buried at Melrose Abbey

ROBIN HOOD

Did Robin Hood really exist? No one can be sure, but his noble cause – stealing from the rich to give to the poor – may have been inspired by the changing economy which led to the PEASANT'S REVOLT of 1381. Robin appears in the late-14th-century poem *PIERS PLOWMAN*, but the earliest surviving tale about him is the anonymous ballad 'Lytell Geste of Robyn Hode' (c.1495), in which he is an outlaw at the time of Edward II, living in the woods of Barnsdale in Yorkshire.

Later legends borrow from traditions such as MAY DAY, which identify Robin with the pageant king. The pageant queen became his romantic interest, Maid Marian. Similar changes inspired today's stories, set in the reign of Richard I, in which Robin leads a band of outlaws in Sherwood forest in Nottingham, fighting authority in the form of the sheriff. The many sites named after Robin throughout England bear witness to his popularity – Robin Hood's Bay in North Yorkshire has been known as such since at least 1544.

CHRISTMAS CHEER Robins are more noticeable in winter when their breast feathers are at their brightest for the mating season

ROB ROY

• **Cattle dealer and outlaw** • **1671-1734**

Scottish clansman Robert Macgregor became a hero of the poor in the style of Robin Hood in Walter SCOTT's novel *Rob Roy* (1818). In reality, he was an astute cattle dealer who knew how to exploit his situation to make a profit.

In the 17th and 18th centuries, the Highlands were dominated by feudal landlords and clan chieftains. The Macgregor land at Balquhidder separated the estates of the rival dukes of Montrose and Argyll. Rob Roy – 'roy' is Gaelic for 'red', from his flame-coloured hair – worked this to his advantage. He kept a private army to protect his own livestock, but was not above stealing cattle. Paying him a fee to guard a herd was the best form of protection.

In 1712 the duke of Montrose turned on Rob Roy. Having lent him money for cattle speculation, he withdrew his aid and seized the Macgregor lands. Rob Roy turned wholly to plundering cattle, becoming notoriously successful during the unrest caused by the JACOBITE rising in 1715. After persistent exploits against Montrose he was arrested in 1727, but was pardoned. He died at Balquhidder.

ROCHESTER

• **Kent (p.495 H5)** • **Pop. 23 970**

In the 2nd century AD, the Roman fort of Durobrivae laid the foundations for Rochester. Its location at the mouth of the River Medway guarded an important river crossing on the road between the south-east coast and London.

The cathedral was established in 604 in the Saxon settlement of Hroffeceaster and is the second oldest see in England after Canterbury. The present building dates mostly from the 11th to the 14th centuries. The Normans built Rochester Castle, the town's dominant landmark, with its 37 m (120 ft) keep.

Rochester and the other Medway towns retain their maritime tradition; Charles DICKENS's father once worked in the navy pay office in nearby Chatham. The novelist grew up in Rochester, which often appears in his books. His home in Gads Hill is now a school; the Charles Dickens Centre on Higher Eastgate recalls his time in Rochester.

ALL THE YOUNG DUDES

For half a century Britain has vied with the USA to rule the world of pop. From rock'n'roll, blues and soul to hip-hop and rap, British bands and singers have given the music an ironic, theatrical twist, and they have contributed some distinctive, home-grown sounds

TOMMY STEELE

NE OF the first British singers to pick up on the new American popular music that emerged in the early 1950s was Lonnie Donegan, a Glasgow-born strummer who played a speeded-up version of folk and blues called 'skiffle'. This sound was easy for keen amateurs to imitate with a cheap guitar and a tea-chest bass. Among the ambitious teenagers who formed their own bedroom skiffle bands was John Lennon. His band was called The Quarry Men until, in punning homage to Buddy Holly's Crickets, he changed it to The BEATLES.

THE YOUNG ONES

Pop music became a national craze with Bill Haley. His 'Rock Around the Clock' (1955) was the first million-selling single in Britain, and it prompted a rash of young British rockers: Tommy Steele, Billy Fury and, in 1959, Cliff RICHARD.

But these were strictly local talents. It was only in 1963 that MERSEYBEAT made Liverpool the international capital of pop. The Beatles led the way, followed by Gerry and the Pacemakers and The Searchers. America was now open to British bands of other persuasions, such as the ROLLING STONES with their raw blues, and the sugary pop of Herman's Hermits. The Stones were imitating a black-American sound, but they were not the only ones. When in 1964 Diana Ross and Martha Reeves infused the charts with soul, Britain responded with Lulu, the barefoot Sandie Shaw, Cilla Black and the husky Dusty Springfield.

By the mid 1960s, when swinging London was the global centre of youth culture, a satirical wit and a touch of anger crept into the music. Ray Davies of The Kinks gently mocked the Carnaby Street culture with 'Dedicated Follower of Fashion', while The Who in 'My Generation' ruffled feathers with the line 'Hope I die before I get old'.

As the heady 1960s came to a close, the highly amplified rock of bands such as Cream and Led Zeppelin came into vogue. The music was deafening at

HERMAN'S HERMITS

DUSTY SPRINGFIELD

SANDIE SHAW

THE KINKS

WIZZARD – ROY WOOD

SLADE

GENESIS – PETER GABRIEL

THE WHO

SIOUXSIE AND THE BANSHEES – SIOUXSIE SIOUX

MADNESS

PULP – JARVIS COCKER

PRODIGY – KEITH FLINT

CULTURE CLUB – BOY GEORGE

THE SPICE GIRLS

ADAM AND THE ANTS

QUEEN – FREDDIE MERCURY

close range, so the venues moved from clubs and theatres to sports stadiums and open-air festivals. Few were bigger than the three Isle of Wight events from 1968 to 1970, which attracted more than 140 000 people.

At the same time, rock music began to acquire grown-up pretensions filtered through songwriters' quasi-religious, drug-fuelled experiences. The resulting 'Progressive rock' wore the garb of high art: the 3 minute dance track gave way to the vast, symphonic compositions of bands such as Yes, Pink Floyd, and Emerson, Lake and Palmer.

This rock theatre reached a peak with Ziggy Stardust, the bizarre stage and recording persona of David BOWIE. It was also reflected in the laser shows, the transformational stage sets and the sheer musicianship of the band Genesis, led by the theatrics of singer Peter Gabriel.

Bowie's spangles and glitter were appropriated by less serious acts, such as Gary Glitter and Slade. To the burlesque of 'glam rock' Queen added an element of razzmatazz. The band's 6 minute single 'Bohemian Rhapsody' spent nine weeks at number one in 1975; its accompanying film heralded the age of the rock video.

NO MORE HEROES

In 1976 the music world was mugged by the very British anarchy of PUNK ROCK. The Sex Pistols, The Damned and The Clash recaptured the spirit of the 1960s by sneering at authority and setting out to shock. Rock music was now stridently political, as The Specials, The Jam and UB40 wrote antigovernment anthems and sang of urban decay.

In the early 1980s New Romanticism (Duran Duran, Adam and the Ants) enjoyed a brief and frilly vogue, but the rest of the decade was filled by American dance music such as hip-hop, house and garage. Then in the 1990s bands such as Blur, Pulp, Suede and Oasis borrowed from earlier decades to create Britpop. Pulp sang of the 'Common People' in an ironic style reminiscent of The Kinks, while Oasis added a punkish leer to their hero worship of The Beatles.

The original teen heroes of pop were by now in comfortable middle age, but the music they pioneered had not lost the ability to re-invent itself.

ART OF THE COVER

The 12 inch canvas of the record sleeve has given rise to some fine popular art. It did not take long for record designers to move beyond a smiling mugshot of the singer, and use the flat, square space to say something more than just 'Buy me'. Sometimes the package was as keenly awaited as its contents. But it was a short-lived art form killed off in the late Seventies and Eighties by the tape in its palm-sized box and the small, fiddly package of the CD.

GANG OF FOUR

The Beatles' Abbey Road *(1969) turned a London zebra crossing into a place of homage. In 1971 The Rolling Stones used Andy Warhol to design the teasing cover of Sticky Fingers, complete with working zip. The Hipgnosis studio designed the unfathomable cover for Pink Floyd's Dark Side Of The Moon (1973), at 25 million copies, the best-selling British album. Yessongs (1973), like many records by Yes, had a cover painted by the artist Roger Dean. The style matched the ethereal weirdness of the band's music.*

Lord ROCHESTER

• Poet • John Wilmot; 1647-80; earl 1658

The nobler parts, which but to name
In our sex would be counted shame,
By age's frozen grasp possessed,
From their ice shall be released:
And soothed by my reviving hand,
In former warmth and vigour stand...
                    'To Her Ancient Lover' (1690)

Many poets – Chaucer, Donne and Shakespeare among them – can be explicit, even bawdy, but John Wilmot, 2nd earl of Rochester, is indisputably England's finest pornographic poet.

Handsome, witty and with irresistible charm, Rochester became the most notorious rake at the court of CHARLES II. He was famed for his dissolute lifestyle, heavy drinking, satirical pen and savage practical jokes. He also had an erudite and serious side. His *Satire Against Mankind* (1675) reveals a deep scorn for moral hypocrisy. He also supported liberal causes in the House of Lords.

In 1679 his health failed as a result of alcohol and venereal disease. He retired to his Oxfordshire estates, where he proved a model landlord, and died a repentant Christian.

ROCK

Two thousand tons of rock, so-called for its tooth-breaking hardness, are sold in Blackpool every year. The lettering that runs the length of the traditionally pink mint stick is a perennial delight but rock also comes in such novel shapes as dummies, fruit and false teeth.

As early as 1800, sugar boilers were turning rough cane sugar into sticks of rock and putting letters and patterns through them. But it was Ben Bullock, a sweetmaker on holiday in Blackpool in 1887, who saw its potential. He went home to Dewsbury, made a batch of 'Blackpool' rock, sold it to the town and then marketed the idea in other resorts. By 1902 rock-making was a cottage industry in Blackpool, where around 15 companies still produce the confection.

Lettered sticks of rock for souvenirs or promotions are now exported worldwide. House of Commons rock complete with portcullis running through the centre sells steadily to visitors and tourists.

ROCK AND POP: *see page 374*

Richard ROGERS

• Architect • b.1933; bn 1996

His uncompromisingly high-tech designs have brought Richard Rogers controversy throughout his career. Unlike much of the

---

ROCKS

The buildings of Britain reflect the rocks below the surface. Britain's geology shows itself in the granite town houses of Aberdeen, the honey-coloured limestone cottages of the Cotswolds and the grey Portland stone houses of the south-west as much as in the shape of the landscape.

ANCIENT BEDROCK

The oldest and hardest rocks are formed from lava and are called igneous, meaning from fire. If the rock cools and hardens below ground, it is known as an intrusive igneous rock – granite is the main example in Britain; if it has erupted from a volcano to cool on the surface it is called extrusive, such as the basalt on the north Antrim coast of Northern Ireland. A fifth of the exposed rocks in Britain are igneous.

LOCAL STONE Many buildings in Aberdeen, sometimes called the Silver City, are made of granite, including Marischal College

HIDDEN VALUE

Rocks contain many different minerals, as the flecks in granite show. Some have industrial uses, others are precious or semiprecious gems. These minerals are all easily found in Britain.

QUARTZ The most common mineral on Earth is quartz. Crystals are often used in electronics and watches

GALENA Silver and lead can be extracted from galena but a ton of it is needed to yield 1 kg (2 lb) of silver

IRON PYRITE A metallic glint earned iron pyrite the name 'fool's gold'. It is often found in Britain but is not valuable

BLUE JOHN The striking, veined Blue John is a type of fluorite found only in Castleton, in Derbyshire

Most of Britain's rocks are sedimentary, which means they were formed from the deposits eroded from exposed igneous rocks. Sandstone and limestone can be seen across Britain and in buildings such as the colleges of Oxford University. Animals and plants are often preserved in the sediments as fossils.

Extreme heat or pressure can change rocks into metamorphic rocks, such as the Purbeck marble found in Dorset.

GRANITE
Lava cooled slowly below ground to form granite, made up of large crystals of minerals such as quartz, feldspar and mica, which make it a hard-wearing material for building and a rich source of gemstones

BASALT
Erupted lava cooled quickly on the surface into small crystals, giving basalt its smooth, regular shape. It is best seen in the hexagonal columns of Northern Ireland's GIANT'S CAUSEWAY

CHALK
Billions of tiny marine animal shells compressed in sediment to form chalk. The rock indicates areas that are, or were, once coastal. It erodes very easily: just rubbing it on a harder surface will leave a white mark

LIMESTONE
The sedimentary rock limestone forms when calcium-rich water evaporates to leave calcium carbonate. It often reveals fossils of plants or animals that were submerged in the water

SLATE
The layers of mud sediments that have been compressed to form slate, a metamorphic rock, mean that it is easily separated into thin sheets, ideal for use as roofing tiles or for flooring

work of his former collaborator Norman FOSTER, Rogers' designs are always forceful, and do not necessarily sit comfortably in their surroundings.

Rogers won international recognition for the Pompidou Centre in Paris, a joint project with Renzo Piano, completed in 1977. The building externalises the usually internal workings: a steel framework, air ducts and water conduits crisscross the glass front and sides, and an external escalator diagonally bisects the façade. He used the same approach with the Lloyd's Building (1978-86) in the City of London (see MODERN BUILDINGS), which has the look of a building still under construction.

The Greenwich Millennium Dome, a structure large enough to house 13 Albert Halls, is Rogers' largest project yet. It includes the development of 120 ha (295 acres) of the Greenwich peninsula, including a river walkway, a piazza, parks, offices, shops and housing.

The ROLLING STONES

• Pop group • Formed 1962

An antiestablishment insolence made the Rolling Stones a daring contrast to The BEATLES in the early 1960s. The band formed in London in 1962 and began to challenge the supremacy of MERSEYBEAT. The founding members, Mick Jagger and Keith Richards, drew on the rhythm and blues music of black Americans such as Muddy Waters and Bo Diddley. They later wrote their own songs, voicing the concerns of disaffected youth in such hits as *(I can't get no) Satisfaction* (1965). In 1969 Brian Jones, the lead guitarist, drowned in his swimming pool – a

STILL ROCKING Bill Wyman left the band after nearly 30 years service in 1992, aged 55, but the Rolling Stones – Keith Richards, Ron Wood, Mick Jagger and Charlie Watts shown here (*left to right*) in 1994 – played on

symbol of ROCK AND POP star excesses; the band were never shy about their drug-taking or sexuality.

Among their finest albums are 1970s classics such as *Sticky Fingers* and *Exile on Main Street* but they performed and recorded throughout the 1980s and 90s.

ROLLS-ROYCE

• Est. 1904

The car produced in 1907 by the dashing pioneer motorist and aviator, Charles S. Rolls, and Henry Royce, a dour engineer and businessman, is still acclaimed by some as the best in the world. The Rolls-Royce Silver Ghost was the first in a series of prestige MOTOR CARS that secured the company's reputation for luxury and quality.

Rolls-Royce began to manufacture aero engines in 1914, and powered the Spitfire fighters and Lancaster bombers of the Second World War. During the 1950s and 60s, they made jet engines for the civilian Comet, Caravelle and Concorde aircraft (see AVIATION).

In 1998 Rolls-Royce Motors, the most British of brands, was sold to the German company Volkswagen for £430 million. Rolls-Royce plc still makes aero engines.

MARKING TIME The vast Millennium Dome at north Greenwich, designed by Richard Rogers, includes some 53 ha (130 acres) of exhibition space. At its apex, the dome is higher than Nelson's Column

PAX ROMANA

When Caesar visited Britain in 55 BC he found a well-fortified land, but its 'cities', he reported, were nothing more than groups of huts in forest clearings. The Roman occupation soon transformed them into urban centres with roads, shops and public buildings, changing the British way of life for four centuries

**MEDUSA'S HEAD
A Roman carving
found in Bath**

WHEN JULIUS CAESAR rounded the coast near Dover in 55 BC with 12 000 legionaries, native British warriors, according to Caesar's account, massed on the white cliffs sounding war trumpets. He returned the next year to defeat the tribes of south-east Britain led by Cassivellaunus, signed a treaty and withdrew, taking hostages and fixing an annual tribute to be paid by the hostile tribes.

The decisive invasion came in AD 43 when some 40 000 troops landed in Kent with Claudius. They crossed the Thames into Essex and expanded west, establishing forts and lines of communication such as the 200 mile Fosse Way linking Devon and Lincoln.

BRAVE REBELLION

Opposition to the Romans was led by CARATACUS of the Catuvellauni. He allied with Welsh tribes but was defeated in AD 51. BOUDICCA, queen of the East Anglian Iceni, led a rebellion in AD 60-61 in which the Roman towns of Camulodonum (Colchester), London and Verulamium (St Albans) were destroyed. But she died defeated and by AD 80 most of Britain,

including Scotland as far north as the River Tay, was under Roman control. However, attacks by Scottish tribes over the next century made it impossible to hold frontiers beyond HADRIAN'S WALL such as the ANTONINE WALL.

Roman rule did not remain brutal. Many Britons adapted to the new way of life, and much of the province was divided into self-governing areas, each known as a *civitas*, based on tribal boundaries and with councils that included native landowners. Towns were established, including *coloniae* for Roman citizens, and within a generation much of lowland Britain was prosperous and peaceful.

IMPERIAL TWILIGHT

Early in the 5th century, problems in the rest of the empire led to the withdrawal of Roman troops from Britain. This, combined with economic collapse and Saxon attacks, marked the beginning of the end of Roman influence, although memories of the Pax Romana – the civilised peace brought by Roman rule – lingered for centuries, and inspired monarchs such as Alfred the Great.

MINERAL WEALTH
Britain's supplies of gold, silver, copper, iron, tin and lead were needed by the Romans to make coins, ornaments, tools and weapons

BUILT TO LAST Many stone Roman roads with good drainage survive, including the road over Wheeldale moor in Yorkshire

CONNECTING THE LANDSCAPE

More than 6000 miles of Roman roads have been traced in Britain – not including lanes and tracks. The army built roads to high standards for the movement of troops and supplies, and the network soon linked garrisons and towns across the province. An efficient postal service was established for official use – messengers could stay at *mansiones* (posting inns) en route. A package could reach London from the northern frontier in a week. Many Roman roads remained in use throughout the medieval period and parts of major routes, such as the A5 (Watling Street) and the A10 (Ermine Street), still follow the Roman layout.

Antonine Wall
Bearsden
Holyhead
Caernarfon
Tomen Y Mur
DEMETAE
MORIDUNUM (Carmarthen)
DUMNON
ISCA DUMNON

A ROMAN ROUTINE
Bathing at the Roman spa in Bath (*far left*) involved the application of oils to the skin from flasks. Scrapers, known as strigils, were used to scrape off dirt caught in the oils (*left*)

KEY

▣	civitas capital	〰	amphitheatre
■	colonia	🏛	bathhouse
▢	town	🏛	gateway
🏛	temple	ICENI	tribe
🏛	villa	▦	remains of road
▦	mosaic	▦	probable road
🏠	house	〰	wall
🏛	fort	▪▪▪	pavement
🏛	tower or lighthouse		

URBAN LIVING

The Romans introduced Britain to a new way of life based on their well-organised economy and the rule of law. In the most developed towns streets were lined with shops and taverns, markets were held in the forum and games in the amphitheatre. Schools provided Latin education, gossip could be exchanged in public baths and courts sat in the basilica, where town councils debated local bye-laws and taxation. Outside the cities, Roman and native dignitaries built agricultural estates on the profits of supplying town dwellers and the army. Villas such as FISHBOURNE and LULLINGSTONE still contain evidence of their luxurious lifestyle.

TALKING POINT The owners of Lullingstone considered themselves wholly Roman. They chose European mythology as a theme for this mosaic floor, in which Jupiter, disguised as a bull, abducts a beautiful Phoenician princess

HOME COMFORTS At Chedworth villa, hypocaust pillars made space for hot air to circulate beneath the floors (right)

SLAVE BOY A Roman lamp discovered at Aldborough

A CHANGING FAITH

The Romans' religious tolerance helped to keep the peace. Woodland spirits on a carving found near Hadrian's Wall suggest that the troops worshipped local deities as well as the Roman pantheon. But Roman patience was sorely tested by the DRUIDS. The high-ranking priestly class, they suspected, were behind Welsh resistance – the Romans accused them of sinister practices and tried to stamp them out. One of the earliest Christian symbols in Britain, painted in Lullingstone villa in the 4th century, shows that the new religion was widespread long before it became the official religion of the Roman Empire in AD 391, replacing pagan cults.

ROMAN RIVER GOD A figurine found at Richborough Castle

Map labels: Birdoswald, Housesteads, Chesters, Hadrian's Wall, South Shields, Vindolanda, Corbridge, ...IUM (isle), BRIGANTES, CARVETII, Ambleside, ...nott, Binchester, Beadlam, Wheeldale Roman Road, ISURIUM (Aldborough), PARISI, EBORACUM (York), Petvaria (Brough), Ribchester, Mamucium (Manchester), Melandra, CORNOVII, Deva (Chester), CORITANI, Lindum (Lincoln), Ermine Street, CONIUM (Wroxeter), Wall, RATAE (Leicester), Watling Street, Great Casterton, ICENI, Caister-on-Sea, Burgh Castle, VENTA ICENORUM (Caistor St Edmund), The Lunt, Hoxne Treasure, DOBUNNI, Fosse Way, CATUVELLAUNI, TRINOVANTES, GLEVUM (Gloucester), Great Witcombe, Chedworth, North Leigh, Stane Street, CAMULODUNUM (Colchester), CORINIUM (Cirencester), VERULAMIUM (St Albans), VENTA SILURUM (Caerwent), King's Weston, Littlecote, ATREBATES, Londinium (London), Orpington, Lullingstone, Richborough, Aquae Sulis (Bath), CALLEVA (Silchester), Stane Street, DUROVERNUM (Canterbury), BELGAE, Sorviodunum (Old Sarum), REGNENSES, CANTI, Portus Dubris (Dover), Lindinis (Ilchester), Ackling Dyke, Rockbourne, VENTA BELGARUM (Winchester), Fishbourne, Bignor, Pevensey, Frampton, Portchester, NOVIOMAGUS (Chichester), Newport, Brading, DURNOVARIA (Dorchester), ...TRIGES

ROMANTIC MOVEMENT

• c.1770-1850

The first stirrings of discontent with 18th-century rationalism were felt as early as the mid century. Thomas GRAY's gently melancholic *Elegy Written in a Country Churchyard* appeared in 1751, and in 1764 Horace WALPOLE wrote *The Castle of Otranto*, the first GOTHIC NOVEL.

These were hardly a serious challenge to Enlightenment values but they paved the way for William BLAKE's *Songs of Innocence* (1789) and *Songs of Experience* (1794), which attacked all that the 18th century revered: reason, order, restraint.

AN AGE OF REVOLT

The year of 1789 also saw the start of the French Revolution. Together with the revolutionary writings of the French philosopher Jean-Jacques Rousseau, it profoundly affected young English poets, including William WORDSWORTH and Samuel Taylor COLERIDGE. 'Bliss was it in that dawn to be alive/But to be young was very heaven', Wordsworth wrote.

The young revolutionaries rejected traditional authority and proclaimed instead the power of individual imagination. Society and city life were seen as corrupt, and nature the true source of moral insight.

The next generation of poets, BYRON, SHELLEY and KEATS, built on the work of Wordsworth and Coleridge but tried to create a new poetic language by returning to what they saw as the true sources of English poetry: Chaucer, Shakespeare and Milton.

LOOKING AT THE WORLD ANEW

Painting, too, was fired with the new spirit. By the end of the 18th century J.M.W. TURNER was producing softly 'romantic' landscapes. Little more than a decade later his paintings had turned into passionate dramas of a sort never seen before. The *Snowstorm: Hannibal and His Army Crossing the Alps*, painted in 1812, seemed like a vision of the end of the world. Other painters, such as John CONSTABLE and Samuel PALMER, took the movement in differing directions. By 1850 Romanticism had exhausted its revolutionary energy and virtually ceased to exist as a movement.

RONNIE SCOTT'S

• Est. 1959

Club Eleven, the first club set up by the saxophonist Ronnie Scott, in 1958, was a brief affair, forced to close after a drugs raid. In 1959 he opened a second club, in Gerrard Street in Soho, where he and fellow musicians could play. It was an immediate success, capitalising on the growing enthusiasm for modern jazz and providing cheap beer in a dim dive-bar.

In the early 1960s, musicians from the USA, such as Sonny Rollins and Stan Getz, topped the bills. When the club moved to larger premises in Frith Street in 1965 it entered a golden age.

Ella Fitzgerald, Dizzy Gillespie and Oscar Peterson appeared regularly, but audiences often came just for the house band, which featured pianist Stan Tracey and Ronnie Scott himself. A second club was opened in Birmingham in 1991. After Scott's death in 1997, his London club remained the hub of British JAZZ.

ROSE

The simple five-petalled wild roses found in our hedgerows – such as the scented sweet-briar and the dog rose – have inspired British poets, gardeners and even soldiers for centuries.

The enduring symbolic association of the rose is with the WARS OF THE ROSES – the struggle for the English throne between the houses of Lancaster and York. In his play *Henry VI, Part 1*, Shakespeare showed Lancastrians and Yorkists plucking white and red roses to reflect their allegiances. Henry Tudor, as HENRY VII, brought the two sides together when he married Elizabeth of York, adding a white Yorkist rose to his red Lancastrian emblem.

ROYAL BADGE English unity was symbolised by the Tudor rose, painted here in c.1574

ROOFS

The universal roofing of the Middle Ages was THATCHING. It still covers some 50 000 houses in Britain but has largely been replaced by clay and stone tiles and, in the 18th century, Welsh slate on Georgian town houses. Today, roofs also make use of imitation slate, concrete tiles and waterproof asphalt.

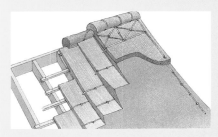

NORFOLK REED THATCH
A Norfolk reed roof lasts about 60 years, twice as long as any other thatch, and can be fireproofed for increased safety

WELSH SLATE
A roof covered with top-quality slate is lighter than both thatch and tiles, and is fireproof, rotproof and waterproof

EAST ANGLIAN PANTILES
Lightweight pantiling came from Holland in the late 17th century, and quickly spread across eastern Britain and into Scotland

PENNINE STONE FLAGS
Thick, heavy sandstone flags are torched with clay and hair on the underside to prevent the Pennine snow from penetrating

Roses appear in poetry, particularly that of Shakespeare, almost as often as in suburban gardens, although in neither case is the association exclusively British. Most of the roses we grow in parks and gardens are of complex parentage, including strains of continental European (especially French), Middle Eastern, Asian (particularly Chinese) and in many cases American roses.

James Clark ROSS

• **Naval officer and explorer** • **1800-62; kt 1843**
A passion for the Poles led James Clark Ross to become the most experienced polar explorer of his time. Between 1818 and 1843 he spent just five years away from the Arctic and Antarctic.

His first major voyage was undertaken with his uncle, John Ross, in 1829, with the purpose of finding a north-west passage to China and the East. But for five years Arctic ice entrapped their boats, during which time Ross discovered the magnetic North Pole (1831). In 1833 he finally ran out of food and escaped with his crew in three small boats, intercepting a whaler off Greenland.

After another abortive Arctic mission, Ross set off in 1839 to find the magnetic South Pole. In the last major exploration made solely under sail, he spent four years in and around Antarctica, naming its two volcanoes after his ships *Erebus* and *Terror*. He also discovered Victoria Land, the Ross Sea and an impenetrable barrier of ice that also bears his name today: the Ross Ice Shelf.

Ronald ROSS

• **Physician** • **1857-1932; kt 1911**
For centuries malaria had been the scourge of the tropics, until a meeting with Patrick 'Mosquito' Manson in 1894 led the Indian-born doctor Ronald Ross to make the breakthrough that produced a cure.

Manson rejected the popular view that malaria was caused by 'bad air' (from the Latin *mal aria*), blaming mosquitoes instead. Ross agreed and in 1898 traced the reproductive cycle of the mosquito-borne parasite that caused the disease.

ROTTEN BUSINESS Rioting demonstrators at the Eatanswill parliamentary election protest at result-rigging in Charles Dickens' novel *The Pickwick Papers,* **published in 1837**

Ross received a Nobel prize for medicine in 1902. The Ross Institute and Hospital for Tropical Diseases, opened in London in 1926, is named in his honour.

ROTHSCHILD FAMILY

The German Jewish banking family came to Britain in 1792 when Mayer Anselm Rothschild sent his third son, Nathan, to open a London branch of the family merchant bank.

During the Napoleonic Wars the bank acquired a reputation for being both bold and shrewd and was soon a powerful economic force. In 1875 under Nathan's son Lionel it lent £4 million to Benjamin Disraeli to purchase control of the Suez Canal for Britain. Lionel's son, Nathaniel, was made a baron in 1885 and became the first Jew to sit in the House of Lords.

Today N.M. Rothschild & Sons Ltd, still located in London, is one of Britain's leading independent merchant banks.

ROTTEN BOROUGHS

Until well into the 19th century Britain had a number of spurious parliamentary constituencies with tiny electorates that nevertheless returned MPs to

Westminster. These notorious 'rotten boroughs' were abused by the rich and powerful to obtain parliamentary seats for themselves and their placemen.

Rotten boroughs came into existence mainly because there was no system of reviewing CONSTITUENCY boundaries and changing them to reflect population shifts. Dunwich in Suffolk continued to send two MPs to Westminster even after most of the once-thriving port had fallen into the sea, leaving a local populace of just 32 voters.

The REFORM ACT of 1832 abolished rotten boroughs by altering constituency boundaries and ensuring fairer representation for urban dwellers.

ROYAL ACADEMY OF ARTS

• **Central London (p.499 B6)** • **Est. 1768**
The model for the Royal Academy of Arts (RA) was the French Academy of Arts, which was already 120 years old when the British institution was founded.

Joshua REYNOLDS, the RA's first president, established its early prestige and classical orientation. Its schools were the first to provide British artists with professional training, and since 1769 it has held an annual Summer Exhibition open to all.

The RA's first home was in Pall Mall but since 1869 it has occupied premises in Burlington House, Piccadilly. There are 80 Academicians from whom full members are recruited.

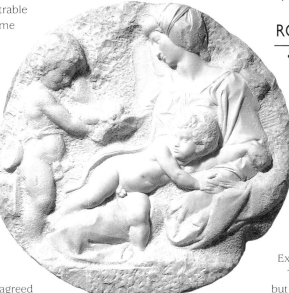

OLD MASTER Michelangelo's marble relief *The Virgin and Child with the Infant St John* **is on display at the Royal Academy in Piccadilly**

ROYAL ACADEMY OF DRAMATIC ART

• **Central London (p.499 D2)** • **Founded 1904**
Generations of fine actors – including John Gielgud, Flora Robson, Anthony Hopkins, Glenda Jackson and Kenneth Branagh – have trained at Britain's most prestigious drama school, the Royal Academy of Dramatic Art (RADA).

Founded by the actor-manager Herbert Beerbohm Tree, the academy was granted a royal charter in 1920. The school was funded by royalties from George Bernard Shaw's play *Pygmalion* (1913), which led to considerable revenue from its musical version *My Fair Lady* (1953). As a tribute, the academy named one of its three theatres after Shaw.

RADA accepts some 30 students annually, after auditions and interview, for its three-year diploma.

ROYAL AIR FORCE

• **Formed 1918**
In April 1918 the Royal Naval Air Service and the Royal Flying Corps merged to form a new armed service, the Royal Air Force (RAF). The greater coordination of forces and resources enabled the RAF to play a decisive role in the First World War. The RAF inherited more than 250 000 personnel and 23 000 aircraft, including Blériots, Bristol Scouts and the Sopwith Pups and Camels, that had performed so ably over the Western Front (*see* AVIATION).

Lack of peacetime funding caused the force to be ill-equipped for the Second World War. Yet for day after day during the Battle of BRITAIN, hastily built Hurricanes and Spitfires repelled the German Luftwaffe from English skies, proving that the RAF had superseded the Royal Navy as Britain's first defence against invasion.

Over the next half century, the RAF took advantage of advances in technology, from the jet engine to air-to-air refuelling, guided missiles and laser-guided bombs. Vulcan bombers and Harrier jump-jets played a decisive role in the Falklands War of 1982, and

THE ROYAL COAT OF ARMS

strike aircraft, particularly the Harrier and Tornado, were used in the Gulf War of 1991 and in the NATO Operation Allied Force against Serbia in 1999.

ROYAL ALBERT HALL

• **Central London (p.499 A3)** • **Built 1867-71**
In 1867 a grieving Queen Victoria came out of mourning to lay the foundation stone of this magnificent memorial to her beloved Prince Albert. Four years later, a red and gold amphitheatre, with seating for 8000, opened to celebrate the prince's patronage of art and science.

Decorated with a high mosaic frieze and surmounted by a glass dome, the grand exterior belied its poor internal acoustics, the 'Albert Hall echo'. After nearly a century of fruitless attempts to rectify the problem, a solution was found in 1969 by hanging 135 glass fibre-filled 'acoustic diffusers' from the ceiling.

The hall has been a venue for boxing matches, circuses and Suffragette meetings, as well as concerts. Since 1941 it has been home to the BBC Henry Wood Promenade concerts (the PROMS).

ROYAL ARMS

The first personal arms of an English sovereign appeared as a trio of lions on a seal of Richard I, the Lionheart, in 1198. Insignia representing new member nations of the Crown have been added to the royal arms, originally embroidered on a surcoat worn in battle, hence known as coat of arms (*see* HERALDRY).

The central shield displays the three lions of England in two quarters, while the upright lion of Scotland and harp of Ireland reflect union with England in 1603 and 1801, respectively. The 1603 union also introduced the shield supports of a crowned lion for England and unicorn for Scotland. Wales is a principality and has its own heraldry in the arms of the PRINCE OF WALES.

The Queen's tradesmen, selected to sell goods to the royal household, may display the coat of arms with the words 'By Appointment'.

ROYAL COMMISSION

A Royal Commission is the most senior committee a government may set up. The first Royal Commission of the 20th century reported on military and civil expenditure in India in 1900. Since then, 157 Commissions have examined subjects as diverse as the death penalty, divorce, trade union reform, gambling and, in 1991, the whole criminal justice system after a string of notorious miscarriages of justice.

On behalf of the monarch, the prime minister appoints members to the commission. They usually include experts as well as eminent people from unrelated fields. Commissions usually take around two years to report, and their role is purely advisory; the government is not bound to act upon any recommendations.

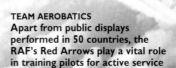

TEAM AEROBATICS
Apart from public displays performed in 50 countries, the RAF's Red Arrows play a vital role in training pilots for active service

SURVIVAL KITS Royal Geographical Society expeditions were well equipped. Lord Curzon's medicine chest (*above*) for India around 1894 contained quinine pills, poison and a guidebook, while John Hunt's Everest supplies in 1953 (*right*) included oxygen cylinders, a water bottle, tent and diary. Both sets are held at the RGS

ROYAL FORESTS

Large tracts of uncultivated land became the first royal forests of England when Saxon and then Norman kings claimed hunting rights over them. Part wooded and part open country, 150 royal forests covered a third of England by 1200.

The forests were a valuable resource, providing game for royal feasts and timber from their woods. But the Magna Carta curtailed the monarch's right to declare new forests in 1216, and many rulers, especially Elizabeth I and the Stuart kings, sold them off to raise funds.

As the 18th-century Enclosure Acts encouraged cultivation and timber was needed for the navy, more ancient woods were felled, leading to a public outcry in the 1890s. Some medieval forests such as Sherwood have almost disappeared, but many remain, including EPPING, EXMOOR and the NEW FOREST.

ROYAL GEOGRAPHICAL SOCIETY

• Founded 1830

Dedicated to expanding geographical knowledge of the world, the Royal Geographical Society (RGS) has sponsored more expeditions to uncharted territory than any other nongovernmental organisation in history. RGS explorations have included the 19th-century African adventures of David LIVINGSTONE and Richard BURTON, the polar voyages of R.F. SCOTT and E.H. SHACKLETON in the early 1900s, and the climbing of Everest in 1953 by Edmund Hillary.

In 1995 the RGS merged with the Institute of British Geographers. It organises three major overseas field research programmes a year and lectures for its 13 000 members; it also publishes the monthly *Geographical* magazine.

ROYAL GREENWICH OBSERVATORY

• **SE London (p.498 D4)** • **Founded 1676**

Charles II commissioned the architect Christopher WREN, himself a professor of astronomy, to build an observatory that could map the sky at night in such detail that ships' officers would be able to calculate precisely their positions at sea.

Wren designed an octagonal observatory with windows 2.5 m (8 ft) high to accommodate large telescopes. Alongside, he built Flamsteed House,

home to the first ASTRONOMER ROYAL, John Flamsteed, who painstakingly compiled a nautical almanac that listed around 3000 angular distances between the Moon and stars through the night.

This exhaustive work established Greenwich as one of the world's leading observatories.

Additions to the Royal Observatory between 1772 and 1858 included a rooftop time ball (1833), which still drops down its mast every day at 1 pm, originally so that ships in the Thames could set their clocks.

When air pollution made observations from Greenwich difficult, its scientific work moved to Herstmonceux in East Sussex in 1946, and to Cambridge in 1990.
See also GREENWICH MEAN TIME

An international conference held at Washington DC in 1884 chose the axis of the Royal Greenwich Observatory as the prime meridian of longitude

ROYAL HORTICULTURAL SOCIETY

• Founded 1804

When exploration of new lands revealed a world of unknown exotic plants, the botanist Joseph BANKS founded Britain's foremost society of gardeners, the Royal Horticultural Society (RHS), to assemble not only information about botanic cultivation but the plants themselves.

The society sent out PLANT COLLECTORS such as David Douglas and Robert Fortune to distant places, and established gardens at Chiswick in west London to nurture the imported specimens. It held its first flower show in 1827, and since 1913 has run the CHELSEA FLOWER SHOW. The society has about 250 000 members. The headquarters are in Westminster but the main experimental and display gardens are at WISLEY in Surrey.

BORN TO RULE

THREE HEIRS Princes Charles, William and Harry are the first Windsors in line to the throne

From Egbert to Elizabeth II, England has been ruled by 62 monarchs. Scotland had 41 kings and queens before James VI joined the two kingdoms. Rightly or wrongly, some rulers are remembered as good, some as bad, and two – Edward the Martyr and Edward the Confessor – are saints

KINGS AND QUEENS OF ENGLAND

Saxon rule in England, interrupted by the Dane Canute and his two sons, ended with the Norman invasion of 1066. Since then nine royal houses have held the throne, all linked by blood. Elizabeth II can claim direct descent from William the Conqueror.

SAXON

Egbert	802-39
Ethelwulf	839-55
Ethelbald	855-60
Ethelbert	860-6
Ethelred I	866-71
Alfred the Great	871-99
Edward the Elder	899-924
Athelstan	924-39
Edmund I	939-46
Eadred	946-55
Eadwig	955-9
Edgar	959-75
Edward the Martyr	975-8
Ethelred II the Unready	978-1016
Edmund II Ironside	1016 (Apr-Nov)

DANISH

Canute	1016-35
Harold I	1035-40
Hardicanute	1040-2

SAXON

Edward the Confessor	1042-66
Harold II	1066 (Jan-Oct)

NORMAN

William I the Conqueror	1066-87
William II Rufus	1087-1100
Henry I	1100-35
Stephen	1135-54

PLANTAGENET

Henry II	1154-89
Richard I the Lionheart	1189-99
John	1199-1216
Henry III	1216-72
Edward I	1272-1307
Edward II	1307-27
Edward III	1327-77
Richard II	1377-99

LANCASTER

Henry IV	1399-1413
Henry V	1413-22
Henry VI	1422-61 and 1470-1

YORK

Edward IV	1461-70 and 1471-83
Edward V	1483 (Apr-June)
Richard III	1483-5

TUDOR

Henry VII	1485-1509
Henry VIII	1509-47
Edward VI	1547-53
Lady Jane Grey	1553 (July 10-19)
Mary I	1553-8
Elizabeth I	1558-1603

STUART

James I	1603-25
Charles I	1625-49
(Commonwealth	1649-60)
Charles II	1660-85
James II	1685-8
William III and Mary II	1689-94
William III	1694-1702
Anne	1702-14

HANOVER

George I	1714-27
George II	1727-60
George III	1760-1820
George IV	1820-30
William IV	1830-7
Victoria	1837-1901

SAXE-COBURG-GOTHA

Edward VII	1901-10

WINDSOR

George V	1910-36
Edward VIII	1936
George VI	1936-52
Elizabeth II	1952-

LOSE SOME, WIN SOME The demise of Richard II (*above*) marked the end of 250 years of rule by the Plantagenets. They were deposed by the House of Lancaster, whose 60 years included the heroics of Henry V (*right*), victor of Agincourt

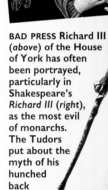

BAD PRESS Richard III (*above*) of the House of York has often been portrayed, particularly in Shakespeare's *Richard III* (*right*), as the most evil of monarchs. The Tudors put about the myth of his hunched back

WRONG DIAGNOSIS George III, played by Nigel Hawthorne (*below*) in the film *The Madness of King George*, was not mad but a sufferer from porphyria, a rare blood disorder

STUART WOMEN Mary, Queen of Scots (*right*) failed to win the English throne, although her son, James, became king of both Scotland and England. Anne (*left*) was the last Stuart. She was pregnant 17 times but left no heir

REGAL VICTIM Deeply moral and a keen patron of the arts, Charles I (*left*) was in many ways a model king. Yet he was the only monarch to be tried and executed. His death was followed by 11 years of republican rule in Britain

HIS MAJESTY'S VOICE George V makes a Christmas Day broadcast from Sandringham House in 1934. He was the first British monarch to take advantage of the new medium of radio to reach his subjects

IN THE SPOTLIGHT On June 2, 1953, a televison audience of about 20 million saw Elizabeth II crowned in Westminster Abbey

KINGS AND QUEENS OF SCOTS

Under Kenneth I, Scots and Picts joined in what became known as the kingdom of Scotia. In 1034 Duncan I added the kingdom of Strathclyde to create a new kingdom of Scotland. The brief periods of Balliol and Bruce rule grew out of the struggle with England, and particularly Edward I – 'the hammer of the Scots'. The Stuart dynasty linked the two kingdoms in 1603.

CANMORE	
Kenneth I Macalpin	843-58
Donald I	858-62
Constantine I	862-77
Aed	877-8
Giric and Eochaid	878-89
Donald II	889-900
Constantine II	900-43
Malcolm I	943-54
Indulf	954-62
Dubh	962-6
Culen	966-71
Kenneth II	971-95
Constantine III	995-7
Kenneth III	997-1005
Malcolm II	1005-34
Duncan I	1034-40
Macbeth	1040-57
Lulach	1057-8
Malcolm III	1058-93
Donald III	1093-4
Duncan II	1094
Donald III (restored)	1094-7
Edgar	1097-1107
Alexander I	1107-24
David I	1124-53
Malcolm IV	1153-65
William I the Lion	1165-1214
Alexander II	1214-49
Alexander III	1249-86
Margaret Maid of Norway	1286-90
(Interregnum	1290-2)

BALLIOL	
John Balliol	1292-6
(Interregnum	1296-1306)

BRUCE	
Robert Bruce	1306-29
David II	1329-71

STEWART (STUART)	
Robert II	1371-90
Robert III	1390-1406
James I	1406-37
James II	1437-60
James III	1460-88
James IV	1488-1513
James V	1513-42
Mary, Queen of Scots	1542-67
James VI	1567-1625

(king of England and Scotland from 1603)

ROYAL MARINES

• Formed 1664

The Royal Marines (RM) were formed under Charles II to furnish the 'Land Soldiers for His Majesty's Fleet', and have served with the ROYAL NAVY ever since. Today's RMs number some 7000 officers and men, representing 15 per cent of the trained strength of the Navy. The training is notoriously demanding: only the toughest recruits qualify.

The marines provide specialist amphibious and mountain warfare expertise for NATO, the Western European Union, as well as other allied and national operations. They are also a core brigade of Britain's Joint Rapid Deployment Force.

The marines served in the FALKLANDS WAR of 1982 and the GULF WAR of 1991, and have contributed to peace-keeping in Iraq and the former Yugoslavia.

ROYAL MILE

• Edinburgh (p.497 D4)

Historic associations press close at every step down EDINBURGH's Royal Mile. It begins in Castlehill, just below the castle, then runs into the Lawnmarket, where country folk once sold their produce. In Gladstone's Land – once the tenement of a merchant called Thomas Gledstanes – two floors have been restored to their 17th-century state. The nearby Lady Stair's House (1622) has been turned into a museum devoted to the writers Robert BURNS, Walter SCOTT and Robert Louis STEVENSON.

Beyond the Lawnmarket is the High Street, dominated by the 14th-century St Giles's Cathedral, with its crown-shaped steeple; here John KNOX was a minister. In Parliament Square a cobblestone heart marks the site of the Old Tolbooth, or prison, the 'Heart of Midlothian' of Scott's novel.

The final section, leading to the gates of Holyrood Palace, is known as Canongate, where the Huntly House Museum (1517) and the Canongate Tolbooth (1591) display different aspects of Edinburgh's rich and colourful history.

ROYAL MINT

• Llantrisant, S Wales (p.494 D4)

The Royal Mint produces the 20 billion coins in circulation in Britain today. It also makes coins for 100 other countries.

Minting began over 1000 years ago but the 'mint' was established in 1300 on a site at the Tower of London. At first it produced only pennies, smaller values being obtained by cutting pennies in half (halfpennies) or quarters (farthings), but other denominations soon followed.

In 1968 a new Royal Mint capable of dealing with the hundreds of millions of new coins required for decimalisation in 1971 was opened at a 12 ha (30 acre) site near Cardiff in South Wales. The life-expectancy of a coin is about 40 years (50 times longer than the nine-month lifespan of a note), which is why in 1983 the Royal Mint began replacing £1 notes with gold-coloured coins.

ROYAL NAVY

Britain's first naval force was created by King Alfred in the 9th century, but the modern navy traces its origins back to Tudor times, when Henry VIII built a series of battleships. The navy earned worldwide respect after Lord NELSON's victory at TRAFALGAR in 1805, and for more than a century 'ruled the waves'.

The Industrial Revolution swept away the sail-driven men-of-war. Iron and steel replaced the wooden hull, and long-range heavy guns superseded muzzle-loading cannon. These changes culminated in the construction of dreadnoughts, the mighty new battleships that were put to use in the First World War. By the end of the Second World War, these ships had been made obsolete by the development of the aircraft carrier.

The Royal Navy, though smaller now than at any time since Nelson, remains a crucial guarantor of national security. Its four ballistic missile submarines carry Britain's nuclear deterrent. The fleet also includes 35 destroyers and frigates, three aircraft carriers and 12 other nuclear-powered submarines, manned and supported by 45 000 uniformed personnel.

SEA POWER HMS *Invincible* **can carry up to 22 aircraft, including potent Sea Harriers**

ROYAL OPERA HOUSE

• **Central London** (p.499 D5) • **Built 1858**

The home of the Royal Opera Company and the Royal Ballet has undergone several reconstructions, the first two as a result of fires in 1808 and 1856, and the most recent to modernise it to the high standards of other international venues.

It has been known as the Royal Opera House only since 1939, spending most of its history as the Theatre Royal Covent Garden. Funding has always been a sensitive issue. In 1763, an audience vandalised the interior over the ending of half-price tickets for late-comers, and in 1810, when the management tried to increase prices to pay for repairs, riots ensued lasting 61 nights.

In 1997 the house was given a £78.5 million National Lottery grant to update the building. For the first time ever, there is adjoining space for the ballet and opera companies to rehearse on site, and the 19th-century Floral Hall next to the house has been restored as a spectacular foyer, open to the public during the day.

ROYAL SHAKESPEARE COMPANY

• **Founded 1961**

The Royal Shakespeare Company (RSC) was set up by the director Peter HALL in 1961, though SHAKESPEARE's work had enjoyed a permanent residence at the Shakespeare Memorial Theatre, Stratford, since 1879. (In 1926 the theatre burned down to be replaced in 1932 by the present Royal Shakespeare Theatre.)

In 1974 The Other Place opened in Stratford as the RSC's experimental theatre and in 1986 the Swan Theatre was built within the shell of the Memorial Theatre. The RSC's London home is the BARBICAN CENTRE and the company also tours the regions.

Under the artistic direction of Peter Hall, Trevor Nunn, Terry Hands and Adrian Noble, the RSC has performed not only Shakespeare's works, but also plays by his contemporaries, modern classics and new drama. Laurence OLIVIER, John GIELGUD, Judi Dench and Kenneth Branagh are among the distinguished British actors who have held audiences in thrall at RSC productions.

ROYAL SOCIETY

• **Est. 1660**

The oldest scientific society in the world currently has 1189 members ('fellows') from the realms of the biological and physical sciences. Early fellows included Christopher WREN and Isaac NEWTON.

The society has always excluded politics and religion from its meetings and has produced many important publications as well as financing expeditions such as Captain COOK's voyage to the Pacific in 1768. Its annual Copley medal, which originated from a £100 legacy left by Godfrey Copley in 1709, is revered as Britain's most prestigious scientific accolade.

ROYAL YACHT

The royal yacht *Britannia* is the last in a line of 35 ships dating back to 1660, when the town officials of Amsterdam presented Charles II with the *Mary* to celebrate the restoration of the British monarchy. In this vessel the king raced anyone who dared, usually for a wager.

Later royal yachts were used for state occasions and in 1843 sail gave way to the paddle steamer *Victoria and Albert I*. George V was so attached to his racing yacht *Britannia*, built in 1892, that she was scuppered off the Isle of Wight at his request after his death.

Britannia, built in 1954 for Elizabeth II, is a ship of 576 tons that once carried a crew of 270. She was retired from royal service in 1997 and opened to the public in 1998 at her berth at Leith in Scotland.

RUGBY

This team sport has its origins at Rugby School, where 'running-in' with the ball (picking it up and running with it), as a variation of football, was allowed from 1841. The game soon spread, leading to the formation of the Rugby Football Union (RFU) in 1871.

International games were initially restricted to teams from England, Wales, Scotland and Ireland (joined by France in 1910, creating the Five Nations tournament), while the British Lions represented Britain abroad, touring

A LEAGUE OF THEIR OWN Karle Hammond goes over for a try as his team, St Helens, take on the Bradford Bulls in the 1997 Rugby League Challenge Cup Final

Australia, South Africa and New Zealand from 1888. The first World Cup was held in New Zealand and Australia in 1987.

In 1895, 21 clubs broke away from the RFU, as it refused to permit them to compensate players for time away from work. They formed the Northern Union (renamed Rugby Football League in 1922), altering the rules and reducing the team size from 15 to 13. They play for the Super League Championship and the 'knockout' Challenge Cup.

The RUMP PARLIAMENT

• **1648-53**

When Oliver CROMWELL heard, in the final throes of the CIVIL WAR, that some members of his parliament were considering a compromise with CHARLES I, he swiftly appointed Colonel Thomas Pride to expel them. 'Pride's Purge' excluded around 40 moderate members, leaving about 60 hard-line Puritans. Collectively and derisively known as 'The Rump', they voted for the execution of the king in 1649.

Cromwell later decided that the country would be better off without them and at 11.15am on April 20, 1653, he entered the House of Commons and ejected them all, saying: 'You have sat too long here for any good you have been doing... In the name of God, go!' When parliament was recalled in 1659 it was to dissolve itself before the Restoration of CHARLES II.

John RUSKIN

• Art critic   • 1819-1900

John Ruskin was the most influential art critic of the 19th century. He learned his subject by travelling abroad, sketching buildings and copying Old Masters, especially Venetian painters whom he praised in *The Stones of Venice* (1851). A romantic, he defended the work of the PRE-RAPHAELITES, championed J.M.W. TURNER and admired Gothic architecture.

With William MORRIS, Ruskin believed that mass production had ruined both individual craftsmanship and human happiness. Ruskin's own life was deeply troubled: an unconsummated marriage ended when his wife ran off with the artist John Everett Millais, and his later years were spent in the shadow of mental illness.

Bertrand RUSSELL

• Philosopher, mathematician and campaigner
• 1872-1970; 3rd earl 1931

One of the towering geniuses of the 20th century, Bertrand Russell contributed to almost every sphere of philosophy and managed to fit in a great deal of social and political activity as well.

His *Principia Mathematica* (1910-13), written with A.N. Whitehead, established the method of 'philosophical logic' – analysis of philosophical propositions in terms of formal logic – that came to dominate Anglo-American philosophy for much of the 20th century. It also attempted to show that the whole of mathematics could be reduced to logic.

Russell applied his mind not just to philosophy but to issues from progressive education to free thinking and feminism, often courting controversy. He was jailed as a pacifist in the First World War and again at nearly 90 for his role in the CAMPAIGN FOR NUCLEAR DISARMAMENT.

Although Russell's main contribution to philosophy was highly technical, he also wrote many popular books, among them *A History of Western Philosophy* (1946). He was awarded the Nobel prize for literature in 1950.

Ernest RUTHERFORD

• Physicist   • 1871-1937; kt 1914; bn 1931

The New Zealand-born and Cambridge-educated Ernest Rutherford made four important discoveries. He showed that radioactivity is created by the disintegration of atoms, and identified the nature of alpha particles (for which he received the Nobel prize for chemistry in 1908). He determined that atoms consist of a nucleus of protons surrounded by electrons and, in 1919, he became the first to change one element into another, bombarding nitrogen with alpha particles to create

ANCIENT HOSTELRY Rye's Mermaid Inn stands at the top of a steep, cobbled street. It has been open for business since 1420

oxygen. Rutherford was a rigorous experimenter and was suspicious of any result that needed statistics to back it up. Yet despite all his ground-breaking discoveries, he was a scientific conservative, decrying Albert Einstein and declaring in 1933 that anybody who expected a source of power from the atom was talking moonshine.

RYE

• East Sussex (p.495 J5)   • Pop. 3710

The steady silting of Rye's rivers has left the town two miles inland today, but when it was first settled in the Middle Ages the sea surrounded it on three sides. From the 12th century, Rye was associated with the CINQUE PORTS, supplying ships for the navy. Its small fortress, the Ypres Tower, now a museum, was built in 1250 to deter the French – latterly without success, as they sacked the town in 1377 and 1448.

In the 18th century Rye was known for its smugglers, who gathered in its inns. Many houses have interconnecting attics, constructed to allow smugglers to escape from revenue officers.

The town has long been popular with writers, notably the novelist Henry James who lived in the fine Georgian Lamb House. The art gallery displays works by Paul NASH and John PIPER, who also frequented the town.

Martin RYLE

• Radio astronomer   • 1918-84; kt 1966; Astronomer Royal 1972

The success of radio telescopes pinpointing sources of radiowaves in space, such as stars and galaxies, had much to do with Martin Ryle. He started his career working on RADAR during the Second World War and later pioneered the use of signals from two or more aerials to give high resolution.

In 1955 Ryle found that the number of radio sources in space increased as the intensity decreased. This implied that the farther one looked into space, and the farther back in time, the more galaxies there were, supporting Edwin Hubble's theory of an evolving Universe that began with a 'Big Bang'. Ryle shared the Nobel prize for physics in 1974 with his colleague Antony Hewish.

Vita SACKVILLE-WEST

- **Writer and gardener** - 1892-1962

A lesbian who had male lovers and a celebrated 49 year marriage; a woman whose grandmother was a Spanish prostitute and father an English lord; a feminist pioneer who was happiest gardening; a rebel proud of ancestors who were courtiers to Elizabeth I – the life of Vita (Victoria) Sackville-West was colourful and contradictory.

Her writing encompassed poetry, travel, gardening and fiction. The novel *The Edwardians* (1930) – written, she said, with the aims of 'making a fortune' and 'annoying everyone' – was loosely based on memories of the family home, KNOLE, and included several characters reflecting aspects of Vita's own multi-faceted personality.

In 1913 Vita married the diplomat and writer Harold Nicolson – a union that lasted despite both having homosexual affairs. One of her lovers was the writer Virginia WOOLF who based the central character in her novel *Orlando* (1928) on Vita. Together with her husband, Vita created the gardens at SISSINGHURST in Kent – their home from 1930.

VITA THE MOTHER Vita enjoyed seeing her two sons, Lionel and Nigel, at 'convenient times'. In his book *Portrait of a Marriage* (1973) Nigel describes his parents' unconventional relationship

SADLER'S WELLS

- **Central London (p.499 E1)** - **Founded 1753**

Sadler's Wells began life as a wooden 'Musick House' in the pleasure garden built up around a medicinal spring discovered by Thomas Sadler in 1683. As a theatre it had a resident company of actors who performed to packed houses until it closed in 1878.

The theatrical manager Lilian BAYLIS rebuilt the theatre in 1931, opening with *Twelfth Night* starring John Gielgud. Within three years Sadler's Wells was almost exclusively devoted to opera and ballet, although by 1946 the ballet company had moved to Covent Garden, and in 1968 the opera relocated to the Coliseum, becoming the English National Opera. Sadler's Wells survived by hosting visiting dance companies from all over the world. In 1996 the theatre closed again for a reconstruction costing £48 million. Under the artistic direction of Christopher Bruce, the theatre's opening gala in October 1998 featured the Rambert Dance Company.

SAINSBURY'S

- **Est. 1869**

Sainsbury's is Britain's oldest food and wine retailer and remains, after Tesco, its second largest. It began in 1869 when John and Mary Sainsbury opened a grocery shop in London's Drury Lane. From the first the shop's hallmarks were order, cleanliness and value for money.

The couple aspired to open a shop for each of their six sons to manage, but the business expanded so rapidly that the boys were soon outnumbered by the stores. By the time John Benjamin, the eldest son, succeeded his father as chairman in the 1920s, there were some 140 branches. By 1999 Sainsbury's had 423 British branches and an operating profit of more than £756 million.

The Sainsbury family have long been patrons of the arts. In 1991 they funded an extension to the NATIONAL GALLERY, known as the Sainsbury Wing.

> Sainsbury's changed the face of shopping when it opened its first self-service branch in Croydon in 1950. The new style of 'Q-less shopping' was an instant success and led the way to modern supermarkets

ST ALBANS

- **Hertfordshire (p.495 G4)** - **Pop. 80 380**

A short walk through the streets of St Albans reveals traces of its 2000 year history. Founded by the Romans as Verulamium in AD 43, the town was sacked by BOUDICCA in *c*.AD 60 and then rebuilt in lavish style. Numerous Roman remains can be seen near the city centre.

In AD 209 a local Roman soldier named Alban was executed for harbouring a Christian priest. Alban, revered as Britain's first saint, gave his name to the Saxon town that replaced Verulamium. An 11th-century cathedral, with the longest nave in England, now stands on the hill where Alban is said to have been beheaded. It was formerly the local monastery's abbey church, while Ye Olde Fighting Cocks – one of several pubs that claim to be the oldest in England – was once the monks' fishing lodge.

St Albans was the site of two battles in the WARS OF THE ROSES: the first, in 1455, when Henry VI was defeated and captured; the second in 1461, when he was released after Margaret of Anjou's victory.

The philosopher Francis BACON lived at the now ruined Verulam House to the west of the town, and is buried in the 10th-century St Michael's Church.

ST ANDREWS

• Fife (p.497 D4) • Pop. 14600

The 800 year history of St Andrews as a seat of learning and religion has been overshadowed by its fame as the world capital of GOLF. The Royal and Ancient Club, founded in 1754, is the game's governing authority, and the Old Course is a place of pilgrimage. The British Golf Museum, opened in 1990 and run by the Royal and Ancient Trust, traces the history of the game.

St Andrews is named after the patron saint of Scotland, whose crucifixion on an X-shaped 'saltire' cross in AD 60 is symbolised in the Scottish national flag. The cathedral dates from the 12th and 13th centuries, but fell into decay after being plundered in 1559 by a mob led by John KNOX.

St Andrews University, founded in 1411, is pre-eminent in liberal arts and chemistry.

ST BARTHOLOMEW'S HOSPITAL

• Central London (p.499 E2)
• Founded 1123

'Bart's', as it is known, is London's oldest hospital, established in the 12th century as part of an Augustinian priory. Nuns and monks of the order cared for the sick, travellers, orphans and the poor until 1537, when the priory was dissolved by Henry VIII; in 1544 a petition led to the refounding of the hospital.

During the 16th century surgeons were appointed, a herb garden planted and an operating theatre built. From 1609 to 1633 William HARVEY served as chief physician.

The hospital was rebuilt (1730-59) by James GIBBS

WEDDING-CAKE STYLE
Legend has it that St Bride's elegant 69 m (226 ft) steeple inspired a local baker to produce the first tiered wedding cake

and grew rapidly in size and reputation. Its distinguished medical school, founded in the early 1700s, became a college of London University in 1900, but in a wave of mergers in the 1980s its title became St Bartholomew's and the Royal London School of Medicine and Dentistry.

In 1998 the government announced plans to convert Bart's into a hospital specialising in cancer and heart disease.

ST BRIDE'S

• Central London (p.499 E2)
• Built c.17th-18th century

Known as the journalists' church (or printers' cathedral), St Bride's has been closely connected with the printing industry since 1500, when Wynkyn de Worde, William CAXTON's apprentice and successor, set up his printing press next door.

The church of that time burned down in the 1666 FIRE OF LONDON and a replacement was designed by Christopher WREN. Wren's church too was burned – after an air raid on December 29, 1940 – though the steeple survived and the building was restored in 1957. The work unearthed traces of buildings on the site dating from Roman and Saxon times.

Memorial services for journalists and printers are still held at St Bride's.

ST CRISPIN'S DAY

• October 25

St Crispin's Day falls on the anniversary of the Battle of Agincourt and it is thanks, at least in part, to Shakespeare's *Henry V* that the saint's name continues to be familiar today. In his speech before the battle Henry mentions St Crispin (or the variant Crispian) no fewer than six times.

St Crispin and his brother St Crispinian lived in the third century. They are believed to have been of Roman origin and to have travelled to Gaul as

missionaries. When they arrived they refused to take alms from the poor and made a living as cobblers. It was said that each night the angels would bring new leather to the brothers while they slept, so that they could continue their work the following day.

Today, St Crispin and St Crispinian are the patron saints of cobblers and leatherworkers. An awl is sometimes referred to as St Crispin's lance.

ST DAVID'S

• Pembrokeshire (p.494 A4) • Pop. 1810

St David's owes its city status to having been a bishop's seat since the 6th century. Unlike other cities, which grew – for geographical or political reasons – it has remained for 1400 years hardly more than a village.

The town was founded by St David, the patron saint of Wales, in about AD 550, but his church and monastery have left no trace. The Welsh remember him on his feast day (March 1) by wearing a leek or a daffodil. Leeks are thought to signify David's asceticism, while the daffodil is thought to be worn because its name sounds like *Dafydd*, which is Welsh for David. The present cathedral, built of the local purple stone, was begun in about 1180, but most of it, including the tall central tower, is in the 14th-century Decorated style.

ST IVES: *see opposite page*

ST JAMES'S PALACE

• Central London (p.499 B7) • Built 1531

After 140 years as the principal royal residence in London, St James's Palace lost its pre-eminence when Queen Victoria abandoned it in favour of BUCKINGHAM PALACE on her accession in 1837. Even so, foreign ambassadors to Britain are to this day accredited 'to the Court of St James's'. Henry VIII built the palace on the site of a former leper hospital dedicated to St James.

The four-storey redbrick gatehouse and Chapel Royal have remained intact since Henry's day. The chapel, with its coffered ceiling attributed to Hans HOLBEIN to commemorate the marriage of Henry VIII and Anne of Cleves, has been the scene of many historic royal events. There Mary I died in 1558 and Charles I received communion before his execution in 1649. It saw the marriage of Victoria and Albert in 1840, and in September 1997 the body of Diana, Princess of Wales, lay there until the eve of her funeral. The Palace's main function today is as apartments for officials of the royal households.

ST MARTIN-IN-THE-FIELDS

• Central London (p.499 D6) • Built 1721-6

A church has existed on this site since at least the 12th century, when fields really did border the Thames between the City and Westminster. By the time the present church was built in the 18th century, the site lay at the heart of a tight network of streets. The architect was James GIBBS, whose portrait hangs at the end of the north aisle.

In the 20th century, the crypt of St Martin's became a focal point of the church's work in the community. It sheltered homeless soldiers after the First World War and Londoners during the Blitz. It has been used as a soup kitchen for many years, and still feeds the hungry – as well as paying visitors in its restaurant. St Martin's hosts regular concerts of classical music, performed by its world famous orchestra and choir.

ST MICHAEL'S MOUNT

• Cornwall (p.494 A7) • NT

The origins of this mysterious island are the stuff of Celtic myth: built by Corcoran the Cornish giant in a forest that the sea submerged, it was perhaps the site of Ictis, famed as a tin-port throughout the ancient world. The abbey was established in 1135 by Benedictine monks from Mont St Michel, a similar granite outcrop off the coast of Normandy. Throughout the Middle Ages its sanctity was compromised because of the site's defensive possibilities. The Mount played its part in every conflict that affected

ST IVES

• Cornwall (p.494 A7) • Pop. 10 090

A combination of tourism, fine art and a rich maritime heritage have shaped St Ives. The town, named after St Ia, an Irish priestess who brought Christianity to the area in the 5th century, was once a fishing and mining centre. These industries declined in the late 19th century but by then St Ives' picturesque harbour and long sandy beaches had started to attract new visitors: painters, sculptors and holidaymakers.

The first recorded visit of a major artist was in 1811, when J.M.W. TURNER painted the town and coast beyond. By 1910, there were over 80 studios and an annual show. The potter Bernard LEACH

the West Country. It was last besieged in 1641 during the Civil War.

After the Restoration, it became home to the St Aubyn family, who extended the old buildings to make a comfortable mansion in the 18th and 19th centuries. The family remains, although the National Trust has been the house's guardian since 1954.

arrived in 1920, and in 1927 the St Ives Society of Artists was formed. In 1949 the Penwith Society of Arts began, whose members specialised in abstract landscapes, strongly influenced by local features. Both societies are still active with regular exhibitions.

The town continues to attract artists and has 17 galleries, including a branch of the TATE, which opened in 1993. It alone draws more than 200 000 visitors each year. Other tourists come to St Ives to swim or surf off Porthmeor Beach, or simply to wander through the town's narrow, cobbled streets.

A BROAD CANVAS St Ives has attracted numerous artists over the years, including James McNeill Whistler, who painted *Cliffs and Breakers* there (*above, left*) in 1884, and the sculptress Barbara Hepworth, who moved to the town in 1939. Her studio is now a museum and its sculpture garden (*right*) displays a collection of her typically abstract creations

ST PANCRAS

• Central London (p.499 D1)

Before 1965, when it became part of Camden, the borough of St Pancras stretched from Oxford Street to Highgate. Now the area is best known for its churches and station.

A 7th-century altar at St Pancras Old Church in Pancras Road suggests that this is probably one of Britain's oldest Christian sites. Restoration in the mid-19th century enlarged and dramatically altered the church, though traces of Norman structure can still be seen.

The New Church stands on Upper Woburn Place. It was designed in 1819 by William

continued on page 393

GRANITE ISLAND The craggy outcrop of St Michael's Mount rises from the sands off Marazion, weathering many seasons in its time – as abbey, fort and country house

LIVES GIVEN TO FAITH

The lives of our saints are shrouded in myth and legend. Some came on missions to convert wild and heathen Britons. Others were local men renowned for holiness or goodness, or martyred for their faith. A few, including St George, had little connection with these islands

ALTHOUGH CHRISTIANITY came relatively late to Britain there is a saint for nearly every day of the year. Some have become national symbols:

ST AIDAN (c.600-51)
The Irish-born Aidan came to the holy island of Iona in about 635 from where he took the Christian message to northern England.

ST ALBAN: *see ST ALBANS*

ST ANDREW: *see ST ANDREWS*

ST AUGUSTINE (d.604)
Augustine was chosen by Pope Gregory I to lead a mission to England and in 597 he landed on the Kentish coast with some 40 monks. King Ethelbert of Kent, though fearful of their 'magic' at first, was won over and allowed the monks to use an ancient church in CANTERBURY. Augustine established his see there as well as founding the monastery of St Peter and St Paul, now St Augustine's.

ST BONIFACE (c.675-754)
The studious monk Boniface compiled the first Latin grammar

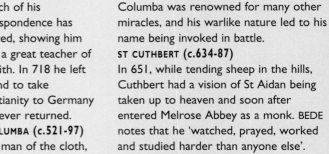

CHURCH LEADER
Augustine was the first archbishop of Canterbury

written in England. He was a prolific letter-writer and much of his correspondence has survived, showing him to be a great teacher of the faith. In 718 he left England to take Christianity to Germany and never returned.

ST COLUMBA (c.521-97)
For a man of the cloth, Columba had a volatile nature and it is said that he left Ireland in disgrace after involvement in a bloody battle. In any event, he came to IONA in 563, where he founded a monastery that became the centre of the CELTIC CHURCH. He quickly set about converting the Picts and impressed the Pictish king Brude

by driving a monster from Loch Ness. Columba was renowned for many other miracles, and his warlike nature led to his name being invoked in battle.

ST CUTHBERT (c.634-87)
In 651, while tending sheep in the hills, Cuthbert had a vision of St Aidan being taken up to heaven and soon after entered Melrose Abbey as a monk. BEDE notes that he 'watched, prayed, worked and studied harder than anyone else'.

Cuthbert later became prior of LINDISFARNE and then bishop. Among the many miracles he performed was healing a dying baby with a kiss.

ST DAVID: *see ST DAVID'S*

ST DUNSTAN (c.909-88)
A severe illness prompted Dunstan to become a monk. He is said to have had

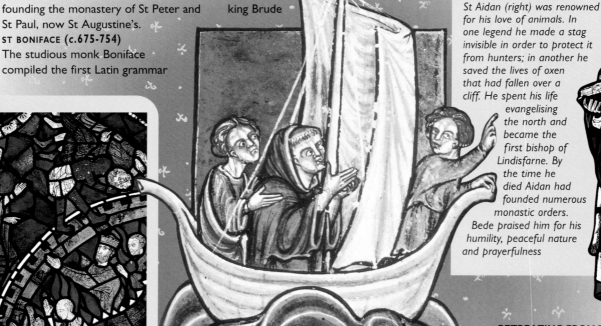

SAVING SOULS *An adviser to all the Wessex kings, St Dunstan saved King Edwy from 'the jaws of hell' (above). In 943 King Edmund made him abbot of Glastonbury, where he set up a monastic community. He founded many other abbeys, rekindling English monasticism*

ANIMAL LOVER
St Aidan (right) was renowned for his love of animals. In one legend he made a stag invisible in order to protect it from hunters; in another he saved the lives of oxen that had fallen over a cliff. He spent his life evangelising the north and became the first bishop of Lindisfarne. By the time he died Aidan had founded numerous monastic orders. Bede praised him for his humility, peaceful nature and prayerfulness

RETREATING FROM THE WORLD
In 676, Cuthbert left northern England and sailed to the remote Farne Islands (left). There he lived as a hermit until 685, when he was called to be bishop of Hexham. Still seeking solitude he exchanged sees with the bishop of Lindisfarne, another island retreat. Cuthbert returned to Inner Farne in 687 to die

DRAGON-SLAYER

The story of St George and the dragon was popularised in the 13th-century Italian Golden Legend. George is said to have saved a Libyan woman from a dragon. Protected by the sign of the Cross, he wounded the monster and promised to kill it if her town converted

an ear for music (he played the harp and had a good voice) as well as being a competent metalworker (his emblem is a pair on tongs) and bell founder.

ST GEORGE (d.303)
The patron saint of England was probably a native of Palestine and a soldier in the Roman army. It is said that George refused to persecute Christians, for which the emperor Diocletian had him tortured and beheaded.

St George's popularity soared in the Middle Ages. Crusaders claimed to have seen him in visions that spurred them on to deeds of bravery. His insignia – a red cross on a white background – was worn to invoke holy protection. Edward III made him patron of the Order of the Garter in 1347, which probably confirmed him as England's patron saint.

ST PATRICK (389-c.461)
The patron saint of Ireland was born in England. He went to Ireland in about 432 and was appointed bishop. Around 444 he founded the diocese of Armagh, which became Ireland's principal Christian centre. Legend says that Patrick expelled snakes from Ireland and explained the doctrine of the Trinity using a shamrock, both of which became his emblems.

Inwood in Greek Revival style, complete with terracotta caryatids (women in classical Greek dress).

St Pancras Station was designed and built by W.H. Barlow and R.M. Ordish in 1867. Its single-arched train shed of glass and iron spans 74 m (243 ft). Fronting the station is a neo-Gothic hotel (1868-74) designed by George Gilbert SCOTT, while next door is the new red-brick home of the BRITISH LIBRARY.

ST PAUL'S CATHEDRAL:
see Christopher WREN

ST SWITHIN'S DAY

• July 15

St Swithin (*c*.800-62) was revered for his compassion, piety and humility. Shortly before his death he asked to be laid where passers-by might tread on him and where the rain from the eaves might fall. He was duly buried in the churchyard of WINCHESTER Cathedral, but in 971, supposedly because of a vision granted to a poor labourer, the monks dug up his remains for reburial inside.

When the move was made, on July 15, there was exceptionally heavy rain, which some said signified St Swithin's displeasure at being transferred from his more humble resting place. From this grew the superstition: 'On Swithin's day, if it doth rain, for forty days it will remain.'

SALISBURY

• Wiltshire (p.495 F5) • Pop. 39 270

The historic capital of Wiltshire stands beside the River Avon 3 miles south of Old Sarum, its medieval forebear. No longer the county's administrative capital, the city is still an important local centre, rich in medieval architecture.

The cathedral is situated in a walled CATHEDRAL CLOSE that covers a third of a square mile and is the largest in Britain. The cathedral's foundation stone was laid in 1220, and the building was almost completed within 40 years, except for its spire, which was a 14th-century addition. Inside, fine medieval carvings have survived 18th-century alterations.

The surrounding streets, laid out like a grid of chequers, centre on the market square, the economic heart of the city for 700 years. Salisbury grew rich trading wool and until the 19th century the plain surrounding it – noted for its prehistoric sites, including STONEHENGE and WOODHENGE – remained a vast, uncultivated sheep-walk. It contains the largest area of grass downland left in Europe, of which the army now uses 100 000 acres for training.

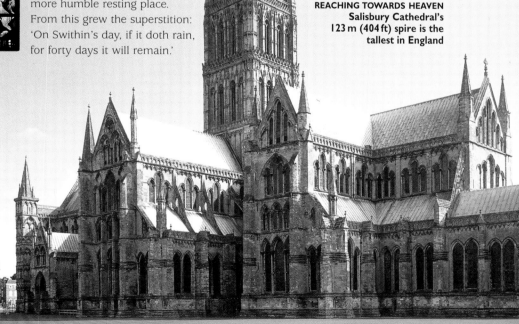

REACHING TOWARDS HEAVEN
Salisbury Cathedral's 123 m (404 ft) spire is the tallest in England

THAT DRESS Although she was fully clothed, the erotically charged *Madame X* caused such a scandal in Paris that John Singer Sargent was driven to settle in England

SANDHURST

• **Founded 1812**

Set in 364 ha (900 acres) on the Surrey-Berkshire border, the Royal Military Academy, Sandhurst, has trained officers for the British army for nearly 200 years. Candidates are mostly men, but women have been admitted since 1984 and make up about a quarter of the intake.

The basic course covers traditional military disciplines such as physical fitness and war studies alongside the more contemporary skills of barricade clearing, vehicle inspection and the patrolling of built-up areas – all part of the modern army's peacetime role in trouble spots such as Northern Ireland.

Training is tough, supervised by regular army sergeant instructors, but it no longer includes the humiliating punishments for which the academy was once notorious – one of which involved 'pupils' pushing pencils with their noses down the majolica-tiled main corridor.

The course ends with the ceremonial Sovereign's Parade but officers are not officially commissioned until midnight of the same day. By this time the training staff have left, avoiding embarrassments such as the occasion when a resentful newly commissioned officer tried to arrest the sergeant who had made his life so miserable during the previous year.

OFFICERS AT LAST The Adjutant of Sandhurst watches new officers complete their 16 week course with the traditional Sovereign's Parade

SANDRINGHAM HOUSE

• **Norfolk (p.495 H2)** • **Built 1867-70**

To George V, Sandringham was 'the place I love better than anywhere else in the world'. He made his historic first Christmas broadcast there in 1932, and died there four years later.

Sandringham has been a royal home since 1861, when Queen Victoria bought it as a shooting lodge for her son the Prince of Wales, later Edward VII. By 1870 the original Georgian house had been rebuilt in Jacobean style, in red brick and local brown carstone, its roofline a medley of gables, cupolas, turrets and tall chimneys.

Inside Sandringham are many royal portraits, collections of porcelain, and Fabergé jewellery and silver from the Russian royal family. The gardens were opened to the public by Edward VII and include a formal North Garden, created for George VI, as well as woodland, glades and landscaped lakes.

Frederick SANGER

• **Biochemist** • **b.1918**

Frederick Sanger is the only British scientist to have won two Nobel prizes, both for chemistry. In 1958 he won the award for his discovery of the sequence of amino acids in insulin. His second award, in 1980, was gained jointly with two Americans, Walter Gilbert and Paul Berg, for his work in determining the structure of nucleic acids.

John Singer SARGENT

• **Painter** • **1856-1925**

'An American born in Italy, educated in France, who ... speaks like an Englishman and paints like a Spaniard,' said a critic of John Singer Sargent.

Sargent's artistic education began in Italy and finished in Spain. An admirer of Velasquez's portraits, he was influenced also by Claude Monet and the works of the Dutch artist Frans Hals.

England eventually became Sargent's home and he was soon famed for stylish and sensual portraits of the aristocracy. He also loved landscapes and in the 1890s decorated Boston Public Library with huge murals. His most surprising work is *Gassed*, which he painted in 1918 as an official war artist – one of the greatest pictures of the First World War.

Malcolm SARGENT

- **Conductor** • **1895-1967; kt 1947**

The flag-waving patriotic fervour associated with the Last Night of the PROMS was largely due to the enthusiasm of Malcolm Sargent. All his life he was an unapologetic advocate of British music, especially choral works, the staple diet of the long amateur choral society tradition, and his devotion was reciprocated by adoring singers of the Royal Choral Society and Huddersfield Choral Society, both of which he led for 25 years.

Sargent was born in Lincolnshire, the son of a coal merchant, organist and choirmaster. During the 1930s he helped Thomas BEECHAM to establish the London Philharmonic Orchestra, which he conducted on morale-boosting tours during the Second World War.

He was principal conductor of the BBC Symphony Orchestra and from 1948 until his death chief conductor of the Proms. He always referred to the audience as 'my beloved promenaders' and his portrait hangs opposite that of the founder Henry WOOD in the lobby of the Royal Albert Hall.

Siegfried SASSOON

- **Writer** • **1886-1967**

If it had not been for the traumatic impact of the First World War, Siegfried Sassoon might have lived out his days as a country gentleman who occasionally wrote pleasing, if unadventurous, poetry.

But the horror of life in the trenches transformed dashing Lieutenant Sassoon, who had volunteered for the army with enthusiasm and won the Military Cross for bravery, into one of the leading war poets. The bleak realism of poems collected in *The Old Huntsman* (1917) and in *Counter-Attack* (1918) revealed his contempt for the military establishment.

Sassoon greatly inspired Wilfred OWEN, whom he met in hospital while supposedly recovering from shell shock. In fact Sassoon had refused to return to the front but the authorities did not want to arrest a war hero.

After the war, he confirmed his poetic reputation with further collections and wrote a semiautobiographical trilogy. The first volume, *Memoirs of a Fox-Hunting Man*, was published in 1928.

MADE TO MEASURE A tailor at Gieves & Hawkes on Savile Row uses large tacking stitches as he begins work on a man's suit – a technique that has hardly changed in 100 years

Thomas SAVERY

- **Engineer** • **c.1650-1715**

The inventor of the world's first effective steam pump was a military engineer who turned to mechanical experiments in his spare time. Thomas Savery invented a machine for polishing glass and a set of paddle wheels to move sailing ships on windless days before devising the steam pump in 1698.

Born at Shilstone in Devon, Savery was familiar with the problem of water in Cornish copper mines, and he named his pump 'The Miner's Friend'. It worked by condensing steam to create a vacuum which sucked up water. Although not itself a great success, it led directly to Thomas NEWCOMEN's 1712 engine.

SAVILE ROW

- **Central London (p.499 A6)**

When it was laid out in the 1730s, Savile Row was a fashionable Mayfair street, and remained so nearly a century later, when playwright Richard Brinsley Sheridan lived there. But then a change took place. By the mid-19th century, Savile Row had become entirely commercial and the number of tailors and gentlemen's outfitters made its name a synonym for understated, impeccable bespoke menswear, particularly suits.

Among the firms whose clientele now includes princes and plutocrats are Gieves & Hawkes, Anderson and Sheppard, Henry Huntsman and Son, and Hardy Amies.

SAVOY HOTEL

- **Central London (p.499 D6)**
- **Opened August 6, 1889**

The Savoy not only set a new standard of luxury for British hotels; it also helped to make dining and entertaining in public socially acceptable. It was built by the impresario Richard D'Oyly Carte as an adjunct to his Savoy Theatre, which opened in 1881.

The hotel had 250 rooms and all the latest technology, including electric lighting, six 'ascending rooms' and 67 bathrooms – unheard-of at the time. But D'Oyly Carte realised that the hotel needed more than this to succeed and early on enticed César Ritz (*see* RITZ HOTEL) as manager, Auguste Escoffier to run the kitchens and the orchestra of Johann Strauss to play at mealtimes. Soon prominent figures from Edward VII to William Gladstone had become regular diners.

The dessert *pêche melba* was invented for the singer Nellie Melba by Auguste Escoffier, who César Ritz persuaded to become chef at the Savoy Hotel

Dorothy L. SAYERS

- **Author** • **1893-1957**

The meticulously researched crime novels of Dorothy Leigh Sayers feature the erudite amateur detective Lord Peter Wimsey and, in later books, the woman investigator Harriet Vane. Her last detective novel, *Busman's Honeymoon*, has them marrying each other.

Sayers also wrote a number of religious plays, including *The Devil to Pay* (1939), and made acclaimed translations of Dante's *Inferno* and *Purgatorio*.

SAFER HARBOUR The sinking of the *Royal Oak* at Scapa Flow led to the hasty construction of the Churchill Barriers, defensive concrete causeways that still block the base's eastern approaches

SCAPA FLOW

• **Orkney (p.497 D1)**

The huge natural anchorage of Scapa Flow, extending over 50 square miles and enclosed by the ORKNEY ISLANDS, was a base for British fleets in both world wars. In 1919, 71 ships of the German fleet interned at Scapa Flow were scuttled by their crews. In 1939, a German submarine slipped past naval defences and sank the British battleship *Royal Oak*, berthed at Scapa Flow. The tragedy cost more than 800 lives – one of the worst so close to home.

SCARBOROUGH

• **North Yorkshire (p.496 D4)** • **Pop. 38 810**

Medieval fortress town, fishing port, Georgian spa and seaside resort – in its long history Scarborough has played many different roles. Long before Henry II built a castle on the headland, it was home to Iron Age tribesmen, and later a Roman signal station. Cromwell's artillery demolished a large part of the castle in the Civil War, and damaged the 12th century parish church of St Mary on the windy plateau beneath, where Anne Brontë was later buried.

Scarborough was one of the first sea bathing resorts. The Grand Hotel above South Bay, built for Victorian visitors in 1865, symbolises the passage of time with 365 rooms, 52 chimneys, 12 floors and four towers. Inland, the curved terrace of The Crescent echoes the architecture of Bath. The poet Edith Sitwell was brought up at nearby Wood End Lodge, now a natural history museum, and the town's Stephen Joseph Theatre is known for premiéres of local Alan AYCKBOURN's plays.

The SCARLET PIMPERNEL

We seek him here, we seek him there,
Those Frenchies seek him everywhere.
Is he in heaven? – Is he in hell?
That demmed, elusive Pimpernel!

Sir Percy Blakeney – aka the Scarlet Pimpernel – took Britain by storm from his first appearance in 1905. A master of disguise, the swashbuckling hero rescued aristocrats from revolutionary France, leaving behind a tiny pimpernel flower.

The author of the nine Pimpernel novels was the Hungarian-born Baroness Orczy, who came to London at 15 and later lived on the Isle of Thanet with her husband, the artist Montague Barstow. Her plots were hardly original – Charles Dickens covered much the same ground in *A Tale of Two Cities* 50 years earlier – but Sir Percy's sheer derring-do was hard to match and spawned a literary genre whose inheritors include James Bond.

SCHOOL UNIFORMS

Until quite recently, school pupils dressed no differently from anyone else. When Christ's Hospital was founded in 1552 as a school for London's poor children, pupils wore a long blue Tudor coat and ruff – and Tudor dress is still the uniform (*see* PUBLIC SCHOOLS). ETON boys, by contrast, wore the latest men's fashions until 1798, when the Eton jacket was adopted as a uniform by the juniors. The Eton suit was a trendsetter, copied by many choir schools and even becoming a general fashion for boys.

A HEALTHY TREND

But most of today's school uniforms come from developments in the 19th century, when sports became part of the curriculum. Team clothes, such as cricket caps, flannels, blazers, and ties in school colours, were believed to promote team spirit, and became everyday wear.

In girls' schools, revolutionary loose-fitting clothes were introduced for games and gymnastics pioneered by headmistresses such as Frances Mary Buss at the North London Collegiate School for Ladies, founded in 1850.

During the 20th century, the gymslip and straw boater, originally a games outfit, became the uniform of private girls' schools. Later, blouses and skirts became fashionable, developed from hockey and lacrosse wear that liberated women from the strictures of corsetry.

SCIENCE MUSEUM

• **W London (p.499 A3)** • **Est. 1909**

The largest of its kind in the world, the Science Museum houses over 15 000 exhibits covering all aspects of science, technology, industry and medicine.

Charles BABBAGE's calculating engines (precursors of the computer) are on display, as is the model used by Crick and Watson to explain the

PERIOD PIECE Leslie Howard (*left*) played the Scarlet Pimpernel in the 1935 film

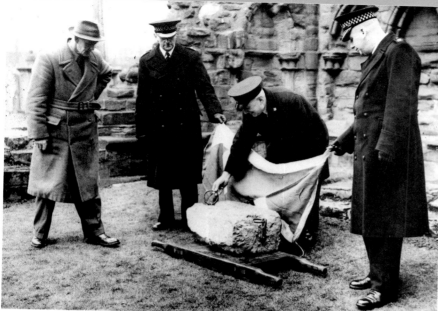

HOT PROPERTY On Christmas Day, 1951, four Scots nationalist students 'liberated' the Stone of Scone from Westminster Abbey. It was found by police not long after at Arbroath Abbey

structure of DNA, and the Apollo 10 command module, which in 1969 made the first manned flight around the moon.

The museum is a world leader in working models and its 2.6 million annual visitors can gain hands-on experience of science from more than 2000 interactive exhibits.

Stone of SCONE

An ancient wrong was righted when the historic coronation stone of Scots kings was taken from Westminster Abbey and placed in Edinburgh Castle on St Andrew's Day, 1996. The stone had been seized in 1296 by Edward I of England from its home at Scone – the Pictish and Scots capital since the 8th century – causing 700 years of Scots resentment.

The stone's history is steeped in legend. According to an 18th century antiquarian, 'The stone, which had first served Jacob for his pillow, was afterwards transported into Spain, where it was used as a seat of justice by Gethalus, contemporary with Moses. It afterwards found its way to Dunstaffnage in Argyllshire, continued there as the Coronation Chair till the reign of Kenneth II who, to secure his empire, removed it to Scone.'

Mystery still surrounds the stone. According to one theory Edward was given a fake, while monks hid the real stone at an abbey on the site of Scone Palace, where it may continue to lie.

SCOTLAND

• **Area 29 795 sq miles** • **Pop. 5.1 million**
The River Tweed, the Cheviots and the Solway Firth form the southern border of Scotland, the second largest of the four countries of the United Kingdom. The Shetland Islands define its northern limit. Industry and towns are largely concentrated in a central belt between Edinburgh and Glasgow, with the sparsely populated Highlands still retaining a distinctive Celtic culture.

A HISTORY OF INVASION
The Romans intermittently occupied the lowlands during the 1st and 2nd centuries AD, but never subdued the indigenous tribes – later known as PICTS. During the Dark Ages Irish tribes called Scots settled in Argyle, while the Anglo-Saxons of Northumbria penetrated to the Firth of Forth. Pictish power was further challenged by Norse conquests and in 843 the Picts recognised a Scots king as their ruler. By the early 11th century all of present Scotland was a sovereign nation, though its English border was disputed and the northern isles were under Norse rule.

TOWARDS A UNITED KINGDOM
Conquest by the English in the early 14th century was successfully resisted by Robert BRUCE, but border wars and religious conflicts continued until James VI of Scotland inherited England's throne in 1603. The two kingdoms were united by the Act of Union in 1707.

SCOTLAND YARD

• **Central London (p.499 C3)**
The popular name for London's Metropolitan Police comes from the site of its former headquarters near the Houses of Parliament. The Scottish connection goes back to the 16th century when lodging houses there were used by Scottish officials attending Westminster. Since 1967 the force has been based at Broadway, London SW1.

George Gilbert SCOTT

• **Architect** • **1811-78; kt 1872**
The soaring spires and curving turrets of George Gilbert Scott's romantic buildings rise high over London, Glasgow and numerous British towns. The foremost architect of the 19th-century GOTHIC REVIVAL, he designed London's effervescent ST PANCRAS station and hotel and Glasgow University. Scott also restored Ely Cathedral and Westminster Abbey, and designed many churches in his trademark late-13th-century Anglo-French style.

To satisfy the prime minister Lord Palmerston, Scott designed the foreign office and India office buildings in Whitehall in Italian Renaissance style. His most prestigious commission was the ALBERT MEMORIAL and in all he worked on more than 700 buildings.

Both Scott's sons became architects. His grandson, Giles, designed Liverpool's neo-Gothic Anglican Cathedral, Battersea Power Station and Waterloo Bridge.

FAMILY AFFAIR
George Gilbert Scott's grandson, Giles Gilbert Scott (1880-1960), designed the classic red telephone box, introduced onto the pavements of Britain in 1926

Robert Falcon
SCOTT

• **Explorer** • 1868-1912; kt 1913 (posthumous)

One of the most tragic names in Antarctic exploration, Robert Falcon Scott was the first Briton to reach the South Pole – but not the first man. He arrived on January 17, 1912, a month behind the Norwegian Roald Amundsen.

HOLLOW TRIUMPH Scott (*back row, centre*), and his team, Oates, Bowers, Wilson and Evans, plant the British flag at the South Pole. Less than three months later they were dead

On the return journey Scott and his four companions suffered from frostbite and exhaustion. Edgar Evans died first. Despite the heroism of Captain Oates who, to give the others a better chance of survival, walked off into a blizzard with the words, 'I may be some time', the rest of the party also died – just 11 miles from their main depot.

Planning of the expedition was fatally flawed. While Amundsen made 25 miles a day on dog-drawn sledges following a line of food depots, Scott's party hauled their sledges themselves, some days struggling to cover 100 yards. Scott's indominitable spirit was no substitute for the Norwegians' professionalism. It was a miracle they reached the Pole at all.

Walter SCOTT

• **Writer** • 1771-1832; bt 1820

Over 250 years Scott's reputation as a writer has been buffeted by constant changes in literary taste. The heyday of Empire saw leather-bound editions of his novels presented to schoolchildren across the world. In the 20th century he has been more often ignored, or condemned for sentimentalising the past.

Born in Edinburgh, Scott spent his early childhood in the Borders, where he developed a romantic view of Scottish landscape and history inspired by ballads, ruined towers and tales of long-dead reivers. He trained as a lawyer, a profession he pursued all his life, but from the age of 30, when he published *Minstrelsy of the Scottish Border*, literature became his vocation.

In an age when classicism was giving way to a more romantic spirit, novels such as *Rob Roy* and *Heart of Midlothian* achieved huge success. But bad business deals and the cost of transforming his farmhouse at Abbotsford into a Gothic fantasy drove Scott to bankruptcy in 1826. He spent his last years writing furiously until he had repaid his debts.

SCOTTISH
NATIONAL PARTY

For more than 70 years the Scottish National Party (SNP) has fought for Scottish independence. It was founded in 1928 as the National Party of Scotland but changed its name in 1934 after merging with another separatist party. The first MP was elected in 1945.

The 1974 general election marked a high point: the SNP won a third of the Scottish vote and 11 seats. A referendum on DEVOLUTION was held in Scotland in 1979 but the Scottish vote in favour was not above the Labour government's requirement of 40 per cent. The SNP lost all but two seats in the 1979 election.

SNP fortunes revived in the 1990s. In the 1997 election the party won six seats and in a referendum the following year a majority of Scots voted for their own parliament. The first Scottish elections were held in May 1999, with the SNP winning 35 out of 129 seats to become the Labour party's main opposition.

SCOUTS AND GUIDES

• Founded 1907

About 25 million children in some 210 countries (1.3 million in Britain alone) belong to the Scouts and Guides.

The Boy Scouts were founded in 1907 by the Boer War hero Robert BADEN-POWELL with the aim, as he explained in *The Times,* 'to benefit the rising generation... to make them good citizens and upright men, and to teach them to put their religion, of whatever form it may be, into practice in their everyday life'.

In 1908, 12-year-old Doris Best was accepted as an affiliate member of her local Scout troop. Within a month 60 more girls had joined the Scouts, and in 1910 Baden-Powell's sister Agnes and his wife Olave officially launched the Girl Guides Association.

Both Scouts and Guides are still taught traditional skills such as tying knots, tracking and cooking on an open fire, and also learn about contemporary issues such as conservation. Scouts can train for badges in computing and public relations, while Guides may turn their hand to car maintenance and audiovisual production.

OUTFITS FOR OUTDOORS Baseball caps, sweatshirts and trousers are part of the uniform for today's Guides – a far cry from the style of 1910 (*right*) worn by the 1st Bollington troop

BESIDE THE SEA

You probably have to be British to appreciate fully the particular pleasures of the traditional seaside resort with its amusement arcades, bandstands and deckchairs on the pier. For 250 years people have come to the coast for the restorative powers of water and sea air

FOUR-LEGGED FUN Once, no seaside holiday was complete without a donkey ride. Now, like Punch and Judy, uniformed bands and toffee apples they can be hard to find

THE BRITISH seaside holiday began as a serious business promoted by the medical profession. As early as the 1730s the spa town of SCARBOROUGH, on Yorkshire's windy coast, was receiving wealthy invalids encouraged by a local doctor, Robert Wittie, to take a dip in the ocean.

In the 1750s Richard Russell, a doctor in Lewes, near the Sussex coast, wrote a popular book on the merits of sea water. He used the money from his book to buy houses in the nearby fishing village of BRIGHTON and established the nucleus of the future resort.

THE PLACE TO BE SEEN

Brighton was within easy reach of London, even by stagecoach, and it soon became popular. When the Prince of Wales (later Prince Regent and George IV) began to visit the town in the 1780s and built the spectacular Pavilion, the future of both Brighton and the seaside holiday were assured.

By the end of the 18th century seaside resorts had sprouted all round the coast of Britain. At first, men and women bathed naked from different sections of the beach – cartoonists of the time delighted in showing clifftop roués studying frolicking girls through telescopes. Scarborough claims to have introduced bathing machines in 1735, and Margate certainly had them by the 1750s.

PIERS OF THE REALM

By the 19th century beaches were becoming crowded and a rash of pleasure piers sprang up to accommodate ever more deckchairs and public entertainments. Brighton led the way in 1823, BLACKPOOL followed in 1863, Bournemouth in 1878 and Southend – at 1⅓ miles the world's longest, with an electric railway – in 1889.

SOUTH EASTERN & CHATHAM RAILWAY
SUNNY
BROADSTAIRS
The Children's Elysium
STELLA MARIS
LONDON WEEK-END FARES
16⁴ 1ˢᵀ Class. 12⁴ 2ᴺᴰ Class. 8⁴ 3ᴿᴰ Class.
FOR ILLUSTRATED GUIDE SEND PENNY STAMP
TO HUGH SMITH, BROADSTAIRS

GETTING AWAY From the mid 19th century railway travel brought a seaside holiday – once the privilege of the wealthy – in reach of all, and ushered in the age of boarding houses

CHANGING TIMES

Victorian holidaymakers went to the beach in crinolines and bonnets, frock coats and top hats, and well into the 1950s many families were still sitting fully clad on the beach.

But such stoic formality ended forever in the 1960s. Cheap Mediterranean holidays with guaranteed sun made people less inhibited, and aroused new expectations. British resorts have responded by reinventing themselves as off-season conference centres or venues for festivals of art, music or theatre.

TAKING TO THE WATER Bathing machines protect the modest at Lowestoft (*left*) in 1887. Cromer pier (*below*) has a slipway at its end from which the lifeboat is launched

SAFER SKIES **RAF** balloon defences against flying bombs over southern Britain in 1944 were the greatest air barrage ever erected

SECOND WORLD WAR

• September 3, 1939 - August 15, 1945

Although conscription was introduced in Britain in May 1939 and war declared four months later, it was not until 1940, with the surrender of France and the Dunkirk evacuation, that the impact was fully felt at home.

A NEW KIND OF WAR
Britain's experience of war was very different than in the last great conflict. Communications were more advanced than in 1914-18, and information was received more quickly. The radio was a common possession and almost everyone tuned in for news and to hear Winston CHURCHILL's speeches. Newspapers, though smaller in size, also carried reliable reports and censored only sensitive material.

FIGHTING ON ALL FRONTS
Everyone played a part in the war. More than 5 million people – nearly a quarter of the working population – joined the armed or auxiliary services. Men who could not fight signed up for the Home Guard or queued in their thousands to join the Air Raid Precautions or fire service. Many women

DOING THEIR BIT By 1944, 1 758 000 men and women had joined the Home Guard ready to repel an invasion

"........ but for Heaven's sake don't say *I* told you!"

CARELESS TALK COSTS LIVES

STATE SECRETS
The Second World War involved the public like no other. Every aspect of life was considered important – even telephone calls

who did not enlist put in long hours on the land, and even children played their part as firewatchers. RATIONING of food was introduced from 1940, and recycling and economy measures of all sorts were practised, from making underwear out of parachutes to collecting meat bones to be made into glycerine for explosives.

THE AFTERMATH OF WAR
When more than five years of total war ended in 1945, Britain was victorious but left exhausted and poor. More than 40 000 civilians died in the Blitz and 264 443 servicemen and women died.

Yet with a sense of common purpose attention immediately turned to building a new society. In 1945 the first ever majority Labour government was elected, ushering in the WELFARE STATE.

SECURITY AND SECRET INTELLIGENCE SERVICES

Britain's domestic and foreign secret security services started in 1916 as MI5 and MI6 – the 'MI' standing for military intelligence, of which they were separate departments. Nowadays MI5 is properly referred to as the Security Service and MI6 as the Secret Intelligence Service.

SECURITY AT HOME
The Security Service specialises in detecting and monitoring people on British soil thought to pose a threat to national security. Suspects range from fringe extremist political parties to agents of foreign governments and potential terrorists – the service took control of anti-IRA intelligence gathering in mainland Britain in 1992.

For years, ministers refused to talk about the service or its cost, but that changed with the Security Services Act 1989 setting out the organisation's function and powers. The service has become more open since 1992 when the name of its director general was made public, but it is not required to publish information about its spending.

PROTECTING BRITISH INTERESTS ABROAD
The Secret Intelligence Service collects information in other countries on possible threats to national security, and makes use of a network of spies.

Like its domestic equivalent, its very existence was shrouded in secrecy until the early 1990s. Now the name of its director general is public knowledge, and the organisation's remit spelled out in the Intelligence Services Act 1994.

Act of SETTLEMENT

• 1701

After the GLORIOUS REVOLUTION of 1688 to 1689, which replaced the Roman Catholic JAMES II with the Protestant WILLIAM AND MARY, parliament set about ensuring that no Roman Catholic monarch should ever rule again.

A Bill of Rights in 1689 limited the succession to the children of William and Mary or Mary's sister Anne, cutting out the deposed James – their father – and his heirs. But in 1700 Anne's only surviving son out of 17 pregnancies died at the age of 11, and the following year

Mary died childless. ANNE became queen after Mary's death, but since she had no heir, the next monarch had to be found elsewhere.

In 1701 parliament passed the Act of Settlement, decreeing that the line pass to the heirs of Sophia, wife of the elector of HANOVER and Protestant granddaughter of James I. When Anne died in 1714, she was succeeded by the first Hanoverian king – GEORGE I, who could not speak a word of English.

The Act also imposed enduring restrictions on the monarchy, requiring every sovereign to be a member of the Church of England and prohibiting foreign monarchs from going to war without the support of parliament.

SETTLE TO CARLISLE RAILWAY

• **Built 1869-75**

In the 1870s the Midland Railway built a 73 mile line from Settle Junction in Yorkshire to Carlisle in Cumbria. The line is the highest in England, more than 305 m (1000 ft) above sea level in places. It runs through spectacular scenery, burrowing into hillsides and cutting across high country. Its complex and costly engineering, which includes 12 viaducts, made it the most expensive stretch of railway ever built in Britain.

The railway's crowning glory is the Ribblehead viaduct, a magnificent engineering achievement, built of brick and locally quarried limestone, with 24 arches. Most of the piers extend 7.5 m (25 ft) below ground to the bedrock and rise 32 m (105 ft).

HIGH VICTORIAN The stupendous engineering of the Ribblehead viaduct carries the Settle to Carlisle railway high above marshy ground at the headwater of the River Ribble

River SEVERN

• **Central Wales and W England (p.494 E4)**
Britain's longest river rises on the slopes of Plynlimon in central Wales and flows for 220 miles through the Vale of Powys, Shrewsbury, Worcester and Gloucester, and into the Bristol Channel.

At flood tide, incoming tidal water from the Bristol Channel fills the narrowing Severn estuary and sweeps upstream in a wall of water up to 3 m (9 ft) high, known as the Severn Bore. The bore sometimes travels as far as Gloucester, 10 miles upstream.

The Severn Road Bridge, a toll bridge linking Wales and England, was opened in 1966. In 1996 the even longer Second Severn Bridge spanning nearly 3 miles was added a little way downstream.

Ernest Henry SHACKLETON

• **Explorer   • 1874-1922; kt 1909**
Overshadowed by his more famous companion Robert SCOTT, Shackleton was nonetheless a South Polar explorer of great capability. Born in Kilkee in Ireland, he saw his first Antarctic service in 1901 when he sailed in the *Discovery* under Scott to reach the South Pole.

The expedition did not reach the Pole but, undeterred, Shackleton mounted a second expedition in 1908. His brusque but determined leadership carried his team across the Ross Ice Shelf, over the Beardmore Glacier and to within 97 miles of the Pole – a record for the time.

Scott's death in 1912 did nothing to diminish Shackleton's enthusiasm and in 1914 he launched a third polar expedition. It was a calamity. His ship, the *Endeavour* was trapped in Antarctic ice and was crushed. Shackleton and his

> On his horrifying 1914 voyage to South Georgia, Shackleton felt himself accompanied by an invisible watcher – an idea T.S. Eliot refers to in his poem *The Waste Land*

companions reached a barren rock called Elephant Island. With no hope of rescue, he took a small boat and with five crew sailed for 800 miles through stormy seas to South Georgia where, after climbing over its highest mountain, he found a whaling station that sent a ship to pick up the men left behind.

A few years later, in 1922, the island of South Georgia in the South Atlantic became his final destination. Shackleton died there of a heart attack, during his fourth and last foray into the Antarctic.

Lord SHAFTESBURY

• **Reformer and philanthropist**
• **1801-85; earl 1851**
Anthony Ashley Cooper, later 7th earl of Shaftesbury, took his seat as a Tory MP in 1826. But he soon eschewed a conventional political career and by 1828 was involved in the first of many good causes: the better treatment of lunatics.

He then focused on employment conditions in mills and factories. The several mid-Victorian Factory Acts limiting women's and children's hours of work owed much to his campaigning.

His next campaign resulted in the Mines Act 1842. After this came 'climbing boys' (apprentice chimney sweeps), ragged schools, housing conditions, the Corn Laws, Florence Nightingale's work at Scutari in the Crimea, animal welfare, Christian missions and other philanthropic causes.

Shaftesbury's reforming zeal was inspired by a compassionate heart and a fervent Christian faith. However, he never questioned the social and political roots of inequality, and those of a more radical disposition criticised his reforms as paternalistic.

A POET FOR ALL TIME

William Shakespeare not only shaped the English language, coining such everyday words and phrases as 'virtue of necessity', 'cold comfort' and 'a foregone conclusion', but helped to forge the identity of modern Britain. His insight into human nature gives his plays a timeless relevance

CHANGE OF SCALE Shakespeare's audiences would have had to imagine the magical world of plays such as *The Tempest*, but modern productions can stage illusions such as Caliban being small enough to hide inside a shell

W HEN THE actor-playwright William Shakespeare (1564-1616) arrived in London around 1590 he found a city alive with optimism. He had left his wife, Anne Hathaway, and children in Stratford-upon-Avon and gone to seek his fortune. With Elizabeth I on the throne, England had seen off the Armada and was a thriving international trade centre.

Behind the glory of London, waves of bubonic plague tore through the city's filthy tenements, yet the population of London had increased by half in 30 years and was hungry for entertainment.

The first purpose-built structure for staging plays, called 'The Theatre', had opened in London in 1576 and attracted large audiences. Professional theatre companies were still relatively new: the most distinguished, such as Shakespeare's company, the Lord Chamberlain's Men, had the patronage of noblemen.

PLEASING THE PEOPLE

Audiences ranged from 'groundlings' — who paid a penny to stand and would talk, eat and provide instant vociferous criticism — to the upper classes, who sat on the stage itself. All demanded an absorbing story, distinctly good or evil characters, passion, fighting, clowning, rhetoric and wit.

Shakespeare had begun as an actor but, with companies performing a different play each day, writers were in demand. Between 1590 and 1600 he penned more than 20 histories and romantic comedies ranging from *Richard III* to *A Midsummer Night's Dream*.

SHAKESPEARE'S LITERARY LEGACY

Many of Shakespeare's plays premiered at the GLOBE, the home of his company from 1599. From 1600 to 1608 he wrote the great tragedies, including *Hamlet* and *Macbeth*, and the 'dark' comedies or 'problem plays' such as *Measure for Measure*. His last plays, including *The Winter's Tale*, were mostly romances. The sonnets, written during the 1590s to a

mysterious 'dark lady', are considered the most sublime examples of the form.

Shakespeare's genius lay in his ability to please his audience, his company and, most importantly, his royal patron, while retaining his own voice. His plays have an enduring universal appeal and he remains the world's most-performed playwright.

THE PLAYS

1591-2	*Henry VI*
1592	*The Comedy of Errors*
1592	*Titus Andronicus*
1592-3	*Richard III*
1593	*The Taming of the Shrew*
1593	*All's Well That Ends Well*
1594	*Love's Labour's Lost*
1594	*The Two Gentlemen of Verona*
1594-5	*Edward III*
1595	*Romeo and Juliet*
1595	*Richard II*
1595	*A Midsummer Night's Dream*
1596	*King John*
1596	*The Merchant of Venice*
1597	*Henry IV*
1598	*The Merry Wives of Windsor*
1598	*Much Ado About Nothing*
1599	*Henry V*
1599	*Julius Caesar*
1599	*As You Like It*
1599	*Twelfth Night*
1600	*Hamlet*
1602	*Troilus and Cressida*
1602	*Othello*
1604	*Measure for Measure*
1604	*Timon of Athens*
1605	*King Lear*
1605	*Macbeth*
1607	*Antony and Cleopatra*
1607-8	*Coriolanus*
1608	*Pericles*
1610	*Cymbeline*
1610	*The Winter's Tale*
1611	*The Tempest*
1613	*The Two Noble Kinsmen*
1613	*Henry VIII*

THE POEMS

1593	*Venus and Adonis*
1594	*The Rape of Lucrece*
1609	Sonnets published

THE GREAT BARD A statue in Westminster Abbey commemorates Shakespeare's life and poetry; the poet Ben Jonson praised his friend's wit in a foreword to a 1623 edition of his work

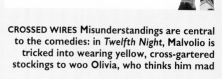

CROSSED WIRES Misunderstandings are central to the comedies: in *Twelfth Night*, Malvolio is tricked into wearing yellow, cross-gartered stockings to woo Olivia, who thinks him mad

OUT OF THE GUTTER George Bernard Shaw's play *Pygmalion* was filmed in 1956 as *My Fair Lady.* It starred Audrey Hepburn (*centre*) and had sets and costumes by Cecil Beaton

George Bernard SHAW

- Playwright and critic
- 1856-1950

'It is by jingling the bells of a jester's cap that I have made people listen to me,' said the playwright George Bernard Shaw. In his plays and their long prefaces he advocated socialism and women's rights – he believed in equality of income and easy divorce – but Shaw was also an avid campaigner for a wide variety of causes, including antivivisection and simplified spelling.

Plays such as *Pygmalion* (1913) and *Heartbreak House* (1920) were witty satires, criticising class distinction and decadent high society. Some provoked opposition: *Mrs Warren's Profession* (1893), in which it is argued that well-paid prostitution was better than long hours, hard work and starvation wages in a factory, was banned until 1925.

Shaw's were plays of ideas, with little action and emotion but a great deal of intelligent talk, and his work was often criticised for being cold and dry. His intellectual approach produced outstanding musical and dramatic criticism during the 1880s and 1890s that is still widely read.

Norman SHAW

- Architect   • 1831-1912

Norman Shaw was the master architect of the late Victorian era. Picturesque, old-English-style country houses made his name but he also designed furniture, interiors, churches, cottages, office buildings and city housing schemes.

In 1858 Shaw became draughtsman to George Street, a church architect, and began his career designing churches in GOTHIC REVIVAL style, such as Holy Trinity in Bingley. His early houses mingled Gothic and Tudor styles with local features such as half-timbering, hung tiles and exterior plasterwork. During the 1870s, Shaw's style matured to more sober brick houses such as those on the Bedford Park Estate in west London. In the 1890s he turned to a monumental classicism, seen at its best in the QUEEN ANNE STYLE Bryanston House in Blandford, Dorset, and the Piccadilly Hotel and New Scotland Yard in London.

SHEEPDOG TRIALS

In 1876, two farmers in south Wales arguing over who had the better dog settled their dispute with a contest – the first sheepdog trial. A popular spectator sport was born; thousands of trials are now held each year in Britain.

The canine competitors are nearly all working farm dogs – mostly border collies – displaying skills they use each day. They must herd sheep between two points, separate two unmarked ewes from a flock (shedding) and herd a flock into a pen (penning). The television programme 'One Man and His Dog', first broadcast in 1976, brought trials to the attention of city folk, attracting an average 5 million viewers at its peak.

Collies have been bred as working dogs since the late 19th century; their speed gave them an advantage over the old English sheepdog used until then. They have an instinct for herding and can be taught to obey signals from the voice, hand and whistle such as 'come by' (go left) and 'away to me' (right).

HOME MADE Norman Shaw designed his own home in Hampstead in 1874 and set a trend for great houses in the fashionable London suburb

SHEFFIELD

- N England (p.496 C5)
- Pop. 431 610

Making cutlery was a major industry in Sheffield as early as the Middle Ages – the Miller in Geoffrey Chaucer's *Canterbury Tales* carries a Sheffield knife. By 1760 the fumes of industry prompted the writer Horace Walpole to describe it as 'the foulest town in England in the most charming situation'. Steel made Sheffield England's fourth largest city during the 1800s as foundries lined the banks of the river Don. The city's development is traced in the Kelham Island Industrial Museum, where exhibits range from knives and sickles to modern precision tools.

The Victorian Renaissance-style town hall is typical of Sheffield's monumental buildings. A giant statue of Vulcan, the blacksmith-god of Roman mythology, crowns the hall, which is lavishly decorated with marble and plasterwork.

As the steel industry declined the city found new roles for its disused foundries. East of the city, 74 ha (183 acres) of land occupied by the Hadfield steel works until 1983 has been redeveloped as Meadowhall, the largest shopping centre in Europe when it opened in 1990. *See also SHEFFIELD STEEL*

WATER WONDERS The four lakes at Sheffield Park Garden are linked by waterfalls and spanned by ornamental bridges. They were laid out by 'Capability' Brown in the 1770s

SHEFFIELD PARK GARDEN

• **East Sussex (p.495 H5)**
• **Created 18th-20th century   • NT**

'Capability' Brown originally landscaped Sheffield Park Garden, but the exotic trees and shrubs that are the garden's most spectacular feature were planted by the Soames family, who acquired the 50 ha (120 acre) estate in 1909.

Majestic North American conifers provide a constant backdrop to the garden's seasonal displays. Spring carpets of daffodils and bluebells are followed by bright splashes of azaleas and rhododendrons, and a blaze of autumn colour from a mass of maples.

Sheffield Park is the southern terminus of the Bluebell Railway, a steam railway with more than 40 locomotives, which opened in 1960.

SHEFFIELD STEEL

The city of SHEFFIELD has been the centre of British steel manufacture and especially cutlery since the 12th century. The innovations of Henry BESSEMER, Thomas Boulsover and Benjamin Huntsman – all local men – helped to make Sheffield steel the world's best.

Boulsover developed Sheffield plate in the 1740s, a sandwich of silver around copper used for small items such as buttons. In the same decade, Huntsman invented the crucible method of steel-making. But in 1856 Bessemer made it possible to produce steel in large quantities and the industry took off.

Stainless steel, a rust-resistant alloy of steel and chromium, was pioneered in Sheffield in the early 1900s, when the city had the highest concentration of steel furnaces in Britain. Although the number of people who

work in Sheffield steel mills today is only a quarter of the 1970 figure, more steel is being produced there now than during the Second World War.

Percy Bysshe SHELLEY and Mary SHELLEY

• **Writers   • Percy Bysshe Shelley 1792-1822**
• **Mary Wollstonecraft Shelley 1797-1851**

From childhood, the poet Percy Shelley betrayed a revolutionary streak. At school he had the nickname the 'Eton Atheist', and he was sent down from Oxford in 1811 for writing a pamphlet called *The Necessity of Atheism*. He was influenced by writers such as the anarchist William Godwin and opposed not just religion but also royalty and meat eating.

When Shelley met Godwin he fell in love with his daughter Mary, whose mother, Mary Wollstonecraft, was the feminist author of *A Vindication of The Rights of Woman* (1792). Together they travelled in Switzerland and stayed with Lord BYRON by Lake Geneva in 1816, where Mary began her GOTHIC NOVEL *Frankenstein*.

Both were inspired by the ROMANTIC MOVEMENT to revel in the force of nature and question the morality of meddling with it: Shelley marvelled at the majesty of the Alps in the poem 'Mont Blanc' (1817). The grim repercussions of Frankenstein's monstrous creation reflected fears of scientific progress.

Dogged by ill health and debts, Shelley preferred not to live in Britain and in 1818 the couple moved to Italy. There, Shelley produced many of his finest poems: 'Prometheus Unbound' (1820), the ode 'To a Skylark' (1820) and 'Epipsychidion' (1821). Shelley drowned in a boating accident near Livorno. His body was burned in a funeral pyre on the beach but his heart is buried with his parents-in-law and wife in Bournemouth.

Thomas SHERATON

• **Furniture designer   • 1751-1806**

Thomas Sheraton was a trained cabinet maker but never had his own workshop. He moved from County Durham to London in 1790 to teach design and published his furniture sketches in the *Cabinet-Maker and Upholsterer's Drawing-Book* (1791-3).

Sheraton's designs – particularly his delicate armchairs, with low backs and downward-sweeping arms – exerted a more lasting influence than those of his contemporary, George HEPPLEWHITE. He used elements of English and French styles, and many of his pieces prefigure the tastes of the REGENCY period.

Today, the name 'Sheraton' is used to distinguish light-coloured, slender furniture in satinwood and mahogany from dark red-wood CHIPPENDALE.

SWEET DREAMS Thomas Sheraton's furniture designs, such as this elaborate canopied bed, inspired many imitators though few of his designs were actually built

Richard Brinsley SHERIDAN

• Playwright and politician • 1751-1816

Two of the most popular comedies in English, *The Rivals* (1775) and *The School for Scandal* (1777), established the Dublin-born Richard Brinsley Sheridan in fashionable society. Full of all the misunderstandings and disguises of romantic comedy, the plays are also witty satires on romance, pretension and gossip-mongering.

Sheridan's most memorable character is the witless Mrs Malaprop in *The Rivals*. Her habit of mixing up words has given a name to ignorant slips of the tongue – 'malapropisms' – such as comparing someone to an 'allegory', not an alligator, 'on the banks of the Nile'.

PLAYING TO A FULL HOUSE

His plays were widely acclaimed by critics and audiences but Sheridan was not satisfied and longed to enter politics. In 1780 he became a Member of Parliament and then under-secretary for foreign affairs. He won a reputation for brilliant and lengthy orations – he once held the floor for more than five hours.

In 1809, while he was the proprietor of the DRURY LANE theatre it burned to the ground, losing him a fortune. Sheridan sat watching the blaze from a café nearby and, when his calm was remarked upon, he reportedly replied, 'A man may surely be allowed to take a glass of wine beside his own fireside'.

SUPER SLEUTH Basil Rathbone played Sherlock Holmes in 14 films between 1939 and 1945

VIKING REVIVAL 'Norsemen' – Shetlanders in costume – revisit the tranquil Shetland Islands every year to celebrate the ancient fire festival **Up-Helly-Aa**

SHERLOCK HOLMES

• Fictional detective

Between *A Study in Scarlet* (1887) and *The Casebook of Sherlock Holmes* (1927) Scotsman Arthur Conan Doyle (1859-1930) wrote 56 stories and four novels about Holmes and his friend Dr Watson. But in none of them did he mention a deerstalker cap or a curved meerschaum pipe, the trademarks for which Holmes was to become so well known in films.

The detective's penetrating power of deduction was inspired by one of Doyle's lecturers at medical school, who claimed to be able to spot a left-handed cobbler from which side of his britches was more worn. It was not until the 1929 film *The Return of Sherlock Holmes* that Holmes, played by Clive Brook uttered the catchphrase that later accompanied all his revelations: 'Elementary, my dear Watson.'

In 1893 Doyle, who wanted to write more serious books, killed off Holmes in a fight with his arch-enemy, Professor Moriarty. Readers protested, and Doyle was forced to bring Holmes back to life.

SHERRY

The drink made around Jerez in southern Spain has been popular in Britain since the 16th century. Sherry, or 'sack' as it was known until the late 17th century, was wine fortified with brandy and sugar as preservatives. In the late 18th century merchants began to blend varieties of sherry, from bone-dry manzanilla to rich oloroso. In the 1860s the Bristol shipper, John Harvey, added a sweeter wine to his imported oloroso to make Bristol Cream, now the world's most popular blend.

In its Victorian heyday, sherry made up nearly half the wine imported into Britain. Its popularity has declined since the 1950s, although more than 4.9 million gallons were imported in 1998.

SHETLAND ISLANDS

• NE Scotland (p.497 D2) • Pop. 17 600

Of the 100 or so Shetland Islands a hundred miles off north-east Scotland, fewer than 20 are inhabited. Some, such as the now-deserted Mousa, were first settled in prehistoric times and there are many ancient remains, such as the Stone Age settlement at JARLSHOF.

On the last Tuesday in January in Lerwick, on Mainland, the largest island, locals re-enact the Norse festival of Up-Helly-Aa. Pagan Vikings settled in the Shetlands in the 9th century and celebrated the end of Christian yuletide with feasting and drinking and by ceremonially burning a longship.

Nowhere in Shetland is more than 3 miles from the sea and shipping has long been the main industry. Many islanders work for North Sea oil companies, notably at Sullom Voe, near Lerwick.

SHIPBUILDING

Portsmouth, and the Thames and Medway rivers, were the main centres of wooden shipbuilding. Lord Nelson's flagship *VICTORY* was launched in 1765 at Chatham. Change came when wood and sail gave way to iron and steam. The first British iron boat, *The Trial*, was launched in 1787 and the first steamer, *Comet*, in 1812. BRUNEL's SS *Great Britain*, the first large iron ship and the first to be screw propelled, set the pattern for the future.

The new technology required access to cheap iron and coal and deeper water, so the industry moved north to the Mersey, Tyne, Belfast and Glasgow, which had particular expertise in engine building. Britain dominated shipbuilding throughout the 19th century: the industry grew more than 15 fold between 1850 and 1870.

BRITANNIA RULES THE WAVES

In the early 20th century, British ships such as the *TITANIC* and *QUEEN MARY* were the world's finest. Passengers crossed the Atlantic in luxury until air transport in the 1960s made travel far faster and cheaper than by sea.

A brief rise in demand after the Second World War could not halt the decline of Britain's shipbuilding, as overseas yards with lower costs and more modern technology increasingly won new orders. By 1977 Britain produced 4 per cent of the world's ships, compared with 60 per cent in 1914. Today few yards survive.

WEATHER MAP There are 30 shipping forecast areas covering the coastal waters around Britain. The boundaries extend inland to include estuaries used by ships

SHIPPING FORECAST

'Viking, North Utsire, South Utsire, south-easterly, gale eight, decreasing six, rain or snow, moderate becoming poor.' The shipping forecast is heard by millions of listeners every day, but understood by only a handful.

To sailors, the bulletins broadcast four times a day on BBC Radio 4 provide vital information. They announce first the areas whose forecast follows (Viking, North Utsire, South Utsire), then the wind direction (south-easterly), its current and predicted strength (gale eight, decreasing six), the weather conditions (rain or snow) and finally the visibility (moderate becoming poor). Many coastal areas are named after a prominent feature, such as the Bay of Biscay, Cape Finisterre, the Dogger Bank and Malin Head. Details of current weather conditions in smaller areas are also available from 50 coastal stations.
See also WEATHER FORECASTING

FORGING A COLOSSUS The *Titanic* (left) was built at Harland and Wolff's Belfast shipyard. The scale of such ships can be imagined from the size of the propellers; the one above, being finished in 1934, weighed 35 tons

SHOP TILL YOU DROP

Leisurely trips to the village store for flour from sacks and tea from chests are memories from a gentler age. Speed and convenience are the bywords of the modern shopping experience

N ANGLO-SAXON Britain people from neighbouring villages met regularly at a bridge or crossroads to exchange livestock and home-produced goods. These meetings became weekly MARKETS during the Middle Ages, controlled by the Church. At the same time, FAIRS became popular meeting places for travelling salesmen.

THE RETAIL REVOLUTION

Shops evolved from market stalls and the earliest were just boxes with flaps that folded out to make a canopy and counter. From the 11th century guilds of merchants formed, dealing in imported or commercially produced goods for profit. Gradually master craftsmen began to sell their wares from shops.

VALUE FOR MONEY The village shop was store and community centre in one. The Co-op gave shoppers a share of the profits in exchange for stamps collected in a 'divvy' book (above)

THE GROWTH OF THE HIGH STREET

By the 18th century shops were an established part of British life and narrow town streets bristled with large signs advertising the goods on sale. Names such as Bread Street, Fish Street, Leather Lane or Cornmarket recall the merchants who traded there. 'Shambles', another common street name, originally meant simply a row of covered stalls.

From the mid to late 19th century chains of stores started to open. Victorian Britain was in the middle of a consumer boom, with more money than ever before being spent in shops, often on 'luxury' items. Shopkeepers could afford to expand into new premises and before long high streets began to look identical from town to town as the chain stores with their distinctive shopfronts arrived.

During this boom time several modern stores had their humble beginnings. In 1848 W.H. SMITH began selling books, and Jesse Boot opened his first chemist shop in 1877. By 1900 Smith had 800 stores and Boot 181. The worldwide chain of MARKS & SPENCER stores began as a penny-goods stall in Leeds market in 1894, and in 1869 Sainsbury's, Britain's oldest supermarket chain, started as a small dairy shop.

In the 19th century shopping became almost a form of recreation. London's West End led the way with elegant, glass-roofed arcades of luxury shops selling anything from books to jewels and silks.

To supply an increasingly prosperous, middle class, a new shopping concept – department stores – emerged. Dickins & Jones and Marshall & Snelgrove sold haberdashery, fabrics and ready-made ladies' fashions. In 1849 Charles Harrod took over a Knightsbridge grocery, which became HARRODS the world's largest store; LIBERTY'S began life in 1875.

SHARE AND SHARE ALIKE

In 1844 a group of socialists from Rochdale founded a 'cooperative' store. They bought goods in bulk and shared the profits; regular customers received a half-yearly dividend, or 'divvy'. More branches opened and the 'Co-op' (Co-operative

Wholesale Society) was founded, buying direct from farmers, importers and manufacturers to keep prices low. Grocers, such as Thomas Lipton who had a chain of stores by 1900, sold the new 'convenience' foods such as pickles, jams and ready-weighed and packaged food in tins and cartons. In the growing industrial cities, large groceries flourished selling cheap, brightly packaged goods from all corners of the Empire.

CATHEDRALS OF COMMERCE

Hypermarkets and shopping malls now offer goods irrespective of season or origin. In 1996, Tesco, Britain's largest food retailer, launched 24 hour opening; others followed suit. In 1998 two SAINSBURY'S stores opened on Christmas Day. Mail order and Internet shopping now also fuel the national passion.

ONE-STOP SHOP In 1863 Britain's first 'department' store opened in west London. Whiteley's slogan promised to supply anything 'from a pin to an elephant'

THE LIVING COASTLINE

**Britain has more than 5000 miles of coastline,
sheltering a diversity of life ranging from giant seaweeds and
rare natterjack toads to huge, noisy colonies of sea birds**

**KITTIWAKE
These sea
birds roam far
and wide over
the open ocean,
but return to
breed on narrow
cliff ledges**

SEA CLIFFS

Britain has some of the world's finest
sea cliffs for breeding sea birds, providing
a variety of nesting sites. Different
species nest at different levels, from the
precipitously slender ledges of the clifftop
to the sea caves near the base.
Seals breed in the more remote
bays and caves, protected from
human interference by tall,
inaccessible cliffs.

**GANNET A goose-sized
bird nesting mostly on
small offshore islands.
About 70 per cent of
the world population
breeds around Britain**

**PUFFIN
This clown-
faced bird
nests in
burrows on
grassy clifftops**

**GREY SEAL About 50 per cent of all grey
seals live around the British coast. Females
come ashore in autumn to give birth to a
single pup each**

A S THE SEA relentlessly erodes
the shore at one point, only
to deposit material at another,
the living things found along the coast
must cope with a constantly changing
environment. Animals and seaweeds are
covered and uncovered by tides, one
moment deluged by salt water, the next
baked by sun and blasted by wind.

COASTAL ZONES

Britain has a variety of coastal habitats.
Cornwall's rocky shores, for example, are
carpeted with seaweed, the many rock
pools teeming with tiny creatures. In
contrast, the sandy shores of eastern
Britain can seem lifeless as most of
their smaller inhabitants are
buried beneath the surface at low
tide. The Lancashire coast has many
examples of well-established dunes,
supporting a mixture of wildlife, while flat,
muddy estuaries, such as The Wash, are
renowned for the waders and wildfowl
that regularly visit.

ESTUARIES

As the tide comes in, estuary plants and
animals are bathed in salt water from the sea,
but when it ebbs, fresh river water reduces
the salinity. The special plants and animals
that are adapted to these dramatic changes
flourish in great numbers. The muddy shores
are teeming with worms, molluscs and other
small creatures beneath the surface. Huge
numbers of wildfowl and waders visit our
estuaries every winter to feast on this
incredibly rich food supply.

**CURLEW With
redshanks and dunlin,
curlews are common waders
of British estuaries. The
numerous species have bills
of different lengths to
probe the mud for food
at various levels, so
avoiding competition**

**RED-BREASTED
MERGANSER This
bird (male)
has taken to
estuary life**

SAND DUNES

Sand dunes begin to form where loose sand is blown inland by winds, building up behind a clump of plants. Colonising plants anchor the sand with a dense network of roots and more sand builds up until the dunes become 'fixed'. On older, more stable dunes, mosses and lichens invade; eventually, as the dune system becomes drier, thickets of hardy trees and shrubs, such as sea buckthorn and creeping willow, spring up.

LITTLE TERN The RSPB has helped to protect little terns from human disturbance. They breed on sandy or shingly beaches

CINNABAR MOTH As bright as any butterfly, this moth flies by day over the dunes

BROWN-LIPPED SNAIL One of a variety of snails that can be found living on sand dunes

NATTERJACK TOAD This rare toad lives in short dune vegetation and breeds in the wet hollows, or 'slacks', between dunes

MARRAM GRASS This grass's strong roots help dunes to stabilise. It is found on dunes throughout Britain

CORD GRASS This grass is quick to colonise bare mud. **SEA ASTER** An estuary plant with fleshy leaves, which can absorb or lose water as necessary

HYDROBIA SNAIL A tiny mud-dweller, living at densities of up to 35 000 per square metre

ROCK POOLS

The creatures that live in rock pools face extreme variations. Temperature changes from season to season, and even during a single day. Salinity fluctuates too, as water evaporates in the heat of the sun or is replenished by rainstorms. Even oxygen and carbon dioxide levels vary widely.

TWO-SPOTTED GOBY Just one of several types of goby adapted to rock-pool life

COMMON BEADLET ANEMONE Calm pool conditions are ideal for this sea creature

SHORE CRAB This common resident of rock pools can be found lurking under seaweed at low tide

SEAWEED Some of the 'wracks' have tiny gas-filled bladders in their fronds to buoy them up so that they receive more sunlight

SHREWSBURY

• **Shropshire (p494 E2)** • **Pop. 64 220**

To guard the WELSH MARCHES, Edward I continued what the Normans had begun and turned the natural defensive site of Shrewsbury into a medieval citadel. A loop of the River Severn protects the town, which can be reached overland only by confronting the sandstone castle, together with remains of the town walls.

The town expanded to fill much of the loop with medieval and Tudor half-timbered houses, including Ancient House, where Henry VII stayed in 1485 before marching south to defeat Richard III at Bosworth Field. Other figures associated with Shrewsbury, the county town of Shropshire, include the naturalist Charles Darwin, born there in 1809, the poet Wilfred Owen, killed in 1918 and commemorated on the war memorial in the abbey church, and Clive of India, the town's MP from 1761-74.

LINE DANCE To capture the vibrancy and frenetic atmosphere of a music hall performance, Walter Sickert learned from the French artist Degas how to paint from sketches and memory

experimented by varying impressionism with more tightly designed compositions, including painting from photographs, developing an intensely personal style.

Returning to England in 1905, Sickert soon became the link between the French avant-garde and progressive British artists, and in 1911 he formed the Camden Town Group of artists.

Rather than fashionable society, Sickert preferred to paint rainy streets and drab, dingy interiors. Typical of his art are his four sombre portraits of a failed marriage, entitled *Ennui* (1914).

Walter SICKERT

• **Painter** • **1860-1942**

Long before French Impressionist art was widely admired in Britain, Walter Sickert was the leading British impressionist painter. His early work shows the subtle tones typical of his first teacher, James McNeill WHISTLER. In Paris in 1883 Sickert met the painter Edgar Degas and

Sarah SIDDONS

• **Actress** • **1755-1831**

'Wherever she sits there is grace and grandeur, there is tragedy personified', said the writer William Hazlitt of the actress Sarah Siddons. After her second stage performance in London in 1782 she was heralded as the peerless queen of tragedy, a status that remained

unchallenged until her retirement three decades later. Her Lady Macbeth was unrivalled and Joshua Reynolds' portrait that hangs in DULWICH PICTURE GALLERY, immortalises her as 'The Tragic Muse'.

Philip SIDNEY

• **Poet, critic and courtier** • **1554-86; kt 1582**

The wide-ranging talents and noble lineage of Philip Sidney – his uncles were the earls of Leicester and Warwick – made him a model Renaissance English gentleman, accomplished as Elizabethan courtier, diplomat, poet, horseman and swordsman. He was greatly mourned after his death from wounds sustained in battle in the Low Countries.

Sidney's writing, none of it published in his lifetime, included the first sonnet sequence in English, *Astrophel and Stella*, which Shakespeare used as a model for his own sonnets; *Arcadia*, a prose pastoral romance, interspersed with elegant lyric verses; and *An Apology for Poetry* – known also as *A Defence of Poetry* – the first major work of literary criticism in English, defending the value of imaginative literature. Sidney was an active patron of scholars and poets, including Edmund SPENSER.

SILBURY HILL

• **Prehistoric site** • **Wiltshire (p.495 F5)** • **EH**

The largest man-made prehistoric mound in Europe – 40 m (130 ft) high and more than 2 ha (5 acres) at the base – forms

MYSTERY MOUND Despite drilling a maze of exploratory tunnels into Silbury Hill, archaeologists are still puzzled about its purpose; ideas range from a celestial observatory to a fertility mound

part of a complex of standing stones and similar monuments around AVEBURY.

The hill conceals sophisticated workmanship by its Neolithic builders. The stepped chalk framework, filled with earth, has remained intact since it was built around 2600 BC. Attempts to find hidden burial chambers and establish the hill's purpose have proved unsuccessful.

SILCHESTER

• Roman site • Hampshire (p.495 G5)
Crumbling walls enclosing empty fields are all that now remain at Silchester, but excavations in the 1890s revealed that the site was one of Britain's first towns. Upon the Roman conquest of Britain from AD 43, the sprawling Celtic centre of Calleva was gradually rebuilt by Roman architects who designed a formal street plan and built temples, baths, a basilica and, outside the town walls, an amphitheatre.

Although Silchester contained impressive houses with painted plaster and mosaic floors, its population may have been no more than 1000 at its height, and the town declined after the Romans left Britain. A museum at Silchester covers the town's history.

SILVER

Silver was mined in Britain as a precious metal as early as Roman times and its first HALLMARKS were struck in around 1300. Tankards decorated with hunting scenes were popular and church silver was often ornate, but it was not until the late 17th century that the demand for decorative silverware expanded. Wealthy Restoration patrons commissioned Continental baroque and rococo styles to give domestic silver an ornate twist and scroll, and Britain its first silver teapot.

Fashionable displays of wealth among the middle classes of the 18th century brought a demand for new articles for use in entertaining at home: wine decanters, tasting cups, coasters, cream jugs, sorbet cups and bottle labels were all made in silver.

Silver was no longer produced only in artisan workshops but on an industrial scale. It has since been shaped and reshaped by fashion – by the Victorians' passion for trophy cups and medals, by

the aesthetics of the Arts and Crafts movement, by art nouveau and art deco. Silver's malleability makes it as suited to fashioning a rococo candelabra as a plain 20th-century fork or spoon.

SILVER STUDIO

• Design studio • 1880-1963
For more than 50 years the Silver Studio was a major influence on British commercial design. Arthur Silver founded the studio in Hammersmith, in London, just as the furnishings market was opening up. He sold designs for upholstery, wallpapers, linoleums and carpets to such manufacturers as LIBERTY, Warner and Sanderson. The studio also offered complete interior

A NEW LEAF The 1930s rise of the suburban home inspired new interior designs from the Silver Studio, including autumn-tint wallpaper to create a cottage atmosphere

design schemes, including plasterwork, stencils, metalware and ceramics. Its style was eclectic and reflected ordinary middle-class tastes in decor.

From 1880 to the Second World War the Silver Studio followed the day's fashion, from Queen Anne revival to Japanese and Cubist patterns for textiles and wallpaper. When Arthur Silver died in 1896, his sons took over the business.

James SIMPSON

• Obstetrician • 1811-70; bt 1866
Contravening Victorian beliefs that it was God's will that women should suffer in childbirth, James Simpson successfully administered ether in 1847 to relieve a mother's pain in a difficult birth. He and his assistants at Edinburgh University went on to experiment with chloroform as an anaesthetic by inhaling it themselves, and found it both effective and more pleasant to take than ether, although it is now known not to be safe.

Simpson's anaesthetic techniques gained the royal seal of approval from Queen Victoria in 1853, and soon revolutionised all kinds of surgery.

SINN FÉIN

• Founded 1905
The words Sinn Féin, Gaelic for 'we alone', reflect the aim of Arthur Griffith, the founder of the political party, to secure home rule for Ireland. Sinn Féin's opposition to Britain's planned partition of Ireland, ardently expressed by Eamon de Valera, its president from 1917, won the party 73 of the 105 Irish seats at Westminster in the 1918 election.

Sinn Féin's subsequent rejection of the 1921 Anglo-Irish treaty, in which Britain retained control over the six counties of ULSTER, and its refusal to recognise the new Irish Assembly, marginalised the party in Irish politics for the next 40 years.

Sinn Féin's close links with the terrorist IRISH REPUBLICAN ARMY (IRA) prompted the British government in 1988 to ban the broadcasting of speeches by its representatives, including its leader Gerry Adams. In return for a ceasefire in 1993, Sinn Féin was allowed to take part in talks on the future of NORTHERN IRELAND.

SISSINGHURST

- **Kent (p.495 J5)** • **Created 1930s** • **NT**

Discovering a derelict pink-brick Tudor manor house surrounded by six acres of tangled wilderness in the Kentish Weald, the author Vita SACKVILLE-WEST wrote in 1930 that she had found 'Sleeping Beauty's garden'. Over the next decade she laboured with her husband, Harold Nicolson, to awaken Sissinghurst from its 200 year slumber, and when they opened it to the public after the Second World War it was recognised as a classic among English gardens.

The Nicolsons made the most of the space by creating a series of intimate themed gardens. There was a cottage garden, rose garden, nut garden, herb garden and – best-known of all – a white garden. They also added a lime walk and a moat walk.

The remains of the manor house are overshadowed by its soaring gate tower. French prisoners-of-war held in the house in the 18th century called it *le château*, after which it became known as Sissinghurst Castle.

SITES OF SPECIAL SCIENTIFIC INTEREST

The story of the rare plant that forced a roadworks company to remove, store and replace top soil around a new road bridge at Hook Moor in Yorkshire

SITWELL STYLE Dressing in voluminous brocaded robes and wearing enormous rings, Edith Sitwell played up her distinctive Gothic looks and medieval family line

in 1998 is no myth but a demonstration of Sites of Special Scientific Interest (SSSIs) at work. These areas of nature conservation – around 4000 across England – are administered by English Nature and protect fragile populations of indigenous plants and animals – such as the thistle broomrape whose habitat was threatened by the road bridge.

SSSIs vary in size, the largest being in the Anglian WASH at more than 62 000 ha (153 000 acres), and are patrolled by 21 teams covering 76 regions. A recovery programme targets species most at risk, such as the lady's slipper orchid, which has been propagated at Kew Gardens for reintroduction to the Pennine woodland sites that are its natural home.

Despite their legal status SSSIs are frequently threatened and require further protection. In 1998 English Nature won the first special conservation order halting unauthorised work damaging an SSSI habitat for moorland birds in the Peak District.

SITWELL FAMILY

- **Writers**
- **Edith 1887-1964; DBE 1954**
- **Osbert 1892-1969; 5th bt 1943**
- **Sacheverell 1897-1988; 6th bt 1969**

The three Sitwell siblings were as self-consciously aristocratic as they were literary. Edith, with a talent for theatrical self-promotion, described herself as a Plantagenet; the family was descended from the medieval royal house.

Edith's poetry went through romantic and antiromantic periods, but was always full of fanciful, unexpected imagery. Interested in the use of sound, she collaborated with the composer William WALTON in setting her poem sequence *Façade* to music. Short lyrics such as 'Still Falls the Rain', about the Blitz, dealt with the horror of war and her long poem 'Gold Coast Customs' the corruption of Western society.

Osbert wrote the text of Walton's *Belshazzar's Feast* and a nostalgic five-volume autobiography describing the Sitwells' Derbyshire childhood. Sacheverell wrote mainly on art and was responsible for reviving interest in European baroque painting.

SKARA BRAE

- **Prehistoric site** • **Orkney (p.497 D1)** • **HS**

In 1850 strong winds blowing across the Orkney Islands dispersed a layer of sand to reveal a largely intact Neolithic village. The site consists of the remains of ten houses – some still containing their original stone beds and furniture – connected by a series of covered passageways, and, set apart from the other buildings, what appears to have been a workshop.

For some 600 years around 3000 BC a village community of about 50 people grazed livestock, grew crops, hunted, fished and gathered shellfish. Though life must have been hard and comforts rudimentary, they had a drainage system, and chambers built into the walls that may have been lavatories.

The villagers were skilled stone-carvers, producing a grooved style of pottery that was copied and found at later henges in southern Britain. The nearby tomb of MAES HOWE exhibits the same sophisticated building skills.

INSIDE OUT The Sissinghurst garden takes the form of a series of outdoor 'rooms', each with its own colour scheme. The celebrated white garden is planted with white roses, artemesias and a silver pear

COUNTRY PURSUIT The old game of ninepin skittles was still an outdoor sport in the early 19th century, and a favourite event around the local inn at sheep-shearing festivals

SKITTLES

Banned by Edward III in the 14th century for lacking aggression, the 'peaceful' game of skittles survives noisily in pubs and clubs, particularly in Wales, the west country and northern England. Rules vary regionally, but a typical game consists of nine pins set out at the end of an alley in a diamond formation. Each player has three turns with wooden or rubber balls and scores points by knocking down as many pins as possible with each ball.

Around 1800, gambling on the game was so widespread that it was outlawed in Britain for a second time. A 19th-century American law banning the playing of ninepins was bypassed by adding one pin to the game, giving rise to modern tenpin bowling.

SKYE

- Highland (p.497 B3)
- Area 643 sq miles • Pop. 11 820

The largest and most spectacular of the Inner Hebrides islands is so deeply indented that no point is further than 5 miles from the sea, yet the jagged Cuillin Hills rise to nearly 1000 m (3258 ft) to provide the finest mountaineering in the British Isles. Strongholds among the remote rocks and moorland that stretch the 50 mile length of the island provided safe refuge for Bonnie Prince Charlie, who escaped to Skye aided by the islander Flora MACDONALD after his defeat by the English at Culloden Moor in 1746.

SKYLARK

The poet Percy Bysshe Shelley's ode *To a Skylark* (1820) commemorates a small brown bird, unremarkable for its looks but by virtue of its song a byword for poetic inspiration.

Hail to thee blithe Spirit!
Bird thou never wert,
That from Heaven, or near it,
Pourest thy full heart
In profuse strains of unpremeditated art.

The male sustains a shrill warbling song for up to 10 minutes in every hour of daylight as he rises several hundred metres in the air, glides on the wind and slowly descends, still singing. As with other birdsong the skylark's is a display warning rival birds off its territory. Skylarks nest on the ground, hidden by tussocks of grass, and modern farming methods have made it one of Britain's ENDANGERED SPECIES.

SLATE MINING

No roofing material rivals slate for its strength, lightness and durability, and no region beats Wales for its quality. But large-scale quarrying began only in the 18th century when the businessman Richard Pennant discovered vast reserves on his estate in Snowdonia.

Pennant bought out the local quarrymen, who used to bring slates down the mountainside on pack ponies, and re-employed them on a huge quarry at Bethesda, serviced by new roads, tramways and a harbour at nearby Port Penrhyn. Pennant's success inspired confidence. Slate quarries opened across north Wales in the second half of the 18th century, the largest at Blaenau Ffestiniog, which became the new slate capital of the world. At its peak, one quarry contained 100 working chambers at 25 different levels up and down the hillside.

Other past slating centres include Collyweston near Stamford in Cambridgeshire, where the local brownish-grey slate roofed cathedrals and black slate made school blackboards. Slate can also be blue, purple, rust red and, in the Lake District, green.

Most slate used in Britain today still comes from north Wales. As well as roofing, slate was once used for making cills, cladding and flooring, but the expense of quarrying now tends to restrict its use to restoration work.

SPLITTING SLATE Skilled workers (*inset*) can chisel a 2.5 cm (1 in) block of stone, cut out of quarries such as Penrhyn in Bethesda, north Wales (*main picture*), into as many as 35 separate sheets of top quality slate

SLAVE TRADE

When the merchant sailor John Hawkins bought slaves on the coast of Guinea in the 1560s and sold them to sugar barons in the Spanish West Indies, he began the most inhumane and lucrative business known to Britain until the slave trade was abolished in the 19th century.

For 250 years merchants sailed with cotton goods from Bristol, Liverpool and London to western Africa, shipped Negro slaves to plantation owners in North America, and returned to Britain with raw cotton, rum, sugar cane and tobacco. The Royal Africa Company ran the British slave trade from 1672 to 1752, while the commerce was at its height. During the 18th century more than 2 million slaves were taken to British colonies.

Thirty-five years of campaigning in Britain to end the slave trade, notably by the MP William WILBERFORCE, succeeded in 1833 when the Abolition Act freed all slaves in British territories and compensated slave owners with British taxpayers' money.

SLIMBRIDGE

• **Gloucestershire (p.494 E4)** • **Est. 1946**
Thousands of geese, swans, ducks, waders and birds of prey have found refuge at Slimbridge wildfowl reserve,

SOMETHING TO READ Every main train station in Britain in the 1920s had a W.H. Smith stall. The company was already international, with branches in Paris and Brussels

on the upper reaches of the River Severn near the village of Slimbridge. In 1945 the ornithologist and painter Peter Scott visited the area and spotted among the flocks of wintering geese the lesser white-fronted goose – a bird recorded in Britain only twice before.

The following year Scott chose Slimbridge to be the headquarters of the Wildfowl and Wetlands Trust, which now has the world's largest collection of captive wildfowl. It is the only place in Europe that has all six types of flamingo. Hides overlook salt marshes, lakes and artificial pools where birds are fed, and in winter, flocks of Bewick's swans from Siberia can be watched under floodlight.

Adam SMITH

• **Economist** • **1723-90**
The idea proposed by the Scottish moral philosopher Adam Smith, that free trade and competition left to take their natural course result in society's progress, laid the foundations of classical economics.

Smith argued in his 1776 work *The Wealth of Nations* that the free play of enlightened self-interest and minimum government interference in the economy

created both wealth and social welfare. It was radical thinking at the time, but his free-market ideals remain influential in the Adam Smith Institute, set up in 1977 to influence government.

Delia SMITH

• **Cookery writer and broadcaster** • **b.1942**
Known to her legions of fans simply as Delia, Smith has won the hearts of the British public with her straightforward recipes intended, she claims, 'to please rather than to dazzle'.

Her initial success as the recipe writer for London's *Evening Standard* from the early 1970s was followed by mixed fortunes on television. When her prime-time series was downgraded for being unexciting she turned to publishing, producing best sellers such as the three-part *Complete Cookery Course* (1978-81). Ever since she has enjoyed phenomenal success in print and on television.

W.H. SMITH

• **Founded 1792**
When Henry and Anna Smith opened their small newspaper shop in 1792 they laid the foundation of what is now one of Britain's largest retail groups. Their son, William Henry Smith, expanded the business by setting up a newspaper

distribution network. His son, also William Henry, opened the first railway stall at Euston Station in 1848. Using this foothold he turned the business into a national retail chain, famed for its 'yellowbacks' – books of guaranteed moral probity. He opened some 150 station shops and in 1905 the chain began to colonise England's high streets. Smith's became a public company in 1949, and has continued to grow. In 1998, when it acquired John Menzies, the chain had 509 stores selling literature and everything from CDs to felt-tip pens.

SMUGGLER'S EPITAPH *'To the Memory of THOs SIVELL who was cruely shot on board his sloop by some officers of the customs of the Port of Portsmouth, 15th June 1785, at the age of 64'*

SMUGGLERS

High import duties, contraband goods, addictive habits and war have all encouraged smuggling in Britain. Ever since the Saxons levied a duty on imported goods, smuggling has occurred on every coast, especially in Cornwall and the north east, where creeks and caves favour concealment.

When tobacco, tea, coffee, beer and cider carried duties in the 17th century, smuggling became a full-scale profession, and was rife when war preoccupied the authorities. The coastguard, set up in 1822, inhibited it until the relatively recent development of drug trafficking.

ALL IN A MOMENT Lord Snowdon's portraits often reveal the character of his subjects in an unexpected context, such as the hard-living Irish actors Richard Harris and Peter O'Toole sharing a pot of tea at the Dorchester Hotel

SNETTISHAM HOARD

• Discovered 1948

In 1948 a Norfolk farmer ploughed what he believed to be a rusted bedstead from a field. Dumped beside a road as scrap, the twisted wires, rings and discs were recognised by local archaeologists as Iron Age jewellery and coins. Subsequent chance finds and excavations at the village of Snettisham have yielded 14 hoards of treasure, the largest Iron Age discovery in Britain.

The finds, kept at the British Museum and the Castle Museum in Norwich, include 175 gold, silver and bronze torcs (neckrings worn by Iron Age elites), and coins which date the hoards to around 70 BC. Why they were buried remains a mystery, but it is likely that they represent the wealth of the Iceni tribe, hidden in a period of turmoil.

SNOOKER

If British officers of the RAJ had not invented snooker in 1875, television may have done so. The advent of colour transmission in the late 1960s transformed the game's sleazy image of idle men in smoky halls. Played with coloured balls on a table of green baize by men in dress suits, snooker appeared tailor-made for the new medium.

The BBC's *Pot Black* programme helped to create cult figures such as Northern Ireland's tempestuous Alex 'Hurricane' Higgins, and paved the way for a professional circuit. The world championship also benefited from this new exposure, as did Sheffield's Crucible Theatre, venue for the finals since 1977.

John SNOW

• Physician and anaesthetist • 1813-58

A water pump without its handle stands in Broadwick Street in London's Soho to commemorate a medical breakthrough made in 1854. A cholera epidemic had gripped the city for six years when the physician John Snow identified a factor common to 500 cases – drinking water taken from the same pump.

Snow disabled the pump by removing its handle, after which new cases of the disease ceased to appear, confirming his theory that infected water was the source of the cholera. His discovery led to vital improvements in city sanitation.

Lord SNOWDON

• Photographer • b.1930; earl 1961

A celebrated fashion photographer, who captured with equal panache the glassily formal society beauties of the 1950s and the 'dolly birds' of 1960s' swinging London, Lord Snowdon (born Antony Armstrong-Jones) is also a skilled photojournalist, an award-winning television producer and the designer of London Zoo's aviary (1965).

Snowdon's best-known work is his society portraiture, which had extended to royalty even before his marriage to Princess Margaret in 1960. His original approach often causes surprise or shock, as with his picture of the almost naked actor Ralph Fiennes, which appeared on a cover of *Vogue* magazine in 1995.

PEAK POWER The Snowdon Mountain Railway was built between 1894 and 1896. Starting from Llanberis Station, it uses a rack-and-pinion system to climb 957 m (3140 ft) towards the summit

SNOWDONIA

• **N Wales (p.494 C1)**   • **Area 827 sq miles**
Mountainous north-west Wales has the highest peak in England and Wales, Snowdon, at 1085 m (3560 ft). The area surrounding it, Snowdonia, became a National Park in 1951. It includes 30 miles of the north Wales coast as well as spectacular hills, forests and lakes.

Mountain roads and narrow-gauge railways traverse this wild landscape. The Snowdon Mountain Railway climbs almost to the summit where, on a clear day, Ireland's Wicklow Mountains and the Lake District peaks can be seen. Locomotives dating from the 1860s run from Porthmadog to Blaenau Ffestiniog on the Ffestiniog Railway.

The region also features castles built by Welsh princes who defied the invading English, and quarries and mines where copper and gold were, and SLATE still is, extracted.

John SOANE

• **Antiquarian and architect**
• **1753-1837; kt 1831**
The English architect John Soane was one of Britain's most original designers. His buildings followed the prevailing homage to the classical forms of ancient Rome and Greece, but Soane also made innovative use of space, lighting and stone and plasterwork, seen to great advantage in his London house in Lincoln's Inn Fields, now a museum. His work on the BANK OF ENGLAND (1788-1828) included domed banking halls, lit from above, and concealed by a windowless façade. He reverted to a less austere style for his design of the DULWICH PICTURE GALLERY (1811-14), Britain's first public art gallery.

MUSEUM PIECE John Soane's curiously eccentric house at 13 Lincoln's Inn Fields, London (1812-13), contains the architect's extensive collection of antiquities and art

SOAP OPERA

Soap operas started on radio in the United States in the 1930s, usually sponsored by soap manufacturers, hence the name. British radio soaps such as *Mrs Dale's Diary* and THE ARCHERS, Britain's longest-running soap, followed in the 1950s. A family was usually at the centre of the plot, as in the first successful TV soap, *The Grove Family*.

Soaps began by reflecting traditional moral attitudes, but gradually challenged social and sexual conventions. In the 1960s and 70s CORONATION STREET and *Crossroads* attracted audiences of up to 15 million. In the 1980s they were made to look old-fashioned by Channel 4's gritty Liverpool-based *Brookside* and the BBC's inner-city soap, *EastEnders*, which dealt with issues such as homosexuality, rape and racial prejudice.

SOCIETY MAGAZINES

The Tatler (circulation 88 000) is an example of the British gift for adapting old institutions to new purposes. Founded in the early 18th century by the literary wits Richard Steel and Joseph Addison, it collapsed after three years. It was revived in 1901 as an illustrated magazine about the doings of 'society' and today combines pictures of the rich and famous at play with lush advertising, reviews and travel writing.

Tatler's rival *Harper's & Queen* (circulation 94 000) resulted from the merger in 1970 of *Queen* (founded in 1861) and *Harper's Bazaar* (founded in 1929). Its regular 'Jennifer's Diary' charts the partygoing of social aspirants. Gentry holed up in London can take comfort in the pages of the weekly-published *Country Life*, founded in 1897.

SOHO

• **Central London (p.499 B5/C5)**
With an all-embracing spirit that celebrates life and exudes energy, Soho is the most entertaining area of central London. At its heart in Old Compton Street are Italian and French cafés and restaurants, while south of Shaftesbury Avenue the

aromatic fragrance of Asia drifts from Gerrard Street in Chinatown.

In the 18th century French, Greek and Italian immigrants gravitated to Soho, and a Bohemian atmosphere developed. Among the restaurants, delicatessens, pubs and clubs came writers, artists and musicians. Mozart, De Quincy, Blake and Shelley all lived near Soho Square.

From the end of the 19th century, restaurants steadily grew in number. Throughout the 20th century, Soho maintained a devotion to life's excesses, be they sexual, alcoholic or culinary.

SOLSTICE

The days that mark midwinter and midsummer – the solstices – are of vital interest to all agricultural societies. In the absence of sophisticated calendars these dates are best calculated by the position of the sunrise, and celebrations have traditionally accompanied both the shortest and the longest days.

The Roman church fixed the date of CHRISTMAS close to the winter solstice to replace the pagan Saturnalia and 'the birthday of the unconquered sun' (*Dies Natalis Solus Invicti*), while Saxons and Norsemen celebrated with the festival of Yule, when the year's rebirth was symbolised by greenery and fires. Such traditions took root in Britain and were later adapted by the Church.

The summer solstice, too, was celebrated with bonfires by the Celts and the longest day has enjoyed a revival as a festival, particularly at STONEHENGE.

Thomas SOPWITH

• **Engineer and aviator** • 1888-1989; kt 1953
As well as supervising the design and construction of some of the most successful planes of two world wars, Thomas Sopwith was also an adventurous sportsman, competing on two occasions in the America's Cup yacht race. On leaving school he tried motor racing at the BROOKLANDS circuit and taught himself to fly. By 1910 he was establishing distance records for flying, and started the Sopwith Aviation Company in 1912.

At the outbreak of the First World War he began manufacturing on a large

scale, including more than 5000 Camel fighter planes. In peacetime, as head of the Hawker Siddeley Group, Sopwith began building the Hurricane fighter even before the government placed an order for them. As a result 300 were available for the Battle of Britain in 1940. *See also* AVIATION

SOTHEBY'S

• **Founded 1744**
Sotheby's was founded 22 years before its great rival CHRISTIE'S but did not auction fine art until the 20th century. It was London's leading book auctioneers of the 18th and 19th centuries and handled the sale of all the great collections, including those of Emperor Napoleon and the polemicists John Wilkes and John Bright. In the mid-19th century Sotheby's expanded into prints, coins, medals and antiquities, and later into the contents of country houses.

Fine art sales became Sotheby's foremost business in the inter-war years of the 20th century. In the 1960s the firm played a significant part in fostering the rise of the market in impressionist and modern paintings, boosted by the flamboyant sale of the Goldschmidt Collection in 1958, conducted in evening

dress. Sotheby's expansion overseas from its base at 34-35 New Bond Street began in 1955 with a New York office.

SOUTHAMPTON

• **Hampshire (p.495 F6)** • **Pop. 210 140**
Ships and sea have dominated the history of Southampton, straddling the River Itchen. The Romans built the fortified port of Bitterne on one bank. In the 8th century, the Saxons set their new town of Hamwich opposite, and the Normans joined the two to form the port of Southampton. Henry V sailed from here to his victory at Agincourt in 1415, and in the 20th century 10 million soldiers left the port to fight in France during two world wars. Some of the world's biggest ocean liners, including the *Queen Mary* and the ill-fated *Titanic*, have docked at Southampton; the *Queen Elizabeth 2* still uses the port on its transatlantic voyages.

The city was heavily bombed during the Second World War, but the medieval entrance, Bargate, and sections of the old city wall survive. The town's maritime history is documented in the 14th-century Wool House. Southampton was made a city in 1964, although it does not have a cathedral.

SALES PITCH Leading international auctioneers Sotheby's has conducted a number of celebrity sales, including the collections of the Duchess of Windsor, Greta Garbo and Andy Warhol

SOUTH BANK CENTRE

- Central London (p.499 E7) • Est. 1951

On a sweep of the Thames by Waterloo Bridge stands the South Bank Centre, a concrete arts complex of concert halls, theatres, art gallery and museum, which attracts more than 6 million visitors a year.

The Royal Festival Hall, built for the FESTIVAL OF BRITAIN in 1951, and the smaller Queen Elizabeth Hall and Purcell Room, opened in 1967, host a variety of musical events, while art is displayed at the Hayward Gallery, opened in 1968. The other buildings include the NATIONAL THEATRE, the NATIONAL FILM THEATRE and the Museum of the Moving Image.

The Richard Rogers Partnership won an architectural competition to enliven the South Bank in 1994. They planned a glass canopy over the Hayward and Queen Elizabeth Hall, but in 1999 the project was shelved due to lack of funds.

SOUTH SEA BUBBLE

In 1720, a speculative boom – later called the South Sea Bubble – plunged Britain into a financial crisis, bringing ruin to many investors. Central to the controversy was the South Sea Company, which had grown prosperous from its participation in the Spanish slave trade.

The company's offer to take over most of the national debt – well over £50 million – and the government's acceptance provoked a frenzy of share buying. The directors used many unorthodox financial manoeuvres and

WORTHLESS BOND By June 1720, South Sea Company stock was worth eight times its February value. Gambling fever hit the nation. In November, the company crashed

even bribed government ministers to help force up the price of shares, but eventually the 'bubble' burst and the stock became worthless.

Robert WALPOLE increased his political power by formulating a rescue scheme for the economy and limiting the scandal's damage to George I.

SOUTHWARK

- Central London (p.499 E3)

The borough of Southwark originated in Roman times, developing at the southern end of a wooden bridge built over the Thames in the 1st century AD. It was for centuries the main southern route to the CITY OF LONDON, and as Southwark grew so did its number of hostelries.

The area by the river – Bankside – was a hotbed of vice in medieval times, with entertainment supplied by bear-baiting, brothels, inns and a notorious annual fair. It was also the theatre district and site of Shakespeare's GLOBE THEATRE. Docks and warehouses of the

18th and 19th centuries were largely converted in the 1980s and 1990s into offices, apartments, shops and the Design Museum.

Other sites in the borough include Southwark Cathedral, dating back in part to the 12th century; the London Dungeon, which re-creates the more bloody moments of British history; and the Bermondsey Antiques Market.

SPANISH ARMADA

On July 19, 1588, 130 galleons of Philip of Spain's invasion force were sighted off Cornwall. Relations between Spain and England had been bad since ELIZABETH I asserted her country's Protestant faith and encouraged attacks on Spanish treasure ships. Though legend has it that Francis DRAKE nonchalantly finished a game of bowls on Plymouth Hoe before setting sail, he was probably waiting for the tide to turn. That night he led out 80 ships of the English fleet.

His small, nimble vessels, armed with guns of a longer range than the Spanish fleet, harried the enemy in running battles up the English Channel. When the Spanish ships anchored off Calais on the night of July 28, fireships filled with explosives were sent among them.

Within ten days, the Spaniards were forced out into the North Sea. No English ships were lost in the conflict.

ENGLISH MIGHT ON THE MAIN The English fleet's superior firepower and a north-west gale reduced the Armada to half its original strength. Elizabeth I had a celebratory medal inscribed 'God blew and they were scattered'

SPEAKER OF THE HOUSE OF COMMONS

Dressed in traditional garb, the Speaker of the House of Commons presides over parliamentary debates and ministerial question-time sessions, uttering the familiar cry 'Order! Order!' whenever proceedings get rowdy. An MP chosen by fellow MPs at the start of each new parliament, or when a vacancy arises, the Speaker must remain, for the term of office, politically neutral.

The Speaker chooses which MPs are called to debate, and keeps the House in order. If there is a tied vote, the Speaker holds the casting vote. Convention dictates that he or she uses it to prevent change in the law and to uphold the status quo.

There have been 186 Speakers; the most recent, Betty Boothroyd, is the first woman to hold the post, which dates from the 14th century. In the past the task could prove dangerous as it included defending parliament as it struggled against the monarch for power.

That the job had its undesirable side is reflected in the initiation ceremony: the candidate pretends to struggle as he or she is dragged to the Speaker's chair.

SPEAKER'S CORNER

• **Central London (p.499 B2)**
Sunday mornings bring Marxists, anarchists, Esperanto speakers, fanatics, philosophers, conspirators – in fact anyone with a message – to the north-east corner of Hyde Park near Marble Arch.

There, often with just a milk crate for a stage, they are free to voice their views, proffer advice, or merely vent their spleen on the imperfections of London transport. Many who are drawn to this unique public stage are eccentric, and the discourses that ensue between hecklers and speakers are often highly entertaining.

This singular tradition is the result of events in the mid-19th century, when crowds gathered in Hyde Park to listen to inflammatory speakers protesting against a series of government bills. Clashes with the police were not uncommon as attempts were made to break up the demonstrations, which in 1866 led to a full-scale battle with supporters of the Reform League. In 1872 an Act of parliament recognised the right of assembly (as long as the speakers were not blasphemous, obscene or seditious).

SPECIAL AIR SERVICE (SAS)

'Who Dares Wins' proclaims the SAS badge, an apposite motto for this highly trained unit of the British army based at Hereford. The force was formed during the Second World War to operate behind enemy lines, conducting raids, sabotaging aircraft and disrupting communications and lines of supply.

It was disbanded in 1945 and reborn in 1949 as the 'Malayan Scouts', then in 1951 as 22 SAS. It was active in Malaya (1950-60) and Oman (1958-9), in Borneo (1963-6), in Aden (1964-7) and was first sent to Northern Ireland in 1969.

On May 5, 1980, the normally clandestine force went on public view as television cameras filmed an SAS team storming the besieged Iranian Embassy in London. Five of the six terrorists were killed with no other casualties.

In 1981, the SAS went into west Africa to put down a coup in The Gambia. They were also active in the FALKLANDS WAR in 1982 and the GULF WAR in 1991.

PITCH IN THE PARK A revivalist preacher proclaims her message at Speaker's Corner. The Methodist minister Lord Soper was a speaker up to his death in 1998 aged 95

YORKSHIRE WATER The elegant pump room was built in 1842 at Harrogate – a favourite spa in Victorian times with a remarkable diversity of healing waters. At its height, a thousand people were treated each day

SPA TOWNS

In the 1st century AD, Romans sampled the mineral waters at Buxton in Derbyshire, and developed a resort around the hot springs that gave BATH in Somerset its name.

Some 1500 years later, in 1630, Henrietta Maria, wife of Charles I, was sent by her physician to take the waters at Tunbridge Wells. Society followed and it became the first of many fashionable and architecturally resplendent spa towns, to the consternation of Puritans who dubbed the springs 'waters of scandal'.

Spa therapy – propounded by doctors and encouraged by developers of the new resorts – bloomed during the Restoration at Epsom, in Surrey, Harrogate in Yorkshire and even at Moffat in the Lowlands of Scotland, which became fashionable for its sulphurous springs.

The vogue continued in the 18th century as Bath and Buxton were rediscovered, CHELTENHAM became an elegant spa town and the Welsh waters of Llandrindod Wells won renown. Wherever mineral springs bubbled up through iron or sulphur-laden rock, new resorts developed throughout the 19th century, from Strathpeffer near Inverness, which drew the European aristocracy, to Leamington, a former royal spa.

The fashion for 'taking the waters' flourished until the First World War but, like holidaying in Britain, later declined as easier travel enhanced the attractions of warmer foreign climes.

STYLE REVIVAL On first viewing Stanley
Spencer's *The Resurrection, Cookham*, a critic
from *The Times* newspaper wrote, 'It is as if a
Pre-Raphaelite had shaken hands with Christ'

Stanley SPENCER

• **Artist**   • 1891-1959; kt 1959

Stanley Spencer was a highly individual
painter, comparable only to William
BLAKE in his visionary naivety. Born in
Cookham, Berkshire, he spent most of
his life there, but trained at the Slade
(1908-12). His experiences in Macedonia
in the First World War inspired his later
work such as the vast murals (1927-32)
in Burghclere Chapel, Hampshire.

Intensely Christian, Spencer felt that
a religious painting did not need to be
strictly limited by religious imagery. He
incorporated elements of everyday life,
quite unchanged, into his works: in his
huge, unfinished *Christ Preaching at
Cookham Regatta* everyone but Christ
is in modern dress.

Edmund SPENSER

• **Poet**   • c.1552-99

Admired by poets as different as Ben
Jonson, John Milton, John Keats and
W.B. Yeats, Spenser is the 'poets' poet'.
His verse is both sensuous and moral,
with a beauty of language and rhythm.

Of quite humble birth, Spenser used
his verse to win powerful friends such as
Philip SIDNEY and Walter RALEIGH. From
1580 he was a civil servant in Ireland.

The Shepheardes Calendar (1579), a series
of pastoral dialogues, marks the debut
of the golden age of Elizabethan lyric
poetry. The 89 sonnets of his *Amoretti*
and the wedding hymn *Epithalamion*
celebrate his second marriage in 1594.

Best known is his unfinished work
The Faerie Queene (1590-6), a complex
allegory in which knights personify
Renaissance virtues. With more than
35 000 lines, it is the longest major
poem in the English language.

SPODE

• **Founded c.1770**

The Staffordshire firm that would
later win world acclaim for its
POTTERY AND PORCELAIN was
established by Josiah Spode
(1733-97). The talented
potter made fine cream
ware and pearl ware and
pioneered a blue and white
transfer printing technique.

His son Josiah II helped to
publicise the company; the
name Spode was impressed
on pieces from 1790. Bone
china was developed around
1800; stone china, a very hard
earthenware, from 1805; and parian, a
marble-like porcelain, from the 1840s.

In 1833, William Taylor Copeland
bought the company. It became known
as Copeland & Garrett, then Copeland.
Since 1970 it has traded as Spode Ltd.

DISH OF BONE An
**1800 dessert dish
is an early piece of
Spode bone china**

SQUASH

Since the 1970s this fast and furious ball
game has experienced a huge surge in
participation, with Britain boasting more
than 3 million players.

It is derived from the game of rackets
that evolved in the mid 19th century at
Harrow School. By the early 1900s there
were private and club courts. Standard
rules were drawn up in the 1920s.

The game is played with a long-
handled strung racket and a rubber ball
in an enclosed court, against whose four
walls the ball is hit. It differs from rackets
in that it is solely a singles game,
played to nine points – rackets
is played to 15 – where only
the serving player may score.

In 1982-91, the British
Open was won a record
ten times by Jahangir Khan
of Pakistan.

SQUIRREL

The native red squirrel, with
its rich russet coat, is now far
rarer than the larger grey
squirrel, which was first
introduced into Britain from
North America in 1876.

Red squirrels are most numerous in
the far north of England and in Scotland
and can be found elsewhere in only a
handful of isolated sites in Wales, the Isle
of Wight and parts of England. Greys

began to displace them in the 1920s but even now naturalists are not sure why. There seems to be no direct conflict between reds and greys, and red squirrels have apparently not succumbed to disease. It may be that, where they live side by side, grey squirrels compete more successfully for food – the tree seeds, fungi and sometimes tree shoots and flowers eaten by both species.

Nowadays red squirrels appear to fare best in deep conifer forests. They are protected by law, and conservation bodies try to keep grey squirrels out of areas where the reds still flourish.

STAGECOACH

The first public stagecoach routes were introduced in the London area during the reign of Charles I. But throughout the 17th century the service was slow and sporadic. In the early 18th century stagecoaches became lighter and more comfortable and better roads led to a rapid increase in routes, with travellers refreshed at coaching inns.

In 1784 John Palmer devised a scheme for carrying the Royal Mail by coaches running to strict schedules. The first such mail coach, with four passengers on board, left Bristol on August 2 at 4 pm, arriving in London at 9 am the following day.

From then on travel times decreased rapidly and journeys that had taken days were reduced to mere hours. By the 1830s, Britain's mail coaches had become the most efficient means of land transport in the world. But the rapid growth of the RAILWAYS network heralded the end of the road for stagecoaches.

STAINED GLASS

Stained glass – coloured and fitted into lead strips to create a design or picture – was first used in Britain in the 11th century. Within 200 years, magnificent windows were illuminating biblical scenes with a jewel-like brilliance in the vast, shadowy interiors of Gothic churches and CATHEDRALS.

The glass was stained either by adding metallic oxides to molten glass or by fusing thin layers of coloured

glass on to plain. Fine details such as features and folds were then painted on in matt enamel. From the 16th century the art form declined, but enjoyed a renaissance with the GOTHIC REVIVAL in the 19th century and the art nouveau movement that began in the 1890s.

Surviving examples of medieval stained glass include the 'Miracle Windows' in Canterbury Cathedral and the 'Tree of Jesse' at York Minster.

STANLEY GIBBONS

Stanley Gibbons at 399 Strand in London's West End is the world's best-known stamp shop, with a global range of 4 million stamps in stock.

Its most valuable treasure – worth £350 000 – is an envelope dated May 6, 1840, the day British stamps were first officially used, that bears ten Penny Blacks, the world's first postage stamps.

The year 1840 was also the year of birth of Edward Stanley Gibbons, founder of the stamp store. He set up business in Plymouth in 1863 with a sack full of rare stamps purchased from a sailor who had won it in a raffle. Moving the business to London, he became the leading British stamp dealer. His first catalogue came out in 1865; today it runs to 22 volumes.

King STEPHEN

- King 1135-54   • c.1097-1154

Most of Stephen's reign was bedevilled by intermittent civil war for dynastic reasons.

Though a grandson – through the female line – of WILLIAM I, and brought up by HENRY I almost as a son, his was a defective claim to the throne,

especially as he had been the first baron to swear an oath recognising Matilda, Henry I's eldest surviving legitimate child, as her father's heir.

Nevertheless, on Henry's death Stephen seized the throne. In 1138 Matilda's half-brother Robert rebelled and the Scots invaded northern England. In 1139 Matilda returned to claim her inheritance. Stephen was taken prisoner in 1141, but when his men in turn seized Robert, the two were exchanged.

The fighting continued but when Stephen's wife and eldest son died in 1153, the king capitulated and reluctantly accepted Matilda's eldest son, the future HENRY II, as his heir.

George and Robert STEPHENSON

- Engineers   • George 1781-1848
- Robert 1803-59

The Stephensons, father and son, were pioneers of the railway age. George was born in the Tyneside village of Wylam and designed his first engine, *Blucher*, in 1814 for use at the local colliery.

In 1821 he was appointed chief engineer to the first steam-powered railway, the Stockton and Darlington, and with his son, Robert, built its locomotives. In 1829 *Rocket*, designed by his son Robert, won a contest set by the Liverpool and Manchester Railway to find the most efficient form of traction.

Robert's later railways included the London and Birmingham, and the Chester and Holyhead with a tubular bridge across the Menai Straits. He used the same design for the even grander bridge over the St Lawrence at Montreal.

STEAM POWER Stephenson's *Rocket* – now in the Science Museum, London – pulled a train of 14 tons at a top speed of 29 mph to win a contest in 1829 on tracks at Rainhill, Merseyside

STERLING

The term, commonly used to distinguish British MONEY from other currencies, originally denoted a Norman silver penny. Its name was probably derived from the small star on the coin. A pound in weight of these silver coins – 240 pence – made up the pound sterling.

From 1931 until the early 1970s, the sterling area was an association of states with close trade links to Britain, which kept their exchange rates in step with sterling rather than let them find their own level against the US dollar.

The word is also used to denote a standard quality for old and new English silver of 92.5 per cent silver to 7.5 per cent base metal. Since 1544, sterling silver has been indicated by the stamped HALLMARK of a lion passant together with date, place and manufacturer's marks.

Robert Louis STEVENSON

• Writer • 1850-94

Though best known for adventure tales such as *Kidnapped* and the children's classic *Treasure Island*, Robert Louis Stevenson was a writer of considerable breadth and sophistication, who combined lightness of touch with an understanding of the darker side of human nature.

Born in Edinburgh, the son of a lighthouse engineer, he sought a more bohemian lifestyle from an early age.

His early works were essays and short stories, while frequent trips abroad inspired him as a travel writer. In 1879, he crossed the USA in pursuit of a divorcee, Fanny Osbourne, whom he married the next year.

For the rest of his life, though a prolific writer, Stevenson's health was blighted by tuberculosis. Unable to endure the cold Scottish winds, he and his family set off to find a warm home.

These restless travels ended when Stevenson moved to a large and beautiful plantation at Vailma in Samoa in 1891. He was working on his most ambitious novel, *Weir of Hermiston*, when he died of a cerebral haemorrhage at the age of 44.

Jackie STEWART

• Motor racing driver • b.1939; OBE 1972

A former British clay pigeon shooting champion, Jackie Stewart went on to become one of Britain's most successful Grand Prix drivers. Between 1969 and 1973, he had 27 Formula One Grand Prix victories, winning three world drivers' titles and finishing runner-up on two further occasions – due partly to his fastidious race preparations.

A charismatic Scot, Stewart conquered the dyslexia that had hindered his education, and gained wide repute for his trenchant views and dry wit.

Unafraid to attack lax safety standards, he retired at his peak but continued to campaign

DRIVING AMBITION In his early career Jackie Stewart, here at Brands Hatch, drove a BRM for the Owen Racing Organisation but became world champion driving for Matra and Tyrrell

for better protection while promoting the sport as a consultant. In 1997, Stewart returned to Formula One with his own team, and has remained at the forefront of British MOTOR RACING.

STIRLING

• Central Scotland (p.497 C4) • Pop. 30510

The city's history is that of its castle – the site of a fortress since Roman times – high on a rocky outcrop guarding the valley of the River Forth.

The present castle, dating back to the 11th century, was taken by the English in 1296 and retaken by the Scots in 1297 at the Battle of Stirling Bridge. On the castle esplanade a statue of ROBERT BRUCE commemorates his victory in 1314 at BANNOCKBURN, which won the Scots independence from EDWARD II. Both Mary, Queen of Scots and her son James VI were crowned in Stirling.

STOCK EXCHANGE

• Central London (p.499 F2)

The London Stock Exchange is Britain's national market for trading stocks and shares and the world's third largest stock market after New York and Tokyo.

In the 18th century, trading in securities was conducted in the City of London's COFFEE HOUSES, notably Garraway's and Jonathan's, the latter of which changed its name to the Stock Exchange in 1773. It acquired its own home in 1801 in Threadneedle Street, on the site of the Hercules Tavern.

PIRATE PLUNDER *Treasure Island* (1883) was conceived by R.L. Stevenson and his stepson, Lloyd Osbourne, while on holiday in Scotland

Although the volume of Stock Exchange business grew rapidly in the 19th and early 20th centuries, bad years outnumbered the good from the start of the First World War to the 1950s. In the 1960s business revived and a new 26-storey Exchange building was opened in Threadneedle Street in 1972.

On October 27, 1986 – dubbed 'big bang' for its explosive impact – the Financial Services Act revolutionised trading practices, abolishing the minimum level of commission and computerising the system. Many stockbrokers were taken over by larger firms, and trading moved from the Stock Exchange floor to large trading floors in City institutions. When the Euro was launched in 1999 the Stock Exchange announced plans to link up with the Frankfurt-based German stock exchange.

STOKE MANDEVILLE HOSPITAL

• Buckinghamshire (p.495 G4)   • Est. c.1920
Originally a fever isolation hospital, Stoke Mandeville was expanded in the Second World War and its doctors developed new techniques in plastic surgery and for treating spinal injuries, which have won world renown. Led by Ludwig Guttman, they also pioneered the use of athletics as a therapy for paraplegics and in 1948 instigated an event for the disabled that became the Paralympic Games.

Following an appeal by Jimmy Savile, the National Spinal Injuries Centre opened in 1983 at the district general hospital, which also serves the local area.

STONEHENGE

• Prehistoric site   • Wiltshire (p.495 F5)   • EH
Centuries of debate and speculation surround Britain's best-known prehistoric monument, which draws 500 000 visitors a year. But beyond a few well-established facts, Stonehenge retains its mystery.

Carbon-dated evidence of huge post holes suggests that some immense structure on wooden supports existed here 10 000 years ago. This vanished long before Neolithic farmers built the first phase of the present monument – a ditch and a 1.8 m (6 ft) bank of earth enclosing a ring of 56 wooden posts –

around 3000 BC. Between 2000 and 1500 BC, 'sarsens', stones from the Marlborough Downs weighing up to 80 tons, were erected around earlier circles of bluestones from Wales.

The stones were repositioned several times. Bronze Age builders added to the monument between 1200 and 1000 BC by extending its ceremonial approach – the Avenue – down to the River Avon.

Marie STOPES

• Birth-control pioneer   • 1880-1958
A disastrous, unconsummated marriage prompted Marie Stopes to write *Married Love*, the book that brought her fame.

Published in 1918, it was frank and controversial – daring to suggest that women should be able to enjoy sexual intercourse. She struggled to find a publisher but her experiences struck a chord. Despite a barrage of criticism after the book's publication, she received so many requests for further information that she followed it up with *Wise Parenthood* later the same year.

In 1921, supported by her second husband, she opened the Centre for Constructive Birth Control in Holloway, London, signalling the start of a gradual acceptance of contraception that would bring unprecedented freedom from serial motherhood for millions of women.

A highly educated woman, Stopes was also an unashamed publicist, astute at turning criticism to her advantage. Through a series of high-profile battles, she brought contraception to the attention of the public. A network of birth control clinics sprang up around the country; there was even a mobile clinic in a horse-drawn caravan until it was burned by a Catholic fanatic in Bradford.

Marie Stopes' British clinics are now part of the National Health Service, but Marie Stopes International is active in raising awareness of contraception in 25 countries in the developing world.

SHROUDED IN MYSTERY The ancient shrine of Stonehenge with its sarsen circles and great altar-like trilithons is a miracle of construction and an enigma that continues to baffle scholars

Tom STOPPARD

• **Playwright** • **b.1937; kt 1997**

It must have taken nerve for the 29-year-old Tom Stoppard to dissect Shakespeare's venerated *Hamlet* and create from it the verbally dazzling *Rosencrantz and Guildenstern are Dead*. But the gamble paid off. From the comedy's first performance in 1966, Stoppard was acknowledged as the most scintillating dramatist in British theatre.

Subsequent plays such as *The Real Inspector Hound* (1968), *Jumpers* (1972), *Travesties* (1974), *Arcadia* (1993) and *The Invention of Love* (1997) have continued to draw critical acclaim, and in 1999 he won an Oscar for his screenplay of the film *Shakespeare in Love*.

Born in Czechoslovakia as Thomas Straussler, Stoppard settled in England in 1946, taking the name of his stepfather.

STORMONT

• **Northern Ireland (p.497 B6)**

Stormont has been associated with the government of NORTHERN IRELAND since the province was created in 1922. Until then, the Stormont estate had been the home of the Cleland family, who turned the house into a baronial castle in 1858.

After the division of Ireland, the castle became the official residence of the Northern Ireland prime minister, and later administrative offices. Stormont became the seat of the Northern Ireland

BALANCING ACT In *Jumpers* **Tom Stoppard parodies academic philosophy by juxtaposing the physical gymnastics of the acrobats and the verbal dexterity of the main character**

government when the parliament building of Portland stone – a gift from Westminster – was completed in 1932.

In 1972, the province came under direct rule from Westminster and the parliament lost its functions. However, since the Good Friday Agreement of 1998, Stormont has again become the meeting place of the shadow Northern Ireland Assembly as the peace process gradually takes shape.

STOURHEAD

• **Wiltshire (p.494 E5)** • **House and gardens created 18th century** • **NT**

Henry Hoare, the son of the 18th-century banker also called Henry Hoare, laid out the grounds of Stourhead, his Wiltshire

estate, to create the illusion of a picturesque natural landscape – anticipating by more than a decade the work of 'Capability' BROWN.

In a valley close to his house he dammed the infant River Stour to create a series of lakes – complete with wooded islands – and planted hundreds of trees around them.

Having set his stage, Hoare then indulged his passion for ancient Greece and Rome by dotting it with classical buildings, including a grotto, a five-arched Palladian bridge and a temple of Apollo. Each was precisely sited to allow it to be seen at its best from one of the garden's vantage points.

Time has softened Hoare's design. Mature trees now shade the buildings, and rhododendrons and azaleas splash the lakeside paths with colour.

The house, built in simple 18th-century Palladian style, contains a picture gallery, Chippendale furniture and family portraits and other paintings.

STOWE

• **Buckinghamshire (p.495 G3)**
• **Gardens created 18th century** • **NT**

The landscaping of Stowe absorbed the talents of three important 18th-century designers: Charles Bridgeman, William Kent and 'Capability' BROWN. Its tally of more than 30 temples, pavilions, monuments, arches and bridges includes twice as many listed buildings as any other garden in Britain.

The garden was created by Richard Temple, 1st viscount Cobham, a soldier and politician who sought to advance his renown by the splendour he conferred on Stowe. In its temples he celebrated classical and national heroes whom he admired for their energy and enterprise; none of Cobham's contemporaries, however, earned a place.

Though further embellished by his nephew and heir Richard Grenville, Stowe fell into a long decline from the 1840s. This process was reversed by a programme of restoration begun by the National Trust in 1989 and the gardens are now reassuming their former glory.

One restored Gothic temple can be rented through the LANDMARK TRUST. The main house (not a National Trust property) is occupied by Stowe School.

EMBELLISHING NATURE One of the many glorious views at Stourhead extends over a Palladian-style bridge across a lake fringed with woodland and rhododendrons to the pantheon beyond

STRANGFORD LOUGH

• Northern Ireland (p.497 B6)

The tidal waters of the Irish Sea surge through a narrow strait into the great sea inlet of Strangford Lough, which extends for some 20 miles between the rolling hills of County Down.

It is a place of dramatic natural beauty with a rocky shoreline to the south and, to the west, long oval mounds or 'drumlins' formed by deposits left behind as a glacier scoured the land during the last Ice Age. Most of its 120 islands are drowned, rounded drumlins, known locally as 'pladdies'.

Archaeological finds indicate that Neolithic people first settled the lough's shores. A key attraction today is its rich marine life, including pilot whales, porpoises and the largest colony of common seals in Ireland. In winter its bird numbers include most of the world's population of pale-bellied brent geese.

STRATFORD-UPON-AVON

• Warwickshire (p.495 F3)   • Pop. 22 230

Stratford has long traded on its claim to fame as the home town of the playwright William SHAKESPEARE, diligently preserving and restoring the Tudor landmarks of the great writer's time.

These include the lovely half-timbered house where he was born, the school he probably attended and, at nearby Shottery, the family home of his wife, Anne Hathaway. The Memorial Theatre, overlooking the River Avon, is now the Royal Shakespeare Theatre; the Swan Theatre adjoins it and the Royal Shakespeare Company performs at both.

Tudor houses line the town's wide streets and its Holy Trinity Church, where Shakespeare was baptised, also holds the tomb where he is buried beside his wife and eldest daughter, Susanna.

The town's more modern attractions include its Motor Museum and an international array of species at the Stratford Butterfly Farm.

STRIP FARMING

Regular grooves on the sides of valleys and hills survive in many parts of Britain as evidence of a medieval system of agriculture known as strip farming. From Anglo-Saxon times to the 18th century, cattle were kept in large open fields or commons but each man was also allocated several long strips of land on which to grow food for his family.

The strips, or lynchets, usually followed the contours of a hill and were ploughed in a characteristic up-and-down pattern with a central ridge. Evidence of the strips was largely erased when old pastures were ploughed up in the Second World War but some can still be seen in Dorset, Wiltshire and the Midlands.

Strip farming started to die out from the late Middle Ages as common land was increasingly enclosed, changing the landscape to its now familiar patchwork of fields and hedges.

STREET VENDORS

The streets of Britain's cities were once much livelier than they are today. They were also much noisier with hundreds of vendors shouting their wares such as 'Dumplins! Dumplins! Diddle, diddle dumplins ho!', 'Hot Baked Warden Pears and Pippins!' or 'Cockles an' Mussels! Alive, alive-O!'

In the Middle Ages hawkers offered seasonal fruit, peascods, hot sheep's feet, mackerel, pies and pasties while Flemish merchants sold hats and spectacles. 'Rushes, fair and clean' (for use on floors) was then a common cry.

Later on, wholesale MARKETS developed and costermongers were the retailers of the day, selling fruit and vegetables from regular pitches and confusing police and customers alike with their own secret language, which had a cryptic vocabulary and often involved saying words backwards.

COLD COMFORT Whatever the weather, the ice-cream man has long been a children's favourite – as here on a frosty morning at St Clements Dane Church, London, in 1912

BLOOMIN' LUVERLY A flower vendor offers his wares at a regular street market in Colombia Road, Shoreditch in East London

Urban Victorians could enjoy breakfast on the street as stalls set up for the day to sell coffee, hot pea soup or hot eels. In the evening, sellers of baked potatoes, ham sandwiches, ginger beer, chestnuts and sugar sticks stationed themselves on street corners and in front of theatres.

The proliferation of shops in the 20th century put paid to much of the old-style street vending. However, in car-free shopping precincts, street sellers are back with a mix of traditional flower barrows and modern food stalls. Long-established London street markets such as Brick Lane, Petticoat Lane and Portobello Road continue to thrive.

EQUINE PASSION George Stubbs used horses from a Lincolnshire tannery for his anatomy studies, assisted by his common-law wife, Mary Spencer. Forty-one of his drawings survive

House of STUART

- **Scottish royal house   • 1371-1603**
- **British royal house   • 1603-1714**

Two childless queens were the making and undoing of the House of Stuart. The virginity of Elizabeth I gave James VI of Scotland, descended from Henry VII, the chance to unite the thrones of England and its northern neighbour as JAMES I. He was succeeded by his son, CHARLES I, then his grandsons, CHARLES II and JAMES II, his great-grandchildren WILLIAM AND MARY, who ruled jointly, and finally his great-granddaughter, ANNE. She died without an heir, leading to the accession of the house of HANOVER.
See also ROYAL HOUSES

George STUBBS

- **Artist   • 1724-1806**

George Stubbs is best remembered and admired for his strikingly realistic paintings of horses, such as the prancing Arabian thoroughbred *Whistlejacket* (1762). He had little formal training and around 1745 moved from Liverpool to York, where he studied anatomy at a local hospital. After visiting Italy in 1754 he stated that 'nature is always superior to Art,

whether Greek or Roman', and began an 18 month period of dissecting and drawing horses. His book of engravings, *The Anatomy of the Horse* (1766), was admired in London society and Stubbs received commissions from noblemen to paint animal entourages, particularly horses and carriages.

Stubbs preferred painting animals alone such as the peaceful *Mares and Foals* (c.1760). The dramatic *Lion and Horse* (1770), with a ghost-white horse terrified by a lion emerging from the darkness, looked forward to the painters of the ROMANTIC MOVEMENT.
MAIN COLLECTIONS • Tate Gallery, London • Walker Art Gallery, Liverpool

SUDBURY HALL

- **Derbyshire (p.495 F2)   • Built 1661-80   • NT**

When George Vernon inherited the Sudbury estate in 1659, he threw off the austerity of the Cromwellian years and built a house using the finest decorative artists of the time. Grinling GIBBONS contributed intricate wood carvings, and Edward Pierce made the Great Staircase, its sides a lace-like filigree of carved wood. The French artist Louis Laguerre added a series of mythological paintings.

In the 1996 BBC television production of Jane Austen's *Pride and Prejudice*, Sudbury Hall provided the grand interiors of 'Pemberley', Mr Darcy's home. A museum of childhood now occupies the former servants' wing.

SUDELEY CASTLE

- **Gloucestershire (p.494 E4)**
- **Built 15th-19th century**

The walls of a banqueting hall and an eight-sided tower holed by cannon survive from the medieval fortress of Sudeley, ruined by the Parliamentarians in the Civil War. The castle was built by Baron Sudeley in the 1400s, and was later the home of Catherine Parr, Henry VIII's sixth wife.

After years of decay, Sudeley was bought in 1837 by the Dent family, Worcester glove-makers. They rebuilt the chapel, in which Catherine Parr lies buried, and collected the arms and armour, furniture, tapestries, china and old

ALL A FAÇADE Sudbury Hall was begun in dignified Jacobean style, but the central cupola hints at the Restoration extravagance of its interior

master paintings that fill the castle's rooms. Mementoes of Catherine Parr include her prayer book and a love letter to her fourth husband, Thomas Seymour.

SUEZ CRISIS

• November 5-6, 1956

On November 5, 1956, British and French forces intervened disastrously in a war between Israel and Egypt. In the guise of peace keepers they seized the Suez Canal, a vital shipping corridor between Europe and Asia. The canal had been nationalised by President Nasser of Egypt, prompting fears that he might close it, cutting off oil supplies to Europe.

Britain and France were condemned by the United Nations, the Soviet Union threatened a nuclear strike and pressure from the USA led to a ceasefire on November 6. By February all foreign troops had been withdrawn. The crisis brought about the resignation of prime minister Anthony EDEN and weakened Britain's international influence.

PUBLIC PROTEST A suffragette is seized after chaining herself to the railings of Buckingham Palace in 1914. Mrs Pankhurst, the suffragette leader, was also arrested outside the palace

SUFFRAGETTES

The battle for women's suffrage – the right to vote – turned into a physical struggle when Emmeline PANKHURST and her daughters Sylvia and Christabel formed the Women's Social and Political Union in 1903. Its supporters attacked MPs and their property and were prepared to risk injury and even death to promote their cause. One suffragette, Emily Davison, was fatally injured in 1913 when she dashed into the path of the king's horse at the Epsom Derby.

Many imprisoned suffragettes went on hunger strike. Some were force-fed, through clamped-open mouths or nasal tubes. One woman killed herself after 49 nasal feeds, leaving the message, 'One big tragedy may save many others'.

The turning point came with the First World War, when women nursed the wounded and worked in factories, steel mills and dockyards. In 1918 women aged over 30 won the vote, extended in 1928 to those of 21 or more.

SURNAMES

Until the 14th century most people managed with a single name. As towns grew, trades developed and people began to pay tax in money rather than goods or services, family names were introduced for more accurate identification.

LIKE FATHER, LIKE SON

In earlier times, someone with the name Alfred Watson had a father called Wat. These names – patronymics – started to be inherited. Often the -son was reduced to -s, or dropped. So, as well as Johnson, there were Johns, John and Jones. There

were also matronymics, like Megson and Betts. The Scots McGregor, Irish MacDermot and Norman-Irish Fitzpatrick are all 'son of' names. The Welsh Powell comes from 'ap Hywel', son of Hywel.

Sometimes a family inherited a man's nickname, referring to hair colour – Black and Russell (red haired); to stature – Lowe and Biggs; to resemblances – Brock (badger-like) and Hogg; or to personal disposition – Sharpe and Jolly.

HOME AND WORK

People might be known by their village or region of origin, or by their 'address' in a village or town (*see below*).

Many names derived from occupations require a knowledge of 14th-century working practices. A Farmer, for instance, was a tax collector; Walkers, like Fullers, were in the business of shrinking cloth; and Plummers made lead roofs rather than pipes.

Names like Clarke, Parsons and Bishop suggest that clerical celibacy was not all it should have been, though names could be applied to members of a man's household as well as to his offspring.

MODEL ARTIST Sutherland used his reflection standing against a cardboard cross to capture the correct pose for *Crucifixion* (1946)

Graham SUTHERLAND

• **Artist** • 1903-80

Graham Sutherland's career as a painter started unusually late. He gave up his railway engineering apprenticeship in the 1920s to begin etching in a neoromantic style inspired by the 19th-century artist Samuel PALMER. Only in 1935 did he begin to paint, adapting abstract shapes and swirling colours into landscapes such as *Entrance to a Lane* (1939).

In the Second World War, Sutherland was employed as an official war artist. His blurred scenes of bombing such as *Devastation 1941: An East End Street* conveyed the aching desolation of the conflict. After the war he concentrated on portraits of the famous, at times with controversial results. His portrait of Somerset Maugham (1949) was said to make the elderly writer look like 'an old Chinese madam in a brothel', while that of Winston Churchill was so disliked by its sitter that it was never exhibited and destroyed by his widow.

Sutherland's many religious works included the gigantic tapestry *Christ in Glory in the Tetramorph* (1962), which hangs in the lady chapel at Coventry Cathedral. He also designed ceramics, stamps and a series of posters for the Shell oil company.

MAIN COLLECTIONS • **Picton Castle, Pembrokeshire** • **Tate Gallery, London** • **Victoria and Albert Museum, London**

SUTTON HOO

• **Suffolk (p.495 J3)**

A 7th-century Anglo-Saxon ship-burial with its treasure was discovered in a field at Sutton Hoo near Woodbridge in 1939. It is the most valuable collection of ANGLO-SAXON artefacts ever found in Britain.

The site had been settled and farmed intermittently for at least 1000 years when a wealthy king, perhaps Raedwald of East Anglia, was laid to rest on board a ship 28 m (90 ft) long, together with the possessions required on his voyage to the afterlife. These included coins, jewels and weapons, drinking horns, cooking pots, silverware, and what may have been a woollen tunic, leather shoes and a fur-lined cap.

The high quality of craftsmanship emphasised the sophistication of early medieval Britain, and its extensive overseas contacts: the king's helmet and shield are Swedish in style, and some of his possessions came from as far afield as Byzantium and Alexandria. The finds are exhibited in the British Museum.

SWALLOW

Swooping, twittering swallows catching insects on the wing are welcome heralds of the British summer. The high-speed birds, with their blue-black upper parts, white rump, red bib and forked tail feathers, rarely settle except to collect nesting materials to incubate their eggs. In autumn, they gather on trees and telephone wires before migrating in great flocks more than 5000 miles to southern Africa. They return in March or April, often to the same nest.

This constancy and association with good weather may be why it has long been considered good luck to have swallows building their cup-shaped mud nests in a barn or other outbuilding.

Joseph SWAN

• **Inventor** • 1828-1914; kt 1904

Few British inventors were as prolific as Joseph Swan, who took out more than 70 patents, including one for his greatest achievement, the electric light.

From the 1840s, when he joined his brother-in-law's Newcastle chemical firm, Swan tried to make an electric lamp based on a glowing filament of carbon inside a glass bulb. He was defeated by the imperfect vacuum in the bulbs, which caused the filaments to burn away. The invention of the mercury vacuum pump in 1865 allowed Swan to make the first bulbs with an appreciable life. He first demonstrated them in 1878 and began to manufacture them in 1881.

An interest in the chemical processes of photography led Swan in 1879 to invent bromide paper, which is still used. Further inventions included a miner's electric safety lamp and artificial silk, which he exhibited in 1885 but never produced.

BRIGHT SPARK A redundant gas bracket was used by Swan to hold this 1884 light bulb

SWANSCOMBE SKULL

A fossil-hunter, A.T. Marston, found skull fragments in gravel-workings on the Thames estuary at Swanscombe in 1935 and 1936. The fragments were probably those of a female of a species of human, *Homo heidelbergensis*, who lived around 300 000 to 250 000 years ago, when sea levels were 30 m (100 ft) higher than today and grassland plains were grazed by wild horses, rhinoceros and elephants. The fragments were found with tools belonging to an early Stone Age culture.

Until discoveries at BOXGROVE in 1984 the fragments represented Britain's oldest identifiable human inhabitant.

SWANSEA

• S Wales (p.494 C4) • Pop. 151 040

The second largest city in Wales is named from the Norse *Sveins Ey*, meaning Swein's Island. Its position at the mouth of the River Tawe gives it its Welsh name of Abertawe. The town grew up around a Norman castle, whose remains survived the Second World War bombing that devastated the city centre.

Abundant local coal made Swansea a centre for copper smelting, steelmaking and tin plating in the 1700s and 1800s. The old docks now house marinas and the Maritime and Industrial Museum. The nearby GOWER PENINSULA provides seafoods such as Pen-clawdd cockles and laver bread for the city's market. The old guildhall houses the Dylan THOMAS centre, dedicated to the Swansea poet.

SWAN UPPING

Every July the five-day ceremony of swan upping, dating from the 16th century, takes place on the River Thames. Swans are lifted from the water and marked by the Queen's Swan Uppers and Swan Marker, accompanied by the Swan Uppers of the Vintners and Dyers livery companies of the City of London. The monarch owns all swans on open waters, but in 1473 Edward IV gave the then powerful companies a number of swans, whose descendants they now mark.

The uppers row between Sunbury and Abingdon in skiffs, led by the Queen's Swan Marker, wearing a red jacket. Swans are examined and cygnets ringed (formerly their beaks were nicked) according to their parentage – all birds on the right leg with a number and the Vintners' and Dyers' birds on the left leg as well with a ring indicating company ownership. The marking is also used to check the welfare of the swans.

Jonathan SWIFT

• Writer and clergyman • 1667-1745

The keen mind and biting wit of Jonathan Swift is remembered today for a work that is sometimes mistaken for a children's book: *Gulliver's Travels* (1726). Swift intended the work, about the fantastical voyages of Lemuel Gulliver, as a satire on the bestiality and stupidity of

LITTLE PEOPLE Lilliputians carry off the possessions of Lemuel Gulliver in Jonathan Swift's *Gulliver's Travels*. The book earned Swift £200, which he gave away to the poor

mankind, and on the politics, philosophy and science of his time.

Born in Ireland of English parents, Swift attended Trinity College, Dublin, and in 1689 moved to England, meeting Esther Johnson – the 'Stella' of *Journal to Stella* (1710-13) and the love of his life. For the next 25 years he divided his time between Ireland and London, where he threw himself into political and literary life, publishing *A Tale of a Tub* (1704), lampooning religious extremism, contributing to *The Spectator* and co-founding the 'Scriblerus Club' with the poets Alexander Pope and John Gay.

When Queen Anne died in 1714 and the Tories, for whom he was a pamphleteer, lost office, Swift returned to Ireland for good as dean of St Patrick's Cathedral in Dublin. He agitated for greater Irish liberty, writing the bitterly ironic *A Modest Proposal* (1729) with its suggestion that the children of the Irish poor be used as food for the rich.

BIRD WATCHING A red-flagged skiff of the Vintners' company and two blue-flagged skiffs of the Dyers' company track a group of swans on the Thames at the swan-upping ceremony

SYNOD OF WHITBY

• Convened AD 664

The Synod of Whitby unified an English church split between the Celtic Christians in the north and west and the followers of Roman CHRISTIANITY in the south.

Leaders of the Celtic and Roman traditions met at Whitby, in the Anglo-Saxon kingdom of Northumbria and the site of an important abbey, to debate their differences – such as the method used for calculating the date of Easter – before King Oswy. The king's decision in favour of Rome was accepted throughout England, and the Church in the north fell into line with CANTERBURY, the centre of the Roman Church in England.

SYON HOUSE

• W London (p.498 B4)
• Built 16th-19th century

The fort-like exterior of the family home of the Percys, dukes of Northumberland, was built in the 1540s by Edward Seymour, duke of Somerset and lord protector to Edward VI. The 18th-century interior is one of the finest works of Robert ADAM. From the ante-room's floor of polished scagliola, an imitation marble, rise 12 gleaming Ionic columns, with 12 gilded Classical figures. Beyond are a dining room set with copies of antique statues, a drawing room hung with crimson silk, and a gallery with painted pilasters and rich plasterwork.

The grounds, created by 'Capability' Brown, now embrace a butterfly house, an aviary and a motor museum.

TABLE TENNIS

The British invention of table tennis is one of the fastest indoor ball games. It developed in the 19th century as a miniaturised indoor version of tennis, played on a 2.7 m (9 ft) by 1.5 m (5 ft) table with a 15 cm (6 in) high net. It was originally given the onomatopoeic name of 'ping pong' by the sports goods company J. Jacques & Son.

At first cork and rubber balls were used. These were replaced with a hollow celluloid ball by an Englishman James Gibb in 1887, and from 1903 the use of pimpled rubber on each surface of a bat enhanced spin and control.

The game's governing body, the International Table Tennis Federation, was formed in 1926. The most successful British player was Hungarian-born Victor Barna. He won a record 15 world titles between 1930 and 1939.

William Henry Fox TALBOT

• **Photograpic pioneer** • **1800-77**

A faded print on silver chloride paper of an oriel window, made by William Henry Fox Talbot at his family home of Lacock Abbey in Wiltshire in 1835, is the world's earliest negative photograph. The announcement by the Frenchman Louis Daguerre of his daguerrotype process in 1839 prompted Talbot to make public his discovery. Two years later he patented the calotype (from kalos, Greek for beauty) as the first process for making positive prints from a negative.

In 1844 Talbot set up a printing works at Reading to produce calotypes, and created the first photographically illustrated book, *The Pencil of Nature*, published in six parts up to 1846.

Talbot was also a Liberal Member of Parliament and a classical scholar, helping to decipher the cuneiform tablets from the ruins of Nineveh, capital of ancient Assyria. His photographic achievements are commemorated in the

INFANTRY HAMMER A Mark I prepares for the first ever tank battle, at Flers-Courcelette on the Somme on September 15, 1916. The British army's latest tank, the Challenger 2 (*right*), built by the Vickers company, has a crew of four and a top speed of 37 mph

Fox Talbot Museum of Photography in a 16th-century barn at Lacock Abbey. The displays include Talbot's first camera and 1500 prints and paper negatives.

Thomas TALLIS

• **Composer** • **c.1505-85**

At the Dissolution of the Monasteries Thomas Tallis lost his job as organist at Waltham Abbey in Essex but gained a position under Henry VIII as a gentleman of the Chapel Royal. He went on to serve in the royal households of Edward VI, Mary I and Elizabeth I, composing some of the finest Renaissance sacred music. His 40-voice masterpiece of complex melodic interplay, *Spem in alium*, was written to be performed on the 40th birthday of Elizabeth I.

Tallis's fame rests partly on his relationship with his pupil William BYRD. In 1575 Elizabeth I granted Tallis and Byrd exclusive rights to publish music in England. Shortly afterwards they produced the *Cantiones Sacrae* which, being published in the 17th year of the queen's reign, contained 17 Latin anthems by each man.

Tallis is remembered in the hymn tune Tallis's Canon and in the *Fantasia on a Theme of Thomas Tallis* by Ralph VAUGHAN WILLIAMS, which sparked a 20th-century English music revival.

TANKS

In October 1914, three months into the First World War, the British War Office started to investigate building a tracked armoured vehicle capable of attacking enemy trenches. A few months later it abandoned the project as impractical.

The idea was kept alive by Ernest Swinton, a Royal Engineers officer, who by February 1916 had come up with the world's first working tank, the lozenge-shaped 'Mother'. In an attempt to keep its purpose secret, those building the vehicle were told it was a mobile water tank and the name 'tank' stuck.

Mother's 'child', the Mark I, was first used in combat in September 1916, but in too small numbers to be effective. The next year 373 Mark IV tanks pierced the German lines at Cambrai, though the breakthrough was poorly supported. Not until the introduction of the swifter 8 mph Whippet in March 1918, did the tank make a real impact.

The British army began the Second World War with the Churchill, a light tank later replaced by the heavier US Sherman. Since the war the army has used British-built tanks: the Centurion, Conqueror, Chieftain and Challenger 2.

> The Royal Armoured Corps Tank Museum at Bovington in Dorset has the world's largest collection of tanks and armoured vehicles — nearly 300 from 26 countries

KILTS, KITH AND KIN

The colourful checked tartan fabric, especially when woven into a kilt, is one of Scotland's most enduring symbols. It was worn in battle, for hunting and for ceremony, the tartan identifying the wearer as a member of one of the many clans, or tribes, that made up the volatile northern kingdom

THE GENEALOGY OF Scotland's clans and the disputed antiquity of their various distinctive tartans arouse passionate debate among a people whose pride in their history can bewilder their Anglo-Saxon neighbours.

The clan system of extended families living under the protection of a chief has its origins in the tribal Celtic society that existed throughout Britain 2000 years ago. Though modified by feudalism and the influence of central government, medieval Scottish history was largely a family affair, while above the Highland line, north and west of the Grampians,

WELL-DRESSED LAIRD Archibald MacNab, 17th chief of the Clan MacNab, is portrayed around 1830 wearing Highland regalia, including the clan tartan, chief's feathers, crest and badge, and carrying his unsheathed *sgean dubh*, or dirk

TARTAN SOLDIERS The 50-strong Atholl Highlanders, a regiment still recruited largely from the estate of the duke of Atholl, Chief of the Clan Murray, is the only private army in Europe. It is based at Blair Castle

the authority of chiefs reigned supreme until the end of the 18th century.

After the Battle of CULLODEN MOOR in 1746, even those chiefs who had fought with the English against the Young Pretender, BONNIE PRINCE CHARLIE, lost their authority, although they remained landowners of large but impoverished estates. Subsequently, during the HIGHLAND CLEARANCES, many clansmen were evicted from their ancestral lands and forced to emigrate.

ROMANCING THE ROOTS

The tradition of weaving multi-coloured checks in specific local patterns was first documented in 1697. When an Act in 1747 banned the wearing of tartan north of the Highland Line, the weaving firm of Wilson at Bannockburn, south of the Line, became the main source of new tartans to families and army regiments, including the Black Watch, the Royal Scots, the Seaforths, the Gordons, and the Argyll and Sutherland Highlanders.

The 19th-century novelist Walter Scott almost single-handedly reinvented tartan as the national costume when he stage-managed George IV's visit to Edinburgh in 1822, the first by a monarch for more than 200 years. Scott urged the people of Edinburgh to appear 'plaided and plumed'. The king donned corsets to enable him to wear a kilt; it is said he fainted several times.

FOUR MIGHTY CLANS

There are 67 original Scottish clans. Each has a crest, a motto and a variety of colours in its tartan. Some clans have a 'hunting' version of dull browns and greens that acts as a camouflage in open country, and a 'dress' version for ceremonial occasions. The four clans below are thought to be the largest.

STEWART

The royal family is descended indirectly from Walter Stewart, High Steward of Scotland under Robert Bruce, who married the Bruce's daughter to found the Stuart dynasty. Elizabeth II often wears the Stewart tartan, which is also the uniform of pipers in the Scots Guards. Motto: 'Courage grows strong at a wound.'

MACDONALD

The clan claims descent from the high kings of Ireland. Clan members fought with Robert Bruce at Bannockburn, and as lords of the isles their chiefs ruled Scotland's western seaboard until the end of the 15th century. Though divided into several branches, it is Scotland's largest clan. Motto: 'By sea and by land.'

CAMPBELL

Originating in the ancient British kingdom of Strathclyde, this clan acquired through force and diplomacy much land that belonged to smaller clans. A feud with the Macdonalds culminated in the 1692 GLEN COE MASSACRE. The clan chiefs, the dukes of Argyll, have lived at Inveraray Castle for more than 500 years. Motto: 'Do not forget.'

MURRAY

The clan, consisting of many branches and headed by the duke of Atholl, is descended from Freskin, a Fleming, who received a grant of land in the 12th century from David I. In the 17th century the earldom of Atholl was joined through marriage to that of Murray with its seat of Blair Castle. Motto: 'Furth fortune and fill the fetters.'

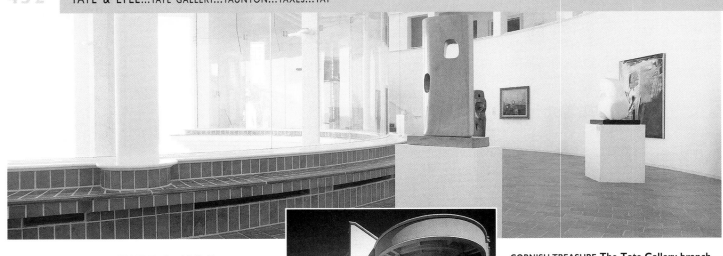

TATE & LYLE

• Founded 1921

Tate & Lyle, synonymous in Britain with sugar, is Europe's largest cane sugar refiner and one of the world's biggest producers of sweeteners, starch products and animal feeds. The company employs some 22 000 people in 50 countries.

It was formed by the merger of two sugar refiners, Henry Tate (1819-90) and Abram Lyle (1820-99), each with a refinery on the Thames. Tate specialised in cubed sugar and Lyle in syrup.

In the 1920s and 1930s, Tate & Lyle developed branded sugar products and expanded overseas into Africa and the West Indies. The company survived sugar rationing in the Second World War, after which it added desserts and jams to its products, making sugar a staple part of the British diet. Sugar consumption in Britain dropped from 2.28 million tons in 1992 to 2.12 million tons in 1997.

SUGAR HERO Tate & Lyle used 'Mr Cube' to fight against nationalisation in 1949 with the slogan 'State control will make a hole in your pocket and my packet'

TATE GALLERY

• Central London (p.499 D4) • Opened 1897

Each year around 2 million people visit the national collections of British and modern art at the Tate Gallery, built on the Thames-side site of the former Millbank prison. The gallery was founded by the sugar magnate Henry Tate, who donated his own impressive collection of painting and sculpture.

In 1988 a satellite Tate Gallery was opened in Liverpool, followed in 1993 by one in ST IVES, Cornwall. In 2000 the

London displays are to be split between the Millbank building, which will become the Tate Gallery of British Art, and the New Tate Gallery of Modern Art in the former Bankside power station.

The Tate's sites cover British art from the 16th century onwards, including works by HOGARTH, CONSTABLE, STUBBS, the PRE-RAPHAELITES, HEPWORTH and MOORE, as well as contemporary artists such as Damien HIRST and Rachel Whiteread. The TURNER Bequest at the London site consists of around 300 oil paintings and 38 000 watercolours and drawings, some on display in the adjoining Clore Gallery, opened in 1987. The Tate's modern collection includes work by Picasso, Matisse and Warhol.

TAUNTON

• Somerset (p.494 D5) • Pop. 55 860

The county town of Somerset is still haunted by the memory of Judge Jeffreys's 'Bloody Assize' in Taunton Castle, which condemned more than 500 supporters of the duke of Monmouth's 1685 rebellion to transportation or death. The Norman castle now houses the Somerset County Museum, with Iron Age and Roman relics. St Mary's Church, built about 1500, is Somerset's largest.

Surrounding the town is the Vale of Taunton Deane, which for centuries has provided the apples for Taunton's CIDER-making, celebrated every October in a cider barrel-rolling race.

CORNISH TREASURE The Tate Gallery branch in St Ives was built on the site of a gasometer. Its semicircular galleries attract some 200 000 people a year to view the work of Barbara Hepworth and other St Ives' school artists

TAXES

The government needs money to pay for everything from schools to missiles. It covers the cost by taxing British people and business on income (direct taxation) and expenditure (indirect taxation).

WHERE THE GOVERNMENT'S MONEY COMES FROM

Government taxes	Year of introduction	£ million 1998-9
Excise duty	1643	35 727
Income tax	1799	84 300
Stamp duty	1891	4600
Inheritance tax	1894 (as estate duty)	1900
Capital gains tax	1965	2200
Corporation tax	1965	30 000
VAT	1973	52 319
Petroleum revenue tax	1975	500
Council tax	1993	10 460
Windfall tax	1997	2600

River TAY

• Central Scotland (p.497 C4)

The 120 mile Tay is Scotland's longest river. It takes its name from Loch Tay, 40 miles from the probable source near Ben Lui, in the foothills of the Highlands. The river, with its fine scenery and salmon fishing, runs through Aberfeldy and Perth into the Firth of Tay on the east coast.

The two-mile long Tay Rail Bridge spans the Firth of Tay, dating from 1887. Beside it can be seen the remains of an earlier bridge that in 1879 collapsed under a train with the loss of 75 lives.

A NICE CUPPA

The Chinese invented tea – or ch'a as they call it – but Britain and Ireland are now the world's biggest consumers. Tea replaced gin and ale in the 18th century as our national drink and has become part of the daily ritual of British life, fuelling the working day and soothing in times of crisis

TEA DRINKING WAS the exclusive preserve of the Chinese, to whose country the plant is native, until as recently as the late 16th century when their nomadic Russian neighbours first came into contact with the drink. The Dutch imported tea to Europe from 1610, but the British love affair with the leaf – first publicly sold by Thomas Garway, a London merchant, in 1657 – developed more rapidly than in any other western country. The huge appetite for tea, officially fed by the tea clippers of the British East India Company, and an import duty of 119 per cent, resulted in the 18th century's most intensive bout of smuggling. By Victorian times much of the imperial economy was underpinned by the tea plantations of India.

As greater quantities were imported, the price of tea fell rapidly. Within 50 years of its first appearance in London the retail price had fallen from up to £10 a pound to about £1 a pound. By the mid 1700s tea was well on its way to becoming a staple beverage of all classes – to the dismay of brewers and the government, which suffered reduced revenues from liquor.

A VERY BRITISH BEVERAGE
Social rituals evolved around the serving of tea, with the mass production of the teapot and tea service from the mid-18th century helping to make the fortunes of Josiah WEDGWOOD and other Stoke potters. The use of milk was not at first general practice, although in China tea was boiled with both milk and butter. European tea drinkers took to milk from the late 17th century, finding it softened the astringency of tannin.

Today, more than 145 million kg (319 million lb) of tea is consumed in Britain every year, less and less of it as loose leaves since the widespread commercial use of the teabag, invented

A TASTE FOR TEA Most British teas are blends of up to 35 varieties. Tea tasters test the pure teas bought at auction to ensure their quality and mix them to obtain the correct blend. They may taste up to 1000 teas in a day

by an American tea merchant in 1904 (the first bags were made of silk). More than three-quarters of Britons over the age of ten drink tea every day, averaging three to four cups each – far more than coffee, alcohol or soft drinks.

TEA TIMES
Afternoon tea, served at 4pm accompanied by cress or cucumber sandwiches and cake, is said to have been invented in the early 1800s by Anna, duchess of Bedford. It was seen as a way of bridging the gap between lunch and a fashionably later dinner at about 8pm.

High tea evolved in Victorian times as the main meal of the day for factory workers. Taken between 5pm and 6pm, it was heartier than afternoon tea but less elaborate than dinner, involving perhaps pies, a fry-up or toad-in-the-hole, cakes and, of course, copious brews.

LIGHT REFRESHMENT A Cambridge maid has a cheering cuppa in 1939. The great British tea break began around 200 years ago, when industrial workers toiling long hours were allowed to stop mid morning for tea and food

A WORLD OF TEA
At least 1500 varieties of tea are grown in more than 25 countries, mainly in Africa and Asia. Most British tea comes from India, Sri Lanka, China and Kenya, reflecting old imperial trading interests.

ASSAM
Assam, in north-east India, the first region to be planted by the British, is the largest tea-growing area on the subcontinent. It produces a drink with a strong malty flavour.

DARJEELING
The pick of Indian teas, delicately flavoured Darjeeling comes from the Himalayan foothills of north India. The original plants were grown from Chinese seeds.

EARL GREY
A black China tea, Earl Grey is scented with oil of zest of bergamot. It was blended for the 2nd earl Grey, British prime minister, after a visit to China in 1830.

FORMOSA OOLONG
Oolong, produced on Formosa, now Taiwan, is only partly exposed to the fermentation process that turns green tea black. It has a delicate aroma and amber colour.

CEYLON ORANGE PEKOE
Tea was first planted on the island of Sri Lanka, then the British colony of Ceylon, in 1867. Ceylon teas have a delicate but distinctive and slightly bitter flavour.

GLUED TO THE BOX

It was a Briton, John Logie Baird, who invented television and Britain that gave the world its first public television service. Today we watch an average of 26 hours a week. Our programmes, quirky and accomplished, cultured, folksy or rebellious, exert a mighty influence on national life

A S EARLY AS the late 1920s, scientists knew that television was an idea whose time was about to come. There were promising experiments in France, Germany and Russia as well as in the USA. The world's first public television service went on air from the BBC's transmitter at Alexandra Palace in London in November 1936.

Less than three years later war broke out. Television closed down until 1946, and became a mass medium only in 1953 when the coronation of Elizabeth II led to a frenzy of set-buying.

TELEVISION LEARNS TO TALK BACK

At first British television – both the BBC and, from 1955, independent television (ITV) – was deferential. Commentators were solemn, dignified and respectful to authority. Drama was either classical or unthreatening, comedy in 'mustn't grumble' music-hall tradition.

That changed in the 1960s with the coming of satire in the form of *That Was the Week that Was* (1962), the absurdist comedy of *Monty Python's Flying Circus* (1969), and gritty working-class dramas such as *CORONATION STREET* (1960) and the Liverpool police series *Z-Cars* (1962).

REVOLUTION IN THE SITTING ROOM

By the 1980s, critics were beginning to denounce the 'comfortable duopoly' of the BBC and ITV. Rupert Murdoch took on the two giants, offering a diet of sport and films on his satellite service, Sky. Under its director-general John Birt, the BBC fought back, beginning a new era in the medium, now ruthlessly competitive, commercially driven and overtly populist.

Hundreds of new pay digital channels are now beginning to compete with the five terrestrial services.

Two questions hang over the industry: how long can the BBC rely on the licence fee? And will the new commercial climate still support news, drama, comedy and sports programmes as well as game shows and sit-coms?

BIGGEST BRITISH AUDIENCES

30 million EastEnders *Christmas episode* December 26, 1986

32 million Funeral of Diana, Princess of Wales September 7, 1997

32 million Chelsea v Leeds Cup Final replay April 28, 1970

32 million England v W Germany World Cup final July 30, 1966

32.5 million Brazil v England World Cup match June 10, 1970

39 million Wedding of Diana Spencer and Prince Charles July 29, 1981

THE JEWEL IN THE TV CROWN A single hour of television drama, particularly a period piece such as *Pride and Prejudice* (below), can cost as much as £1 million to make – eight times as much as a documentary and more than 20 times the cost of a daily news programme

LONGEST RUNS

PROGRAMME	FIRST BROADCAST
Come Dancing	Sept 29, 1950
Panorama	Nov 11, 1953
What the Papers Say	Nov 5, 1956
The Sky at Night	Apr 24, 1957
Grandstand	Oct 11, 1958
Blue Peter	Oct 16, 1958
Coronation Street	Dec 9, 1960
Songs of Praise	Oct 1, 1961
Dr Who	Nov 23, 1963
Top of the Pops	Jan 1, 1964

ETERNAL YOUTH Jimmy Savile presented *Top of the Pops* for 20 years, from 1964 to 1984

ALL-TIME FAVOURITES
(*Radio Times* viewers' poll, Sept 1998)

Comedy: *Morecambe and Wise*

Period drama: *I, Claudius*

Police drama: *Inspector Morse*

Soap opera: *Coronation Street*

One-off drama: *Cathy Come Home*

Documentary: *Around the World in 80 Days*

Sit-com: *Only Fools and Horses*

Preschool programme: *Playschool*

Drama series: *All Creatures Great and Small*

FORCE FOR GOOD Ken Loach's *Cathy Come Home* brought homelessness to public attention in 1966

PLAY TIME By 1930 the BBC was preparing the first ever televison drama, *The Man with a Flower in his Mouth* (in rehearsal, left)

TELEVISION TIMETABLE

1897 Cathode-ray tube invented

1900 Constantin Perskyi reads paper in Paris outlining the theory of television

1908 A.C. Swinton proposes the use of a cathode-ray tube to transmit as well as receive pictures

1923 First electronic camera made using a cathode-ray tube

1926 J.L. Baird conducts experimental broadcast in a Soho laboratory

1928 Baird demonstrates colour television system

1929 Baird opens world's first television studio in Long Acre, London

1936 BBC initiates public broadcasting from Alexandra Palace

1937 Marconi electronic system wins out over Baird's mechanical one

1946 BBC returns to the air after the Second World War

1953 Surge in television ownership owing to coronation of Elizabeth II

1955 Independent television goes on air

1960 Transistors make sets smaller

1962 First satellite transmissions of television programmes

1964 BBC2 launched

1967 Colour introduced on BBC2

1982 Channel 4 starts broadcasting

1989 Rupert Murdoch launches Sky, which in 1990 takes over BSatB to become BSkyB

1993 Reorganisation of commercial television under Broadcasting Act 1990, which also paves way for new terrestrial service, Channel 5 (launched 1997)

1998 Digital television introduced, with potential for hundreds of channels

TEDDY BOYS

The 1950s fashion phenomenon of the Teddy Boy, or Ted, seems to have started as a south London sub-culture. The name comes from 'Edwardians', and although it was a working-class cult, it mimicked a retrospective style of dress popular with upper-class young men in the 1940s.

A MONTH'S WAGES FOR AN OUTFIT

Teds wore drainpipe trousers, bootlace ties, square-cut 'drape' jackets, and crepe-soled 'beetle-crusher' or 'brothel-creeper' shoes. They frequented coffee bars, listened to rock'n'roll, and splashed out £17 to £20, three or four weeks' wages, on a single outfit.

Although Teds acted tough and were said to carry knives or coshes, the most serious disturbance was in September 1956 when police were called to cinemas showing *Rock Around the Clock* to stop Teddy Boys dancing in the aisles to Bill Haley and the Comets.

River TEES

• **N England (p.496 C3)**

No river in Britain passes through such changes of character and landscape as the Tees in its short 70 miles. It rises on Cross Fell in a country of moorland and old lead workings and flows eastward to Caldron Snout and High Force in Teesdale where it cascades over basalt sills in spectacular waterfalls. It meanders on through a picturesque plain, joined by the Greta in a rocky reach painted by J.M.W. Turner and John Cotman.

HITCHING A RIDE The 1911 Transporter Bridge across the Tees at Middlesbrough is one of only two 'flying ferry' bridges in Britain. Cars and pedestrians make the crossing on a platform suspended on cables

After tortuous bends, the Tees reaches the conurbations of Stockton, Thornaby and Middlesbrough. It was the need to ship coal mined at Darlington and further north that led to the opening of the world's first passenger steam railway, the Darlington to Stockton, in 1825.

The neat grid of Middlesbrough was laid out in the 1830s by the railway company. When iron ore was found nearby shipbuilding yards sprang up and Teesside was born. The river ends in a broad five-mile estuary on the North Sea between Redcar and Hartlepool.

TELEGRAPH NEWSPAPERS

The Daily Telegraph appeared on the streets in 1855 and as the first penny newspaper rapidly acquired a large readership. In 1939 it replaced front-page advertisements with news – a first among broadsheets.

Its sister title, *The Sunday Telegraph*, was launched 1961 and in 1987 the two papers were among the first to move from Fleet Street to the Docklands area of East London. During the 1990s, their Canadian-born proprietor Conrad Black modernised the papers' image, vastly increasing their circulation.

Despite their conservative image and politics, the NEWSPAPERS of the Telegraph group have been a consistently innovative force in British journalism.

TELEVISION: *see opposite page*

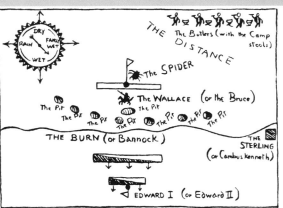

Thomas TELFORD

• Engineer • 1757-1834

Born a Scottish shepherd's son and trained as a stone mason, Thomas Telford brought about a Georgian transport revolution. He was appointed surveyor of public works for Shropshire in 1787 but soon turned to inland waterways, working on projects ranging from the Ellesmere Canal, with its dramatic 37 m (121 ft) high Pontcysyllte aqueduct, to the Gotha Canal in Sweden and St Katharine Dock on the River Thames.

Telford built roads, bridges and harbours throughout Scotland, bringing transport links to the impoverished Highlands. His greatest road work began in 1815 with the reconstruction of the London-Holyhead route and the building of its two pioneering suspension bridges at Conwy and across the Menai Straits.

TENNIS

The outdoor racquet sport associated with such typically English institutions as the country-house weekend and WIMBLEDON began as a French handball game played by monks. Real ('royal') tennis crossed the Channel no later than the 14th century.

The game was adapted for outdoor play as 'lawn tennis' in Victorian times. The chief pioneer was Major Wingfield, who staged a game of 'Sphairistike' in 1873. It remained a predominantly middle-class sport and professionals were not allowed to compete in major tournaments until 1968. No British man has equalled the success of the three-times Wimbledon champion FRED PERRY in the 1930s, although Tim Henman and Greg Ruzedski both reached the top ten in the world rankings in 1998.

Today local authorities across Britain provide courts and coaching, and an estimated 5 million people play, many as members of the 2500 clubs affiliated to the Lawn Tennis Association.

Alfred, Lord TENNYSON

• Poet • 1809-92; bn 1884; poet laureate 1850

Was he a parlour poet or an incisive chronicler of his times? Lord Tennyson's reputation is still in the balance. He was hugely popular in his day, succeeding William Wordsworth as poet laureate and producing such patriotic verses as 'The Charge of the Light Brigade'.

But Tennyson's passion was the rhythm and musicality of language, expressed in the sensuality of poems such as 'The Lady of Shalott' and 'Maud':

> *Come into the garden, Maud*
> *For the black bat, night, has flown,*
> *Come into the garden, Maud,*
> *I am here at the gate alone;*
> *And the woodbine spices are wafted abroad,*
> *And the musk of the rose is blown.*

Longer works such as *In Memoriam*, an elegy on the death of his friend, Arthur Hallam, show a more philosophical Tennyson. The lengthy Arthurian *Idylls of the King* reflects Victorian anxieties, chronicling the downfall of a society founded on idealism.

UNOFFICIAL VERSION Sellar and Yeatman satirised textbook treatment of the Battle of Bannockburn in *1066 And All That* 'A History of England . . . including 103 Good Things, 5 Bad Kings, and 2 Genuine Dates'

1066 AND ALL THAT

• Published 1930

The 'Charge of the Fire Brigade' was led by 'gallant men armed with Cardigans'; the motto of the royal family *Honi soie qui mal y pense* really means 'Honey, your silk stocking's hanging down'; Holland's colonial possessions included Lumbago and the Laxative Islands – revelations such as these spring from every page of *1066 And All That*.

The book, a joyous jumble of jokes, puns, anachronisms and deliberate misunderstandings, was the brainchild of W.C. Sellar and R.J. Yeatman, two demobbed First World War subalterns who met while studying history at Oxford University in 1920.

Their intention was to send up English smugness and the teaching of history by rote. Yet ironically *1066* itself became a historical icon, symbolising the values of Edwardian England, the last days of the British Empire and an education system that is no more.

TEST MATCH CRICKET

Spanning up to five 6 hour days, Test match cricket consumes more time than any other ball game. England and Australia played the inaugural 'Test' at Melbourne in 1877. South Africa joined in 1888 (excluded 1970-92), the West Indies in 1928, New Zealand in 1929, India in 1932, Pakistan in 1948, Sri Lanka in 1982 and Zimbabwe in 1992.

ENGLAND RESULTS 1877-1999

	FIRST PLAYED	WON	LOST	DRAWN
v. Australia	1877	93	117	86
v. South Africa	1889	49	21	45
v. West Indies	1928	28	51	42
v. New Zealand	1929	37	6	39
v. India	1932	32	14	38
v. Pakistan	1954	14	9	32
v. Sri Lanka	1982	3	2	1
v. Zimbabwe	1996	0	0	2
TOTAL		761	256	220	285

BEST PERFORMANCES FOR ENGLAND

Highest team score:	903 for 7 declared (v. Australia, 1938)
Most runs in career:	8900 by Graham Gooch (1975-95)
Most runs in match:	456 by Graham Gooch (v. India, 1990)
Highest individual score:	364 by Len Hutton (v. Australia, 1938)
Most centuries in career:	22 by Walter Hammond (1927-47), Colin Cowdrey (1954-75), Geoff Boycott (1964-82)
Highest-scoring partnership:	411 by Peter May and Colin Cowdrey (v. West Indies, 1957)
Most wickets in career:	383 by Ian Botham (1977-92)
Most wickets in match:	19 by Jim Laker (v. Australia, 1956)

WARP AND WEFT

Making cloth was once a fireside occupation, women and children cleaning and spinning the fibre and men weaving it into fabric on handlooms. Mechanisation changed all that, bringing in less than 100 years a revolution that transformed not just the industry but a whole way of life

COMPANY HOUSING New Lanark, created in 1783, became a model village for millworkers under the management of the philanthropic millowner Robert Owen, who also set an example by refusing to employ young children

I N THE 19th century, Edward Baines, historian of the cotton industry, calculated that if all the cotton spun in Britain in one year was made into a single thread, it would go around the world 200 000 times. Yet a century before, cotton was scarcely manufactured and wool, which clothed rich and poor alike, was still produced as a cottage industry.

IMPORTS AND INVENTIONS

Change came in the 18th century when colourful cotton cloth from India started to appear in Britain. It was soon in great demand and manufacturers began to import raw cotton – at first from India and later from America. In 1733, a Bury craftsman, John Kay, invented the 'flying' shuttle, which greatly increased the output of a loom. Suddenly there was both a demand for new material and fast looms to produce it. But yarn itself was still slow and laborious to make.

SOLVING THE SPINNING CONUNDRUM

Around 1764 the inventor James Hargreaves produced a spinning jenny, which enabled one spinner to work up to 16 spindles instead of just one. But the

great breakthrough was made by Richard ARKWRIGHT, a Preston barber, in 1768 when he designed the water frame, a spinning machine worked by water wheel instead of by hand. By the end of the century, another improved spinning machine, the mule, had appeared and the first power looms had been built.

With the 19th century came efficient steam power and mill towns were born, as mills, no longer needing running water, were built near sources of cheap coal.

CLOTHING THE WORLD

By 1900 Britain was supplying two-thirds of the world's manufactured cotton either as yarn or cloth, and a large amount of woollen goods. But British mills began to decline in the 1930s and the decline has continued in the face of new synthetic materials and cheap imports from abroad. In 1998, the UK exported £3472 million worth of textiles but imported goods worth £5180 million.

A TRIP INTO THE PAST

These museums display remnants of the great age of textile manufacture, some incorporating working mills.

- **Armley Mills Industrial Museum, Leeds:** one of the world's biggest wool mills
- **Bradford Industrial Museum:** mill with working machinery.
- **Colne Valley Museum, Golcar:** handloom weaving
- **Helmshore Textile Museum, Helmshore:** working mill machinery
- **Piece Hall and Calderdale Industrial Museum, Halifax:** 18th-century cloth market and museum
- **Quarry Bank Mill, Styal:** 18th-century cotton mill and village
- **Wigan Pier, Greater Manchester:** huge working mill steam engine

INDUSTRIAL DINOSAURS The restored weaving room at Quarry Bank Mill in Styal, Cheshire, preserves ranks of traditional Lancashire looms as they would have been in their heyday

ON THE JOB Children as young as seven worked in the first textile mills – precariously untangling thread and yarn from massive machines. In 1909 they were still operating machines such as the spinning mule (*below*)

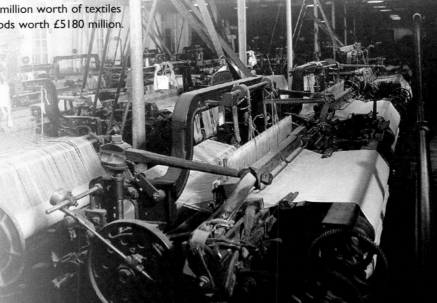

William Makepeace THACKERAY

• Novelist • 1811-63

Few English novelists have written as graphically as Thackeray or constructed better stories. Considered second only to Dickens in his time, he wrote one masterpiece, *Vanity Fair* (1847-8), several other fine novels, journalism, essays and a children's book.

Vanity Fair follows the fortunes of two women, the respectable and virtuous Amelia Smedley and the more disreputable and self-interested Becky Sharp. In Becky, Thackeray created one of the most credible women in English literature – a remarkable achievement for an author who himself said it was his misfortune to have been born when you could not tell the truth about women.

Margaret THATCHER

• Prime minister 1979-90 • b.1925; bn 1992

In 1979 Margaret Hilda Thatcher became Britain's first woman prime minister, head of a nation demoralised by strikes, inflation and economic weakness. Her renegotiation of Britain's contribution to the EEC budget and her handling of the Argentinian invasion of the Falkland Islands in 1982 led to her re-election in 1983 despite severe economic recession and high unemployment figures.

Margaret Thatcher is the only British prime minister to have been a science graduate. She left Oxford University in 1947 with a second class Chemistry degree

By 1988 she had become the century's longest-serving prime minister, and the only one to have given her name to a set of policies: monetarism, the control of the money supply to reduce inflation; privatisation; and the doctrine of self-help. She championed home and share ownership, and small business.

Thatcherite policies created a boom in the 1980s, but by 1989 further economic recession, an increasing gap between rich and poor, an unpopular POLL TAX and key Cabinet resignations caused her popularity to plummet.

The first 20th-century prime minister to win three successive elections, she was forced out of office in 1990, having broken the mould of postwar politics.

THATCHING

Thatching is one of the oldest forms of roofing; in Britain archaeologists have discovered evidence of its use dating

LAYING THATCH The thatcher's basic skills and tools have changed relatively little since the Romans first discovered Britons living in basic dwellings with thatched roofs

from 500 BC. It was common throughout the Middle Ages, though thatched houses built in close proximity contributed to many disastrous fires; thatch was banned in many towns by the 16th century.

Thatchers traditionally work alone or in small teams. They use different materials to achieve specific effects: longstraw for smoothness, durable Norfolk reed for a close-cropped brush-like texture, or combed wheat reed for a rowed design. Traditional styles vary from one region to another according to locally available thatching material and have become popular again as a result of effective modern fire retardants.

River THAMES

• S England (p.495 G4)

The 210 mile River Thames rises in the Cotswold Hills in Gloucestershire, and flows roughly eastwards past Oxford (where it is also known as the Isis), into the Chilterns and on through London to the North Sea. The river has been an important trade and transport route since prehistoric times; the many large houses lining its banks include seven past or present palaces, at Windsor, Hampton Court, Richmond, Kew, Westminster, the Tower of London and Greenwich.

RIVER GOD A statue of Old Father Thames stands at St John's Lock below Lechlade

ANCIENT CROSSING Radcot had a bridge in Saxon times. Today's 14th-century crossing is the river's oldest

LITERARY PUB The Barley Mow at Clifton Hampden features in Jerome K. Jerome's *Three Men in a Boat*

PORT MEADOW The riverside Oxford common has been free-grazing since the 11th century

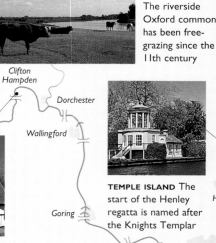

TEMPLE ISLAND The start of the Henley regatta is named after the Knights Templar

KEY
〜 Bridge
< Lock

Thames Head, Lechlade, Kelmscot, Radcot, Bampton, Newbridge, Bablockhythe, Eynsham, Oxford, Abingdon, Clifton Hampden, Dorchester, Wallingford, Goring, Pangbourne, Reading

Dylan THOMAS

• Writer • 1914-1953

A wild and roistering Welsh poet, Dylan Thomas wrote poetry full of vitality, power and passion. His work is notable for its bold lyricism, vivid imagery and sense of awe at the human processes of procreation, birth and death.

In one poem he celebrates 'the force that through the green fuse drives the flower'; in another he urges his dying father not to accept death meekly but to 'Rage, rage against the dying of the light'.

Thomas also wrote stories and the autobiographical *Portrait of the Artist as a Young Dog* (1940). His most popular work was the radio play *Under Milk Wood* (1953), which dramatises the lives and dreams of the people of the imaginary village of Llareggub (which can also be read in reverse). He spent most of his last years in the United States, where he died after much hard drinking and partying.

ON THE AIR Radio broadcasts took Dylan Thomas's work to a wide audience. Alongside the play *Under Milk Wood*, many of his short stories had originally been written for radio

J. J. THOMSON

• Physicist • 1856-1940; kt 1908

Universally known as J.J., Joseph John Thomson discovered the electron, the sub-atomic particle whose movement creates electricity. He was born in Manchester and went to Cambridge on a scholarship in 1876, remaining there for the rest of his life. In 1884, aged only 27, he became professor of physics and head of the CAVENDISH LABORATORY.

Thomson studied cathode rays, and was able to show that they consisted of charged particles about one-thousandth the mass of the smallest known particle, the hydrogen ion. This was the first clear evidence for the existence of sub-atomic particles. Thomson went on to demonstrate the existence of isotopes, forms of elements that are chemically identical but of different mass.

He was awarded the Nobel prize for physics in 1906 and the department he established at the Cavendish Laboratory led the world of sub-atomic physics for the first 30 years of the 20th century, seven of his research assistants also winning Nobel prizes.

THREE CHOIRS FESTIVAL

• August

In 1715 the three cathedral cities of Gloucester, Hereford and Worcester agreed to share in rotation a week-long annual music festival, the 'Three Choirs'. Initially the emphasis was on sacred choral works, dominated in the 18th century by Handel and in the 19th by Mendelssohn. However, from 1902 to 1933, under the influence of the composer Edward ELGAR, the festival became central in the movement to revive British musical creativity.

The festival continues to be a success, attracting a large international audience. It includes not only much secular music but also wide-ranging cultural events such as art exhibitions and drama. Proceeds from the concerts are donated to charity just as they have been since the festival's inception.

Ocean-going ships once sailed up to the Pool of London in the heart of the city but today most ships berth at modern ports such as Tilbury on the river's lower reaches. The Thames used to flood at exceptionally high water, but since 1982 the Thames Barrier at Woolwich has protected the capital.

Upstream from London, boating has become a popular attraction, and many riverside towns, notably Henley-on-Thames, hold summer regattas. In the spring Oxford and Cambridge universities hold an annual BOAT RACE on the river between Putney Bridge to Mortlake.

For the millenium a new footbridge, designed by Norman FOSTER, is to span the river just south of St Paul's Cathedral.

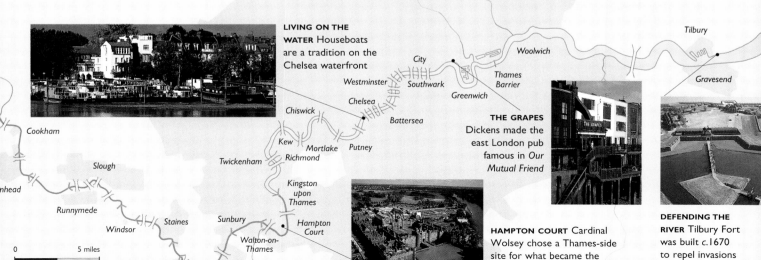

LIVING ON THE WATER Houseboats are a tradition on the Chelsea waterfront

THE GRAPES Dickens made the east London pub famous in *Our Mutual Friend*

HAMPTON COURT Cardinal Wolsey chose a Thames-side site for what became the largest palace in England

DEFENDING THE RIVER Tilbury Fort was built c.1670 to repel invasions

THRUSH

*That's the wise thrush; he sings
each song twice over,
Lest you should think he never
could recapture,
The first fine careless rapture!*

The poet Robert Browning
was enchanted by the melody
of the song thrush, one of the
leaders of the dawn chorus,
and he noted its repeated phrasing. But
it is not the only British thrush to sing.
The blackbird – a true thrush, despite
the lack of breast spots – sings almost
as well, and the less melodious but more
conspicuously spotted mistle thrush sings
even on blustery late winter days, giving
it the alternative name 'storm cock'.

All three resident thrushes have
distinctive feeding habits, the blackbird
cocking its head, probably to watch for
movement with its sideways-set eyes,
and the song thrush breaking snail shells
on an 'anvil' stone. The mistle thrush
prefers the sticky berries of mistletoe
and helps to spread the seeds by
cleaning its beak on the bark of trees.

Three other thrushes come as visitors:
the ring ouzel in summer and the
fieldfare and redwing in winter.

**SONG THRUSH A
single song can last
5 minutes or more**

THRUST

ThrustSSC (SuperSonic Car) was built to
be the first car to establish a land speed
record beyond the sound barrier. It was

**FASTEST MACHINE ON EARTH In 1997 the
British-built *Thrust* broke the sound barrier
by 15 mph, setting a land-speed record that
still stands at the end of the century**

devised by Richard Noble, who in
1983 had set a record speed of
633 mph in an earlier jet
car, *Thrust2*.

In 1993, joined by
the aerodynamicist and
former missile designer Ron
Ayers, Noble built a new car
to a revolutionary design.
The cockpit was housed in
a long, slender body, flanked
by two Rolls-Royce Spey turbo-jet
engines. On October 15, 1997, in the
Black Rock Desert in Nevada, USA, with
RAF pilot Andy Green at the controls it
reached 763 mph, a supersonic record.

The TIMES

- **Est. 1785**

In the years after its foundation as *The
Daily Universal Register*, the paper soon
known as *The Times* was courageous,
innovative and progressive. It espoused
causes like Catholic emancipation, the
abolition of slavery and the Reform Act.

The Victorian *Times* was called 'The
Thunderer' because of the moral and
political authority of two editors, Thomas
Barnes and John Delane. It pioneered
the use of foreign correspondents and
new print technology.

In the late 19th century *The Times* fell
behind its rivals technically and lost its
competitive edge, but the status of the
paper as the voice of the Establishment
ensured its survival. Rupert Murdoch,
the current proprietor of *The Times*,
has doubled its daily sales to 750 000
through astute promotion.
See also NEWSPAPERS

TINTAGEL

- **Cornwall (p.494 B6)**

High on a promontory in north Cornwall
looking out over the Atlantic lie the ruins
of Tintagel, a medieval castle probably
built on the site of a much earlier British
stronghold. Nearby, archaeologists have
uncovered what might have been a Celtic
monastery dating from around AD 500.

Tintagel's shadowy history together
with its awe-inspiring setting have
steeped the place in legend. One tale
tells how the castle, said to have been a
magnificent blue and green chequered
edifice built by giants, became invisible
for two days of each year.

Other legends claim Tintagel as the
place of King Arthur's conception, his
birth or his court. In some accounts the
legendary lovers Tristan and Isolde are
supposed to lie side by side at Tintagel: a
vine is said to have grown from Tristan's
grave and a rose-tree from Isolde's, their
branches now densely intertwined.

TINTERN ABBEY

- **Monmouthshire (p.494 E4)**
- **Built 12th century** • **Cadw**

The gaunt, empty windows of this once
prosperous abbey frame densely wooded
hills sloping down to the River Wye.

Cistercian monks founded the
monastery in 1131. Originally an order
devoted to a simple, pastoral existence,
they acquired a reputation as shrewd
farmers with an eye for the potential of
undeveloped land, and within 500 years
their estates extended 5 miles east and
west of Tintern.

EVOCATIVE RUINS Wordsworth wrote about Tintern Abbey in his *Lyrical Ballads* of 1798. Two hundred years on, the abbey retains its haunting presence

The lord of Chepstow manor, Roger Bigood, financed the building of the abbey church in the late 13th and early 14th centuries but Tintern suffered a gradual decline. By its dissolution in 1536 only 12 brothers remained.

The buildings crumbled in obscurity until romantic tourism brought visitors such as William Wordsworth, who described them in his poetry, and J.M.W. Turner, who painted their Gothic arches.

Michael TIPPETT

• Composer • 1905-98; kt 1966; OM 1983

Michael Tippett's life spanned the 20th century. The son of a suffragette, he was from the outset a political figure. During the 1930s he taught music at a work camp in Yorkshire where he saw at first hand the plight of the unemployed. He was a conscientious objector during the Second World War and was sentenced to three months in prison.

The composer's most celebrated work is the cantata *A Child of Our Time*, first performed in 1944. The child in question is the 17-year-old Jew who shot a Nazi officer in Paris and became the excuse for the persecutions of Kristallnacht.

Tippett's output was relatively small and some of it notoriously difficult to perform. As well as symphonies and string quartets he wrote operas, many dealing with complex social, ethical and psychological problems. He despised middle-class values. The critic Meirion Bowen was his long-time companion and also his biographer.

TITANIC

• Launched 1911

For all its fame the *Titanic*, built in Belfast, had one of shipping's shortest careers. The vessel sank in the early hours of April 15, 1912, after striking an iceberg off Newfoundland. It was the fifth day of the ship's maiden voyage from Southampton to New York.

At 46 329 tons the *Titanic* was the largest passenger liner in the world and branded 'unsinkable'

because of her innovative watertight construction. Even so, 1513 people died, including the captain and the designer.

The wreck was discovered in 1985 and has been extensively investigated and filmed, but without conclusively explaining how such a disaster occurred to such a well-appointed vessel.

TODAY PROGRAMME

• First broadcast 1957

Margaret Thatcher disliked *Today* but she listened just the same, and it would be a brave politician who did not tune into its three hours of news from 6 am to 9 am.

Today is the flagship programme of BBC Radio 4, with its biggest audience (6 million) and its most aggressive interviewing. The formula, with 'Thought for the Day' at exactly 7.48 am and two

MAYDAY The *Titanic* sank in 3 hours. No one knows why it was travelling so fast or why ice warnings were not heeded. Lifeboats for all passengers were thought unnecessary

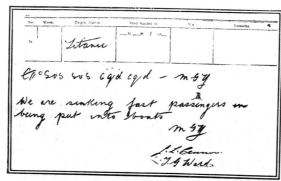

racing tips every morning, may be rigid but the journalism is efficient and exacting. *Today* can 'drop a word in the nation's ear', as the former presenter Brian Redhead put it, making it the most influential news show in the land.

J.R.R. TOLKIEN

• Writer and philologist • 1892-1973

Although his fantasy novels *The Hobbit* and *The Lord of the Rings* sold millions of copies, John Ronald Reuel Tolkien followed an academic career all his life.

His speciality was Old English, which he taught at Oxford University, holding the position of Merton Professor of English (1945-59). Everything he wrote – both scholarly and literary – is full of his profound knowledge of ancient northern European languages, myths and legends.

Tolkien believed Britain should have its own mythology and applied his fertile imagination to inventing one. From 1912 he created a language, 'Elvish', and a place, 'Middle Earth', to go with it. Gradually characters, events, places and histories formed in his mind.

In 1937 Tolkien published *The Hobbit*, and in 1954-5 a more ambitious sequel, the three-volume *The Lord of the Rings*. This complex fable of good and evil achieved cult status in the 1960s, its concern with the fate of the world and the abuse of power striking a chord in the nuclear age.

OPEN SESAME Tower Bridge opened in 1998 for the Royal Yacht *Britannia* to sail through on her final voyage. The high-level walkway provides visitors with panoramic views of London

From the Middle Ages condemned prisoners were brought by boat to Traitors' Gate to be executed on nearby Tower Hill. Aristocratic victims, including Anne Boleyn and Catherine Howard, wives of Henry VIII, were beheaded on Tower Green, within the castle walls. From 1326, prisoners were held in the custody of Yeoman Warders, nicknamed BEEFEATERS, who still patrol the grounds.

The 'Bloody Tower' housed many distinguished prisoners, including Walter RALEIGH, who lived in comfortable rooms with his family for his 13 years' captivity from 1603. The tower earned its bleak name after the two sons of Edward IV, the PRINCES IN THE TOWER, were probably murdered there in 1483.

A Royal Menagerie was started at the Tower by Henry III in the 13th century. At its height there were an alligator, an elephant, lions, leopards, a polar bear and snakes. These animals formed the basis of the London Zoo in 1828. Now only seven ravens inhabit the Tower.

TOLPUDDLE MARTYRS

• **Agricultural unionists**

When in the early 1830s six farm workers in the Dorset village of Tolpuddle had their already low wages cut by three shillings a year by their employer, they founded a branch of the Friendly Society of Agricultural Labourers to protest.

The government feared the power of such TRADE UNIONS but had been forced to repeal the laws that made them illegal in 1824. Since the Tolpuddle men could not be prosecuted for being in a trade union, the Mutiny Law of 1749 was invoked and they were found guilty of 'administering unlawful oaths'.

In 1834, the six men, brothers George and James Loveless, James Brine, James Hammett, Thomas Stanfield and his son John, were all sentenced to seven years' transportation to Australia. There was a public outcry at the sentence and the men became known as 'martyrs'.

Two years later the sentences were remitted and the men pardoned. All six returned to England, but only one stayed; the others emigrated to Canada.

TOWER BRIDGE

• **Central London (p.499 F3)**   • **Built 1894**

Linking Tower Hill to Bermondsey, Tower Bridge is the farthest bridge downstream in London. The engineer John Wolfe Barry was commissioned to design a bridge to allow ships to travel upriver as far as London Bridge, so it would have to open to let through large sailing vessels. Barry's design had two

leaves, each weighing 1000 tons, which could be raised to create a 60 m (200 ft) opening. Electric machinery housed in the twin Gothic towers designed by the architect Horace Jones powers the leaves.

In its early years the bridge was opened up to 50 times a day but pedestrians could cross, uninterrupted, on an upper level reached by lifts. Today few large ships come so far upriver and the bridge has become a popular tourist attraction, offering panoramic views of London from the walkway.

TOWER OF LONDON

• **Central London (p.499 F3)**
• **Built 11th-13th century**

William I, the Conqueror, ordered the construction of the central 'White Tower' of the Tower of London on the banks of the River Thames outside the city walls. It had a dual purpose: to deter attack and to impress upon the public the power of their new king.

Charles TOWNSHEND

• **Politician and farmer**   • **1674-1738; visc. 1687**

Charles, 2nd viscount Townshend, will always be better known as 'Turnip' Townshend. He earned his nickname in retirement, when he developed a system of crop rotation on his Norfolk estate. He advocated growing four different crops in turn to prevent the soil from being sapped of the same nutrients year after year. Turnips played an important part in the system and it is said that they were Townshend's only topic of conversation.

Townshend had served in the Whig administration under George I, directing foreign affairs from 1721 to 1730. He never achieved the high political prominence of his brother-in-law and prime minister Robert Walpole and his government work was soon overshadowed by his farming experiments.

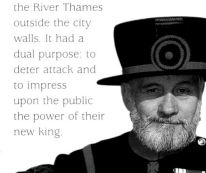

KEEPING THE PEACE Legend says that if the ravens leave the Tower of London the kingdom will fall. The Raven Master ensures that the birds' wings are clipped

PLAYTIME PURSUITS

Hoops, kites and skipping ropes have entertained children since Tudor times; marbles, rocking horses and dolls' houses since the 1700s; and teddy bears since the early 1900s. But for generations of 20th-century children, the toys invented by one man, Frank Hornby, eclipsed them all

BY TRADE, Frank Hornby was a Liverpool book-keeper. In about 1900, he made his sons a kit of hole-punched metal strips that could be assembled with nuts and bolts. The toy was simple but they liked it, and in his spare time Hornby began producing 'Mechanics Made Easy' kits for sale.

The kits came with instructions for making models such as bridges, the Eiffel Tower and a windmill, but extra pieces could be purchased to open up endless possibilities. Hornby registered the kits under a new name, Meccano, in 1907. He launched *Meccano Magazine* in 1916, in which he lectured his young readers on uprightness, honesty and initiative while giving them new construction ideas.

TRANSPORT TOYS
In the 1920s, already a millionaire, Hornby branched out into clockwork trains and during the 1930s, when the Meccano kits were at the height of their popularity, he introduced two more best sellers: Dublo, an electric train set, and Dinky Toys, a range of miniature cars.

The 1930s were the heyday of steam railways and Hornby's train sets brought a little of their thrill and glamour into the home. Children and adults were hooked, and many a loft housed a scale model of an English landscape, with trains weaving through trees and tunnels, over bridges and past fields of Dinky sheep and cows.

TOY TOOLS Many engineers – male and female – started careers with Meccano construction sets

Dinky Toys were the first British toy cars to be made with the advanced die-casting techniques used for real cars, and were known originally as Modelled Miniatures. In 1933 six vehicles were launched, priced at between 6d and 1s. The full set of sports car, sports coupé, truck, delivery van, tractor and tank can now sell for thousands of pounds.

By the 1950s the glamour of motor racing had superseded the excitement of steam, and in 1952 the Hornby company launched a clockwork racing car game, Scalex. Within four years, rubber tracks with a metal groove allowed the cars to run on electricity and the game was renamed Scalextric. Although attention to detail distinguishes most Hornby models, in a principled stand worthy of its founder, the company banned tobacco advertising from its Formula One Grand Prix models in 1972.

REINVENTED FOR THE MODERN AGE
Today, a hundred years after Hornby first experimented with his kits, his toys are entertaining a fifth generation of children. Post-railway privatisation Virgin trains and the Eurostar run on Hornby's 00-gauge rails and Formula One racing cars in Williams' colours hurtle around the Scalextric track.

BUSY INTERCHANGE Hornby accessories make elaborate miniature landscapes with tunnels, signal boxes and stations. As in real life, sets of points avert collisions

BRITISH BY DESIGN
'Must have' toys change with the seasons. These three – not just made in Britain but quintessentially British in character – are among the most enduring.

WHODUNNIT?
Cluedo?, the English country house murder-mystery game, was devised in 1946 by a Birmingham solicitor's clerk, Anthony E. Pratt. The challenge to deduce who murdered Dr Black, how and where, has been taken up in more than 20 countries and has spawned computer games, a film and even real-life role-playing versions

NATIONAL GAME *Wherever there is football there is Subbuteo, with 5 million dedicated players worldwide. The game was created in 1947 and early versions included chalk to mark out pitches on army blankets. Modern sets have floodlights and grandstands. From bedroom battles to international tournaments the inch-high figures are flicked to hit a ball almost as big*

DRESS ME UP *The teenage doll 'Sindy' was first produced in 1963 as a competitor to the American 'Barbie'. Sindy was the epitome of the wholesome girl-next-door in comparison with her curvaceous transatlantic cousin but she and her 'boyfriend', Paul, had a range of clothes that trace a miniature history of late-20th century fashion. Sindy was discontinued in 1997 but revived in 1999. Some 50 million dolls have been sold*

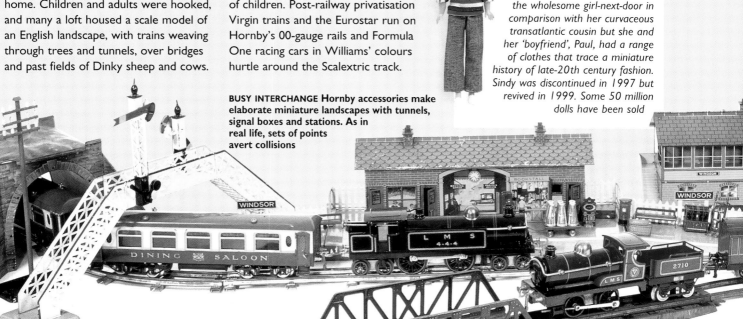

John TRADESCANT

• Botanist   • c.1570-1638

Many favourite garden flowers, such as cornflowers and lupins, first bloomed in Britain thanks to John Tradescant. He was one of the first PLANT COLLECTORS and introduced more than 90 plant species from around the world to British soil.

Tradescant took expeditions to northern Russia in 1616 and north Africa in 1620. He kept his finds – artefacts and animals, including a stuffed dodo – in a garden and museum of curiosities at his home in Lambeth, London.

His son, also John (1608-62), expanded the collection with specimens from the American colony, Virginia. He is said to have been the first person to grow a pineapple in Britain and stone carvings of the fruit decorate Lambeth bridge in his honour.

On the younger Tradescant's death, the collection passed, against his will and by uncertain means, to Elias Ashmole, an aquaintance. Ashmole gave it to Oxford University to found the ASHMOLEAN MUSEUM, the name forever disguising the Tradescants' part in the collection.

TRADE UNIONS

Trade unions, which represent workers in negotiations with employers over issues such as wages, hours, safety at work and other conditions of service, grew up as

UNITY IS STRENGTH The motto of the railwaymen's union, displayed on their banner, emphasises the benefits of solidarity that are fundamental to all trade unions

FOREIGN FRUIT The 'Tradescant Black Heart Cherry' was brought back from the Netherlands by John Tradescant the Elder for Robert Cecil's garden at Hatfield

GUILDS declined. Although they came into their own during the industrial revolution, unions or 'combinations' were emerging before 1700 and continued to do so despite government efforts to suppress them with the Combination Acts (1799-1800).

Ten years after the 1824 Act, which legalised trade unions, a group of farm labourers known as the TOLPUDDLE MARTYRS were prosecuted when they formed a union to protest against a cut in their wages; the ensuing outcry only served to fuel the union movement.

Unions grew rapidly in the early 20th century, rising from 2.5 million members in 1910 to 8 million a decade later. The unsuccessful GENERAL STRIKE of 1926 was a setback but by the late 1970s over half the working population was in a trade union; from this peak of 13 million membership had declined to around 7 million by the end of the century.

The Trades Union Congress (TUC), established in 1868, is the national organisation for unions. It lobbies the government on labour legislation and in 1906 helped to form the LABOUR PARTY.

Battle of TRAFALGAR

• October 21, 1805

On the morning of October 21, 1805, the Franco-Spanish fleet commanded by Admiral Villeneuve faced the British ships of Admiral Lord NELSON at Cape Trafalgar, off the coast of south-west Spain. In 1803, war had resumed between Britain and France, whose ruler Napoleon needed mastery of the sea if he was to prevail.

Villeneuve's 33 ships formed a double line described in the diary of a young British officer, Midshipman Badcock: 'It was a beautiful sight when the line was completed: their broadsides turned towards us showing their iron teeth.'

The 27 British ships, including Nelson's flagship, VICTORY, formed two columns, to break at right angles through the long curve of Villeneuve's fleet. The British ships smashed through the enemy line and overwhelmed them with their superior rate of fire.

At about 1.15pm Nelson was hit by a sniper's ball but he survived long enough to hear news of victory: one French ship blown up and 18 enemy ships captured with the rest in retreat. No British ship had been lost. The Napoleonic wars continued until 1815 but Britain was never threatened with invasion.

TRAFALGAR SQUARE

• Central London (p.499 C6)

On New Year's Eve in Trafalgar Square thousands of midnight revellers throng around the Christmas tree that has been given to Britain every year since the Second World War by the people of Oslo. For more than 100 years the square has also been a popular venue for political demonstrations, from the union-led rallies of the 1880s to the 1989 Poll Tax riots.

The square was the idea of John NASH and laid out in the 1830s and 40s by the architect Charles Barry. It commemorates

the Battle of TRAFALGAR both in name and by its principal monument, the Nelson Column, erected in the 1840s. Four bronze lions, designed by Edwin LANDSEER, were added at the base of the monument in 1867. Busts along the north side of the square pay tribute to other naval commanders, including John Rushworth Jellicoe and David Beatty.

Under consideration is the World Squares for All scheme, backed by the architect Norman FOSTER, which aims to reclaim Trafalgar Square for pedestrians with a £50 million facelift that will divert traffic from the northern side, where the NATIONAL GALLERY stands.

TRANSPORTATION OF CONVICTS

Until the 19th century it was common for people to be sentenced to death for crimes as minor as stealing sheep. Jails were few and overcrowded and imprisoning all felons was impractical. Transportation to the colonies was an alternative to facing the gallows and many had their sentences commuted.

Transportation of offenders began around 1650 with convicts sold as slaves in America. The Transportation Act of 1718 formalised the practice of exiling felons, normally for seven or 14 years. Criminals had their lives and a chance for self-improvement, and the colonies had almost free labour. By 1777 around 1000 convicts a year were being transported to America.

After American independence, Australia became the main destination, with 700 convicts shipped to Botany Bay in 1788. In all, 167 000 prisoners were transported to Australia for the next 80 years to work in gruelling conditions as labourers. By the 1850s transportation was seen as inhumane and expensive both in Australia and Britain and the practice was abolished in 1868. This led to PRISONS being built to house offenders who might once have been transported.

TREASURE

Identifying the rightful owner of buried treasure is almost impossible. Until 1996 coroners had the task of deciding whether treasure had been deliberately hidden with the intention of retrieving it, or whether it had simply been lost. Buried treasure was defined as 'treasure trove' and was judged the property of the Crown; lost items belonged to the finder.

In 1997 the law was simplified. A gold or silver find more than 300 years old must now be reported to the local coroner. It is then offered to the BRITISH MUSEUM or other national and local collections. If a public institution takes it, the finder receives a reward; if not, the treasure becomes the property of the finder.

TREASURY

Control of the nation's purse strings makes the treasury the most powerful of government departments. From offices in WHITEHALL the treasury raises revenue from taxation collected by the INLAND REVENUE and customs and excise service.

The Treasury evolved in the late 17th century to raise funds to repay the NATIONAL DEBT incurred by wars and overseas commitments. The department now controls public spending and economic policy.

Each year departmental ministers meet with the Treasury to negotiate their annual BUDGET, which is then announced in parliament by the CHANCELLOR OF THE EXCHEQUER, head of the Treasury.

River TRENT

• **Midlands and N England (p.495 G1)**
At 170 miles the Trent is the third-longest river in England. Rising in Biddulph Moor in north Staffordshire, it sweeps south in a great loop through the Midlands, then up through North Lincolnshire where it joins the Yorkshire Ouse to form the River Humber.

The river is part of a waterway network stretching through the Midlands and south to London. The Trent and Mersey canal gives sea access through Liverpool.

As a result, industry flourished in towns such as Nottingham along the river's length; Stoke-on-Trent became the headquarters of pottery manufacture and beer companies such as Bass grew up at Burton upon Trent.

NAVAL GIANT The 5 m (17 ft) high statue of Nelson towers 52 m (172 ft) above Trafalgar Square. Reliefs around the base of the column record his battles and his death at Trafalgar

SUBTROPICAL PARADISE A statue of **Gaia,** the Greek earth goddess, in Tresco Abbey Gardens sits naturally among the palm trees and exotic plants that flourish there

Richard TREVITHICK

• Engineer • 1771-1833

As a child Richard Trevithick watched steam engines pump water from the deep tin and copper mines in Cornwall, where his father was a mine engineer. He saw the potential for a more versatile design than those of James WATT and as an adult developed smaller engines with stronger boilers able to generate higher pressure and therefore more power.

In 1801 Trevithick installed his compact engine in a steam carriage, which was one of the first road vehicles to move under its own power. It blew up, however, while he was celebrating in a nearby inn. Three years later he built the first engine to run on rails. Despite public displays of his inventions, Trevithick could not persuade investors to finance their production.

Trevithick never lived to see his innovations realise their full potential and died poor, but his designs helped usher in the age of the RAILWAYS.

TRISTRAM SHANDY

• Published 1759-67

Blank pages, chapters out of order, running jokes and wild digressions make one of the earliest English novels – *The Life and Opinions of Tristram Shandy* – also one of the most eccentric. With his affectionate celebration of human oddity, Laurence Sterne (1713-68) laid the foundations for a new literary form.

The narrator, Tristram, has an earthy sense of humour and a love of absurdity that does not seem out of place beside *The Goon Show* and *Monty Python's Flying Circus* of 200 years on. His erratic narration prefigures thought processes developed by 20th-century 'stream of consciousness' writers such as Virginia Woolf. In its self-conscious artificiality the book would later, like James Joyce's *Ulysses*, have been called an 'antinovel'.

When Sterne wrote *Tristram Shandy* he was a clergyman in Yorkshire. The book brought him instant fame and he became a flamboyant figure in London society. He followed his novel with a parody of travel writing, *A Sentimental Journey through France and Italy*, in 1768.

Anthony TROLLOPE

• Writer • 1815-82

In his autobiography, published posthumously in 1883, Anthony Trollope declared that he could write 250 words in 15 minutes before leaving for work each morning. His books were extremely popular – by 1879 Trollope had earned £70 000 from his writing – but this display of his workaday attitude to his creative talent dismayed his admirers.

Trollope was a civil servant in the post office (*see* POSTAL SYSTEM) from 1834 to 1867 but began writing in his spare time and published his first novel, *The Macdermots of Ballycloran*, in 1847.

In 1855 he wrote *The Warden*, the first of the six 'Barchester Chronicles', set in a cathedral close, which made his name. In these and the six political 'Palliser' novels (1864-80), named after Plantaganet Palliser who appears in all of them, he gave an accurate picture of English provincial life in the middle and upper-middle classes.

Trollope published 47 novels and other works that give a valuable and perceptive historical insight into the period in which he lived and wrote.

TRESCO ABBEY GARDENS

• Isles of Scilly (p.494 A6) • Est. 1834

Spring comes early on Tresco. The gardens in the grounds of the ruined 12th-century abbey are in full bloom while the rest of Britain is still in winter. Augustus Smith, lord proprietor of the ISLES OF SCILLY off south-west Cornwall, began to create the garden in 1834, building walls and growing conifers as shelter from the Atlantic winds.

As the temperature in the Scillies seldom falls below 10°C (50°F) thanks to the warm Gulf Stream ocean current, subtropical plants flourish there that do not grow naturally anywhere else in the Northern Hemisphere.

In the 7 ha (17 acres) of gardens are more than 3000 varieties of plants, from Mexican yuccas and desert agaves and aloes to South African proteas and New Zealand ironwoods.

PERPETUAL MOTION Richard Trevithick demonstrated his steam locomotive 'Catch me who can' on a circular track in Euston Square, London, in 1808

TROOPING THE COLOUR

• **Second Saturday in June**

The original reason for Trooping the Colour was to ensure that soldiers would recognise their regimental 'colour' (or flag) on the battlefield. Since 1748, the ceremony has celebrated the sovereign's official birthday and has been an annual event since 1805.

All seven regiments of the household division – the troops responsible for guarding and escorting the royal family – take part, but only one colour is trooped each year. The five regiments of the foot guards – the Coldstream Guards, Grenadier Guards and Irish, Scots and Welsh Guards – take the honour in turn.

The Queen processes down the Mall from Buckingham Palace to Horse Guards' Parade, where she inspects some 500 guardsmen. Until 1987 she attended on horseback in her role as colonel-in-chief of the household division, and dressed in the uniform of the regiment whose colour was being trooped. She now drives to the parade in a carriage.

Regimental bands accompany the marching soldiers in their full military regalia. The parade culminates in the actual trooping, when the colour is slowly carried along the ranks of guardsmen.

HOWZAT? 'Fiery Fred' Trueman combined fearsome speed with immaculate technique to make himself a formidable figure to face at the wicket

ROYAL SALUTE The Queen, dressed in the uniform of the Grenadier Guards, salutes the regimental colour at the Trooping of the Colour parade

TROSSACHS

• **Stirling (p.497 C4)**

The name 'Trossachs' translates from Gaelic as 'the bristled country' and is an apt description of the narrow, heathery glen between Loch Achray and Loch Katrine in the GRAMPIAN MOUNTAINS of Scotland. The region is often also taken to include the wider area between Callander, Crianlarich and Loch Lomond.

Though frequently described as 'the Highlands in miniature', there is nothing small about the landscape, which was the homeland of the legendary cattle thief Rob Roy; Ben More tops 1174 m (3852 ft) and Ben Ledi 878 m (2882 ft).

Fred TRUEMAN

• **Cricketer** • **b.1931; OBE 1989**

Seldom one for showing false modesty, the Yorkshire cricketer Fred Trueman described himself as 't' finest bloody fast bowler that ever drew breath'. During the late 1950s and early 1960s, at least, it was difficult to disagree.

During his first Test series for England in 1952 against India Trueman took 29 wickets, including a spell of eight for just 31 runs. His bullet-like delivery made him the first bowler to claim 300 Test victims and he might have played in more than his 67 Tests had he not incurred the wrath of the selectors with his disdain for authority.

Trueman played for Yorkshire for 20 years between 1949 and 1968 and took 2304 wickets in his first-class career.

The pace of his bowling slackened as the years advanced, but by concentrating on swing he continued to outwit the world's best batsmen into his thirties. 'The difference between a fast bowler and a good fast bowler,' he maintained, 'is not extra muscle but extra brains.'

TRUSTHOUSE FORTE

• **Est. 1970**

The Italian Forte family arrived in Britain in the 1870s to find work, after having to pay a ransom demand for a kidnapped family member. They opened ice-cream parlours and cafés, the first in Dundee in the early 1880s. Charles, son of one of the original immigrants, started a chain of milk bars in London in the 1940s and by 1952 had made his first million.

Over the next 18 years, Charles Forte built an empire of restaurants, hotels and leisure complexes around Europe. In 1970 Forte merged with Trust Houses, a chain of temperance hotels established in 1904 to cater for commercial travellers. Trust Houses Forte – Trusthouse Forte (THF) from 1979 – became one of the world's largest hotel and catering groups.

In 1996 the company left Forte hands in a takeover by Granada. Rocco Forte, son of Charles, then set up a new hotel group – RF Hotels.

ISLAND RACE Every June motorcyclists gather on the Isle of Man to take on the challenging public-road circuit of the **TT**. Their bikes range in size from 125 cc to 1000 cc

TT RACES

• **Motorcycle races** • **June**

For one week of the year the normally peaceful air of the Isle of Man hums with the whirr of engines as the best and bravest of the world's motorcyclists – amateur racers as well as professionals – tackle the sport's most dangerous course made up entirely of public roads.

Commonly referred to as the TT, the RAC Tourist Trophy was first staged on the Isle of Man in 1907 when road racing was prohibited on the mainland for safety reasons. With its mountainous terrain and absence of speed restrictions outside towns and villages, the island provided challenging racing conditions.

In 1911 the organisers formed a full, round-the-island circuit of 37¾ miles, open to all types of touring motorcycle. As machines became bigger and more powerful, the races were classified by engine size, with a top capacity of 500 cc. The most successful rider to date is Joey Dunlop (b.1952), a publican from County Antrim, who won his 21st TT race in 1996.

A discouraging element of the event is the fatality rate, with total deaths now well past 160, largely due to the lack of safety barriers on a demanding course, which includes mountain hairpin bends.

Jethro TULL

• **Agriculturist** • **1674-1741**

Modern agriculture owes much to Jethro Tull's decision to quit the Bar in order to work on his father's farm in Oxfordshire. About 1701, he developed a prototype seed drill on wheels that was later to revolutionise crop cultivation.

Although primitive seed drills had appeared at the end of the 17th century, most farmers still scattered seed by hand. Tull's device, pulled by a horse, sowed seed in three rows at a time, thereby saving seed and, of more importance, allowing room for weeding between the rows to increase the nourishment a crop can draw from the soil. He also devised a horse-drawn mechanical hoe to do the weeding.

For 30 years Tull struggled to gain acceptance for his ideas, publishing his classic book *The New Horse-houghing Husbandry* in 1731. Ahead of his time, he also advocated the need for farmers to raise productivity beyond the demands of the immediate community.

House of TUDOR

• **British royal house** • **1485-1603**

The Tudor dynasty that oversaw England's transition from a feudal medieval society to a powerful trading nation was strong and pragmatic. Recognising that possession was the surest claim to the throne in the bitter aftermath of the WARS OF THE ROSES, its founder, the Lancastrian Henry Tudor seized the crown by defeating Richard III at the Battle of BOSWORTH in 1485.

Henry, a direct descendant of Edward III through his mother, Margaret Beaufort, then married Elizabeth of York – thus uniting the warring houses of Lancaster and York to safeguard his position as the first Tudor king of all England.

He proved an able monarch, bequeathing a secure kingdom to his flamboyant son HENRY VIII, whose break with the Church of Rome prompted profound religious and political change. Henry VIII's only son, EDWARD VI, died in

QUEUE TO REIGN In an allegorical painting of the 1570s, Mary I and her husband Philip II of Spain watch while Henry VIII passes the sword of succession to Edward VI, with Elizabeth I in waiting

his youth in 1553 and was succeeded by his half-sister MARY I (known as 'Bloody' Mary), who died in 1558 after a childless marriage to Philip II of Spain. She was succeeded by her younger half-sister, ELIZABETH I, whose stable 45 year reign nurtured England's military and economic growth. She never married and at her death in 1603 James VI of Scotland came south to become the first STUART king.

SOLID SPACE Rachel Whiteread's *House*, a plaster cast of the inside of an east London council tenement, won the 1993 Turner Prize. Her object was to represent in solid form the space inhabited by the building's tenants

Alan TURING

- **Mathematician** • 1912-1954

Government secrecy over wartime code-breaking activity at BLETCHLEY PARK long obscured Alan Turing's achievements as a computer pioneer. His 1937 paper 'On Computable Numbers' foreshadowed the use of automated machines to solve mathematical problems.

After the outbreak of the Second World War, Turing joined the Bletchley Park team assigned to break coded messages sent by the German Enigma cypher machine. To do so, they built one of the first computers, Colossus.

After the war, Turing helped to design ACE – the Automatic Computing Engine – for the National Physical Laboratory in London and later worked on the Manchester Automatic Digital Machine, which then had the largest memory in the world. But following a prosecution for homosexual activities, he committed suicide.

J.M.W. TURNER

- **Artist** • 1775-1851

'The Sun is God', announced Joseph Mallord William Turner on his deathbed. The shifting effects of sun, light and colour dominate his landscape paintings and convey the mood of a scene, anticipating impressionism by 50 years.

Turner entered the Royal Academy Schools aged 14, exhibiting watercolours there the following year. At 18 he began a series of sketching tours around Britain and the Continent, during which his delight in unfamiliar scenes and growing appreciation of European art encouraged him to develop his own style.

His early paintings such as *The Fifth Plague of Egypt* (1800) reflect the influence of Claude and Poussin, but Turner's work became increasingly concerned with the effects of light and colour, and he virtually abandoned formal composition in favour of dramatic atmospheric effects. Such shadowy, luminous, near-abstract paintings as *The Fighting Téméraire* (1839) and *Rain,*

Steam and Speed (1844) are more experimental even than those of the Impressionists who followed him. But it was a style at variance with early Victorian taste and during his later life Turner fell from fashion.
MAIN COLLECTION: Tate Gallery, London

TURNER PRIZE

The best-known and most controversial British art prize, the Turner, founded in 1984 and worth £20 000, is awarded to an artist under the age of 50 for 'the greatest contribution to art in Britain in the previous 12 months'.

Winning entries have mostly been conceptual art – that is art not involving painting, drawing or sculpture. They include Gilbert and George's *Living Sculptures* in 1986, Damien HIRST's *Mother and Child, Divided* in 1995, and Gillian Wearing's 1997 video, *60 Minutes Silence*, showing police officers staying motionless for an hour.

To its supporters, the Turner Prize shows the cutting edge of British art. To its critics, the prize is devalued by ignoring traditional art forms, since conceptual art is concerned principally with the idea behind a work, rather than the skill involved in creating it.

The Tate Gallery founded the Turner Prize to try to do for contemporary art what the Booker Prize does for fiction – make the public aware of its existence

Dick TURPIN

- **Highwayman** • 1706-39

The legend of the highwayman who made a dramatic ride from London to York on his mare Black Bess, to escape justice after killing his accomplice Tom King, is just that – a legend.

The 15 hour ride recounted in the novel *Rookwood* by Harrison Ainsworth in 1834 had previously been attributed to another highwayman, John Nevison (Swift Nicks), 30 years before Turpin was born, but may never have taken place.

The truth about Turpin's life was less romantic. The son of a publican and apprenticed as a butcher, he was outlawed for stealing cattle. He joined a gang of deer rustlers and smugglers, and took part in several brutal robberies in rural Essex. Turpin joined up with Tom King in 1735, but killed him accidentally with a shot aimed at a police constable arresting King.

Turpin fled to York – but not in the dramatic way told by Ainsworth – where he set up as a horse dealer. In 1739 he was arrested for stealing horses, tried, and hanged on what is now York racecourse. The prison cell where Turpin spent his last night can be visited at York Castle Museum.
See also HIGHWAYMEN

TWEED

Tweed cloth takes its name not from the mill towns on the River Tweed, but from a 19th-century misreading of 'tweel', the old Scots word for twill – the heavy woollen cloth that was then becoming popular for use as country clothing in many parts of Britain.

Scottish cloths, particularly the twill weaves produced on the Isle of Harris in the Outer Hebrides, acquired a special cachet, attracting orders from SAVILE ROW tailors in London. Harris tweed is still woven at home on handlooms and remains an important local industry.

The enormous range of twill weaves now produced include checks, chevrons, diamonds and a variety of stripe and fleck patterns in natural tones. For both men's and women's fashions tweed is now highly valued as a luxury material.

In the 1990s the avant-garde Vivienne Westwood and other designers such as Paul Smith reinvented tweed as a fashionable material for their cutting-edge collections at FASHION shows.

RATTLE AND ROLL About 400 weavers in Scotland's Outer Hebrides still use traditional methods to produce a greater range of Harris tweeds than ever before for the world market

Wat TYLER

• Rebel leader   • d.1381

Wat Tyler – a man of lowly birth – led the Kentish part of the PEASANTS' REVOLT against a high poll tax. His supporters took Canterbury in June 1381 and marched on London where a large force confronted the 14-year-old Richard II at Smithfield. Tyler presented a list of radical demands, including the abolition of serfdom and the distribution of the church's wealth among the poor. A scuffle with the

MULTIPLE CROSSINGS Six bridges span the Tyne at Newcastle, including the red Swing Bridge that pivots at its centre to allow ships to pass on either side, and inventor Robert Stephenson's two-tier rail and road bridge

mayor of London ensued in which he wounded Tyler, and not long after had him beheaded. The revolt collapsed.

River TYNE

• N England (p.496 B2)

The North and South Tynes tumble from the slopes of Peel Fell in the Cheviot Hills and Cross Fell in Cumberland before they meet at Hexham. Upstream the North Tyne has been dammed to form Kielder Water, Britain's most capacious reservoir.

The latter half of the Tyne's 30 mile course to NEWCASTLE UPON TYNE tells much of Tyneside's industrial history as shipbuilders and coalmine owners crammed wharves and jetties along its banks. The Tyne provided transport from coalfields to shipyards and the North Sea, and in the 17th century became the main artery for supplying most of London's fuel. Its industries declined sharply after the Second World War, resulting in severe unemployment on Tyneside but a cleaner river.

ULSTER

The northernmost of the four ancient kingdoms of Ireland was Ulster, which extended south to Louth and west to the Donegal Atlantic coast. It was colonised by Protestant Scots and English in the 16th and 17th centuries causing strife with the local Catholic population and initiating centuries of bitter conflict in Ireland (*see* IRISH QUESTION).

When Ireland was divided by the Government of Ireland Act 1920-1, six of Ulster's nine counties – Antrim, Armagh, Fermanagh, Down, Londonderry and Tyrone – remained within the United Kingdom as the province of NORTHERN IRELAND while the other three – Donegal, Monaghan and Cavan – became part of what is now the Republic of Ireland. 'Ulster' is sometimes loosely used to refer to Northern Ireland, particularly by the Protestant community.

UNEMPLOYMENT

In modern times, Britain's worst period of mass unemployment came with the DEPRESSION of the 1930s, which saw one in five workers without a job, and only ended with rearmament and the coming of war. Postwar regeneration brought joblessness down to around 3 per cent in the 1950s and 60s, but it began to rise again in the 1970s.

By the early 1980s a shift away from manufacturing coupled with the withdrawal of government support from uncompetitive heavy industries was causing widespread joblessness in the industrial heartlands of the Midlands and the north. In 1986 unemployment stood at 12 per cent, a post-Depression record. The general level of unemployment fell in the 1990s but job losses continued to deplete the manufacturing industries.

UNIONISTS

• Northern Irish Protestant political parties
Irish politicians who campaign for Northern Ireland to remain a part of the United Kingdom are called Unionists or Loyalists. The largest of their political parties, the Ulster Unionist Party headed by James Molyneaux, was founded in 1904 to resist all-Ireland devolution. Ian PAISLEY's more hardline Democratic Unionist Party was established in 1971 to represent working-class opinion.

Unionists are Protestant and have traditionally shared political views on Ireland with the Conservative party – a relationship dented in 1972 when, as a result of tensions between Unionists and the Catholic minority, a Conservative government imposed direct rule.

Following the Good Friday peace agreement signed in 1998, Unionists and representatives of the Catholic minority are seeking political consensus and the return of a devolved assembly.

UNITED KINGDOM

• Area 93 891 sq miles • Pop. 57.5 million
When the Act of Union of 1801 united Ireland with Britain, the resulting realm was called the United Kingdom of GREAT BRITAIN and Ireland. Wales had already been united with England by Henry VIII in two Acts of Parliament in 1536 and 1542, and when James VI of Scotland became also James I of England in 1603, he united the two crowns. Scotland retained its own parliament and law until the Act of Union of 1707, which was prompted by English fears that Scotland might acknowledge a Stuart not a Hanoverian successor to Queen Anne.

The rise of Catholic nationalism was partly responsible for the Act of Union with Ireland. The Irish Parliament was dismissed and Westminster took control.

When southern Ireland became the Irish Free State in 1921, the UK's full title became the United Kingdom of Great Britain and Northern Ireland. The Channel Islands and the Isle of Man are crown dependencies but not part of the United Kingdom.

UNKNOWN WARRIOR

On November 11, 1920, two years after the end of the First World War, a coffin containing the body of an unknown British soldier who fell on the Western Front was interred in Westminster Abbey. The coffin was buried in battlefield soil, in tribute to the servicemen who died without trace during the conflict – more than 150 000 from the battles of the Somme and Ypres alone.

The idea for the tomb came from an army chaplain who in 1916 saw on a rough cross set above a makeshift grave in a French garden the words 'An Unknown British Soldier'.

AMONG THE ILLUSTRIOUS Westminster Abbey, the traditional burial site of English kings, is also the resting place of the Unknown Warrior. Mourners file past the tomb to pay their respects

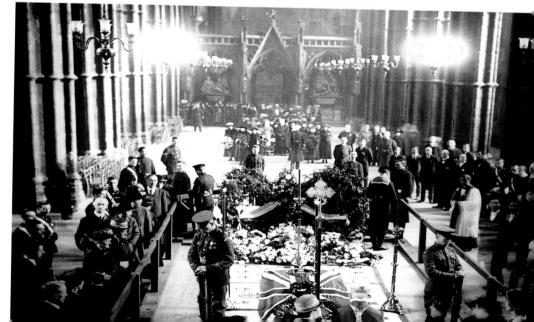

UPPARK

- **West Sussex (p.495 G5)**
- **Built 1690, restored 1995 • NT**

The painstaking six-year restoration of Uppark – gutted by fire in 1989 – demanded an unusual approach. The house in red brick and stone was built in the 17th century by the 1st earl of Tankerville, but most of the interior was the work of its mid-18th-century owner, Matthew Fetherstonhaugh, and had remained untouched by the Victorian age. So there was no attempt to bring the building back to a pristine state; instead the house was returned as closely as possible to its condition the day before the fire, even to the extent of reproducing faded wallpaper and 200-year-old curtains.

In 1816 the house was offered to the Duke of Wellington, but he declined because the steep approach to the crest of the South Downs on which it stands would be too expensive in horses.

John VANBRUGH

- **Architect and dramatist • 1664-1726; kt 1714**

When John Vanbrugh turned his hand to architecture at the age of 35, he was already a successful playwright turning out bawdy Restoration drama. By the time of his death, he had become a master of English baroque architecture.

Taking up an invitation to design CASTLE HOWARD in Yorkshire, Vanbrugh, with no formal training but assisted by the architect Nicholas HAWKSMOOR, combined his sense of theatricality with baroque styles he had seen while living abroad. Vanbrugh's partnership with Hawksmoor continued most successfully with the immense BLENHEIM PALACE in Oxfordshire (1705-16).

GIANT JIGSAW After the fire at Uppark, restorers laid out the surviving bits and pieces of plaster fragments on a full-sized ceiling plan. The gaps were filled by modern master craftsmen

Ralph VAUGHAN WILLIAMS

- **Composer • 1872-1958**

Determination to become a composer drove Ralph Vaughan Williams across Europe to study under such musicians as Bruch and Ravel before coming to the conclusion that the future of British music lay in rediscovering its own past.

After touring the countryside collecting folk songs and studying the church and court music of Tudor times, Vaughan Williams found his own musical identity. His first successful piece was the *Fantasia on a Theme of Thomas Tallis* (1910). Major works followed, including the operas *Riders to the Sea* (1932) and *Pilgrim's Progress* (1951), the popular *Fantasia on Greensleeves* (1929), and his romance for violins and orchestra, *The Lark Ascending* (1929).

Vaughan Williams composed a total of nine symphonies, the last three written after his second marriage at the age of 81.

VAUXHALL GARDENS

- **Opened 1660**

On summer evenings the well-to-do of Georgian London amused themselves by visiting one of about 100 fashionable pleasure gardens in the capital. The oldest and one of the largest was Vauxhall Gardens, which occupied 5 ha (12 acres) south of the River Thames, opposite the Houses of Parliament.

Vauxhall was reopened in 1732, with scented walks, triumphal arches and benches set in leafy arbours – the whole scene lit by 3000 lamps. Orchestras played in a covered rotunda, where food and drink were served, while musicians concealed in pits behind bushes provided more intimate entertainment.

Rich and poor rubbed shoulders there, but pickpockets and prostitutes also prospered, and after 1742 the smarter set migrated across the river to the newly

ELEGANT EXUBERANCE John Vanbrugh's massing of sculptured walls, rising to a climax in the dome at Castle Howard, is a fine English example of the dramatic quality of baroque architecture

opened Ranelagh Gardens, where an eight-year-old Mozart gave a concert in 1764. Vauxhall closed in 1859.

VE DAY and VJ DAY

• **VE (Victory in Europe) Day May 8, 1945**
• **VJ (Victory in Japan) Day August 15, 1945**

A drizzly morning across much of Britain on May 8, 1945, did nothing to dampen the spirits of soldiers and civilians celebrating the end of the SECOND WORLD WAR in Europe after almost six years of fighting. The German leader, Adolf Hitler, was dead, and the previous day all German forces had surrendered.

Winston CHURCHILL and the US president Truman declared the day a public holiday. Everywhere, crowds celebrated in the streets with singing, dancing and drinking. In Westminster, Churchill was mobbed deliriously while attending a thanksgiving service, and for the first time since the blackout began in 1939, street lights were switched on. Bonfires and fireworks lit up the sky.

The Pacific war against Japan rumbled on for another three months before the new prime minister, Clement Atlee, went on air at midnight to announce Japan's surrender after atom bombs destroyed Hiroshima and Nagasaki. Throughout the night crowds again partied in the streets.

VICKERS

• **Founded 1828**

Although founded as a Sheffield steel-maker, Vickers became Britain's leading supplier of armaments in two world wars. As the Anglo-German arms race gathered pace from the 1880s, Vickers built battleships and cruisers, submarines, machine guns, small arms and munitions.

In AVIATION, a Vickers Vimy wartime bomber took ALCOCK AND BROWN across the Atlantic in 1919, and its Spitfire fighters and Wellington bombers played a crucial role for Britain in the Second World War.

After the war, Vickers diversified into mechanical engineering and in

RIDING HIGH VE Day brought spontaneous celebrations up and down the country, although many were still waiting to hear from loved ones fighting on in the **Far East**

1980 acquired Rolls-Royce Motors, selling the company to Volkswagen in 1998. Vickers' 1990s battle TANK Challenger 2 remains one of the world's most efficient fighting vehicles.

VICTORIA

• **Queen 1837-1901; Empress of India from 1877**
• **1819-1901**

'I will be good,' declared the 12-year-old Victoria on hearing she would one day inherit the throne. Despite losing her father Edward, fourth son of George III, when she was a baby and being brought up in virtual isolation in Kensington Palace by her mother, Princess Victoria of Saxe-Coburg-Gotha, Victoria was a confident woman when crowned at 18.

She married ALBERT of Saxe-Coburg-Gotha three years later in 1840 and came increasingly to depend on his advice, giving him a prominent role and turning his values of hard work and high moral standards into Victorian bywords.

Devastated by Albert's death in 1861, Victoria went into seclusion and for the remaining 40 years of her life wore

black, earning her the nickname 'the widow of Windsor'. It is thought that her Scottish gillie John Brown helped her to regain self-confidence, and in 1877 the prime minister Benjamin Disraeli conferred on her the title of Empress of India in recognition of her commitment to the RAJ. By the 1880s the Queen had become a national symbol, not only in Britain but throughout the Empire, which spanned a quarter of the globe.

Through the marriages of her nine children, she formed many alliances overseas, and became fondly known as the matriarch of royal Europe.
See also VICTORIAN AGE

VICTORIA AND ALBERT MUSEUM

• **Central London (p.499 B4)** • **Founded 1852**
One of the world's greatest museums of fine and decorative arts, the Victoria and Albert (or 'V&A') grew out of the Great Exhibition of 1851. It was created to encourage excellence in art and design, and the museum houses an extensive collection of sculpture, furniture, fashion and textiles, paintings, silver, glass, ceramics, jewellery, books, prints and photographs from all over the world.

Highlights include Raphael tapestry cartoons, Renaissance sculpture, a large collection of paintings by John CONSTABLE, Oriental art and the Great Bed of Ware (1580-90).

VICTORIA CROSS

Russian guns captured at Sebastopol in the Crimean War provided the bronze used to fashion medals for the Victoria Cross, Britain's highest military honour. The medal was instituted by Queen Victoria in 1856 and inscribed 'for valour'. It is awarded to British or Commonwealth citizens for acts of selfless courage in the face of the enemy.

A total of 1354 people have received a Victoria Cross, three of them twice. However, only one of the double VC recipients, Charles Upham, who received his in the Second World War, actually lived to enjoy the glory.

BRITANNIA RULES

During Queen Victoria's 64 year reign Britain reached a peak of wealth, power and confidence. And yet Victorians also had to face widespread poverty and the undermining of old beliefs brought about by industrial and scientific progress

IN A SPECIAL colour edition to mark the Diamond Jubilee of Queen VICTORIA in 1897, *The Illustrated London News* printed a series of pictures showing what had been achieved over the six decades of her reign. In 1837 steamships still had masts, sails and paddles; by 1897 screw-driven, iron-hulled steamers were plying the Atlantic. The stagecoaches that ruled the road had been overtaken by 22 000 miles of railway track, and bicycles and early motor cars competed for space beneath electric street lights.

By the end of the century the Victorians' belief in progress through technology, epitomised by the GREAT EXHIBITION, had given Britain cinefilms, gramophones, electric light bulbs, sewing machines, telephones, typewriters, submarines and underground railways.

A ROYAL EXAMPLE

Queen Victoria and her husband Prince ALBERT set the tone of the times. They tried to lead ordinary family lives, setting an example by their dignity, piety and sense of moral duty, and an unquestioning patriotic devotion. Their somewhat sentimental devotion to the family appealed to the expanding middle classes, who were rapidly becoming the new

economic backbone of Britain. Land was no longer the main source of wealth: self-made traders and industrialists were reaching the upper rungs of the social ladder, and living in purpose-built neo-Gothic castles as well as leaving their mark by endowing new universities, museums and public libraries.

The royal family projected its domesticated image through one of the wonders of the age – photography. Prince Albert was one of the first public figures to embrace the new medium, and his enthusiasm helped to provoke a mania for portrait photographs in the 1860s. For the first time people could own believable images not only of themselves and their families, but also of the famous personalities of the day.

The queen was also the figurehead of the vast and growing BRITISH EMPIRE, which fed the Victorian sense of superiority tempered by Christian duty towards their colonial subjects.

But Victorians also knew how to enjoy themselves, and entertainment boomed from MUSIC HALLS, funfairs, fetes and galas to PUBS, dance halls and drinking dens, and newly organised sports such as FOOTBALL, RUGBY and TENNIS.

The mass market had arrived and put within reach of much of the population such novelties as popular NEWSPAPERS and COMICS, holidays at SEASIDE

ON THE MOVE William Frith's *The Railway Station* (1862) caught the excitement of rapid travel and the engineering prowess of the age

RESORTS, board games, china ornaments, and high street chain stores.

A SENSE OF DOUBT

Behind the outward confidence, however, was a growing anxiety at the sweeping away of the old way of life and its certainties. In 1837 the population of Britain stood at about 20 million, 80 per cent of whom lived in the countryside; by 1900 the population had doubled and 75 per cent were now urban dwellers.

Mechanisation brought rapid change to rural areas, pushing thousands of agricultural workers into cities in search of work. Many lived in appalling conditions, with large families sharing one or two rooms and even young children working long hours. According to Charles Booth's survey of London's East End, published at the end of the century, 30 per cent of the London population could not afford basic food and clothing.

Domestic service, which employed more than a million workers, and the armed forces offered more comfortable alternatives to some. Those who failed

GIVE US A SMILE! The stiff appearance of early photographic subjects had more to do with the problem of staying still over a long exposure time than their sense of propriety

FRESH START The engineer Joseph Bazalgette (*top right*) views the building of a new sewer, part of his London drainage system, in 1862. The modern flushing toilet, or water closet, was an invention of the 1870s

clutter of factory-produced knick-knacks, came under fire. William MORRIS attacked the kind of elaborate industrial products promoted by the Great Exhibition and ushered in a simpler approach to manufacture and design and that led to the ARTS AND CRAFTS movement.

Meanwhile the certainties of the Bible held dear by God-fearing Victorians were under attack from scientists such as Charles DARWIN, whose anthropological work *On the Origin of Species* (1859) argued for a quite different explanation of the world's creation. Suddenly, man, whose ingenuity had transformed 19th-century Britain, seemed to be challenging even the omnipotence of the Almighty.

THE UNDERCLASS These slums in the centre of Newcastle upon Tyne in about 1880 were typical of the ramshackle conditions endured by many inhabitants of British industrial cities

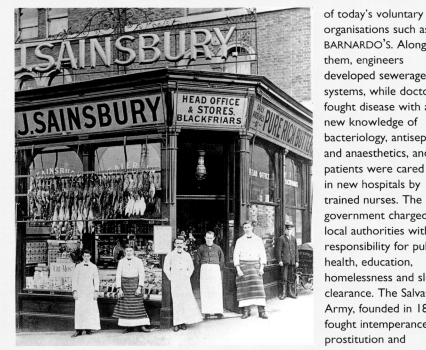

NEW BREED J. Sainsbury had 47 provision stores by 1900. This and other chains foreshadowed the demise of the high street grocer

of today's voluntary organisations such as BARNARDO'S. Alongside them, engineers developed sewerage systems, while doctors fought disease with a new knowledge of bacteriology, antiseptics and anaesthetics, and patients were cared for in new hospitals by trained nurses. The government charged local authorities with responsibility for public health, education, homelessness and slum clearance. The Salvation Army, founded in 1878, fought intemperance, prostitution and destitution with military-style vigour; and radical politicians explored

to find a niche, and the old, infirm and indigent, ended up in the workhouse. The plight of the poor led to a spate of charity-founding – the origin of many concepts such as trade unionism, republicanism and anarchism.

Even the sumptuous, overstuffed look of the Victorian living room, with its

VICTORIA STATION

• Central London (p.499 C4) • Built 1860-2

Strictly speaking, there is not one station at Victoria but three. The first was built for the London, Brighton and South Coast Railway Company in 1860. A second, smaller station was built next door in 1862 for the London, Chatham and Dover Railway. The third is the London Underground station, one of the capital's busiest, which opened in 1907.

In 1900 the Brighton line redesigned its terminus in an exuberant baroque style. From 1913 the Chatham side boasted the romance of foreign travel when a direct service to Paris began. Today an average of 200 000 people use the mainline station every day.

HMS *VICTORY*

• Lord Nelson's flagship • Built 1765

Some 69 m (227 ft) long and weighing 2100 tons, HMS *Victory* was launched from Chatham on May 7, 1765, later becoming Lord NELSON's flagship. Its finest hour was in the Battle of TRAFALGAR. Carrying 821 men and armed with 104 guns on four decks, it led 27 ships to victory against a joint Spanish and French fleet of 33 ships.

HMS *Victory* was retired from service in 1812 and berthed in Portsmouth, where it remains (now in dry dock). Today it is used by the Royal Navy for official entertaining and is open daily to the public.

VIKINGS

• c.800-1100

The best shipbuilders and sailors of the early Middle Ages, the Vikings – a collective term for the maritime Scandinavian peoples who raided much of northern and western Europe from the 8th to the 12th centuries – were probably driven by population pressures to leave their native lands.

They sailed to Britain as plunderers, starting with attacks on eastern coastal villages and monasteries such as LINDISFARNE in 793, but soon became colonists. Despite their warlike reputation, the Vikings had a code of honour, which forbade them to attack traders, farmers or women.

Those from Norway accepted the harsh climate of the Scottish islands and colonised the Shetlands and the Faeroes as well as Ireland. Danes invaded parts of northern and eastern England and by the 870s had conquered East Anglia, Mercia and Northumbria, although ALFRED THE GREAT kept them out of Wessex. In 886 he agreed to a peace treaty, which allowed the DANES to rule the north and east.

Battles continued, and Danes ruled all England from 1016 to 1042. But as time went by, the Vikings settled and started to work the land, becoming part of the population they had conquered.

VILLAGE GREEN: *see opposite page*

VIOLET

There used to be a considerable trade from country to town in sweet violets (*Viola odorata*), Britain's most strongly scented native wild flower. The sweet violet is the only scented type among the dozen or so species of violets and closely related pansies that grow in British woods, hedgerows and grasslands.

The flowers were used medicinally and in cooking, as well as to distil

SWEET AROMA Violet-scented toiletries were popularised by the Victorians, yet this strong perfume has more ancient associations

perfumes; they were also strewn on the floors of homes, churches and other buildings to mask smells. Botanists now know that the flowers' efficacy is due not only to their scent but also to a substance called ionine, which temporarily dulls the sense of smell.

The sweet violet was the flower of Aphrodite, the Greek goddess of love, and William Shakespeare often mentions violets in a romantic context. In *A Midsummer Night's Dream*, Oberon anoints the sleeping Titania's eyes with the juice of heartsease – a folk name for pansy – causing her to fall in love with Bottom, who is transformed into an ass.

VORTICISM

Vorticism is the only avant-garde British art movement with a recognised leader: Wyndham Lewis (1882-1957), painter, poet and novelist. In June 1914 the first issue of the movement's magazine, *Blast*, declared: 'We only want the world to live, and to feel its crude energy flowing through us.'

Vorticism was distinguished by a hard-edged, aggressive and energetic style that looked to the world of machinery and industry for inspiration. It was influenced by Continental movements such as French Cubism and Italian futurism and briefly attracted noted British painters such as David Bomberg and C.R.W. Nevinson. Though the movement was short-lived – the group broke up during the First World War and did not reform afterwards – it successfully opened British art to Continental modernism.

MACHINE-AGE ART The magazine *Blast* revelled in the brutal vigour of vorticism, but the British art movement collapsed soon after the second – and final – edition

HEART OF THE VILLAGE

From maypoles to public floggings, village life has centred on the green for centuries. Serving the changing needs of its community through the years, it is as much a part of local history as any church or manor house

THE OPEN SPACE that forms the heart of some 1400 English villages may, in many cases, have existed for much longer than any of the buildings that surround it. The oldest greens are thought to be relics of Anglo-Saxon settlements, designed as pounds where livestock could be safely gathered, or were laid out as common grazing land when new manors were created during later centuries. The village green was the obvious site for the communal water pump as well as the local lock-up or stocks, and it later became a place of recreation, fairs and markets.

Various festivals are still celebrated on village greens throughout Britain. Ceremonies to welcome spring, including MORRIS DANCING and the 'dressing' of a maypole, are held on many greens on MAY DAY. In Whalton, Northumberland, fires are lit on the green on July 4 to celebrate midsummer (ignoring changes to the calendar made in 1752), and similar fire-ceremonies are held on New Year's Eve in Allendale, Northumberland.

Village greens were always a communal resource and today the question of ownership is often confused. Common rights and ancient customs have helped preserve them even in the heart of London where examples such as Paddington Green and Parsons Green survive. Most village greens are now in the care of parish councils.

CRIME AND PUNISHMENT
The behaviour of villagers, until the 19th century, was regulated by the squire, the rector and frequently by local bullies masquerading as upholders of morality. Ducking-stools no longer stand beside their ponds, but many greens still have whipping-posts and stocks used for the punishment and humiliation of offenders. Drunkards were incarcerated in the village lock-up, a bare cell that was generally clearly visible from the windows of the inn. The stocks at Painswick in Gloucestershire (above) are unusual in being made of iron – most stocks were wooden. Stocks can also be seen at Aldbury in Hertfordshire and Eyam in Derbyshire. Harrold in Bedfordshire has a fine example of a village lock-up.

THE POND
Most village ponds are man-made, being lined with compacted clay and straw. Apart from horses and livestock, domestic ducks and geese also grazed the green, and occasionally wildfowl that added some variety to the cooking pot. Many ponds were neglected when horses were replaced by tractors, but they are now valued as habitats for wildlife and as picturesque features of the local landscape. Some outstanding examples

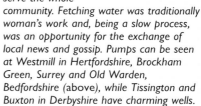

include Finchingfield in Essex, Ashmore in Dorset and Aldbury in Hertfordshire.

THE PARISH PUMP
In the days before piped water, a well or pump on the green would often serve the whole community. Fetching water was traditionally woman's work and, being a slow process, was an opportunity for the exchange of local news and gossip. Pumps can be seen at Westmill in Hertfordshire, Brockham Green, Surrey and Old Warden, Bedfordshire (above), while Tissington and Buxton in Derbyshire have charming wells.

GAMES AND SPORTS
The skill of English archers at Agincourt was learnt at butts on village greens. People of higher birth might also practise tilting with a lance against a revolving 'quintain' or tilting pole. 'Club-ball', condemned by Edward III for distracting young archers, may have been an early form of cricket, a game that has been linked with many greens in Surrey, Kent and Hampshire for the past 300 years. Marbles was a game for Lent and at Tinsley Green, Kent, championships are still held on Good Friday. England's only original quintain post (left) survives at Offham, Kent.

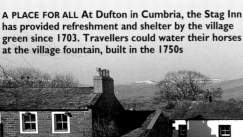

A PLACE FOR ALL At Dufton in Cumbria, the Stag Inn has provided refreshment and shelter by the village green since 1703. Travellers could water their horses at the village fountain, built in the 1750s

Virginia WADE

- **Tennis player** • **b.1945**

The peak of Virginia Wade's career came in 1977. At the height of the celebrations for Elizabeth II's Silver Jubilee, this Bournemouth-born, South African-raised daughter of the archdeacon of Durban satisfied a nation's yearnings by winning the ladies' singles championship in Wimbledon's centenary year. 'It was like playing the queen,' the American Chris Evert mused ruefully after Wade had beaten her in the semifinals.

Talented but wayward and prone to unaccountable lapses in concentration, it had taken Wade 15 years to win the title. Overseas, she was more assured, winning the US and Australian Opens in 1968 and 1972. The most durable female competitor in Wimbledon history (she competed for 25 successive years), it was fitting that in 1983 she became the first woman to be elected to the Championships committee.

WALES

- **Area 8019 sq miles**
- **Pop. 1.5 million**

A country and principality within the mainland of Britain, Wales lies to the west of England, encompassing about a 12th of the United Kingdom's total area and a 20th of its people. CARDIFF is the capital and Newport and SWANSEA the main industrial cities. Most of inner Wales is mountainous and sparsely inhabited.

The Romans left little mark on Wales. Later British refugees from the Anglo-Saxon invasions settled there (the name Wales comes from the Saxon word for foreigner) and in the 8th century an

THE LAUGHING CAVALIER Frans Hals' 17th-century portrait of an unknown 26-year-old was given its popular title in the 1870s when it was first exhibited as part of the Wallace Collection

earthwork boundary, OFFA'S DYKE, was built along the length of its border.

EDWARD I took control of Wales and so started many years of conflict. In 1301 he appointed his son the PRINCE OF WALES, a title given to the male heir to the throne ever since. Owain GLYNDWR's 1401 rebellion failed to topple the English regime, which was succeeded by the part-Welsh Tudors in 1485. An Act of Union finally came in 1536.

Today Wales retains a distinct cultural identity, as displayed at EISTEDDFODs. The WELSH LANGUAGE is spoken by about half a million people, while religious nonconformity and trade unionism are stronger than in other parts of Britain. In 1999 Wales gained its own national assembly as part of the Labour government's policy of DEVOLUTION.

Alfred Russel WALLACE

- **Biologist** • **1823-1913**

At the same time as Charles DARWIN, Alfred Russel Wallace independently developed the idea of evolution by means of natural selection. Although papers by the two men were published jointly in 1858, Wallace had less supporting evidence and it was Darwin's name that became associated with the theory.

William WALLACE

- **Scottish freedom fighter** • **1270-1305**

A martyr to the cause of independence for Scotland, William Wallace was a brave warrior with a character marred by a streak of brutality. From an early age he displayed a deep hatred of the English forces who occupied his country following the invasion by EDWARD I.

At the age of 27 he was declared an outlaw for killing the sheriff of Lanark. Taking to the hills, he displayed his genius as a guerrilla general by uniting Scotland's ill-disciplined resistance fighters under his command. In September 1297 he won a victory over a larger English force at Stirling. But in July 1298 he was defeated at Falkirk by Edward's army. He was captured and executed in 1305.

> The independence movement led by William Wallace was continued after his death in 1305 by Robert Bruce, who triumphed at Bannockburn in 1314

WALLACE COLLECTION

- **Central London (p.499 B2)**
- **Est. 18th-19th century**

On the death of Julie Amélie Charlotte Wallace in 1897, an art collection amassed over five generations by the Seymour-Conway family was bequeathed to the nation. Francis Seymour-Conway had begun the collection in the mid 18th century, but it was Richard Seymour-Conway, and his son, Richard Wallace (Julie's husband), in the following century who were principally responsible for gathering the largest private collection to remain intact from the Georgian period.

The collection includes the best holding of French 18th-century paintings outside France, including works by Watteau, Boucher and Fragonard.

Barnes WALLIS

- **Aeronautical engineer** • **1887-1979**

Barnes Wallis began his career as a marine engineer at Cowes. In 1913 he took a job with the giant VICKERS company, working in the newly formed airship division. He designed the R-100 in 1924, but after its successor, the R-101, was destroyed in a horrific explosion, airship development was halted.

Wallis moved on to aircraft, designing the Wellington bomber and the bouncing bombs used in the 'Dambuster' raid of May 1943. After the war he began work on the variable geometry or 'swing wing' aircraft, which later became the Tornado. Wallis also undertook research into oil transportation by submarine.

WALPOLE FAMILY

- **Robert; politician; 1676-1745; kt 1725**
- **Horace; novelist; 1717-97**

Robert Walpole dominated British politics in the first half of the 18th century. In 1720, as paymaster general, he helped to calm public panic after the SOUTH SEA BUBBLE scandal. He became Britain's first prime minister in 1721, remaining in office until 1742, partly through good relations with GEORGE I – with whom he corresponded in Latin, the German king speaking little English – and GEORGE II. His premiership was marked by a long period of peace and growing prosperity, but in 1739 Walpole

was drawn into conflict with Spain in the War of JENKINS' EAR. He resigned in 1742, charged with corruption.

His youngest son, Horace, although briefly an MP, made his reputation as a gifted man of letters. In 1764, inspired by a nightmare, he wrote *The Castle of Otranto*. A melodramatic tale, it was one of the first 'Gothic' novels and a harbinger of the ROMANTIC MOVEMENT.

Ernest WALTON

- **Physicist** • **1903-95**

Working with John Cockcroft in Cambridge's CAVENDISH LABORATORY, Ernest Walton achieved the first artificial disintegration of an atom by bombarding it with particles from an accelerator. They used protons at an energy of 500 000 electron volts to smash lithium atoms. The two scientists shared the 1951 Nobel prize for physics for this achievement.

Izaak WALTON

- **Writer and angler** • **1593-1683**

'Fishing is an Art, or at least, it is an Art to catch fish.' So said Izaak Walton in *The Compleat Angler* (1653), which has since become the ANGLING bible. Walton spent his youth in Staffordshire before settling in London in 1621 and working as an ironmonger. The outbreak of the Civil War forced him to return

GENTLE ART Izaak Walton's *The Compleat Angler* was more than just a fishing manual – it included practical advice on how best to cook the fish as well as how to catch them

to Staffordshire, where he wrote several biographies in addition to his fishing manual. 'I love any discourse of rivers, and fish and fishing,' he enthused. His book is still in print some 350 years after its first publication.

William WALTON

- **Composer** • **1902-83; kt 1951**

William Walton's parents thought that he mixed with the wrong crowd at Oxford, but he could hardly have made better friends than the wealthy brothers Osbert and Sacheverell Sitwell. It was the SITWELL FAMILY who introduced Walton to affluent London society in the 1920s and encouraged him to compose free of all financial cares.

His most popular piece was the jazzy *Façade* (1926), a setting of Edith Sitwell's poetry. Walton sometimes spent weeks composing a single chord, but the results justified the effort. His Symphony No.1 (1935) is considered the finest of all British 20th-century symphonies, while his Viola Concerto (1929) is revered as one of the best works for the instrument. His music is perhaps best known from film scores, including *Henry V* (1946) and *Richard III* (1955). He also wrote the march 'Orb and Sceptre' for the coronation of Elizabeth II.

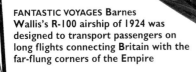

FANTASTIC VOYAGES Barnes Wallis's R-100 airship of 1924 was designed to transport passengers on long flights connecting Britain with the far-flung corners of the Empire

WARS OF THE ROSES

• 1455-87

For 32 years, a bitter struggle for the English throne was waged between two branches of the PLANTAGENET family, the House of LANCASTER and the House of YORK, both descended from EDWARD III. It began after 1453 when HENRY VI's mental collapse caused a power vacuum that ambitious nobles were keen to fill. Richard of York, grandson of Edward III's fourth son, saw his chance to claim the throne. The first fighting broke out in May 1455, when Richard confronted Henry VI at the Battle of St Albans, taking the king captive. Intermittent clashes occurred, with power alternating between the Lancastrians and the Yorkists until 1460, when Richard was killed in a surprise attack at Wakefield.

Richard's son Edward then took up the cause, defeating the Lancastrians and in 1461 declaring himself king as EDWARD IV. In 1471 Henry's heir, Prince Edward, died in the Battle of Tewkesbury, and Henry VI was murdered in the Tower of London.

Edward IV continued to rule until his death in 1483. His 12-year-old son Edward V was briefly king before his uncle RICHARD III imprisoned him and his younger brother in the Tower. It is said that Richard had the boys murdered to secure his own claim to the throne.

The Wars of the Roses – a term first used in the 19th century – began to come to an end when Henry Tudor defeated Richard III at BOSWORTH (1485) and the following year, as HENRY VII united the two warring houses by marrying Edward IV's daughter, Elizabeth of York.

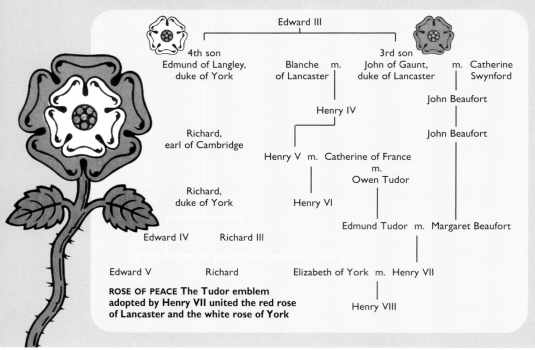

ROSE OF PEACE The Tudor emblem adopted by Henry VII united the red rose of Lancaster and the white rose of York

WARKWORTH CASTLE

• **Northumberland (p.496 C2)**
• **Built 12-14th century** • **EH**

Along with nearby ALNWICK CASTLE, Warkworth Castle was one of the strongholds of the mighty Percy family. An eight-towered keep, built in the shape of a cross, contains a maze of separate chambers. The keep and a curtain wall with towers at each corner were added by the Percys in the 14th century to a castle begun two centuries earlier, on a site high above the River Coquet. The impressive gatehouse has a vaulted entry passage and guardrooms on either side.

A famous owner of Warkworth was Harry Hotspur, who with his father Henry Percy, 1st earl of Northumberland, helped to place HENRY IV on the throne.

WARWICK

• **Warwickshire (p.495 F3)** • **Pop. 22 480**

To the novelist Walter Scott, the turrets and walls of Warwick Castle reflected in the River Avon provided one of England's most beautiful views. The castle and its park, laid out by 'Capability' Brown, dominate the town, but Warwick has far more to offer, including a grand medieval church and Tudor and Georgian houses.

Warwick Castle dates mainly from the 14th century, but the Victorians reconstructed a good deal of it, including the vast Great Hall. The Avon curves around the castle, which now belongs to Madame Tussaud's and has waxworks exhibited in some rooms.

St Mary's Church has superb 15th-century stained glass and ornate tombs of the earls of Warwick. Their emblem, a bear and ragged staff, has given its name to pubs throughout England. One of the earls, Richard Neville, features prominently in William Shakespeare's historical plays. Neville was so influential during the Wars of the Roses that he was nicknamed 'Warwick the kingmaker'. In 1450 he built Warwick's superb timber-framed guildhall.

An even more successful soldier, Field Marshal MONTGOMERY, was colonel of the Royal Warwickshire Regiment. His characteristic Second World War beret and uniform are displayed in the Warwickshire County Museum.

The WASH

• **E England (p.495 H2)** • **Area 300 sq miles**

This shallow inlet of the NORTH SEA divides the counties of Lincolnshire and Norfolk on the east coast of England. The Great Ouse, Nene, Welland and Witham rivers empty into the bay after travelling across flat, fertile FENS and marshes.

The sea is dangerous here for sailors unfamiliar with the turmoil caused by the north-easterly winds. Rising out of this expansive landscape the major landmarks include: prosperous Boston's 82 m (272 ft) tower, known as the 'stump' and visible for up to 20 miles; the handsome profile of KING'S LYNN; Hunstanton, whose conspicuous colour-banded cliffs mark the end of The Wash coast; and outstanding village churches.

Seals, waders, wildfowl and some opportunist birds of prey make abundant use of the mud flats.

NATURE INTO ART

Perhaps it is our climate of mist, cloud and shifting light effects or the soft evanescent tones of land, water and sky that have turned so many native artists into watercolourists. Whatever the reason, British painters have been in thrall to the subtle, fluid medium for more than 200 years

KEEPING NOTE Samuel Palmer's sketchbook is full of miniature watercolours

FINELY CRAFTED Girtin's *The White House at Chelsea* is one of the most perfect English watercolours. Turner is quoted as saying: 'Had Tom Girtin lived, I should have starved'

ALTHOUGH ARTISTS such as Albrecht Dürer and Anthony Van Dyck had used colour washes for sketches, watercolours were generally considered inferior to oils until painters in mid 18th-century England realised their potential. The soft, pastel shades were found to be particularly suited to LANDSCAPE PAINTING.

Watercolour paints are soluble pigments that are thinned with water to achieve lighter tones. They are quick-drying and the equipment is more portable than oil paints, allowing artists to sketch easily and spontaneously.

TRAVELLING LIGHT Part of the appeal of watercolour painting is the direct connection of the artist with the subject matter and the simplicity and portability of the materials used

One early exponent was Alexander Cozens (1717-86), whose innovative works include *Classical Landscape*, a pen and ink sketch with a colour wash.

His son, J.R. Cozens (1752-97), was the first English artist to make a marked transition from topographical scenes to romantic watercolours, using sketches of Alpine scenes as the basis for dramatic works such as his *Pays du Valais*.

He was, according to John CONSTABLE, 'the greatest genius that ever touched landscape'. His work influenced the brilliantly atmospheric water-colourist Thomas Girtin (1775-1802) and J.M.W. TURNER, who excelled in this medium. Turner

adapted it in unorthodox ways to achieve unique effects of light in views such as *Salisbury Cathedral*.

Other 19th-century watercolourists include Richard Bonington (1802-28), who painted in vivid tones that influenced French impressionist painters, and Samuel PALMER, who infused his watercolour landscapes with a Christian vision. In the 20th century, war artists John PIPER and Paul NASH are among those who have used the medium to dramatic effect.

FIRST IMPRESSIONS *The Institut seen from the Quai, Paris*, by Richard Parkes Bonington, is more concerned with light than architecture

BITTER VICTORY The Scots cavalry charges the French at the Battle of Waterloo. A veteran of the battle said: 'Nothing met my eye except the mangled remains of men and horses'

Evelyn WAUGH

• Novelist • 1903-1966

The most blackly humorous of English novelists, Evelyn Waugh satirised fashionable society in a string of early novels, including *Decline and Fall* (1928), *Vile Bodies* (1930) and the brilliant parody of the newspaper industry, *Scoop* (1938). *A Handful of Dust* (1934) was crafted out of the early breakdown of his first marriage.

Brideshead Revisited (1945) remains Waugh's most popular novel despite his own repudiation of it for sentimentality. Later works include masterpieces such as the *Sword of Honour* trilogy (1952-61), whose tone is bleaker and more bitter, reflecting the increasing abhorrence felt by Waugh, a fastidious Catholic convert, for the vulgarity of the modern democratic age.

Battle of WATERLOO

• Belgium • June 18, 1815

The final battle of the Napoleonic Wars, in which the Duke of WELLINGTON and the Prussian marshal Blücher defeated Napoleon's French army and checked his imperialist ambitions, took place on a ridge 12 miles south of Brussels. Wellington commanded an Anglo-Dutch army of 68 000 men against Napoleon's 72 000-strong French Grand Army.

The French assault on the squares of allied infantry was relentless. 'Hard pounding, this, gentlemen,' Wellington observed, 'let's see who will pound longest.' The French had a reputation as the finest troops in Europe, and there is little doubt that Napoleon would have won had not Blücher's Prussian army, numbering 89 000 men, arrived from Namur to save the day. By dusk the French had fled, abandoning their guns.

The dead numbered roughly 25 000 French, 7000 Prussian, and 15 000 of the Anglo-Dutch forces.

WATERLOO STATION

• Central London (p.499 E7/F7) • Opened 1848

Anyone trying to catch a rush-hour commuter train from Waterloo, used by 120 000 travellers a day and London's main gateway to the south-west, will know why it was named after a famous battle. Back in the 1870s crowding was even worse, as piecemeal enlargement had turned the station into London's most confusing railway terminus. One line even crossed the main concourse and disappeared through a hole in the wall to join a substation across the road.

The initial station was a wooden-roofed building constructed in 1848. The forecourt was redesigned in the 1920s, reducing congestion and allowing access to the underground station, opened in 1898. By the 1960s Waterloo was Britain's largest terminus, with more than 20 platforms. In 1994 an international terminus designed by Nicholas GRIMSHAW was opened, with trains travelling through the CHANNEL TUNNEL direct to Brussels, Lisle and Paris.

WATER MILLS AND WINDMILLS:

see opposite page

James WATT

• Engineer • 1736-1819

In the 1760s, through a series of crucial innovations, the instrument maker James Watt began to develop a uniquely effective steam engine. After repairing a NEWCOMEN engine, he worked out that its efficiency could be greatly improved by adding a separate steam condenser.

In partnership with the Birmingham manufacturer Matthew Boulton, Watt went on during the 1780s to patent sun-and-planet rotary motion, reciprocation and parallel motion, which gave him control over steam engine development until his patents expired in 1800.

WAYLAND

In the late 9th century the Saxon king ALFRED THE GREAT noted the passing of pagan belief with the words: 'Where are the wise Weland's bones, the goldsmith that was formerly most famous?'

The story of Wayland, a giant smith of Norse legend, was well known in England by the 8th century. Whatever the words of Alfred, Wayland lived on in folk belief and in myths about the magical swords he made, including that with which BEOWULF was said to have slain the monster Grendel.

A megalithic tomb on the Ridgeway near the WHITE HORSE has been known as Wayland's Smithy since the 800s.

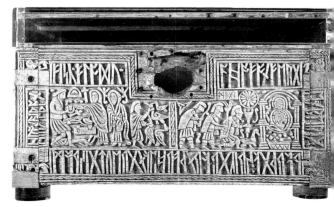

ANCIENT LEGEND A 9th-century whalebone casket at the British Museum depicts the story of Wayland, the giant smith

WHEELS OF INDUSTRY

For almost 2000 years the only source of power available to man, apart from domesticated animals, was provided by the force of water and wind. Mills ground the grain and were later used to run machinery

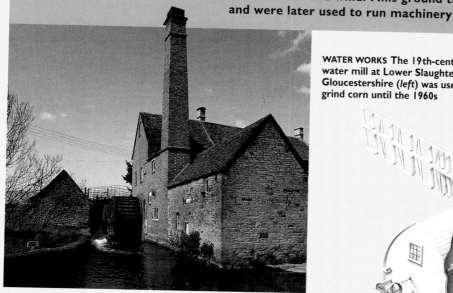

WATER WORKS The 19th-century water mill at Lower Slaughter in Gloucestershire (*left*) was used to grind corn until the 1960s

SAILS The four sails carry hinged shutters or 'vanes', which can be closed or opened depending on the wind speed

WINDSHAFT As the sails turn in the wind, the windshaft turns with them

BRAKE WHEEL Mounted on the windshaft, the brake wheel connects to the cogs that turn the runner stones

FANTAIL OR FLY The blades of the small fantail are set at an angle so that when the main sails are facing into the wind only the edge of the fantail blades catch the breeze. As the wind changes direction it hits the fantail at an angle, swivelling it around

MILLSTONES The lower 'bed stones' are fixed and rest in the floor, while the upper 'runner stones' spin against them, milling the grain. The gap between runner and bed stones can be altered to vary the fineness of meal

THE POST The body of the mill rotates around a timber post clad in iron. The post is secured at its base by two horizontal timber crossbeams and at its crown by a heavy horizontal beam called the 'crown tree'

FAN CARRIAGE The fantail is mounted on a fan carriage that runs on wheels on a track around the mill. As the wind moves the fantail the carriage moves, rotating the body of the mill so that the sails face into the wind again

AN ENDURING STYLE The 18th-century post mill, in use well into the 20th century, was a refinement of the earliest medieval wooden post mills

T HE ROMANS WERE the first to bring water wheels to Britain, and archaeologists have found remains on the Witham at Lincoln and at Chesters fort on HADRIAN'S WALL.

These were grain mills and so much more efficient than the old method of grinding by hand that, unlike many aspects of Roman civilisation, the system remained in use throughout the Dark Ages. By the time the Domesday Book was compiled in 1086 there were more than 5000 mills at work in England.

MILLS MOVE NORTH

The Romans never took the new technology to northern Scotland, but the Norse invaders and settlers of the 8th century brought their own versions of the grain mill to the region.

Where Roman mills had a vertical wheel and gearing to turn horizontal millstones, Norse mills had curved blades set directly in the stream and a vertical shaft turning the wheels directly. Dounby Click Mill in Orkney is one example.

HARNESSING THE WIND

The earliest known reference to a windmill is to a mill in Lincolnshire in 1179. These older mills have long since gone, but medieval illustrations show that they were post mills, in which the body of the mill revolves on a post according to the wind's direction, as in the surviving Bourne Mill in Cambridgeshire and Pitstone Mill in Buckinghamshire.

Over the centuries, more sophisticated mills developed and wind and water power found new uses. The water mill became the main power source for industry until the arrival of the steam engine. Finch's Foundry in Sticklepath, Devon, made agricultural tools.

Windmills called tower mills if made of brick or stone, or smock mills if of wood, were used to mill grain, but many were devised for land drainage – Cambridgeshire's Wicken Fen windpump was used for this.

THE MILLER'S TALE

Medieval villagers had to pay a toll to their lord to have their grain milled. The charge – one-sixteenth of the flour – was measured by the miller.

The dubious honesty of millers was a popular joke, which Geoffrey Chaucer exploited in The Canterbury Tales. 'He felt [grain] with his thumb and ... took three times his due – A thumb of gold, by God, to gauge an oat!'

LIFE ON THE EDGE

Railway cuttings, canal banks and motorway verges constitute an important habitat for British wildlife. These unruly strips of land have become sanctuaries for the plant and animal refugees of urban sprawl and commercial farming

NTENSIVE AGRICULTURE has had a devastating effect on Britain's flower-meadows, helping to reduce them to 3 per cent of what they were before the Second World War. As a result, less intensively managed waysides have come to be a valuable sanctuary for many native plants, often preserving rarities such as violet helleborine, clove-scented broomrape and field eryngium.

Animals also thrive on the fringes of man-made landscapes. Foxes can sometimes be seen boldly strolling along railway embankments in broad daylight. The railways gave them access to towns, where they have adapted to living on any quiet piece of wasteground. They even make their dens in large gardens.

Railway embankments are also home to rabbits, which prefer to build their warrens in warm, south-facing banks. Adders and slow-worms can sometimes be seen basking on the hot concrete of quieter, more remote platforms.

ON THE ROAD

The verges of Britain's motorways support numerous animals. As in any other habitat, there is a complex foodchain. The kestrel occupies the apex, a deadly hunter that preys on mice and voles seeking cover in the vegetation. Foxes also hunt small mammals, which in turn, feed on seeds, insects and berries.

But a roadside habitat is not without its dangers. An average of 50 000 badgers and 100 000 foxes are killed by traffic each year. Plants are threatened by the huge tonnage of salt spread over freezing roads: most plants cannot tolerate it and suffer dieback. But salt-tolerant species, such as sea plantain, sea aster and sea spurrey, thrive in limited local areas and can be seen slowly advancing along Kent motorways from the coast.
See also HEDGEROWS, MEADOWLAND

REED BUNTING
This reedbed resident has a distinctive squeaky, staccato song

ORANGE BALSAM
Since its arrival in England in 1822, this plant has spread along canals and rivers

CANAL BANKS

Like motorway verges, canals connect countryside and town, allowing plants and animals to spread. The reedbeds are sprinkled with flowers such as marsh marigold, bulrush, yellow iris and yellow loosestrife, while the slow-moving water supports a diverse aquatic community of invertebrates, plants and fish.

AQUATIC SNAILS
Several species of aquatic snail enjoy the tranquil waters of canals

WATER VOLE
The shy water vole is a fast swimmer and likes the quiet canal-side environment

HEMLOCK WATER DROPWORT *This deadly poisonous plant grows on wet verges. Its parsley-like scent can induce giddiness*

Lesser celandine

Yellow archangel

ROADSIDE FLOWERS

These pretty wild plants have some unpleasant qualities. Yellow archangel has a 'polecat' stench, lesser celandine is poisonous and the crushed leaves of jack-by-the-hedge smell strongly of garlic

Jack-by-the-hedge

HEDGEHOG *Road deaths have little impact on overall hedgehog population size. The greatest threat is winter starvation*

MOTORWAY VERGES

Roadsides act as corridors along which plants and animals may extend their range. Seeds and spores travel in the air currents caused by moving traffic and can hitch a ride in the fur of animals or be distributed in the droppings of birds. The result is great diversity. Around a quarter of Britain's wildflowers and a third of its grasses have been found along motorway verges and embankments.

CROW *Along with rooks and ants, crows clean up the roadsides by feeding on decaying animals*

RAILWAY EMBANKMENTS

The overgrown swathes of land next to railway tracks generally support more plant species than motorway verges. Animals have taken advantage of the shelter of the relatively inaccessible banks, too. Plants even utilise the gaps between the rails.

BRAMBLES
A tangled mess of brambles gives shelter to birds and mice, while the berries provide them with food

YELLOW MEADOW ANT *The presence of these tiny creatures is signalled by mounds up to a metre across*

OXFORD RAGWORT *The spread of this plant closely followed the growth of the railway network*

FIREWEED *This widespread plant is one of the first to spring up on railway sidings that have been cleared by fire*

FOX *The railways gave foxes safe ground and a way into towns*

WEATHER FORECASTING

A tragic decision to ride out a storm rather than head for port led to the sinking of the *Royal Charter* in 1859, with the loss of 400 lives – and the beginning of official weather forecasting. Robert Fitzroy, who headed Britain's first meteorological service in 1854, began issuing storm warnings in 1861.

But knowledge of weather systems was still in its infancy and forecasts of storms were so unreliable that the service was abandoned from 1867 to 1874. Forecasting improved slowly but it was not until the First World War and the involvement of the armed forces that predictions became widely used.

Today, Met Office forecasters use measurements collected from ships, buoys, balloons, aircraft, ground sites and satellites. Computers generate predictions up to ten days ahead, each involving many trillions of calculations.

Beatrice and Sidney WEBB

- **Social reformers** • **Beatrice 1858-1943**
- **Sidney 1859-1947; bn 1929**

The marriage in 1892 of Beatrice Potter – a wealthy debutante with a social conscience – to Sidney Webb forged one of the most influential partnerships of the early socialist movement.

Sidney – a socialist pioneer and FABIAN SOCIETY essayist – served on the London County Council and as a Labour MP. With Beatrice he founded the London School of Economics in 1895 and the *New Statesman* magazine in 1913 and helped to draw up the Labour party constitution.

Sincere and self-sacrificing, the Webbs steadfastly shunned the luxury their fame could have brought. The prime minister Ramsay Macdonald persuaded Sidney to accept a peerage in order to serve in the second Labour government, but Beatrice insisted on being known as plain Mrs Webb.

John WEBSTER

- **Playwright** • **c.1580-c.1633**

A contemporary of William Shakespeare and like him fascinated by revenge and retribution, John Webster wrote two powerful tragedies: *The White Devil*

A FAIR MEASURE OF WINE

In 1707, during the reign of Queen Anne, wine measures dating back to the Middle Ages were standardised in terms of the 'wine gallon' – 231 cu in (3.785 litres or 0.8325 of the Imperial British gallon) as opposed to the 282 cu in ale gallon. This wine measure was abolished in Britain in 1824.

1 anker	10 wine gallons
1 barrel	31 ½ wine gallons
1 tierce	42 wine gallons
1 hogshead	63 wine gallons
1 puncheon	84 wine gallons (2 tierces)
1 butt or pipe	126 wine gallons (1 ½ puncheons)
1 tun	252 wine gallons (2 butts or pipes)

BRONZE STANDARD Every large town kept a set of weights and measures to regulate trade and solve disputes. The 1707 wine gallon was defined as a cylinder 7 inches across and 6 inches deep

(*c.*1612) and *The Duchess of Malfi* (*c.*1614). Both were based on Italian Renaissance court intrigues, and both centre on a woman who maintains her dignity in the face of terrifying ordeals.

Disembodied hands, madmen, poisoning, strangulation and other horrors infuse the action, which is fast-paced and highly visual, punctuated by passages of sublime poetry that still have the power to move modern audiences.

Josiah WEDGWOOD

- **Potter** • **1730-95**

'The greatest man who ever ... applied himself to the important work of uniting art and industry,' William Gladstone said of Josiah Wedgwood.

Wedgwood opened his first factory in Burslem, Staffordshire, in 1759, creating pottery with greater 'elegance of form' and improved designs, colours and glazes. His cream-ware, known later as Queen's Ware, made his fortune when it found favour with Queen Charlotte.

From the 1760s he began making 'overmantel' ware, principally black basalt and jasper stonewares. In 1769 he established Etruria, the largest pottery manufactory in the world. The principles he established there came to be followed by all English potters.

Wedgwood was a philanthropist, building houses for his workers and campaigning against slavery. At his death the company passed to his sons and still produces many of his original designs.

TRY AND TRY AGAIN Josiah Wedgwood spent four years copying the Roman glass Portland Vase in black-and-white jasper ware – a fine-grained stoneware with bas-relief decoration

WEIGHTS AND MEASURES

Before Britain went metric in 1972, measures such as ounces, furlongs and acres dating back to the 8th century were still in use. In 1305 Edward I standardised the foot at 12 inches, and a 16 ounce pound was introduced in 1340 to bring Britain into line with Florence, a major trading partner.

The Imperial Measure introduced in 1824 created precise standard measures, placed in the Houses of Parliament for safekeeping. They were unchallenged until 1972 when impending membership of the metric-based European Economic Community (EEC) required Britain to start metrication. Imperial measures are being phased out gradually to bring Britain in line with the European Union.

WELFARE STATE

The idea that the State should be responsible for the welfare of citizens, ensuring a basic standard of care for all 'from cradle to grave', was turned into explicit policy under the Labour government of 1945-51.

William Beveridge prepared the ground during the Second World War. His Beveridge Report of 1942 proposed a NATIONAL HEALTH SERVICE and a system of NATIONAL INSURANCE to fund payments such as unemployment benefit and old age pensions. From the start the issue of funding bedevilled the welfare state, though the basic premise remained unquestioned until the 1980s. Since then, concern about 'dependency' – reliance on the State rather than personal initiative – has led successive governments to attempt reforms.

The Labour government elected in 1997 committed itself to reviewing the social security system, a mainstay of the welfare state that costs the country £100 billion a year.

WELLCOME INSTITUTE

• Est. 1968

The Wellcome Institute for the History of Medicine in Euston Road, London, is part of the world's largest medical research charity. Affiliated to London University, it was founded with money bequeathed by the American-born millionaire Henry Wellcome, who died in 1938.

The son of a travelling preacher from Wisconsin, Wellcome made a fortune in pharmaceuticals. He settled in England, where with Silas Burroughs he founded a company that became Burroughs Wellcome (now Glaxo Wellcome).

Wellcome left a priceless collection of medical books and instruments amassed over 40 years. The books are part of the Institute library, which contains some 600 000 printed works and many rare manuscripts. The instruments are on permanent loan to the SCIENCE MUSEUM.

WELL DRESSING

The tradition of decorating wells on special occasions began in ancient times when many wells were regarded as the source of sacred power and dedicated

WATERS OF LIFE According to one local legend, the Ascension Day well-dressing ceremony at Tissington in Derbyshire dates back to 1350, when clean water saved villagers from plague

to pagan deities. With the arrival of Christianity, these holy wells were rededicated to saints, but the custom of well-dressing ceremonies to give thanks for the gift of water remained widespread throughout the Middle Ages. Though condemned by Protestant reformers it has survived into the present day, particularly in Derbyshire.

On a chosen day each year – usually either the well's saint's day or Ascension Day – the well is decorated with leaves, pebbles, petals and moss, and blessed by a member of the clergy. The associated festivities can last for several days.

Duke of WELLINGTON

• Soldier; prime minister 1828-30, 1834
• 1769-1852; kt 1804; visc. 1809; 1st duke 1814

The future heroic duke was born Arthur Wellesley, into an aristocratic Irish family. After schooling at Eton, he bought a commission in the army, and a series of spectacular victories in India, where his brother was governor-general, made his reputation and earned him a baronetcy.

> Queen Victoria once asked Wellington how to control the sparrow population in the Crystal Palace exhibition hall. 'Try sparrowhawks Ma'am,' he replied

By 1808 the French under Napoleon Bonaparte dominated most of Europe, and were determined to conquer the Iberian Peninsular. Wellesley was sent to command the British troops in Portugal, where two years later he masterminded the defence of Lisbon. Turning defence into attack, he drove the French from Spain by 1813. His victories in the 'Peninsular War' turned him into the most famous British general of his time.

Despite his skill and experience, his defeat of Napoleon at the Battle of WATERLOO in 1815 was a desperate struggle: he called it 'the nearest run thing you ever saw in your life'.

Rewarded with a dukedom and the Hampshire estate of Stratfield Saye, Wellington returned to politics – he had already served as MP for Rye. In 1828 he became Tory prime minister. Although conservative, he was not an ideological politician and accepted the need for Catholic emancipation and – after mobs twice stoned Apsley House, his London home – electoral reform. He retired from public life in 1846 but remained an influential elder statesman.

H.G. WELLS

• Writer   • 1866-1946

The vast literary output of the science fiction pioneer Herbert George Wells depicts the lives of ordinary people and an extraordinary view of the future. Wells's own life is reflected in his novels. *Kipps* (1905) is apprenticed to a draper, as was Wells when he left school at 14. *Love and Mr Lewisham* (1900) describes the life of a struggling schoolteacher – Wells's next job.

As a scholarship student at the Normal School of Science – now Imperial College – in London in 1884, Wells studied under the biologist T.H. HUXLEY, whose influence is seen in Wells's preoccupation with the transforming powers of science.

Wells's desire to anticipate the future is revealed in science fiction works such as *The Time Machine* (1895), *The Invisible Man* (1897), *The War of the Worlds* (1898) and *The First Men in the Moon* (1901).

WELLS CATHEDRAL

• Somerset (p.494 E5)   • Begun 1180

Medieval visitors to Wells Cathedral would have gasped in amazement as its west front burst upon their view. They would have been faced by a giant stone tableau containing more than 400 brilliantly painted statues – a microcosm of the Christian world both sacred and profane, with Christ, the Apostles and angels at the apex, above rows of the kings, bishops and knights. The 300

ALIEN ARRIVAL H.G. Wells's *The War of the Worlds* describes Martians landing on Earth. Their circular bodies contain huge brains and need the blood of other creatures to live

surviving figures, repaired in the 1970s and 1980s, form the largest collection of medieval statuary in the world.

Inside, giant stone arches, shaped like pairs of open scissors, support the central tower. The graceful octagonal chapter house is lined with seats for the canons, and there is an astronomical clock constructed in about 1390.

WELSH LANGUAGE

Alone among the CELTIC LANGUAGES of Britain, Welsh still holds firm in its strongholds of rural north-west Wales and in towns such as Aberystwyth and Caernarfon. Its origins lie in the language spoken throughout southern Britain from before Roman times and up to the Anglo-Saxon invasions. Welsh literature flowered in the Middle Ages, notably in the mythological and Arthurian tales of *The MABINOGION*.

After centuries of decline following the Act of Union with England in 1536, the number of Welsh speakers is rising and stands at about 500 000. The language was given official status in 1993: government documents are bilingual, there are television and radio broadcasts in Welsh, and all pupils at Welsh state schools study the language.

WELSH MARCHES

• English-Welsh border area (p.494 D3)

For centuries the hilly country that links England and Wales was disputed territory. In the 8th century, King Offa of Mercia raised his mighty OFFA'S DYKE to keep Welsh cattle raiders at bay.

Following the Norman Conquest the Anglo-Welsh Marches fell under the sway of Roger de Mortimer, a kinsman of William I. From him the earls of March were descended, based at Ludlow Castle.

By the 12th century the lords enjoyed great freedom, but their relationship with government broke down in the 15th century when they sided with the Welsh rebel Owain GLYNDWR against Henry IV. They lost their ruling powers in the Acts of Union of 1536 and 1543 that joined Wales with England.

BORDER COUNTRY The Welsh Marches, especially the area now covered by Shropshire and Herefordshire, was until the 16th century an area of battles and raids as the Welsh and English made claims on each other's territory

WEMBLEY STADIUM...WESLEY...WESSEX...WEST END...WEST KENNET LONG BARROW...WESTMINSTER

WEMBLEY STADIUM

• **NW London (p.498 B3)**   • **Opened 1924**

With its distinctive twin towers, Wembley is the world's most famous sporting arena. Spectators from around the globe have experienced the euphoria and despair of the dramas enacted on its field of play: highlights include England's winning goal of the 1966 WORLD CUP final, and the annual battle for the FA CUP, held here for more than 75 years.

The stadium was built in 1923 for the British Empire Exhibition of 1924-5. Nearby, the Empire Pool, built in 1934, is a popular venue for ice shows and concerts. An adjacent Conference Hall was added to the complex in 1976. In 1999 Wembley Stadium closed for redevelopment to create a new national arena, with a capacity of 90 000.

Charles and John WESLEY

• **Evangelists and founders of Methodism**
• **John 1703-91**   • **Charles 1707-88**

Brought up by their strict High Church father, the Wesley brothers were to remain staunch companions throughout their lives. Together at Oxford they shared the same earnest approach to religion and good works and formed what some called the Holy Club. Their methodical approach to prayer and study earned them the nickname 'methodists'.

John was ordained into the CHURCH OF ENGLAND in 1725. On a voyage to North America, he was deeply influenced by the Moravian belief that people could reach salvation only by faith – it was not enough just to do or be good. It was this message that John and his younger brother preached the length and breadth of England. John founded the first Methodist chapel in Bristol in 1739.

As well as travelling 200 000 miles in 50 years and preaching 40 000 sermons, he and Charles produced the first hymn book and together wrote 7500 hymns.

WESSEX

The ANGLO-SAXON kingdom's name has been used by writers, archaeologists and mystics to describe a part of south-west England that has acquired legendary status. According to tradition, Saxon Wessex was established by two princes,

FAMINE RELIEF In July 1985 Wembley Stadium was the scene of the Live Aid concert, part of the most ambitious musical event ever. It was watched by 1.5 billion people worldwide

Cerdic and Cynric, who landed on the south coast around AD 495. Under their descendants, who included ALFRED THE GREAT, its influence expanded and its royal house ruled all of Saxon England at the time of the Norman Conquest.

For archaeologists, 'Wessex Culture' defines the rich Bronze Age burials found on southern downland. As a land of the imagination Wessex is most powerfully evoked in the novels of Thomas HARDY.

WEST END

• **Central London**

Covering MAYFAIR, SOHO and COVENT GARDEN, the West End is London's playground of shops, theatres, cinemas, restaurants, bars, cafés and pubs.

OXFORD STREET offers the greatest variety of shopping on any street in London, from Selfridges' grand emporium to bargain-basement stores. PICCADILLY and Bond Street offer more upmarket shopping for food, clothes, jewellery and a host of collectables, including antiques and contemporary art.

Charing Cross Road is famed for its bookshops and musical-instrument retailers. To the east, Covent Garden,

once the biggest fruit and vegetable market in London, is now filled with craft stalls, street performers and purveyors of fashion. The ROYAL OPERA HOUSE is located here.

Cinema-goers fill Leicester Square; theatres are on Haymarket, Shaftesbury Avenue, Charing Cross Road and St Martin's Lane. Clubs and music venues cohabit with the many restaurants, pubs and bars of Soho.

WEST KENNET LONG BARROW

• **Prehistoric site**   • **Wiltshire (p.495 F5)**   • **EH**

The cavernous barrow, or tomb, lies near the RIDGEWAY track close to AVEBURY, SILBURY HILL and many other prehistoric sites. Built by Neolithic Britons in the 4th millennium BC, West Kennet Long Barrow consists of a chalk mound 100 m (340 ft) long, with a forecourt and façade of sarsens at its eastern end.

The entrance leads into a stone-built passage with chambers to each side that, when excavated in the 1950s, contained the skeletons and bones of at least 46 adults and children, together with deposits of pottery and flint.

After more than 1000 years of use, the barrow was sealed during the BEAKER period, when old burial traditions began to give way to new funerary practices.

WESTMINSTER

• **Central London (p.499 C8)**

London's richest borough is also the capital's commercial, social and political centre. Within Westminster's borders lie BUCKINGHAM PALACE, the HOUSES OF PARLIAMENT, OXFORD STREET, SOHO and the government offices of WHITEHALL.

Westminster emerged from the swampy land of Thorney Island when Edward the Confessor moved his court here in 1050. From then until Henry VIII moved his court to Whitehall in 1532 it was the main royal residence. In 1834 a fire destroyed most of the palace, which was by then the seat of government, making way for the construction of the present Houses of Parliament.

WESTMINSTER HALL

The magnificent rectangular hall, built by William II in 1097 as an extension to the

WHISKY

The distillation of fermented grains can be traced back at least as far as the 15th century in the British Isles. Whisky, named after the Gaelic for 'water of life' (*uisge beatha* in the Scots variant, *usque baugh* in the Irish) became the staple spirit in a climate too cool for making grape wine for distilling into brandy.

In the early 18th century, English authorities attempted to stamp out the

widespread illicit home distillation of whisky in Scotland, but do-it-yourself distillers simply fled into the Highlands. Today, the spirit is a pillar of the Scots economy, its styles varying from the pungent, peaty spirits of the Western Isles to the gently smoky versions made at Speyside, east of Inverness.

HIGHLAND INGREDIENTS
The unique flavour of Scotch whisky is a combination of malted barley, yeast, the peat that is burnt in the drying kilns and spring water – a deceptively simple formula that has proved wholly resistant to attempts to replicate it elsewhere.

Single malts are especially prized. They are the unblended products of individual distilleries, many aged in casks for more than a decade. Most whisky – 90 per cent of sales – is blended.

The Irish version, also made with barley and almost entirely blended, is spelt 'whiskey'; American and Canadian whiskeys are distilled from maize or rye.

WATER OF LIFE Blair Athol distillery, near Pitlochry, was founded in 1798. Traditionally, whisky was drunk three times a day in Highland homes as a break-time beverage

royal palace, is dominated by Hugh Herland's 14th-century oak hammer-beam roof. Until the 19th century the hall was the chief English law court. Charles I was condemned to death here in 1649. A brass plate embedded in the southern steps marks the spot where he sat through his trial, refusing to acknowledge the validity of the parliamentary court. The hall survived the fire of 1834 and has since served as a place for monarchs and dignitaries to lie in state.

WESTMINSTER ABBEY
Founded by Edward the Confessor and consecrated in 1065, Henry III rebuilt Westminster Abbey in 1245 as the resting place for the canonised Edward. Every English monarch from William I has been crowned there, except for Edward V and Edward VIII. The abbey includes the fan-vaulted Henry VII's Chapel and POETS' CORNER, resting place of revered British writers.

WESTMINSTER CATHEDRAL
The most important Roman Catholic cathedral in Britain, Westminster Cathedral has a startling neo-Byzantine

red brick and white limestone façade. It was designed in 1894 by John Francis Bentley. The Italianate belltower rises 86.5 m (284 ft) above the main body of the church. The top offers wide views over London.

Mortimer WHEELER

• **Archaeologist** • **1890-1976; kt 1952**
The dashing and dynamic Mortimer Wheeler brought glamour to the world of archaeology. In digs at Verulamium (St Albans) and elsewhere Wheeler trained a generation of archaeologists in scientific excavation methods, such as the 'box-grid' system, whereby he dug out squares of earth leaving vertical sections between them, allowing for more detailed study of the layers.

In the 1940s, as director-general of archaeology in India, he uncovered Mohenjo-Daro and Harappa, the twin cities of the Indus Valley civilisation. Wheeler later became a television presenter and wrote for the public; his excavations at MAIDEN CASTLE in Dorset, in particular, received much interest.

WHIGS AND TORIES

Vociferous opposition to the idea of Charles II's Roman Catholic brother, James, duke of York, succeeding him to the throne in the 17th century gave rise to the first political parties in England – Whigs and Tories. Supporters of the duke, the future James II, were nicknamed 'Tories', an Irish Gaelic name for bandits. The Tories thought up 'Whiggamore', a Scottish Gaelic name given to a group of canting presbyterian rebels in 1648, for the opposition.

The Tories were essentially conservative country gentry, while the Whigs came from both the nobility and the growing urban professional class.

In the 19th century the Whigs evolved into the Liberal party and the Tories, increasingly identified with business interests, became known by their alternative name, Conservatives.

WHIP

In parliament, a member of a political party responsible for discipline is known as a 'whip', as in the 'whipper-in of the hounds' in fox-hunting. His or her job is to ensure the attendance and supervise the voting behaviour of party members in important debates.

The government chief whip, who lives at 12 Downing Street, works with the opposition chief whip to organise day-to-day parliamentary business in both HOUSES OF PARLIAMENT. Every week, whips, of whom there are more than 30, send members of their party a schedule of forthcoming debates, underlining each item according to its importance.

A 'three-line whip', when an item is underlined three times, indicates the greatest urgency. An MP who fails to attend could 'have the whip withdrawn' and face suspension from the party.

James McNeill WHISTLER

• **Artist** • **1834-1903**
In 1877 James McNeill Whistler sued the critic John RUSKIN for saying of his picture *Nocturne in Black and Gold – Falling Rocket* that he had 'flung a pot of paint in the public's face'. Whistler won the case but, gaining damages of one farthing only, was bankrupted and left

WHITBREAD ROUND THE WORLD RACE

• **Every four years, usually September-May**
When Colonel Bill Whitbread, the brewing magnate, and Admiral Otto Steiner of the Royal Naval Sailing Association met over a pint of beer in 1972 to plan a round-the-world yacht race, part of the impetus was an attempt to re-create the exploits of the explorers Ferdinand Magellan and Vasco da Gama.

The nine-leg, 31 600 mile voyage from Southampton around the Cape of Good Hope, Australia, Cape Horn and back, has had its share of tragedy and heroism since its inaugural race of 17 boats in 1973-4. Today, competitors all sail in identical yachts, the W60 class, to ensure an equal contest. The 1997-8 race was the last under the Whitbread name. For 2001-2 it has been renamed the Volvo Ocean Race.

WHITBY

• **North Yorkshire (p.496 D3)**   • **Pop. 13 640**
The River Esk carves through the cliffs to create at Whitby a natural harbour and a dramatic setting of narrow streets leading down to the sea. The abbey, dominating East Cliff, was founded by St Hilda in AD 657. It was destroyed by the Danes in 867, but was refounded by the Benedictines in 1087, and rebuilt for a third time in the 13th and 14th centuries. The gaunt ruins, reached by a flight of 199 steps, featured in the novel *Dracula* by Bram Stoker (1897).

The old fishing port was once a shipbuilding centre. Captain James COOK set off from here on his epic voyage to Australia in 1768 aboard the Whitby-built *Endeavour*. The house where he worked as an apprentice is now a museum.

Gilbert WHITE

• **Naturalist**   • **1720-93**
The idyllic image of bygone English village life owes a great deal to one man: the naturalist Reverend Gilbert White. He was born and lived for almost all his life (between travels) in the Hampshire village of Selborne, while working as a curate in the area.

White was one of the first systematic observers of natural history and noted his sightings, whether the appearance of wildflowers or the migration of swifts, in letters to friends. These later formed his hugely successful book *The Natural History and Antiquities of Selborne*, published in 1788, since when it has never been out of print.

White's descriptions of the Hampshire countryside are so vivid that they strike as much of a chord with readers today as they did 200 years ago. His home, The Wakes, is now a museum.

England for Venice. There he soon recouped his losses and returned to London. Such flamboyance was typical of the artist, who counted among his friends Oscar WILDE and was a leading member of the AESTHETIC MOVEMENT.

Whistler was probably the most influential painter in Britain in the late 19th century. Born in the USA, he grew up in Russia and studied in Paris. He was particularly inspired by Japanese art, with its flat decorative colours. His desire to replace the belief that 'every picture tells a story' with the radical idea that the harmony of forms and colours were what mattered bemused the public.

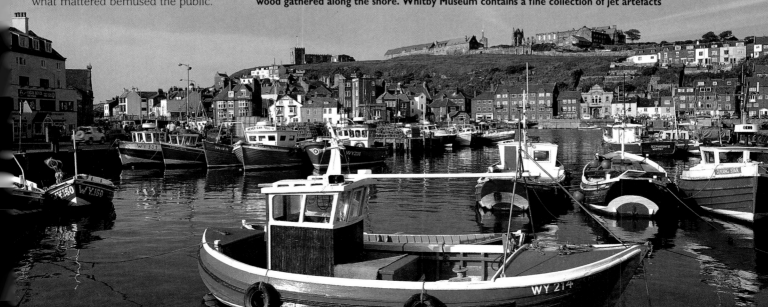

JEWELS OF THE SEA Whitby is noted for its kippers and for its jet jewellery made from fossilised wood gathered along the shore. Whitby Museum contains a fine collection of jet artefacts

KEY
1   Treasury
2   Department of Health
3   Foreign Office
4   10 Downing Street
5   Ministry of Defence
6   Horse Guards Parade

OFFICE POLITICS The ministerial edifices of Whitehall hug the eastern fringes of London's St James's Park. Horse Guards Parade is the site of the annual Trooping the Colour ceremony

WHITEHALL

• Central London (p.499 C7/D7)

The ministerial buildings now lining the broad ceremonial street of Whitehall stand on the site of a sprawling royal palace, developed by Henry VIII and his successors after a fire at Westminster. Whitehall Palace was in turn burnt down in 1698, leaving only Inigo JONES's Banqueting Hall of 1619-22 standing.

Since the 18th century, Whitehall has been the bureaucratic heart of British government. In a modest side road just off the main thoroughfare is Number 10 DOWNING STREET, which has been home to prime ministers since the time of Robert Walpole in 1735.

Along Whitehall's length, a medley of historical figures are remembered in stone and bronze, from the Elizabethan adventurer Walter Raleigh in dandyish pose to the more robust figures of military leaders such as Earl Haig, Viscount Montgomery and Viscount Slim.

Those who fought and died in the two world wars are commemorated by the Cenotaph – a simple stone obelisk designed by Edwin Lutyens. It is the focus for an annual memorial service on the first Sunday in November.

Vale of the WHITE HORSE

• Oxfordshire (p.495 F4)
• Prehistoric site   • EH

Carved into chalk downland just below the RIDGEWAY near Uffington and visible for many miles, abstract lines depict a galloping horse. The 107 m (350 ft) long figure was carved between 1400 and 600 BC and may represent the Celtic horse-goddess Epona, protector of the dead, but the site itself has a far longer history. Neolithic and Bronze Age and later remains nearby suggest it was a funerary complex for at least 4000 years.

In Saxon and medieval times the horse acquired associations with both King Alfred and St George, said to have slain the dragon on the nearby Dragon Hill, and its ancient outline has, through generations, been scoured and cleaned by local people. There are patches where grass will not grow – said to be where the dragon's blood was spilled. Uffington Castle, an Iron Age fort, crowns White Horse Hill.

Dick WHITTINGTON

• Mayor and folklore figure   • c.1358-1423

Richard 'Dick' Whittington was mayor of London on three occasions. He came of rich parents and worked as a textile dealer. But popular legend says he was a kitchen servant, ill-used by his superiors but loved by his master's daughter. He ventured his only possession, a cat, on a trading voyage. The cat was sold for a high price to a Moorish merchant whose palace was plagued with rats. Meanwhile Dick had run away, but turned back when he heard the Bow bells calling 'Turn again, Whittington, Lord Mayor of London'. He discovered that the sale of the cat had made his fortune and that he was rich enough to marry his sweetheart.

This romantic story first appeared in print in 1605. Fairy tales about cats as bringers of good fortune are recorded from the 13th century.

Frank WHITTLE

• Aeronautical engineer and inventor
• 1907-96; kt 1948

The pioneer of the jet engine first proposed it in 1930, but had to wait 11 years to see it take off. His first paper on the subject, in which he pointed out the value of the gas turbine as a form of propulsion, was written while he was an RAF cadet. There was no initial interest.

While studying mechanical sciences at Cambridge in the mid 1930s he formed Power Jets Ltd. A prototype jet engine was built and on the eve of the Second World War the company received government backing. The Gloster Meteor, powered by a Whittle engine, made its first flight on May 15, 1941. Whittle lived on to see his engine dominate air travel.

SUPER JET Twin-engined Meteor aeroplanes powered by Frank Whittle's engines in the 1940s achieved speeds of up to 400 mph

BELOW DECKS In his successful campaign to abolish slavery in the early 19th century, William Wilberforce took this model of a slave trader before parliament to show the method by which slaves were stowed

WHO'S WHO

Nothing indicates that a person has 'made it' quite like an entry in the reference book *Who's Who*.

In 1849 the first edition simply listed peers, MPs, judges and archbishops. Later, newspaper editors, head teachers and police chiefs joined the pantheon of 'the great and the good', which today includes sports, film and rock stars.

A new edition is produced each year by the publishing company Adam and Charles Black. In the late 1890s, the book contained some 5500 entries; today's average of 30 000 entries follow a time-honoured, compact format – full name, official title and present post, then date of birth, family details, education, career, publications, recreation and finally address. 'Biographees' merit inclusion 'by invitation only', and most entries are updated annually.

William WILBERFORCE

• **Anti-slavery campaigner and philanthropist**
• **1759-1833**

Born into a wealthy Hull merchant family, William Wilberforce was to spend his life fighting to end the SLAVE TRADE, and then slavery itself. He was only 21 years old when he was returned as MP for his home town, and he became a close friend of the prime minister Pitt the Younger.

Wilberforce was an evangelical Christian with strong views on the evils of the slave trade. Pitt persuaded him to pursue his campaign in parliament, which itself contained many who owned plantations or represented cities whose prosperity had been built on the trade. With staunch support from the Quakers and others outside the House

of Commons Wilberforce succeeded in getting his bill to abolish the trade passed in 1807. It had taken 19 years of campaigning. He retired through ill-health in 1825 but lived to see slavery abolished throughout the British Empire in 1833.

Oscar WILDE

• **Writer** • **1854-1900**

While still at Oxford University, Oscar Wilde created what many regard as his greatest work of art – himself. A flamboyant proselytiser for the AESTHETIC MOVEMENT, Wilde's appearance as a dandy and his teasing wit made him a social hit. He won literary recognition with *The Picture of Dorian Grey*, first published in 1891 in a magazine. His sparklingly witty plays included *Lady Windermere's Fan* (1892), *A Woman of No Importance* (1893), *An Ideal Husband* (1894) and his best known, *The Importance of Being Earnest* (1895).

Imprisonment for homosexual practices ruined his career but inspired his best-known poem *The Ballad of Reading Gaol* (1898).

WILLIAM I, The Conqueror

• **King 1066-87** • **c.1028-87**

An illegitimate child just eight years old when he became duke of Normandy, William's early

TALK OF THE TOWN 'I have nothing to declare except my genius,' said Irish playwright and poet Oscar Wilde to a customs official on arriving in America to lecture on beauty and art in 1882

years were a precarious struggle against rival claimants. But by 1066 he was free to pursue his claim to the English throne, promised him by EDWARD THE CONFESSOR. Crossing the Channel with a powerful force, he defeated HAROLD II at the Battle of HASTINGS and was crowned king on Christmas Day.

It took five years of brutal campaigning to subdue resistance and impose a Norman ruling class. Many of the intimidating series of castles he built – including the TOWER OF LONDON's White Tower – still bear witness to the NORMAN CONQUEST. In 1085 he commissioned DOMESDAY BOOK, the first economic survey of England.

His final years were spent dealing with his rebellious elder son, Robert Curthose, and warring with neighbours. On his deathbed he bequeathed Robert his duchy and his second son, WILLIAM II 'Rufus', his English crown.

WILLIAM I, The Lion

• **King of Scotland 1165-1214** • **c.1143-1214**

William I of Scotland was known to his contemporaries as 'the brawny'. Historians call him 'the Lion', possibly because he had been referred to in an obituary as 'the lion of justice'.

Unwisely invading the north of England in 1174 in pursuit of a claim to Northumberland, William was captured and taken before Henry II. By the Treaty of Falaise Henry forced William to recognise English lordship over the kingdom and church of Scotland. Fortunately for William, two powerful figures reversed this humiliation. The first was Henry's son Richard I, who by the Quit Claim of Canterbury in 1189 allowed William to buy back his independence in return for 10 000 marks, which Richard needed for his Crusade.

Three years later the pope declared the Scottish church independent under direct papal jurisdiction and William was back where he had started – master of an independent Christian kingdom.

WILLIAM II, 'Rufus'

• King 1087-1100 • c.1056-1100

The son of WILLIAM I, the Conqueror, William II was feared as a tyrant, and met a mysterious death while hunting in the New Forest. His nickname, 'Rufus', the Latin for 'red', referred to the colour of his hair and ruddy complexion.

William's great unpopularity was largely caused by his extortions of money, from the Church in particular. He quarelled with his archbishop of Canterbury, St Anselm, and enraged his nobles. In 1096 he won a long struggle to gain control of the Duchy of Normandy from his brother Robert. William's death by an arrow fired apparently accidentally by a courtier, Walter Tirel, may have been arranged by his brother HENRY I.

WILLIAM IV

• King 1830-37 • 1765-1837

GEORGE IV had reduced the monarchy to ridicule by his behaviour, and his brother William, duke of Clarence, seemed ill-endowed to raise its standing. William was 65 when he came to the throne after a life in the navy, which he had joined aged 13. 'Ignorance, weakness and levity put him in a miserable light, and prove him to be one of the silliest old gentlemen in his dominions,' observed the diarist Charles Greville.

Nevertheless the 'Sailor King' ('Silly Billy') had a reputation for fairness. Change was in the air: he put pressure on the Tory party to get the REFORM bill of 1832 through the House of Lords; the POOR LAWS were reformed; and in 1833 slaves in the West Indies were freed. William had ten illegitimate children by an actress, Dorothea Jordan, but failed to father an heir, despite his marriage in 1818 to Adelaide of Saxe-Meiningen. He was succeeded by his niece, VICTORIA.

WILLIAM AND MARY

• William III 1689-1702 and Mary II 1689-94
• William 1650-1702 • Mary 1662-94

A struggle to protect Protestant Holland against Louis XIV's Catholic France dominated the life of William III. A grandson of Charles I, he drew England into a closer alliance with his own country in 1677 by marrying JAMES II's 15-year-old daughter Mary, who, unlike her father, shared his Protestant beliefs.

In 1688 English political leaders, fearing that James was planning to impose Catholicism on England, invited William to take the crown. He landed at Torbay with 40 000 men on November 5. James fled to France, and William and Mary were jointly proclaimed king and queen. James's resistance in Ireland was crushed at the Battle of the BOYNE, leaving William free to campaign against France and secure the Protestant line for Mary's sister ANNE.

> During the reign of William and Mary, the British constitution was established, the Bank of England founded and the National Debt had its beginnings

WILLIAM OF OCKHAM

• Theologian and philosopher • c.1285-1347

William of Ockham is remembered for the philosophical principle known as 'Ockham's razor' – 'entities are not to be multiplied beyond necessity' – his bid to bring economy and clarity to complex assumptions, terms and theories.

After completing his training with the Franciscans in Oxford in 1323, he was prevented from teaching theology in the university, when the chancellor denounced him for heresy. Ockham travelled to the papal court in Avignon to conduct his defence, where he engaged in a bitter dispute with Pope John XXII over the importance of evangelical poverty in the church. He fled to the protection of Emperor Louis of Bavaria, dying in Munich.

WILLOW

Lining streams, river banks and hedgerows, the willow is one of our most numerous trees. There are about 300 varieties, the commonest being the crack willow (*Salix fragilis*), so named because its twigs crack easily; the white willow (*Salix alba*); the weeping willow (*Salix chrysocoma*); and the cricket bat willow (*Salix corulea*), an extra-fast-growing form planted in East Anglia to provide wood for making cricket bats.

The Celts thought willows sacred to the moon, and 'willow-stripping' festivals are still held on the first full moon in May. Infusions of willow bark – a source of acetylsalicyclic acid – were used to treat fevers long before the substance was synthesised as aspirin in 1899. Today, because willows grow so fast – up to 2 m (6 ft) a year – coppiced willow is a promising source of renewable energy.

Harold WILSON

• Prime minister 1964-70, 1974-6
• 1916-95; bn 1983

The first Labour prime minister for 13 years came to power just as the idea of the 'Swinging Sixties' was becoming

SMOKE SIGNALS At an election rally in 1966 Harold Wilson draws on the pipe that lent him an air of calm authority. Wilson was the first prime minister since Gladstone to win four general elections

WATER FEATURE The Palladian bridge in the grounds of Wilton House was built by the 9th earl of Pembroke (The Architect Earl) and Roger Morris, clerk of works, in 1737

fashionable. Wilson was a generation younger than the Tories he replaced. An Oxford economics lecturer who had become a Cabinet minister at only 31, he had risen rapidly through the Labour ranks to become leader in 1963. But Wilson's promises of a bright future 'forged in the white heat' of scientific revolution proved impossible to deliver.

His socialism was more pragmatic than ideological, guided mainly by the need to keep his party and the powerful trade unions united through a period of rapid social change and industrial decline. In this limited ambition he was successful, winning four general elections, but he left the fundamental problems of the country untackled and the Labour party unreformed.

Wilson's tendency to sacrifice ideals to short term needs is summed up in his best-known saying: 'A week is a long time in politics.'

WILTON HOUSE

- **Wiltshire (p.495 F5)**
- **Built 16th-19th century**

The most celebrated feature of Wilton House is its Double Cube Room, 18 m (60 ft) in length and 9 m (30 ft) in height and width. Its elegant proportions are enhanced by sumptuous Italianate decoration, including a white marble fireplace, a painted ceiling, a wealth of gilding around old master paintings and superb family and royal portraits by Van Dyck. An adjoining Single Cube Room is 9 m (30 ft) in each dimension.

These and other state rooms were designed by Inigo JONES and his assistant John Webb as part of their reconstruction of the house after a fire in 1647. A long and beautifully proportioned south front overlooks wide lawns and ancient cedars to the River Nadder, spanned by a Palladian bridge.

Begun in the 1540s, Wilton House has been the home of the Herbert family, earls of Pembroke, for 400 years. When the 2nd earl lived at Wilton, his third wife, Mary, sister of the statesman-poet Philip Sidney, made it a meeting place of the nation's leading intellectual

figures: the writers Edmund Spenser and Ben Jonson were frequent visitors. Shakespeare's First Folio was dedicated to Mary's sons, William, the third earl, and Philip, the 4th earl of Pembroke.

WIMBLEDON LAWN TENNIS CHAMPIONSHIPS

- **June-July • Founded 1877**

To many, Britain's passion for tennis begins and ends with the Wimbledon fortnight. In stark contrast to the remainder of the year, finding a free public court during the All England Championships – held during the last week of June and the first week of July – is nigh-on impossible.

Strawberries, champagne and unchoreographed events such as pop star Cliff Richard enlivening a rain delay by leading a Centre Court sing-song, have made the championships not just a feast of tennis but also a rite of summer, a symbol of Englishness. Staged behind the ivy-clad walls of south London's All

LOCAL HERO British tennis player Tim Henman contests the 1998 Wimbledon singles semi-final. The last British man to win a Wimbledon singles title was Fred Perry in 1936

England Lawn Tennis Club, they are one of tennis' four Grand Slam events and the only one still played on grass.

In 1968 Wimbledon became the first major tennis tournament to admit professionals. Outstanding players since then have included Sweden's Bjorn Borg (winner of five consecutive men's singles crowns 1976-80) and the Czech-American, Martina Navratilova (nine times women's champion, 1978-90). The last British victor in a Wimbledon singles final was Virginia WADE in 1977.

WINCHESTER

- **Hampshire (p.495 F5) • Pop 36 120**

The city of Winchester, the county town of Hampshire, lying 50 miles south-west of London, was the capital of the Saxon kingdom of WESSEX until the 7th century. Remains exist of the Roman city of Venta Belgarum, and of a Norman castle, but Winchester's best-known landmark is its Norman cathedral, begun in 1079. At 170 m (556 ft), it is Europe's longest medieval church.

Around the cathedral are the ruins of two bishop's palaces and parts of Winchester College, founded in 1382 by the churchman William of Wykeham. The college is the oldest boys' PUBLIC SCHOOL in England and was the model for Eton. The belief that if it rains on ST SWITHIN'S DAY (July 15) it will rain for 40 days is connected to a 9th-century bishop of Winchester, St Swithin: in 971 his remains were transferred from the churchyard to the cathedral, and it is said that rain did indeed fall for 40 days.

FIRM FRIENDS Kenneth Grahame's characters from *The Wind in the Willows*, Mole and Rat, escort a traumatised Toad from the scene of yet another of his escapades

The WIND IN THE WILLOWS

• **Published 1908**
The writer Kenneth Grahame (1859-1932) never intended the children's book *The Wind in the Willows* – a story invented for his son – to be published. The book did not become popular until A.A. Milne dramatised it in 1930. Today both story and play – re-adapted in 1990 by Alan BENNETT for the National Theatre – are regarded as classics.

Grahame combined close observation of real animals' habits with fantastic characterisations in his tale of sensible Mole, Rat and Badger and the spoilt, naughty, lazy Toad. The wealthiest of the animals, Toad lives in a grand house on the river, eating lobster and trifle, and cannot keep away from automobiles, though he is a terrible driver. Toad's incorrigible behaviour lands him in jail, but he disguises himself and escapes, and his friends help him to drive away the horrid stoats and weasels from the Wild Wood who have been squatting in his house during his absence. He then repents and promises, 'Henceforth I will be a very different Toad'.

WINDOW TAX

• **Introduced 1695**
The window tax was intended as a temporary measure, although it lasted more than 150 years until 1851. In 1695 England's silver coinage had become debased by the habit of clipping coins, and the subsequent new coinage had to be paid for: the window tax was seen as a way of raising extra cash.

The tax was first levied on houses with a rental value in excess of £5 a year and with six windows or more. Windows were soon blocked up and new houses built with fewer. A rhyme of the day said: 'We'll tell them we pay for the light of the sun, /For the flash of a candle to cheer the dark night, /For a hole in the wall if it let in the light.' Many windows on pre-1851 houses are still bricked up.

House of WINDSOR

• **British royal house**   • **Founded 1917**
During the First World War, in a climate of revulsion against all things German, GEORGE V agreed to change his German name – Saxe-Coburg-Gotha, inherited from his grandfather, Prince Albert of Saxe-Coburg-Gotha – to a more British-sounding version. He chose 'Windsor' because Edward III had once used the title 'Edward of Windsor'.

The king and his queen, Mary, continued their popular reign, but their son EDWARD VIII caused a constitutional crisis by abdicating in 1936 to marry an American divorcee. Edward's brother GEORGE VI and Queen ELIZABETH dedicated their reign to restoring the Windsors' image, with great success; and their daughter, ELIZABETH II, has earned lasting respect, leading the House of Windsor through difficult times in the 1990s, especially those surrounding the divorce of the heir apparent, Prince CHARLES, from DIANA, Princess of Wales.

WINDSOR CASTLE

• **Berkshire (p.495 G4)**
• **Built 11th-20th century**

Windsor town, on the south bank of the Thames, is dominated by its castle, home of English monarchs since William I built a fortress there in the 11th century. England's largest inhabited castle, it was built in stages, with numerous additions made by later monarchs. The most elaborate building among the vast complex of towers and apartments is St George's Chapel, the resting place of ten sovereigns, which was begun in 1475.

A fire in 1992 caused extensive damage to the state apartments, including St George's Hall, site of royal banquets.

Some furniture and paintings were saved from the fire, but for many rooms all that remained were charred fragments.

An ambitious restoration project was soon underway, with a team of 1500 architects, craftsmen and contractors. Five years later, at a cost of £37 million, the remarkable renovation was complete. To the north and east of the castle is the Home Park where the annual Royal Windsor Horse Show is held in May. South of the castle and town lies the vast Windsor Great Park, which now includes the Legoland theme park.

ROYAL RESIDENCE The centrepiece of Windsor Castle is the Round Tower, built by Henry II in the 12th century. It stands on the site of William the Conqueror's original stronghold

WINE GROWING

Grapes and viticulture were introduced to Britain by the Romans. The Domesday Book of 1086 recorded 38 vineyards in England, a number increased during the Middle Ages by French orders of monks, whose monasteries produced wine for the church mass and for profit.

A cooling of the English climate during the 14th century destroyed many vineyards, and with the Dissolution of the Monasteries under Henry VIII in the late 1530s as well as an increase in the wine trade with France, winemaking expertise in Britain was lost.

A WINE REBIRTH

In 1951 a retired Major-General, Guy Salisbury-Jones, planted 0.6 ha (1.5 acres) of vines at Hambledon in Hampshire and so began a winegrowing revival in southern England. By 1973 around 81 ha (200 acres) of vines had been planted.

There are around 900 ha (2250 acres) of vines now under cultivation in Britain, mostly in the south of England and parts of Wales. The mild English climate, with limited sunshine, is best suited to producing white wines from grape varieties selected from northern Europe. The 1997 crop was devastated by late spring frosts, with the consequence that this is a small vintage.

VINE HARVEST The Harewood vineyard in Cornwall's Tamar Valley is one of about 400 vineyards in England and Wales. They produce more than 18 000 hl (396 000 gallons) of wine a year

WINNIE-THE-POOH

A 'bear of very little brain' who lives with his friends in a forest is the subject of A.A. Milne's books, *Winnie-the-Pooh* (1926) and *The House at Pooh Corner* (1928). Milne's son, Christopher Robin, had a teddy bear and a collection of other animals that inspired the stories.

Milne's gift for characterisation resulted in the memorable cast of creatures, including the tiny, anxious and determined Piglet, the gloomy old donkey Eeyore and the irrepressibly bouncy Tigger. The rotund Pooh, driven by his love of honey, bumbles through many adventures, humming poems and seeking Christopher Robin's help. Often the humour is ironic and appeals to adults with lines such as, 'Once upon a time, a very long time ago now, about last Friday...'.

The stories have proved popular the world over, having been translated into 30 languages, including Chinese, Russian and Latin.

LOST TOYS In 1947 the original Winnie-the-Pooh and friends toured America never to return. They are now on show in the New York Public Library

WISDEN

• Cricket almanack • Founded 1864

It is hard to quibble with the poster that once heralded a new edition of *Wisden Cricketers' Almanack* as the world's best-known sports book. Published at the start of every English cricket season, the cricketers' 'Bible' is an expansive annual of more than 1300 pages of records and dates of birth of cricketers, although its heart has always been the detailed scores and reports of recent matches.

OFF HIS OWN BAT

First published in 1864 (price a shilling), *Wisden* was the brainchild of John 'Little Wonder' Wisden, a feared bowler who later ran a tobacconist's and sports equipment store in London's Leicester Square. To generate advertising revenue, he decided to publish a mostly statistical record of the summer's cricket. Mirroring the game's love of tradition and distrust of change, the format between the yellow covers altered little over the ensuing century.

The advent of the journalist Matthew Engel to the editorship in 1993 proved a watershed. He brought in humour, increased overseas coverage and reduced the space afforded to results from the public schools.

WITCHES

Britain's peak witch-hunting frenzy between 1563 and 1736 resulted in the execution of nearly 1000 'witches' in England, while in Scotland 4400 were killed. The self-proclaimed Witch-Hunter General Matthew Hopkins led a campaign that alone resulted in the execution of several hundred individuals accused of witchcraft in Essex, Suffolk and Norfolk.

During the previous 500 years, a mere half dozen 'witches' had been executed. The sudden upsurge in witch-hunting was the result of several factors, including the destabilisation of religious and social values after the establishment of Protestantism under Elizabeth I, James I's personal fear of sorcery and the Civil War of 1642-51.

The first Witchcraft Act was passed in 1542 by Henry VIII. Records exist of only one case being brought to trial. The law was repealed in 1547, but in 1563 Elizabeth I passed a second Witchcraft Act, in which 'murder by witchcraft' carried a death penalty. A tougher Act introduced by James I in 1604 called for death by hanging for 'harmful witchcraft'.

Many of the accused were rejected by society because they were poor, ugly or simply different. Witches were believed to possess a 'familiar' imp or devil who would take the shape of a common animal such as a cat, dog, toad or rabbit. It was thought that they could be identified by the telltale witch's mark – supposedly an extra nipple for suckling familiars, but in reality almost any mole or blemish. If arrested, a woman accused of witchcraft would often be tortured until she 'confessed'.

The last person hanged for witchcraft in England was Alice Molland at Exeter in

HIGH FLIERS It is thought that witches themselves may have believed they could fly as a result of using potions containing hallucinogens such as hemlock

1684. By the beginning of the 18th century the public had become sceptical about the reality of magic. In 1736 the Witchcraft Act of 1604 was repealed and replaced with milder measures, although women thought to be witches were occasionally lynched by mobs until the late 19th century. In 1951 the Witchcraft Act of 1736 was replaced by the Fraudulent Mediums Act.

Modern 'white' witches tend to be worshippers of the powers of nature rather than believers in the occult, although their initiation ceremonies and occasional rites draw on pagan tradition.

... if they will confess nothing but upon the rack of torture: their apparel must be changed, and every hair in their body must be shaved off with a sharp razor ... she must be told that she is detected, and accused by other of her companions: although in truth there be no such matter: and so perhaps she will confess, the rather to be revenged upon her adversaries and accusers.

REGINALD SCOT, *DISCOVERIE OF WITCHCRAFT* (1584)

BEWITCHED A white witch – one of thousands in Britain – is initiated at an open-air ceremony in the south of England

• Surrey (p.495 G5)

WISLEY

• Royal Horticultural Society garden
• Surrey (p.495 G5)

The ROYAL HORTICULTURAL SOCIETY's principal garden at Wisley, which was given to the society in 1903, has been called 'the gardener's garden'. Its displays are designed to epitomise the best of British GARDENING, and to provide help and inspiration for visitors.

In 97 ha (240 acres) the garden includes numerous self-contained model, or demonstration, gardens and areas. They range from a formal walled garden, glasshouses and an arboretum to a bonsai-filled, Japanese-style 'garden of the senses' and a huge mixed border designed to give continuous colour from June to September.

Wisley's second main function is to research and advise on gardening techniques, materials such as soils and fertilisers, and plants. Part of the garden is devoted to trials of new varieties of plants, fruit and vegetables. Nearly three-quarters of a million people – members and non-members of the society – visit Wisley each year.

Ludwig WITTGENSTEIN

• Philosopher • 1889-1951

Like Sigmund Freud and Karl Marx, Ludwig Wittgenstein was a defining genius of the modern age whom Britain inherited from the Continent. Born into a wealthy Viennese family, he came to England in 1908 as an engineer but soon became distracted by worries about the nature of mathematical truth.

In 1912 he began working with Bertrand Russell at Cambridge. While serving in the Austrian army during the First World War he completed the *Tractatus Logico-Philosophicus* (1921), a brief but austerely beautiful work aimed at dissolving traditional philosophical problems by analysing the logical structure of language.

Wittgenstein gave away his fortune and worked in humble jobs before returning to Cambridge in 1929, where he later became Professor of Philosophy. Between 1936 and 1949, he developed the notion of a 'language game' and claimed that the philosopher's task was to examine linguistic usage – a view

REGAL BREED Père David's deer, descended from the Imperial Herd of China, graze in front of Woburn Abbey. The house has been home to the earls and dukes of Bedford for 350 years

that revolutionised 20th-century thought even though nothing more was published until his *Philosophical Investigations* two years after his death.

WOBURN ABBEY

- **Bedfordshire (p.495 G4)**
- **Built 17th-19th century**

Now an abbey only in name, Woburn has been the home of the Russell family, earls and later dukes of Bedford, since 1547. In the 18th century the monastic building, given to the Russells by Henry VIII and rebuilt in the 17th century by Isaac de Caux, was turned into a mansion by various architects, including John Sanderson and Henry Holland.

Behind its imposing frontage lie state rooms rich in porcelain, sculpture and silver. Paintings include portraits by Reynolds, scenes of Venice by Canaletto and the *Armada* portrait of Elizabeth I watching over the Spanish defeat.

Woburn's huge parkland, landscaped by Humphry REPTON, has a safari park where visitors can drive through territory roamed by lions, giraffes, elephants and other exotic animal species.

LAUGHING AT OURSELVES From the unflappable Jeeves to the sartorially impeccable Rupert Psmith, P.G. Wodehouse's comic creations poked affectionate fun at English stereotypes

P.G. WODEHOUSE

- **Writer • 1881-1975; kt 1975**

The novels and short stories of Pelham Grenville Wodehouse are an enchanting mixture of gentle satire and romantic comedy. In his sunny world of grown-up children, a sex problem is how to get the girl you love to kiss you, and a money problem is persuading your rich guardian to increase your allowance.

Classic Wodehouse characters include Jeeves, valet of the good-natured but incompetent Bertie Wooster, Bertie's friend Gussie Fink-Nottle, and Lord Emsworth and his prize sow, the Empress of Blandings. The dialogue is a mixture of jaunty Edwardian slang ('Egad!', 'Dash it!', 'Toodle-pip!') and distinctive word-play and analogy.

Wodehouse published more than 120 novels and short-story collections. His fiction has been described as 'musical comedy without music', aptly so for a writer who was also the foremost English lyricist between W.S. Gilbert and Noël Coward. He lived mostly in America and became a US citizen in 1955, having fallen foul of British public opinion when he made broadcasts from Germany as an internee during the Second World War.

James WOLFE

- **Soldier • 1727-59**

One of the major triumphs of the Seven Years' War (1756-63) with the French was the British capture of Quebec by General James Wolfe, who died in his hour of triumph at the age of 32. Wolfe was a popular commander who had a skill for combining discipline with friendliness and humanity and would quote poetry to his officers.

When he sailed up the St Lawrence River with 9000 soldiers in 1759, the French general Montcalm's position on the fortified heights of Quebec seemed impregnable. On the night of September 12, Wolfe led his men in a climb up a precipitous escarpment. By dawn half the British army had reached the top: by 8 am it was in battle with the French. By 11 am the French had surrendered. Wolfe died from his wounds that day and Montcalm, who was also fatally wounded, died the next morning.

WOLLATON HALL

• **Nottinghamshire (p.495 F2)** • **Built 1580-8**

The elaborate Gothic-style ornamentation of Wollaton Hall, with its towers, turrets, pinnacles and Ionic pilasters, shows the architect Robert Smythson in more extravagant vein than in his other creations at LONGLEAT and HARDWICK HALL. Unusually for an Elizabethan house, which was generally built around an open courtyard, Wollaton has as its centrepiece a 15 m (50 ft) high Great Hall, rising like a tower with a turret at each corner. Inside, its hammerbeam roof is carved and coloured to look like stone. Other towers, with pinnacles, stand at each corner of the house itself. The building is lit by huge windows – one for each day of the year.

Two storeys of Wollaton Hall are the home of Nottingham's Natural History Museum. The former stable block houses Nottingham's Industrial Museum, covering the city's activity in industries ranging from lace-making and tobacco to pharmaceuticals and coach-building.

Cardinal Thomas WOLSEY

• **Chancellor to Henry VIII** • **1475-1530**

The very name Cardinal Wolsey conjures an image of a gross, venal and menacing presence, which aptly describes the man. As adviser to HENRY VIII for some 20

POWER WITHOUT GLORY Cardinal Wolsey accumulated great wealth and made many enemies. He was compelled to give his palace at Hampton Court to a jealous Henry VIII

years, Wolsey enriched not only his king but himself. His taxation policies, his ambition, gluttony and nepotism made him deeply unpopular.

The son of a prosperous butcher, Wolsey studied at Magdalen College, Oxford. His rise was swift. He became chaplain to Henry VII in 1507, and with the accession of Henry VIII in 1509 he took over the administration of much of the king's private business. As lord chancellor from 1515 he successfully enhanced the power and prestige of the monarch, at home and in Europe. But

when he failed to arrange a papal annulment of Henry's marriage with Catherine of Aragon, the king turned on him. He was prosecuted and his property forfeited to the Crown. Wolsey retired to his archbishopric of York, but was later charged with high treason and would probably have been executed had he not died on the journey to London.

National Federation of WOMEN'S INSTITUTES

• **Est. in Britain 1915**

Britain's largest women's voluntary organisation, known as the WI, defies its cosy village-hall image. It has more than 260 000 members in 8000 local groups, engaged in sport and leisure activities, in education and training, the promotion of its values and the exercise of influence upon policy-makers on issues such as health and conservation.

The non-sectarian, non-political, fiercely independent WI was founded in 1897, in Canada, when Adelaide Hoodless lost her child and blamed the death on her ignorance of good hygiene. Determined that other women should not suffer such a tragedy, she set up classes to teach basic skills. The first British WI was established on Anglesey.

'Lifelong learning' remains to this day a central concern for the federation, which holds more than 500 courses each year, in subjects ranging from crafts and cookery to science and technology, at Denman College in Oxfordshire.

Henry WOOD

• **Conductor** • **1869-1944**

Henry Wood was in his 20s when the impresario Robert Newman suggested he run a series of 'promenade' concerts – the PROMS – at the newly built Queen's Hall in London. The idea appealed to Wood because it allowed him to indulge his enthusiasm for new music.

In the early years of the Proms, Wood programmed works by Sibelius and Schoenberg. During rehearsals for the latter's *Five Easy Pieces* in 1912, he told

HOME PRODUCE Fruit bottled by the Women's Institute attracts visitors at a coronation rally in Kent in 1953. The tradition of selling produce made by members still thrives

his players, 'Stick at it, gentlemen: it is nothing to what you will be playing in 25 years'. By then, the Proms had been bought out by the BBC, and since Wood's death they have borne his name. He conducted at festivals, was committed to bringing on young musicians and was the first British conductor to direct the New York Philharmonic Orchestra.

WOODHENGE

• **Prehistoric site** • **Wiltshire (p.495 F5)** • **EH**

The Neolithic henge, 2 miles north-east of STONEHENGE and dating from around 2300 BC, was first discovered by aerial photography in 1925. Its circular enclosure is defined within a bank and an internal ditch, originally 2.2 m (7 ft) deep. Six concentric ovals of timber posts, some 1 m (3 ft) in diameter, stood inside the henge, possibly as supports for an enormous building. Close by, the crouched skeleton of a child was found.

In common with Durrington Walls, a nearby henge that also featured large timber settings, Woodhenge is thought to have been a centre for trade or ritual. Its alignment with the sun may have had some special astronomical significance.

WOODLAND: *see page 482*

WOOKEY HOLE

• **Somerset (p.494 E5)**

The River Axe flows through Wookey Hole, a series of limestone caverns deep in the MENDIP HILLS. Exploration of the system continues, but in caves open to the public, stalactites and stalagmites, lakes and islands form an unfamiliar landscape. The caves were inhabited from Palaeolithic times around 35 000 BC until about AD 450, and were used for burials and perhaps for stranger rituals.

Archaeologists' finds include the broken skull of a girl and cannibalised bones. Local villagers, even in the 19th century, left metal pins as offerings to the Witch of Wookey, a legendary figure who may have been an Anglo-Saxon woman whose skeleton was found in 1912. The river was harnessed in the 19th century for a paper mill that still operates.

PERFECT PROSE In her fiction Virginia Woolf employed innovative techniques that inspired and influenced many later 20th-century writers

Virginia WOOLF

• **Novelist** • **1882-1941**

The English novelist Virginia Woolf is noted both as a mistress of the stylised reverie that depicts character through mood, and also for her stream-of-consciousness technique, which attempts to convey the fragmentary thoughts and impressions of the human mind. This is most effectively used in *Mrs Dalloway* (1925), a single day in the life of the heroine; the autobiographical *To the Lighthouse* (1927); and the poetic *The Waves* (1931), a series of soliloquies. Her novel *Orlando* (1928) shows an advanced awareness of latent bisexuality in men and women and of women's desire for liberation.

Woolf was married to the publisher Leonard Woolf. Together they set up the Hogarth Press in 1917 and became the centre of the literary and artistic BLOOMSBURY GROUP. With a history of depression and poor health throughout her life, Woolf eventually committed suicide.

WOOL TOWNS

Since the 14th century the LORD CHANCELLOR has sat on the Woolsack in the House of Lords – a square red bag, stuffed with wool, symbolising the source of England's medieval wealth. This came from the vast flocks of sheep that grazed on the Cotswolds and the Lincolnshire Wolds, or on Romney Marsh in Kent and the Fenland of East Anglia. Many places connected with sheep-rearing have names which go back to Saxon times. Sheppey in Kent means 'island of sheep', Shiplake in Oxfordshire means 'stream where sheep were washed', and Shipton, a name found all over England, means 'sheep farm'.

MEDIEVAL MONEY-SPINNER

During the Middle Ages huge quantities of wool were sold to the Continent, and the profits used to build towns such as Saffron Walden in Essex and Stow-on-the-Wold in the Cotswolds, which still has a Sheep Street. Most of these places have fine churches financed by those who excelled in the trade such as William Grevel (died 1401), whose memorial brass in Chipping Campden church dubbs him 'the flower of the wool merchants of all England'.

By the 18th century the wool trade was in decline and sheep were being reared for meat rather than wool to feed the populations of the industrial towns.

WOOL WEALTH Houses of honey-coloured Cotswold stone at Chipping Campden, Gloucestershire, are typical of the substantial architecture of wool towns, endowed by the wool trade of the Middle Ages

BRITAIN'S LIVING FORESTS

The woodland habitat is multi-layered, each level supporting its own ecosystem. All kinds of creatures live in Britain's uniquely varied forests, from badgers and squirrels to the rarer pine marten and capercaillie

AFTER THE last ice age, Britain was covered in a vast primeval forest, traces of which survive in the majestic pinewoods of the Scottish Highlands. Farther south, patches of prehistoric, broad-leaved seminatural woodland can be glimpsed in land avoided by farmers, such as areas of heavy soils or steep slopes.

Today, woodland covers just 10 per cent of the British Isles, but despite their reduction, British woods have a variety and heritage that cannot be matched. Britain boasts some of the oldest trees in Europe, and this unique and valuable resource requires careful management.

Most woodland shows signs of human intervention, sometimes dating back centuries. In the Middle Ages almost every village would have had a wood within the boundaries of its manor, managed by foresters to satisfy the demand for timber, firewood and charcoal.

With growing imports of foreign timber in the 19th century, domestic woodlands became less important and many were built upon. Today, we are coming to see our woodlands as more than a source of timber. They are precious havens where wildlife can thrive undisturbed.

CRESTED TIT *This bird lives on seeds and insects picked from pine trees in the Highlands. The female often excavates a hole in a rotten stump in which to make her nest and is fed throughout the incubation period by her devoted mate*

GREY SQUIRREL *Pinewoods are the natural domain of our native red squirrel, but greys are displacing the reds, especially in plantations. Since their introduction from the USA in the 19th century, greys have gone on to colonise most of Britain. They feed off buds and tree bark and can cause serious damage*

PINE MARTEN *Gamekeepers have hunted pine martens almost to extinction over the past 200 years, even though the eggs they steal are generally those of wild birds. Pine martens also eat small birds, mice, beetles and berries*

PINEWOOD

Today, most of Britain's coniferous woods consist of exotic species such as Norway spruce that have been introduced over the past 300 years as fast-growing timber crops. Monotonous rows of these tall, straight conifers have replaced the graceful Scots pines and birches of the great Caledonian Forest, which until the 18th century carpeted the Highlands of Scotland to 600 m (2000 ft) above sea level.

The felling of trees to fuel iron foundries with charcoal, combined with land clearances, led to the disappearance of huge swathes of virgin pinewood, yet some areas do remain, notably in Scotland's Beinn Eighe, Glen Affric and Glen More.

WOODLAND WILDLIFE

The few remaining natural pinewoods are home to some of Britain's rarest wild animals, such as the pine marten and capercaillie.

The exotic conifers found in plantations support far fewer species, since native wildlife is not adapted to feeding on them. Even so, these areas do play a role by providing valuable shelter for birds and mammals, particularly deer, during winter when the broadleaved woods are bare.

CAPERCAILLIE *This large bird can weigh up to 7 kg (15 lb). Its distinctive 'song' has been described as 'sounding like a rattle, followed by the drawing of a cork and liquid pouring from a bottle before a final knife-grinding noise'*

CANOPY

The topmost leafy branches of the trees provide nesting sites for birds and squirrels. In plantations all the trees are the same age so they are all a similar height. In natural woodland, trees are all different ages and heights. Spaces in the canopy form as old trees die, allowing more light to penetrate

SHRUB LAYER

Saplings, shrubs and the lower branches of mature trees make up this layer. Tree trunks are home to many insect species, such as bark beetles. In deciduous woods ivies may entwine the trees while hazel and bramble flourish. In natural pinewoods, this layer holds juniper and bilberry

FIELD LAYER

Primrose, bluebell and wild garlic thrive in the dappled light of the deciduous woodland floor. Pinewoods – especially plantations – are so densely packed and dark that there is little vegetation in this layer apart from bracken and ferns

GROUND LAYER

The fallen needles and leaves that cover the ground provide shelter for invertebrates, such as wood ants, beetles and slugs. Fungi, such as fly agaric in pinewoods and ceps in broadleaved woods, feed on decaying matter. Mosses and lichens grow over roots and fallen branches

BROADLEAVED WOODLAND

Mixed woodlands of native oak, ash, beech, elm, hornbeam, holly, lime and hazel are found throughout lowland Britain. These broadleaved trees support a greater diversity of wildlife and plants than any other habitat in the world outside the tropics.

In some areas a single tree species predominates, depending on the soil and climate as well as the activities of humans. Beech, for example, is a timber crop and has been widely cultivated.

PRESERVING ANCIENT FORESTS

Because broadleaved woods, unlike pine forests, have continued to be planted and maintained, large areas of pristine woodland still exist in Epping Forest, Wyre Forest, Savernake Forest and Sherwood Forest.

Even so, the decline in woodmanship over the past century has allowed aggressive species such as sycamore to intrude in many places. The Forestry Commission and the National Trust are working to reverse the decades of neglect with schemes to bring back traditional techniques such as coppicing, and to balance commercial, ecological and leisure needs.

TAWNY OWL *The most common owl in Britain, the tawny is the deadliest of woodland hunters thanks to its keen eyesight, hearing and silent flight. Beetles, mice and small birds are all acceptable food*

LESSER SPOTTED WOODPECKER *A tiny, secretive bird that is found only in deciduous woodland, its presence is indicated by the hammering of beak on wood as it chisels away chips of bark to reach grubs and insects with its long tongue*

ROE DEER *These delicate creatures are known as 'Fairies of the Woods' from the way they flit, silent and half seen, between the trees. Their taste for tender saplings makes them a woodland pest*

BADGER *The elaborate burrows or 'setts' built by badgers can be occupied by several families. Extended and re-excavated over generations, they develop into a maze of tunnels 300 m (1000 ft) or more long and with a dozen exits*

WORCESTER

• **Worcestershire (p.494 E3)**   • **Pop. 82 660**
The Civil War ended in 1651 with the Battle of Worcester. Its support for the Royalists earned Worcester, then one of England's largest towns, the motto *Civitas fidelis*: the faithful city. A figure of Cromwell is nailed by his ears at the entrance to the 18th-century guildhall.

A 7th-century cathedral was replaced in 1084 by Bishop Wulfstan. The current building contains the tomb of King John and, in turn with Gloucester and Hereford, hosts the annual THREE CHOIRS FESTIVAL.

Local industries have included the making of gloves and porcelain but

SPORTING SCENERY Worcester cathedral, with its 14th-century tower, is a familiar sight to cricket lovers. It adorns the county ground, which is regarded as one of the loveliest in England

the best-known export is the piquant mixture of soy sauce, vinegar and spices known as Worcestershire sauce. The secret concoction based on an Indian recipe was first made during the 1830s by two local chemists, John Wheeley Lee and William Perrins.

Worcester is home also to the world's oldest surviving newspaper, the *Berrow's Journal*, first published in 1690, and Royal Worcester Porcelain, established in 1751 – the oldest company still making porcelain in England. The composer Edward ELGAR was born nearby and lived in the area for much of his life.

William WORDSWORTH

• **Poet**   • **1770-1850; poet laureate 1843**
The landscape and plain-spoken people of his native Lake District inspired William Wordsworth throughout his life. He grew up in Cumbria and returned there in 1799 with his sister Dorothy, also a writer, to live at Dove Cottage in Grasmere. The peace and calm of the country life compared with the stresses

of the city is a recurring theme in his poetry. During the social unrest in Europe sparked by the French Revolution his affinity with the common man led him to support the revolutionaries.

In his preface to the second edition of *Lyrical Ballads* (1800), which he wrote with his friend Samuel Taylor COLERIDGE Wordsworth called for poetry to reflect the language of everyday speech. He contributed to the collection poems such as 'The Idiot Boy' that some critics regarded as banal, while Coleridge developed supernatural themes, most famously in the 'Ancient Mariner'.

Wordsworth's masterpiece is the long poem *The Prelude*, completed in 1805 but not published until 1850, after the poet's death. It was intended as a preface to an autobiographical poem that was never completed and relates his poetic development in intensely introspective and lyrical style.

WORKHOUSES

The POOR LAW of 1601 placed the duty for the care of the needy into the hands of the PARISH. Alms were dispensed to those who needed them in their own homes and shelter offered to the homeless. The able-bodied homeless worked for their keep in workhouses. Vagrants who refused to work were sent to houses of correction.

Under the Poor Law Amendment Act of 1834, groups of parishes, known as Unions, were required to provide a workhouse as the only form of poor relief. The act reflected the view that poverty was avoidable and should not be indulged, and stipulated that conditions within workhouses should be worse than conditions endured by paid labourers outside. Receiving poor relief was seen as shameful and the prospect of the workhouse instilled fear in even the most wretched.

A PUNISHING REGIME

Inmates were housed according to sex and age, and families were separated. Medical facilities were primitive, living quarters crowded and treatment could be cruel, driving some to begging or prostitution. The social security system, introduced in the early 20th century, put an end to an institution that had come to be seen as inhumane.

WORKING MEN'S CLUBS

Victorian workers regularly toiled 12 hours a day, followed by a drink with their mates in the local working men's club – women strictly not admitted. The middle classes, convinced that drink was the curse of the 'lower orders', tried to take over these institutions and 'improve' the membership by urging temperance upon them. They failed.

Founded in 1862, the Working Men's Clubs and Institutes Union is Britain's largest non-profit-making entertainment organisation, with 3000 affiliated clubs. Although no longer exclusively open to 'working men' – women were first admitted in the 1930s – Britain's social clubs still offer the traditional games of cribbage, darts, dominoes and snooker. The 'club circuit' is also a notoriously tough training ground for would-be comedians and musicians.

WORLD CUP 1966

No year is etched more indelibly in the minds of England FOOTBALL fans than 1966. On June 30, the national team beat West Germany 4-2 in the World Cup final at Wembley Stadium. It was the first time the tournament had been won by the founders of the game. Three months before the final the Jules Rimet trophy had been stolen and held for ransom. A dog called Pickles found the cup a fortnight later in a south London garden.

LOCAL HEROES

England played all their matches at Wembley, with the enthusiastic support of home crowds. The goalkeeper, Gordon Banks, and captain Bobby MOORE – voted the player of the tournament – were staunch in defence; Bobby CHARLTON dazzled in attack.

When the team reached the final the nation was gripped: millions watched the game live on television and 100 000 were in the stadium. Geoff Hurst's three goals constituted the first and only hat-trick to date in a World Cup final.

ENGLAND'S WINNING TEAM

Gordon Banks Leicester City
George Cohen Fulham
Ray Wilson Huddersfield Town
Nobby Stiles Manchester United
Jack Charlton Leeds United
Bobby Moore West Ham United
Alan Ball Blackpool
Roger Hunt Liverpool
Bobby Charlton Manchester United
Geoff Hurst West Ham United
Martin Peters West Ham United

WORLD SERVICE

'When I come home', wrote a listener to the BBC Russian service during the Cold War, 'I open the window to receive oxygen for my lungs and turn on the BBC for oxygen for my mind.' For more than 143 million people in 130 countries the World Service still represents unbiased reporting on news and current affairs in one of 43 languages.

During the Second World War, the BBC's call sign, the Morse code 'V' for victory, was a signal for many in Nazi-occupied Europe that freedom was not dead. The service sometimes transmitted code messages, such as two quotations from the poet Verlaine broadcast on June 1, 1944, to alert the French Resistance that invasion was imminent.

The World Service evolved out of the Empire Service, which went on the air in December 1932, and it is still funded by the Foreign Office, not the licence fee. It is no longer just a radio service but broadcasts television news via satellite and provides hourly news bulletins on the World Wide Web.

Christopher WREN: *see page 486*

John WYCLIFFE

• **Religious reformer** • **c.1328-84**

The Oxford academic and priest John Wycliffe published radical attacks on church doctrines and practices, for which he was denounced by Pope Gregory XI in 1377. And yet he survived, protected by the patronage of John of Gaunt, son of Edward III.

Wycliffe believed the pope could not claim authority from scripture, and was highly critical of the religious orders, such as monks and friars. He got into deeper trouble when in 1381 he questioned the Catholic doctrine of transubstantiation – the belief that the bread and wine of the mass became the body and blood of Christ.

Wycliffe asserted each person's right to study the BIBLE, which was then only

BEND IN THE RIVER Below Symond's Yat Rock, a 122 m (400 ft) cliff near Monmouth, the meandering River Wye flows towards Goodrich. Five miles on it loops back to within half a mile of the same point

available in Latin, and is said to have made its first translation into English. In 1415 Wycliffe was condemned as a heretic and in 1428 his remains were dug up and burnt.

River WYE

• **S Wales and Herefordshire (p.494 D3)**

From its source on Mount Plynlimon in Wales, the River Wye winds 130 miles through the book-buyer's Mecca, Hay, then Hereford, Ross and Monmouth to join the Severn Estuary near Chepstow. At Symond's Yat the river flows below cliffs of 450 million-year-old sandstone.

For most of its route, the river is surrounded by rich farmland, with cider-apple orchards in Herefordshire and the sloping woodlands of the Forest of Dean. The final stretch, below Monmouth, passes the haunting shell of Tintern Abbey and the barbican of Chepstow Castle. Varying from rapids to slow meanders, the Wye is one of Britain's most popular fishing and canoeing rivers, offering all grades of challenge.

ONE MAN'S SKYLINE

The Great Fire of 1666 swept away medieval London, destroying St Paul's Cathedral and 87 other churches. The task of constructing a new city fell to Christopher Wren, a distinguished mathematician who had only recently begun to design buildings. His work over the next 50 years made him Britain's greatest architect

PRAISED BY Isaac Newton as one of the 'leading geometers of this age', a professor of astronomy by the age of 25, co-founder of the Royal Society and twice a member of parliament – these achievements alone would earn Christopher Wren (1632-1723) a place in history. Yet it was as an architect that he towered above his peers for 50 years. No other person has had such a defining effect upon the fabric of the capital.

BOLD BEGINNINGS

Wren's first foray into architecture came almost casually in 1663 when his uncle, the bishop of Ely, asked him to apply his scientific mind to the task of creating a classical temple for Pembroke College, Cambridge. At about the same time Wren designed his first major building, the Sheldonian Theatre in Oxford, based on a Roman theatre. The wide flat ceiling below its skilfully constructed roof was painted to mimic the open sky.

Wren spent several months in Paris studying buildings in the newly fashionable neoclassical style, which was still little known in England. He was subsequently invited – in competition with four other architects – to devise plans to restore the medieval cathedral of St Paul's, ravaged by Cromwell's soldiers during the Civil War of 1642-51. His ambitious proposal included restyling the building along classical lines and the addition of a large dome. It was accepted by Charles II in 1666, shortly before the FIRE OF LONDON consumed most of the City – furnishing Wren with an even greater opportunity to display his architectural skills.

FROM THE ASHES

Although Wren's redevelopment plan for London, with Continental piazzas and avenues, was rejected, the immense task of constructing St Paul's remained.

Parliament raised funds by taxing coal from 1667, and Wren, who has been knighted in 1672, submitted proposals in 1673 that greatly pleased the king. In 1675 work finally began on St Paul's.

At the same time as he worked on the cathedral, Wren supervised the rebuilding of more than 50 churches, designing about 25 of them himself. Their exteriors, built too close to neighbouring houses to be seen properly, are generally plain, but the upper parts amply demonstrate his gift for versatility and architectural invention. Medieval London had been dominated by Gothic church

SIR CHRISTOPHER WREN in 1711, the year after the dome of St Paul's was completed

STEEPLE ORNAMENT Corner pieces of lively scrollwork topped by urns rise up from the steeple's square belfry tower and carry the eye to the 12 columned rotunda above

HIGH WINDS weather van[e] in the shape a dragon sits on a copper ball above a[n] obelisk spire to complete the 68 m (222 ft) high steeple

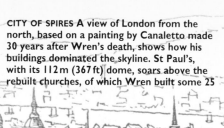

CITY OF SPIRES A view of London from the north, based on a painting by Canaletto made 30 years after Wren's death, shows how his buildings dominated the skyline. St Paul's, with its 112 m (367 ft) dome, soars above the rebuilt churches, of which Wren built some 25

MAKING A CLASSICAL STEEPLE Before Wren, no one had thought of making a traditional church steeple with elements of classical architecture. St Mary-le-Bow (1680) was his first experiment with the style

ROYAL VISTA Wren's 1695 design for the Royal Naval Hospital in Greenwich would have obscured the Queen's House, built by Inigo Jones as the centrepiece of a royal palace. The existing version preserves the view

spires, and Wren set out to reinvent this traditional form in the new style. He replaced the solid spire with a series of diminishing tiers, each richly ornamented with classical detail.

NEW HOME FOR BOW BELLS

At St Mary-le-Bow, Ionic pilasters adorn the bell-stage of the tower. Above them a balustraded platform is completed at each corner by classical urns that recall the pinnacles of the medieval church. The next stage is composed of a rotunda of extravagant Corinthian columns that support a cluster of buttress-like arches, another hint of the old church. At the top is a lantern surrounded by yet more columns, culminating in an obelisk.

The entire ensemble, which must have looked bizarre to those who first saw it, is now recognised as one of Wren's finest steeples, displaying his command of engineering, geometric proportion and stylistic harmony.

The interiors of Wren's churches resembled more closely the basilicas of ancient Rome than the narrow Catholic churches they replaced. Their focus had shifted from the mysteries

LOOKING BACK In 1682 Wren designed Tom Tower, the entrance to the Great Quadrangle at Christ Church, Oxford, in Gothic style to blend with Cardinal Wolsey's college buildings

of the altar to the words of the pulpit. Most interiors were richly decorated with classical motifs in wood and plaster created by the finest craftsmen of the day, such as Grinling GIBBONS.

Apart from his masterpieces, St Paul's, and the surrounding churches, Wren's position as court architect involved him in many of the grandest projects of the reigns of five monarchs. They included hospitals for the army at Chelsea and the navy at Greenwich, a major extension of Hampton Court Palace, and additions to colleges at Oxford and Cambridge. So influential was his adaptation of classical architecture to British tastes that he set the style of public building until the emergence of Victorian Gothic.

MONUMENT TO GENIUS Wren's dream of giving London a dome to rival St Peter's in Rome drew on engineering as well as architectural expertise. A brick cone was built inside the outer dome (34 m/112 ft across) to disperse the weight of the 850 ton lantern topping the dome

A TALE OF TWO CHURCHES

Wren's classical vision for the new St Paul's clashed with the preferences of his ecclesiastical patrons, who wanted a traditional cruciform plan (shaped like a cross, with a long nave and choir, and two equal transepts).

Wren was forced to compromise, but exploited a clause in the contract allowing for alterations to the accepted plan 'more ornamental than structural'. With the strong support of Charles II, a puny dome topped by a spindly spire evolved into today's familiar broad dome above the transept, dividing the nave (right) and chancel into equal lengths.

Wren took 35 years to complete his cathedral, and at his death was one of the first people to be buried in it. His tomb is marked with a simple Latin inscription: 'Reader, if you seek a monument, look around you.'

YEOMEN OF THE GUARD

• Founded 1485

The oldest military corps in Britain, the Yeomen of the Guard were created by Henry VII. They were recruited from the lesser landowning classes to serve as royal bodyguards.

Today their role is more symbolic, and they form a colourful presence at state occasions such as the opening of parliament, which they attend clad in the distinctive uniform of scarlet doublet, breeches and black velvet hat.

The captain is appointed by the government; officer posts are held by retired army officers; and the 81 Yeomen

are former warrant officers and NCOs from the army, marines and air force. They should not be confused with the Yeomen Warders (BEEFEATERS), whose role is to guard the Tower of London.

LIVING ARMOURY Yew trees were a source of wood for medieval longbows. Yews were planted in churchyards as a symbol of the Resurrection and to protect cattle from their poisonous roots

YEW

Growing midnight black in many a churchyard, the common yew (*Taxus baccata*) is Britain's most mysterious tree. One of three native conifers (juniper and Scots pine are the others), slow-growing yews are among our oldest trees – some grand examples are thought to be more than 1000 years old.

Yew wood, hard and dense, has many uses, including furniture-making. Most notably, it was carved into the LONGBOW, a masterpiece of medieval weaponry.

Yew's magical associations are strong, as the witches in Shakespeare's *Macbeth* knew, adding to their cauldron 'slips of yew sliver'd in the moon's eclipse'. But above all, yew is associated with death. 'My shroud of white, stuck all with yew/ O! prepare it!' sang Viola in *Twelfth Night*, and although shrouds are seldom stuck with yew today, it is still used in funeral wreaths. More positively, yew was found in 1981 to produce an alkaloid that can be used to fight ovarian cancer.

YORK

• N England (p.496 C4)   • Pop. 124 610

Situated on the River Ouse in North Yorkshire, the city of York was known as Eboracum to the Romans and Jorvik to the Vikings. It is surrounded by a 3 mile long medieval wall and the centre still has a medieval street layout, overhung by half-timbered houses. In the Middle Ages, York was the capital of northern England and an important religious centre.

The city's crowning glory is York Minster, the largest medieval church in northern Europe. The building of the cathedral – the fourth to

occupy the site – began in 1220 and continued for more than 250 years. Its magnificent 14th-century stained-glass windows survived a fire in 1984 that badly damaged the roof.

York has a modern university. Among its many museums, the National Railway Museum reflects the importance of York as a railway centre in the 19th century. The Jorvik Viking Festival, which includes longship races, is held annually in February. York is noted also for its production of chocolates and other confectionery.

ACT OF GOD The fire in 1984 followed a £2 million restoration project to strengthen York Minster's foundations. The cathedral's crowning glory is its central 60 m (198 ft) high lantern tower, the tallest in England

House of YORK

• English royal house   • 1461-85

The first Yorkist king was EDWARD IV, great-grandson of Edmund Langley, duke of York, the third of Edward III's sons. Both Edward and the king whom he deposed, the Lancastrian HENRY VI, were descended from sons of Edward III, and it was their bitter rivalry that gave rise to the WARS OF THE ROSES.

Second of the Yorkist kings was EDWARD V, elder son of Edward IV and the queen he had married secretly, Elizabeth Woodville. Edward IV's younger brother Richard, duke of Gloucester, seized power in 1483 and declared the marriage invalid and Edward's sons illegitimate. The 12-year-old Edward V and his younger brother – the PRINCES IN THE TOWER – vanished, and the duke of Gloucester was proclaimed RICHARD III.

Richard died at the hands of a rival from the House of LANCASTER, Henry Tudor, at the Battle of BOSWORTH in 1485. Henry was crowned HENRY VII, marking the end of the House of York and the start of the House of TUDOR.

John Zachary YOUNG

• Zoologist • 1907-97

The Anatomy of the Nervous System of Octopus vulgaris is one of several books that Young published in a life devoted to the study of cephalopods – squids and octopuses – from which he made a major contribution to the understanding of animal and human brains.

Young also wrote other masterly texts about the human and animal worlds, including *The Life of Vertebrates* (1951), *The Life of Mammals* (1957) and *An Introduction to the Study of Man* (1971).

Thomas YOUNG

• Physicist • 1773-1829

An infant prodigy who was reading at the age of two, Thomas Young was the first to demonstrate the wave nature of light. His findings were greeted with scepticism because they contradicted Isaac NEWTON, who had declared light to be made up of particles. Today it is known that light has the properties both of waves and particles.

Young was a physician. He was the first to describe several faults of vision, including astigmatism. He made important discoveries in elasticity, and from 1815 concentrated on Egyptology. He established the hieroglyphic vocabulary, beginning with his work on deciphering the Rosetta stone.

WAR CRIES **In one of the dramas of the Zulu War, 139 British soldiers repulsed six attacks from a 4000-strong Zulu force in one night on their garrison at Rorke's Drift in 1879**

ZOOS

Zoos no longer keep animals simply to entertain, but to educate and help to protect endangered species by running breeding programmes.

London Zoo (1828) Endangered species in its breeding programmes include the Mexican bird-eating spider

Bristol Zoo Gardens (1836) More than 80 conservation breeding programmes, are conducted, especially of raptors

Edinburgh Zoo (1913) Europe's largest colony of penguins and rare cold-climate mammals are bred there

Chester Zoo (1931) Among its 5000 animals the zoo has Europe's biggest colony of chimpanzees

Whipsnade Zoo (1931) This outstation of London Zoo specialises in breeding endangered rhinos and hippos

Jersey Zoo (1959) Founded by Gerald Durrell, the zoo aims to save the world's rarest species from extinction

Twycross Zoo Park (1963) In 20 ha (50 acres) of parkland, the zoo specialises in conserving endangered primates

Longleat (1966) The first drive-through safari park outside Africa is set in the estate of the 7th marquess of Bath

Woburn Safari Park (1970) Exotic animals, such as Bengal tigers, rhesus monkeys and black bears, roam free

Knowsley Safari Park (1971) The safari-style habitat contains white rhinoceros, buffalo, cheetahs and antelopes

Highland Wildlife Park (1986) Species native to Scotland are bred, including bison, bears, wolves and red deer

ZULU WAR

• 1879

Britain's attempt to gain control over southern Africa in the late 19th century met with strong resistance from the Zulus. At the battle of Isandhlwana 20 000 Zulus, with amazing speed and secrecy, attacked and decimated a British force of 1200 men.

The war arose after Britain annexed the South African republic of Transvaal in April 1877, and inherited the border disputes between the Boers (Dutch farmer settlers) and the Zulu nation.

Zulu warriors, of whom their king, Cetshwayo, had 40 000, were brave, professional fighters, but ultimately they were no match for the disciplined firepower of British troops. At the Battle of Nkambule some 2000 warriors fell to a British army that lost only 18 men. Cetshwayo fled the field and the Zulus surrendered in July 1879.

ANIMAL MAGIC **Gerald Durrell, founder of Jersey Zoo, fell in love with animals when living on the Greek island of Corfu as a child. In** *My Family and Other Animals* **(1956) he vividly evokes his island life**

Whig	Conservative
Tory	Labour
Coalition	Liberal

BRITISH PRIME MINISTERS

1721-42	Robert Walpole
1742-3	Earl of Wilmington
1743-54	Henry Pelham
1754-6	Duke of Newcastle
1756-7	Duke of Devonshire
1757-62	Duke of Newcastle
1762-3	Earl of Bute
1763-5	George Grenville
1765-6	Marquis of Rockingham
1766-8	Pitt the Elder, Earl of Chatham
1768-70	Duke of Grafton
1770-82	Lord North
1782	Marquis of Rockingham
1782-3	Earl of Shelburne
1783	Duke of Portland
1783-1801	Pitt the Younger
1801-4	Henry Addington
1804-6	Pitt the Younger
1806-7	Lord William Grenville
1807-9	Duke of Portland
1809-12	Spencer Perceval
1812-27	Earl of Liverpool
1827	George Canning
1827-8	Viscount Goderich
1828-30	Duke of Wellington
1830-4	Earl Grey
1834	Viscount Melbourne
1834	Duke of Wellington
1834-5	Robert Peel
1835-41	Viscount Melbourne
1841-6	Robert Peel
1846-52	Lord John Russell
1852	Earl of Derby
1852-5	Earl of Aberdeen
1855-8	Viscount Palmerston
1858-9	Earl of Derby
1859-65	Viscount Palmerston
1865-6	Earl Russell

1866-8	Earl of Derby
1868	Benjamin Disraeli
1868-74	William Gladstone
1874-80	Benjamin Disraeli
1880-5	William Gladstone
1885-6	Marquis of Salisbury
1886	William Gladstone
1886-92	Marquis of Salisbury
1892-4	William Gladstone
1894-5	Earl of Rosebery
1895-1902	Marquis of Salisbury
1902-5	A.J. Balfour
1905-8	H. Campbell-Bannerman
1908-16	Herbert Asquith
1916-22	David Lloyd George
1922-3	Andrew Bonar Law
1923-4	Stanley Baldwin
1924	Ramsay MacDonald
1924-9	Stanley Baldwin
1929-35	Ramsay MacDonald
1935-7	Stanley Baldwin
1937-40	Neville Chamberlain
1940-5	Winston Churchill
1945-51	Clement Attlee
1951-5	Winston Churchill
1955-7	Anthony Eden
1957-63	Harold Macmillan
1963-4	Alec Douglas-Home
1964-70	Harold Wilson
1970-4	Edward Heath
1974-6	Harold Wilson
1976-9	James Callaghan
1979-90	Margaret Thatcher
1990-7	John Major
1997-	Tony Blair

PREMIER GOVERNOR Walpole became the first 'prime minister' when he took over the day-to-day running of the country from George I, who had little interest in the issues of domestic politics

PAY AS YOU EARN In 1799, William Pitt, Britain's youngest prime minister ever, introduced income tax to fund a war with France. He never intended the tax to last

A SOFTER SIDE Wellington famously defeated Napoleon at Waterloo but hated the brutality of war. In 1829 he broadened religious tolerance in Britain by granting full emancipation to Catholics

EARLY REFORMER Grey's government passed the 1832 Reform Act, which abolished corrupt 'rotten boroughs' and increased the number of people in Britain eligible to vote by 50 per cent

When the first Reform Act was passed in 1832, under Earl Grey, the electorate of Scotland rose from 5000 to 65 000

SOCIAL CONSCIENCE Disraeli legislated to clear slums, improve factory conditions and reform trade unions. He also wrote novels, such as *Sybil*, which reflected his concern with social reform

EDUCATION FOR ALL Balfour introduced free secondary education, including state funded grammar school

LABOUR LEADER The first Labour prime minister was James Ramsay MacDonald. During his second term in power, from 1929 to 1935, nine members of the Cabinet resigned over his proposals to reduce unemployment benefit

CARING STATE The welfare state, created under Clement Attlee, promised medical care and social support for all

ECONOMIC CRISIS Escalating inflation led Edward Heath to freeze workers' wages in 1973. Miners walked out in protest and a three-day week was introduced to conserve coal

MILK SNATCHER In her first government post, as minister for education, Margaret Thatcher controversially withdrew free milk from schools. She went on to become Britain's first woman prime minister and the longest-serving premier of the 20th century

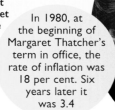

In 1980, at the beginning of Margaret Thatcher's term in office, the rate of inflation was 18 per cent. Six years later it was 3.4

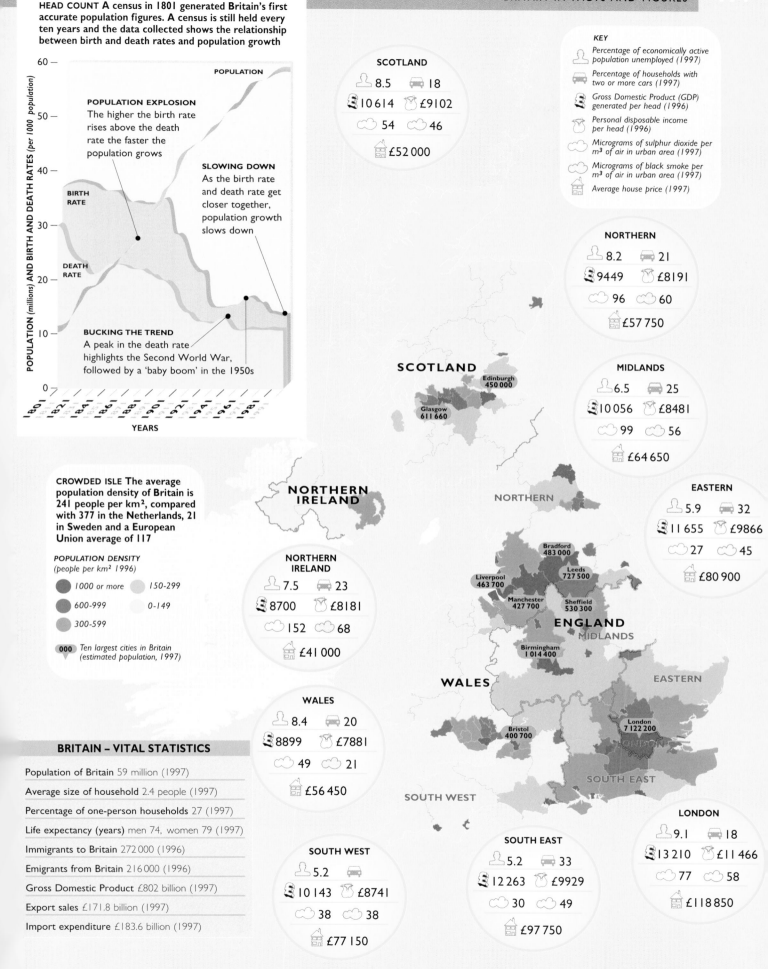

HEAD COUNT A census in 1801 generated Britain's first accurate population figures. A census is still held every ten years and the data collected shows the relationship between birth and death rates and population growth

POPULATION (millions) AND BIRTH AND DEATH RATES (per 1000 population)

POPULATION

POPULATION EXPLOSION
The higher the birth rate rises above the death rate the faster the population grows

SLOWING DOWN
As the birth rate and death rate get closer together, population growth slows down

BIRTH RATE

DEATH RATE

BUCKING THE TREND
A peak in the death rate highlights the Second World War, followed by a 'baby boom' in the 1950s

YEARS

KEY

Percentage of economically active population unemployed (1997)

Percentage of households with two or more cars (1997)

Gross Domestic Product (GDP) generated per head (1996)

Personal disposable income per head (1996)

Micrograms of sulphur dioxide per m³ of air in urban area (1997)

Micrograms of black smoke per m³ of air in urban area (1997)

Average house price (1997)

SCOTLAND
8.5 | 18
£10614 | £9102
54 | 46
£52 000

NORTHERN
8.2 | 21
9449 | £8191
96 | 60
£57 750

MIDLANDS
6.5 | 25
10 056 | £8481
99 | 56
£64 650

EASTERN
5.9 | 32
11 655 | £9866
27 | 45
£80 900

SCOTLAND

Edinburgh 450 000

Glasgow 611 660

NORTHERN IRELAND

NORTHERN

Bradford 483 000

Leeds 727 500

Liverpool 463 700

Manchester 427 700

Sheffield 530 300

ENGLAND
MIDLANDS

Birmingham 1 014 400

WALES

EASTERN

Bristol 400 700

London 7 122 200

SOUTH EAST

SOUTH WEST

CROWDED ISLE The average population density of Britain is 241 people per km², compared with 377 in the Netherlands, 21 in Sweden and a European Union average of 117

POPULATION DENSITY (people per km² 1996)

- 1000 or more
- 600-999
- 300-599
- 150-299
- 0-149

000 Ten largest cities in Britain (estimated population, 1997)

NORTHERN IRELAND
7.5 | 23
8700 | £8181
152 | 68
£41 000

WALES
8.4 | 20
8899 | £7881
49 | 21
£56 450

BRITAIN – VITAL STATISTICS

Population of Britain 59 million (1997)

Average size of household 2.4 people (1997)

Percentage of one-person households 27 (1997)

Life expectancy (years) men 74, women 79 (1997)

Immigrants to Britain 272 000 (1996)

Emigrants from Britain 216 000 (1996)

Gross Domestic Product £802 billion (1997)

Export sales £171.8 billion (1997)

Import expenditure £183.6 billion (1997)

SOUTH WEST
5.2 |
10 143 | £8741
38 | 38
£77 150

SOUTH EAST
5.2 | 33
12 263 | £9929
30 | 49
£97 750

LONDON
9.1 | 18
13 210 | £11 466
77 | 58
£118 850

ADMINISTRATIVE AREAS OF BRITAIN

GOVERNING THE COUNTRY Britain has two systems of local government. Most of England is governed by county authorities – many of which follow the ancient county boundaries – and these are subdivided into districts. The whole of Northern Ireland is also divided into districts. Wales, Scotland and other areas in England are controlled by unitary authorities, which have no second level.

p.497
p.496
p.494   p.495 □
London pp.498/9

Shetland Islands

Orkney Islands

BRITAIN – VITAL STATISTICS

Length of coastline
3209 miles

Miles of road
229 800 (1997)

Miles of motorway
2019 (1997)

Miles of railway track
20 000 (1997)

Biggest forested area
Kielder Forest, 200 sq miles

Tallest building
One Canada Square, Canary Wharf, London, 240 m (787 ft)

Longest bridge
Humber Bridge, 1410 m (4625 ft)

MAJOR ARTERY Motorways carry 17 per cent of Britain's traffic – 49 billion motorway miles were travelled in 1997

SCOTLAND

Aberdeen

Moray

Aberdeenshire

Angus

Dundee

Fife

East Lothian

Midlothian

Perthshire and Kinross

Scottish Borders

Stirling

9

8

11

10

7

6

5

4

3

2

1

South Lanarkshire

East Ayrshire

Dumfries and Galloway

North Ayrshire

South Ayrshire

Argyll and Bute

Highland

Western Isles

Northumberland

Newcastle upon Tyne

North Tyneside

South Tyneside

NORTHERN

Moyle

Ballymoney

Coleraine

Limavady

Derry

SCOTLAND

1 Inverclyde
2 West Dunbartonshire
3 Refrewshire
4 East Refrewshire
5 Glasgow
6 East Dunbartonshire
7 North Lanarkshire
8 Falkirk
9 Clackmannan
10 West Lothian
11 Edinburgh

NORTHERN IRELAND

12 Newtonabbey
13 Carrickfergus
14 Belfast
15 Castlereagh
16 North Down

ENGLAND

Norfolk

Suffolk

Kent

East Riding of Yorkshire

Kingston upon Hull

North East Lincolnshire

North Lincolnshire

Lincolnshire

Cambridgeshire

Peterborough

Essex

GREATER LONDON

Brighton and Hove

East Sussex

ENGLAND

Rutland

Leicestershire

Leicester

Coventry

Warwickshire Northamptonshire

Bedfordshire

Luton

Milton Keynes

Hertfordshire

Surrey

West Sussex

Isle of Wight

Darlington 17 18

York

North Yorkshire

Bradford Leeds

Calderdale

Wakefield

Kirklees

27

26 28 33 32
22 25 31
19 21 24 30
20 23 29

Barnsley Doncaster

Sheffield Rotherham

Nottinghamshire

Derbyshire

Nottingham

Derby

Stoke-on-Trent

Staffordshire

34 36
35 37 38
39

Buckinghamshire

Oxfordshire

Swindon

Newbury 40
41 42
43 44
45

Hampshire

50

51

Lancashire

Blackpool

Sefton

Liverpool

Wirral

Flintshire

Cheshire

Denbighshire

Wrexham

The Wrekin

Shropshire

Herefordshire

Worcestershire

Gloucestershire

South Gloucestershire

Bristol

Bath and North East Somerset

North Somerset

Wiltshire

Dorset

48 49

Torbay

Cumbria

Conwy

Gwynedd

Powys

Ceredigion

WALES

Monmouthshire

54 56 57
53 55 58
52

Cardiff

Vale of Glamorgan

Bridgend

Somerset

Devon

Plymouth

Isle of Anglesey

Carmarthenshire

Swansea

Pembrokeshire

Cornwall

Ards

Lisburn

Dungannon Craigavon

Armagh Banbridge Down

Newry and Mourne

Fermanagh

Isles of Scilly

ENGLAND
17 Stockton-on-Tees
18 Middlesbrough
19 Knowsley
20 Halton
21 St Helens
22 Wigan
23 Warrington
24 Trafford
25 Salford
26 Bolton
27 Blackburn with Darwen
28 Bury
29 Manchester
30 Stockport
31 Tameside
32 Oldham
33 Rochdale
34 Wolverhampton
35 Dudley
36 Walsall
37 Sandwell
38 Birmingham
39 Solihull
40 Reading
41 Wokingham
42 Bracknell Forest
43 Windsor and Maidenhead
44 Slough
45 Thurrock
46 Medway Towns
47 Southend-on-Sea
48 Poole
49 Bournemouth
50 Southampton
51 Portsmouth

WALES
52 Neath-Port Talbot
53 Rhondda-Cynon-Taff
54 Merthyr Tydfil
55 Caerphilly
56 Blaneau-Gwent
57 Torfaen
58 Newport

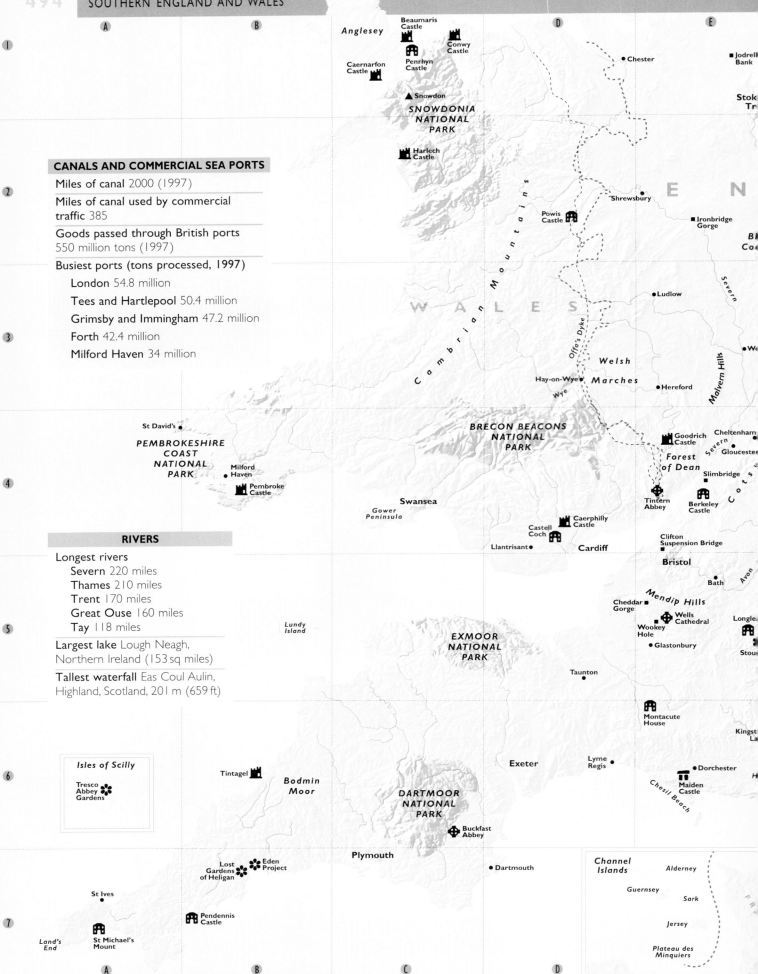

CANALS AND COMMERCIAL SEA PORTS

Miles of canal 2000 (1997)

Miles of canal used by commercial traffic 385

Goods passed through British ports 550 million tons (1997)

Busiest ports (tons processed, 1997)

London 54.8 million

Tees and Hartlepool 50.4 million

Grimsby and Immingham 47.2 million

Forth 42.4 million

Milford Haven 34 million

RIVERS

Longest rivers

Severn 220 miles

Thames 210 miles

Trent 170 miles

Great Ouse 160 miles

Tay 118 miles

Largest lake Lough Neagh, Northern Ireland (153 sq miles)

Tallest waterfall Eas Coul Aulin, Highland, Scotland, 201 m (659 ft)

Isles of Scilly

Tresco Abbey Gardens

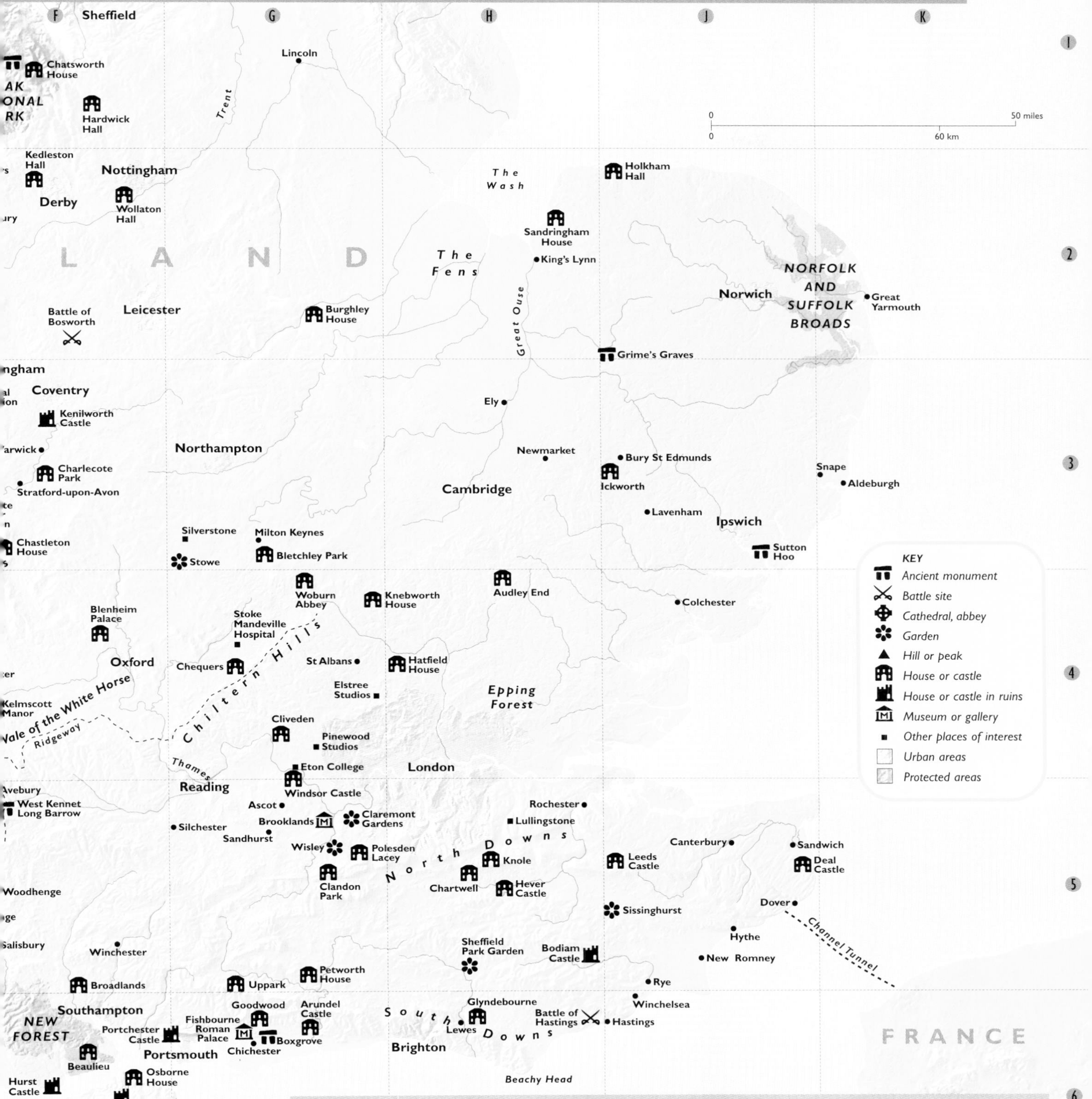

F Sheffield
G
H
J
K

1

Chatsworth House
AK
ONAL
RK
Lincoln

Trent

Hardwick Hall

Kedleston Hall

Nottingham

The Wash

Holkham Hall

50 miles

60 km

2

Derby

Wollaton Hall

L A N D

The Fens

Sandringham House

King's Lynn

Great Ouse

NORFOLK AND SUFFOLK BROADS

Norwich

Great Yarmouth

Battle of Bosworth

Leicester

Burghley House

Grime's Graves

ngham

Coventry

Kenilworth Castle

Northampton

Cambridge

Ely

Newmarket

Bury St Edmunds

Snape

Aldeburgh

3

arwick

Charlecote Park

Stratford-upon-Avon

Ickworth

Lavenham

Ipswich

Chastleton House

Silverstone

Milton Keynes

Stowe

Bletchley Park

Sutton Hoo

Colchester

Woburn Abbey

Knebworth House

Audley End

KEY

Blenheim Palace

Stoke Mandeville Hospital

Ancient monument

Battle site

Oxford

Chequers

Chiltern Hills

St Albans

Hatfield House

Epping Forest

Cathedral, abbey

Garden

4

Kelmscott Manor

Vale of the White Horse

Ridgeway

Elstree Studios

Cliveden

Pinewood Studios

London

Hill or peak

House or castle

House or castle in ruins

Thames

Eton College

Reading

Windsor Castle

Rochester

Museum or gallery

Other places of interest

Avebury

West Kennet Long Barrow

Ascot

Silchester

Sandhurst

Brooklands

Claremont Gardens

Lullingstone

Canterbury

Sandwich

Deal Castle

Urban areas

Protected areas

Woodhenge

Wisley

Polesden Lacey

North Downs

Knole

Leeds Castle

5

age

Clandon Park

Chartwell

Hever Castle

Sissinghurst

Dover

Channel Tunnel

Salisbury

Winchester

Sheffield Park Garden

Bodiam Castle

Hythe

New Romney

Broadlands

Petworth House

Rye

Southampton

Uppark

Goodwood

Arundel Castle

South Downs

Glyndebourne

Battle of Hastings

Winchelsea

Hastings

FRANCE

NEW FOREST

Portchester Castle

Fishbourne Roman Palace

Boxgrove

Lewes

Brighton

Beaulieu

Osborne House

Portsmouth

Chichester

Beachy Head

6

Hurst Castle

emouth

Carisbrooke Castle

Isle of Wight

WORLD HERITAGE SITES

Giant's Causeway and Causeway Coast (est. 1986)

Durham Castle and Cathedral (est. 1986)

Ironbridge Gorge (est. 1986)

Fountains Abbey and Studley Royal Gardens (est. 1986)

Stonehenge, Avebury and associated sites (est. 1986)

Castles and town walls of Edward I in Gwynedd (est. 1986)

St Kilda (est. 1986)

Blenheim Palace (est. 1987)

City of Bath (est. 1987)

Palace of Westminster, Westminster Abbey and St Margaret's Church (est. 1987)

Hadrian's Wall (est. 1987)

Tower of London (est. 1988)

Canterbury Cathedral, St Augustine's Abbey and St Martin's Church (est. 1988)

Old and new towns of Edinburgh (est. 1995)

Maritime Greenwich, London (est. 1997)

7

F
G
H
J
K

MOST VISITED TOURIST ATTRACTIONS
(number of visitors, 1997)

Blackpool Pleasure Beach 7.8 million

British Museum, London 6 million

National Gallery, London 4.8 million

Palace Pier, Brighton 3.5 million

Madame Tussaud's, London 2.8 million

NATIONAL PARKS

Lake District 885 sq miles (est. 1951)

Snowdonia 827 sq miles (est. 1951)

Yorkshire Dales 683 sq miles (est. 1954)

Peak 555 sq miles (est. 1951)

North York Moors 554 sq miles (est. 1952)

Brecon Beacons 519 sq miles (est. 1957)

Northumberland 405 sq miles (est. 1956)

Dartmoor 368 sq miles (est. 1951)

Exmoor 268 sq miles (est. 1954)

Pembrokeshire Coast 226 sq miles (est. 1952)

New Forest 223 sq miles (Heritage area, est. 1994)

Norfolk and Suffolk Broads 117 sq miles (Special protected area, est. 1989)

STILL WATERS At 10½ miles long and a mile wide, Windermere is England's largest lake

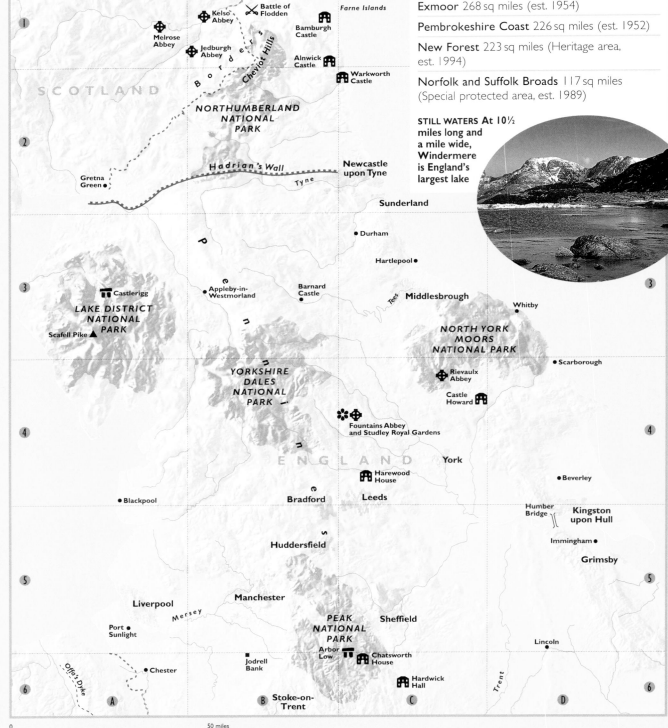

Lindisfarne

Battle of Flodden

Farne Islands

Kelso Abbey

Melrose Abbey

Jedburgh Abbey

Bamburgh Castle

SCOTLAND

B o r d e r s

Cheviot Hills

Alnwick Castle

Warkworth Castle

NORTHUMBERLAND NATIONAL PARK

Hadrian's Wall

Gretna Green

Tyne

Newcastle upon Tyne

Sunderland

Durham

Hartlepool

Castlerigg

LAKE DISTRICT NATIONAL PARK

Scafell Pike

Appleby-in-Westmorland

Barnard Castle

Tees

Middlesbrough

Whitby

NORTH YORK MOORS NATIONAL PARK

Scarborough

YORKSHIRE DALES NATIONAL PARK

Rievaulx Abbey

Castle Howard

Fountains Abbey and Studley Royal Gardens

E N G L A N D

York

Beverley

Harewood House

Blackpool

Bradford

Leeds

Humber Bridge

Kingston upon Hull

Immingham

Huddersfield

Grimsby

Liverpool

Manchester

Mersey

Sheffield

Port Sunlight

PEAK NATIONAL PARK

Lincoln

Arbor Low

Chatsworth House

Jodrell Bank

Chester

Offa's Dyke

Hardwick Hall

Trent

Stoke-on-Trent

0   50 miles

0   60 km

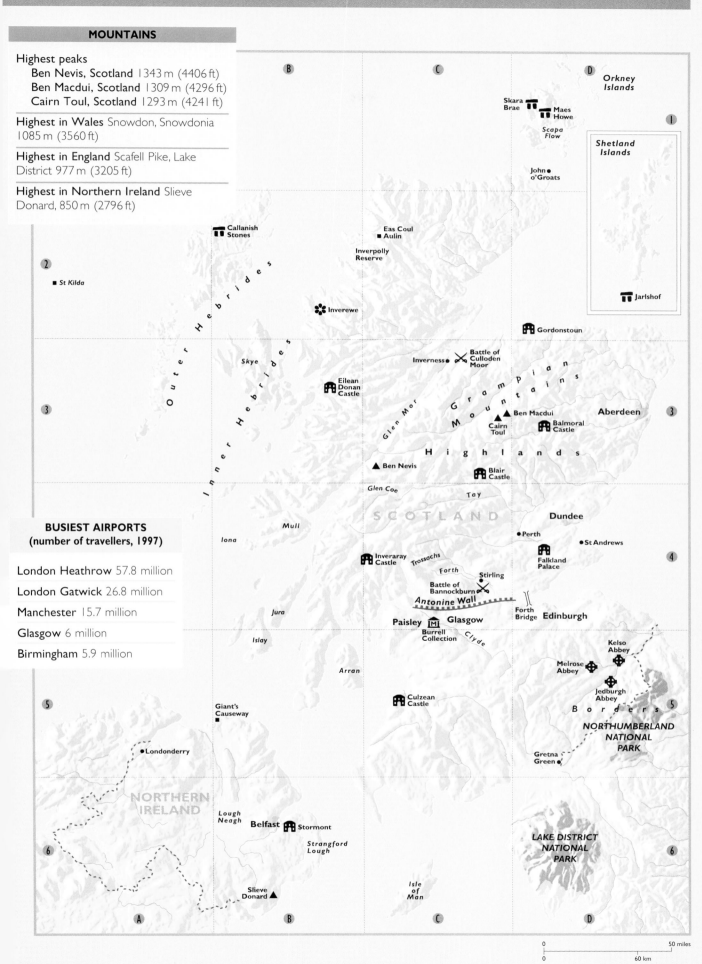

MOUNTAINS

Highest peaks
  Ben Nevis, Scotland 1343 m (4406 ft)
  Ben Macdui, Scotland 1309 m (4296 ft)
  Cairn Toul, Scotland 1293 m (4241 ft)

Highest in Wales Snowdon, Snowdonia
1085 m (3560 ft)

Highest in England Scafell Pike, Lake
District 977 m (3205 ft)

Highest in Northern Ireland Slieve
Donard, 850 m (2796 ft)

BUSIEST AIRPORTS
(number of travellers, 1997)

London Heathrow 57.8 million

London Gatwick 26.8 million

Manchester 15.7 million

Glasgow 6 million

Birmingham 5.9 million

Orkney
Islands

Skara
Brae
Maes
Howe

Scapa
Flow

Shetland
Islands

John
o'Groats

Jarlshof

Callanish
Stones

Eas Coul
Aulin

Inverpolly
Reserve

St Kilda

Inverewe

Gordonstoun

Outer Hebrides

Skye

Battle of
Culloden
Moor

Inverness

Eilean
Donan
Castle

Inner Hebrides

Glen Mor

Grampian Mountains

Ben Macdui

Cairn
Toul

Balmoral
Castle

Aberdeen

H i g h l a n d s

Ben Nevis

Blair
Castle

Glen Coe

Tay

Mull

SCOTLAND

Dundee

Iona

Perth

St Andrews

Inveraray
Castle

Trossachs

Falkland
Palace

Forth

Stirling

Battle of
Bannockburn

Jura

Antonine Wall

Forth
Bridge

Edinburgh

Paisley

Glasgow

Burrell
Collection

Clyde

Islay

Kelso
Abbey

Melrose
Abbey

Arran

Jedburgh
Abbey

Culzean
Castle

B o r d e r s

NORTHUMBERLAND
NATIONAL
PARK

Giant's
Causeway

Gretna
Green

Londonderry

NORTHERN
IRELAND

Lough
Neagh

Belfast

Stormont

LAKE DISTRICT
NATIONAL
PARK

Strangford
Lough

Slieve
Donard

Isle
of
Man

0		50 miles
0		60 km

LONDON – VITAL STATISTICS

Largest borough Bromley, 58.7 sq miles

Smallest borough City of London, 1.9 sq miles

Most densely populated borough Kensington and Chelsea, 5142 people per sq mile (1997)

Least densely populated borough City of London, 731 people per sq mile (1997)

Percentage of one-person households 33.4 (1997)

Gross Domestic Product generated in London £99.9 billion (1995)

Miles of London Underground track 243

Busiest underground station Oxford Circus, 87.8 million passengers (1998)

Longest underground tunnel Northern Line from East Finchley to Morden, 17.3 miles

CITY LIVING Greater London is the most densely populated area in **Britain**, at more than 18 times the national average. Even more people commute in each day to work, and **16.7** per cent of the United Kingdom's Gross Domestic Product is generated in the city

LARGEST ROYAL PARKS

Richmond Park 1012 ha (2500 acres)

Bushy Park 445 ha (1099 acres)

Regent's Park 197 ha (487 acres)

Hyde Park 142 ha (350 acres)

Kensington Gardens 111 ha (275 acres)

MAP A LONDON BOROUGHS

MAP B CENTRAL LONDON

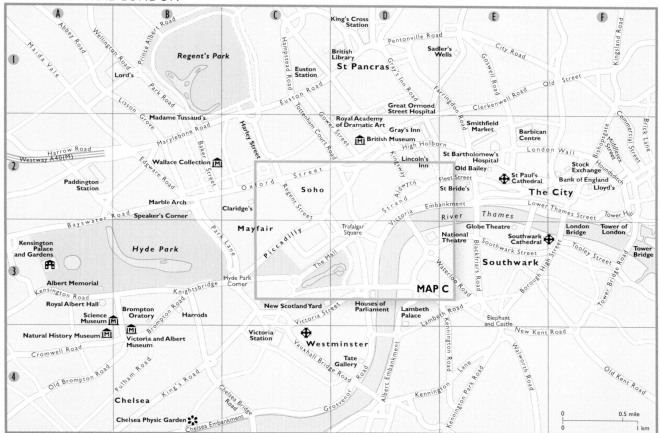

MAP C WEST END

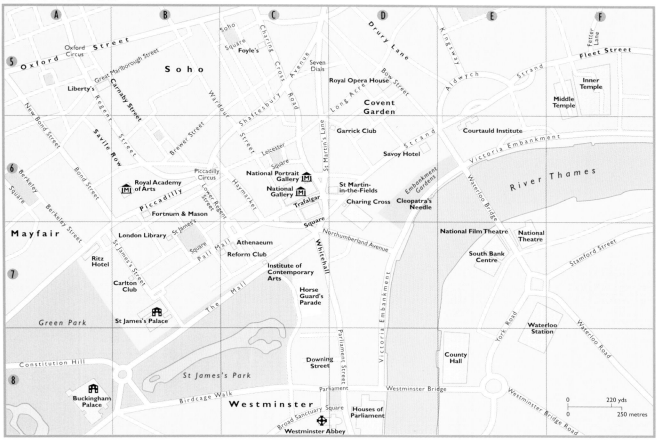

Photographs in ***The Illustrated Encyclopedia of Britain*** came from the following sources; those credited in *italics* are copyright of The Reader's Digest Association Limited. The position of photographs and illustrations on each page is indicated by letters after the page number: **b** bottom; **c** centre; **t** top; **l** left; **r** right. Every effort has been made to trace copyright holders of the illustrations but this has not always been possible. To make a claim, contact the Picture Research Editor, Reader's Digest General Books, 11 Westferry Circus, Canary Wharf, London E14 4HE.

front cover t-b Telegraph Colour Library; Bridgeman Art Library; London/ Museum of London; (castle) Tim Woodcock; Rex Features Ltd • **spine** Allsport UK Ltd • **back cover t-b** Robert Harding/C. Bowman; (gorse) Bruce Coleman Ltd/ Derek Croucher; (angel) The Image Bank/Anthony Edwards; Action Plus/Glyn Kirk **1** The Society of Apothecaries • **2-3** The Scotsman • **4-5** Robert Harding/Raj Kamal • **8** Action Plus/Colin Jarman • **9 tl** Bridgeman Art Library, London/Peter Willi **br** Arcaid/Niall Clutton • **10** National Portrait Gallery, London • **11 t** Hulton Getty Images **c** RAF Museum Hendon **b** London Metropolitan Archives • **12** Ashmolean Museum **b** Aspect/Robin Higginson • **13** Bridgeman Art Library, London/City of Bristol Museum & Art Gallery • **14 tr** Hulton Getty Images **bl** Mick Sharp and Jean Williamson • **15 tr** *White Backgrounds* **c** Robert Harding/Adam Woolfitt **b** Match Angling Plus/Tom Bailey • **16 bl (t)** Permission of the Board of the British Library, London/(Ms. Cot. Tib. BV f.3) **bl (b)** Permission of the Board of the British Library, London/(Ms. Cot. Tib. BV f.6) • **16-17** *Arcand Digital Ltd* • **17** (horn mount) Colour Centre Slides; (king) *Illustrated Arts Ltd*; (pin) Colour Centre Slides; (buckle) Colour Centre Slides; (pommel) Colour Centre Slides **br** *Andrew Thompson* • **18 bl** The Edinburgh Photographic Library/Richard Turpin • **19 t** Ron Arad & Associates **b** BBC • **20 tl** Michael Holford/British Museum **cl** The Board of Trustees of the Royal Armouries/(IV. 470) **c** ©The Trustees of the National Museums of Scotland 1999 **r** Bridgeman Art Library, London/Christie's London **bl** The Board of Trustees of the Royal Armouries/(IV. 174,547) **21** Bridgeman Art Library, London/Musée Conde, Chantilly • **22** Bridgeman Art Library, London/Cheltenham Art Gallery • **23 tl** Hulton Getty Images **br** Hulton Getty Images • **24 tl** Colorsport **b** The John Frost Historical Newspaper Service • **25 tr** Duncan Waldron **bl** Katz Pictures Limited/Alfred Eisenstaedt/LIFE MAGAZINE ©Time Warner Inc. • **26 cl** TRH Pictures **cr** Mike Vines Photo Link **bl** Mike Vines Photo Link • **26-27** Mike Vines Photo Link • **27** (flying boat) Quadrant (Supermarine S6) Aviation Picture Library (Lancaster) Mike Vines Photo Link (Meteor) Mike Vines Photo Link (Comet) Aviation Picture Library (Sea King) Mike Vines Photo Link (Concorde) Telegraph Colour Library • **28** Chorley & Handford Ltd • **29** Marlborough Fine Art (London) Ltd • **30 tl** Hulton Getty Images **r** Permission of the Board of the British Library, London/(Add. Ms. 42130 f.176) • **31** Hulton Getty Images • **32 t** Dee Conway **r** Dominic Photography/Catherine Ashmore **bl** Bill Cooper • **33 t** Network/ Jonathan Olley **b** Popperfoto • **34 tl** Trustees of the British Museum (Natural History) **br** Chamberlain, Powell and Bon/Geremy Butler/Guildhall Library • **35** Barnardos • **36 tr** National Portrait Gallery, London **cl** Robert Harding/ R. Rainford **c** Robert Harding/R. Rainford (map) *Andrew Thompson* • **37 t** NHPA/ Stephen Dalton **b** BBC • **38 t** BBC News & Current Affairs Publicity **b** Images Colour Library • **39** Hulton Getty Images • **40 t** Ken Garland Associates **b** Courtesy of the Trustees of the Victoria and Albert Museum, London • **41** ET Archive, London • **42** (beer glasses) *White Backgrounds* **bl** Archie Miles • **43 tl** Katz Pictures Limited/Mansell/Time inc./Permission of the estate of Max Beerbohm, London Management & Representation Ltd **br** Science Photo Library/Library of Congress • **44** Patricia Macdonald • **45 tl** Permission of the Board of the British Library, London/(Ms. Cott. Vit. A. XV. f.132) **br** Action Plus • **46** The Conde Nast Publications Limited/Sarah Moon ©Vogue • **47 t** Robert Opie **b** Rex Features Ltd • **48 c** *David Ritchie* (background) Aquila Photographics/Hans Gebuil • **49** (map) Mountain High (birds) *David Ritchie* • **50** Dominic Photography • **51 t** Images Colour Library/Charles Walker Collection **r** Robert Harding/Andy Williams • **52** Bridgeman Art Library, London/Fitzwilliam Museum, University of Cambridge • **53 t** National Maritime Museum, London **b** Henry Moore Foundation • **54 tc** Hulton Getty Images **tr** Hodder & Stoughton/from 'Five Run Away Together' by Enid Blyton **c** English Heritage **b** Action Plus/Steve Bardens • **55** Inverness Museum/*Neil Holmes* • **56** Network/Roger Hutchings • **57** London Features International • **58** Mary Evans Picture Library • **59 t** PA News **b** Hulton Getty Images/Bill Brandt • **60 tl** Robert Harding/R. Rainford **b** Robert Harding/Dave Jacobs • **61** Popperfoto • **62 tr** Permission of the Board of the British Library, London **bl** *Andrew Thompson* • **63 cr** AKG London **bl** ©The British Museum • **64 t** National Portrait Gallery, London **b** Popperfoto • **65** Garden Picture Library/John Bethell • **66 tl** Brunel University Library **tc** Brunel University Library **b** Science and Society Picture Library • **67 t** The Royal Collection ©Her Majesty The Queen/Jeremy Whitaker **c** Camera Press/Earl Beesley **b** Frank Spooner/David Gaywood/Gamma • **68** The Kobal Collection • **69 t** The Calouste Gulbenkian Foundation, Lisbon **b** ET Archive, London/Richmond Borough Council • **70** Dee Conway • **71 tl** NHPA/A P Barnes (large blue) Bruce Coleman Ltd/Dennis Green **tr** *Illustrated Arts Ltd* **cl** NHPA/ Michael Leach **c** NHPA/Laurie Campbell **cr** NHPA/A.P. Barnes **bl** NHPA/L. Hugh Newman (caterpillar) NHPA/G.I. Bernard **bc** NHPA/Stephen Dalton **br** NHPA/ Alberto Nardi • **72** Cadbury Limited • **73 tr** Neil Holmes **bl** The John Frost Historical Newspaper Service • **74 tr** Popperfoto **bl** (all) Topham Picture Library • **75 t** Sonia Halliday **b** Det Nationalhistoriske Museum pa Frederiksborg, Hillerod • **76** Skyscan • **76-77** *Ed Stuart (International Artworks)* • **77 tr** Derek Pratt **br** Mary Evans Picture Library • **78 l** Guildhall Library, Corporation of London/Worshipful Company of Playing Card Makers **r** Sporting Pictures (UK) Ltd. • **79 tc** Permission of the Board of the British Library, London/(Ms. Add. 46700 f.18) **tr** Mary Evans Picture Library • **80 tl** The Kobal Collection **bl** Popperfoto • **81 tr** ©Steve Bell **cl** 'Punch' **cr** Matthew Pritchett/Daily Telegraph **bl** Bridgeman Art Library, London/ Guildhall Library, Corporation of London • **82** Tim Woodcock • **83 tr** Popperfoto **cl** AKG London • **84-85** *Ed Stuart (International Artworks)* • **86 tl** National Monuments Record, ©Crown Copyright **tr** Clive Hicks **bl** Angelo Hornak **br** Permission of the Dean and Chapter of Lincoln Cathedral • **86-87** *Ed Stuart (International Artworks)* • **87 tl** National Monuments Record, ©Crown Copyright **tc** Reproduced by kind permission of the Dean and Chapter of York/Jim Kershaw **tr** Michael Holford **tc** Britain On View/Stockwave • **88** Mick Sharp and Jean Williamson • **89 tr** Mick Sharp and Jean Williamson **cr** ©The British Museum **bl** Emilio Segre Visual Archives **bc** Science Photo Library/A. Barrington Brown • **90** QA Photos • **91** ET Archive, London • **92 t** Bridgeman Art Library, London/Bolton Museum and Art Gallery **b** Popperfoto • **93 t** Scottish Tourist Board/S.J. Taylor (rest) The Anthony Blake Photo Library/Milk Marque • **94 t** Network/Homer Sykes **b** Rex Features Ltd/Ashley Coombes • **95** Archie Miles • **96 tr** Images Colour Library **bl** Hulton Getty Images • **97 tr** Courtesy of the Trustees of the Victoria and Albert Museum, London **b** *Digital Wisdom Publishing Ltd* • **98 t** By permission of the Trustees of the Chatsworth Settlement/ Devonshire Collection Chatsworth **b** Mary Evans Picture Library • **99** Popperfoto • **100** Jacqui Hurst • **101 t** Michael Holford/Corinium Museum **b** *Andrew Thompson* • **102 tl** Bridgeman Art Library, London/Imperial Defence College, Camberley **cl** National Portrait Gallery, London **cr** Bridgeman Art Library, London/Private Collection **bc** Images Colour Library **br** By permission of the Earl of Rosebery/ Scottish National Portrait Gallery (map) *Andrew Thompson* • **103 cl** Peter Newark's Pictures **br** Robert Harding • **104 t** Bridgeman Art Library, London/Dreweatt Neate Fine Art Auctioneers, Newbury **b** Mary Evans Picture Library • **105 l** Science Photo Library/NRSC Ltd **tr** *Andrew Thompson* **br** Thanet Times • **106 l** Bridgeman Art Library, London/Bonhams, London **r** Mick Sharp and Jean Williamson • **107 t** *Andrew Thompson* **bl** Topham Picture Library **br** Network/John Sturrock • **108** Lloyd's of London • **109 bl** D.C. Thomson & Co. Ltd./'The Beano' **bc** The John Frost Historical Newspaper Service **br** The John Frost Historical Newspaper Service • **110** (Leno) Hulton Getty Images; (Miller) Popperfoto; (Tate) Hulton Getty Images; (Cooper) BBC; (ITMA) Hulton Getty Images; (Dodd) Popperfoto; (Izzard) David Corio, New York; (Horne) BBC • **111** (Fawlty Towers) BBC; (Only Fools...) BBC; (Dad's Army) BBC; (Rag Trade) BBC; (Hill) The Ronald Grant Archive/Thames Television; (Till Death...) BBC; (Good Life) BBC; (Hancock) Pictorial Press/Polygram; (Emery) BBC; (One Foot...) BBC; (Blackadder) BBC; (Thatcher) Spitting Image; (Everett) BBC; (AbFab) BBC; (Enfield) BBC • **112 t** The Advertising Archives **b** Slide File • **113 t** Courtesy of the Trustees of the Victoria and Albert Museum, London/Habitat Press Office **b** NHPA/David Woodfall • **114** National Gallery of Victoria, Melbourne, Australia/E. Phillips Fox 1865-1915 Australia 'The Landing of Captain Cook at Botany Bay 1770' 1902, oil on canvas, 226 x 194.7 cm, Gilbee Bequest 1902 • **115 t** Allsport UK Ltd **b** Thomas Cook Travel Archive • **116** Bridgeman Art Library, London/Guildhall Library, Corporation of London • **117 t** Christie's Images **b** Hulton Getty Images • **118** Robert Harding/ Ian Griffiths • **119 t** The John Frost Historical Newspaper Service **tr** permission of the Syndics of Cambridge University Library/(Ms. Ee 3.59, f.30) **b** Judges Postcards • **120** PPL Ltd/Barry Pickthall • **121 t** Patrick Eagar **c** Paul Barker **b** Allsport UK Ltd/Adrian Murrell • **122** Tate Gallery, London 1999 • **123 t** Hulton Getty Images **b** Impact/Jeremy Nicholl • **124 tl** Bridgeman Art Library, London/British Library **tr** Bridgeman Art Library, London/British Library **c** Museum of the Order of St. John **b** Michael Holford • **125 t** NHPA/John Buckingham **b** Crown copyright: Public Record Office • **126 t** Scottish Tourist Board **b** Action Plus/Glyn Kirk • **127** from 'Dirty Beasts' by Roald Dahl, Jonathan Cape • **128 tl** Topham Picture Library **tr** Royal College of Art, London • **129 t** Skyscan **b** Imperial War Museum • **130 cl** National Portrait Gallery, London **bc** Hulton Getty Images • **131** Rex Features Ltd/David Hartley • **132 tl** Museum In Docklands, PLA Collection **tc** Popperfoto **tr** Hulton Getty Images **br** Collections • **133** Bridgeman Art Library, London/Private collection • **134** Images Colour Library/CPRE • **135 t** Network/Homer Sykes **b** Christie's Images • **136 tc** The Advertising Archives **tr** Hulton Getty Images • **137** Dyson Appliances • **138** The Kobal Collection • **139 c** Collections/Brian Shuel **b** Ove Arup & Partners/The Eden Project • **140 tr** Rex Features Ltd **cr** Dundee City Council, Arts and Heritage Dept. **bl** Hulton Getty Images • **141** Dean and Chapter of Westminster • **142 tl** The Edinburgh Photographic Library **tr** The Edinburgh Photographic Library **cl** Doug Corrance **bl** The Edinburgh Photographic Library • **142-3** Skyscan • **143 tl** Doug Corrance **tc** Doug Corrance; (juggler) Perfoming Arts Library/ Marcelo Bendahan; (pipers) Rex Features Ltd **bc** Rex Features Ltd • **144 t** Katz Pictures Limited/Life Magazine ©Time Warner Inc./David Scherman **b** Hulton Getty Images • **145** Robert Harding/R. Rainford • **146 bl** Michael Holford/British Museum **br** Michael Holford/British Museum • **147 tr** National Portrait Gallery, London/(detail) **c** The Fotomas Index/By permission of the Marquess of Salisbury

cr by kind permission of the Marquess of Tavistock, and the Trustees of the Bedford Estates **br** Private Collection • **148 tc** British Film Institute **cl** British Film Institute **cr** National Portrait Gallery, London **bl** British Film Institute • **149** Tim Woodcock • **150** (dormouse) NHPA/Stephen Dalton **cl** NHPA/Derek Carp **c** NHPA/Laurie Campbell **cr** NHPA/A.P. Barnes **bl** NHPA/Mike Lane **br** Planet Earth Pictures/Martin Rugner • **151 tl** Bruce Coleman Ltd/Petr Zabransky **cl** NHPA/Manfred Danegger **bl** Bruce Coleman Ltd/Kim Taylor **br** David Hare Photography • **152 r** By kind permission of Historic Scotland **bl** 'Punch' • **153 tl** Mary Evans Picture Library **tr** Hulton Getty Images **br** Allsport UK Ltd/Julian Herbert • **154** Impact/Piers Cavendish • **155 t** National Monuments Record, ©Crown copyright **b** Tim Woodcock • **156-7** Richard and Sally Greenhill • **157 t** Format/Roshini Kempadoo **c** Network/Barry Lewis **b** Collections/Liba Taylor • **158 tr** NHPA/Andy Rouse **bl** Permission of the National Museum of Labour History • **159 t** Collections/Brian Shuel **b** The National Fairground Archive (NFA) • **160 tr** *Andrew Thompson*; (background) Comstock Photofile Limited **b** *Raymond Turvey* • **161 t** Skyscan **cr** *Raymond Turvey* **b** Julian Cotton Picture Library/Jason Hawkes Aerial Collection; (all artwork) *Raymond Turvey* • **162** The National Trust/Charlie Waite • **163 tr** Crown copyright: Public Record Office **c** Hulton Getty Images • **164 bl** Popperfoto **bc** Robert Harding/Adam Woolfitt **br** Camera Press/John Young **b** (background) Mary Quant • **164-5 t** (background) Courtesy of the Trustees of the Victoria and Albert Museum, London/Jean Muir Ltd • **165 tl** Camera Press/Anthony Crickmay **cr** Camera Press/Niall McInerney **bl** The Conde Nast Publications Limited/Henry Clarke ©Vogue **bc** Niall McInerney **br** Camera Press/Ben Coster • **166 tr** The Ronald Grant Archive/20th Century Fox **bl** *Andrew Thompson* • **167 cr** *John Vigurs* **br** Museum of London • **168 tc** Imperial War Museum **tr** Imperial War Museum **br** Imperial War Museum • **169 l** *Illustrated Arts Ltd* **c** *Ian Atkinson* • **170 tl** Hulton Getty Images **br** Andrew Lawson • **171 tr** The National Trust/Vera Collingwood **cl** Painshill Park Trust/Jane Tubbs **cr** Sheila & Oliver Mathews **b** Robert Estall/Donald Buchanan • **172 tc** Allsport UK Ltd **cl** ©Onyx Photos **cl** ©Onyx Photos **bl** Popperfoto • **172-3** Colorsport • **173 tl** Popperfoto; (Francis) Colorsport; (Jennings) Colorsport; (Owen) Colorsport **r** Camera Press/Cecil Beaton • **174** Royal Commission on the Ancient and Historical Monuments of Scotland/Crown Copyright • **175 t** *Neil Holmes* **b** Foster & Partners/Ken Kirkwood • **176 tr** *Andrew Thompson* **cl** Geoscience Features; (fern) Trustees of the British Museum (Natural History) **c** Trustees of the British Museum (Natural History); (urchin) Trustees of the British Museum (Natural History) **cr** Geoscience Features • **177 t** Bridgeman Art Library, London/Private Collection **b** The Freud Museum • **178 tr** Christie's Images **br** ET Archive, London • **178-9** (sofa) *RDPL Iain Stuart* • **179 l** Lovegrove/Jose Lasheras; (lacquering) Christie's Images; (marquetry) Courtesy of the Trustees of the Victoria and Albert Museum, London; (veneer) Bridgeman Art Library, London/Musée des Beaux-Arts, Nantes; (rococo) Bridgeman Art Library, London/Mallet and Son, London; (bamboo) Christie's Images; (Art Deco) Bridgeman Art Library, London/Dan Klein Collection, London **bc (l)** Bridgeman Art Library, London/The Stapleton Collection **bc (r)** Bridgeman Art Library, London/Scottish National Portrait Gallery **br** Ron Arad & Associates • **180 cl** The National Gallery, London **bc** Permission of the Board of the British Library, London/(08275 i 25) • **181 tl** Andrew Lawson **tr** Garden Picture Library/Geoff Dann **b** Garden Picture Library/Erika Craddock • **182 t** Hulton Getty Images **tr** Hulton Getty Images **bl** Allsport UK Ltd/David Cannon • **183** The Royal Collection ©Her Majesty The Queen • **184 t** John Cleare/Mountain Camera **l** John Cleare/Mountain Camera **b** John Cleare/Mountain Camera • **184-5** *Andrew Thompson* • **185 tr** Hulton Getty Images **cl** Geoscience Features **cr** Bridgeman Art Library, London/Imperial War Museum, London **bl** Environmental Images/Jim Hodson • **186 tl** ET Archive, London/V&A Museum **tr** Stapleton Collection/Bridgeman Art Library **cl** Christie's Images **c** *Ed Stuart (International Artworks)* **cr** Edifice **bl** Christie's Images; (background) The National Trust/Jeremy Whitaker • **187 t** 'Punch' **b** Aspect/Gavin Hellier • **188 t** The Raymond Mander & Joe Mitchenson Theatre Collection **bl** Permission of the estate of Eric Gill **bc** Angelo Hornak • **189 t** Bridgeman Art Library, London/Private collection **b** Bridgeman Art Library, London/Private collection • **190 t** Christie's Images **b** Skyscan • **191 tl** Rex Features Ltd/Gill Allen/Times **tc** Bridgeman Art Library, London/Private collection **br** Mick Sharp and Jean Williamson • **192 t** Richard Davies **b** Bridgeman Art Library, London/Guildhall Library, Corporation of London • **193** The Ronald Grant Archive • **194** BBC • **195 t** Bridgeman Art Library, London/Private Collection **b** Mary Evans Picture Library • **196 tl** Angelo Hornak **br** John Freeman • **197 tr** Popperfoto **cr** *Andrew Lawson* **bl** Hulton Getty Images • **198 tr** National Portrait Gallery, London **cr** The Penguin Group **b** Colorsport • **199 tr** Topham Picture Library/Picturepoint **c** Topham Picture Library **bl** Ecclesiastical & Ephemera Picture Library **bc(r)** Archie Miles **bc (l)** Topham Picture Library/Picturepoint **br** Arcaid/Lucinda Lambton • **200 t** ET Archive, London **b** Hulton Getty Images • **201 tr** The John Frost Historical Newspaper Service **cl** Frank Spooner/Gaywood • **202 tl** The Royal Collection ©Her Majesty The Queen/Mark Fiennes **bc** Hulton Getty Images **br** Hulton Getty Images • **203** Jo Reid & John Peck • **204 tr** Rex Features Ltd/SIPA **bl** Museum of London/By permission of the Worshipful Company of Framework Knitters • **205 t** Bridgeman Art Library, London **b** Norman Thelwell • **206 tr** Dominic Photography **cl** English Heritage/Jeremy Richards **cr** English Heritage /Corbridge Museum **bc** Mick Sharp and Jean Williamson **br** The National Trust/Charlie Waite • **206-7** *Andrew Thompson* • **207 tr** Science Photo Library/ Ronald Royer **cr** Mick Sharp and Jean Williamson; (lion) English Heritage **bl** The National Trust/Andy Williams **br** Mick Sharp and Jean Williamson • **208 bl** Courtesy of the Trustees of the Victoria and Albert Museum, London **bc** Courtesy of the Trustees of the Victoria and Albert Museum, London • **208-9** The National Trust/Bill Batten • **209** National Portrait Gallery, London • **210 tl** Permission of the Board of the British Library, London/(Man: R. M. 20.E.9. F.91v) **tc** National Portrait Gallery, London **br** Hulton Getty Images • **211** Skyscan • **212** Harrods • **212-13** Michael Holford/Musée de Bayeux • **213 l** Mary Evans Picture Library **r** Archie Miles • **214 c** London Metropolitan Archives **r** National Portrait Gallery, London • **215** *Eric Meacher* • **216 tl** Bruce Coleman Ltd/Dennis Green **tr** Bruce Coleman Ltd; (grouse) Bruce Coleman Ltd/Gordon Langsbury; (hare) Bruce Coleman Ltd/Gordon Langsbury; (stag) Bruce Coleman Ltd/John Cancalosi; (lizard) Bruce Coleman Ltd/George McCarthy; (snake) Bruce Coleman Ltd/George McCarthy **bl** Bruce Coleman Ltd/Jane Burton **bc** Bruce Coleman Ltd/Jose Luis Gonzalez Grande **br** Bruce Coleman Ltd/Colin Varndell • **217 bc** David Hastilow Picture Library **br** David Hastilow Picture Library • **218 tl** Bruce Coleman Ltd/Werner Layer **tr** Bruce Coleman Ltd/Jens Rydell **cl** Bruce Coleman Ltd/P. Clement **cr** Bruce Coleman Ltd/Colin Varndell; (vole) Bruce Coleman Ltd/P. Clement; (spider) Bruce Coleman Ltd/Geoff Dore **bl** Bruce Coleman Ltd/Colin Varndell **bc** Bruce Coleman Ltd/Michael McKavett • **218-19** Biofotos/Heather Angel • **219 tl** Frank Lane Picture Agency/David Grewcock **cr** Bridgeman Art Library, London/Lambeth Palace Library • **220 tr** Christie's Images **b** Bridgeman Art Library, London/Walker Art Gallery, Liverpool • **221** *Illustrated Arts Ltd* • **222 l** Tate Gallery, London 1999/Copyright ©Alan Bowness, Hepworth Estate **tr** Hulton Getty Images • **222-3** The National Trust/Nick Meers • **223 tr** Friends of Highgate Cemetery/John Gay **c** Friends of Highgate Cemetery/John Gay • **224 t** Scotland in Focus/Wilbir **b** Scotland in Focus • **225** (blunderbuss) The Board of Trustees of the Royal Armouries/(XII 1042); (pistol) The Board of Trustees of the Royal Armouries/(XII 1644); (pistol) The Board of Trustees of the Royal Armouries/(XII 1661) **cr** *Angelo Hornak* **bl** *Eric Fraser* **bc** *Angelo Hornak* • **226 t** Anthony Oliver/©Damien Hirst **c** Courtesy of the Trustees of the Victoria and Albert Museum, London • **227** United Northern Photographers • **228** The National Gallery, London • **229 t** Hulton Getty Images **cr** Popperfoto • **230** Gerry Cranham • **230-1** Allsport UK Ltd/Ben Radford • **231 cr** Trevor Jones **br** Alison Hamilton-Russell • **232 tl** Images Colour Library/Charles Walker Collection **c** ©The Trustees of the National Galleries of Scotland 1999 **b** Bruce Coleman Ltd/Allan G. Potts • **233 t** private collection **b** ©The British Museum • **234 tl** Courtesy of the Trustees of the Victoria and Albert Museum, London **tr** Courtesy of the Trustees of the Victoria and Albert Museum, London **c** Rex Features Ltd/Nils Jorgansen **bl** Reproduced by permission of the Palace of Westminster • **234-5** Julian Cotton Picture Library/*Line and Line* • **235 tc** Woodmansterne Ltd **tr** Angelo Hornak **cr** Angelo Hornak **bl** The World of Interiors/Christopher Simon-Sykes • **236** Courtesy of the Trustees of the Victoria and Albert Museum, London • **236-7** Aspect/Archie Miles • **237** Hulton Getty Images • **238 tr** Hulton Getty Images **bl** Allsport UK Ltd/Hulton Getty • **239 t** The National Trust/F.A.H. Bloemendal **bl** *Andrew Thompson* **b** John Cleare/Mountain Camera • **240** By Permission of the Dean and Chapter of Winchester/Miki Slingsby • **241 tl** Bridgeman Art Library, London/Wolverhampton Art Gallery **br** Andrew Butler • **242 tl** Natural Science Photos/N.K.D. Miller **tc** NHPA/Wernwer Zepf **tr** Bruce Coleman Ltd/Kim Taylor; (rose aphids) Natural Science Photos/Jeremy Burgess; (ants) BBC Natural History Unit; (fly) NHPA/N.A. Callow; (grasshopper) Natural Science Photos/Richard Revels; (wasp) NHPA/Stephen Dalton; (silverfish) NHPA/Stephen Dalton; (woodlouse) Natural Science Photos/Richard Revels **bl** Bruce Coleman Ltd/Andy Purcell **bc** Natural Science Photos/Richard Revels **br** NHPA/E.A. Janes • **243 tr** Scotland in Focus/R. Weir **cr** Mick Sharp and Jean Williamson **b** Scotland in Focus/D. Burrows • **244 c** Ironbridge Gorge Museum/Neil Jinkerson **bl** English Heritage • **245 t** Tim Woodcock **cr** Christie's Images **br** Quadrant • **246 cl** Allsport UK Ltd/Simon Bruty **br** National Portrait Gallery, London • **247 tr** The Ronald Grant Archive/Eon Productions **cr** ©Ian Fleming, 1953. By permission of the Fleming family & Ian Fleming (Glidrose) Publications Ltd/First published in the UK by Jonathan Cape **bc** The Kobal Collection **br** The Ronald Grant Archive/Eon Productions • **248 c** Royal Institute of British Architects/By permission of Jane Ridley **bl** Popperfoto • **249 t** Science Photo Library/Martin Bond **b** Tate Gallery, London 1999/©Estate of Gwen John 2000. All rights reserved DACS • **250** Rex Features Ltd/Julian Makey • **251 t** Hulton Getty Images **b** John Freeman • **252** Universal Pictorial Press and Agency • **253 tr** Hulton Getty Images **bl** Walter Keeler • **254** Topham Picture Library • **255 cr** Biofotos **b** Robert Harding/C. Bowman • **256 tl** Science and Society Picture Library/National Railway Museum **br** Tim Woodcock • **257 c** British Standards Institution **br** Hulton Getty Images • **258 t** Universal Pictorial Press and Agency **b** Bridgeman Art Library, London/British Library • **259 tr** The Landmark Trust/M. Campbell Cole **cr** Royal Horticultural Society, Lindley Library **b** Royal Horticultural Society, Lindley Library • **260-1** Bridgeman Art Library, London/Ipswich Borough Council, Museums and Art Galleries • **261 tl** ©The British Museum Bridgeman Art Library, London/

Imperial War Museum, London • **262 t** Chris Barker **b** (background) Skyscan • **263** Imperial War Museum • **264** Christie's Images • **264-5** The Kobal Collection • **265** Angelo Hornak • **266** John Freeman • **267 t** Hulton Getty Images **b** *Lee Peters, International Arts* • **268 cl** Thames and Hudson, London/Photo John Caine, from 'The House of Liberty' Ed. Stephen Calloway, 1992 **bl** Thames and Hudson, London/Higgs & Hill PLC, from 'The House of Liberty' Ed. Stephen Calloway 1992 • **269 tr** English Heritage **bc** English Heritage/Kim Williams **br** English Heritage • **270 tl** The National Trust/Mark Fiennes **tr** ET Archive, London; (cross) Collections/Gary Smith **cl** Scotland in Focus/C. K. Robeson **c** Scotland in Focus/G. Satterley **bl** British Film Institute • **270-1** *Andrew Thompson* • **271 tl** *Eric Meacher* **cr** ET Archive, London/V&A Museum; (arch) Collections/Gena Davis; (inn) Collections/Paul Watts **bc** Collections/Alain Le Garsmeur **br** Collections/Paul Watts • **272 tr** Topham Picture Library **b** *Neil Holmes* • **273 t** ZEFA/Douglas MacLennan **b** Tom Kidd • **274-5** (inserts) *Line and Line*; (map) *Andrew Thompson* • **276** ET Archive, London/Bibliothèque Nationale, Paris • **277** *Andrew Thompson* • **278** Aspect/Richard Turpin • **279** Tate Gallery, London 1999/(detail) • **280** The National Trust/Joe Cornish • **281 tr** ©The British Museum **bl** Bridgeman Art Library, London/Collection of The Royal Shakespeare Theatre • **282-3 t** National Trust for Scotland/Allan Forbes **b** Permission of the Board of the British Library, London/(7943d. 8 128) • **284 t** John Makepeace **b** Colorific/Nigel Trotter • **285 tr** Oldham Evening Chronicle **cr** Manchester United Merchandising Ltd • **286 t** Britain On View/Stockwave **b** Britain On View/Stockwave • **287 t** Reproduced by kind permission of His Grace the Duke of Marlborough **b** GEC-Marconi Ltd • **288 t** The Landmark Trust **b** Christopher Dalton • **289 t** The Royal Collection ©Her Majesty The Queen **br** Mary Rose Trust • **290** Magnum/Burt Glinn • **291 tr** Collections/Brian Shuel **c** Collections/Brian Shuel **b** Collections/Brian Shuel • **292 tl** Bruce Coleman Ltd/Kim Taylor **tr** Natural Science Photos/Richard Revels **c** Bruce Coleman Ltd/John Markham **bl** Bruce Coleman Ltd/N.G. Blake **bc** Natural Science Photos/Richard Revels • **292-3** (background) Bruce Coleman Ltd/Granville Harris • **293 tl** Premaphotos/K.G. Preston-Mafham; (fritillaries) Bruce Coleman Ltd/Hans Reinhard; (orchid) Natural Science Photos/Andrew Watts; (Quaking grass) Natural Science Photos/Richard Revels **bl** Bruce Coleman Ltd/Norbert Schwirtz **br** Skyscan • **294** Magnum/Martine Franck • **295 t** The Ronald Grant Archive/Merchant Ivory **b** Images Colour Library • **296 cl** (background) Foster & Partners **c** Foster & Partners/Dennis Gilbert **bl** Richard Davies **br** Richard Davies • **297 tl** Richard Davies **tc** (background) Future Systems **tr** Arcaid/Richard Bryant/Architect Seth Stein **c** (background) Richard Rogers Partnership **bl** Arcaid/Richard Bryant **br** Philip Bier/View Pictures • **298** Robert Harding • **299 cr** Magnum/Chris Steele-Perkins **br** Popperfoto • **300 t** Permission of the Board of the British Library, London/(Ms. 39942 f.20) **c** Buckfast Abbey, Devon **b** private collection • **300-1** Skyscan • **301 tr** *Ian Atkinson* **cr** Camera Press/Homer Sykes **bl** Times Newspapers Ltd/Paul Rogers • **302** (all) ©The British Museum • **303 tl** BBC **br** Camera Press/Gemma Levine • **304 tr** Christie's Images **bl** Hulton Getty Images • **305 tr** Hulton Getty Images **bl** Allsport UK Ltd • **306 tl** Quadrant/Ken McKay • **306-7** Neill Bruce: Motoring Photolibrary/Peter Roberts • **307 tl** The National Motor Museum, Beaulieu **tr** Science and Society Picture Library; (lights) Hulton Getty Images; (Land Rover) Neill Bruce: Motoring Photolibrary; (E-type) Quadrant; (Lotus) Quadrant/Phil Talbot; (M1) Quadrant; (wardens) Topham Picture Library; (camera) Robert Harding • **308 tr** Scotland in Focus/B. Chapple **bl** Topham Picture Library • **309** (field mushroom) NHPA/E.A. Janes; (puffball) Oxford Scientific Films/David Thomson; (cep) Biofotos; (death cap) NHPA/G. Bernard **b** Oxford Scientific Films/David Boag • **310 tr** Science and Society Picture Library **bl** Hulton Getty Images • **311** Arcaid/Mark Fiennes • **312 c** British Film Institute **bl** Topham Picture Library • **313 t** Popperfoto **b** National Museum of Photography Film & Television • **314** Dominic Photography • **315** Trustees of the British Museum (Natural History) • **316** The Black Country Living Museum, Dudley • **317 t** Sunday Times Syndication **tr** The John Frost Historical Newspaper Service; (Observer) The John Frost Historical Newspaper Service; (Mirror) The John Frost Historical Newspaper Service; (supplement) The John Frost Historical Newspaper Service; (Today) The John Frost Historical Newspaper Service; (background) Financial Times Pictures • **318 tl** The Bodleian Library, Oxford/permission of the Warden and Fellows, New College, Oxford/(Ms. New College 361/2, f.45v.) **c** *Eileen Tweedy* • **319 t** Popperfoto **b** Hulton Getty Images • **320 tl** ©The British Museum **cl** Bridgeman Art Library, London/British Library **bc** Crown copyright: Public Record Office • **320-1 t** Glasgow Museums: The Burrell Collection **b** Bibliothèque de Dijon • **321 tl** Michael Holford/Musée de Bayeux **tr** *Andrew Thompson* **cl** ET Archive, London **cr** Robert Hallmann **bl** The Bodleian Library, Oxford/(Ms. Auct. D.2.6, f16v) **bc** Michael Holford **br** English Heritage • **322** Christopher Hill Photographic/Jill Jennings • **323 tl** The Hutchison Picture Library/Philip Wolmuth **tc(l)** The Hutchison Picture Library/Michael MacIntyre **tc(r)** Impact/Ben Edwards **tr** Format/Jenny Matthews **br** BMIHT/Rover Group • **324** *Digital Wisdom Publishing Ltd* • **325 tc** The Harvard Theatre Collection, The Houghton Library, Fredric Woodbridge Wilson, Curator **cr** Colorsport **br** Allsport UK Ltd/Ross Kinnaird • **326** Pacemaker Press International • **327 t** Popperfoto **b** (background) Ordnance Survey/©Crown Copyright **bl** Ordnance Survey/ ©Crown Copyright **br** Ordnance Survey/©Crown Copyright • **328 tl** Sheila & Oliver Mathews **cl** Hulton Getty Images • **329 t** Popperfoto **b** Oxford Picture Library/Chris Andrews • **330 tr** The National Trust/Martin Charles **b** Paisley Museum & Art Galleries • **331 tr** The Raymond Mander & Joe Mitchenson Theatre Collection **cr** Dominic Photography/Catherine Ashmore • **332 tl** Airborne Forces Museum **br** ©Aardman Animations Ltd • **333** Network/B. Hermann/Rapho • **334** ET Archive, London/Jarrold • **335 tr** Tim Woodcock **cl** The Penguin Group • **336 tr** Bridgeman Art Library, London/Manchester City Art Galleries **bl** Allsport UK Ltd • **337** ©The Petrie Museum of Egyptian Archaeology, University College London • **338** Tony Stone Photo Library, London/Martin Rogers • **339 c** *Andrew Thompson* **cr** Museum of London **br** Southampton City Museum • **340** permission of Charles Staffell • **341 tl** June Osborne **tc (l)** June Osborne **tc (r)** June Osborne **tr** June Osborne • **342 tc** ET Archive, London **c** Science and Society Picture Library **bl** Museum of London • **343** (creeper) *RDPL*; (lily) *RDPL*; (rhododendron) *RDPL*; (orchid) *RDPL*; (pelargonium) Garden Picture Library/Chris Burrows; (tulips) *RDPL* **cr** *Andrew Thompson* **cr** Royal Horticultural Society, Lindley Library **br** Royal Horticultural Society, Lindley Library • **344 tl** *Kate Harris* **b** Angelo Hornak • **345 tr** The National Trust/Nick Meers **bc** Hulton Getty Images **br** Topham Picture Library • **346 t** Network/Paul Lowe **b** Network/Homer Sykes • **347** Bridgeman Art Library, London/Kunsthalle, Tubingen/© Richard Hamilton 2000 All Rights Reserved DACS • **348 tl** Unilever **tr** *Neil Holmes* **cr** ©The Post Office Reproduced by Kind Permission of The Post Office All Rights Reserved **bl** Neil Holmes **br** ©The Post Office Reproduced by Kind Permission of The Post Office All Rights Reserved • **349 t** Copyright ©F. Warne & Co./1902,1987 **b** The Kobal Collection • **350 tc** ET Archive, London/Stoke Museum **tr** Christie's Images **cr** Christie's Images **bl** Christie's Images **bc** Christie's Images • **350-1** Christie's Images • **351 tl** Christie's Images **tc** Christie's Images **tr** ET Archive, London/Stoke Museum **cl** Christie's Images **cr** Christie's Images **bl** Courtesy of the Trustees of the Victoria and Albert Museum, London **bc** Dartington Pottery **br** By Courtesy of the Wedgwood Museum Trustees, Barlaston, Stoke-on-Trent, Staffordshire • **352 c** *Jim Lindsay* **br** Environmental Images/Martin Bond **b** Science Photo Library/Sheila Terry • **353** Tate Gallery, London 1999 • **354 tl** By Kind Permission of Historic Scotland **tc** By Kind Permission of Historic Scotland **tr** Charles Tait **bl** Charles Tait **bc** Mick Sharp and Jean Williamson **br** Robert Estall • **354-5** *Andrew Thompson* • **355 tl** Trustees of the British Museum (Natural History) **tc** ©The British Museum **tr** Skyscan **c** English Heritage **bl** Robert Harding **bc** ©The British Museum **br** English Heritage • **356 t** Robert Opie **b** Colorific/Anthony Howarth • **357 tr** Popperfoto **c** Topham Picture Library **b** Rex Features Ltd • **358 t** Rex Features Ltd/Ilpo Musto **c** (Eton) Eton College-New & Lingwood Ltd; (Winchester) Wykehamist Society; (Rugby) Salters of Rugby; (Charterhouse) Dr Caroline Harcourt; (Fettes) Aitkin & Niven; (Harrow) Harrow School-Billings & Edmonds Ltd **bl** Arcaid/Lucinda Lambton • **359 tr** The National Trust/Will Webster **cr** The National Trust/Will Webster; (Swan) Edifice **bl** Retna Pictures/Ray Stevenson **br** (Royal Oak) Corbis-Bettmann/Patrick Ward; (Red Lion) Corbis-Bettmann/Rupert Horrox; (The Bull) Archie Miles • **360 tr** Christie's Images **bl** RMS Foundation Inc • **361** Elizabeth Whiting & Associates/Tom Leighton • **362 t** Crown copyright: Public Record Office **bl** Hulton Getty Images • **363 tr** Robert Opie **cr** Hulton Getty Images • **364 bl** Science and Society Picture Library/National Railway Museum **bc** Science and Society Picture Library/National Railway Museum • **364-5** Science and Society Picture Library/National Railway Museum • **365 tc** Milepost Ninety-Two and a Half; (tickets) Science and Society Picture Library/National Railway Museum **br** Milepost Ninety-Two and a Half • **366** The Kobal Collection • **367** Images Colour Library • **368 tl** John Cleare/Mountain Camera **br** Topham Picture Library • **369** Tate Gallery, London 1999 • **370 tr** Barbican Art Gallery **bl** Camera Press/The Times • **371** Comstock Photofile Limited • **372** (artwork) *Raymond Turvey* **t** Planet Earth Pictures/Martin Rugner **c** John Cleare/Mountain Camera **b** Skyscan • **373 t** Tom Scott **b** Bridgeman Art Library, London/Private collection • **374** (Steele) Pictorial Press; (Herman's Hermits) Pictorial Press/Polygram; (Kinks) Popperfoto; (Genesis) London Features International; (Slade) London Features International; (Springfield) London Features International; (The Who) Redferns/Richie Aaron; (Wizzard) Pictorial Press/Pietar Mazel; (Shaw) Redferns/David Redfern • **375** (Madness) London Features International/Simon Fowler; (George) London Features International; (Cocker) Redferns/Barbara Steinwehe; (Flint) Redferns/Jon Super; (Siouxsie) London Features International/Simon Fowler; (Adam) London Features International/Kevin Cummins; (Spice) Popperfoto; (Queen) Redferns/Fin Costello; (Beatles) Iain Macmillan/Apple Corps Ltd; (Stones) Virgin Records; (Pink Floyd) Pink Floyd Music Ltd; (Yes) ©1973 Elektra Entertainment Group Inc • **376** (quartz) Dorling Kindersley/Colin Keats; (galena) Dorling Kindersley; (pyrite) Dorling Kindersley/Colin Keates; (Blue John) Trustees of the British Museum (Natural History); (granite) Trustees of the British Museum (Natural History); (basalt) Dorling Kindersley/Andreas von Einsiedel; (chalk) Trustees of the British Museum (Natural History); (limestone) Dorling Kindersley/Harry Taylor; (slate) Trustees of the British Museum (Natural History) **bl** Doug Corrance • **377 tl** Star File Photo Agency Ltd **br** New Millennium Experience/QA Photos • **378 tl** Mick Sharp and Jean Williamson **tr** English Heritage **c** ©The British Museum **c** ©The British Museum **bl** *Neil Holmes* **bc** Museum of London • **378-9** *Andrew Thompson* • **379 tc** English Heritage **c** English Heritage **cr** The National Trust/Ian Shaw **br** English Heritage/Jonathan

Bailey • 380 (Roofs) *Ron Hayward* **bl** Bridgeman Art Library, London/Walker Art Gallery, Liverpool • 381 **tr** The Dickens House Museum, London **b** Royal Academy of Arts, London • 382 **t** The Royal Warrant Holders Association **b** Richard Cooke • 383 **tl** Royal Geographical Society **tc** Royal Geographical Society • 384 **tr** Camera Press/Richard Gillard **tr** National Portrait Gallery, London; (Henry V) National Portrait Gallery, London; (Richard III) National Portrait Gallery, London; (Richard III) Donald Cooper **br** The Kobal Collection/Keith Hamshere/The Samuel Goldwyn Co • 384-5 Hulton Getty Images • 385 **tl** National Portrait Gallery, London **tc** National Portrait Gallery, London **cl** National Portrait Gallery, London **c** Hulton Getty Images • 386 MOD, Department of the Royal Navy • 387 Colorsport • 388 Robert Harding/Ruth Tomlinson • 389 Hulton Getty Images • 390 London Metropolitan Archives • 391 **tc** Hunterian Art Gallery, University of Glasgow **cr** Tate Gallery, St Ives **b** Robert Harding • 392 **l** Sonia Halliday **tc** Bridgeman Art Library, London/Philip Mould Historical Portraits Ltd, London **c** Bridgeman Art Library, London/British Library/Add 39943 f.2b **r** Sonia Halliday • 393 **tl** Sonia Halliday **br** Bridgeman Art Library, London/John Bethell • 394 **t** Metropolitan Museum of Art/Arthur Hoppock Hern Fund, 1916 (16.53) **b** Rex Features Ltd/Dave Hartley • 395 Network • 396 **t** Charles Tait **b** The Kobal Collection • 397 **tl** Popperfoto **br** BT Archives • 398 **tl** Popperfoto/Ponting **bl** Geoffrey Sturdy **bc** The Guide Association • 399 **tl** Neil Holmes **tr** Crown copyright: Public Record Office **cl** Crown copyright: Public Record Office **b** Neil Holmes • 400 **tl** Imperial War Museum **c** Imperial War Museum **bl** Hulton Getty Images • 401 Leslie Garland Picture Library • 402 **tl** Performing Arts Library/Clive Barda **bl** Angelo Hornak **bc** Courtesy of the Trustees of the Victoria and Albert Museum, London **br** Mark Douet • 403 **t** The Ronald Grant Archive **br** National Monuments Record, ©Crown Copyright • 404 **t** Sheila & Oliver Mathews **b** Courtesy of the Trustees of the Victoria and Albert Museum, London • 405 **tc** Scotland in Focus/James Weir **tr** Charles Tait **bl** The Ronald Grant Archive • 406 **t** *Andrew Thompson* **bl** ©National Galleries of Northern Ireland, Ulster Folk & Transport Museum/Harland And Wolff Collection **bl** Hulton Getty Images • 407 **tc** private collection **tr** Robert Opie **br** Mary Evans Picture Library • 408 **l** Oxford Scientific Films/David Tipling **tc** *Raymond Turvey* **br** *Raymond Turvey* • 408-9 Skyscan • 409 **tl** *Raymond Turvey* **tr** Bruce Coleman Ltd/John Worrall **cr** *Raymond Turvey* **br** Planet Earth Pictures/Mark Mattock • 410 **tr** Bridgeman Art Library, London/Scottish National Gallery of Modern Art, Edinburgh/© Estate of Walter Sickert 2000 All Rights Reserved DACS **bl** Images Colour Library • 411 Silver Studio Collection, University of Middlesex/Chris Barker • 412 **t** Popperfoto **b** Garden Picture Library/John Miller • 413 **t** ET Archive, London **bc** Celtic Picture Library **br** Celtic Picture Library • 414 Hulton Getty Images • 415 **t** Sheila & Oliver Mathews **b** Camera Press/Lord Snowdon • 416 **tl** Collections/Alain Le Garsmeur **b** Courtesy of the Trustees of Sir John Soane's Museum • 417 Sotheby's, London • 418 **t** Brian Mills **b** The Society of Apothecaries • 419 **t** Collections/Mike Kipling **b** Rex Features Ltd/Rick Colls • 420 **t** Tate Gallery, London 1999 **c** Robert Copeland • 421 Science and Society Picture Library/National Railway Museum • 422 **tr** Allsport UK Ltd **bl** The Fotomas Index **bc** Mary Evans Picture Library • 423 Julian Cotton Picture Library/Jason Hawkes Aerial Collection • 424 **t** Dominic Photography **b** The National Trust/Oliver Benn • 425 **cr** Network/Jenny Matthews **br** Hulton Getty Images • 426 **tl** Royal Academy of Arts, London **tc (l)** Royal Academy of Arts, London **tc (r)** Royal Academy of Arts, London **tr** Royal Academy of Arts, London **bc** The National Trust/Andrew Butler • 427 **t** Popperfoto **b** *Lee Peters* • 428 **tl** Bridgeman Art Library, London/St Matthew's Church, Northampton **cr** Science and Society Picture Library • 429 **t** Mary Evans Picture Library **b** Biofotos/Heather Angel • 430 **tr** Imperial War Museum **cr** TRH Pictures/E. Nevill • 431 (background) Scottish Tartan Society **tr** AA **bl** Scottish National Portrait Gallery (detail); (all tartans) Scottish Tartan Society; (all badges) Romilly Squire, Heraldic Artist at the Court of King Lyon and Deputy Secretary of the Standing Council of Scottish Chiefs • 432 **t** Tate Gallery, St Ives **cl** Tate & Lyle **c** Tate Gallery, St Ives • 433 **tr** The Tea Council **bc** Hulton Getty Images **br** *White Backgrounds* • 434 **c** Photograph by Tim Graham **cr** BBC **bl** ©The Making of Pride & Prejudice by Sue Birtwistle & Susie Conklin (Penguin/BBC) **br** BBC • 435 **tl** BBC **bl** Spectrum Colour Library **br** United Northern Photographers • 436 **t** From '1066 and All That' by W.C. Sellar & R.J. Yeatman/Methuen Publishers Ltd 1930 **br** Empics/Adam Davy • 437 **t** New Lanark Conservation **bl** Hulton Getty Images **br** The National Trust/Mike Williams • 438 **tr** Collections/Andy Hibbert; (river god) Oxford Picture Library/Chris Andrews; (meadow) Robert Hallmann **bl** Robert Hallmann **bc** Robert Harding **br** *Neil Holmes* • 439 **t** National Portrait Gallery, London **b** Richard Turpin **bc** (l) Skyscan **bc (r)** Robert Hallmann **br** Skyscan • 440 **t** *Raymond Harris Ching* **b** Rex Features Ltd/Charles Ommanney • 441 **t** Mick Sharp and Jean Williamson **b** Popperfoto • 442 **tl** Skyscan **bc** Collections/James Bartholomew • 443 **tl** Robert Opie **tr** Robert Opie **c** Robert Opie **cr** Rex Features Ltd/J. Sutton-Hibbert **b** New Cavendish Books • 444 **t** Department of Rare Books and Special Collections, University Library, Rochester, New York **b** Permission of the National Museum of Labour History • 445 **tl** Timothy Millet, A.H. Baldwin and Sons, London **b** Aspect/Phil Conrad • 446 **tl** Robert Harding/Adam Woolfitt **bc** Science and Society Picture Library • 447 **tr** Colorsport **bl** Anwar Hussein • 448 **tl** Action Plus/Mike Hewitt **br** National Museum of Wales • 449 Artangel/Edward Woodman

• 450 **tr** The Image Bank/A. Edwards **cl** Scotland in Focus/P. Davies **bl** Scotland in Focus/R.G. Elliot • 451 Hulton Getty Images • 452 **t** Christopher Cormack **b** Castle Howard, York • 453 Popperfoto • 454 **bl** Hulton Getty Images **bc** Courtesy of the Trustees of the Victoria and Albert Museum, London • 454-5 Bridgeman Art Library, London/Royal Holloway and New Bedford College • 455 **tr** Hulton Getty Images **cr** The Advertising Archives **bl** J. Sainsbury plc **br** Hulton Getty Images • 456 **t** Robert Opie **b** The Mayor Gallery • 457 *S&O Mathews* **tc** Sheila & Oliver Mathews **tr** Neil Holmes **cl** Robert Hallmann **b** Val Corbett • 458 Bridgeman Art Library, London/Wallace Collection, London • 459 **tr** The Fotomas Index **bl** Hulton Getty Images/Edward Malindine • 460 **t** ET Archive, London/V&A **l** ET Archive, London/V&A • 461 (background) Exclusivity/Richard Dunkley **tl** Tate Gallery, London 1999 **tr** ©The British Museum **cr** ©The British Museum • 462 **t** Bridgeman Art Library, London/City Art Gallery, Leeds, UK **b** Michael Holford/British Museum • 463 **tl** Collections/Robert Hallmann **c** *Pavel Kostal, International Artworks* **br** The Bodleian Library, Oxford/ (Ms. Bod. 264 f.81) • 464 **bl** Frank Lane Picture Agency/Joan Hutchings • 464-5 (artwork) *Raymond Turvey* • 465 **tr** NHPA/Michael Leach **br** Frank Lane Picture Agency/Ray Bird • 466 **tr** Science and Society Picture Library **br** Castle Museum, Nottingham • 467 Andrew Lawson • 468 **t** Mary Evans Picture Library **b** *Simon McComb* • 469 Redferns • 470 Scotland in Focus • 471 **tl** Tate Gallery, London 1999 **b** David Tarn • 472 **tl** London Aerial Photo Library **br** Hulton Getty Images • 473 **t** Bridgeman Art Library, London/Wilberforce House Museum, Hull **b** National Portrait Gallery, London • 474 Paul Hill • 475 **tr** Wilton House Trust **b** Allsport UK Ltd/Gary Prior • 476 **t** Line drawing by E.H. Shepard © under the Berne Convention, colouring copyright ©1970 by E.H. Shepard/and Methuen Children's Books, permission of Curtis Brown, London **b** Aerofilms • 477 **t** Collections/Paul Watts **b** The New York Public Library/Don Hamerman/ Central Children's Room, Donnell Library Center • 478 **t** Bibliothèque Nationale, Paris/(Ms.Fr.12476 f.105v) **b** Fortean Picture Library/Kevin Carlyon • 479 **t** By kind permission of the Marquess of Tavistock, and the Trustees of the Bedford Estates **bl** ET Archive, London **bc** ET Archive, London **br** ET Archive, London • 480 **t** National Portrait Gallery, London **b** Hulton Getty Images • 481 **c** Hulton Getty Images **b** Images Colour Library • 482 (background) Bruce Coleman Ltd/Jules Cowan **tl** Bruce Coleman Ltd **c** NHPA/Stephen Dalton **cr** Bruce Coleman Ltd/Robert Maier **br** Bruce Coleman Ltd/Felix Labhardt • 483 (background) Biofotos/Heather Angel **tl** Bruce Coleman Ltd/Kim Taylor **cl** Bruce Coleman Ltd/George McCarthy **cr** Bruce Coleman Ltd/George McCarthy **bl** Bruce Coleman Ltd/Hans Reinhard • 484 'The Independent'/David Ashdown • 485 Mick Sharp and Jean Williamson • 486 **l** National Portrait Gallery, London **r** Guildhall Library, Corporation of London • 486-7 **b** Mary Evans Picture Library • 487 **l** Angelo Hornak **tl** Arcaid/John Stuart Miller **tr** Guildhall Library, Corporation of London **br** Angelo Hornak • 488 **t** Weidenfeld and Nicolson/Thomas Pakenham **b** Topham Picture Library • 489 **t** The Royal Collection ©Her Majesty The Queen **b** Jersey Wildlife Preservation Trust/Peter Trenchard • 490 **tl** English Heritage **tr** Mary Evans Picture Library **c** Popperfoto **bl** Mary Evans Picture Library **br** Popperfoto/EMP • 491 *Andrew Thompson* 'Regional Trends', Office of National Statistics ©Crown Copyright 1998/General Register Office, Scotland/Northern Ireland Statistics and Research Agency • 492 **tr** Skyscan **c** Telegraph Colour Library/Malcolm Sanders • 492-3 *Cartographic Solutions Ltd* • 494-5 *Digital Wisdom Publishing Ltd* • 496 **cr** Telegraph Colour Library/D Noton • 496-7 *Digital Wisdom Publishing Ltd* • 498 **t** Telegraph Colour Library/Malcolm Sanders **b** *Cartographic Solutions Ltd* • 499 *Andrew Thompson*

The publishers would also like to thank the following for their help in the preparation of this book: Clive Adamson, Michael Bailey, Tony Bastow, Professor Jeremy Black, Christopher Breward, Colin Bruce, John Burnett, John Chesshyre, Lloyd Clark, Dave Clegg, William Dodd, Peter Dolman, Kate Evans, Geographical Research Associates, The Georgian Group, Miranda Goodby, The Reverend Peter Green, Prue Grice, Mike Hill, Robin Hildyard, Eleanor John, Father Kennedy, Sophia Kingshill, Sandy Malcolm, Glen Miller, Clare Mitchell, John Moore, Kevin More, Navy Board Historical Branch, Ronan Paterson, Sarah Paterson, Helen Phillips, Stephanie Pickering, Mark Rowland-Jones, Derek Salter, Alexander Schulenburg, James Spilling, Graham Sussum, Emma Wager, Robin Walton, Dave Welsh, Abigail Wheatley, Jackie Wilson, Jacqueline Wyer.

Book Production Manager Chris Reynolds
Assistant Book Production Manager Fiona McIntosh
Pre-press Manager Howard Reynolds
Pre-press Technical Analyst Martin Hendrick

Origination Studio One Ltd, London, England
Paper Townsend Hook Ltd, Snodland, England
Printing and binding Brepols Graphic Industries NV, Turnhout, Belgium

40-587-01